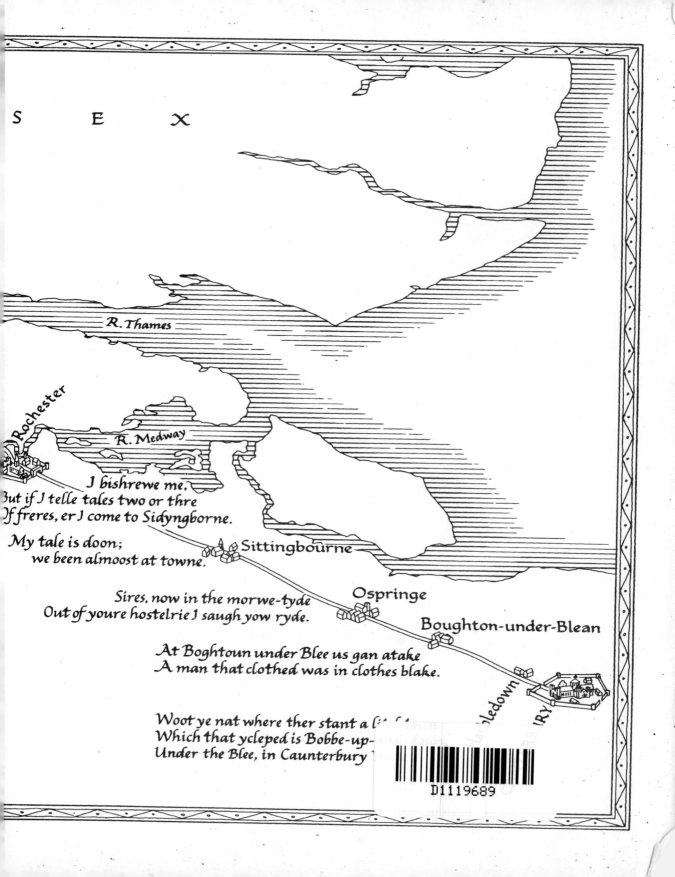

S E X

R. Thames

Rochester

R. Medway

J bishrewe me,
But if J telle tales two or thre
Of freres, er J come to Sidyngborne.

My tale is doon;
    we been almoost at towne.

Sittingbourne

Sires, now in the morwe-tyde
Out of youre hostelrie J saugh yow ryde.

Ospringe

Boughton-under-Blean

At Boghtoun under Blee us gan atake
A man that clothed was in clothes blake.

edown

RY

Woot ye nat where ther stant a [...]
Which that ycleped is Bobbe-up-
Under the Blee, in Caunterbury

GEOFFREY CHAUCER

From an early painting on wood (artist unknown),
by permission of the Houghton Library, Harvard University.

2

GEOFFREY CHAUCER

The Canterbury Tales

COMPLETE

EDITED BY

Larry D. Benson, *Harvard University*

BASED ON
The Riverside Chaucer,
Third Edition

Houghton Mifflin Company   Boston   New York

Senior Sponsoring Editor: Dean Johnson
Editorial Associate: Bruce Cantley
Senior Editorial Production Coordinator: Carla Thompson
Senior Production/Design Coordinator: Sarah Ambrose
Senior Cover Design Coordinator: Deborah Azerrad Savona
Senior Manufacturing Coordinator: Priscilla Bailey
Senior Marketing Manager: Nancy Lyman

Cover Design: Sarah Ho
Cover Image: Chaucer's Canterbury Pilgrims, engraved and published by the artist, 1810 (engraving), William Blake

Title page art and details on pp. xiii, 1, 311, 333: Taz Sibley

Printed in the U.S.A.

Library of Congress Catalog Card Number: 99-72033

ISBN: 0-395-97823-8

56789-CRS-04 03

Contents

Preface

THIS EDITION of *The Canterbury Tales* has been adapted from *The Riverside Chaucer,* Third Edition, with the aim of producing a text suited to the needs of beginning students while retaining as much material suitable to more advanced students as space allowed.

The text is that of *The Riverside Chaucer* (incorporating, as copies of the Riverside now do, a few minor corrections made in early reprintings), and the glosses on the pages are (with a few corrections) the same as those in the Riverside and, like those, they include a few definitions taken from F. N. Robinson's notes (indicated by the abbreviation "R.").

In the Introduction, a section on the life of Chaucer has been retained largely unchanged, and a chronology of Chaucer's life and times has been added (it incorporates the received dates of Chaucer's works in the Riverside note on canon and chronology, omitted from this edition). The section on Chaucer's language and versification has been revised to focus solely on the language of the Canterbury Tales rather on all of Chaucer's works, and the same is true of the Glossary and the Index of Proper Names. The Textual Notes have been omitted (or in a very few cases moved to the Explanatory Notes), and the Explanatory Notes have been extensively revised and provided with an index to the principal matters treated in the notes.

The Preface to *The Riverside Chaucer,* Third Edition, sets out the general principles that guided the making of the Explanatory Notes for that edition, explaining that even in 1957 Robinson had to abandon the inclusive bibliographical references that marked his 1933 edition:

> Such comprehensive treatments were no longer possible [and] Robinson had to restrict his new citations to only the most notable contributions that had appeared since the First Edition. The volume of scholarship and criticism has increased even more rapidly in the thirty years since the Second Edition. Our notes therefore do not and cannot provide full bibliographies or complete histories of opinion and scholarship on the problems of the particular works; they are intended rather to supply the reader with the information needed to begin the study of the work and to provide references for further investigation. The emphasis has been on the factual rather than the speculative, although important critical interpretations and problems are not ignored. Every effort has been made to represent impartially the diversity of viewpoints.

In adapting and revising those notes for the present edition the same principles were observed, though with new emphases. The aim has been to make the Explanatory Notes more accessible to undergraduate students: all quotations from foreign languages are translated into modern English (the original is retained when a comparison of the original to Chaucer's text is relevant); translations (when available) are cited for all works in languages other than English; and difficult passages from Middle English in the citations have often been regularized or translated. Moreover, an attempt has been made to render the notes self-contained; that is, references to short passages in the Bible, literary works, or historical sources, or even to works of Chaucer other than the Canterbury Tales, are quoted rather than merely cited, thus providing the reader with immediate access to the relevant parts of the references.

The Explanatory Notes have also been brought up to date by including citations of critical and scholarly works that have appeared since about 1985, which was in most cases the cut-off date for references in *The Riverside Chaucer* (published in 1987). The citation of such works has been even more selective than in the Riverside edition, since space is limited and the attempt to render the notes more accessible often resulted in a considerable expansion of individual notes. To make room for this, much older scholarship had to be omitted, along with materials of interest primarily to advanced students (such as the ultimate sources of ideas and motifs, studies in languages other than English, citations of works relevant to the history of criticism rather than immediately to the text, and purely linguistic matters). More recent scholarship had to be cited selectively, with even less of an attempt to survey critical opinion than was possible in the Riverside edition. However, full surveys of critical opinions may be even less necessary today than they were in 1987, since the bibliographical resources now available (both in print and on-line) are greatly expanded from what they were even a dozen or so years ago. Nevertheless, the new references are selected with an intention to reflect the varieties of approaches in the critical works of the past decade or so and to direct students to the most useful and accessible of those works.

The notes should be frequently consulted, even by beginning readers. Page glosses are provided to explain difficult words and constructions, and they usually suffice for a first reading, but some matters necessary even to an initial understanding of the texts require more explanation than brief glosses allow. These are ordinarily indicated in the glosses by "see n.," directing the reader to the relevant entry in the Explanatory Notes. Even when there is no such indication, the beginning reader as well as the more advanced student will profit from consulting these notes.

ACKNOWLEDGMENTS

THIS VOLUME is, of course, almost totally dependent on the work of the contributors to The Riverside Chaucer whose notes have been adapted for this edition; acknowledgments to their works are made in the text. However, special thanks are due to those who supplied corrections and suggestions for this edition: J. A. Burrow, Vincent J. DiMarco, Warren S. Ginsberg, Douglas Gray, John Reidy, Sharon Hiltz Romino, V. J. Scattergood, M. Teresa Tavoramina, and Siegfried Wenzel. I am especially indebted to C. David Benson and Florence H. Ridley, who generously supplied materials for sets of notes beyond those that they originally wrote.

I owe thanks as well to Henry Ansgar Kelly, who kindly shared with me some of his recent works, and to Traugott Lawler for corrections he has supplied over the years that are incorporated in this volume. Stephen B. Partridge, whose help was crucial to the production of *The Riverside Chaucer,* was again most helpful indeed, providing me with the latest version of his study of the glosses in the manuscripts of the Tales (which is soon to appear as a book).

For help in the final stages of preparing this edition, I am indebted to Scott-Morgan Straker and Gustavo P. Secchi, whose learning and hard work cleared the notes of many errors. So too did the patience and expertise of the staff at Houghton Mifflin, most especially Carla Thompson and Dean Johnson.

With all this help one would expect the following text to be flawless. I am keenly aware that is not the case and that the errors remaining are all my own.

L. D. B.

Introduction

CHAUCER'S LIFE

Chaucer's Life was written for The Riverside Chaucer *by Martin M. Crow and Virginia E. Leland. It has been slightly condensed and occasionally revised for use in this volume.*

IN COMPARISON with other major English writers of his time, Chaucer left abundant records of his life. We have no official documents for the life of the author of *Piers Plowman* or for the *Gawain*-poet; records of Gower's life are few and confused. But Chaucer, because he was a public servant, can be traced in the records of his offices. Publication of *Chaucer Life-Records* in 1966 brought together the 493 known items and provided a substantial basis for a Chaucer biography. These records of official acts rarely touch on his personal affairs and never mention his poetry; they do not give the year of his birth or the exact date of his marriage or death. But they do document a useful and eventful life.

Chaucer was a soldier, an esquire of the king's household, a member of diplomatic missions, a controller of customs, a justice of the peace, a member of Parliament, the clerk of the king's works in charge of building and repair at ten royal residences, and a forest official. On the king's business he traveled over much of southeast England, to France a number of times, to Spain, and at least twice to Italy. Chaucer yet found time to write thousands of lines, among them some of the best poetry in English.

The Chaucer Family

Chaucer came from a well-to-do merchant family that had lived for several generations in Ipswich, some seventy miles northeast of London. The city exported wool to Flanders and imported wine from France. The family were vintners, wholesale dealers in wine, and also held positions in the customs service. As often happened in medieval families, they did not always use the same surname. Geoffrey Chaucer's paternal great-grandfather was called Andrew de Dinnington; Andrew's son, Robert Malyn le Chaucer; Robert's son, John Chaucer. The name Chaucer, from the French, meant maker of shoes or hose; but none of Chaucer's ancestors was, so far as is known, a shoemaker or a hosier.

By the late thirteenth century Robert Chaucer, the grandfather, and his wife Mary had settled in London. Prosperous people, they continued to hold property in Ipswich. In 1324, John, son of Robert and Mary, was kidnapped by an aunt, who intended to marry him to her daughter in order to keep the Ipswich holdings in the family. Instead, the twelve-year-old boy was freed; the aunt and her accomplices went to prison and paid a heavy fine, proof that they were wealthy.

John later married Agnes, daughter of one John Copton and niece of Hamo de Copton, "moneyer" at the mint in the Tower of London. The couple continued to accumulate property. After Hamo's death in 1349, a plague year, Agnes inherited, with Hamo's other London property, twenty-four shops and two gardens. In the same year, John Chaucer inherited property from his half brother, Thomas Heyron. John and Agnes were, then, owners of substantial London property. John Chaucer was a vintner, as his father, stepfather, and half brother had been; like his father, stepfather, and cousins, he also held positions in the customs service.

Geoffrey Chaucer's parentage is clearly established; he described himself in a deed of 19 June 1381 as "son of John Chaucer, vintner, of London." But the date and place of his birth are not precisely known. For the date, the clearest evidence comes from his deposition of 15 October 1386 in the famous Scrope-Grosvenor trial (discussed below). There he testified that he was forty years old "et plus" (and more), making the date of his birth no later than 1345. Some witnesses in that case guessed inaccurately at their ages; but Chaucer added a verifiable statement that supports his testimony. He said that he had borne arms twenty-seven years; he had in fact served in France in the campaign of 1359. It is usual, then, to accept a birth date in the early 1340s.

Fourteenth- and fifteenth-century records tell something of Chaucer's descendants. A London lawsuit of Michaelmas term, 1396, identified "Thomas Chaucer, esquire, son of Geoffrey Chaucer, esquire." Additional evidence that Thomas was the son of Geoffrey rests upon a statement by Dr. Gascoigne, chancellor of Oxford and a neighbor of Thomas, and on the use by Thomas of a seal with Geoffrey Chaucer's coat of arms and name. A retinue roll compiled at Carmarthen Castle in 1403 lists Thomas Chaucer with Lewis Chaucer. Lewis seems to have been the *lyte Lowys my sone* of the *tendir age of ten year* for whom in 1391 the poet composed *A Treatise on the Astrolabe*. Two presumed daughters of Geoffrey Chaucer are also sometimes mentioned, Elizabeth Chaucy, a nun at Barking in 1381, and Agnes, an attendant at the coronation of Henry IV; but the records do not clearly identify them as daughters of the poet.

Nothing more is known of Lewis, Agnes, or Elizabeth, but many records attest to the distinguished career of Thomas Chaucer, as he became one of the wealthiest and most influential men in England. Enriched by marriage to a great heiress and by annuities from John of Gaunt, Richard II, and Henry IV, he served as chief butler to four kings, envoy to France, and, often, speaker of the House of Commons. His daughter Alice married as her third husband William de la Pole, Duke of Suffolk; their grandson John, Earl of Lincoln, was designated heir to the throne of his uncle, Richard III. Richard's defeat and death at Bosworth Field in 1485 effec-

tively ended the possibility that a nephew of his could gain the crown. But John de la Pole and, after him, three of his brothers continued to assert the claim until the last of them died in about 1539, a prisoner in the Tower of London, thus ending the line of Chaucer's male descendants.

Chaucer's Early Home and Youth

Though Chaucer's birthplace is unknown, it is known that his parents, Agnes and John Chaucer, held property in Vintry Ward, one of the two wealthiest wards in medieval London, and in what the sixteenth-century antiquary John Stow called "the middes and hart of the city." One Chaucer "tenement" (property holding, not tenement in the modern sense) lay on Thames Street, which ran parallel to the river and a block north. It was largely inhabited by vintners, since wine landed at the quays on the Thames could easily be brought to their cellars for storage. Some of London's leading merchants, among the richest men in the city, lived in the ward as well. Two of them, John Stodeye and Henry Picard, served as mayors and lent thousands of pounds to the king. John Chaucer's name is associated with theirs in such records as wills and deeds. Nobles as well as merchants lived in Vintry Ward. Queen Philippa owned a dwelling there called Tower Royal; after her death it passed to her daughter-in-law, mother of Richard II, Joan of Kent, who took refuge there in 1381. Among the people living nearby were Gascon wine merchants, an Italian family, and Flemings; London in Chaucer's boyhood was a cosmopolitan city.

Wills of neighbors, deeds, and inventories give some idea of the probable plan and furnishings of the Chaucer home. Above the cellars were the hall (not a passageway, but the principal room), the kitchen, a latrine, and upper rooms called "solars." They were furnished comfortably with hangings for the walls and cushions for the benches, and such luxuries as heavy silver pitchers and cups engraved with the owners' coats of arms.

No school records for Chaucer have survived, but it is possible to account for some of the knowledge of Latin classics shown in his works. London merchants' sons in his time could receive a good education. Near the Chaucer home on Thames Street were three schools, among them the almonry school of St. Paul's Cathedral, which has preserved the inventory of books left in 1358 by a schoolmaster, William de Ravenstone, for the use of the pupils. As well as Latin grammars, treatises on theology, and a few music textbooks, there were classics—Virgil's *Georgics;* Claudian's *Rape of Proserpina,* cited three times in Chaucer's poems; ten books of Lucan; the *Thebaid* of Statius, quoted at the beginning of The Knight's Tale and partly summarized in *Troilus and Criseyde;* and the *Metamorphoses* of Ovid, Chaucer's favorite classical Latin source. Chaucer paid tribute, near the end of *Troilus and Criseyde* (5.1792) to five of the great poets of antiquity, *Virgile, Ovide, Omer, Lucan, and Stace.* Chaucer probably did not know Homer directly, but, as Ravenstone's bequest makes clear, works of the four others were available at St. Paul's school.

The earliest known document actually naming Geoffrey Chaucer is a fragmentary household account book, June 1356 to April 1359, kept for Elizabeth de Burgh, Countess of Ulster and wife of Lionel, a son of Edward III. It records purchases in April 1357 for Geoffrey Chaucer—a short jacket, a pair of red and black hose (?), and a pair of shoes; and, "for necessaries at Christmas," there was recorded a gift to him of 2 shillings, 6 pence. The relative modesty of the gifts suggests that Chaucer was among the youngest and least important of the retainers of the countess, perhaps in his early teens, and perhaps a page.

Life in the countess's household would offer a young attendant a rich variety of experiences if he accompanied her on her almost constant travels. During the time covered by the accounts, she spent Christmas at Hatfield for a royal hunting party, along with her young brother-in-law John of Gaunt, who later became the richest and most powerful man in England; she purchased mourning in London for the funeral of the dowager queen, Isabella; she visited a royal relative at the convent of Stratford-atte-Bowe (where the Prioress learned her French; General Prologue I.125); and she was a guest at King Edward's Great Feast of St. George at Windsor, the king's favorite castle.

Journeys and the Royal Court

From the household of the countess Chaucer seems to have followed her husband, Prince Lionel, into the king's army. In September 1359 King Edward and his sons, with a large expeditionary force, were invading France. The king, who held King John of France prisoner, hoped to take the city of Reims and to be crowned king of France in Reims Cathedral, traditional site of the coronation of French kings. Chaucer, according to his testimony in the Scrope-Grosvenor case (see below), was at the town of "Retters" (Réthel), near Reims, which Edward was besieging in December and early January 1359–60. Chaucer testified that he was captured, but the captivity was short. By 1 March 1360 the king had contributed 16 pounds to help pay Chaucer's ransom, and he was free. Edward's forces were at that date in the village of Brétigny, in the vicinity of Chartres. The campaign had brought Chaucer within sight of the great cathedrals of Reims and probably Chartres.

The last record of Chaucer in the service of Prince Lionel dates from the peace negotiations at Calais in October 1360, when the prince paid Chaucer for carrying letters from Calais to England.

The expedition and messenger service of 1359–60 were the first of many journeys and commissions for Chaucer. No records have yet been found for him, however, for the years between 1360 and 1366. After the gap in the records the first document concerning Chaucer is a safe-conduct for the period of 22 February to 24 May 1366, granted to Chaucer by Charles II (Charles the Bad) of Navarre; it permitted "Geffroy de Chausserre" with three companions, their servants, horses, and luggage, to travel through Navarre. Perhaps Chaucer was on a pilgrimage, like many others (and like the Wife of Bath; General Prologue I.466), to the popular shrine of Compostela *in Galice at Seint-Jame;* the customary pilgrimage route crossed Navarre. Or Chaucer may have been sent by the Black Prince to recall English mercenaries from the forces of Henry of Trastamara, against whom the prince was mounting an expedition. Another possible explanation for Chaucer's journey is that it was connected with arrangements for the later passage of English troops through Navarre into Castile, where in April of 1367 the prince was to win the battle of Nájera and restore to his throne Pedro the Cruel, called in The Monk's Tale (VII.2375) *O noble, O worthy Petro, glorie of Spayne.*

Other events of 1366 may have been more important to Chaucer than the Navarrese journey: the evidence indicates that Chaucer's father died in that year and that Chaucer married. The last record of John Chaucer is dated 16 January 1366, when he and his wife Agnes signed a deed; on 13 July 1366 Agnes was referred to as the wife of Bartholomew atte Chapel. Chaucer's marriage is implied by the record of a grant, on 12 September 1366, of an exchequer annuity of 10 marks to one Philippa Chaucer, damoiselle of the queen. This annuity was often collected for her "by the hands of" Geoffrey Chaucer. Philippa may have been a member of the Ulster household during Chaucer's service there; the accounts note in 1356 and 1358 clothing bought for one "Philippa Pan." Chaucer's wife seems to have been the daughter of Sir Gilles, called "Paon," de Roet, a knight of Hainault and one of Queen Philippa's countrymen who had accompanied her to England, and who became Guienne King of Arms, that is, chief herald of Aquitaine, when that region was ruled by the Black Prince. Another of the Roet daughters, Katherine Swynford, was for more than twenty years the mistress of John of Gaunt; he married her in 1396. Philippa Chaucer was in attendance on three members of the royal family: King Edward's daughter-in-law, Elizabeth; the queen, Philippa; and, after the queen's death, another daughter-in-law, Constance of Castile, the second wife of John of Gaunt. As Philippa Chaucer had received a royal annuity in 1366, so she also received in 1372 an annuity from the revenues of John of Gaunt.

Geoffrey Chaucer is first recorded as a member of the royal household on 20 June 1367, when he received a royal annuity. One record of that date described him as *valettus;* another of the same date called him *esquier*. At any rate, he was one of a group of some forty young men in the king's service, not personal servants, but expected to make themselves useful around the court. Like Chaucer, other esquires of Edward III did not come from the great noble families. They were often sent about England on the king's business, sometimes performed military service, and occasionally journeyed overseas on the king's behalf. In return, they received rewards such as were given to Chaucer: summer and winter robes, daily wages, annuities, and appointments to office. Geoffrey and Philippa Chaucer, among others, received liveries of mourning for Queen Philippa in 1369.

During the years when Chaucer was in the king's service, he may also have been studying among the lawyers of the Inner Temple, one of the Inns of Court. The tradition that he had received such training arose from a statement by Thomas Speght in his Chaucer edition of 1598 that "Master Buckley" had seen an

Inner Temple record "where Geffrye Chaucer was fined two shillings for beatinge a Franciscane Fryer in fletestreate." It is now known that Master Buckley was at that time the keeper of the Inner Temple records, and that the fine was a customary amount. His testimony is accepted as very probably true. Mention of the Manciple (General Prologue I.567) and of the career of the Man of Law (General Prologue I.309–30) seems to show familiarity with the Inns of Court and the lawyers there. In addition, Chaucer's later official positions, as controller of the customs and clerk of the king's works, demanded that he keep records in Chancery hand, and use French and Latin legal formulas, skills taught in the Inns of Court.

During this time Chaucer may have been experimenting with various popular verse forms, in French as well as in English. By their nature, most of them were likely ephemeral, but recent publication of fifteen French lyrics, with the siglum "Ch," from a fourteenth-century French manuscript (Wimsatt, *Chaucer and the Poems of "Ch"*) raises the intriguing possibility that these poems might be by Chaucer. Even if they are not, they represent the kind of French verse Chaucer may well have written during his early years at court.

While he was the king's esquire and, presumably, studying among the lawyers, Chaucer also made a number of journeys overseas. Two years after the Navarre safe-conduct of 1366, he "passed at Dover" on 17 July 1368 and was absent from England for at most 106 days; in that length of time the king's envoys had been able to make the journey to Rome and return. It has, accordingly, been suggested that Chaucer was sent as a messenger to Prince Lionel in Milan. There, in May 1368, the prince had married a daughter of the immensely powerful Visconti family, despots of Milan. Chaucer may, however, have gone no farther than to France or Flanders on this journey.

The Book of the Duchess, Chaucer's first major poem, belongs to this period. It is an elegy for Blanche, Duchess of Lancaster, John of Gaunt's first wife, who died, it is now believed, on 12 September 1368. The duke remarried in 1371; but he continued to remember Blanche, paying 30 pounds on 12 September 1379 for memorial masses on the anniversary of her death and ten silver marks in 1382 to each of the chaplains chanting masses at her tomb in St. Paul's. In his will of 1398 he directed that he be buried beside his "very dear late consort, Blanche." It seems significant, then, that on 13 June 1374 John of Gaunt granted a life annuity of 10 pounds to Chaucer "in consideration of the services rendered by Chaucer to the grantor" and "by the grantee's wife Philippa to the grantor's late mother and to his consort." A few days later, on 18 June 1374, the duke ordered alabaster from which the master mason, Henry Yevele, was to erect a tomb for Blanche. It is clear that in 1374 John of Gaunt was remembering Blanche; by his grant to Chaucer he may have been rewarding the author of *The Book of the Duchess.*

Another Lancaster connection was recorded in 1369, when Chaucer received 10 pounds as one of the members of the king's household who were to accompany John of Gaunt on a military expedition to Picardy (where the Squire of the General Prologue [I.86] served part of his military apprenticeship). There is no record of Chaucer's part in the 1369 campaign. Nor is it known what was the king's business that took Chaucer to "parts beyond the seas" in 1370.

Having made four journeys abroad in four years, 1366–70, Chaucer undertook in 1372–73 a commission that gave him his first recorded contact with Italy. He accompanied two Italian merchants, Giovanni di Mari and Sir Jacopo di Provano, then residents of London, to negotiate on the king's behalf with the doge and people of Genoa, who wanted the use of an English port. The business discussed may have been partly military; Giovanni di Mari, Chaucer's associate, was in the same year hiring Genoese mercenaries for King Edward.

The commission given Chaucer before his departure did not name Florence; yet the expense account submitted on his return, 23 May 1373, recorded treating of the affairs of the king "in Genoa and Florence." The visit to Florence has seemed significant to Chaucer scholars because Petrarch and Boccaccio, still living, were in that region. Chaucer, if he did not meet them, could hardly have avoided hearing a great deal about them and about Dante, who, though he had died in exile fifty years earlier, was now revered in Florence. Quite possibly Chaucer obtained manuscripts of some of these authors' works on this visit. It is customary in this connection to mention the reference to Petrarch in The Clerk's Prologue (IV.31–33), but with the warning that it is the Clerk, and not Chaucer, who claims to have heard the story in The Clerk's Tale from Petrarch.

The journey of 1372–73, it was once thought, gave Chaucer his first acquaintance with the language and literature of Italy; but it is now agreed that Chaucer might well have been chosen for that mission because he already knew some Italian. The hundred days allowed by the 1372–73 journey would hardly have given Chaucer time to learn a language. London in Chaucer's youth provided better opportunities; many Italian families lived in London, some near the Chaucer house in the Vintry; Chaucer's father and grandfather had business dealings with Italians. In any event, Italy had become, by 1373, a part of Chaucer's firsthand experience.

A few months after his return from Florence, he had occasion to deal with Italians again. He was sent by the king to deliver a Genoese ship, detained at Dartmouth, to her master, a merchant of Genoa and an associate of Chaucer's fellow envoy, Giovanni di Mari. This commission has been taken as additional proof of Chaucer's knowledge of Italian. (It is also of interest because the piratical Shipman of the General Prologue [I.389] was *of Dertemouthe.*)

Other Journeys and the Customhouse

Chaucer seems to have had good fortune during the year after his return from Italy. On 23 April 1374, St. George's Day, while the king was celebrating the feast at Windsor, he made an unusual grant to Chaucer. Almost no other business was done on that holiday, but King Edward granted the poet a gallon pitcher of wine daily for life. The wine, it is sometimes suggested, may have been the reward for a poem presented to the king during the festivities. Chaucer collected the wine until the death of Edward III in 1377; Richard II, on his accession, immediately confirmed the gift and, on 18 April 1378, permitted Chaucer to commute it for an annuity of 20 marks, a respectable income.

In 1374, also, Chaucer obtained a home in London. On 10 May, Adam de Bury, mayor of London, and the aldermen leased to Chaucer, rent-free for life, the dwelling over Aldgate, one of the six gates in the city wall. Chaucer was to keep the apartment in good repair, to allow entry for purposes of defense in time of war, and he was not to sublet. Such a lease was not unusual; the city owned dwellings over other gates and sometimes leased them to city officials. Ralph Strode, Chaucer's friend, had a similar apartment over Aldersgate. Adam de Bury, whose name appears on Chaucer's lease, had been an associate of Chaucer's father, had been sent abroad on a mission by the king, and had held a customs office himself. It was once suggested that Chaucer owed the lease to the influence of King Edward's mistress, Alice Perrers, who owned property near Aldgate; but it is more likely that Adam de Bury, because of his contact with the Chaucer family, did, as the lease states, make the arrangement.

The dwelling over Aldgate became, as it turned out, very convenient, just a few minutes walk from the customhouse, where Chaucer was to be employed for the next twelve years. On 8 June 1374 Edward III appointed Chaucer controller of the export tax, or customs, on wool, sheepskins, and leather, in the port of London, and of the subsidy, a heavier tax on the same merchandise. He was to receive an annual salary of 10 pounds. Chaucer, the son and grandson of men who had held minor offices in the customs service, was taking up a family occupation.

His task was essential. Because wool was England's principal export, much depended on the wool customs and subsidy. These taxes had helped to finance King Edward's wars in the 1340s and 1350s and were paying for the smaller military expeditions of the 1370s and 1380s. Wool taxes paid the daily costs of government, including, often, royal grants and annuities, and supported the costly court of King Edward and, later, of his grandson, Richard II.

As controller, Chaucer worked with the collectors, the nominal heads of the customs organization for the port of London. The collectors were merchants and were making the king large loans on the security of the revenue from the customs. Among these collector-creditors while Chaucer was in office were the immensely rich Nicholas Brembre, John Philipot, and William Walworth, neighbors of the Chaucer family in Vintry Ward. These three men were leaders of the politically powerful victualers' guilds, *riche and selleres of vitaille,* like the friends of the Friar (General Prologue I.248). At the customhouse the collectors were expected to record each day's shipments and the amount of customs or subsidy collected. The controller, Chaucer, kept the "counter-rolls," independent lists against which theirs were checked. The controller had to monitor the honesty and efficiency of the collectors. Under these conditions, Chaucer's position at the customhouse demanded tact and astuteness.

He had a heavy responsibility because customs receipts while he was in office were large, averaging over a ten-year period 24,600 pounds a year. Dealing with such sums, the controller was, reasonably enough, expected to keep the rolls "with his own hand" and to exercise the office "in his own person." At the end of the fiscal year, at Michaelmas, controller and collectors were summoned to the "view," or audit, a complex and arduous process.

An incident connected with the customs gave Chaucer a sizable reward. He was granted, on 12 July 1376, the value (71 pounds, 4 shillings, and 6 pence) of wool forfeited by one John Kent, who had exported it without paying customs. The sum was important, more than seven times Chaucer's annual salary.

Chaucer seems to have been successful as controller. He was appointed on 20 April 1382 to the additional controllership of the petty customs, import and export duties on wine and other merchandise not assessed under the wool customs. He managed to collect his annual salary regularly, a considerable feat in itself. He remained in office twelve years, longer than any other controller of his time; and he received in most years an additional reward for his "unremitting labor and diligence."

One detail from his experience at the customhouse explains the background of the line from the General Prologue (I.277) in which we learn that the Merchant wants the sea protected from pirates *bitwixe Middelburgh and Orewelle:* customed merchandise was, after 1384, shipped to a central "staple" at Middelburg across the sea from Orwell, the seaport for the Chaucers' home city of Ipswich.

While he held the office as controller, Chaucer was pursuing his literary interests. According to the Eagle in *The House of Fame* (653–57), *Geffrey,* when he had made his *rekenynges,* went to his house to sit *at another book.* Presumably the reckonings were at the customhouse, and Chaucer went home to Aldgate to read and write. It is generally believed that during the years when he lived over Aldgate Chaucer was writing major poems: *The Parliament of Fowls, The House of Fame,* and *Troilus and Criseyde.* In addition he was translating the *Consolation of Philosophy* of Boethius from the Latin. It has been observed that Chaucer was most prolific as a writer when he was apparently most busy with other affairs.

But he was too experienced an envoy to be allowed to devote himself entirely to his books and to the customhouse. In 1376, the year when Edward III and his heir, the Black Prince, were both dying, Sir John Burley, knight, and Chaucer, esquire of the king, received payment for journeys "on secret business of the king." The records do not show where they went or what matters they discussed. During 1377 Chaucer was sent overseas several times on royal business. In February he and Sir Thomas Percy were advanced sums for a mission to Flanders, also described as "the king's secret business." But the expense accounts submitted on their return do not mention Flanders. Instead, they note payment to Chaucer for travel to Paris and Montreuil, 17 February to 25 March, and to "parts of France," 30 April to 26 June 1377. The French poet Eustache Deschamps, who in 1386 was to send Chaucer a well-known ballade in his praise, may have been in Paris at that time.

According to Froissart, Chaucer was a member of a mission attempting to negotiate a marriage between Richard and a French princess; but Froissart is frequently inaccurate, and no known English record names Chaucer as a member of such a mission until after the death of Edward III, 21 June 1377. In fact, the only official note concerning the purpose of Chaucer's series of journeys to France is dated 6 March 1381. It speaks of Chaucer as having been in France "to treat of peace in time of Edward III and in time of Richard II to discuss a marriage between the king and a daughter [not named] of his adversary of France." A French marriage did not take place, and war with France was renewed.

Chaucer's next mission gave him another opportunity to visit Italy. He and Sir Edward Berkeley received funds on 28 May 1378 from "the king's treasurers for war," William Walworth and John Philipot, collectors of the London customs, for a journey to Lombardy to discuss "certain business concerning the king's war" with Bernabò Visconti, lord of Milan, and Sir John Hawkwood, the Englishman who was Bernabò's son-in-law and commander of mercenaries. Official records do not give the result of these secret negotiations, but they do indicate that Lombardy maintained relations with England. Exchequer accounts of December 1378 show King Richard's rich gifts to messengers from Bernabò and Hawkwood.

For Chaucer the journey meant a renewal of his acquaintance with Italian literature. The Visconti owned famous libraries and had been patrons of Petrarch. The strong impression they made on Chaucer was recorded in his poems. Bernabò himself, *God of delit, and scourge of Lumbardye,* appears in The Monk's Tale (VII.2399–2400). Observation of Bernabò and his brother, notorious tyrants, may have suggested to Chaucer the phrase *tirauntz of Lumbardye* (LGWPro F 374).

By 19 September 1378 Chaucer had returned to London. He did not go overseas again until his work at the customhouse had ended.

While he was still controller, his name appeared in a record which is not yet fully understood. One Cecilia Chaumpaigne, daughter of a London baker, William Chaumpaigne, and his wife Agnes, acknowledged, on 4 May 1380, a release to Geoffrey Chaucer of all kinds of actions (i.e., legal procedures seeking redress) in respect of her *raptus* as well as of any other matter. The definition of the word *raptus* in the context of this 1380 incident has been discussed repeatedly. It could have meant physical rape; or it could have meant abduction, as it did in the account of John Chaucer's kidnapping and in the case Chaucer was appointed to investigate in 1387, the abduction of a young heiress, Isabella atte Halle. The record, however, is clear; it means that Cecilia Chaumpaigne clears Chaucer of all responsibility. Additional facts, equally ambiguous, further complicate interpretation of these events. On 30 June 1380 Robert Goodchild, cutler, and John Grove, armorer, citizens of London, acknowledged a general release to Chaucer of all actions of law. On the same day Cecilia Chaumpaigne acknowledged a similar release to Goodchild and Grove. Then, in a recognizance dated 2 July 1380 Grove agreed to pay Cecilia at Michaelmas 10 pounds, a sum equivalent to Chaucer's annual salary at the customhouse. It has been suggested that Grove served as an intermediary to bring about a settlement between Chaucer and Cecilia. It has also been suggested that Grove, because of his financial involvement, was the principal in the case and Chaucer only an accessory.

Students of medieval English law disagree on the interpretation of the records. What is undeniable is the high social standing of the witnesses to Chaucer's release: Sir William Beauchamp, chamberlain of the king's household; Sir William Neville, admiral of the king's fleet; Neville's friend, Sir John Clanvowe, author of a religious treatise; John Philipot, collector of customs; and Richard Morel, a merchant and member of Parliament who lived near Chaucer in Aldgate Ward.

The next year was marked by an event of much wider significance than the Chaumpaigne case: the Rising of 1381, the Peasants' Revolt. No record tells us whether Chaucer was at Aldgate when thousands of rebels entered London through that gate or whether he saw them burn John of Gaunt's palace, the Savoy, or whether he saw them behead Simon Sudbury, archbishop of Canterbury and chancellor of the kingdom. A number of the victims came from Vintry Ward, where Chaucer still owned his father's house; they included Richard Lyons, merchant, who had profited by lending thousands of pounds to the king; and scores of Flemings, whose headless bodies were, according to the chroniclers, left piled in the streets near the river. When the Nun's Priest speaks casually of the noise made by the mob *whan that they wolden any Flemyng kille* (NPT VII.3396), Chaucer was talking of events that may once have been of a good deal more than casual importance to him.

The mob was brought under control with the help of John Philipot, Nicholas Brembre, and William Walworth, with all of whom Chaucer had worked at the customhouse. These "gode and worthi men of the city of London," as they were called in a popular account of the revolt, were immediately knighted by the king.

Chaucer, on 19 June 1381, four days after the suppression of the revolt, quit-claimed his father's holdings on Thames Street to Henry Herbury, a merchant and a man of means.

Chaucer may have been gradually ending his connections with London. He was beginning to entrust the work of the customs to deputies. The terms of his appointment as controller of the petty customs on 20 April 1382 allowed him to name a deputy. During his earlier absences, in France, 1377, and in Italy, 1378, his work had been carried on by deputies. He was permitted to employ a deputy at the wool customs from 23 June to 1 November 1383, and again for a month beginning 25 November 1384. Finally, on 17 February 1385 he was given leave to appoint a permanent deputy.

Chaucer and Kent

The changes at the customhouse have been taken to suggest that Chaucer had already left London for nearby Kent, a county with which he had had earlier associations. In 1375 King Edward had granted him the wardship of two Kentish heirs, William Soles and Edmund Staplegate. Such wardships, often granted to the king's retainers, could be lucrative. Staplegate's father had left large holdings in Canterbury, and Chaucer's profit from the estate was 104 pounds.

By 1388, records described Chaucer as "of Kent." He may have been living in Greenwich. The Host's reference in the Reeve's Prologue (I.3907) to *Grenewych, ther many a shrewe* [rascal] *is inne* has often been taken to mean that Chaucer himself was living in Greenwich and making one of his customary self-deprecating jokes.

Knowledge of two official positions Chaucer held in the 1380s strengthens the theory that he was then living in Kent. He was added on 12 October 1385 to a sixteen-member commission of peace for Kent. Other members were Sir Simon Burley, the Black Prince's friend, sometimes called the most influential man in the kingdom of the prince's son, King Richard II; representatives of leading Kentish families, Cobham, Culpepper, and Devereux; and six sergeants-at-law, men of the same high legal rank as Chaucer's Man of Law (General Prologue I.309). Membership on a Kentish peace commission in 1385–86 entailed a special responsibility because the French were at that time threatening to invade the south coast of England. In 1386 Cobham and Devereux were also appointed members of a "great and continual council given comprehensive powers over all matters of state" in the kingdom. Chaucer remained a member of the peace commission, with one brief and apparently accidental break, until 15 July 1389, a few days after he had been given another position.

Even more important than Chaucer's appointment as a justice of the peace was his election to Parliament in 1386 as one of the two "knights of the shire" (members of the House of Commons) to represent Kent. The Parliament to which he was sent was a turning point in King Richard's reign and in the history of medieval England. When it convened in October, troops had been called up to defend London against the threatened French invasion. But there were no funds to pay them; they were wandering the London streets searching for food and loot. In the sessions of Parliament, powerful noblemen, led by the king's youngest uncle, Thomas of Gloucester, attacked the chancellor and the treasurer of the realm and compelled Richard to dismiss them. Gloucester and his allies may have threatened to depose Richard if he did not comply. Though knights of the shire took a prominent part in the attack, there is no record that Chaucer was more than a quiet observer. He had ties with both sides.

While he was at Westminster attending Parliament, Chaucer, on 15 October 1386, gave his often-cited deposition in the Scrope-Grosvenor case. He was testifying that his friends, the Scrope family, had long borne the coat of arms that the Grosvenors were attempting to make theirs. Chaucer had, he said, seen the device on Scrope armor at the time of the siege of Reims in 1359–60.

Personal Matters

One of the first tributes to Chaucer as poet came from France in 1385–86. Though France at that time was preparing to invade England, Chaucer's friend, Sir Lewis Clifford, returned from France bringing Chaucer a poem of generous praise, written by the leading French poet of the time, Eustache Deschamps. Deschamps's ballade, with the refrain "great translator, noble Geoffrey Chaucer," stressed Chaucer's role as a cultural intermediary who had made *Le roman de la rose* accessible to English readers. The poem praised Chaucer extravagantly for his brevity of speech, his wisdom, his practical learning. Deschamps himself, he wrote, would be only a nettle in Chaucer's garden of poetry.

At about the same time, two English writers were commenting on Chaucer's poetry. In late 1385, Thomas Usk, a London clerk, in his prose *Testament of Love* called Chaucer "the noble philosophical poete." He declared that Chaucer surpassed all other poets in "goodnes of manliche speche" and in sound sense. John Gower's praise in his *Confessio amantis* (1390), in which he remarked that Chaucer had filled the land with "ditees" and "songes glade," was less emphatic. The remark disappears in the course of Gower's later revision of the *Confessio*, but for structural reasons, it is now thought, not because of a quarrel between the poets.

On 19 February 1386, Philippa Chaucer was admitted to the fraternity of Lincoln Cathedral. In the same company were the future Henry IV, Henry of Derby, the oldest son of John of Gaunt, and Thomas Swynford and John Beaufort, sons of Philippa's sister, Katherine Swynford. Both John of Gaunt and the Swynford family had been long associated with the cathedral.

Membership in the fraternity was something of a custom with the royal family. King Richard and Queen Anne themselves were enrolled on 26 March 1387 when they visited the cathedral, site of the shrine of the boy martyr, St. Hugh of Lincoln, who is mentioned in The Prioress's Tale (VII.684). It has been argued that this tale was first read on that occasion.

In the late 1380s an important period of Chaucer's life came to an end. On 5 October 1386 he gave up the lease of the Aldgate dwelling, where he had lived for twelve years. New controllers took his positions at the customhouse. Philippa Chaucer, to whom he had been married for at least twenty-one years, disappeared from the records after 18 June 1387 and is presumed to have died. When Chaucer was given a safe-conduct on 5 July 1387 to accompany his friend, Sir William Beauchamp, to Calais, he was making the last of a series of journeys overseas that he had begun in 1359, almost thirty years before. He had apparently reached a low point in his career.

Chaucer lived safely through 1388 when the king's enemies, the Appellants, who dominated Parliament, caused the execution of three men with whom Chaucer had worked, Sir Nicholas Brembre of the customhouse, and two members of the Kent peace commission, Sir Simon Burley and Chief Justice Robert Tresilian. Whether or not Chaucer saw them moving through the London streets to their deaths, he described such a scene memorably in The Man of Law's Tale (II.645–50):

Have ye nat seyn somtyme a pale face,
Among a prees, of hym that hath be lad
Toward his deeth, wher as hym gat no grace,
And swich a colour in his face hath had
Men myghte knowe his face that was bistad
Amonges alle the faces in that route?

Chaucer himself seems to have been harmed during this time only by suits for debt. Twice, 16 and 25 April 1388, he was sued by John Churchman, collector of the customs at London. It is, therefore, sometimes believed that when he made over his annuities to a certain John Scalby on 1 May 1388, he was exchanging future income for cash with which to settle present debts.

Chaucer was not entirely free from official duties; he was still a member of the Kent peace commission.

But between 1386 and 1389 he had leisure in which he could work on the General Prologue of *The Canterbury Tales* and a number of the tales themselves.

Clerk of the Works and Forester

New official tasks, however, soon demanded his attention. King Richard, who had regained power in May 1389, appointed Chaucer on 12 July 1389 to what was possibly his most arduous position: he became clerk of the king's works. He had responsibility for construction and repair at ten royal residences and other holdings of the king. One was the Tower of London, serving at that time as palace, fortress, prison, armory, mint, and place of safekeeping for records. Among other "works" he oversaw were Westminster Palace, center of government as well as occasional dwelling for the royal family; the castle of Berkhamsted; and seven of Richard's favorite manors, including Eltham and Sheen, mentioned in *The Legend of Good Women* (Pro F 497). He was also overseer of hunting lodges in royal forests, the mews at Charing Cross for the king's falcons, parks (hunting preserves), gardens, mills, pools, and fences. He had purveyors who assisted him at most of these places and a controller who checked his accounts as he had checked those of the customs collectors.

Chaucer's clerkship represented a heavier and more direct responsibility than did the controllership. He was not dealing with such large sums of money as he had checked at the customhouse, but he supervised a great number of craftsmen and arranged for the purchase, transportation, and storage of large quantities of supplies. He had to find and pay the men, pursue them if they ran away, and, if necessary, imprison them; he had to choose, purchase, and store building materials, and to see that they were not stolen. Chaucer's wages, at 2 shillings a day, amounted to more than three and one-half times his base salary at the customhouse.

The importance of Chaucer's position is suggested by the achievements of the king's craftsmen on his payroll. One of them, master mason Henry Yeveley, planned the rebuilding of the naves of Westminster Abbey and Canterbury Cathedral, designed the tombs of Richard II and Queen Anne in the Abbey, and devised the rebuilding of Westminster Hall, sometimes called "the handsomest building in Europe."

Special occasions made special demands. After a storm that caused great damage along the Thames,

Chaucer was appointed on 12 March 1390 to a royal commission "of walls and ditches" for the extensive marshes between Woolwich and Greenwich; he may then have been living in the latter town. In May and October of 1390, when King Richard invited knights from overseas to take part in his tournaments, Chaucer was in charge of putting up "scaffolds," seating for the royal and noble spectators, and lists for the combats at Smithfield. Construction of lists in The Knight's Tale (I.1882–84, 1908, 2087–88) has sometimes been compared to Chaucer's task at Smithfield. One of the October guests was to be installed as a Knight of the Garter in St. George's Chapel at Windsor Castle, where the order had been founded; accordingly, on 12 July 1390, Chaucer was commissioned to repair the chapel, described as "ruinous and like to fall to the ground."

No large building projects were under way during Chaucer's clerkship. Average spending by his successors was two and one-half times as great as his. But one useful project, undertaken before Chaucer took office, continued throughout his term and beyond. It was the rebuilding and enlarging of the wharf beside the Tower of London, where wool was brought for customs levy. The wharf repairs and other works near the Tower cost more than half of all the money spent by Chaucer in the works office; and, appropriately, they were paid for by the revenue from wool customs. Chaucer's previous work as controller of customs had brought him daily to the wharf, and he knew well what improvements were needed.

At least once during his clerkship he encountered danger. In early September 1390, probably while traveling from one royal manor to another with money for payrolls, he was attacked by a gang of highwaymen and robbed. The robbers were caught, tried, and convicted. But the legal records differ so widely that it is not possible to determine whether there was one robbery or three; whether the loss was 10 pounds, or 20 pounds, 6 shillings, and 8 pence, or 9 pounds, 43 pence; whether the place was Westminster or Hatcham or the "Foule Oke," a place name or a tree, in Surrey or in Kent. It is certain, however, that Chaucer was not required to repay the king's money.

Chaucer's clerkship of the works ended on 17 June 1391. The robbery, in which he was said to have been wounded, may have caused him to give up the office. Or he may have found the financial situation unsatisfactory; when Chaucer left office, the audit of his account showed more than 87 pounds still owing to him. This was a large sum; it exceeded by 17 pounds the total amount of his wages during the entire term of his appointment.

When Chaucer left the clerkship, another place was waiting for him: at some time before 22 June 1391 he was appointed deputy forester of the royal forest at North Petherton in Somerset. Other royal servants received similar appointments.

The forestership, like Chaucer's earlier positions, was a responsible one, demanding skill in handling money and men, because forests in late medieval England were sources of revenue. Royal forests comprised entire regions that could, and at North Petherton did, include moor, marsh, pastureland, cultivated fields, and villages and their churches, as well as wooded areas. Royal forests yielded many kinds of income, such as fees for pasturing cattle and for allowing swine to feed on acorns and beech mast, and tolls for traveling forest roads.

According to tradition, Chaucer as deputy forester lived at Park House in the forest, though it is not clear whether his duties required that he live there. Wherever he lived, he did not lose touch with the court. In 1393 Chaucer received from King Richard a gift of 10 pounds "for good service." The next year Richard granted him an annuity of 20 pounds. Henry of Derby gave Chaucer fur to trim a gown of scarlet (a fine cloth) during the year 1395–96. In the same year, Chaucer delivered 10 pounds to Henry from the royal exchequer. King Richard, reminded of an earlier grant, certified to Chaucer in 1398 the yearly gift of a tun of wine.

Last Years

The mood of the court changed in 1397. After several years of peace and moderation Richard moved suddenly to take revenge on the Appellants, who had in 1388 caused the exile or death of a group of his friends. The king arrested his enemies, charged them with treason, and caused them to be imprisoned, exiled, or put to death. Henry, John of Gaunt's son, had been one of the Appellants; he was exiled in 1398. When John of Gaunt died in 1399, Richard seized his estates; Henry returned to claim them and took advantage of the opportunity to depose Richard and have himself crowned as Henry IV.

Of Chaucer in these years we know little. We know that his Petherton appointment was renewed, and that he may have taken his last recorded journey. A royal protection was issued on 4 May 1398 to "Geoffrey

Chaucer, our beloved esquire going about divers parts of England on the king's arduous and pressing business."

Henry's accession seems at first glance to have made little difference in Chaucer's life. The poet and his wife had received annuities from Henry's father; Chaucer had written *The Book of the Duchess* as a memorial to Henry's mother; and during the last decade Chaucer had received a gift from Henry himself. As king, Henry renewed the grants Chaucer had received from Richard II and granted an additional 40 marks yearly for life. The envoy of a late poem, The Complaint of Chaucer to His Purse, hailed Henry as true king by right of conquest, birth, and *free eleccion* (line 23), though the Complaint itself suggests that the grants approved by the new king had not yet been paid.

Chaucer now provided himself with a home near the court. On 24 December 1399 he took a fifty-three-year lease of a house near the Lady Chapel of Westminster Abbey, on a site now occupied by the Chapel of King Henry VII. For a few months he collected, or others collected for him, his royal grants: on 21 February and 5 June 1400 he received partial payments of the arrears due on his exchequer annuities. No life records of later date have been found.

The inscription on Chaucer's tomb in Westminster Abbey gives the date of his death as 25 October 1400. The tomb may, however, have been erected as late as 1555, and there is no other evidence as to the exact date of his death. He was buried in the Abbey for several reasons, none of them, so far as we know, related to his being a poet. He had a right to burial there because he was a tenant of the Abbey and a member of the parish. Moreover, commoners who had been royal servants were beginning to be buried near the tombs of the kings they had served. No one in England in 1400 could foresee that Chaucer's tomb would be the beginning of Poets' Corner and that Chaucer would become the "stremes hede" of poetry in English.

A CHRONOLOGY OF CHAUCER'S LIFE AND TIMES

Note: The dates of birth and of the composition or publication of literary works are often approximations and should be used with caution.

1300 Dante's *Divine Comedy.*

1300 Birth of Guillaume de Machaut, French musician and poet.

1304 Birth of Francis Petrarch (Francesco Petrarca).

1313 Birth of Giovanni Boccaccio.

1321 Death of Dante Alighieri. (b. 1265).

1330 Birth of John Gower (d. 1408).

1335 Boccaccio begins *Il Filostrato* (source of *Troilus*).

1337 Hundred Years War begins (ends 1453).

1337 Birth of Jean Froissart, French poet and chronicler (d. 1404).

1339 Boccaccio begins *Il Teseida delle Nozze d'Emilia* (source of The Knight's Tale).

Early 1340s Birth of Chaucer.

1346 English victory at Crecy.

1346 Birth of Eustache Deschamps, French poet (d. 1406).

1348–50 The Black Death.

1350–53 Boccaccio writes the *Decameron*.

1356 English victory at Poitiers.

1357 Chaucer serves in the household of the Countess of Ulster.

1359–60 Chaucer serves in the war in France.

1360 Chaucer, captured by the French, is ransomed (for 16 pounds).

1360 Peace with France, Treaty of Bretigny (lull in Hundred Years War; resumes in 1369).

1361–62 Severe recurrence of the Black Death.

1360s Langland's *Piers Plowman* (the "A text").

1361–67 Jean Froissart serves in household of Queen Philippa.

1366 Chaucer marries Philippa Roet, "damoiselle" of the Queen.

1366 John Chaucer, Chaucer's father, dies; his mother, Agnes, remarries.

1366 Chaucer travels to Spain.

1367 Birth of Chaucer's son, Thomas.

1367 Chaucer serves as a "valettus" and then squire in the court of Edward III; granted a payment of 20 marks per annum for life.

1368 Chaucer travels to the continent on "the King's service."

1368 Birth of Thomas Hoccleve, a poetic "disciple" of Chaucer (d. 1450).

1368–72 Chaucer writes "Fragment A" of *The Romaunt of the Rose, The Book of the Duchess,* probably a good many lyrics in French and English, now lost, and such lyrics as The Complaint unto Pity and A Complaint to His Lady.

1369 Chaucer serves with John of Gaunt's army in France.

1370 Birth of John Lydgate, admirer and imitator of Chaucer (d. 1449).

1370 Chaucer again serves with the army in France.

1372 Chaucer's wife, Philippa, serves in the household of John of Gaunt's wife.

1372 Chaucer travels to Italy (Genoa and Florence) on a diplomatic mission.

1374 Death of Petrarch.

1374 Chaucer granted a gallon pitcher of wine daily for life.

1374 Chaucer appointed controller of the customs; granted a lease on a dwelling over Aldgate.

1375 Death of Boccaccio.

1375 Chaucer and Otho de Graunson (French knight and poet on whose poems Chaucer drew for The Complaint of Venus) both receive grants from John of Gaunt.

1376–77 Chaucer makes several trips to France, negotiating for peace and the marriage of Richard.

1377 Edward III dies; Richard II becomes king.

1377 Pope Gregory XI condemns doctrines of John Wycliffe (d. 1384); Lollard movement grows.

1378 The "Great Schism"—rival popes in Rome (Urban) and Avignon (Clement); the schism ends 1409.

1378 Chaucer travels to Italy (Milan) on diplomatic mission.

1378 John Gower and Richard Forester have Chaucer's power of attorney while he travels abroad.

Late 1370s Chaucer writes *Saint Cecelia* (possibly later); *The House of Fame, Anelida and Arcite.*

1380 Cecily Chaumpaigne signs a document, releasing Chaucer from all actions "in the case of my rape" (*de raptu meo*).

1380 Birth of Chaucer's second son, Lewis.

1380–82 Chaucer writes *The Parliament of Fowls.*

1381 The Peasants' Revolt.

1381 Death of Chaucer's mother, Agnes.

1382 Chaucer's controllership of the customs renewed, with permission to have a deputy.

1382 The Bible is translated into English (the "Wyclif Bible"; a later version is made in 1388).

1382–86 Chaucer writes *Boece, Troilus and Criseyde.*

1385 Chaucer granted a permanent deputy in the customs.

1385 Eustache Deschamps sends Chaucer a poem of praise, hailing him as "great translator, noble Geoffrey Chaucer."

1385–87 Chaucer writes *Palamoun and Arcite* (later used as The Knight's Tale) and *The Legend of Good Women* (though some parts may be earlier and the Prologue was later revised).

1385–89 Chaucer serves as justice of peace for Kent.

1386 Chaucer gives up the house in Aldgate; resigns from customs.

1386 Chaucer serves as member of Parliament for Kent (where he now probably lives).

1386–87 Chaucer praised as a poet of love and philosophy by Thomas Usk (1350–88), author of *The Testament of Love.*

1387–92 Chaucer begins *The Canterbury Tales.*

1388 Some of Richard II's closest supporters removed by the Lords Appellant; some (including Thomas Usk, an admirer of Chaucer) are executed.

1389 Chaucer appointed clerk of the works, with responsibility for Westminster, Tower of London, and other royal estates.

1390 John Gower "publishes" his *Confessio amantis* (later revised).

1390 As clerk of the works, Chaucer has scaffolds built for jousts in Smithfield.

1390 Chaucer is robbed of horse, goods, and a considerable amount of money at Hacham, Surrey (perhaps robbed again a bit later).

1391–92 Chaucer writes *A Treatise on the Astrolabe* (with additions 1393 and later).

1392–95 Chaucer writes most of *The Canterbury Tales,* including probably the "Marriage Group."

1394 King Richard II grants Chaucer an annuity of 20 pounds a year.

1396–1400 Chaucer writes the latest of the *Tales,* including probably The Nun's Priest's Tale, The Canon's Yeoman's Tale (though part is probably earlier), and The Parson's Tale, and several short poems, such as Lenvoy to Scogan and Lenvoy to Bukton, in which Bukton is urged to read "The Wife of Bath."

1398 Chaucer is granted a tun of wine a year.

1399 Richard II deposed; Henry IV becomes king.

1399 Henry IV confirms, and adds to, Chaucer's royal annuities.

1399 Chaucer leases a tenement, for 53 years, in the garden of the Lady Chapel at Westminster Abbey.

1400 Chaucer writes The Complaint of Chaucer to His Purse.

1400 Chaucer's death (on 25 October, according to tradition).

LANGUAGE AND VERSIFICATION

The following is an adaptation of the section on language and versification written by Norman Davis for The Riverside Chaucer. *The section on language is heavily revised (since it now deals only with* The Canterbury Tales*); that on versification has few changes.*

The English language had been used in poetry and prose for centuries before Chaucer began to write, and by the tenth century Old English, partially standardized in the form now called Late West Saxon, had become the language of law, government, and literature. That tradition was destroyed by the great political and cultural upheaval of the Norman Conquest in 1066: first Latin and then French became the language of official record, and French (or Anglo-Norman), spoken by most of the upper classes, was the language of aristocratic literature and social prestige. For several generations writing in English was not much cultivated. When it was revived as a literary language, in the late twelfth century and after, English had no prestige dialect; French had that function. Chaucer himself probably spoke French from his earliest years and when he went to school construed his Latin in that language.

For a variety of reasons, the use of French declined in the late thirteenth and fourteenth centuries, and English became the language of the upper classes and the royal court. The Mercer's Petition to Parliament in 1386, the first such document in English, is the culmination of a long development and marks the reestablishment of the language; less than a decade later Chaucer in his *Treatise on The Astrolabe* could refer to the King's English—"God save the king that is lord of this language." The king's language was that of London, which Chaucer naturally spoke and wrote. After the Conquest, commerce had become increasingly centered in London, and government administration and courts of law were concentrated at nearby Westminster. The London area attracted a varied population from many parts of the country, especially the east and central midlands, and this led eventually to a blend of linguistic elements recognizable as characteristic of the capital, though considerable variation in particular features was accepted until long after Chaucer's time.

In the centuries that followed, this dialect became the basis of Standard English, and later writers such as Spenser regarded Chaucer as the founder of their language—the "well of English undefiled." That is something of an overstatement. Chaucer was a great literary innovator, and a substantial number of words and phrases, many of French origin, are first recorded in his work. He had a tremendous effect on the literary language, but forces other than literature determined the development of our language, and Chaucer's example cannot have had much effect in determining what kind of English would later develop into the generally accepted written standard.

Pronunciation

An author as interested in language as Chaucer obviously cannot be appreciated without attention to the effect of reading aloud. Mastering the pronunciation is thus a necessity. That may seem daunting on one's first encounter with Middle English, but it is not as difficult as it may at first seem.

Much of the apparent difficulty is only a matter of spelling, for in Chaucer's time English had not yet developed a standardized orthography, and common words can appear with different spellings even in the work of a single writer. A variety of words have such alternative spellings, notably the largely free variation between *i* and *y* as in *lif* and *lyf* (life), or between *ou* and *ow* as in *you* or *yow*. Long vowels are sometimes represented by doubling (*hooly, deedly*) and sometimes not (*holy, dedly*), and short -*on*- and -*an*- sometimes vary freely, as in *hond* (I.1603) and *hand* (I.1930). These and other minor variations are matters of spelling rather than changes in pronunciation, and reading the text aloud will most often clarify any problems they may present.

The main difficulty for a beginning reader is presented by the long vowels and diphthongs. English, like other European vernaculars, was first written with its sounds represented by the Latin alphabet. Early writers, who had learned to read and write Latin, not their native tongues, in effect transcribed the sounds of their vernaculars, assigning them the equivalent Latin representations. The letter *i* thus had the same sounds (or nearly so) in written Latin, German, French, or English. Today there are striking differences between modern English and the continental languages in the way in which letters representing the long vowels and diphthongs are pronounced. This arose after Chaucer's time and marks the major difference between Middle

English and the modern language. By the late fifteenth century the spelling of English words was largely (though by no means universally) fixed, and this was the spelling adopted (and further regularized) by the early printers who so influenced the orthography of our language. However, even before the printers began work and for reasons no one understands, the sounds of English had changed. This is called the "Great Vowel Shift," and it affected in a regular fashion all the Middle English long vowels and diphthongs. For example, Middle English *mete* (which sounded something like modern *mate*) became our "meet," and Middle English *mate* (which had a vowel like that in the first syllable of *father*) became our *mate*.

The change affected only long vowels in stressed syllables; thus, in a word like modern English *lively,* the first syllable changed (from sounding like modern English *leaf*) but the second, unstressed syllable retains the old sound. Because the Great Vowel Shift was a regular change in English and had no equivalent in the European vernaculars, the modern reader can recover the pronunciation of Chaucer's English, however partially and approximately, by giving the the long vowels the values they would have in, say, modern German, Spanish, or Italian.

In general, though there are many exceptions, vowels that are long in modern English were long in Middle English. The same does not apply to short vowels; a good many long Middle English vowels have been shortened in modern English.

Chaucer's language distinguishes between "close" and "open" *ē* and *ō* (this refers to the way they are pronounced—with the jaw relatively closed or more widely opened). The difference was not expressed in spelling when most Chaucerian manuscripts were written. The appropriate sound of *o* or *oo* can usually be deduced from the modern forms of the words concerned, for the sounds remained distinct and the descendant of close *ō* came in modern English to be spelled usually *oo* (e.g., modern *boot*), that of open *ō* often *oa* (modern *boat*). The history of close and open *e* is much the same: some fifteenth-century scribes and sixteenth-century printers represented close *ē* by *ee,* and the open sound by *ea,* and the inherited modern spellings are usually a good indication of the earlier difference in such pairs as *meet* (formerly close) and *meat* (open). (The sound in modern *break* and *great* is due to a different sound relation.) Chaucer does not carefully distinguish open

e from close *e* (he frequently rhymes the two sounds). He does observe the distinction between open and close *o*, which he never rhymes with one another.

The short vowels of Middle English are much like those in modern English: short *u* was often written *o*, especially next to letters consisting of short vertical strokes like *m, n,* and *v,* as in *comen, sonne,* and *love*—pronounced /cumən/, /sunə/, /luvə/. Short *a* had a sound like that of French *patte,* not that sound now general in words like English *bat; o* was a rounded vowel more like that of the British *hot* or the first sound in *auction* than the unrounded sound now general in American speech; *u* was always rounded as in modern English *put,* not unrounded as in *putt.* Unstressed *e* is pronounced, as in modern English, with the sound in the final syllables of *horses* and *wanted;* when final ("silent *e*" in modern English), it is usually pronounced, though it is elided before a vowel or *h.*

The consonants of Chaucer's English were mostly the same as those used in the modern language and were represented by the same letters. A number of consonants since lost in pronunciation were still sounded (see chart on page XXVIII):

g, k, and *w* as initial clusters (with *n, l, r*): *gnawen, knowen, wlatsom, writen.*

l before consonants, as in *half, folk.*

r in all positions, and it was probably trilled, at least between vowels, as in *faren.*

wh- was still always distinct from *w-.*

g in *-ng* the *g* was probably sounded as in *finger;* in the combination *gn* in words derived from French, such as *signe* and *benigne,* the *g* was not pronounced.

h-, initial, in French-derived words (e.g., *honour*) was not pronounced.

ch, cch represented the sound (like modern *tch*) that it still has in *church,* and not the sound (like *sh*) that developed in French, as in modern *machine.*

-cio(u)n, the equivalent of modern English monosyllabic *-tion,* always has two syllables, and *-cc-* was the normal spelling in words like *accioun* (action).

	Sound	Pronunciation	Spelling	ME Examples
ā	/a:/	*a in* father *(but fronted)*	a, aa	name, caas
ă	/a/	*a in Fr.* patte *or Ger.* Mann	a	can, that
ē *(close)*	/e:/	*e in Fr.* café *or in* fate *(but a pure vowel)*	e, ee	grene, sweete
ę *(open)*	/ɛ:/	*e in Fr.* fête *or in* there *(but a pure vowel)*	e, ee	teche, heeth
ĕ	/ɛ/	*e in* set	e	tendre
e *(in unstressed syllables)*	/ə/	*e in* hors*es*	e	sonne
ī	/i:/	*i in* machine	i, y	shires, ryden
ĭ	/i/	*i in* sit	i, y	this, thyng
ō *(close)*	/o:/	*o in* note *(but a pure vowel)*	o, oo	bote, good
ǫ *(open)*	/ɔ:/	*oa in* broad	o, oo	holy, goon
ŏ	/o/	*o in* hot *(but not unrounded)*	o	oft, folk
ū	/u:/	*oo in* boot *(but a pure vowel)*	ou, ow, ogh	flour, fowles, droghte
ŭ	/u/	*u in* put	u, o	but, yong
ü	/y:/	*u in Fr.* lune *or Ger.* grün	u, eu, ew, uw	vertu, seur, salewe, muwe
au	/au/	*ou in* house	au, aw	cause, lawe
ęi	/ai/ or /æi/	*e + i or a + i*	ay, ai, ey, ei	sayle, day, wey, heir
ēu	/iu/	*i + u*	eu, ew	knew, newe
ęu	/ɛu/	*e + u*	eu, ew	lewed, fewe
oi	/ɔi/	*oy in* boy	oi, oy	coy
ōu	/ɔu/	*o + u*	ou, ow	growen, soule
ŏu	/ɔu/	*o + u*	o, ou *(before* -gh*)*	thoght, foughte

-gg- could represent a stop, as in *bigge* (big), or in *brigge* it could represent the sound in modern "bridge." (The spelling *dg* was not yet in use.)

-gh- in words such as *ought* represents the sound in German *Bach* and Scots *loch*, and in words such as *knight* the sound in German *ich*. The nearest sound in modern English is perhaps a strongly articulated initial consonant as in *hue*. The sound may be approximated in modern English by saying "raggedy" or "rickety" very fast.

-s, final, was ordinarily voiceless; that is, the word *is* rhymed with *this* and *was* rhymed with *alas*.

In Chaucer's usage a distinction is maintained between long and short consonants; that is, both elements of a doubled consonant are pronounced—*sonne* rather than *sonn-e*. Thus *sone* (son) rhymes only with *wone*, noun or verb, which historically had a single -n-, whereas *sonne* (sun) rhymes with words such as *yronne, conne, bigonne,* with historical double *n*.

STRESS   In Middle English, as in modern English, the main word stress falls on the root syllable, which may be the first syllable (as in *sýllable*) or may follow a prefix (as in *undó*). Foreign words taken into the language may initially retain a differing pattern of stress, though when the words are fully assimilated they will usually follow the English pattern. Chaucer's recent borrowings from French were often still accented in the French way. For example, *licour* (I.3) has the stress on the final syllable, to rhyme with *flour* (I.4). However, French borrowings were rapidly assimilating, and the stress pattern could alternate between French and English: *servýse* (I.250) takes the stress on the second syllable, as modern French *service* still does, and rhymes with *arise*. Elsewhere it has the native English stress on the root syllable: *For wel I woot my sérvyce is in vayn* (V.972).

Inflections

NOUNS   Most Middle English nouns have the same simple inflection as modern English: the genitive (possessive) and plural are formed by the addition of -*(e)s:*

Singular, nominative and objective:	freend
Genitive:	freendes
Plural (all cases):	freendes

Nouns with stems ending in a consonant, as above, add -*es;* those that end in a vowel (*see*) or an unstressed -*e* (*ende, space*) add -*s.* (Note that in modern English some of these endings develop into /z/; that is not the case in Middle English.)

"Irregular" declensions are much the same as in modern English, though more numerous:

A small group of nouns form their plurals with -*(e)n: asshen* (ashes), *been* (bees), *doghtren* (daughters), *(e)yen* (eyes), *hosen* (hose), *shoon* (shoes), *oxen, sustren* (sisters), *toon* (toes); all but *(e)ye* and *ox* also have plurals in -*s.*

Those nouns that form the plural by change of vowel (as in modern English) are *men, wommen, feet, gees, teeth, mys* (mice). A few nouns show plurality by both a change in the root vowel and the addition of -*n: bretheren, keen* (cows); *children* combines the -*n* with an older pluralization with -*r.*

Some nouns are unchanged in the plural. These are (a) animals: *deer, hors, neet* (cattle), *sheep;* (b) words of measurement, qualified by numerals, such as *foot, myle, pound, night, winter, yeer;* (c) words of French origin ending in -*s*, notably *ca(a)s* and *pa(a)s.*

A few nouns are unchanged in the possessive. These are mainly nouns of relation ending in -*r*, such as *fader* and *brother;* alternative forms with -*s* are also found. A few others, such as *lady*, descend from Old English genitives in -*an.* Proper names ending in -*s* add no suffix in the possessive: *lusty Venus children.*

In most nouns the objective (dative and accusative) case is the same as the nominative. However, in prepositional phrases a singular noun may add the ending -*e* (and double a final consonant after a short vowel): *to bedde, to shippe, on fire, with childe,* and most frequently *on live* (alive).

ADJECTIVES   Like nouns, adjectives may have a stem with an -*e*, whether of Old English origin, as *grene, sweete,* or French, as *amiable, debonaire, rude.* Monosyllabic adjectives ending with a consonant retain some traces of the Old English "strong" and "weak" declensions of the adjective.

Strong declension: The strong declension has no -*e* in the singular; the final -*e* is used in all other cases:

Singular:	a **yong** knight (II.585)
Plural:	Two **yonge** knightes (I.1011)

Weak declension: The weak (or "definite") declension has -*e* in the singular under certain conditions:

Following a defining word	
Definite article:	the **yonge** sonne (I.7)
Demonstrative:	this **yonge** Monk (VII.28)
Possessive:	hir **yonge** suster (I.972)
Vocative expressions:	O **yonge** Hugh (VII.684)
Prepositional phrases:	with **harde** grace (III.2228)

The weak declension, like the strong, marks the plural with e: *Bothe hire* **yonge** *children* (IV.181).

The regular suffixes for the comparison of adjectives are the same as in modern English, *-er* and *-est*, sometimes in the weak forms *-re* and *-este*. Monosyllables ending in a consonant double it before the comparative ending, and a long vowel in the stem syllable is then shortened, as *gretter* from *greet*. The short vowel is extended to the superlative *grettest*. The irregular comparative and superlative forms are similar to those that survive in modern English:

	Comparative	Superlative
good	bet, bettre	beste
litel	lasse, lesse	leeste
long	lenger	lengest
muche, muchel	moore	mooste
neigh, nye	neer, ner	nexte
oold	elder	eldeste
strong	strenger	strengest
yvel, bad	worse, werse	worste, werste

Comparison may also be expressed by the adverbs *moore* and *mooste*, as *the moore mury* (I.802), *the moore noble* (I.2888), *the mooste stedefast* (IV.1551).

ADVERBS   Many adverbs of manner were derived from adjectives, often by means of the suffix *-e*, as *faire, faste, hoote, lowe*. Such forms may be compared in the same way as adjectives, with suffixes *-er(e)* and *-est(e)*, as *The fastere shette* (shut) *they* (VII.2532), *the faireste hewed* (VII.2869).

Irregular comparison appears in the same group of words as with adjectives:

	Comparative	Superlative
baddely, yvele	wors(e)	worst(e)
fer	ferre, ferrer	ferrest
litel, lite	lesse, lasse	leest
muche, muchel	mo, moore	moost(e)
ny	neer	next
wel	bet, bettre	best

New adverbs were derived from adjectives of whatever origin (French or native) by the addition of *-ly* or *-liche*: e.g., *myrily, playnly, rudeliche*. Such forms are mostly compared by means of *moore* and *moost*, as *the moore lightly* (X.1041), *moost felyngly* (I.2203). *Murierly* (I.714) is the only example of the addition of the comparative suffix before the ending.

PRONOUNS

Personal:

Singular	1st person	2nd person	3rd person
Nominative:	I, ich	thou, thow	he, she, hit
Genitive:	my, myn(e)	thy, thyn(e)	his(e), hir(e)
Objective:	me	the(e)	him, hir(e), hit

Plural	1st person	2nd person	3rd person
Nominative:	we	ye	thei
Genitive:	our(e)	your(e)	hir(e)
Objective:	us	you	hem

The second person nominative *thou* is often suffixed to a verb; this occurs most frequently with lightly stressed modal and copulative verbs, as in *artow, wiltow*, but also occasionally with other verbs, as *cridestow* (I.1083).

The possessives *myn* and *thyn* have that form when preceding a word beginning with a vowel or *-h*; they have the form *my* and *thy* when any consonant save *-h* follows: *Alas, myn hertes queene! Alas, my wyf!* (I.2775).

Indefinite pronoun: men, an unstressed form of the noun, functions as the indefinite pronoun *one* (see below).

Relative pronouns: The relative pronouns *that, which, which that*, and *the which (that)* are all used for both persons and things. *Who* is not used in the nominative as a relative pronoun; it is the usual interrogative with reference to persons. But the possessive *whos* and objective *whom* are often relative, as *bifore whos child* (II.642), *whom that we diden wo* (III.1491).

VERBS   Like modern English, Middle English has "weak" verbs (those that form their preterite with *-ed*), "strong" verbs (which form the preterite by a change in the root vowel), and a number of irregular conjugations, such as *ben* in the chart on page XXXI.

	"Weak"	"Strong"	"To be"
Infinitive	love(n)	singe(n)	be(n)
Present indicative:			
1st pers. sing. **ich**	love	sing	am
2nd pers. sing. **thou**	lovest	singeth	art
3rd pers. sing. **he,** etc.	loveth	singeth	beth
1st–3rd pers. pl. **we**	love(n)	singe(n)	be(n)
Present participle	lovyng(e)	syngyng(e)	(not found)
Preterite indicative:			
1st pers. sing.	loved	song	was
2nd pers. sing.	lovedest	songe	were, weere
3rd pers. sing.	loved(e)	song(e), soong	was
1st–3rd pers. pl.	lovede(n)	songe(n)	were(n)
Past participle	(y)loved	songe(n)	(y)be(n), (y)been
Imperative (sing.)	love	sing	be
Imperative (pl.)	loveth	singeth	beth, beeth, be

The subjunctive usually has -*e* (though it is often not pronounced): *wher-so she wepe or synge* (II.294), *Ne that thy tale ne make us not to slepe* (IV.14), *Welcome be the cut* (present tense, I.854), *if it were deed or bledde* (preterite, I.145).

Negative forms occur for parts of *been*: *nam, nart, nis, nas, nere(n)*; of *haven*: *nath, nad(de)*; of *wil*: *nil, nilt, nolde*; of *witen*: *noot* (I know not), *niste* (he, she knows not).

Monosyllabic verbs with stems ending in a dental consonant (-*d, -t, -th,* or -*s*) may take an alternative form in the present 3rd singular: the -*eth* and final dental of the stem coalesce to form a monosyllabic form ending in -*t*: as *bit* for *biddeth* (I.187), *rit* for *rideth* (I.974), *rist* for *riseth* (I.3688), *fynt* for *fyndeth* (I.4071), *worth* for *wortheth* (VII.751). The vowel *o* in the stems of *holden* and *stonden* is also replaced by *a* in the short form, as *halt* (V.61) for *holdeth* (IV.1189), *stant* (V.171) for *stondeth* (V.190).

An exceptional contracted form of the 2nd singular is *lixt* for *liest* (III.1618, 1761).

Some weak verbs change the vowel of the stem in the past tense and participle. Most are like the forms in modern English, as *solde* from *sellen* and *taughte* from *techen*, but some have not survived, as *dreynte* from *drenchen* (drown), *queynte* from *quenchen* (quench), and *straughte* from *strecchen* (stretch). An exceptionally irregular verb, having features of both strong and weak conjugations, is *hoten*, past *highte* (which has both the active sense "promise" and the passive "be called"), and abnormal forms such as *heet(e)* in the preterite singular and past participle.

As in modern English, "modal" verbs, such as *shall, will, can,* and *may*, have past forms like weak verbs, but (like strong verbs) the present 3rd person singular has a zero ending (we say "he goes," with an -*s* on "go," but "he shall go," with no ending on the modal "shall").

	shullen	*willen*	*konnen*	*mowen*	*witen*
Present:					
1st pers.	shal	wol, wil	kan	may	woot, wot
2nd pers.	shul, shalt	wolt	kanst	mowe, mayst	woost
3rd pers.	shal	wol, wil	kan	may	woot
plural:	shul(en)	wol, wil	konne(n)	mowe(n)	wite(n), woot, wot
Preterite:					
1st pers.	sholde	wolde	koude	myghte	wiste
2nd pers.	sholdest	woldest	koudest	myghtest	wistest
3rd pers.	sholde	wolde	koude, kouthe	myghte	wiste
plural:	sholde(n)	wolde(n)	koude	myghte(n)	wiste(n)

Other irregular verb forms are:

	don	*gon*	*haven*
Present:			
1st pers.	do	go	have
2nd pers.	doost	goost	hast
3rd pers.	dooth	gooth	hath
plural:	do, doon	goon, go(n)	han, have
Preterite:			
1st pers.	dide	went(e)	hadde
2nd pers.	didest	wentest	haddest
3rd pers.	dide	wente	hadde
plural:	dide(n)	wente(n)	hadde(n)
ppl:	ydo(on), doon	goon, go(n), ygo	had, yhad

The past forms for *gon* are the preterite of *wenden* (to go); the historical past form (*yede*) appears but rarely in Chaucer (only twice, VIII.1141 and VIII.1281, in *The Canterbury Tales*).

Some Features of Syntax and Idiom

NOUNS   *Number:* An object or attribute possessed separately by each member of a group may have a singular form: *the colour in hir face* (their faces, I.1637). *Thus shal mankynde drenche, and lese hir lyf* (their life, I.3521); but the plural may also be used, as *han lost hir lyves* (III.1997).

Case: Some genitive forms in *-es* are used as adjectives, notably *lyves* (living), in *lyves creature* (I.2395, IV.903), *shames* (shameful), as *shames deeth* (II.819, IV.2377). The same ending may also have an adverbial function, as in *algates* (at any rate), *nedes* (necessarily), *ones* (once), and in phrases having *thankes* with a possessive pronoun, meaning "willingly," as *hir thankes* (I.2114).

As in modern English, a noun that is the indirect object of a verb may be preceded by *to*, but may also be simply in the common form: *Men moote yeve silver to the povre freres* (I.232), but *pynnes, for to yeven faire wyves* (I.234).

ADJECTIVES   Adjectives normally precede the nouns they qualify but they may also follow: *his shoures soote* (I.1), *hir fyngres smale* (IV.380), *Jerusalem celestial* (X.80). Certain set phrases regularly have this order: *the blood roial* (I.1018, 1546, II.657, etc.).

Occasionally (usually in French phrases or when translating from French or Latin, most often in prose) a plural adjective will be inflected: *places delitables* (V.899); *goodes temporels* (VII.998).

A rare survival of a genitive plural ending is *-er* in *aller* (of all; Old English *(e)alra*) in phrases such as *oure aller cost* (I.799); it also functions as an intensive of the superlative in the form *alder* as in *alderbest* (I.710), and *alderfirst* (V.550)

In the predicate, superlatives are sometimes reinforced by *oon*: *she was oon the faireste* (IV.212 and V.734). The sense is "the very fairest," differing from the later common use "one of the fairest," though that usage is also found: *oon of the worthieste/ Of al Ytaille* (IV.1131–32).

An adjective may function as a noun, not only with a plural referent, such as "the poor" in modern English, or *thise olde wyse* (VIII.1067), but also with a singular, *the nye slye* (I.3392).

The demonstrative *this* is used idiomatically to draw attention to a character in a narrative, as *This gentil duc* (I.952), sometimes by name, as *This Nicholas* (I.3288). It may more generally imply familiarity with, or understanding of, persons or things referred to: *Thise noble wyves and thise loveris* (II.59).

ARTICLES   The definite article is sometimes used with abstract nouns, as *Th'experience so preveth* (IV.2238), and with other words that seldom have it in modern English, e.g., *the deeth* (I.1716).

The indefinite article may be used with a numeral to indicate an approximate figure: *Wel ny an eighte busshels* (VI.771).

PRONOUNS   In Chaucer's time, sophisticated writers began imitating the French custom of using the singular pronouns *thee, thou, thy* with the corresponding singular verb forms (the "familiar" forms) when addressing a child, intimate, or inferior, and the "plurals of respect" *ye, you, your* with the corresponding plural verb forms when addressing superiors and equals. This was a literary usage that only slowly made its way into actual speech. Writing to his friends and acquaintances, Chaucer uses both the singular and plural forms in Lenvoy de Chaucer a Bukton (Buk 17: *lest thou do worse, take a wyf,* 29: *The Wyf of Bath I pray yow that ye rede*). In Lenvoy de Chaucer a Scogan he uses singular forms throughout (Scog 49: *Farewel, and loke thou never eft Love diffye*). Addressing King Richard in the Envoy to Lak of Stedfastnesse, Chaucer uses the singular only: *Wed thy folk agein to stedfastnesse,* Sted 28; addressing King Henry IV in the Envoy to the Complaint of Chaucer to His Purse, he uses the plural: *Ye, that mowen alle our harmes amende/ Have mynde upon my supplicacioun* (Purse 25–26). Chaucer is seldom completely consistent when employing the "plural of respect"; nevertheless, the use of the "polite" and "familiar" forms allows for subtle definitions of the relations between the characters (see, for example, ClT IV.890n.).

A personal pronoun is occasionally used with a proper name, both in the nominative—*he Jakke Straw and his meynee* (VII.3394), *he Julius, the conquerour* (VII.2673)—and in the objective—*Of hire Philologie and hym Mercurie* (IV.1734), *To sleen hym Olofernus in his tente* (II.940). It seems to function somewhat like the demonstrative *this* with a proper name (see above).

The personal pronoun is also occasionally used as an indefinite pronoun (that one, that fellow): *Somme helden with hym with the blake berd, . . . Somme seyde he looked grymme, and he wolde fighte* (I.2517–19).

The indefinite pronoun *men* (equivalent to modern English *one*) is singular and takes the appropriate singular verb forms: *What asketh men to have?* (I.2777), *"Unhardy is unseely," thus men sayth* (I.4210). However, the plural of *man* may be used in much the same sense (like modern English *they*): *In ydel, as men seyn, ye no thing make* (V.867).

The pronouns *who* and *what*, which are mainly interrogative, also function as indefinites: *Bityde what bityde* (whatever may happen; VII.874). They may imply an antecedent: *Who hath no wyf* (he who has no wife; I.3152). Especially when reinforced by *so*, the indefinite often suggests condition: *whoso wel the stories soghte* (if anyone were to investigate; VI.488).

ADVERBS AND CONJUNCTIONS   **As** is used in a number of ways that were later largely or wholly lost. It may introduce an imperative (*As lene it me*, I.3777) or subjunctive (*as help me God*, III.201). It begins many expressions of time: *as now* (I.2264), *As in his tyme* (VII.2498), *as for a certein tyme* (VII.977). It may intensify an adverb: *as swithe* (as quickly as possible; II.637). It may form a conjunction: *ther as I yow devyse* (I.34).

Ther often introduces a wish, blessing, or the like: *ther Mars his soule gye* (I.2815), *ther God his bones corse* (IV.1308).

Ther and *ther as* are also sometimes used in contexts modern English would use *where* or *wherever*: *Unto the bed ther as the millere lay* (I.4258), *for over al ther he cam* (I. 547).

Many conjunctions incorporate a redundant **that**: *Whan that* (I.1), *though that* (I.68), *if that* (I.144).

PREPOSITIONS   Some prepositions have, in addition to senses still current, others that are now obsolete:

After in *after hir degree* (according to their rank; I.2573), *after oon* (alike; I.341).

At in *at ye* (plainly; I.3016), *at o word* (briefly; II.428), *at regard of* (in comparison with; X.180).

By in *by the morwe* (in the morning; I.334), *by wyves that been wyse* (about, concerning wives; III.229).

For, besides its common expression of cause or aim, may signify intention or purpose to avoid a certain result, as *For lesynge of richesse* (for fear of losing wealth; VII.2560). When followed by an adjective or past participle, *for* expresses reason, as if constructed with the corresponding noun: *for old* (with, because of age; I.2142), *for swoot* (because of, to avoid sweat; VIII.578). *For* is often used with *to* and an infinitive (see below, under "Infinitives").

Of often signifies an agent: *I wolde nat of hym corrected be* (by him; III.661), *he was slayn of Achilles* (by Achilles; VII.3148). It appears in numerous phrases, such as *of kynde* (by nature), *of newe* (newly), *of youre curteisye* (by your courtesy, please; I.725), and is equivalent to *over* in *To have victorie of hem* (I.2246). It sometimes expresses the idea of *some*, an indefinite amount: *Of smale houndes* (some little dogs; I.146), *of youre wolle* (some of your wool; VI.910).

Out of is equivalent to *without* in *out of doute* (doubtless; I.487), *out of mesure* (without restraint, VII.1417).

To indicates function in *to borwe* (as a pledge; I.1622), *to wyve* (as a wife, I.1289). It is also used with the infinitive (see below).

Toward is sometimes divided, with the object between the parts: *To Rome-ward* (II.968), *To scoleward* (VII.549); the construction with *-ward* is also found with prepositions other than *to*: *Fro Burdeux-ward* (I.397), *Unto the gardyn-ward* (I.3572).

Up is equivalent to *upon* in *up peyne of* (on pain of; I.1707), *up peril of* (VII.2944).

Prepositions may follow the nouns or pronouns they govern: *al the fyr aboute* (I.2952), *Rood hym agayns* (II.999), *seyde his maister to* (VIII.1449).

When the preposition *in* is at the end of the line, it has the form *inne*: *in what array that they were inne* (I.41). With an infinitive, a preposition defining the relation of an object to the infinitive is normally placed before the object: *to shorte with oure weye* (with which to shorten our journey; I.791), *To saffron with my predicacioun* (with which to season my preaching; VI.345).

An infinitive with an adjective or noun may be preceded by a preposition with a semi-adverbial function: *moore blisful on to see* (more delightful to look at; I.3247).

VERBS   Modal auxiliary verbs are often the same as in modern English but with some additional meanings that have now been lost. Certain verbs that in the later language are only auxiliaries may be used as full verbs:

Conne (present **kan**, past **koude**) is most often a modal verb, meaning "can, know how to." But it also is sometimes used as a transitive verb meaning "know": *She koude muchel of wandrynge by the weye* (I.467), *And konne he letterure or konne he noon* (VIII.846). Sometimes it is used as a verb meaning "learn": *I wol it konne Oure Lady for to honoure!* (VII.543).

Do/did usually have their modern senses, though they appear only rarely as auxiliaries, as in *why do ye wepe*, and *Is ther no morsel breed that ye do kepe?* (VII.2432, 2434), and probably

Nicholas . . . dooth ful softe unto his chambre carie (I.3409–10). However, it is also used as a causative followed by an infinitive: *And for oure owene tresor doon us honge* (have us hanged; VI.790), *Ne nevere myghte hir foomen doon hem flee* (make them flee; VII.2317).

Gan, gonne, singular and plural of *ginnen,* are used mainly in periphrastic forms of the preterite, somewhat like modern *do* and *did*: *Dyane gan appeere* (Diane did appear, appeered, I.2346), *and homward gonne they ride* (did they ride, rode, I.1879). The infinitive in such constructions may appear without the partitive *to* or with it, though sometimes the *to* seems to add an inchoative sense: *gan to crie* (began to cry; I.2342).

May, might usually have their modern meanings, as in *He nolde answere for thyng that myghte falle* (I.3418), though sometimes they carry the older sense "can, be able": *Now help me, lady, sith ye may and kan* (I.2312); *"I se," quod he, "as wel as evere I myghte"* (IV.2384).

Let, leet usually have the modern meaning (allow, permit), but they may be used as causatives: *For which anon duc Theseus leet crye* (had announced; I.2731), *leet maken a statue of gold* (had made; VII.2159).

Mo(o)t has two almost contrary senses, "may" and "must": *Also moote I thee* (as I may prosper; VII.817), *A man moot nedes love* (a man must of necessity love; I.1169). The past tense *moste* expresses past time: *As forward was, right there he moste abyde* (had to remain; I.2619). However, it is also used with reference to present time, like its descendant, modern *must*: *We moste endure it* (I.1091).

Shal as an auxiliary often retains the older sense of obligation, necessity, or destiny, as *He moot be deed, the kyng as shal a page* (I.3030), but it may also indicate simple futurity, as *I am agast ye shul it nat susteene* (IV.1760).

Thar ("need") has not survived in modern English. It is used impersonally, always the third person form with a pronoun in the objective case: *what thar thee recche* (why need you care; III.329), *yet thar ye nat accomplice thilke ordinaunce* (you need not complete that undertaking; VII.1068).

Wil/wol and the past **wolde** usually designate simple futurity, like modern *will* and *would*, but they also often have the older sense of "wish, desire": *I wol nat do no labour* (VI.444). More rarely they carry the sense of regular or customary action: *Mordre wol out, certeyn, it wol nat faille* (VII.576).

Impersonal constructions: Impersonal constructions are more common in Chaucer's language than they are in modern English. They are found with some modal verbs, such as *thar* (above), *Us moste* (we must; VIII.946), and *as him oghte* (as he ought; II.1097).

They also occur frequently with a number of other verbs, sometimes with the subject pronoun *it,* as *Me thynketh it* (it seems to me; I.37), *it reweth me* (I regret it; VII.3097), and sometimes without, as *if yow liketh* (if it pleases you; I.777), *hire liste nat* (she had no wish; II.1048), and *Hym deigned nat* (he did not deign; VII.3181).

Infinitives: Infinitives may be used in their "plain" form or with a preceding particle *to* or *for to. To* and *for to* are often simple alternatives without distinction of meaning, even in adjacent phrases, as *Thanne longen folk to goon on pilgrimages,/ And palmeres for to seken straunge strondes* (I.12–13). As in modern English, the plain infinitive occurs principally after auxiliary verbs such as *can, may, shal, wil.* It sometimes occurs also after *oghte,* as in *I oghte avyse me right wel* (IV.1526) or *as it oghte be* (VIII.1182).

The infinitive with *(for) to* has a wide range of use, largely in the same functions as the modern infinitive with *to.* Thus, for example, it may express purpose as in *for to seke* (I.17), *for to tellen* (I.73), *for to doon* (I.78), *To make his Englissh sweete* (I.265), *sooth to seyn* (I.284).

In some phrases the infinitive has a passive sense: *to blame* (to be blamed; I.3710), *to preyse* (to be praised; VI.42), *to drede* (to be feared; VII.3063). This is related to the use of the inherited "inflected infinitive" in *ye woot what is to doone* (what is to be done; III.2194). A concessive use of the *for to* infinitive appears in usages such as *for to dyen in the peyne* (though we were to die under torture; I.1133), *for to be deed* (even if I were to die; IV.364).

Participles: As in modern English, a present or past participle may function as an adjective, a usage

Chaucer frequently employs: e.g., *a whistlynge wynd* (I.170), *a spiced conscience* (I.526), *That slidynge science* (VIII.732).

Mood: The subjunctive is much more common in Middle English than it is in the modern language. In main clauses it may express a wish, as *God yelde yow* (may God reward you; III.2177), an imperative of the first person plural, as *go we dyne* (VII.223), and concession, as *Bityde what bityde* (VII.874), *Be as be may* (VII.2129).

The subjunctive is also used in conditional sentences, most often following *if*, as *if gold ruste* (I.500), *if thou telle it* (I.3505), and especially in the frequent tag *if so be/were*, with a subordinate clause also using a subjunctive, as *if so be that thou my lady wynne* (I.1617). It extends naturally to clauses introduced by *but if* (unless): *Who may been a fool but if he love?* (I.1799); *al* (although): *Al speke he never so rudeliche and large* (I.734); and *as though*: *As though he stongen were* (as though he had been stabbed; I.1079).

The subjunctive is also used in anticipation of a future event, as *er that thou go henne* (I.2356), *til that it dye* (III.1145). It implies the uncertainty of information in *Where that he be I kan nat soothly seyn* (I.3670), and the unwillingness of a speaker to vouch for a report in *I trowe that he be went* (I.3665), though it is likely that in such dependent clauses the use of the subjunctive was at least to some extent conventional after verbs expressing belief (*That wenen wisly that it be nat so,* IV.2114) or advice (*I rede that thou apparaille thee therto,* VII.1346), after imperatives (*But looke that it have his spokes alle,* III.2256), and in other hypothetical or contrary-to-fact clauses. In all these, the verb is usually subjunctive, but not invariably: e.g., *Though in this toun is noon apothecarie* (VII.2948).

Tense: "Expanded" or "progressive" forms of present and past tenses (those made up of a part of the verb *be* and a present participle) are infrequent in comparison with the later language: *My newe wyf is comynge* (IV.805), *As Canacee was pleyyng in hir walk* (V.410), *We han ben waitynge* (I.929). The simple forms sometimes function like the modern progressive: *Ye goon to Caunterbury* (you are going; I.769). A simple past, rather than a construction with *have,* is used in expressions like *A fairer saugh I nevere* (I have never seen anyone more beautiful; IV.1033).

The perfect and pluperfect tenses are formed, as in modern English, with *be* and *have,* though intransitive verbs commonly use *be* rather than *have: The constable of the castel doun is fare* (II.512), *been they kist* (II.1074), *be they went* (IV.1701), *At nyght was come* (I.23).

A characteristic feature of Chaucer's narrative style is the use of present forms to refer to past time (the historical present), often with parallel past forms closely following: *She walketh up and doun . . . And as an aungel hevenysshly she soong* (I.1052–55), *He taketh his leve, and she astoned stood* (V.1339).

Future time is expressed mainly by the auxiliaries *shal* and *wil,* pretty much as in modern English.

Negation: The primary negative adverb is *ne,* placed before the verb (or incorporated in it in those contracted forms noted above in the description of verb forms), is sufficient to mark a sentence as negative: *she ne wiste what it signyfied* (I.2343), *I noot how men hym calle* (I.284). It is often reinforced by another negative, most frequently *nat* or *nought: he ne lefte nat* (I.492), *Ne studieth noght* (I.841). *Nat* or *nought* alone, following the verb, may also suffice, as in *His arwes drouped noght* (I.107), *It is nat honest; it may nat avaunce* (I.246); exceptionally, the negative form precedes the finite verb, as in *Nat greveth us youre glorie* (I.917). Sometimes a series of words in a passage, pronouns as well as adverbs, are all given negative forms: *He nevere yet no vileynye ne sayde . . . unto no maner wight* (I.70–71).

Interrogation: A positive sentence is normally converted into a question by inversion of verb and subject: *Wostow not wel?* (I.1163). When the question concerns two alternatives, the interrogative may be intensified by beginning the sentence with *whether,* as *Wheither seistow this in ernest or in pley?* (I.1125). After interrogative words such as *why,* or *what* as object, inversion is also normal: *Why cridestow?* (I.1083), *What do ye?* (I.3437), *how thynke ye?* (III.2204).

Versification

Verse in English in the fourteenth century was composed in two distinct traditions. One descended from Old English alliterative verse, which ordinarily used no rhyme and is characterized by alliteration, the repetition of the initial sounds of the stressed syllables.

The other tradition began in the twelfth century and was imitated from French and Latin models; this depended partly on the number of syllables in each line and partly on the linking of lines in couplets or groups by rhyming final sounds. This form as used by French writers regularly had eight or nine syllables, and the syllable count determined the line. Syllable stress is more prominent in English than in French, and when this form was imitated in English, syllables bearing stress usually alternated with syllables of less weight, so that the line was characterized by four stresses, or beats. The number of unstressed syllables was less restricted than in French, probably owing to the influence of the native type of line. This form was used in many English poems from the early thirteenth century onward, and it was well established long before Chaucer began to write.

Chaucer drew upon this tradition in his early poems *The Book of the Duchess* and *The House of Fame*. (Four-stress lines also form part of the "tail-rhyme" stanzas of The Tale of Sir Thopas.) In his other poetry, however, Chaucer used a longer line, containing five stresses, or beats, which before his time had appeared only rarely, in a few anonymous poems. It is likely that this form was suggested by the decasyllabic line often used in French, especially arranged in groups to form stanzas, but in part also by the eleven-syllable line used in Italian verse, which is of similar length but freer in rhythm. Chaucer took up the five-stress line early in his writing career, in the eight-line stanza of the ABC (a French form), and used it again in The Monk's Tale. He used the same kind of line in seven-line stanzas (later called "rime royal") in *The Parliament of Fowls*, *Troilus and Criseyde*, and the tales told by the Man of Law, the Clerk, the Prioress, and the Second Nun, as well as in much of *Anelida and Arcite* and some minor poems. His greatest contribution to the technique of English verse was the arrangement of this five-stress line in rhyming couplets, which he adopted in *The Legend of Good Women* and most of *The Canterbury Tales*. No earlier model for this has been found; it may well have been his own adaptation of the familiar English four-stress couplet to the more expansive five-stress form.

Chaucer wrote rhymed verse in all his poetical works. He clearly knew the alliterative form (see the Parson's comment in X.42–44), and he exploited features of it in a few passages (such as I.2605–16), but the alliterative form is never essential to the structure of his verse. His rhymes are in general careful, matching sounds that must have corresponded exactly in the type of English he wrote. In some words, or groups of words, he took advantage of the existence of alternative pronunciations (much as a modern versifier may rhyme *again* either with *main* or with *men*). Thus the verb *dien* (die) most often appears as *dye*, rhyming with such words as *crye* (e.g., I.3813–14), but it appears sometimes as *deye*, rhyming with words like *weye* (e.g., I.3033–34).

The most significant difference between Chaucer's verse and that of later centuries lies in the greater number of light syllables required or permitted by the inflectional system of his language. In modern English we frequently elide inflections—*worked* becomes *workt*. In Chaucer's English -*ed* is pronounced as a separate syllable whenever it appears; if we elide the vowel as we do in *workt*, we ruin the meter. For the sake of the meter we must also take care in our treatment of final -*e*. This vowel may function as a grammatical inflection (indicating, for example, case, number, mood, or tense) or it may be an integral part of a word; thus in *the yonge sonne* (I.7) the *e* of *yonge* is the mark of the definite ("weak") form of the adjective, while that of *sonne* had been part of the word already in its Old English form *sunne*. Pronunciation of these endings is, for the most part, necessary to the rhythm of the lines. A good indication that these final vowels were indeed sounded appears in such rhymes as *Rome* = *to me* (I.671–72), where the *to* must be stressed and *Rome* must have two syllables.

Though final -*e* was usually pronounced, there are many exceptions within the line. In particular, when a final -*e* is followed by a word beginning with a vowel or with an *h* that is either silent (as in French words like *honour*) or in weak stress (as often in such words as *he, his, hem, hire*), it is normally elided. Thus in *So hoote he lovede* (I.97), the -*e* of the adverb *hoote*, grammatically correct, is not pronounced before *he*. The final -*e* is also silent in many short unstressed words such as *hadde, hire, oure*, and it is sometimes slurred in polysyllables such as *mesurable* (I.435), *benefice* (I.507). Likewise, the inflection -*es* is slurred in polysyllabic words when the preceding syllable is light (*lordynges, pilgrymes*).

A regular line contains five stressed and five unstressed syllables. The stresses may vary a good deal in strength according to the sense, and indeed may often be potential rather than essential to a natural reading. Usually a light syllable precedes each of the stressed syllables. In

Bifíl that ín that séson ón a dáy,
In Sóuthwerk át the Tábard ás I láy (I.19–20)

a normal reading gives a regular rhythm. But the order of stressed and light syllables is often reversed, as in the next line,

Rédy to wénden ón my pílgrymáge (I.21)

and, more notably, there is sometimes no initial light syllable at all, and the line may be called "headless":

Twénty bóokes, clád in blák or réed (I.294)

A small number of lines lack a light syllable after the second stressed syllable, giving a "broken-backed" effect that some fifteenth-century poets, especially Lydgate, much favored, so that the line may be called "Lydgatian":

Hirȩ grétteste óoth wás but bý Seintȩ Lóy (I.120)

On the other hand, there are sometimes more light syllables (mostly only one) than regular rhythm requires. An extra light syllable may occur at the end of the line (see the many examples in the passages below). Within the line a light syllable may precede a natural pause:

For hé was láte ycóme   from hís viáge (I.77)
That nó drópe   ne fíllȩ upón hirȩ brést (I.131)
And fórth we ríden   a lítel móorȩ than páas (I.825)

But in numerous lines it clearly does not do so:

Of cóurt, and to béen estátlich óf manére (I.140)
Men móote yeve sílver tó the póvre fréres (I.232)
With a thrédbare cópe, as ís a póvre scolér (I.260)
Pékke hem up ríght as they grówe and éte hem ýn (VII.2967)

(Chaucer did not divide his lines by a regular caesura after a set number of syllables.)

By such means Chaucer gave his verse great freedom and variety of movement. To illustrate these qualities with a characteristic passage, the following extract from the General Prologue (I.285–308) is marked to show metrical stresses and the probable treatment of unstressed syllables. Stressed syllables are marked by accents, but the degree of stress must, of course, have varied with individual readers. Unstressed -*e* pronounced in final syllables has a dieresis (ë); when it is elided or slurred, it is underdotted (ȩ).

A Clérk ther wás of Óxenfórd alsó,
That únto lógyk háddë lóngȩ ygó.
As léenë wás his hórs as ís a rákë,
And hé nas nát right fát, I úndertákë,
But lóokëd hólwë, and thérto sóbrelȳ.
Ful thrédbarȩ wás his óverestȩ cóurtepȳ,
For hé haddȩ gétȩn hym yét no bénefícë,
Ne wás so wórldly fór to hávȩ officë.
For hým was lévȩrȩ hávȩ at his béddës héed,
Twénty bóokës, clád in blák or réed,
Of Áristótlȩ and hís philósophië,
Than róbës ríchȩ, or fíthelȩ, or gáy sautrië.
But ál be thát hé wás a phílosóphrë,
Yet háddë hé but lítel góld in cófrë;
But ál that hé mýght of his fréendës héntë,
On bóokes ánd on lérnynge hé it spéntë,
And bísilȳ gán for the sóulës préyȩ
Of hém that yáf hym whérwith tó scoléyȩ.
Of stúdië tóok he móost cúrȩ and móost héedë.
Noght ó word spák he móorë thán was néedë,
And thát was séyd in fórmȩ and réveréncë,
And shórt and qúyk and fúl of hȳ senténcë.
Sównyngȩ in móral vértu wás his spéchë,
And gládly wóldȩ he lérnȩ and gládly téchë.

The
Canterbury Tales

THE CANTERBURY TALES contains a wide variety of subjects and literary genres, from racy fabliaux to sober tales of Christian suffering, in accents that range from the elegant opening sentence of the General Prologue to the thumping doggerel of Sir Thopas and the solemn prose of the Parson.  The whole is lent coherence and verisimilitude by a framing narrative: a pilgrimage provides the occasion for gathering a broadly diverse group of characters to tell a series of tales intercalated with narrative links, in which the pilgrims argue, interrupt one another, or comment on the tales that have been told as they move through the fourteenth-century countryside to their common goal.

It is not known exactly when Chaucer began the *Tales*. The pilgrimage is traditionally dated 1387, but that date is based on a number of doubtful assumptions—that The Man of Law's Tale is told on the second day, that the pilgrimage could not have taken place in Holy Week, and, most important, that Chaucer must have had some specific year in mind. The composition of the *Tales* extended over a considerable length of time, and perhaps the idea of the *Tales* evolved rather than originated at a specific moment. Some of the tales—certainly the Knight"s, the Second Nun's, probably the Monk's, and perhaps others—were in existence in some form before Chaucer conceived the idea of *The Canterbury Tales*. They show that he had been interested in short narrative for some time, and The Monk's Tale and *The Legend of Good Women* show a further interest in composing a collection of short narratives. Sometime in the late 1380s he hit upon the idea of a pilgrimage to Canterbury as a framework for his collection.

The use of a narrative framework for a collection of tales was as ancient as *The Thousand and One Nights* and as contemporary as the *Confessio amantis*, on which Chaucer's friend John Gower was still working (it was completed, in its first form, in 1390). Chaucer doubtless knew Gower's work, as well as other collections such as *The Seven Sages of Rome*, but by far the most suggestive analogue to *The Canterbury Tales* is Boccaccio's *Decameron*.

There is no proof that Chaucer knew the *Decameron*. He never quotes it, and though he and Boccaccio narrate a number of similar tales, in no case has it been clearly demonstrated that Chaucer drew directly on Boccaccio's version. Yet Chaucer must have at least heard of the most famous prose work of his favorite Italian poet, even if he did not have a chance to read it or to acquire a copy of his own, and he most likely did receive from the *Decameron*, however indirectly, some suggestion that helped shape his own narrative framework.

If so, it was only a suggestion, for Chaucer's work differs greatly from Boccaccio's. In the *Decameron*, ten elegant young ladies and gentlemen, accompanied by their servants, journey from villa to villa through the countryside around Florence to avoid the plague then raging in the city. They amuse themselves by telling tales. Each in turn serves as leader for a day and sets the subject for that day's tales. After two weeks' sojourn and ten days of storytelling (Fridays and Saturdays being devoted to preparations for religious observance and other activities), exactly one hundred tales (ten *decades*, hence the title) have been told, and the party returns to Florence.

The resemblances between the *Tales* and the *Decameron* are obvious. Boccaccio, like Chaucer, uses a journey as the occasion for a collection of tales ostensibly told by the travelers (though the tales are told at the villas in which they stay, rather than on the road). The tales vary in tone and attitude, but the device of the leader's setting a common subject provides for their unity and lends each day's tales something of the nature of a debate, like those that develop in Chaucer's work. Boccaccio's tellers, however, are all young aristocrats of the same age and social status, and though they are to some extent individualized, they form a homogeneous group of equals. Their servants provide comic interludes in the framing narrative, but none tells a tale; in the *Decameron*, telling tales is an elegant and well-ordered aristocratic pastime.

That may have been what Harry Bailly, the Host of the Tabard Inn, had in mind when he proposed the storytelling competition and appointed himself leader. Chaucer's pilgrims, however, represent a wide range of social levels, ages, and occupations, and they are apparently gathered not by prior agreement but by mere chance. They have little in common except the goal of their pilgrimage, and the comic disputes that Boccaccio had restricted to the servants in Chaucer break out among the tellers themselves. Despite the Host's attempts to control the situation, the storytelling seems often to develop of its own volition as the pilgrims squabble, interrupt one another, and tell tales that the author would prefer not to relate but that must be told, he helplessly protests, if he is to give a true report of what was actually said and done.

The Canterbury Tales has the air of actuality because it is based on actuality. A pilgrimage was one of the few occasions in medieval life when so diverse a group of people might have gathered on a basis of temporary equality and might have told tales to pass the time on their journey. Chaucer had no literary precedent for this (Sercambi's *Novelle*, once regarded as a possible model, was probably not written until after Chaucer's death), and the journey to Canterbury gains much of its realistic tone from the fact that it was modeled on life.

This is not to say that Chaucer attempts to represent an actual Canterbury pilgrimage. Since the pilgrims are on their way to give thanks for help "whan that they were seeke," we expect some of the jollity that the Wife of Bath associates with religious festivals and relatively little of those penitential aspects of pilgrimage of which the Parson later reminds us. Yet most of these characters seem pure holiday merrymakers. None goes "naked in pilgrimages, or barefoot" (X.105), and even the Parson rides, lean though his nag may be. We are never told that the pilgrims attend Mass, even on the morning of their departure (in contrast to Boccaccio's characters, who scrupulously attend to their religious duties, though they are not on a pilgrimage), nor that they take any notice of the famous shrines and relics along the way—the miraculous cross at Rochester or St. Thomas's shoe at Boughton under Blee, which pilgrims customarily stopped to kiss. And they are an unlikely set of pilgrims, including not only those, like the Monk, who probably should not have been on a pilgrimage, but a good many rascals who probably would not have wanted to be on such a journey. Chaucer, in short, does not describe a real pilgrimage; rather, he uses the idea of the journey as a likely occasion and as a metaphor for the world, in which "we been pilgrymes, passynge to and fro" (I.2848). In the manner of the best late medieval art, he presents his metaphor with such a palpably concrete representation of actuality that it seems to come alive.

Much of this lifelike quality is due to Chaucer's eye for authenticating detail and his ear for the rhythms of colloquial speech, but, even more, it is the product of his dramatic method. Chaucer pretends merely to report what he sees and hears; he is content to let his characters speak for themselves, and when he does tell a tale in his own person, he does so as their equal, merely another teller.

Moreover, in many cases the tales are so suited to their tellers that they seem like dramatic soliloquies, further revelations of the characters we first encounter in the General Prologue, though the tales are sometimes unexpected and never completely predictable. The portrait in the General Prologue, the speeches and actions of the character in the links, and the tale he or she tells are, in many cases, all of a piece and cannot be fully understood in isolation from one another.

This celebrated dramatic principle extends to the larger structure of the work, in the creation of a dramatic interplay between the tales. Some, such as the tales of the Friar and the Summoner, function as parts of arguments that develop between the pilgrims. Others, such as those of the Wife of Bath, the Clerk, the Merchant, and the Franklin, are parts of continuing debates between the pilgrims, with each using his or her tale to express his or her viewpoint on a common theme or problem. Still others, such as those of the Second Nun and Canon's Yeoman, are related in subtler ways, and the recurrence of common themes and subjects throughout the *Tales*—love, justice, the relations between men and women, the proper conduct of life—add reverberations of meaning and reference that extend beyond the limits of the individual tales and groups of tales and provide a sense of coherence and fullness for the whole work, despite the absence of a completed narrative framework.

The Order of the Tales

For reasons unknown, Chaucer left *The Canterbury Tales* incomplete and without final revision. The work survives in ten fragments, labeled with Roman numerals in this edition (the alphabetical designations added in parentheses are those of the Chaucer Society, adopted by Skeat in his edition). These fragments are editorial units determined by the existence of internal signs of linkage—bits of conversation or narrative that explicitly refer to a tale just told or to one that immediately follows. There are no explicit connections between the fragments (save for IX–X and, in the tradition of the Ellesmere manuscript, IV–V) and, consequently, no explicit indication of the order in which Chaucer intended the fragments to be read. (Indeed, there is no explicit indication that he had made a final decision in this matter.) Consequently, modern editions differ in the order in which the tales are presented. Skeat's edition has them in the order followed by the Chaucer Society, with the "shift" proposed by Henry Bradshaw, whereby Fragment VII (B^2) is printed following Fragment II (B), and with Fragment VI following next, so that the complete arrangement is as follows: I (A), II (B), VII (B^2), VI (C), III (D), IV (E), V (F), VIII (G), IX (H), X (I). Baugh and Pratt follow this order except for the position of Fragment VI, which they print following Fragment V. Donaldson and Fisher print the tales in the order followed here. Robinson chose that order even though he believed it probable that the "Bradshaw shift" was indeed what Chaucer intended; nevertheless, he wrote, "in the present edition the inconsistent arrangement of the best manuscripts" (by which he meant the Ellesmere and related manuscripts) "is followed and no attempt is made to correct discrepancies left standing by the author."

The Canterbury Tales

FRAGMENT I (GROUP A)

General Prologue

Here bygynneth the Book of the Tales of Caunterbury.

Whan that Aprill with his shoures soote
The droghte of March hath perced to the roote,
And bathed every veyne in swich licour
Of which vertu engendred is the flour;
Whan Zephirus eek with his sweete breeth   5
Inspired hath in every holt and heeth
The tendre croppes, and the yonge sonne
Hath in the Ram his half cours yronne,
And smale foweles maken melodye,
That slepen al the nyght with open ye   10
(So priketh hem Nature in hir corages),
Thanne longen folk to goon on pilgrimages,
And palmeres for to seken straunge strondes,
To ferne halwes, kowthe in sondry londes;
And specially from every shires ende   15
Of Engelond to Caunterbury they wende,

The hooly blisful martir for to seke,
That hem hath holpen whan that they were seeke.
    Bifil that in that seson on a day,
In Southwerk at the Tabard as I lay   20
Redy to wenden on my pilgrymage
To Caunterbury with ful devout corage,
At nyght was come into that hostelrye
Wel nyne and twenty in a compaignye
Of sondry folk, by aventure yfalle   25
In felaweshipe, and pilgrimes were they alle,
That toward Caunterbury wolden ryde.
The chambres and the stables weren wyde,
And wel we weren esed atte beste.
And shortly, whan the sonne was to reste,   30
So hadde I spoken with hem everichon
That I was of hir felaweshipe anon,
And made forward erly for to ryse,
To take oure wey ther as I yow devyse.

This text was revised by RALPH HANNA III and LARRY D. BENSON, with materials provided by ROBERT A. PRATT.

1 **his:** its **shoures soote:** sweet, fragrant showers
2 **droghte:** dryness **perced:** pierced
3 **veyne:** vein (of the plants) **swich licour:** such liquid
4 **Of which vertu:** by which power
5 **Zephirus:** the west wind (which blows in Spring)
6 **Inspired:** breathed life into **holt and heeth:** grove and field
7 **croppes:** shoots, new leaves **yonge:** young, because the solar year has just begun with the vernal equinox. The sun has passed through the second half of the zodiacal sign Aries (the Ram); the time is thus late April. April 18 is specified in IntrMLT (II.5).
10 **ye:** eye
11 **priketh hem:** spurs, incites them **hir corages:** their spirits, hearts
13 **palmeres:** professional pilgrims who had been to the Holy Land and carried a palm frond as their emblem **straunge strondes:** foreign shores
14 **ferne halwes:** distant shrines **kowthe in sondry londes:** known in various lands (i.e., famous)

17 **blisful martir:** blessed martyr, St. Thomas à Becket
18 **hem hath holpen:** helped them **seeke:** sick
19 **Bifil:** it happened **seson:** season
20 **Southwerk:** Southwark, across the Thames from London **Tabard:** the Tabard Inn
22 **corage:** spirit, feelings
25 **sondry folk:** various sorts of people
25–26 **by aventure yfalle In felaweshipe:** fallen by chance into fellowship
27 **wolden:** desired, intended to
28 **chambres:** bedrooms
29 **esed atte beste:** accommodated in the best way
30 **shortly:** in brief
31 **everichon:** every one
32 **anon:** straightway
33 **forward:** agreement
34 **devyse:** tell

But nathelees, whil I have tyme and space,   35
Er that I ferther in this tale pace,
Me thynketh it acordaunt to resoun
To telle yow al the condicioun
Of ech of hem, so as it semed me,
And whiche they weren, and of what degree,   40
And eek in what array that they were inne;
And at a knyght than wol I first bigynne.

A KNYGHT ther was, and that a worthy man,
That fro the tyme that he first bigan
To riden out, he loved chivalrie,   45
Trouthe and honour, fredom and curteisie.
Ful worthy was he in his lordes werre,
And therto hadde he riden, no man ferre,
As wel in cristendom as in hethenesse,
And evere honoured for his worthynesse;   50
At Alisaundre he was whan it was wonne.
Ful ofte tyme he hadde the bord bigonne
Aboven alle nacions in Pruce;
In Lettow hadde he reysed and in Ruce,
No Cristen man so ofte of his degree.   55
In Gernade at the seege eek hadde he be
Of Algezir, and riden in Belmarye.
At Lyeys was he and at Satalye,
Whan they were wonne, and in the Grete See
At many a noble armee hadde he be.   60
At mortal batailles hadde he been fiftene,
And foughten for oure feith at Tramyssene
In lystes thries, and ay slayn his foo.

This ilke worthy knyght hadde been also
Somtyme with the lord of Palatye   65
Agayn another hethen in Turkye;
And everemoore he hadde a sovereyn prys.
And though that he were worthy, he was wys,
And of his port as meeke as is a mayde.
He nevere yet no vileynye ne sayde   70
In al his lyf unto no maner wight.
He was a verray, parfit gentil knyght.
But for to tellen yow of his array,
His hors were goode, but he was nat gay.
Of fustian he wered a gypon   75
Al bismotered with his habergeon,
For he was late ycome from his viage,
And wente for to doon his pilgrymage.

With hym ther was his sone, a yong SQUIER,
A lovyere and a lusty bacheler,   80
With lokkes crulle as they were leyd in presse.
Of twenty yeer of age he was, I gesse.
Of his stature he was of evene lengthe,
And wonderly delyvere, and of greet strengthe.
And he hadde been somtyme in chyvachie   85
In Flaundres, in Artoys, and Pycardie,
And born hym weel, as of so litel space,
In hope to stonden in his lady grace.
Embrouded was he, as it were a meede
Al ful of fresshe floures, whyte and reede.   90
Syngynge he was, or floytynge, al the day;
He was as fressh as is the month of May.

---

64 **ilke:** same
65 **Somtyme:** once, at one time   **Palatye:** Balat (in modern Turkey)
66 **Agayn:** against
67 **sovereyn prys:** outstanding reputation
68 Although he was a distinguished knight (i.e., brave), he was prudent.
69 **port:** bearing, manner
70 **vileynye:** rudeness
71 **no maner wight:** any sort of person
72 **verray:** true   **parfit:** perfect (complete)   **gentil:** noble
73 **array:** equipment
74 **gay:** gaily dressed, richly attired
75 **fustian:** coarse cloth   **gypon:** tunic
76 **bismotered with his habergeon:** stained by (rust from) his coat of mail
77 **viage:** journey, expedition
79 **Squier:** squire, a young knight in the service of another knight
80 **lovyere:** lover   **lusty:** lively   **bacheler:** young knight, not yet a knight banneret
81 **crulle:** curled   **presse:** press (curler)
82 **yeer:** years
83 **evene lengthe:** moderate height
84 **wonderly:** marvelously   **delyvere:** agile
85 **somtyme:** for a time, once   **in chyvachie:** on a cavalry expedition
86 **Flaundres, Artoys, Pycardie:** Flanders and parts of northern France, where English armies fought
87 **born hym weel:** conducted himself well   **space:** time
88 **stonden in his lady grace:** find favor with his lady
89 **Embrouded:** embroidered   **meede:** meadow
90 **reede:** red
91 **floytynge:** piping, playing the flute

35 **nathelees:** nonetheless   **space:** opportunity
36 **pace:** go, proceed
37 **Me thynketh it:** it seems to me, I think it   **acordaunt to resoun:** in accord with proper order
38 **condicioun:** state, circumstances
39 **ech:** each (one)
40 **degree:** social rank
41 **array:** dress
42 **wol:** will
45 **chivalrie:** prowess
46 **Trouthe:** fidelity   **honour:** good reputation   **fredom:** generosity of spirit
curteisie: refinement of manners
47 **werre:** war
48 **ferre:** farther
49 **hethenesse:** heathen lands
51 **Alisaundre:** Alexandria. The places named in lines 51–66 are those where English knights campaigned in the fourteenth century.
52 **bord bigonne:** sat in the place of honor
53 **Aboven alle nacions:** above knights from all nations   **Pruce:** Prussia
54 **Lettow:** Lithuania   **reysed:** ridden on raids   **Ruce:** Russia
56 **Gernade:** Granada   **seege:** siege   **eek:** also   **be:** been
57 **Algezir:** Algeciras, in Spain   **Belmarye:** Morocco (Benmarin)
58 **Lyeys:** Ayash (in modern Turkey)   **Satalye:** Atalia (in modern Turkey)
59 **Grete See:** Mediterranean
60 **armee:** military expedition
62 **Tramyssene:** Tlemcen (near Morocco)
63 **In lystes:** in formal duels   **ay:** always

Short was his gowne, with sleves longe and wyde.
Wel koude he sitte on hors and faire ryde.
He koude songes make and wel endite,   95
Juste and eek daunce, and weel purtreye and write.
So hoote he lovede that by nyghtertale
He sleep namoore than dooth a nyghtyngale.
Curteis he was, lowely, and servysable,
And carf biforn his fader at the table.   100
    A YEMAN hadde he and servantz namo
At that tyme, for hym liste ride so,
And he was clad in cote and hood of grene.
A sheef of pecok arwes, bright and kene,
Under his belt he bar ful thriftily   105
(Wel koude he dresse his takel yemanly;
His arwes drouped noght with fetheres lowe),
And in his hand he baar a myghty bowe.
A not heed hadde he, with a broun visage.
Of wodecraft wel koude he al the usage.   110
Upon his arm he baar a gay bracer,
And by his syde a swerd and a bokeler,
And on that oother syde a gay daggere
Harneised wel and sharp as point of spere;
A Cristopher on his brest of silver sheene.   115
An horn he bar, the bawdryk was of grene;
A forster was he, soothly, as I gesse.
    Ther was also a Nonne, a PRIORESSE,
That of hir smylyng was ful symple and coy;
Hire gretteste ooth was but by Seinte Loy;   120
And she was cleped madame Eglentyne.
Ful weel she soong the service dyvyne,
Entuned in hir nose ful semely;

And Frenssh she spak ful faire and fetisly,
After the scole of Stratford atte Bowe,   125
For Frenssh of Parys was to hire unknowe.
At mete wel ytaught was she with alle;
She leet no morsel from hir lippes falle,
Ne wette hir fyngres in hir sauce depe;
Wel koude she carie a morsel and wel kepe   130
That no drope ne fille upon hire brest.
In curteisie was set ful muchel hir lest.
Hir over-lippe wyped she so clene
That in hir coppe ther was no ferthyng sene
Of grece, whan she dronken hadde hir draughte.   135
Ful semely after hir mete she raughte.
And sikerly she was of greet desport,
And ful plesaunt, and amyable of port,
And peyned hire to countrefete cheere
Of court, and to been estatlich of manere,   140
And to ben holden digne of reverence.
But for to speken of hire conscience,
She was so charitable and so pitous
She wolde wepe, if that she saugh a mous
Kaught in a trappe, if it were deed or bledde.   145
Of smale houndes hadde she that she fedde
With rosted flessh, or milk and wastel-breed.
But soore wepte she if oon of hem were deed,
Or if men smoot it with a yerde smerte;
And al was conscience and tendre herte.   150
Ful semyly hir wympul pynched was,
Hir nose tretys, hir eyen greye as glas,
Hir mouth ful smal, and therto softe and reed.

[handwritten margin note: there are stairving people but she feeds her dogs]

94 **koude:** knew how to
96 **Juste:** joust   **eek:** also   **weel:** well   **purtreye:** draw
97 **hoote:** passionately   **by nyghtertale:** at nighttime
98 **sleep:** slept
99 **lowely:** modest (humble)   **servysable:** willing to serve, attentive
100 **carf:** carved
101 **Yeman:** yeoman, freeborn servant   **he:** the Knight   **namo:** no other
102 **hym liste:** he preferred to
104 **sheef:** sheaf
105 **bar ful thriftily:** bore very properly
106 **koude:** knew how to   **dresse his takel:** care for his arrows, equipment for archery   **yemanly:** skillfully, as a good yeoman should
107 **drouped noght with fetheres lowe:** did not fall short because of poorly adjusted feathers
109 **not heed:** close-cropped head   **broun:** very dark
111 **gay:** bright   **bracer:** archer's arm guard
112 **bokeler:** buckler, small shield
114 **Harneised:** ornamented
115 **Cristopher:** image of St. Christopher   **sheene:** bright
116 **bar:** bore   **bawdryk:** baldric, shoulder strap for the horn
117 **forster:** forester, game-keeper
119 **ful:** very   **symple and coy:** unaffected and quiet
120 **ooth:** oath   **Seinte Loy:** St. Eligius
121 **cleped:** called
122 **soong:** sang   **service dyvyne:** liturgy
123 **Entuned:** intoned   **ful semely:** in a very seemly manner

124 **fetisly:** elegantly
125 in the manner of (*After the scole of*) Stratford atte Bowe (rather than that of the royal court)
127 **At mete:** at dinner   **with alle:** indeed
128 **leet:** allowed
130 **koude:** knew how to   **wel kepe:** take good care
131 **no drope ne fille:** no drop fell
132 Her greatest pleasure (*lest*) was in good manners (*curteisie*).
133 **over-lippe:** upper lip
134 **coppe:** cup   **ferthyng:** speck (spot the size of a farthing)
135 **grece:** grease
136 **after hir mete she raughte:** she reached for her food
137 **sikerly:** truly   **greet desport:** excellent deportment
138 **port:** bearing, manner
139 **peyned hire:** took pains   **countrefete:** imitate
139–140 **cheere Of court:** the manners of the court
140 **estatlich of manere:** dignified in behavior
141 **digne of reverence:** worthy of respect
142 **conscience:** moral sense and solicitude
143 **pitous:** compassionate
144 **saugh:** saw
147 **rosted flessh:** roasted meat   **wastel-breed:** expensive fine white bread
148 **soore:** sorely, bitterly
149 **smoot:** beat   **yerde:** switch   **smerte:** smartly, painfully
151 **Ful semyly:** very properly   **wympul:** wimple, a head dress that covers all but the face   **pynched:** pleated
152 **tretys:** well formed   **greye:** gray (?); the exact color intended is uncertain.
153 **smal:** small, elegant   **therto:** moreover   **reed:** red

But sikerly she hadde a fair forheed;
It was almoost a spanne brood, I trowe; 155
For, hardily, she was nat undergrowe.
Ful fetys was hir cloke, as I was war.
Of smal coral aboute hire arm she bar
A peire of bedes, gauded al with grene,
And theron heng a brooch of gold ful sheene, 160
On which ther was first write a crowned A,
And after *Amor vincit omnia.*

    Another NONNE with hire hadde she,
That was hir chapeleyne, and preestes thre.

    A MONK ther was, a fair for the maistrie, 165
An outridere, that lovede venerie,
A manly man, to been an abbot able.
Ful many a deyntee hors hadde he in stable,
And whan he rood, men myghte his brydel heere
Gynglen in a whistlynge wynd als cleere 170
And eek as loude as dooth the chapel belle
Ther as this lord was kepere of the celle.
The reule of Seint Maure or of Seint Beneit—
By cause that it was old and somdel streit
This ilke Monk leet olde thynges pace, 175
And heeld after the newe world the space.
He yaf nat of that text a pulled hen,
That seith that hunters ben nat hooly men,
Ne that a monk, whan he is recchelees,
Is likned til a fissh that is waterlees— 180
This is to seyn, a monk out of his cloystre.
But thilke text heeld he nat worth an oystre;
And I seyde his opinion was good.

What sholde he studie and make hymselven wood,
Upon a book in cloystre alwey to poure, 185
Or swynken with his handes, and laboure,
As Austyn bit? How shal the world be served?
Lat Austyn have his swynk to hym reserved!
Therfore he was a prikasour aright:
Grehoundes he hadde as swift as fowel in flight; 190
Of prikyng and of huntyng for the hare
Was al his lust, for no cost wolde he spare.
I seigh his sleves purfiled at the hond
With grys, and that the fyneste of a lond;
And for to festne his hood under his chyn, 195
He hadde of gold ywroght a ful curious pyn;
A love-knotte in the gretter ende ther was.
His heed was balled, that shoon as any glas,
And eek his face, as he hadde been enoynt.
He was a lord ful fat and in good poynt; 200
His eyen stepe, and rollynge in his heed,
That stemed as a forneys of a leed;
His bootes souple, his hors in greet estaat.
Now certeinly he was a fair prelaat;
He was nat pale as a forpyned goost. 205
A fat swan loved he best of any roost.
His palfrey was as broun as is a berye.

    A FRERE ther was, a wantowne and a merye,
A lymytour, a ful solempne man.
In alle the ordres foure is noon that kan 210
So muchel of daliaunce and fair langage.
He hadde maad ful many a mariage
Of yonge wommen at his owene cost.
Unto his ordre he was a noble post.

---

154 **sikerly:** certainly
155 **spanne brood:** about seven to nine inches wide **trowe:** believe
156 **hardily:** certainly
157 **Ful fetys:** very elegant, well made **war:** aware
159 **peire:** set **gauded:** divided by large beads (*gaudes*) marking the Paternosters
160 **sheene:** bright
161 **crowned A:** an A surmounted by a crown
162 **Amor vincit omnia:** love conquers all; the phrase could apply to either divine or earthly love.
164 **chapeleyne:** a nun serving as a secretary to a prioress **preestes thre:** three priests; see n.
165 **a fair for the maistrie:** an extremely fine or handsome one
166 **outridere:** monk with business outside the monastery **venerie:** hunting
167 **manly:** generous, virile
168 **deyntee:** fine
169 **myghte his brydel heere:** could hear his bridle
170 **Gynglen:** jingle **als cleere:** as clearly
172 **celle:** a subordinate monastery
173 **reule of Seint Maure . . . Seint Beneit:** the Benedictine Rule, established by St. Benedict and introduced into France by his follower St. Maurus
174 **somdel streit:** somewhat narrow, strict
175–76 This same monk let old things pass away (*pace*) and followed the customs of modern times.
177 **yaf:** gave **text:** authoritative written statement **pulled:** plucked
179 **recchelees:** heedless of rules
180 **til:** to **waterlees:** out of water
182 **thilke:** that **nat worth an oystre:** i.e., worth nothing

184 **wood:** crazy, mad
185 **alwey:** always **poure:** pore over
186 **swynken:** work
187 **Austyn:** St. Augustine, supposed author of a monastic rule **bit** = *biddeth,* commands
189 **prikasour:** horseman, hunter on horseback **aright:** certainly
190 **Grehoundes:** greyhounds
191 **prikyng:** tracking
192 **lust:** pleasure
193 **seigh:** saw **purfiled:** lined with fur
194 **grys:** expensive squirrel fur **fyneste of a lond:** best to be had
196 **curious:** skillfully made
197 **love-knotte:** elaborate knot **gretter:** larger
198 **balled:** bald
199 **enoynt:** anointed, rubbed with oil
200 **in good poynt:** in good condition
201 **stepe:** prominent or bright
202 His eyes gleamed like a furnace under a cauldron (R.).
203 **souple:** pliant **greet estaat:** excellent condition
204 **prelaat:** ecclesiastical dignitary
205 **forpyned goost:** tormented spirit
208 **wantowne:** jovial, pleasure-loving **merye:** merry
209 **lymytour:** friar licensed (by his order) to beg in a specific district **solempne:** dignified, important
210 **ordres foure:** the four orders of friars **kan:** knows
211 **muchel:** much **daliaunce:** sociability
214 **post:** supporter (pillar of the Church)

Ful wel biloved and famulier was he   215
With frankeleyns over al in his contree,
And eek with worthy wommen of the toun;
For he hadde power of confessioun,
As seyde hymself, moore than a curat,
For of his ordre he was licenciat.   220
Ful swetely herde he confessioun,
And plesaunt was his absolucioun:
He was an esy man to yeve penaunce,
Ther as he wiste to have a good pitaunce.
For unto a povre ordre for to yive   225
Is signe that a man is wel yshryve;
For if he yaf, he dorste make avaunt,
He wiste that a man was repentaunt;
For many a man so hard is of his herte,
He may nat wepe, althogh hym soore smerte.   230
Therfore in stede of wepynge and preyeres
Men moote yeve silver to the povre freres.
His typet was ay farsed ful of knyves
And pynnes, for to yeven faire wyves.
And certeinly he hadde a murye note: 235
Wel koude he synge and pleyen on a rote;
Of yeddynges he baar outrely the pris.
His nekke whit was as the flour-de-lys;
Therto he strong was as a champioun.
He knew the tavernes wel in every toun   240
And everich hostiler and tappestere
Bet than a lazar or a beggestere,
For unto swich a worthy man as he
Acorded nat, as by his facultee,
To have with sike lazars aqueyntaunce.   245
It is nat honest; it may nat avaunce,
For to deelen with no swich poraille,
But al with riche and selleres of vitaille.

And over al, ther as profit sholde arise,
Curteis he was and lowely of servyse;   250
Ther nas no man nowher so vertuous.
He was the beste beggere in his hous;
[And yaf a certeyn ferme for the graunt;
Noon of his bretheren cam ther in his haunt;]
For thogh a wydwe hadde noght a sho,
So plesaunt was his *In principio,*
Yet wolde he have a ferthyng, er he wente.   255
His purchas was wel bettre than his rente.
And rage he koude, as it were right a whelp.
In love-dayes ther koude he muchel help,
For ther he was nat lyk a cloysterer
With a thredbare cope, as is a povre scoler,   260
But he was lyk a maister or a pope.
Of double worstede was his semycope,
That rounded as a belle out of the presse.
Somwhat he lipsed, for his wantownesse,
To make his Englissh sweete upon his tonge;   265
And in his harpyng, whan that he hadde songe,
His eyen twynkled in his heed aryght
As doon the sterres in the frosty nyght.
This worthy lymytour was cleped Huberd.

A MARCHANT was ther with a forked berd,   270
In mottelee, and hye on horse he sat;
Upon his heed a Flaundryssh bever hat,
His bootes clasped faire and fetisly.
His resons he spak ful solempnely,
Sownynge alwey th'encrees of his wynnyng.   275
He wolde the see were kept for any thyng
Bitwixe Middelburgh and Orewelle.

216 **frankeleyns:** landowners   **over al:** everywhere
217 **eek:** also
220 **licenciat:** licensed to hear confessions
223 **esy:** lenient   **yeve:** give
224 **wiste:** expected   **pitaunce:** gift (literally food allowed to a member of a religious house)
225 **povre:** poor
226 **yshryve:** confessed, penitent
227 For if a man gave, he (the Friar) dared to assert (R.)
228 **wiste:** knew
230 **may nat:** cannot, is not able to   **hym soore smerte:** he sorely, painfully, suffers
232 **moote yeve:** must give
233 **typet:** the dangling tip of the hood   **farsed:** stuffed
234 **yeven:** give
235 **murye:** merry, pleasing   **note:** voice
236 **rote:** stringed instrument
237 For reciting ballads (*yeddynges*), he absolutely (*outrely*) took the prize.
238 **flour-de-lys:** lily
239 **champioun:** champion, representative in a judicial duel
241 **everich:** every   **hostiler:** innkeeper   **tappestere:** barmaid
242 **Bet:** better   **lazar:** leper   **beggestere:** beggar-woman
243 **swich:** such
244 It was not suitable, in view of his official position.
245 **sike:** sick
246 **honest:** honorable, respectable   **may nat avaunce:** cannot be profitable
247 **swich poraille:** such poor people
248 **vitaille:** victuals, provisions

249 **ther as:** where
250 **lowely of servyse:** graciously humble
251 **nas** = *ne was,* was not   **vertuous:** capable
252a **ferme:** fee, fixed payment   **graunt:** grant (of an exclusive territory for begging)
252b **haunt:** territory
253 **sho:** shoe
254 **In principio:** in the beginning (the opening words of Gen. 1 and John 1, popular for devotions)
255 **ferthyng:** farthing
256 **purchas:** total income   **rente:** proper income
257 **rage:** romp, sport (or flirt)   **whelp:** pup
258 **love-dayes:** days on which disputes were reconciled
260 **povre scoler:** poor scholar, student
262 **double worstede:** a very wide (hence expensive) cloth   **semycope:** short cloak
263 **rounded:** was round   **presse:** casting mold
264 **lipsed:** lisped   **wantownesse:** affectation
266 **songe:** sung
267 **aryght:** exactly
268 **sterres:** stars
269 **cleped:** called
271 **mottelee:** parti-colored cloth   **hye on horse:** in a high saddle
272 **Flaundryssh:** Flemish
273 **fetisly:** elegantly, neatly
274 **resons:** remarks, opinions   **solempnely:** ceremoniously, solemnly
275 **Sownynge:** concerned with, or, making known   **wynnyng:** profit
276 **see:** sea   **kept for any thyng:** protected at all costs
277 **Middelburgh:** a Dutch port   **Orewelle:** Orwell, on the English coast

Wel koude he in eschaunge sheeldes selle.
This worthy man ful wel his wit bisette:
Ther wiste no wight that he was in dette,   280
So estatly was he of his governaunce
With his bargaynes and with his chevyssaunce.
For sothe he was a worthy man with alle,
But, sooth to seyn, I noot how men hym calle.
    A CLERK ther was of Oxenford also,   285
That unto logyk hadde longe ygo.
As leene was his hors as is a rake,
And he nas nat right fat, I undertake,
But looked holwe, and therto sobrely.
Ful thredbare was his overeste courtepy,   290
For he hadde geten hym yet no benefice,
Ne was so worldly for to have office.
For hym was levere have at his beddes heed
Twenty bookes, clad in blak or reed,
Of Aristotle and his philosophie   295
Than robes riche, or fithele, or gay sautrie.
But al be that he was a philosophre,
Yet hadde he but litel gold in cofre;
But al that he myghte of his freendes hente,
On bookes and on lernynge he it spente,   300
And bisily gan for the soules preye
Of hem that yaf hym wherwith to scoleye.
Of studie took he moost cure and moost heede.
Noght o word spak he moore than was neede,
And that was seyd in forme and reverence,   305
And short and quyk and ful of hy sentence;
Sownynge in moral vertu was his speche,

And gladly wolde he lerne and gladly teche.
    A SERGEANT OF THE LAWE, war and wys,
That often hadde been at the Parvys,   310
Ther was also, ful riche of excellence.
Discreet he was and of greet reverence—
He semed swich, his wordes weren so wise.
Justice he was ful often in assise,
By patente and by pleyn commissioun.   315
For his science and for his heigh renoun,
Of fees and robes hadde he many oon.
So greet a purchasour was nowher noon:
Al was fee symple to hym in effect;
His purchasyng myghte nat been infect.   320
Nowher so bisy a man as he ther nas,
And yet he semed bisier than he was.
In termes hadde he caas and doomes alle
That from the tyme of kyng William were falle.   324
Therto he koude endite and make a thyng,
Ther koude no wight pynche at his writyng;
And every statut koude he pleyn by rote.
He rood but hoomly in a medlee cote,
Girt with a ceint of silk, with barres smale;
Of his array telle I no lenger tale.   330
    A FRANKELEYN was in his compaignye.
Whit was his berd as is the dayesye;
Of his complexioun he was sangwyn.
Wel loved he by the morwe a sop in wyn;
To lyven in delit was evere his wone,   335
For he was Epicurus owene sone,

---

278 **sheeldes:** A *sheeld* was a unit of exchange; selling shields was a way of borrowing money, often at a cost to the seller.
279 **his wit bisette:** used his wits
281 **estatly:** dignified   **governaunce:** behavior, management
282 **bargaynes:** buying and selling   **chevyssaunce:** financial arrangements, borrowing
283 **For sothe:** truly   **with alle:** indeed
284 **noot** = *ne woot,* do not know
285 **Clerk:** university student, scholar
286 **unto logyk hadde longe ygo:** had taken (studied) logic a long time
288 **right:** very   **undertake:** affirm, declare
289 **holwe:** emaciated   **sobrely:** grave, serious
290 **overeste:** uppermost   **courtepy:** short coat
291 **benefice:** ecclesiastical living
292 **office:** secular employment
293 **hym was levere:** he would rather   **his beddes heed:** head of his bed
296 **fithele:** fiddle   **gay sautrie:** elegant psaltry (a harp-like instrument)
297 **al be that:** even though   **philosophre:** the word can mean either philosopher or alchemist
299 **myghte of his freendes hente:** could get from his friends
301 **gan . . . preye:** did pray, prayed
302 **scoleye:** attend the schools of the university
303 **cure:** care
304 **o:** one   **neede:** necessary
305 **in forme and reverence:** with due formality and respect (R.)
306 **quyk:** vivid, lively   **hy sentence:** elevated content
307 **Sownynge in:** consonant with

309 **Sergeant of the Lawe:** a lawyer who belonged to the highest order in his profession
war: prudent
310 **Parvys:** the porch of St. Paul's Cathedral
311 **ful riche of excellence:** well endowed with superior qualities
312 **Discreet . . . and of greet reverence:** judicious and with much dignity
314 **Justice:** judge   **assise:** the court of assizes
315 **patente:** letter of appointment from the king   **pleyn commissioun:** full jurisdiction
316 **science:** knowledge
317 **fees and robes:** grants of yearly income (a legal formula)   **many oon:** many a one
318 **purchasour:** land-buyer
319 **fee symple:** unrestricted possession
320 **been infect:** be invalidated
323–24 He had in Year Books all the cases (*caas* a*nd* judicial decisions (*doomes*) from the time of William I.
325 **endite and make a thyng:** draft and draw up a legal document
326 **pynche at:** find a flaw in
327 And he knew every statute entirely by heart.
328 **hoomly:** simply   **medlee:** parti-colored
329 **Girt:** girded   **ceint:** belt   **barres:** stripes
330 **array:** dress
331 **Frankeleyn:** landowner
332 **dayesye:** daisy
333 **complexioun:** temperament, balance of the body's fluids, the four "humors"—blood, phlegm, red or yellow bile (choler), black bile (melancholy)   **sangwyn:** of the sanguine humor (dominated by blood)
334 **sop in wyn:** piece of bread in wine
335 **delit:** delight, pleasure   **wone:** custom, wont
336 **Epicurus owene sone:** an Epicurean

That heeld opinioun that pleyn delit
Was verray felicitee parfit.
An housholdere, and that a greet, was he;
Seint Julian he was in his contree.   340
His breed, his ale, was alweys after oon;
A bettre envyned man was nowher noon.
Withoute bake mete was nevere his hous,
Of fissh and flessh, and that so plentevous
It snewed in his hous of mete and drynke;   345
Of alle deyntees that men koude thynke,
After the sondry sesons of the yeer,
So chaunged he his mete and his soper.
Ful many a fat partrich hadde he in muwe,
And many a breem and many a luce in stuwe.   350
Wo was his cook but if his sauce were
Poynaunt and sharp, and redy al his geere.
His table dormant in his halle alway
Stood redy covered al the longe day.
At sessiouns ther was he lord and sire;   355
Ful ofte tyme he was knyght of the shire.
An anlaas and a gipser al of silk
Heeng at his girdel, whit as morne milk.
A shirreve hadde he been, and a contour.
Was nowher swich a worthy vavasour.   360
    AN HABERDASSHERE and a CARPENTER,
A WEBBE, a DYERE, and a TAPYCER—
And they were clothed alle in o lyveree
Of a solempne and a greet fraternitee.
Ful fressh and newe hir geere apiked was;   365
Hir knyves were chaped noght with bras
But al with silver, wroght ful clene and weel,

Hire girdles and hir pouches everydeel.
Wel semed ech of hem a fair burgeys
To sitten in a yeldehalle on a deys.   370
Everich, for the wisdom that he kan,
Was shaply for to been an alderman.
For catel hadde they ynogh and rente,
And eek hir wyves wolde it wel assente;
And elles certeyn were they to blame.   375
It is ful fair to been ycleped "madame,"
And goon to vigiliies al bifore,
And have a mantel roialliche ybore.
    A COOK they hadde with hem for the nones
To boille the chiknes with the marybones,   380
And poudre-marchant tart and galyngale.
Wel koude he knowe a draughte of Londoun ale.
He koude rooste, and sethe, and broille, and frye,
Maken mortreux, and wel bake a pye.
But greet harm was it, as it thoughte me,   385
That on his shyne a mormal hadde he.
For blankmanger, that made he with the beste.
    A SHIPMAN was ther, wonynge fer by weste;
For aught I woot, he was of Dertemouthe.
He rood upon a rouncy, as he kouthe,   390
In a gowne of faldyng to the knee.
A daggere hangynge on a laas hadde he
Aboute his nekke, under his arm adoun.
The hoote somer hadde maad his hewe al broun;
And certeinly he was a good felawe.   395
Ful many a draughte of wyn had he ydrawe

337 **That:** who   **pleyn delit:** pure pleasure
338 **verray felicitee parfit:** true perfect happiness
340 **Seint Julian:** patron saint of hospitality
341 **after oon:** of the same (good) quality
342 **envyned:** stocked with wine
343 **bake mete:** pie of meat, fowl, or fish
344 **plentevous:** plenteous
345 **snewed:** snowed
346 **deyntees:** fine food and drink
347 **After the sondry sesons:** according to the various seasons. Seasonal adjustment of the diet was a health measure.
349 **partrich:** partridge   **muwe:** pen for birds
350 **breem:** bream (a freshwater fish)   **luce:** pike   **stuwe:** fish pond
351 **but if:** unless
352 **Poynaunt:** spicy, piercing   **geere:** utensils
353 **table dormant:** table permanently in place (rather than taken down between meals)
355 He presided at court sessions.
356 **knyght of the shire:** member of Parliament
357 **anlaas:** broad, two-edged dagger   **gipser:** purse
359 **shirreve:** sheriff   **contour:** auditor
360 **vavasour:** feudal landholder
361 **Haberdasshere:** a dealer in hats or small wares
362 **Webbe:** weaver   **Tapycer:** weaver of tapestries, rugs, etc.
363 **o lyveree:** one livery, distinctive dress worn by members of a guild
364 **solempne:** dignified, important   **fraternitee:** parish guild
365 **geere:** equipment   **apiked:** trimmed, adorned
366 **chaped:** mounted

368 **girdles:** belts   **pouches:** purses   **everydeel:** every bit
369 **ech:** each (one)   **burgeys:** citizen of a city (tradesman)
370 **yeldehalle:** guildhall   **deys:** dais
371 **kan:** knows
372 **shaply:** suitable, fit   **alderman:** city official
373 **catel:** property   **rente:** income
375 **elles:** otherwise
376 **ycleped "madame":** called "my lady"
377 **vigiliies:** vigils, feasts held on the eve of a holy day   **al bifore:** in front of everyone, heading the procession
378 **roialliche ybore:** royally carried
379 **for the nones:** for the occasion
380 **chiknes:** chickens   **marybones:** marrow bones
381 **poudre-marchant tart:** a tart spice   **galyngale:** powdered aromatic root used as a sweet spice
383 **sethe:** simmer
384 **mortreux:** stews or hashes
385 **harm:** pity   **it thoughte me:** it seemed to me
386 **mormal:** ulcer; see n.
387 **blankmanger:** a thick stew or mousse of chopped chicken or fish boiled with rice **with the beste:** excellently
388 **wonynge:** dwelling   **fer by weste:** far in the west
389 **For aught I woot:** for all I know   **Dertemouthe:** Dartmouth, in Devon, in the south west
390 **rouncy:** carthorse, nag   **as he kouthe:** as best he could
391 **faldyng:** coarse woolen cloth
392 **laas:** cord
393 **under his arm adoun:** down under his arm
395 **good felawe:** good companion; see n.

Fro Burdeux-ward, whil that the chapman sleep.
Of nyce conscience took he no keep.
If that he faught and hadde the hyer hond,
By water he sente hem hoom to every lond.   400
But of his craft to rekene wel his tydes,
His stremes, and his daungers hym bisides,
His herberwe, and his moone, his lodemenage,
Ther nas noon swich from Hulle to Cartage.
Hardy he was and wys to undertake;   405
With many a tempest hadde his berd been shake.
He knew alle the havenes, as they were,
Fro Gootlond to the cape of Fynystere,
And every cryke in Britaigne and in Spayne.
His barge ycleped was the Maudelayne.   410

    With us ther was a DOCTOUR OF PHISIK;
In al this world ne was ther noon hym lik,
To speke of phisik and of surgerye,
For he was grounded in astronomye.
He kepte his pacient a ful greet deel   415
In houres by his magyk natureel.
Wel koude he fortunen the ascendent
Of his ymages for his pacient.
He knew the cause of everich maladye,
Were it of hoot, or coold, or moyste, or drye,   420
And where they engendred, and of what humour.
He was a verray, parfit praktisour:
The cause yknowe, and of his harm the roote,
Anon he yaf the sike man his boote.
Ful redy hadde he his apothecaries   425
To sende hym drogges and his letuaries,
For ech of hem made oother for to wynne—
Hir frendshipe nas nat newe to bigynne.

Wel knew he the olde Esculapius,
And Deyscorides, and eek Rufus,   430
Olde Ypocras, Haly, and Galyen,
Serapion, Razis, and Avycen,
Averrois, Damascien, and Constantyn,
Bernard, and Gatesden, and Gilbertyn.
Of his diete mesurable was he,   435
For it was of no superfluitee,
But of greet norissyng and digestible.
His studie was but litel on the Bible.
In sangwyn and in pers he clad was al,
Lyned with taffata and with sendal.   440
And yet he was but esy of dispence;
He kepte that he wan in pestilence.
For gold in phisik is a cordial,
Therefore he lovede gold in special.

    A good WIF was ther OF biside BATHE,   445
But she was somdel deef, and that was scathe.
Of clooth-makyng she hadde swich an haunt
She passed hem of Ypres and of Gaunt.
In al the parisshe wif ne was ther noon
That to the offrynge bifore hire sholde goon;   450
And if ther dide, certeyn so wrooth was she
That she was out of alle charitee.
Hir coverchiefs ful fyne weren of ground;
I dorste swere they weyeden ten pound
That on a Sonday weren upon hir heed.   455
Hir hosen weren of fyn scarlet reed,
Ful streite yteyd, and shoes ful moyste and newe.
Boold was hir face, and fair, and reed of hewe.
She was a worthy womman al hir lyve:
Housbondes at chirche dore she hadde fyve,   460
Withouten oother compaignye in youthe—

397 **Burdeux-ward:** the direction of Bordeaux   **chapman:** merchant   **sleep:** slept
398 **nyce:** scrupulous   **took he no keep:** he took no notice
399 **If that:** if   **the hyer hond:** the upper hand
401 **craft to rekene:** skill to reckon
402 **stremes:** currents   **daungers hym bisides:** perils near at hand
403 **herberwe:** harbors, anchorages   **moone:** positions of the moon   **lodemenage:** skill in navigation. See n. to lines 401–9.
404 **Hulle:** Hull, on the Yorkshire Coast   **Cartage:** Carthage, Tunisia, or Cartagena, Spain
405 **wys to undertake:** prudent in his undertakings
408 **Gootlond . . . cape of Fynystere:** Probably Gotland and Cape Finistere
409 **cryke:** inlet   **Britaigne:** Brittany
410 **barge:** sailing vessel; see n.
411 **Phisik:** medicine
414 **grounded:** instructed   **astronomye:** the science of astrology; see n.
416 **houres:** astronomical hours   **magyk natureel:** science
417 **fortunen the ascendent:** calculate the planetary position
418 **ymages:** talismanic figures in astrology
420 **hoot, coold, moyste, drye:** the elemental qualities; see n.
421 **humour:** kind of bodily fluid
422 **verray:** true   **parfit:** perfect, complete   **praktisour:** practitioner
424 **Anon:** at once   **boote:** remedy
426 **drogges:** drugs   **letuaries:** electuaries, medicinal mixtures
427 **ech:** each (one)   **wynne:** profit
428 **newe to bigynne:** recently begun

429–34 The physician knows the standard medical authorities, from the Greeks (Aesculapius) to the contemporary English Gilbertus Anglicus; see n.
435 **mesurable:** moderate
439 **sangwyn:** red   **pers:** blue or bluish gray
440 **taffata, sendal:** varieties of silk
441 **but esy of dispence:** moderate in (careful about) spending
442 **wan:** gained
443 **cordial:** medicine for the heart
444 **in special:** in particular
446 **somdel deef:** somewhat deaf   **that was scathe:** that was a pity. See WBPro III.668.
447 **haunt:** skill
448 **Ypres, Gaunt:** Ypres, Ghent, cloth-making centers in modern Belgium
450 **offrynge:** offering (when the people go to the altar with their offerings at Mass)
451 **wrooth:** angry
452 **out of alle charitee:** deeply upset
453 **coverchiefs:** linen coverings for the head   **fyne weren of ground:** were fine in texture
454 **dorste swere:** dare swear   **weyeden:** weighed
456 **hosen:** stockings
457 **streite yteyd:** closely laced   **moyste:** supple
460 **chirche dore:** door of the church
461 **Withouten:** not counting; see n.

But thereof nedeth nat to speke as nowthe.
And thries hadde she been at Jerusalem;
She hadde passed many a straunge strem;
At Rome she hadde been, and at Boloigne,   465
In Galice at Seint-Jame, and at Coloigne.
She koude muchel of wandrynge by the weye.
Gat-tothed was she, soothly for to seye.
Upon an amblere esily she sat,
Ywympled wel, and on hir heed an hat   470
As brood as is a bokeler or a targe;
A foot-mantel aboute hir hipes large,
And on hir feet a paire of spores sharpe.
In felaweshipe wel koude she laughe and carpe.
Of remedies of love she knew per chaunce,   475
For she koude of that art the olde daunce.

  A good man was ther of religioun,
And was a povre PERSOUN OF A TOUN,
But riche he was of hooly thoght and werk.
He was also a lerned man, a clerk,   480
That Cristes gospel trewely wolde preche;
His parisshens devoutly wolde he teche.
Benygne he was, and wonder diligent,
And in adversitee ful pacient,
And swich he was ypreved ofte sithes.   485
Ful looth were hym to cursen for his tithes,
But rather wolde he yeven, out of doute,
Unto his povre parisshens aboute
Of his offryng and eek of his substaunce.
He koude in litel thyng have suffisaunce.   490
Wyd was his parisshe, and houses fer asonder,
But he ne lefte nat, for reyn ne thonder,
In siknesse nor in meschief to visite

The ferreste in his parisshe, muche and lite,
Upon his feet, and in his hand a staf.   495
This noble ensample to his sheep he yaf,
That first he wroghte, and afterward he taughte.
Out of the gospel he tho wordes caughte,
And this figure he added eek therto,
That if gold ruste, what shal iren do?   500
For if a preest be foul, on whom we truste,
No wonder is a lewed man to ruste;
And shame it is, if a prest take keep,
A shiten shepherde and a clene sheep.
Wel oghte a preest ensample for to yive,   505
By his clennesse, how that his sheep sholde lyve.
He sette nat his benefice to hyre
And leet his sheep encombred in the myre
And ran to Londoun unto Seinte Poules
To seken hym a chaunterie for soules,   510
Or with a bretherhed to been withholde;
But dwelte at hoom, and kepte wel his folde,
So that the wolf ne made it nat myscarie;
He was a shepherde and noght a mercenarie.
And though he hooly were and vertuous,   515
He was to synful men nat despitous,
Ne of his speche daungerous ne digne,
But in his techyng discreet and benygne.
To drawen folk to hevene by fairnesse,
By good ensample, this was his bisynesse.   520
But it were any persone obstinat,
What so he were, of heigh or lough estat,
Hym wolde he snybben sharply for the nonys.
A bettre preest I trowe that nowher noon ys.
He waited after no pompe and reverence,   525
Ne maked him a spiced conscience,

462 **as nowthe:** now
463–66 Jerusalem, Rome, *Boloigne* (Boulogne in France)*, in Galice at Seint-Jame*
(St. James of Compostella in Galicia, Spain), and *Coloigne (*Cologne) were celebrated
places of pilgrimage.
464 **straunge strem:** foreign sea
468 **Gat-tothed:** with teeth set wide apart (R.)
469 **amblere:** a pacing horse   **esily:** comfortably
470 **Ywympled wel:** wearing a large wimple, a head dress that covers all but the face
471 **brood as is a bokeler or a targe:** broad as a buckler or shield
472 **foot-mantel:** an apron-like overskirt
473 **spores:** spurs
474 **carpe:** chatter
475 **remedies of love:** remedies for love-sickness   **per chaunce:** as it happened
476 **olde daunce:** tricks of the trade, game of love
478 **povre Persoun:** poor parson
482 **parisshens:** parishioners
483 **Benygne:** gracious
485 **ypreved:** proven   **ofte sithes:** many times
486 He was very reluctant (*Ful looth*) to excommunicate (*cursen*) those who did not
pay the tithes (one-tenth of their income) legally due their priest.
489 **offryng:** voluntary offerings of the people at Mass   **substaunce:** fixed income
(from property of the Church)
491 **asonder:** apart
492 **ne lefte nat:** did not omit
493 **meschief:** trouble

494 **ferreste:** those farthest away   **muche and lite:** great and small, everyone
496 **ensample:** model
498 **tho:** those
499 **figure:** metaphor
501 **foul:** evil
502 **lewed man:** uneducated man, layman
503 **take keep:** is concerned
504 **shiten:** defiled, foul
506 **clennesse:** purity
507 **sette nat . . . to hyre:** did not farm out
508 **leet:** left   **encombred:** stuck
509 **Seinte Poules:** St. Paul's Cathedral
510 **chaunterie:** appointment as a chantry priest, to serve in a chapel endowed for
prayers for the soul of its patron
511 **bretherhed to been withholde:** to be retained, hired, as its chaplain by a guild
513 **myscarie:** go wrong
516 **despitous:** scornful
517 **daungerous:** domineering   **digne:** haughty
518 **discreet:** courteous
519 **fairnesse:** graciousness, kindness
522 **heigh or lough estat:** high or low rank
523 **snybben:** rebuke   **for the nonys:** then, at that time
524 **trowe:** believe
525 **waited after:** expected   **reverence:** ceremony
526 **spiced:** over-fastidious; see n.

But Cristes loore and his apostles twelve
He taughte; but first he folwed it hymselve.
    With hym ther was a PLOWMAN, was his brother,
That hadde ylad of dong ful many a fother;   530
A trewe swynkere and a good was he,
Lyvynge in pees and parfit charitee.
God loved he best with al his hoole herte
At alle tymes, thogh him gamed or smerte,
And thanne his neighebor right as hymselve.   535
He wolde thresshe, and therto dyke and delve,
For Cristes sake, for every povre wight,
Withouten hire, if it lay in his myght.
His tithes payde he ful faire and wel,
Bothe of his propre swynk and his catel.   540
In a tabard he rood upon a mere.
    Ther was also a REVE, and a MILLERE,
A SOMNOUR, and a PARDONER also,
A MAUNCIPLE, and myself—ther were namo.
    The MILLERE was a stout carl for the nones;   545
Ful byg he was of brawn, and eek of bones.
That proved wel, for over al ther he cam,
At wrastlynge he wolde have alwey the ram.
He was short-sholdred, brood, a thikke knarre;
Ther was no dore that he nolde heve of harre,   550
Or breke it at a rennyng with his heed.
His berd as any sowe or fox was reed,
And therto brood, as though it were a spade.
Upon the cop right of his nose he hade
A werte, and theron stood a toft of herys,   555
Reed as the brustles of a sowes erys;
His nosethirles blake were and wyde.
A swerd and a bokeler bar he by his syde.
His mouth as greet was as a greet forneys.

He was a janglere and a goliardeys,   560
And that was moost of synne and harlotries.
Wel koude he stelen corn and tollen thries;
And yet he hadde a thombe of gold, pardee.
A whit cote and a blew hood wered he.
A baggepipe wel koude he blowe and sowne,   565
And therwithal he broghte us out of towne.
    A gentil MAUNCIPLE was ther of a temple,
Of which achatours myghte take exemple
For to be wise in byynge of vitaille;
For wheither that he payde or took by taille,   570
Algate he wayted so in his achaat
That he was ay biforn and in good staat.
Now is nat that of God a ful fair grace
That swich a lewed mannes wit shal pace
The wisdom of an heep of lerned men?   575
Of maistres hadde he mo than thries ten,
That weren of lawe expert and curious,
Of which ther were a duszeyne in that hous
Worthy to been stywardes of rente and lond
Of any lord that is in Engelond,   580
To make hym lyve by his propre good
In honour dettelees (but if he were wood),
Or lyve as scarsly as hym list desire;
And able for to helpen al a shire
In any caas that myghte falle or happe.   585
And yet this Manciple sette hir aller cappe.
    The REVE was a sclendre colerik man.
His berd was shave as ny as ever he kan;

530 Who had hauled (*ylad*) full many a cartload (*fother*) of dung (*dong*)
531 **swynkere:** worker
532 **pees:** peace
534 **thogh him gamed or smerte:** whether it pleased or pained him
535 **right as:** exactly as
536 **therto:** moreover   **dyke and delve:** make ditches and dig
537 **wight:** person
538 **hire:** payment   **myght:** power
540 **propre swynk:** own labor   **catel:** possessions
541 **tabard:** workman's loose, sleeveless outer garment   **mere:** mare
544 **namo:** no others
545 **carl:** fellow   **for the nones:** indeed
546 **byg:** strong   **brawn:** muscle
547 **over al:** wherever
548 **have alwey the ram:** always win the ram (given as a prize)
549 **short-sholdred:** stoutly built (with a thick neck)   **thikke knarre:** stout fellow
550 **nolde** = *ne wolde,* would not   **heve of harre:** lift off its hinges
551 **at a rennyng:** by running against it
554 **cop:** top
555 **werte:** wart   **toft of herys:** tuft of hairs
556 **brustles:** bristles   **sowes erys:** sow's ears
557 **nosethirles:** nostrils
559 **greet forneys:** large cauldron

560 **janglere:** a teller of dirty stories   **goliardeys:** buffoon
561 **harlotries:** deeds of harlotry, obscenities
562 **stelen corn:** steal grain   **tollen thries:** take toll (payment) three times
563 **thombe of gold:** golden thumb; an ironic reference to a proverb, with the implication that there are no honest millers   **pardee:** indeed
564 **blew:** blue
565 **sowne:** play
567 **Maunciple . . . of a temple:** business agent, purchaser of provisions for a *temple,*
an Inn of Court (school of law)
568 **achatours:** buyers   **myghte:** could
569 **byynge of vitaille:** purchase of victuals, provisions
570 **by taille:** on credit
571 **Algate:** always   **wayted so in his achaat:** watched so carefully (for his opportunity)
in his purchases
572 **ay biforn:** always ahead
574 **lewed:** uneducated   **pace:** surpass
576 **mo:** more
577 **curious:** skillful
578 **duszeyne:** dozen
579 **stywardes:** stewards   **rente:** income
581 **propre good:** own wealth
582 **dettelees:** without debts   **but if he were wood:** unless he was crazy
583 **as scarsly as hym list desire:** as economically as he pleased
585 **caas:** case, circumstances   **happe:** occur by chance
586 **sette hir aller cappe:** deceived them all
587 **Reve:** reeve, manager of an estate or farm   **sclendre:** lean   **colerik:** dominated
by the humor choler
588 **ny:** close   **kan:** can

His heer was by his erys ful round yshorn;
His top was dokked lyk a preest biforn.　590
Ful longe were his legges and ful lene,
Ylyk a staf; ther was no calf ysene.
Wel koude he kepe a gerner and a bynne;
Ther was noon auditour koude on him wynne.
Wel wiste he by the droghte and by the reyn　595
The yeldynge of his seed and of his greyn.
His lordes sheep, his neet, his dayerye,
His swyn, his hors, his stoor, and his pultrye
Was hoolly in this Reves governynge,
And by his covenant yaf the rekenynge,　600
Syn that his lord was twenty yeer of age.
Ther koude no man brynge hym in arrerage.
Ther nas baillif, ne hierde, nor oother hyne,
That he ne knew his sleighte and his covyne;
They were adrad of hym as of the deeth.　605
His wonyng was ful faire upon an heeth;
With grene trees yshadwed was his place.
He koude bettre than his lord purchace.
Ful riche he was astored pryvely.
His lord wel koude he plesen subtilly,　610
To yeve and lene hym of his owene good,
And have a thank, and yet a cote and hood.
In youthe he hadde lerned a good myster:
He was a wel good wrighte, a carpenter.
This Reve sat upon a ful good stot　615
That was al pomely grey and highte Scot.
A long surcote of pers upon he hade,
And by his syde he baar a rusty blade.
Of Northfolk was this Reve of which I telle,
Biside a toun men clepen Baldeswelle.　620

Tukked he was as is a frere aboute,
And evere he rood the hyndreste of oure route.
　A SOMONOUR was ther with us in that place,
That hadde a fyr-reed cherubynnes face,
For saucefleem he was, with eyen narwe.　625
As hoot he was and lecherous as a sparwe,
With scalled browes blake and piled berd.
Of his visage children were aferd.
Ther nas quyk-silver, lytarge, ne brymstoon,
Boras, ceruce, ne oille of tartre noon,　630
Ne oynement that wolde clense and byte,
That hym myghte helpen of his whelkes white,
Nor of the knobbes sittynge on his chekes.
Wel loved he garleek, oynons, and eek lekes,
And for to drynken strong wyn, reed as blood;　635
Thanne wolde he speke and crie as he were wood.
And whan that he wel dronken hadde the wyn,
Thanne wolde he speke no word but Latyn.
A fewe termes hadde he, two or thre,
That he had lerned out of som decree—　640
No wonder is, he herde it al the day;
And eek ye knowen wel how that a jay
Kan clepen "Watte" as wel as kan the pope.
But whoso koude in oother thyng hym grope,
Thanne hadde he spent al his philosophie;　645
Ay "Questio quid iuris" wolde he crie.
He was a gentil harlot and a kynde;
A bettre felawe sholde men noght fynde.
He wolde suffre for a quart of wyn
A good felawe to have his concubyn　650
A twelf month, and excuse hym atte fulle;
Ful prively a fynch eek koude he pulle.

589 erys: ears　round yshorn: closely cropped
590 top: top of his head　dokked: cut short　biforn: in the front
592 Ylyk a staf: like a stick
593 gerner: granary　bynne: bin (for storing grain)
594 on him wynne: earn anything (by catching him out)
597 neet: cattle　dayerye: herd of dairy cattle
598 hors: horses　stoor: livestock　pultrye: poultry
600 covenant: agreement, contract
601 Syn that: since　yeer: years
602 arrerage: arrears
603 nas = ne was, was not　baillif: manager of a farm　hierde: herdsman　hyne: servant
604 sleighte: trickery　covyne: treachery
605 adrad: afraid　the deeth: the plague (?); see n.
606 wonyng: dwelling
608 purchace: buy property
609 riche: richly　astored: provided　pryvely: secretly
610–12 He could please his lord by lending him some of his (the lord's) own possessions (i.e., what he had stolen from him) and thus obtain thanks and a reward besides (R.).
613 myster: craft
615 stot: horse
616 pomely: dapple　highte: was called
617 surcote: outer coat　pers: dark blue
620 clepen: call

621 Tukked he was as is a frere: having his long coat hitched up and held by a girdle (R.), like a friar
622 hyndreste: last　route: company
623 Somonour: a server of summonses for an ecclesiastical court
624 fyr-reed: fire-red　cherubynnes: cherub's
625 saucefleem: pimpled　eyen narwe: swollen eyelids
627 scalled: infected with the scall, a skin disease; cf. Adam 3　piled: with hair fallen out
629–30 Mercury, lead monoxide (lytarge), sulphur (brymstoon), borax (boras), white lead (ceruce), and cream of tartar were all used in medicine.
631 oynement: ointment　byte: burn
632 whelkes: pimples, pustules
633 knobbes: swellings
634 garleek, oynons, lekes: garlic, onions, leeks
636 wood: crazy
639 termes: technical terms
640 decree: decretal, text of ecclesiastical law
643 clepen "Watte": say "Walter"
644 grope: examine
644–45 But anyone who knew how to test him further found that to be the extent of his learning.
646 Questio quid iuris: The question is, what point of the law (applies)?
647 harlot: buffoon, jester
649 suffre: allow
651 atte fulle: completely
652 Secretly (discreetly) he also knew how to pluck a finch (trick or swindle someone).

And if he foond owher a good felawe,
He wolde techen him to have noon awe
In swich caas of the ercedekenes curs,   655
But if a mannes soule were in his purs;
For in his purs he sholde ypunysshed be.
"Purs is the ercedekenes helle," seyde he.
But wel I woot he lyed right in dede;
Of cursyng oghte ech gilty man him drede,   660
For curs wol slee right as assoillyng savith,
And also war hym of a *Significavit*.
In daunger hadde he at his owene gise
The yonge girles of the diocise,
And knew hir conseil, and was al hir reed.   665
A gerland hadde he set upon his heed,
As greet as it were for an ale-stake.
A bokeleer hadde he maad hym of a cake.

  With hym ther rood a gentil PARDONER
Of Rouncivale, his freend and his compeer,   670
That streight was comen fro the court of Rome.
Ful loude he soong "Com hider, love, to me!"
This Somonour bar to hym a stif burdoun;
Was nevere trompe of half so greet a soun.
This Pardoner hadde heer as yelow as wex,   675
But smothe it heeng as dooth a strike of flex;
By ounces henge his lokkes that he hadde,
And therwith he his shuldres overspradde;
But thynne it lay, by colpons oon and oon.
But hood, for jolitee, wered he noon,   680
For it was trussed up in his walet.
Hym thoughte he rood al of the newe jet;
Dischevelee, save his cappe, he rood al bare.

Swiche glarynge eyen hadde he as an hare.
A vernycle hadde he sowed upon his cappe;   685
His walet, biforn hym in his lappe,
Bretful of pardoun comen from Rome al hoot.
A voys he hadde as smal as hath a goot.
No berd hadde he, ne nevere sholde have;
As smothe it was as it were late shave.   690
I trowe he were a geldyng or a mare.
But of his craft, fro Berwyk into Ware
Ne was ther swich another pardoner.
For in his male he hadde a pilwe-beer,
Which that he seyde was Oure Lady veyl;   695
He seyde he hadde a gobet of the seyl
That Seint Peter hadde, whan that he wente
Upon the see, til Jhesu Crist hym hente.
He hadde a croys of latoun ful of stones,
And in a glas he hadde pigges bones.   700
But with thise relikes, whan that he fond
A povre person dwellynge upon lond,
Upon a day he gat hym moore moneye
Than that the person gat in monthes tweye;
And thus, with feyned flaterye and japes,   705
He made the person and the peple his apes.
But trewely to tellen atte laste,
He was in chirche a noble ecclesiaste.
Wel koude he rede a lessoun or a storie,
But alderbest he song an offertorie;   710
For wel he wiste, whan that song was songe,
He moste preche and wel affile his tonge
To wynne silver, as he ful wel koude;
Therefore he song the murierly and loude.

  Now have I toold you soothly, in a clause,   715
Th'estaat, th'array, the nombre, and eek the cause

---

653 **owher:** anywhere
655 **caas:** case, circumstances   **ercedekenes curs:** excommunication
656 **But if:** unless
659 **woot:** know
660 **cursyng:** archdeacon's curse, excommunication   **him drede:** be afraid
661 **wol slee:** will slay   **assoillyng:** absolution
662 **war hym:** let him beware   **Significavit:** order for imprisonment
663 **In daunger:** in (his) control   **at his owene gise:** as he pleased
664 **girles:** young women or young people
665 **conseil:** secrets   **al hir reed:** adviser of them all
666 **gerland:** wreath
667 **ale-stake:** sign of an alehouse
668 **cake:** loaf of bread
669 **Pardoner:** a seller of indulgences
670 **Rouncivale:** a hospital at Charing Cross   **compeer:** companion
671 **court of Rome:** papal court
672 **"Com hider . . .":** Probably the refrain of a popular song
673 **stif burdoun:** strong bass
674 **trompe:** trumpet   **soun:** sound
675 **heer:** hair   **wex:** wax
676 **strike:** clump, hank   **flex:** flax
677 **ounces:** small strands
679 **colpons:** strands   **oon and oon:** one by one
680 **for jolitee:** to make an attractive appearance
681 **trussed:** packed   **walet:** pouch, knapsack
682 **Hym thoughte:** it seemed to him, he thought   **al of the newe jet:** in the very latest fashion
683 **Dischevelee:** with hair unbound, hanging loose   **save:** save for, except

684 **glarynge eyen:** staring eyes
685 **vernycle:** Veronica, a reproduction of St. Veronica's cloth, bearing the imprint of Christ's face; a badge of the pilgrimage to Rome   **sowed:** sewn
686 **walet:** pouch, knapsack   **lappe:** large pocket (in a fold of his clothing)
687 **Bretful:** brimful   **pardoun:** papal indulgences
688 **voys:** voice   **smal:** high   **goot:** goat
691 **trowe:** believe   **geldyng or a mare:** a eunuch or a homosexual
692 **fro Berwyk into Ware:** from one end of England to the other
694 **male:** pouch, bag   **pilwe-beer:** pillow-case
695 **Oure Lady veyl:** Our Lady's veil
696 **gobet of the seyl:** piece of the sail
698 **see:** sea   **til:** until   **hente:** took
699 **croys:** cross   **latoun:** a brass-like alloy
702 **person:** parson   **upon lond:** in the countryside
703 **gat hym:** got himself
704 **tweye:** two
705 **japes:** tricks
706 He made fools (*apes*) of the parson and the people.
707 **atte laste:** at the last, finally
709 **lessoun, storie:** liturgical texts, often from the Bible, read during Mass
710 **alderbest:** best of all   **offertorie:** Offertory (said or sung when offerings are made at Mass)
712 **affile his tonge:** smooth his speech
714 **song:** sang   **murierly:** more merrily
715 **in a clause:** briefly

Why that assembled was this compaignye
In Southwerk at this gentil hostelrye
That highte the Tabard, faste by the Belle.
But now is tyme to yow for to telle   720
How that we baren us that ilke nyght,
Whan we were in that hostelrie alyght;
And after wol I telle of our viage
And al the remenaunt of oure pilgrimage.
But first I pray yow, of youre curteisye,   725
That ye n'arette it nat my vileynye,
Thogh that I pleynly speke in this mateere,
To telle yow hir wordes and hir cheere,
Ne thogh I speke hir wordes proprely.
For this ye knowen al so wel as I: 730
Whoso shal telle a tale after a man,
He moot reherce as ny as evere he kan
Everich a word, if it be in his charge,
Al speke he never so rudeliche and large,
Or ellis he moot telle his tale untrewe,   735
Or feyne thyng, or fynde wordes newe.
He may nat spare, althogh he were his brother;
He moot as wel seye o word as another.
Crist spak hymself ful brode in hooly writ,   *christ is involved in*
And wel ye woot no vileynye is it.   *the way he speaks*   740
Eek Plato seith, whoso kan hym rede,
The wordes moote be cosyn to the dede.
Also I prey yow to foryeve it me,
Al have I nat set folk in hir degree
Heere in this tale, as that they sholde stonde.   745
My wit is short, ye may wel understonde.
  Greet chiere made oure Hoost us everichon,
And to the soper sette he us anon.
He served us with vitaille at the beste;
Strong was the wyn, and wel to drynke us leste.   750

A semely man OURE HOOSTE was withalle
For to been a marchal in an halle.
A large man he was with eyen stepe—
A fairer burgeys was ther noon in Chepe—
Boold of his speche, and wys, and wel ytaught,   755
And of manhod hym lakkede right naught.   *manly man*
Eek therto he was right a myrie man;
And after soper pleyen he bigan,
And spak of myrthe amonges othere thynges,
Whan that we hadde maad oure rekenynges,   760
And seyde thus: "Now, lordynges, trewely,
Ye been to me right welcome, hertely;
For by my trouthe, if that I shal nat lye,
I saugh nat this yeer so myrie a compaignye
Atones in this herberwe as is now.   765
Fayn wolde I doon yow myrthe, wiste I how.
And of a myrthe I am right now bythoght,
To doon yow ese, and it shal coste noght.
  "Ye goon to Caunterbury—God yow speede,
The blisful martir quite yow youre meede!   770
And wel I woot, as ye goon by the weye,
Ye shapen yow to talen and to pleye;
For trewely, confort ne myrthe is noon
To ride by the weye doumb as a stoon;
And therfore wol I maken yow disport,   775
As I seyde erst, and doon yow som confort.
And if yow liketh alle by oon assent
For to stonden at my juggement,
And for to werken as I shal yow seye,
Tomorwe, whan ye riden by the weye,   780
Now, by my fader soule that is deed,
But ye be myrie, I wol yeve yow myn heed!
Hoold up youre hondes, withouten moore speche."
  Oure conseil was nat longe for to seche.
Us thoughte it was noght worth to make it wys,   785
And graunted hym withouten moore avys,

719 **faste by:** close to   **Belle:** a tavern
721 **baren us:** behaved   **ilke:** same
722 **alyght:** arrived
723 **wol:** will   **viage:** journey
726 **n'arette it nat:** do not attribute it to   **vileynye:** rudeness
728 **cheere:** behavior
730 **al so:** as
731 **Whoso:** whoever   **shal:** must
732 **moot reherce:** must repeat   **ny:** close   **kan:** knows how
733 **Everich a:** every   **in his charge:** his responsibility
734 **Al speke he:** although he may speak   **rudeliche:** ignorantly, crudely   **large:** freely
735 **moot:** must   **untrewe:** inaccurately
736 **feyne thyng:** make up things
738 **o:** one
739 **brode:** plainly
740 **woot:** know   **vileynye:** rudeness
741 **kan hym rede:** knows how to interpret him
742 **cosyn:** cousin, closely related
744 **Al:** although   **degree:** social rank
746 **may:** can
747 **Greet chiere:** good cheer   **us everichon:** every one of us
749 **vitaille:** victuals, provisions   **at the beste:** of the best sort
750 **wel to drynke us leste:** we were well pleased to drink

751 **semely:** seemly, impressive   **withalle:** indeed
752 **marchal:** master of ceremonies
753 **eyen stepe:** bright or large eyes; see n.
754 **burgeys:** citizen of a city (tradesman)   **Chepe:** Cheapside
756 **manhod:** manliness, qualities proper to a good man   **right naught:** nothing at all
758 **pleyen:** to play, provide amusement
760 **maad oure rekenynges:** paid our bills
763 **trouthe:** faith
764 **saugh:** saw
765 **Atones:** at one time   **herberwe:** lodging
766 **Fayn:** gladly   **doon yow myrthe:** make you happy   **wiste I:** if I knew
767 **am . . . bythoght:** have thought
768 **doon yow ese:** give you pleasure
769 **yow speede:** give you success
770 **quite yow youre meede:** give you your reward
772 **shapen yow:** you intend   **talen:** tell tales   **pleye:** amuse yourselves
776 **erst:** before
777 **yow liketh alle:** it pleases all of you   **by oon assent:** unanimously
779 **werken:** do
781 Now by the soul of my father, who is dead
782 **But ye be:** unless you are, if you are not
784 **conseil:** decision   **nat longe for to seche:** i.e., ready at hand
785 **worth:** worthwhile   **make it wys:** deliberate on it, raise difficulties
786 **avys:** discussion

in the morning

And bad him seye his voirdit as hym leste.
"Lordynges," quod he, "now herkneth for the beste;
But taak it nought, I prey yow, in desdeyn.
This is the poynt, to speken short and pleyn,   790
That ech of yow, to shorte with oure weye,
In this viage shal telle tales tweye
To Caunterbury-ward, I mene it so,
And homward he shal tellen othere two,
Of aventures that whilom han bifalle.   795
And which of yow that bereth hym best of alle—
That is to seyn, that telleth in this caas
Tales of best sentence and moost solaas—
Shal have a soper at oure aller cost
Heere in this place, sittynge by this post,   800
Whan that we come agayn fro Caunterbury.
And for to make yow the moore mury,
I wol myselven goodly with yow ryde,
Right at myn owene cost, and be youre gyde;
And whoso wole my juggement withseye   805
Shal paye al that we spenden by the weye.
And if ye vouche sauf that it be so,
Tel me anon, withouten wordes mo,
And I wol erly shape me therfore."   809
   This thyng was graunted, and oure othes swore
With ful glad herte, and preyden hym also
That he wolde vouche sauf for to do so,
And that he wolde been oure governour,
And of oure tales juge and reportour,
And sette a soper at a certeyn pris,   815
And we wol reuled been at his devys
In heigh and lough; and thus by oon assent
We been acorded to his juggement.
And therupon the wyn was fet anon;
We dronken, and to reste wente echon,   820
Withouten any lenger taryynge.

woot them / Hoost / woke up

Amorwe, whan that day bigan to sprynge,
Up roos oure Hoost, and was oure aller cok,
And gadrede us togidre alle in a flok,
And forth we riden a litel moore than paas   825
Unto the Wateryng of Seint Thomas;
And there oure Hoost bigan his hors areste
And seyde, "Lordynges, herkneth, if yow leste.
Ye woot youre foreward, and I it yow recorde.
If even-song and morwe-song accorde,   830
Lat se now who shal telle the firste tale.
As evere mote I drynke wyn or ale,
Whoso be rebel to my juggement
Shal paye for al that by the wey is spent.
Now draweth cut, er that we ferrer twynne;   835
He which that hath the shorteste shal bigynne.
Sire Knyght," quod he, "my mayster and my lord,
Now draweth cut, for that is myn accord.
Cometh neer," quod he, "my lady Prioresse.
And ye, sire Clerk, lat be youre shamefastnesse,   840
Ne studieth noght; ley hond to, every man!"
Anon to drawen every wight bigan,
And shortly for to tellen as it was,
Were it by aventure, or sort, or cas,
The sothe is this: the cut fil to the Knyght,   845
Of which ful blithe and glad was every wyght,
And telle he moste his tale, as was resoun,
By foreward and by composicioun,
As ye han herd; what nedeth wordes mo?
And whan this goode man saugh that it was so,   850
As he that wys was and obedient
To kepe his foreward by his free assent,
He seyde, "Syn I shal bigynne the game,
What, welcome be the cut, a Goddes name!
Now lat us ryde, and herkneth what I seye."   855
And with that word we ryden forth oure weye,
And he bigan with right a myrie cheere
His tale anon, and seyde as ye may heere.

787 **voirdit:** verdict
788 **quod:** said   **for the beste:** the best course of action
790 **short and pleyn:** clearly and briefly
791 **to shorte with:** in order (with which) to shorten
792 **shal:** must   **tweye:** two
794 **othere two:** two others
795 **whilom:** once, in former times   **han bifalle:** have happened
796 **bereth hym best:** does best
798 **sentence:** meaning, significance   **solaas:** pleasure
799 **at oure aller cost:** at the cost of all of us
803 **goodly:** gladly
804 **gyde:** guide
805 **withseye:** gainsay
806 **Shal:** must
807 **vouche sauf:** grant, agree
808 **anon:** straightway   **mo:** more
809 **shape me:** get ready
811 **preyden:** The understood subject is "we."
814 **juge:** judge   **reportour:** record keeper
815 **pris:** price
816 **at his devys:** as he wishes
817 **In heigh and lough:** in every respect   **by oon assent:** unanimously
819 **fet:** fetched
820 **echon:** each one

823 **oure aller cok:** rooster of us all (awakened us all)
825 **paas:** walk, the slowest gait of a horse
826 **the Wateryng of Seint Thomas:** a brook about two miles from London
827 **areste:** stop
828 **if yow leste:** if you please
829 **foreward:** agreement   **recorde:** recall, bring to mind
830 *That is,* if you still agree this morning with what you said last night.
832 **mote:** may
835 **draweth cut:** draw lots   **ferrer twynne:** depart further (from London)
838 **accord:** decision
839 **neer:** nearer
840 **lat be:** leave off   **shamefastnesse:** modesty
844 **aventure, or sort, or cas:** chance, luck, or destiny
845 **sothe:** truth
847 **resoun:** reasonable, just
848 **composicioun:** agreement
853 **Syn:** since   **shal:** must
854 **a:** in
857 **cheere:** expression

The Knight's Tale

Heere bigynneth the Knyghtes Tale.

Iamque domos patrias, Scithice post aspera gentis
prelia, laurigero, &c.

Whilom, as olde stories tellen us,
Ther was a duc that highte Theseus; 860
Of Atthenes he was lord and governour,
And in his tyme swich a conquerour
That gretter was ther noon under the sonne.
Ful many a riche contree hadde he wonne;
What with his wysdom and his chivalrie, 865
He conquered al the regne of Femenye,
That whilom was ycleped Scithia,
And weddede the queene Ypolita,
And broghte hire hoom with hym in his contree
With muchel glorie and greet solempnytee, 870
And eek hir yonge suster Emelye.
And thus with victorie and with melodye
Lete I this noble duc to Atthenes ryde,
And al his hoost in armes hym bisyde.

   And certes, if it nere to long to heere, 875
I wolde have toold yow fully the manere
How wonnen was the regne of Femenye
By Theseus and by his chivalrye;
And of the grete bataille for the nones
Bitwixen Atthenes and Amazones; 880
And how asseged was Ypolita,
The faire, hardy queene of Scithia;
And of the feste that was at hir weddynge,
And of the tempest at hir hoom-comynge;
But al that thyng I moot as now forbere. 885
I have, God woot, a large feeld to ere,
And wayke been the oxen in my plough.

The remenant of the tale is long ynough.
I wol nat letten eek noon of this route;
Lat every felawe telle his tale aboute, 890
And lat se now who shal the soper wynne;
And ther I lefte, I wol ayeyn bigynne.

   This duc, of whom I make mencioun,
Whan he was come almoost unto the toun,
In al his wele and in his mooste pride, 895
He was war, as he caste his eye aside,
Where that ther kneled in the heighe weye
A compaignye of ladyes, tweye and tweye,
Ech after oother clad in clothes blake;
But swich a cry and swich a wo they make 900
That in this world nys creature lyvynge
That herde swich another waymentynge;
And of this cry they nolde nevere stenten
Til they the reynes of his brydel henten. 904

   "What folk been ye, that at myn homcomynge
Perturben so my feste with criynge?"
Quod Theseus. "Have ye so greet envye
Of myn honour, that thus compleyne and crye?
Or who hath yow mysboden or offended?
And telleth me if it may been amended, 910
And why that ye been clothed thus in blak."

   The eldeste lady of hem alle spak,
Whan she hadde swowned with a deedly cheere,
That it was routhe for to seen and heere;
She seyde, "Lord, to whom Fortune hath yiven 915
Victorie, and as a conqueror to lyven,

859 **Whilom:** once   **stories:** histories
860 **duc:** duke   **highte:** was called
866 **regne of Femenye:** country of the Amazons, land of women
870 **solempnytee:** splendor, ceremony
871 **suster:** sister
875 **certes:** certainly   **nere** = *ne were,* were not   **heere:** hear
878 **chivalrye:** knights
881 **asseged:** besieged
883 **feste:** festivity
884 **tempest:** storm
885 **moot as now forbere:** must now forgo
886 **ere:** plow
887 **wayke:** weak

889 **letten:** hinder   **route:** company
890 **aboute:** in turn
892 **ther:** where   **ayeyn:** again
895 **wele:** prosperity
896 **war:** aware
898 **tweye and tweye:** two by two
901 **nys** = *ne ys,* is not
902 **waymentynge:** lamentation
903 **nolde** = *ne wolde,* would not   **stenten:** cease
904 **Til:** until   **henten:** siezed
906 **Perturben:** disturb   **feste:** festival
908 **compleyne:** lament
909 **mysboden:** injured
913 **swowned:** swooned, fainted   **deedly cheere:** deathlike look
914 **routhe:** pity, a sorrowful matter
915 **yiven:** given

Nat greveth us youre glorie and youre honour,
But we biseken mercy and socour.
Have mercy on oure wo and oure distresse!
Som drope of pitee, thurgh thy gentillesse,   920
Upon us wrecched wommen lat thou falle,
For, certes, lord, ther is noon of us alle
That she ne hath been a duchesse or a queene.
Now be we caytyves, as it is wel seene,
Thanked be Fortune and hire false wheel,   925
That noon estaat assureth to be weel.
And certes, lord, to abyden youre presence,
Heere in this temple of the goddesse Clemence
We han ben waitynge al this fourtenyght.
Now help us, lord, sith it is in thy myght.   930
    "I, wrecche, which that wepe and wayle thus,
Was whilom wyf to kyng Cappaneus,
That starf at Thebes—cursed be that day!—
And alle we that been in this array
And maken al this lamentacioun,   935
We losten alle oure housbondes at that toun,
Whil that the seege theraboute lay.
And yet now the olde Creony—weylaway!—
That lord is now of Thebes the citee,
Fulfild of ire and of iniquitee,   940
He, for despit and for his tirannye,
To do the dede bodyes vileynye
Of alle oure lordes whiche that been yslawe,
Hath alle the bodyes on an heep ydrawe,
And wol nat suffren hem, by noon assent,   945
Neither to been yburyed nor ybrent,
But maketh houndes ete hem in despit."
    And with that word, withouten moore respit,
They fillen gruf and criden pitously,
"Have on us wrecched wommen som mercy,   950
And lat oure sorwe synken in thyn herte."
    This gentil duc doun from his courser sterte

With herte pitous, whan he herde hem speke.
Hym thoughte that his herte wolde breke,
Whan he saugh hem so pitous and so maat,   955
That whilom weren of so greet estaat;
And in his armes he hem alle up hente,
And hem conforteth in ful good entente,
And swoor his ooth, as he was trewe knyght,
He wolde doon so ferforthly his myght   960
Upon the tiraunt Creon hem to wreke
That al the peple of Grece sholde speke
How Creon was of Theseus yserved
As he that hadde his deeth ful wel deserved.
And right anoon, withouten moore abood,   965
His baner he desplayeth, and forth rood
To Thebes-ward, and al his hoost biside.
No neer Atthenes wolde he go ne ride,
Ne take his ese fully half a day,
But onward on his wey that nyght he lay,   970
And sente anon Ypolita the queene,
And Emelye, hir yonge suster sheene,
Unto the toun of Atthenes to dwelle,
And forth he rit; ther is namoore to telle.
    The rede statue of Mars, with spere and targe,   975
So shyneth in his white baner large
That alle the feeldes glyteren up and doun;
And by his baner born is his penoun
Of gold ful riche, in which ther was ybete
The Mynotaur, which that he wan in Crete.   980
Thus rit this duc, thus rit this conquerour,
And in his hoost of chivalrie the flour,
Til that he cam to Thebes and alighte
Faire in a feeld, ther as he thoughte to fighte.
But shortly for to speken of this thyng,   985
With Creon, which that was of Thebes kyng,
He faught, and slough hym manly as a knyght
In pleyn bataille, and putte the folk to flyght;
And by assaut he wan the citee after,

917 **Nat greveth us:** does not grieve us
918 **biseken:** beseech, ask for
920 **thurgh:** through, because of
924 **caytyves:** miserable wretches
926 **weel:** well
927 **abyden:** wait for
929 **han ben:** have been
930 **sith:** since
933 **starf:** died
934 **array:** state
937 **seege:** siege
938 **weylaway:** alas
941 **despit:** spite
942 **vileynye:** shame, dishonor
943 **yslawe:** slain
944 **on an heep ydrawe:** dragged in a heap
945 **suffren hem:** allow them
946 **yburyed nor ybrent:** buried nor burned, cremated
947 **in despit:** in spite
948 **respit:** delay, respite
949 **fillen gruf:** fell face down
951 **sorwe:** sorrow
952 **gentil:** noble   **courser:** charger, warhorse   **sterte:** leapt

953 **pitous:** compassionate
955 **pitous:** pitiful   **maat:** dejected
956 **whilom:** once, formerly   **so greet estaat:** such high rank
957 **hem alle up hente:** picked them all up
958 **in ful good entente:** with a good will, kindly
959 **trewe:** faithful
960 **so ferforthly:** so completely
961 **wreke:** avenge
963 **of Theseus yserved:** served, treated by Theseus
965 **right anoon:** immediately   **abood:** delay
967 **To Thebes-ward:** toward Thebes
968 **neer:** nearer   **go ne ride:** walk nor ride
970 **on his wey that nyght he lay:** he spent the night on the road
972 **sheene:** bright
974 **rit** = *rideth,* rides
975 **targe:** shield
977 **feeldes glyteren up and doun:** fields glitter all about
979 **ybete:** embroidered
980 **Mynotaur:** the monster slain by Theseus; see LGW 1886–2227.   **wan:** conquered
984 **thoughte:** intended
988 **pleyn bataille:** open battle
989 **assaut:** assault

And rente adoun bothe wall and sparre and rafter;
And to the ladyes he restored agayn 991
The bones of hir freendes that were slayn,
To doon obsequies, as was tho the gyse.
But it were al to longe for to devyse
The grete clamour and the waymentynge 995
That the ladyes made at the brennynge
Of the bodies, and the grete honour
That Theseus, the noble conquerour,
Dooth to the ladyes, whan they from hym wente;
But shortly for to telle is myn entente. 1000
    Whan that this worthy duc, this Theseus,
Hath Creon slayn and wonne Thebes thus,
Stille in that feeld he took al nyght his reste,
And dide with al the contree as hym leste.
    To ransake in the taas of bodyes dede, 1005
Hem for to strepe of harneys and of wede,
The pilours diden bisynesse and cure
After the bataille and disconfiture.
And so bifel that in the taas they founde, 1009
Thurgh-girt with many a grevous blody wounde,
Two yonge knyghtes liggynge by and by,
Bothe in oon armes, wroght ful richely,
Of whiche two Arcita highte that oon,
And that oother knyght highte Palamon.
Nat fully quyke, ne fully dede they were, 1015
But by hir cote-armures and by hir gere
The heraudes knewe hem best in special
As they that weren of the blood roial
Of Thebes, and of sustren two yborn.
Out of the taas the pilours han hem torn, 1020
And han hem caried softe unto the tente
Of Theseus; and he ful soone hem sente
To Atthenes, to dwellen in prisoun
Perpetuelly—he nolde no raunsoun.
    And whan this worthy duc hath thus ydon, 1025

He took his hoost, and hoom he rit anon
With laurer crowned as a conquerour;
And ther he lyveth in joye and in honour
Terme of his lyf; what nedeth wordes mo?
And in a tour, in angwissh and in wo, 1030
This Palamon and his felawe Arcite
For everemoore; ther may no gold hem quite.
    This passeth yeer by yeer and day by day,
Till it fil ones, in a morwe of May,
That Emelye, that fairer was to sene 1035
Than is the lylie upon his stalke grene,
And fressher than the May with floures newe—
For with the rose colour stroof hire hewe,
I noot which was the fyner of hem two—
Er it were day, as was hir wone to do, 1040
She was arisen and al redy dight,
For May wole have no slogardie anyght.
The sesoun priketh every gentil herte,
And maketh it out of his slep to sterte,
And seith "Arys, and do thyn observaunce." 1045
This maked Emelye have remembraunce
To doon honour to May, and for to ryse.
Yclothed was she fressh, for to devyse:
Hir yelow heer was broyded in a tresse
Bihynde hir bak, a yerde long, I gesse. 1050
And in the gardyn, at the sonne upriste,
She walketh up and doun, and as hire liste
She gadereth floures, party white and rede,
To make a subtil gerland for hire hede;
And as an aungel hevenysshly she soong. 1055
The grete tour, that was so thikke and stroong,
Which of the castel was the chief dongeoun
(Ther as the knyghtes weren in prisoun
Of which I tolde yow and tellen shal),
Was evene joynant to the gardyn wal 1060
Ther as this Emelye hadde hir pleyynge.

990 **rente adoun:** tore down   **sparre:** beam
992 **freendes:** husbands
993 **tho the gyse:** then the custom
994 **devyse:** tell
995 **waymentynge:** lamentation
996 **brennynge:** burning
1000 **entente:** intention
1004 **as hym leste:** as he pleased
1005 **ransake:** search   **taas:** heap
1006 **strepe:** strip   **harneys:** armor   **wede:** clothing
1007 **pilours:** scavengers   **diden bisynesse and cure:** took great pains, worked hard
1008 **disconfiture:** defeat
1010 **Thurgh-girt:** pierced through
1011 **liggynge by and by:** lying side by side
1012 **in oon armes:** with the same heraldic device
1015 **quyke:** living
1016 **cote-armures:** tunics embroidered with heraldic devices, worn over the armor
gere: armor
1017 **heraudes:** heralds   **in special:** in particular
1019 **sustren:** sisters
1021 **softe:** gently
1024 **nolde no raunsoun:** would not accept any ransom

1026 **rit** = *rideth*, rides
1027 **laurer:** laurel
1029 **Terme:** for the duration
1030 **tour:** tower
1032 **may . . . hem quite:** can ransom them
1034 **fil ones:** once happened
1035 **to sene:** to be seen, to look upon
1038 **stroof hire hewe:** her hue strove (vied with)
1039 **noot** = *ne woot*, do not know
1040 **wone:** custom, wont
1041 **dight:** prepared
1042 **slogardie:** sluggishness, laziness   **anyght:** at night
1043 **sesoun:** season   **priketh:** spurs, incites
1044 **sterte:** move suddenly, awake
1049 **broyded:** braided
1050 **yerde:** yard
1051 **sonne upriste:** rising of the sun
1052 **hire liste:** it pleased her, she liked
1054 **subtil gerland:** ingenious, skillfully made, wreath
1055 **hevenysshly:** in a heavenly manner
1057 **dongeoun:** keep, main fortification of a castle
1060 **evene joynant:** just next to
1061 **pleyynge:** amusement

Bright was the sonne and cleer that morwenynge,
And Palamoun, this woful prisoner,
As was his wone, by leve of his gayler,
Was risen and romed in a chambre an heigh,   1065
In which he al the noble citee seigh,
And eek the gardyn, ful of braunches grene,
Ther as this fresshe Emelye the shene
Was in hire walk, and romed up and doun.
This sorweful prisoner, this Palamoun,   1070
Goth in the chambre romynge to and fro
And to hymself compleynynge of his wo.
That he was born, ful ofte he seyde, "allas!"
And so bifel, by aventure or cas,
That thurgh a wyndow, thikke of many a barre   1075
Of iren greet and square as any sparre,
He cast his eye upon Emelya,
And therwithal he bleynte and cride, "A!"
As though he stongen were unto the herte.
And with that cry Arcite anon up sterte   1080
And seyde, "Cosyn myn, what eyleth thee,
That art so pale and deedly on to see?
Why cridestow? Who hath thee doon offence?
For Goddes love, taak al in pacience
Oure prisoun, for it may noon oother be.   1085
Fortune hath yeven us this adversitee.
Som wikke aspect or disposicioun
Of Saturne, by som constellacioun,
Hath yeven us this, although we hadde it sworn;
So stood the hevene whan that we were born.   1090
We moste endure it; this is the short and playn."
    This Palamon answerde and seyde agayn,
"Cosyn, for sothe, of this opinioun
Thow hast a veyn ymaginacioun.
This prison caused me nat for to crye,   1095
But I was hurt right now thurghout myn ye
    Into myn herte, that wol my bane be.
The fairnesse of that lady that I see

Yond in the gardyn romen to and fro
Is cause of al my criyng and my wo.   1100
I noot wher she be womman or goddesse,
But Venus is it soothly, as I gesse."
And therwithal on knees doun he fil,
And seyde, "Venus, if it be thy wil
Yow in this gardyn thus to transfigure   1105
Bifore me, sorweful, wrecched creature,
Out of this prisoun help that we may scapen.
And if so be my destynee be shapen
By eterne word to dyen in prisoun,
Of oure lynage have som compassioun,   1110
That is so lowe ybroght by tirannye."
And with that word Arcite gan espye
Wher as this lady romed to and fro,
And with that sighte hir beautee hurte hym so,
That, if that Palamon was wounded sore,   1115
Arcite is hurt as muche as he, or moore.
And with a sigh he seyde pitously,
"The fresshe beautee sleeth me sodeynly
Of hire that rometh in the yonder place;
And but I have hir mercy and hir grace,   1120
That I may seen hire atte leeste weye,
I nam but deed; ther nis namoore to seye."
    This Palamon, whan he tho wordes herde,
Dispitously he looked and answerde,
"Wheither seistow this in ernest or in pley?"   1125
    "Nay," quod Arcite, "in ernest, by my fey!
God helpe me so, me list ful yvele pleye."
    This Palamon gan knytte his browes tweye.
"It nere," quod he, "to thee no greet honour
For to be fals, ne for to be traitour   1130
To me, that am thy cosyn and thy brother
Ysworn ful depe, and ech of us til oother,
That nevere, for to dyen in the peyne,
Til that the deeth departe shal us tweyne,
Neither of us in love to hyndre oother,   1135
Ne in noon oother cas, my leeve brother,

1064 **by leve of his gayler:** with permission of his jailer
1065 **an heigh:** on high
1066 **seigh:** saw
1068 **shene:** bright
1072 **compleynynge of:** lamenting
1074 And so it happened by chance or accident
1075 **thurgh:** through   **thikke of:** thick(ly set) with
1076 **sparre:** wooden beam
1078 **bleynte:** turned pale
1080 **sterte:** leapt up
1081 **Cosyn:** kinsman   **eyleth:** ails
1082 **on to see:** to look upon
1083 **cridestow** = *cridest thow,* did you cry out
1087–89 Some evil aspect or disposition of the planet Saturn, by arrangement of the
heavenly bodies (*constellacioun*) has given us this (fate, which we must suffer)
although we had sworn the contrary (would befall).
1091 **this is:** pronounced as one syllable
1092 **agayn:** in reply
1094 **veyn ymaginacioun:** idle, foolish conception
1096 **ye:** eye
1097 **bane:** killer

1101 **noot** = *ne woot,* know not   **wher:** whether
1107 **scapen:** escape
1108 **shapen:** ordained
1110 **lynage:** noble birth
1112 **gan espye:** did espy, saw
1118 **sodeynly:** suddenly
1120 **but:** unless
1121 **atte leeste weye:** at least
1122 **I nam but deed:** I am as good as dead
1123 **tho:** those
1124 **Dispitously:** angrily
1125 **Wheither seistow:** tell me whether you say (*seistow* = *seiest thow*) this
1126 **fey:** faith
1127 **me list ful yvele pleye:** I have very little desire to play
1129 **nere** = *ne were,* would not be (subj.)
1131–32 **brother Ysworn:** sworn brother
1132 **ful depe:** very deeply, sincerely   **til:** to
1133 Never, though we had to die by torture (*in the peyne*)
1136 **leeve:** dear

But that thou sholdest trewely forthren me
In every cas, as I shal forthren thee—
This was thyn ooth, and myn also, certeyn;
I woot right wel, thou darst it nat withseyn.　　　1140
Thus artow of my conseil, out of doute,
And now thow woldest falsly been aboute
To love my lady, whom I love and serve,
And evere shal til that myn herte sterve.
Nay, certes, false Arcite, thow shalt nat so.　　　1145
I loved hire first, and tolde thee my wo
As to my conseil and my brother sworn
To forthre me, as I have toold biforn.
For which thou art ybounden as a knyght
To helpen me, if it lay in thy myght,　　　1150
Or elles artow fals, I dar wel seyn."
　　This Arcite ful proudly spak ageyn:
"Thow shalt," quod he, "be rather fals than I;
And thou art fals, I telle thee outrely,
For paramour I loved hire first er thow.　　　1155
What wiltow seyen? Thou woost nat yet now
Wheither she be a womman or goddesse!
Thyn is affeccioun of hoolynesse,
And myn is love as to a creature;
For which I tolde thee myn aventure　　　1160
As to my cosyn and my brother sworn.
I pose that thow lovedest hire biforn;
Wostow nat wel the olde clerkes sawe,
That "who shal yeve a lovere any lawe?"
Love is a gretter lawe, by my pan,　　　1165
Than may be yeve to any erthely man;
And therfore positif lawe and swich decree
Is broken al day for love in ech degree.
A man moot nedes love, maugree his heed;
He may nat fleen it, thogh he sholde be deed,　　　1170
Al be she mayde, or wydwe, or elles wyf.
And eek it is nat likly al thy lyf
To stonden in hir grace; namoore shal I;
For wel thou woost thyselven, verraily,

That thou and I be dampned to prisoun　　　1175
Perpetuelly; us gayneth no raunsoun.
We stryve as dide the houndes for the boon;
They foughte al day, and yet hir part was noon.
Ther cam a kyte, whil that they were so wrothe,
And baar awey the boon bitwixe hem bothe.　　　1180
And therfore, at the kynges court, my brother,
Ech man for hymself, ther is noon oother.
Love, if thee list, for I love and ay shal;
And soothly, leeve brother, this is al.
Heere in this prisoun moote we endure,　　　1185
And everich of us take his aventure."
　　Greet was the strif and long bitwix hem tweye,
If that I hadde leyser for to seye;
But to th'effect. It happed on a day,
To telle it yow as shortly as I may,　　　1190
A worthy duc that highte Perotheus,
That felawe was unto duc Theseus
Syn thilke day that they were children lite,
Was come to Atthenes his felawe to visite,
And for to pleye as he was wont to do;　　　1195
For in this world he loved no man so,
And he loved hym als tendrely agayn.
So wel they lovede, as olde bookes sayn,
That whan that oon was deed, soothly to telle,
His felawe wente and soughte hym doun in helle—
But of that storie list me nat to write.　　　1201
Duc Perotheus loved wel Arcite,
And hadde hym knowe at Thebes yeer by yere,
And finally at requeste and preyere
Of Perotheus, withouten any raunsoun,　　　1205
Duc Theseus hym leet out of prisoun
Frely to goon wher that hym liste over al,
In swich a gyse as I you tellen shal.
　　This was the forward, pleynly for t'endite,
Bitwixen Theseus and hym Arcite:　　　1210
That if so were that Arcite were yfounde
Evere in his lif, by day or nyght, oo stounde
In any contree of this Theseus,
And he were caught, it was acorded thus,
That with a swerd he sholde lese his heed.　　　1215

1137 **forthren:** help
1140 **darst it nat withseyn:** dare not deny it
1141 Thus you are (artow = art thow, you are) in my confidence without doubt (*out of doute*); i.e., you know of my love.
1144 **sterve:** die
1152 **ageyn:** in return
1154 **outrely:** utterly, flatly
1155 **paramour:** mistress, human love
1156 **woost:** know
1158 **affeccioun of hoolynesse:** religious feeling, love of a deity
1162 **pose:** posit, suppose for the sake of argument
1163 **clerkes' sawe:** scholars' saying
1165 **by my pan:** by my skull
1167 **positif lawe:** man-made, legislated (as opposed to natural) law
1168 **al day:** daily
1169 **moot nedes:** must necessarily　　**maugree his heed:** despite his care, in spite of all he could do about it
1170 **fleen:** escape
1171 **Al be she:** whether she be
1173 **stonden in hir grace:** be in her good favor
1174 **verraily:** truly

1175 **dampned:** condemned
1176 **us gayneth no raunsoun:** no ransom avails (can help) us
1179 **wrothe:** angry
1182 **noon oother:** no other (way)
1183 **ay:** always
1184 **leeve:** dear
1186 **everich:** each
1189 **th'effect:** the point
1193 **Syn:** since　　**thilke:** that　　**lite:** little
1203 **yeer by yere:** year after year, for a long time
1208 **gyse:** manner
1209 **forward:** agreement
1210 **hym Arcite:** this Arcite
1212 **oo stounde:** at one (i.e., any) moment
1215 **lese:** lose

Ther nas noon oother remedie ne reed;
But taketh his leve, and homward he him spedde.
Lat hym be war! His nekke lith to wedde.

How greet a sorwe suffreth now Arcite!
The deeth he feeleth thurgh his herte smyte;   1220
He wepeth, wayleth, crieth pitously;
To sleen hymself he waiteth prively.
He seyde, "Allas that day that I was born!
Now is my prisoun worse than biforn;
Now is me shape eternally to dwelle   1225
Noght in purgatorie, but in helle.
Allas, that evere knew I Perotheus!
For elles hadde I dwelled with Theseus,
Yfetered in his prisoun everemo.
Thanne hadde I been in blisse and nat in wo.   1230
Oonly the sighte of hire whom that I serve,
Though that I nevere hir grace may deserve,
Wolde han suffised right ynough for me.
O deere cosyn Palamon," quod he,
"Thyn is the victorie of this aventure.   1235
Ful blisfully in prison maistow dure—
In prison? Certes nay, but in paradys!
Wel hath Fortune yturned thee the dys,
That hast the sighte of hire, and I th'absence.
For possible is, syn thou hast hire presence,   1240
And art a knyght, a worthy and an able,
That by som cas, syn Fortune is chaungeable,
Thow maist to thy desir somtyme atteyne.
But I, that am exiled and bareyne
Of alle grace, and in so greet dispeir   1245
That ther nys erthe, water, fir, ne eir,
Ne creature that of hem maked is,
That may me helpe or doon confort in this,
Wel oughte I sterve in wanhope and distresse.
Farwel my lif, my lust, and my gladnesse!   1250

"Allas, why pleynen folk so in commune
On purveiaunce of God, or of Fortune,
That yeveth hem ful ofte in many a gyse
Wel bettre than they kan hemself devyse?
Som man desireth for to han richesse,   1255

That cause is of his mordre or greet siknesse;
And som man wolde out of his prisoun fayn,
That in his hous is of his meynee slayn.
Infinite harmes been in this mateere.
We witen nat what thing we preyen heere;   1260
We faren as he that dronke is as a mous.
A dronke man woot wel he hath an hous,
But he noot which the righte wey is thider,
And to a dronke man the wey is slider.
And certes, in this world so faren we;   1265
We seken faste after felicitee,
But we goon wrong ful often, trewely.
Thus may we seyen alle, and namely I,
That wende and hadde a greet opinioun
That if I myghte escapen from prisoun,   1270
Thanne hadde I been in joye and parfit heele,
Ther now I am exiled fro my wele.
Syn that I may nat seen you, Emelye,
I nam but deed; ther nys no remedye."

Upon that oother syde Palamon,   1275
Whan that he wiste Arcite was agon,
Swich sorwe he maketh that the grete tour
Resouneth of his youlyng and clamour.
The pure fettres on his shynes grete
Weren of his bittre, salte teeres wete.   1280
"Allas," quod he, "Arcita, cosyn myn,
Of al oure strif, God woot, the fruyt is thyn.
Thow walkest now in Thebes at thy large,
And of my wo thow yevest litel charge.   1284
Thow mayst, syn thou hast wisdom and man-hede,
Assemblen alle the folk of oure kynrede,
And make a werre so sharp on this citee
That by som aventure or some tretee
Thow mayst have hire to lady and to wyf
For whom that I moste nedes lese my lyf.   1290
For, as by wey of possibilitee,
Sith thou art at thy large, of prisoun free,

1216 **reed:** course of action
1217 **him spedde:** hurried
1218 **lith to wedde:** lies as a pledge
1222 **sleen:** slay, kill   **waiteth:** awaits an occasion   **prively:** secretly
1225 **is me shape:** I am destined
1236 **maistow dure:** you can live
1237 **Certes nay:** certainly not
1238 **yturned thee the dys:** cast the dice for you
1242 **by som cas, syn:** by some chance, since
1244 **bareyne:** barren
1246 **nys** = *ne ys,* is not   **erthe, water, fir, ne eir:** earth, water, fire, nor air (the four elements; i.e., all creation)
1249 **sterve:** die   **wanhope:** despair
1250 **lust:** delight
1251 **pleynen:** complain
1252 **purveiaunce:** foresight, providence
1253 **yeveth:** gives
1254 **devyse:** imagine

1256 **mordre:** murder
1257 **wolde . . . fayn:** eagerly desires (to be)
1258 **of his meynee:** by the members of his household
1260 **witen:** know
1261 **faren:** act
1263 **thider:** thither, there
1264 **slider:** slippery
1265 **certes:** certainly
1269 **wende:** supposed
1271 **heele:** well-being
1272 **wele:** prosperity
1274 **I nam but deed:** I am as good as dead   **nys** = *ne ys,* is not
1278 **Resouneth of:** resounded with   **youlyng:** howling
1279 **pure fettres:** very fetters   **grete:** large (probably to be construed with *fetters*)
1283 **at thy large:** freely
1284 **yevest litel charge:** give little care
1286 **kynrede:** family
1287 **werre:** war
1289 **to:** as
1290 **moste nedes lese:** must necessarily lose

And art a lord, greet is thyn avauntage
Moore than is myn, that sterve here in a cage.
For I moot wepe and wayle, whil I lyve, 1295
With al the wo that prison may me yive,
And eek with peyne that love me yeveth also,
That doubleth al my torment and my wo."
Therwith the fyr of jalousie up sterte
Withinne his brest, and hente him by the herte 1300
So woodly that he lyk was to biholde
The boxtree or the asshen dede and colde.

Thanne seyde he, "O crueel goddes that governe
This world with byndyng of youre word eterne,
And writen in the table of atthamaunt 1305
Youre parlement and youre eterne graunt,
What is mankynde moore unto you holde
Than is the sheep that rouketh in the folde?
For slayn is man right as another beest,
And dwelleth eek in prison and arreest, 1310
And hath siknesse and greet adversitee,
And ofte tymes giltelees, pardee.

"What governance is in this prescience,
That giltelees tormenteth innocence?
And yet encresseth this al my penaunce, 1315
That man is bounden to his observaunce,
For Goddes sake, to letten of his wille,
Ther as a beest may al his lust fulfille.
And whan a beest is deed he hath no peyne;
But man after his deeth moot wepe and pleyne, 1320
Though in this world he have care and wo.
Withouten doute it may stonden so.
The answere of this lete I to dyvynys,
But wel I woot that in this world greet pyne ys.
Allas, I se a serpent or a theef, 1325
That many a trewe man hath doon mescheef,
Goon at his large, and where hym list may turne.
But I moot been in prisoun thurgh Saturne,
And eek thurgh Juno, jalous and eek wood,

That hath destroyed wel ny al the blood 1330
Of Thebes with his waste walles wyde;
And Venus sleeth me on that oother syde
For jalousie and fere of hym Arcite."

Now wol I stynte of Palamon a lite,
And lete hym in his prisoun stille dwelle, 1335
And of Arcita forth I wol yow telle.

The somer passeth, and the nyghtes longe
Encressen double wise the peynes stronge
Bothe of the lovere and the prisoner.
I noot which hath the wofuller mester. 1340
For, shortly for to seyn, this Palamoun
Perpetuelly is dampned to prisoun,
In cheynes and in fettres to been deed;
And Arcite is exiled upon his heed
For everemo, as out of that contree, 1345
Ne nevere mo ne shal his lady see.

Yow loveres axe I now this questioun:
Who hath the worse, Arcite or Palamoun?
That oon may seen his lady day by day,
But in prison he moot dwelle alway; 1350
That oother wher hym list may ride or go,
But seen his lady shal he nevere mo.
Now demeth as yow liste, ye that kan,
For I wol telle forth as I bigan. 1354

Explicit prima pars

Sequitur pars secunda

Whan that Arcite to Thebes comen was,
Ful ofte a day he swelte and seyde "Allas!"
For seen his lady shal he nevere mo.
And shortly to concluden al his wo,
So muche sorwe hadde nevere creature
That is, or shal, whil that the world may dure. 1360
His slep, his mete, his drynke, is hym biraft,
That lene he wex and drye as is a shaft;
His eyen holwe and grisly to biholde,
His hewe falow and pale as asshen colde,
And solitarie he was and evere allone, 1365

1293 **avauntage**: advantage
1301 **woodly**: madly, passionately **lyk was to biholde**: to look upon was like
1304 **eterne**: eternal
1305 **table of atthamaunt**: tablet of adamant (hardest of stones)
1306 **parlement**: decision **graunt**: decree
1307 **holde**: obligated
1308 **rouketh**: cowers
1310 **arreest**: restraint
1312 **giltelees**: innocent **pardee**: indeed
1313–14 What (sort of) governance is there in this (providential) foreknowledge (*prescience*) that (thus) torments guiltless innocence?
1315 **penaunce**: suffering
1316 **observaunce**: duty
1317 **to letten of his wille**: to refrain from his desire (R.)
1318 **Ther as**: whereas **lust**: desire
1320 **pleyne**: lament
1323 **lete**: leave **dyvynys**: theologians
1324 **pyne**: pain
1326 **trewe**: honest **mescheef**: wrong
1327 **at his large**: freely
1328 **thurgh**: through, because of

1331 **waste**: wasted, devastated
1333 **fere**: fear **hym Arcite**: this Arcite
1334 **stynte of**: cease (speaking) of
1340 **mester**: occupation
1344 **upon his heed**: on threat of losing his head
1345 **as out of**: (to be) out of
1347 **questioun**: logical problem (of love); see n.
1351 **ride or go**: ride or walk
1353 **demeth**: judge **kan**: know how
Explicit, *etc.*: Here ends the first part. **Sequitur**, *etc.*: Here follows the second part.
1356 **swelte**: grew faint
1360 **dure**: last
1361 **biraft**: taken away from
1362 **lene he wex**: he became lean **shaft**: stick
1363 **holwe**: sunken
1364 **falow**: sickly yellow

And waillynge al the nyght, makynge his mone;
And if he herde song or instrument,
Thanne wolde he wepe, he myghte nat be stent.
So feble eek were his spiritz, and so lowe,
And chaunged so, that no man koude knowe   1370
His speche nor his voys, though men it herde.
And in his geere for al the world he ferde
Nat oonly lik the loveris maladye
Of Hereos, but rather lyk manye,
Engendred of humour malencolik   1375
Biforen, in his celle fantastik.
And shortly, turned was al up so doun
Bothe habit and eek disposicioun
Of hym, this woful lovere daun Arcite.
    What sholde I al day of his wo endite?   1380
Whan he endured hadde a yeer or two
This crueel torment and this peyne and wo,
At Thebes, in his contree, as I seyde,
Upon a nyght in sleep as he hym leyde,   1384
Hym thoughte how that the wynged god Mercurie
Biforn hym stood and bad hym to be murie.
His slepy yerde in hond he bar uprighte;
An hat he werede upon his heris brighte.
Arrayed was this god, as he took keep,
As he was whan that Argus took his sleep;   1390
And seyde hym thus: "To Atthenes shaltou wende,
Ther is thee shapen of thy wo an ende."
And with that word Arcite wook and sterte.
"Now trewely, hou soore that me smerte,"
Quod he, "to Atthenes right now wol I fare,   1395
Ne for the drede of deeth shal I nat spare
To se my lady, that I love and serve.
In hire presence I recche nat to sterve."
    And with that word he caughte a greet mirour,

And saugh that chaunged was al his colour,   1400
And saugh his visage al in another kynde.
And right anon it ran hym in his mynde,
That, sith his face was so disfigured
Of maladye the which he hadde endured,
He myghte wel, if that he bar hym lowe,   1405
Lyve in Atthenes everemoore unknowe,
And seen his lady wel ny day by day.
And right anon he chaunged his array,
And cladde hym as a povre laborer,
And al allone, save oonly a squier   1410
That knew his privetee and al his cas,
Which was disgised povrely as he was,
To Atthenes is he goon the nexte way.
And to the court he wente upon a day,
And at the gate he profreth his servyse   1415
To drugge and drawe, what so men wol devyse.
And shortly of this matere for to seyn,
He fil in office with a chamberleyn
The which that dwellynge was with Emelye,
For he was wys and koude soone espye,   1420
Of every servaunt, which that serveth here.
Wel koude he hewen wode, and water bere,
For he was yong and myghty for the nones,
And therto he was long and big of bones
To doon that any wight kan hym devyse.   1425
A yeer or two he was in this servyse,
Page of the chambre of Emelye the brighte,
And Philostrate he seyde that he highte.
But half so wel biloved a man as he
Ne was ther nevere in court of his degree;   1430
He was so gentil of condicioun
That thurghout al the court was his renoun.
They seyden that it were a charitee
That Theseus wolde enhauncen his degree,
And putten hym in worshipful servyse,   1435

1366 **makynge his mone:** lamenting
1368 **stent:** stopped
1371 **voys:** voice
1372 **geere:** behavior   **ferde:** behaved
1373–74 **loveris maladye Of Hereos:** love-sickness; see n. to lines 1355–76.
1374 **manye:** mania
1375 **humour malencolik:** melancholy humor
1376 **celle fantastik:** the part of the brain that controls the imagination
1377 **up so doun:** topsy turvy
1378 **habit:** physical condition
1379 **daun:** sir
1380 **al day:** at length   **endite:** write
1385 **Mercurie:** Mercury
1387 **slepy yerde:** sleep-inducing staff
1389 **he took keep:** Arcite took heed, noticed
1390 **Argus:** mythical guardian of Io, whom Mercury put to sleep and then killed
1392 **shapen:** destined
1394 **hou soore that me smerte:** however sorely it may pain me
1395 **fare:** go
1398 **recche nat to sterve:** care not if I die

1401 **in another kynde:** (changed) into another sort
1403 **sith:** since
1404 **Of maladye:** by illness
1405 **myghte:** could   **bar hym lowe:** conducted himself humbly
1408 **right anon:** at once
1411 **privetee:** private affairs   **cas:** situation
1412 **disgised povrely:** dressed poorly
1413 **nexte:** nearest
1415 **profreth:** offers
1416 **drugge and drawe:** drudge and draw water   **devyse:** command
1418 **fil in office:** fell in service, was employed   **chamberleyn:** household attendant
1420–21 **espye, Of:** take notice, take the measure of
1422 **bere:** bear, carry
1424 **long:** tall   **big:** strong
1425 **wight:** person
1427 **Page of the chambre:** personal servant
1428 **highte:** was called
1431 **condicioun:** disposition, manner
1432 **renoun:** fame, renown
1434 **enhauncen his degree:** advance, enhance his rank
1435 **worshipful servyse:** honorable, noble employment

Ther as he myghte his vertu excercise.
And thus withinne a while his name is spronge,
Bothe of his dedes and his goode tonge,
That Theseus hath taken hym so neer
That of his chambre he made hym a squier,   1440
And gaf hym gold to mayntene his degree.
And eek men broghte hym out of his contree,
From yeer to yeer, ful pryvely his rente;
But honestly and slyly he it spente,
That no man wondred how that he it hadde.   1445
And thre yeer in this wise his lif he ladde,
And bar hym so, in pees and eek in werre,
Ther was no man that Theseus hath derre.
And in this blisse lete I now Arcite,
And speke I wole of Palamon a lite.   1450
    In derknesse and horrible and strong prisoun
Thise seven yeer hath seten Palamoun
Forpyned, what for wo and for distresse.
Who feeleth double soor and hevynesse
But Palamon, that love destreyneth so   1455
That wood out of his wit he goth for wo?
And eek therto he is a prisoner
Perpetuelly, noght oonly for a yer.
    Who koude ryme in Englyssh proprely
His martirdom? For sothe it am nat I;   1460
Therfore I passe as lightly as I may.
    It fel that in the seventhe yer, of May
The thridde nyght (as olde bookes seyn,
That al this storie tellen moore pleyn),
Were it by aventure or destynee—   1465
As, whan a thyng is shapen, it shal be—
That soone after the mydnyght Palamoun,
By helpyng of a freend, brak his prisoun
And fleeth the citee faste as he may go.
For he hadde yeve his gayler drynke so   1470
Of a clarree maad of a certeyn wyn,
With nercotikes and opie of Thebes fyn,
That al that nyght, thogh that men wolde him shake,
The gayler sleep; he myghte nat awake.
And thus he fleeth as faste as evere he may.   1475

The nyght was short and faste by the day
That nedes cost he moot hymselven hyde,
And til a grove faste ther bisyde
With dredeful foot thanne stalketh Palamon.
For, shortly, this was his opinion: 1480
That in that grove he wolde hym hyde al day,
And in the nyght thanne wolde he take his way
To Thebes-ward, his freendes for to preye
On Theseus to helpe him to werreye;
And shortly, outher he wolde lese his lif   1485
Or wynnen Emelye unto his wyf.
This is th'effect and his entente pleyn.
    Now wol I turne to Arcite ageyn,
That litel wiste how ny that was his care,
Til that Fortune had broght him in the snare.   1490
    The bisy larke, messager of day,
Salueth in hir song the morwe gray,
And firy Phebus riseth up so bright
That al the orient laugheth of the light,
And with his stremes dryeth in the greves   1495
The silver dropes hangynge on the leves.
And Arcita, that in the court roial
With Theseus is squier principal,
Is risen and looketh on the myrie day.
And for to doon his observaunce to May,   1500
Remembrynge on the poynt of his desir,
He on a courser, startlynge as the fir,
Is riden into the feeldes hym to pleye,
Out of the court, were it a myle or tweye.
And to the grove of which that I yow tolde   1505
By aventure his wey he gan to holde
To maken hym a gerland of the greves,
Were it of wodebynde or hawethorn leves,
And loude he song ayeyn the sonne shene:
"May, with alle thy floures and thy grene,   1510
Welcome be thou, faire, fresshe May,
In hope that I som grene gete may."
And from his courser, with a lusty herte,
Into the grove ful hastily he sterte,
And in a path he rometh up and doun,   1515
Ther as by aventure this Palamoun
Was in a bussh, that no man myghte hym se,
For soore afered of his deeth was he.

1436 **vertu:** abilities
1437 **name:** reputation
1439 **neer:** near (though this is usually the comparative *nearer*)
1446 **wise:** manner
1447 **pees:** peace
1448 **hath derre:** holds dearer
1449 **lete:** leave
1453 **Forpyned:** wasted by suffering
1454 **soor:** pain   **hevynesse:** sadness
1455 **destreyneth:** afflicts
1465 **aventure or destynee:** chance or fate
1470 **gayler:** jailer
1471 **clarree:** a spiced and sweetened wine
1472 **opie:** opium
1474 **sleep:** slept
1475 **fleeth:** flees, hastens

1477 **nedes cost:** necessarily
1478 **faste:** close
1479 **dredeful:** fearful
1484 **werreye:** wage war
1485 **outher:** either
1487 **th'effect:** the purpose
1495 **stremes:** rays   **greves:** groves
1502 **courser:** warhorse, charger   **startlynge:** leaping about
1506 **gan to holde:** did hold, held (took his way)
1507 **greves:** branches
1509 **ayeyn the sonne:** in the sun
1512 **som grene:** something green
1514 **sterte:** rushed

No thyng ne knew he that it was Arcite;
God woot he wolde have trowed it ful lite.   1520
But sooth is seyd, go sithen many yeres,
That "feeld hath eyen and the wode hath eres."
It is ful fair a man to bere hym evene,
For al day meeteth men at unset stevene.
Ful litel woot Arcite of his felawe,   1525
That was so ny to herknen al his sawe,
For in the bussh he sitteth now ful stille.

    Whan that Arcite hadde romed al his fille,
And songen al the roundel lustily,
Into a studie he fil sodeynly,   1530
As doon thise loveres in hir queynte geres,
Now in the crope, now doun in the breres,
Now up, now doun, as boket in a welle.
Right as the Friday, soothly for to telle,
Now it shyneth, now it reyneth faste,   1535
Right so kan geery Venus overcaste
The hertes of hir folk; right as hir day
Is gereful, right so chaungeth she array.
Selde is the Friday al the wowke ylike.

    Whan that Arcite had songe, he gan to sike   1540
And sette hym doun withouten any moore.
"Allas," quod he, "that day that I was bore!
How longe, Juno, thurgh thy crueltee,
Woltow werreyen Thebes the citee?
Allas, ybroght is to confusioun   1545
The blood roial of Cadme and Amphioun—
Of Cadmus, which that was the firste man
That Thebes bulte, or first the toun bigan,
And of the citee first was crouned kyng.
Of his lynage am I and his ofspryng   1550
By verray ligne, as of the stok roial,
And now I am so caytyf and so thral,
That he that is my mortal enemy,
I serve hym as his squier povrely.

And yet dooth Juno me wel moore shame,   1555
For I dar noght biknowe myn owene name;
But ther as I was wont to highte Arcite,
Now highte I Philostrate, noght worth a myte.
Allas, thou felle Mars! Allas, Juno!
Thus hath youre ire oure lynage al fordo,   1560
Save oonly me and wrecched Palamoun,
That Theseus martireth in prisoun.
And over al this, to sleen me outrely
Love hath his firy dart so brennyngly
Ystiked thurgh my trewe, careful herte   1565
That shapen was my deeth erst than my sherte.
Ye sleen me with youre eyen, Emelye!
Ye been the cause wherfore that I dye.
Of al the remenant of myn oother care
Ne sette I nat the montance of a tare,   1570
So that I koude doon aught to youre plesaunce."
And with that word he fil doun in a traunce
A longe tyme, and after he up sterte.

    This Palamoun, that thoughte that thurgh his herte
He felte a coold swerd sodeynliche glyde,   1575
For ire he quook; no lenger wolde he byde.
And whan that he had herd Arcites tale,
As he were wood, with face deed and pale,
He stirte hym up out of the buskes thikke
And seide: "Arcite, false traytour wikke,   1580
Now artow hent, that lovest my lady so,
For whom that I have al this peyne and wo,
And art my blood, and to my conseil sworn,
As I ful ofte have told thee heerbiforn,
And hast byjaped heere duc Theseus,   1585
And falsly chaunged hast thy name thus!
I wol be deed, or elles thou shalt dye.
Thou shalt nat love my lady Emelye,
But I wol love hire oonly and namo;
For I am Palamon, thy mortal foo.   1590

1521 **go sithen many yeres**: since many years ago
1523 **bere hym evene**: act calmly, moderately
1524 **meeteth men**: people meet   **at unset stevene**: with an unexpected (not set) time
1526 **sawe**: speech
1529 **roundel**: a short poetic and musical form; for an example, see PF 680–92.
1530 **sodeynly**: suddenly
1531 **thise loveres**: lovers in general   **queynte geres**: strange manners
1532 **crope**: leaves (top)   **breres**: briars
1533 **boket**: bucket
1536 **geery**: fickle   **overcaste**: sadden
1538 **gereful**: changeable
1539 Friday is seldom like all the rest of the week.
1540 **sike**: sigh
1544 **werreyen**: wage war on
1545 **confusioun**: ruin
1546 **Cadme and Amphioun**: Cadmus and Amphion, founders of Thebes
1548 **or**: ere
1551 **verray ligne**: true lineage   **stok**: stock, family
1552 **caytyf**: wretched captive   **thral**: enslaved
1554 **povrely**: lowly, meekly

1556 **biknowe**: acknowledge
1557 **highte**: be called
1558 **myte**: a small Flemish coin of little value
1559 **felle**: fierce
1560 **fordo**: destroyed
1562 **martireth**: torments
1563 **sleen**: slay, kill
1564 **brennyngly**: ardently
1565 **Ystiked**: struck, stabbed   **trewe**: faithful   **careful**: sorrowful
1566 My death was destined before my first garment was made for me (before my birth).
1570 **montance**: amount, value   **tare**: weed (i.e., nothing)
1571 **plesaunce**: pleasure
1576 **quook**: trembled
1579 **buskes**: bushes
1580 **wikke**: wicked
1585 **byjaped**: tricked
1589 **namo**: no others

And though that I no wepene have in this place,
But out of prison am astert by grace,
I drede noght that outher thow shalt dye,
Or thow ne shalt nat loven Emelye.
Chees which thou wolt, or thou shalt nat asterte!" 1595
    This Arcite, with ful despitous herte,
Whan he hym knew, and hadde his tale herd,
As fiers as leon pulled out his swerd,
And seyde thus: "By God that sit above,
Nere it that thou art sik and wood for love,   1600
And eek that thow no wepne hast in this place,
Thou sholdest nevere out of this grove pace,
That thou ne sholdest dyen of myn hond.
For I defye the seurete and the bond
Which that thou seist that I have maad to thee.   1605
What! Verray fool, thynk wel that love is free,
And I wol love hire maugree al thy myght!
But for as muche thou art a worthy knyght
And wilnest to darreyne hire by bataille,
Have heer my trouthe; tomorwe I wol nat faille,   1610
Withoute wityng of any oother wight,
That heere I wol be founden as a knyght,
And bryngen harneys right ynough for thee;
And ches the beste, and leef the worste for me.
And mete and drynke this nyght wol I brynge   1615
Ynough for thee, and clothes for thy beddynge.
And if so be that thou my lady wynne,
And sle me in this wode ther I am inne,
Thow mayst wel have thy lady as for me."
    This Palamon answerde, "I graunte it thee."   1620
And thus they been departed til amorwe,
Whan ech of hem had leyd his feith to borwe.
    O Cupide, out of alle charitee!
O regne, that wolt no felawe have with thee!
Ful sooth is seyd that love ne lordshipe   1625
Wol noght, his thankes, have no felaweshipe.
Wel fynden that Arcite and Palamoun.

Arcite is riden anon unto the toun,
And on the morwe, er it were dayes light,
Ful prively two harneys hath he dight,   1630
Bothe suffisaunt and mete to darreyne
The bataille in the feeld bitwix hem tweyne;
And on his hors, allone as he was born,
He carieth al the harneys hym biforn.
And in the grove, at tyme and place yset,   1635
This Arcite and this Palamon ben met.
To chaungen gan the colour in hir face;
Right as the hunters in the regne of Trace,
That stondeth at the gappe with a spere,
Whan hunted is the leon or the bere,   1640
And hereth hym come russhyng in the greves,
And breketh bothe bowes and the leves,
And thynketh, "Heere cometh my mortal enemy!
Withoute faille, he moot be deed, or I,
For outher I moot sleen hym at the gappe,   1645
Or he moot sleen me, if that me myshappe."
So ferden they in chaungyng of hir hewe,
As fer as everich of hem oother knewe.
    Ther nas no good day, ne no saluyng,
But streight, withouten word or rehersyng,   1650
Everich of hem heelp for to armen oother
As freendly as he were his owene brother;
And after that, with sharpe speres stronge
They foynen ech at oother wonder longe.
Thou myghtest wene that this Palamon   1655
In his fightyng were a wood leon,
And as a crueel tigre was Arcite;
As wilde bores gonne they to smyte,
That frothen whit as foom for ire wood.
Up to the ancle foghte they in hir blood.   1660
And in this wise I lete hem fightyng dwelle,
And forth I wole of Theseus yow telle.
    The destinee, ministre general,
That executeth in the world over al
The purveiaunce that God hath seyn biforn,   1665
So strong it is that, though the world had sworn
The contrarie of a thyng by ye or nay,

1591 **wepene:** weapons
1592 **astert:** escaped
1593 **drede:** doubt **outher:** either
1595 **Chees:** choose
1596 **despitous:** scornful
1599 **sit** = *sitteth,* sits
1600 **sik:** sick
1604 **defye:** repudiate **seurete:** pledge
1606 **What!:** Lo!
1607 **maugree:** in spite of
1609 **wilnest:** desire **darreyne hire:** decide the right to her
1610 **trouthe:** pledge
1611 **wityng:** knowledge
1613 **harneys:** armor
1614 **leef:** leave
1618 **ther:** where
1620 **graunte it thee:** agree
1622 **to borwe:** as a pledge
1626 **his thankes:** willingly **felaweshipe:** equal partnership

1630 **two harneys:** two suits of armor **dight:** prepared
1631 **mete:** suitable, fitting
1631–32 **darreyne The bataille:** engage in, decide the battle
1638 **regne of Trace:** kingdom of Thrace
1639 **gappe:** gap (toward which the game is driven)
1646 **me myshappe:** I should suffer misfortune
1649 **saluyng:** greeting
1650 **rehersyng:** conversation
1654 **foynen:** thrust **ech at oother:** at each other
1655 **wene:** suppose
1658 **bores:** boars
1659 **frothen:** foam at the mouth
1664 **executeth:** administers
1665 **purveiaunce:** foresight, providence

Yet somtyme it shal fallen on a day
That falleth nat eft withinne a thousand yeer.
For certeinly, oure appetites heer,   1670
Be it of werre, or pees, or hate, or love,
Al is this reuled by the sighte above.
    This mene I now by myghty Theseus,
That for to hunten is so desirus,
And namely at the grete hert in May,   1675
That in his bed ther daweth hym no day
That he nys clad, and redy for to ryde
With hunte and horn and houndes hym bisyde.
For in his huntyng hath he swich delit
That it is al his joye and appetit   1680
To been hymself the grete hertes bane,
For after Mars he serveth now Dyane.
    Cleer was the day, as I have toold er this,
And Theseus with alle joye and blis,
With his Ypolita, the faire queene,   1685
And Emelye, clothed al in grene,
On huntyng be they riden roially.
And to the grove that stood ful faste by,
In which ther was an hert, as men hym tolde,
Duc Theseus the streighte wey hath holde.   1690
And to the launde he rideth hym ful right,
For thider was the hert wont have his flight,
And over a brook, and so forth on his weye.
This duc wol han a cours at hym or tweye
With houndes swiche as that hym list comaunde.   1695
    And whan this duc was come unto the launde,
Under the sonne he looketh, and anon
He was war of Arcite and Palamon,
That foughten breme as it were bores two.
The brighte swerdes wenten to and fro   1700
So hidously that with the leeste strook
It semed as it wolde felle an ook.
But what they were, no thyng he ne woot.
This duc his courser with his spores smoot,
And at a stert he was bitwix hem two,   1705
And pulled out a swerd and cride, "Hoo!

Namoore, up peyne of lesynge of youre heed!
By myghty Mars, he shal anon be deed
That smyteth any strook that I may seen.
But telleth me what myster men ye been,   1710
That been so hardy for to fighten heere
Withouten juge or oother officere,
As it were in a lystes roially."
    This Palamon answerde hastily
And seyde, "Sire, what nedeth wordes mo?   1715
We have the deeth disserved bothe two.
Two woful wrecches been we, two caytyves,
That been encombred of oure owene lyves;
And as thou art a rightful lord and juge,
Ne yif us neither mercy ne refuge,   1720
But sle me first, for seinte charitee!
But sle my felawe eek as wel as me;
Or sle hym first, for though thow knowest it lite,
This is thy mortal foo, this is Arcite,
That fro thy lond is banysshed on his heed,   1725
For which he hath deserved to be deed.
For this is he that cam unto thy gate
And seyde that he highte Philostrate.
Thus hath he japed thee ful many a yer,
And thou hast maked hym thy chief squier;   1730
And this is he that loveth Emelye.
For sith the day is come that I shal dye,
I make pleynly my confessioun
That I am thilke woful Palamoun
That hath thy prisoun broken wikkedly.   1735
I am thy mortal foo, and it am I
That loveth so hoote Emelye the brighte
That I wol dye present in hir sighte.
Wherfore I axe deeth and my juwise;
But sle my felawe in the same wise,   1740
For bothe han we deserved to be slayn."
    This worthy duc answerde anon agayn,
And seyde, "This is a short conclusioun.
Youre owene mouth, by youre confessioun,
Hath dampned yow, and I wol it recorde;   1745
It nedeth noght to pyne yow with the corde.
Ye shal be deed, by myghty Mars the rede!"

1669 **eft:** again
1672 **sighte:** foresight
1673 **mene:** say   **by:** concerning
1675 **grete hert:** large hart, worthy of hunting
1676 **daweth hym:** dawns for him
1678 **hunte:** huntsman
1681 **bane:** killer
1682 **after Mars:** next to Mars, the god of war   **Dyane:** Diana, goddess of hunting
1688 **ful faste by:** very close by
1692 **thider:** thither, there
1694 **cours:** run
1696 **launde:** clearing
1697 **Under the sonne:** in the direction of the sun
1699 **breme:** fiercely
1705 **at a stert:** with a sudden movement, instantly
1706 **Hoo!:** stop!

1707 **up peyne of:** on the penalty of
1710 **what myster men:** what sort of men
1712 **juge or oother officere:** judge or some other officer, as in a properly conducted legal duel (*in a lystes roially*)
1717 **caytyves:** wretches
1718 **encombred:** burdened
1721 **for seinte charitee:** by holy charity (*seinte* is pronounced with two syllables)
1729 **japed:** tricked
1734 **thilke:** that
1737 **hoote:** passionately
1739 **axe:** ask   **juwise:** judicial sentence
1745 **dampned:** condemned   **recorde:** pronounce
1746 **to pyne yow with the corde:** to torture you (to force a confession) with a cord (twisted about your heads)

The queene anon, for verray wommanhede,
Gan for to wepe, and so dide Emelye,
And alle the ladyes in the compaignye.   1750
Greet pitee was it, as it thoughte hem alle,
That evere swich a chaunce sholde falle,
For gentil men they were of greet estaat,
And no thyng but for love was this debaat;
And saugh hir blody woundes wyde and soore,   1755
And alle crieden, bothe lasse and moore,
"Have mercy, Lord, upon us wommen alle!"
And on hir bare knees adoun they falle
And wolde have kist his feet ther as he stood;
Til at the laste aslaked was his mood,   1760
For pitee renneth soone in gentil herte.
And though he first for ire quook and sterte,
He hath considered shortly, in a clause,
The trespas of hem bothe, and eek the cause,
And although that his ire hir gilt accused,   1765
Yet in his resoun he hem bothe excused,
As thus: he thoghte wel that every man
Wol helpe hymself in love, if that he kan,
And eek delivere hymself out of prisoun.
And eek his herte hadde compassioun   1770
Of wommen, for they wepen evere in oon,
And in his gentil herte he thoughte anon,
And softe unto hymself he seyde, "Fy
Upon a lord that wol have no mercy,
But been a leon, bothe in word and dede,   1775
To hem that been in repentaunce and drede,
As wel as to a proud despitous man
That wol mayntene that he first bigan.
That lord hath litel of discrecioun,
That in swich cas kan no divisioun   1780
But weyeth pride and humblesse after oon."
And shortly, whan his ire is thus agoon,
He gan to looken up with eyen lighte
And spak thise same wordes al on highte:

"The god of love, a benedicite!   1785
How myghty and how greet a lord is he!
Ayeyns his myght ther gayneth none obstacles.
He may be cleped a god for his myracles,

For he kan maken, at his owene gyse,
Of everich herte as that hym list divyse.   1790
Lo heere this Arcite and this Palamoun,
That quitly weren out of my prisoun,
And myghte han lyved in Thebes roially,
And witen I am hir mortal enemy,
And that hir deth lith in my myght also,   1795
And yet hath love, maugree hir eyen two,
Broght hem hyder bothe for to dye.
Now looketh, is nat that an heigh folye?
Who may been a fool but if he love?
Bihoold, for Goddes sake that sit above,   1800
Se how they blede! Be they noght wel arrayed?
Thus hath hir lord, the god of love, ypayed
Hir wages and hir fees for hir servyse!
And yet they wenen for to been ful wyse
That serven love, for aught that may bifalle.   1805
But this is yet the beste game of alle,
That she for whom they han this jolitee
Kan hem therfore as muche thank as me.
She woot namoore of al this hoote fare,
By God, than woot a cokkow or an hare!   1810
But all moot ben assayed, hoot and coold;
A man moot ben a fool, or yong or oold—
I woot it by myself ful yore agon,
For in my tyme a servant was I oon.
And therfore, syn I knowe of loves peyne   1815
And woot hou soore it kan a man distreyne,
As he that hath ben caught ofte in his laas,
I yow foryeve al hoolly this trespaas,
At requeste of the queene, that kneleth heere,
And eek of Emelye, my suster deere.   1820
And ye shul bothe anon unto me swere
That nevere mo ye shal my contree dere,
Ne make werre upon me nyght ne day,
But been my freendes in all that ye may,
I yow foryeve this trespas every deel."   1825

1748 **wommanhede:** womanliness (having the qualities proper to a woman)
1760 **aslaked:** calmed
1761 **renneth:** moves
1762 **quook:** shook **sterte:** trembled
1763 **in a clause:** briefly
1771 **evere in oon:** continually
1773 **softe:** quietly
1778 **mayntene:** persist in
1779 **discrecioun:** sound judgment
1780 **kan no divisioun:** knows no distinctions
1781 **weyeth:** weighs **after oon:** alike
1784 **on highte:** aloud
1785 **benedicite:** (the Lord) bless you
1787 **gayneth:** avail

1789 **at his owene gyse:** after his own fashion
1790 **divyse:** command
1792 **quitly:** freely
1794 **witen:** know
1796 **maugree:** in spite of anything she could do
1799 Who can be a fool unless (*but if*) he is in love?
1800 **sit** = *sitteth,* sits
1802 **ypayed:** paid
1804 **wenen for to been:** think themselves
1806 **game:** joke
1807 **jolitee:** passion
1808 Owes them as much gratitude for this as she owes me
1809 **hoote fare:** rash conduct
1810 **cokkow:** cuckoo
1811 **assayed:** experienced
1813 **yore agon:** long ago
1814 **servant:** servant of Love, lover
1816 **distreyne:** afflict
1817 **laas:** snare
1821 **shul:** must
1822 **dere:** harm
1825 **every deel:** completely

And they hym sworen his axyng faire and weel,
And hym of lordshipe and of mercy preyde,
And he hem graunteth grace, and thus he seyde:
    "To speke of roial lynage and richesse,
Though that she were a queene or a princesse,   1830
Ech of you bothe is worthy, doutelees,
To wedden whan tyme is; but nathelees—
I speke as for my suster Emelye,
For whom ye have this strif and jalousye—
Ye woot yourself she may nat wedden two   1835
Atones, though ye fighten everemo,
That oon of you, al be hym looth or lief,
He moot go pipen in an yvy leef;
This is to seyn, she may nat now han bothe,
Al be ye never so jalouse ne so wrothe.   1840
And forthy I yow putte in this degree,
That ech of yow shal have his destynee
As hym is shape, and herkneth in what wyse;
Lo, heere youre ende of that I shal devyse.
    My wyl is this, for plat conclusioun,   1845
Withouten any repplicacioun—
If that you liketh, take it for the beste:
That everich of you shal goon where hym leste
Frely, withouten raunson or daunger,
And this day fifty wykes, fer ne ner,   1850
Everich of you shal brynge an hundred knyghtes
Armed for lystes up at alle rightes,
Al redy to darreyne hire by bataille.
And this bihote I yow withouten faille,
Upon my trouthe, and as I am a knyght,   1855
That wheither of yow bothe that hath myght—
This is to seyn, that wheither he or thow
May with his hundred, as I spak of now,
Sleen his contrarie, or out of lystes dryve,
Thanne shal I yeve Emelya to wyve   1860
To whom that Fortune yeveth so fair a grace.
The lystes shal I maken in this place,
And God so wisly on my soule rewe

As I shal evene juge been and trewe.
Ye shul noon oother ende with me maken,   1865
That oon of yow ne shal be deed or taken.
And if yow thynketh this is weel ysayd,
Seyeth youre avys, and holdeth you apayd.
This is youre ende and youre conclusioun."
    Who looketh lightly now but Palamoun?   1870
Who spryngeth up for joye but Arcite?
Who kouthe telle, or who kouthe it endite,
The joye that is maked in the place
Whan Theseus hath doon so fair a grace?
But doun on knees wente every maner wight,   1875
And thonked hym with al hir herte and myght,
And namely the Thebans often sithe.
And thus with good hope and with herte blithe
They taken hir leve, and homward gonne they ride
To Thebes with his olde walles wyde.   1880

Explicit secunda pars

Sequitur pars tercia

    I trowe men wolde deme it necligence
If I foryete to tellen the dispence
Of Theseus, that gooth so bisily
To maken up the lystes roially,
That swich a noble theatre as it was   1885
I dar wel seyen in this world ther nas.
The circuit a myle was aboute,
Walled of stoon, and dyched al withoute.
Round was the shap, in manere of compas,
Ful of degrees, the heighte of sixty pas,   1890
That whan a man was set on o degree,
He letted nat his felawe for to see.
    Estward ther stood a gate of marbul whit,
Westward right swich another in the opposit.
And shortly to concluden, swich a place   1895
Was noon in erthe, as in so litel space;
For in the lond ther was no crafty man
That geometrie or ars-metrike kan,
Ne portreyour, ne kervere of ymages,

1827 **of lordshipe:** to be their lord, protector
1829 **richesse:** wealth
1832 **nathelees:** none the less
1836 **Atones:** at once, at the same time
1837 **al be hym looth or lief:** whether he likes it or not
1838 He may as well go whistle (for consolation).
1840 **wrothe:** angry
1841 **forthy:** therefore   **degree:** situation
1843 **wyse:** manner
1845 **plat:** flat, blunt
1846 **repplicacioun:** reply
1849 **daunger:** resistance
1850 **fer ne ner:** more or less; see n.
1852 **for lystes:** for battle in the lists   **at alle rightes:** in all respects
1853 **darreyne hire:** decide the right to her
1854 **bihote:** promise
1856 **wheither:** whichever
1860 **to wyve:** as a wife
1863 **rewe:** have mercy

1864 **evene:** impartial
1865 **shul:** shall
1868 **avys:** opinion   **apayd:** satisfied
1870 **lightly:** cheerfully
1872 **endite:** describe in writing
1874 **doon so fair a grace:** behaved so graciously   **Explicit,** *etc.*: Here ends the second part.   **Sequitur,** *etc.*: Here follows the third part.
1882 **dispence:** expenditures
1888 **dyched:** surrounded by a ditch
1889 **manere of compas:** the shape of a circle
1890 **degrees:** tiers, rows of seats   **pas:** paces
1892 **letted:** hindered
1896 **space:** time
1897 **crafty:** skillful, ingenious
1898 **ars-metrike:** art of measurement (arithmetic)   **kan:** knows
1899 **portreyour:** painter   **kervere of ymages:** sculptor

That Theseus ne yaf him mete and wages   1900
The theatre for to maken and devyse.
And for to doon his ryte and sacrifise,
He estward hath, upon the gate above,
In worshipe of Venus, goddesse of love,
Doon make an auter and an oratorie;   1905
And on the gate westward, in memorie
Of Mars, he maked hath right swich another,
That coste largely of gold a fother.
And northward, in a touret on the wal,
Of alabastre whit and reed coral,   1910
An oratorie, riche for to see,
In worshipe of Dyane of chastitee,
Hath Theseus doon wroght in noble wyse.

But yet hadde I foryeten to devyse
The noble kervyng and the portreitures,   1915
The shap, the contenaunce, and the figures
That weren in thise oratories thre.

First in the temple of Venus maystow se
Wroght on the wal, ful pitous to biholde,
The broken slepes, and the sikes colde,   1920
The sacred teeris, and the waymentynge,
The firy strokes of the desirynge
That loves servantz in this lyf enduren;
The othes that hir covenantz assuren;
Plesaunce and Hope, Desir, Foolhardynesse,   1925
Beautee and Youthe, Bauderie, Richesse,
Charmes and Force, Lesynges, Flaterye,
Despense, Bisynesse, and Jalousye,
That wered of yelewe gooldes a gerland,
And a cokkow sittynge on hir hand;   1930
Festes, instrumentz, caroles, daunces,
Lust and array, and alle the circumstaunces
Of love, which that I rekned and rekne shal,
By ordre weren peynted on the wal,
And mo than I kan make of mencioun.   1935
For soothly al the mount of Citheroun,

Ther Venus hath hir principal dwellynge,
Was shewed on the wal in portreyynge,
With al the gardyn and the lustynesse.
Nat was foryeten the porter, Ydelnesse,   1940
Ne Narcisus the faire of yore agon,
Ne yet the folye of kyng Salomon,
Ne yet the grete strengthe of Ercules—
Th'enchauntementz of Medea and Circes—
Ne of Turnus, with the hardy fiers corage,   1945
The riche Cresus, kaytyf in servage.
Thus may ye seen that wysdom ne richesse,
Beautee ne sleighte, strengthe ne hardynesse,
Ne may with Venus holde champartie,
For as hir list the world than may she gye.   1950
Lo, alle thise folk so caught were in hir las,
Til they for wo ful ofte seyde "allas!"
Suffiseth heere ensamples oon or two,
And though I koude rekene a thousand mo.

The statue of Venus, glorious for to se,   1955
Was naked, fletynge in the large see,
And fro the navele doun al covered was
With wawes grene, and brighte as any glas.
A citole in hir right hand hadde she,
And on hir heed, ful semely for to se,   1960
A rose gerland, fressh and wel smellynge;
Above hir heed hir dowves flikerynge.
Biforn hire stood hir sone Cupido;
Upon his shuldres wynges hadde he two,
And blynd he was, as it is often seene;   1965
A bowe he bar and arwes brighte and kene.

Why sholde I noght as wel eek telle yow al
The portreiture that was upon the wal
Withinne the temple of myghty Mars the rede?
Al peynted was the wal, in lengthe and brede,   1970
Lyk to the estres of the grisly place
That highte the grete temple of Mars in Trace,
In thilke colde, frosty regioun
Ther as Mars hath his sovereyn mansioun.

1901 **devyse:** contrive
1905 **auter:** altar   **oratorie:** shrine, chapel
1908 **fother:** cartload
1909 **touret:** turret
1912 **Dyane of chastitee:** the chaste Diana
1913 **doon wroght:** had made
1915 **kervyng:** sculpture   **portreitures:** paintings
1916 **contenaunce:** appearance
1920 **sikes:** sighs
1921 **waymentynge:** lamentation
1924 **covenantz:** agreements
1925 **Plesaunce:** Pleasure, amusement
1926 **Bauderie:** Mirth, jollity
1927 **Lesynges:** Falsehood, deceit
1928 **Despense:** expenditures   **Bisynesse:** attentiveness
1929 **yelewe:** yellow   **gooldes:** marigolds
1930 **cokkow:** cuckoo (a symbol of cuckoldry)
1931 **caroles:** dance-songs
1934 **By ordre:** sequentially
1936 **Citheroun:** Cithaeron, here confused with the island Cytherea

1939 **lustynesse:** pleasure
1941 **Narcisus:** Narcissus, for whom the nymph Echo died; for the story, see Rom 1469–1638.
1942 **folye:** lechery   **Salomon:** Solomon, who had many wives
1943 **Ercules:** Hercules, whose beloved killed him; see MkT VII.2095–142.
1944 **Medea and Circes:** famous sorceresses, who tried to hold their loves by magic
1945 **Turnus:** whose love for Lavinia led to his fatal duel with Aeneas; cf. HF 457–58.
1946 **Cresus, kaytyf in servage:** Croesus, wretched in captivity; see MkT VII.2727–66.
1948 **sleighte:** trickery   **hardynesse:** bravery
1949 **champartie:** partnership in power
1950 **gye:** rule
1951 **las:** snare
1956 **fletynge:** floating
1958 **wawes:** waves
1959 **citole:** a stringed instrument, like a zither
1962 **flikerynge:** fluttering
1967 **eek:** also
1970 **brede:** breadth
1971 **estres:** interior apartments
1974 **sovereyn:** best, most excellent

First on the wal was peynted a forest,   1975
In which ther dwelleth neither man ne best,
With knotty, knarry, bareyne trees olde,
Of stubbes sharpe and hidouse to biholde,
In which ther ran a rumbel in a swough,
As though a storm sholde bresten every bough.   1980
And dounward from an hille, under a bente,
Ther stood the temple of Mars armypotente,
Wroght al of burned steel, of which the entree
Was long and streit, and gastly for to see.
And therout came a rage and swich a veze   1985
That it made al the gate for to rese.
The northren lyght in at the dores shoon,
For wyndowe on the wal ne was ther noon,
Thurgh which men myghten any light discerne.
The dore was al of adamant eterne,   1990
Yclenched overthwart and endelong
With iren tough; and for to make it strong,
Every pyler, the temple to sustene,
Was tonne-greet, of iren bright and shene.
    Ther saugh I first the derke ymaginyng   1995
Of Felonye, and al the compassyng;
The crueel Ire, reed as any gleede;
The pykepurs, and eek the pale Drede;
The smylere with the knyf under the cloke;
The shepne brennynge with the blake smoke;   2000
The tresoun of the mordrynge in the bedde;
The open werre, with woundes al bibledde;
Contek, with blody knyf and sharp manace.
Al ful of chirkyng was that sory place.
The sleere of hymself yet saugh I ther—   2005
His herte-blood hath bathed al his heer—
The nayl ydryven in the shode anyght;

The colde deeth, with mouth gapyng upright.
Amyddes of the temple sat Meschaunce,
With disconfort and sory contenaunce.   2010
Yet saugh I Woodnesse, laughynge in his rage,
Armed Compleint, Outhees, and fiers Outrage;
The careyne in the busk, with throte ycorve;
A thousand slayn, and nat of qualm ystorve;
The tiraunt, with the pray by force yraft;   2015
The toun destroyed, ther was no thyng laft.
Yet saugh I brent the shippes hoppesteres;
The hunte strangled with the wilde beres;
The sowe freten the child right in the cradel;
The cook yscalded, for al his longe ladel.   2020
Noght was foryeten by the infortune of Marte:
The cartere overryden with his carte—
Under the wheel ful lowe he lay adoun.
Ther were also, of Martes divisioun,
The barbour, and the bocher, and the smyth,   2025
That forgeth sharpe swerdes on his styth.
And al above, depeynted in a tour,
Saugh I Conquest, sittynge in greet honour,
With the sharpe swerd over his heed
Hangynge by a soutil twynes threed.   2030
Depeynted was the slaughtre of Julius,
Of grete Nero, and of Antonius;
Al be that thilke tyme they were unborn,
Yet was hir deth depeynted ther-biforn
By manasynge of Mars, right by figure;   2035
So was it shewed in that portreiture,
As is depeynted in the sterres above
Who shal be slayn or elles deed for love.
Suffiseth oon ensample in stories olde;
I may nat rekene hem alle though I wolde.   2040
    The statue of Mars upon a carte stood
Armed, and looked grym as he were wood;

1977 **knarry**: gnarled   **bareyne**: barren
1978 **stubbes**: stumps
1979 **rumbel**: rumbling noise   **swough**: sound of wind
1980 **bresten**: burst
1981 **under**: close to   **bente**: grassy slope
1982 **armypotente**: powerful in arms
1983 **burned**: burnished
1984 **streit**: narrow, small   **gastly**: terrifying
1985 **rage**: rush of wind   **veze**: rush, blast
1986 **rese**: shake
1987 **northren lyght**: light from the north
1990 **adamant**: the hardest of stones
1991 **Yclenched**: bound, clinched   **overthwart**: crosswise   **endelong**: lengthwise
1993 **pyler**: pillar   **sustene**: sustain, support
1994 **tonne-greet**: big around as a large barrel
1995 **derke ymaginyng**: malicious plotting
1996 **Felonye**: Wickedness   **compassyng**: scheming
1997 **gleede**: glowing coal
1998 **pykepurs**: pick-purse, thief   **Drede**: Fear
2000 **shepne**: stable
2001 **mordrynge**: murder
2002 **with woundes al bibledde**: all covered with blood from wounds
2003 **Contek**: strife
2004 **chirkyng**: groaning, creaking   **sory**: sorry, wretched
2005 **sleere**: slayer
2007 **shode**: parting of the hair, temple

2008 **upright**: upwards
2009 **Meschaunce**: Misfortune
2011 **Woodnesse**: Madness
2012 **Compleint**: Grievance, discontent   **Outhees**: Outcry, alarm   **Outrage**: Violence, excessive cruelty
2013 **careyne**: corpse   **busk**: woods   **ycorve**: cut
2014 **of qualm ystorve**: killed by the plague
2015 **pray**: prey   **yraft**: taken away
2017 **brent**: burned   **hoppesteres**: dancing (on a stormy sea)
2018 **hunte**: hunter   **strangled with**: killed by
2019 **freten**: devour
2020 **for al his longe ladel**: despite his long-handled spoon
2021 **infortune of Marte**: evil influence of Mars
2022 **overryden with**: run over by
2024 **Martes divisioun**: those influenced by Mars
2025 **bocher**: butcher
2026 **styth**: anvil
2027 **depeynted**: painted
2030 **soutil twynes threed**: thin thread of twine
2031–32 **Julius, Nero, Antonius**: the Roman emperors
2035 **manasynge**: menace, threat   **by figure**: according to the configuration of the planets; "perhaps a technical reference to a horoscope" (R.)
2036 **portreiture**: painting
2039 **ensample**: illustrative story   **stories**: histories
2041 **carte**: chariot

And over his heed ther shynen two figures
Of sterres, that been cleped in scriptures,
That oon Puella, that oother Rubeus—   2045
This god of armes was arrayed thus.
A wolf ther stood biforn hym at his feet
With eyen rede, and of a man he eet;
With soutil pencel was depeynted this storie
In redoutynge of Mars and of his glorie.   2050
  Now to the temple of Dyane the chaste,
As shortly as I kan, I wol me haste,
To telle yow al the descripsioun.
Depeynted been the walles up and doun
Of huntyng and of shamefast chastitee.   2055
Ther saugh I how woful Calistopee,
Whan that Diane agreved was with here,
Was turned from a womman til a bere,
And after was she maad the loode-sterre.
Thus was it peynted; I kan sey yow no ferre.   2060
Hir sone is eek a sterre, as men may see.
Ther saugh I Dane, yturned til a tree—
I mene nat the goddesse Diane,
But Penneus doghter, which that highte Dane.
Ther saugh I Attheon an hert ymaked,   2065
For vengeaunce that he saugh Diane al naked;
I saugh how that his houndes have hym caught
And freeten hym, for that they knewe hym naught.
Yet peynted was a litel forther moor
How Atthalante hunted the wilde boor,   2070
And Meleagre, and many another mo,
For which Dyane wroghte hym care and wo.
Ther saugh I many another wonder storie,
The which me list nat drawen to memorie.
  This goddesse on an hert ful hye seet,   2075
With smale houndes al aboute hir feet,
And undernethe hir feet she hadde a moone—
Wexynge it was and sholde wanye soone.
In gaude grene hir statue clothed was,
With bowe in honde and arwes in a cas.   2080
Hir eyen caste she ful lowe adoun

Ther Pluto hath his derke regioun.
A womman travaillynge was hire biforn;
But for hir child so longe was unborn,
Ful pitously Lucyna gan she calle   2085
And seyde, "Help, for thou mayst best of alle!"
Wel koude he peynten lifly that it wroghte;
With many a floryn he the hewes boghte.
  Now been thise lystes maad, and Theseus,
That at his grete cost arrayed thus   2090
The temples and the theatre every deel,
Whan it was doon, hym lyked wonder weel.
But stynte I wole of Theseus a lite,
And speke of Palamon and of Arcite.
  The day approcheth of hir retournynge,   2095
That everich sholde an hundred knyghtes brynge
The bataille to darreyne, as I yow tolde.
And til Atthenes, hir covenant for to holde,
Hath everich of hem broght an hundred knyghtes,
Wel armed for the werre at alle rightes.   2100
And sikerly ther trowed many a man
That nevere, sithen that the world bigan,
As for to speke of knyghthod of hir hond,
As fer as God hath maked see or lond,
Nas of so fewe so noble a compaignye.   2105
For every wight that lovede chivalrye
And wolde, his thankes, han a passant name,
Hath preyed that he myghte been of that game;
And wel was hym that therto chosen was,
For if ther fille tomorwe swich a cas,   2110
Ye knowen wel that every lusty knyght
That loveth paramours and hath his myght,
Were it in Engelond or elleswhere,
They wolde, hir thankes, wilnen to be there—
To fighte for a lady, benedicitee!   2115
It were a lusty sighte for to see.
  And right so ferden they with Palamon.
With hym ther wenten knyghtes many on;
Som wol ben armed in an haubergeoun,
And in a brestplate and a light gypoun;   2120

2044 **scriptures:** books
2045 **Puella, Rubeus:** figures in geomancy; see n.
2048 **eet:** ate
2050 **redoutynge:** reverence
2055 **shamefast:** modest
2056 **Calistopee:** Callisto, who was metamorphosed into Ursa Major
2057 **agreved:** angered
2059 **loode-sterre:** polestar, North star
2060 **ferre:** further
2062 **Dane:** Daphne, pursued by Apollo and metamorphosed into the laurel tree
2065 **Attheon:** Actaeon, metamorphosed into a hart by Diana
2068 **freeten:** devoured
2070 **Atthalante:** Atalanta, for whom Meleager (*Meleagre*) hunted the Calydonian
boar; see Tr 5.1464–84.
2075 **seet:** sat
2078 **Wexynge:** waxing   **wanye:** wane
2079 **gaude:** yellowish

2083 **travaillynge:** in labor
2085 **Lucyna:** Lucina, Diana as goddess of childbirth
2086 **thou mayst best:** you are best able, have most power
2088 **floryn:** florin, a gold coin   **hewes:** pigments
2090 **arrayed:** prepared
2091 **every deel:** in all respects
2097 **darreyne:** decide
2100 **at alle rightes:** in all respects
2101 **sikerly:** truly   **trowed:** believed
2103 **of hir hond:** of the deeds of their hand, their prowess
2107 **his thankes:** willingly   **passant name:** outstanding reputation
2112 **paramours:** passionately
2114 **wilnen:** desire
2116 **lusty:** pleasing
2119 **Som:** a certain one   **haubergeoun:** coat of mail
2120 **gypoun:** tunic

And som wol have a paire plates large;
And som wol have a Pruce sheeld or a targe;
Som wol ben armed on his legges weel,
And have an ax, and som a mace of steel—
Ther is no newe gyse that it nas old.   2125
Armed were they, as I have yow told,
Everych after his opinioun.

    Ther maistow seen, comynge with Palamoun,
Lygurge hymself, the grete kyng of Trace.
Blak was his berd, and manly was his face;   2130
The cercles of his eyen in his heed,
They gloweden bitwixen yelow and reed,
And lik a grifphon looked he aboute,
With kempe heeris on his browes stoute;
His lymes grete, his brawnes harde and stronge,   2135
His shuldres brode, his armes rounde and longe;
And as the gyse was in his contree,
Ful hye upon a chaar of gold stood he,
With foure white boles in the trays.
In stede of cote-armure over his harnays,   2140
With nayles yelewe and brighte as any gold,
He hadde a beres skyn, col-blak for old.
His longe heer was kembd bihynde his bak;
As any ravenes fethere it shoon for blak;
A wrethe of gold, arm-greet, of huge wighte,   2145
Upon his heed, set ful of stones brighte,
Of fyne rubyes and of dyamauntz.
Aboute his chaar ther wenten white alauntz,
Twenty and mo, as grete as any steer,
To hunten at the leoun or the deer,   2150
And folwed hym with mosel faste ybounde,
Colered of gold, and tourettes fyled rounde.
An hundred lordes hadde he in his route,
Armed ful wel, with hertes stierne and stoute.

    With Arcita, in stories as men fynde,   2155
The grete Emetreus, the kyng of Inde,

Upon a steede bay trapped in steel,
Covered in clooth of gold, dyapred weel,
Cam ridynge lyk the god of armes, Mars.
His cote-armure was of clooth of Tars   2160
Couched with perles white and rounde and grete;
His sadel was of brend gold newe ybete;
A mantelet upon his shulder hangynge,
Bret-ful of rubyes rede as fyr sparklynge;
His crispe heer lyk rynges was yronne,   2165
And that was yelow, and glytered as the sonne.
His nose was heigh, his eyen bright citryn,
His lippes rounde, his colour was sangwyn;
A fewe frakenes in his face yspreynd,
Bitwixen yelow and somdel blak ymeynd;   2170
And as a leon he his lookyng caste.
Of fyve and twenty yeer his age I caste.
His berd was wel bigonne for to sprynge;
His voys was as a trompe thonderynge.
Upon his heed he wered of laurer grene   2175
A gerland, fressh and lusty for to sene.
Upon his hand he bar for his deduyt
An egle tame, as any lilye whyt.
An hundred lordes hadde he with hym there,
Al armed, save hir heddes, in al hir gere,   2180
Ful richely in alle maner thynges.
For trusteth wel that dukes, erles, kynges
Were gadered in this noble compaignye,
For love and for encrees of chivalrye.
Aboute this kyng ther ran on every part   2185
Ful many a tame leon and leopart.
And in this wise thise lordes, alle and some,
Been on the Sonday to the citee come
Aboute pryme, and in the toun alight.

    This Theseus, this duc, this worthy knyght,   2190
Whan he had broght hem into his citee,
And inned hem, everich at his degree,
He festeth hem, and dooth so greet labour
To esen hem and doon hem al honour

2121 **paire plates**: set of plate armor
2122 **Pruce**: Prussian
2125 There is no new fashion (*gyse*) that has not been old. (R.)
2127 **after**: according to
2129 **Lygurge**: Lycurgus
2133 **grifphon**: griffin (mythical beast with the body of a lion and the head of an eagle)
2134 **kempe**: shaggy
2135 **lymes greet**: large limbs   **brawnes**: muscles
2138 **chaar**: chariot
2139 **boles**: bulls   **trays**: traces, harness
2140 **cote-armure**: a tunic embroidered with a heraldic device, worn over the armor
2141 **nayles**: rivets   **yelewe**: yellow
2142 **col-blak**: coal-black   **for old**: because of age
2143 **kembd**: combed
2144 **for blak**: because of blackness
2145 **arm-greet**: thick as an arm   **wighte**: weight
2147 **dyamauntz**: diamonds
2148 **alauntz**: wolfhounds
2151 **mosel**: muzzle
2152 **Colered**: wearing collars   **tourettes**: rings for leashes   **fyled**: smoothed
2153 **route**: company
2154 **stierne**: stern, cruel
2156 **Inde**: India

2157 **bay**: reddish-brown   **trapped**: equipped with trappings
2158 **dyapred**: decorated with small geometric patterns
2160 **clooth of Tars**: silk from Tarsia in Turkestan
2161 **Couched**: adorned   **perles**: pearls
2162 **brend gold**: refined (pure) gold   **ybete**: adorned
2163 **mantelet**: short cloak
2164 **Bret-ful**: brimful
2165 **crispe**: curly   **yronne**: fashioned (literally, *run*)
2167 **citryn**: lemon-colored
2168 **sangwyn**: ruddy
2169 **frakenes**: freckles   **yspreynd**: sprinkled
2170 **ymeynd**: mingled
2171 **lookyng caste**: looked about
2177 **deduyt**: delight
2184 **encrees**: increase
2185 **on every part**: on all sides
2187 **alle and some**: one and all, everyone
2189 **pryme**: around 9 A.M.   **alight**: dismounted, arrived
2192 **inned hem**: provided them lodging
2193 **dooth so greet labour**: makes such an effort
2194 **esen**: accommodate, entertain

That yet men wenen that no mannes wit   2195
Of noon estaat ne koude amenden it.
    The mynstralcye, the service at the feeste,
The grete yiftes to the meeste and leeste,
The riche array of Theseus paleys,
Ne who sat first ne last upon the deys,   2200
What ladyes fairest been or best daunsynge,
Or which of hem kan dauncen best and synge,
Ne who moost felyngly speketh of love;
What haukes sitten on the perche above,
What houndes liggen on the floor adoun—   2205
Of al this make I now no mencioun,
But al th'effect; that thynketh me the beste.
Now cometh the point, and herkneth if yow leste.
    The Sonday nyght, er day bigan to sprynge,
Whan Palamon the larke herde synge   2210
(Although it nere nat day by houres two,
Yet song the larke) and Palamon right tho
With hooly herte and with an heigh corage,
He roos to wenden on his pilgrymage
Unto the blisful Citherea benigne—   2215
I mene Venus, honurable and digne.
And in hir houre he walketh forth a pas
Unto the lystes ther hire temple was,
And doun he kneleth, and with humble cheere
And herte soor he seyde as ye shal heere: 2220
    "Faireste of faire, O lady myn, Venus,
Doughter to Jove and spouse of Vulcanus,
Thow gladere of the mount of Citheron,
For thilke love thow haddest to Adoon,
Have pitee of my bittre teeris smerte,   2225
And taak myn humble preyere at thyn herte.
Allas! I ne have no langage to telle
Th'effectes ne the tormentz of myn helle;
Myn herte may myne harmes nat biwreye;
I am so confus that I kan noght seye   2230
But "Mercy, lady bright, that knowest weele
My thought and seest what harmes that I feele!'

Considere al this and rewe upon my soore,
As wisly as I shal for everemoore,
Emforth my myght, thy trewe servant be,   2235
And holden werre alwey with chastitee.
That make I myn avow, so ye me helpe!
I kepe noght of armes for to yelpe,
Ne I ne axe nat tomorwe to have victorie,
Ne renoun in this cas, ne veyne glorie   2240
Of pris of armes blowen up and doun;
But I wolde have fully possessioun
Of Emelye, and dye in thy servyse.
Fynd thow the manere hou and in what wyse:
I recche nat but it may bettre be   2245
To have victorie of hem, or they of me,
So that I have my lady in myne armes.
For though so be that Mars is god of armes,
Youre vertu is so greet in hevene above
That if yow list, I shal wel have my love.   2250
Thy temple wol I worshipe everemo,
And on thyn auter, where I ride or go,
I wol doon sacrifice and fires beete.
And if ye wol nat so, my lady sweete,
Thanne preye I thee, tomorwe with a spere   2255
That Arcita me thurgh the herte bere.
Thanne rekke I noght, whan I have lost my lyf,
Though that Arcita wynne hire to his wyf.
This is th'effect and ende of my preyere:
Yif me my love, thow blisful lady deere."   2260
    Whan the orison was doon of Palamon,
His sacrifice he dide, and that anon,
Ful pitously, with alle circumstaunces,
Al telle I noght as now his observaunces;
But atte laste the statue of Venus shook,   2265
And made a signe, wherby that he took
That his preyere accepted was that day.
For thogh the signe shewed a delay,
Yet wiste he wel that graunted was his boone,
And with glad herte he wente hym hoom ful soone.
    The thridde houre inequal that Palamon   2271
Bigan to Venus temple for to gon,

2195 **wenen:** suppose
2197 **mynstralcye:** music
2198 **yiftes:** gifts   **to the meeste and leeste:** to everyone
2199 **array:** adornment
2200 **deys:** dais
2203 **moost felyngly:** with the most delicate understanding
2205 **liggen:** lie   **adoun:** below
2207 **th'effect:** the substance
2212 **tho:** then
2215 **Citherea:** a name for Venus, who rose from the sea at the island Cythera
benigne: gracious
2216 **digne:** worthy of honor
2217 **houre:** planetary hour; see n.   **a pas:** slowly
2219 **cheere:** expression
2223 **gladere:** one who brings joy
2224 **Adoon:** Adonis
2228 **tormentz:** tortures
2229 **biwreye:** reveal
2232 **harmes:** sorrows

2233 **rewe:** have mercy   **soore:** pain, misery
2234 **As wisly as:** as surely as
2235 **Emforth:** according to
2237 **so ye me helpe:** providing you help me
2238 **kepe noght:** care nothing   **yelpe:** boast
2239 **Ne I:** to be pronounced as one syllable (n'I)
2241 **pris of armes blowen:** praise for deeds of arms proclaimed
2245 **recche nat but:** care not if
2249 **vertu:** power
2252 **where I ride or go:** wherever I ride or walk (whatever I do)
2253 **beete:** kindle
2260 **Yif:** give
2263 **circumstaunces:** ceremony, due propriety
2264 **Al:** although
2269 **boone:** request
2271 **houre inequal:** planetary hour; see n.

Up roos the sonne, and up roos Emelye
And to the temple of Dyane gan hye.
Hir maydens, that she thider with hire ladde,   2275
Ful redily with hem the fyr they hadde,
Th'encens, the clothes, and the remenant al
That to the sacrifice longen shal;
The hornes fulle of meeth, as was the gyse—
Ther lakked noght to doon hir sacrifise.   2280
Smokynge the temple, ful of clothes faire,
This Emelye, with herte debonaire,
Hir body wessh with water of a welle.
But hou she dide hir ryte I dar nat telle,
But it be any thing in general;   2285
And yet it were a game to heeren al.
To hym that meneth wel it were no charge;
But it is good a man been at his large.
Hir brighte heer was kembd, untressed al;
A coroune of a grene ook cerial   2290
Upon hir heed was set ful fair and meete.
Two fyres on the auter gan she beete,
And dide hir thynges, as men may biholde
In Stace of Thebes and thise bookes olde.
Whan kyndled was the fyr, with pitous cheere   2295
Unto Dyane she spak as ye may heere:
    "O chaste goddesse of the wodes grene,
To whom bothe hevene and erthe and see is sene,
Queene of the regne of Pluto derk and lowe,
Goddesse of maydens, that myn herte hast knowe
Ful many a yeer, and woost what I desire,   2301
As keepe me fro thy vengeaunce and thyn ire,
That Attheon aboughte cruelly.
Chaste goddesse, wel wostow that I
Desire to ben a mayden al my lyf,   2305
Ne nevere wol I be no love ne wyf.
I am, thow woost, yet of thy compaignye,
A mayde, and love huntynge and venerye,
And for to walken in the wodes wilde,
And noght to ben a wyf and be with childe.   2310

Noght wol I knowe compaignye of man.
Now help me, lady, sith ye may and kan,
For tho thre formes that thou hast in thee.
And Palamon, that hath swich love to me,
And eek Arcite, that loveth me so soore,   2315
This grace I preye thee withoute moore,
As sende love and pees bitwixe hem two,
And fro me turne awey hir hertes so
That al hire hoote love and hir desir,
And al hir bisy torment, and hir fir   2320
Be queynt, or turned in another place.
And if so be thou wolt nat do me grace,
Or if my destynee be shapen so
That I shal nedes have oon of hem two,
As sende me hym that moost desireth me.   2325
Bihoold, goddesse of clene chastitee,
The bittre teeris that on my chekes falle.
Syn thou art mayde and kepere of us alle,
My maydenhede thou kepe and wel conserve,
And whil I lyve, a mayde I wol thee serve."   2330
    The fires brenne upon the auter cleere,
Whil Emelye was thus in hir preyere.
But sodeynly she saugh a sighte queynte,
For right anon oon of the fyres queynte
And quyked agayn, and after that anon   2335
That oother fyr was queynt and al agon;
And as it queynte it made a whistelynge,
As doon thise wete brondes in hir brennynge,
And at the brondes ende out ran anon
As it were blody dropes many oon;   2340
For which so soore agast was Emelye
That she was wel ny mad and gan to crye,
For she ne wiste what it signyfied,
But oonly for the feere thus hath she cried,
And weep that it was pitee for to heere.   2345
And therwithal Dyane gan appeere,
With bowe in honde, right as an hunteresse,
And seyde, "Doghter, stynt thyn hevynesse.
Among the goddes hye it is affermed,
And by eterne word writen and confermed,   2350

2274 **gan hye:** hurried
2278 **longen:** belong
2279 **meeth:** mead
2281 **Smokynge:** censing
2282 **debonaire:** gentle
2283 **wessh:** washed
2287 **charge:** burden
2288 **at his large:** without restriction
2289 **kembd:** combed   **untressed:** loose
2290 **ook cerial:** an evergreen oak of southern Europe (Quercus Cerris)
2291 **meete:** suitable, fitting
2292 **beete:** kindle, feed
2293 **thynges:** business, duties
2294 **Stace of Thebes:** Statius's *Thebaid* (quoted as an epigraph to this tale)
2298 **sene:** visible
2299 **Pluto:** god of the underworld
2302 **As keepe:** keep (*as* is not translated)
2303 **Attheon aboughte:** Actaeon paid for
2308 **venerye:** hunting

2311 **compaignye of man:** sexual intercourse
2313 **tho thre formes:** those three forms (as goddess of the chase, the moon, the underworld—cf. 2297–99 above)
2320 **bisy:** intense
2321 **queynt:** extinguished
2324 **nedes:** of necessity
2333 **queynte:** curious
2334 **queynte:** went out, was extinguished
2335 **quyked:** rekindled
2336 **queynt:** extinguished
2337 **whistelynge:** roaring sound
2341 **agast:** frightened
2345 **weep:** wept
2348 **stynt:** cease

Thou shalt ben wedded unto oon of tho
That han for thee so muchel care and wo,
But unto which of hem I may nat telle.
Farwel, for I ne may no lenger dwelle.
The fires which that on myn auter brenne   2355
Shulle thee declaren, er that thou go henne,
Thyn aventure of love, as in this cas."
And with that word, the arwes in the caas
Of the goddesse clateren faste and rynge,
And forth she wente and made a vanysshynge;   2360
For which this Emelye astoned was,
And seyde, "What amounteth this, allas?
I putte me in thy proteccioun,
Dyane, and in thy disposicioun."
And hoom she goth anon the nexte weye.   2365
This is th'effect; ther is namoore to seye.

    The nexte houre of Mars folwynge this,
Arcite unto the temple walked is
Of fierse Mars to doon his sacrifise,
With alle the rytes of his payen wyse.   2370
With pitous herte and heigh devocioun,
Right thus to Mars he seyde his orisoun:

    "O stronge god, that in the regnes colde
Of Trace honoured art and lord yholde,
And hast in every regne and every lond   2375
Of armes al the brydel in thyn hond,
And hem fortunest as thee lyst devyse,
Accepte of me my pitous sacrifise.
If so be that my youthe may deserve,
And that my myght be worthy for to serve   2380
Thy godhede, that I may been oon of thyne,
Thanne preye I thee to rewe upon my pyne.
For thilke peyne and thilke hoote fir
In which thow whilom brendest for desir,
Whan that thow usedest the beautee   2385
Of faire, yonge, fresshe Venus free,
And haddest hire in armes at thy wille—
Although thee ones on a tyme mysfille,
Whan Vulcanus hadde caught thee in his las
And foond thee liggynge by his wyf, allas!—   2390
For thilke sorwe that was in thyn herte,
Have routhe as wel upon my peynes smerte.
I am yong and unkonnynge, as thow woost,

And, as I trowe, with love offended moost
That evere was any lyves creature,   2395
For she that dooth me al this wo endure
Ne reccheth nevere wher I synke or fleete.
And wel I woot, er she me mercy heete,
I moot with strengthe wynne hire in the place,
And wel I woot, withouten help or grace   2400
Of thee ne may my strengthe noght availle.
Thanne help me, lord, tomorwe in my bataille,
For thilke fyr that whilom brente thee,
As wel as thilke fyr now brenneth me,
And do that I tomorwe have victorie.   2405
Myn be the travaille, and thyn be the glorie!
Thy sovereyn temple wol I moost honouren
Of any place, and alwey moost labouren
In thy plesaunce and in thy craftes stronge,
And in thy temple I wol my baner honge   2410
And alle the armes of my compaignye,
And everemo, unto that day I dye,
Eterne fir I wol bifore thee fynde.
And eek to this avow I wol me bynde:
My beerd, myn heer, that hongeth long adoun,   2415
That nevere yet ne felte offensioun
Of rasour nor of shere, I wol thee yive,
And ben thy trewe servant whil I lyve.
Now, lord, have routhe upon my sorwes soore;
Yif me [victorie]; I aske thee namoore."   2420

    The preyere stynt of Arcita the stronge,
The rynges on the temple dore that honge,
And eek the dores, clatereden ful faste,
Of which Arcita somwhat hym agaste.
The fyres brenden upon the auter brighte   2425
That it gan al the temple for to lighte;
A sweete smel the ground anon up yaf,
And Arcita anon his hand up haf,
And moore encens into the fyr he caste,
With othere rytes mo; and atte laste   2430
The statue of Mars bigan his hauberk rynge,
And with that soun he herde a murmurynge
Ful lowe and dym, and seyde thus, "Victorie!"

2351 **tho:** those
2356 **henne:** hence, away
2361 **astoned:** astonished
2365 **nexte:** nearest
2367 **houre:** planetary hour
2370 **payen wyse:** pagan manner (of worship)
2377 **hem fortunest:** grant them fortune, control their destinies
2382 **pyne:** pain
2388 **mysfille:** things went wrong (for) you
2389 **Vulcanus:** Vulcan
2390 **liggynge:** lying
2393 **unkonnynge:** ignorant, unskillful

2394 **with:** by
2395 **lyves:** living
2396 **dooth:** makes
2397 **wher I synke or fleete:** whether I sink or float
2398 **heete:** promise
2399 **place:** area where the action takes place, i.e., lists
2405 **do:** cause, bring about
2406 **travaille:** labor
2407 **sovereyn:** best, most excellent
2413 **fynde:** provide
2416 **offensioun:** injury
2417 **shere:** scissors
2421 **stynt:** stinted, stopped
2424 **hym agaste:** was afraid
2428 **haf:** raised
2431 **hauberk:** coat of mail
2432 **soun:** sound

For which he yaf to Mars honour and glorie.
And thus with joye and hope wel to fare   2435
Arcite anon unto his in is fare,
As fayn as fowel is of the brighte sonne.

    And right anon swich strif ther is bigonne,
For thilke grauntyng, in the hevene above,
Bitwixe Venus, the goddesse of love,   2440
And Mars, the stierne god armypotente,
That Juppiter was bisy it to stente,
Til that the pale Saturnus the colde,
That knew so manye of aventures olde,
Foond in his olde experience an art   2445
That he ful soone hath plesed every part.
As sooth is seyd, elde hath greet avantage;
In elde is bothe wysdom and usage;
Men may the olde atrenne and noght atrede.
Saturne anon, to stynten strif and drede,   2450
Al be it that it is agayn his kynde,
Of al this strif he gan remedie fynde.
    "My deere doghter Venus," quod Saturne,
"My cours, that hath so wyde for to turne,
Hath moore power than woot any man.   2455
Myn is the drenchyng in the see so wan;
Myn is the prison in the derke cote;
Myn is the stranglyng and hangyng by the throte,
The murmure and the cherles rebellyng,
The groynynge, and the pryvee empoysonyng;   2460
I do vengeance and pleyn correccioun,
Whil I dwelle in the signe of the leoun.
Myn is the ruyne of the hye halles,
The fallynge of the toures and of the walles
Upon the mynour or the carpenter.   2465
I slow Sampsoun, shakynge the piler;
And myne be the maladyes colde,
The derke tresons, and the castes olde;
My lookyng is the fader of pestilence.
Now weep namoore; I shal doon diligence   2470

That Palamon, that is thyn owene knyght,
Shal have his lady, as thou hast him hight.
Though Mars shal helpe his knyght, yet nathelees
Bitwixe yow ther moot be som tyme pees,
Al be ye noght of o compleccioun,   2475
That causeth al day swich divisioun.
I am thyn aiel, redy at thy wille;
Weep now namoore; I wol thy lust fulfille."
    Now wol I stynten of the goddes above,
Of Mars, and of Venus, goddesse of love,   2480
And telle yow as pleynly as I kan
The grete effect, for which that I bygan.

Explicit tercia pars

Sequitur pars quarta

    Greet was the feeste in Atthenes that day,
And eek the lusty seson of that May
Made every wight to been in swich plesaunce   2485
That al that Monday justen they and daunce,
And spenden it in Venus heigh servyse.
But by the cause that they sholde ryse
Eerly, for to seen the grete fight,
Unto hir reste wenten they at nyght.   2490
And on the morwe, whan that day gan sprynge,
Of hors and harneys noyse and claterynge
Ther was in hostelryes al aboute,
And to the paleys rood ther many a route
Of lordes upon steedes and palfreys.   2495
Ther maystow seen devisynge of harneys
So unkouth and so riche, and wroght so weel
Of goldsmythrye, of browdynge, and of steel;
The sheeldes brighte, testeres, and trappures,
Gold-hewen helmes, hauberkes, cote-armures;   2500
Lordes in parementz on hir courseres,
Knyghtes of retenue, and eek squieres
Nailynge the speres, and helmes bokelynge;
Giggynge of sheeldes, with layneres lacynge—
There as nede is they weren no thyng ydel;   2505

2436 **in:** inn, lodgings
2437 **fayn:** glad
2441 **stierne:** stern, cruel   **armypotente:** powerful in arms
2443 **Saturnus the colde:** Saturn the hostile
2445 **art:** plan
2446 **part:** party, side
2447 **elde:** old age
2448 **usage:** experience
2449 One can outrun the old but not outwit them.
2451 **kynde:** nature
2453 **quod:** said
2454 **cours:** orbit
2456 **drenchyng:** drowning   **wan:** dark
2457 **cote:** cell
2459 **murmure:** grumbling   **cherles:** peasants'
2460 **groynynge:** grumbling   **pryvee:** secret   **empoysonyng:** poisoning
2461 **do . . . correccioun:** punish
2462 **leoun:** the zodiacal sign Leo
2465 **mynour:** miner, digging under the walls
2466 **slow:** slew   **Sampsoun:** Sampson, the biblical hero; cf. MkT VII.2015–94.
2468 **derke:** malicious   **castes:** plots
2469 **lookyng is the fader:** (astrological) aspect is the cause

2472 **hight:** promised
2473 **nathelees:** nonetheless
2475 **o compleccioun:** the same temperament (as determined by the humors)
2477 **aiel:** grandfather
2478 **lust:** desire
Explicit, *etc.*: Here ends the third part.   **Sequitur,** *etc.*: Here follows the fourth part.
2485 **plesaunce:** delight
2486 **justen:** joust
2496 **devisynge of harneys:** preparation of armor
2497 **unkouth:** exotic
2498 **browdynge:** embroidery
2499 **testeres:** head-armor for war horses   **trappures:** horse armor
2500 **Gold-hewen:** gold-colored
2501 **parementz:** richly decorated robes
2502 **of retenue:** in his service
2503 **Nailynge the speres:** fastening the heads to the shafts (R.)   **helmes bokelynge:** buckling on helms
2504 **Giggynge of sheeldes:** fitting the shields with straps (OF *guige*, thong) (R.)
layneres lacynge: fastening of straps

The fomy steedes on the golden brydel
Gnawynge, and faste the armurers also
With fyle and hamer prikynge to and fro;
Yemen on foote, and communes many oon
With shorte staves, thikke as they may goon;   2510
Pypes, trompes, nakers, clariounes,
That in the bataille blowen blody sounes;
The paleys ful of peple up and doun,
Heere thre, ther ten, holdynge hir questioun,
Dyvynynge of thise Thebane knyghtes two.   2515
Somme seyden thus, somme seyde "it shal be so";
Somme helden with hym with the blake berd,
Somme with the balled, somme with the thikke herd;
Somme seyde he looked grymme, and he wolde fighte:
"He hath a sparth of twenty pound of wighte."   2520
Thus was the halle ful of divynynge,
Longe after that the sonne gan to sprynge.

    The grete Theseus, that of his sleep awaked
With mynstralcie and noyse that was maked,
Heeld yet the chambre of his paleys riche   2525
Til that the Thebane knyghtes, bothe yliche
Honured, were into the paleys fet.
Duc Theseus was at a wyndow set,
Arrayed right as he were a god in trone.
The peple preesseth thiderward ful soone   2530
Hym for to seen, and doon heigh reverence,
And eek to herkne his heste and his sentence.
An heraud on a scaffold made an "Oo!"
Til al the noyse of peple was ydo,
And whan he saugh the peple of noyse al stille,   2535
Tho shewed he the myghty dukes wille:

    "The lord hath of his heigh discrecioun
Considered that it were destruccioun
To gentil blood to fighten in the gyse
Of mortal bataille now in this emprise.   2540
Wherfore, to shapen that they shal nat dye,
He wol his firste purpos modifye.

No man therfore, up peyne of los of lyf,
No maner shot, ne polax, ne short knyf
Into the lystes sende or thider brynge;   2545
Ne short swerd, for to stoke with poynt bitynge,
No man ne drawe, ne bere it by his syde.
Ne no man shal unto his felawe ryde
But o cours with a sharpe ygrounde spere;
Foyne, if hym list, on foote, hymself to were.   2550
And he that is at meschief shal be take
And noght slayn, but be broght unto the stake
That shal ben ordeyned on either syde;
But thider he shal by force, and there abyde.
And if so falle the chieftayn be take   2555
On outher syde, or elles sleen his make,
No lenger shal the turneiynge laste.
God spede you! Gooth forth and ley on faste!
With long swerd and with mace fighteth youre fille.
Gooth now youre wey; this is the lordes wille."   2560
    The voys of peple touchede the hevene,
So loude cride they with murie stevene,
"God save swich a lord, that is so good
He wilneth no destruccion of blood!"
Up goon the trompes and the melodye,   2565
And to the lystes rit the compaignye,
By ordinance, thurghout the citee large,
Hanged with clooth of gold, and nat with sarge.
    Ful lik a lord this noble duc gan ryde,
Thise two Thebans upon either syde,   2570
And after rood the queene and Emelye,
And after that another compaignye
Of oon and oother, after hir degree.
And thus they passen thurghout the citee,
And to the lystes come they by tyme.   2575
It nas nat of the day yet fully pryme
Whan set was Theseus ful riche and hye,
Ypolita the queene, and Emelye,
And othere ladys in degrees aboute.
Unto the seetes preesseth al the route.   2580

2506 **fomy:** frothing
2509 **communes:** common soldiers
2510 **goon:** walk
2511 **nakers:** kettle drums   **clariounes:** bugles
2512 **blody:** warlike   **sounes:** sounds
2514 **holdynge hir questioun:** debating
2515 **Dyvynynge of:** conjecturing about
2518 **balled:** bald   **thikke herd:** thickly haired (man)
2519 **he:** that fellow
2520 **sparth:** battle-axe   **wighte:** weight
2521 **divynynge:** speculation
2526 **yliche:** alike
2527 **fet:** fetched, brought
2529 **trone:** throne
2530 **preesseth:** push   **thiderward:** thither, toward there
2532 **heste:** command   **sentence:** decision
2537 **discrecioun:** sound judgment
2540 **emprise:** undertaking
2542 **firste:** previous

2543 **up:** on
2544 **shot:** arrow   **polax:** battle axe
2546 **stoke:** stab, jab
2549 **But o:** only one   **cours:** run (in a joust)
2550 **Foyne:** let him thrust   **were:** protect
2551 **at meschief:** in distress, at a disadvantage
2554 **abyde:** remain
2556 **make:** opponent
2557 **turneiynge:** tournament
2558 **spede you:** give you success
2562 **stevene:** voice
2568 **sarge:** serge
2573 **after hir degree:** according to their rank
2576 **pryme:** 9 A.M.
2577 **riche:** splendidly
2579 **degrees:** tiers, rows of seats

And westward, thurgh the gates under Marte,
Arcite, and eek the hondred of his parte,
With baner reed is entred right anon;
And in that selve moment Palamon
Is under Venus, estward in the place,   2585
With baner whyt and hardy chiere and face.
In al the world, to seken up and doun,
So evene, withouten variacioun,
Ther nere swiche compaignyes tweye,
For ther was noon so wys that koude seye   2590
That any hadde of oother avauntage
Of worthynesse, ne of estaat, ne age,
So evene were they chosen, for to gesse.
And in two renges faire they hem dresse.
Whan that hir names rad were everichon,   2595
That in hir nombre gyle were ther noon,
Tho were the gates shet, and cried was loude:
"Do now youre devoir, yonge knyghtes proude!"
    The heraudes lefte hir prikyng up and doun;
Now ryngen trompes loude and clarioun.   2600
Ther is namoore to seyn, but west and est
In goon the speres ful sadly in arrest;
In gooth the sharpe spore into the syde.
Ther seen men who kan juste and who kan ryde;
Ther shyveren shaftes upon sheeldes thikke;   2605
He feeleth thurgh the herte-spoon the prikke.
Up spryngen speres twenty foot on highte;
Out goon the swerdes as the silver brighte;
The helmes they tohewen and toshrede;
Out brest the blood with stierne stremes rede;   2610
With myghty maces the bones they tobreste.
He thurgh the thikkeste of the throng gan threste;
Ther stomblen steedes stronge, and doun gooth al,
He rolleth under foot as dooth a bal;
He foyneth on his feet with his tronchoun,   2615
And he hym hurtleth with his hors adoun;
He thurgh the body is hurt and sithen ytake,
Maugree his heed, and broght unto the stake;

As forward was, right there he moste abyde.
Another lad is on that oother syde.   2620
And some tyme dooth hem Theseus to reste,
Hem to refresshe and drynken, if hem leste.
Ful ofte a day han thise Thebanes two
Togydre ymet, and wroght his felawe wo;
Unhorsed hath ech oother of hem tweye.   2625
Ther nas no tygre in the vale of Galgopheye,
Whan that hir whelp is stole whan it is lite,
So crueel on the hunte as is Arcite
For jelous herte upon this Palamon.
Ne in Belmarye ther nys so fel leon,   2630
That hunted is, or for his hunger wood,
Ne of his praye desireth so the blood,
As Palamon to sleen his foo Arcite.
The jelous strokes on hir helmes byte;
Out renneth blood on bothe hir sydes rede.   2635
    Som tyme an ende ther is of every dede.
For er the sonne unto the reste wente,
The stronge kyng Emetreus gan hente
This Palamon, as he faught with Arcite,
And made his swerd depe in his flessh to byte,   2640
And by the force of twenty is he take
Unyolden, and ydrawen to the stake.
And in the rescus of this Palamoun
The stronge kyng Lygurge is born adoun,
And kyng Emetreus, for al his strengthe,   2645
Is born out of his sadel a swerdes lengthe,
So hitte him Palamoun er he were take.
But al for noght; he was broght to the stake.
His hardy herte myghte hym helpe naught:
He moste abyde, whan that he was caught,   2650
By force and eek by composicioun.
    Who sorweth now but woful Palamoun,
That moot namoore goon agayn to fighte?
And whan that Theseus hadde seyn this sighte,
Unto the folk that foghten thus echon   2655
He cryde, "Hoo! namoore, for it is doon!
I wol be trewe juge, and no partie.

2582 **parte:** party, side
2584 **selve:** same
2593 **evene:** equally   **for to gesse:** as an estimate
2594 **renges:** ranks   **hem dresse:** arrange themselves
2595 **rad:** read
2596 **gyle:** deception
2597 **shet:** shut
2598 **devoir:** duty
2602 **sadly:** firmly   **arrest:** lance rest (on the breast plate)
2603 **spore into the syde:** spur into the flank
2605 **shyveren:** shiver, break
2606 **herte-spoon:** the spoon-shaped hollow at the end of the breastbone
2609 **tohewen and toshrede:** hew to pieces and cut into shreds
2610 **brest:** burst   **stierne:** strong
2611 **tobreste:** break to pieces
2612, 2614 **He:** one, another (*indef. pron.*)
2615 **foyneth:** stabs   **tronchoun:** spear shaft
2616 **hurtleth . . . adoun:** knocks down
2618 **Maugree his heed:** despite all he can do

2619 **forward:** agreement
2621 **dooth hem Theseus to reste:** Theseus makes them rest
2626 **Galgopheye:** probably Gargaphia, a valley in Boeotia (Greece)
2627 **whelp:** cub
2630 **Belmarye:** Benmarin (Morocco)
2632 **praye:** prey
2634 **jelous:** fervent, vigorous
2635 **renneth:** runs
2642 **Unyolden:** without having surrendered
2643 **rescus:** rescue
2651 **composicioun:** agreement (that he had made)
2652 **sorweth:** grieves
2655 **echon:** each one
2656 **Hoo!:** stop!
2657 **partie:** partisan

Arcite of Thebes shal have Emelie,
That by his fortune hath hire faire ywonne."
Anon ther is a noyse of peple bigonne   2660
For joye of this, so loude and heighe withalle
It semed that the lystes sholde falle.

What kan now faire Venus doon above?
What seith she now? What dooth this queene of love,
But wepeth so, for wantynge of hir wille,   2665
Til that hir teeres in the lystes fille?
She seyde, "I am ashamed, doutelees."

Saturnus seyde, "Doghter, hoold thy pees!
Mars hath his wille, his knyght hath al his boone,
And, by myn heed, thow shalt been esed soone."

The trompours, with the loude mynstralcie,   2671
The heraudes, that ful loude yelle and crie,
Been in hire wele for joye of daun Arcite.
But herkneth me, and stynteth noyse a lite,
Which a myracle ther bifel anon.   2675

This fierse Arcite hath of his helm ydon,
And on a courser, for to shewe his face,
He priketh endelong the large place
Lokynge upward upon this Emelye;
And she agayn hym caste a freendlich ye   2680
(For wommen, as to speken in comune,
Thei folwen alle the favour of Fortune)
And was al his chiere, as in his herte.

Out of the ground a furie infernal sterte,
From Pluto sent at requeste of Saturne,   2685
For which his hors for fere gan to turne,
And leep aside, and foundred as he leep;
And er that Arcite may taken keep,
He pighte hym on the pomel of his heed,
That in the place he lay as he were deed,   2690
His brest tobrosten with his sadel-bowe.
As blak he lay as any cole or crowe,
So was the blood yronnen in his face.
Anon he was yborn out of the place,

With herte soor, to Theseus paleys.   2695
Tho was he korven out of his harneys
And in a bed ybrought ful faire and blyve,
For he was yet in memorie and alyve,
And alwey criynge after Emelye.

Duc Theseus, with al his compaignye,   2700
Is comen hoom to Atthenes his citee,
With alle blisse and greet solempnitee.
Al be it that this aventure was falle,
He nolde noght disconforten hem alle.
Men seyde eek that Arcite shal nat dye;   2705
He shal been heeled of his maladye.
And of another thyng they weren as fayn,
That of hem alle was ther noon yslayn,
Al were they soore yhurt, and namely oon,
That with a spere was thirled his brest boon. 2710
To othere woundes and to broken armes
Somme hadden salves, and somme hadden charmes;
Fermacies of herbes, and eek save
They dronken, for they wolde hir lymes have.
For which this noble duc, as he wel kan,   2715
Conforteth and honoureth every man,
And made revel al the longe nyght
Unto the straunge lordes, as was right.
Ne ther was holden no disconfitynge
But as a justes or a tourneiynge;   2720
For soothly ther was no disconfiture.
For fallyng nys nat but an aventure,
Ne to be lad by force unto the stake
Unyolden, and with twenty knyghtes take,
O persone allone, withouten mo,   2725
And haryed forth by arme, foot, and too,
And eke his steede dryven forth with staves
With footmen, bothe yemen and eek knaves—
It nas arretted hym no vileynye;
Ther may no man clepen it cowardye.   2730
For which anon duc Theseus leet crye,
To stynten alle rancour and envye,

2665 **wantynge:** lack
2666 **teeres in the lystes fille:** i.e., it rained
2667 **ashamed:** disgraced
2669 **boone:** request
2670 **esed:** relieved
2671 **trompours:** trumpeters
2673 **wele:** prosperity
2675 **Which a:** what a
2676 **of his helm ydon:** taken off his helmet
2677 **shewe:** show
2678 **endelong:** from end to end
2680 **agayn:** toward
2681 **in comune:** in general
2683 **chiere:** source of pleasure
2687 **foundred:** stumbled **leep:** leapt
2688 **taken keep:** take heed
2689 **pighte:** threw **pomel:** top
2691 **tobrosten:** shattered
2692 **cole:** coal

2696 **Tho:** then **korven:** cut
2697 **blyve:** quickly
2698 **in memorie:** conscious
2699 **after:** for
2704 **disconforten:** distress
2707 **fayn:** happy
2709 **namely:** especially
2710 whose breastbone was pierced (*thirled*) by a spear
2713 **Fermacies:** medicines **save:** sage, in a concoction
2718 **straunge:** foreign
2719 **disconfitynge:** defeat, dishonor
2720 **justes or a tourneiynge:** joust or a tournament
2721 **disconfiture:** dishonor
2724 **Unyolden:** without having surrendered
2725 **mo:** others
2726 **haryed:** dragged **too:** toe
2728 **knaves:** male servants
2729 He incurred no shameful blame for it
2731 **leet crye:** had proclaimed
2732 **envye:** ill-will

The gree as wel of o syde as of oother,
And eyther syde ylik as ootheres brother;
And yaf hem yiftes after hir degree,   2735
And fully heeld a feeste dayes three,
And conveyed the kynges worthily
Out of his toun a journee largely.
And hoom wente every man the righte way.
Ther was namoore but "Fare wel, have good day!"
Of this bataille I wol namoore endite,   2741
But speke of Palamon and of Arcite.
    Swelleth the brest of Arcite, and the soore
Encreesseth at his herte moore and moore.
The clothered blood, for any lechecraft,   2745
Corrupteth, and is in his bouk ylaft,
That neither veyne-blood, ne ventusynge,
Ne drynke of herbes may ben his helpynge.
The vertu expulsif, or animal,
Fro thilke vertu cleped natural   2750
Ne may the venym voyden ne expelle.
The pipes of his longes gonne to swelle,
And every lacerte in his brest adoun
Is shent with venym and corrupcioun.
Hym gayneth neither, for to gete his lif,   2755
Vomyt upward, ne dounward laxatif.
Al is tobrosten thilke regioun;
Nature hath now no dominacioun.
And certeinly, ther Nature wol nat wirche,
Fare wel phisik! Go ber the man to chirche!   2760
This al and som, that Arcita moot dye;
For which he sendeth after Emelye,
And Palamon, that was his cosyn deere.
Thanne seyde he thus, as ye shal after heere:
"Naught may the woful spirit in myn herte   2765
Declare o point of alle my sorwes smerte
To yow, my lady, that I love moost,
But I biquethe the servyce of my goost
To yow aboven every creature,

Syn that my lyf may no lenger dure.   2770
Allas, the wo! Allas, the peynes stronge,
That I for yow have suffred, and so longe!
Allas, the deeth! Allas, myn Emelye!
Allas, departynge of oure compaignye!
Allas, myn hertes queene! Allas, my wyf,   2775
Myn hertes lady, endere of my lyf!
What is this world? What asketh men to have?
Now with his love, now in his colde grave
Allone, withouten any compaignye.
Fare wel, my sweete foo, myn Emelye!   2780
And softe taak me in youre armes tweye,
For love of God, and herkneth what I seye.
    "I have heer with my cosyn Palamon
Had strif and rancour many a day agon
For love of yow, and for my jalousye.   2785
And Juppiter so wys my soule gye,
To speken of a servaunt proprely,
With alle circumstances trewely—
That is to seyen, trouthe, honour, knyghthede,
Wysdom, humblesse, estaat, and heigh kynrede,
Fredom, and al that longeth to that art—   2791
So Juppiter have of my soule part,
As in this world right now ne knowe I non
So worthy to ben loved as Palamon,
That serveth yow, and wol doon al his lyf.   2795
And if that evere ye shul ben a wyf,
Foryet nat Palamon, the gentil man."
And with that word his speche faille gan,
For from his feet up to his brest was come
The coold of deeth, that hadde hym overcome,   2800
And yet mooreover, for in his armes two
The vital strengthe is lost and al ago.
Oonly the intellect, withouten moore,
That dwelled in his herte syk and soore,
Gan faillen whan the herte felte deeth.   2805
Dusked his eyen two, and failled breeth,
But on his lady yet caste he his ye;
His laste word was, "Mercy, Emelye!"
His spirit chaunged hous and wente ther,
As I cam nevere, I kan nat tellen wher.   2810
Therfore I stynte; I nam no divinistre;
Of soules fynde I nat in this registre,
Ne me ne list thilke opinions to telle

2733 **gree:** victory
2735 **yiftes:** gifts
2738 **journee:** day's journey
2741 **endite:** write
2743–56 The sense is that Arcite's breast swells, increasing the pain at his heart. The
clotted blood left in the trunk of the body, despite the efforts of medical science in letting blood and administering herbs, cannot be voided by the expulsive spirit. The tubes
of the lungs begin to swell, and every muscle in the breast is destroyed by the venom.
Neither purgatives to induce vomiting nor laxatives help.
2745 **clothered:** clotted
2746 **Corrupteth:** decays   **bouk:** trunk
2747 **veyne-blood:** blood-letting at a vein   **ventusynge:** cupping
2749 **expulsif:** expulsive
2751 **venym:** poison   **voyden:** remove
2752 **longes:** lungs
2753 **lacerte:** muscle
2754 **shent:** destroyed   **corrupcioun:** decayed matter
2755 **Hym gayneth:** it avails him   **gete:** preserve
2759 **wirche:** work
2760 **phisik:** medicine
2761 **This** = *this is*

2770 **dure:** last
2777 **asketh men:** does one ask
2781 **softe:** gently
2786 **gye:** guide
2790 **heigh kynrede:** noble lineage
2791 **Fredom:** nobility of character
2792 **So:** as   **of my soule part:** interest in, concern for, my soul
2798 **faille gan:** began to fail
2806 **Dusked:** grew dark
2811 **nam** = *ne am,* am not   **divinistre:** theologian

Of hem, though that they writen wher they dwelle.
Arcite is coold, ther Mars his soule gye! 　　　2815
Now wol I speken forth of Emelye.

　　Shrighte Emelye, and howleth Palamon,
And Theseus his suster took anon
Swownynge, and baar hire fro the corps away.
What helpeth it to tarien forth the day 　　　2820
To tellen how she weep bothe eve and morwe?
For in swich cas wommen have swich sorwe,
Whan that hir housbondes ben from hem ago,
That for the moore part they sorwen so,
Or ellis fallen in swich maladye 　　　2825
That at the laste certeinly they dye.

　　Infinite been the sorwes and the teeres
Of olde folk and folk of tendre yeeres
In al the toun for deeth of this Theban.
For hym ther wepeth bothe child and man; 　　　2830
So greet wepyng was ther noon, certayn,
Whan Ector was ybroght, al fressh yslayn,
To Troye. Allas, the pitee that was ther,
Cracchynge of chekes, rentynge eek of heer.
"Why woldestow be deed," thise wommen crye, 　　　2835
"And haddest gold ynough, and Emelye?"

　　No man myghte gladen Theseus,
Savynge his olde fader Egeus,
That knew this worldes transmutacioun,
As he hadde seyn it chaunge bothe up and doun, 2840
Joye after wo, and wo after gladnesse,
And shewed hem ensamples and liknesse.

　　"Right as ther dyed nevere man," quod he,
"That he ne lyvede in erthe in some degree,
Right so ther lyvede never man," he seyde, 　　　2845
"In al this world, that som tyme he ne deyde.
This world nys but a thurghfare ful of wo,
And we been pilgrymes, passynge to and fro.
Deeth is an ende of every worldly soore."
And over al this yet seyde he muchel moore 　　　2850
To this effect, ful wisely to enhorte
The peple that they sholde hem reconforte.

　　Duc Theseus, with al his bisy cure,
Caste now wher that the sepulture
Of goode Arcite may best ymaked be, 　　　2855

And eek moost honurable in his degree.
And at the laste he took conclusioun
That ther as first Arcite and Palamoun
Hadden for love the bataille hem bitwene,
That in that selve grove, swoote and grene, 　　　2860
Ther as he hadde his amorouse desires,
His compleynte, and for love his hoote fires,
He wolde make a fyr in which the office
Funeral he myghte al accomplice.
And leet comande anon to hakke and hewe 　　　2865
The okes olde, and leye hem on a rewe
In colpons wel arrayed for to brenne.
His officers with swifte feet they renne
And ryde anon at his comandement.
And after this, Theseus hath ysent 　　　2870
After a beere, and it al overspradde
With clooth of gold, the richeste that he hadde.
And of the same suyte he cladde Arcite;
Upon his hondes hadde he gloves white,
Eek on his heed a coroune of laurer grene, 　　　2875
And in his hond a swerd ful bright and kene.
He leyde hym, bare the visage, on the beere;
Therwith he weep that pitee was to heere.
And for the peple sholde seen hym alle,
Whan it was day, he broghte hym to the halle, 　　　2880
That roreth of the criyng and the soun.

　　Tho cam this woful Theban Palamoun,
With flotery berd and ruggy, asshy heeres,
In clothes blake, ydropped al with teeres;
And, passynge othere of wepynge, Emelye, 　　　2885
The rewefulleste of al the compaignye.
In as muche as the servyce sholde be
The moore noble and riche in his degree,
Duc Theseus leet forth thre steedes brynge,
That trapped were in steel al gliterynge, 　　　2890
And covered with the armes of daun Arcite.
Upon thise steedes, that weren grete and white,
Ther seten folk, of whiche oon baar his sheeld,
Another his spere up on his hondes heeld,
The thridde baar with hym his bowe Turkeys 　　　2895
(Of brend gold was the caas and eek the harneys);

2815 **ther Mars his soule gye:** may Mars guide his soul
2817 **Shrighte:** shrieked
2821 **weep:** wept
2824 **for the moore part:** mostly
2834 **Cracchynge:** scratching
2837 **gladen:** comfort
2838 **Savynge:** except for
2849 **soore:** pain, misery
2851 **enhorte:** encourage
2852 **hem reconforte:** take heart
2853 **bisy cure:** careful attention
2854 **Caste:** considered

2860 **selve:** same　**swoote:** sweet-smelling
2862 **compleynte:** lament
2865 **leet comande:** ordered
2866 **on a rewe:** in a row
2867 **colpons:** piles　**arrayed:** arranged
2871 **beere:** funeral bier　**overspradde:** overspread
2883 **flotery:** waving　**ruggy:** rough
2886 **rewefulleste:** most pitiful
2889 **leet forth . . . brynge:** had brought forth
2890 **trapped:** equipped with trappings
2891 **armes:** heraldic devices
2895 **bowe Turkeys:** Turkish bow
2896 **brend gold:** refined (pure) gold

And riden forth a paas with sorweful cheere
Toward the grove, as ye shul after heere.
The nobleste of the Grekes that ther were
Upon hir shuldres caryeden the beere, 2900
With slakke paas and eyen rede and wete,
Thurghout the citee by the maister strete,
That sprad was al with blak, and wonder hye
Right of the same is the strete ywrye.
Upon the right hond wente olde Egeus, 2905
And on that oother syde duc Theseus,
With vessels in hir hand of gold ful fyn,
Al ful of hony, milk, and blood, and wyn;
Eek Palamon, with ful greet compaignye;
And after that cam woful Emelye, 2910
With fyr in honde, as was that tyme the gyse,
To do the office of funeral servyse.

Heigh labour and ful greet apparaillynge
Was at the service and the fyr-makynge,
That with his grene top the hevene raughte; 2915
And twenty fadme of brede the armes straughte—
This is to seyn, the bowes weren so brode.
Of stree first ther was leyd ful many a lode.
But how the fyr was maked upon highte,
Ne eek the names that the trees highte, 2920
As ook, firre, birch, aspe, alder, holm, popler,
Wylugh, elm, plane, assh, box, chasteyn, lynde, laurer,
Mapul, thorn, bech, hasel, ew, whippeltree—
How they weren feld shal nat be toold for me;
Ne hou the goddes ronnen up and doun, 2925
Disherited of hire habitacioun,
In which they woneden in reste and pees,
Nymphes, fawnes and amadrides;
Ne hou the beestes and the briddes alle
Fledden for fere, whan the wode was falle; 2930
Ne how the ground agast was of the light,
That was nat wont to seen the sonne bright;
Ne how the fyr was couched first with stree,
And thanne with drye stikkes cloven a thre,

And thanne with grene wode and spicerye, 2935
And thanne with clooth of gold and with perrye,
And gerlandes, hangynge with ful many a flour;
The mirre, th'encens, with al so greet odour;
Ne how Arcite lay among al this,
Ne what richesse aboute his body is; 2940
Ne how that Emelye, as was the gyse,
Putte in the fyr of funeral servyse;
Ne how she swowned whan men made the fyr,
Ne what she spak, ne what was hir desir;
Ne what jeweles men in the fyre caste, 2945
Whan that the fyr was greet and brente faste;
Ne how somme caste hir sheeld, and somme hir spere,
And of hire vestimentz, whiche that they were,
And coppes fulle of wyn, and milk, and blood,
Into the fyr, that brente as it were wood; 2950
Ne how the Grekes, with an huge route,
Thries riden al the fyr aboute
Upon the left hand, with a loud shoutynge,
And thries with hir speres claterynge;
And thries how the ladyes gonne crye; 2955
And how that lad was homward Emelye;
Ne how Arcite is brent to asshen colde;
Ne how that lyche-wake was yholde
Al thilke nyght; ne how the Grekes pleye
The wake-pleyes; ne kepe I nat to seye 2960
Who wrastleth best naked with oille enoynt,
Ne who that baar hym best, in no disjoynt.
I wol nat tellen eek how that they goon
Hoom til Atthenes, whan the pley is doon;
But shortly to the point thanne wol I wende 2965
And maken of my longe tale an ende.

By processe and by lengthe of certeyn yeres,
Al stynted is the moornynge and the teres
Of Grekes, by oon general assent.
Thanne semed me ther was a parlement 2970
At Atthenes, upon certein pointz and caas;
Among the whiche pointz yspoken was,
To have with certein contrees alliaunce,
And have fully of Thebans obeisaunce.
For which this noble Theseus anon 2975
Leet senden after gentil Palamon,
Unwist of hym what was the cause and why,
But in his blake clothes sorwefully

2897 **a paas:** slowly
2900 **beere:** funeral bier
2901 **slakke:** slow
2902 **maister strete:** main street
2904 **ywrye:** covered
2913 **apparaillynge:** preparation
2915 **raughte:** reached to
2916 **fadme of brede:** fathoms broad   **armes straughte:** sides projected
2918 **stree:** straw   **lode:** load
2921 **holm:** probably the holm oak
2922 **Wylugh:** willow   **chasteyn:** chestnut tree   **laurer:** laurel
2923 **bech:** beech   **ew:** yew   **whippeltree:** cornel-tree, dogwood
2925 **ronnen:** ran
2927 **woneden:** dwelt
2928 **fawnes:** fauns   **amadrides:** Hamadryads (wood nymphs)
2931 **agast was of:** was frightened by
2933 **couched:** laid   **stree:** straw
2934 **stikkes cloven a thre:** branches cleft in thirds

2935 **spicerye:** mixture of spices
2936 **perrye:** precious stones
2938 **mirre:** myrrh
2948 **vestimentz:** costumes, garbs
2958 **lyche-wake:** wake
2960 **wake-pleyes:** funeral games
2962 **disjoynt:** difficulty
2967 **processe:** course of events
2970 **parlement:** parliament
2977 **Unwist of:** unknown by

He cam at his comandement in hye.
Tho sente Theseus for Emelye.   2980
Whan they were set, and hust was al the place,
And Theseus abiden hadde a space
Er any word cam fram his wise brest,
His eyen sette he ther as was his lest.
And with a sad visage he siked stille,   2985
And after that right thus he seyde his wille:
     "The Firste Moevere of the cause above,
Whan he first made the faire cheyne of love,
Greet was th'effect, and heigh was his entente.
Wel wiste he why, and what thereof he mente,   2990
For with that faire cheyne of love he bond
The fyr, the eyr, the water, and the lond
In certeyn boundes, that they may nat flee.
That same Prince and that Moevere," quod he,
"Hath stablissed in this wrecched world adoun   2995
Certeyne dayes and duracioun
To al that is engendred in this place,
Over the whiche day they may nat pace,
Al mowe they yet tho dayes wel abregge.
Ther nedeth noght noon auctoritee t'allegge,   3000
For it is preeved by experience,
But that me list declaren my sentence.
Thanne may men by this ordre wel discerne
That thilke Moevere stable is and eterne.
Wel may men knowe, but it be a fool,   3005
That every part dirryveth from his hool,
For nature hath nat taken his bigynnyng
Of no partie or cantel of a thyng,
But of a thyng that parfit is and stable,
Descendynge so til it be corrumpable.   3010
And therfore, of his wise purveiaunce,
He hath so wel biset his ordinaunce
That speces of thynges and progressiouns
Shullen enduren by successiouns,
And nat eterne, withouten any lye.   3015
This maystow understonde and seen at ye.

"Loo the ook, that hath so long a norisshynge
From tyme that it first bigynneth to sprynge,
And hath so long a lif, as we may see,
Yet at the laste wasted is the tree.   3020
     "Considereth eek how that the harde stoon
Under oure feet, on which we trede and goon,
Yet wasteth it as it lyth by the weye.
The brode ryver somtyme wexeth dreye;
The grete tounes se we wane and wende.   3025
Thanne may ye se that al this thyng hath ende.
     "Of man and womman seen we wel also
That nedes, in oon of thise termes two—
This is to seyn, in youthe or elles age—
He moot be deed, the kyng as shal a page;   3030
Som in his bed, som in the depe see,
Som in the large feeld, as men may see;
Ther helpeth noght; al goth that ilke weye.
Thanne may I seyn that al this thyng moot deye.
     "What maketh this but Juppiter, the kyng,   3035
That is prince and cause of alle thyng,
Convertynge al unto his propre welle
From which it is dirryved, sooth to telle?
And heer-agayns no creature on lyve,
Of no degree, availleth for to stryve.   3040
     "Thanne is it wysdom, as it thynketh me,
To maken vertu of necessitee,
And take it weel that we may nat eschue,
And namely that to us alle is due.
And whoso gruccheth ought, he dooth folye,   3045
And rebel is to hym that al may gye.
And certeinly a man hath moost honour
To dyen in his excellence and flour,
Whan he is siker of his goode name;   3049
Thanne hath he doon his freend, ne hym, no shame.
And gladder oghte his freend been of his deeth,
Whan with honour up yolden is his breeth,
Than whan his name apalled is for age,
For al forgeten is his vassellage.
Thanne is it best, as for a worthy fame,   3055
To dyen whan that he is best of name.
     "The contrarie of al this is wilfulnesse.
Why grucchen we, why have we hevynesse,
That goode Arcite, of chivalrie flour,

2979 **in hye:** in haste
2981 **hust:** quiet
2982 **abiden:** waited
2984 **lest:** pleasure
2986 **seyde his wille:** pronounced his decision
2989 **entente:** plan
2992 The four elements—fire, air, water, earth
2993 **certeyn:** definite, specific
2995 **adoun:** below
2999 **mowe:** can   **abregge:** abridge, shorten
3000 **noon auctoritee t'allegge:** to cite no written authorities
3001 **preeved:** proven
3002 Unless I wish to make my meaning more clear
3006 **his:** its
3008 **partie:** part   **cantel:** portion
3010 **corrumpable:** corruptible
3011 **of his wise purveiaunce:** by his wise foresight
3012 **biset:** established
3013 **speces:** species (types of being)   **progressiouns:** natural processes
3014 **by successiouns:** one after another
3016 **at ye:** plainly

3024 **wexeth:** becomes
3028 **termes:** periods of time
3030 **page:** servant boy
3033 **ilke:** same
3037 Causing everything to return to its own source (*welle*)
3039 **heer-agayns:** against this
3043 **eschue:** escape
3045 **gruccheth ought:** complains in any way
3049 **siker:** sure
3052 **up yolden:** given up (died)
3053 **apalled:** faded
3054 **vassellage:** prowess

d is with duetee and honour   3060
Out of this foule prisoun of this lyf?
Why grucchen heere his cosyn and his wyf
Of his welfare, that loved hem so weel?
Kan he hem thank? Nay, God woot, never a deel,
That both his soule and eek hemself offende,   3065
And yet they mowe hir lustes nat amende.
    "What may I conclude of this longe serye,
But after wo I rede us to be merye
And thanken Juppiter of al his grace?
And er that we departen from this place   3070
I rede that we make of sorwes two
O parfit joye, lastynge everemo.
And looketh now, wher moost sorwe is herinne,
Ther wol we first amenden and bigynne.
    "Suster," quod he, "this is my fulle assent, 3075
With al th'avys heere of my parlement,
That gentil Palamon, youre owene knyght,
That serveth yow with wille, herte, and myght,
And ever hath doon syn ye first hym knewe,
That ye shul of youre grace upon hym rewe,   3080
And taken hym for housbonde and for lord.
Lene me youre hond, for this is oure accord.
Lat se now of youre wommanly pitee.
He is a kynges brother sone, pardee;

And though he were a povre bacheler,   3085
Syn he hath served yow so many a yeer,
And had for yow so greet adversitee,
It moste been considered, leeveth me,
For gentil mercy oghte to passen right."   3089
    Thanne seyde he thus to Palamon the knight:
"I trowe ther nedeth litel sermonyng
To make yow assente to this thyng.
Com neer, and taak youre lady by the hond."
    Bitwixen hem was maad anon the bond
That highte matrimoigne or mariage,   3095
By al the conseil and the baronage.
And thus with alle blisse and melodye
Hath Palamon ywedded Emelye.
And God, that al this wyde world hath wroght,
Sende hym his love that hath it deere abogh;   3100
For now is Palamon in alle wele,
Lyvynge in blisse, in richesse, and in heele,
And Emelye hym loveth so tendrely,
And he hire serveth so gentilly,
That nevere was ther no word hem bitwene   3105
Of jalousie or any oother teene.
Thus endeth Palamon and Emelye;
And God save al this faire compaignye! Amen.

Heere is ended the Knyghtes Tale.

The Miller's Prologue

Heere folwen the wordes bitwene the Hoost and the Millere.

Whan that the Knyght had thus his tale ytoold,
In al the route nas ther yong ne oold   3110
That he ne seyde it was a noble storie
And worthy for to drawen to memorie,
And namely the gentils everichon.

Oure Hooste lough and swoor, "So moot I gon,
This gooth aright; unbokeled is the male.   3115
Lat se now who shal telle another tale;
For trewely the game is wel bigonne.
Now telleth ye, sir Monk, if that ye konne,
Somwhat to quite with the Knyghtes tale."

3060 **with duetee and honour:** with all proper honor
3064 **Kan he hem thank?:** Can he show them his gratitude?   **never a deel:** not a bit, not at all
3067 **serye:** process of thought, argument
3068 **rede:** advise
3074 **amenden:** make amends
3075 **assent:** opinion
3076 **parlement:** parliament, assembly

3112 **drawen to memorie:** remember
3113 **gentils:** gentlefolk

3085 **bacheler:** young knight
3089 Noble mercy ought to prevail over justice
3091 **sermonyng:** discourse
3100 **deere abogh:** dearly paid for
3101 **alle wele:** complete happiness
3102 **heele:** health, well-being
3106 **teene:** vexation

3115 **unbokeled is the male:** the pouch is opened; i.e., the game is well begun
3118 **konne:** know
3119 **quite with:** with which to repay, or match

The Millere, that for dronken was al pale, 3120
So that unnethe upon his hors he sat,
He nolde avalen neither hood ne hat,
Ne abyde no man for his curteisie,
But in Pilates voys he gan to crie,
And swoor, "By armes, and by blood and bones, 3125
I kan a noble tale for the nones, 3126
With which I wol now quite the Knyghtes tale."
Oure Hooste saugh that he was dronke of ale,
And seyde, "Abyd, Robyn, my leeve brother;
Som bettre man shal telle us first another. 3130
Abyd, and lat us werken thriftily."

  "By Goddes soule," quod he, "that wol nat I;
For I wol speke or elles go my wey."
Oure Hoost answerde, "Tel on, a devel wey!
Thou art a fool; thy wit is overcome." 3135
  "Now herkneth," quod the Millere, "alle and some!
But first I make a protestacioun
That I am dronke; I knowe it by my soun.
And therfore if that I mysspeke or seye,
Wyte it the ale of Southwerk, I you preye. 3140
For I wol telle a legende and a lyf
Bothe of a carpenter and of his wyf,
How that a clerk hath set the wrightes cappe."

  The Reve answerde and seyde, "Stynt thy clappe!
Lat be thy lewed dronken harlotrye. 3145
It is a synne and eek a greet folye
To apeyren any man, or hym defame,
And eek to bryngen wyves in swich fame.
Thou mayst ynogh of othere thynges seyn."
  This dronke Millere spak ful soone ageyn 3150
And seyde, "Leve brother Osewold,

Who hath no wyf, he is no cokewold.
But I sey nat therfore that thou art oon;
Ther been ful goode wyves many oon, 3154
And evere a thousand goode ayeyns oon badde.
That knowestow wel thyself, but if thou madde.
Why artow angry with my tale now?
I have a wyf, pardee, as wel as thow;
Yet nolde I, for the oxen in my plogh,
Take upon me moore than ynogh, 3160
As demen of myself that I were oon;
I wol bileve wel that I am noon.
An housbonde shal nat been inquisityf
Of Goddes pryvetee, nor of his wyf.
So he may fynde Goddes foyson there, 3165
Of the remenant nedeth nat enquere."

  What sholde I moore seyn, but this Millere
He nolde his wordes for no man forbere,
But tolde his cherles tale in his manere.
M'athynketh that I shal reherce it heere. 3170
And therfore every gentil wight I preye,
For Goddes love, demeth nat that I seye
Of yvel entente, but for I moot reherce
Hir tales alle, be they bettre or werse,
Or elles falsen som of my mateere. 3175
And therfore, whoso list it nat yheere,
Turne over the leef and chese another tale;
For he shal fynde ynowe, grete and smale,
Of storial thyng that toucheth gentillesse,
And eek moralitee and hoolynesse. 3180
Blameth nat me if that ye chese amys.
The Millere is a cherl; ye knowe wel this.
So was the Reve eek and othere mo,
And harlotrie they tolden bothe two.
Avyseth yow, and put me out of blame; 3185
And eek men shal nat maken ernest of game.

3120 **for dronken:** because of being drunk
3121 **unnethe:** hardly
3122 **avalen:** take off
3124 **Pilates voys:** a loud, ranting voice
3125 By the arms, blood, and bones of Christ
3127 **quite:** pay back, requite
3129 **Abyd:** wait **leeve:** dear
3131 **thriftily:** properly
3134 **a devel wey:** in the Devil's name
3136 **alle and some:** one and all
3139 **mysspeke or seye:** The prefix *mys-* applies to both verbs.
3140 **Wyte it:** blame it on
3141 **legende:** saint's life
3143 **set the wrightes cappe:** deceived, made a fool of the carpenter
3144 **Stynt thy clappe:** stop your noisy talk, hold your tongue
3145 **harlotrye:** ribaldry
3147 **apeyren:** injure, slander
3150 **ageyn:** in reply

3152 **cokewold:** cuckold
3155 **ayeyns:** as opposed to
3156 **madde:** go mad
3161 **demen of:** to judge, believe of   **oon:** i.e., a cuckold
3162 **wol bileve:** want to believe
3164 **pryvetee:** secrets
3165 **Goddes foyson:** God's plenty
3169 **cherles:** low-born fellows'
3170 **M'athynketh:** it displeases me, I regret   **reherce:** repeat, narrate
3177 **chese:** choose
3178 **grete and smale:** of every sort
3179 **storial:** historical, true   **toucheth:** concerns
3184 **harlotrie:** ribaldry, dirty stories
3185 **Avyseth yow:** consider, think about (this)
3186 **maken ernest of game:** take a joke seriously

The Miller's Tale

Heere bigynneth the Millere his tale.

Whilom ther was dwellynge at Oxenford
A riche gnof, that gestes heeld to bord,
And of his craft he was a carpenter.
With hym ther was dwellynge a poure scoler,   3190
Hadde lerned art, but al his fantasye
Was turned for to lerne astrologye,
And koude a certeyn of conclusiouns,
To demen by interrogaciouns,
If that men asked hym, in certein houres   3195
Whan that men sholde have droghte or elles shoures,
Or if men asked hym what sholde bifalle
Of every thyng; I may nat rekene hem alle.
This clerk was cleped hende Nicholas.
Of deerne love he koude and of solas;   3200
And therto he was sleigh and ful privee,
And lyk a mayden meke for to see.
A chambre hadde he in that hostelrye
Allone, withouten any compaignye,
Ful fetisly ydight with herbes swoote;   3205
And he hymself as sweete as is the roote
Of lycorys or any cetewale.
His Almageste, and bookes grete and smale,
His astrelabie, longynge for his art,
His augrym stones layen faire apart,   3210
On shelves couched at his beddes heed;
His presse ycovered with a faldyng reed;
And al above ther lay a gay sautrie,
On which he made a-nyghtes melodie

So swetely that all the chambre rong;   3215
And *Angelus ad virginem* he song;
And after that he song the Kynges Noote.
Ful often blessed was his myrie throte.
And thus this sweete clerk his tyme spente
After his freendes fyndyng and his rente.   3220
This carpenter hadde wedded newe a wyf,
Which that he lovede moore than his lyf;
Of eighteteene yeer she was of age.
Jalous he was, and heeld hire narwe in cage,
For she was wylde and yong, and he was old   3225
And demed hymself been lik a cokewold.
He knew nat Catoun, for his wit was rude,
That bad man sholde wedde his simylitude.
Men sholde wedden after hire estaat,
For youthe and elde is often at debaat.   3230
But sith that he was fallen in the snare,
He moste endure, as oother folk, his care.
Fair was this yonge wyf, and therwithal
As any wezele hir body gent and smal.
A ceynt she werede, barred al of silk,   3235
A barmclooth as whit as morne milk
Upon hir lendes, ful of many a goore.
Whit was hir smok, and broyden al bifoore
And eek bihynde, on hir coler aboute,
Of col-blak silk, withinne and eek withoute.   3240
The tapes of hir white voluper
Were of the same suyte of hir coler;

3187 **Oxenford:** Oxford
3188 **gnof:** churl   **gestes:** lodgers   **to bord:** as boarders
3190 **poure scoler:** impoverished student
3191 **art:** the arts curriculum at the university, esp. logic   **fantasye:** fancy, desire
3193 **koude:** knew   **a certeyn of conclusiouns:** a certain number of astrological operations
3194 To determine by scientific calculations
3195 **in certein houres:** at specific (astrological) hours
3199 **hende:** courteous
3200 **deerne:** secret   **solas:** pleasure, satisfaction (of sexual desires)
3201 **sleigh:** sly   **privee:** discreet, secretive
3205 Very elegantly adorned with sweet-smelling herbs
3207 **cetewale:** zedoary (a spice resembling ginger, used as a condiment and stimulant)
3208 **Almageste:** Ptolemy's treatise on astrology
3209 **astrelabie:** astrolabe   **longynge for:** belonging to, necessary for (his *art,* astronomy)
3210 **augrym stones:** counters, for use on an abacus
3211 **couched:** arranged
3212 **presse:** cupboard, linen press   **faldyng reed:** coarse red woolen cloth
3213 **sautrie:** psaltry
3214 **a-nyghtes:** at night

3216 **Angelus ad virginem:** "The angel to the virgin [Mary]"
3217 **the Kynges Noote:** the King's Tune (not identified)
3220 According to what his friends provided (*freendes fyndyng*) and his income (*rente*)
3224 **narwe:** closely
3226 **lik:** like (?)
3227 **Catoun:** Cato, author of an elementary school text   **rude:** ignorant, unlearned
3228 **bad:** bade, enjoined   **simylitude:** equal, counterpart
3230 **elde:** old age
3231 **snare:** trap
3234 **wezele:** weasel   **gent:** delicate   **smal:** slender
3235 **ceynt:** belt   **barred:** with decorative strips
3236 **barmclooth:** apron   **morne:** morning
3237 **lendes:** loins   **goore:** flounce
3238 **smok:** shift, undergarment (over which aprons and more elaborate items of clothing are worn)   **broyden:** embroidered
3239 **coler:** collar
3241 **tapes:** ribbons   **voluper:** cap
3242 **same suyte of:** same color as

Hir filet brood of silk, and set ful hye.
And sikerly she hadde a likerous ye;
Ful smale ypulled were hire browes two,　　3245
And tho were bent and blake as any sloo.
She was ful moore blisful on to see
Than is the newe pere-jonette tree,
And softer than the wolle is of a wether.
And by hir girdel heeng a purs of lether,　　3250
Tasseled with silk and perled with latoun.
In al this world, to seken up and doun,
There nys no man so wys that koude thenche
So gay a popelote or swich a wenche.
Ful brighter was the shynyng of hir hewe　　3255
Than in the Tour the noble yforged newe.
But of hir song, it was as loude and yerne
As any swalwe sittynge on a berne.
Therto she koude skippe and make game,
As any kyde or calf folwynge his dame.　　3260
Hir mouth was sweete as bragot or the meeth,
Or hoord of apples leyd in hey or heeth.
Wynsynge she was, as is a joly colt,
Long as a mast, and upright as a bolt.
A brooch she baar upon hir lowe coler,　　3265
As brood as is the boos of a bokeler.
Hir shoes were laced on hir legges hye.
She was a prymerole, a piggesnye,
For any lord to leggen in his bedde,
Or yet for any good yeman to wedde.　　3270
　　Now, sire, and eft, sire, so bifel the cas
That on a day this hende Nicholas
Fil with this yonge wyf to rage and pleye,
Whil that hir housbonde was at Oseneye,
As clerkes ben ful subtile and ful queynte;　　3275
And prively he caughte hire by the queynte,

And seyde, "Ywis, but if ich have my wille,
For deerne love of thee, lemman, I spille."
And heeld hire harde by the haunchebones,
And seyde, "Lemman, love me al atones,　　3280
Or I wol dyen, also God me save!"
And she sproong as a colt dooth in the trave,
And with hir heed she wryed faste awey,
And seyde, "I wol nat kisse thee, by my fey!
Why, lat be!" quod she. "Lat be, Nicholas,　　3285
Or I wol crie 'out, harrow' and 'allas'!
Do wey youre handes, for youre curteisye!"
　　This Nicholas gan mercy for to crye,
And spak so faire, and profred him so faste,
That she hir love hym graunted atte laste,　　3290
And swoor hir ooth, by Seint Thomas of Kent,
That she wol been at his comandement,
Whan that she may hir leyser wel espie.
"Myn housbonde is so ful of jalousie
That but ye wayte wel and been privee,　　3295
I woot right wel I nam but deed," quod she.
"Ye moste been ful deerne, as in this cas."
　　"Nay, therof care thee noght," quod Nicholas.
"A clerk hadde litherly biset his whyle,
But if he koude a carpenter bigyle."　　3300
And thus they been accorded and ysworn
To wayte a tyme, as I have told biforn.
　　Whan Nicholas had doon thus everideel
And thakked hire aboute the lendes weel,
He kiste hire sweete and taketh his sawtrie,　　3305
And pleyeth faste, and maketh melodie.
　　Thanne fil it thus, that to the paryssh chirche,
Cristes owene werkes for to wirche,
This goode wyf went on an haliday.
Hir forheed shoon as bright as any day,　　3310
So was it wasshen whan she leet hir werk.
Now was ther of that chirche a parissh clerk,
The which that was ycleped Absolon.
Crul was his heer, and as the gold it shoon,

3243 **filet:** headband
3244 **sikerly:** truly　**likerous:** flirtatious
3245 **ypulled:** plucked
3246 **sloo:** sloe (a plum-like fruit)
3247 **blisful:** pleasing
3248 **pere-jonette:** early-ripe pear
3249 **wolle:** wool　**wether:** sheep (ram)
3250 **girdel:** belt
3251 **perled:** adorned　**latoun:** a brass-like alloy
3253 **thenche:** imagine
3254 **popelote:** little doll　**wenche:** lower-class woman
3256 **Tour:** Tower of London (the mint)　**noble:** a gold coin (6 shillings, 8 pence)
3257 **yerne:** eager, lively
3258 **swalwe:** swallow　**berne:** barn
3260 **dame:** mother (dam)
3261 **bragot:** country drink　**meeth:** mead
3263 **Wynsynge:** skittish　**joly:** spirited
3264 **upright:** straight　**bolt:** cross-bow bolt
3266 **boos of a bokeler:** raised center of a shield
3268 **prymerole, piggesnye:** primrose, "pig's eye," names of flowers
3269 **leggen:** lay
3271 **eft:** again
3273 **rage:** sport (sexually)
3274 **Oseneye:** Osney
3275 **queynte:** ingenious, clever
3276 **queynte:** elegant, pleasing (thing); i.e., pudendum

3277 **Ywis:** truly, indeed
3278 **deerne:** secret　**lemman:** my love, sweetheart　**spille:** die
3279 **haunchebones:** thighs
3280 **al atones:** at once, immediately
3281 **also:** as
3282 **sproong:** sprang　**trave:** frame for holding a horse to be shod
3283 **wryed faste:** turned rapidly, twisted
3286 **out, harrow:** help
3289 **profred him:** pressed his suit
3291 **Seint Thomas of Kent:** Thomas Becket
3293 **leyser:** opportunity
3295 **wayte:** await, watch for (an opportunity)　**privee:** discreet
3297 **deerne:** secretive
3299 **litherly biset his whyle:** wasted his time
3304 **thakked:** patted　**lendes:** loins
3309 **haliday:** holy day
3311 **leet:** left
3314 **Crul:** curled

And strouted as a fanne large and brode;   3315
Ful streight and evene lay his joly shode.
His rode was reed, his eyen greye as goos.
With Poules wyndow corven on his shoos,
In hoses rede he wente fetisly.
Yclad he was ful smal and proprely   3320
Al in a kirtel of a lyght waget;
Ful faire and thikke been the poyntes set.
And therupon he hadde a gay surplys
As whit as is the blosme upon the rys.
A myrie child he was, so God me save.   3325
Wel koude he laten blood, and clippe and shave,
And maken a chartre of lond or acquitaunce.
In twenty manere koude he trippe and daunce
After the scole of Oxenforde tho,
And with his legges casten to and fro,   3330
And pleyen songes on a smal rubible;
Therto he song som tyme a loud quynyble;
And as wel koude he pleye on a giterne.
In al the toun nas brewhous ne taverne
That he ne visited with his solas,   3335
Ther any gaylard tappestere was.
But sooth to seyn, he was somdeel squaymous
Of fartyng, and of speche daungerous.
    This Absolon, that jolif was and gay,
Gooth with a sencer on the haliday,   3340
Sensynge the wyves of the parisshe faste;
And many a lovely look on hem he caste,
And namely on this carpenteris wyf.
To looke on hire hym thoughte a myrie lyf,
She was so propre and sweete and likerous.   3345
I dar wel seyn, if she hadde been a mous,

And he a cat, he wolde hire hente anon.
This parissh clerk, this joly Absolon,
Hath in his herte swich a love-longynge
That of no wyf took he noon offrynge;   3350
For curteisie, he seyde, he wolde noon.
    The moone, whan it was nyght, ful brighte shoon,
And Absolon his gyterne hath ytake;
For paramours he thoghte for to wake.
And forth he gooth, jolif and amorous,   3355
Til he cam to the carpenteres hous
A litel after cokkes hadde ycrowe,
And dressed hym up by a shot-wyndowe
That was upon the carpenteris wal.
He syngeth in his voys gentil and smal,   3360
"Now, deere lady, if thy wille be,
I praye yow that ye wole rewe on me,"
Ful wel acordaunt to his gyternynge.
This carpenter awook, and herde him synge,
And spak unto his wyf, and seyde anon,   3365
"What! Alison! Herestow nat Absolon,
That chaunteth thus under oure boures wal?"
And she answerde hir housbonde therwithal,
"Yis, God woot, John, I heere it every deel."
    This passeth forth; what wol ye bet than weel?
Fro day to day this joly Absolon   3371
So woweth hire that hym is wo bigon.
He waketh al the nyght and al the day;
He kembeth his lokkes brode, and made hym gay;
He woweth hire by meenes and brocage,   3375
And swoor he wolde been hir owene page;
He syngeth, brokkynge as a nyghtyngale;
He sente hire pyment, meeth, and spiced ale,
And wafres, pipyng hoot out of the gleede;
And, for she was of town, he profred meede;   3380
For som folk wol ben wonnen for richesse,
And somme for strokes, and somme for gentillesse.

3315 **strouted as a fanne:** stretched out like a fan
3316 **joly:** pretty   **shode:** parted hair
3317 **rode:** complexion
3318 **Poules wyndow:** window of St. Paul's   **corven:** carved
3319 **fetisly:** elegantly
3320 **smal:** tightly, in close-fitting clothes
3321 **kirtel:** tunic   **lyght waget:** light blue
3322 **poyntes:** laces
3323 **surplys:** surplice (ecclesiastical gown)
3324 **blosme:** blossom   **rys:** twig
3325 **child:** young man   **so:** as
3326 **laten blood:** let blood (as a medical treatment)   **clippe:** cut hair
3327 **chartre:** deed   **acquitaunce:** quitance (legal release of property)
3328 **twenty manere:** twenty ways
3329 **After the scole:** in the style, fashion   **tho:** then
3330 **casten:** move quickly
3331 **rubible:** rebeck, a kind of fiddle
3332 **quynyble:** high treble
3333 **giterne:** cithern, a stringed instrument
3335 **solas:** entertainment
3336 **gaylard tappestere:** merry   barmaid
3337 **somdeel squaymous:** somewhat squeamish
3338 **daungerous:** fastidious
3339 **jolif:** pretty, lively
3340 **sencer:** censer
3341 **Sensynge:** censing   **so:** as
3342 **lovely:** loving

3354 **For paramours:** for the sake of love   **wake:** remain awake
3358 **dressed hym:** took his place   **shot-wyndowe:** hinged window (one that opens and closes)
3360 **smal:** high
3362 **rewe:** have mercy
3363 **acordaunt to:** in harmony with   **gyternynge:** playing on the cithern
3367 **chaunteth:** sings   **under oure boures:** next to our bed chamber's
3369 **Yis:** yes, indeed   **every deel:** every bit
3370 **bet than weel:** better than well (i.e., what more would you have?)
3374 **kembeth:** combs
3375 **meenes:** go-betweens   **brocage:** use of an agent
3376 **page:** servant
3377 **brokkynge:** trilling
3378 **pyment:** spiced, sweetened wine   **meeth:** mead
3379 **wafres:** cakes   **pipyng:** whistling, hissing   **gleede:** fire
3380 **profred meede:** offered money
3382 **for strokes:** i.e., by force

Somtyme, to shewe his lightnesse and maistrye,
He pleyeth Herodes upon a scaffold hye.
But what availleth hym as in this cas?   3385
She loveth so this hende Nicholas
That Absolon may blowe the bukkes horn;
He ne hadde for his labour but a scorn.
And thus she maketh Absolon hire ape,
And al his ernest turneth til a jape.   3390
Ful sooth is this proverbe, it is no lye,
Men seyn right thus: "Alwey the nye slye
Maketh the ferre leeve to be looth."
For though that Absolon be wood or wrooth,
By cause that he fer was from hire sight,   3395
This nye Nicholas stood in his light.

      Now ber thee wel, thou hende Nicholas,
For Absolon may waille and synge "allas."
And so bifel it on a Saterday,
This carpenter was goon til Osenay;   3400
And hende Nicholas and Alisoun
Acorded been to this conclusioun,
That Nicholas shal shapen hym a wyle
This sely jalous housbonde to bigyle;
And if so be the game wente aright,   3405
She sholde slepen in his arm al nyght,
For this was his desir and hire also.
And right anon, withouten wordes mo,
This Nicholas no lenger wolde tarie,
But dooth ful softe unto his chambre carie   3410
Bothe mete and drynke for a day or tweye,
And to hire housbonde bad hire for to seye,
If that he axed after Nicholas,
She sholde seye she nyste where he was;
Of al that day she saugh hym nat with ye;   3415
She trowed that he was in maladye,
For, for no cry hir mayde koude hym calle,
He nolde answere for thyng that myghte falle.

      This passeth forth al thilke Saterday,
That Nicholas stille in his chambre lay,   3420
And eet and sleep, or dide what hym leste,
Til Sonday, that the sonne gooth to reste.
This sely carpenter hath greet merveyle
Of Nicholas, or what thyng myghte hym eyle,

And seyde, "I am adrad, by Seint Thomas,   3425
It stondeth nat aright with Nicholas.
God shilde that he deyde sodeynly!
This world is now ful tikel, sikerly.
I saugh today a cors yborn to chirche   3429
That now, on Monday last, I saugh hym wirche.
      "Go up," quod he unto his knave anoon,
"Clepe at his dore, or knokke with a stoon.
Looke how it is, and tel me boldely."
      This knave gooth hym up ful sturdily,
And at the chambre dore whil that he stood,   3435
He cride and knokked as that he were wood,
"What, how! What do ye, maister Nicholay?
How may ye slepen al the longe day?"
      But al for noght; he herde nat a word.
An hole he foond, ful lowe upon a bord,   3440
Ther as the cat was wont in for to crepe,
And at that hole he looked in ful depe,
And at the laste he hadde of hym a sight.
This Nicholas sat evere capyng upright,
As he had kiked on the newe moone.   3445
Adoun he gooth, and tolde his maister soone
In what array he saugh this ilke man.
      This carpenter to blessen hym bigan,
And seyde, "Help us, Seinte Frydeswyde!
A man woot litel what hym shal bityde.   3450
This man is falle, with his astromye,
In some woodnesse or in som agonye.
I thoghte ay wel how that it sholde be!
Men sholde nat knowe of Goddes pryvetee.
Ye, blessed be alwey a lewed man   3455
That noght but oonly his bileve kan!
So ferde another clerk with astromye;
He walked in the feeldes for to prye
Upon the sterres, what ther sholde bifalle,
Til he was in a marle-pit yfalle;   3460
He saugh nat that. But yet, by Seint Thomas,

3383 **lightnesse:** agility   **maistrye:** skill
3384 **Herodes:** the part of Herod   **scaffold hye:** stage
3387 **blowe the bukkes horn:** go whistle
3389 **ape:** fool, dupe
3390 **jape:** joke
3392 **nye slye:** nigh (at hand) sly one
3393 **ferre leeve to be looth:** distant loved one to be disliked
3396 **in his light:** in his way (i.e., prevented his being seen)
3403 **wyle:** trick
3404 **sely:** innocent, simple, hapless
3416 **trowed:** believed   **in maladye:** ill
3418 **falle:** befall, happen
3421 **eet:** ate   **sleep:** slept
3423–24 **hath greet merveyle Of:** wondered about
3424 **eyle:** ail

3427 God forbid (*shilde*) that he should die suddenly.
3428 **tikel:** unstable, ticklish
3429 **cors:** corpse
3430 **That . . . hym:** whom   **wirche:** work
3431 **knave:** servant
3432 **Clepe:** call out
3434 **sturdily:** boldly
3444 **capyng upright:** gaping straight up
3445 **kiked:** gazed
3446 **soone:** immediately
3447 **array:** condition
3449 **Seinte Frydeswyde:** St. Frideswide, noted for her healing powers
3451 **astromye:** astronomy
3452 **agonye:** fit
3454 **Goddes pryvetee:** God's secrets
3455 **Ye:** yes
3456 Who knows nothing but his creed (*bileve*)
3457 **ferde:** fared
3458 **prye:** gaze
3460 **marle-pit:** clay pit

Me reweth soore of hende Nicholas.
He shal be rated of his studiyng,
If that I may, by Jhesus, hevene kyng!
Get me a staf, that I may underspore,   3465
Whil that thou, <u>Robyn</u>, hevest up the dore.
He shal out of his studiyng, as I gesse."
And to the chambre dore he gan hym dresse.
His knave was a strong carl for the nones,
And by the haspe he haaf it of atones;   3470
Into the floor the dore fil anon.
This Nicholas sat ay as stille as stoon,
And evere caped upward into the eir.
This carpenter wende he were in despeir,
And hente hym by the sholdres myghtily,   3475
And shook hym harde, and cride spitously,
"What! Nicholay! What, how! What, looke adoun!
Awak, and thenk on Cristes passioun!
I crouche thee from elves and fro wightes."
Therwith the nyght-spel seyde he anon-rightes   3480
On foure halves of the hous aboute,
And on the thresshfold of the dore withoute:
"Jhesu Crist and Seinte Benedight,
Blesse this hous from every wikked wight,
For nyghtes verye, the white *pater-noster!*   3485
Where wentestow, Seinte Petres soster?"
    And atte laste this hende Nicholas
Gan for to sik soore, and seyde, "Allas!
Shal al the world be lost eftsoones now?"
    This carpenter answerde, "What seystow?   3490
What! Thynk on God, as we doon, men that swynke."
    This Nicholas answerde, "Fecche me drynke,
And after wol I speke in pryvetee
Of certeyn thyng that toucheth me and thee.
I wol telle it noon oother man, certeyn."   3495

This carpenter goth doun, and comth ageyn,
And broghte of myghty ale a large quart;
And whan that ech of hem had dronke his part,
This Nicholas his dore faste shette,
And doun the carpenter by hym he sette.   3500
    He seyde, "John, myn hooste, lief and deere,
Thou shalt upon thy trouthe swere me heere
That to no wight thou shalt this conseil wreye,
For it is Cristes conseil that I seye,
And if thou telle it man, thou art forlore;   3505
For this vengeaunce thou shalt han therfore,
That if thou wreye me, thou shalt be wood."
"Nay, Crist forbede it, for his hooly blood!"
Quod tho this sely man, "I nam no labbe,
Ne, though I seye, I nam nat lief to gabbe.   3510
Sey what thou wolt, I shal it nevere telle
To child ne wyf, by hym that harwed helle!"
    "Now John," quod Nicholas, "I wol nat lye;
I have yfounde in myn astrologye,
As I have looked in the moone bright,   3515
That now a Monday next, at quarter nyght,
Shal falle a reyn, and that so wilde and wood
That half so greet was nevere Noes flood.
This world," he seyde, "in lasse than an hour
Shal al be dreynt, so hidous is the shour.   3520
Thus shal mankynde drenche, and lese hir lyf."
    This carpenter answerde, "Allas, my wyf!
And shal she drenche? Allas, myn Alisoun!"
For sorwe of this he fil almoost adoun,
And seyde, "Is ther no remedie in this cas?"   3525
    "Why, yis, for Gode," quod hende Nicholas,
"If thou wolt werken after loore and reed.
Thou mayst nat werken after thyn owene heed;
For thus seith Salomon, that was ful trewe,
'Werk al by conseil, and thou shalt nat rewe.'   3530
And if thou werken wolt by good conseil,
I undertake, withouten mast and seyl,
Yet shal I saven hire and thee and me.
Hastow nat herd hou saved was Noe,   3534
Whan that oure Lord hadde warned hym biforn

3462 **Me reweth soore of:** I feel sorry for
3463 **rated of:** scolded for
3465 **underspore:** pry up from under
3467 **shal:** shall come (verb of motion is understood)
3469 **carl:** fellow
3470 **haaf it of:** heaved it off   **atones:** at once, immediately
3473 **caped:** gaped
3474 **wende he were:** supposed he was
3476 **spitously:** vigorously, loudly
3479 **crouche:** make the sign of the cross as a blessing over   **elves:** evil spirits
wightes: (evil) creatures
3480 **nyght-spel:** a charm   **anon-rightes:** straightaway
3481 **halves:** sides
3482 **thresshfold:** threshold
3483 **Seinte Benedight:** St. Benedict
3484 **wight:** creature
3485 **For nyghtes verye:** against the evil spirits of the night (?)   **white pater-noster:**
a charm
3486 **wentestow:** did you go   **Seinte Petres soster:** St. Peter's sister
3488 **sik:** sigh
3489 **eftsoones now:** right now
3491 **swynke:** work
3493 **in pryvetee:** in secret, confidentially
3494 **toucheth:** concerns

3497 **myghty:** strong   **large:** full
3499 **shette:** shut
3501 **lief:** beloved
3503 **wreye:** reveal
3505 **forlore:** lost
3507 **wreye:** betray
3509 **sely:** innocent, ignorant, hapless   **labbe:** blabbermouth
3510 **nam nat lief to gabbe:** do not like to gab
3512 **hym that harwed helle:** Christ, who despoiled Hell of its captives
3516 **a:** on   **quarter nyght:** a quarter way through the night; in April, after midnight
3518 **Noes:** Noah's
3520 **dreynt:** drowned
3521 **drenche:** drown   **hir lyf:** their lives
3526 **yis:** yes indeed
3527 **loore:** learning   **reed:** (good) advice
3528 **heed:** head (i.e., ideas)
3530 **rewe:** be sorry
3532 **undertake:** affirm, declare

That al the world with water sholde be lorn?"
    "Yis," quod this Carpenter, "ful yoore ago."
    "Hastou nat herd," quod Nicholas, "also
The sorwe of Noe with his felaweshipe,
Er that he myghte gete his wyf to shipe?   3540
Hym hadde be levere, I dar wel undertake,
At thilke tyme, than alle his wetheres blake
That she hadde had a ship hirself allone.
And therfore, woostou what is best to doone?
This asketh haste, and of an hastif thyng   3545
Men may nat preche or maken tariyng.
    "Anon go gete us faste into this in
A knedyng trogh, or ellis a kymelyn,
For ech of us, but looke that they be large,
In which we mowe swymme as in a barge,   3550
And han therinne vitaille suffisant
But for a day—fy on the remenant!
The water shal aslake and goon away
Aboute pryme upon the nexte day.
But Robyn may nat wite of this, thy knave,   3555
Ne eek thy mayde Gille I may nat save;
Axe nat why, for though thou aske me,
I wol nat tellen Goddes pryvetee.
Suffiseth thee, but if thy wittes madde,
To han as greet a grace as Noe hadde.   3560
Thy wyf shal I wel saven, out of doute.
Go now thy wey, and speed thee heer-aboute.
    "But whan thou hast, for hire and thee and me,
Ygeten us thise knedyng tubbes thre,
Thanne shaltow hange hem in the roof ful hye,   3565
That no man of oure purveiaunce espye.
And whan thou thus hast doon as I have seyd,
And hast oure vitaille faire in hem yleyd,
And eek an ax to smyte the corde atwo,
Whan that the water comth, that we may go   3570
And breke an hole an heigh, upon the gable,
Unto the gardyn-ward, over the stable,
That we may frely passen forth oure way,

Whan that the grete shour is goon away.
Thanne shaltou swymme as myrie, I undertake,
As dooth the white doke after hire drake.   3576
Thanne wol I clepe, 'How, Alison! How, John!
Be myrie, for the flood wol passe anon.'
And thou wolt seyn, 'Hayl, maister Nicholay!
Good morwe, I se thee wel, for it is day.'   3580
And thanne shul we be lordes al oure lyf
Of al the world, as Noe and his wyf.
    "But of o thyng I warne thee ful right:
Be wel avysed on that ilke nyght
That we ben entred into shippes bord,   3585
That noon of us ne speke nat a word,
Ne clepe, ne crie, but be in his preyere;
For it is Goddes owene heeste deere.
    "Thy wyf and thou moote hange fer atwynne,
For that bitwixe yow shal be no synne,   3590
Namoore in lookyng than ther shal in deede.
This ordinance is seyd. Go, God thee speede!
Tomorwe at nyght, whan men ben alle aslepe,
Into oure knedyng-tubbes wol we crepe,
And sitten there, abidyng Goddes grace.   3595
Go now thy wey; I have no lenger space
To make of this no lenger sermonyng.
Men seyn thus, 'sende the wise, and sey no thyng.'
Thou art so wys, it needeth thee nat teche.
Go, save oure lyf, and that I the biseche."   3600
    This sely carpenter goth forth his wey.
Ful ofte he seide "Allas and weylawey,"
And to his wyf he tolde his pryvetee,
And she was war, and knew it bet than he,
What al this queynte cast was for to seye.   3605
But nathelees she ferde as she wolde deye,
And seyde, "Allas! go forth thy wey anon,
Help us to scape, or we been dede echon!
I am thy trewe, verray wedded wyf;
Go, deere spouse, and help to save oure lyf."   3610
    Lo, which a greet thyng is affeccioun!
Men may dyen of ymaginacioun,
So depe may impressioun be take.
This sely carpenter bigynneth quake;
Hym thynketh verraily that he may see   3615

3536 **lorn:** lost
3537 **yoore ago:** long ago
3539 **Noe:** Noah, here as a character in the popular mystery plays
3541–43 He would have preferred (*Hym hadde be levere*), I dare affirm, that she had a ship all to herself, than have all his black sheep (*wetheres*); i.e., he would have given all his sheep for this.
3547 **in:** house
3548 **knedyng trogh:** large trough for kneading dough   **kymelyn:** large tub for brewing beer
3550 **swymme:** float   **barge:** sailing vessel
3551 **vitaille suffisant:** enough food
3553 **aslake:** subside
3554 **pryme:** around 9 A.M.
3559 **madde:** go mad
3562 **speed thee:** hurry   **heer-aboute:** about this matter
3566 **purveiaunce:** preparations
3569 **atwo:** in two
3571 **an heigh:** above
3572 **Unto the gardyn-ward:** toward the garden

3584 **wel avysed:** well warned
3588 **heeste:** commandment
3589 **atwynne:** apart
3592 **ordinance:** command
3595 **abidyng:** awaiting
3596 **space:** time
3597 **sermonyng:** talk
3604 **bet:** better
3605 **queynte cast:** ingenious plot   **seye:** mean
3608 **scape:** escape   **echon:** each one
3611 **which a:** what a   **affeccioun:** emotion
3612 **ymaginacioun:** fantasy
3614 **quake:** tremble

Noees flood come walwynge as the see
To drenchen Alisoun, his hony deere.
He wepeth, weyleth, maketh sory cheere;
He siketh with ful many a sory swogh;
He gooth and geteth hym a knedyng trogh,   3620
And after that a tubbe and a kymelyn,
And pryvely he sente hem to his in,
And heng hem in the roof in pryvetee.
His owene hand he made laddres thre,
To clymben by the ronges and the stalkes   3625
Unto the tubbes hangynge in the balkes,
And hem vitailled, bothe trogh and tubbe,
With breed, and chese, and good ale in a jubbe,
Suffisynge right ynogh as for a day.
But er that he hadde maad al this array,   3630
He sente his knave, and eek his wenche also,
Upon his nede to London for to go.
And on the Monday, whan it drow to nyght,
He shette his dore withoute candel-lyght,
And dressed alle thyng as it sholde be.   3635
And shortly, up they clomben alle thre;
They seten stille wel a furlong way.
    "Now, *Pater-noster,* clom!" seyde Nicholay,
And "Clom!" quod John, and "Clom!" seyde Alisoun.
This carpenter seyde his devocioun,   3640
And stille he sit, and biddeth his preyere,
Awaitynge on the reyn, if he it heere.
    The dede sleep, for wery bisynesse,
Fil on this carpenter right, as I gesse,
Aboute corfew-tyme, or litel moore;   3645
For travaille of his goost he groneth soore,
And eft he routeth, for his heed myslay.
Doun of the laddre stalketh Nicholay,
And Alisoun ful softe adoun she spedde;
Withouten wordes mo they goon to bedde,   3650
Ther as the carpenter is wont to lye.
Ther was the revel and the melodye;

And thus lith Alison and Nicholas,
In bisynesse of myrthe and of solas,
Til that the belle of laudes gan to rynge,   3655
And freres in the chauncel gonne synge.
    This parissh clerk, this amorous Absolon,
That is for love alwey so wo bigon,
Upon the Monday was at Oseneye
With compaignye, hym to disporte and pleye,   3660
And axed upon cas a cloisterer
Ful prively after John the carpenter;
And he drough hym apart out of the chirche,
And seyde, "I noot; I saugh hym heere nat wirche
Syn Saterday; I trowe that he be went   3665
For tymber, ther oure abbot hath hym sent;
For he is wont for tymber for to go
And dwellen at the grange a day or two;
Or elles he is at his hous, certeyn.
Where that he be, I kan nat soothly seyn."   3670
    This Absolon ful joly was and light,
And thoghte, "Now is tyme to wake al nyght,
For sikirly I saugh hym nat stirynge
Aboute his dore, syn day bigan to sprynge.
    "So moot I thryve, I shal, at cokkes crowe,   3675
Ful pryvely knokken at his wyndowe
That stant ful lowe upon his boures wal.
To Alison now wol I tellen al
My love-longynge, for yet I shal nat mysse
That at the leeste wey I shal hire kisse.   3680
Som maner confort shal I have, parfay.
My mouth hath icched al this longe day;
That is a signe of kissyng atte leeste.
Al nyght me mette eek I was at a feeste.
Therfore I wol go slepe an houre or tweye,   3685
And al the nyght thanne wol I wake and pleye."
    Whan that the firste cok hath crowe, anon
Up rist this joly lovere Absolon,
And hym arraieth gay, at poynt-devys.
But first he cheweth greyn and lycorys,   3690
To smellen sweete, er he hadde kembd his heer.

3616 **walwynge:** surging
3618 **maketh sory cheere:** looks sad, wretched
3619 **swogh:** groan
3624 **His owene hand:** by himself
3625 **stalkes:** uprights (of the ladder)
3626 **balkes:** beams
3627 **vitailled:** stocked with provisions
3628 **jubbe:** large container, jug
3630 **array:** preparation
3631 **wenche:** servant girl
3632 **nede:** business
3635 **dressed:** arranged
3637 **furlong way:** a couple of minutes
3638 Now say a Paternoster (Lord's Prayer) and then hush (*clom*).
3641 **sit** = *sitteth,* sits   **biddeth:** prays
3643 **for wery bisynesse:** wearied by this work
3645 **corfew-tyme:** dusk
3646 **travaille of his goost:** suffering of his spirit, mental anguish
3647 **eft:** likewise   **routeth:** snores   **myslay:** lay wrong
3651 **Ther as:** where   **wont:** accustomed

3655 **laudes:** an early morning service, before daybreak
3661 **upon cas:** by chance
3663 **drough:** drew
3668 **grange:** outlying farm
3671 **light:** happy
3672 **wake:** remain awake
3675 **So moot I thryve:** as I may prosper
3677 **stant** = *stondith,* stands
3679 **mysse:** fail
3680 **at the leeste wey:** at least
3681 **parfay:** indeed, by my faith
3682 **icched:** itched
3684 **me mette:** I dreamed
3688 **rist** = *riseth,* rises
3689 **hym arraieth gay:** dresses himself handsomely   **at poynt-devys:** in every detail, completely
3690 **greyn:** Grain of Paradise, cardamom seed, a breath-sweetener

Under his tonge a trewe-love he beer,
For therby wende he to ben gracious.
He rometh to the carpenteres hous,
And stille he stant under the shot-wyndowe—　3695
Unto his brest it raughte, it was so lowe—
And softe he cougheth with a semy soun:
"What do ye, hony-comb, sweete Alisoun,
My faire bryd, my sweete cynamome?
Awaketh, lemman myn, and speketh to me!　3700
Wel litel thynken ye upon my wo,
That for youre love I swete ther I go.
No wonder is thogh that I swelte and swete;
I moorne as dooth a lamb after the tete.
Ywis, lemman, I have swich love-longynge　3705
That lik a turtel trewe is my moornynge.
I may nat ete na moore than a mayde."
　　"Go fro the wyndow, Jakke fool," she sayde;
"As help me God, it wol nat be 'com pa me.'
I love another—and elles I were to blame—　3710
Wel bet than thee, by Jhesu, Absolon.
Go forth thy wey, or I wol caste a ston,
And lat me slepe, a twenty devel wey!"
　　"Allas," quod Absolon, "and weylawey,
That trewe love was evere so yvel biset!　3715
Thanne kysse me, syn it may be no bet,
For Jhesus love, and for the love of me."
　　"Wiltow thanne go thy wey therwith?" quod she.
　　"Ye, certes, lemman," quod this Absolon.
　　"Thanne make thee redy," quod she, "I come anon."　
And unto Nicholas she seyde stille,　3721
"Now hust, and thou shalt laughen al thy fille."
　　This Absolon doun sette hym on his knees
And seyde, "I am a lord at alle degrees;
For after this I hope ther cometh moore.　3725
Lemman, thy grace, and sweete bryd, thyn oore!"
　　The wyndow she undoth, and that in haste.

"Have do," quod she, "com of, and speed the faste,
Lest that oure neighebores thee espie."
　　This Absolon gan wype his mouth ful drie.　3730
Derk was the nyght as pich, or as the cole,
And at the wyndow out she putte hir hole,
And Absolon, hym fil no bet ne wers,
But with his mouth he kiste hir naked ers
Ful savourly, er he were war of this.　3735
Abak he stirte, and thoughte it was amys,
For wel he wiste a womman hath no berd.
He felte a thyng al rough and long yherd,
And seyde, "Fy! allas! what have I do?"
　　"Tehee!" quod she, and clapte the wyndow to,
And Absolon gooth forth a sory pas.　3741
　　"A berd! A berd!" quod hende Nicholas,
"By Goddes corpus, this goth faire and weel."
　　This sely Absolon herde every deel,
And on his lippe he gan for anger byte,　3745
And to hymself he seyde, "I shal thee quyte."
　　Who rubbeth now, who froteth now his lippes
With dust, with sond, with straw, with clooth, with
　　　chippes,
But Absolon, that seith ful ofte, "Allas!"
"My soule bitake I unto Sathanas,　3750
But me were levere than al this toun," quod he,
"Of this despit awroken for to be.
Allas," quod he, "allas, I ne hadde ybleynt!"
His hoote love was coold and al yqueynt;
For fro that tyme that he hadde kist hir ers,　3755
Of paramours he sette nat a kers,
For he was heeled of his maladie.
Ful ofte paramours he gan deffie,
And weep as dooth a child that is ybete.
A softe paas he wente over the strete　3760
Until a smyth men cleped daun Gerveys,
That in his forge smythed plough harneys;

3692 **trewe-love:** a four-leafed sprig of herb paris (Paris quadrifolia) in the shape of a fourfold true-love knot
3693 **gracious:** attractive
3695 **stant** = *stondeth*, stands　**under:** next to　**shot-wyndowe:** hinged window
3696 **raughte:** reached
3697 **semy soun:** small, gentle sound
3699 **bryd:** bird (i.e., sweetheart)　**cynamome:** cinnamon
3700 **lemman:** sweetheart
3703 **swelte:** grow faint　**swete:** sweat
3704 **moorne:** yearn
3705 **Ywis:** truly, indeed
3706 **turtel:** turtledove
3708 **Jakke fool:** you idiot
3709 **com pa me:** come kiss me
3713 **a twenty devel wey:** in the name of twenty devils
3715 **so yvel biset:** in such miserable circumstances
3722 **hust:** be quiet
3724 **at alle degrees:** in every way
3726 **bryd:** bird (i.e., sweetheart)　**oore:** mercy, grace
3727 **undoth:** opens

3728 **Have do:** finish up　**com of:** hurry up　**speed the faste:** be quick
3731 **pich:** pitch
3733 **wers:** worse
3735 **savourly:** with relish
3738 **long yherd:** long-haired
3741 **a sory pas:** sadly
3742 **A berd! A berd!:** a beard! a trick!
3743 **corpus:** body
3744 **every deel:** every bit
3746 **quyte:** pay back (revenge)
3747 **froteth:** rubs
3750 **bitake:** give
3751 If I would not rather than (own) all this town
3752 **despit:** insult　**awroken:** avenged
3753 **ybleynt:** turned away
3754 **yqueynt:** quenched
3756 **kers:** cress (i.e., something of no value)
3758 **deffie:** repudiate
3761 **Until:** to　**daun:** sir
3762 **plough harneys:** ploughing equipment

He sharpeth shaar and kultour bisily.
This Absolon knokketh al esily,
And seyde, "Undo, Gerveys, and that anon."   3765
    "What, who artow?" "It am I, Absolon."
"What, Absolon! for Cristes sweete tree,
Why rise ye so rathe? Ey, benedicitee!
What eyleth yow? Som gay gerl, God it woot,
Hath broght yow thus upon the viritoot.   3770
By Seinte Note, ye woot wel what I mene."
    This Absolon ne roghte nat a bene
Of al his pley; no word agayn he yaf;
He hadde moore tow on his distaf   3774
Than Gerveys knew, and seyde, "Freend so deere,
That hoote kultour in the chymenee heere,
As lene it me; I have therwith to doone,
And I wol brynge it thee agayn ful soone."
    Gerveys answerde, "Certes, were it gold,
Or in a poke nobles alle untold,   3780
Thou sholdest have, as I am trewe smyth.
Ey, Cristes foo! What wol ye do therwith?"
    "Therof," quod Absolon, "be as be may.
I shal wel telle it thee to-morwe day"—
And caughte the kultour by the colde stele.   3785
Ful softe out at the dore he gan to stele,
And wente unto the carpenteris wal.
He cogheth first, and knokketh therwithal
Upon the wyndowe, right as he dide er.
    This Alison answerde, "Who is ther   3790
That knokketh so? I warante it a theef."
    "Why, nay," quod he, "God woot, my sweete leef,
I am thyn Absolon, my deerelyng.
Of gold," quod he, "I have thee broght a ryng.
My mooder yaf it me, so God me save;   3795
Ful fyn it is, and therto wel ygrave.
This wol I yeve thee, if thou me kisse."

    This Nicholas was risen for to pisse,
And thoughte he wolde amenden al the jape;
He sholde kisse his ers er that he scape.   3800
And up the wyndowe dide he hastily,
And out his ers he putteth pryvely
Over the buttok, to the haunche-bon;
And therwith spak this clerk, this Absolon,
"Spek, sweete bryd, I noot nat where thou art."   3805
    This Nicholas anon leet fle a fart
As greet as it had been a thonder-dent,
That with the strook he was almoost yblent;
And he was redy with his iren hoot,
And Nicholas amydde the ers he smoot.   3810
    Of gooth the skyn an hande-brede aboute,
The hoote kultour brende so his toute,
And for the smert he wende for to dye.
As he were wood, for wo he gan to crye,
"Help! Water! Water! Help, for Goddes herte!"   3815
    This carpenter out of his slomber sterte,
And herde oon crien "water!" as he were wood,
And thoughte, "Allas, now comth Nowelis flood!"
He sit hym up withouten wordes mo,
And with his ax he smoot the corde atwo,   3820
And doun gooth al; he foond neither to selle,
Ne breed ne ale, til he cam to the celle
Upon the floor, and ther aswowne he lay.
    Up stirte hire Alison and Nicholay,
And criden "Out" and "Harrow" in the strete.   3825
The neighebores, bothe smale and grete,
In ronnen for to gauren on this man,
That yet aswowne lay, bothe pale and wan,
For with the fal he brosten hadde his arm.
But stonde he moste unto his owene harm;   3830
For whan he spak, he was anon bore doun
With hende Nicholas and Alisoun.
They tolden every man that he was wood;
He was agast so of Nowelis flood

3763 **sharpeth:** sharpens   **shaar:** ploughshare   **kultour:** vertical blade at the front of the plough
3764 **esily:** gently
3765 **Undo:** open up
3767 **sweete tree:** dear cross
3768 **rathe:** early
3769 **gay gerl:** good-looking girl
3770 **upon the viritoot:** astir (?)
3771 **Seinte Note:** St. Neot
3772 **roghte nat a bene:** cared not a bean (i.e., nothing)
3774 **tow on his distaf:** flax on his distaff (i.e., more business on hand)
3776 **chymenee:** hearth
3777 **As lene:** lend (*as* is not translated)
3780 **poke:** bag   **nobles:** gold coins   **untold:** countless
3782 **Ey, Cristes foo!:** Ah, by Christ's foe (i.e., the Devil)
3783 **be as be may:** whatever may be
3785 **stele:** handle
3791 **warante:** swear
3792 **leef:** beloved
3793 **deerelyng:** darling
3796 **ygrave:** engraved

3799 **amenden al the jape:** make the joke even better
3803 **haunche-bon:** thigh
3806 **leet fle:** let fly
3807 **thonder-dent:** thunderstroke
3808 **yblent:** blinded
3811 **Of:** off   **hande-brede aboute:** width of a hand all around
3812 **toute:** rump
3813 **smert:** pain   **wende for to dye:** thought he would die
3818 **Nowelis:** Noah's
3821–22 He did not stop to sell bread or ale on the way (i.e., he wasted no time).
3822 **celle:** floor
3823 **aswowne:** in a faint
3826 **smale and grete:** i.e., everyone
3827 **ronnen:** ran   **gauren on:** stare at
3829 **brosten:** broken
3830 But he had to stand up (for himself), though it turned out badly for him.
3832 **With:** by
3834 **agast:** frightened

Thurgh fantasie that of his vanytee   3835
He hadde yboght hym knedyng tubbes thre,
And hadde hem hanged in the roof above;
And that he preyed hem, for Goddes love,
To sitten in the roof, *par compaignye.*

   The folk gan laughen at his fantasye;   3840
Into the roof they kiken and they cape,
And turned al his harm unto a jape.
For what so that this carpenter answerde,
It was for noght; no man his reson herde.

With othes grete he was so sworn adoun   3845
That he was holde wood in al the toun;
For every clerk anonright heeld with oother.
They seyde, "The man is wood, my leeve brother";
And every wight gan laughen at this stryf.
Thus swyved was this carpenteris wyf,   3850
For al his kepyng and his jalousye,
And Absolon hath kist hir nether ye,
And Nicholas is scalded in the towte.
This tale is doon, and God save al the rowte!

Heere endeth the Millere his tale.

The Reeve's Prologue

The prologe of the Reves Tale.

   Whan folk hadde laughen at this nyce cas   3855
Of Absolon and hende Nicholas,
Diverse folk diversely they seyde,
But for the moore part they loughe and pleyde.
Ne at this tale I saugh no man hym greve,
But it were oonly Osewold the Reve.   3860
By cause he was of carpenteris craft,
A litel ire is in his herte ylaft;
He gan to grucche, and blamed it a lite.

   "So theek," quod he, "ful wel koude I thee quite
With bleryng of a proud milleres ye,   3865
If that me liste speke of ribaudye.
But ik am oold; me list not pley for age;
Gras tyme is doon; my fodder is now forage;
This white top writeth myne olde yeris;
Myn herte is also mowled as myne heris,   3870

But if I fare as dooth an open-ers—
That ilke fruyt is ever lenger the wers,
Til it be roten in mullok or in stree.
We olde men, I drede, so fare we:
Til we be roten, kan we nat be rype;   3875
We hoppen alwey whil that the world wol pype.
For in oure wyl ther stiketh evere a nayl,
To have an hoor heed and a grene tayl,
As hath a leek; for thogh oure myght be goon,
Oure wyl desireth folie evere in oon.   3880
For whan we may nat doon, than wol we speke;
Yet in oure asshen olde is fyr yreke.

   "Foure gleedes han we, which I shal devyse—
Avauntyng, liyng, anger, coveitise;
Thise foure sparkles longen unto eelde.   3885

3835 **vanytee:** foolishness
3839 **par compaignye:** for fellowship's sake, to keep him company
3841 **kiken:** stare   **cape:** gape
3845 **sworn adoun:** overcome by oaths

3855 **nyce cas:** foolish business
3859 **hym greve:** get angry
3863 **grucche:** complain
3864 **So theek:** as I may prosper (I swear)
3865 **bleryng of a proud milleres ye:** deluding, tricking a proud miller
3866 **ribaudye:** ribaldry, coarse jesting
3867 **ik:** I
3868 I have left the pasture for the stable.
3869 My white hairs declare my old age.
3870 **also:** as   **mowled:** molded

3847 **anonright:** immediately   **heeld:** held, agreed
3850 **swyved:** copulated with
3851 **kepyng:** guarding
3852 **nether ye:** lower eye

3871 **open-ers:** fruit of the medlar
3872 **ever lenger the wers:** increasingly worse
3873 **roten:** rotten   **mullok:** mullock (rubbish, refuse)   **stree:** straw
3876 **hoppen:** dance
3877 We are always goaded by desire (*nayl* = nail).
3878 **hoor:** white-haired
3880 **evere in oon:** continually
3882 Still in our old ashes, fire is raked over (*yreke;* i.e., covered).
3883 **gleedes:** embers, live coals
3884 **Avauntyng:** boasting   **coveitise:** greed, avarice
3885 **eelde:** old age

Oure olde lemes mowe wel been unweelde,
But wyl ne shal nat faillen, that is sooth.
And yet ik have alwey a coltes tooth,
As many a yeer as it is passed henne
Syn that my tappe of lif bigan to renne. 3890
For sikerly, whan I was bore, anon
Deeth drough the tappe of lyf and leet it gon,
And ever sithe hath so the tappe yronne
Til that almoost al empty is the tonne.
The streem of lyf now droppeth on the chymbe. 3895
The sely tonge may wel rynge and chymbe
Of wrecchednesse that passed is ful yoore;
With olde folk, save dotage, is namoore!"
    Whan that oure Hoost hadde herd this sermonyng,
He gan to speke as lordly as a kyng. 3900
He seide, "What amounteth al this wit?
What shul we speke alday of hooly writ?
The devel made a reve for to preche,

Or of a soutere a shipman or a leche.
Sey forth thy tale, and tarie nat the tyme. 3905
Lo Depeford, and it is half-wey pryme!
Lo Grenewych, ther many a shrewe is inne!
It were al tyme thy tale to bigynne."
    "Now, sires," quod this Osewold the Reve,
"I pray yow alle that ye nat yow greve, 3910
Thogh I answere, and somdeel sette his howve;
For leveful is with force force of-showve.
    "This dronke Millere hath ytoold us heer
How that bigyled was a carpenteer,
Peraventure in scorn, for I am oon. 3915
And, by youre leve, I shal hym quite anoon;
Right in his cherles termes wol I speke.
I pray to God his nekke mote to-breke;
He kan wel in myn eye seen a stalke,
But in his owene he kan nat seen a balke." 3920

The Reeve's Tale

Heere bigynneth the Reves Tale.

At Trumpyngtoun, nat fer fro Cantebrigge,
Ther gooth a brook, and over that a brigge,
Upon the whiche brook ther stant a melle;
And this is verray sooth that I yow telle:
A millere was ther dwellynge many a day. 3925
As any pecok he was proud and gay.
Pipen he koude and fisshe, and nettes beete,
And turne coppes, and wel wrastle and sheete;
Ay by his belt he baar a long panade,
And of a swerd ful trenchant was the blade. 3930

A joly poppere baar he in his pouche;
Ther was no man, for peril, dorste hym touche.
A Sheffeld thwitel baar he in his hose.
Round was his face, and camus was his nose;
As piled as an ape was his skulle. 3935
He was a market-betere atte fulle.
Ther dorste no wight hand upon hym legge,

3886 **lemes:** limbs   **unweelde:** feeble
3887 **wyl:** will, desire
3888 **coltes tooth:** young man's desires
3889 **henne:** hence, away
3892 **drough the tappe:** drew the tap, turned on the spigot
3894 **tonne:** barrel, cask
3895 **chymbe:** rim
3896 **chymbe:** chime
3897 **ful yoore:** long ago
3901 What does all this wisdom amount to? (R.)
3902 **What:** why   **alday:** all day

3921 **Trumpyngtoun:** Trumpington   **Cantebrigge:** Cambridge
3922 **brigge:** bridge
3923 **stant** = *stondith,* stands   **melle:** mill
3927 **Pipen:** play the bagpipes   **beete:** mend
3928 **turne coppes:** turn up the cups (?), play a drinking game   **sheete:** shoot (arrows)
3929 **panade:** cutlass
3930 **trenchant:** sharp

3904 **soutere:** cobbler   **leche:** physician
3906 **Depeford:** Deptford, about five miles from London   **half-wey pryme:** about 7:30 A.M. (?)
3907 **Grenewych:** Greenwich (where Chaucer was probably living), about a half mile past Deptford   **shrewe:** scoundrel
3908 **al tyme:** high time
3911 **somdeel:** somewhat   **sette his howve:** tip his hood, make a fool of him; cf. GP I.586.
3912 For it is permitted (*leveful*) to repel (*of-showve*) force with force
3914 **bigyled:** tricked
3915 **Peraventure:** perhaps   **oon:** one (i.e., a carpenter)
3916 **quite:** pay back, exact vengeance on (him)
3917 **cherles termes:** churlish words, rude expressions
3918 **to-breke:** break in pieces
3919 **stalke:** piece of straw
3920 **balke:** beam

3931 **poppere:** small dagger   **pouche:** pocket
3932 **dorste:** dared
3933 **Sheffeld thwitel:** Sheffield knife
3934 **camus was his nose:** he had a pug nose
3935 **piled:** bald
3936 **market-betere:** bully, quarrelsome swaggerer
3937 **legge:** lay

That he ne swoor he sholde anon abegge.
A theef he was for sothe of corn and mele,
And that a sly, and usaunt for to stele.
His name was hoote deynous Symkyn. 3940
A wyf he hadde, ycomen of noble kyn;
The person of the toun hir fader was.
With hire he yaf ful many a panne of bras,
For that Symkyn sholde in his blood allye. 3945
She was yfostred in a nonnerye;
For Symkyn wolde no wyf, as he sayde,
But she were wel ynorissed and a mayde,
To saven his estaat of yomanrye.
And she was proud, and peert as is a pye. 3950
A ful fair sighte was it upon hem two;
On halydayes biforn hire wolde he go
With his typet wounde aboute his heed,
And she cam after in a gyte of reed;
And Symkyn hadde hosen of the same. 3955
Ther dorste no wight clepen hire but "dame";
Was noon so hardy that wente by the weye
That with hire dorste rage or ones pleye,
But if he wolde be slayn of Symkyn
With panade, or with knyf, or boidekyn. 3960
For jalous folk ben perilous everemo—
Algate they wolde hire wyves wenden so.
And eek, for she was somdel smoterlich,
She was as digne as water in a dich,
And ful of hoker and of bisemare. 3965
Hir thoughte that a lady sholde hire spare,
What for hire kynrede and hir nortelrie
That she hadde lerned in the nonnerie.
    A doghter hadde they bitwixe hem two
Of twenty yeer, withouten any mo, 3970
Savynge a child that was of half yeer age;
In cradel it lay and was a propre page.

This wenche thikke and wel ygrowen was,
With kamus nose and eyen greye as glas,
With buttokes brode and brestes rounde and hye.
But right fair was hire heer; I wol nat lye. 3976
    This person of the toun, for she was feir,
In purpos was to maken hire his heir,
Bothe of his catel and his mesuage,
And straunge he made it of hir mariage. 3980
His purpos was for to bistowe hire hye
Into som worthy blood of auncetrye;
For hooly chirches good moot been despended
On hooly chirches blood, that is descended.
Therfore he wolde his hooly blood honoure, 3985
Though that he hooly chirche sholde devoure.
    Greet sokene hath this millere, out of doute,
With whete and malt of al the land aboute;
And nameliche ther was a greet collegge
Men clepen the Soler Halle at Cantebregge; 3990
Ther was hir whete and eek hir malt ygrounde.
And on a day it happed, in a stounde,
Sik lay the maunciple on a maladye;
Men wenden wisly that he sholde dye. 3994
For which this millere stal bothe mele and corn
An hundred tyme moore than biforn;
For therbiforn he stal but curteisly,
But now he was a theef outrageously,
For which the wardeyn chidde and made fare.
But therof sette the millere nat a tare; 4000
He craketh boost, and swoor it was nat so.
    Thanne were ther yonge povre scolers two,
That dwelten in this halle, of which I seye.
Testif they were, and lusty for to pleye,
And, oonly for hire myrthe and revelrye, 4005
Upon the wardeyn bisily they crye
To yeve hem leve, but a litel stounde,
To goon to mille and seen hir corn ygrounde;

3938 **abegge:** pay for (it)
3939 **corn:** grain **mele:** ground meal
3940 **sly:** sly one **usaunt for to stele:** accustomed to stealing
3941 **hoote:** called **deynous:** haughty
3943 **person:** parson, priest
3945 **in his blood allye:** make an alliance with his family
3946 **yfostred:** raised
3948 **But:** unless **ynorissed:** raised, educated **mayde:** virgin
3949 To maintain his state of free (rather than servile) birth
3950 **peert:** impudent **pye:** magpie
3953 **typet:** the dangling tip of the hood
3954 **gyte:** gown, mantle
3956 **dame:** lady
3958 **rage:** flirt
3960 **panade:** cutlass **boidekyn:** dagger
3961 **everemo:** always
3962 At least they would like their wives to think so.
3963 **smoterlich:** besmirched, sullied (in reputation, by her illegitimacy)
3964 **as digne as water in a dich:** literally, as haughty as ditch-water (OED: "stinking with pride")
3965 **hoker:** disdain **bisemare:** scorn
3966 **hire spare:** be aloof
3967 **kynrede:** lineage **nortelrie:** nurture, education
3972 **page:** boy

3974 **kamus nose:** pug nose
3978 **In purpos was:** intended
3979 **catel:** property **mesuage:** house and its contents
3980 And he made difficulties about her marriage.
3981 **hye:** nobly
3982 **auncetrye:** noble lineage
3987 **Greet sokene:** large, profitable monopoly (*sokene* = exclusive right to grind grain in a given area)
3990 **Soler Halle:** a name for King's Hall, a college at Cambridge
3992 **in a stounde:** at a time, once
3994 **wisly:** surely
3995 **stal:** stole
3997 **therbiforn:** previously
3998 **outrageously:** to excess
3999 **wardeyn:** master of the college **chidde and made fare:** chided and made a fuss
4000 **tare:** weed (i.e., nothing)
4001 **craketh boost:** blustered fiercely
4002 **povre scolers:** impoverished students
4004 **Testif:** testy, headstrong
4005 **revelrye:** pleasure, delight
4007 **stounde:** time, while

And hardily they dorste leye hir nekke
The millere sholde not stele hem half a pekke   4010
Of corn by sleighte, ne by force hem reve;
And at the laste the wardeyn yaf hem leve.
John highte that oon, and Aleyn highte that oother;
Of o toun were they born, that highte Strother,
Fer in the north; I kan nat telle where.   4015
    This Aleyn maketh redy al his gere,
And on an hors the sak he caste anon.
Forth goth Aleyn the clerk, and also John,
With good swerd and with bokeler by hir syde.
John knew the weyy—hem nedede no gyde—   4020
And at the mille the sak adoun he layth.
Aleyn spak first: "Al hayl, Symond, y-fayth!
Hou fares thy faire doghter and thy wyf?"
    "Aleyn, welcome," quod Symkyn, "by my lyf!
And John also, how now, what do ye heer?"   4025
    "Symond," quod John, "by God, nede has na peer.
Hym boes serve hymself that has na swayn,
Or elles he is a fool, as clerkes sayn.
Oure manciple, I hope he wil be deed,
Swa werkes ay the wanges in his heed;   4030
And forthy is I come, and eek Alayn,
To grynde oure corn and carie it ham agayn;
I pray yow spede us heythen that ye may."
    "It shal be doon," quod Symkyn, "by my fay!
What wol ye doon whil that it is in hande?"   4035
    "By God, right by the hopur wil I stande,"
Quod John, "and se howgates the corn gas in.
Yet saugh I nevere, by my fader kyn,
How that the hopur wagges til and fra."
    Aleyn answerde, "John, and wiltow swa?   4040
Thanne wil I be bynethe, by my croun,
And se how that the mele falles doun

Into the trough; that sal be my disport.
For John, y-faith, I may been of youre sort;
I is as ille a millere as ar ye."   4045
    This millere smyled of hir nycetee,
And thoghte, "Al this nys doon but for a wyle.
They wene that no man may hem bigyle,
But by my thrift, yet shal I blere hir ye,
For al the sleighte in hir philosophye.   4050
The moore queynte crekes that they make,
The moore wol I stele whan I take.
In stide of flour yet wol I yeve hem bren.
'The gretteste clerkes been noght wisest men,'
As whilom to the wolf thus spak the mare.   4055
Of al hir art counte I noght a tare."
    Out at the dore he gooth ful pryvely,
Whan that he saugh his tyme, softely.
He looketh up and doun til he hath founde
The clerkes hors, ther as it stood ybounde   4060
Bihynde the mille, under a levesel;
And to the hors he goth hym faire and wel;
He strepeth of the brydel right anon.
And whan the hors was laus, he gynneth gon
Toward the fen, ther wilde mares renne,   4065
And forth with "wehee," thurgh thikke and thurgh
            thenne.
    This millere gooth agayn, no word he seyde,
But dooth his note, and with the clerkes pleyde
Til that hir corn was faire and weel ygrounde.
And whan the mele is sakked and ybounde,   4070
This John goth out and fynt his hors away,
And gan to crie "Harrow!" and "Weylaway!
Oure hors is lorn, Alayn, for Goddes banes,
Step on thy feet! Com of, man, al atanes!
Allas, our wardeyn has his palfrey lorn."   4075
This Aleyn al forgat, bothe mele and corn;

4009 **hardily:** certainly   **leye:** wager
4011 **sleighte:** trickery   **reve:** rob
4014 **Strother:** a town in the North of England
4020 **hem nedede:** they needed
4022 The clerks speak a Northern dialect; see n.
4026 **nede has na peer:** need has no equal (i.e., necessity knows no law)
4027 **Hym boes:** he must (Nth)   **swayn:** servant
4029 **hope:** expect
4030 **Swa werkes:** so ache (Nth)   **wanges:** teeth
4032 **ham:** home (Nth)
4033 **heythen:** hence (Nth)   **that ye may:** (as fast) as you can
4035 **in hande:** in process
4036 **hopur:** hopper (of the mill)
4037 **howgates:** how (Nth)   **gas:** goes (Nth)
4038 **by my fader kyn:** (I swear) by my father's kin (i.e., on my family's honor)
4039 **wagges til and fra:** wags to and fro (Nth)
4040 **wiltow swa:** will you (do) so (*swa* Nth)
4041 **by my croun:** by my head

4043 **sal:** shall (Nth)   **disport:** amusement
4045 **ille:** poor
4046 **nycetee:** foolishness
4047 **wyle:** trick
4049 **by my thrift:** by my welfare (I swear)   **blere hir ye:** trick them
4050 **philosophye:** learning
4051 **queynte:** ingenious, clever   **crekes:** tricks
4053 **In stide of:** instead of   **bren:** bran
4056 **noght a tare:** not a weed (i.e., nothing)
4061 **levesel:** arbor
4063 **strepeth of:** strips off
4064 **laus:** loose
4065 **fen:** probably Lingay Fen, south of Trumpington
4068 **note:** task, business
4070 **sakked:** put in a sack
4071 **fynt** = *fyndeth,* finds
4072 **Weylaway:** alas
4073 **banes:** bones (Nth)
4074 **Com of:** hurry   **al atanes:** at once (Nth)

Al was out of his mynde his housbondrie.
"What, whilk way is he geen?" he gan to crie.
    The wyf cam lepynge inward with a ren.
She seyde, "Allas! youre hors goth to the fen   4080
With wilde mares, as faste as he may go.
Unthank come on his hand that boond hym so,
And he that bettre sholde han knyt the reyne!"
    "Allas," quod John, "Aleyn, for Cristes peyne
Lay doun thy swerd, and I wil myn alswa.   4085
I is ful wight, God waat, as is a raa;
By Goddes herte, he sal nat scape us bathe!
Why ne had thow pit the capul in the lathe?
Ilhayl! By God, Alayn, thou is a fonne!"
    Thise sely clerkes han ful faste yronne   4090
Toward the fen, bothe Aleyn and eek John.
    And whan the millere saugh that they were gon,
He half a busshel of hir flour hath take,
And bad his wyf go knede it in a cake.
He seyde, "I trowe the clerkes were aferd.   4095
Yet kan a millere make a clerkes berd,
For al his art; now lat hem goon hir weye!
Lo, wher he gooth! Ye, lat the children pleye.
They gete hym nat so lightly, by my croun."
    Thise sely clerkes rennen up and doun   4100
With "Keep! Keep! Stand! Stand! Jossa, warderere,
Ga whistle thou, and I shal kepe hym heere!"
But shortly, til that it was verray nyght,
They koude nat, though they dide al hir myght,
Hir capul cacche, he ran alwey so faste,   4105
Til in a dych they caughte hym atte laste.
    Wery and weet, as beest is in the reyn,
Comth sely John, and with him comth Aleyn.
"Allas," quod John, "the day that I was born!
Now are we dryve til hethyng and til scorn.   4110
Oure corn is stoln; men wil us fooles calle,
Bathe the wardeyn and oure felawes alle,
And namely the millere, weylaway!"
    Thus pleyneth John as he gooth by the way

Toward the mille, and Bayard in his hond.   4115
The millere sittynge by the fyr he fond,
For it was nyght, and forther myghte they noght;
But for the love of God they hym bisoght
Of herberwe and of ese, as for hir peny.
    The millere seyde agayn, "If ther be eny,   4120
Swich as it is, yet shal ye have youre part.
Myn hous is streit, but ye han lerned art;
Ye konne by argumentes make a place
A myle brood of twenty foot of space.
Lat se now if this place may suffise,   4125
Or make it rowm with speche, as is youre gise."
    "Now, Symond," seyde John, "by Seint Cutberd,
Ay is thou myrie, and this is faire answerd.
I have herd seyd, "Man sal taa of twa thynges:
Slyk as he fyndes, or taa slyk as he brynges.'   4130
But specially I pray thee, hooste deere,
Get us som mete and drynke, and make us cheere,
And we wil payen trewely atte fulle.
With empty hand men may na haukes tulle;
Loo, heere oure silver, redy for to spende."   4135
    This millere into toun his doghter sende
For ale and breed, and rosted hem a goos,
And boond hire hors, it sholde namoore go loos,
And in his owene chambre hem made a bed,
With sheetes and with chalons faire yspred   4140
Noght from his owene bed ten foot or twelve.
His doghter hadde a bed, al by hirselve,
Right in the same chambre by and by.
It myghte be no bet, and cause why?
Ther was no roumer herberwe in the place.   4145
They soupen and they speke, hem to solace,
And drynken evere strong ale atte beste.
Aboute mydnyght wente they to reste.
    Wel hath this millere vernysshed his heed;
Ful pale he was for dronken, and nat reed.   4150
He yexeth, and he speketh thurgh the nose
As he were on the quakke, or on the pose.

4078 **whilk:** which (Nth)   **geen:** gone (Nth)
4079 **with a ren:** at a run, running
4082 **Unthank:** curses
4083 **knyt:** tied
4085 **alswa:** also (Nth)
4086 **wight:** strong   **waat:** knows (Nth)   **raa:** roe (Nth)
4087 **sal:** shall (Nth)   **bathe:** both (Nth)
4088 **pit:** put   **capul:** horse   **lathe:** barn (Nth)
4089 **Ilhayl:** bad luck   **fonne:** fool
4094 **cake:** loaf of bread
4095 **aferd:** leery
4096 **make a . . . berd:** outwit, fool
4100 **Thise sely clerkes:** these poor, hapless clerks
4101 **Keep:** stay   **Jossa:** down here   **warderere:** watch out behind
4102 **Ga:** go (Nth)
4110 **til hethyng:** to contempt

4119 **herberwe:** lodging   **ese:** refreshment, food
4122 **streit:** narrow, small   **art:** the arts curriculum at the university, esp. logic
4123 **konne by argumentes make:** know how by logical disputation to make
4126 **rowm:** large, roomy
4127 **Seint Cutberd:** St. Cuthbert
4129–30 Of two things one must take (*taa*) such (*Slyk*) as he finds or take such as he brings.
4134 **tulle:** lure
4140 **chalons:** blankets   **yspred:** spread
4143 **by and by:** side by side
4145 **roumer:** larger   **herberwe:** lodging
4147 **atte beste:** of the best sort
4149 **vernysshed his heed:** made his head shine (from drinking)
4151 **yexeth:** belches
4152 **on the quakke:** had hoarseness   **on the pose:** had a cold

To bedde he goth, and with hym goth his wyf.
As any jay she light was and jolyf,
So was hir joly whistle wel ywet.   4155
The cradel at hir beddes feet is set,
To rokken, and to yeve the child to sowke.
And whan that dronken al was in the crowke,
To bedde wente the doghter right anon;
To bedde goth Aleyn and also John;   4160
Ther nas na moore—hem nedede no dwale.
This millere hath so wisely bibbed ale
That as an hors he fnorteth in his sleep,
Ne of his tayl bihynde he took no keep.
His wyf bar hym a burdon, a ful strong;   4165
Men myghte hir rowtyng heere two furlong;
The wenche rowteth eek, *par compaignye*.

    Aleyn the clerk, that herde this melodye,
He poked John, and seyde, "Slepestow?
Herdestow evere slyk a sang er now?   4170
Lo, swilk a complyn is ymel hem alle;
A wilde fyr upon thair bodyes falle!
Wha herkned evere slyk a ferly thyng?
Ye, they sal have the flour of il endyng.
This lange nyght ther tydes me na reste;   4175
But yet, na fors, al sal be for the beste.
For, John," seyde he, "als evere moot I thryve,
If that I may, yon wenche wil I swyve.
Som esement has lawe yshapen us,
For, John, ther is a lawe that says thus: 4180
That gif a man in a point be agreved,
That in another he sal be releved.
Oure corn is stoln, sothly, it is na nay,
And we han had an il fit al this day;
And syn I sal have neen amendement   4185
Agayn my los, I will have esement.
By Goddes sale, it sal neen other bee!"

This John answerde, "Alayn, avyse thee!
The millere is a perilous man," he seyde,
"And gif that he out of his sleep abreyde,   4190
He myghte doon us bathe a vileynye."
    Aleyn answerde, "I counte hym nat a flye."
And up he rist, and by the wenche he crepte.
This wenche lay uprighte and faste slepte,
Til he so ny was, er she myghte espie,   4195
That it had been to late for to crie,
And shortly for to seyn, they were aton.
Now pley, Aleyn, for I wol speke of John.

    This John lith stille a furlong wey or two,
And to hymself he maketh routhe and wo.   4200
"Allas!" quod he, "this is a wikked jape;
Now may I seyn that I is but an ape.
Yet has my felawe somwhat for his harm;
He has the milleris doghter in his arm.
He auntred hym, and has his nedes sped,   4205
And I lye as a draf-sak in my bed;
And when this jape is tald another day,
I sal been halde a daf, a cokenay!
I wil arise and auntre it, by my fayth!
'Unhardy is unseely,' thus men sayth."   4210
And up he roos, and softely he wente
Unto the cradel, and in his hand it hente,
And baar it softe unto his beddes feet.
    Soone after this the wyf hir rowtyng leet,
And gan awake, and wente hire out to pisse,   4215
And cam agayn, and gan hir cradel mysse,
And groped heer and ther, but she foond noon.
"Allas!" quod she, "I hadde almoost mysgoon;
I hadde almoost goon to the clerkes bed.
Ey, benedicite! Thanne hadde I foule ysped!"   4220
And forth she gooth til she the cradel fond.
She gropeth alwey forther with hir hond,
And foond the bed, and thoghte noght but good,
By cause that the cradel by it stood,
And nyste wher she was, for it was derk;   4225

4157 **sowke:** suck
4158 **crowke:** crock
4161 **hem nedede:** they needed   **dwale:** sleeping potion
4162 **wisely:** surely   **bibbed:** imbibed
4163 **fnorteth:** snorts
4165 **burdon:** bass accompaniment
4166 **rowtyng:** snoring
4167 **rowteth:** snores   **par compaignye:** for fellowship's sake, to keep them company
4170 **slyk a sang:** such a song (Nth)
4171 **swilk a complyn:** such a compline, last service of the day   **ymel:** among (Nth)
4172 **wilde fyr:** erysipelas, an acute inflammation of the skin (?)
4173 **Wha:** who (Nth)   **ferly:** amazing
4174 **flour of il endyng:** the best (i.e., worst) of a bad end
4175 **lange:** long (Nth)   **tydes me na reste:** I get no sleep
4176 **na fors:** no matter
4178 **swyve:** copulate with
4179 **esement:** compensation, redress
4181 **gif:** if   **a point:** one point   **agreved:** injured
4182 **sal be releved:** shall be compensated
4183 **it is na nay:** it cannot be denied
4184 **il fit:** hard time
4185 **neen:** none, no (Nth)
4186 **Agayn:** in return for
4187 **sale:** soul (Nth)

4188 **avyse thee:** think carefully
4190 **abreyde:** start, awake
4191 **vileynye:** injury
4192 **nat a flye:** i.e., not at all
4197 **aton:** at one, together
4199 **a furlong wey or two:** five minutes or so
4200 **maketh routhe:** pities (feels sorry for himself)
4201 **jape:** trick
4202 **ape:** fool
4205 **auntred hym:** took a risk   **his nedes sped:** accomplished his purpose
4206 **draf-sak:** sack of chaff or rubbish
4208 **halde a daf:** considered a fool   **cokenay:** weakling
4210 **Unhardy is unseely:** the timid one is unlucky   **men sayth:** it is said (*men* = one)
4214 **hir rowtyng leet:** stopped her snoring
4218 **mysgoon:** gone astray
4225 **nyste** = *ne wiste,* did not know

But faire and wel she creep in to the clerk,
And lith ful stille, and wolde han caught a sleep.
Withinne a while this John the clerk up leep,
And on this goode wyf he leith on soore.
So myrie a fit ne hadde she nat ful yoore;   4230
He priketh harde and depe as he were mad.
This joly lyf han thise two clerkes lad
Til that the thridde cok bigan to synge.

 Aleyn wax wery in the dawenynge,
For he had swonken al the longe nyght,   4235
And seyde, "Fare weel, Malyne, sweete wight!
The day is come; I may no lenger byde;
But everemo, wher so I go or ryde,
I is thyn awen clerk, swa have I seel!"   4239
 "Now, deere lemman," quod she, "go, far weel!
But er thow go, o thyng I wol thee telle:
Whan that thou wendest homward by the melle,
Right at the entree of the dore bihynde
Thou shalt a cake of half a busshel fynde
That was ymaked of thyn owene mele,   4245
Which that I heelp my sire for to stele.
And, goode lemman, God thee save and kepe!"
And with that word almoost she gan to wepe.

 Aleyn up rist, and thoughte, "Er that it dawe,
I wol go crepen in by my felawe,"   4250
And fond the cradel with his hand anon.
"By God," thoughte he, "al wrang I have mysgon.
Myn heed is toty of my swynk to-nyght,
That makes me that I ga nat aright.
I woot wel by the cradel I have mysgo;   4255
Heere lith the millere and his wyf also."
And forth he goth, a twenty devel way,
Unto the bed ther as the millere lay.
He wende have cropen by his felawe John,
And by the millere in he creep anon,   4260
And caughte hym by the nekke, and softe he spak.

He seyde, "Thou John, thou swynes-heed, awak,
For Cristes saule, and heer a noble game.
For by that lord that called is Seint Jame,
As I have thries in this shorte nyght   4265
Swyved the milleres doghter bolt upright,
Whil thow hast, as a coward, been agast."
 "Ye, false harlot," quod the millere, "hast?
A, false traitour! False clerk!" quod he,
"Thow shalt be deed, by Goddes dignitee!   4270
Who dorste be so boold to disparage
My doghter, that is come of swich lynage?"
And by the throte-bolle he caughte Alayn,
And he hente hym despitously agayn,
And on the nose he smoot hym with his fest.   4275
Doun ran the blody streem upon his brest;
And in the floor, with nose and mouth tobroke,
They walwe as doon two pigges in a poke;
And up they goon, and doun agayn anon,
Til that the millere sporned at a stoon,   4280
And doun he fil bakward upon his wyf,
That wiste no thyng of this nyce stryf;
For she was falle aslepe a lite wight
With John the clerk, that waked hadde al nyght,
And with the fal out of hir sleep she breyde.   4285
"Help! hooly croys of Bromeholm," she seyde,
"*In manus tuas!* Lord, to thee I calle!
Awak, Symond! The feend is on me falle.
Myn herte is broken; help! I nam but deed!
Ther lyth oon upon my wombe and on myn heed.   4290
Help, Symkyn, for the false clerkes fighte!"
 This John stirte up as faste as ever he myghte,
And graspeth by the walles to and fro,
To fynde a staf; and she stirte up also,
And knew the estres bet than dide this John,   4295
And by the wal a staf she foond anon,
And saugh a litel shymeryng of a light,

For at an hole in shoon the moone bright,
And by that light she saugh hem bothe two,
But sikerly she nyste who was who,   4300
But as she saugh a whit thyng in hir ye.
And whan she gan this white thyng espye,
She wende the clerk hadde wered a volupeer,
And with the staf she drow ay neer and neer,
And wende han hit this Aleyn at the fulle,   4305
And smoot the millere on the pyled skulle,
That doun he gooth, and cride, "Harrow! I dye!"
Thise clerkes beete hym weel and lete hym lye,
And greythen hem, and tooke hir hors anon,
And eek hire mele, and on hir wey they gon.   4310
And at the mille yet they tooke hir cake

Of half a busshel flour, ful wel ybake.
    Thus is the proude millere wel ybete,
And hath ylost the gryndynge of the whete,
And payed for the soper everideel   4315
Of Aleyn and of John, that bette hym weel.
His wyf is swyved, and his doghter als.
Lo, swich it is a millere to be fals!
And therfore this proverbe is seyd ful sooth,
"Hym thar nat wene wel that yvele dooth."   4320
A gylour shal hymself bigyled be.
And God, that sitteth heighe in magestee,
Save al this compaignye, grete and smale!
Thus have I quyt the Millere in my tale.   4324

Heere is ended the Reves Tale.

The Cook's Prologue

The prologe of the Cokes Tale.

    The Cook of Londoun, whil the Reve spak,
For joye him thoughte he clawed him on the bak.
"Ha! ha!" quod he, "For Cristes passion,
This millere hadde a sharp conclusion
Upon his argument of herbergage!
Wel seyde Salomon in his langage,   4330
'Ne bryng nat every man into thyn hous,'
For herberwynge by nyghte is perilous.
Wel oghte a man avysed for to be
Whom that he broghte into his pryvetee.
I pray to God, so yeve me sorwe and care   4335
If evere, sitthe I highte Hogge of Ware,
Herde I a millere bettre yset a-werk.
He hadde a jape of malice in the derk.

But God forbede that we stynte heere;
And therfore, if ye vouche-sauf to heere   4340
A tale of me, that am a povre man,
I wol yow telle, as wel as evere I kan,
A litel jape that fil in oure citee."
    Oure Hoost answerde and seide, "I graunte it thee.
Now telle on, Roger; looke that it be good,   4345
For many a pastee hastow laten blood,
And many a Jakke of Dovere hastow soold
That hath been twies hoot and twies coold.
Of many a pilgrym hastow Cristes curs,
For of thy percely yet they fare the wors,   4350
That they han eten with thy stubbel goos,
For in thy shoppe is many a flye loos.

4303 **volupeer:** nightcap
4305 **at the fulle:** squarely
4306 **pyled:** bald
4307 **Harrow!:** Help!
4309 **greythen hem:** dress
4311 **cake:** loaf

4326 **clawed him on the bak:** scratched his back (he so enjoyed the tale it seemed as if the Reeve were scratching his back)
4328–29 **conclusion Upon his argument:** proposition derived from disputation
4332 **herberwynge:** providing lodging
4333 **avysed for to be:** to take heed
4336 **Hogge of Ware:** Roger of Ware (a town in Hertfordshire, some thirty miles from London)
4337 **yset a-werk:** tricked (cf. III.215)

4316 **bette:** beat
4320 One who does evil should not (literally, need not) expect good.
4321 **gylour:** deceiver
4324 **quyt:** repaid

4340 **vouche-sauf:** grant, agree
4344 **graunte it thee:** agree
4346 **pastee:** meat pie   **laten blood:** let blood (draw off the gravy from unsold pies to make them keep longer)
4347 **Jakke of Dovere:** a kind of pie
4349 **Cristes curs:** damnation
4350 **percely:** parsley
4351 **stubbel goos:** fat goose that had been fed on stubble

Now telle on, gentil Roger by thy name.
But yet I pray thee, be nat wroth for game;
A man may seye ful sooth in game and pley."   4355
    "Thou seist ful sooth," quod Roger, "by my fey!
But 'sooth pley, quaad pley,' as the Flemyng seith.
And therfore, Herry Bailly, by thy feith,

Be thou nat wrooth, er we departen heer,
Though that my tale be of an hostileer.   4360
But nathelees I wol nat telle it yit;
But er we parte, ywis, thou shalt be quit."
And therwithal he lough and made cheere,
And seyde his tale, as ye shul after heere.

The Cook's Tale

Heere bigynneth the Cookes Tale.

A prentys whilom dwelled in oure citee,   4365
And of a craft of vitailliers was hee.
Gaillard he was as goldfynch in the shawe,
Broun as a berye, a propre short felawe,
With lokkes blake, ykembd ful fetisly.
Dauncen he koude so wel and jolily   4370
That he was cleped Perkyn Revelour.
He was as ful of love and paramour
As is the hyve ful of hony sweete;
Wel was the wenche with hym myghte meete.
At every bridale wolde he synge and hoppe;   4375
He loved bet the taverne than the shoppe.
For whan ther any ridyng was in Chepe,
Out of the shoppe thider wolde he lepe—
Til that he hadde al the sighte yseyn,
And daunced wel, he wolde nat come ayeyn—   4380
And gadered hym a meynee of his sort
To hoppe and synge and maken swich disport;
And ther they setten stevene for to meete,
To pleyen at the dys in swich a streete.
For in the toune nas ther no prentys   4385
That fairer koude caste a paire of dys
Than Perkyn koude, and therto he was free
Of his dispense, in place of pryvetee.
That fond his maister wel in his chaffare,

For often tyme he foond his box ful bare.   4390
For sikerly a prentys revelour
That haunteth dys, riot, or paramour,
His maister shal it in his shoppe abye,
Al have he no part of the mynstralcye.
For thefte and riot, they been convertible,   4395
Al konne he pleye on gyterne or ribible.
Revel and trouthe, as in a lowe degree,
They been ful wrothe al day, as men may see.
    This joly prentys with his maister bood,
Til he were ny out of his prentishood,   4400
Al were he snybbed bothe erly and late,
And somtyme lad with revel to Newegate.
But atte laste his maister hym bithoghte,
Upon a day, whan he his papir soghte,
Of a proverbe that seith this same word: 4405
"Wel bet is roten appul out of hoord
Than that it rotie al the remenaunt."
So fareth it by a riotous servaunt;

4360 **hostileer:** innkeeper
4363 **lough:** laughed

4390 **box:** strongbox
4391 **revelour:** reveller, profligate
4392 **haunteth:** makes a habit of   **dys:** dicing, gambling   **riot:** debauchery
paramour: womanizing
4393 **abye:** pay for
4394 **he:** the master   **mynstralcye:** entertainment (for which he pays)
4395 **convertible:** interchangeable
4396 Even though he knows how to play a cithern (*gyterne*) or fiddle (*ribible*, rebeck)
4397–98 Revelling and honesty, in a man of low rank, are always angry (i.e., incompatible) with each other.
4399 **bood:** remained
4400 **prentishood:** apprenticeship
4401 **snybbed:** rebuked
4402 **Newegate:** Newgate prison
4404 **he:** Perkyn   **papir:** probably his written certificate of release
4407 **rotie:** rot
4408 **by:** with respect to, with   **riotous:** dissolute

4357 **sooth pley, quaad pley:** A true jest is a bad jest.

4365 **prentys:** apprentice
4366 **vitailliers:** victuallers, sellers of food
4367 **Gaillard:** merry   **shawe:** wood, thicket
4368 **Broun as a berye:** very dark-complexioned
4372 **paramour:** wenching
4375 **bridale:** wedding party   **hoppe:** dance
4377 **ridyng:** procession, equestrian display   **Chepe:** Cheapside
4381 **meynee:** company
4383 **setten stevene:** made an appointment
4388 **place of pryvetee:** a private place
4389 **chaffare:** business

It is ful lasse harm to lete hym pace,
Than he shende alle the servantz in the place.   4410
Therfore his maister yaf hym acquitance,
And bad hym go, with sorwe and with meschance!
And thus this joly prentys hadde his leve.
Now lat hym riote al the nyght or leve.
And for ther is no theef withoute a lowke,   4415

That helpeth hym to wasten and to sowke
Of that he brybe kan or borwe may,
Anon he sente his bed and his array
Unto a compeer of his owene sort,
That lovede dys, and revel, and disport,   4420
And hadde a wyf that heeld for contenance
A shoppe, and swyved for hir sustenance.

4409 **pace:** go away
4410 **shende:** corrupt
4412 **meschance:** bad luck to him
4413 **leve:** permission to leave
4414 **riote:** revel, engage in debauchery
4415 There is no thief without an accomplice (*lowke*).

4416 **sowke:** suck (expend)
4417 **brybe:** steal
4419 **compeer:** companion
4421 **contenance:** the sake of appearances
4422 **swyved for hir sustenance:** copulated for a living

Introduction to the Man of Law's Tale

The wordes of the Hoost to the compaignye.

Oure Hooste saugh wel that the brighte sonne
The ark of his artificial day hath ronne
The ferthe part, and half an houre and moore,
And though he were nat depe ystert in loore,
He wiste it was the eightetethe day   5
Of Aprill, that is messager to May;
And saugh wel that the shadwe of every tree
Was as in lengthe the same quantitee
That was the body erect that caused it.
And therfore by the shadwe he took his wit   10
That Phebus, which that shoon so clere and brighte,
Degrees was fyve and fourty clombe on highte,
And for that day, as in that latitude,
It was ten of the clokke, he gan conclude,
And sodeynly he plighte his hors aboute.   15
    "Lordynges," quod he, "I warne yow, al this route,
The fourthe party of this day is gon.
Now for the love of God and of Seint John,
Leseth no tyme, as ferforth as ye may.
Lordynges, the tyme wasteth nyght and day,   20
And steleth from us, what pryvely slepynge,
And what thurgh necligence in oure wakynge,
As dooth the streem that turneth nevere agayn,
Descendynge fro the montaigne into playn.
Wel kan Senec and many a philosophre   25
Biwaillen tyme moore than gold in cofre;
For 'Los of catel may recovered be,
But los of tyme shendeth us,' quod he.
It wol nat come agayn, withouten drede,
Namoore than wole Malkynes maydenhede,   30

Whan she hath lost it in hir wantownesse.
Lat us nat mowlen thus in ydelnesse.
    "Sire Man of Lawe," quod he, "so have ye blis,
Telle us a tale anon, as forward is.
Ye been submytted, thurgh youre free assent,   35
To stonden in this cas at my juggement.
Acquiteth yow now of youre biheeste;
Thanne have ye do youre devoir atte leeste."
    "Hooste," quod he, "*depardieux*, ich assente;
To breke forward is nat myn entente.   40
Biheste is dette, and I wole holde fayn
Al my biheste, I kan no bettre sayn.
For swich lawe as a man yeveth another wight,
He sholde hymselven usen it, by right;
Thus wole oure text. But nathelees, certeyn,   45
I kan right now no thrifty tale seyn
That Chaucer, thogh he kan but lewedly
On metres and on rymyng craftily,
Hath seyd hem in swich Englissh as he kan
Of olde tyme, as knoweth many a man;   50
And if he have noght seyd hem, leve brother,
In o book, he hath seyd hem in another.
For he hath toold of loveris up and doun
Mo than Ovide made of mencioun
In his Episteles, that been ful olde.   55
What sholde I tellen hem, syn they been tolde?
    "In youthe he made of Ceys and Alcione,
And sitthen hath he spoken of everichone,
Thise noble wyves and thise loveris eke.
Whoso that wole his large volume seke,   60

---

2 **ark of his artificial day:** the time the sun is above the horizon; see n. for the Host's calculation of time.
3 **ferthe:** fourth
4 **depe ystert in loore:** far advanced in learning
5 **eightetethe:** eighteenth
10 **took his wit:** judged
11 **Phebus:** the sun
12 **was . . . clombe:** had climbed
15 **plighte:** pulled
17 **party:** part
19 **as ferforth as:** insofar as
21 **what:** what with
28 **shendeth:** ruins
29 **drede:** doubt
30 **Malkynes maydenhede:** Malkin's virginity

32 **mowlen:** grow moldy
37 **Acquiteth yow . . . of:** acquit yourself of (fulfill)   **biheeste:** promise
38 **devoir:** duty
39 **depardieux:** in God's name
41 **Biheste is dette:** A promise is an obligation
45 **wole:** says
46 **thrifty:** suitable
47–8 **kan but lewedly On:** knows little about
49 **Hath** = *nath*, has not
50 **Of olde tyme:** long ago
54 **made of mencioun:** made mention of
55 **Episteles:** Ovid's *Heroides*
57 **made of Ceys and Alcione:** wrote about Ceyx and Alcion; see BD 62–220.
59 **eke:** also
60 **seke:** examine

Cleped the Seintes Legende of Cupide,
Ther may he seen the large woundes wyde
Of Lucresse, and of Babilan Tesbee;
The swerd of Dido for the false Enee;
The tree of Phillis for hire Demophon;   65
The pleinte of Dianire and of Hermyon,
Of Adriane, and of Isiphilee—
The bareyne yle stondynge in the see—
The dreynte Leandre for his Erro;
The teeris of Eleyne, and eek the wo   70
Of Brixseyde, and of the, Ladomya;
The crueltee of the, queene Medea,
Thy litel children hangynge by the hals,
For thy Jason, that was of love so fals!
O Ypermystra, Penelopee, Alceste,   75
Youre wifhod he comendeth with the beste!

    "But certeinly no word ne writeth he
Of thilke wikke ensample of Canacee,
That loved hir owene brother synfully—
Of swiche cursed stories I sey fy!—   80
Or ellis of Tyro Appollonius,
How that the cursed kyng Antiochus
Birafte his doghter of hir maydenhede,
That is so horrible a tale for to rede,
Whan he hir threw upon the pavement.   85
And therfore he, of ful avysement,
Nolde nevere write in none of his sermons
Of swiche unkynde abhomynacions,
Ne I wol noon reherce, if that I may.

    "But of my tale how shal I doon this day?   90
Me were looth be likned, doutelees,
To Muses that men clepe Pierides—
Methamorphosios woot what I mene;
But nathelees, I recche noght a bene
Though I come after hym with hawebake.   95

I speke in prose, and lat him rymes make."
And with that word he, with a sobre cheere,
Bigan his tale, as ye shal after heere.

The prologe of the Mannes Tale of Lawe.

    O hateful harm, condicion of poverte!   99
With thurst, with coold, with hunger so confoundid!
To asken help thee shameth in thyn herte;
If thou noon aske, with nede artow so woundid
That verray nede unwrappeth al thy wounde hid!
Maugree thyn heed, thou most for indigence
Or stele, or begge, or borwe thy despence!   105

Thow blamest Crist and seist ful bitterly
He mysdeparteth richesse temporal;
Thy neighebor thou wytest synfully,
And seist thou hast to lite and he hath al.
"Parfay," seistow, "somtyme he rekene shal,   110
Whan that his tayl shal brennen in the gleede,
For he noght helpeth needfulle in hir neede."

    Herkne what is the sentence of the wise:
"Bet is to dyen than have indigence";
"Thy selve neighebor wol thee despise."   115
If thou be povre, farwel thy reverence!
Yet of the wise man take this sentence:
"Alle the dayes of povre men been wikke."
Be war, therfore, er thou come to that prikke!

If thou be povre, thy brother hateth thee,   120
And alle thy freendes fleen from thee, allas!
O riche marchauntz, ful of wele been yee,
O noble, o prudent folk, as in this cas!
Youre bagges been nat fild with ambes as,
But with sys cynk, that renneth for youre chaunce;
At Cristemasse myrie may ye daunce!   126

61 **the Seintes Legende of Cupide:** the Legend of Good Women
63 **Lucresse, and of Babilan Tesbee:** Lucretia, Thisbe of Babylon; see LGW for the
stories of the women listed in lines 63–76, except for *Dianire* (Deianira; see MkT
VII.2119–35), *Hermyon* (Hermione, the lover of Orestes), *Erro* (Hero, the lover of
Leandre, Leander), *Eleyne* (Helen of Troy), *Brixseyde* (Briseyde, the lover of Achilles;
see HF 398), *Ladomya* (Laodomia, who killed herself on the death of her husband
Protesilaus), and *Penelopee* (Penelope, faithful wife of Ulysses).
66 **pleinte:** complaint, lament
68 **bareyne:** barren
69 **dreynte:** drowned
73 **hals:** neck
76 **wifhod:** fidelity as a wife
78 **Canacee:** heroine of a tale of incest told by Gower; see n. to lines 77–89.
81 **Tyro Appollonius:** Apollonius of Tyre, hero of a popular story, also involving
incest, told in Gower's *Confessio Amantis*
83 **Birafte:** deprived
86 **of ful avysement:** after careful consideration
88 **unkynde:** unnatural
91 **Me were looth:** I would hate
92 **Pierides:** the Muses; see n. to lines 91–92.
93 **Methamorphosios:** Ovid's *Metamorphoses*
94 **recche noght a bene:** don't care a bean
95 **hawebake:** baked hawthorn berries (a poor dish)

97 **a sobre cheere:** a solemn expression
99 **harm:** misfortune
100 **confoundid:** distressed
103 **unwrappeth:** discloses
104 **Maugree thyn heed:** against your will, despite all you can do
105 **Or . . . or:** either . . . or   **despence:** living expenses
107 **mysdeparteth:** wrongly allots
108 **wytest:** accuse
109 **to lite:** too little
110 **Parfay:** by my faith   **rekene:** take account (of it)
111 **brennen in the gleede:** burn in the live coals
112 **needfulle:** the needy
115 **selve:** very
116 **reverence:** respect (that others show you)
118 **wikke:** miserable
119 **prikke:** point
124 **ambes as:** two ones, a losing throw in dice
125 **sys cynk:** six and five, a winning throw   **renneth for youre chaunce:** runs in
favor of your luck (*chaunce* = winning number)

Ye seken lond and see for yowre wynnynges;
As wise folk ye knowen al th'estaat
Of regnes; ye been fadres of tidynges
And tales, bothe of pees and of debaat.   130

I were right now of tales desolaat,
Nere that a marchant, goon is many a yeere,
Me taughte a tale, which that ye shal heere.

The Man of Law's Tale

Heere begynneth the Man of Lawe his tale.

In Surrye whilom dwelte a compaignye
Of chapmen riche, and therto sadde and trewe,   135
That wyde-where senten hir spicerye,
Clothes of gold, and satyns riche of hewe.
Hir chaffare was so thrifty and so newe
That every wight hath deyntee to chaffare
With hem, and eek to sellen hem hire ware.   140

Now fil it that the maistres of that sort
Han shapen hem to Rome for to wende;
Were it for chapmanhod or for disport,
Noon oother message wolde they thider sende,
But comen hemself to Rome; this is the ende.   145
And in swich place as thoughte hem avantage
For hire entente, they take hir herbergage.

Sojourned han thise merchantz in that toun
A certein tyme, as fil to hire plesance.
And so bifel that th'excellent renoun   150
Of the Emperoures doghter, dame Custance,
Reported was, with every circumstance,
Unto thise Surryen marchantz in swich wyse,
Fro day to day, as I shal yow devyse.

This was the commune voys of every man: 155
"Oure Emperour of Rome—God hym see!—

A doghter hath that, syn the world bigan,
To rekene as wel hir goodnesse as beautee,
Nas nevere swich another as is shee.
I prey to God in honour hire susteene,   160
And wolde she were of al Europe the queene.

"In hire is heigh beautee, withoute pride,
Yowthe, withoute grenehede or folye;
To alle hire werkes vertu is hir gyde;
Humblesse hath slayn in hire al tirannye.   165
She is mirour of alle curteisye;
Hir herte is verray chambre of hoolynesse,
Hir hand, ministre of fredam for almesse."

And al this voys was sooth, as God is trewe.
But now to purpos lat us turne agayn.   170
Thise marchantz han doon fraught hir shippes newe,
And whan they han this blisful mayden sayn,
Hoom to Surrye been they went ful fayn,
And doon hir nedes as they han doon yoore,
And lyven in wele; I kan sey yow namoore.   175

Now fil it that thise marchantz stode in grace
Of hym that was the Sowdan of Surrye;
For whan they cam from any strange place,
He wolde, of his benigne curteisye,
Make hem good chiere, and bisily espye   180

---

130 **debaat:** conflict

134 **Surrye:** Syria
135 **chapmen:** merchants   **sadde:** trustworthy
136 **wyde-where:** far and wide   **spicerye:** oriental goods (spices, cloths, and such)
138 **chaffare:** merchandise   **thrifty:** serviceable
139 **hath deyntee to chaffare:** is eager to do business
140 **ware:** wares
142 **shapen hem:** arranged
143 **chapmanhod:** business dealings   **disport:** amusement
144 **message:** messenger
146 **avantage:** advantageous
147 **herbergage:** lodging
148 **Sojourned:** remained
149 **fil to hire plesance:** accorded with their desires
152 **circumstance:** detail
155 **voys:** opinion
156 **God hym see:** may God look after him

131 **of tales desolaat:** lacking in tales
132 **Nere** = *ne were,* were (it) not

160 **susteene:** sustain
163 **grenehede:** immaturity
168 **fredam for almesse:** generosity in giving alms
169 **voys:** report
170 **to purpos:** to the point
171 **han doon fraught:** have had loaded   **newe:** anew
172 **sayn:** seen
174 **doon hir nedes:** conducted their business   **yoore:** formerly
176 **grace:** the good graces
177 **Sowdan:** sultan
178 **strange:** foreign
179 **benigne:** gracious

Tidynges of sondry regnes, for to leere
The wondres that they myghte seen or heere.

Amonges othere thynges, specially,
Thise marchantz han hym toold of dame Custance
So greet noblesse in ernest, ceriously,   185
That this Sowdan hath caught so greet plesance
To han hir figure in his remembrance,
That al his lust and al his bisy cure
Was for to love hire while his lyf may dure.

Paraventure in thilke large book   190
Which that men clepe the hevene ywriten was
With sterres, whan that he his birthe took,
That he for love sholde han his deeth, allas!
For in the sterres, clerer than is glas,
Is writen, God woot, whoso koude it rede,   195
The deeth of every man, withouten drede.

In sterres, many a wynter therbiforn,
Was writen the deeth of Ector, Achilles,
Of Pompei, Julius, er they were born;
The strif of Thebes; and of Ercules,   200
Of Sampson, Turnus, and of Socrates
The deeth; but mennes wittes ben so dulle
That no wight kan wel rede it atte fulle.

    This Sowdan for his privee conseil sente,
And, shortly of this matiere for to pace,   205
He hath to hem declared his entente,
And seyde hem, certein, but he myghte have grace
To han Custance withinne a litel space,
He nas but deed; and charged hem in hye
To shapen for his lyf som remedye.   210

    Diverse men diverse thynges seyden;
They argumenten, casten up and doun;
Many a subtil resoun forth they leyden;
They speken of magyk and abusioun.

But finally, as in conclusioun,   215
They kan nat seen in that noon avantage,
Ne in noon oother wey, save mariage.

Thanne sawe they therinne swich difficultee
By wey of reson, for to speke al playn,
By cause that ther was swich diversitee   220
Bitwene hir bothe lawes, that they sayn
They trowe that no "Cristen prince wolde fayn
Wedden his child under oure lawe sweete
That us was taught by Mahoun, oure prophete."

    And he answerde, "Rather than I lese   225
Custance, I wol be cristned, douteles.
I moot been hires; I may noon oother chese.
I prey yow hoold youre argumentz in pees;
Saveth my lyf, and beth noght recchelees
To geten hire that hath my lyf in cure,   230
For in this wo I may nat longe endure."

    What nedeth gretter dilatacioun?
I seye, by tretys and embassadrie,
And by the popes mediacioun,
And al the chirche, and al the chivalrie,   235
That in destruccioun of mawmettrie,
And in encrees of Cristes lawe deere,
They been acorded, so as ye shal heere:

How that the Sowdan and his baronage
And alle his liges sholde ycristned be,   240
And he shal han Custance in mariage,
And certein gold, I noot what quantitee;
And heer-to founden sufficient suretee.
This same accord was sworn on eyther syde;
Now, faire Custance, almyghty God thee gyde!   245

    Now wolde som men waiten, as I gesse,
That I sholde tellen al the purveiance
That th'Emperour, of his grete noblesse,
Hath shapen for his doghter, dame Custance.
Wel may men knowen that so greet ordinance   250
May no man tellen in a litel clause
As was arrayed for so heigh a cause.

181 **sondry:** various   **leere:** learn
185 **ceriously:** in detail
186 **plesance:** desire
187 **figure:** image
188 **lust:** pleasure   **bisy cure:** intent concern
190 **Paraventure:** perhaps
195 **rede:** interpret
198 **Ector, Achilles:** Hector and Achilles, the Greek heroes
199 **Pompei, Julius:** Pompey the Great, Julius Caesar; see MkT VII.2671–2726.
200 **strif of Thebes:** the siege of Thebes, told in part in Tr 5.1457–1512   **Ercules:** Hercules; see MkT VII.2095–2142.
201 **Sampson:** the biblical hero; see MkT VII.2015–94.   **Turnus:** opponent of Aeneas; see HF 457–58.   **Socrates:** the philosopher; see Bo 1.pr3.26–28.
204 **privee conseil:** privy council, confidential advisors
205 **pace:** pass over
208 **space:** time
209 **nas but deed:** was as good as dead   **charged:** commanded   **in hye:** in haste
212 **argumenten:** dispute, argue   **casten up and doun:** consider alternatives
214 **abusioun:** deception

221 **hir bothe lawes:** religions of both parties
222 **trowe:** suppose, judge
224 **Mahoun:** Mohammed
229 **recchelees:** negligent
230 **in cure:** in her keeping
232 **dilatacioun:** increase of words
233 **tretys:** treaty   **embassadrie:** negociation
236 **mawmettrie:** idolatry
243 **heer-to founden:** for this provided
246 **waiten:** expect
247 **purveiance:** preparations
250 **ordinance:** preparations

Bisshopes been shapen with hire for to wende,
Lordes, ladies, knyghtes of renoun,
And oother folk ynowe; this is th'ende; 255
And notified is thurghout the toun
That every wight, with greet devocioun,
Sholde preyen Crist that he this mariage
Receyve in gree and spede this viage.

    The day is comen of hir departynge; 260
I seye, the woful day fatal is come,
That ther may be no lenger tariynge,
But forthward they hem dressen, alle and some.
Custance, that was with sorwe al overcome,
Ful pale arist, and dresseth hire to wende; 265
For wel she seeth ther is noon oother ende.

Allas, what wonder is it thogh she wepte,
That shal be sent to strange nacioun
Fro freendes that so tendrely hire kepte,
And to be bounden under subjeccioun 270
Of oon, she knoweth nat his condicioun?
Housbondes been alle goode, and han ben yoore;
That knowen wyves; I dar sey yow na moore.

    "Fader," she seyde, "thy wrecched child Custance,
Thy yonge doghter fostred up so softe, 275
And ye, my mooder, my soverayn plesance
Over alle thyng, out-taken Crist on-lofte,
Custance youre child hire recomandeth ofte
Unto youre grace, for I shal to Surrye,
Ne shal I nevere seen yow moore with ye. 280

"Allas, unto the Barbre nacioun
I moste anoon, syn that it is youre wille;
But Crist, that starf for our redempcioun
So yeve me grace his heestes to fulfille!
I, wrecche womman, no fors though I spille! 285
Wommen are born to thraldom and penance,
And to been under mannes governance."

I trowe at Troye, whan Pirrus brak the wal
Or Ilion brende, at Thebes the citee,
N'at Rome, for the harm thurgh Hanybal 290
That Romayns hath venquysshed tymes thre,
Nas herd swich tendre wepyng for pitee
As in the chambre was for hire departynge;
But forth she moot, wher-so she wepe or synge.

O firste moevyng! Crueel firmament, 295
With thy diurnal sweigh that crowdest ay
And hurlest al from est til occident
That naturelly wolde holde another way,
Thy crowdyng set the hevene in swich array
At the bigynnyng of this fiers viage, 300
That crueel Mars hath slayn this mariage.

Infortunat ascendent tortuous,
Of which the lord is helplees falle, allas,
Out of his angle into the derkeste hous!
O Mars, o atazir, as in this cas! 305
O fieble moone, unhappy been thy paas!
Thou knyttest thee ther thou art nat receyved;
Ther thou were weel, fro thennes artow weyved.

Imprudent Emperour of Rome, allas!
Was ther no philosophre in al thy toun? 310
Is no tyme bet than oother in swich cas?
Of viage is ther noon eleccioun,
Namely to folk of heigh condicioun?
Noght whan a roote is of a burthe yknowe?
Allas, we been to lewed or to slowe! 315

256 **notified:** made known
259 **in gree:** favorably
263 **hem dressen:** prepare themselves **alle and some:** one and all
265 **arist** = *ariseth*, arises
271 **condicioun:** disposition
272 **yoore:** long since
275 **softe:** tenderly
277 **out-taken:** except **on-lofte:** on high
278 **hire recomandeth:** commends herself
279 **shal:** must go (the verb of motion is understood)
281 **Barbre nacioun:** pagan world
282 **moste:** must go
283 **starf:** died
285 **wrecche:** exiled **no fors:** no matter **spille:** die
286 **penance:** suffering
287 **governance:** control

288 **Pirrus:** Pyrrhus, one of the Greek warriors at Troy
289 **Or:** ere **Ilion:** the citadel of Troy **Thebes:** destroyed in a siege
290 **Hanybal:** Hannibal, the Carthaginian general who attacked Rome
294 **wher-so:** whether
295 **firste moevyng:** primum mobile, the outermost of the nine heavenly spheres; see n. to lines 295–301.
296 **diurnal sweigh:** daily motion **crowdest:** pushes
297 **est til occident:** east to west
298 The stars are naturally inclined to move from west to east (see n. to lines 295–301 for the astronomical details).
299 **array:** arrangement
300 **fiers:** dangerous
302–8 According to the theory of judicial astronomy, at the time of Custance's departure the position of the heavenly bodies was unfavorable, especially because of the evil influence of Mars. See n. for a detailed analysis of the technical vocabulary.
302 **Infortunat ascendent tortuous:** inauspicious oblique ascending sign
303 **lord:** the "lord of the ascendent" (see n. to lines 302–8)
304 **angle:** a "house" at one of the cardinal compass points
305 **atazir:** the dominant planetary influence
306 **unhappy:** unfortunate **paas:** steps
307 You move into conjunction (*knyttest thee*) where you are not welcomed (by an auspicious planet).
308 **weyved:** banished
310 **philosophre:** astrologer
312 **eleccioun:** choice of an astrologically favorable time
313 **condicioun:** social position
314 **roote . . . of a burthe:** exact time of birth, which provides a date (*roote*) from which an astrological calculation can be made

To shippe is brought this woful faire mayde
Solempnely, with every circumstance.
"Now Jhesu Crist be with yow alle!" she sayde;
Ther nys namoore, but "Farewel, faire Custance!"
She peyneth hire to make good contenance;   320
And forth I lete hire saille in this manere,
And turne I wole agayn to my matere.

   The mooder of the Sowdan, welle of vices,
Espied hath hir sones pleyn entente,
How he wol lete his olde sacrifices;   325
And right anon she for hir conseil sente,
And they been come to knowe what she mente.
And whan assembled was this folk in-feere,
She sette hire doun, and seyde as ye shal heere.

   "Lordes," quod she, "ye knowen everichon,   330
How that my sone in point is for to lete
The hooly lawes of our Alkaron,
Yeven by Goddes message Makomete.
But oon avow to grete God I heete,
The lyf shal rather out of my body sterte   335
Or Makometes lawe out of myn herte!

"What sholde us tyden of this newe lawe
But thraldom to oure bodies and penance,
And afterward in helle to be drawe,
For we reneyed Mahoun oure creance?   340
But, lordes, wol ye maken assurance,
As I shal seyn, assentynge to my loore,
And I shal make us sauf for everemoore?"

   They sworen and assenten, every man,
To lyve with hire and dye, and by hire stonde,   345
And everich, in the beste wise he kan,
To strengthen hire shal alle his frendes fonde;
And she hath this emprise ytake on honde,
Which ye shal heren that I shal devyse,
And to hem alle she spak right in this wyse: 350

"We shul first feyne us cristendom to take—
Coold water shal nat greve us but a lite!—
And I shal swich a feeste and revel make
That, as I trowe, I shal the Sowdan quite.
For thogh his wyf be cristned never so white,   355
She shal have nede to wasshe awey the rede,
Thogh she a font-ful water with hire lede."

O Sowdanesse, roote of iniquitee!
Virago, thou Semyrame the secounde!
O serpent under femynynytee,   360
Lik to the serpent depe in helle ybounde!
O feyned womman, al that may confounde
Vertu and innocence, thurgh thy malice,
Is bred in thee, as nest of every vice!

O Sathan, envious syn thilke day   365
That thou were chaced from oure heritage,
Wel knowestow to wommen the olde way!
Thou madest Eva brynge us in servage;
Thou wolt fordoon this Cristen mariage.
Thyn instrument—so weylawey the while!—   370
Makestow of wommen, whan thou wolt bigile.

   This Sowdanesse, whom I thus blame and warye,
Leet prively hire conseil goon hire way.
What sholde I in this tale lenger tarye?
She rydeth to the Sowdan on a day,   375
And seyde hym that she wolde reneye hir lay,
And cristendom of preestes handes fonge,
Repentynge hire she hethen was so longe,

Bisechynge hym to doon hire that honour,
That she moste han the Cristen folk to feeste—   380
"To plesen hem I wol do my labour."
The Sowdan seith, "I wol doon at youre heeste,"
And knelynge thanketh hire of that requeste.
So glad he was, he nyste what to seye.
She kiste hir sone, and hoom she gooth hir weye.   385

Explicit prima pars.

---

317 **circumstance:** ceremony
320 **peyneth hire:** takes pains
325 **lete:** abandon
328 **in-feere:** together
331 **in point . . . for to lete:** on the point of leaving, forsaking
332 **Alkaron:** the Koran
333 **message:** messenger   **Makomete:** Mohammed
334 **heete:** promise
336 **Or:** before
337 **tyden:** happen to
340 **reneyed:** renounced   **creance:** belief
341 **maken assurance:** pledge
342 **loore:** teaching, advice
343 **sauf:** safe
346 **wise:** way
347 **fonde:** try (i.e., persuade to support her)
348 **emprise:** enterprise

351 **feyne us:** feign
357 **font-ful:** baptismal font full of   **lede:** bring
359 **Virago:** woman usurping man's office; see n.   **Semyrame:** Semiramis, a queen famed for her wickedness
360 **under femynynytee:** in a female form
361 **serpent:** Satan
362 **confounde:** destroy
369 **fordoon:** destroy
372 **warye:** curse
376 **reneye:** renounce   **lay:** religion
377 **fonge:** receive
381 **do my labour:** make an effort
382 **doon at youre heeste:** act according to your command   **Explicit,** *etc.*: Here ends the first part.

Sequitur pars secunda.

    Arryved been this Cristen folk to londe
In Surrye, with a greet solempne route,
And hastifliche this Sowdan sente his sonde
First to his mooder, and al the regne aboute,
And seyde his wyf was comen, out of doute,   390
And preyde hire for to ryde agayn the queene,
The honour of his regne to susteene.

Greet was the prees, and riche was th'array
Of Surryens and Romayns met yfeere;
The mooder of the Sowdan, riche and gay,   395
Receyveth hire with also glad a cheere
As any mooder myghte hir doghter deere,
And to the nexte citee ther bisyde
A softe paas solempnely they ryde.

    Noght trowe I the triumphe of Julius,   400
Of which that Lucan maketh swich a boost,
Was roialler ne moore curius
Than was th'assemblee of this blisful hoost.
But this scorpioun, this wikked goost,
The Sowdanesse, for al hire flaterynge,   405
Caste under this ful mortally to stynge.

    The Sowdan comth hymself soone after this
So roially that wonder is to telle,
And welcometh hire with alle joye and blis.
And thus in murthe and joye I lete hem dwelle;   410
The fruyt of this matiere is that I telle.
Whan tyme cam, men thoughte it for the beste
That revel stynte, and men goon to hir reste.

    The tyme cam, this olde Sowdanesse
Ordeyned hath this feeste of which I tolde,   415
And to the feeste Cristen folk hem dresse
In general, ye, bothe yonge and olde.
Heere may men feeste and roialtee biholde,
And deyntees mo than I kan yow devyse;
But al to deere they boghte it er they ryse.   420

    O sodeyn wo, that evere art successour
To worldly blisse, spreynd with bitternesse,

The ende of the joye of oure worldly labour!
Wo occupieth the fyn of oure gladnesse.
Herke this conseil for thy sikernesse: 425
Upon thy glade day have in thy mynde
The unwar wo or harm that comth bihynde.

    For shortly for to tellen, at o word,
The Sowdan and the Cristen everichone
Been al tohewe and stiked at the bord,   430
But it were oonly dame Custance allone.
This olde Sowdanesse, cursed krone,
Hath with hir freendes doon this cursed dede,
For she hirself wolde al the contree lede.

    Ne ther was Surryen noon that was converted,   435
That of the conseil of the Sowdan woot,
That he nas al tohewe er he asterted.
And Custance han they take anon, foot-hoot,
And in a ship al steerelees, God woot,
They han hir set, and bidde hire lerne saille   440
Out of Surrye agaynward to Ytaille.

    A certein tresor that she thider ladde,
And, sooth to seyn, vitaille greet plentee
They han hire yeven, and clothes eek she hadde,
And forth she sailleth in the salte see.   445
O my Custance, ful of benignytee,
O Emperoures yonge doghter deere,
He that is lord of Fortune be thy steere!

    She blesseth hire, and with ful pitous voys
Unto the croys of Crist thus seyde she: 450
"O cleere, o welful auter, hooly croys,
Reed of the Lambes blood ful of pitee,
That wessh the world fro the olde iniquitee,
Me fro the feend and fro his clawes kepe,
That day that I shal drenchen in the depe.   455

    "Victorious tree, proteccioun of trewe,
That oonly worthy were for to bere
The Kyng of Hevene with his woundes newe,
The white Lamb, that hurt was with a spere,

Sequitur, *etc.*: The second part follows.
388 **sonde:** message
391 **agayn:** toward
393 **prees:** crowd
394 **met yfeere:** met together
399 **A softe paas:** slowly
400 **triumphe:** triumphal procession   **Julius:** Julius Caesar
401 **Lucan:** author of the Pharsalia   **boost:** boast
402 **curius:** elaborate
404 **goost:** demon
406 **Caste:** planned
411 **fruyt:** essential part
419 **deyntees:** delicacies
420 **al to deere they boghte it:** they paid only too dearly for it
422 **spreynd:** sprinkled

424 **fyn:** end
425 **sikernesse:** safety
427 **unwar:** unexpected
430 **tohewe:** cut to pieces   **stiked:** stabbed   **bord:** table
431 **But it were:** except for
432 **krone:** hag
437 **asterted:** escaped
438 **foot-hoot:** immediately
439 **steerelees:** without a rudder
441 **agaynward to:** back again to
442 **tresor:** treasure
443 **vitaille:** food
446 **benignytee:** goodness
448 **lord of Fortune:** i.e., God   **steere:** rudder, guide
451 **welful auter:** blessed altar
452 **Reed of:** red with
453 **wessh:** washed

Flemere of feendes out of hym and here   460
On which thy lymes feithfully extenden,
Me kepe, and yif me myght my lyf t'amenden."

Yeres and dayes fleet this creature
Thurghout the See of Grece unto the Strayte
Of Marrok, as it was hire aventure.   465
On many a sory meel now may she bayte;
After hir deeth ful often may she wayte,
Er that the wilde wawes wol hire dryve
Unto the place ther she shal arryve.

Men myghten asken why she was nat slayn   470
Eek at the feeste? Who myghte hir body save?
And I answere to that demande agayn,
Who saved Danyel in the horrible cave
Ther every wight save he, maister and knave,
Was with the leon frete er he asterte?   475
No wight but God that he bar in his herte.

God liste to shewe his wonderful myracle
In hire, for we sholde seen his myghty werkis;
Crist, which that is to every harm triacle,
By certeine meenes ofte, as knowen clerkis,   480
Dooth thyng for certein ende that ful derk is
To mannes wit, that for oure ignorance
Ne konne noght knowe his prudent purveiance.

Now sith she was nat at the feeste yslawe,
Who kepte hire fro the drenchyng in the see?   485
Who kepte Jonas in the fisshes mawe
Til he was spouted up at Nynyvee?
Wel may men knowe it was no wight but he
That kepte peple Ebrayk from hir drenchynge,
With drye feet thurghout the see passynge.   490

Who bad the foure spirites of tempest
That power han t'anoyen lond and see,
Bothe north and south, and also west and est,

"Anoyeth neither see, ne land, ne tree"?
Soothly, the comandour of that was he   495
That fro the tempest ay this womman kepte
As wel whan she wook as whan she slepte.

Where myghte this womman mete and drynke have
Thre yeer and moore? How lasteth hire vitaille?
Who fedde the Egipcien Marie in the cave,   500
Or in desert? No wight but Crist, sanz faille.
Fyve thousand folk it was as greet mervaille
With loves fyve and fisshes two to feede.
God sente his foyson at hir grete neede.

She dryveth forth into oure occian   505
Thurghout oure wilde see, til atte laste
Under an hoold that nempnen I ne kan,
Fer in Northhumberlond the wawe hire caste,
And in the sond hir ship stiked so faste
That thennes wolde it noght of al a tyde;   510
The wyl of Crist was that she sholde abyde.

The constable of the castel doun is fare
To seen this wrak, and al the ship he soghte,
And foond this wery womman ful of care;
He foond also the tresor that she broghte.   515
In hir langage mercy she bisoghte,
The lyf out of hir body for to twynne,
Hire to delivere of wo that she was inne.

A maner Latyn corrupt was hir speche,
But algates therby was she understonde.   520
The constable, whan hym lyst no longer seche,
This woful womman broghte he to the londe.
She kneleth doun and thanketh Goddes sonde;
But what she was she wolde no man seye,
For foul ne fair, thogh that she sholde deye.   525

She seyde she was so mazed in the see
That she forgat hir mynde, by hir trouthe.

460–61 Banisher of evil spirits from the man and woman over whom thy limbs faithfully extend (i.e., on whom the sign of the Cross has been made)
463 **fleet** = *fleeteth*, drifts
464 **See of Grece:** the eastern Mediterranean
464–65 **Strayte Of Marrok:** the strait of Gibraltar
466 **bayte:** feed
467 **After:** for
468 **wawes:** waves
472 **demande:** question
475 **frete:** devoured
479 **triacle:** medicine
481 **derk:** mysterious
483 **purveiance:** providence
486 **Jonas:** Jonah
487 **Nynyvee:** Nineveh
489 **peple Ebrayk:** Hebrews
491 **spirites:** angels

500 **Egipcien Marie:** St. Mary the Egyptian
501 **sanz faille:** doubtless
503 **loves:** loaves
504 **foyson:** plenty
505 **occian:** ocean
507 **hoold:** castle   **nempnen:** name
508 **wawe:** wave
509 **stiked:** stuck
510 **of al a tyde:** for the duration of an entire tide
513 **wrak:** wreck   **soghte:** searched
517 **twynne:** separate
519 **Latyn corrupt:** corrupted Latin (?); see n.
520 **algates:** nevertheless
521 **seche:** look about
523 **Goddes sonde:** divine providence (literally, God's sending, what He sends)
525 **For foul ne fair:** under any circumstances
526 **mazed:** bewildered
527 **forgat hir mynde:** lost her memory

The constable hath of hire so greet pitee,
And eek his wyf, that they wepen for routhe.
She was so diligent, withouten slouthe,   530
To serve and plesen everich in that place
That alle hir loven that looken in hir face.

This constable and dame Hermengyld, his wyf,
Were payens, and that contree everywhere;
But Hermengyld loved hire right as hir lyf,   535
And Custance hath so longe sojourned there,
In orisons, with many a bitter teere,
Til Jhesu hath converted thurgh his grace
Dame Hermengyld, constablesse of that place.

In al that lond no Cristen dorste route;   540
Alle Cristen folk been fled fro that contree
Thurgh payens, that conquereden al aboute
The plages of the north, by land and see.
To Walys fledde the Cristyanytee
Of olde Britons dwellynge in this ile;   545
Ther was hir refut for the meene while.

But yet nere Cristene Britons so exiled
That ther nere somme that in hir privetee
Honoured Crist and hethen folk bigiled,
And ny the castel swiche ther dwelten three.   550
That oon of hem was blynd and myghte nat see,
But it were with thilke eyen of his mynde
With whiche men seen, after that they ben blynde.

Bright was the sonne as in that someres day,
For which the constable and his wyf also   555
And Custance han ytake the righte way
Toward the see a furlong wey or two,
To pleyen and to romen to and fro,
And in hir walk this blynde man they mette,
Croked and oold, with eyen faste yshette.   560

"In name of Crist," cride this blinde Britoun,
"Dame Hermengyld, yif me my sighte agayn!"
This lady weex affrayed of the soun,
Lest that hir housbonde, shortly for to sayn,
Wolde hire for Jhesu Cristes love han slayn,   565

Til Custance made hire boold, and bad hire wirche
The wyl of Crist, as doghter of his chirche.

The constable weex abasshed of that sight,
And seyde, "What amounteth al this fare?"
Custance answerde, "Sire, it is Cristes myght,   570
That helpeth folk out of the feendes snare."
And so ferforth she gan oure lay declare
That she the constable, er that it was eve
Converteth, and on Crist made hym bileve.

This constable was nothyng lord of this place   575
Of which I speke, ther he Custance fond,
But kepte it strongly many a wyntres space
Under Alla, kyng of al Northhumbrelond,
That was ful wys, and worthy of his hond
Agayn the Scottes, as men may wel heere;   580
But turne I wole agayn to my mateere.

Sathan, that evere us waiteth to bigile,
Saugh of Custance al hire perfeccioun,
And caste anon how he myghte quite hir while,
And made a yong knyght that dwelte in that toun
Love hire so hoote, of foul affeccioun,   586
That verraily hym thoughte he sholde spille,
But he of hire myghte ones have his wille.

He woweth hire, but it availleth noght;
She wolde do no synne, by no weye.   590
And for despit he compassed in his thoght
To maken hire on shameful deeth to deye.
He wayteth whan the constable was aweye,
And pryvely upon a nyght he crepte
In Hermengyldes chambre, whil she slepte.   595

Wery, forwaked in hire orisouns,
Slepeth Custance, and Hermengyld also.
This knyght, thurgh Sathanas temptaciouns,
Al softely is to the bed ygo,
And kitte the throte of Hermengyld atwo,   600
And leyde the blody knyf by dame Custance,
And wente his wey, ther God yeve hym meschance!

530 **slouthe:** sloth
534 **payens:** pagans
537 **orisons:** prayers
540 **route:** assemble
543 **plages:** coastal regions
544 **Cristyanytee:** Christian community
546 **refut:** refuge
557 **furlong wey:** about an eighth of a mile
563 **weex:** became **affrayed:** frightened

568 **abasshed:** troubled
569 **fare:** commotion
572 **so ferforth:** to such an extent
579 **worthy of his hond:** brave in battle
582 **waiteth:** seeks an occasion
584 **caste:** plotted **quite hir while:** repay her
586 **of . . . affeccioun:** with passion
587 **spille:** die
591 **compassed:** plotted
596 Exhausted from lack of sleep because of praying
600 **kitte:** cut **atwo:** in two

Soone after cometh this constable hoom agayn,
And eek Alla, that kyng was of that lond,
And saugh his wyf despitously yslayn,   605
For which ful ofte he weep and wroong his hond,
And in the bed the blody knyf he fond
By Dame Custance. Allas, what myghte she seye?
For verray wo hir wit was al aweye.

To kyng Alla was toold al this meschance,   610
And eek the tyme, and where, and in what wise
That in a ship was founden this Custance,
As heer-biforn that ye han herd devyse.
The kynges herte of pitee gan agryse,
Whan he saugh so benigne a creature   615
Falle in disese and in mysaventure.

For as the lomb toward his deeth is broght,
So stant this innocent bifore the kyng.
This false knyght, that hath this tresoun wroght,
Berth hire on hond that she hath doon thys thyng. 620
But nathelees, ther was greet moornyng
Among the peple, and seyn they kan nat gesse
That she had doon so greet a wikkednesse,

For they han seyn hire evere so vertuous,
And lovynge Hermengyld right as hir lyf.   625
Of this baar witnesse everich in that hous,
Save he that Hermengyld slow with his knyf.
This gentil kyng hath caught a greet motyf
Of this witnesse, and thoghte he wolde enquere
Depper in this, a trouthe for to lere.   630

Allas! Custance, thou hast no champioun,
Ne fighte kanstow noght, so weylaway!
But he that starf for our redempcioun,
And boond Sathan (and yet lith ther he lay),
So be thy stronge champion this day!   635

For, but if Crist open myracle kithe,
Withouten gilt thou shalt be slayn as swithe.

She sette hire doun on knees, and thus she sayde:
"Immortal God, that savedest Susanne
Fro false blame, and thou, merciful mayde,   640
Marie I meene, doghter to Seint Anne,
Bifore whos child angeles synge Osanne,
If I be giltlees of this felonye,
My socour be, for ellis shal I dye!"

Have ye nat seyn somtyme a pale face,   645
Among a prees, of hym that hath be lad
Toward his deeth, wher as hym gat no grace,
And swich a colour in his face hath had
Men myghte knowe his face that was bistad
Amonges alle the faces in that route?   650
So stant Custance, and looketh hire aboute.

O queenes, lyvynge in prosperitee,
Duchesses, and ye ladyes everichone,
Haveth som routhe on hire adversitee!
An Emperoures doghter stant allone;   655
She hath no wight to whom to make hir mone.
O blood roial, that stondest in this drede,
Fer been thy freendes at thy grete nede!

This Alla kyng hath swich compassioun,
As gentil herte is fulfild of pitee,   660
That from his eyen ran the water doun.
"Now hastily do fecche a book," quod he,
"And if this knyght wol sweren how that she
This womman slow, yet wol we us avyse
Whom that we wole that shal been oure justise." 665

A Britoun book, written with Evaungiles,
Was fet, and on this book he swoor anoon
She gilty was, and in the meene whiles
An hand hym smoot upon the nekke-boon,
That doun he fil atones as a stoon,   670

605 **despitously:** cruelly
613 **herd devyse:** heard tell
614 **gan agryse:** trembled
616 **disese:** distress
618 **stant** = *stondith*, stands
620 **Berth hire on hond:** accuses her falsely
622 **seyn:** say
624 **seyn:** seen
627 **slow:** slew
628 **caught a greet motyf:** was deeply moved
630 **Depper:** more deeply   **lere:** learn
631 **champioun:** champion, representative in a judicial duel
633 **starf:** died

636 **kithe:** reveal
637 **Withouten gilt:** guiltless   **as swithe:** immediately
639 **Susanne:** Susannah (falsely accused by the Elders in the apocryphal Book of Susannah)
641 **Seint Anne:** the mother of the Virgin
642 **Osanne:** Hosanna
646 **prees:** crowd
649 **bistad:** in trouble
656 **make hir mone:** lament
658 **Fer:** far away
662 **do fecche a book:** have a book brought
664 **us avyse:** think over carefully
667 **fet:** fetched

And bothe his eyen broste out of his face
In sighte of every body in that place.

   A voys was herd in general audience,
And seyde, "Thou hast desclaundred, giltelees,
The doghter of hooly chirche in heigh presence; 675
Thus hastou doon, and yet holde I my pees!"
Of this mervaille agast was al the prees;
As mazed folk they stoden everichone,
For drede of wreche, save Custance allone.

   Greet was the drede and eek the repentance
Of hem that hadden wrong suspecioun   681
Upon this sely innocent, Custance;
And for this miracle, in conclusioun,
And by Custances mediacioun,
The kyng—and many another in that place— 685
Converted was, thanked be Cristes grace!

   This false knyght was slayn for his untrouthe
By juggement of Alla hastifly;
And yet Custance hadde of his deeth greet routhe.
And after this Jhesus, of his mercy,   690
Made Alla wedden ful solempnely
This hooly mayden, that is so bright and sheene;
And thus hath Crist ymaad Custance a queene.

But who was woful, if I shal nat lye,
Of this weddyng but Donegild, and namo, 695
The kynges mooder, ful of tirannye?
Hir thoughte hir cursed herte brast atwo.
She wolde noght hir sone had do so;
Hir thoughte a despit that he sholde take
So strange a creature unto his make. 700

   Me list nat of the chaf, ne of the stree,
Maken so long a tale as of the corn.
What sholde I tellen of the roialtee
At mariage, or which cours goth biforn;
Who bloweth in a trumpe or in an horn? 705
The fruyt of every tale is for to seye:

They ete, and drynke, and daunce, and synge, and
   pleye.

They goon to bedde, as it was skile and right;
For thogh that wyves be ful hooly thynges,
They moste take in pacience at nyght   710
Swiche manere necessaries as been plesynges
To folk that han ywedded hem with rynges,
And leye a lite hir hoolynesse aside,
As for the tyme—it may no bet bitide.

On hire he gat a knave child anon,   715
And to a bisshop, and his constable eke,
He took his wyf to kepe, whan he is gon
To Scotlond-ward, his foomen for to seke.
Now faire Custance, that is so humble and meke,
So longe is goon with childe, til that stille 720
She halt hire chambre, abidyng Cristes wille.

The tyme is come a knave child she beer;
Mauricius at the fontstoon they hym calle.
This constable dooth forth come a messageer,
And wroot unto his kyng, that cleped was Alle,
How that this blisful tidyng is bifalle, 726
And othere tidynges spedeful for to seye.
He taketh the lettre, and forth he gooth his weye.

   This messager, to doon his avantage,
Unto the kynges mooder rideth swithe, 730
And salueth hire ful faire in his langage:
"Madame," quod he, "ye may be glad and blithe,
And thanketh God an hundred thousand sithe!
My lady queene hath child, withouten doute,
To joye and blisse to al this regne aboute. 735

"Lo, heere the lettres seled of this thyng,
That I moot bere with al the haste I may.
If ye wol aught unto youre sone the kyng,
I am youre servant, bothe nyght and day."

671 **broste:** burst
673 **in general audience:** in the hearing of all
674 **desclaundred:** slandered
675 **in heigh presence:** in presence of the High One (God)
677 **prees:** crowd
678 **mazed:** bewildered, dazed
679 **wreche:** vengeance
682 **sely:** blessed
687 **untrouthe:** perjury
697 **brast atwo:** broke in two
700 **unto his make:** as his spouse
701 **chaf:** chaff (husks)   **stree:** straw
702 **corn:** fruit, essential part, of the story

708 **skile:** reasonable
711 **necessaries:** necessities
715 **gat:** begot   **knave child:** boy
717 **took:** gave
718 **to Scotlond-ward:** towards Scotland
721 **halt** = *holdeth,* holds, keeps to
723 **fontstoon:** baptismal font
726 **tidyng:** event
727 **spedeful:** useful
729 **to doon his avantage:** to do himself good
730 **swithe:** quickly
733 **sithe:** times
736 **seled:** marked with his seal
738 **wol aught:** want (to send) anything

Donegild answerde, "As now at this tyme, nay;   740
But heere al nyght I wol thou take thy reste.
To-morwe wol I seye thee what me leste."

This messager drank sadly ale and wyn,
And stolen were his lettres pryvely
Out of his box, whil he sleep as a swyn;   745
And countrefeted was ful subtilly
Another lettre, wroght ful synfully,
Unto the kyng direct of this mateere
Fro his constable, as ye shal after heere.

The lettre spak the queene delivered was   750
Of so horrible a feendly creature
That in the castel noon so hardy was
That any while dorste ther endure.
The mooder was an elf, by aventure
Ycomen, by charmes or by sorcerie,   755
And every wight hateth hir compaignye.

Wo was this kyng whan he this lettre had sayn,
But to no wight he tolde his sorwes soore,
But of his owene hand he wroot agayn,
"Welcome the sonde of Crist for everemoore   760
To me that am now lerned in his loore!
Lord, welcome be thy lust and thy plesaunce;
My lust I putte al in thyn ordinaunce.

"Kepeth this child, al be it foul or feir,
And eek my wyf, unto myn hoom-comynge.   765
Crist, whan hym list, may sende me an heir
Moore agreable than this to my likynge."
This lettre he seleth, pryvely wepynge,
Which to the messager was take soone,
And forth he gooth; ther is na moore to doone.   770

O messager, fulfild of dronkenesse,
Strong is thy breeth, thy lymes faltren ay,
And thou biwreyest alle secreenesse.
Thy mynde is lorn, thou janglest as a jay,
Thy face is turned in a newe array.   775
Ther dronkenesse regneth in any route,

Ther is no conseil hyd, withouten doute.

O Donegild, I ne have noon Englissh digne
Unto thy malice and thy tirannye!
And therfore to the feend I thee resigne;   780
Lat hym enditen of thy traitorie!
Fy, mannysh, fy!—o nay, by God, I lye—
Fy, feendlych spirit, for I dar wel telle,
Thogh thou heere walke, thy spirit is in helle!

This messager comth fro the kyng agayn,   785
And at the kynges moodres court he lighte,
And she was of this messager ful fayn,
And plesed hym in al that ever she myghte.
He drank, and wel his girdel underpighte;
He slepeth, and he fnorteth in his gyse   790
Al nyght, til the sonne gan aryse.

Eft were his lettres stolen everychon,
And countrefeted lettres in this wyse:
"The king comandeth his constable anon,
Up peyne of hangyng, and on heigh juyse,   795
That he ne sholde suffren in no wyse
Custance in-with his reawme for t'abyde
Thre dayes and o quarter of a tyde;

"But in the same ship as he hire fond,
Hire, and hir yonge sone, and al hir geere,   800
He sholde putte, and croude hire fro the lond,
And charge hire that she never eft coome theere."
O my Custance, wel may thy goost have feere,
And, slepynge, in thy dreem been in penance,
Whan Donegild cast al this ordinance.   805

This messager on morwe, whan he wook,
Unto the castel halt the nexte way,
And to the constable he the lettre took;
And whan that he this pitous lettre say,
Ful ofte he seyde, "Allas and weylaway!"   810
"Lord Crist," quod he, "how may this world endure,
So ful of synne is many a creature?

743 **sadly:** steadily
748 **direct:** addressed
754 **elf:** evil spirit
757 **sayn:** seen
760 **sonde:** dispensation
763 **in thyn ordinaunce:** in your control
768 **seleth:** marks with his seal
769 **take:** given
772 **faltren:** are unsteady
773 **biwreyest:** betray   **secreenesse:** secret information
774 **lorn:** lost   **janglest:** chatter

778 **digne:** fit
780 **resigne:** consign
781 **enditen:** write   **traitorie:** treachery
786 **lighte:** alighted, dismounted
789 **his girdel underpighte:** stuffed (drink) under his belt
790 **fnorteth:** snores
792 **Eft:** again
795 **Up peyne of:** on the penalty of   **juyse:** judicial sentence
797 **reawme:** realm
798 **tyde:** hour, or duration of a tide (ebb and flow)
801 **croude:** push
802 **charge:** command
807 **halt the nexte way:** takes (*halt* = *holdeth*) the shortest (literally, nearest) way
808 **took:** gave
809 **say:** saw

"O myghty God, if that it be thy wille,
Sith thou art rightful juge, how may it be
That thou wolt suffren innocentz to spille,   815
And wikked folk regne in prosperitee?
O goode Custance, allas, so wo is me
That I moot be thy tormentour, or deye
On shames deeth; ther is noon oother weye."

Wepen bothe yonge and olde in al that place   820
Whan that the kyng this cursed lettre sente,
And Custance, with a deedly pale face,
The ferthe day toward hir ship she wente.
But nathelees she taketh in good entente
The wyl of Crist, and knelynge on the stronde,   825
She seyde, "Lord, ay welcome be thy sonde!

"He that me kepte fro the false blame
While I was on the lond amonges yow,
He kan me kepe from harm and eek fro shame
In salte see, althogh I se noght how.   830
As strong as evere he was, he is yet now.
In hym triste I, and in his mooder deere,
That is to me my seyl and eek my steere."

Hir litel child lay wepyng in hir arm,
And knelynge, pitously to hym she seyde,   835
"Pees, litel sone, I wol do thee noon harm."
With that hir coverchief of hir heed she breyde,
And over his litel eyen she it leyde,
And in hir arm she lulleth it ful faste,
And into hevene hire eyen up she caste.   840

"Mooder," quod she, "and mayde bright, Marie,
Sooth is that thurgh wommanes eggement
Mankynde was lorn, and damned ay to dye,
For which thy child was on a croys yrent.
Thy blisful eyen sawe al his torment;   845
Thanne is ther no comparison bitwene
Thy wo and any wo man may sustene.

"Thow sawe thy child yslayn bifore thyne yen,
And yet now lyveth my litel child, parfay!
Now, lady bright, to whom alle woful cryen,   850
Thow glorie of wommanhede, thow faire may,

Thow haven of refut, brighte sterre of day,
Rewe on my child, that of thy gentillesse
Rewest on every reweful in distresse.

"O litel child, allas! What is thy gilt,   855
That nevere wroghtest synne as yet, pardee?
Why wil thyn harde fader han thee spilt?
O mercy, deere constable," quod she,
"As lat my litel child dwelle heer with thee;
And if thou darst nat saven hym, for blame,   860
So kys hym ones in his fadres name!"

Therwith she looked bakward to the londe,
And seyde, "Farewel, housbonde routhelees!"
And up she rist, and walketh doun the stronde
Toward the ship—hir folweth al the prees—   865
And evere she preyeth hire child to holde his pees;
And taketh hir leve, and with an hooly entente
She blisseth hire, and into ship she wente.

Vitailled was the ship, it is no drede,
Habundantly for hire ful longe space,   870
And othere necessaries that sholde nede
She hadde ynogh—heryed be Goddes grace!
For wynd and weder almyghty God purchace,
And brynge hire hoom! I kan no bettre seye,
But in the see she dryveth forth hir weye.   875

Explicit secunda pars.

Sequitur pars tercia.

Alla the kyng comth hoom soone after this
Unto his castel, of the which I tolde,
And asketh where his wyf and his child is.
The constable gan aboute his herte colde,
And pleynly al the manere he hym tolde   880
As ye han herd—I kan telle it no bettre—
And sheweth the kyng his seel and eek his lettre,

And seyde, "Lord, as ye comanded me
Up peyne of deeth, so have I doon, certein."
This messager tormented was til he   885

852 **refut**: refuge   **sterre**: star
853 **Rewe**: take pity
857 **spilt**: put to death
863 **routhelees**: without compassion
869 **Vitailled**: stocked with provisions
870 **space**: time
871 **necessaries**: necessities   **nede**: be needed
872 **heryed**: praised
873 **weder**: weather   **purchace**: provide
Explicit, *etc.*: Here ends the second part.   **Sequitur**, *etc.*: The third part follows.
880 **al the manere**: the whole affair
884 **Up peyne of**: on the penalty of
885 **tormented**: tortured

815 **spille**: die
823 **ferthe**: fourth
825 **stronde**: strand, shore
826 **sonde**: dispensation
832 **triste**: trust
833 **steere**: rudder, guide
837 **coverchief**: kerchief   **of . . . breyde**: drew off
842 **eggement**: instigation
844 **yrent**: stretched (literally, *torn*)
849 **parfay**: by my faith
851 **wommanhede**: femininity   **may**: maid

Moste biknowe and tellen, plat and pleyn,
Fro nyght to nyght, in what place he had leyn;
And thus, by wit and sotil enquerynge,
Ymagined was by whom this harm gan sprynge.

The hand was knowe that the lettre wroot,   890
And al the venym of this cursed dede,
But in what wise, certeinly, I noot.
Th'effect is this: that Alla, out of drede,
His mooder slow—that may men pleynly rede—
For that she traitour was to hire ligeance.   895
Thus endeth olde Donegild, with meschance!

The sorwe that this Alla nyght and day
Maketh for his wyf, and for his child also,
Ther is no tonge that it telle may.
But now wol I unto Custance go,   900
That fleteth in the see, in peyne and wo,
Fyve yeer and moore, as liked Cristes sonde,
Er that hir ship approched unto londe.

Under an hethen castel, atte laste,
Of which the name in my text noght I fynde,   905
Custance, and eek hir child, the see up caste.
Almyghty God, that saveth al mankynde,
Have on Custance and on hir child som mynde,
That fallen is in hethen hand eft soone,
In point to spille, as I shal telle yow soone.   910

Doun fro the castel comth ther many a wight
To gauren on this ship and on Custance.
But shortly, from the castel, on a nyght,
The lordes styward—God yeve hym meschance!—
A theef, that hadde reneyed oure creance,   915
Cam into ship allone, and seyde he sholde
Hir lemman be, wher-so she wolde or nolde.

Wo was this wrecched womman tho bigon;
Hir child cride, and she cride pitously.
But blisful Marie heelp hire right anon;   920
For with hir struglyng wel and myghtily

The theef fil over bord al sodeynly,
And in the see he dreynte for vengeance;
And thus hath Crist unwemmed kept Custance.

O foule lust of luxurie, lo, thyn ende!   925
Nat oonly that thou feyntest mannes mynde,
But verraily thou wolt his body shende.
Th'ende of thy werk, or of thy lustes blynde,
Is compleynyng. Hou many oon may men fynde
That noght for werk somtyme, but for th'entente   930
To doon this synne, been outher slayn or shente!

How may this wayke womman han this strengthe
Hire to defende agayn this renegat?
O Golias, unmesurable of lengthe,
Hou myghte David make thee so maat,   935
So yong and of armure so desolaat?
Hou dorste he looke upon thy dredful face?
Wel may men seen, it nas but Goddes grace.

Who yaf Judith corage or hardynesse
To sleen hym Olofernus in his tente,   940
And to deliveren out of wrecchednesse
The peple of God? I seye, for this entente,
That right as God spirit of vigour sente
To hem and saved hem out of meschance,
So sente he myght and vigour to Custance.   945

Forth gooth hir ship thurghout the narwe mouth
Of Jubaltare and Septe, dryvynge ay
Somtyme west, and somtyme north and south,
And somtyme est, ful many a wery day,
Til Cristes mooder—blessed be she ay!—   950
Hath shapen, thurgh hir endelees goodnesse,
To make an ende of al hir hevynesse.

Now lat us stynte of Custance but a throwe,
And speke we of the Romayn Emperour,

886 **biknowe:** reveal   **plat:** bluntly
888 **wit:** knowledge   **sotil enquerynge:** subtle, skillful questioning
889 **Ymagined:** deduced
891 **venym:** poison
893 **out of drede:** doubtless
895 **ligeance:** allegiance
901 **fleteth:** floats
908 **mynde:** thought
909 **eft soone:** again
910 **In point to:** on the point of
912 **gauren on:** stare at
914 **styward:** steward
915 **reneyed:** renounced   **creance:** belief
917 **lemman:** lover   **wher-so:** whether
918 **Wo . . . bigon:** in a sad plight

924 **unwemmed:** undefiled
925 **luxurie:** lechery
926 **feyntest:** weaken
927 **shende:** destroy
929 **compleynyng:** lamentation
930 **werk:** the deed
932 **wayke:** weak
934 **Golias:** Goliath, the biblical giant slain by David
935 **maat:** defeated
936 **of armure so desolaat:** so lacking in arms and armor
937 **dredful:** frightening
939–40 Judith slew the lecherous Holofernes (*Olofernus*); for the story see MkT
VII.2551–74.
946 **narwe mouth:** the narrow strait between Gibraltar (*Jubaltare*) and Morocco
(*Septe*)
952 **hevynesse:** sadness
953 **throwe:** short while

That out of Surrye hath by lettres knowe   955
The slaughtre of cristen folk, and dishonour
Doon to his doghter by a fals traytour,
I mene the cursed wikked Sowdanesse
That at the feeste leet sleen bothe moore and lesse.

For which this Emperour hath sent anon   960
His senatour, with roial ordinance,
And othere lordes, God woot, many oon,
On Surryens to taken heigh vengeance.
They brennen, sleen, and brynge hem to meschance
Ful many a day; but shortly—this is th'ende—   965
Homward to Rome they shapen hem to wende.

This senatour repaireth with victorie
To Rome-ward, saillynge ful roially,
And mette the ship dryvynge, as seith the storie,
In which Custance sit ful pitously.   970
Nothyng ne knew he what she was, ne why
She was in swich array, ne she nyl seye
Of hire estaat, althogh she sholde deye.

He bryngeth hire to Rome, and to his wyf
He yaf hire, and hir yonge sone also;   975
And with the senatour she ladde hir lyf.
Thus kan Oure Lady bryngen out of wo
Woful Custance, and many another mo.
And longe tyme dwelled she in that place,
In hooly werkes evere, as was hir grace.   980

The senatoures wyf hir aunte was,
But for al that she knew hire never the moore.
I wol no lenger tarien in this cas,
But to kyng Alla, which I spak of yoore,
That for his wyf wepeth and siketh soore,   985
I wol retourne, and lete I wol Custance
Under the senatoures governance.

Kyng Alla, which that hadde his mooder slayn,
Upon a day fil in swich repentance
That, if I shortly tellen shal and playn,   990
To Rome he comth to receyven his penance;
And putte hym in the Popes ordinance
In heigh and logh, and Jhesu Crist bisoghte
Foryeve his wikked werkes that he wroghte.

The fame anon thurgh Rome toun is born,   995
How Alla kyng shal comen in pilgrymage,
By herbergeours that wenten hym biforn;
For which the senatour, as was usage,
Rood hym agayns, and many of his lynage,
As wel to shewen his heighe magnificence   1000
As to doon any kyng a reverence.

Greet cheere dooth this noble senatour
To kyng Alla, and he to hym also;
Everich of hem dooth oother greet honour.
And so bifel that in a day or two   1005
This senatour is to kyng Alla go
To feste, and shortly, if I shal nat lye,
Custances sone wente in his compaignye.

Som men wolde seyn at requeste of Custance
This senatour hath lad this child to feeste;   1010
I may nat tellen every circumstance—
Be as be may, ther was he at the leeste.
But sooth is this, that at his moodres heeste
Biforn Alla, durynge the metes space,
The child stood, lookynge in the kynges face.   1015

This Alla kyng hath of this child greet wonder,
And to the senatour he seyde anon,
"Whos is that faire child that stondeth yonder?"
"I noot," quod he, "by God, and by Seint John!
A mooder he hath, but fader hath he noon   1020
That I of woot"—and shortly, in a stounde,
He tolde Alla how that this child was founde.

"But God woot," quod this senatour also,
"So vertuous a lyvere in my lyf
Ne saugh I nevere as she, ne herde of mo,   1025
Of worldly wommen, mayde, ne of wyf.
I dar wel seyn hir hadde levere a knyf
Thurghout hir brest, than ben a womman wikke;
There is no man koude brynge hire to that prikke."

---

959 **leet sleen:** had (caused to be) slain
972 **nyl** = *ne wyl,* will not
992 **ordinance:** governance
993 **In heigh and logh:** in all things

997 **herbergeours:** servants who travel ahead to arrange lodging
999 **hym agayns:** toward him
1000 **his heighe magnificence:** his own noble state
1012 **Be as be may:** whatever may be
1014 **metes space:** dinner time
1021 **stounde:** little time
1024 **lyvere:** being
1028 **wikke:** evil
1029 **prikke:** point

Now was this child as lyk unto Custance   1030
As possible is a creature to be.
This Alla hath the face in remembrance
Of dame Custance, and ther on mused he
If that the childes mooder were aught she
That is his wyf, and pryvely he sighte,   1035
And spedde hym fro the table that he myghte.

"Parfay," thoghte he, "fantome is in myn heed!
I oghte deme, of skilful juggement,
That in the salte see my wyf is deed."
And afterward he made his argument: 1040
"What woot I if that Crist have hyder ysent
My wyf by see, as wel as he hire sente
To my contree fro thennes that she wente?"

And after noon, hoom with the senatour
Goth Alla, for to seen this wonder chaunce.   1045
This senatour dooth Alla greet honour,
And hastifly he sente after Custaunce.
But trusteth weel, hire liste nat to daunce
Whan that she wiste wherfore was that sonde;
Unnethe upon hir feet she myghte stonde.   1050

    Whan Alla saugh his wyf, faire he hire grette,
And weep that it was routhe for to see;
For at the firste look he on hire sette
He knew wel verraily that it was she.
And she, for sorwe, as doumb stant as a tree,   1055
So was hir herte shet in hir distresse,
Whan she remembred his unkyndenesse.

Twyes she swowned in his owene sighte;
He weep, and hym excuseth pitously.
"Now God," quod he, "and his halwes brighte   1060
So wisly on my soule as have mercy,
That of youre harm as giltelees am I
As is Maurice my sone, so lyk youre face;
Elles the feend me fecche out of this place!"

    Long was the sobbyng and the bitter peyne,   1065
Er that hir woful hertes myghte cesse;
Greet was the pitee for to heere hem pleyne,

Thurgh whiche pleintes gan hir wo encresse.
I pray yow alle my labour to relesse;
I may nat telle hir wo until to-morwe,   1070
I am so wery for to speke of sorwe.

But finally, whan that the sothe is wist
That Alla giltelees was of hir wo,
I trowe an hundred tymes been they kist,
And swich a blisse is ther bitwix hem two   1075
That, save the joye that lasteth everemo,
Ther is noon lyk that any creature
Hath seyn or shal, whil that the world may dure.

Tho preyde she hir housbonde mekely,
In relief of hir longe, pitous pyne,   1080
That he wolde preye hir fader specially
That of his magestee he wolde enclyne
To vouche sauf som day with hym to dyne.
She preyde hym eek he sholde by no weye
Unto hir fader no word of hire seye.   1085

    Som men wolde seyn how that the child Maurice
Dooth this message unto this Emperour;
But, as I gesse, Alla was nat so nyce
To hym that was of so sovereyn honour
As he that is of Cristen folk the flour,   1090
Sente any child, but it is bet to deeme
He wente hymself, and so it may wel seeme.

    This Emperour hath graunted gentilly
To come to dyner, as he hym bisoughte;
And wel rede I he looked bisily   1095
Upon this child, and on his doghter thoghte.
Alla goth to his in, and as hym oghte,
Arrayed for this feste in every wise
As ferforth as his konnyng may suffise.

    The morwe cam, and Alla gan hym dresse,   1100
And eek his wyf, this Emperour to meete;
And forth they ryde in joye and in gladnesse.
And whan she saugh hir fader in the strete,
She lighte doun, and falleth hym to feete.   1104
"Fader," quod she, "youre yonge child Custance
Is now ful clene out of youre remembrance.

1034 **aught:** in any way
1035 **sighte:** sighed
1036 **that he myghte:** as soon as he could
1037 **fantome:** hallucination
1038 **skilful:** discerning
1048 **hire liste nat to daunce:** she did not want to dance (for joy)
1050 **Unnethe:** hardly
1051 **grette:** greeted
1052 **routhe:** pity
1056 **shet:** shut up, pressed by emotion
1060 **halwes:** saints
1061 **So wisly:** surely
1066 **cesse:** cease

1069 **relesse:** release (me from my labors)
1074 **been they kist:** they kissed each other
1080 **pyne:** pain
1083 **vouche sauf:** grant
1088 **nyce:** foolish
1091 **Sente:** to have sent
1095 **rede I:** I read (in my source)   **bisily:** intently
1104 **hym to feete:** at his feet
1106 **ful clene:** completely

"I am youre doghter Custance," quod she,
"That whilom ye han sent unto Surrye.
It am I, fader, that in the salte see
Was put allone and dampned for to dye.   1110
Now, goode fader, mercy I yow crye!
Sende me namoore unto noon hethenesse,
But thonketh my lord heere of his kyndenesse."

    Who kan the pitous joye tellen al
Bitwixe hem thre, syn they been thus ymette?   1115
But of my tale make an ende I shal;
The day goth faste, I wol no lenger lette.
This glade folk to dyner they hem sette;
In joye and blisse at mete I lete hem dwelle
A thousand foold wel moore than I kan telle.   1120

    This child Maurice was sithen Emperour
Maad by the Pope, and lyved cristenly;
To Cristes chirche he dide greet honour.
But I lete al his storie passen by;
Of Custance is my tale specially.   1125
In the olde Romayn geestes may men fynde
Maurices lyf; I bere it noght in mynde.

    This kyng Alla, whan he his tyme say,
With his Custance, his hooly wyf so sweete,
To Engelond been they come the righte way,   1130
Wher as they lyve in joye and in quiete.
But litel while it lasteth, I yow heete,
Joye of this world, for tyme wol nat abyde;
Fro day to nyght it changeth as the tyde.

Who lyved euere in swich delit o day   1135
That hym ne moeved outher conscience,
Or ire, or talent, or som kynnes affray,
Envye, or pride, or passion, or offence?
I ne seye but for this ende this sentence,
That litel while in joye or in plesance   1140
Lasteth the blisse of Alla with Custance.

For Deeth, that taketh of heigh and logh his rente,
Whan passed was a yeer, evene as I gesse,
Out of this world this kyng Alla he hente,
For whom Custance hath ful greet hevynesse.   1145
Now lat us prayen God his soule blesse!
And dame Custance, finally to seye,
Toward the toun of Rome goth hir weye.

    To Rome is come this hooly creature,
And fyndeth hire freendes hoole and sounde;   1150
Now is she scaped al hire aventure.
And whan that she hir fader hath yfounde,
Doun on hir knees falleth she to grounde;
Wepynge for tendrenesse in herte blithe,
She heryeth God an hundred thousand sithe.   1155

    In vertu and in hooly almus-dede
They lyven alle, and nevere asonder wende;
Til deeth departeth hem, this lyf they lede.
And fareth now weel! my tale is at an ende.
Now Jhesu Crist, that of his myght may sende   1160
Joye after wo, governe us in his grace,
And kepe us alle that been in this place! Amen

Heere endeth the tale of the Man of Lawe.

The Epilogue of the Man of Law's Tale

[Owre Hoost upon his stiropes stood anon,
And seyde, "Goode men, herkeneth everych on!
This was a thrifty tale for the nones!   1165
Sir Parisshe Prest," quod he, "for Goddes bones,
Telle us a tale, as was thi forward yore.

I se wel that ye lerned men in lore
Can moche good, by Goddes dignitee!"
    The Parson him answerde, "Benedicite!   1170
What eyleth the man, so synfully to swere?"

1117 **lette:** delay
1126 **Romayn geestes:** Roman histories
1128 **say:** saw
1130 **righte way:** direct route

1165 **thrifty:** worthwhile

1136 **moeved:** moved   **outher:** either
1137 **som kynnes:** some kind of   **affray:** fear
1138 **Envye:** ill-will
1144 **hente:** snatched
1155 **heryeth:** praises   **sithe:** times
1156 **almus-dede:** charitable works
1157 **asonder wende:** parted

1169 **Can moche good:** know what you are about

Oure Host answerde, "O Jankin, be ye there?
I smelle a Lollere in the wynd," quod he.
"Now! goode men," quod oure Hoste, "herkeneth
     me;
Abydeth, for Goddes digne passioun,   1175
For we schal han a predicacioun;
This Lollere heer wil prechen us somwhat."
     "Nay, by my fader soule, that schal he nat!"
Seyde the Shipman, "Heer schal he nat preche;
He schal no gospel glosen here ne teche.   1180

We leven alle in the grete God," quod he;
"He wolde sowen som difficulte,
Or springen cokkel in our clene corn.
And therfore, Hoost, I warne thee biforn,
My joly body schal a tale telle,   1185
And I schal clynken you so mery a belle,
That I schal waken al this compaignie.
But it schal not ben of philosophie,
Ne phislyas, ne termes queinte of lawe.
Ther is but litel Latyn in my mawe!"]   1190

1172 **Jankin:** derisive name for a priest
1173 **Lollere:** Lollard, a heretic
1176 **predicacioun:** sermon
1179 **Shipman:** The identity of the speaker is uncertain; see n.
1180 **glosen:** interpret

1181 **leven:** believe
1183 **springen:** sprinkle   **cokkel:** corn cockle (a weed)
1189 **phislyas:** files, cases (?); see n.   **queinte:** learned, complex

The Wife of Bath's Prologue

The Prologe of the Wyves Tale of Bathe.

"Experience, though noon auctoritee
Were in this world, is right ynogh for me
To speke of wo that is in mariage;
For, lordynges, sith I twelve yeer was of age,
Thonked be God that is eterne on lyve,   5
Housbondes at chirche dore I have had fyve—
If I so ofte myghte have ywedded bee—
And alle were worthy men in hir degree.
But me was toold, certeyn, nat longe agoon is,
That sith that Crist ne wente nevere but onis   10
To weddyng, in the Cane of Galilee,
That by the same ensample taughte he me
That I ne sholde wedded be but ones.
Herkne eek, lo, which a sharp word for the nones,
Biside a welle, Jhesus, God and man,   15
Spak in repreeve of the Samaritan:
'Thou hast yhad fyve housbondes,' quod he,
'And that ilke man that now hath thee
Is noght thyn housbonde,' thus seyde he certeyn.
What that he mente therby, I kan nat seyn;   20
But that I axe, why that the fifthe man
Was noon housbonde to the Samaritan?
How manye myghte she have in mariage?
Yet herde I nevere tellen in myn age
Upon this nombre diffinicioun.   25
Men may devyne and glosen, up and doun,
But wel I woot, expres, withoute lye,
God bad us for to wexe and multiplye;
That gentil text kan I wel understonde.
Eek wel I woot, he seyde myn housbonde   30
Sholde lete fader and mooder and take to me.
But of no nombre mencion made he,
Of bigamye, or of octogamye;

Why sholde men thanne speke of it vileynye?
    Lo, heere the wise kyng, daun Salomon;   35
I trowe he hadde wyves mo than oon.
As wolde God it leveful were unto me
To be refreshed half so ofte as he!
Which yifte of God hadde he for alle his wyvys!
No man hath swich that in this world alyve is.   40
God woot, this noble kyng, as to my wit,
The firste nyght had many a myrie fit
With ech of hem, so wel was hym on lyve.
Yblessed be God that I have wedded fyve!
[Of whiche I have pyked out the beste,   44a
Bothe of here nether purs and of here cheste.
Diverse scoles maken parfyt clerkes,
And diverse practyk in many sondry werkes
Maketh the werkman parfyt sekirly;
Of fyve husbondes scoleiyng am I.]   44f
Welcome the sixte, whan that evere he shal.
For sothe, I wol nat kepe me chaast in al.   46
Whan myn housbonde is fro the world ygon,
Som Cristen man shal wedde me anon,
For thanne th'apostle seith that I am free
To wedde, a Goddes half, where it liketh me.   50
He seith that to be wedded is no synne;
Bet is to be wedded than to brynne.
What rekketh me, thogh folk seye vileynye
Of shrewed Lameth and his bigamye?
I woot wel Abraham was an hooly man,   55
And Jacob eek, as ferforth as I kan;
And ech of hem hadde wyves mo than two,

1 **auctoritee:** written authority
10 **onis:** once
11 **Cane:** the town of Cana
14 **Herkne:** listen
16 **repreeve:** reproof
21 **axe:** ask
26 **devyne:** conjecture   **glosen, up and doun:** interpret in every way
27 **expres:** clearly
28 **wexe:** increase (breed)
31 **lete:** leave
33 **octogamye:** marrying eight times

34 **vileynye:** in reproach
35 **daun:** sir   **Salomon:** Solomon
37 **leveful:** lawful, permissible
39 **Which yifte:** what a gift
41 **wit:** judgment
44b **nether:** lower
44d **practyk:** practice
44e **sekirly:** certainly
44f **scoleiyng:** schooling
46 **chaast:** chaste
49 **th'apostle:** St. Paul
50 **a Goddes half:** by God's side, by God
52 **brynne:** burn
53 **rekketh me:** do I care
54 **shrewed:** cursed, evil   **Lameth:** the biblical Lamech, the first bigamist
55–56 **Abraham, Jacob:** the biblical patriarchs

And many another holy man also.
Wher can ye seye, in any manere age,
That hye God defended mariage   60
By expres word? I pray yow, telleth me.
Or where comanded he virginitee?
I woot as wel as ye, it is no drede,
Th'apostel, whan he speketh of maydenhede,
He seyde that precept therof hadde he noon.   65
Men may conseille a womman to been oon,
But conseillyng is no comandement.
He putte it in oure owene juggement;
For hadde God comanded maydenhede,
Thanne hadde he dampned weddyng with the dede.
And certes, if ther were no seed ysowe,   71
Virginitee, thanne wherof sholde it growe?
Poul dorste nat comanden, atte leeste,
A thyng of which his maister yaf noon heeste.
The dart is set up for virginitee;   75
Cacche whoso may, who renneth best lat see.

   But this word is nat taken of every wight,
But ther as God lust gyve it of his myght.
I woot wel that th'apostel was a mayde;
But nathelees, thogh that he wroot and sayde   80
He wolde that every wight were swich as he,
Al nys but conseil to virginitee.
And for to been a wyf he yaf me leve
Of indulgence; so nys it no repreve
To wedde me, if that my make dye,   85
Withouten excepcion of bigamye.
Al were it good no womman for to touche—
He mente as in his bed or in his couche,
For peril is bothe fyr and tow t'assemble;
Ye knowe what this ensample may resemble.   90
This is al and som: he heeld virginitee
Moore parfit than weddyng in freletee.
Freletee clepe I, but if that he and she
Wolde leden al hir lyf in chastitee.

   I graunte it wel; I have noon envie,   95
Thogh maydenhede preferre bigamye.
It liketh hem to be clene, body and goost;
Of myn estaat I nyl nat make no boost,
For wel ye knowe, a lord in his houshold,
He nath nat every vessel al of gold;   100
Somme been of tree, and doon hir lord servyse.
God clepeth folk to hym in sondry wyse,
And everich hath of God a propre yifte—
Som this, som that, as hym liketh shifte.

   Virginitee is greet perfeccion,   105
And continence eek with devocion,
But Crist, that of perfeccion is welle,
Bad nat every wight he sholde go selle
Al that he hadde, and gyve it to the poore,
And in swich wise folwe hym and his foore.   110
He spak to hem that wolde lyve parfitly;
And lordynges, by youre leve, that am nat I.
I wol bistowe the flour of al myn age
In the actes and in fruyt of mariage.

   Telle me also, to what conclusion   115
Were membres maad of generacion,
And of so parfit wys a [wright] ywroght?
Trusteth right wel, they were nat maad for noght.
Glose whoso wole, and seye bothe up and doun
That they were maked for purgacioun   120
Of uryne, and oure bothe thynges smale
Were eek to knowe a femele from a male,
And for noon oother cause—say ye no?
The experience woot wel it is noght so.
So that the clerkes be nat with me wrothe,   125
I sey this: that they maked ben for bothe;
That is to seye, for office and for ese
Of engendrure, ther we nat God displese.
Why sholde men elles in hir bookes sette
That man shal yelde to his wyf hire dette?   130
Now wherwith sholde he make his paiement,
If he ne used his sely instrument?
Thanne were they maad upon a creature
To purge uryne, and eek for engendrure.

61 **expres:** explicit
63 **drede:** doubt
64 **Th'apostel:** St. Paul
73 **Poul:** St. Paul
74 **of which his maister yaf noon heeste:** about which his Master made no
commandment
75 **dart:** dart offered as a prize
76 **Cacche whoso may:** catch it whoever can
77 **is nat taken of:** does not apply to
78 **lust:** it pleases (God)
79 **mayde:** virgin
82 **Al nys but:** all is only
84 **Of indulgence:** by permission   **repreve:** shame
85 **make:** mate
86 **excepcion of:** objection on the grounds of
89 **tow:** flax
91 **al and som:** the entire matter
92 **in freletee:** because of weakness
93 **but if that:** unless
94 **chastitee:** abstinence from sexual intercourse

96 **preferre:** may have precedence over   **bigamye:** in this instance, marriage by or
with a widower or widow
98 **nyl** = *ne wyl,* will not
101 **of tree:** made of wood
103 **propre yifte:** special, individual gift
104 **hym liketh shifte:** it pleases God to provide
110 **foore:** footsteps
111 **parfitly:** perfectly
115 **conclusion:** purpose
117 And made by so perfectly wise a maker
119 **Glose:** interpret   **up and doun:** in all respects
125 **So that:** providing that
127 **office:** function (of urination)   **ese:** pleasure
128 **engendrure:** procreation
130 **yelde:** pay   **dette:** marital debt (obligation to engage in intercourse; see ParsT X.940)
132 **sely instrument:** blessed, innocent tool

But I seye noght that every wight is holde,   135
That hath swich harneys as I to yow tolde,
To goon and usen hem in engendrure.
Thanne sholde men take of chastitee no cure.
Crist was a mayde and shapen as a man,
And many a seint, sith that the world bigan;   140
Yet lyved they evere in parfit chastitee.
I nyl envye no virginitee.
Lat hem be breed of pured whete-seed,
And lat us wyves hoten barly-breed;
And yet with barly-breed, Mark telle kan,   145
Oure Lord Jhesu refresshed many a man.
In swich estaat as God hath cleped us
I wol persevere; I nam nat precius.
In wyfhod I wol use myn instrument
As frely as my Makere hath it sent.   150
If I be daungerous, God yeve me sorwe!
Myn housbonde shal it have bothe eve and morwe,
Whan that hym list come forth and paye his dette.
An housbonde I wol have—I wol nat lette—
Which shal be bothe my dettour and my thral,   155
And have his tribulacion withal
Upon his flessh, whil that I am his wyf.
I have the power durynge al my lyf
Upon his propre body, and noght he.
Right thus the Apostle tolde it unto me,   160
And bad oure housbondes for to love us weel.
Al this sentence me liketh every deel"—
    Up stirte the Pardoner, and that anon;
"Now, dame," quod he, "by God and by Seint John!
Ye been a noble prechour in this cas.   165
I was aboute to wedde a wyf; allas!
What sholde I bye it on my flessh so deere?
Yet hadde I levere wedde no wyf to-yeere!"
    "Abyde!" quod she, "my tale is nat bigonne.
Nay, thou shalt drynken of another tonne,   170
Er that I go, shal savoure wors than ale.
And whan that I have toold thee forth my tale
Of tribulacion in mariage,

Of which I am expert in al myn age—
This is to seyn, myself have been the whippe—   175
Than maystow chese wheither thou wolt sippe
Of thilke tonne that I shal abroche.
Be war of it, er thou to ny approche;
For I shal telle ensamples mo than ten.
'Whoso that nyl be war by othere men,   180
By hym shul othere men corrected be.'
The same wordes writeth Ptholomee;
Rede in his Almageste, and take it there."
    "Dame, I wolde praye yow, if youre wyl it were,"
Seyde this Pardoner, "as ye bigan,   185
Telle forth youre tale, spareth for no man,
And teche us yonge men of youre praktike."
    "Gladly," quod she, "sith it may yow like;
But yet I praye to al this compaignye,
If that I speke after my fantasye,   190
As taketh not agrief of that I seye,
For myn entente nys but for to pleye.
    Now, sire, now wol I telle forth my tale.
As evere moote I drynken wyn or ale,
I shal seye sooth; tho housbondes that I hadde,   195
As thre of hem were goode, and two were badde.
The thre were goode men, and riche, and olde;
Unnethe myghte they the statut holde
In which that they were bounden unto me.
Ye woot wel what I meene of this, pardee!   200
As help me God, I laughe whan I thynke
How pitously a-nyght I made hem swynke!
And, by my fey, I tolde of it no stoor.
They had me yeven hir lond and hir tresoor;
Me neded nat do lenger diligence   205
To wynne hir love, or doon hem reverence.
They loved me so wel, by God above,
That I ne tolde no deyntee of hir love!
A wys womman wol bisye hire evere in oon
To gete hire love, ye, ther as she hath noon.   210

135 **holde:** obligated
143 **pured:** refined
144 **hoten:** be called   **barly-breed:** an inexpensive bread
148 **precius:** fussy, fastidious
151 **daungerous:** grudging, niggardly
154 **lette:** leave off, desist
155 **thral:** servant, slave
156 **withal:** also
165 **prechour:** preacher
167 **What:** why   **bye it on:** pay for it with
168 **to-yeere:** this year
170 **tonne:** barrel
171 **savoure:** taste

177 **abroche:** open
178 **to ny:** too close
180–81 He who will not (*nyl* = *ne wyll*) be admonished by examples offered by others must himself become an example for the correction of others.
182 **Ptholomee:** Ptolemy, the Greek mathematician and astronomer, author of the *Almageste* (cf. MilT I.3208)
187 **praktike:** practice
190 **after my fantasye:** according to my fancy, desire
191 **As taketh not agrief of:** do not be annoyed with (*as* is not translated)
198 **Unnethe:** hardly   **statut:** the conjugal debt (see 130 above)
202 **a-nyght:** at night   **swynke:** work
203 **fey:** faith   **tolde of it no stoor:** set no store by it, regarded it as useless
204 **tresoor:** treasure
208 **ne tolde no deyntee of:** did not value, reckoned little of
209 **bisye hire evere in oon:** be constantly busy

But sith I hadde hem hoolly in myn hond,   211
And sith they hadde me yeven al hir lond,
What sholde I taken keep hem for to plese,
But it were for my profit and myn ese?
I sette hem so a-werke, by my fey,   215
That many a nyght they songen 'Weilawey!'
The bacon was nat fet for hem, I trowe,
That som men han in Essex at Dunmowe.
I governed hem so wel, after my lawe,
That ech of hem ful blisful was and fawe   220
To brynge me gaye thynges fro the fayre.
They were ful glad whan I spak to hem faire,
For, God it woot, I chidde hem spitously.
     Now herkneth hou I baar me proprely,
Ye wise wyves, that kan understonde.   225
Thus shulde ye speke and bere hem wrong on honde,
For half so boldely kan ther no man
Swere and lyen, as a womman kan.
I sey nat this by wyves that been wyse,
But if it be whan they hem mysavyse.   230
A wys wyf, if that she kan hir good,
Shal beren hym on honde the cow is wood,
And take witnesse of hir owene mayde
Of hir assent. But herkneth how I sayde:
     'Sire olde kaynard, is this thyn array?   235
Why is my neighebores wyf so gay?
She is honoured overal ther she gooth;
I sitte at hoom; I have no thrifty clooth.
What dostow at my neighebores hous?
Is she so fair? Artow so amorous?   240
What rowne ye with oure mayde? Benedicite!
Sire olde lecchour, lat thy japes be!
And if I have a gossib or a freend,
Withouten gilt, thou chidest as a feend,
If that I walke or pleye unto his hous!   245
Thou comest hoom as dronken as a mous,
And prechest on thy bench, with yvel preef!
Thou seist to me it is a greet meschief

To wedde a povre womman, for costage;
And if that she be riche, of heigh parage,   250
Thanne seistow that it is a tormentrie
To soffre hire pride and hire malencolie.
And if that she be fair, thou verray knave,
Thou seyst that every holour wol hire have;
She may no while in chastitee abyde,   255
That is assailled upon ech a syde.
     Thou seyst som folk desiren us for richesse,
Somme for oure shap, and somme for oure fairnesse,
And som for she kan outher synge or daunce,
And som for gentillesse and daliaunce;   260
Som for hir handes and hir armes smale;
Thus goth al to the devel, by thy tale.
Thou seyst men may nat kepe a castel wal,
It may so longe assailled been overal.
     And if that she be foul, thou seist that she   265
Coveiteth every man that she may se,
For as a spanyel she wol on hym lepe,
Til that she fynde som man hire to chepe.
Ne noon so grey goos gooth ther in the lake
As, sëistow, wol been withoute make.   270
And seyst it is an hard thyng for to welde
A thyng that no man wole, his thankes, helde.
Thus seistow, lorel, whan thow goost to bedde,
And that no wys man nedeth for to wedde,
Ne no man that entendeth unto hevene.   275
With wilde thonder-dynt and firy levene
Moote thy welked nekke be tobroke!
     Thow seyst that droppyng houses, and eek smoke,
And chidyng wyves maken men to flee
Out of hir owene houses; a, benedicitee!   280
What eyleth swich an old man for to chide?
     Thow seyst we wyves wol oure vices hide
Til we be fast, and thanne we wol hem shewe—
Wel may that be a proverbe of a shrewe!

213 **taken keep:** take care
215 **sette hem so a-werke:** worked them so hard (or, tricked them; cf. I.4337)
217–18 **bacon . . . in Essex at Dunmowe:** side of bacon awarded to spouses who lived a year and a day without quarrelling
220 **fawe:** eager
223 **chidde hem spitously:** chided, scolded them cruelly
226 **bere hem wrong on honde:** accuse them wrongfully
229 **by:** concerning, about
231 **kan hir good:** knows what's good for her
232 **beren hym on honde:** deceive him by swearing   **cow:** chough, a crow-like bird, which can talk (see n.)
234 **Of hir assent:** of her agreement (i.e., the maid agrees with what she says)
235 **kaynard:** dotard
237 **overal ther:** wherever
238 **thrifty clooth:** serviceable clothing
241 **rowne:** whisper
243 **gossib:** close friend
244 **chidest as:** scold like
247 **with yvel preef:** bad luck to you

249 **costage:** expense
250 **heigh parage:** high birth
251 **tormentrie:** torture
252 **malencolie:** anger, sullenness (due to an excess of the humor)
254 **holour:** lecher
256 **ech a:** every
260 **daliaunce:** socializing
261 **smale:** slender
262 **by thy tale:** according to what you say
268 **chepe:** buy (i.e., take)
270 **make:** mate
271 **welde:** control
272 **his thankes:** willingly   **helde:** holde
273 **lorel:** scoundrel
275 **entendeth unto:** hopes (to go) to
276 **thonder-dynt:** thunderstroke   **levene:** lightning
277 **welked:** withered   **tobroke:** broken to pieces
278 **droppyng:** dripping, leaky
279 **chidyng:** scolding
283 **fast:** securely tied (in marriage)
284 **shrewe:** scoundrel

Thou seist that oxen, asses, hors, and houndes,
They been assayed at diverse stoundes;   286
Bacyns, lavours, er that men hem bye,
Spoones and stooles, and al swich housbondrye,
And so been pottes, clothes, and array;
But folk of wyves maken noon assay,   290
Til they be wedded—olde dotard shrewe!—
And thanne, seistow, we wol oure vices shewe.
    Thou seist also that it displeseth me
But if that thou wolt preyse my beautee,
And but thou poure alwey upon my face,   295
And clepe me "faire dame" in every place.
And but thou make a feeste on thilke day
That I was born, and make me fressh and gay;
And but thou do to my norice honour,
And to my chamberere withinne my bour,   300
And to my fadres folk and his allyes—
Thus seistow, olde barel-ful of lyes!
    And yet of oure apprentice Janekyn,
For his crispe heer, shynynge as gold so fyn,
And for he squiereth me bothe up and doun,   305
Yet hastow caught a fals suspecioun.
I wol hym noght, thogh thou were deed tomorwe!
    But tel me this: why hydestow, with sorwe,
The keyes of thy cheste awey fro me?
It is my good as wel as thyn, pardee!   310
What, wenestow make an ydiot of oure dame?
Now by that lord that called is Seint Jame,
Thou shalt nat bothe, thogh that thou were wood,
Be maister of my body and of my good;
That oon thou shalt forgo, maugree thyne yen.   315
What helpith it of me to enquere or spyen?
I trowe thou woldest loke me in thy chiste!
Thou sholdest seye, "Wyf, go wher thee liste;
Taak youre disport; I wol nat leve no talys.
I knowe yow for a trewe wyf, dame Alys."   320
We love no man that taketh kep or charge
Wher that we goon; we wol ben at oure large.

Of alle men yblessed moot he be,
The wise astrologien, Daun Ptholome,
That seith this proverbe in his Almageste: 325
"Of alle men his wysdom is the hyeste
That rekketh nevere who hath the world in honde."
By this proverbe thou shalt understonde,
Have thou ynogh, what thar thee recche or care
How myrily that othere folkes fare?   330
For, certeyn, olde dotard, by youre leve,
Ye shul have queynte right ynogh at eve.
He is to greet a nygard that wolde werne
A man to lighte a candle at his lanterne;
He shal have never the lasse light, pardee.   335
Have thou ynogh, thee thar nat pleyne thee.
    Thou seyst also, that if we make us gay
With clothyng, and with precious array,
That it is peril of oure chastitee;
And yet—with sorwe!—thou most enforce thee,   340
And seye thise wordes in the Apostles name:
"In habit maad with chastitee and shame
Ye wommen shul apparaille yow," quod he,
"And noght in tressed heer and gay perree,
As perles, ne with gold, ne clothes riche."   345
After thy text, ne after thy rubriche,
I wol nat wirche as muchel as a gnat.
    Thou seydest this, that I was lyk a cat;
For whoso wolde senge a cattes skyn,
Thanne wolde the cat wel dwellen in his in;   350
And if the cattes skyn be slyk and gay,
She wol nat dwelle in house half a day,
But forth she wole, er any day be dawed,
To shewe hir skyn and goon a-caterwawed.
This is to seye, if I be gay, sire shrewe,   355
I wol renne out my borel for to shewe.
    Sire olde fool, what helpeth thee to spyen?
Thogh thou preye Argus with his hundred yen
To be my warde-cors, as he kan best,

286 **diverse stoundes:** different times
287 **Bacyns:** basins   **lavours:** wash bowls   **bye:** pay for, buy
288 **housbondrye:** household equipment
290 **assay:** trial
291 **dotard shrewe:** senile scoundrel
295 **poure:** gaze intently
299 **norice:** nurse
300 **chamberere:** chambermaid   **bour:** bedchamber
301 **allyes:** kinsmen
302 **lyes:** lees (dregs)
304 **crispe:** curly
305 **squiereth:** formally attends
308 **hydestow:** do you hide   **with sorwe:** bad luck to you
311 **wenestow:** do you expect   **oure dame:** the lady of our house (me)
312 **Seint Jame:** St. James of Compostella
317 **loke:** lock   **chiste:** strongbox, coffer
319 **leve:** believe
322 **at oure large:** free to act as we wish

327 **in honde:** in his control
329 **thar:** need
331 **dotard:** senile fool
332 **queynte:** my elegant, pleasing thing (sexual favors)
333 **werne:** refuse
336 **thar nat pleyne thee:** need not complain
340 **enforce thee:** make an effort
341 **Apostles:** St. Paul's
342 **habit:** clothing
343 **apparaille yow:** dress yourselves
344 **tressed heer:** carefully arranged hair   **perree:** precious stones
346 **rubriche:** words written in red as a heading to a text
349 **senge:** singe
350 **wolde the cat:** the cat would want   **in:** dwelling-place
351 **slyk:** sleek, shining
353 **dawed:** dawned
354 **a-caterwawed:** caterwauling
356 **borel:** coarse, poor cloth (of which my clothes are made)
358 **Argus:** the mythical guardian of Io, one of Zeus's loves
359 **warde-cors:** bodyguard

In feith, he shal nat kepe me but me lest;   360
Yet koude I make his berd, so moot I thee!
    Thou seydest eek that ther been thynges thre,
The whiche thynges troublen al this erthe,
And that no wight may endure the ferthe.
O leeve sire shrewe, Jhesu shorte thy lyf!   365
Yet prechestow and seyst an hateful wyf
Yrekened is for oon of thise meschances.
Been ther none othere maner resemblances
That ye may likne youre parables to,
But if a sely wyf be oon of tho?   370
    Thou liknest eek wommenes love to helle,
To bareyne lond, ther water may nat dwelle.
Thou liknest it also to wilde fyr;
The moore it brenneth, the moore it hath desir
To consume every thyng that brent wole be.   375
Thou seyest, right as wormes shende a tree,
Right so a wyf destroyeth hire housbonde;
This knowe they that been to wyves bonde.'
    Lordynges, right thus, as ye have understonde,
Baar I stifly myne olde housbondes on honde   380
That thus they seyden in hir dronkenesse;
And al was fals, but that I took witnesse
On Janekyn, and on my nece also.
O Lord! The peyne I dide hem and the wo,
Ful giltelees, by Goddes sweete pyne!   385
For as an hors I koude byte and whyne.
I koude pleyne, and yit was in the gilt,
Or elles often tyme hadde I been spilt.
Whoso that first to mille comth, first grynt;
I pleyned first, so was oure werre ystynt.   390
They were ful glade to excuse hem blyve
Of thyng of which they nevere agilte hir lyve.
Of wenches wolde I beren hem on honde,
Whan that for syk unnethes myghte they stonde.
    Yet tikled I his herte, for that he   395
Wende that I hadde of hym so greet chiertee!

I swoor that al my walkynge out by nyghte
Was for t'espye wenches that he dighte;
Under that colour hadde I many a myrthe.
For al swich wit is yeven us in oure byrthe;   400
Deceite, wepyng, spynnyng God hath yive
To wommen kyndely, whil that they may lyve.
And thus of o thyng I avaunte me:
Atte ende I hadde the bettre in ech degree,
By sleighte, or force, or by som maner thyng,   405
As by continueel murmur or grucchyng.
Namely abedde hadden they meschaunce:
Ther wolde I chide and do hem no plesaunce;
I wolde no lenger in the bed abyde,
If that I felte his arm over my syde,   410
Til he had maad his raunson unto me;
Thanne wolde I suffre hym do his nycetee.
And therfor every man this tale I telle,
Wynne whoso may, for al is for to selle;
With empty hand men may none haukes lure.   415
For wynnyng wolde I al his lust endure,
And make me a feyned appetit;
And yet in bacon hadde I nevere delit.
That made me that evere I wolde hem chide,
For thogh the pope hadde seten hem biside,   420
I wolde nat spare hem at hir owene bord,
For, by my trouthe, I quitte hem word for word.
As helpe me verray God omnipotent,
Though I right now sholde make my testament,
I ne owe hem nat a word that it nys quit.   425
I broghte it so aboute by my wit
That they moste yeve it up, as for the beste,
Or elles hadde we nevere been in reste;
For thogh he looked as a wood leon,
Yet sholde he faille of his conclusion.   430
    Thanne wolde I seye, 'Goode lief, taak keep
How mekely looketh Wilkyn, oure sheep!
Com neer, my spouse, lat me ba thy cheke!
Ye sholde been al pacient and meke,

---

361 **make his berd:** deceive him   **so moot I thee:** as I may prosper
373 **wilde fyr:** Greek fire, an inflammable mixture, used in warfare
376 **shende:** destroy
378 **bonde:** bound
380 **Baar I stifly . . . on honde:** I firmly swore
382 **but that:** except that
383 **nece:** kinswoman
385 **pyne:** suffering
386 **whyne:** whinny, whine
387 **in the gilt:** in the wrong
388 **spilt:** ruined
389 **grynt** *gryndeth,* grinds
391 **blyve:** quickly
392 **agilte hir lyve:** been guilty in their lives
393 **beren hem on honde:** accuse them
394 **syk:** illness   **unnethes:** hardly
395 **tikled:** tickled, pleased
396 **chiertee:** fondness

398 **dighte:** copulated with
399 **colour:** pretense
402 **kyndely:** naturally
403 **avaunte me:** boast
404 **in ech degree:** in all respects
406 **murmur:** grumbling   **grucchyng:** complaining
407 **abedde:** in bed
411 **maad his raunson:** paid his penalty
412 **nycetee:** foolishness, lust
416 **wynnyng:** profit
417 **feyned:** pretended
418 **bacon:** bacon (i.e., preserved old meat)
421 **bord:** table
422 **quitte:** repaid
424 **testament:** will
430 **faille of his conclusion:** fail to attain his goal
431 **Goode lief:** sweetheart
432 **mekely:** meekly   **Wilkyn:** Willie
433 **neer:** nearer   **ba:** kiss

And han a sweete spiced conscience,   435
Sith ye so preche of Jobes pacience.
Suffreth alwey, syn ye so wel kan preche;
And but ye do, certein we shal yow teche
That it is fair to have a wyf in pees.
Oon of us two moste bowen, doutelees,   440
And sith a man is moore resonable
Than womman is, ye moste been suffrable.
What eyleth yow to grucche thus and grone?
Is it for ye wolde have my queynte allone?
Wy, taak it al! Lo, have it every deel!   445
Peter! I shrewe yow, but ye love it weel;
For if I wolde selle my *bele chose,*
I koude walke as fressh as is a rose;
But I wol kepe it for youre owene tooth.
Ye be to blame, by God! I sey yow sooth.'   450
     Swiche manere wordes hadde we on honde.
Now wol I speken of my fourthe housbonde.

     My fourthe housbonde was a revelour—
This is to seyn, he hadde a paramour—
And I was yong and ful of ragerye,   455
Stibourn and strong, and joly as a pye.
How koude I daunce to an harpe smale,
And synge, ywis, as any nyghtyngale,
Whan I had dronke a draughte of sweete wyn!
Metellius, the foule cherl, the swyn,   460
That with a staf birafte his wyf hir lyf,
For she drank wyn, thogh I hadde been his wyf,
He sholde nat han daunted me fro drynke!
And after wyn on Venus moste I thynke,
For al so siker as cold engendreth hayl,   465
A likerous mouth moste han a likerous tayl.
In wommen vinolent is no defence—
This knowen lecchours by experience.
     But—Lord Crist!—whan that it remembreth me
Upon my yowthe, and on my jolitee,   470

It tikleth me aboute myn herte roote.
Unto this day it dooth myn herte boote
That I have had my world as in my tyme.
But age, allas, that al wole envenyme,
Hath me biraft my beautee and my pith.   475
Lat go. Farewel! The devel go therwith!
The flour is goon; ther is namoore to telle;
The bren, as I best kan, now moste I selle;
But yet to be right myrie wol I fonde.
Now wol I tellen of my fourthe housbonde.   480
     I seye, I hadde in herte greet despit
That he of any oother had delit.
But he was quit, by God and by Seint Joce!
I made hym of the same wode a croce;
Nat of my body, in no foul manere,   485
But certeinly, I made folk swich cheere
That in his owene grece I made hym frye
For angre, and for verray jalousye.
By God, in erthe I was his purgatorie,
For which I hope his soule be in glorie.   490
For, God it woot, he sat ful ofte and song,
Whan that his shoo ful bitterly hym wrong.
Ther was no wight, save God and he, that wiste,
In many wise, how soore I hym twiste.
He deyde whan I cam fro Jerusalem,   495
And lith ygrave under the roode beem,
Al is his tombe noght so curyus
As was the sepulcre of hym Daryus,
Which that Appelles wroghte subtilly;
It nys but wast to burye hym preciously.   500
Lat hym fare wel; God yeve his soule reste!
He is now in his grave and in his cheste.
     Now of my fifthe housbonde wol I telle.
God lete his soule nevere come in helle!
And yet was he to me the mooste shrewe;   505
That feele I on my ribbes al by rewe,

435 **spiced:** scrupulous
436 **Jobes:** (the biblical Job's
442 **suffrable:** able to bear suffering
444 **queynte:** elegant, pleasing thing (sexual favors)
445 **have it every deel:** have every bit of it
446 **Peter!:** by, in the name of, St. Peter   **shrewe yow, but ye:** curse you unless you (if you do not)
447 **bele chose:** beautiful thing (sexual favors)
449 **tooth:** taste, pleasure
450 **I sey yow sooth:** I am telling you the truth
453 **revelour:** reveller, profligate
454 **paramour:** lady-love, concubine
455 **ragerye:** wantonness
456 **Stibourn:** stubborn   **pye:** magpie
460 **Metellius:** Egnatius Metellius   **cherl:** villain
461 **birafte:** took away from
462 **thogh:** although if
463 **daunted:** frightened
465 **al so siker as:** as surely as
466 **likerous mouth:** a gluttonous mouth   **likerous tayl:** lecherous tail
467 **vinolent:** drunken
469 **it remembreth me:** I remember

471 **herte roote:** the bottom of my heart
472 **dooth myn herte boote:** does my heart good
474 **envenyme:** poison
475 **biraft:** taken away   **pith:** vigor
478 **bren:** bran
479 **fonde:** try
483 **Seint Joce:** St. Judocus
484 **croce:** cross
487 **grece:** grease
490 **hope:** suppose
492 **wrong:** pinched
493 **wiste:** knew
494 **twiste:** tortured
495 **deyde:** died
496 **ygrave:** buried   **roode beem:** beam supporting the cross at the entrance to the choir of the church
498 **sepulcre:** sepulcher   **hym Daryus:** that Darius
499 **Appelles:** the Jewish craftsman supposedly responsible for Darius's tomb
500 **preciously:** expensively
502 **cheste:** coffin
505 **mooste shrewe:** greatest scoundrel
506 **by rewe:** in a row, one after another

And evere shal unto myn endyng day.
But in oure bed he was so fressh and gay,
And therwithal so wel koude he me glose,
Whan that he wolde han my *bele chose;*   510
That thogh he hadde me bete on every bon,
He koude wynne agayn my love anon.
I trowe I loved hym best, for that he
Was of his love daungerous to me.
We wommen han, if that I shal nat lye,   515
In this matere a queynte fantasye:
Wayte what thyng we may nat lightly have,
Therafter wol we crie al day and crave.
Forbede us thyng, and that desiren we;
Preesse on us faste, and thanne wol we fle.   520
With daunger oute we al oure chaffare;
Greet prees at market maketh deere ware,
And to greet cheep is holde at litel prys:
This knoweth every womman that is wys.   524
    My fifthe housbonde—God his soule blesse!—
Which that I took for love, and no richesse,
He som tyme was a clerk of Oxenford,
And hadde left scole, and wente at hom to bord
With my gossib, dwellynge in oure toun;
God have hir soule! Hir name was Alisoun.   530
She knew myn herte, and eek my privetee,
Bet than oure parisshe preest, so moot I thee!
To hire biwreyed I my conseil al.
For hadde myn housbonde pissed on a wal,
Or doon a thyng that sholde han cost his lyf,   535
To hire, and to another worthy wyf,
And to my nece, which that I loved weel,
I wolde han toold his conseil every deel.
And so I dide ful often, God it woot,
That made his face often reed and hoot   540
For verray shame, and blamed hymself for he
Had toold to me so greet a pryvetee.
    And so bifel that ones in a Lente—
So often tymes I to my gossyb wente,
For evere yet I loved to be gay,   545
And for to walke in March, Averill, and May,
Fro hous to hous, to heere sondry talys—
That Jankyn clerk, and my gossyb dame Alys,

And I myself, into the feeldes wente.
Myn housbonde was at Londoun al that Lente;   550
I hadde the bettre leyser for to pleye,
And for to se, and eek for to be seye
Of lusty folk. What wiste I wher my grace
Was shapen for to be, or in what place?
Therfore I made my visitaciouns   555
To vigilies and to processiouns,
To prechyng eek, and to thise pilgrimages,
To pleyes of myracles, and to mariages,
And wered upon my gaye scarlet gytes.
Thise wormes, ne thise motthes, ne thise mytes, 560
Upon my peril, frete hem never a deel;
And wostow why? For they were used weel.
    Now wol I tellen forth what happed me.
I seye that in the feeldes walked we,
Til trewely we hadde swich daliance,   565
This clerk and I, that of my purveiance
I spak to hym and seyde hym how that he,
If I were wydwe, sholde wedde me.
For certeinly—I sey for no bobance—
Yet was I nevere withouten purveiance   570
Of mariage, n'of othere thynges eek.
I holde a mouses herte nat worth a leek
That hath but oon hole for to sterte to,
And if that faille, thanne is al ydo.
    I bar hym on honde he hadde enchanted me—   575
My dame taughte me that soutiltee—
And eek I seyde I mette of hym al nyght,
He wolde han slayn me as I lay upright,
And al my bed was ful of verray blood;
'But yet I hope that ye shal do me good,   580
For blood bitokeneth gold, as me was taught.'
And al was fals; I dremed of it right naught,
But as I folwed ay my dames loore,
As wel of this as of othere thynges moore.
    But now, sire, lat me se what I shal seyn.   585
A ha! By God, I have my tale ageyn.
    Whan that my fourthe housbonde was on beere,

509 **glose:** flatter
510 **bele chose:** beautiful thing (sexual favors)
514 **daungerous:** standoffish, hard to get
516 **queynte fantasye:** curious, strange inclination
517 **Wayte what:** note that whatever   **lightly:** easily
520 **Preesse:** press, entreat
521 With niggardliness (*daunger*) we spread out (*oute*) all our merchandise (*chaffare*).
522 **prees:** crowd   **deere:** expensive
523 **to greet cheep:** too good a bargain
527 **som tyme:** once, formerly
529 **gossib:** close friend
533 **biwreyed:** revealed
542 **pryvetee:** secret

551 **leyser:** leisure, opportunity
552 **seye:** seen
554 **shapen:** destined
556 **vigilies:** gatherings on the evenings before religious holidays
558 **pleyes of myracles:** popular dramas on religious subjects
559 **gytes:** robes
560 **motthes:** moths   **mytes:** small insects
561 **Upon my peril:** (I swear) on peril (of my soul)   **frete:** devoured   **never a deel:** not a bit
565 **daliance:** flirtation
566 **purveiance:** foresight, provision
569 **bobance:** boast
576 **dame:** mother   **soutiltee:** subtlety, trick
577 **mette:** dreamed
582 **right naught:** not at all
587 **beere:** bier

I weep algate, and made sory cheere,
As wyves mooten, for it is usage,
And with my coverchief covered my visage,   590
But for that I was purveyed of a make,
I wepte but smal, and that I undertake.

   To chirche was myn housbonde born a-morwe
With neighebores, that for hym maden sorwe;
And Jankyn, oure clerk, was oon of tho.   595
As help me God, whan that I saugh hym go
After the beere, me thoughte he hadde a paire
Of legges and of feet so clene and faire
That al myn herte I yaf unto his hoold.
He was, I trowe, twenty wynter oold,   600
And I was fourty, if I shal seye sooth;
But yet I hadde alwey a coltes tooth.
Gat-tothed I was, and that bicam me weel;
I hadde the prente of seinte Venus seel.
As help me God, I was a lusty oon,   605
And faire, and riche, and yong, and wel bigon,
And trewely, as myne housbondes tolde me,
I hadde the beste *quoniam* myghte be.
For certes, I am al Venerien
In feelynge, and myn herte is Marcien.   610
Venus me yaf my lust, my likerousnesse,
And Mars yaf me my sturdy hardynesse;
Myn ascendent was Taur, and Mars therinne.
Allas, allas! That evere love was synne!
I folwed ay myn inclinacioun   615
By vertu of my constellacioun;
That made me I koude noght withdrawe
My chambre of Venus from a good felawe.
Yet have I Martes mark upon my face,
And also in another privee place.   620
For God so wys be my savacioun,

I ne loved nevere by no discrecioun,
But evere folwede myn appetit,
Al were he short, or long, or blak, or whit;
I took no kep, so that he liked me,   625
How poore he was, ne eek of what degree.

   What sholde I seye but, at the monthes ende,
This joly clerk, Jankyn, that was so hende,
Hath wedded me with greet solempnytee,
And to hym yaf I al the lond and fee   630
That evere was me yeven therbifoore.
But afterward repented me ful soore;
He nolde suffre nothyng of my list.
By God, he smoot me ones on the lyst,
For that I rente out of his book a leef,   635
That of the strook myn ere wax al deef.
Stibourn I was as is a leonesse,
And of my tonge a verray jangleresse,
And walke I wolde, as I had doon biforn,
From hous to hous, although he had it sworn;   640
For which he often tymes wolde preche,
And me of olde Romayn geestes teche;
How he Symplicius Gallus lefte his wyf,
And hire forsook for terme of al his lyf,
Noght but for open-heveded he hir say   645
Lookynge out at his dore upon a day.

   Another Romayn tolde he me by name,
That, for his wyf was at a someres game
Withouten his wityng, he forsook hire eke.
And thanne wolde he upon his Bible seke   650
That ilke proverbe of Ecclesiaste
Where he comandeth and forbedeth faste
Man shal nat suffre his wyf go roule aboute.
Thanne wolde he seye right thus, withouten doute:

   'Whoso that buyldeth his hous al of salwes,   655
And priketh his blynde hors over the falwes,

588 **algate:** continuously
591 **purveyed of:** provided with beforehand
592 **smal:** little   **undertake:** affirm, declare
593 **a-morwe:** next morning
599 **hoold:** keeping
600 **wynter:** years
602 **coltes tooth:** youthful tastes, desires
603 **Gat-tothed:** with teeth set wide apart
604 **prente:** imprint, mark   **Venus seel:** Venus's mark, a birthmark
606 **wel bigon:** in a good situation
608 **quoniam:** whatsit (literally, *because* or *whereas*), a euphemism
609 **Venerien:** dominated by the planet Venus
610 **Marcien:** dominated by the planet Mars
612 **hardynesse:** boldness
613 **ascendent was Taur:** ascending sign was Taurus, the bull; see n. for the astro.
details in lines 613–20.
615 **inclinacioun:** astrologically determined inclination
616 **constellacioun:** configuration of the heavenly bodies, horoscope
617 **withdrawe:** withhold
619 **Martes mark:** mark of Mars, a reddish birthmark
620 **privee:** secret
621 **God so wys be:** as may God surely be   **savacioun:** salvation

622 **discrecioun:** moderation, prudence
625 **so that:** providing that
628 **hende:** courteous
630 **fee:** property
633 **list:** desires
634 **lyst:** ear
635 **rente:** tore
637 **Stibourn:** stubborn
638 **jangleresse:** chatterbox
640 **it sworn:** sworn the contrary
642 **geestes:** stories
643 **Symplicius Gallus:** His story is told by Valerius Maximus, as is the incident in
647 below.
645 **open-heveded:** bareheaded   **say:** saw
647 **Another Romayn:** See 643 above.
648 **someres game:** midsummer revels
649 **wityng:** knowledge
651 **Ecclesiaste:** Ecclesiasticus
652 **he:** the author of Ecclesiasticus
653 **roule:** wander
655 **salwes:** willow branches
656 **falwes:** open fields (idle land)

And suffreth his wyf to go seken halwes,
Is worthy to been hanged on the galwes!'
But al for noght, I sette noght an hawe
Of his proverbes n'of his olde sawe,   660
Ne I wolde nat of hym corrected be.
I hate hym that my vices telleth me,
And so doo mo, God woot, of us than I.
This made hym with me wood al outrely;
I nolde noght forbere hym in no cas.   665
    Now wol I seye yow sooth, by Seint Thomas,
Why that I rente out of his book a leef,
For which he smoot me so that I was deef.
    He hadde a book that gladly, nyght and day,
For his desport he wolde rede alway;   670
He cleped it Valerie and Theofraste,
At which book he lough alwey ful faste.
And eek ther was somtyme a clerk at Rome,
A cardinal, that highte Seint Jerome,
That made a book agayn Jovinian;   675
In which book eek ther was Tertulan,
Crisippus, Trotula, and Helowys,
That was abbesse nat fer fro Parys,
And eek the Parables of Salomon,
Ovides Art, and bookes many on,   680
And alle thise were bounden in o volume.
And every nyght and day was his custume,
Whan he hadde leyser and vacacioun
From oother worldly occupacioun,
To reden on this book of wikked wyves.   685
He knew of hem mo legendes and lyves
Than been of goode wyves in the Bible.
For trusteth wel, it is an impossible
That any clerk wol speke good of wyves,
But if it be of hooly seintes lyves,   690
Ne of noon oother womman never the mo.
Who peyntede the leon, tel me who?

By God, if wommen hadde writen stories,
As clerkes han withinne hire oratories,
They wolde han writen of men moore wikkednesse
Than al the mark of Adam may redresse.   696
The children of Mercurie and of Venus
Been in hir wirkyng ful contrarius;
Mercurie loveth wysdam and science,
And Venus loveth ryot and dispence.   700
And, for hire diverse disposicioun,
Ech falleth in otheres exaltacioun.
And thus, God woot, Mercurie is desolat
In Pisces, wher Venus is exaltat,
And Venus falleth ther Mercurie is reysed.   705
Therfore no womman of no clerk is preysed.
The clerk, whan he is oold, and may noght do
Of Venus werkes worth his olde sho,
Thanne sit he doun, and writ in his dotage
That wommen kan nat kepe hir mariage!   710
    But now to purpos, why I tolde thee
That I was beten for a book, pardee!
Upon a nyght Jankyn, that was oure sire,
Redde on his book, as he sat by the fire,
Of Eva first, that for hir wikkednesse   715
Was al mankynde broght to wrecchednesse,
For which that Jhesu Crist hymself was slayn,
That boghte us with his herte blood agayn.
Lo, heere expres of womman may ye fynde
That womman was the los of al mankynde.   720
    Tho redde he me how Sampson loste his heres:
Slepynge, his lemman kitte it with hir sheres;
Thurgh which treson loste he bothe his yen.
    Tho redde he me, if that I shal nat lyen,
Of Hercules and of his Dianyre,   725
That caused hym to sette hymself afyre.
    No thyng forgat he the care and the wo
That Socrates hadde with his wyves two,

657 **seken halwes:** go on pilgrimages
659 **hawe:** haw, hawthorn berry (i.e., nothing)
664 **al outrely:** entirely
665 **forbere:** put up with
671–80 **Valerie and Theofraste:** Valerius, supposed author of the *Dissuasio* (or *Epistola*) *ad Rufinum,* and Theophrastus, author of the *Golden Book on Marriage,* both works attacking marriage. Jankyn's book of "wicked wives" also contains passages from the book by *Jerome* (a father of the Church) *agayn Jovinian* (an unorthodox monk who denied that virginity was necessarily superior to marriage), *Tertulan* (Tertullian, whose works contain misogynist and anti-marriage passages), *Crisippus* (mentioned by Jerome but otherwise unknown), *Trotula* (probably Trotula di Ruggiero, a female physician and author), *Helowys* (Heloïse, lover of Abelard), the *Parables of Salomon* (Prov. 10.1 to 22.16 in the Vulgate), and *Ovides Art* (Ovid's *Ars amatoria*). For further information see n. to lines 669–75.
673 **clerk:** scholar
683 **vacacioun:** spare time
688 **impossible:** impossibility
689 **clerk:** learned man, clergyman
691 **never the mo:** in any way
692 The lion's question when he saw a picture of a man killing a lion

693 **stories:** histories
694 **oratories:** chapels
696 **mark of Adam:** male sex
697 **children of Mercurie:** those dominated by the planet Mercury (scholars)
of Venus: those dominated by Venus, lovers
698 **wirkyng ful contrarius:** actions directly contrary
699 **science:** knowledge
700 **ryot:** debauchery   **dispence:** extravagant expenditures
702 **exaltacioun:** the zodiacal sign in which a planet is most powerful
703 **desolat:** powerless
704 **Pisces:** the zodiacal sign   **exaltat:** exalted (has her exaltation, is most powerful)
711 **now to purpos:** now to the point
713 **oure sire:** master of our house
715 **Eva:** Eve
719 **expres:** clearly
721 **Sampson:** For the story see MkT VII.2015–94.
725 **Hercules and . . . Dianyre:** For the story see MkT VII.2119–35.

How Xantippa caste pisse upon his heed.
This sely man sat stille as he were deed;   730
He wiped his heed, namoore dorste he seyn,
But 'Er that thonder stynte, comth a reyn!'

    Of Phasipha, that was the queene of Crete,
For shrewednesse, hym thoughte the tale swete;
Fy! Spek namoore—it is a grisly thyng—   735
Of hire horrible lust and hir likyng.

    Of Clitermystra, for hire lecherye,
That falsly made hire housbonde for to dye,
He redde it with ful good devocioun.

    He tolde me eek for what occasioun   740
Amphiorax at Thebes loste his lyf.
Myn housbonde hadde a legende of his wyf,
Eriphilem, that for an ouche of gold
Hath prively unto the Grekes told
Wher that hir housbonde hidde hym in a place,   745
For which he hadde at Thebes sory grace.

    Of Lyvia tolde he me, and of Lucye:
They bothe made hir housbondes for to dye,
That oon for love, that oother was for hate.
Lyvia hir housbonde, on an even late,   750
Empoysoned hath, for that she was his fo;
Lucia, likerous, loved hire housbonde so
That, for he sholde alwey upon hire thynke,
She yaf hym swich a manere love-drynke
That he was deed er it were by the morwe;   755
And thus algates housbondes han sorwe.

    Thanne tolde he me how oon Latumyus
Compleyned unto his felawe Arrius
That in his gardyn growed swich a tree
On which he seyde how that his wyves thre   760
Hanged hemself for herte despitus.
'O leeve brother,' quod this Arrius,
'Yif me a plante of thilke blissed tree,
And in my gardyn planted shal it bee.'

    Of latter date, of wyves hath he red   765
That somme han slayn hir housbondes in hir bed,
And lete hir lecchour dighte hire al the nyght,

Whan that the corps lay in the floor upright.
And somme han dryve nayles in hir brayn,
Whil that they slepte, and thus they had hem slayn.   770
Somme han hem yeve poysoun in hire drynke.
He spak moore harm than herte may bithynke,
And therwithal he knew of mo proverbes
Than in this world ther growen gras or herbes.
'Bet is,' quod he, 'thyn habitacioun   775
Be with a leon or a foul dragoun,
Than with a womman usynge for to chyde.
Bet is,' quod he, 'hye in the roof abyde,
Than with an angry wyf doun in the hous;
They been so wikked and contrarious,   780
They haten that hir housbondes loven ay.'
He seyde, 'A womman cast hir shame away,
Whan she cast of hir smok'; and forthermo,
'A fair womman, but she be chaast also,
Is lyk a gold ryng in a sowes nose.'   785
Who wolde wene, or who wolde suppose,
The wo that in myn herte was, and pyne?

    And whan I saugh he wolde nevere fyne
To reden on this cursed book al nyght,
Al sodeynly thre leves have I plyght   790
Out of his book, right as he radde, and eke
I with my fest so took hym on the cheke
That in oure fyr he fil bakward adoun.
And he up stirte as dooth a wood leoun,
And with his fest he smoot me on the heed   795
That in the floor I lay as I were deed.
And whan he saugh how stille that I lay,
He was agast and wolde han fled his way,
Til atte laste out of my swogh I breyde.
'O! hastow slayn me, false theef?' I seyde,   800
'And for my land thus hastow mordred me?
Er I be deed, yet wol I kisse thee.'

    And neer he cam, and kneled faire adoun,
And seyde, 'Deere suster Alisoun,
As help me God, I shal thee nevere smyte!   805
That I have doon, it is thyself to wyte.
Foryeve it me, and that I thee biseke!'
And yet eftsoones I hitte hym on the cheke,

---

729 **Xantippa:** Xantippe, shrewish wife of *Socrates,* the Greek philosopher
733 **Phasipha:** Pasiphae, mother of the Minotaur, fathered on her by a bull
734 **shrewednesse:** malignancy
737 **Clitermystra:** Clytemnestra murdered her husband Agamemnon, the Greek king
who waged war against Troy.
741 **Amphiorax:** Amphiaraus died at Thebes because he took the advice of his wife
Eriphyle (*Eriphilem*).
743 **ouche:** brooch
746 **sory grace:** misfortune
747 **Lyvia:** Livia, lover of Sejanus   **Lucye:** Lucia, wife of the Roman poet Lucretius
751 **Empoysoned:** poisoned
756 **algates:** always
757–58 **Latumyus, Arrius:** see n.
767 **dighte:** copulate with

772 **harm:** slander   **bithynke:** imagine
777 **usynge for to:** used to
783 **smok:** shift, undergarment
788 **fyne:** cease
790 **plyght:** plucked
791 **radde:** read
792 **took hym:** gave him (a blow)
799 **swogh:** swoon   **breyde:** started up, awoke
806 **to wyte:** to blame
808 **eftsoones:** immediately

And seyde, 'Theef, thus muchel am I wreke;
Now wol I dye, I may no lenger speke.'   810
But atte laste, with muchel care and wo,
We fille acorded by us selven two.
He yaf me al the bridel in myn hond,
To han the governance of hous and lond,
And of his tonge, and of his hond also;   815
And made hym brenne his book anon right tho.
And whan that I hadde geten unto me,
By maistrie, al the soveraynetee,
And that he seyde, 'Myn owene trewe wyf,
Do as thee lust the terme of al thy lyf;   820
Keep thyn honour, and keep eek myn estaat'—
After that day we hadden never debaat.
God helpe me so, I was to hym as kynde
As any wyf from Denmark unto Ynde,
And also trewe, and so was he to me.   825
I prey to God, that sit in magestee,
So blesse his soule for his mercy deere.
Now wol I seye my tale, if ye wol heere."

Biholde the wordes bitwene the
Somonour and the Frere.

The Frere lough, whan he hadde herd al this;
"Now dame," quod he, "so have I joye or blis,   830
This is a long preamble of a tale!"

And whan the Somonour herde the Frere gale,
"Lo," quod the Somonour, "Goddes armes two!
A frere wol entremette hym everemo.
Lo, goode men, a flye and eek a frere   835
Wol falle in every dyssh and eek mateere.
What spekestow of preambulacioun?
What! amble, or trotte, or pees, or go sit doun!
Thou lettest oure disport in this manere."
     "Ye, woltow so, sire Somonour?" quod the Frere;
"Now, by my feith I shal, er that I go,   841
Telle of a somonour swich a tale or two
That alle the folk shal laughen in this place."
     "Now elles, Frere, I bishrewe thy face,"
Quod this Somonour, "and I bishrewe me,   845
But if I telle tales two or thre
Of freres er I come to Sidyngborne
That I shal make thyn herte for to morne,
For wel I woot thy pacience is gon."
     Oure Hooste cride "Pees! And that anon!"   850
And seyde, "Lat the womman telle hire tale.
Ye fare as folk that dronken ben of ale.
Do, dame, telle forth youre tale, and that is best."
     "Al redy, sire," quod she, "right as yow lest,
If I have licence of this worthy Frere."   855
     "Yis, dame," quod he, "tel forth, and I wol heere."

Heere endeth the Wyf of Bathe hir Prologe.

The Wife of Bath's Tale

Heere bigynneth the Tale of the Wyf of Bathe.

In th'olde dayes of the Kyng Arthour,
Of which that Britons speken greet honour,
Al was this land fulfild of fayerye.
The elf-queene, with hir joly compaignye,   860
Daunced ful ofte in many a grene mede.
This was the olde opinion, as I rede;
I speke of manye hundred yeres ago.
But now kan no man se none elves mo,

For now the grete charitee and prayeres   865
Of lymytours and othere hooly freres,
That serchen every lond and every streem,

809 **wreke:** avenged
818 **soveraynetee:** sovereignty, mastery
824 **Denmark unto Ynde:** throughout the whole world

859 The whole country was filled with fairies.
860 **elf-queene:** fairy queen

832 **gale:** cry out
834 **entremette hym:** interfere
837 **preambulacioun:** making a preamble
838 **amble, or trotte, or pees:** amble (an easy lateral walk on horseback; i.e., go slow), trot (i.e., go fast), or keep still
839 **lettest:** hinder
844 **bishrewe:** curse
847 **Sidyngborne:** Sittingbourne, a town between Rochester and Canterbury, about 40 miles from London
848 **morne:** mourn
852 **fare:** act
856 **Yis:** yes indeed

866 **lymytours:** friars (see GP I.209)
867 **serchen:** haunt

As thikke as motes in the sonne-beem,
Blessynge halles, chambres, kichenes, boures,
Citees, burghes, castels, hye toures,   870
Thropes, bernes, shipnes, dayeryes—
This maketh that ther ben no fayeryes.
For ther as wont to walken was an elf
Ther walketh now the lymytour hymself
In undermeles and in morwenynges,   875
And seyth his matyns and his hooly thynges
As he gooth in his lymytacioun.
→ Wommen may go saufly up and doun.
In every bussh or under every tree
Ther is noon oother incubus but he,   880
And he ne wol doon hem but dishonour.

   And so bifel that this kyng Arthour
Hadde in his hous a lusty bacheler,
That on a day cam ridynge fro ryver,
And happed that, allone as he was born,   885
He saugh a mayde walkynge hym biforn,
Of which mayde anon, maugree hir heed,
By verray force, he rafte hire maydenhed;
For which oppressioun was swich clamour
And swich pursute unto the kyng Arthour   890
That dampned was this knyght for to be deed,
By cours of lawe, and sholde han lost his heed—
Paraventure swich was the statut tho—
But that the queene and other ladyes mo
So longe preyeden the kyng of grace   895
Til he his lyf hym graunted in the place,
And yaf hym to the queene, al at hir wille,
To chese wheither she wolde hym save or spille.

   The queene thanketh the kyng with al hir myght,
And after this thus spak she to the knyght,   900
Whan that she saugh hir tyme, upon a day:
"Thou standest yet," quod she, "in swich array
That of thy lyf yet hastow no suretee.

I grante thee lyf, if thou kanst tellen me
What thyng is it that wommen moost desiren.   905
Be war, and keep thy nekke-boon from iren!
And if thou kanst nat tellen it anon,
Yet wol I yeve thee leve for to gon
A twelf-month and a day, to seche and leere
An answere suffisant in this mateere;   910
And suretee wol I han, er that thou pace,
Thy body for to yelden in this place."

   Wo was this knyght, and sorwefully he siketh;
But what! He may nat do al as hym liketh.
And at the laste he chees hym for to wende   915
And come agayn, right at the yeres ende,
With swich answere as God wolde hym purveye;
And taketh his leve, and wendeth forth his weye.

   He seketh every hous and every place
Where as he hopeth for to fynde grace   920
To lerne what thyng wommen loven moost,
But he ne koude arryven in no coost
Wher as he myghte fynde in this mateere
Two creatures accordynge in-feere.
Somme seyde wommen loven best richesse,   925
Somme seyde honour, somme seyde jolynesse,
Somme riche array, somme seyden lust abedde,
And oftetyme to be wydwe and wedde.
Somme seyde that oure hertes been moost esed
Whan that we been yflatered and yplesed.   930
He gooth ful ny the sothe, I wol nat lye.
A man shal wynne us best with flaterye,
And with attendance and with bisynesse
Been we ylymed, bothe moore and lesse.

   And somme seyen that we loven best   935
For to be free and do right as us lest,
And that no man repreve us of oure vice,
But seye that we be wise and no thyng nyce.
For trewely ther is noon of us alle,
If any wight wol clawe us on the galle,   940
That we nel kike, for he seith us sooth.
Assay, and he shal fynde it that so dooth;

---

868 **motes:** specks of dust
869 **boures:** bedrooms
870 **burghes:** boroughs
871 **Thropes:** villages **bernes:** barns **shipnes:** stables **dayeryes:** dairies
875 **undermeles:** late mornings (from 9 to 12) **morwenynges:** mornings
876 **matyns:** matins, morning prayers
877 **lymytacioun:** territory
878 **saufly:** safely
880 **incubus:** evil spirit, said to copulate with women
883 **bacheler:** young knight
884 **ryver:** hawking for waterfowl
887 **maugree hir heed:** against her will, despite all she could do
888 **rafte:** took
889 **oppressioun:** wrong
890 **pursute:** suing for justice
893 **Paraventure:** perhaps
898 **spille:** put to death
903 **suretee:** security

906 **iren:** iron (i.e., the executioner's axe)
909 **seche:** search **leere:** learn
911 **suretee:** pledge
912 **yelden:** surrender
917 **purveye:** provide
922 **coost:** coast (region)
924 **accordynge in-feere:** agreeing together, in agreement
931 **gooth ful ny the sothe:** gets very close to the truth
933 **attendance:** attention
934 **ylymed:** caught (as with bird-lime)
936 **us lest:** we please
937 **repreve:** reprove
940 **clawe us on the galle:** rub a sore spot
941 **nel kike:** will not (*nel = ne wil*) kick back

For, be we never so vicious withinne,
We wol been holden wise and clene of synne.
 And somme seyn that greet delit han we 945
For to been holden stable, and eek secree,
And in o purpos stedefastly to dwelle,
And nat biwreye thyng that men us telle.
But that tale is nat worth a rake-stele.
Pardee, we wommen konne no thyng hele; 950
Witnesse on Myda—wol ye heere the tale?
 Ovyde, amonges othere thynges smale,
Seyde Myda hadde, under his longe heres,
Growynge upon his heed two asses eres,
The whiche vice he hydde as he best myghte 955
Ful subtilly from every mannes sighte,
That, save his wyf, ther wiste of it namo.
He loved hire moost, and trusted hire also;
He preyede hire that to no creature
She sholde tellen of his disfigure. 960
 She swoor him, "Nay"; for al this world to wynne,
She nolde do that vileynye or synne,
To make hir housbonde han so foul a name.
She nolde nat telle it for hir owene shame.
But nathelees, hir thoughte that she dyde 965
That she so longe sholde a conseil hyde;
Hir thoughte it swal so soore aboute hir herte
That nedely som word hire moste asterte;
And sith she dorste telle it to no man,
Doun to a mareys faste by she ran— 970
Til she cam there hir herte was afyre—
And as a bitore bombleth in the myre,
She leyde hir mouth unto the water doun:
"Biwreye me nat, thou water, with thy soun,"
Quod she; "to thee I telle it and namo; 975
Myn housbonde hath longe asses erys two!
Now is myn herte al hool; now is it oute.
I myghte no lenger kepe it, out of doute."
Heere may ye se, thogh we a tyme abyde,
Yet out it moot; we kan no conseil hyde. 980

The remenant of the tale if ye wol heere,
Redeth Ovyde, and ther ye may it leere.
 This knyght, of which my tale is specially,
Whan that he saugh he myghte nat come therby—
This is to seye, what wommen love moost— 985
Withinne his brest ful sorweful was the goost.
But hoom he gooth; he myghte nat sojourne;
The day was come that homward moste he tourne.
And in his wey it happed hym to ryde,
In al this care, under a forest syde, 990
Wher as he saugh upon a daunce go
Of ladyes foure and twenty, and yet mo;
Toward the whiche daunce he drow ful yerne,
In hope that som wysdom sholde he lerne.
But certeinly, er he cam fully there, 995
Vanysshed was this daunce, he nyste where.
No creature saugh he that bar lyf,
Save on the grene he saugh sittynge a wyf—
A fouler wight ther may no man devyse.
Agayn the knyght this olde wyf gan ryse, 1000
And seyde, "Sire knyght, heer forth ne lith no wey.
Tel me what that ye seken, by youre fey!
Paraventure it may the bettre be;
Thise olde folk kan muchel thyng," quod she.
 "My leeve mooder," quod this knyght, "certeyn
I nam but deed but if that I kan seyn 1006
What thyng it is that wommen moost desire.
Koude ye me wisse, I wolde wel quite youre hire."
 "Plight me thy trouthe heere in myn hand,"
  quod she,
"The nexte thyng that I requere thee, 1010
Thou shalt it do, if it lye in thy myght,
And I wol telle it yow er it be nyght."
 "Have heer my trouthe," quod the knyght,
  "I grante."
 "Thanne," quod she, "I dar me wel avante
Thy lyf is sauf, for I wol stonde therby; 1015
Upon my lyf, the queene wol seye as I.

944 **holden:** considered
946 **secree:** discreet, able to keep a secret
948 **biwreye:** betray, reveal
949 **rake-stele:** rake handle (i.e., nothing)
950 **hele:** keep secret
951 **Witnesse on:** take the evidence of   **Myda:** Midas
952 **Ovyde:** Ovid, the Roman poet
960 **disfigure:** deformity
965 **dyde:** would die
966 **conseil:** secret
967 **swal:** swelled
968 **nedely:** of necessity   **asterte:** escape
970 **mareys:** marsh
972 **bitore bombleth in the myre:** bittern bumbles (booms) in the mire
974 **Biwreye:** betray   **soun:** sound

982 **leere:** learn
987 **sojourne:** remain
989 **it happed hym:** he chanced
990 **under:** by, near
993 **yerne:** eagerly
998 **wyf:** woman
999 **devyse:** imagine
1000 **Agayn:** toward (to meet)
1008 **wisse:** inform, instruct   **quite youre hire:** reward your efforts
1009 **Plight:** pledge
1010 **requere:** ask
1013 **grante:** consent
1014 **avante:** boast
1015 **sauf:** safe
1016 **seye as I:** say as I do, agree with me

Lat se which is the proudeste of hem alle
That wereth on a coverchief or a calle
That dar seye nay of that I shal thee teche.
Lat us go forth withouten lenger speche." 1020
Tho rowned she a pistel in his ere,
And bad hym to be glad and have no fere.

    Whan they be comen to the court, this knyght
Seyde he had holde his day, as he hadde hight,
And redy was his answere, as he sayde. 1025
Ful many a noble wyf, and many a mayde,
And many a wydwe, for that they been wise,
The queene hirself sittynge as a justise,
Assembled been, his answere for to heere;
And afterward this knyght was bode appeere. 1030

    To every wight comanded was silence,
And that the knyght sholde telle in audience
What thyng that worldly wommen loven best.
This knyght ne stood nat stille as doth a best,
But to his questioun anon answerde 1035
With manly voys, that al the court it herde:

    "My lige lady, generally," quod he,
"Wommen desiren to have sovereynetee
As wel over hir housbond as hir love,
And for to been in maistrie hym above. 1040
This is youre mooste desir, thogh ye me kille.
Dooth as yow list; I am heer at youre wille."
In al the court ne was ther wyf, ne mayde,
Ne wydwe that contraried that he sayde,
But seyden he was worthy han his lyf. 1045
And with that word up stirte the olde wyf,
Which that the knyght saugh sittynge on the grene:
"Mercy," quod she, "my sovereyn lady queene!
Er that youre court departe, do me right.
I taughte this answere unto the knyght; 1050
For which he plighte me his trouthe there,
The firste thyng that I wolde hym requere
He wolde it do, if it lay in his myghte.
Bifore the court thanne preye I thee, sir knyght,"
Quod she, "that thou me take unto thy wyf, 1055
For wel thou woost that I have kept thy lyf.
If I seye fals, sey nay, upon thy fey!"
    This knyght answerde, "Allas and weylawey!

I woot right wel that swich was my biheste.
For Goddes love, as chees a newe requeste! 1060
Taak al my good and lat my body go."
    "Nay, thanne," quod she, "I shrewe us bothe two!
For thogh that I be foul, and oold, and poore
I nolde for al the metal, ne for oore
That under erthe is grave or lith above, 1065
But if thy wyf I were, and eek thy love."
    "My love?" quod he, "nay, my dampnacioun!
Allas, that any of my nacioun
Sholde evere so foule disparaged be!"
But al for noght; the ende is this, that he 1070
Constreyned was; he nedes moste hire wedde,
And taketh his olde wyf, and gooth to bedde.

    Now wolden som men seye, paraventure,
That for my necligence I do no cure
To tellen yow the joye and al th'array 1075
That at the feeste was that ilke day.
To which thyng shortly answeren I shal:
I seye ther nas no joye ne feeste at al;
Ther nas but hevynesse and muche sorwe.
For prively he wedded hire on morwe, 1080
And al day after hidde hym as an owle,
So wo was hym, his wyf looked so foule.

    Greet was the wo the knyght hadde in his thoght,
Whan he was with his wyf abedde ybroght;
He walweth and he turneth to and fro. 1085
His olde wyf lay smylynge everemo,
And seyde, "O deere housbonde, benedicitee!
Fareth every knyght thus with his wyf as ye?
Is this the lawe of kyng Arthures hous?
Is every knyght of his so dangerous? 1090
I am youre owene love and youre wyf;
I am she which that saved hath youre lyf,
And, certes, yet ne dide I yow nevere unright;
Why fare ye thus with me this firste nyght?
Ye faren lyk a man had lost his wit. 1095
What is my gilt? For Goddes love, tel it,
And it shal been amended, if I may."
    "Amended?" quod this knyght, "Allas, nay, nay!
It wol nat been amended nevere mo.
Thou art so loothly, and so oold also, 1100

1018 **calle:** hairnet worn as a headdress
1021 **rowned:** whispered   **pistel:** message
1024 **hight:** promised
1030 **bode appeere:** commanded to appear
1034 **best:** beast
1044 **contraried:** denied
1051 **plighte:** pledged

1059 **biheste:** promise
1060 **as chees:** choose
1064 **oore:** ore
1068 **nacioun:** family
1069 **disparaged:** degraded by a union with someone of lower birth
1075 **array:** rich display
1085 **walweth:** writhes
1096 **gilt:** offense
1100 **loothly:** loathsome

And therto comen of so lough a kynde,
That litel wonder is thogh I walwe and wynde.
So wolde God myn herte wolde breste!"
　　"Is this," quod she, "the cause of youre unreste?"
　　"Ye, certeinly," quod he, "no wonder is."　　1105
　　"Now, sire," quod she, "I koude amende al this,
If that me liste, er it were dayes thre,
So wel ye myghte bere yow unto me.
　　"But, for ye speken of swich gentillesse
As is descended out of old richesse,　　1110
That therfore sholden ye be gentil men,
Swich arrogance is nat worth an hen.
Looke who that is moost vertuous alway,
Pryvee and apert, and moost entendeth ay
To do the gentil dedes that he kan;　　1115
Taak hym for the grettest gentil man.
Crist wole we clayme of hym oure gentillesse,
Nat of oure eldres for hire old richesse.
For thogh they yeve us al hir heritage,
For which we clayme to been of heigh parage,　　1120
Yet may they nat biquethe for no thyng
To noon of us hir vertuous lyvyng,
That made hem gentil men ycalled be,
And bad us folwen hem in swich degree.
　　"Wel kan the wise poete of Florence,　　1125
That highte Dant, speken in this sentence.
Lo, in swich maner rym is Dantes tale:
'Ful selde up riseth by his branches smale
Prowesse of man, for God, of his goodnesse,
Wole that of hym we clayme oure gentillesse';　　1130
For of oure eldres may we no thyng clayme
But temporel thyng, that man may hurte and mayme.
　　"Eek every wight woot this as wel as I,
If gentillesse were planted natureelly
Unto a certeyn lynage doun the lyne,　　1135
Pryvee and apert thanne wolde they nevere fyne
To doon of gentillesse the faire office;
They myghte do no vileynye or vice.
　　"Taak fyr and ber it in the derkeste hous

Bitwix this and the mount of Kaukasous,　　1140
And lat men shette the dores and go thenne;
Yet wole the fyr as faire lye and brenne
As twenty thousand men myghte it biholde;
His office natureel ay wol it holde,
Up peril of my lyf, til that it dye.　　1145
　　"Heere may ye se wel how that genterye
Is nat annexed to possessioun,
Sith folk ne doon hir operacioun
Alwey, as dooth the fyr, lo, in his kynde.
For, God it woot, men may wel often fynde　　1150
A lordes sone do shame and vileynye;
And he that wole han pris of his gentrye,
For he was boren of a gentil hous
And hadde his eldres noble and vertuous,
And nel hymselven do no gentil dedis　　1155
Ne folwen his gentil auncestre that deed is,
He nys nat gentil, be he duc or erl,
For vileyns synful dedes make a cherl.
For gentillesse nys but renomee
Of thyne auncestres, for hire heigh bountee,　　1160
Which is a strange thyng to thy persone.
Thy gentillesse cometh fro God allone.
Thanne comth oure verray gentillesse of grace;
It was no thyng biquethe us with oure place.
　　"Thenketh hou noble, as seith Valerius,　　1165
Was thilke Tullius Hostillius,
That out of poverte roos to heigh noblesse.
Reedeth Senek, and redeth eek Boece;
Ther shul ye seen expres that it no drede is
That he is gentil that dooth gentil dedis.　　1170
And therfore, leeve housbonde, I thus conclude:
Al were it that myne auncestres were rude,
Yet may the hye God, and so hope I,
Grante me grace to lyven vertuously.
Thanne am I gentil, whan that I bigynne　　1175
To lyven vertuously and weyve synne.
　　"And ther as ye of poverte me repreeve,
The hye God, on whom that we bileeve,

1101 **comen of so lough a kynde:** descended from such base-born lineage
1102 **wynde:** twist about
1104 **unreste:** distress
1108 **so:** so that　　**bere yow unto me:** behave towards me
1109 **gentillesse:** nobility
1114 **Pryvee and apert:** in private and public, in all circumstances　　**entendeth:** strives
1120 **heigh parage:** noble lineage
1126 **Dant:** Dante Alighieri
1130 **Wole:** desires
1132 **mayme:** injure
1136 **fyne:** cease
1137 **office:** duties

140 **Kaukasous:** the Caucasus mountains
1141 **thenne:** thence
1142 **lye:** blaze
1146 **genterye:** gentility
1147 **annexed to:** joined with
1148 **ne doon hir operacioun:** do not behave as they should
1152 **pris of his gentrye:** praise for his noble birth
1155 **nel** = *ne wyl*, will not
1159 **renomee:** renown
1160 **bountee:** goodness
1161 **strange thyng:** a thing foreign to, not naturally part of
1165 **Valerius:** Valerius Maximus, the Roman author
1166 **Tullius Hostillius:** legendary third king of Rome
1168 **Senek:** Seneca, Roman author　　**Boece:** Boethius (see, e.g., Boece 3.pr4)
1172 **Al were:** even though　　**rude:** humble
1176 **weyve:** abandon

In wilful poverte chees to lyve his lyf.
And certes every man, mayden, or wyf   1180
May understonde that Jhesus, hevene kyng,
Ne wolde nat chese a vicious lyvyng.
Glad poverte is an honest thyng, certeyn;
This wole Senec and othere clerkes seyn.
Whoso that halt hym payd of his poverte,   1185
I holde hym riche, al hadde he nat a sherte.
He that coveiteth is a povre wight,
For he wolde han that is nat in his myght;
But he that noght hath, ne coveiteth have,
Is riche, although ye holde hym but a knave.   1190
Verray poverte, it syngeth proprely;
Juvenal seith of poverte myrily:
'The povre man, whan he goth by the weye,
Bifore the theves he may synge and pleye.'
Poverte is hateful good and, as I gesse,   1195
A ful greet bryngere out of bisynesse;
A greet amendere eek of sapience
To hym that taketh it in pacience.
Poverte is this, although it seme alenge:
Possessioun that no wight wol chalenge.   1200
Poverte ful ofte, whan a man is lowe,
Maketh his God and eek hymself to knowe.
Poverte a spectacle is, as thynketh me,
Thurgh which he may his verray freendes see.
And therfore, sire, syn that I noght yow greve,   1205
Of my poverte namoore ye me repreve.
    "Now, sire, of elde ye repreve me;
And certes, sire, thogh noon auctoritee
Were in no book, ye gentils of honour
Seyn that men sholde an oold wight doon favour   1210
And clepe hym fader, for youre gentillesse;
And auctours shal I fynden, as I gesse.
    "Now ther ye seye that I am foul and old,
Than drede you noght to been a cokewold;
For filthe and eelde, also moot I thee,   1215
Been grete wardeyns upon chastitee.
But nathelees, syn I knowe youre delit,

I shal fulfille youre worldly appetit.
    "Chese now," quod she, "oon of thise thynges tweye:
To han me foul and old til that I deye,   1220
And be to yow a trewe, humble wyf,
And nevere yow displese in al my lyf,
Or elles ye wol han me yong and fair,
And take youre aventure of the repair
That shal be to youre hous by cause of me,   1225
Or in som oother place, may wel be.
Now chese yourselven, wheither that yow liketh."
    This knyght avyseth hym and sore siketh,
But atte laste he seyde in this manere:
"My lady and my love, and wyf so deere,   1230
I put me in youre wise governance;
Cheseth youreself which may be moost plesance
And moost honour to yow and me also.
I do no fors the wheither of the two,
For as yow liketh, it suffiseth me."   1235
    "Thanne have I gete of yow maistrie," quod she,
"Syn I may chese and governe as me lest?"
    "Ye, certes, wyf," quod he, "I holde it best."
    "Kys me," quod she, "we be no lenger wrothe,
For, by my trouthe, I wol be to yow bothe—   1240
This is to seyn, ye, bothe fair and good.
I prey to God that I moote sterven wood,
But I to yow be also good and trewe
As evere was wyf, syn that the world was newe.
And but I be to-morn as fair to seene   1245
As any lady, emperice, or queene,
That is bitwixe the est and eke the west,
Dooth with my lyf and deth right as yow lest.
Cast up the curtyn, looke how that it is."
    And whan the knyght saugh verraily al this,   1250
That she so fair was, and so yong therto,
For joye he hente hire in his armes two.
His herte bathed in a bath of blisse.
A thousand tyme a-rewe he gan hire kisse,
And she obeyed hym in every thyng   1255
That myghte doon hym plesance or likyng.
    And thus they lyve unto hir lyves ende
In parfit joye; and Jhesu Crist us sende
Housbondes meeke, yonge, and fressh abedde,

1179 **wilful:** willing, voluntary
1185 **halt hym payd:** is satisfied
1189 **have:** to have (anything)
1190 **knave:** peasant
1192 **Juvenal:** the Roman poet
1196 **bryngere out of bisynesse:** remover of cares
1197 **amendere:** improver   **sapience:** wisdom
1199 **alenge:** miserable
1200 **chalenge:** claim
1203 **spectacle:** eyeglass
1209 **gentils:** nobles
1212 **auctours:** authoritative writers   **fynden:** find (to support this)
1214 **cokewold:** cuckold
1215 **thee:** prosper
1216 **wardeyns:** guardians
1217 **delit:** desire

1224 **aventure:** chances   **repair:** resort, visitors
1227 **wheither:** which
1234 **I do no fors:** I don't care
1235 **suffiseth me:** is sufficient for me
1242 **sterven wood:** die insane
1245 **to-morn:** in the morning
1253 **bathed:** basked
1254 **a-rewe:** in succession

And grace t'overbyde hem that we wedde;   1260
And eek I praye Jhesu shorte hir lyves
That noght wol be governed by hir wyves;

And olde and angry nygardes of dispence,
God sende hem soone verray pestilence!

Heere endeth the Wyves Tale of Bathe.

The Friar's Prologue

⑨

The Prologe of the Freres Tale.

This worthy lymytour, this noble Frere,   1265
He made alwey a maner louryng chiere
Upon the Somonour, but for honestee
No vileyns word as yet to hym spak he.
But atte laste he seyde unto the wyf,
"Dame," quod he, "God yeve yow right good lyf!   1270
Ye han heer touched, also moot I thee,
In scole-matere greet difficultee.
Ye han seyd muche thyng right wel, I seye;
But, dame, heere as we ryde by the weye,
Us nedeth nat to speken but of game,   1275
And lete auctoritees, on Goddes name,
To prechyng and to scoles of clergye.
But if it lyke to this compaignye,
I wol yow of a somonour telle a game.
Pardee, ye may wel knowe by the name   1280
That of a somonour may no good be sayd;
I praye that noon of you be yvele apayd.

A somonour is a rennere up and doun
With mandementz for fornicacioun,
And is ybet at every townes ende."   1285
    Oure Hoost tho spak, "A, sire, ye sholde be hende
And curteys, as a man of youre estaat;
In compaignye we wol have no debaat.
Telleth youre tale, and lat the Somonour be."   1289
    "Nay," quod the Somonour, "lat hym seye to me
What so hym list; whan it comth to my lot,
By God, I shal hym quiten every grot.
I shal hym tellen which a greet honour
It is to be a flaterynge lymytour,
And of many another manere cryme   1295
Which nedeth nat rehercen at this tyme;
And his office I shal hym telle, ywis."
    Oure Hoost answerde, "Pees, namoore of this!"
And after this he seyde unto the Frere,
"Tel forth youre tale, leeve maister deere."   1300

1260 **t'overbyde:** to outlive

1266 **a maner louryng chiere:** a kind of scowling face
1267 **honestee:** propriety
1268 **vileyns:** rude, churlish
1271 **also moot I thee:** as I may prosper (I swear)
1272 **scole-matere:** subject for debate at the universities
1276 **auctoritees:** quoting from authoritative texts
1278 **lyke:** is pleasing
1282 **yvele apayd:** displeased

1263 **nygardes of dispence:** misers in spending

1283 **rennere:** runner
1284 **mandementz:** summonses
1285 **ybet:** beaten
1292 **grot:** groat, silver coin worth four pence
1297 **office:** i.e., how he performs his duties

The Friar's Tale

Heere bigynneth the Freres Tale.

Whilom ther was dwellynge in my contree
An erchedeken, a man of heigh degree,
That boldely dide execucioun
In punysshynge of fornicacioun,
Of wicchecraft, and eek of bawderye,   1305
Of diffamacioun, and avowtrye,
Of chirche reves, and of testamentz,
Of contractes and of lakke of sacramentz,
Of usure, and of symonye also.
But certes, lecchours dide he grettest wo;   1310
They sholde syngen if that they were hent;
And smale tytheres weren foule yshent,
If any persoun wolde upon hem pleyne.
Ther myghte asterte hym no pecunyal peyne.
For smale tithes and for smal offrynge   1315
He made the peple pitously to synge,
For er the bisshop caughte hem with his hook,
They weren in the erchedeknes book.
Thanne hadde he, thurgh his jurisdiccioun,
Power to doon on hem correccioun.   1320
He hadde a somonour redy to his hond;
A slyer boye nas noon in Engelond;
For subtilly he hadde his espiaille,
That taughte hym wel wher that hym myghte availle.
He koude spare of lecchours oon or two,   1325
To techen hym to foure and twenty mo.
For thogh this Somonour wood were as an hare,
To telle his harlotrye I wol nat spare;

For we been out of his correccioun.
They han of us no jurisdiccioun,   1330
Ne nevere shullen, terme of alle hir lyves.
    "Peter! so been wommen of the styves,"
Quod the Somonour, "yput out of oure cure!"
    "Pees! with myschance and with mysaventure!"
Thus seyde oure Hoost, "and lat hym telle his tale.   1335
Now telleth forth, thogh that the Somonour gale;
Ne spareth nat, myn owene maister deere."
    This false theef, this somonour, quod the Frere,
Hadde alwey bawdes redy to his hond,
As any hauk to lure in Engelond,   1340
That tolde hym al the secree that they knewe,
For hire acqueyntance was nat come of newe.
They weren his approwours prively.
He took hymself a greet profit therby;
His maister knew nat alwey what he wan.   1345
Withouten mandement a lewed man
He koude somne, on peyne of Cristes curs,
And they were glade for to fille his purs
And make hym grete feestes atte nale.
And right as Judas hadde purses smale,   1350
And was a theef, right swich a theef was he;
His maister hadde but half his duetee.
He was, if I shal yeven hym his laude,
A theef, and eek a somnour, and a baude.
He hadde eek wenches at his retenue,   1355
That, wheither that sir Robert or sir Huwe,

1302 **erchedeken:** archdeacon
1303 **dide execucioun:** carried out the law
1305 **wicchecraft:** witchcraft   **bawderye:** pandering
1306 **diffamacioun:** slander   **avowtrye:** adultery
1307 **chirche reves:** robbing of churches
1307–8 **testamentz, contractes:** violations relating to wills and marriage contracts
lakke of sacramentz: failure to observe any of the sacraments, here probably
confession and communion
1309 **usure:** taking interest on loans   **symonye:** buying or selling church positions
1312 **smale tytheres:** those who did not pay their full tithes   **yshent:** punished
1313 **persoun:** parson
1314 **asterte:** escape   **pecunyal peyne:** monetary punishment, fine
1317 **hook:** bishop's staff
1320 **doon . . . correccioun:** punish them
1322 **boye:** knave
1323 **espiaille:** network of spies
1326 **techen:** direct, lead
1328 **harlotrye:** wickedness

1329 **out of his correccioun:** exempt from his authority
1332 **Peter!:** by St. Peter   **styves:** brothels; see n.
1333 **cure:** jurisdiction
1334 **with myschance and with mysaventure:** bad luck to you
1336 **gale:** complain loudly
1339 **bawdes:** pimps
1340 **lure:** a device to reclaim (call back) hawks
1341 **secree:** secret information
1342 **of newe:** recently
1343 **approwours:** agents
1346 **mandement:** summons
1347 **somne:** summon   **Cristes curs:** excommunication
1349 **atte nale:** at an ale-house
1350 **purses smale:** small amount of money belonging to the Apostles, entrusted to *Judas*
1352 **duetee:** amount due to him
1353 **laude:** due praise
1355 **at his retenue:** in his service

Or Jakke, or Rauf, or whoso that it were
That lay by hem, they tolde it in his ere.
Thus was the wenche and he of oon assent,
And he wolde fecche a feyned mandement,   1360
And somne hem to chapitre bothe two,
And pile the man, and lete the wenche go.
Thanne wolde he seye, "Freend, I shal for thy sake
Do striken hire out of oure lettres blake;
Thee thar namoore as in this cas travaille.   1365
I am thy freend, ther I thee may availle."
Certeyn he knew of briberyes mo
Than possible is to telle in yeres two.
For in this world nys dogge for the bowe
That kan an hurt deer from an hool yknowe   1370
Bet than this somnour knew a sly lecchour,
Or an avowtier, or a paramour.
And for that was the fruyt of al his rente,
Therfore on it he sette al his entente.

          And so bifel that ones on a day   1375
This somnour, evere waityng on his pray,
Rood for to somne an old wydwe, a ribibe,
Feynynge a cause, for he wolde brybe.
And happed that he saugh bifore hym ryde
A gay yeman, under a forest syde.   1380
A bowe he bar, and arwes brighte and kene;
He hadde upon a courtepy of grene,
An hat upon his heed with frenges blake.
     "Sire," quod this somnour, "hayl, and wel atake!"
     "Welcome," quod he, "and every good felawe!
Wher rydestow, under this grene-wode shawe?"
Seyde this yeman, "Wiltow fer to day?"   1387
     This somnour hym answerde and seyde, "Nay;
Heere faste by," quod he, "is myn entente
To ryden, for to reysen up a rente   1390
That longeth to my lordes duetee."

"Artow thanne a bailly?" "Ye," quod he.
He dorste nat, for verray filthe and shame
Seye that he was a somonour, for the name.
     "*Depardieux*," quod this yeman, "deere broother,
Thou art a bailly, and I am another.   1396
I am unknowen as in this contree;
Of thyn aqueyntance I wolde praye thee,
And eek of bretherhede, if that yow leste.
I have gold and silver in my cheste;   1400
If that thee happe to comen in oure shire,
Al shal be thyn, right as thou wolt desire."
     "Grant mercy," quod this somonour, "by my feith!"
Everych in ootheres hand his trouthe leith,
For to be sworne bretheren til they deye.   1405
In daliance they ryden forth and pleye.
     This somonour, which that was as ful of jangles
As ful of venym been thise waryangles
And evere enqueryng upon every thyng,
"Brother," quod he, "where is now youre dwellyng
Another day if that I sholde yow seche?"   1411
This yeman hym answerde in softe speche,
     "Brother," quod he, "fer in the north contree,
Whereas I hope som tyme I shal thee see.
Er we departe, I shal thee so wel wisse   1415
That of myn hous ne shaltow nevere mysse."
     "Now, brother," quod this somonour, "I yow preye,
Teche me, whil that we ryden by the weye,
Syn that ye been a baillif as am I,
Som subtiltee, and tel me feithfully   1420
In myn office how that I may moost wynne;
And spareth nat for conscience ne synne,
But as my brother tel me, how do ye."
     "Now, by my trouthe, brother deere," seyde he,
"As I shal tellen thee a feithful tale,   1425
My wages been ful streite and ful smale.
My lord is hard to me and daungerous,
And myn office is ful laborous,

1359 **of oon assent:** agreed, in league together
1361 **chapitre:** a session of the archdeacon's court
1362 **pile:** rob
1364 **Do striken hire out:** cause her to be struck out
1365 **thar:** need   **travaille:** trouble yourself
1367 **briberyes:** ways of stealing
1369 **dogge for the bowe:** dog trained to hunt with an archer
1370 **hool:** whole, unhurt
1373 **fruyt of al his rente:** the best portion of his income
1376 **pray:** prey
1377 **Rood:** rode   **ribibe:** fiddle, old woman
1378 **cause:** charge   **brybe:** extort money
1380 **yeman:** yeoman
1382 **courtepy:** jacket
1383 **frenges:** ornamental fringes
1384 **wel atake:** well met
1386 **shawe:** wood, thicket
1391 **duetee:** what is due (to my lord)

1392 **bailly:** bailiff, an agent for a lord's estate who collected revenues and administered justice
1394 **for the name:** because the name itself was so odious
1395 **Depardieux:** by God
1399 **bretherhede:** sworn brotherhood
1403 **Grant mercy:** thank you
1404 **trouthe:** pledge (i.e., they shook hands on it)
1407 **jangles:** gossip
1408 **waryangles:** shrikes, butcher-birds
1415 **wisse:** inform, instruct
1427 **daungerous:** demanding
1428 **laborous:** laborious

And therfore by extorcions I lyve.
For sothe, I take al that men wol me yive.   1430
Algate, by sleyghte or by violence,
Fro yeer to yeer I wynne al my dispence.
I kan no bettre telle, feithfully."
    "Now certes," quod this Somonour, "so fare I.
I spare nat to taken, God it woot,   1435
But if it be to hevy or to hoot.
What I may gete in conseil prively,
No maner conscience of that have I.
Nere myn extorcioun, I myghte nat lyven,
Ne of swiche japes wol I nat be shryven.   1440
Stomak ne conscience ne knowe I noon;
I shrewe thise shrifte-fadres everychoon.
Wel be we met, by God and by Seint Jame!
But, leeve brother, tel me thanne thy name,"
Quod this somonour. In this meene while   1445
This yeman gan a litel for to smyle.
    "Brother," quod he, "wiltow that I thee telle?
I am a feend; my dwellyng is in helle,
And heere I ryde aboute my purchasyng,
To wite wher men wol yeve me any thyng.   1450
My purchas is th'effect of al my rente.
Looke how thou rydest for the same entente,
To wynne good, thou rekkest nevere how;
Right so fare I, for ryde wolde I now
Unto the worldes ende for a preye."   1455
    "A!" quod this somonour, "benedicite! What sey ye?
I wende ye were a yeman trewely.
Ye han a mannes shap as wel as I;
Han ye a figure thanne determinat
In helle, ther ye been in youre estat?"   1460
    "Nay, certeinly," quod he, "ther have we noon;
But whan us liketh we kan take us oon,
Or elles make yow seme we been shape;
Somtyme lyk a man, or lyk an ape,
Or lyk an angel kan I ryde or go.   1465
It is no wonder thyng thogh it be so;
A lowsy jogelour kan deceyve thee,
And pardee, yet kan I moore craft than he."

"Why," quod this somonour, "ryde ye thanne or
      goon
In sondry shap, and nat alwey in oon?"   1470
    "For we," quod he, "wol us swiche formes make
As moost able is oure preyes for to take."
    "What maketh yow to han al this labour?"
    "Ful many a cause, leeve sire somonour,"
Seyde this feend, "but alle thyng hath tyme.   1475
The day is short, and it is passed pryme,
And yet ne wan I nothyng in this day.
I wol entende to wynnyng, if I may,
And nat entende oure wittes to declare.
For, brother myn, thy wit is al to bare   1480
To understonde, althogh I tolde hem thee.
But, for thou axest why labouren we—
For somtyme we been Goddes instrumentz
And meenes to doon his comandementz,
Whan that hym list, upon his creatures,   1485
In divers art and in diverse figures.
Withouten hym we have no myght, certayn,
If that hym list to stonden ther-agayn.
And somtyme, at oure prayere, han we leve
Oonly the body and nat the soule greve;   1490
Witnesse on Job, whom that we diden wo.
And somtyme han we myght of bothe two—
This is to seyn, of soule and body eke.
And somtyme be we suffred for to seke
Upon a man and doon his soule unreste   1495
And nat his body, and al is for the beste.
Whan he withstandeth oure temptacioun,
It is a cause of his savacioun,
Al be it that it was nat oure entente
He sholde be sauf, but that we wolde hym hente.   1500
And somtyme be we servant unto man,
As to the erchebisshop Seint Dunstan,
And to the apostles servant eek was I."
    "Yet tel me," quod the somonour, "feithfully,
Make ye yow newe bodies thus alway   1505
Of elementz?" The feend answerde, "Nay.
Somtyme we feyne, and somtyme we aryse
With dede bodyes, in ful sondry wyse,
And speke as renably and faire and wel
As to the Phitonissa dide Samuel.   1510

1431 **Algate:** anyhow
1432 **dispence:** living expenses
1440 **shryven:** confessed
1441 **Stomak:** stomach (compassion)
1442 **shrifte-fadres:** confessors
1449 **purchasyng:** acquisition of profits
1451 **purchas:** what is acquired (in this way)   **th'effect:** the sum and substance
rente: income
1459 **figure . . . determinat:** definite shape (as opposed to the shapes devils assume
on earth)
1467 **jogelour:** conjurer

1472 **able:** suitable
1480 **al to bare:** entirely inadequate
1486 **art:** methods
1491 **Witnesse on Job:** take the evidence of the Biblical Job
1494–95 **seke Upon:** harass
1495 **unreste:** distress
1502 **Seint Dunstan:** St. Dunstan was said to control devils
1509 **renably:** readily
1510 **Phitonissa:** the Biblical Witch of Endor

(And yet wol som men seye it was nat he;
I do no fors of youre dyvynytee.)
But o thyng warne I thee, I wol nat jape:
Thou wolt algates wite how we been shape;
Thou shalt herafterward, my brother deere,   1515
Come there thee nedeth nat of me to leere,
For thou shalt, by thyn owene experience,
Konne in a chayer rede of this sentence
Bet than Virgile, while he was on lyve,
Or Dant also. Now lat us ryde blyve,   1520
For I wole holde compaignye with thee
Til it be so that thou forsake me."
    "Nay," quod this somonour, "that shal nat bityde!
I am a yeman, knowen is ful wyde;
My trouthe wol I holde, as in this cas.   1525
For though thou were the devel Sathanas,
My trouthe wol I holde to my brother,
As I am sworn, and ech of us til oother,
For to be trewe brother in this cas;
And bothe we goon abouten oure purchas.   1530
Taak thou thy part, what that men wol thee yive,
And I shal myn; thus may we bothe lyve.
And if that any of us have moore than oother,
Lat hym be trewe and parte it with his brother."
    "I graunte," quod the devel, "by my fey."   1535
And with that word they ryden forth hir wey.
And right at the entryng of the townes ende,
To which this somonour shoop hym for to wende,
They saugh a cart that charged was with hey,
Which that a cartere droof forth in his wey.   1540
Deep was the wey, for which the carte stood.
The cartere smoot and cryde as he were wood,
"Hayt, Brok! Hayt, Scot! What spare ye for the
        stones?
The feend," quod he, "yow fecche, body and bones,

As ferforthly as evere were ye foled,   1545
So muche wo as I have with yow tholed!
The devel have al, bothe hors and cart and hey!"
    This somonour seyde, "Heere shal we have
        a pley."
And neer the feend he drough, as noght ne were,
Ful prively, and rowned in his ere: 1550
"Herkne, my brother, herkne, by thy feith!
Herestow nat how that the cartere seith?
Hent it anon, for he hath yeve it thee,
Bothe hey and cart, and eek his caples thre."   1554
    "Nay," quod the devel, "God woot, never a deel!
It is nat his entente, trust me weel.
Axe hym thyself, if thou nat trowest me;
Or elles stynt a while, and thou shalt see."
    This cartere thakketh his hors upon the croupe,
And they bigonne to drawen and to stoupe.   1560
"Heyt! Now," quod he, "ther Jhesu Crist yow blesse,
And al his handwerk, bothe moore and lesse!
That was wel twight, myn owene lyard boy.
I pray God save thee, and Seinte Loy!
Now is my cart out of the slow, pardee!"   1565
    "Lo, brother," quod the feend, "what tolde I thee?
Heere may ye se, myn owene deere brother,
The carl spak oo thing, but he thoghte another.
Lat us go forth abouten oure viage;
Heere wynne I nothyng upon cariage."   1570
    Whan that they coomen somwhat out of towne,
This somonour to his brother gan to rowne:
"Brother," quod he, "heere woneth an old rebekke
That hadde almoost as lief to lese hire nekke

1512 **do no fors of:** care nothing for   **dyvynytee:** theology
1513 **jape:** deceive (you)
1514 **algates:** surely
1518 **in a chayer rede of:** in a (professorial) chair lecture on
1519–20 **Virgile, Dant:** Virgil, Dante, poets who described Hell
1520 **blyve:** quickly
1530 **purchas:** acquisition
1534 **parte:** share
1538 **shoop hym:** prepared himself
1539 **charged:** loaded
1541 **Deep was the wey:** the road was deep in mud (cf. 1565)
1543 **Hayt:** giddap   **spare ye:** spare yourselves, stop pulling

1545 **As ferforthly as:** as sure as   **foled:** foaled (i.e., born)
1546 **tholed:** suffered
1549 **as noght ne were:** as if it were nothing (i.e., as if he had no particular purpose)
1550 **rowned:** whispered
1554 **caples:** horses
1559 **thakketh:** pats   **croupe:** hindquarters
1561 **Heyt!:** giddap   **ther Jhesu Crist yow blesse:** may Jesus Christ bless you
1563 **twight:** pulled   **lyard:** dappled
1564 **Seinte Loy:** St. Eligius
1565 **slow:** mud, mire
1568 **carl:** fellow
1569 **viage:** undertaking
1570 **cariage:** a feudal lord's right to the use of a tenant's horses and cart, waived for a money payment
1572 **rowne:** whisper
1573 **woneth:** dwells   **rebekke:** fiddle, old woman
1574 **That hadde almoost as lief:** who would be almost as willing

As for to yeve a peny of hir good.   1575
I wole han twelf pens, though that she be wood,
Or I wol sompne hire unto oure office;
And yet, God woot, of hire knowe I no vice.
But for thou kanst nat, as in this contree,
Wynne thy cost, taak heer ensample of me."   1580
   This somonour clappeth at the wydwes gate.
"Com out," quod he, "thou olde virytrate!
I trowe thou hast som frere or preest with thee."
   "Who clappeth?" seyde this wyf, "benedicitee!
God save you, sire, what is youre sweete wille?"   1585
   "I have," quod he, "of somonce here a bille;
Up peyne of cursyng, looke that thou be
Tomorn bifore the erchedeknes knee
T'answere to the court of certeyn thynges."
   "Now, Lord," quod she, "Crist Jhesu, kyng of
      kynges,   1590
So wisly helpe me, as I ne may.
I have been syk, and that ful many a day.
I may nat go so fer," quod she, "ne ryde,
But I be deed, so priketh it in my syde.
May I nat axe a libel, sire somonour,   1595
And answere there by my procuratour
To swich thyng as men wole opposen me?"
   "Yis," quod this somonour, "pay anon—lat se—
Twelf pens to me, and I wol thee acquite.
I shal no profit han therby but lite;   1600
My maister hath the profit and nat I.
Com of, and lat me ryden hastily;
Yif me twelf pens, I may no lenger tarye."
   "Twelf pens!" quod she, "Now, lady Seinte Marie
So wisly help me out of care and synne,   1605
This wyde world thogh that I sholde wynne,
Ne have I nat twelf pens withinne myn hoold.
Ye knowen wel that I am povre and oold;
Kithe youre almesse on me, povre wrecche."   1609
   "Nay thanne," quod he, "the foule feend me fecche
If I th'excuse, though thou shul be spilt!"

"Allas!" quod she, "God woot, I have no gilt."
   "Pay me," quod he, "or by the sweete Seinte Anne,
As I wol bere awey thy newe panne
For dette which thou owest me of old.   1615
Whan that thou madest thyn housbonde cokewold,
I payde at hoom for thy correccioun."
   "Thou lixt!" quod she, "by my savacioun,
Ne was I nevere er now, wydwe ne wyf,
Somoned unto youre court in al my lyf;   1620
Ne nevere I nas but of my body trewe!
Unto the devel blak and rough of hewe
Yeve I thy body and my panne also!"
   And whan the devel herde hire cursen so
Upon hir knees, he seyde in this manere,   1625
"Now, Mabely, myn owene mooder deere,
Is this youre wyl in ernest that ye seye?"
   "The devel," quod she, "so fecche hym er he deye,
And panne and al, but he wol hym repente!"
   "Nay, olde stot, that is nat myn entente,"   1630
Quod this somonour, "for to repente me
For any thyng that I have had of thee.
I wolde I hadde thy smok and every clooth!"
   "Now, brother," quod the devel, "be nat wrooth;
Thy body and this panne been myne by right.   1635
Thou shalt with me to helle yet tonyght,
Where thou shalt knowen of oure privetee
Moore than a maister of dyvynytee."
And with that word this foule feend hym hente;
Body and soule he with the devel wente   1640
Where as that somonours han hir heritage.
And God, that maked after his ymage
Mankynde, save and gyde us, alle and some,
And leve thise somonours goode men bicome!
   Lordynges, I koude han toold yow, quod this Frere,
Hadde I had leyser for this Somnour heere,   1646
After the text of Crist, Poul, and John,
And of oure othere doctours many oon,
Swiche peynes that youre hertes myghte agryse,
Al be it so no tonge may it devyse,   1650
Thogh that I myghte a thousand wynter telle

1579 **But for:** since
1580 **cost:** expenses
1581 **clappeth:** knocks
1582 **virytrate:** hag
1586 **of somonce . . . a bille:** a writ of summons to court
1587 **cursyng:** excommunication
1588 **Tomorn:** in the morning
1591 **So wisly:** surely
1595 **axe a libel:** ask for a written copy of the indictment
1596 **procuratour:** representative
1597 **opposen:** bring against
1602 **Com of:** come on, hurry up
1607 **hoold:** possession
1609 **Kithe:** show **almesse:** charity

1613 **Seinte Anne:** St. Anne, mother of Mary
1617 **correccioun:** fine
1618 **lixt:** lie
1622 **hewe:** appearance
1630 **stot:** cow, old woman
1644 **leve:** allow
1648 **doctours:** authorities on church doctrine
1649 **agryse:** cause to tremble
1651 **wynter:** years

The peynes of thilke cursed hous of helle.
But for to kepe us fro that cursed place,
Waketh and preyeth Jhesu for his grace
So kepe us fro the temptour Sathanas.   1655
Herketh this word! Beth war, as in this cas:
"The leoun sit in his awayt alway
To sle the innocent, if that he may."

Disposeth ay youre hertes to withstonde   1659
The feend, that yow wolde make thral and bonde.
He may nat tempte yow over youre myght,
For Crist wol be youre champion and knyght.
And prayeth that thise somonours hem repente
Of hir mysdedes, er that the feend hem hente!

Heere endeth the Freres Tale.

The Summoner's Prologue

⑥

The Prologe of the Somonours Tale.

This Somonour in his styropes hye stood;   1665
Upon this Frere his herte was so wood
That lyk an aspen leef he quook for ire.
    "Lordynges," quod he, "but o thyng I desire;
I yow biseke that, of youre curteisye,
Syn ye han herd this false Frere lye,   1670
As suffreth me I may my tale telle.
This Frere bosteth that he knoweth helle,
And God it woot, that it is litel wonder;
Freres and feendes been but lyte asonder.
For, pardee, ye han ofte tyme herd telle   1675
How that a frere ravysshed was to helle
In spirit ones by a visioun;
And as an angel ladde hym up and doun,
To shewen hym the peynes that ther were,
In al the place saugh he nat a frere;   1680
Of oother folk he saugh ynowe in wo.
Unto this angel spak the frere tho:
    'Now, sire,' quod he, 'han freres swich a grace
That noon of hem shal come to this place?'
    'Yis,' quod this angel, 'many a millioun!'   1685
And unto Sathanas he ladde hym doun.

'And now hath Sathanas,' seith he, 'a tayl
Brodder than of a carryk is the sayl.
Hold up thy tayl, thou Sathanas!' quod he;
'Shewe forth thyn ers, and lat the frere se   1690
Where is the nest of freres in this place!'
And er that half a furlong wey of space,
Right so as bees out swarmen from an hyve,
Out of the develes ers ther gonne dryve
Twenty thousand freres on a route,   1695
And thurghout helle swarmed al aboute,
And comen agayn as faste as they may gon,
And in his ers they crepten everychon.
He clapte his tayl agayn and lay ful stille.
This frere, whan he looked hadde his fille   1700
Upon the tormentz of this sory place,
His spirit God restored, of his grace,
Unto his body agayn, and he awook.
But natheles, for fere yet he quook,
So was the develes ers ay in his mynde,   1705
That is his heritage of verray kynde.
God save yow alle, save this cursed Frere!
My prologe wol I ende in this manere."

1657 **in . . . awayt:** in ambush

1667 **quook:** trembled
1685 **Yis:** yes indeed

1660 **bonde:** enslaved
1662 **champion:** champion, representative in a judicial duel
1664 **mysdedes:** sins

1688 **carryk:** large sailing ship
1692 **half a furlong wey of space:** in a couple of minutes

The Summoner's Tale

Heere bigynneth the Somonour his Tale.

Lordynges, ther is in Yorkshire, as I gesse,
A mersshy contree called Holdernesse, 1710
In which ther wente a lymytour aboute
To preche, and eek to begge, it is no doute.
And so bifel that on a day this frere
Hadde preched at a chirche in his manere,
And specially, aboven every thyng, 1715
Excited he the peple in his prechyng
To trentals, and to yeve, for Goddes sake,
Wherwith men myghte hooly houses make,
Ther as divine servyce is honoured,
Nat ther as it is wasted and devoured, 1720
Ne ther it nedeth nat for to be yive,
As to possessioners, that mowen lyve,
Thanked be God, in wele and habundaunce.
"Trentals," seyde he, "deliveren fro penaunce
Hir freendes soules, as wel olde as yonge— 1725
Ye, whan that they been hastily ysonge,
Nat for to holde a preest joly and gay—
He syngeth nat but o masse in a day.
Delivereth out," quod he, "anon the soules!
Ful hard it is with flesshhook or with oules 1730
To been yclawed, or to brenne or bake.
Now spede yow hastily, for Cristes sake!"
And whan this frere had seyd al his entente,
With *qui cum patre* forth his wey he wente.
    Whan folk in chirche had yeve him what hem leste,
He wente his wey; no lenger wolde he reste. 1736
With scrippe and tipped staf, ytukked hye,
In every hous he gan to poure and prye,
And beggeth mele and chese, or elles corn.
His felawe hadde a staf tipped with horn, 1740

A peyre of tables al of yvory,
And a poyntel polysshed fetisly,
And wroot the names alwey, as he stood,
Of alle folk that yaf hym any good,
Ascaunces that he wolde for hem preye. 1745
"Yif us a busshel whete, malt, or reye,
A Goddes kechyl, or a trype of chese,
Or elles what yow lyst, we may nat cheese;
A Goddes halfpeny, or a masse peny,
Or yif us of youre brawn, if ye have eny; 1750
A dagon of youre blanket, leeve dame,
Oure suster deere—lo! Heere I write youre name—
Bacon or beef, or swich thyng as ye fynde."
    A sturdy harlot wente ay hem bihynde,
That was hir hostes man, and bar a sak, 1755
And what men yaf hem, leyde it on his bak.
And whan that he was out at dore, anon
He planed awey the names everichon
That he biforn had writen in his tables;
He served hem with nyfles and with fables. 1760
    "Nay, ther thou lixt, thou Somonour!" quod the Frere.
    "Pees," quod oure Hoost, "for Cristes mooder deere!
Tel forth thy tale, and spare it nat at al."
    "So thryve I," quod this Somonour, "so I shal!"
    So longe he wente, hous by hous, til he 1765
Cam til an hous ther he was wont to be
Refresshed moore than in an hundred placis.
Syk lay the goode man whos that the place is;
Bedrede upon a couche lowe he lay.

1710 **mersshy:** marshy **Holdernesse:** a district in Yorkshire
1711 **lymytour:** friar
1717 **trentals:** office of thirty requiem Masses sung for a soul in Purgatory
1722 **possessioners:** secular and monastic clergy living on endowments **mowen:** are able
1730 **flesshhook:** meat-hook **oules:** awls
1731 **yclawed:** torn, lacerated **brenne:** burn
1734 **qui cum patre:** "Who with the Father" (beginning of a closing formula for a prayer or sermon)
1737 **scrippe:** bag, satchel **tipped staf:** staff tipped with metal, a symbol of his authority **ytukked hye:** with the skirts of his coat tucked up under his belt
1738 **poure and prye:** pore (look intently) and peer

1741 **peyre of tables:** folding set of writing tablets
1742 **poyntel:** stylus (for writing on wax)
1745 **Ascaunces:** as if
1746 **reye:** rye
1747 **A Goddes kechyl:** a little cake given as alms **trype:** bit
1749 **Goddes halfpeny:** a halfpenny given as alms **masse peny:** money offered for the singing of a Mass
1750 **brawn:** meat
1751 **dagon:** piece **blanket:** undyed woolen cloth
1754 **harlot:** servant
1755 **hostes man:** servant of the host at their inn
1760 **nyfles:** trifles, silly stories **fables:** falsehoods
1761 **lixt:** lie
1768 **goode man:** goodman, head of the household
1769 **Bedrede:** bedridden

"*Deus hic!*" quod he, "O Thomas, freend, good day!"
Seyde this frere, curteisly and softe.   1771
"Thomas," quod he, "God yelde yow! Ful ofte
Have I upon this bench faren ful weel;
Heere have I eten many a myrie meel."
And fro the bench he droof awey the cat,   1775
And leyde adoun his potente and his hat,
And eek his scrippe, and sette hym softe adoun.
His felawe was go walked into toun
Forth with his knave, into that hostelrye
Where as he shoop hym thilke nyght to lye.   1780
    "O deere maister," quod this sike man,
"How han ye fare sith that March bigan?
I saugh yow noght this fourtenyght or moore."
"God woot," quod he, "laboured I have ful soore,
And specially for thy savacion   1785
Have I seyd many a precious orison,
And for oure othere freendes, God hem blesse!
I have to day been at youre chirche at messe,
And seyd a sermon after my symple wit—
Nat al after the text of hooly writ,   1790
For it is hard to yow, as I suppose,
And therfore wol I teche yow al the glose.
Glosynge is a glorious thyng, certeyn,
For lettre sleeth, so as we clerkes seyn—
There have I taught hem to be charitable,   1795
And spende hir good ther it is resonable;
And there I saugh oure dame—A! Where is she?"
    "Yond in the yerd I trowe that she be,"
Seyde this man, "and she wol come anon."
    "Ey, maister, welcome be ye, by Seint John!"
Seyde this wyf, "How fare ye, hertely?"   1801
    The frere ariseth up ful curteisly,
And hire embraceth in his armes narwe,
And kiste hire sweete, and chirketh as a sparwe
With his lyppes: "Dame," quod he, "right weel,
As he that is youre servant every deel,   1806
Thanked be God, that yow yaf soule and lyf!
Yet saugh I nat this day so fair a wyf
In al the chirche, God so save me!"

"Ye, God amende defautes, sire," quod she.   1810
"Algates, welcome be ye, by my fey!"
    "Graunt mercy, dame, this have I founde alwey.
But of youre grete goodnesse, by youre leve,
I wolde prey yow that ye nat yow greve,
I wole with Thomas speke a litel throwe.   1815
Thise curatz been ful necligent and slowe
To grope tendrely a conscience
In shrift; in prechyng is my diligence,
And studie in Petres wordes and in Poules.
I walke and fisshe Cristen mennes soules   1820
To yelden Jhesu Crist his propre rente;
To sprede his word is set al myn entente."
    "Now, by youre leve, o deere sire," quod she,
"Chideth him weel, for seinte Trinitee!
He is as angry as a pissemyre,   1825
Though that he have al that he kan desire;
Though I hym wrye a-nyght and make hym warm,
And over hym leye my leg outher myn arm,
He groneth lyk oure boor, lith in oure sty.
Oother desport right noon of hym have I;   1830
I may nat plese hym in no maner cas."
    "O Thomas, *je vous dy*, Thomas! Thomas!
This maketh the feend; this moste ben amended.
Ire is a thyng that hye God defended,
And therof wol I speke a word or two."   1835
    "Now, maister," quod the wyf, "er that I go,
What wol ye dyne? I wol go theraboute."
    "Now, dame," quod he, "now *je vous dy sanz
            doute*,
Have I nat of a capon but the lyvere,
And of youre softe breed nat but a shyvere,   1840
And after that a rosted pigges heed—
But that I nolde no beest for me were deed—
Thanne hadde I with yow hoomly suffisaunce.

1770 **Deus hic!**: God be here
1772 **yelde**: reward
1776 **potente**: walking stick
1778 **was go walked**: was gone
1780 **shoop hym**: intended
1792 **glose**: interpretation
1798 **yerd**: enclosed garden
1801 **hertely**: cordially (I ask it)
1803 **narwe**: closely, tightly
1804 **chirketh**: makes a chirping sound
1806 **every deel**: every bit, completely

1810 **amende defautes**: correct my faults (a self-deprecating response)
1814 **yow greve**: get angry
1815 **throwe**: while
1817 **grope**: examine (a penitent's conscience)
1818 **shrift**: confession
1821 **yelden**: pay
1825 **pissemyre**: ant
1827 **wrye**: cover
1829 **boor**: boar, pig   **lith**: that lies
1832 **je vous dy**: I tell you
1834 **Ire**: the deadly sin of wrath (see ParsT X.533–676)   **defended**: forbad
1837 **theraboute**: (see) about it
1838 **je vous dy sanz doute**: I say to you indeed
1839 **lyvere**: liver
1840 **shyvere**: sliver
1843 **hoomly suffisaunce**: enough plain food, family fare

I am a man of litel sustenaunce;
My spirit hath his fostryng in the Bible.   1845
The body is ay so redy and penyble
To wake, that my stomak is destroyed.
I prey yow, dame, ye be nat anoyed,
Though I so freendly yow my conseil shewe.
By God! I wolde nat telle it but a fewe."   1850
    "Now, sire," quod she, "but o word er I go.
My child is deed withinne thise wykes two,
Soone after that ye wente out of this toun."
    "His deeth saugh I by revelacioun,"
Seide this frere, "at hoom in oure dortour.   1855
I dar wel seyn that, er that half an hour
After his deeth, I saugh hym born to blisse
In myn avision, so God me wisse!
So dide oure sexteyn and oure fermerer,
That han been trewe freres fifty yeer;   1860
They may now—God be thanked of his loone!—
Maken hir jubilee and walke allone.
And up I roos, and al oure covent eke,
With many a teere trillyng on my cheke,
Withouten noyse or claterynge of belles;   1865
Te Deum was oure song, and nothyng elles,
Save that to Crist I seyde an orison,
Thankynge hym of his revelacion.
For, sire and dame, trusteth me right weel,
Oure orisons been moore effectueel,   1870
And moore we seen of Cristes secree thynges,
Than burel folk, although they weren kynges.
We lyve in poverte and in abstinence,
And burell folk in richesse and despence
Of mete and drynke, and in hir foul delit.   1875
We han this worldes lust al in despit.
Lazar and Dives lyveden diversly,
And divers gerdon hadden they therby.
Whoso wol preye, he moot faste and be clene,
And fatte his soule, and make his body lene.   1880
We fare as seith th'apostle; clooth and foode

Suffisen us, though they be nat ful goode.
The clennesse and the fastynge of us freres
Maketh that Crist accepteth oure preyeres.
    "Lo, Moyses fourty dayes and fourty nyght   1885
Fasted, er that the heighe God of myght
Spak with hym in the mountayne of Synay.
With empty wombe, fastynge many a day,
Receyved he the lawe that was writen
With Goddes fynger; and Elye, wel ye witen,   1890
In mount Oreb, er he hadde any speche
With hye God, that is oure lyves leche,
He fasted longe and was in contemplaunce.
    "Aaron, that hadde the temple in governaunce,
And eek the othere preestes everichon,   1895
Into the temple whan they sholde gon
To preye for the peple and do servyse,
They nolden drynken in no maner wyse
No drynke which that myghte hem dronke make,
But there in abstinence preye and wake,   1900
Lest that they deyden. Taak heede what I seye!
But they be sobre that for the peple preye,
War that—I seye namoore, for it suffiseth.
    "Oure Lord Jhesu, as hooly writ devyseth,
Yaf us ensample of fastynge and preyeres.   1905
Therfore we mendynantz, we sely freres,
Been wedded to poverte and continence,
To charite, humblesse, and abstinence,
To persecucioun for rightwisnesse,
To wepynge, misericorde, and clennesse.   1910
And therfore may ye se that oure preyeres—
I speke of us, we mendynantz, we freres—
Been to the hye God moore acceptable
Than youres, with youre feestes at the table.
Fro Paradys first, if I shal nat lye,   1915
Was man out chaced for his glotonye;
And chaast was man in Paradys, certeyn.
    "But herkne now, Thomas, what I shal seyn.
I ne have no text of it, as I suppose,
But I shal fynde it in a maner glose,   1920
That specially oure sweete Lord Jhesus
Spak this by freres, whan he seyde thus:
'Blessed be they that povere in spirit been.'

1844 **a man of litel sustenaunce:** one who eats little
1845 **fostryng:** nourishment
1846 **penyble:** accustomed to suffering
1847 **wake:** spend the night in prayer and meditation
1855 **dortour:** dormitory (in the convent)
1857 **born to blisse:** carried to heaven
1858 **wisse:** guide
1859 **sexteyn:** sacristan, friar in charge of the liturgical vestments and vessels
fermerer: friar in charge of the infirmary
1861 **loone:** grace
1862 **jubilee:** fiftieth anniversary
1864 **trillyng:** trickling
1866 **Te Deum:** "To You O God" (a hymn of praise)
1872 **burel:** lay, secular
1877 **Lazar and Dives:** the poor man and rich man of the New Testament
1878 **gerdon:** reward

1883 **clennesse:** purity
1885 **Moyses:** Moses
1890 **Elye:** the biblical Elijah
1891 **Oreb:** Horeb
1892 **leche:** healer
1906 **mendynantz:** mendicants   **sely:** good, blessed
1909 **rightwisnesse:** righteousness
1910 **misericorde:** charity, mercy
1919 **text:** biblical text
1920 **in a maner glose:** in some interpretation

And so forth al the gospel may ye seen,
Wher it be likker oure professioun,   1925
Or hirs that swymmen in possessioun.
Fy on hire pompe and on hire glotonye!
And for hir lewednesse I hem diffye.
    "Me thynketh they been lyk Jovinyan,
Fat as a whale, and walkynge as a swan,   1930
Al vinolent as botel in the spence.
Hir preyere is of ful greet reverence,
Whan they for soules seye the psalm of Davit:
Lo, 'buf!' they seye, '*cor meum eructavit!*'
Who folweth Cristes gospel and his foore,   1935
But we that humble been, and chaast, and poore,
Werkeris of Goddes word, nat auditours?
Therfore, right as an hauk up at a sours
Up springeth into th'eir, right so prayeres
Of charitable and chaste bisy freres   1940
Maken hir sours to Goddes eres two.
Thomas, Thomas! So moote I ryde or go,
And by that lord that clepid is Seint Yve,
Nere thou oure brother, sholdestou nat thryve.
In our chapitre praye we day and nyght   1945
To Crist, that he thee sende heele and myght
Thy body for to weelden hastily."
    "God woot," quod he, "no thyng therof feele I!
As help me Crist, as I in fewe yeres,
Have spent upon diverse manere freres   1950
Ful many a pound; yet fare I never the bet.
Certeyn, my good have I almoost biset.
Farwel, my gold, for it is al ago!"
    The frere answerde, "O Thomas, dostow so?
What nedeth yow diverse freres seche?   1955
What nedeth hym that hath a parfit leche
To sechen othere leches in the toun?
Youre inconstance is youre confusioun.
Holde ye thanne me, or elles oure covent,
To praye for yow been insufficient?   1960
Thomas, that jape nys nat worth a myte.

Youre maladye is for we han to lyte.
A, yif that covent half a quarter otes!
A, yif that covent foure and twenty grotes!
A, yif that frere a peny, and lat hym go!   1965
Nay, nay, Thomas, it may no thyng be so!
What is a ferthyng worth parted in twelve?
Lo, ech thyng that is oned in himselve
Is moore strong than whan it is toscatered.
Thomas, of me thou shalt nat been yflatered;   1970
Thou woldest han oure labour al for noght.
The hye God, that al this world hath wroght,
Seith that the werkman worthy is his hyre.
Thomas, noght of youre tresor I desire
As for myself, but that al oure covent   1975
To preye for yow is ay so diligent,
And for to buylden Cristes owene chirche.
Thomas, if ye wol lernen for to wirche,
Of buyldynge up of chirches may ye fynde
If it be good in Thomas lyf of Inde.   1980
Ye lye heere ful of anger and of ire,
With which the devel set youre herte afyre,
And chiden heere the sely innocent,
Youre wyf, that is so meke and pacient.
And therfore, Thomas, trowe me if thee leste,   1985
Ne stryve nat with thy wyf, as for thy beste;
And ber this word awey now, by thy feith;
Touchynge swich thyng, lo, what the wise seith:
'Withinne thyn hous ne be thou no leon;
To thy subgitz do noon oppression,   1990
Ne make thyne aqueyntances nat to flee.'
And, Thomas, yet eft-soones I charge thee,
Be war from Ire that in thy bosom slepeth;
War fro the serpent that so slily crepeth
Under the gras and styngeth subtilly.   1995
Be war, my sone, and herkne paciently
That twenty thousand men han lost hir lyves
For stryvyng with hir lemmans and hir wyves.
Now sith ye han so hooly meke a wyf,
What nedeth yow, Thomas, to maken stryf?   2000
Ther nys, ywys, no serpent so cruel,
Whan man tret on his tayl, ne half so fel,

1925 **it be likker:** it (the Gospel) more closely resembles   **professioun:** religious order
1928 **lewednesse:** ignorance   **diffye:** repudiate
1929 **Jovinyan:** Jovinianus, who provoked St. Jerome's *Adversus Jovinianum*
1930 **walkynge as:** waddling like
1931 Full of wine as a bottle in the pantry
1934 **buf!:** the sound of a belch   **cor meum eructavit:** "My heart has uttered (a good word)," the opening of Psalm 45
1935 **foore:** tracks, path (i.e., example)
1937 **auditours:** hearers (who merely listen)
1938 **sours:** upward flight
1944 **brother:** lay member of our order (see 2126–28)
1945 **chapitre:** assembly of the members of the convent
1946 **heele:** health
1947 **weelden:** move with ease
1952 **biset:** disposed of
1958 **confusioun:** ruin
1961 **myte:** a small Flemish coin of little value

1962 **to lyte:** too little
1963 **otes:** oats
1964 **grotes:** groats, silver coins worth four pence
1967 **ferthyng:** farthing
1968 **oned:** united
1969 **toscatered:** scattered, dispersed
1978 **for to wirche:** i.e., to do good works
1980 **Thomas lyf of Inde:** the life of St. Thomas of India
1988 **Touchynge:** concerning   **the wise:** the wise man (i.e., Jesus, son of Sirach, author of the Vulgate Ecclesiasticus)
1992 **eft-soones:** again   **charge:** command
1998 **lemmans:** sweethearts
2000 **maken stryf:** cause trouble
2002 **tret** = *tredeth,* steps

As womman is, whan she hath caught an ire;
Vengeance is thanne al that they desire.
Ire is a synne, oon of the grete of sevene,   2005
Abhomynable unto the God of hevene;
And to hymself it is destruccion.
This every lewed viker or person
Kan seye, how ire engendreth homycide.
Ire is, in sooth, executour of pryde.   2010
I koude of ire seye so muche sorwe,
My tale sholde laste til to-morwe.
And therfore preye I God bothe day and nyght
An irous man, God sende hym litel myght!
It is greet harm and certes greet pitee   2015
To sette an irous man in heigh degree.

    "Whilom ther was an irous potestat,
As seith Senek, that, durynge his estaat,
Upon a day out ryden knyghtes two,
And as Fortune wolde that it were so,   2020
That oon of hem cam hoom, that oother noght.
Anon the knyght bifore the juge is broght,
That seyde thus, 'Thou hast thy felawe slayn,
For which I deme thee to the deeth, certayn.'
And to another knyght comanded he,   2025
'Go lede hym to the deeth, I charge thee.'
And happed, as they wente by the weye
Toward the place ther he sholde deye,
The knyght cam which men wenden had be deed.
Thanne thoughte they it were the beste reed   2030
To lede hem bothe to the juge agayn.
They seiden, 'Lord, the knyght ne hath nat slayn
His felawe; heere he standeth hool alyve.'
'Ye shul be deed,' quod he, 'so moot I thryve!
That is to seyn, bothe oon, and two, and thre!'   2035
And to the firste knyght right thus spak he,
'I dampned thee; thou most algate be deed.
And thou also most nedes lese thyn heed,
For thou art cause why thy felawe deyth.'
And to the thridde knyght right thus he seith,   2040
'Thou hast nat doon that I comanded thee.'
And thus he dide doon sleen hem alle thre.

    "Irous Cambises was eek dronkelewe,
And ay delited hym to been a shrewe.
And so bifel, a lord of his meynee   2045

That loved vertuous moralitee
Seyde on a day bitwix hem two right thus:
    "'A lord is lost, if he be vicius;
And dronkenesse is eek a foul record
Of any man, and namely in a lord.   2050
Ther is ful many an eye and many an ere
Awaityng on a lord, and he noot where.
For Goddes love, drynk moore attemprely!
Wyn maketh man to lesen wrecchedly
His mynde and eek his lymes everichon.'   2055
    "'The revers shaltou se,' quod he, 'anon,
And preve it by thyn owene experience,
That wyn ne dooth to folk no swich offence.
Ther is no wyn bireveth me my myght
Of hand ne foot, ne of myne eyen sight.'   2060
And for despit he drank ful muchel moore,
An hondred part, than he hadde don bifoore;
And right anon this irous, cursed wrecche
Leet this knyghtes sone bifore hym fecche,
Comandynge hym he sholde bifore hym stonde.
And sodeynly he took his bowe in honde,   2066
And up the streng he pulled to his ere,
And with an arwe he slow the child right there.
'Now wheither have I a siker hand or noon?'
Quod he; 'Is al my myght and mynde agon?   2070
Hath wyn bireved me myn eyen sight?'
What sholde I telle th'answere of the knyght?
His sone was slayn; ther is namoore to seye.
Beth war, therfore, with lordes how ye pleye.
Syngeth Placebo and 'I shal, if I kan,'   2075
But if it be unto a povre man.
To a povre man men sholde his vices telle,
But nat to a lord, thogh he sholde go to helle.

    "Lo irous Cirus, thilke Percien,
How he destroyed the ryver of Gysen,   2080
For that an hors of his was dreynt therinne,
Whan that he wente Babiloigne to wynne.
He made that the ryver was so smal
That wommen myghte wade it over al.
Lo, what seyde he that so wel teche kan?   2085
'Ne be no felawe to an irous man,
Ne with no wood man walke by the weye,
Lest thee repente;' I wol no ferther seye.

2003 **caught an ire:** become angry
2008 **lewed:** ignorant, uneducated   **viker:** vicar
2010 **executour of pryde:** one who carries out Pride's orders
2016 **irous:** angry
2017 **potestat:** potentate
2018 **Senek:** Seneca   **estaat:** term of office
2030 **reed:** plan
2042 **dide doon sleen:** had (caused to be) slain
2043 **Cambises:** king of Persia, son of Cyrus the Elder (line 2079)   **dronkelewe:** addicted to drink
2045 **meynee:** household

2049 **record:** reputation
2052 **Awaityng on:** observing
2053 **attemprely:** moderately
2054 **lesen:** lose
2064 **Leet . . . fecche:** had fetched
2068 **slow:** slew
2069 **wheither:** tell me whether
2075 **Placebo:** "I shall please" (Psalm 114:9)
2079 **Cirus:** Cyrus the Elder (the Great)   **Percien:** Persian
2080 **Gysen:** the river Gyndes
2081 **dreynt:** drowned
2082 **Babiloigne:** Babylon
2085 **he:** Solomon

"Now, Thomas, leeve brother, lef thyn ire;
Thou shalt me fynde as just as is a squyre.   2090
Hoold nat the develes knyf ay at thyn herte—
Thyn angre dooth thee al to soore smerte—
But shewe to me al thy confessioun."
     "Nay," quod the sike man, "by Seint Symoun!
I have be shryven this day at my curat.   2095
I have hym toold hoolly al myn estat;
Nedeth namoore to speken of it," seith he,
"But if me list, of myn humylitee."
     "Yif me thanne of thy gold, to make oure cloystre,"
Quod he, "for many a muscle and many an oystre,   2100
Whan othere men han ben ful wel at eyse,
Hath been oure foode, our cloystre for to reyse.
And yet, God woot, unnethe the fundement
Parfourned is, ne of our pavement
Nys nat a tyle yet withinne oure wones.   2105
By God, we owen fourty pound for stones.
     "Now help, Thomas, for hym that harwed helle!
For elles moste we oure bookes selle.
And if yow lakke oure predicacioun,
Thanne goth the world al to destruccioun.   2110
For whoso wolde us fro this world bireve,
So God me save, Thomas, by youre leve,
He wolde bireve out of this world the sonne.
For who kan teche and werchen as we konne?
And that is nat of litel tyme," quod he,   2115
"But syn Elye was, or Elise,
Han freres been—that fynde I of record—
In charitee, ythanked be oure Lord!
Now Thomas, help, for seinte charitee!"
And doun anon he sette hym on his knee.   2120
     This sike man wax wel ny wood for ire;
He wolde that the frere had been on-fire
With his false dissymulacioun.
"Swich thyng as is in my possessioun,"
Quod he, "that may I yeve, and noon oother.   2125

Ye sey me thus, how that I am youre brother?"
     "Ye, certes," quod the frere, "trusteth weel.
I took oure dame oure lettre with oure seel."
     "Now wel," quod he, "and somwhat shal I yive
Unto youre hooly covent whil I lyve;   2130
And in thyn hand thou shalt it have anon,
On this condicion, and oother noon,
That thou departe it so, my deere brother,
That every frere have also muche as oother.
This shaltou swere on thy professioun,   2135
Withouten fraude or cavillacioun."
     "I swere it," quod this frere, "by my feith!"
And therwithal his hand in his he leith,
"Lo, heer my feith; in me shal be no lak."   2139
     "Now thanne, put in thyn hand doun by my bak,"
Seyde this man, "and grope wel bihynde.
Bynethe my buttok there shaltow fynde
A thyng that I have hyd in pryvetee."
     "A!" thoghte this frere, "That shal go with me!"
And doun his hand he launcheth to the clifte   2145
In hope for to fynde there a yifte.
And whan this sike man felte this frere
Aboute his tuwel grope there and heere,
Amydde his hand he leet the frere a fart;
Ther nys no capul, drawynge in a cart,   2150
That myghte have lete a fart of swich a soun.
     The frere up stirte as dooth a wood leoun—
"A, false cherl," quod he, "for Goddes bones!
This hastow for despit doon for the nones.
Thou shalt abye this fart, if that I may!"   2155
     His meynee, whiche that herden this affray,
Cam lepynge in and chaced out the frere;
And forth he gooth, with a ful angry cheere,
And fette his felawe, ther as lay his stoor.
He looked as it were a wilde boor;   2160
He grynte with his teeth, so was he wrooth.
A sturdy paas doun to the court he gooth,
Wher as ther woned a man of greet honour,
To whom that he was alwey confessour.

2090 **just:** true, exact   **squyre:** carpenter's square
2094 **Seint Symoun:** unidentified; possibly Simon Magus, the false apostle; see n.
2095 **shryven:** confessed
2100 **muscle:** mussel
2102 **reyse:** build
2103 **fundement:** foundation
2104 **Parfourned:** completed
2105 **wones:** dwelling place
2107 **hym that harwed helle:** Christ, who despoiled Hell of its captives
2109 **predicacioun:** preaching
2111 **bireve:** take away
2113 **sonne:** sun
2116 **Elye, Elise:** Elijah, Elisha; see n.

2126 **youre brother:** lay member of your order
2133 **departe:** share, divide
2134 **also:** as
2135 **professioun:** religious vows
2136 **cavillacioun:** quibbling
2139 **lak:** flaw
2145 **launcheth:** thrusts   **clifte:** cleft of the buttocks
2148 **tuwel:** anus
2150 **capul:** horse
2155 **abye:** pay for
2156 **affray:** disturbance
2159 **fette:** fetched   **stoor:** store (what he had collected)
2161 **grynte with:** ground
2162 **sturdy paas:** quick pace   **court:** manor house
2163 **woned:** dwelt

This worthy man was lord of that village.   2165
This frere cam as he were in a rage,
Where as this lord sat etyng at his bord;
Unnethes myghte the frere speke a word,
Til atte laste he seyde, "God yow see!"   2169
　　This lord gan looke, and seide, "Benedicitee!
What, frere John, what maner world is this?
I se wel that som thyng ther is amys;
Ye looken as the wode were ful of thevys.
Sit doun anon, and tel me what youre grief is,
And it shal been amended, if I may."   2175
　　"I have," quod he, "had a despit this day,
God yelde yow, adoun in youre village,
That in this world is noon so povre a page
That he nolde have abhomynacioun
Of that I have receyved in youre toun.   2180
And yet ne greveth me nothyng so soore,
As that this olde cherl with lokkes hoore
Blasphemed hath oure hooly covent eke."
　　"Now, maister," quod this lord, "I yow biseke—"
　　"No maister, sire," quod he, "but servitour,   2185
Thogh I have had in scole that honour.
God liketh nat that 'Raby' men us calle,
Neither in market ne in youre large halle."
　　"No fors," quod he, "but tel me al youre grief."
　　"Sire," quod this frere, "an odious meschief   2190
This day bityd is to myn ordre and me,
And so, *per consequens*, to ech degree
Of hooly chirche—God amende it soone!"
　　"Sire," quod the lord, "ye woot what is to doone.
Distempre yow noght; ye be my confessour;   2195
Ye been the salt of the erthe and the savour.
For Goddes love, youre pacience ye holde!
Tel me youre grief." And he anon hym tolde,
As ye han herd biforn—ye woot wel what.
　　The lady of the hous ay stille sat   2200
Til she had herd what the frere sayde.
"Ey, Goddes mooder," quod she, "Blisful mayde!
Is ther oght elles? Telle me feithfully."

"Madame," quod he, "how thynke ye herby?"
"How that me thynketh?" quod she. "So God me
　　speede,   2205
I seye a cherl hath doon a cherles dede.
What shold I seye? God lat hym nevere thee!
His sike heed is ful of vanytee;
I holde hym in a manere frenesye."
　　"Madame," quod he, "by God, I shal nat lye,   2210
But I on oother wyse may be wreke,
I shal disclaundre hym over al ther I speke,
This false blasphemour that charged me
To parte that wol nat departed be
To every man yliche, with meschaunce!"   2215
　　The lord sat stille as he were in a traunce,
And in his herte he rolled up and doun,
"How hadde this cherl ymaginacioun
To shewe swich a probleme to the frere?
Nevere erst er now herde I of swich mateere.   2220
I trowe the devel putte it in his mynde.
In ars-metrike shal ther no man fynde,
Biforn this day, of swich a question.
Who sholde make a demonstracion
That every man sholde have yliche his part   2225
As of the soun or savour of a fart?
O nyce, proude cherl, I shrewe his face!
Lo, sires," quod the lord, "with harde grace!
Who evere herde of swich a thyng er now?
To every man ylike? Tel me how.   2230
It is an inpossible; it may nat be.
Ey, nyce cherl, God lete him nevere thee!
The rumblynge of a fart, and every soun,
Nis but of eir reverberacioun,
And evere it wasteth litel and litel awey.   2235
Ther is no man kan deemen, by my fey,
If that it were departed equally.
What, lo, my cherl, lo, yet how shrewedly
Unto my confessour to-day he spak!
I holde hym certeyn a demonyak!   2240
Now ete youre mete, and lat the cherl go pleye;

2168 **Unnethes:** hardly
2169 **God yow see!:** may God look after you
2171 **what maner world:** what sort of carrying on
2182 **hoore:** white
2185 **servitour:** servant
2186 **that honour:** Master of Arts degree
2187 **Raby:** rabbi
2189 **No fors:** no matter
2192 **per consequens:** consequently
2195 **Distempre yow noght:** do not be angry
2196 **savour:** delight

2204 **herby:** about this
2207 **lat hym nevere thee:** never allow him to prosper
2209 **frenesye:** madness
2211 **wreke:** avenged
2212 **disclaundre:** defame
2214 **parte:** share, divide
2215 **yliche:** equally
2217 **rolled up and doun:** pondered
2218 **ymaginacioun:** the ingenuity
2219 **probleme:** logical problem
2222 **ars-metrike:** art of measurement (arithmetic)
2223 **question:** logical problem
2224 **make a demonstracion:** prove
2226 **savour:** odor
2228 **with harde grace:** bad luck to him
2231 **inpossible:** impossibility, a logical exercise; see n.
2240 **demonyak:** possessed by a demon

Lat hym go honge hymself a devel weye!"

The wordes of the lordes squier and
his kervere for departynge of the
fart on twelve.

Now stood the lordes squier at the bord,
That karf his mete, and herde word by word
Of alle thynges whiche I have yow sayd.   2245
"My lord," quod he, "be ye nat yvele apayd,
I koude telle, for a gowne-clooth,
To yow, sire frere, so ye be nat wrooth,
How that this fart sholde evene deled be
Among youre covent, if it lyked me."   2250
"Tel," quod the lord, "and thou shalt have anon
A gowne-clooth, by God and by Seint John!"
"My lord," quod he, "whan that the weder is fair,
Withouten wynd or perturbynge of air,
Lat brynge a cartwheel heere into this halle;   2255
But looke that it have his spokes alle—
Twelve spokes hath a cartwheel comunly.
And bryng me thanne twelve freres. Woot ye why?
For thrittene is a covent, as I gesse.
Youre confessour heere, for his worthynesse,   2260
Shal parfourne up the nombre of his covent.
Thanne shal they knele doun, by oon assent,
And to every spokes ende, in this manere,
Ful sadly leye his nose shal a frere.   2264
Youre noble confessour—there God hym save!—
Shal holde his nose upright under the nave.

Thanne shal this cherl, with bely stif and toght
As any tabour, hyder been ybroght;
And sette hym on the wheel right of this cart,
Upon the nave, and make hym lete a fart.   2270
And ye shul seen, up peril of my lyf,
By preeve which that is demonstratif,
That equally the soun of it wol wende,
And eke the stynk, unto the spokes ende,
Save that this worthy man, youre confessour,   2275
By cause he is a man of greet honour,
Shal have the firste fruyt, as resoun is.
The noble usage of freres yet is this,
The worthy men of hem shul first be served;
And certeinly he hath it weel disserved.   2280
He hath to-day taught us so muche good
With prechyng in the pulpit ther he stood,
That I may vouche sauf, I sey for me,
He hadde the firste smel of fartes thre;
And so wolde al his covent hardily,   2285
He bereth hym so faire and hoolily."
The lord, the lady, and ech man, save the frere,
Seyde that Jankyn spak, in this matere,
As wel as Euclide [dide] or Ptholomee.
Touchynge the cherl, they seyde, subtiltee   2290
And heigh wit made hym speken as he spak;
He nys no fool, ne no demonyak.
And Jankyn hath ywonne a newe gowne—
My tale is doon; we been almoost at towne.

Heere endeth the Somonours Tale.

2242 **a devel weye:** in the name of the Devil
2246 **yvele apayd:** displeased
2249 **evene deled:** evenly divided out
2253 **weder:** weather
2254 **perturbynge:** disturbance
2255 **Lat brynge:** have brought
2261 **parfourne up:** complete
2264 **sadly:** firmly

2267 **toght:** taut
2268 **tabour:** drum
2270 **nave:** hub
2272 **demonstratif:** demonstrable, logical
2289 **Euclide:** Euclid, the Greek mathematician **Ptholomee:** Ptolemy, the astronomer
2291 **wit:** intelligence

The Clerk's Prologue

Heere folweth the Prologe of the Clerkes Tale of Oxenford.

"Sire Clerk of Oxenford," oure Hooste sayde,
"Ye ryde as coy and stille as dooth a mayde
Were newe spoused, sittynge at the bord;
This day ne herde I of youre tonge a word.
I trowe ye studie aboute som sophyme; 5
But Salomon seith 'every thyng hath tyme.'
   "For Goddes sake, as beth of bettre cheere!
It is no tyme for to studien heere.
Telle us som myrie tale, by youre fey!
For what man that is entred in a pley, 10
He nedes moot unto the pley assente.
But precheth nat, as freres doon in Lente,
To make us for oure olde synnes wepe,
Ne that thy tale make us nat to slepe.
   "Telle us som murie thyng of aventures. 15
Youre termes, youre colours, and youre figures,
Keepe hem in stoor til so be ye endite
Heigh style, as whan that men to kynges write.
Speketh so pleyn at this tyme, we yow preye,
That we may understonde what ye seye." 20
   This worthy clerk benignely answerde:
"Hooste," quod he, "I am under youre yerde;
Ye han of us as now the governance,
And therfore wol I do yow obeisance,
As fer as resoun axeth, hardily. 25
I wol yow telle a tale which that I
Lerned at Padowe of a worthy clerk,
As preved by his wordes and his werk.
He is now deed and nayled in his cheste;
I prey to God so yeve his soule reste! 30

   "Fraunceys Petrak, the lauriat poete,
Highte this clerk, whos rethorike sweete
Enlumyned al Ytaille of poetrie,
As Lynyan dide of philosophie,
Or lawe, or oother art particuler; 35
But Deeth, that wol nat suffre us dwellen heer,
But as it were a twynklyng of an ye,
Hem bothe hath slayn, and alle shul we dye.
   "But forth to tellen of this worthy man
That taughte me this tale, as I bigan, 40
I seye that first with heigh stile he enditeth,
Er he the body of his tale writeth,
A prohemye, in the which discryveth he
Pemond and of Saluces the contree,
And speketh of Apennyn, the hilles hye, 45
That been the boundes of West Lumbardye,
And of Mount Vesulus in special,
Where as the Poo out of a welle smal
Taketh his firste spryngyng and his sours,
That estward ay encresseth in his cours 50
To Emele-ward, to Ferrare, and Venyse,
The which a long thyng were to devyse.
And trewely, as to my juggement,
Me thynketh it a thyng impertinent,
Save that he wole conveyen his mateere; 55
But this his tale, which that ye may heere."

2 **coy**: quiet, demure
3 **bord**: dinner table
5 **sophyme**: sophism, plausible but fallacious argument
7 **as beth**: be (*as* is not translated)
11 **pley**: rules of the game
16 **termes**: technical terms   **colours**: figures of speech   **figures**: rhetorical devices
17 **in stoor**: in stock, in reserve
18 **Heigh style**: elaborate, ornamented style
22 **under youre yerde**: under your authority
24 **do obeisance**: obey
27 **Padowe**: Padua
29 **cheste**: coffin

31 **Fraunceys Petrak**: Petrarch, who was crowned with laurel in 1341
33 **Enlumyned**: made illustrious
34 **Lynyan**: Giovanni da Lignano, professor of canon law at Padua
35 **art particuler**: specialized area of study
43 **prohemye**: proem, introduction   **discryveth**: describes
44 **Pemond**: Piedmont, an area in northern Italy west of Lombardy   **Saluces**: Saluzzo, a region and town in Piedmont
45 **Apennyn**: the Apennines
46 **Lumbardye**: Lombardy, east of the Apennines
47 **Vesulus**: Monte Viso or Monviso, highest of the Italian Alps
48 **Poo**: the river Po   **welle**: spring
49 **sours**: source
51 **To Emele-ward**: toward Emilia, the area of eastern Italy south of Lombardy
Ferrare: Ferrara, a town and area in Emilia   **Venyse**: Venice, where the Po empties into the Adriatic Sea
54 **impertinent**: irrelevant
55 **conveyen**: introduce

The Clerk's Tale

Heere bigynneth the Tale of the Clerk of Oxenford.

Ther is, at the west syde of Ytaille,
Doun at the roote of Vesulus the colde,
A lusty playn, habundant of vitaille,
Where many a tour and toun thou mayst biholde,   60
That founded were in tyme of fadres olde,
And many another delitable sighte,
And Saluces this noble contree highte.

A markys whilom lord was of that lond,
As were his worthy eldres hym bifore;   65
And obeisant, ay redy to his hond,
Were alle his liges, bothe lasse and moore.
Thus in delit he lyveth, and hath doon yoore,
Biloved and drad, thurgh favour of Fortune,
Bothe of his lordes and of his commune.   70

Therwith he was, to speke as of lynage,
The gentilleste yborn of Lumbardye,
A fair persone, and strong, and yong of age,
And ful of honour and of curteisye;
Discreet ynogh his contree for to gye,   75
Save in somme thynges that he was to blame;
And Walter was this yonge lordes name.

I blame hym thus: that he considered noght
In tyme comynge what myghte hym bityde,
But on his lust present was al his thoght,   80
As for to hauke and hunte on every syde.
Wel ny alle othere cures leet he slyde,
And eek he nolde—and that was worst of alle—
Wedde no wyf, for noght that may bifalle.

Oonly that point his peple bar so soore   85
That flokmeele on a day they to hym wente,
And oon of hem, that wisest was of loore—
Or elles that the lord best wolde assente
That he sholde telle hym what his peple mente,

Or elles koude he shewe wel swich mateere—   90
He to the markys seyde as ye shul heere:

"O noble markys, youre humanitee
Asseureth us and yeveth us hardinesse,
As ofte as tyme is of necessitee,
That we to yow mowe telle oure hevynesse.   95
Accepteth, lord, now of youre gentillesse
That we with pitous herte unto yow pleyne,
And lat youre eres nat my voys desdeyne.

"Al have I noght to doone in this mateere
Moore than another man hath in this place,   100
Yet for as muche as ye, my lord so deere,
Han alwey shewed me favour and grace
I dar the bettre aske of yow a space
Of audience to shewen oure requeste,
And ye, my lord, to doon right as yow leste.   105

"For certes, lord, so wel us liketh yow
And al youre werk, and evere han doon, that we
Ne koude nat us self devysen how
We myghte lyven in moore felicitee,
Save o thyng, lord, if it youre wille be,   110
That for to been a wedded man yow leste;
Thanne were youre peple in sovereyn hertes reste.

"Boweth youre nekke under that blisful yok
Of soveraynetee, noght of servyse,
Which that men clepe spousaille or wedlok;   115
And thenketh, lord, among youre thoghtes wyse
How that oure dayes passe in sondry wyse,
For thogh we slepe, or wake, or rome, or ryde,
Ay fleeth the tyme; it nyl no man abyde.   119

"And thogh youre grene youthe floure as yit,   120
In crepeth age alwey, as stille as stoon,

---

58 **roote of Vesulus:** foot of Monte Viso
59 **habundant of vitaille:** rich in agricultural produce
64 **markys:** marquis
69 **drad:** feared, respected
70 **commune:** citizenry
75 **gye:** govern
80 **lust present:** immediate pleasure
82 **slyde:** slip away
85 **bar so soore:** took so badly
86 **flokmeele:** in groups

92 **humanitee:** graciousness
93 **Asseureth us:** makes us confident   **hardinesse:** boldness
98 **desdeyne:** disdain, scorn
104 **audience:** hearing
105 **yow leste:** it may please you
106–7 **so wel us liketh yow . . . han doon:** you and your work so well please us and ever have done so
108 **us self:** ourselves
115 **spousaille:** marriage

And deeth manaceth every age, and smyt
In ech estaat, for ther escapeth noon;
And al so certein as we knowe echoon
That we shul deye, as uncerteyn we alle   125
Been of that day whan deeth shal on us falle.

"Accepteth thanne of us the trewe entente,
That nevere yet refuseden youre heeste,
And we wol, lord, if that ye wole assente,
Chese yow a wyf, in short tyme atte leeste,   130
Born of the gentilleste and of the meeste
Of al this land, so that it oghte seme
Honour to God and yow, as we kan deeme.

"Delivere us out of al this bisy drede,
And taak a wyf, for hye Goddes sake!   135
For if it so bifelle, as God forbede,
That thurgh youre deeth youre lyne sholde slake,
And that a straunge successour sholde take
Youre heritage, O wo were us alyve!
Wherfore we pray you hastily to wyve."   140

Hir meeke preyere and hir pitous cheere
Made the markys herte han pitee.
"Ye wol," quod he, "myn owene peple deere,
To that I nevere erst thoughte streyne me.
I me rejoysed of my liberte,   145
That seelde tyme is founde in mariage;
Ther I was free, I moot been in servage.

"But nathelees I se youre trewe entente,
And truste upon youre wit, and have doon ay;
Wherfore of my free wyl I wole assente   150
To wedde me, as soone as evere I may.
But ther as ye han profred me to-day
To chese me a wyf, I yow relesse
That choys and prey yow of that profre cesse.

"For God it woot, that children ofte been   155
Unlyk hir worthy eldres hem bifore;
Bountee comth al of God, nat of the streen
Of which they been engendred and ybore.

I truste in Goddes bountee, and therfore
My mariage and myn estaat and reste   160
I hym bitake; he may doon as hym leste.

"Lat me allone in chesynge of my wyf—
That charge upon my bak I wole endure.
But I yow preye, and charge upon youre lyf,
What wyf that I take, ye me assure   165
To worshipe hire, whil that hir lyf may dure,
In word and werk, bothe heere and everywheere,
As she an emperoures doghter weere.

"And forthermoore, this shal ye swere: that ye
Agayn my choys shul neither grucche ne stryve;
For sith I shal forgoon my libertee   171
At youre requeste, as evere moot I thryve,
Ther as myn herte is set, ther wol I wyve;
And but ye wole assente in swich manere,
I prey yow, speketh namoore of this matere."   175

With hertely wyl they sworen and assenten
To al this thyng—ther seyde no wight nay—
Bisekynge hym of grace, er that they wenten,
That he wolde graunten hem a certein day
Of his spousaille, as soone as evere he may;   180
For yet alwey the peple somwhat dredde,
Lest that the markys no wyf wolde wedde.

He graunted hem a day, swich as hym leste,
On which he wolde be wedded sikerly,
And seyde he dide al this at hir requeste.   185
And they, with humble entente, buxomly,
Knelynge upon hir knees ful reverently,
Hym thonken alle; and thus they han an ende
Of hire entente, and hoom agayn they wende.

And heerupon he to his officeres   190
Comaundeth for the feste to purveye,
And to his privee knyghtes and squieres
Swich charge yaf as hym liste on hem leye;
And they to his comandement obeye,
And ech of hem dooth al his diligence   195
To doon unto the feeste reverence.

Explicit prima pars.

122 **smyt** = *smyteth,* smites, strikes
131 **meeste:** greatest (in rank)
134 **bisy drede:** constant fear
137 **slake:** diminish, fail
140 **wyve:** take a wife
143 **wol:** want
144 **To that:** that to which   **streyne me:** force, constrain myself
146 **seelde tyme:** seldom
152 **profred:** offered
153 **yow relesse:** set you free from
154 **profre:** offer   **cesse:** cease
157 **Bountee:** goodness   **streen:** strain, family

161 **hym bitake:** entrust to him
163 **charge:** responsibility
173 **wyve:** take a wife
174 **And but:** unless
180 **spousaille:** wedding
186 **buxomly:** obediently
188–89 **ende Of hire entente:** conclusion in accord with their wishes
191 **purveye:** prepare
192 **privee:** personal, of his own household
Explicit, *etc.*: Here ends the first part.

Incipit secunda pars.

Noght fer fro thilke paleys honurable,
Wher as this markys shoop his mariage,
There stood a throop, of site delitable,
In which that povre folk of that village   200
Hadden hir beestes and hir herbergage,
And of hire labour tooke hir sustenance,
After that the erthe yaf hem habundance.

Amonges thise povre folk ther dwelte a man
Which that was holden povrest of hem alle;   205
But hye God somtyme senden kan
His grace into a litel oxes stalle;
Janicula men of that throop hym calle.
A doghter hadde he, fair ynogh to sighte,
And Grisildis this yonge mayden highte.   210

But for to speke of vertuous beautee,
Thanne was she oon the faireste under sonne;
For povreliche yfostred up was she,
No likerous lust was thurgh hire herte yronne.
Wel ofter of the welle than of the tonne   215
She drank, and for she wolde vertu plese,
She knew wel labour but noon ydel ese.

But thogh this mayde tendre were of age,
Yet in the brest of hire virginitee
Ther was enclosed rype and sad corage;   220
And in greet reverence and charitee
Hir olde povre fader fostred shee.
A fewe sheep, spynnynge, on feeld she kepte;
She wolde noght been ydel til she slepte.

And whan she homward cam, she wolde brynge 225
Wortes or othere herbes tymes ofte,
The whiche she shredde and seeth for hir lyvynge,
And made hir bed ful hard and nothyng softe;
And ay she kepte hir fadres lyf on-lofte
With everich obeisaunce and diligence   230
That child may doon to fadres reverence.

Upon Grisilde, this povre creature,
Ful ofte sithe this markys sette his ye
As he on huntyng rood paraventure;
And whan it fil that he myghte hire espye,   235
He noght with wantown lookyng of folye
His eyen caste on hire, but in sad wyse
Upon hir chiere he wolde hym ofte avyse,

Commendynge in his herte hir wommanhede,
And eek hir vertu, passynge any wight   240
Of so yong age, as wel in chiere as dede.
For thogh the peple have no greet insight
In vertu, he considered ful right
Hir bountee, and disposed that he wolde
Wedde hire oonly, if evere he wedde sholde.   245

The day of weddyng cam, but no wight kan
Telle what womman that it sholde be;
For which merveille wondred many a man,
And seyden, whan they were in privetee,
"Wol nat oure lord yet leve his vanytee?   250
Wol he nat wedde? Allas! Allas, the while!
Why wole he thus hymself and us bigile?"

But nathelees this markys hath doon make
Of gemmes, set in gold and in asure,
Brooches and rynges, for Grisildis sake;   255
And of hir clothyng took he the mesure
By a mayde lyk to hire stature,
And eek of othere aornementes alle
That unto swich a weddyng sholde falle.

The time of undren of the same day   260
Approcheth, that this weddyng sholde be,
And al the paleys put was in array,
Bothe halle and chambres, ech in his degree;
Houses of office stuffed with plentee
Ther maystow seen, of deyntevous vitaille   265
That may be founde as fer as last Ytaille.

This roial markys, richely arrayed,
Lordes and ladyes in his compaignye,
The whiche that to the feeste weren yprayed,
And of his retenue the bachelrye,   270

Incipit, *etc.*: Here begins the second part.
199 **throop:** village
201 **herbergage:** lodging
209 **to sighte:** in appearance
212 **oon the faireste:** the fairest of all
213 **povreliche:** in poverty
214 **likerous lust:** sensual desire
215 **tonne:** wine barrel
216 **vertu plese:** satisfy the demands of virtue
220 **rype and sad:** mature and steadfast
222 **fostred:** supported
223 **spynnynge:** while spinning
226 **Wortes:** cabbages
227 **shredde:** cut up   **seeth:** boiled
229 **kepte . . . on-lofte:** sustained

234 **paraventure:** by chance
236 **wantown:** lecherous
237 **sad:** serious
239 **wommanhede:** femininity, womanly qualities
244 **disposed:** decided
258 **aornementes:** ornaments
260 **undren:** midmorning, about 9 A.M.
264 **Houses of office:** outbuildings
265 **deyntevous:** delicious
266 **last Ytaille:** farthest Italy, as far as Italy extends
269 **yprayed:** invited
270 And the knights in his service

With many a soun of sondry melodye,
Unto the village of the which I tolde
In this array the righte wey han holde.

Grisilde of this, God woot, ful innocent,
That for hire shapen was al this array,   275
To fecchen water at a welle is went,
And cometh hoom as soone as ever she may;
For wel she hadde herd seyd that thilke day
The markys sholde wedde, and if she myghte,
She wolde fayn han seyn som of that sighte.   280

She thoghte, "I wole with othere maydens stonde,
That been my felawes, in oure dore and se
The markysesse, and therfore wol I fonde
To doon at hoom, as soone as it may be,
The labour which that longeth unto me,   285
And thanne I may at leyser hire biholde,
If she this wey unto the castel holde."

And as she wolde over hir thresshfold gon,
The markys cam and gan hire for to calle;
And she set doun hir water pot anon,   290
Biside the thresshfold, in an oxes stalle,
And doun upon hir knes she gan to falle,
And with sad contenance kneleth stille,
Til she had herd what was the lordes wille.

This thoghtful markys spak unto this mayde   295
Ful sobrely, and seyde in this manere:
"Where is youre fader, O Grisildis?" he sayde.
And she with reverence, in humble cheere,
Answerde, "Lord, he is al redy heere."
And in she gooth withouten lenger lette,   300
And to the markys she hir fader fette.

He by the hand thanne took this olde man,
And seyde thus, whan he hym hadde asyde:
"Janicula, I neither may ne kan
Lenger the plesance of myn herte hyde.   305
If that thou vouche sauf, what so bityde,
Thy doghter wol I take, er that I wende,
As for my wyf, unto hir lyves ende.

"Thou lovest me, I woot it wel certeyn,
And art my feithful lige man ybore,   310
And al that liketh me, I dar wel seyn

It liketh thee, and specially therfore
Tel me that poynt that I have seyd bifore,
If that thou wolt unto that purpos drawe,
To take me as for thy sone-in-lawe."   315

This sodeyn cas this man astonyed so
That reed he wax; abayst and al quakynge
He stood; unnethes seyde he wordes mo,
But oonly thus: "Lord," quod he, "my willynge
Is as ye wole, ne ayeynes youre likynge   320
I wol no thyng, ye be my lord so deere;
Right as yow lust, governeth this mateere."

"Yet wol I," quod this markys softely,
"That in thy chambre I and thou and she
Have a collacioun, and wostow why?   325
For I wol axe if it hire wille be
To be my wyf and reule hire after me.
And al this shal be doon in thy presence;
I wol noght speke out of thyn audience."

And in the chambre, whil they were aboute   330
Hir tretys, which as ye shal after heere,
The peple cam unto the hous withoute,
And wondred hem in how honest manere
And tentifly she kepte hir fader deere.
But outrely Grisildis wondre myghte,   335
For nevere erst ne saugh she swich a sighte.

No wonder is thogh that she were astoned
To seen so greet a gest come in that place;
She nevere was to swiche gestes woned,
For which she looked with ful pale face.   340
But shortly forth this matere for to chace,
Thise arn the wordes that the markys sayde
To this benigne, verray, feithful mayde:

"Grisilde," he seyde, "ye shal wel understonde
It liketh to youre fader and to me   345
That I yow wedde, and eek it may so stonde,
As I suppose, ye wol that it so be.
But thise demandes axe I first," quod he,

314 **unto that purpos drawe:** agree with that proposal
317 **abayst:** embarrassed
319 **willynge:** desire
325 **collacioun:** discussion, colloquy
327 **reule hire after me:** conduct herself as I decide
329 **audience:** hearing
331 **tretys:** negotiation
333 **how honest:** what a virtuous
334 **tentifly:** attentively
339 **woned:** accustomed
341 **chace:** pursue
342 **arn:** are
348 **demandes:** questions

273 **righte:** direct
283 **markysesse:** marchioness   **fonde:** try
288 **thresshfold:** threshold
299 **al redy:** right
300 **lette:** delay
306 **If that thou vouche sauf:** if you agree
310 **ybore:** born

"That, sith it shal be doon in hastif wyse,
Wol ye assente, or elles yow avyse?   350

"I seye this: be ye redy with good herte
To al my lust, and that I frely may,
As me best thynketh, do yow laughe or smerte,
And nevere ye to grucche it, nyght ne day?
And eek whan I sey 'ye,' ne sey nat 'nay,'   355
Neither by word ne frownyng contenance?
Swere this, and heere I swere oure alliance."

Wondrynge upon this word, quakynge for drede,
She seyde, "Lord, undigne and unworthy
Am I to thilke honour that ye me beede,   360
But as ye wole youreself, right so wol I.
And heere I swere that nevere willyngly,
In werk ne thoght, I nyl yow disobeye,
For to be deed, though me were looth to deye."

"This is ynogh, Grisilde myn," quod he.   365
And forth he gooth with a ful sobre cheere
Out at the dore, and after that cam she,
And to the peple he seyde in this manere:
"This is my wyf," quod he, "that standeth heere.
Honoureth hire and loveth hire, I preye,   370
Whoso me loveth; ther is namoore to seye."

And for that no thyng of hir olde geere
She sholde brynge into his hous, he bad
That wommen sholde dispoillen hire right theere;
Of which thise ladyes were nat right glad   375
To handle hir clothes, wherinne she was clad.
But nathelees, this mayde bright of hewe
Fro foot to heed they clothed han al newe.

Hir heris han they kembd, that lay untressed
Ful rudely, and with hir fyngres smale   380
A corone on hire heed they han ydressed,
And sette hire ful of nowches grete and smale.
Of hire array what sholde I make a tale?
Unnethe the peple hir knew for hire fairnesse
Whan she translated was in swich richesse.   385
This markys hath hire spoused with a ryng
Broght for the same cause, and thanne hire sette

Upon an hors, snow-whit and wel amblyng,
And to his paleys, er he lenger lette,
With joyful peple that hire ladde and mette,   390
Conveyed hire; and thus the day they spende
In revel, til the sonne gan descende.

And shortly forth this tale for to chace,
I seye that to this newe markysesse
God hath swich favour sent hire of his grace   395
That it ne semed nat by liklynesse
That she was born and fed in rudenesse,
As in a cote or in an oxe-stalle,
But norissed in an emperoures halle.

To every wight she woxen is so deere   400
And worshipful that folk ther she was bore,
And from hire birthe knewe hire yeer by yeere,
Unnethe trowed they—but dorste han swore—
That to Janicle, of which I spak bifore,
She doghter were, for, as by conjecture,   405
Hem thoughte she was another creature.

For though that evere vertuous was she,
She was encressed in swich excellence
Of thewes goode, yset in heigh bountee,
And so discreet and fair of eloquence,   410
So benigne and so digne of reverence,
And koude so the peples herte embrace,
That ech hire lovede that looked on hir face.

Noght oonly of Saluces in the toun
Publiced was the bountee of hir name,   415
But eek biside in many a regioun,
If oon seide wel, another seyde the same;
So spradde of hire heighe bountee the fame
That men and wommen, as wel yonge as olde,
Goon to Saluce upon hire to biholde.   420

Thus Walter lowely—nay, but roially—
Wedded with fortunat honestetee,
In Goddes pees lyveth ful esily
At hoom, and outward grace ynogh had he;
And for he saugh that under low degree   425
Was ofte vertu hid, the peple hym heelde
A prudent man, and that is seyn ful seelde.

---

350 **yow avyse:** consider the matter further (with the implication of refusal)
359 **undigne:** unsuitable
360 **beede:** offer
374 **dispoillen:** undress
379 **untressed:** unkempt
380 **rudely:** roughly   **hir fyngres smale:** their elegant fingers
381 **corone:** crown, nuptial garland
382 **nowches:** brooches, jewelled ornaments   **grete and smale:** of every sort
385 **translated:** transformed

388 **wel amblyng:** with a gentle pace
394 **markysesse:** marchioness
397 **rudenesse:** humble, unsophisticated conditions
398 **cote:** peasant's hut
400 **woxen is:** has grown, has become
409 **thewes:** morals, personal qualities
422 **honestetee:** honor, virtue
427 **seelde:** seldom

Nat oonly this Grisildis thurgh hir wit
Koude al the feet of wyfly hoomlinesse,
But eek, whan that the cas required it, 430
The commune profit koude she redresse.
Ther nas discord, rancour, ne hevynesse
In al that land that she ne koude apese,
And wisely brynge hem alle in reste and ese.

Though that hire housbonde absent were anon, 435
If gentil men or othere of hire contree
Were wrothe, she wolde bryngen hem aton;
So wise and rype wordes hadde she,
And juggementz of so greet equitee,
That she from hevene sent was, as men wende, 440
Peple to save and every wrong t'amende.

Nat longe tyme after that this Grisild
Was wedded, she a doghter hath ybore,
Al had hire levere have born a knave child;
Glad was this markys and the folk therfore, 445
For though a mayde child coome al bifore,
She may unto a knave child atteyne
By liklihede, syn she nys nat bareyne.

Explicit secunda pars.

Incipit tercia pars.

Ther fil, as it bifalleth tymes mo,
Whan that this child had souked but a throwe, 450
This markys in his herte longeth so
To tempte his wyf, hir sadnesse for to knowe,
That he ne myghte out of his herte throwe
This merveillous desir his wyf t'assaye; 454
Nedelees, God woot, he thoghte hire for t'affraye.

He hadde assayed hire ynogh bifore,
And foond hire evere good; what neded it
Hire for to tempte, and alwey moore and moore,
Though som men preise it for a subtil wit?
But as for me, I seye that yvele it sit 460

To assaye a wyf whan that it is no nede,
And putten hire in angwyssh and in drede.

For which this markys wroghte in this manere:
He cam allone a-nyght, ther as she lay,
With stierne face and with ful trouble cheere, 465
And seyde thus: "Grisilde," quod he, "that day
That I yow took out of youre povere array,
And putte yow in estaat of heigh noblesse—
Ye have nat that forgeten, as I gesse?

"I seye, Grisilde, this present dignitee, 470
In which that I have put yow, as I trowe,
Maketh yow nat foryetful for to be
That I yow took in povre estaat ful lowe,
For any wele ye moot youreselven knowe.
Taak heede of every word that y yow seye; 475
Ther is no wight that hereth it but we tweye.

"Ye woot youreself wel how that ye cam heere
Into this hous, it is nat longe ago;
And though to me that ye be lief and deere,
Unto my gentils ye be no thyng so. 480
They seyn, to hem it is greet shame and wo
For to be subgetz and been in servage
To thee, that born art of a smal village.

"And namely sith thy doghter was ybore
Thise wordes han they spoken, doutelees. 485
But I desire, as I have doon bifore,
To lyve my lyf with hem in reste and pees.
I may nat in this caas be recchelees;
I moot doon with thy doghter for the beste,
Nat as I wolde, but as my peple leste. 490

"And yet, God woot, this is ful looth to me;
But nathelees withoute youre wityng
I wol nat doon; but this wol I," quod he,
"That ye to me assente as in this thyng.
Shewe now youre pacience in youre werkyng, 495
That ye me highte and swore in youre village
That day that maked was oure mariage."

Whan she had herd al this, she noght ameved
Neither in word, or chiere, or contenaunce,
For, as it semed, she was nat agreved. 500
She seyde, "Lord, al lyth in youre plesaunce.

429 **feet of wyfly hoomlinesse:** feats, skills of a housewife's duties
431 **commune profit:** common good, welfare of the state **redresse:** amend, promote
433 **apese:** pacify
437 **aton:** to agreement
444 **levere:** rather **knave child:** baby boy
Explicit, *etc.*: Here ends the second part.
Incipit, *etc.*: Here begins the third part.
449 **tymes mo:** often
450 **souked:** sucked, fed on the breast **throwe:** short while
452 **tempte:** test **sadnesse:** constancy
454 **t'assaye:** to test
455 **t'affraye:** to frighten
460 **yvele it sit:** it ill befits one (sit = *sitteth*)

465 **trouble:** troubled
470 **dignitee:** high social position
480 **gentils:** nobles
483 **smal:** humble
488 **recchelees:** careless
492 **wityng:** knowledge
498 **ameved:** changed

My child and I, with hertely obeisaunce,
Been youres al, and ye mowe save or spille
Youre owene thyng; werketh after youre wille.

"Ther may no thyng, God so my soule save,   505
Liken to yow that may displese me;
Ne I desire no thyng for to have,
Ne drede for to leese, save oonly yee.
This wyl is in myn herte, and ay shal be;
No lengthe of tyme or deeth may this deface,   510
Ne chaunge my corage to another place."

Glad was this markys of hire answeryng,
But yet he feyned as he were nat so;
Al drery was his cheere and his lookyng,
Whan that he sholde out of the chambre go.   515
Soone after this, a furlong wey or two,
He prively hath toold al his entente
Unto a man, and to his wyf hym sente.

A maner sergeant was this privee man,
The which that feithful ofte he founden hadde   520
In thynges grete, and eek swich folk wel kan
Doon execucioun in thynges badde.
The lord knew wel that he hym loved and dradde;
And whan this sergeant wiste his lordes wille,
Into the chambre he stalked hym ful stille.   525

"Madame," he seyde, "ye moote foryeve it me,
Though I do thyng to which I am constreyned.
Ye been so wys that ful wel knowe ye
That lordes heestes mowe nat been yfeyned;
They mowe wel been biwailled or compleyned,   530
But men moote nede unto hire lust obeye,
And so wol I; ther is namoore to seye.

"This child I am comanded for to take"—
And spak namoore, but out the child he hente
Despitously, and gan a cheere make   535
As though he wolde han slayn it er he wente.
Grisildis moot al suffre and al consente,
And as a lamb she sitteth meke and stille,
And leet this crueel sergeant doon his wille.

Suspecious was the diffame of this man,   540
Suspect his face, suspect his word also;
Suspect the tyme in which he this bigan.
Allas! Hir doghter that she loved so,

She wende he wolde han slawen it right tho.
But nathelees she neither weep ne syked,   545
Conformynge hire to that the markys lyked.

But atte laste to speken she bigan,
And mekely she to the sergeant preyde,
So as he was a worthy gentil man,
That she moste kisse hire child er that it deyde.   550
And in hir barm this litel child she leyde
With ful sad face, and gan the child to blisse,
And lulled it, and after gan it kisse.

And thus she seyde in hire benigne voys,
"Fareweel my child! I shal thee nevere see.   555
But sith I thee have marked with the croys
Of thilke Fader—blessed moote he be!—
That for us deyde upon a croys of tree,
Thy soule, litel child, I hym bitake,
For this nyght shaltow dyen for my sake."   560

I trowe that to a norice in this cas
It had been hard this reuthe for to se;
Wel myghte a mooder thanne han cryd "allas!"
But nathelees so sad stidefast was she
That she endured al adversitee,   565
And to the sergeant mekely she sayde,
"Have heer agayn youre litel yonge mayde.

"Gooth now," quod she, "and dooth my lordes
        heeste;
But o thyng wol I prey yow of youre grace,
That, but my lord forbad yow, atte leeste   570
Burieth this litel body in som place
That beestes ne no briddes it torace."
But he no word wol to that purpos seye,
But took the child and wente upon his weye.

This sergeant cam unto his lord ageyn,   575
And of Grisildis wordes and hire cheere
He tolde hym point for point, in short and pleyn,
And hym presenteth with his doghter deere.
Somwhat this lord hadde routhe in his manere,
But nathelees his purpos heeld he stille,   580
As lordes doon, whan they wol han hir wille;

And bad this sergeant that he pryvely
Sholde this child softe wynde and wrappe,

---

510 **deface:** obliterate
519 **sergeant:** servant whose duty is to enforce the law   **privee man:** confidential
servant
529 **yfeyned:** evaded (by dissembling)
540 **diffame:** bad reputation

544 **slawen:** slain
551 **barm:** lap
552 **blisse:** bless
558 **tree:** wood
561 **norice:** nurse
562 **reuthe:** pitiful situation
564 **sad stidefast:** firmly steadfast
572 **briddes:** birds   **torace:** tear to pieces

With alle circumstances tendrely,
And carie it in a cofre or in a lappe;   585
But, upon peyne his heed of for to swappe,
That no man sholde knowe of his entente,
Ne whenne he cam, ne whider that he wente;

But at Boloigne to his suster deere,
That thilke tyme of Panik was countesse,   590
He sholde it take and shewe hire this mateere,
Bisekynge hire to doon hire bisynesse
This child to fostre in alle gentillesse;
And whos child that it was he bad hire hyde
From every wight, for oght that may bityde.   595

The sergeant gooth, and hath fulfild this thyng;
But to this markys now retourne we.
For now gooth he ful faste ymaginyng
If by his wyves cheere he myghte se,
Or by hire word aperceyve, that she   600
Were chaunged; but he nevere hire koude fynde
But evere in oon ylike sad and kynde.

As glad, as humble, as bisy in servyse,
And eek in love, as she was wont to be,
Was she to hym in every maner wyse;   605
Ne of hir doghter noght a word spak she.
Noon accident, for noon adversitee,
Was seyn in hire, ne nevere hir doghter name
Ne nempned she, in ernest nor in game.

Explicit tercia pars.

Sequitur pars quarta.

In this estaat ther passed been foure yeer   610
Er she with childe was, but, as God wolde,
A knave child she bar by this Walter,
Ful gracious and fair for to biholde.
And whan that folk it to his fader tolde,
Nat oonly he but al his contree merye   615
Was for this child, and God they thanke and herye.

Whan it was two yeer old, and fro the brest
Departed of his norice, on a day

This markys caughte yet another lest
To tempte his wyf yet ofter, if he may.   620
O nedelees was she tempted in assay!
But wedded men ne knowe no mesure,
Whan that they fynde a pacient creature.

"Wyf," quod this markys, "ye han herd er this
My peple sikly berth oure mariage;   625
And namely sith my sone yboren is,
Now is it worse than evere in al oure age.
The murmur sleeth myn herte and my corage,
For to myne eres comth the voys so smerte
That it wel ny destroyed hath myn herte.   630

"Now sey they thus: 'Whan Walter is agon,
Thanne shal the blood of Janicle succede
And been oure lord, for oother have we noon.'
Swiche wordes seith my peple, out of drede.
Wel oughte I of swich murmur taken heede,   635
For certeinly I drede swich sentence,
Though they nat pleyn speke in myn audience.

"I wolde lyve in pees, if that I myghte;
Wherfore I am disposed outrely,
As I his suster servede by nyghte,   640
Right so thenke I to serve hym pryvely.
This warne I yow, that ye nat sodeynly
Out of youreself for no wo sholde outreye;
Beth pacient, and therof I yow preye."

"I have," quod she, "seyd thus, and evere shal: 645
I wol no thyng, ne nyl no thyng, certayn,
But as yow list. Naught greveth me at al,
Though that my doughter and my sone be slayn—
At youre comandement, this is to sayn.
I have noght had no part of children tweyne   650
But first siknesse, and after, wo and peyne.

"Ye been oure lord; dooth with youre owene thyng
Right as yow list; axeth no reed at me.
For as I lefte at hoom al my clothyng,
Whan I first cam to yow, right so," quod she,   655
"Lefte I my wyl and al my libertee,

584 **alle circumstances:** every care
585 **lappe:** large pocket (made by a fold in the clothing)
586 **swappe:** strike
588 **whenne:** whence   **whider:** whither
590 **Panik:** Panico, near Bologna
598 **ymaginyng:** considering
607 **accident:** accidental (external) sign (of change)
609 **nempned:** named
Explicit, *etc.*: Here ends the third part.
Sequitur, *etc.*: Here follows the fourth part.
616 **herye:** praise

619 **lest:** desire
622 **mesure:** moderation
625 **sikly berth:** dislike, take ill
627 **al oure age:** all our lives
628 **murmur:** grumbling
629 **smerte:** sharply
636 **sentence:** opinion
639 **disposed:** decided
643 **outreye:** break out in a passion

And took youre clothyng; wherfore I yow preye,
Dooth youre plesaunce; I wol youre lust obeye.

"And certes, if I hadde prescience
Youre wyl to knowe, er ye youre lust me tolde,   660
I wolde it doon withouten necligence;
But now I woot youre lust, and what ye wolde,
Al youre plesance ferme and stable I holde;
For wiste I that my deeth wolde do yow ese,
Right gladly wolde I dyen, yow to plese.   665

"Deth may noght make no comparisoun
Unto youre love." And whan this markys say
The constance of his wyf, he caste adoun
His eyen two, and wondreth that she may
In pacience suffre al this array;   670
And forth he goth with drery contenance,
But to his herte it was ful greet plesance.

This ugly sergeant, in the same wyse
That he hire doghter caughte, right so he—
Or worse, if men worse kan devyse—   675
Hath hent hire sone, that ful was of beautee.
And evere in oon so pacient was she
That she no chiere maade of hevynesse,
But kiste hir sone, and after gan it blesse;

Save this, she preyede hym that, if he myghte,   680
Hir litel sone he wolde in erthe grave
His tendre lymes, delicaat to sighte,
Fro foweles and fro beestes for to save.
But she noon answere of hym myghte have.
He wente his wey, as hym no thyng ne roghte,   685
But to Boloigne he tendrely it broghte.

This markys wondred, evere lenger the moore,
Upon hir pacience, and if that he
Ne hadde soothly knowen therbifoore
That parfitly hir children loved she,   690
He wolde have wend that of som subtiltee,
And of malice, or for crueel corage,
That she hadde suffred this with sad visage.

But wel he knew that next hymself, certayn,
She loved hir children best in every wyse.   695
But now of wommen wolde I axen fayn
If thise assayes myghte nat suffise?
What koude a sturdy housbonde moore devyse
To preeve hir wyfhod and hir stedefastnesse,
And he continuynge evere in sturdinesse?   700

But ther been folk of swich condicion
That whan they have a certein purpos take,
They kan nat stynte of hire entencion,
But, right as they were bounden to that stake,
They wol nat of that firste purpos slake.   705
Right so this markys fulliche hath purposed
To tempte his wyf as he was first disposed.

He waiteth if by word or contenance
That she to hym was changed of corage,
But nevere koude he fynde variance.   710
She was ay oon in herte and in visage,
And ay the forther that she was in age,
The moore trewe, if that it were possible,
She was to hym in love, and moore penyble.

For which it semed thus: that of hem two   715
Ther nas but o wyl, for as Walter leste,
The same lust was hire plesance also.
And, God be thanked, al fil for the beste.
She shewed wel, for no worldly unreste
A wyf, as of hirself, nothing ne sholde   720
Wille in effect, but as hir housbonde wolde.

The sclaundre of Walter ofte and wyde spradde,
That of a crueel herte he wikkedly,
For he a povre womman wedded hadde,
Hath mordred bothe his children prively.   725
Swich murmur was among hem comunly.
No wonder is, for to the peples ere
Ther cam no word but that they mordred were.

For which, where as his peple therbifore
Hadde loved hym wel, the sclaundre of his diffame   730
Made hem that they hym hatede therfore.

---

659 **prescience:** foreknowledge
663 **ferme and stable I holde:** I obey unswervingly
667 **say:** saw
681 **grave:** bury
682 **delicaat to sighte:** pleasing in appearance
685 **roghte:** cared
690 **parfitly:** perfectly, completely
691 **subtiltee:** treachery

698 **sturdy:** harsh, cruel
700 **sturdinesse:** harshness, cruelty
705 **slake:** desist
706 **purposed:** decided
714 **penyble:** painstaking, attentive
719 **for no worldly unreste:** on account of no earthly discomfort
721 **Wille in effect:** desire in fact   **but:** except
722 **sclaundre:** ill fame
730 **diffame:** bad reputation

To been a mordrere is an hateful name;
But nathelees, for ernest ne for game,
He of his crueel purpos nolde stente;
To tempte his wyf was set al his entente.   735

Whan that his doghter twelve yeer was of age,
He to the court of Rome, in subtil wyse
Enformed of his wyl, sente his message,
Comaundynge hem swiche bulles to devyse
As to his crueel purpos may suffyse—   740
How that the pope, as for his peples reste,
Bad hym to wedde another, if hym leste.

I seye, he bad they sholde countrefete
The popes bulles, makynge mencion
That he hath leve his firste wyf to lete,   745
As by the popes dispensacion,
To stynte rancour and dissencion
Bitwixe his peple and hym; thus seyde the bulle,
The which they han publiced atte fulle.

The rude peple, as it no wonder is,   750
Wenden ful wel that it hadde be right so;
But whan thise tidynges came to Grisildis,
I deeme that hire herte was ful wo.
But she, ylike sad for everemo,
Disposed was, this humble creature,   755
The adversitee of Fortune al t'endure,

Abidynge evere his lust and his plesance,
To whom that she was yeven herte and al,
As to hire verray worldly suffisance.
But shortly if this storie I tellen shal,   760
This markys writen hath in special
A lettre, in which he sheweth his entente,
And secreely he to Boloigne it sente.

To the Erl of Panyk, which that hadde tho
Wedded his suster, preyde he specially   765
To bryngen hoom agayn his children two
In honurable estaat al openly.
But o thyng he hym preyede outrely,
That he to no wight, though men wolde enquere,
Sholde nat telle whos children that they were,   770

But seye the mayden sholde ywedded be
Unto the Markys of Saluce anon.
And as this erl was preyed, so dide he;
For at day set he on his wey is goon
Toward Saluce, and lordes many oon   775
In riche array, this mayden for to gyde,
Hir yonge brother ridynge hire bisyde.

Arrayed was toward hir mariage
This fresshe mayde, ful of gemmes cleere;
Hir brother, which that seven yeer was of age,   780
Arrayed eek ful fressh in his manere.
And thus in greet noblesse and with glad cheere,
Toward Saluces shapynge hir journey,
Fro day to day they ryden in hir wey.

Explicit quarta pars.

Sequitur pars quinta.

Among al this, after his wikke usage,   785
This markys, yet his wyf to tempte moore
To the outtreste preeve of hir corage,
Fully to han experience and loore
If that she were as stidefast as bifoore,
He on a day in open audience   790
Ful boistously hath seyd hire this sentence:

"Certes, Grisilde, I hadde ynogh plesance
To han yow to my wyf for youre goodnesse,
As for youre trouthe and for youre obeisance,
Noght for youre lynage, ne for youre richesse;   795
But now knowe I in verray soothfastnesse
That in greet lordshipe, if I wel avyse,
Ther is greet servitute in sondry wyse.

"I may nat doon as every plowman may.
My peple me constreyneth for to take   800
Another wyf, and crien day by day;
And eek the pope, rancour for to slake,
Consenteth it—that dar I undertake—
And trewely thus muche I wol yow seye:
My newe wyf is comynge by the weye.   805

"Be strong of herte, and voyde anon hir place;
And thilke dowere that ye broghten me,

738 **message:** messenger
739 **bulles:** papal edicts
745 **lete:** desert
750 **rude:** ignorant, unlearned
763 **secreely:** secretly

Explicit, *etc.:* Here ends the fourth part.
Sequitur, *etc.:* Here follows the fifth part.
785 **Among al this:** meanwhile
787 **outtreste preve:** utmost, final test
788 **loore:** knowledge
797 **wel avyse:** judge rightly
803 **undertake:** assert
806 **voyde:** vacate

Taak it agayn; I graunte it of my grace.
Retourneth to youre fadres hous," quod he;
"No man may alwey han prosperitee.   810
With evene herte I rede yow t'endure
The strook of Fortune or of aventure."

And she agayn answerde in pacience:
"My lord," quod she, "I woot, and wiste alway,
How that bitwixen youre magnificence   815
And my poverte no wight kan ne may
Maken comparison; it is no nay.
I ne heeld me nevere digne in no manere
To be youre wyf, no, ne youre chamberere.

"And in this hous, ther ye me lady maade—   820
The heighe God take I for my witnesse,
And also wysly he my soule glaade—
I nevere heeld me lady ne mistresse,
But humble servant to youre worthynesse,
And evere shal, whil that my lyf may dure,   825
Aboven every worldly creature.

"That ye so longe of youre benignitee
Han holden me in honour and nobleye,
Where as I was noght worthy for to bee,
That thonke I God and yow, to whom I preye   830
Foryelde it yow; ther is namoore to seye.
Unto my fader gladly wol I wende,
And with hym dwelle unto my lyves ende.

"Ther I was fostred of a child ful smal,
Til I be deed my lyf ther wol I lede,   835
A wydwe clene in body, herte, and al.
For sith I yaf to yow my maydenhede,
And am youre trewe wyf, it is no drede,
God shilde swich a lordes wyf to take
Another man to housbonde or to make!   840

"And of youre newe wyf God of his grace
So graunte yow wele and prosperitee!
For I wol gladly yelden hire my place,
In which that I was blisful wont to bee.
For sith it liketh yow, my lord," quod shee,   845
"That whilom weren al myn hertes reste,
That I shal goon, I wol goon whan yow leste.

"But ther as ye me profre swich dowaire
As I first broghte, it is wel in my mynde
It were my wrecched clothes, nothyng faire,   850
The whiche to me were hard now for to fynde.
O goode God! How gentil and how kynde
Ye semed by youre speche and youre visage
The day that maked was oure mariage!

"But sooth is seyd—algate I fynde it trewe,   855
For in effect it preeved is on me—
Love is noght oold as whan that it is newe.
But certes, lord, for noon adversitee,
To dyen in the cas, it shal nat bee
That evere in word or werk I shal repente   860
That I yow yaf myn herte in hool entente.

"My lord, ye woot that in my fadres place
Ye dide me streepe out of my povre weede,
And richely me cladden, of youre grace.
To yow broghte I noght elles, out of drede,   865
But feith, and nakednesse, and maydenhede;
And heere agayn your clothyng I restoore,
And eek your weddyng ryng, for everemore.

"The remenant of youre jueles redy be
Inwith youre chambre, dar I saufly sayn.   870
Naked out of my fadres hous," quod she,
"I cam, and naked moot I turne agayn.
Al youre plesance wol I folwen fayn;
But yet I hope it be nat youre entente
That I smoklees out of youre paleys wente.   875

"Ye koude nat doon so dishonest a thyng,
That thilke wombe in which youre children leye
Sholde biforn the peple, in my walkyng,
Be seyn al bare; wherfore I yow preye,
Lat me nat lyk a worm go by the weye.   880
Remembre yow, myn owene lord so deere,
I was youre wyf, though I unworthy weere.

"Wherfore, in gerdon of my maydenhede,
Which that I broghte, and noght agayn I bere,
As voucheth sauf to yeve me, to my meede,   885
But swich a smok as I was wont to were,

---

811 **evene:** tranquil   **rede:** advise
817 **is no nay:** cannot be denied
818 **in no manere:** in no way
819 **chamberere:** chambermaid
822 **also wysly:** as surely as   **glaade:** may gladden
828 **nobleye:** noble state
831 **Foryelde:** may he repay
839 **shilde:** forbid

848 **dowaire:** dowry
857 When love is old it is not the same as when it was new.
859 **To dyen:** even if I were to die
863 **dide me streepe:** had me stripped   **weede:** clothing
870 **Inwith:** within   **saufly:** confidently
875 **smoklees:** without a smock (i.e., naked)
876 **dishonest:** shameful
883 **gerdon:** requital
885 **to my meede:** as my compensation
886 **smok:** simple garment, undergarment

That I therwith may wrye the wombe of here
That was youre wyf. And heer take I my leeve
Of yow, myn owene lord, lest I yow greve." 889

"The smok," quod he, "that thou hast on thy bak,
Lat it be stille, and bere it forth with thee."
But wel unnethes thilke word he spak,
But wente his wey, for routhe and for pitee.
Biforn the folk hirselven strepeth she,
And in hir smok, with heed and foot al bare, 895
Toward hir fadre hous forth is she fare.

The folk hire folwe, wepynge in hir weye,
And Fortune ay they cursen as they goon;
But she fro wepyng kepte hire eyen dreye,
Ne in this tyme word ne spak she noon. 900
Hir fader, that this tidynge herde anoon,
Curseth the day and tyme that Nature
Shoop hym to been a lyves creature.

For out of doute this olde poure man
Was evere in suspect of hir mariage; 905
For evere he demed, sith that it bigan,
That whan the lord fulfild hadde his corage,
Hym wolde thynke it were a disparage
To his estaat so lowe for t'alighte,
And voyden hire as soone as ever he myghte. 910

Agayns his doghter hastily goth he,
For he by noyse of folk knew hire comynge,
And with hire olde coote, as it myghte be
He covered hire, ful sorwefully wepynge.
But on hire body myghte he it nat brynge, 915
For rude was the clooth, and moore of age
By dayes fele than at hire mariage.

Thus with hire fader for a certeyn space
Dwelleth this flour of wyfly pacience,
That neither by hire wordes ne hire face, 920
Biforn the folk, ne eek in hire absence,
Ne shewed she that hire was doon offence;
Ne of hire heighe estaat no remembraunce
Ne hadde she, as by hire contenaunce.

No wonder is, for in hire grete estaat 925
Hire goost was evere in pleyn humylitee;
No tendre mouth, noon herte delicaat,

No pompe, no semblant of roialtee,
But ful of pacient benyngnytee,
Discreet and pridelees, ay honurable, 930
And to hire housbonde evere meke and stable.

Men speke of Job, and moost for his humblesse,
As clerkes, whan hem list, konne wel endite,
Namely of men, but as in soothfastnesse,
Though clerkes preise wommen but a lite, 935
Ther kan no man in humblesse hym acquite
As womman kan, ne kan been half so trewe
As wommen been, but it be falle of newe.

[PART VI.]

Fro Boloigne is this Erl of Panyk come,
Of which the fame up sprang to moore and lesse, 940
And to the peples eres, alle and some,
Was kouth eek that a newe markysesse
He with hym broghte, in swich pompe and richesse
That nevere was ther seyn with mannes ye
So noble array in al West Lumbardye. 945

The markys, which that shoop and knew al this,
Er that this erl was come, sente his message
For thilke sely povre Grisildis;
And she with humble herte and glad visage,
Nat with no swollen thoght in hire corage, 950
Cam at his heste, and on hire knees hire sette,
And reverently and wisely she hym grette.

"Grisilde," quod he, "my wyl is outrely
This mayden, that shal wedded been to me,
Received be to-morwe as roially 955
As it possible is in myn hous to be,
And eek that every wight in his degree
Have his estaat, in sittyng and servyse
And heigh plesaunce, as I kan best devyse.

"I have no wommen suffisaunt, certayn, 960
The chambres for t'arraye in ordinaunce
After my lust, and therfore wolde I fayn
That thyn were al swich manere governaunce.
Thou knowest eek of old al my plesaunce;

887 **wrye:** cover
908 **disparage:** degradation
910 **voyden:** get rid of
917 **fele:** many
927 **delicaat:** self-indulgent

928 **semblant:** outward appearance
930 **pridelees:** humble, without pride
938 **of newe:** recently
940 **moore and lesse:** great and humble, everyone
941 **alle and some:** one and all
958 **sittyng:** seating arrangement at the table

Thogh thyn array be badde and yvel biseye,   965
Do thou thy devoir at the leeste weye."

"Nat oonly, lord, that I am glad," quod she,
"To doon youre lust, but I desire also
Yow for to serve and plese in my degree
Withouten feyntyng, and shal everemo;   970
Ne nevere, for no wele ne no wo,
Ne shal the goost withinne myn herte stente
To love yow best with al my trewe entente."

And with that word she gan the hous to dighte,
And tables for to sette, and beddes make;   975
And peyned hire to doon al that she myghte,
Preyynge the chambereres, for Goddes sake,
To hasten hem, and faste swepe and shake;
And she, the mooste servysable of alle,
Hath every chambre arrayed and his halle.   980

Abouten undren gan this erl alighte,
That with hym broghte thise noble children tweye,
For which the peple ran to seen the sighte
Of hire array, so richely biseye;
And thanne at erst amonges hem they seye   985
That Walter was no fool, thogh that hym leste
To chaunge his wyf, for it was for the beste.

For she is fairer, as they deemen alle,
Than is Grisilde, and moore tendre of age,
And fairer fruyt bitwene hem sholde falle,   990
And moore plesant, for hire heigh lynage.
Hir brother eek so fair was of visage
That hem to seen the peple hath caught plesaunce,
Commendynge now the markys governaunce.

"O stormy peple! Unsad and evere untrewe!   995
Ay undiscreet and chaungynge as a fane!
Delitynge evere in rumbul that is newe,
For lyk the moone ay wexe ye and wane!

Ay ful of clappyng, deere ynogh a jane!   999
Youre doom is fals, youre constance yvele preeveth;
A ful greet fool is he that on yow leeveth."

Thus seyden sadde folk in that citee,
Whan that the peple gazed up and doun,
For they were glad, right for the noveltee,
To han a newe lady of hir toun.   1005
Namoore of this make I now mencioun,
But to Grisilde agayn wol I me dresse,
And telle hir constance and hir bisynesse.

Ful bisy was Grisilde in every thyng
That to the feeste was apertinent.   1010
Right noght was she abayst of hire clothyng,
Thogh it were rude and somdeel eek torent;
But with glad cheere to the yate is went
With oother folk to greete the markysesse,
And after that dooth forth hire bisynesse.   1015

With so glad chiere his gestes she receyveth,
And so konnyngly, everich in his degree,
That no defaute no man aperceyveth,
But ay they wondren what she myghte bee
That in so povre array was for to see,   1020
And koude swich honour and reverence,
And worthily they preisen hire prudence.

In al this meene while she ne stente
This mayde and eek hir brother to commende
With al hir herte, in ful benyngne entente,   1025
So wel that no man koude hir pris amende.
But atte laste, whan that thise lordes wende
To sitten doun to mete, he gan to calle
Grisilde, as she was bisy in his halle.

"Grisilde," quod he, as it were in his pley,   1030
"How liketh thee my wyf and hire beautee?"
"Right wel," quod she, "my lord; for, in good fey,
A fairer saugh I nevere noon than she.
I prey to God yeve hire prosperitee;
And so hope I that he wol to yow sende   1035
Plesance ynogh unto youre lyves ende.

965 **yvel biseye:** ill-looking
966 **devoir:** duty
970 **feyntyng:** flagging, weakening
974 **dighte:** prepare
976 **peyned hire:** took pains
977 **chambereres:** chambermaids
979 **servysable:** willing to serve, attentive
981 **undren:** the third hour, about 9 A.M.
984 **richely biseye:** rich in appearance, splendid
985 **at erst:** for the first time
995 **Unsad:** inconstant
996 **undiscreet:** undiscerning   **fane:** weathervane
997 **rumbul:** rumor
998 **wexe:** wax

999 **clappyng:** chattering   **deere ynogh a jane:** expensive enough at a halfpenny
(i.e., worthless)
1000 **doom:** judgment   **preeveth:** proves
1001 **leeveth:** believes, trusts
1010 **apertinent:** suitable
1012 **torent:** ragged
1017 **konnyngly:** skillfully
1018 **defaute:** fault
1026 **pris amende:** improve her praise, praise them more highly

"O thyng biseke I yow, and warne also,
That ye ne prikke with no tormentynge
This tendre mayden, as ye han doon mo;
For she is fostred in hire norissynge   1040
Moore tendrely, and, to my supposynge,
She koude nat adversitee endure
As koude a povre fostred creature."

    And whan this Walter saugh hire pacience,
Hir glade chiere, and no malice at al,   1045
And he so ofte had doon to hire offence,
And she ay sad and constant as a wal,
Continuynge evere hire innocence overal,
This sturdy markys gan his herte dresse
To rewen upon hire wyfly stedfastnesse.   1050

    "This is ynogh, Grisilde myn," quod he;
"Be now namoore agast ne yvele apayed.
I have thy feith and thy benyngnytee,
As wel as evere womman was, assayed,
In greet estaat and povreliche arrayed.   1055
Now knowe I, dere wyf, thy stedfastnesse"—
And hire in armes took and gan hire kesse.

    And she for wonder took of it no keep;
She herde nat what thyng he to hire seyde;
She ferde as she had stert out of a sleep,   1060
Til she out of hire mazednesse abreyde.
"Grisilde," quod he, "by God, that for us deyde,
Thou art my wyf, ne noon oother I have,
Ne nevere hadde, as God my soule save!

    "This is thy doghter, which thou hast supposed
To be my wyf; that oother feithfully   1066
Shal be myn heir, as I have ay disposed;
Thou bare hym in thy body trewely.
At Boloigne have I kept hem prively;
Taak hem agayn, for now maystow nat seye   1070
That thou hast lorn noon of thy children tweye.

    "And folk that ootherweys han seyd of me,
I warne hem wel that I have doon this deede
For no malice, ne for no crueltee,
But for t'assaye in thee thy wommanheede,   1075

And nat to sleen my children—God forbeede!—
But for to kepe hem pryvely and stille,
Til I thy purpos knewe and al thy wille."

    Whan she this herde, aswowne doun she falleth
For pitous joye, and after hire swownynge   1080
She bothe hire yonge children to hire calleth,
And in hire armes, pitously wepynge,
Embraceth hem, and tendrely kissynge
Ful lyk a mooder, with hire salte teeres
She bathed bothe hire visage and hire heeres.   1085

    O which a pitous thyng it was to se
Hir swownyng, and hire humble voys to heere!
"Grauntmercy, lord, God thanke it yow," quod she,
"That ye han saved me my children deere!
Now rekke I nevere to been deed right heere;   1090
Sith I stonde in youre love and in youre grace,
No fors of deeth, ne whan my spirit pace!

    "O tendre, o deere, o yonge children myne!
Youre woful mooder wende stedfastly
That crueel houndes or som foul vermyne   1095
Hadde eten yow; but God of his mercy
And youre benyngne fader tendrely
Hath doon yow kept"—and in that same stounde
Al sodeynly she swapte adoun to grounde.

    And in hire swough so sadly holdeth she   1100
Hire children two, whan she gan hem t'embrace,
That with greet sleighte and greet difficultee
The children from hire arm they gonne arace.
O many a teere on many a pitous face
Doun ran of hem that stooden hire bisyde;   1105
Unnethe abouten hire myghte they abyde.

    Walter hire gladeth and hire sorwe slaketh;
She riseth up, abaysed, from hire traunce,
And every wight hire joye and feeste maketh
Til she hath caught agayn hire contenaunce.   1110
Walter hire dooth so feithfully plesaunce

1040 **norissynge:** nurture
1041 **to my supposynge:** as I believe
1047 **sad:** firm, steadfast
1048 **overal:** in every way
1049 **sturdy:** harsh, cruel   **dresse:** prepare
1052 **yvele apayed:** displeased
1055 **povreliche:** poorly
1057 **kesse:** kiss
1061 **mazednesse:** bewilderment   **abreyde:** awakened quickly

1092 **pace:** pass (away)
1095 **vermyne:** animal pests
1098 **Hath doon yow kept:** has had you protected   **stounde:** moment
1099 **swapte:** dropped suddenly
1100 **swough:** swoon   **sadly:** tightly
1103 **arace:** tear away
1108 **abaysed:** disconcerted
1110 **caught . . . hire contenaunce:** composed herself

That it was deyntee for to seen the cheere
Bitwixe hem two, now they been met yfeere.

Thise ladyes, whan that they hir tyme say,
Han taken hire and into chambre gon,   1115
And strepen hire out of hire rude array,
And in a clooth of gold that brighte shoon,
With a coroune of many a riche stoon
Upon hire heed, they into halle hire broghte,
And ther she was honured as hire oghte.   1120

Thus hath this pitous day a blisful ende,
For every man and womman dooth his myght
This day in murthe and revel to dispende
Til on the welkne shoon the sterres lyght.
For moore solempne in every mannes syght   1025
This feste was, and gretter of costage,
Than was the revel of hire mariage.

Ful many a yeer in heigh prosperitee
Lyven thise two in concord and in reste,
And richely his doghter maryed he   1130
Unto a lord, oon of the worthieste
Of al Ytaille; and thanne in pees and reste
His wyves fader in his court he kepeth,
Til that the soule out of his body crepeth.

His sone succedeth in his heritage   1135
In reste and pees, after his fader day,
And fortunat was eek in mariage,
Al putte he nat his wyf in greet assay.
This world is nat so strong, it is no nay,
As it hath been in olde tymes yoore,   1140
And herkneth what this auctour seith therfoore.

This storie is seyd nat for that wyves sholde
Folwen Grisilde as in humylitee,
For it were inportable, though they wolde,
But for that every wight, in his degree,   1145
Sholde be constant in adversitee
As was Grisilde; therfore Petrak writeth
This storie, which with heigh stile he enditeth.

For sith a womman was so pacient
Unto a mortal man, wel moore us oghte   1150
Receyven al in gree that God us sent;

For greet skile is he preeve that he wroghte.
But he ne tempteth no man that he boghte,
As seith Seint Jame, if ye his pistel rede;
He preeveth folk al day, it is no drede,   1155

And suffreth us, as for oure excercise,
With sharpe scourges of adversitee
Ful ofte to be bete in sondry wise;
Nat for to knowe oure wyl, for certes he,
Er we were born, knew al oure freletee;   1160
And for oure beste is al his governaunce.
Lat us thanne lyve in vertuous suffraunce.

But o word, lordynges, herkneth er I go:
It were ful hard to fynde now-a-dayes
In al a toun Grisildis thre or two;   1165
For if that they were put to swiche assayes,
The gold of hem hath now so badde alayes
With bras, that thogh the coyne be fair at ye,
It wolde rather breste a-two than plye.

For which heere, for the Wyves love of Bathe—
Whos lyf and al hire secte God mayntene   1171
In heigh maistrie, and elles were it scathe—
I wol with lusty herte, fressh and grene,
Seyn yow a song to glade yow, I wene;
And lat us stynte of ernestful matere.   1175
Herkneth my song that seith in this manere:

Lenvoy de Chaucer.

Grisilde is deed, and eek hire pacience,
And bothe atones buryed in Ytaille;
For which I crie in open audience
No wedded man so hardy be t'assaille   1180
His wyves pacience in trust to fynde
Grisildis, for in certein he shal faille.

O noble wyves, ful of heigh prudence,
Lat noon humylitee youre tonge naille,
Ne lat no clerk have cause or diligence   1185
To write of yow a storie of swich mervaille
As of Grisildis pacient and kynde,
Lest Chichevache yow swelwe in hire entraille!

1113 **met yfeere:** met together
1124 **welkne:** sky
1126 **costage:** cost, expense
1136 **fader:** father's
1141 **therfoore:** concerning this (tale)
1144 **inportable:** intolerable
1151 **in gree:** graciously   **sent** = *sendeth*, sends

1152 **For greet skile is:** it is very reasonable that
1154 **pistel:** epistle
1157 **scourges:** whips
1160 **freletee:** weakness
1162 **suffraunce:** patience, forbearance
1167 **alayes:** alloys
1168 **at ye:** to look at
1169 **plye:** bend
1170 **the Wyves love of Bathe:** the love of the Wife of Bath
1171 **secte:** sex, or school, those of her persuasion
1172 **scathe:** pity
1188 **Chichevache:** a legendary lean cow who feeds on patient wives, and so has little to eat   **swelwe:** swallow

Folweth Ekko, that holdeth no silence,
But evere answereth at the countretaille.　1190
Beth nat bidaffed for youre innocence,
But sharply taak on yow the governaille.
Emprenteth wel this lessoun in youre mynde,
For commune profit sith it may availle.

Ye archewyves, stondeth at defense,　1195
Syn ye be strong as is a greet camaille;
Ne suffreth nat that men yow doon offense.
And sklendre wyves, fieble as in bataille,
Beth egre as is a tygre yond in Ynde;
Ay clappeth as a mille, I yow consaille.　1200

Ne dreed hem nat; doth hem no reverence,
For though thyn housbonde armed be in maille,
The arwes of thy crabbed eloquence
Shal perce his brest and eek his aventaille.
In jalousie I rede eek thou hym bynde,　1205

And thou shalt make hym couche as doth a quaille.
　If thou be fair, ther folk been in presence,
Shewe thou thy visage and thyn apparaille;
If thou be foul, be fre of thy dispence;
To gete thee freendes ay do thy travaille;　1210
Be ay of chiere as light as leef on lynde,
And lat hym care, and wepe, and wrynge, and waille!

[The following stanza appears after the Envoy in
　most of the manuscripts that preserve it.

Bihoold the murye words of the Hoost.

　This worthy Clerk, whan ended was his tale,　1212A
Oure Hooste seyde, and swoor, "By Goddes bones,
Me were levere than a barel ale
My wyf at hoom had herd this legende ones!
This is a gentil tale for the nones,
As to my purpos, wiste ye my wille;
But thyng that wol nat be, lat it be stille."]　1212G

Heere endeth the Tale of the Clerk of Oxenford.

The Merchant's Prologue

☉

The Prologe of the Marchantes Tale.

"Wepyng and waylyng, care and oother sorwe
I knowe ynogh, on even and a-morwe,"
Quod the Marchant, "and so doon other mo　1215
That wedded been. I trowe that it be so,
For wel I woot it fareth so with me.
I have a wyf, the worste that may be;
For thogh the feend to hire ycoupled were,

She wolde hym overmacche, I dar wel swere.　1220
What sholde I yow reherce in special
Hir hye malice? She is a shrewe at al.
Ther is a long and large difference
Bitwix Grisildis grete pacience
And of my wyf the passyng crueltee.　1225
Were I unbounden, also moot I thee,
I wolde nevere eft comen in the snare.
We wedded men lyven in sorwe and care.
Assaye whoso wole, and he shal fynde
That I seye sooth, by Seint Thomas of Ynde,　1230

1189 **Ekko:** Echo
1190 **at the countretaille:** in reply (countertally)
1191 **bidaffed:** fooled, cowed, deafened (?)
1192 **governaille:** control
1194 **commune profit:** common good, welfare of all
1195 **archewyves:** quintessential women　**at defense:** ready for battle
1196 **camaille:** camel; see n.
1198 **sklendre:** slender
1199 **egre:** fierce
1200 **clappeth:** wag your tongues
1202 **maille:** mail, armor
1203 **crabbed:** spiteful, angry
1204 **perce:** pierce　**aventaille:** a piece of chain mail forming the neck-guard of the helmet

1209 **be fre of thy dispence:** spend freely
1211 **leef on lynde:** leaf on a linden tree
1212 **care:** grieve　**wrynge:** wring his hands
1212c **barel ale:** barrel of ale

1220 **overmacche:** outmatch, defeat
1222 **at al:** in every way
1226 **unbounden:** free (of marriage)
1230 **Seint Thomas of Ynde:** St. Thomas of India (the Apostle)

As for the moore part—I sey nat alle.   1231
God shilde that it sholde so bifalle!

   "A, goode sire Hoost, I have ywedded bee
Thise monthes two, and moore nat, pardee;
And yet, I trowe, he that al his lyve   1235
Wyflees hath been, though that men wolde him ryve
Unto the herte, ne koude in no manere
Tellen so muchel sorwe as I now heere

Koude tellen of my wyves cursednesse!"
   "Now," quod oure Hoost, "Marchaunt, so God
      yow blesse,   1240
Syn ye so muchel knowen of that art
Ful hertely I pray yow telle us part."
   "Gladly," quod he, "but of myn owene soore,
For soory herte, I telle may namoore."

The Merchant's Tale

Heere bigynneth the Marchantes Tale.

Whilom ther was dwellynge in Lumbardye   1245
A worthy knyght, that born was of Pavye,
In which he lyved in greet prosperitee;
And sixty yeer a wyflees man was hee,
And folwed ay his bodily delyt
On wommen, ther as was his appetyt,   1250
As doon thise fooles that been seculeer.
And whan that he was passed sixty yeer,
Were it for hoolynesse or for dotage
I kan nat seye, but swich a greet corage
Hadde this knyght to been a wedded man   1255
That day and nyght he dooth al that he kan
T'espien where he myghte wedded be,
Preyinge oure Lord to graunten him that he
Mighte ones knowe of thilke blisful lyf
That is bitwixe an housbonde and his wyf,   1260
And for to lyve under that hooly boond
With which that first God man and womman bond.
"Noon oother lyf," seyde he, "is worth a bene,
For wedlok is so esy and so clene,
That in this world it is a paradys."   1265
Thus seyde this olde knyght, that was so wys.

   And certeinly, as sooth as God is kyng,
To take a wyf it is a glorious thyng,
And namely whan a man is oold and hoor;

Thanne is a wyf the fruyt of his tresor.   1270
Thanne sholde he take a yong wyf and a feir,
On which he myghte engendren hym an heir,
And lede his lyf in joye and in solas,
Where as thise bacheleris synge "allas,"
Whan that they fynden any adversitee   1275
In love, which nys but childyssh vanytee.
And trewely it sit wel to be so,
That bacheleris have often peyne and wo;
On brotel ground they buylde, and brotelnesse
They fynde whan they wene sikernesse.   1280
They lyve but as a bryd or as a beest,
In libertee and under noon arreest,
Ther as a wedded man in his estaat
Lyveth a lyf blisful and ordinaat
Under this yok of mariage ybounde.   1285
Wel may his herte in joy and blisse habounde,
For who kan be so buxom as a wyf?
Who is so trewe, and eek so ententyf
To kepe hym, syk and hool, as is his make?
For wele or wo she wole hym nat forsake;   1290
She nys nat wery hym to love and serve,
Though that he lye bedrede til he sterve.
And yet somme clerkes seyn it nys nat so,
Of whiche he Theofraste is oon of tho.

1231 **moore part:** greater part, majority
1236 **ryve:** stab, pierce
1237 **in no manere:** in no way

1245 **Lumbardye:** Lombardy
1246 **Pavye:** Pavia
1249 **delyt:** pleasure, desire
1251 **seculeer:** of the laity (?)
1262 **bond:** bound
1269 **hoor:** white-haired

1270 **fruyt:** the best part
1277 **sit wel:** is fitting, well suits
1279 **brotel:** brittle, insecure
1280 **wene sikernesse:** expect safety, security
1282 **arreest:** restraint
1284 **ordinaat:** orderly
1287 **buxom:** obedient
1288 **ententyf:** eager, diligent
1289 **make:** mate
1292 **bedrede:** bedridden
1294 **Theofraste:** Theophrastus, author of the *Golden Book on Marriage*, a tract attacking marriage

What force though Theofraste liste lye?   1295
"Ne take no wyf," quod he, "for housbondrye,
As for to spare in houshold thy dispence.
A trewe servant dooth moore diligence
Thy good to kepe than thyn owene wyf,
For she wol clayme half part al hir lyf.   1300
And if thou be syk, so God me save,
Thy verray freendes, or a trewe knave,
Wol kepe thee bet than she that waiteth ay
After thy good and hath doon many a day.
And if thou take a wyf unto thyn hoold   1305
Ful lightly maystow been a cokewold."
This sentence, and an hundred thynges worse,
Writeth this man, ther God his bones corse!
But take no kep of al swich vanytee;
Deffie Theofraste, and herke me.   1310
    A wyf is Goddes yifte verraily;
Alle othere manere yiftes hardily,
As londes, rentes, pasture, or commune,
Or moebles—alle been yiftes of Fortune
That passen as a shadwe upon a wal.   1315
But drede nat, if pleynly speke I shal:
A wyf wol laste, and in thyn hous endure,
Wel lenger than thee list, paraventure.
    Mariage is a ful greet sacrement.
He which that hath no wyf, I holde hym shent;   1320
He lyveth helplees and al desolat—
I speke of folk in seculer estaat.
And herke why—I sey nat this for noght—
That womman is for mannes helpe ywroght.
The hye God, whan he hadde Adam maked,   1325
And saugh him al allone, bely-naked,
God of his grete goodnesse seyde than,
"Lat us now make an helpe unto this man
Lyk to hymself"; and thanne he made him Eve.
Heere may ye se, and heerby may ye preve,   1330
That wyf is mannes helpe and his confort,
His paradys terrestre, and his disport.
So buxom and so vertuous is she,
They moste nedes lyve in unitee.
O flessh they been, and o fleesh, as I gesse,   1335
Hath but oon herte, in wele and in distresse.

A wyf! a, Seinte Marie, benedicite!
How myghte a man han any adversitee
That hath a wyf? Certes, I kan nat seye.
The blisse which that is bitwixe hem tweye   1340
Ther may no tonge telle, or herte thynke.
If he be povre, she helpeth hym to swynke;
She kepeth his good, and wasteth never a deel;
Al that hire housbonde lust, hire liketh weel;
She seith nat ones "nay," whan he seith "ye."   1345
"Do this," seith he; "Al redy, sire," seith she.
O blisful ordre of wedlok precious,
Thou art so murye, and eek so vertuous,
And so commended and appreved eek
That every man that halt hym worth a leek   1350
Upon his bare knees oughte al his lyf
Thanken his God that hym hath sent a wyf,
Or elles preye to God hym for to sende
A wyf to laste unto his lyves ende.
For thanne his lyf is set in sikernesse;   1355
He may nat be deceyved, as I gesse,
So that he werke after his wyves reed.
Thanne may he boldely beren up his heed,
They been so trewe and therwithal so wyse;
For which, if thou wolt werken as the wyse,   1360
Do alwey so as wommen wol thee rede.
    Lo, how that Jacob, as thise clerkes rede,
By good conseil of his mooder Rebekke,
Boond the kydes skyn aboute his nekke,
For which his fadres benyson he wan.   1365
    Lo Judith, as the storie eek telle kan,
By wys conseil she Goddes peple kepte,
And slow hym Olofernus, whil he slepte.
    Lo Abigayl, by good conseil how she
Saved hir housbonde Nabal whan that he   1370
Sholde han be slayn; and looke, Ester also
By good conseil delyvered out of wo
The peple of God, and made hym Mardochee
Of Assuere enhaunced for to be.
    Ther nys no thyng in gree superlatyf,   1375
As seith Senek, above an humble wyf.

1343 **never a deel:** not a bit, not at all
1349 **appreved:** tested, proven
1361 **rede:** advise
1362 **rede:** tell, advise
1363 **Rebekke:** Rebecca, who counselled Jacob to trick his father, Isaac, into blessing him
1365 **benyson:** blessing
1368 **Olofernus:** Holofernes, slain by Judith; for the story see MkT VII.2551–74.
1369 **Abigayl:** Abigail saved Nabal from the wrath of King David (cf. VII.1100).
1371 **Ester:** Esther, who saved her uncle Mordecai (*Mardochee*) and her people by an appeal to her husband Ahasuerus (*Assuere*)
1374 **enhaunced:** exalted, advanced
1375 **in gree superlatyf:** superior (in degree of virtue)
1376 **Senek:** Seneca

1295 **What force:** what does it matter
1296 **housbondrye:** domestic economy
1297 **spare:** be sparing of   **dispence:** expenditures
1302 **knave:** male servant
1306 **cokewold:** cuckold
1308 **ther:** i.e., may (*ther* is not translated; it is used to introduce the subjunctive)
1312 **hardily:** certainly
1313 **commune:** right to use land held in common
1314 **moebles:** personal property
1316 **drede:** doubt
1320 **shent:** ruined
1326 **bely-naked:** stark naked
1332 **paradys terrestre:** earthly paradise
1333 **buxom:** obedient

Suffre thy wyves tonge, as Catoun bit;
She shal comande, and thou shalt suffren it,
And yet she wole obeye of curteisye.
A wyf is kepere of thyn housbondrye;   1380
Wel may the sike man biwaille and wepe,
Ther as ther nys no wyf the hous to kepe.
I warne thee, if wisely thou wolt wirche,
Love wel thy wyf, as Crist loved his chirche.
If thou lovest thyself, thou lovest thy wyf;   1385
No man hateth his flessh, but in his lyf
He fostreth it, and therfore bidde I thee
Cherisse thy wyf, or thou shalt nevere thee.
Housbonde and wyf, what so men jape or pleye,
Of worldly folk holden the siker weye;   1390
They been so knyt ther may noon harm bityde,
And namely upon the wyves syde.
For which this Januarie, of whom I tolde,
Considered hath, inwith his dayes olde,
The lusty lyf, the vertuous quyete,   1395
That is in mariage hony-sweete,
And for his freendes on a day he sente,
To tellen hem th'effect of his entente.

   With face sad his tale he hath hem toold.
He seyde, "Freendes, I am hoor and oold,   1400
And almoost, God woot, on my pittes brynke;
Upon my soule somwhat moste I thynke.
I have my body folily despended;
Blessed be God that it shal been amended!
For I wol be, certeyn, a wedded man,   1405
And that anoon in al the haste I kan.
Unto som mayde fair and tendre of age,
I prey yow, shapeth for my mariage
Al sodeynly, for I wol nat abyde;
And I wol fonde t'espien, on my syde,   1410
To whom I may be wedded hastily.
But forasmuche as ye been mo than I,
Ye shullen rather swich a thyng espyen
Than I, and where me best were to allyen.

   "But o thyng warne I yow, my freendes deere,
I wol noon oold wyf han in no manere.   1416
She shal nat passe twenty yeer, certayn;
Oold fissh and yong flessh wolde I have fayn.
Bet is," quod he, "a pyk than a pykerel,

And bet than old boef is the tendre veel.   1420
I wol no womman thritty yeer of age;
It is but bene-straw and greet forage.
And eek thise olde wydwes, God it woot,
They konne so muchel craft on Wades boot,
So muchel broken harm, whan that hem leste,   1425
That with hem sholde I nevere lyve in reste.
For sondry scoles maken sotile clerkis;
Womman of manye scoles half a clerk is.
But certeynly, a yong thyng may men gye,
Right as men may warm wex with handes plye.   1430
Wherfore I sey yow pleynly, in a clause,
I wol noon oold wyf han right for this cause.
For if so were I hadde swich myschaunce
That I in hire ne koude han no plesaunce,
Thanne sholde I lede my lyf in avoutrye   1435
And go streight to the devel whan I dye.
Ne children sholde I none upon hire geten;
Yet were me levere houndes had me eten
Than that myn heritage sholde falle
In straunge hand, and this I telle yow alle.   1440
I dote nat; I woot the cause why
Men sholde wedde, and forthermoore woot I
Ther speketh many a man of mariage
That woot namoore of it than woot my page
For whiche causes man sholde take a wyf.   1445
If he ne may nat lyven chaast his lyf,
Take hym a wyf with greet devocioun,
By cause of leveful procreacioun
Of children to th'onour of God above,
And nat oonly for paramour or love;   1450
And for they sholde leccherye eschue,
And yelde hir dette whan that it is due;
Or for that ech of hem sholde helpen oother
In meschief, as a suster shal the brother,
And lyve in chastitee ful holily.   1455
But sires, by youre leve, that am nat I.
For—God be thanked!—I dar make avaunt
I feele my lymes stark and suffisaunt
To do al that a man bilongeth to;
I woot myselven best what I may do.   1460

1420 **boef:** beef   **veel:** veal
1422 **bene-straw:** dried beanstalks   **greet forage:** coarse fodder
1424 **Wades boot:** boat of Wade, an obscure legendary figure, perhaps associated with deception
1425 **So muchel broken harm:** do so much harm, make such mischief
1427 **sotile:** subtle, clever
1429 **gye:** guide
1430 **wex:** wax   **plye:** bend, mold
1435 **avoutrye:** adultery
1437 **geten:** beget
1448 **leveful:** lawful
1452 **dette:** the marital debt, obligation to engage in intercourse; see ParsT X.940.
1455 **in chastitee:** under a vow to abstain from sex
1458 **stark:** strong

1377 **Suffre:** endure, forbear   **Catoun:** Cato   **bit** = *biddeth,* commands
1389 **what so:** however much
1390 **worldly:** lay, secular   **siker:** sure, safe
1391 **knyt:** united
1392 **syde:** behalf
1394 **inwith:** in
1398 **th'effect:** the substance
1401 **pittes:** grave's
1403 **folily despended:** foolishly wasted
1410 **fonde t'espien:** try to discover
1414 **allyen:** ally myself, marry
1419 **pykerel:** young pike

Though I be hoor, I fare as dooth a tree
That blosmeth er that fruyt ywoxen bee;
And blosmy tree nys neither drye ne deed.
I feele me nowhere hoor but on myn heed;
Myn herte and alle my lymes been as grene   1465
As laurer thurgh the yeer is for to sene.
And syn that ye han herd al myn entente,
I prey yow to my wyl ye wole assente."
      Diverse men diversely hym tolde
Of mariage manye ensamples olde.   1470
Somme blamed it, somme preysed it, certeyn,
But atte laste, shortly for to seyn,
As al day falleth altercacioun
Bitwixen freendes in disputisoun,
Ther fil a stryf bitwixe his bretheren two,   1475
Of whiche that oon was cleped Placebo;
Justinus soothly called was that oother.
      Placebo seyde, "O Januarie, brother,
Ful litel nede hadde ye, my lord so deere,
Conseil to axe of any that is heere,   1480
But that ye been so ful of sapience
That yow ne liketh, for youre heighe prudence,
To weyven fro the word of Salomon.
This word seyde he unto us everychon:
'Wirk alle thyng by conseil,' thus seyde he,   1485
'And thanne shaltow nat repente thee.'
But though that Salomon spak swich a word,
Myn owene deere brother and my lord,
So wysly God my soule brynge at reste,
I holde youre owene conseil is the beste.   1490
For, brother myn, of me taak this motyf:
I have now been a court-man al my lyf,
And God it woot, though I unworthy be,
I have stonden in ful greet degree
Abouten lordes of ful heigh estaat;   1495
Yet hadde I nevere with noon of hem debaat.
I nevere hem contraried, trewely;
I woot wel that my lord kan moore than I.
What that he seith, I holde it ferme and stable;
I seye the same, or elles thyng semblable.   1500
A ful greet fool is any conseillour
That serveth any lord of heigh honour,
That dar presume, or elles thenken it,
That his conseil sholde passe his lordes wit.
Nay, lordes been no fooles, by my fay!   1505

Ye han youreselven shewed heer to-day
So heigh sentence, so holily and weel,
That I consente and conferme everydeel
Youre wordes alle and youre opinioun.
By God, ther nys no man in al this toun,   1510
Ne in Ytaille, that koude bet han sayd!
Crist halt hym of this conseil ful wel apayd.
And trewely, it is an heigh corage
Of any man that stapen is in age
To take a yong wyf; by my fader kyn,   1515
Youre herte hangeth on a joly pyn!
Dooth now in this matiere right as yow leste,
For finally I holde it for the beste."
      Justinus, that ay stille sat and herde,
Right in this wise he to Placebo answerde: 1520
"Now, brother myn, be pacient, I preye,
Syn ye han seyd, and herkneth what I seye.
Senek, amonges othere wordes wyse,
Seith that a man oghte hym right wel avyse
To whom he yeveth his lond or his catel.   1525
And syn I oghte avyse me right wel
To whom I yeve my good awey fro me,
Wel muchel moore I oghte avysed be
To whom I yeve my body for alwey.
I warne yow wel, it is no childes pley   1530
To take a wyf withouten avysement.
Men moste enquere—this is myn assent—
Wher she be wys, or sobre, or dronkelewe,
Or proud, or elles ootherweys a shrewe,
A chidestere, or wastour of thy good,   1535
Or riche, or poore, or elles mannyssh wood.
Al be it so that no man fynden shal
Noon in this world that trotteth hool in al,
Ne man, ne beest, swich as men koude devyse;
But nathelees it oghte ynough suffise   1540
With any wyf, if so were that she hadde
Mo goode thewes than hire vices badde;
And al this axeth leyser for t'enquere.
For, God it woot, I have wept many a teere
Ful pryvely, syn I have had a wyf.   1545
Preyse whoso wole a wedded mannes lyf,
Certein I fynde in it but cost and care
And observances, of alle blisses bare.

1462 blosmeth: blooms   ywoxen: grown
1463 blosmy: filled with blooms
1466 laurer: laurel, an evergreen   for to sene: to be seen
1476 Placebo: "I shall please" (Psalm 114:9)
1477 Justinus: "the just one"
1483 weyven fro: depart from
1491 motyf: idea, advice
1492 court-man: courtier
1499 I holde it ferme and stable: I view it as unshakably true
1500 semblable: similar

1507 heigh sentence: good judgment
1512 halt hym = holdeth hym, considers himself   ful wel apayd: very well satisfied
1513 an heigh corage: a bold act
1514 stapen is in age: is advanced (literally stepped) in years
1516 hangeth on a joly pyn: is lively, merry
1531 avysement: deliberation
1532 assent: opinion
1533 dronkelewe: addicted to drink, habitually drunk
1535 chidestere: scolding woman   wastour: waster
1536 mannyssh wood: fierce as a man, man-crazy (?); see n.
1538 trotteth hool in al: trots perfectly, is perfect in everything
1542 thewes: personal traits
1548 observances: duties

And yet, God woot, my neighebores aboute,
And namely of wommen many a route,   1550
Seyn that I have the mooste stedefast wyf,
And eek the mekeste oon that bereth lyf;
But I woot best where wryngeth me my sho.
Ye mowe, for me, right as yow liketh do;
Avyseth yow—ye been a man of age—   1555
How that ye entren into mariage,
And namely with a yong wyf and a fair.
By hym that made water, erthe, and air,
The yongeste man that is in al this route
Is bisy ynough to bryngen it aboute   1560
To han his wyf allone. Trusteth me,
Ye shul nat plesen hire fully yeres thre—
This is to seyn, to doon hire ful plesaunce.
A wyf axeth ful many an observaunce.
I prey yow that ye be nat yvele apayd."   1565
    "Wel," quod this Januarie, "and hastow ysayd?
Straw for thy Senek, and for thy proverbes!
I counte nat a panyer ful of herbes
Of scole-termes. Wyser men than thow,
As thou hast herd, assenteden right now   1570
To my purpos. Placebo, what sey ye?"
    "I seye it is a cursed man," quod he,
"That letteth matrimoigne, sikerly."
And with that word they rysen sodeynly,
And been assented fully that he sholde   1575
Be wedded whanne hym liste and where he wolde.

    Heigh fantasye and curious bisynesse
Fro day to day gan in the soule impresse
Of Januarie aboute his mariage.
Many fair shap and many a fair visage   1580
Ther passeth thurgh his herte nyght by nyght,
As whoso tooke a mirour, polisshed bryght,
And sette it in a commune market-place,
Thanne sholde he se ful many a figure pace
By his mirour; and in the same wyse   1585
Gan Januarie inwith his thoght devyse
Of maydens whiche that dwelten hym bisyde.
He wiste nat wher that he myghte abyde.
For if that oon have beaute in hir face,
Another stant so in the peples grace   1590
For hire sadnesse and hire benyngnytee

That of the peple grettest voys hath she;
And somme were riche and hadden badde name.
But nathelees, bitwixe ernest and game,
He atte laste apoynted hym on oon,   1595
And leet alle othere from his herte goon,
And chees hire of his owene auctoritee;
For love is blynd alday, and may nat see.
And whan that he was in his bed ybroght,
He purtreyed in his herte and in his thoght   1600
Hir fresshe beautee and hir age tendre,
Hir myddel smal, hire armes longe and sklendre,
Hir wise governaunce, hir gentillesse,
Hir wommanly berynge, and hire sadnesse.
And whan that he on hire was condescended,   1605
Hym thoughte his choys myghte nat ben amended.
For whan that he hymself concluded hadde,
Hym thoughte ech oother mannes wit so badde
That inpossible it were to repplye
Agayn his choys; this was his fantasye.   1610
His freendes sente he to, at his instaunce,
And preyed hem to doon hym that plesaunce,
That hastily they wolden to hym come;
He wolde abregge hir labour, alle and some.
Nedeth namoore for hym to go ne ryde;   1615
He was apoynted ther he wolde abyde.

    Placebo cam, and eek his freendes soone,
And alderfirst he bad hem alle a boone,
That noon of hem none argumentes make
Agayn the purpos which that he hath take,   1620
Which purpos was plesant to God, seyde he,
And verray ground of his prosperitee.
    He seyde ther was a mayden in the toun,
Which that of beautee hadde greet renoun,
Al were it so she were of smal degree;   1625
Suffiseth hym hir yowthe and hir beautee.
Which mayde, he seyde, he wolde han to his wyf,
To lede in ese and hoolynesse his lyf;
And thanked God that he myghte han hire al,
That no wight his blisse parten shal.   1630

1553 **wryngeth**: pinches
1561 **han his wyf allone**: have his wife to himself
1565 **yvele apayd**: displeased
1568 **panyer**: bread basket
1569 **scole-termes**: scholastic (philosophical) terms
1573 **letteth**: hinders
1577 **Heigh fantasye**: exaggerated fancy, imagination   **curious bisynesse**: painstaking attention, constant thought (of this)
1578 **gan . . . impresse**: made a mark, became fixed
1591 **sadnesse**: seriousness

1592 **voys**: praise
1595 **apoynted hym on**: decided on
1596 **othere**: others
1598 **alday**: always
1602 **sklendre**: slender
1605 **was condescended**: had decided, settled
1611 **instaunce**: request
1614 **abregge**: abridge, shorten
1616 **was apoynted**: had decided
1618 **alderfirst**: first of all   **bad . . . a boone**: asked a favor
1621 **plesant**: pleasing
1625 **Al were it so**: although   **smal degree**: low rank
1630 **parten**: share

And preyed hem to laboure in this nede,
And shapen that he faille nat to spede;
For thanne, he seyde, his spirit was at ese.
"Thanne is," quod he, "no thyng may me displese,
Save o thyng priketh in my conscience,   1635
The which I wol reherce in youre presence.

   "I have," quod he, "herd seyd, ful yoore ago,
Ther may no man han parfite blisses two—
This is to seye, in erthe and eek in hevene.
For though he kepe hym fro the synnes sevene,   1640
And eek from every branche of thilke tree,
Yet is ther so parfit felicitee
And so greet ese and lust in mariage
That evere I am agast now in myn age
That I shal lede now so myrie a lyf,   1645
So delicat, withouten wo and stryf,
That I shal have myn hevene in erthe heere.
For sith that verray hevene is boght so deere
With tribulacion and greet penaunce,
How sholde I thanne, that lyve in swich plesaunce
As alle wedded men doon with hire wyvys,   1651
Come to the blisse ther Crist eterne on lyve ys?
This is my drede, and ye, my bretheren tweye,
Assoilleth me this question, I preye."

   Justinus, which that hated his folye,   1655
Answerde anon right in his japerye;
And for he wolde his longe tale abregge,
He wolde noon auctoritee allegge,
But seyde, "Sire, so ther be noon obstacle
Oother than this, God of his hygh myracle   1660
And of his mercy may so for yow wirche
That, er ye have youre right of hooly chirche,
Ye may repente of wedded mannes lyf,
In which ye seyn ther is no wo ne stryf.
And elles, God forbede but he sente   1665
A wedded man hym grace to repente
Wel ofte rather than a sengle man!
And therfore, sire—the beste reed I kan—
Dispeire yow noght, but have in youre memorie,
Paraunter she may be youre purgatorie!   1670
She may be Goddes meene and Goddes whippe;

Thanne shal youre soule up to hevene skippe
Swifter than dooth an arwe out of a bowe.
I hope to God, herafter shul ye knowe
That ther nys no so greet felicitee   1675
In mariage, ne nevere mo shal bee,
That yow shal lette of youre savacion,
So that ye use, as skile is and reson,
The lustes of youre wyf attemprely,
And that ye plese hire nat to amorously,   1680
And that ye kepe yow eek from oother synne.
My tale is doon, for my wit is thynne.
Beth nat agast herof, my brother deere,
But lat us waden out of this mateere.
The Wyf of Bathe, if ye han understonde,   1685
Of mariage, which we have on honde,
Declared hath ful wel in litel space.
Fareth now wel. God have yow in his grace."

   And with this word this Justyn and his brother
Han take hir leve, and ech of hem of oother.   1690
For whan they saughe that it moste nedes be,
They wroghten so, by sly and wys tretee,
That she, this mayden which that Mayus highte,
As hastily as evere that she myghte
Shal wedded be unto this Januarie.   1695
I trowe it were to longe yow to tarie,
If I yow tolde of every scrit and bond
By which that she was feffed in his lond,
Or for to herknen of hir riche array.
But finally ycomen is the day   1700
That to the chirche bothe be they went
For to receyve the hooly sacrement.
Forth comth the preest, with stole aboute his nekke,
And bad hire be lyk Sarra and Rebekke
In wysdom and in trouthe of mariage;   1705
And seyde his orisons, as is usage,
And croucheth hem, and bad God sholde hem blesse,
And made al siker ynogh with hoolynesse.

   Thus been they wedded with solempnitee,
And at the feeste sitteth he and she   1710
With othere worthy folk upon the deys.

1632 **shapen:** arrange
1641 **thilke tree:** the tree of the seven deadly sins (see ParsT X.387–90).
1646 **delicat:** pleasing
1654 **Assoilleth me this question:** resolve this problem
1656 **japerye:** mockery
1657 **abregge:** abridge, shorten
1658 **allegge:** cite, adduce
1662 **right of hooly chirche:** the last sacraments
1665 **God forbede but he sente:** God forbid that he should not send
1667 **sengle:** single
1671 **meene:** means, instrument

1677 **lette of:** keep from
1678 **skile:** reasonable, proper
1679 **attemprely:** moderately
1684 **waden:** wade, go
1692 **tretee:** negotiation
1697 **scrit:** writ, legal document
1698 **feffed in:** enfeoffed, endowed with
1702 **the hooly sacrement:** i.e., marriage
1704 **Sarra and Rebekke:** Sarah and Rebecca, biblical exemplars of faithfulness and wisdom
1707 **croucheth:** makes the sign of the cross over
1711 **deys:** dais

Al ful of joye and blisse is the paleys,
And ful of instrumentz and of vitaille,
The mooste deyntevous of al Ytaille.
Biforn hem stoode instrumentz of swich soun   1715
That Orpheus, ne of Thebes Amphioun,
Ne maden nevere swich a melodye.
At every cours thanne cam loud mynstralcye
That nevere tromped Joab for to heere,
Nor he Theodomas, yet half so cleere   1720
At Thebes whan the citee was in doute.
Bacus the wyn hem shynketh al aboute,
And Venus laugheth upon every wight,
For Januarie was bicome hir knyght
And wolde bothe assayen his corage   1725
In libertee, and eek in mariage;
And with hire fyrbrond in hire hand aboute
Daunceth biforn the bryde and al the route.
And certeinly, I dar right wel seyn this,
Ymeneus, that god of weddyng is,   1730
Saugh nevere his lyf so myrie a wedded man.
Hoold thou thy pees, thou poete Marcian,
That writest us that ilke weddyng murie
Of hire Philologie and hym Mercurie,
And of the songes that the Muses songe!   1735
To smal is bothe thy penne, and eek thy tonge,
For to descryven of this mariage.
Whan tendre youthe hath wedded stoupyng age,
Ther is swich myrthe that it may nat be writen.
Assayeth it youreself; thanne may ye witen   1740
If that I lye or noon in this matiere.
    Mayus, that sit with so benyngne a chiere,
Hire to biholde it semed fayerye.
Queene Ester looked nevere with swich an ye
On Assuer, so meke a look hath she.   1745
I may yow nat devyse al hir beautee.
But thus muche of hire beautee telle I may,
That she was lyk the brighte morwe of May,
Fulfild of alle beautee and plesaunce.
    This Januarie is ravysshed in a traunce   1750
At every tyme he looked on hir face;

But in his herte he gan hire to manace
That he that nyght in armes wolde hire streyne
Harder than evere Parys dide Eleyne.
But nathelees yet hadde he greet pitee   1755
That thilke nyght offenden hire moste he,
And thoughte, "Allas! O tendre creature,
Now wolde God ye myghte wel endure
Al my corage, it is so sharp and keene!
I am agast ye shul it nat susteene.   1760
But God forbede that I dide al my myght!
Now wolde God that it were woxen nyght,
And that the nyght wolde lasten everemo.
I wolde that al this peple were ago."
And finally he dooth al his labour,   1765
As he best myghte, savynge his honour,
To haste hem fro the mete in subtil wyse.
    The tyme cam that resoun was to ryse;
And after that men daunce and drynken faste,
And spices al aboute the hous they caste,   1770
And ful of joye and blisse is every man—
Al but a squyer, highte Damyan,
Which carf biforn the knyght ful many a day.
He was so ravysshed on his lady May
That for the verray peyne he was ny wood.   1775
Almoost he swelte and swowned ther he stood,
So soore hath Venus hurt hym with hire brond,
As that she bar it daunsynge in hire hond;
And to his bed he wente hym hastily.
Namoore of hym at this tyme speke I,   1780
But there I lete hym wepe ynogh and pleyne
Til fresshe May wol rewen on his peyne.
    O perilous fyr, that in the bedstraw bredeth!
O famulier foo, that his servyce bedeth!
O servant traytour, false hoomly hewe,   1785
Lyk to the naddre in bosom sly untrewe,
God shilde us alle from youre aqueyntaunce!
O Januarie, dronken in plesaunce
In mariage, se how thy Damyan,
Thyn owene squier and thy borne man,   1790
Entendeth for to do thee vileynye.
God graunte thee thyn hoomly fo t'espye!
For in this world nys worse pestilence
Than hoomly foo al day in thy presence.

1714 **deyntevous:** delicious
1716 **Orpheus:** the legendary musician   **Amphioun:** king of Thebes and a famous harper
1719 **tromped:** trumpeted   **Joab:** one of David's generals, who sounded trumpets to direct his army
1720 **Theodomas:** the augur of the army at Thebes
1721 **doute:** danger
1722 **Bacus:** Bacchus, god of wine   **shynketh:** pours out
1723 **Venus:** goddess of love
1727 **fyrbrond:** torch
1730 **Ymeneus:** Hymen
1731 **his lyf:** in his life
1732 **Marcian:** Martianus Capella, author of the *Marriage of Philology and Mercury*
1743 **fayerye:** something enchanting
1744 **Ester:** Esther, whose meekness and beauty won the love of King Ahasuerus (*Assuer*)

1752 **manace:** menace, threaten
1753 **streyne:** press
1754 **Eleyne:** Helen of Troy, whose ravishment by Paris (*Parys*) caused the Trojan War
1759 **corage:** ardor, sexual desire   **keene:** eager
1765 **dooth al his labour:** takes all possible pains
1776 **swelte:** fainted
1777 **brond:** torch
1784 **famulier foo:** enemy in one's own household   **bedeth:** offers
1785 **hoomly hewe:** domestic servant
1786 **naddre:** adder, serpent
1792 **hoomly fo:** foe in the household

Parfourned hath the sonne his ark diurne;   1795
No lenger may the body of hym sojurne
On th'orisonte, as in that latitude.
Night with his mantel, that is derk and rude,
Gan oversprede the hemysperie aboute;
For which departed is this lusty route   1800
Fro Januarie, with thank on every syde.
Hoom to hir houses lustily they ryde,
Where as they doon hir thynges as hem leste,
And whan they sye hir tyme, goon to reste.
Soone after that, this hastif Januarie   1805
Wolde go to bedde; he wolde no lenger tarye.
He drynketh ypocras, clarree, and vernage
Of spices hoote t'encreessen his corage;
And many a letuarie hath he ful fyn,
Swiche as the cursed monk, daun Constantyn,   1810
Hath writen in his book *De Coitu*;
To eten hem alle he nas no thyng eschu.
And to his privee freendes thus seyde he:
"For Goddes love, as soone as it may be,
Lat voyden al this hous in curteys wyse."   1815
And they han doon right as he wol devyse.
Men drynken and the travers drawe anon.
The bryde was broght abedde as stille as stoon;
And whan the bed was with the preest yblessed,
Out of the chambre hath every wight hym dressed,
And Januarie hath faste in armes take   1821
His fresshe May, his paradys, his make.
He lulleth hire; he kisseth hire ful ofte;
With thikke brustles of his berd unsofte,
Lyk to the skyn of houndfyssh, sharp as brere—
For he was shave al newe in his manere—   1826
He rubbeth hire aboute hir tendre face,
And seyde thus, "Allas! I moot trespace
To yow, my spouse, and yow greetly offende
Er tyme come that I wil doun descende.   1830
But nathelees, considereth this," quod he,
"Ther nys no werkman, whatsoevere he be,
That may bothe werke wel and hastily;
This wol be doon at leyser parfitly.

It is no fors how longe that we pleye;   1835
In trewe wedlok coupled be we tweye,
And blessed be the yok that we been inne,
For in oure actes we mowe do no synne.
A man may do no synne with his wyf,
Ne hurte hymselven with his owene knyf,   1840
For we han leve to pleye us by the lawe."
Thus laboureth he til that the day gan dawe;
And thanne he taketh a sop in fyn clarree,
And upright in his bed thanne sitteth he,
And after that he sang ful loude and cleere,   1845
And kiste his wyf, and made wantown cheere.
He was al coltissh, ful of ragerye,
And ful of jargon as a flekked pye.
The slakke skyn aboute his nekke shaketh
Whil that he sang, so chaunteth he and craketh.   1850
But God woot what that May thoughte in hir herte,
Whan she hym saugh up sittynge in his sherte,
In his nyght-cappe, and with his nekke lene;
She preyseth nat his pleyyng worth a bene.
Thanne seide he thus, "My reste wol I take;   1855
Now day is come, I may no lenger wake."
And doun he leyde his heed and sleep til pryme.
And afterward, whan that he saugh his tyme,
Up ryseth Januarie; but fresshe May
Heeld hire chambre unto the fourthe day,   1860
As usage is of wyves for the beste.
For every labour somtyme moot han reste,
Or elles longe may he nat endure;
This is to seyn, no lyves creature,
Be it of fyssh, or bryd, or beest, or man.   1865
    Now wol I speke of woful Damyan,
That langwissheth for love, as ye shul heere;
Therfore I speke to hym in this manere:
I seye, "O sely Damyan, allas!
Andswere to my demaunde, as in this cas.   1870
How shaltow to thy lady, fresshe May,
Telle thy wo? She wole alwey seye nay.
Eek if thou speke, she wol thy wo biwreye.
God be thyn helpe! I kan no bettre seye."
    This sike Damyan in Venus fyr   1875
So brenneth that he dyeth for desyr,
For which he putte his lyf in aventure.

1795 **Parfourned:** completed   **ark diurne:** daily transit from horizon to horizon
1796 **sojurne:** remain
1797 **th'orisonte:** the horizon
1799 **hemysperie:** hemisphere (the half of the heavens above the earth)
1801 **on every syde:** from all sides
1804 **sye:** saw
1807 **ypocras, clarree:** strong spiced and sweetened wines;   **vernage:** sweet Italian white wine, Vernaccia
1809 **letuarie:** electuary, medical mixture
1810 **Constantyn:** Constantinus Africanus (Afer), author of a work on sexual intercourse containing recipes for aphrodisiacs
1812 **eschu:** averse
1815 **Lat voyden:** clear out
1817 **travers:** curtain (dividing the room)
1825 **houndfyssh:** dogfish, a small shark   **brere:** briar

1835 **It is no fors:** it doesn't matter
1843 **sop in fyn clarree:** a bit of bread soaked in wine
1846 **wantown:** lecherous
1847 **coltissh:** frisky as a colt   **ragerye:** wantonness
1848 **jargon:** chatter   **flekked pye:** spotted magpie
1849 **slakke:** slack, loose
1850 **chaunteth:** sings   **craketh:** croaks
1857 **pryme:** the first canonical hour (part) of the day (from about 6 to 9 A.M.)
1870 **demaunde:** question
1873 **biwreye:** reveal
1877 **in aventure:** at risk

No lenger myghte he in this wise endure,
But prively a penner gan he borwe,
And in a lettre wroot he al his sorwe,   1880
In manere of a compleynt or a lay,
Unto his faire, fresshe lady May;
And in a purs of sylk heng on his sherte
He hath it put, and leyde it at his herte.

    The moone, that at noon was thilke day   1885
That Januarie hath wedded fresshe May
In two of Tawr, was into Cancre glyden;
So longe hath Mayus in hir chambre abyden,
As custume is unto thise nobles alle.
A bryde shal nat eten in the halle   1890
Til dayes foure, or thre dayes atte leeste,
Ypassed been; thanne lat hire go to feeste.
The fourthe day compleet fro noon to noon,
Whan that the heighe masse was ydoon,
In halle sit this Januarie and May,   1895
As fressh as is the brighte someres day.
And so bifel how that this goode man
Remembred hym upon this Damyan,
And seyde, "Seynte Marie! how may this be,
That Damyan entendeth nat to me?   1900
Is he ay syk, or how may this bityde?"
His squieres, whiche that stooden ther bisyde,
Excused hym by cause of his siknesse,
Which letted hym to doon his bisynesse;
Noon oother cause myghte make hym tarye.   1905
    "That me forthynketh," quod this Januarie,
"He is a gentil squier, by my trouthe!
If that he deyde, it were harm and routhe.
He is as wys, discreet, and as secree
As any man I woot of his degree,   1910
And therto manly, and eek servysable,
And for to been a thrifty man right able.
But after mete, as soone as evere I may,
I wol myself visite hym, and eek May,
To doon hym al the confort that I kan."   1915
And for that word hym blessed every man,
That of his bountee and his gentillesse
He wolde so conforten in siknesse
His squier, for it was a gentil dede.
"Dame," quod this Januarie, "taak good hede,   1920

At after-mete ye with youre wommen alle,
Whan ye han been in chambre out of this halle,
That alle ye go se this Damyan.
Dooth hym disport—he is a gentil man;
And telleth hym that I wol hym visite,   1925
Have I no thyng but rested me a lite;
And spede yow faste, for I wole abyde
Til that ye slepe faste by my syde."
And with that word he gan to hym to calle
A squier, that was marchal of his halle,   1930
And tolde hym certeyn thynges, what he wolde.
    This fresshe May hath streight hir wey yholde
With alle hir wommen unto Damyan.
Doun by his beddes syde sit she than,
Confortynge hym as goodly as she may.   1935
This Damyan, whan that his tyme he say,
In secree wise his purs and eek his bille,
In which that he ywriten hadde his wille,
Hath put into hire hand, withouten moore,
Save that he siketh wonder depe and soore,   1940
And softely to hire right thus seyde he:
"Mercy! And that ye nat discovere me,
For I am deed if that this thyng be kyd."
This purs hath she inwith hir bosom hyd
And wente hire wey; ye gete namoore of me.   1945
But unto Januarie ycomen is she,
That on his beddes syde sit ful softe.
He taketh hire, and kisseth hire ful ofte,
And leyde hym doun to slepe, and that anon.
She feyned hire as that she moste gon   1950
Ther as ye woot that every wight moot neede;
And whan she of this bille hath taken heede,
She rente it al to cloutes atte laste,
And in the pryvee softely it caste.
    Who studieth now but faire fresshe May?   1955
Adoun by olde Januarie she lay,
That sleep til that the coughe hath hym awaked.
Anon he preyde hire strepen hire al naked;
He wolde of hire, he seyde, han som plesaunce;
He seyde hir clothes dide hym encombraunce,   1960
And she obeyeth, be hire lief or looth.
But lest that precious folk be with me wrooth,
How that he wroghte, I dar nat to yow telle,

1879 **penner:** writing case, with pen and ink
1881 **compleynt:** poetic lament (for examples see the Short Poems)   **lay:** song
1883 **heng:** which hung
1885–87 The moon was in the second degree of the zodiacal sign of Taurus and has now moved into the sign of Cancer.
1893 **compleet:** completed
1900 **entendeth nat to:** does not attend, wait on
1906 **That me forthynketh:** that grieves me, I am sorry
1909 **secree:** discreet
1911 **servysable:** willing to serve, attentive
1912 **thrifty:** proper, successful
1917 **bountee:** goodness

1921 **after-mete:** the time after dinner
1926 **Have I no thyng but:** when I have merely
1930 **marchal:** master of ceremonies (cf. I.751–52)
1936 **say:** saw
1937 **bille:** letter
1943 **kyd:** known
1953 **cloutes:** tatters
1960 **dide hym encombraunce:** got in his way
1962 **precious:** fastidious, prudish

Or wheither hire thoughte it paradys or helle.
But heere I lete hem werken in hir wyse 1965
Til evensong rong and that they moste aryse.
　　Were it by destynee or by aventure,
Were it by influence or by nature,
Or constellacion, that in swich estaat
The hevene stood that tyme fortunaat 1970
Was for to putte a bille of Venus werkes—
For alle thyng hath tyme, as seyn thise clerkes—
To any womman for to gete hire love,
I kan nat seye; but grete God above,
That knoweth that noon act is causelees, 1975
He deme of al, for I wole holde my pees.
But sooth is this, how that this fresshe May
Hath take swich impression that day
Of pitee of this sike Damyan
That from hire herte she ne dryve kan 1980
The remembrance for to doon hym ese.
"Certeyn," thoghte she, "whom that this thyng displese
I rekke noght, for heere I hym assure
To love hym best of any creature,
Though he namoore hadde than his sherte." 1985
Lo, pitee renneth soone in gentil herte!
　　Heere may ye se how excellent franchise
In wommen is, whan they hem narwe avyse.
Som tyrant is, as ther be many oon
That hath an herte as hard as any stoon, 1990
Which wolde han lat hym sterven in the place
Wel rather than han graunted hym hire grace,
And hem rejoysen in hire crueel pryde,
And rekke nat to been an homycide.
　　This gentil May, fulfilled of pitee, 1995
Right of hire hand a lettre made she,
In which she graunteth hym hire verray grace.
Ther lakketh noght oonly but day and place
Wher that she myghte unto his lust suffise,
For it shal be right as he wole devyse. 2000
And whan she saugh hir tyme, upon a day
To visite this Damyan gooth May,
And sotilly this lettre doun she threste
Under his pilwe; rede it if hym leste.
She taketh hym by the hand and harde hym twiste 2005

So secrely that no wight of it wiste,
And bad hym been al hool, and forth she wente
To Januarie, whan that he for hire sente.
　　Up riseth Damyan the nexte morwe;
Al passed was his siknesse and his sorwe. 2010
He kembeth hym, he preyneth hym and pyketh,
He dooth al that his lady lust and lyketh,
And eek to Januarie he gooth as lowe
As evere dide a dogge for the bowe.
He is so plesant unto every man 2015
(For craft is al, whoso that do it kan)
That every wight is fayn to speke hym good,
And fully in his lady grace he stood.
Thus lete I Damyan aboute his nede,
And in my tale forth I wol procede. 2020
　　Somme clerkes holden that felicitee
Stant in delit, and therfore certeyn he,
This noble Januarie, with al his myght,
In honest wyse, as longeth to a knyght,
Shoop hym to lyve ful deliciously. 2025
His housynge, his array, as honestly
To his degree was maked as a kynges.
Amonges othere of his honeste thynges,
He made a gardyn, walled al with stoon;
So fair a gardyn woot I nowher noon. 2030
For, out of doute, I verraily suppose
That he that wroot the Romance of the Rose
Ne koude of it the beautee wel devyse;
Ne Priapus ne myghte nat suffise,
Though he be god of gardyns, for to telle 2035
The beautee of the gardyn and the welle
That stood under a laurer alwey grene.
Ful ofte tyme he Pluto and his queene,
Proserpina, and al hire fayerye,
Disporten hem and maken melodye 2040
Aboute that welle, and daunced, as men tolde.
　　This noble knyght, this Januarie the olde,
Swich deyntee hath in it to walke and pleye,
That he wol no wight suffren bere the keye
Save he hymself; for of the smale wyket 2045
He baar alwey of silver a clyket,
With which, whan that hym leste, he it unshette.

1968 **influence:** power (transmitted by rays from heavenly bodies)
1969 **constellacion:** configuration of the heavenly bodies
1971 **putte a bille:** present a petition
1976 **He deme:** may he judge
1987 **franchise:** generosity of spirit
1988 **hem narwe avyse:** consider carefully
1999 **unto his lust suffise:** satisfy his desires
2003 **sotilly:** craftily　**threste:** thrust
2004 **pilwe:** pillow

2011 **kembeth:** combs　**preyneth hym:** preens himself, makes himself neat
pyketh: cleans, adorns
2013 **lowe:** humbly
2014 **dogge for the bowe:** dog trained to hunt with an archer
2024 **honest:** honorable, respectable
2025 **deliciously:** voluptuously
2032 **he:** Guillaume de Lorris (cf. Rom 49–728)
2034 **Priapus:** a phallic god (cf. PF 253–59)
2038–39 **Pluto, Proserpina:** king and queen of the underworld
2043 **deyntee hath:** takes pleasure
2045 **wyket:** wicket gate
2046 **clyket:** latchkey
2047 **unshette:** unlocked

And whan he wolde paye his wyf hir dette
In somer seson, thider wolde he go,
And May his wyf, and no wight but they two;   2050
And thynges whiche that were nat doon abedde,
He in the gardyn parfourned hem and spedde.
And in this wyse, many a murye day,
Lyved this Januarie and fresshe May.
But worldly joye may nat alwey dure   2055
To Januarie, ne to no creature.
    O sodeyn hap! O thou Fortune unstable!
Lyk to the scorpion so deceyvable,
That flaterest with thyn heed whan thou wolt stynge;
Thy tayl is deeth, thurgh thyn envenymynge.   2060
O brotil joye! O sweete venym queynte!
O monstre, that so subtilly kanst peynte
Thy yiftes under hewe of stidefastnesse,
That thou deceyvest bothe moore and lesse!
Why hastow Januarie thus deceyved,   2065
That haddest hym for thy fulle freend receyved?
And now thou hast biraft hym bothe his yen,
For sorwe of which desireth he to dyen.
    Allas, this noble Januarie free,
Amydde his lust and his prosperitee,   2070
Is woxen blynd, and that al sodeynly.
He wepeth and he wayleth pitously;
And therwithal the fyr of jalousie,
Lest that his wyf sholde falle in som folye,
So brente his herte that he wolde fayn   2075
That som man bothe hire and hym had slayn.
For neither after his deeth nor in his lyf
Ne wolde he that she were love ne wyf,
But evere lyve as wydwe in clothes blake,
Soul as the turtle that lost hath hire make.   2080
But atte laste, after a month or tweye,
His sorwe gan aswage, sooth to seye;
For whan he wiste it may noon oother be,
He paciently took his adversitee,
Save, out of doute, he may nat forgoon   2085
That he nas jalous everemoore in oon;
Which jalousye it was so outrageous
That neither in halle, n'yn noon oother hous,
Ne in noon oother place, neverthemo,
He nolde suffre hire for to ryde or go,   2090

But if that he had hond on hire alway;
For which ful ofte wepeth fresshe May,
That loveth Damyan so benyngnely
That she moot outher dyen sodeynly
Or elles she moot han hym as hir leste.   2095
She wayteth whan hir herte wolde breste.
    Upon that oother syde Damyan
Bicomen is the sorwefulleste man
That evere was, for neither nyght ne day
Ne myghte he speke a word to fresshe May,   2100
As to his purpos, of no swich mateere,
But if that Januarie moste it heere,
That hadde an hand upon hire everemo.
But nathelees, by writyng to and fro
And privee signes wiste he what she mente,   2105
And she knew eek the fyn of his entente.
    O Januarie, what myghte it thee availle,
Thogh thou myghtest se as fer as shippes saille?
For as good is blynd deceyved be
As to be deceyved whan a man may se.   2110
    Lo, Argus, which that hadde an hondred yen,
For al that evere he koude poure or pryen,
Yet was he blent, and, God woot, so been mo
That wenen wisly that it be nat so.
Passe over is an ese, I sey namoore.   2115
    This fresshe May, that I spak of so yoore,
In warm wex hath emprented the clyket
That Januarie bar of the smale wyket,
By which into his gardyn ofte he wente;
And Damyan, that knew al hire entente,   2120
The cliket countrefeted pryvely.
Ther nys namoore to seye, but hastily
Som wonder by this clyket shal bityde,
Which ye shul heeren, if ye wole abyde.
    O noble Ovyde, ful sooth seystou, God woot,
What sleighte is it, thogh it be long and hoot, 2126
That Love nyl fynde it out in som manere?
By Piramus and Tesbee may men leere;
Thogh they were kept ful longe streite overal,
They been accorded, rownynge thurgh a wal,   2130
Ther no wight koude han founde out swich a sleighte.

2048 **dette:** marital debt (obligation to engage in intercourse)
2057 **hap:** chance
2058 **deceyvable:** deceitful
2061 **brotil:** uncertain
2062 **peynte:** disguise
2063 **hewe:** pretense
2080 **Soul:** solitary   **turtle:** turtledove
2085 **Save:** except that
2085–86 **forgoon That he nas:** i.e., refrain from being
2087 **outrageous:** excessive
2089 **neverthemo:** no longer

2096 **wayteth:** expects (the time)
2111 **Argus:** mythical guardian of Io
2112 **poure:** look intently, pore   **pryen:** gaze, see
2113 **blent:** blinded, deceived
2114 **wenen wisly:** confidently suppose, believe
2115 **Passe over is an ese:** to overlook is an advantage (what you don't know won't hurt you)
2117 **emprented the clyket:** made an impression of the key
2118 **wyket:** wicket gate
2125 **Ovyde:** Ovid
2126 **sleighte:** trick
2128 **Piramus and Tesbee:** Pyramus and Thisbe; see LGW 706–923.
2129 **streite:** strictly
2130 **rownynge:** whispering

But now to purpos: er that dayes eighte
Were passed [of] the month of [Juyn], bifil
That Januarie hath caught so greet a wil,
Thurgh eggyng of his wyf, hym for to pleye   2135
In his gardyn, and no wight but they tweye,
That in a morwe unto his May seith he:
"Rys up, my wyf, my love, my lady free!
The turtles voys is herd, my dowve sweete;
The wynter is goon with alle his reynes weete. 2140
Com forth now, with thyne eyen columbyn!
How fairer been thy brestes than is wyn!
The gardyn is enclosed al aboute;
Com forth, my white spouse! Out of doute
Thou hast me wounded in myn herte, O wyf!   2145
No spot of thee ne knew I al my lyf.
Com forth, and lat us taken oure disport;
I chees thee for my wyf and my confort."
    Swiche olde lewed wordes used he.
On Damyan a signe made she,   2150
That he sholde go biforn with his cliket.
This Damyan thanne hath opened the wyket,
And in he stirte, and that in swich manere
That no wight myghte it se neither yheere,
And stille he sit under a bussh anon.   2155
    This Januarie, as blynd as is a stoon,
With Mayus in his hand, and no wight mo,
Into his fresshe gardyn is ago,
And clapte to the wyket sodeynly.
    "Now wyf," quod he, "heere nys but thou and I,
That art the creature that I best love.   2161
For by that Lord that sit in hevene above,
Levere ich hadde to dyen on a knyf
Than thee offende, trewe deere wyf!
For Goddes sake, thenk how I thee chees,   2165
Noght for no coveitise, doutelees,
But oonly for the love I had to thee.
And though that I be oold and may nat see,
Beth to me trewe, and I wol telle yow why.
Thre thynges, certes, shal ye wynne therby: 2170
First, love of Crist, and to youreself honour,
And al myn heritage, toun and tour;
I yeve it yow, maketh chartres as yow leste;
This shal be doon to-morwe er sonne reste,
So wisly God my soule brynge in blisse.   2175
I prey yow first, in covenant ye me kisse;

And though that I be jalous, wyte me noght.
Ye been so depe enprented in my thoght
That, whan that I considere youre beautee
And therwithal the unlikly elde of me,   2180
I may nat, certes, though I sholde dye,
Forbere to been out of youre compaignye
For verray love; this is withouten doute.
Now kys me, wyf, and lat us rome aboute."
    This fresshe May, whan she thise wordes herde,
Benyngnely to Januarie answerde,   2186
But first and forward she bigan to wepe.
"I have," quod she, "a soule for to kepe
As wel as ye, and also myn honour,
And of my wyfhod thilke tendre flour,   2190
Which that I have assured in youre hond,
Whan that the preest to yow my body bond;
Wherfore I wole answere in this manere,
By the leve of yow, my lord so deere:
I prey to God that nevere dawe the day   2195
That I ne sterve, as foule as womman may,
If evere I do unto my kyn that shame,
Or elles I empeyre so my name,
That I be fals; and if I do that lak,
Do strepe me and put me in a sak,   2200
And in the nexte ryver do me drenche.
I am a gentil womman and no wenche.
Why speke ye thus? But men been evere untrewe,
And wommen have repreve of yow ay newe.
Ye han noon oother contenance, I leeve,   2205
But speke to us of untrust and repreeve."
    And with that word she saugh wher Damyan
Sat in the bussh, and coughen she bigan,
And with hir fynger signes made she
That Damyan sholde clymbe upon a tree   2210
That charged was with fruyt, and up he wente.
For verraily he knew al hire entente,
And every signe that she koude make,
Wel bet than Januarie, hir owene make,
For in a lettre she hadde toold hym al   2215
Of this matere, how he werchen shal.
And thus I lete hym sitte upon the pyrie,
And Januarie and May romynge myrie.
    Bright was the day, and blew the firmament;
Phebus hath of gold his stremes doun ysent   2220

2132–33 On or shortly before June 8
2135 **eggyng:** incitement
2141 **columbyn:** dovelike
2150 **On:** to
2166 **coveitise:** greed
2173 **chartres:** contracts, deeds
2176 **in covenant:** to seal the contract

2177 **wyte:** blame
2180 **unlikly:** unsuitable
2187 **first and forward:** first of all
2191 **assured:** entrusted
2198 **empeyre:** damage
2199 **do that lak:** commit that offence
2201 **do me drenche:** have me drowned
2204 **ay newe:** always
2205 **contenance:** manner of behavior
2206 **But:** except   **untrust:** distrust   **repreeve:** reproof
2217 **pyrie:** pear tree

To gladen every flour with his warmnesse.   2221
He was that tyme in Geminis, as I gesse,
But litel fro his declynacion
Of Cancer, Jovis exaltacion.
And so bifel, that brighte morwe-tyde   2225
That in that gardyn, in the ferther syde,
Pluto, that is kyng of Fayerye,
And many a lady in his compaignye,
Folwynge his wyf, the queene Proserpyna,
Which that he ravysshed out of [Ethna]   2230
Whil that she gadered floures in the mede—
In Claudyan ye may the stories rede,
How in his grisely carte he hire fette—
This kyng of Fairye thanne adoun hym sette
Upon a bench of turves, fressh and grene,   2235
And right anon thus seyde he to his queene:
    "My wyf," quod he, "ther may no wight seye nay;
Th'experience so preveth every day
The tresons whiche that wommen doon to man.
Ten hondred thousand [tales] tellen I kan   2240
Notable of youre untrouthe and brotilnesse.
O Salomon, wys, and richest of richesse,
Fulfild of sapience and of worldly glorie,
Ful worthy been thy wordes to memorie
To every wight that wit and reson kan.   2245
Thus preiseth he yet the bountee of man:
'Amonges a thousand men yet foond I oon,
But of wommen alle foond I noon.'
    "Thus seith the kyng that knoweth youre
        wikkednesse.
And Jhesus, filius Syrak, as I gesse,   2250
Ne speketh of yow but seelde reverence.
A wylde fyr and corrupt pestilence
So falle upon youre bodyes yet to-nyght!
Ne se ye nat this honurable knyght,
By cause, allas, that he is blynd and old,   2255
His owene man shal make hym cokewold.
Lo, where he sit, the lecchour, in the tree!
Now wol I graunten, of my magestee,
Unto this olde, blynde, worthy knyght
That he shal have ayen his eyen syght,   2260
Whan that his wyf wold doon hym vileynye.

Thanne shal he knowen al hire harlotrye,
Bothe in repreve of hire and othere mo."
    "Ye shal?" quod Proserpyne, "wol ye so?
Now by my moodres sires soule I swere   2265
That I shal yeven hire suffisant answere,
And alle wommen after, for hir sake,
That, though they be in any gilt ytake,
With face boold they shulle hemself excuse,
And bere hem doun that wolden hem accuse.   2270
For lak of answere noon of hem shal dyen.
Al hadde man seyn a thyng with bothe his yen,
Yit shul we wommen visage it hardily,
And wepe, and swere, and chyde subtilly,
So that ye men shul been as lewed as gees.   2275
    "What rekketh me of youre auctoritees?
I woot wel that this Jew, this Salomon,
Foond of us wommen fooles many oon.
But though that he ne foond no good womman,
Yet hath ther founde many another man   2280
Wommen ful trewe, ful goode, and vertuous.
Witnesse on hem that dwelle in Cristes hous;
With martirdom they preved hire constance.
The Romayn geestes eek make remembrance
Of many a verray, trewe wyf also.   2285
But, sire, ne be nat wrooth, al be it so,
Though that he seyde he foond no good womman,
I prey yow take the sentence of the man;
He mente thus, that in sovereyn bontee
Nis noon but God, but neither he ne she.   2290
    "Ey! for verray God that nys but oon,
What make ye so muche of Salomon?
What though he made a temple, Goddes hous?
What though he were riche and glorious?
So made he eek a temple of false goddis.   2295
How myghte he do a thyng that moore forbode is?
Pardee, as faire as ye his name emplastre,
He was a lecchour and an ydolastre,
And in his elde he verray God forsook;
And if God ne hadde, as seith the book,   2300
Yspared him for his fadres sake, he sholde
Have lost his regne rather than he wolde.
I sette right noght, of al the vileynye
That ye of wommen write, a boterflye!

2222–24 The sun was in the sign of Gemini (Geminis), not far from the summer solstice, after which the sun begins to decline in its apparent altitude (his declynacion);
this is at the beginning of Cancer, the sign in which Jupiter exerts its greatest influence a1(Jovis exaltacion).
2230 Ethna: Mt. Etna
2232 Claudyan: Claudian, author of the Rape of Proserpina
2235 turves: pieces of turf
2241 brotilnesse: frailty, fickleness
2242 Salomon: Solomon
2250 Jhesus, filius Syrak: author of Ecclesiasticus
2251 seelde: seldom
2252 wylde fyr: erysipelas, an acute inflammation of the skin   corrupt: infectious

2262 harlotrye: wickedness
2265 my moodres sires soule: the soul of Saturn, father of Ceres
2273 visage it hardily: face it out boldly
2284 Romayn geestes: Roman history   make remembrance: remind
2289 sovereyn bontee: perfect goodness
2290 he ne she: man nor woman
2297 emplastre: apply a medicinal plaster (i.e., gloss over)
2298 ydolastre: idolater
2302 rather: sooner

I am a womman, nedes moot I speke,   2305
Or elles swelle til myn herte breke.
For sithen he seyde that we been jangleresses,
As evere hool I moote brouke my tresses,
I shal nat spare, for no curteisye,
To speke hym harm that wolde us vileynye."   2310
    "Dame," quod this Pluto, "be no lenger wrooth;
I yeve it up! But sith I swoor myn ooth
That I wolde graunten hym his sighte ageyn,
My word shal stonde, I warne yow certeyn.
I am a kyng; it sit me noght to lye."   2315
    "And I," quod she, "a queene of Fayerye!
Hir answere shal she have, I undertake.
Lat us namoore wordes heerof make;
For sothe, I wol no lenger yow contrarie."
    Now lat us turne agayn to Januarie,   2320
That in the gardyn with his faire May
Syngeth ful murier than the papejay,
"Yow love I best, and shal, and oother noon."
So longe aboute the aleyes is he goon,
Til he was come agaynes thilke pyrie   2325
Where as this Damyan sitteth ful myrie
An heigh among the fresshe leves grene.
    This fresshe May, that is so bright and sheene,
Gan for to syke, and seyde, "Allas, my syde!
Now sire," quod she, "for aught that may bityde,
I moste han of the peres that I see,   2331
Or I moot dye, so soore longeth me
To eten of the smale peres grene.
Help, for hir love that is of hevene queene!
I telle yow wel, a womman in my plit   2335
May han to fruyt so greet an appetit
That she may dyen but she of it have."
    "Allas," quod he, "that I ne had heer a knave
That koude clymbe! Allas, allas," quod he,
"For I am blynd!" "Ye, sire, no fors," quod she;   2340
"But wolde ye vouche sauf, for Goddes sake,
The pyrie inwith youre armes for to take,
For wel I woot that ye mystruste me,
Thanne sholde I clymbe wel ynogh," quod she,
"So I my foot myghte sette upon youre bak."   2345

"Certes," quod he, "theron shal be no lak,
Mighte I yow helpen with myn herte blood."
He stoupeth doun, and on his bak she stood,
And caughte hire by a twiste, and up she gooth—
Ladyes, I prey yow that ye be nat wrooth;   2350
I kan nat glose, I am a rude man—
And sodeynly anon this Damyan
Gan pullen up the smok, and in he throng.
    And whan that Pluto saugh this grete wrong,
To Januarie he gaf agayn his sighte,   2355
And made hym se as wel as evere he myghte.
And whan that he hadde caught his sighte agayn,
Ne was ther nevere man of thyng so fayn,
But on his wyf his thoght was everemo.
Up to the tree he caste his eyen two,   2360
And saugh that Damyan his wyf had dressed
In swich manere it may nat been expressed,
But if I wolde speke uncurteisly;
And up he yaf a roryng and a cry,
As dooth the mooder whan the child shal dye: 2365
"Out! Help! Allas! Harrow!" he gan to crye,
"O stronge lady stoore, what dostow?"
    And she answerde, "Sire, what eyleth yow?
Have pacience and resoun in youre mynde.
I have yow holpe on bothe youre eyen blynde.   2370
Up peril of my soule, I shal nat lyen,
As me was taught, to heele with youre eyen,
Was no thyng bet, to make yow to see,
Than strugle with a man upon a tree.
God woot, I dide it in ful good entente."   2375
    "Strugle?" quod he, "Ye, algate in it wente!
God yeve yow bothe on shames deth to dyen!
He swyved thee; I saugh it with myne yen,
And elles be I hanged by the hals!"
    "Thanne is," quod she, "my medicyne fals;   2380
For certeinly, if that ye myghte se,
Ye wolde nat seyn thise wordes unto me.
Ye han som glymsyng, and no parfit sighte."
    "I se," quod he, "as wel as evere I myghte,
Thonked be God! With bothe myne eyen two,   2385
And by my trouthe, me thoughte he dide thee so."
    "Ye maze, maze, goode sire," quod she;
"This thank have I for I have maad yow see.

2307 **jangleresses:** chattering women
2308 **brouke my tresses:** remain alive (literally, *enjoy my hair*)
2315 **sit** = *sitteth,* suits, befits
2319 **contrarie:** contradict
2322 **papejay:** parrot
2324 **aleyes:** alleys, garden paths
2325 **agaynes:** in front of **pyrie:** pear tree
2331 **of the peres:** some of the pears
2335 **plit:** condition

2349 **twiste:** branch
2351 **glose:** use circumlocutions
2353 **throng:** thrust
2361 **dressed:** treated
2363 **uncurteisly:** crudely
2366 **Harrow!:** help!
2367 **stronge lady stoore:** bold, crude woman
2370 **holpe:** helped
2378 **swyved:** copulated with
2379 **hals:** neck
2383 **glymsyng:** glimpse
2387 **maze:** are bewildered, dazed

Allas," quod she, "that evere I was so kynde!"
  "Now, dame," quod he, "lat al passe out of mynde.
Com doun, my lief, and if I have myssayd,   2391
God helpe me so, as I am yvele apayd.
But, by my fader soule, I wende han seyn
How that this Damyan hadde by thee leyn,
And that thy smok hadde leyn upon his brest." 2395
  "Ye, sire," quod she, "ye may wene as yow lest.
But, sire, a man that waketh out of his sleep,
He may nat sodeynly wel taken keep
Upon a thyng, ne seen it parfitly,
Til that he be adawed verraily.   2400
Right so a man that longe hath blynd ybe,
Ne may nat sodeynly so wel yse,
First whan his sighte is newe come ageyn,

As he that hath a day or two yseyn.
Til that youre sighte ysatled be a while   2405
Ther may ful many a sighte yow bigile.
Beth war, I prey yow, for by hevene kyng,
Ful many a man weneth to seen a thyng,
And it is al another than it semeth.
He that mysconceyveth, he mysdemeth."   2410
And with that word she leep doun fro the tree.
  This Januarie, who is glad but he?
He kisseth hire and clippeth hire ful ofte,
And on hire wombe he stroketh hire ful softe,
And to his palays hoom he hath hire lad.   2415
Now, goode men, I pray yow to be glad.
Thus endeth heere my tale of Januarie;
God blesse us, and his mooder Seinte Marie!

Heere is ended the Marchantes Tale of Januarie.

Epilogue to the Merchant's Tale

  "Ey! Goddes mercy!" seyde oure Hooste tho,
"Now swich a wyf I pray God kepe me fro!   2420
Lo, whiche sleightes and subtilitees
In wommen been! For ay as bisy as bees
Been they, us sely men for to deceyve,
And from the soothe evere wol they weyve;
By this Marchauntes tale it preveth weel.   2425
But doutelees, as trewe as any steel
I have a wyf, though that she povre be,
But of hir tonge, a labbyng shrewe is she,
And yet she hath an heep of vices mo;

Therof no fors! Lat alle swiche thynges go.   2430
But wyte ye what? In conseil be it seyd,
Me reweth soore I am unto hire teyd.
For and I sholde rekenen every vice
Which that she hath, ywis I were to nyce.
And cause why? It sholde reported be   2435
And toold to hire of somme of this meynee—
Of whom, it nedeth nat for to declare,
Syn wommen konnen outen swich chaffare;
And eek my wit suffiseth nat therto
To tellen al; wherfore my tale is do."   2440

2405 **ysatled:** settled
2409 **al another:** completely otherwise
2410 **mysconceyveth:** misapprehends, misunderstands   **mysdemeth:** misjudges
2413 **clippeth:** embraces

2431 **In conseil:** confidentially
2432 **Me reweth:** I repent   **teyd:** tied
2433 **and:** if
2436 **meynee:** company
2438 **outen:** display   **chaffare:** wares

2393 **wende han seyn:** thought to have seen, thought I saw
2400 **adawed verraily:** fully awakened
2402 **yse:** see

2424 **weyve:** deviate
2428 **labbyng:** blabbing

Introduction to the Squire's Tale

Squier, com neer, if it youre wille be,
And sey somwhat of love, for certes ye
Konnen theron as muche as any man."
  "Nay, sire," quod he, "but I wol seye as I kan

With hertly wyl, for I wol nat rebelle 5
Agayn youre lust; a tale wol I telle.
Have me excused if I speke amys;
My wyl is good, and lo, my tale is this."

The Squire's Tale

Here bigynneth the Squieres Tale.

At Sarray, in the land of Tartarye,
Ther dwelte a kyng that werreyed Russye, 10
Thurgh which ther dyde many a doughty man.
This noble kyng was cleped Cambyuskan,
Which in his tyme was of so greet renoun
That ther was nowher in no regioun
So excellent a lord in alle thyng: 15
Hym lakked noght that longeth to a kyng.
As of the secte of which that he was born
He kepte his lay, to which that he was sworn;
And therto he was hardy, wys, and riche,
And pitous and just, alwey yliche; 20
Sooth of his word, benigne, and honurable;
Of his corage as any centre stable;
Yong, fressh, and strong, in armes desirous
As any bacheler of al his hous.
A fair persone he was and fortunat, 25
And kept alwey so wel roial estat
That ther was nowher swich another man.
  This noble kyng, this Tartre Cambyuskan,
Hadde two sones on Elpheta his wyf,
Of whiche the eldeste highte Algarsyf; 30
That oother sone was cleped Cambalo.
A doghter hadde this worthy kyng also,
That yongest was, and highte Canacee.
But for to telle yow al hir beautee,

It lyth nat in my tonge, n'yn my konnyng; 35
I dar nat undertake so heigh a thyng.
Myn Englissh eek is insufficient.
It moste been a rethor excellent
That koude his colours longynge for that art,
If he sholde hire discryven every part. 40
I am noon swich, I moot speke as I kan.
  And so bifel that whan this Cambyuskan
Hath twenty wynter born his diademe,
As he was wont fro yeer to yeer, I deme,
He leet the feeste of his nativitee 45
Doon cryen thurghout Sarray his citee,
The laste Idus of March, after the yeer.
Phebus the sonne ful joly was and cleer,
For he was neigh his exaltacioun
In Martes face and in his mansioun 50
In Aries, the colerik hoote signe.
Ful lusty was the weder and benigne,
For which the foweles, agayn the sonne sheene,
What for the sesoun and the yonge grene,
Ful loude songen hire affecciouns. 55
Hem semed han geten hem protecciouns
Agayn the swerd of wynter, keene and coold.

38 **rethor:** rhetorician, master of eloquence
39 **colours longynge for:** rhetorical devices belonging to
45–46 **leet . . . Doon cryen:** had proclaimed
47 Exactly 15 March, in the ordinary course of the year
48–51 The sun is near the position where it has its strongest influence (*his exaltacioun*), in the first ten degrees of Aries (*Martes face*); Aries is a hot and dry sign, like the *colerik* humor.
53 **agayn:** facing toward, in response to
54 **What for:** what with

9 **Sarray:** Tsarev **Tartarye:** the Mongol Empire
10 **werreyed:** waged war on
12 **Cambyuskan:** Genghis (Chengiz) Khan
17 **As of the secte:** in accord with the religion
18 **lay:** religious laws
24 **bacheler:** young knight

This Cambyuskan, of which I have yow toold,
In roial vestiment sit on his deys,
With diademe, ful heighe in his paleys,   60
And halt his feeste so solempne and so ryche
That in this world ne was ther noon it lyche;
Of which if I shal tellen al th'array,
Thanne wolde it occupie a someres day,
And eek it nedeth nat for to devyse   65
At every cours the ordre of hire servyse.
I wol nat tellen of hir strange sewes,
Ne of hir swannes, ne of hire heronsewes.
Eek in that lond, as tellen knyghtes olde,
Ther is som mete that is ful deynte holde   70
That in this lond men recche of it but smal;
Ther nys no man that may reporten al.
I wol nat taryen yow, for it is pryme
And for it is no fruyt but los of tyme;
Unto my firste I wole have my recours.   75

    And so bifel that after the thridde cours,
Whil that this kyng sit thus in his nobleye,
Herknynge his mynstralles hir thynges pleye
Biforn hym at the bord deliciously,
In at the halle dore al sodeynly   80
Ther cam a knyght upon a steede of bras,
And in his hand a brood mirour of glas.
Upon his thombe he hadde of gold a ryng,
And by his syde a naked swerd hangyng;
And up he rideth to the heighe bord.   85
In al the halle ne was ther spoken a word
For merveille of this knyght; hym to biholde
Ful bisily they wayten, yonge and olde.

    This strange knyght, that cam thus sodeynly,
Al armed, save his heed, ful richely,   90
Saleweth kyng and queene and lordes alle,
By ordre, as they seten in the halle,
With so heigh reverence and obeisaunce,
As wel in speche as in contenaunce,
That Gawayn, with his olde curteisye,   95
Though he were comen ayeyn out of Fairye,
Ne koude hym nat amende with a word.
And after this, biforn the heighe bord,
He with a manly voys seide his message,
After the forme used in his langage,   100
Withouten vice of silable or of lettre;
And for his tale sholde seme the bettre,

Accordant to his wordes was his cheere,
As techeth art of speche hem that it leere.
Al be that I kan nat sowne his stile,   105
Ne kan nat clymben over so heigh a style,
Yet seye I this, as to commune entente:
Thus muche amounteth al that evere he mente,
If it so be that I have it in mynde.

    He seyde, "The kyng of Arabe and of Inde,   110
My lige lord, on this solempne day
Saleweth yow, as he best kan and may,
And sendeth yow, in honour of youre feeste,
By me, that am al redy at youre heeste,
This steede of bras, that esily and weel   115
Kan in the space of o day natureel—
This is to seyn, in foure and twenty houres—
Wher-so yow lyst, in droghte or elles shoures,
Beren youre body into every place
To which youre herte wilneth for to pace,   120
Withouten wem of yow, thurgh foul or fair;
Or, if yow lyst to fleen as hye in the air
As dooth an egle whan hym list to soore,
This same steede shal bere yow evere moore,
Withouten harm, til ye be ther yow leste,   125
Though that ye slepen on his bak or reste,
And turne ayeyn with writhyng of a pyn.
He that it wroghte koude ful many a gyn.
He wayted many a constellacion
Er he had doon this operacion,   130
And knew ful many a seel and many a bond.
    "This mirour eek, that I have in myn hond,
Hath swich a myght that men may in it see
Whan ther shal fallen any adversitee
Unto youre regne or to youreself also,   135
And openly who is youre freend or foo.
    "And over al this, if any lady bright
Hath set hire herte on any maner wight,
If he be fals, she shal his tresoun see,
His newe love, and al his subtiltee,   140
So openly that ther shal no thyng hyde.
Wherfore, ageyn this lusty someres tyde,
This mirour and this ryng, that ye may see,
He hath sent to my lady Canacee,
Youre excellente doghter that is heere.   145

67 **sewes:** stews, broths
68 **heronsewes:** young herons
73 **pryme:** the first hour of the day, from about 6 to 9 A.M.
74 **no fruyt:** not an essential part of the tale
75 **have my recours:** return
77 **nobleye:** noble state
79 **deliciously:** delightfully
85 **heighe bord:** high table
91 **Saleweth:** greets
92 **By ordre:** sequentially   **seten:** sat

105 **sowne:** repeat, imitate
110 **of Arabe and of Inde:** of Arabia and India
112 **kan and may:** knows how and can
116 **day natureel:** twenty-four hours; see Astr 2.7.
121 **wem:** harm
123 **soore:** soar
127 **writhyng:** turning
128 **gyn:** ingenious contrivance
129 **constellacion:** configuration of the heavenly bodies
131 **seel:** seal   **bond:** controlling force (see n.)
142 **ageyn:** in anticipation of

"The vertu of the ryng, if ye wol heere,
Is this: that if hire lust it for to were
Upon hir thombe or in hir purs it bere,
Ther is no fowel that fleeth under the hevene
That she ne shal wel understonde his stevene,   150
And knowe his menyng openly and pleyn,
And answere hym in his langage ageyn;
And every gras that groweth upon roote
She shal eek knowe, and whom it wol do boote,
Al be his woundes never so depe and wyde.   155
   "This naked swerd, that hangeth by my syde,
Swich vertu hath that what man so ye smyte
Thurghout his armure it wole kerve and byte,
Were it as thikke as is a branched ook;
And what man that is wounded with the strook   160
Shal never be hool til that yow list, of grace,
To stroke hym with the plat in thilke place
Ther he is hurt; this is as muche to seyn,
Ye moote with the platte swerd ageyn
Stroke hym in the wounde, and it wol close.   165
This is a verray sooth, withouten glose;
It failleth nat whils it is in youre hoold."
   And whan this knyght hath thus his tale toold,
He rideth out of halle and doun he lighte.
His steede, which that shoon as sonne brighte,   170
Stant in the court, stille as any stoon.
This knyght is to his chambre lad anoon,
And is unarmed, and to mete yset.
   The presentes been ful roially yfet—
This is to seyn, the swerd and the mirour—   175
And born anon into the heighe tour
With certeine officers ordeyned therfore;
And unto Canacee this ryng is bore
Solempnely, ther she sit at the table.
But sikerly, withouten any fable,   180
The hors of bras, that may nat be remewed,
It stant as it were to the ground yglewed.
Ther may no man out of the place it dryve
For noon engyn of wyndas or polyve;
And cause why? For they kan nat the craft.   185
And therfore in the place they han it laft
Til that the knyght hath taught hem the manere
To voyden hym, as ye shal after heere.

Greet was the prees that swarmeth to and fro
To gauren on this hors that stondeth so,   190
For it so heigh was, and so brood and long,
So wel proporcioned for to been strong,
Right as it were a steede of Lumbardye;
Therwith so horsly, and so quyk of ye,
As it a gentil Poilleys courser were.   195
For certes, fro his tayl unto his ere
Nature ne art ne koude hym nat amende
In no degree, as al the people wende.
But everemoore hir mooste wonder was
How that it koude gon, and was of bras;   200
It was a fairye, as the peple semed.
Diverse folk diversely they demed;
As many heddes, as manye wittes ther been.
They murmureden as dooth a swarm of been,
And maden skiles after hir fantasies,   205
Rehersynge of thise olde poetries,
And seyden it was lyk the Pegasee,
The hors that hadde wynges for to flee;
Or elles it was the Grekes hors Synon,
That broghte Troie to destruccion,   210
As men in thise olde geestes rede.
"Myn herte," quod oon, "is everemoore in drede;
I trowe som men of armes been therinne,
That shapen hem this citee for to wynne.
It were right good that al swich thyng were knowe."   215
Another rowned to his felawe lowe,   216
And seyde, "He lyeth, for it is rather lyk
An apparence ymaad by som magyk,
As jogelours pleyen at thise feestes grete."
Of sondry doutes thus they jangle and trete,   220
As lewed peple demeth comunly
Of thynges that been maad moore subtilly
Than they kan in hir lewednesse comprehende;
They demen gladly to the badder ende.
   And somme of hem wondred on the mirour,   225
That born was up into the maister-tour,
Hou men myghte in it swiche thynges se.
   Another answerde and seyde it myghte wel be

---

150 **stevene:** voice, speech
154 **do boote:** cure
162 **plat:** blunt side
166 **withouten glose:** without deception
171 **court:** courtyard
173 **mete:** meal
180 **fable:** falsehood
181 **remewed:** moved
182 **yglewed:** glued
184 **wyndas:** windlass   **polyve:** pulley
188 **voyden:** move

190 **gauren:** stare
194 **horsly:** with the best qualities of a horse   **quyk:** lively
195 **Poilleys:** Apulian
201 **a fairye:** a marvel
204 **been:** bees
205 **skiles:** reasons, arguments
206 **poetries:** poems
207 **Pegasee:** Pegasus
209 **the Grekes hors Synon:** the horse of Synon the Greek; i.e., the Trojan horse
218 **apparence:** illusion
219 **jogelours:** conjurers
220 **doutes:** doubts (conjectures)   **jangle:** chatter   **trete:** discuss, debate
224 **gladly:** habitually
226 **maister-tour:** chief, principal tower

Naturelly, by composiciouns
Of anglis and of slye reflexiouns,   230
And seyde that in Rome was swich oon.
They speken of Alocen, and Vitulon,
And Aristotle, that writen in hir lyves
Of queynte mirours and of perspectives,
As knowen they that han hir bookes herd.   235
  And oother folk han wondred on the swerd
That wolde percen thurghout every thyng,
And fille in speche of Thelophus the kyng,
And of Achilles with his queynte spere,
For he koude with it bothe heele and dere,   240
Right in swich wise as men may with the swerd
Of which right now ye han youreselven herd.
They speken of sondry hardyng of metal,
And speke of medicynes therwithal,
And how and whanne it sholde yharded be,   245
Which is unknowe, algates unto me.
  Tho speeke they of Canacees ryng,
And seyden alle that swich a wonder thyng
Of craft of rynges herde they nevere noon,
Save that he Moyses and kyng Salomon   250
Hadde a name of konnyng in swich art.
Thus seyn the peple and drawen hem apart.
But nathelees somme seiden that it was
Wonder to maken of fern-asshen glas,
And yet nys glas nat lyk asshen of fern;   255
But, for they han yknowen it so fern,
Therfore cesseth hir janglyng and hir wonder.
As soore wondren somme on cause of thonder,
On ebbe, on flood, on gossomer, and on myst,
And alle thyng, til that the cause is wyst.   260
Thus jangle they, and demen, and devyse
Til that the kyng gan fro the bord aryse.
  Phebus hath laft the angle meridional,
And yet ascendynge was the beest roial,
The gentil Leon, with his Aldiran,   265
Whan that this Tartre kyng, Cambyuskan,

Roos fro his bord, ther as he sat ful hye.
Toforn hym gooth the loude mynstralcye
Til he cam to his chambre of paramentz,
Ther as they sownen diverse instrumentz   270
That it is lyk an hevene for to heere.
Now dauncen lusty Venus children deere,
For in the Fyssh hir lady sat ful hye,
And looketh on hem with a freendly ye.
  This noble kyng is set upon his trone.   275
This strange knyght is fet to hym ful soone,
And on the daunce he gooth with Canacee.
Heere is the revel and the jolitee
That is nat able a dul man to devyse.
He moste han knowen love and his servyse   280
And been a feestlych man as fressh as May,
That sholde yow devysen swich array.
  Who koude telle yow the forme of dlaunces
So unkouthe, and swiche fresshe contenaunces,
Swich subtil lookyng and dissymulynges   285
For drede of jalouse mennes aperceyvynges?
No man but Launcelot, and he is deed.
Therfore I passe of al this lustiheed;
I sey namoore, but in this jolynesse
I lete hem til men to the soper dresse.   290
  The styward bit the spices for to hye,
And eek the wyn, in al this melodye.
The usshers and the squiers been ygoon,
The spices and the wyn is come anoon.
They ete and drynke, and whan this hadde an ende,
Unto the temple, as reson was, they wende.   296
The service doon, they soupen al by day.
What nedeth yow rehercen hire array?
Ech man woot wel that a kynges feeste
Hath plentee to the meeste and to the leeste,   300
And deyntees mo than been in my knowyng.
At after-soper gooth this noble kyng
To seen this hors of bras, with al a route
Of lordes and of ladyes hym aboute.
  Swich wondryng was ther on this hors of bras   305
That syn the grete sege of Troie was,
Theras men wondreden on an hors also,

229 **composiciouns:** arrangements
231 **swich oon:** such a one (magic mirror)
232 **Alocen:** Alhazen, an authority on optics   **Vitulon:** Vitello, an authority on
perspective
233 **Aristotle:** probably mentioned because of his explanation of rainbows   **writen in
hir lyves:** wrote during their lifetimes
234 **perspectives:** optical lenses
237 **percen:** pierce
238 **Thelophus:** Telephus, wounded by Achilles's spear
240 **dere:** harm
243 **hardyng:** hardening, tempering
244 **medicynes:** chemicals
250 **he Moyses:** that (famous) Moses, noted, like Solomon, for his skill in magic
254 **fern-asshen:** ashes of fern
256 **fern:** long ago
257 **cesseth:** stops
259 **gossomer:** spider web
263–65 The sun (*Phebus*) has left the *angle meridional*, through which it passes from
10 to 12 A.M., and the *beest roial* (the constellation Leo, *Leon*) and the star *Aldiran* are
rising above the horizon (*ascendynge*); see n.

269 **chambre of paramentz:** the Presence Chamber, hung with tapestries
(*paramentz*), where a sovereign receives official visitors
272 **Venus children:** those under the influence of the planet Venus; i.e., lovers
273 **Fyssh:** the zodiacal sign Pisces, in which Venus (*hir lady*) has her exaltation and
is especially powerful
281 **feestlych:** convivial
284 **unkouthe:** strange, exotic   **contenaunces:** expressions
285 **dissymulynges:** dissimulations
287 **Launcelot:** Lancelot, lover of Guinevere in the Arthurian romances
288 **lustiheed:** pleasure
290 **dresse:** go
291 **styward:** steward   **spices:** spiced cakes   **hye:** hurry, be quickly brought
297 **by day:** in daylight
300 **Hath plentee to:** there is plenty for
306 **sege:** siege

Ne was ther swich a wondryng as was tho.
But fynally the kyng axeth this knyght
The vertu of this courser and the myght,   310
And preyde hym to telle his governaunce.

This hors anoon bigan to trippe and daunce,
Whan that this knyght leyde hand upon his reyne,
And seyde, "Sire, ther is namoore to seyne,
But, whan yow list to ryden anywhere,   315
Ye mooten trille a pyn, stant in his ere,
Which I shal yow telle bitwix us two.
Ye moote nempne hym to what place also,
Or to what contree, that yow list to ryde.
And whan ye come ther as yow list abyde,   320
Bidde hym descende, and trille another pyn,
For therin lith th'effect of al the gyn,
And he wol doun descende and doon youre wille,
And in that place he wol abyde stille.
Though al the world the contrarie hadde yswore,   325
He shal nat thennes been ydrawe ne ybore.
Or, if yow liste bidde hym thennes goon,
Trille this pyn, and he wol vanysshe anoon
Out of the sighte of every maner wight,
And come agayn, be it by day or nyght,   330
Whan that yow list to clepen hym ageyn
In swich a gyse as I shal to yow seyn
Bitwixe yow and me, and that ful soone.
Ride whan yow list; ther is namoore to doone."

Enformed whan the kyng was of that knyght,   335
And hath conceyved in his wit aright
The manere and the forme of al this thyng,
Ful glad and blithe, this noble doughty kyng
Repeireth to his revel as biforn.
The brydel is unto the tour yborn   340
And kept among his jueles leeve and deere.
The hors vanysshed, I noot in what manere,
Out of hir sighte; ye gete namoore of me.
But thus I lete in lust and jolitee
This Cambyuskan his lordes festeiynge   345
Til wel ny the day bigan to sprynge.

Explicit prima pars.

Sequitur pars secunda.

The norice of digestioun, the sleep,
Gan on hem wynke and bad hem taken keep

That muchel drynke and labour wolde han reste;
And with a galpyng mouth hem alle he keste,   350
And seyde that it was tyme to lye adoun,
For blood was in his domynacioun.
"Cherisseth blood, natures freend," quod he.
They thanken hym galpynge, by two, by thre,
And every wight gan drawe hym to his reste,   355
As sleep hem bad; they tooke it for the beste.

Hire dremes shul nat now been toold for me;
Ful were hire heddes of fumositee,
That causeth dreem of which ther nys no charge.
They slepen til that it was pryme large,   360
The mooste part, but it were Canacee.
She was ful mesurable, as wommen be;
For of hir fader hadde she take leve
To goon to reste soone after it was eve.
Hir liste nat appalled for to be,   365
Ne on the morwe unfeestlich for to se,
And slepte hire firste sleep, and thanne awook.
For swich a joye she in hir herte took
Bothe of hir queynte ryng and hire mirour,
That twenty tyme she changed hir colour;   370
And in hire sleep, right for impressioun
Of hire mirour, she hadde a visioun.
Wherfore, er that the sonne gan up glyde,
She cleped on hir maistresse hire bisyde,
And seyde that hire liste for to ryse.   375

Thise olde wommen that been gladly wyse,
As is hire maistresse, answerde hire anon,
And seyde, "Madame, whider wil ye goon
Thus erly, for the folk been alle on reste?"

"I wol," quod she, "arise, for me leste   380
Ne lenger for to slepe, and walke aboute."
Hire maistresse clepeth wommen a greet route,
And up they rysen, wel a ten or twelve;
Up riseth fresshe Canacee hireselve,
As rody and bright as dooth the yonge sonne,   385
That in the Ram is foure degrees up ronne—
Noon hyer was he whan she redy was—
And forth she walketh esily a pas,

311 **his governaunce:** how to make it work
316 **trille:** turn
318 **nempne:** name, tell
322 **gyn:** device
331 **clepen hym ageyn:** call him back
332 **gyse:** manner
Explicit, *etc.*: Here ends the first part.
Sequitur, *etc.*: Here follows the second part.

350 **galpyng:** yawning   **keste:** kissed
352 **blood:** the humor blood; see n.
358 **fumositee:** fumes deriving from wine drinking
359 **charge:** weight, significance
360 **pryme large:** fully prime, 9 A.M.
362 **mesurable:** moderate
365 **appalled:** faded, pale-looking
366 **unfeestlich:** unfestive   **for to se:** to be seen, in appearance
377 **maistresse:** governess
378 **whider:** whither
385 **rody:** ruddy, fresh-looking   **yonge:** young because the solar year has just begun; cf. 49–51 above and I.7–8.
386 **Ram:** the zodiacal sign Aries

Arrayed after the lusty seson soote
Lightly, for to pleye and walke on foote,   390
Nat but with fyve or sixe of hir meynee;
And in a trench forth in the park gooth she.

  The vapour which that fro the erthe glood
Made the sonne to seme rody and brood;
But nathelees it was so fair a sighte   395
That it made alle hire hertes for to lighte,
What for the seson and the morwenynge,
And for the foweles that she herde synge.
For right anon she wiste what they mente
Right by hir song, and knew al hire entente.   400

  The knotte why that every tale is toold,
If it be taried til that lust be coold
Of hem that han it after herkned yoore,
The savour passeth ever lenger the moore,
For fulsomnesse of his prolixitee;   405
And by the same resoun, thynketh me,
I sholde to the knotte condescende,
And maken of hir walkyng soone an ende.

  Amydde a tree, for drye as whit as chalk,
As Canacee was pleyyng in hir walk,   410
Ther sat a faucon over hire heed ful hye,
That with a pitous voys so gan to crye
That all the wode resouned of hire cry.
Ybeten hadde she hirself so pitously
With bothe hir wynges til the rede blood   415
Ran endelong the tree ther-as she stood.
And evere in oon she cryde alwey and shrighte,
And with hir beek hirselven so she prighte
That ther nys tygre, ne noon so crueel beest
That dwelleth outher in wode or in forest,   420
That nolde han wept, if that he wepe koude,
For sorwe of hire, she shrighte alwey so loude.
For ther nas nevere yet no man on lyve,
If that I koude a faucon wel discryve,
That herde of swich another of fairnesse,   425
As wel of plumage as of gentillesse
Of shap, of al that myghte yrekened be.
A faucon peregryn thanne semed she
Of fremde land; and everemoore, as she stood,
She swowneth now and now for lak of blood,   430

Til wel neigh is she fallen fro the tree.

  This faire kynges doghter, Canacee,
That on hir fynger baar the queynte ryng,
Thurgh which she understood wel every thyng
That any fowel may in his leden seyn,   435
And koude answeren hym in his ledene ageyn,
Hath understonde what this faucon seyde,
And wel neigh for the routhe almoost she deyde.
And to the tree she gooth ful hastily,
And on this faukon looketh pitously,   440
And heeld hir lappe abrood, for wel she wiste
The faukon moste fallen fro the twiste,
Whan that it swowned next, for lak of blood.
A longe whil to wayten hire she stood
Til atte laste she spak in this manere   445
Unto the hauk, as ye shal after heere:

  "What is the cause, if it be for to telle,
That ye be in this furial pyne of helle?"
Quod Canacee unto this hauk above.
"Is this for sorwe of deeth or los of love?   450
For, as I trowe, thise been causes two
That causen moost a gentil herte wo;
Of oother harm it nedeth nat to speke.
For ye yourself upon yourself yow wreke,
Which proveth wel that outher ire or drede   455
Moot been enchesoun of youre cruel dede,
Syn that I see noon oother wight yow chace.
For love of God, as dooth youreselven grace,
Or what may been youre help? For west nor est
Ne saugh I nevere er now no bryd ne beest   460
That ferde with hymself so pitously.
Ye sle me with youre sorwe verraily,
I have of yow so greet compassioun.
For Goddes love, com fro the tree adoun;
And as I am a kynges doghter trewe,   465
If that I verraily the cause knewe
Of youre disese, if it lay in my myght,
I wolde amenden it er that it were nyght,
As wisly helpe me grete God of kynde!
And herbes shal I right ynowe yfynde   470
To heel with youre hurtes hastily."

  Tho shrighte this faucon yet moore pitously
Than ever she dide, and fil to grounde anon,
And lith aswowne, deed and lyk a stoon,
Til Canacee hath in hire lappe hire take   475
Unto the tyme she gan of swough awake.

389 **soote:** sweet-smelling, fragrant
392 **trench:** path
393 **glood:** rose
394 **rody:** red
401 **knotte:** gist, main point
404 **savour:** taste
409 **for drye:** very dry (or because of dryness)
413 **resouned of:** resounded with
416 **endelong:** down the length of
417 **shrighte:** shrieked
418 **prighte:** stabbed
428 **faucon peregryn:** peregrine falcon
429 **fremde:** foreign
430 **now and now:** every now and then

435 **leden:** language
441 **heeld hir lappe abrood:** spread wide the skirt of her dress
442 **twiste:** branch
448 **furial pyne:** pain such as the Furies suffer
454 **wreke:** avenge
456 **enchesoun:** reason
458 **dooth youreselven grace:** spare yourself
467 **disese:** distress

And after that she of hir swough gan breyde,
Right in hir haukes ledene thus she seyde:
"That pitee renneth soone in gentil herte,
Feelynge his similitude in peynes smerte, 480
Is preved alday, as men may it see,
As wel by werk as by auctoritee;
For gentil herte kitheth gentillesse.
I se wel that ye han of my distresse
Compassion, my faire Canacee, 485
Of verray wommanly benignytee
That Nature in youre principles hath set.
But for noon hope for to fare the bet,
But for to obeye unto youre herte free,
And for to maken othere be war by me, 490
As by the whelp chasted is the leon,
Right for that cause and that conclusion,
Whil that I have a leyser and a space,
Myn harm I wol confessen er I pace."

    And evere, whil that oon hir sorwe tolde, 495
That oother weep as she to water wolde
Til that the faucon bad hire to be stille,
And, with a syk, right thus she seyde hir wille:
    "Ther I was bred—allas, that ilke day!—
And fostred in a roche of marbul gray 500
So tendrely that no thyng eyled me,
I nyste nat what was adversitee
Til I koude flee ful hye under the sky.
Tho dwelte a tercelet me faste by,
That semed welle of alle gentillesse; 505
Al were he ful of treson and falsnesse,
It was so wrapped under humble cheere,
And under hewe of trouthe in swich manere,
Under plesance, and under bisy peyne,
That no wight koude han wend he koude feyne, 510
So depe in greyn he dyed his coloures.
Right as a serpent hit hym under floures
Til he may seen his tyme for to byte,
Right so this god of loves ypocryte
Dooth so his cerymonyes and obeisaunces, 515
And kepeth in semblaunt alle his observaunces
That sownen into gentillesse of love.

As in a toumbe is al the faire above,
And under is the corps, swich as ye woot,
Swich was this ypocrite, bothe coold and hoot. 520
And in this wise he served his entente
That, save the feend, noon wiste what he mente,
Til he so longe hadde wopen and compleyned,
And many a yeer his service to me feyned,
Til that myn herte, to pitous and to nyce, 525
Al innocent of his crouned malice,
Forfered of his deeth, as thoughte me,
Upon his othes and his seuretee,
Graunted hym love, upon this condicioun,
That everemoore myn honour and renoun 530
Were saved, bothe privee and apert;
This is to seyn, that after his desert,
I yaf hym al myn herte and al my thoght—
God woot and he, that ootherwise noght—
And took his herte in chaunge of myn for ay. 535
But sooth is seyd, goon sithen many a day,
'A trewe wight and a theef thenken nat oon.'
And whan he saugh the thyng so fer ygoon
That I hadde graunted hym fully my love
In swich a gyse as I have seyd above, 540
And yeven hym my trewe herte as free
As he swoor he yaf his herte to me,
Anon this tigre, ful of doublenesse,
Fil on his knees with so devout humblesse,
With so heigh reverence, and, as by his cheere, 545
So lyk a gentil lovere of manere,
So ravysshed, as it semed, for the joye
That nevere Jason ne Parys of Troye—
Jason? certes, ne noon oother man
Syn Lameth was, that alderfirst bigan 550
To loven two, as writen folk biforn—
Ne nevere, syn the firste man was born,
Ne koude man, by twenty thousand part,
Countrefete the sophymes of his art,
Ne were worthy unbokelen his galoche, 555
Ther doublenesse or feynyng sholde approche,

477 **gan breyde:** started up
480 **similitude:** counterpart
482 **werk:** experience
483 **kitheth:** makes known
487 **principles:** natural disposition
491 **chasted:** chastised
493 **leyser:** leisure, time   **space:** opportunity
500 **roche:** rock
501 **eyled:** troubled
503 **flee:** fly
504 **tercelet:** male falcon
511 So deeply in a fast dye (*in greyn*) he disguised (*dyed his coloures*) his true feelings
512 **hit hym** = *hideth hym,* hides himself
514 **ypocryte:** hypocrite
516 **semblaunt:** outward appearance

523 **wopen:** wept
525 **nyce:** foolish
526 **crouned:** sovereign, consummate
527 **Forfered of his deeth:** very frightened that he might die (for love)
531 **privee and apert:** in private and in public, in all circumstances
534 **ootherwise noght:** on any other terms (I would) not at all (have agreed)
543 **doublenesse:** duplicity
548 **Jason:** Jason deserted Medea (see LGW 1580–1679) **Parys:** Paris deserted the nymph Oënone for Helen (see Tr I.652–56)
550 **Lameth:** the biblical Lamech, the first bigamist **alderfirst:** first of all
554 **sophymes:** sophisms, deceitful arguments
555 **unbokelen his galoche:** unbuckle his sandal
556 **approche:** be concerned

Ne so koude thonke a wight as he dide me!
His manere was an hevene for to see
Til any womman, were she never so wys,
So peynted he and kembde at point-devys   560
As wel his wordes as his contenaunce.
And I so loved hym for his obeisaunce,
And for the trouthe I demed in his herte,
That if so were that any thyng hym smerte,
Al were it never so lite, and I it wiste,   565
Me thoughte I felte deeth myn herte twiste.
And shortly, so ferforth this thyng is went
That my wyl was his willes instrument;
This is to seyn, my wyl obeyed his wyl
In alle thyng, as fer as reson fil,   570
Kepynge the boundes of my worshipe evere.
Ne nevere hadde I thyng so lief, ne levere,
As hym, God woot, ne nevere shal namo.
    "This laste lenger than a yeer or two,
That I supposed of hym noght but good.   575
But finally, thus atte laste it stood,
That Fortune wolde that he moste twynne
Out of that place which that I was inne.
Wher me was wo, that is no questioun;
I kan nat make of it discripsioun.   580
For o thyng dar I tellen boldely:
I knowe what is the peyne of deeth therby;
Swich harm I felte for he ne myghte bileve.
So on a day of me he took his leve,
So sorwefully eek that I wende verraily   585
That he had felt as muche harm as I,
Whan that I herde hym speke and saugh his hewe.
But nathelees, I thoughte he was so trewe,
And eek that he repaire sholde ageyn
Withinne a litel while, sooth to seyn;   590
And resoun wolde eek that he moste go
For his honour, as ofte it happeth so,
That I made vertu of necessitee,
And took it wel, syn that it moste be.
As I best myghte, I hidde fro hym my sorwe,   595
And took hym by the hond, Seint John to borwe,
And seyde hym thus: 'Lo, I am youres al;
Beth swich as I to yow have been and shal.'
What he answerde, it nedeth noght reherce;

Who kan sey bet than he, who kan do werse?   600
Whan he hath al wel seyd, thanne hath he doon.
'Therfore bihoveth hire a ful long spoon
That shal ete with a feend,' thus herde I seye.
So atte laste he moste forth his weye,
And forth he fleeth til he cam ther hym leste.   605
Whan it cam hym to purpos for to reste,
I trowe he hadde thilke text in mynde,
That 'alle thyng, repeirynge to his kynde,
Gladeth hymself;' thus seyn men, as I gesse.
Men loven of propre kynde newefangelnesse,   610
As briddes doon that men in cages fede.
For though thou nyght and day take of hem hede,
And strawe hir cage faire and softe as silk,
And yeve hem sugre, hony, breed and milk,
Yet right anon as that his dore is uppe   615
He with his feet wol spurne adoun his cuppe,
And to the wode he wole and wormes ete;
So newefangel been they of hire mete,
And loven novelries of propre kynde,
No gentillesse of blood ne may hem bynde.   620
    "So ferde this tercelet, allas the day!
Though he were gentil born, and fressh and gay,
And goodlich for to seen, and humble and free,
He saugh upon a tyme a kyte flee,
And sodeynly he loved this kyte so   625
That al his love is clene fro me ago,
And hath his trouthe falsed in this wyse.
Thus hath the kyte my love in hire servyse,
And I am lorn withouten remedie!"
And with that word this faucon gan to crie   630
And swowned eft in Canacees barm.
    Greet was the sorwe for the haukes harm
That Canacee and alle hir wommen made;
They nyste hou they myghte the faucon glade.
But Canacee hom bereth hire in hir lappe,   635
And softely in plastres gan hire wrappe,
Ther as she with hire beek hadde hurt hirselve.
Now kan nat Canacee but herbes delve
Out of the ground, and make salves newe
Of herbes preciouse and fyne of hewe   640
To heelen with this hauk. Fro day to nyght

560 **peynted:** painted, disguised   **kembde:** arranged (literally *combed*)   **at point-**
devys: in every detail, perfectly
566 **twiste:** twist, wring
571 **worshipe:** honor
572 I never loved anything more, or even as much
573 **namo:** no more, never again
574 **laste:** lasted
577 **twynne:** depart
579 **Wher:** whether
583 **bileve:** stay, remain
589 **repaire:** return
596 **Seint John to borwe:** with St. John as my guarantor

602 **bihoveth hire:** it behooves her, she needs
605 **fleeth:** flies
607 **thilke text:** Boece 3 m2.39–42; see n.
610 **of propre kynde:** by nature   **newefangelnesse:** novelty
615 **right anon as:** as soon as   **uppe:** up, open
616 **spurne:** kick
618 **newefangel:** fond of novelty
619 **novelries:** novelties
624 **kyte:** kite, a scavenger bird
631 **eft:** immediately   **barm:** lap
636 **plastres:** bandages

She dooth hire bisynesse and al hire myght,
And by hire beddes heed she made a mewe
And covered it with veluettes blewe,
In signe of trouthe that is in wommen sene.   645
And al withoute, the mewe is peynted grene,
In which were peynted alle thise false fowles,
As ben thise tidyves, tercelettes, and owles;
Right for despit were peynted hem bisyde,
Pyes, on hem for to crie and chyde.   650
     Thus lete I Canacee hir hauk kepyng;
I wol namoore as now speke of hir ryng
Til it come eft to purpos for to seyn
How that this faucon gat hire love ageyn
Repentant, as the storie telleth us,   655
By mediacion of Cambalus,
The kynges sone, of which I yow tolde.
But hennesforth I wol my proces holde
To speken of aventures and of batailles
That nevere yet was herd so grete mervailles.   660
     First wol I telle yow of Cambyuskan,
That in his tyme many a citee wan;
And after wol I speke of Algarsif,
How that he wan Theodora to his wif,
For whom ful ofte in greet peril he was,   665
Ne hadde he ben holpen by the steede of bras;
And after wol I speke of Cambalo,
That faught in lystes with the bretheren two
For Canacee er that he myghte hire wynne.
And ther I lefte I wol ayeyn bigynne.

Explicit secunda pars.

Incipit pars tercia.

     Appollo whirleth up his chaar so hye
Til that the god Mercurius hous, the slye—

3 months have passed

.   .   .

*Heere folwen the wordes of the
Frankeleyn to the Squier, and the
wordes of the Hoost to the Frankeleyn.*

"In feith, Squier, thow hast thee wel yquit
And gentilly. I preise wel thy wit,"
Quod the Frankeleyn, "consideringe thy yowthe,   675
So feelyngly thou spekest, sire, I allow the!
As to my doom, ther is noon that is heere
Of eloquence that shal be thy peere,
If that thou lyve; God yeve thee good chaunce,
And in vertu sende thee continuaunce,   680
For of thy speche I have greet deyntee.
I have a sone, and by the Trinitee,
I hadde levere than twenty pound worth lond,
Though it right now were fallen in myn hond,
He were a man of swich discrecioun   685
As that ye been! Fy on possessioun,
But if a man be vertuous withal!
I have my sone snybbed, and yet shal,
For he to vertu listeth nat entende;
But for to pleye at dees, and to despende   690
And lese al that he hath is his usage.
And he hath levere talken with a page
Than to comune with any gentil wight
Where he myghte lerne gentillesse aright."
     "Straw for youre gentillesse!" quod oure Hoost.   695
"What, Frankeleyn! Pardee, sire, wel thou woost
That ech of yow moot tellen atte leste
A tale or two, or breken his biheste."
     "That knowe I wel, sire," quod the Frankeleyn.
"I prey yow, haveth me nat in desdeyn,   700
Though to this man I speke a word or two."
     "Telle on thy tale withouten wordes mo."
     "Gladly, sire Hoost," quod he, "I wole obeye
Unto your wyl; now herkneth what I seye.
I wol yow nat contrarien in no wyse   705
As fer as that my wittes wol suffyse.
I prey to God that it may plesen yow;
Thanne woot I wel that it is good ynow."

---

643 **mewe:** pen
644 **veluettes:** velvet cloths
648 **tidyves:** small birds (cf. LGW 154)   **tercelettes:** male falcons
650 **Pyes:** magpies, chatterers
Explicit, *etc.*: Here ends the second part.
Incipit, *etc.*: Here begins the third part.
671 **chaar:** chariot

673 **thee wel yquit:** conducted yourself well
676 **So feelyngly:** with such delicate understanding   **allow:** praise
677 **As to my doom:** in my judgment
680 **continuaunce:** perseverance
681 **have greet deyntee:** take great pleasure
683 **twenty pound worth lond:** land yielding an annual income of twenty pounds
687 **vertuous:** accomplished, able   **withal:** also
688 **snybbed:** rebuked
692 **page:** servant boy
693 **comune:** have conversation with
698 **breken his biheste:** break his promise

The Franklin's Prologue

The Prologe of the Frankeleyns Tale.

Thise olde gentil Britouns in hir dayes
Of diverse aventures maden layes, 710
Rymeyed in hir firste Briton tonge,
Whiche layes with hir instrumentz they songe
Or elles redden hem for hir plesaunce;
And oon of hem have I in remembraunce,
Which I shal seyn with good wyl as I kan. 715
But, sires, by cause I am a burel man,
At my bigynnyng first I yow biseche,
Have me excused of my rude speche.

I lerned nevere rethorik, certeyn;
Thyng that I speke, it moot be bare and pleyn. 720
I sleep nevere on the Mount of Pernaso,
Ne lerned Marcus Tullius Scithero.
Colours ne knowe I none, withouten drede,
But swiche colours as growen in the mede,
Or elles swiche as men dye or peynte. 725
Colours of rethoryk been to me queynte;
My spirit feeleth noght of swich mateere.
But if yow list, my tale shul ye heere

The Franklin's Tale

Here bigynneth the Frankeleyns Tale.

In Armorik, that called is Britayne,
Ther was a knyght that loved and dide his payne 730
To serve a lady in his beste wise;
And many a labour, many a greet emprise,
He for his lady wroghte er she were wonne.
For she was oon the faireste under sonne,
And eek therto comen of so heigh kynrede 735
That wel unnethes dorste this knyght, for drede,
Telle hire his wo, his peyne, and his distresse.
But atte laste she, for his worthynesse,
And namely for his meke obeysaunce,
Hath swich a pitee caught of his penaunce 740
That pryvely she fil of his accord
To take hym for hir housbonde and hir lord,

Of swich lordshipe as men han over hir wyves.
And for to lede the moore in blisse hir lyves,
Of his free wyl he swoor hire as a knyght 745
That nevere in al his lyf he, day ne nyght,
Ne sholde upon hym take no maistrie
Agayn hir wyl, ne kithe hire jalousie,
But hire obeye, and folwe hir wyl in al,
As any lovere to his lady shal, 750
Save that the name of soveraynetee,
That wolde he have for shame of his degree.
She thanked hym, and with ful greet humblesse
She seyde, "Sire, sith of youre gentillesse
Ye profre me to have so large a reyne, 755
Ne wolde nevere God bitwixe us tweyne,

---

709 **Britouns:** Bretons
710 **layes:** Breton lays, brief romances; see n.
711 **Rymeyed:** rhymed, versified
716 **burel man:** unlearned man, layman

729 **Armorik:** Armorica, ancient name of coastal Brittany
732 **emprise:** chivalric exploit
734 **oon the faireste:** the fairest of all
740 **penaunce:** distress, suffering

721 **Pernaso:** Mt. Parnassus, sacred to the muses
722 **Marcus Tullius Scithero:** Cicero, author of authoritative works on rhetoric
723 **Colours:** rhetorical ornaments

748 **kithe:** show
752 **for shame of his degree:** in order not to bring shame on his status
755 **so large a reyne:** so loose a rein, such freedom from restraint

As in my gilt, were outher werre or stryf.
Sire, I wol be youre humble trewe wyf—
Have heer my trouthey—til that myn herte breste."
Thus been they bothe in quiete and in reste.   760

　For o thyng, sires, saufly dar I seye,
That freendes everych oother moot obeye,
If they wol longe holden compaignye.
Love wol nat been constreyned by maistrye.
Whan maistrie comth, the God of Love anon   765
Beteth his wynges, and farewel, he is gon!
Love is a thyng as any spirit free.
Wommen, of kynde, desiren libertee,
And nat to been constreyned as a thral;
And so doon men, if I sooth seyen shal.   770
Looke who that is moost pacient in love,
He is at his avantage al above.
Pacience is an heigh vertu, certeyn,
For it venquysseth, as thise clerkes seyn,
Thynges that rigour sholde nevere atteyne.   775
For every word men may nat chide or pleyne.
Lerneth to suffre, or elles, so moot I goon,
Ye shul it lerne, wher so ye wole or noon;
For in this world, certein, ther no wight is
That he ne dooth or seith somtyme amys.   780
Ire, siknesse, or constellacioun,
Wyn, wo, or chaungynge of complexioun
Causeth ful ofte to doon amys or speken.
On every wrong a man may nat be wreken.
After the tyme moste be temperaunce   785
To every wight that kan on governaunce.
And therfore hath this wise, worthy knyght,
To lyve in ese, suffrance hire bihight,
And she to hym ful wisly gan to swere
That nevere sholde ther be defaute in here.   790

　Heere may men seen an humble, wys accord;
Thus hath she take hir servant and hir lord—
Servant in love, and lord in mariage.
Thanne was he bothe in lordshipe and servage.
Servage? Nay, but in lordshipe above,   795
Sith he hath bothe his lady and his love;
His lady, certes, and his wyf also,
The which that lawe of love acordeth to.
And whan he was in this prosperitee,
Hoom with his wyf he gooth to his contree,   800

Nat fer fro Pedmark, ther his dwellyng was,
Where as he lyveth in blisse and in solas.
　Who koude telle, but he hadde wedded be,
The joye, the ese, and the prosperitee
That is bitwixe an housbonde and his wyf?   805
A yeer and moore lasted this blisful lyf,
Til that the knyght of which I speke of thus,
That of Kayrrud was cleped Arveragus,
Shoop hym to goon and dwelle a yeer or tweyne
In Engelond, that cleped was eek Briteyne,   810
To seke in armes worshipe and honour—
For al his lust he sette in swich labour—
And dwelled there two yeer; the book seith thus.
　Now wol I stynten of this Arveragus,
And speken I wole of Dorigen his wyf,   815
That loveth hire housbonde as hire hertes lyf.
For his absence wepeth she and siketh,
As doon thise noble wyves whan hem liketh.
She moorneth, waketh, wayleth, fasteth, pleyneth;
Desir of his presence hire so destreyneth   820
That al this wyde world she sette at noght.
Hire freendes, whiche that knewe hir hevy thoght,
Conforten hire in al that ever they may.
They prechen hire, they telle hire nyght and day
That causelees she sleeth hirself, allas!   825
And every confort possible in this cas
They doon to hire with al hire bisynesse,
Al for to make hire leve hire hevynesse.
　By proces, as ye knowen everichoon,
Men may so longe graven in a stoon   830
Til som figure therinne emprented be.
So longe han they conforted hire til she
Receyved hath, by hope and by resoun,
The emprentyng of hire consolacioun,
Thurgh which hir grete sorwe gan aswage;   835
She may nat alwey duren in swich rage.
　And eek Arveragus, in al this care,
Hath sent hire lettres hoom of his welfare,
And that he wol come hastily agayn;
Or elles hadde this sorwe hir herte slayn.   840
　Hire freendes sawe hir sorwe gan to slake
And preyde hire on knees, for Goddes sake,
To come and romen hire in compaignye,

---

757 **As in my gilt:** through my fault
761 **saufly:** confidently
769 **thral:** servant, slave
772 **at his avantage:** in the best position　**above:** superior
782 **complexioun:** temperament, balance of the humors in one's body
785 **After the tyme:** according to the time, occasion
786 **kan on:** knows about
788 **suffrance:** patience, forbearance　**bihight:** promised
790 **defaute:** flaw
795 **above:** superior

811 **worshipe:** good reputation
820 **destreyneth:** afflicts, presses upon
821 **sette at noght:** reckoned as worth nothing
822 **hevy:** gloomy
834 **emprentyng:** impression
836 **duren:** continue　**rage:** passionate grief

Awey to dryve hire derke fantasye.
And finally she graunted that requeste,   845
For wel she saugh that it was for the beste.
    Now stood hire castel faste by the see,
And often with hire freendes walketh shee
Hire to disporte upon the bank an heigh,
Where as she many a ship and barge seigh   850
Seillynge hir cours, where as hem liste go.
But thanne was that a parcel of hire wo,
For to hirself ful ofte, "Allas!" seith she,
"Is ther no ship, of so manye as I se,
Wol bryngen hom my lord? Thanne were myn herte
Al warisshed of his bittre peynes smerte."   856
    Another tyme ther wolde she sitte and thynke,
And caste hir eyen dounward fro the brynke.
But whan she saugh the grisly rokkes blake,
For verray feere so wolde hir herte quake   860
That on hire feet she myghte hire noght sustene.
Thanne wolde she sitte adoun upon the grene,
And pitously into the see biholde,
And seyn right thus, with sorweful sikes colde:
    "Eterne God, that thurgh thy purveiaunce   865
Ledest the world by certein governaunce,
In ydel, as men seyn, ye no thyng make.
But, Lord, thise grisly feendly rokkes blake,
That semen rather a foul confusion
Of werk than any fair creacion   870
Of swich a parfit wys God and a stable,
Why han ye wroght this werk unresonable?
For by this werk, south, north, ne west, ne eest,
Ther nys yfostred man, ne bryd, ne beest;
It dooth no good, to my wit, but anoyeth.   875
Se ye nat, Lord, how mankynde it destroyeth?
An hundred thousand bodyes of mankynde
Han rokkes slayn, al be they nat in mynde,
Which mankynde is so fair part of thy werk
That thou it madest lyk to thyn owene merk.   880
Thanne semed it ye hadde a greet chiertee
Toward mankynde; but how thanne may it bee
That ye swiche meenes make it to destroyen,
Whiche meenes do no good, but evere anoyen?

I woot wel clerkes wol seyn as hem leste,   885
By argumentz, that al is for the beste,
Though I ne kan the causes nat yknowe.
But thilke God that made wynd to blowe
As kepe my lord! This my conclusion.
To clerkes lete I al disputison.   890
But wolde God that alle thise rokkes blake
Were sonken into helle for his sake!
Thise rokkes sleen myn herte for the feere."
Thus wolde she seyn, with many a pitous teere.
    Hire freendes sawe that it was no disport   895
To romen by the see, but disconfort,
And shopen for to pleyen somwher elles.
They leden hire by ryveres and by welles,
And eek in othere places delitables;
They dauncen and they pleyen at ches and tables. 900
    So on a day, right in the morwe-tyde,
Unto a gardyn that was ther bisyde,
In which that they hadde maad hir ordinaunce
Of vitaille and of oother purveiaunce,
They goon and pleye hem al the longe day.   905
And this was on the sixte morwe of May,
Which May hadde peynted with his softe shoures
This gardyn ful of leves and of floures;
And craft of mannes hand so curiously
Arrayed hadde this gardyn, trewely,   910
That nevere was ther gardyn of swich prys
But if it were the verray paradys.
The odour of floures and the fresshe sighte
Wolde han maked any herte lighte
That evere was born, but if to greet siknesse   915
Or to greet sorwe helde it in distresse,
So ful it was of beautee with plesaunce.
At after-dyner gonne they to daunce,
And synge also, save Dorigen allone,
Which made alwey hir compleint and hir moone, 920
For she ne saugh hym on the daunce go
That was hir housbonde and hir love also.
But nathelees she moste a tyme abyde
And with good hope lete hir sorwe slyde.
    Upon this daunce, amonges othere men,   925
Daunced a squier biforn Dorigen,

---

844 **fantasye:** imaginings
850 **barge:** sailing vessel
852 **parcel:** portion
856 **warisshed:** cured
865 **purveiaunce:** providence
867 **In ydel:** in vain
869 **confusion:** chaos
874 **nys yfostred:** is not supported (i.e., benefited)
880 **merk:** image
881 **chiertee:** love
884 **anoyen:** cause trouble

886 **argumentz:** logical reasoning
889 **conclusion:** conclusion, inference derived from logical argumentation
890 **disputison:** logical disputation
892 **sonken:** sunk
899 **delitables:** delightful
900 **ches:** chess   **tables:** backgammon
909 **curiously:** skillfully
924 **slyde:** slip away
926 **squier:** young knight

That fressher was and jolyer of array,
As to my doom, than is the month of May.
He syngeth, daunceth, passynge any man
That is, or was, sith that the world bigan. 930
Therwith he was, if men sholde hym discryve,
Oon of the beste farynge man on lyve;
Yong, strong, right vertuous, and riche, and wys,
And wel biloved, and holden in greet prys.
And shortly, if the sothe I tellen shal, 935
Unwityng of this Dorigen at al,
This lusty squier, servant to Venus,
Which that ycleped was Aurelius,
Hadde loved hire best of any creature
Two yeer and moore, as was his aventure, 940
But nevere dorste he tellen hire his grevaunce.
Withouten coppe he drank al his penaunce.
He was despeyred; no thyng dorste he seye,
Save in his songes somwhat wolde he wreye
His wo, as in a general compleynyng; 945
He seyde he lovede and was biloved no thyng.
Of swich matere made he manye layes,
Songes, compleintes, roundels, virelayes,
How that he dorste nat his sorwe telle,
But langwissheth as a furye dooth in helle; 950
And dye he moste, he seyde, as dide Ekko
For Narcisus, that dorste nat telle hir wo.
In oother manere than ye heere me seye,
Ne dorste he nat to hire his wo biwreye,
Save that, paraventure, somtyme at daunces, 955
Ther yonge folk kepen hir observaunces,
It may wel be he looked on hir face
In swich a wise as man that asketh grace;
But nothyng wiste she of his entente.
Nathelees it happed, er they thennes wente, 960
By cause that he was hire neighebour,
And was a man of worshipe and honour,
And hadde yknowen hym of tyme yoore,
They fille in speche; and forth, moore and moore,
Unto his purpos drough Aurelius, 965
And whan he saugh his tyme, he seyde thus:
  "Madame," quod he, "by God that this world made,

So that I wiste it myghte youre herte glade,
I wolde that day that youre Arveragus
Wente over the see, that I, Aurelius, 970
Hadde went ther nevere I sholde have come agayn.
For wel I woot my servyce is in vayn;
My gerdon is but brestyng of myn herte.
Madame, reweth upon my peynes smerte;
For with a word ye may me sleen or save. 975
Heere at youre feet God wolde that I were grave!
I ne have as now no leyser moore to seye;
Have mercy, sweete, or ye wol do me deye!"
  She gan to looke upon Aurelius;
"Is this youre wyl," quod she, "and sey ye thus? 980
Nevere erst," quod she, "ne wiste I what ye mente.
But now, Aurelie, I knowe youre entente,
By thilke God that yaf me soule and lyf,
Ne shal I nevere been untrewe wyf
In word ne werk, as fer as I have wit; 985
I wol been his to whom that I am knyt.
Taak this for fynal answere as of me."
But after that in pley thus seyde she:
  "Aurelie," quod she, "by heighe God above,
Yet wolde I graunte yow to been youre love, 990
Syn I yow se so pitously complayne.
Looke what day that endelong Britayne
Ye remoeve alle the rokkes, stoon by stoon,
That they ne lette ship ne boot to goon—
I seye, whan ye han maad the coost so clene 995
Of rokkes that ther nys no stoon ysene,
Thanne wol I love yow best of any man;
Have heer my trouthe, in al that evere I kan."
  "Is ther noon oother grace in yow?" quod he.
  "No, by that Lord," quod she, "that maked me! 1000
For wel I woot that it shal never bityde.
Lat swiche folies out of youre herte slyde.
What deyntee sholde a man han in his lyf
For to go love another mannes wyf,
That hath hir body whan so that hym liketh?" 1005
  Aurelius ful ofte soore siketh;
Wo was Aurelie whan that he this herde,
And with a sorweful herte he thus answerde:
  "Madame," quod he, "this were an inpossible!
Thanne moot I dye of sodeyn deth horrible." 1010
And with that word he turned hym anon.

932 **beste farynge:** most handsome
936 **Unwityng of:** unknown to
942 He suffered intensely; see n.
944 **wreye:** reveal
947 **layes:** songs, brief poems
948 **compleintes:** poems lamenting misfortune in love; see the Short Poems for examples.
  roundels: brief poems or songs with refrains; see PF 680–92 for an example
  virelayes: a form of the roundel
951 **Ekko:** Echo, the nymph who loved Narcisus (*Narcisus*); see Rom 1469–1538.
956 **observaunces:** customs (of courtship)
962 **worshipe:** good reputation

973 **gerdon:** reward, requital
991 **complayne:** lament
994 **lette:** prevent **boot:** boat
1009 **an inpossible:** an impossibility

Tho coome hir othere freendes many oon,
And in the aleyes romeden up and doun,
And nothyng wiste of this conclusioun,
But sodeynly bigonne revel newe   1015
Til that the brighte sonne loste his hewe;
For th'orisonte hath reft the sonne his lyght—
This is as muche to seye as it was nyght—
And hoom they goon in joye and in solas,
Save oonly wrecche Aurelius, allas!   1020
He to his hous is goon with sorweful herte.
He seeth he may nat fro his deeth asterte;
Hym semed that he felte his herte colde.
Up to the hevene his handes he gan holde,
And on his knowes bare he sette hym doun,   1025
And in his ravyng seyde his orisoun.
For verray wo out of his wit he breyde.
He nyste what he spak, but thus he seyde;
With pitous herte his pleynt hath he bigonne
Unto the goddes, and first unto the sonne: 1030
     He seyde, "Appollo, god and governour
Of every plaunte, herbe, tree, and flour,
That yevest, after thy declinacion,
To ech of hem his tyme and his seson,
As thyn herberwe chaungeth lowe or heighe,   1035
Lord Phebus, cast thy merciable eighe
On wrecche Aurelie, which that am but lorn.
Lo, lord! My lady hath my deeth ysworn
Withoute gilt, but thy benignytee
Upon my dedly herte have som pitee.   1040
For wel I woot, lord Phebus, if yow lest,
Ye may me helpen, save my lady, best.
Now voucheth sauf that I may yow devyse
How that I may been holpen and in what wyse.
     "Youre blisful suster, Lucina the sheene,   1045
That of the see is chief goddesse and queene
(Though Neptunus have deitee in the see,
Yet emperisse aboven hym is she),
Ye knowen wel, lord, that right as hir desir
Is to be quyked and lighted of youre fir,   1050
For which she folweth yow ful bisily,
Right so the see desireth naturelly
To folwen hire, as she that is goddesse
Bothe in the see and ryveres moore and lesse.
Wherfore, lord Phebus, this is my requeste—   1055

Do this miracle, or do myn herte breste—
That now next at this opposicion
Which in the signe shal be of the Leon,
As preieth hire so greet a flood to brynge
That fyve fadme at the leeste it oversprynge   1060
The hyeste rokke in Armorik Briteyne;
And lat this flood endure yeres tweyne.
Thanne certes to my lady may I seye,
'Holdeth youre heste, the rokkes been aweye.'
     "Lord Phebus, dooth this miracle for me.   1065
Preye hire she go no faster cours than ye;
I seye, preyeth your suster that she go
No faster cours than ye thise yeres two.
Thanne shal she been evene atte fulle alway,
And spryng flood laste bothe nyght and day.   1070
And but she vouche sauf in swich manere
To graunte me my sovereyn lady deere,
Prey hire to synken every rok adoun
Into hir owene dirke regioun
Under the ground, ther Pluto dwelleth inne,   1075
Or nevere mo shal I my lady wynne.
Thy temple in Delphos wol I barefoot seke.
Lord Phebus, se the teeris on my cheke,
And of my peyne have som compassioun."
And with that word in swowne he fil adoun,   1080
And longe tyme he lay forth in a traunce.
     His brother, which that knew of his penaunce,
Up caughte hym and to bedde he hath hym broght.
Dispeyred in this torment and this thoght
Lete I this woful creature lye;   1085
Chese he, for me, wheither he wol lyve or dye.
     Arveragus, with heele and greet honour,
As he that was of chivalrie the flour,
Is comen hoom, and othere worthy men.
O blisful artow now, thou Dorigen,   1090
That hast thy lusty housbonde in thyne armes,
The fresshe knyght, the worthy man of armes,
That loveth thee as his owene hertes lyf.
No thyng list hym to been ymaginatyf,
If any wight hadde spoke, whil he was oute,   1095
To hire of love; he hadde of it no doute.
He noght entendeth to no swich mateere,

1057 **opposicion:** the position of the sun and moon when they are directly opposite one another, a time of the highest tides; see n.
1058 **Leon:** the zodiacal sign Leo
1060 **fadme:** fathoms   **oversprynge:** rise above
1064 **Holdeth youre heste:** keep your promise
1066 **go no faster cours:** go at the same speed
1069 **evene atte fulle:** fully even (with you), in exact opposition
1075 **Pluto:** god of the underworld
1077 **Delphos:** Delphi, in Greece
1080 **swowne:** faint
1087 **heele:** well-being
1094 **ymaginatyf:** suspicious

1013 **aleyes:** garden paths
1017 **th'orisonte:** the horizon   **reft:** taken away
1025 **knowes:** knees
1033 **after thy declinacion:** according to your angular distance from the celestial equator (i.e., the height of the sun in each season); see n.
1035 **herberwe:** (astrological) house, position in the zodiac
1036 **Phebus:** Phoebus Apollo, the sun
1040 **dedly:** dying
1045 **Lucina:** goddess of the moon
1047 **Neptunus:** Neptune   **deitee:** divine power
1050 **quyked:** kindled

But daunceth, justeth, maketh hire good cheere;
And thus in joye and blisse I lete hem dwelle,
And of the sike Aurelius wol I telle.   1100
    In langour and in torment furyus
Two yeer and moore lay wrecche Aurelyus,
Er any foot he myghte on erthe gon;
Ne confort in this tyme hadde he noon,
Save of his brother, which that was a clerk.   1105
He knew of al this wo and al this werk,
For to noon oother creature, certeyn,
Of this matere he dorste no word seyn.
Under his brest he baar it moore secree
Than evere dide Pamphilus for Galathee.   1110
His brest was hool, withoute for to sene,
But in his herte ay was the arwe kene.
And wel ye knowe that of a sursanure
In surgerye is perilous the cure,
But men myghte touche the arwe or come therby.   1115
His brother weep and wayled pryvely,
Til atte laste hym fil in remembraunce,
That whiles he was at Orliens in Fraunce—
As yonge clerkes that been lykerous
To reden artes that been curious   1120
Seken in every halke and every herne
Particuler sciences for to lerne—
He hym remembred that, upon a day,
At Orliens in studie a book he say
Of magyk natureel, which his felawe,   1125
That was that tyme a bacheler of lawe,
Al were he ther to lerne another craft,
Hadde prively upon his desk ylaft;
Which book spak muchel of the operaciouns
Touchynge the eighte and twenty mansiouns   1130
That longen to the moone, and swich folye
As in oure dayes is nat worth a flye—
For hooly chirches feith in oure bileve
Ne suffreth noon illusioun us to greve.
And whan this book was in his remembraunce,   1135
Anon for joye his herte gan to daunce,
And to hymself he seyde pryvely:
"My brother shal be warisshed hastily;
For I am siker that ther be sciences

By whiche men make diverse apparences,   1140
Swiche as thise subtile tregetoures pleye.
For ofte at feestes have I wel herd seye
That tregetours withinne an halle large
Have maad come in a water and a barge,
And in the halle rowen up and doun.   1145
Somtyme hath semed come a grym leoun;
And somtyme floures sprynge as in a mede;
Somtyme a vyne, and grapes white and rede;
Somtyme a castel, al of lym and stoon;
And whan hem lyked, voyded it anon.   1150
Thus semed it to every mannes sighte.
    "Now thanne conclude I thus: that if I myghte
At Orliens som oold felawe yfynde
That hadde thise moones mansions in mynde,
Or oother magyk natureel above,   1155
He sholde wel make my brother han his love.
For with an apparence a clerk may make,
To mannes sighte, that alle the rokkes blake
Of Britaigne weren yvoyded everichon,
And shippes by the brynke comen and gon,   1160
And in swich forme enduren a wowke or two.
Thanne were my brother warisshed of his wo;
Thanne moste she nedes holden hire biheste,
Or elles he shal shame hire atte leeste."
    What sholde I make a lenger tale of this?   1165
Unto his brotheres bed he comen is,
And swich confort he yaf hym for to gon
To Orliens that he up stirte anon,
And on his wey forthward thanne is he fare
In hope for to been lissed of his care.   1170
    Whan they were come almoost to that citee,
But if it were a two furlong or thre,
A yong clerk romynge by hymself they mette,
Which that in Latyn thriftily hem grette,
And after that he seyde a wonder thyng: 1175
"I knowe," quod he, "the cause of youre comyng."
And er they ferther any foote wente,
He tolde hem al that was in hire entente.
    This Briton clerk hym asked of felawes
The whiche that he had knowe in olde dawes,   1180
And he answerde hym that they dede were,
For which he weep ful ofte many a teere.
    Doun of his hors Aurelius lighte anon,
And with this magicien forth is he gon

1101 **langour:** suffering   **furyus:** like that of the furies in Hell
1110 **Pamphilus, Galathee:** lovers in the thirteenth-century poem *Pamphilus de Amore*
1113 **sursanure:** wound healed only on the surface
1118 **Orliens:** Orleans
1119 **lykerous:** eager
1120 **curious:** arcane
1121 **every halke and every herne:** every nook and cranny
1122 **Particuler sciences:** specialized branches of learning
1124 **in studie:** in a study hall   **say:** saw
1125 **magyk natureel:** natural science
1130 **mansiouns:** stations of the moon; see n.

1140 **apparences:** illusions
1141 **tregetoures:** illusionists, magicians
1149 **lym:** lime (mortar)
1150 **voyded:** caused it to disappear
1155 **above:** in addition to
1161 **wowke:** week
1162 **warisshed:** cured
1170 **lissed:** relieved
1174 **thriftily:** suitably, politely

Hoom to his hous, and maden hem wel at ese.   1185
Hem lakked no vitaille that myghte hem plese.
So wel arrayed hous as ther was oon
Aurelius in his lyf saugh nevere noon.

He shewed hym, er he wente to sopeer,
Forestes, parkes ful of wilde deer;   1190
Ther saugh he hertes with hir hornes hye,
The gretteste that evere were seyn with ye.
He saugh of hem an hondred slayn with houndes,
And somme with arwes blede of bittre woundes.
He saugh, whan voyded were thise wilde deer,   1195
Thise fauconers upon a fair ryver,
That with hir haukes han the heron slayn.

Tho saugh he knyghtes justyng in a playn;
And after this he dide hym swich plesaunce
That he hym shewed his lady on a daunce,   1200
On which hymself he daunced, as hym thoughte.
And whan this maister that this magyk wroughte
Saugh it was tyme, he clapte his handes two,
And farewel! Al oure revel was ago.
And yet remoeved they nevere out of the hous,   1205
Whil they saugh al this sighte merveillous,
But in his studie, ther as his bookes be,
They seten stille, and no wight but they thre.

To hym this maister called his squier,
And seyde hym thus: "Is redy oure soper?   1210
Almoost an houre it is, I undertake,
Sith I yow bad oure soper for to make,
Whan that thise worthy men wenten with me
Into my studie, ther as my bookes be."
"Sire," quod this squier, "whan it liketh yow,   1215
It is al redy, though ye wol right now."
"Go we thanne soupe," quod he, "as for the beste.
Thise amorous folk somtyme moote han hir reste."

At after-soper fille they in tretee
What somme sholde this maistres gerdon be   1220
To remoeven alle the rokkes of Britayne,
And eek from Gerounde to the mouth of Sayne.

He made it straunge, and swoor, so God hym save,
Lasse than a thousand pound he wolde nat have,
Ne gladly for that somme he wolde nat goon.   1225

Aurelius, with blisful herte anoon,
Answerde thus: "Fy on a thousand pound!
This wyde world, which that men seye is round,
I wolde it yeve, if I were lord of it.
This bargayn is ful dryve, for we been knyt.   1230
Ye shal be payed trewely, by my trouthe!
But looketh now, for no necligence or slouthe
Ye tarie us heere no lenger than to-morwe."
"Nay," quod this clerk, "have heer my feith to
     borwe."
To bedde is goon Aurelius whan hym leste,   1235
And wel ny al that nyght he hadde his reste.
What for his labour and his hope of blisse,
His woful herte of penaunce hadde a lisse.

Upon the morwe, whan that it was day,
To Britaigne tooke they the righte way,   1240
Aurelius and this magicien bisyde,
And been descended ther they wolde abyde.
And this was, as thise bookes me remembre,
The colde, frosty seson of Decembre.

Phebus wax old, and hewed lyk laton,   1245
That in his hoote declynacion
Shoon as the burned gold with stremes brighte;
But now in Capricorn adoun he lighte,
Where as he shoon ful pale, I dar wel seyn.
The bittre frostes, with the sleet and reyn,   1250
Destroyed hath the grene in every yerd.
Janus sit by the fyr, with double berd,
And drynketh of his bugle horn the wyn;
Biforn hym stant brawen of the tusked swyn,
And "Nowel" crieth every lusty man.   1255
Aurelius in al that evere he kan
Dooth to this maister chiere and reverence,
And preyeth hym to doon his diligence
To bryngen hym out of his peynes smerte,
Or with a swerd that he wolde slitte his herte. 1260
This subtil clerk swich routhe had of this man
That nyght and day he spedde hym that he kan

1196 **fauconers:** hunters with falcons   **ryver:** hawking ground
1219 **tretee:** negotiation
1222 **Gerounde, Sayne:** the rivers Gironde and Seine
1223 **made it straunge:** raised difficulties

1232 **slouthe:** sloth, laziness
1234 **to borwe:** as a pledge
1238 **lisse:** respite
1240 **righte:** direct
1245 **Phebus wax old:** the sun grew old (reached the end of the solar year)   **laton:** a
brass-like alloy grayish-silver in color
1246 **hoote declynacion:** the sign of Cancer, when the sun's northern declination is
greatest (in summer)
1248 **Capricorn:** the sign of the winter solstice (December 13), the lowest altitude of
the sun
1251 **yerd:** enclosed garden
1252 **Janus:** god of entries and of the month of January   **double berd:** i.e., two faces
(one looking forward, the other backward)
1253 **bugle horn:** drinking vessel made from the horn of the bugle, buffalo
1254 **brawen:** meat   **tusked swyn:** boar
1255 **Nowel:** Noel

To wayten a tyme of his conclusioun;
This is to seye, to maken illusioun,
By swich an apparence or jogelrye—   1265
I ne kan no termes of astrologye—
That she and every wight sholde wene and seye
That of Britaigne the rokkes were aweye,
Or ellis they were sonken under grounde.
So atte laste he hath his tyme yfounde   1270
To maken his japes and his wrecchednesse
Of swich a supersticious cursednesse.
His tables Tolletanes forth he brought,
Ful wel corrected, ne ther lakked nought,
Neither his collect ne his expans yeeris,   1275
Ne his rootes, ne his othere geeris,
As been his centris and his argumentz
And his proporcioneles convenientz
For his equacions in every thyng.
And by his eighte speere in his wirkyng   1280
He knew ful wel how fer Alnath was shove
Fro the heed of thilke fixe Aries above,
That in the ninthe speere considered is;
Ful subtilly he kalkuled al this.

Whan he hadde founde his firste mansioun,   1285
He knew the remenaunt by proporcioun,
And knew the arisyng of his moone weel,
And in whos face, and terme, and everydeel;
And knew ful weel the moones mansioun
Acordaunt to his operacioun,   1290
And knew also his othere observaunces
For swiche illusiouns and swiche meschaunces
As hethen folk useden in thilke dayes.
For which no lenger maked he delayes,
But thurgh his magik, for a wyke or tweye,   1295
It semed that alle the rokkes were aweye.

Aurelius, which that yet despeired is
Wher he shal han his love or fare amys,

Awaiteth nyght and day on this myracle;
And whan he knew that ther was noon obstacle, 1300
That voyded were thise rokkes everychon,
Doun to his maistres feet he fil anon,
And seyde, "I woful wrecche, Aurelius,
Thanke yow, lord, and lady myn Venus,
That me han holpen fro my cares colde."   1305
And to the temple his wey forth hath he holde,
Where as he knew he sholde his lady see.
And whan he saugh his tyme, anon-right hee,
With dredful herte and with ful humble cheere,
Salewed hath his sovereyn lady deere: 1310
"My righte lady," quod this woful man,
"Whom I moost drede and love as I best kan,
And lothest were of al this world displese,
Nere it that I for yow have swich disese
That I moste dyen heere at youre foot anon,   1315
Noght wolde I telle how me is wo bigon.
But certes outher moste I dye or pleyne;
Ye sle me giltelees for verray peyne.
But of my deeth thogh that ye have no routhe,
Avyseth yow er that ye breke youre trouthe.   1320
Repenteth yow, for thilke God above,
Er ye me sleen by cause that I yow love.
For, madame, wel ye woot what ye han hight—
Nat that I chalange any thyng of right
Of yow, my sovereyn lady, but youre grace—   1325
But in a gardyn yond, at swich a place,
Ye woot right wel what ye bihighten me;
And in myn hand youre trouthe plighten ye
To love me best—God woot, ye seyde so,
Al be that I unworthy am therto.   1330
Madame, I speke it for the honour of yow
Moore than to save myn hertes lyf right now—
I have do so as ye comanded me;
And if ye vouche sauf, ye may go see.
Dooth as yow list; have youre biheste in mynde, 1335
For, quyk or deed, right there ye shal me fynde.
In yow lith al to do me lyve or deye—
But wel I woot the rokkes been aweye."

He taketh his leve, and she astoned stood;
In al hir face nas a drope of blood.   1340
She wende nevere han come in swich a trappe.
"Allas," quod she, "that evere this sholde happe!
For wende I nevere by possibilitee
That swich a monstre or merveille myghte be!
It is agayns the proces of nature."   1345

1263 **conclusioun:** astronomical operation
1265 **jogelrye:** conjurer's trick
1273 **tables Tolletanes:** astrological tables corrected for a given latitude, with tables of a planet's positions in single years (*expans yeeris*) and in twenty-year periods (*collect*); see the Expl. Notes for the technical vocabulary in lines 1263–84.
1276 **rootes:** dates from which astronomical calculations are made   **geeris:** apparatus
1277 **centris:** table of distances between certain parts of an equator   **argumentz:** angles used in calulating astronomical positions
1278 **proporcioneles convenientz:** tables for computing planetary motions
1279 **equacions:** divisions of the sphere into astronomical houses
1280 **eighte speere:** sphere of the fixed stars
1281 **Alnath:** a star in the constellation Aries (*fixed Aries*); see 1280 n.
1283 **considered:** observed
1285 **mansioun:** position of the moon
1286 He could calculate the positions of the other mansions by astronomical tables (*by proporcioun;* cf. 1278 above).
1288 **face, terme:** divisions of the zodiacal signs, each of which was assigned to a planet; see n.
1290 **Acordaunt to:** consonant with
1292 **meschaunces:** evil practices
1295 **wyke:** week
1298 **amys:** badly

1309 **dredful:** fearful
1314 **disese:** distress
1323 **hight:** promised
1324 **chalange:** claim   **of right:** as a legal right
1325 **but youre grace:** (I ask) only your favor
1327 **bihighten:** promised
1336 **quyk:** living

And hoom she goth a sorweful creature;
For verray feere unnethe may she go.
She wepeth, wailleth, al a day or two,
And swowneth, that it routhe was to see.
But why it was to no wight tolde shee,   1350
For out of towne was goon Arveragus.
But to hirself she spak, and seyde thus,
With face pale and with ful sorweful cheere,
In hire compleynt, as ye shal after heere:
    "Allas," quod she, "on thee, Fortune, I pleyne,   1355
That unwar wrapped hast me in thy cheyne,
Fro which t'escape woot I no socour,
Save oonly deeth or elles dishonour;
Oon of thise two bihoveth me to chese.
But nathelees, yet have I levere to lese   1360
My lif than of my body to have a shame,
Or knowe myselven fals, or lese my name;
And with my deth I may be quyt, ywis.
Hath ther nat many a noble wyf er this,
And many a mayde, yslayn hirself, allas,   1365
Rather than with hir body doon trespas?
    "Yis, certes, lo, thise stories beren witnesse:
Whan thritty tirauntz, ful of cursednesse,
Hadde slayn Phidon in Atthenes atte feste,
They comanded his doghtres for t'areste   1370
And bryngen hem biforn hem in despit,
Al naked, to fulfille hir foul delit,
And in hir fadres blood they made hem daunce
Upon the pavement, God yeve hem meschaunce!
For which thise woful maydens, ful of drede,   1375
Rather than they wolde lese hir maydenhede,
They prively been stirt into a welle
And dreynte hemselven, as the bookes telle.
    "They of Mecene leete enquere and seke
Of Lacedomye fifty maydens eke,   1380
On whiche they wolden doon hir lecherye.
But was ther noon of al that compaignye
That she nas slayn, and with a good entente
Chees rather for to dye than assente
To been oppressed of hir maydenhede.   1385
Why sholde I thanne to dye been in drede?
Lo, eek, the tiraunt Aristoclides,
That loved a mayden, heet Stymphalides,
Whan that hir fader slayn was on a nyght,
Unto Dianes temple goth she right,   1390
And hente the ymage in hir handes two,
Fro which ymage wolde she nevere go.

No wight ne myghte hir handes of it arace
Til she was slayn, right in the selve place.
    "Now sith that maydens hadden swich despit 1395
To been defouled with mannes foul delit,
Wel oghte a wyf rather hirselven slee
Than be defouled, as it thynketh me.
What shal I seyn of Hasdrubales wyf,
That at Cartage birafte hirself hir lyf?   1400
For whan she saugh that Romayns wan the toun,
She took hir children alle, and skipte adoun
Into the fyr, and chees rather to dye
Than any Romayn dide hire vileynye.
Hath nat Lucresse yslayn hirself, allas,   1405
At Rome, whan that she oppressed was
Of Tarquyn, for hire thoughte it was a shame
To lyven whan she hadde lost hir name?
The sevene maydens of Milesie also
Han slayn hemself, for verrey drede and wo,   1410
Rather than folk of Gawle hem sholde oppresse.
Mo than a thousand stories, as I gesse,
Koude I now telle as touchynge this mateere.
Whan Habradate was slayn, his wyf so deere
Hirselven slow, and leet hir blood to glyde   1415
In Habradates woundes depe and wyde,
And seyde, "My body, at the leeste way,
Ther shal no wight defoulen, if I may.'
    "What sholde I mo ensamples heerof sayn,
Sith that so manye han hemselven slayn   1420
Wel rather than they wolde defouled be?
I wol conclude that it is bet for me
To sleen myself than been defouled thus.
I wol be trewe unto Arveragus,
Or rather sleen myself in som manere,   1425
As dide Demociones doghter deere
By cause that she wolde nat defouled be.
O Cedasus, it is ful greet pitee
To reden how thy doghtren deyde, allas,
That slowe hemself for swich manere cas.   1430
As greet a pitee was it, or wel moore,
The Theban mayden that for Nichanore
Hirselven slow, right for swich manere wo.
Another Theban mayden dide right so;
For oon of Macidonye hadde hire oppressed,   1435
She with hire deeth hir maydenhede redressed.
What shal I seye of Nicerates wyf,
That for swich cas birafte hirself hir lyf?
How trewe eek was to Alcebiades

1356 **unwar:** unexpectedly
1363 **quyt:** free from blame
1370 **t'areste:** seize
1379 **Mecene:** Messene
1380 **Lacedomye:** Lacedaemon (Sparta)

1393 **arace:** pull away
1405 **Lucresse:** Lucretia; see LGW 1680–1885
1409 **Milesie:** Miletus
1411 **Gawle:** Galatia
1428 **Cedasus:** Scedasus
1430 **cas:** cause
1435 **Macidonye:** Macedonia

His love, that rather for to dyen chees   1440
Than for to suffre his body unburyed be.
Lo, which a wyf was Alceste," quod she.
"What seith Omer of goode Penalopee?
Al Grece knoweth of hire chastitee.
Pardee, of Laodomya is writen thus,   1445
That whan at Troie was slayn Protheselaus,
Ne lenger wolde she lyve after his day.
The same of noble Porcia telle I may;
Withoute Brutus koude she nat lyve,
To whom she hadde al hool hir herte yive.   1450
The parfit wyfhod of Arthemesie
Honured is thurgh al the Barbarie.
O Teuta, queene, thy wyfly chastitee
To alle wyves may a mirour bee.
The same thyng I seye of Bilyea,   1455
Of Rodogone, and eek Valeria."

    Thus pleyned Dorigen a day or tweye,
Purposynge evere that she wolde deye.
But nathelees, upon the thridde nyght,
Hoom cam Arveragus, this worthy knyght,   1460
And asked hire why that she weep so soore;
And she gan wepen ever lenger the moore.
"Allas," quod she, "that evere was I born!
Thus have I seyd," quod she, "thus have I sworn"—
And toold hym al as ye han herd bifore;   1465
It nedeth nat reherce it yow namoore.
This housbonde, with glad chiere, in freendly wyse
Answerde and seyde as I shal yow devyse:
"Is ther oght elles, Dorigen, but this?"

    "Nay, nay," quod she, "God helpe me so as wys!
This is to muche, and it were Goddes wille."   1471

    "Ye, wyf," quod he, "lat slepen that is stille.
It may be wel, paraventure, yet to day.
Ye shul youre trouthe holden, by my fay!
For God so wisly have mercy upon me,   1475
I hadde wel levere ystiked for to be
For verray love which that I to yow have,
But if ye sholde youre trouthe kepe and save.
Trouthe is the hyeste thyng that man may kepe"—

But with that word he brast anon to wepe,   1480
And seyde, "I yow forbede, up peyne of deeth,
That nevere, whil thee lasteth lyf ne breeth,
To no wight telle thou of this aventure—
As I may best, I wol my wo endure—
Ne make no contenance of hevynesse,   1485
That folk of yow may demen harm or gesse."

    And forth he cleped a squier and a mayde:
"Gooth forth anon with Dorigen," he sayde,
"And bryngeth hire to swich a place anon."
They take hir leve, and on hir wey they gon,   1490
But they ne wiste why she thider wente.
He nolde no wight tellen his entente.

    Paraventure an heep of yow, ywis,
Wol holden hym a lewed man in this
That he wol putte his wyf in jupartie.   1495
Herkneth the tale er ye upon hire crie.
She may have bettre fortune than yow semeth;
And whan that ye han herd the tale, demeth.

    This squier, which that highte Aurelius,
On Dorigen that was so amorus,   1500
Of aventure happed hire to meete
Amydde the toun, right in the quykkest strete,
As she was bown to goon the wey forth right
Toward the gardyn ther as she had hight.
And he was to the gardyn-ward also;   1505
For wel he spyed whan she wolde go
Out of hir hous to any maner place.
But thus they mette, of aventure or grace,
And he saleweth hire with glad entente,
And asked of hire whiderward she wente;   1510
And she answerde, half as she were mad,
"Unto the gardyn, as myn housbonde bad,
My trouthe for to holde—allas, allas!"

    Aurelius gan wondren on this cas,
And in his herte hadde greet compassioun   1515
Of hire and of hire lamentacioun,
And of Arveragus, the worthy knyght,
That bad hire holden al that she had hight,
So looth hym was his wyf sholde breke hir trouthe;
And in his herte he caughte of this greet routhe,
Considerynge the beste on every syde,   1521
That fro his lust yet were hym levere abyde

1442 **which a**: what a **Alceste**: Alcestis, heroine of the Prologue of LGW, where the story is told briefly (LGW F 511–16)
1443 **Omer**: Homer **Penalopee**: faithful wife of Ulysses
1448 **Porcia**: Portia committed suicide rather than survive her husband, Brutus.
1451 **Arthemesie**: Famed for her chastity, she built a magnificent tomb for her husband.
1452 **Barbarie**: heathendom
1453 **Teuta**: queen of Ilyrica and famous for chastity
1455 **Bilyea**: Bilia, famed for innocent chastity
1456 **Rodogone, Valeria**: Rhodogune and Valeria refused to remarry after the deaths of their husbands.
1458 **Purposynge**: intending

1480 **brast ... to wepe**: burst into tears
1486 **of yow**: concerning you
1495 **jupartie**: jeopardy
1502 **quykkest strete**: busiest street
1503 **bown**: ready, prepared
1505 **to the gardyn-ward**: (going) toward the garden
1510 **whiderward**: whither
1522 He would prefer to desist from attaining his desire

Than doon so heigh a cherlyssh wrecchednesse
Agayns franchise and alle gentillesse;
For which in fewe wordes seyde he thus: 1525
    "Madame, seyth to youre lord Arveragus
That sith I se his grete gentillesse
To yow, and eek I se wel youre distresse,
That him were levere han shame (and that were
        routhe)
Than ye to me sholde breke thus youre trouthe, 1530
I have wel levere evere to suffre wo
Than I departe the love bitwix yow two.
I yow relesse, madame, into youre hond
Quyt every serement and every bond
That ye han maad to me as heerbiforn,   1535
Sith thilke tyme which that ye were born.
My trouthe I plighte, I shal yow never repreve
Of no biheste, and heere I take my leve,
As of the treweste and the beste wyf
That evere yet I knew in al my lyf.   1540
But every wyf be war of hire biheeste!
On Dorigen remembreth, atte leeste.
Thus kan a squier doon a gentil dede
As wel as kan a knyght, withouten drede."
    She thonketh hym upon hir knees al bare,   1545
And hoom unto hir housbonde is she fare,
And tolde hym al, as ye han herd me sayd;
And be ye siker, he was so weel apayd
That it were impossible me to wryte.
What sholde I lenger of this cas endyte?   1550
    Arveragus and Dorigen his wyf
In sovereyn blisse leden forth hir lyf.
Nevere eft ne was ther angre hem bitwene.
He cherisseth hire as though she were a queene,
And she was to hym trewe for everemoore.   1555
Of thise two folk ye gete of me namoore.
    Aurelius, that his cost hath al forlorn,
Curseth the tyme that evere he was born:
"Allas!" quod he. "Allas, that I bihighte
Of pured gold a thousand pound of wighte   1560
Unto this philosophre! How shal I do?
I se namoore but that I am fordo.
Myn heritage moot I nedes selle,
And been a beggere; heere may I nat dwelle
And shamen al my kynrede in this place,   1565
But I of hym may gete bettre grace.

But nathelees, I wole of hym assaye,
At certeyn dayes, yeer by yeer, to paye,
And thanke hym of his grete curteisye.
My trouthe wol I kepe, I wol nat lye."   1570
    With herte soor he gooth unto his cofre,
And broghte gold unto this philosophre,
The value of fyve hundred pound, I gesse,
And hym bisecheth, of his gentillesse,
To graunte hym dayes of the remenaunt;   1575
And seyde, "Maister, I dar wel make avaunt,
I failled nevere of my trouthe as yit.
For sikerly my dette shal be quyt
Towardes yow, howevere that I fare
To goon a-begged in my kirtle bare.   1580
But wolde ye vouche sauf, upon seuretee,
Two yeer or thre for to respiten me,
Thanne were I wel; for elles moot I selle
Myn heritage; ther is namoore to telle."
    This philosophre sobrely answerde,   1585
And seyde thus, whan he thise wordes herde:
"Have I nat holden covenant unto thee?"
    "Yes, certes, wel and trewely," quod he.
"Hastow nat had thy lady as thee liketh?"
    "No, no," quod he, and sorwefully he siketh. 1590
    "What was the cause? Tel me if thou kan."
    Aurelius his tale anon bigan,
And tolde hym al, as ye han herd bifoore;
It nedeth nat to yow reherce it moore.
    He seide, "Arveragus, of gentillesse,   1595
Hadde levere dye in sorwe and in distresse
Than that his wyf were of hir trouthe fals."
The sorwe of Dorigen he tolde hym als;
How looth hire was to been a wikked wyf,
And that she levere had lost that day hir lyf, 1600
And that hir trouthe she swoor thurgh innocence,
She nevere erst hadde herde speke of apparence.
"That made me han of hire so greet pitee;
And right as frely as he sente hire me,
As frely sente I hire to hym ageyn.   1605
This al and som; ther is namoore to seyn."
    This philosophre answerde, "Leeve brother,
Everich of yow dide gentilly til oother.
Thou art a squier, and he is a knyght;
But God forbede, for his blisful myght,   1610
But if a clerk koude doon a gentil dede
As wel as any of yow, it is no drede!

1524 **franchise:** nobility of character
1529 **him were levere:** he would rather
1533 **relesse:** release, set free
1534 **serement:** oath, pledge
1537 **plighte:** pledge
1544 **withouten drede:** doubtless
1547 **sayd:** say
1548 **apayd:** satisfied
1557 **forlorn:** forfeited
1560 **pured:** refined   **wighte:** weight

1575 **dayes of the remenaunt:** additional time to pay the balance
1580 **a-begged:** a-begging   **kirtle:** tunic
1582 **respiten me:** grant me a respite, additional time
1602 **apparence:** illusion
1606 **al and som:** the entire matter

"Sire, I releesse thee thy thousand pound,
As thou right now were cropen out of the ground,
Ne nevere er now ne haddest knowen me.   1615
For, sire, I wol nat taken a peny of thee
For al my craft, ne noght for my travaille.
Thou hast ypayed wel for my vitaille.

It is ynogh, and farewel, have good day!"
And took his hors, and forth he goth his way.   1620
Lordynges, this question, thanne, wol I aske now,
Which was the mooste fre, as thynketh yow?
Now telleth me, er that ye ferther wende.
I kan namoore; my tale is at an ende.

Heere is ended the Frankeleyns Tale.

1613 **releesse thee:** set you free from
1614 **cropen:** crept

The Physician's Tale

Heere folweth the Phisiciens Tale.

Ther was, as telleth Titus Livius,
A knyght that called was Virginius,
Fulfild of honour and of worthynesse,
And strong of freendes, and of greet richesse.
This knyght a doghter hadde by his wyf; 5
No children hadde he mo in al his lyf.
Fair was this mayde in excellent beautee
Aboven every wight that man may see;
For Nature hath with sovereyn diligence
Yformed hire in so greet excellence, 10
As though she wolde seyn, "Lo! I, Nature,
Thus kan I forme and peynte a creature,
Whan that me list; who kan me countrefete?
Pigmalion noght, though he ay forge and bete,
Or grave, or peynte; for I dar wel seyn 15
Apelles, Zanzis, sholde werche in veyn
Outher to grave, or peynte, or forge, or bete,
If they presumed me to countrefete.
For He that is the formere principal
Hath maked me his vicaire general, 20
To forme and peynten erthely creaturis
Right as me list, and ech thyng in my cure is
Under the moone, that may wane and waxe,
And for my werk right no thyng wol I axe;
My lord and I been ful of oon accord. 25
I made hire to the worshipe of my lord;
So do I alle myne othere creatures,
What colour that they han or what figures."
Thus semeth me that Nature wolde seye.
This mayde of age twelve yeer was and tweye, 30
In which that Nature hadde swich delit.
For right as she kan peynte a lilie whit,
And reed a rose, right with swich peynture
She peynted hath this noble creature,
Er she were born, upon hir lymes fre, 35
Where as by right swiche colours sholde be;

And Phebus dyed hath hire tresses grete
Lyk to the stremes of his burned heete.
And if that excellent was hire beautee,
A thousand foold moore vertuous was she. 40
In hire ne lakked no condicioun
That is to preyse, as by discrecioun.
As wel in goost as body chast was she,
For which she floured in virginitee
With alle humylitee and abstinence, 45
With alle attemperaunce and pacience,
With mesure eek of beryng and array.
Discreet she was in answeryng alway;
Though she were wis as Pallas, dar I seyn,
Hir facound eek ful wommanly and pleyn, 50
No countrefeted termes hadde she
To seme wys, but after hir degree
She spak, and alle hire wordes, moore and lesse,
Sownynge in vertu and in gentillesse.
Shamefast she was in maydens shamefastnesse, 55
Constant in herte, and evere in bisynesse
To dryve hire out of ydel slogardye.
Bacus hadde of hir mouth right no maistrie;
For wyn and youthe dooth Venus encresse,
As men in fyr wol casten oille or greesse. 60
And of hir owene vertu, unconstreyned,
She hath ful ofte tyme syk hire feyned,
For that she wolde fleen the compaignye
Where likly was to treten of folye,
As is at feestes, revels, and at daunces, 65
That been occasions of daliaunces.
Swich thynges maken children for to be
To soone rype and boold, as men may se,

37 **Phebus:** Phoebus Apollo, the sun
38 **burned heete:** burnished heat (rays of the sun)
42 **as by discrecioun:** concerning moral discernment
43 **goost:** spirit
46 **attemperaunce:** temperance, moderation
47 **mesure:** moderation   **beryng:** bearing, demeanor
49 **Pallas:** Pallas Athena, goddess of wisdom
50 **facound:** way of speaking
54 **Sownynge:** conducing to
55 **Shamefast:** modest
57 **slogardye:** sluggishness, laziness
58 **Bacus:** Bacchus, god of wine
59 **Venus:** i.e., sexual desire
64 **treten of:** speak about

1 **Titus Livius:** Livy, the Roman historian
14 **Pigmalion:** the famous Greek sculptor
15 **grave:** carve
16 **Apelles:** legendary sculptor of the tomb of Darius the Great   **Zanzis:** Zeuxis, an Athenian artist
20 **vicaire general:** chief deputy
25 **ful of oon accord:** completely in accord
33 **peynture:** painting, coloration

Which is ful perilous and hath been yoore.
For al to soone may she lerne loore   70
Of booldnesse, whan she woxen is a wyf.
    And ye maistresses, in youre olde lyf,
That lordes doghtres han in governaunce,
Ne taketh of my wordes no displesaunce.
Thenketh that ye been set in governynges   75
Of lordes doghtres oonly for two thynges:
Outher for ye han kept youre honestee,
Or elles ye han falle in freletee,
And knowen wel ynough the olde daunce,
And han forsaken fully swich meschaunce   80
For everemo; therfore, for Cristes sake,
To teche hem vertu looke that ye ne slake.
    A theef of venysoun, that hath forlaft
His likerousnesse and al his olde craft,
Kan kepe a forest best of any man.   85
Now kepeth wel, for if ye wole, ye kan.
Looke wel that ye unto no vice assente,
Lest ye be dampned for youre wikke entente;
For whoso dooth, a traitour is, certeyn.
And taketh kep of that that I shal seyn: 90
Of alle tresons sovereyn pestilence
Is whan a wight bitrayseth innocence.
    Ye fadres and ye moodres eek also,
Though ye han children, be it oon or mo,
Youre is the charge of al hir surveiaunce,   95
Whil that they been under youre governaunce.
Beth war, if by ensample of youre lyvynge,
Or by youre necligence in chastisynge,
That they ne perisse; for I dar wel seye
If that they doon, ye shul it deere abeye.   100
Under a shepherde softe and necligent
The wolf hath many a sheep and lamb torent.
Suffiseth oon ensample now as heere,
For I moot turne agayn to my matere.
    This mayde, of which I wol this tale expresse,   105
So kepte hirself hir neded no maistresse,
For in hir lyvyng maydens myghten rede,
As in a book, every good word or dede

That longeth to a mayden vertuous,
She was so prudent and so bountevous.   110
For which the fame out sprong on every syde,
Bothe of hir beautee and hir bountee wyde,
That thurgh that land they preised hire echone
That loved vertu, save Envye allone,
That sory is of oother mennes wele   115
And glad is of his sorwe and his unheele.
(The Doctour maketh this descripcioun.)
    This mayde upon a day wente in the toun
Toward a temple, with hire mooder deere,
As is of yonge maydens the manere.   120
Now was ther thanne a justice in that toun,
That governour was of that regioun.
And so bifel this juge his eyen caste
Upon this mayde, avysynge hym ful faste,
As she cam forby ther as this juge stood.   125
Anon his herte chaunged and his mood,
So was he caught with beautee of this mayde,
And to hymself ful pryvely he sayde,
"This mayde shal be myn, for any man!"
    Anon the feend into his herte ran,   130
And taughte hym sodeynly that he by slyghte
The mayden to his purpos wynne myghte.
For certes, by no force ne by no meede,
Hym thoughte, he was nat able for to speede;
For she was strong of freendes, and eek she   135
Confermed was in swich soverayn bountee
That wel he wiste he myghte hire nevere wynne
As for to make hire with hir body synne.
For which, by greet deliberacioun,
He sente after a cherl, was in the toun,   140
Which that he knew for subtil and for boold.
This juge unto this cherl his tale hath toold
In secree wise, and made hym to ensure
He sholde telle it to no creature,
And if he dide, he sholde lese his heed.   145
Whan that assented was this cursed reed,
Glad was this juge, and maked him greet cheere,
And yaf hym yiftes preciouse and deere.
    Whan shapen was al hire conspiracie
Fro point to point, how that his lecherie   150
Parfourned sholde been ful subtilly,

71 **woxen is:** has become
72 **maistresses:** governesses
74 **taketh . . . no displesaunce:** do not take offense
77 **honestee:** chastity
78 **freletee:** frailty
79 **olde daunce:** tricks of the trade, game of love
80 **meschaunce:** misconduct
82 **slake:** be slack, desist
83 **venysoun:** game, venison   **forlaft:** abandoned
84 **likerousnesse:** greedy appetite
86 **kepeth wel:** take good care
91 **sovereyn pestilence:** the supreme wickedness
92 **bitrayseth:** betrays
95 **surveiaunce:** surveillance (protection)
99 **perisse:** perish
100 **it deere abeye:** pay dearly for it
102 **torent:** torn to pieces

110 **bountevous:** full of goodness
116 **unheele:** misery
117 **The Doctour:** St. Augustine
125 **forby ther as:** past where
129 **for:** despite
131 **slyghte:** trickery
143 **ensure:** assure, give assurance
147 **maked him greet cheere:** was very friendly to him
151 **Parfourned:** performed, accomplished

As ye shul heere it after openly,
Hoom gooth the cherl, that highte Claudius.
This false juge, that highte Apius,
(So was his name, for this is no fable,   155
But knowen for historial thyng notable;
The sentence of it sooth is, out of doute),
This false juge gooth now faste aboute
To hasten his delit al that he may.
And so bifel soone after, on a day,   160
This false juge, as telleth us the storie,
As he was wont, sat in his consistorie,
And yaf his doomes upon sondry cas.
This false cherl cam forth a ful greet pas,
And seyde, "Lord, if that it be youre wille,   165
As dooth me right upon this pitous bille,
In which I pleyne upon Virginius;
And if that he wol seyn it is nat thus,
I wol it preeve, and fynde good witnesse,
That sooth is that my bille wol expresse."   170
    The juge answerde, "Of this, in his absence,
I may nat yeve diffynytyf sentence.
Lat do hym calle, and I wol gladly heere;
Thou shalt have al right, and no wrong heere."
    Virginius cam to wite the juges wille,   175
And right anon was rad this cursed bille;
The sentence of it was as ye shul heere:
    "To yow, my lord, sire Apius so deere,
Sheweth youre povre servant Claudius
How that a knyght, called Virginius,   180
Agayns the lawe, agayn al equitee,
Holdeth, expres agayn the wyl of me,
My servant, which that is my thral by right,
Which fro myn hous was stole upon a nyght,
Whil that she was ful yong; this wol I preeve   185
By witnesse, lord, so that it nat yow greeve.
She nys his doghter nat, what so he seye.
Wherfore to yow, my lord the juge, I preye,
Yeld me my thral, if that it be youre wille."
Lo, this was al the sentence of his bille.   190
    Virginius gan upon the cherl biholde,
But hastily, er he his tale tolde,
And wolde have preeved it as sholde a knyght,

And eek by witnessyng of many a wight,
That al was fals that seyde his adversarie,   195
This cursed juge wolde no thyng tarie,
Ne heere a word moore of Virginius,
But yaf his juggement, and seyde thus:
    "I deeme anon this cherl his servant have;
Thou shalt no lenger in thyn hous hir save.   200
Go bryng hire forth, and put hire in oure warde.
The cherl shal have his thral, this I awarde."
    And whan this worthy knyght Virginius
Thurgh sentence of this justice Apius
Moste by force his deere doghter yiven   205
Unto the juge, in lecherie to lyven,
He gooth hym hoom, and sette him in his halle,
And leet anon his deere doghter calle,
And with a face deed as asshen colde
Upon hir humble face he gan biholde,   210
With fadres pitee stikynge thurgh his herte,
Al wolde he from his purpos nat converte.
    "Doghter," quod he, "Virginia, by thy name,
Ther been two weyes, outher deeth or shame,
That thou most suffre; allas, that I was bore!   215
For nevere thou deservedest wherfore
To dyen with a swerd or with a knyf.
O deere doghter, endere of my lyf,
Which I have fostred up with swich plesaunce
That thou were nevere out of my remembraunce!   220
O doghter, which that art my laste wo,
And in my lyf my laste joye also,
O gemme of chastitee, in pacience
Take thou thy deeth, for this is my sentence.
For love, and nat for hate, thou most be deed;   225
My pitous hand moot smyten of thyn heed.
Allas, that evere Apius the say!
Thus hath he falsly jugged the to-day"—
And tolde hire al the cas, as ye bifore
Han herd; nat nedeth for to telle it moore.   230
    "O mercy, deere fader!" quod this mayde,
And with that word she bothe hir armes layde
Aboute his nekke, as she was wont to do.
The teeris bruste out of hir eyen two,
And seyde, "Goode fader, shal I dye?   235
Is ther no grace, is ther no remedye?"
    "No, certes, deere doghter myn," quod he.
    "Thanne yif me leyser, fader myn," quod she,
"My deeth for to compleyne a litel space;

155 **fable:** fiction
156 **historial:** historical
162 **consistorie:** court
163 **doomes:** judgments, decisions
164 **ful greet pas:** at a rapid pace, hurriedly
166 **As dooth me right:** do justice for me **bille:** formal charge
167 **pleyne upon:** make complaint against
173 **Lat do hym calle:** have him called
176 **rad:** read
182 **expres agayn:** clearly against
183 **thral:** servant, slave
189 **Yeld:** give back
193 **as sholde a knyght:** i.e., in a trial by battle

194 **witnessyng:** testimony
200 **save:** keep
201 **warde:** custody
208 **leet . . . calle:** had . . . called
221 **laste:** greatest
227 **the say:** saw you

For, pardee, Jepte yaf his doghter grace   240
For to compleyne, er he hir slow, allas!
And, God it woot, no thyng was hir trespas,
But for she ran hir fader first to see,
To welcome hym with greet solempnitee."
And with that word she fil aswowne anon,   245
And after, whan hir swownyng is agon,
She riseth up, and to hir fader sayde,
"Blissed be God that I shal dye a mayde!
Yif me my deeth, er that I have a shame;
Dooth with youre child youre wyl, a Goddes name!"
    And with that word she preyed hym ful ofte   251
That with his swerd he wolde smyte softe;
And with that word aswowne doun she fil.
Hir fader, with ful sorweful herte and wil,
Hir heed of smoot, and by the top it hente,   255
And to the juge he gan it to presente,
As he sat yet in doom in consistorie.
And whan the juge it saugh, as seith the storie,
He bad to take hym and anhange hym faste;
But right anon a thousand peple in thraste,   260
To save the knyght, for routhe and for pitee,
For knowen was the false iniquitee.
The peple anon had suspect in this thyng,

By manere of the cherles chalangyng,
That it was by the assent of Apius;   265
They wisten wel that he was lecherus.
For which unto this Apius they gon
And caste hym in a prisoun right anon,
Ther as he slow hymself; and Claudius,
That servant was unto this Apius,   270
Was demed for to hange upon a tree,
But that Virginius, of his pitee,
So preyde for hym that he was exiled;
And elles, certes, he had been bigyled.
The remenant were anhanged, moore and lesse,   275
That were consentant of this cursednesse.
    Heere may men seen how synne hath his merite.
Beth war, for no man woot whom God wol smyte
In no degree, ne in which manere wyse;
The worm of conscience may agryse   280
Of wikked lyf, though it so pryvee be
That no man woot therof but God and he.
For be he lewed man, or ellis lered,
He noot how soone that he shal been afered.
Therfore I rede yow this conseil take: 285
Forsaketh synne, er synne yow forsake.

Heere is ended the Phisiciens Tale.

The Introduction to the Pardoner's Tale

The wordes of the Hoost to the Phisicien and the Pardoner.

Oure Hooste gan to swere as he were wood;
"Harrow!" quod he, "by nayles and by blood!
This was a fals cherl and a fals justise.
As shameful deeth as herte may devyse   290
Come to thise juges and hire advocatz!
Algate this sely mayde is slayn, allas!
Allas, to deere boughte she beautee!

Wherfore I seye al day that men may see
That yiftes of Fortune and of Nature   295
Been cause of deeth to many a creature.
Hire beautee was hire deth, I dar wel sayn.
Allas, so pitously as she was slayn!
Of bothe yiftes that I speke of now
Men han ful ofte moore for harm than prow.   300
But trewely, myn owene maister deere,

---

240 **Jepte:** the biblical Jephtha; see n.
257 **in doom in consistorie:** giving judgment in court
259 **anhange:** hang
260 **in thraste:** thrust, pushed in
263 **suspect:** suspicions

287 **wood:** mad
288 "Alas," said he, "by the nails and blood of Christ!"
292 **Algate:** at any rate

264 **By manere of:** by reason of   **chalangyng:** claim
274 **bigyled:** betrayed (i.e., killed)
277 **merite:** reward
280 **agryse:** tremble for fear
285 **rede:** advise

300 **prow:** profit, benefit

This is a pitous tale for to heere.
But nathelees, passe over; is no fors.
I pray to God so save thy gentil cors,
And eek thyne urynals and thy jurdones,　305
Thyn ypocras, and eek thy galiones,
And every boyste ful of thy letuarie;
God blesse hem, and oure lady Seinte Marie!
So moot I theen, thou art a propre man,
And lyk a prelat, by Seint Ronyan!　310
Seyde I nat wel? I kan nat speke in terme;
But wel I woot thou doost myn herte to erme,
That I almoost have caught a cardynacle.
By corpus bones! but I have triacle,
Or elles a draughte of moyste and corny ale,　315

Or but I heere anon a myrie tale,
Myn herte is lost for pitee of this mayde.
Thou beel amy, thou Pardoner," he sayde,
"Telle us som myrthe or japes right anon."
　"It shal be doon," quod he, "by Seint Ronyon!　320
But first," quod he, "heere at this alestake
I wol bothe drynke and eten of a cake."
　But right anon thise gentils gonne to crye,
"Nay, lat hym telle us of no ribaudye!
Telle us som moral thyng, that we may leere　325
Som wit, and thanne wol we gladly heere."
　"I graunte, ywis," quod he, "but I moot thynke
Upon som honest thyng while that I drynke."

The Pardoner's Prologue

Heere folweth the Prologe of the Pardoners Tale.

Radix malorum est Cupiditas: Ad Thimotheum, 6°.

　"Lordynges," quod he, "in chirches whan I preche,
I peyne me to han an hauteyn speche,　330
And rynge it out as round as gooth a belle,
For I kan al by rote that I telle.
My theme is alwey oon, and evere was—
Radix malorum est Cupiditas.
　"First I pronounce whennes that I come,　335
And thanne my bulles shewe I, alle and some.
Oure lige lordes seel on my patente,

That shewe I first, my body to warente,
That no man be so boold, ne preest ne clerk,
Me to destourbe of Cristes hooly werk.　340
And after that thanne telle I forth my tales;
Bulles of popes and of cardynales,
Of patriarkes and bishopes I shewe,
And in Latyn I speke a wordes fewe,
To saffron with my predicacioun,　345
And for to stire hem to devocioun.
Thanne shewe I forth my longe cristal stones,
Ycrammed ful of cloutes and of bones—
Relikes been they, as wenen they echoon.
Thanne have I in latoun a sholder-boon　350
Which that was of an hooly Jewes sheep.
'Goode men,' I seye, 'taak of my wordes keep;
If that this boon be wasshe in any welle,
If cow, or calf, or sheep, or oxe swelle
That any worm hath ete, or worm ystonge,　355

303 **passe over:** let it be　**is no fors:** it does not matter
305 **urynals:** vessels for analyzing urine　**jurdones:** glass vessels used by physicians
306 **ypocras, galiones:** medicinal drinks named after Hippocrates and Galen, ancient medical authorities
307 **boyste:** container　**letuarie:** medicine
309 **theen:** prosper
310 **Seint Ronyan:** probably St. Ronan, a Scottish saint
311 **in terme:** in technical language
312 **erme:** grieve
313 **cardynacle:** probably the Host's error for *cardiacle,* heart attack
314 **By corpus bones!:** by God's bones!　**triacle:** medicine
315 **moyste:** fresh, new　**corny:** malty, strong

Radix malorum, *etc.:* Greed is the root of [all] evils, 1 Timothy 6.10
330 **hauteyn:** impressive, loud
332 **by rote:** by heart
333 **theme:** biblical text for a sermon
336 **bulles:** papal bulls (here indulgences)
337 **lige lordes seel:** seal of our liege lord (the bishop)　**patente:** letter patent (authorizing his sale of pardons)

318 **beel amy:** fair friend (perhaps used derisively)
321 **alestake:** pole hung with a garland, the sign of an alehouse
322 **cake:** loaf of bread
324 **ribaudye:** ribaldry, coarse jesting

338 **warente:** protect
345 **saffron:** flavor with saffron, season　**predicacioun:** sermon
347 **cristal stones:** glass cases; cf. GP I.700.
348 **cloutes:** rags
350 **in latoun:** mounted in latten, a brass-like alloy
355 **worm:** snake

Taak water of that welle and wassh his tonge,
And it is hool anon; and forthermoore,
Of pokkes and of scabbe, and every soore
Shal every sheep be hool that of this welle
Drynketh a draughte. Taak kep eek what I telle: 360
If that the good-man that the beestes oweth
Wol every wyke, er that the cok hym croweth,
Fastynge, drynken of this welle a draughte,
As thilke hooly Jew oure eldres taughte,
His beestes and his stoor shal multiplie.   365
    'And, sires, also it heeleth jalousie;
For though a man be falle in jalous rage,
Lat maken with this water his potage,
And nevere shal he moore his wyf mystriste,
Though he the soothe of hir defaute wiste,   370
Al had she taken prestes two or thre.
    'Heere is a miteyn eek, that ye may se.
He that his hand wol putte in this mitayn,
He shal have multipliyng of his grayn,
Whan he hath sowen, be it whete or otes,   375
So that he offre pens, or elles grotes.
    'Goode men and wommen, o thyng warne I yow:
If any wight be in this chirche now
That hath doon synne horrible, that he
Dar nat, for shame, of it yshryven be,   380
Or any womman, be she yong or old,
That hath ymaked hir housbonde cokewold,
Swich folk shal have no power ne no grace
To offren to my relikes in this place.
And whoso fyndeth hym out of swich blame,   385
He wol come up and offre a Goddes name,
And I assoille him by the auctoritee
Which that by bulle ygraunted was to me.'
    "By this gaude have I wonne, yeer by yeer,
An hundred mark sith I was pardoner.   390
I stonde lyk a clerk in my pulpet,
And whan the lewed peple is doun yset,
I preche so as ye han herd bifoore
And telle an hundred false japes moore.
Thanne peyne I me to strecche forth the nekke,   395
And est and west upon the peple I bekke,
As dooth a dowve sittynge on a berne.

Myne handes and my tonge goon so yerne
That it is joye to se my bisynesse.
Of avarice and of swich cursednesse   400
Is al my prechyng, for to make hem free
To yeven hir pens, and namely unto me.
For myn entente is nat but for to wynne,
And nothyng for correccioun of synne.
I rekke nevere, whan that they been beryed,   405
Though that hir soules goon a-blakeberyed!
For certes, many a predicacioun
Comth ofte tyme of yvel entencioun;
Som for plesance of folk and flaterye,
To been avaunced by ypocrisye,   410
And som for veyne glorie, and som for hate.
For whan I dar noon oother weyes debate,
Thanne wol I stynge hym with my tonge smerte
In prechyng, so that he shal nat asterte
To been defamed falsly, if that he   415
Hath trespased to my bretheren or to me.
For though I telle noght his propre name,
Men shal wel knowe that it is the same,
By signes, and by othere circumstances.
Thus quyte I folk that doon us displesances;   420
Thus spitte I out my venym under hewe
Of hoolynesse, to semen hooly and trewe.
    "But shortly myn entente I wol devyse:
I preche of no thyng but for coveityse.
Therfore my theme is yet, and evere was,   425
Radix malorum est Cupiditas.
Thus kan I preche agayn that same vice
Which that I use, and that is avarice.
But though myself be gilty in that synne,
Yet kan I maken oother folk to twynne   430
From avarice and soore to repente.
But that is nat my principal entente;
I preche nothyng but for coveitise.
Of this mateere it oghte ynogh suffise.
    "Thanne telle I hem ensamples many oon   435
Of olde stories longe tyme agoon.
For lewed peple loven tales olde;
Swiche thynges kan they wel reporte and holde.
What, trowe ye, that whiles I may preche,
And wynne gold and silver for I teche,   440

---

358 **pokkes:** pocks, pustules
361 **good-man:** goodman, head of the household   **oweth:** owns
365 **stoor:** stock, possessions
368 **potage:** soup
370 **defaute:** misdeed
372 **miteyn:** mitten
375 **otes:** oats
376 **pens:** pence, pennies   **grotes:** groats, silver coins worth four pence
380 **yshryven:** confessed and forgiven
387 **assoille:** absolve
389 **gaude:** trick
390 **hundred mark:** about sixty-six pounds
396 **bekke:** nod
397 **berne:** barn

398 **yerne:** quickly
405 **beryed:** buried
406 **goon a-blakeberyed:** go blackberry picking
414 **asterte:** escape
420 **quyte:** pay back (revenge)   **doon us displesances:** make trouble for us (pardoners)
421 **hewe:** pretense
424 **coveityse:** greed
427 **agayn:** against
430 **twynne:** depart, turn away from
435 **ensamples:** exempla, illustrative anecdotes
437 **lewed:** ignorant, unlearned

That I wol lyve in poverte wilfully?
Nay, nay, I thoghte it nevere, trewely!
For I wol preche and begge in sondry landes;
I wol nat do no labour with myne handes,
Ne make baskettes and lyve therby,   445
By cause I wol nat beggen ydelly.
I wol noon of the apostles countrefete;
I wol have moneie, wolle, chese, and whete,
Al were it yeven of the povereste page,
Or of the povereste wydwe in a village,   450
Al sholde hir children sterve for famyne.

Nay, I wol drynke licour of the vyne
And have a joly wenche in every toun.
But herkneth, lordynges, in conclusioun:
Youre likyng is that I shal telle a tale.   455
Now have I dronke a draughte of corny ale,
By God, I hope I shal yow telle a thyng
That shal by reson been at youre likyng.
For though myself be a ful vicious man,
A moral tale yet I yow telle kan,   460
Which I am wont to preche for to wynne.
Now hoold youre pees! My tale I wol bigynne."

The Pardoner's Tale

Heere bigynneth the Pardoners Tale.

In Flaundres whilom was a compaignye
Of yonge folk that haunteden folye,
As riot, hasard, stywes, and tavernes,   465
Where as with harpes, lutes, and gyternes,
They daunce and pleyen at dees bothe day and nyght,
And eten also and drynken over hir myght,
Thurgh which they doon the devel sacrifise
Withinne that develes temple in cursed wise   470
By superfluytee abhomynable.
Hir othes been so grete and so dampnable
That it is grisly for to heere hem swere.
Oure blissed Lordes body they totere—
Hem thoughte that Jewes rente hym noght ynough—
And ech of hem at otheres synne lough.   476
And right anon thanne comen tombesteres
Fetys and smale, and yonge frutesteres,
Syngeres with harpes, baudes, wafereres,
Whiche been the verray develes officeres   480
To kyndle and blowe the fyr of lecherye,
That is annexed unto glotonye.

The hooly writ take I to my witnesse
That luxurie is in wyn and dronkenesse.
   Lo, how that dronken Looth, unkyndely,   485
Lay by his doghtres two, unwityngly;
So dronke he was, he nyste what he wroghte.
   Herodes, whoso wel the stories soghte,
Whan he of wyn was repleet at his feeste,
Right at his owene table he yaf his heeste   490
To sleen the Baptist John, ful giltelees.
   Senec seith a good word doutelees;
He seith he kan no difference fynde
Bitwix a man that is out of his mynde
And a man which that is dronkelewe,   495
But that woodnesse, yfallen in a shrewe,
Persevereth lenger than doth dronkenesse.
O glotonye, ful of cursednesse!
O cause first of oure confusioun!
O original of oure dampnacioun,   500
Til Crist hadde boght us with his blood agayn!
Lo, how deere, shortly for to sayn,
Aboght was thilke cursed vileynye!
Corrupt was al this world for glotonye.

441 **in poverte wilfully:** in voluntary poverty (like a monk)
446 **ydelly:** in vain
448 **wolle:** wool
449 **povereste:** poorest

464 **haunteden:** made a habit of
465 **riot:** debauchery   **hasard:** dicing   **stywes:** brothels
466 **gyternes:** citterns (guitar-like instruments)
467 **dees:** dice
474 **totere:** tear in pieces
476 **lough:** laughed
477 **tombesteres:** dancing girls
478 **Fetys:** elegantly shaped   **smale:** slim   **frutesteres:** girls who sell fruit
479 **wafereres:** sellers of wafers

456 **corny:** malty, strong

483 **hooly writ:** the Bible
484 **luxurie:** lechery
485 **Looth:** Lot   **unkyndely:** unnaturally
486 **unwityngly:** unknowingly
487 **nyste** = *ne wiste*, did not know
488 **Herodes:** Herod   **stories:** histories (or possibly the gospel narratives in Matthew 14 and Mark 6)
489 **repleet:** filled
492 **Senec:** Seneca
495 **dronkelewe:** addicted to drink
497 **Persevereth:** lasts
499 **confusioun:** ruin

Adam oure fader, and his wyf also, 505
Fro Paradys to labour and to wo
Were dryven for that vice, it is no drede.
For whil that Adam fasted, as I rede,
He was in Paradys; and whan that he
Eet of the fruyt deffended on the tree, 510
Anon he was out cast to wo and peyne.
O glotonye, on thee wel oghte us pleyne!
O, wiste a man how manye maladyes
Folwen of excesse and of glotonyes,
He wolde been the moore mesurable 515
Of his diete, sittynge at his table.
Allas, the shorte throte, the tendre mouth,
Maketh that est and west and north and south,
In erthe, in eir, in water, men to swynke
To gete a glotoun deyntee mete and drynke! 520
Of this matiere, O Paul, wel kanstow trete:
"Mete unto wombe, and wombe eek unto mete,
Shal God destroyen bothe," as Paulus seith.
Allas, a foul thyng is it, by my feith,
To seye this word, and fouler is the dede, 525
Whan man so drynketh of the white and rede
That of his throte he maketh his pryvee
Thurgh thilke cursed superfluitee.
  The apostel wepyng seith ful pitously,
"Ther walken manye of whiche yow toold have I—
I seye it now wepyng, with pitous voys— 531
They been enemys of Cristes croys,
Of whiche the ende is deeth; wombe is hir god!"
O wombe! O bely! O stynkyng cod,
Fulfilled of dong and of corrupcioun! 535
At either ende of thee foul is the soun.
How greet labour and cost is thee to fynde!
Thise cookes, how they stampe, and streyne, and
      grynde,
And turnen substaunce into accident
To fulfille al thy likerous talent! 540
Out of the harde bones knokke they
The mary, for they caste noght awey
That may go thurgh the golet softe and swoote.

Of spicerie of leef, and bark, and roote
Shal been his sauce ymaked by delit, 545
To make hym yet a newer appetit.
But, certes, he that haunteth swiche delices
Is deed, whil that he lyveth in tho vices.
  A lecherous thyng is wyn, and dronkenesse
Is ful of stryvyng and of wrecchednesse. 550
O dronke man, disfigured is thy face,
Sour is thy breeth, foul artow to embrace,
And thurgh thy dronke nose semeth the soun
As though thou seydest ay "Sampsoun,
      Sampsoun!"
And yet, God woot, Sampsoun drank nevere no wyn.
Thou fallest as it were a styked swyn; 556
Thy tonge is lost, and al thyn honeste cure,
For dronkenesse is verray sepulture
Of mannes wit and his discrecioun.
In whom that drynke hath dominacioun 560
He kan no conseil kepe; it is no drede.
Now kepe yow fro the white and fro the rede,
And namely fro the white wyn of Lepe
That is to selle in Fysshstrete or in Chepe.
This wyn of Spaigne crepeth subtilly 565
In othere wynes, growynge faste by,
Of which ther ryseth swich fumositee
That whan a man hath dronken draughtes thre,
And weneth that he be at hoom in Chepe,
He is in Spaigne, right at the toune of Lepe— 570
Nat at the Rochele, ne at Burdeux toun—
And thanne wol he seye "Sampsoun, Sampsoun!"
  But herkneth, lordynges, o word, I yow preye,
That alle the sovereyn actes, dar I seye,
Of victories in the Olde Testament, 575
Thurgh verray God, that is omnipotent,
Were doon in abstinence and in preyere.
Looketh the Bible, and ther ye may it leere.
  Looke, Attilla, the grete conquerour,
Deyde in his sleep, with shame and dishonour, 580
Bledynge ay at his nose in dronkenesse.
A capitayn sholde lyve in sobrenesse.
And over al this, avyseth yow right wel

510 **deffended:** forbidden
515 **mesurable:** temperate
519 **swynke:** labor
521 **Paul:** St. Paul the apostle   **trete:** treat, discuss
522 **wombe:** belly
526 **white and rede:** wines
529 **The apostel:** St. Paul
534 **cod:** bag, belly
535 **corrupcioun:** decayed matter
537 **thee to fynde:** to provide food for you
538 **stampe:** pound
539 **substaunce into accident:** the inner reality into the outward appearance
540 **likerous:** greedy   **talent:** desire, inclination
542 **mary:** marrow
543 **golet:** gullet   **swoote:** sweet

545 **by:** for
547 **delices:** delicacies
550 **stryvyng:** strife, quarrelling
554 **Sampsoun:** Samson (cf. VII.2055)
556 **styked swyn:** stuck pig
557 **honeste cure:** care for decency, self-respect
563 **Lepe:** wine-growing district in Spain
564 **Fysshstrete, Chepe:** streets in London
567 **fumositee:** vapors (rising from the stomach to the head)
571 **Rochele, Burdeux toun:** La Rochelle, Bordeaux, wine-growing districts in France
579 **Attilla:** king of the Huns
582 **sobrenesse:** sobriety

What was comaunded unto Lamuel—
Nat Samuel, but Lamuel, seye I;   585
Redeth the Bible, and fynde it expresly
Of wyn-yevyng to hem that han justise.
Namoore of this, for it may wel suffise.
   And now that I have spoken of glotonye,
Now wol I yow deffenden hasardrye.   590
Hasard is verray mooder of lesynges,
And of deceite, and cursed forswerynges,
Blaspheme of Crist, manslaughtre, and wast also
Of catel and of tyme; and forthermo,
It is repreeve and contrarie of honour   595
For to ben holde a commune hasardour.
And ever the hyer he is of estaat,
The moore is he yholden desolaat.
If that a prynce useth hasardrye,
In alle governaunce and policye   600
He is, as by commune opinioun,
Yholde the lasse in reputacioun.
   Stilboun, that was a wys embassadour,
Was sent to Corynthe in ful greet honour
Fro Lacidomye to make hire alliaunce.   605
And whan he cam, hym happede, par chaunce,
That alle the gretteste that were of that lond,
Pleyynge atte hasard he hem fond.
For which, as soone as it myghte be,
He stal hym hoom agayn to his contree,   610
And seyde, "Ther wol I nat lese my name,
Ne I wol nat take on me so greet defame,
Yow for to allie unto none hasardours.
Sendeth othere wise embassadours;
For, by my trouthe, me were levere dye   615
Than I yow sholde to hasardours allye.
For ye, that been so glorious in honours,
Shul nat allyen yow with hasardours
As by my wyl, ne as by my tretee."
This wise philosophre, thus seyde hee.   620
   Looke eek that to the kyng Demetrius
The kyng of Parthes, as the book seith us,
Sente him a paire of dees of gold in scorn,
For he hadde used hasard ther-biforn;
For which he heeld his glorie or his renoun   625
At no value or reputacioun.

Lordes may fynden oother maner pley
Honest ynough to dryve the day awey.
   Now wol I speke of othes false and grete
A word or two, as olde bookes trete.   630
Gret sweryng is a thyng abhominable,
And fals sweryng is yet moore reprevable.
The heighe God forbad sweryng at al,
Witnesse on Mathew; but in special
Of sweryng seith the hooly Jeremye,   635
"Thou shalt swere sooth thyne othes, and nat lye,
And swere in doom and eek in rightwisnesse";
But ydel sweryng is a cursednesse.
Bihoold and se that in the firste table
Of heighe Goddes heestes honurable,   640
Hou that the seconde heeste of hym is this:
"Take nat my name in ydel or amys."
Lo, rather he forbedeth swich sweryng
Than homycide or many a cursed thyng;
I seye that, as by ordre, thus it stondeth;   645
This knoweth, that his heestes understondeth,
How that the seconde heeste of God is that.
And forther over, I wol thee telle al plat
That vengeance shal nat parten from his hous
That of his othes is to outrageous.   650
"By Goddes precious herte," and "By his nayles,"
And "By the blood of Crist that is in Hayles,
Sevene is my chaunce, and thyn is cynk and treye!"
"By Goddes armes, if thou falsly pleye,
This daggere shal thurghout thyn herte go!"—   655
This fruyt cometh of the bicched bones two,
Forsweryng, ire, falsnesse, homycide.
Now, for the love of Crist, that for us dyde,
Lete youre othes, bothe grete and smale.
But, sires, now wol I telle forth my tale.   660
   Thise riotoures thre of whiche I telle,
Longe erst er prime rong of any belle,

---

584 **Lamuel:** Lemuel, biblical king of Massa
587 **wyn-yevyng:** giving wine   **justise:** the duty of rendering justice
590 **deffenden:** forbid   **hasardrye:** gambling
591 **Hasard:** dicing   **lesynges:** lies
592 **forswerynges:** perjuries
594 **catel:** property
603 **Stilboun:** possibly the Greek philosopher Stilbo
604 **Corynthe:** Corinth, a Peloponnesian city noted for luxury
605 **Lacidomye:** Lacedaemon, Sparta
622 **Parthes:** Parthia, northern Persia

631 **Gret sweryng:** frequent swearing
632 **reprevable:** blameworthy
634 **Mathew:** St. Matthew
635 **Jeremye:** Jeremiah the prophet
637 **rightwisnesse:** justice
638 **ydel sweryng:** profanity
639 **firste table:** the first three commandments
641 **seconde heeste:** second commandment
643 **rather:** earlier (in the ten commandments)
646 **that:** he who
648 **forther over:** furthermore   **al plat:** flatly
650 **outrageous:** excessive
651 **nayles:** nails
652 **Hayles:** Hales Abbey in Gloucestershire
653 **chaunce:** a call in dicing (the number the shooter is trying to roll)   **cynk:** five
treye: three
656 **bicched bones:** cursed dice
661 **riotoures:** debauchers, profligates
662 **erst er:** before   **prime:** first hour of the day, beginning about 6 A.M.

Were set hem in a taverne to drynke,
And as they sat, they herde a belle clynke
Biforn a cors, was caried to his grave. 665
That oon of hem gan callen to his knave:
"Go bet," quod he, "and axe redily
What cors is this that passeth heer forby;
And looke that thou reporte his name weel."
    "Sire," quod this boy, "it nedeth never-a-deel; 670
It was me toold er ye cam heer two houres.
He was, pardee, an old felawe of youres,
And sodeynly he was yslayn to-nyght,
Fordronke, as he sat on his bench upright.
Ther cam a privee theef men clepeth Deeth, 675
That in this contree al the peple sleeth,
And with his spere he smoot his herte atwo,
And wente his wey withouten wordes mo.
He hath a thousand slayn this pestilence.
And, maister, er ye come in his presence, 680
Me thynketh that it were necessarie
For to be war of swich an adversarie.
Beth redy for to meete hym everemoore;
Thus taughte me my dame; I sey namoore."
"By Seinte Marie!" seyde this taverner, 685
"The child seith sooth, for he hath slayn this yeer,
Henne over a mile, withinne a greet village,
Bothe man and womman, child, and hyne, and page;
I trowe his habitacioun be there.
To been avysed greet wysdom it were, 690
Er that he dide a man a dishonour."
    "Ye, Goddes armes!" quod this riotour,
"Is it swich peril with hym for to meete?
I shal hym seke by wey and eek by strete,
I make avow to Goddes digne bones! 695
Herkneth, felawes, we thre been al ones;
Lat ech of us holde up his hand til oother,
And ech of us bicomen otheres brother,
And we wol sleen this false traytour Deeth.
He shal be slayn, he that so manye sleeth, 700
By Goddes dignitee, er it be nyght!"
    Togidres han thise thre hir trouthes plight
To lyve and dyen ech of hem for oother,

As though he were his owene ybore brother.
And up they stirte, al dronken in this rage, 705
And forth they goon towardes that village
Of which the taverner hadde spoke biforn.
And many a grisly ooth thanne han they sworn,
And Cristes blessed body they torente—
Deeth shal be deed, if that they may hym hente! 710
    Whan they han goon nat fully half a mile,
Right as they wolde han troden over a stile,
An oold man and a povre with hem mette.
This olde man ful mekely hem grette,
And seyde thus, "Now, lordes, God yow see!" 715
    The proudeste of thise riotoures three
Answerde agayn, "What, carl, with sory grace!
Why artow al forwrapped save thy face?
Why lyvestow so longe in so greet age?"
    This olde man gan looke in his visage, 720
And seyde thus: "For I ne kan nat fynde
A man, though that I walked into Ynde,
Neither in citee ne in no village,
That wolde chaunge his youthe for myn age;
And therfore moot I han myn age stille, 725
As longe tyme as it is Goddes wille.
Ne Deeth, allas, ne wol nat han my lyf.
Thus walke I, lyk a restelees kaityf,
And on the ground, which is my moodres gate,
I knokke with my staf, bothe erly and late, 730
And seye, 'Leeve mooder, leet me in!
Lo how I vanysshe, flessh, and blood, and skyn!
Allas, whan shul my bones been at reste?
Mooder, with yow wolde I chaunge my cheste
That in my chambre longe tyme hath be, 735
Ye, for an heyre clowt to wrappe me!'
But yet to me she wol nat do that grace,
For which ful pale and welked is my face.
    "But, sires, to yow it is no curteisye
To speken to an old man vileynye, 740
But he trespasse in word or elles in dede.
In Hooly Writ ye may yourself wel rede:
'Agayns an oold man, hoor upon his heed,
Ye sholde arise;' wherfore I yeve yow reed,
Ne dooth unto an oold man noon harm now, 745
Namoore than that ye wolde men did to yow

665 **cors:** corpse
667 **Go bet:** go quickly
670 **boy:** servant   **it nedeth never-a-deel:** it is not at all necessary
674 **Fordronke:** very drunk
675 **men clepeth:** one calls, is called
679 **this pestilence:** during this plague
684 **dame:** mother
687 **Henne:** hence, from here
688 **hyne:** hind, farm worker   **page:** serving boy
690 **avysed:** forewarned
698 **brother:** sworn brother
702 **plight:** pledged

709 **torente:** tore to pieces
715 **God yow see:** may God look after you
717 **carl:** fellow   **with sory grace:** bad luck to you
718 **forwrapped:** completely wrapped up
722 **Ynde:** India; i.e., the most remote place on earth
728 **kaityf:** wretch
731 **Leeve:** dear
732 **vanysshe:** waste away
734 **cheste:** strongbox for valuables
736 **heyre clowt:** haircloth
738 **welked:** withered

In age, if that ye so longe abyde.
And God be with yow, where ye go or ryde!
I moot go thider as I have to go."
    "Nay, olde cherl, by God, thou shalt nat so,"   750
Seyde this oother hasardour anon;
"Thou partest nat so lightly, by Seint John!
Thou spak right now of thilke traytour Deeth,
That in this contree alle oure freendes sleeth.
Have heer my trouthe, as thou art his espye,   755
Telle where he is or thou shalt it abye,
By God and by the hooly sacrement!
For soothly thou art oon of his assent
To sleen us yonge folk, thou false theef!"
    "Now, sires," quod he, "if that yow be so leef   760
To fynde Deeth, turne up this croked wey,
For in that grove I lafte hym, by my fey,
Under a tree, and there he wole abyde;
Noght for youre boost he wole him no thyng hyde.
Se ye that ook? Right there ye shal hym fynde.   765
God save yow, that boghte agayn mankynde,
And yow amende!" Thus seyde this olde man;
And everich of thise riotoures ran
Til he cam to that tree, and ther they founde
Of floryns fyne of gold ycoyned rounde   770
Wel ny an eighte busshels, as hem thoughte.
No lenger thanne after Deeth they soughte,
But ech of hem so glad was of that sighte,
For that the floryns been so faire and brighte,
That doun they sette hem by this precious hoord.   775
The worste of hem, he spak the firste word.
    "Bretheren," quod he, "taak kep what that I seye;
My wit is greet, though that I bourde and pleye.
This tresor hath Fortune unto us yiven
In myrthe and jolitee oure lyf to lyven,   780
And lightly as it comth, so wol we spende.
Ey, Goddes precious dignitee! Who wende
To-day that we sholde han so fair a grace?
But myghte this gold be caried fro this place
Hoom to myn hous, or elles unto youres—   785
For wel ye woot that al this gold is oures—
Thanne were we in heigh felicitee.
But trewely, by daye it may nat bee.

Men wolde seyn that we were theves stronge,
And for oure owene tresor doon us honge.   790
This tresor moste ycaried be by nyghte
As wisely and as slyly as it myghte.
Wherfore I rede that cut among us alle
Be drawe, and lat se wher the cut wol falle;
And he that hath the cut with herte blithe   795
Shal renne to the town, and that ful swithe,
And brynge us breed and wyn ful prively.
And two of us shul kepen subtilly
This tresor wel; and if he wol nat tarie,
Whan it is nyght, we wol this tresor carie,   800
By oon assent, where as us thynketh best."
That oon of hem the cut broghte in his fest,
And bad hem drawe and looke where it wol falle;
And it fil on the yongeste of hem alle,
And forth toward the toun he wente anon.   805
And also soone as that he was gon,
That oon of hem spak thus unto that oother:
"Thow knowest wel thou art my sworen brother;
Thy profit wol I telle thee anon.
Thou woost wel that oure felawe is agon.   810
And heere is gold, and that ful greet plentee,
That shal departed been among us thre.
But nathelees, if I kan shape it so
That it departed were among us two,
Hadde I nat doon a freendes torn to thee?"   815
    That oother answerde, "I noot hou that may be.
He woot that the gold is with us tweye;
What shal we doon? What shal we to hym seye?"
    "Shal it be conseil?" seyde the firste shrewe,
"And I shal tellen in a wordes fewe   820
What we shal doon, and brynge it wel aboute."
    "I graunte," quod that oother, "out of doute,
That, by my trouthe, I wol thee nat biwreye."
    "Now," quod the firste, "thou woost wel we be
        tweye,
And two of us shul strenger be than oon.   825
Looke whan that he is set, that right anoon
Arys as though thou woldest with hym pleye,
And I shal ryve hym thurgh the sydes tweye
Whil that thou strogelest with hym as in game,
And with thy daggere looke thou do the same;   830

---

747 **abyde:** remain (alive)
758 **oon of his assent:** in league with him
765 **ook:** oak
766 **boghte agayn:** redeemed
770 **floryns:** gold coins
778 **bourde:** jest
779 **tresor:** treasure

789 **theves stronge:** arrant thieves
790 **doon us honge:** have us hanged
793–94 **cut . . . Be drawe:** lots be drawn
796 **ful swithe:** very quickly
815 **freendes torn:** friend's turn, friendly act
823 **biwreye:** betray
828 **ryve:** stab

And thanne shal al this gold departed be,
My deere freend, bitwixen me and thee.
Thanne may we bothe oure lustes all fulfille,
And pleye at dees right at oure owene wille."
And thus acorded been thise shrewes tweye   835
To sleen the thridde, as ye han herd me seye.
        This yongeste, which that wente to the toun,
Ful ofte in herte he rolleth up and doun
The beautee of thise floryns newe and brighte.
"O Lord!" quod he, "if so were that I myghte   840
Have al this tresor to myself allone,
Ther is no man that lyveth under the trone
Of God that sholde lyve so murye as I!"
And atte laste the feend, oure enemy,
Putte in his thought that he sholde poyson beye,   845
With which he myghte sleen his felawes tweye;
For-why the feend foond hym in swich lyvynge
That he hadde leve him to sorwe brynge.
For this was outrely his fulle entente,
To sleen hem bothe and nevere to repente.   850
And forth he gooth, no lenger wolde he tarie,
Into the toun, unto a pothecarie,
And preyde hym that he hym wolde selle
Som poyson, that he myghte his rattes quelle;
And eek ther was a polcat in his hawe,   855
That, as he seyde, his capouns hadde yslawe,
And fayn he wolde wreke hym, if he myghte,
On vermyn that destroyed hym by nyghte.
        The pothecarie answerde, "And thou shalt have
A thyng that, also God my soule save,   860
In al this world ther is no creature
That eten or dronken hath of this confiture
Noght but the montance of a corn of whete,
That he ne shal his lif anon forlete;
Ye, sterve he shal, and that in lasse while   865
Than thou wolt goon a paas nat but a mile,
This poysoun is so strong and violent."
        This cursed man hath in his hond yhent
This poysoun in a box, and sith he ran
Into the nexte strete unto a man,   870
And borwed [of] hym large botelles thre,
And in the two his poyson poured he;

The thridde he kepte clene for his drynke.
For al the nyght he shoop hym for to swynke
In cariynge of the gold out of that place.   875
And whan this riotour, with sory grace,
Hadde filled with wyn his grete botels thre,
To his felawes agayn repaireth he.
        What nedeth it to sermone of it moore?
For right as they hadde cast his deeth bifoore,   880
Right so they han hym slayn, and that anon.
And whan that this was doon, thus spak that oon:
"Now lat us sitte and drynke, and make us merie,
And afterward we wol his body berie."
And with that word it happed hym, par cas,   885
To take the botel ther the poyson was,
And drank, and yaf his felawe drynke also,
For which anon they storven bothe two.
        But certes, I suppose that Avycen
Wroot nevere in no canon, ne in no fen,   890
Mo wonder signes of empoisonyng
Than hadde thise wrecches two, er hir endyng.
Thus ended been thise homycides two,
And eek the false empoysonere also.
        O cursed synne of alle cursednesse!   895
O traytours homycide, O wikkednesse!
O glotonye, luxurie, and hasardrye!
Thou blasphemour of Crist with vileynye
And othes grete, of usage and of pride!
Allas, mankynde, how may it bitide   900
That to thy creatour, which that the wroghte
And with his precious herte-blood thee boghte,
Thou art so fals and so unkynde, allas?
        Now, goode men, God foryeve yow youre trespas,
And ware yow fro the synne of avarice!   905
Myn hooly pardoun may yow alle warice,
So that ye offre nobles or sterlynges,
Or elles silver broches, spoones, rynges.
Boweth youre heed under this hooly bulle!
Cometh up, ye wyves, offreth of youre wolle!   910
Youre names I entre heer in my rolle anon;
Into the blisse of hevene shul ye gon.

838 **rolleth up and doun:** meditates on
842 **trone:** throne
848 **leve:** permission
852 **pothecarie:** apothecary
854 **quelle:** kill
855 **polcat:** weasel   **hawe:** yard
857 **wreke hym:** revenge himself
858 **vermyn:** animal pests   **destroyed:** were ruining
862 **confiture:** concoction
863 **montance:** amount, size   **corn:** grain
864 **forlete:** lose
865 **sterve:** die   **while:** time
866 **a paas:** at a walk

874 **shoop hym:** intended
885 **par cas:** by chance
889 **Avycen:** Avicenna, Arabic author of a medical treatise
890 **canon:** set of rules   **fen:** a division of Avicenna's book
891 **empoisonyng:** poisoning
894 **empoysonere:** poisoner
897 **luxurie:** lechery
899 **usage:** habit
903 **unkynde:** unnatural
906 **warice:** cure, save
907 **nobles:** gold coins   **sterlynges:** silver pennies
910 **wolle:** wool

I yow assoille, by myn heigh power,
Yow that wol offre, as clene and eek as cleer
As ye were born.—And lo, sires, thus I preche.   915
And Jhesu Crist, that is oure soules leche,
So graunte yow his pardoun to receyve,
For that is best; I wol yow nat deceyve.
   But, sires, o word forgat I in my tale:
I have relikes and pardoun in my male,   920
As faire as any man in Engelond,
Whiche were me yeven by the popes hond.
If any of yow wole, of devocion,
Offren and han myn absolucion,
Com forth anon, and kneleth heere adoun,   925
And mekely receyveth my pardoun;
Or elles taketh pardoun as ye wende,
Al newe and fressh at every miles ende,
So that ye offren, alwey newe and newe,
Nobles or pens, whiche that be goode and trewe.   930
It is an honour to everich that is heer
That ye mowe have a suffisant pardoneer
T'assoille yow in contree as ye ryde,
For aventures whiche that may bityde.
Paraventure ther may fallen oon or two   935
Doun of his hors and breke his nekke atwo.
Looke which a seuretee is it to yow alle
That I am in youre felaweshipe yfalle,
That may assoille yow, bothe moore and lasse,
Whan that the soule shal fro the body passe.   940
I rede that oure Hoost heere shal bigynne,

For he is moost envoluped in synne.
Com forth, sire Hoost, and offre first anon,
And thou shalt kisse the relikes everychon,
Ye, for a grote! Unbokele anon thy purs."   945
   "Nay, nay!" quod he, "thanne have I Cristes
     curs!
Lat be," quod he, "it shal nat be, so theech!
Thou woldest make me kisse thyn olde breech,
And swere it were a relyk of a seint,
Though it were with thy fundement depeint!   950
But, by the croys which that Seint Eleyne fond,
I wolde I hadde thy coillons in myn hond
In stide of relikes or of seintuarie.
Lat kutte hem of, I wol thee helpe hem carie;
They shul be shryned in an hogges toord!"   955
   This Pardoner answerde nat a word;
So wrooth he was, no word ne wolde he seye.
   "Now," quod oure Hoost, "I wol no lenger pleye
With thee, ne with noon oother angry man."
But right anon the worthy Knyght bigan,   960
Whan that he saugh that al the peple lough,
"Namoore of this, for it is right ynough!
Sire Pardoner, be glad and myrie of cheere;
And ye, sire Hoost, that been to me so deere,
I prey yow that ye kisse the Pardoner.   965
And Pardoner, I prey thee, drawe thee neer,
And, as we diden, lat us laughe and pleye."
Anon they kiste, and ryden forth hir weye.

Heere is ended the Pardoners Tale.

913 **assoille:** absolve
916 **leche:** physician
917 **graunte:** allow
920 **pardoun:** pardons, papal indulgences   **male:** pouch, bag
937 **which a:** what a   **seuretee:** safeguard

942 **envoluped:** enveloped
945 **grote:** groat, a silver coin worth four pence
946 **Cristes curs:** damnation
947 **so theech** = *so thee ich,* as I may prosper (I swear)
948 **breech:** underpants
950 **fundement:** anus   **depeint:** stained
951 **croys:** cross   **Seint Eleyne:** St. Helen, discoverer of the true cross
952 **coillons:** testicles
953 **seintuarie:** sanctuary, box for relics
955 **shryned:** enshrined   **toord:** turd
968 **ryden:** rode

⑤

The Shipman's Tale

⑤

Heere bigynneth the Shipmanne's Tale.

A marchant whilom dwelled at Seint-Denys,
That riche was, for which men helde him wys.
A wyf he had of excellent beautee;
And compaignable and revelous was she,
Which is a thyng that causeth more dispence   5
Than worth is al the chiere and reverence
That men hem doon at festes and daunces.
Swiche salutaciouns and countenaunces
Passen as dooth a shadwe upon the wal;
But wo is hym that payen moot for al!   *1200
The sely housbonde, algate he moot paye,
He moot us clothe, and he moot us arraye,
Al for his owene worshipe richely,
In which array we daunce jolily.
And if that he noght may, par aventure,   15
Or ellis list no swich dispence endure,
But thynketh it is wasted and ylost,
Thanne moot another payen for oure cost,
Or lene us gold, and that is perilous.
   This noble marchaunt heeld a worthy hous, *1210
For which he hadde alday so greet repair
For his largesse, and for his wyf was fair,
That wonder is; but herkneth to my tale.
Amonges alle his gestes, grete and smale,
Ther was a monk, a fair man and a boold—   25
I trowe a thritty wynter he was oold—
That evere in oon was drawynge to that place.
This yonge monk, that was so fair of face,
Aqueynted was so with the goode man,

Sith that hir firste kноweliche bigan,   *1220
That in his hous as famulier was he
As it is possible any freend to be.
   And for as muchel as this goode man,
And eek this monk of which that I bigan,
Were bothe two yborn in o village,   35
The monk hym claymeth as for cosynage,
And he agayn; he seith nat ones nay,
But was as glad therof as fowel of day,
For to his herte it was a greet plesaunce.
Thus been they knyt with eterne alliaunce,   *1230
And ech of hem gan oother for t'assure
Of bretherhede whil that hir lyf may dure.
   Free was daun John, and manly of dispence,
As in that hous, and ful of diligence
To doon plesaunce, and also greet costage.   45
He noght forgat to yeve the leeste page
In al that hous; but after hir degree,
He yaf the lord, and sitthe al his meynee,
Whan that he cam, som manere honest thyng,
For which they were as glad of his comyng   *1240
As fowel is fayn whan that the sonne up riseth.
Na moore of this as now, for it suffiseth.
   But so bifel, this marchant on a day
Shoop hym to make redy his array
Toward the toun of Brugges for to fare,   55
To byen there a porcioun of ware;
For which he hath to Parys sent anon
A messager, and preyed hath daun John
That he sholde come to Seint-Denys to pleye
With hym and with his wyf a day or tweye,   *1250
Er he to Brugges wente, in alle wise.
   This noble monk, of which I yow devyse,
Hath of his abbot, as hym list, licence,
By cause he was a man of heigh prudence

*For the convenience of the reader in finding references, the tra-
ditional numbering of Group B², marked with asterisks, is carried
alternately with that of Fragment VII.

1 **Seint-Denys:** a town north of Paris
4 **compaignable:** sociable   **revelous:** convivial, fond of revelry
5 **dispence:** expense
6 **chiere:** attention
8 **contenaunces:** courtesies
11 **sely:** poor
13 **worshipe:** honor
20 **heeld a worthy hous:** maintained his household generously
21 **alday:** daily   **so greet repair:** so many visitors
22 **largesse:** generosity
26 **a thritty wynter:** about thirty years
27 **evere in oon:** always
29 **aqueynted:** acquainted with   **goode man:** the goodman, head of the household

30 **knoweliche:** acquaintance
36 **cosynage:** kinship
42 **bretherhede:** sworn brotherhood
43 **manly:** generous
45 **doon . . . greet costage:** spend much money
54 **Shoop hym:** prepared
55 **Brugges:** Bruges, now in Belgium
56 **porcioun:** quantity   **ware:** goods

And eek an officer, out for to ryde,   65
To seen hir graunges and hire bernes wyde,
And unto Seint-Denys he comth anon.
Who was so welcome as my lord daun John,
Oure deere cosyn, ful of curteisye?
With hym broghte he a jubbe of malvesye,   *1260
And eek another ful of fyn vernage,
And volatyl, as ay was his usage.
And thus I lete hem ete and drynke and pleye,
This marchant and this monk, a day or tweye.

    The thridde day, this marchant up ariseth,   75
And on his nedes sadly hym avyseth,
And up into his countour-hous gooth he
To rekene with hymself, wel may be,
Of thilke yeer how that it with hym stood,
And how that he despended hadde his good,   *1270
And if that he encressed were or noon.
His bookes and his bagges many oon
He leith biforn hym on his countyng-bord.
Ful riche was his tresor and his hord,
For which ful faste his countour-dore he shette;   85
And eek he nolde that no man sholde hym lette
Of his acountes, for the meene tyme;
And thus he sit til it was passed pryme.

    Daun John was rysen in the morwe also,
And in the gardyn walketh to and fro,   *1280
And hath his thynges seyd ful curteisly.

    This goode wyf cam walkynge pryvely
Into the gardyn, there he walketh softe,
And hym saleweth, as she hath doon ofte.
A mayde child cam in hire compaignye,   95
Which as hir list she may governe and gye,
For yet under the yerde was the mayde.
"O deere cosyn myn, daun John," she sayde,
"What eyleth yow so rathe for to ryse?"

    "Nece," quod he, "it oghte ynough suffise   *1290
Fyve houres for to slepe upon a nyght,
But it were for an old appalled wight,
As been thise wedded men, that lye and dare

As in a fourme sit a wery hare,
Were al forstraught with houndes grete and smale.
But deere nece, why be ye so pale?   106
I trowe, certes, that oure goode man
Hath yow laboured sith the nyght bigan
That yow were nede to resten hastily."
And with that word he lough ful murily,   *1300
And of his owene thought he wax al reed.

    This faire wyf gan for to shake hir heed
And seyde thus, "Ye, God woot al," quod she.
"Nay, cosyn myn, it stant nat so with me;
For, by that God that yaf me soule and lyf,   115
In al the reawme of France is ther no wyf
That lasse lust hath to that sory pley.
For I may synge 'allas and weylawey
That I was born,' but to no wight," quod she,
"Dar I nat telle how that it stant with me.   *1310
Wherfore I thynke out of this land to wende,
Or elles of myself to make an ende,
So ful am I of drede and eek of care."

    This monk bigan upon this wyf to stare,
And seyde, "Allas, my nece, God forbede   125
That ye, for any sorwe or any drede,
Fordo youreself; but telleth me youre grief.
Paraventure I may, in youre meschief,
Conseille or helpe; and therfore telleth me
Al youre anoy, for it shal been secree.   *1320
For on my portehors I make an ooth
That nevere in my lyf, for lief ne looth,
Ne shal I of no conseil yow biwreye."

    "The same agayn to yow," quod she, "I seye.
By God and by this portehors I swere,   135
Though men me wolde al into pieces tere,
Ne shal I nevere, for to goon to helle,
Biwreye a word of thyng that ye me telle,
Nat for no cosynage ne alliance,
But verraily for love and affiance."   *1330
Thus been they sworn, and heerupon they kiste,
And ech of hem tolde oother what hem liste.

    "Cosyn," quod she, "if that I hadde a space,
As I have noon, and namely in this place,
Thanne wolde I telle a legende of my lyf,   145

---

65 **officer:** probably cellarer
66 **graunges:** outlying farms
69 **cosyn:** kinsman
70 **jubbe:** a large container, jug   **malvesye:** malmsey
71 **vernage:** white Italian wine (vernaccia)
72 **volatyl:** game fowl
76 **nedes:** business duties
86 **lette:** disturb
88 **pryme:** 9 A.M.
91 **thynges:** devotions
97 **under the yerde:** subject to (adult) authority
99 **rathe:** early
100 **Nece:** kinswoman
102 **appalled:** pallid, feeble
103 **dare:** lie motionless or dozing

104 **fourme:** form (a grassy, often sheltered, hollow)
105 **forstraught:** distraught
108 **laboured:** put to work
116 **reawme:** realm
117 **lust:** pleasure
130 **anoy:** trouble
131 **portehors:** breviary
133 **biwreye:** expose, betray
139 **cosynage:** kinship
140 **affiance:** trust
143 **space:** time, space of time
145 **legende:** saint's life, tale of suffering

What I have suffred sith I was a wyf
With myn housbonde, al be he youre cosyn."
  "Nay," quod this monk, "by God and Seint
      Martyn,
He is na moore cosyn unto me
Than is this leef that hangeth on the tree! *1340
I clepe hym so, by Seint Denys of Fraunce,
To have the moore cause of aqueyntaunce
Of yow, which I have loved specially
Aboven alle wommen, sikerly.
This swere I yow on my professioun. 155
Telleth youre grief, lest that he come adoun;
And hasteth yow, and gooth youre wey anon."
  "My deere love," quod she, "O my daun John,
Ful lief were me this conseil for to hyde,
But out it moot; I may namoore abyde. *1350
Myn housbonde is to me the worste man
That evere was sith that the world bigan.
But sith I am a wyf, it sit nat me
To tellen no wight of oure privetee,
Neither abedde ne in noon oother place; 165
God shilde I sholde it tellen, for his grace!
A wyf ne shal nat seyn of hir housbonde
But al honour, as I kan understonde;
Save unto yow thus muche I tellen shal:
As helpe me God, he is noght worth at al *1360
In no degree the value of a flye.
But yet me greveth moost his nygardye.
And wel ye woot that wommen naturelly
Desiren thynges sixe as wel as I:
They wolde that hir housbondes sholde be 175
Hardy and wise, and riche, and therto free,
And buxom unto his wyf and fressh abedde.
But by that ilke Lord that for us bledde,
For his honour, myself for to arraye,
A Sonday next I moste nedes paye *1370
An hundred frankes, or ellis I am lorn.
Yet were me levere that I were unborn
Than me were doon a sclaundre or vileynye;
And if myn housbonde eek it myghte espye,
I nere but lost; and therfore I yow preye, 185
Lene me this somme, or ellis moot I deye.

Daun John, I seye, lene me thise hundred frankes.
Pardee, I wol nat faille yow my thankes,
If that yow list to doon that I yow praye.
For at a certeyn day I wol yow paye, *1380
And doon to yow what plesance and service
That I may doon, right as yow list devise.
And but I do, God take on me vengeance
As foul as evere hadde Genylon of France."
  This gentil monk answerde in this manere: 195
"Now trewely, myn owene lady deere,
I have," quod he, "on yow so greet a routhe
That I yow swere, and plighte yow my trouthe,
That whan youre housbonde is to Flaundres fare,
I wol delyvere yow out of this care; *1390
For I wol brynge yow an hundred frankes."
And with that word he caughte hire by the flankes,
And hire embraceth harde, and kiste hire ofte.
"Gooth now youre wey," quod he, "al stille and softe,
And lat us dyne as soone as that ye may; 205
For by my chilyndre it is pryme of day.
Gooth now, and beeth as trewe as I shal be."
  "Now elles God forbede, sire," quod she;
And forth she gooth as jolif as a pye,
And bad the cookes that they sholde hem hye, *1400
So that men myghte dyne, and that anon.
Up to hir housbonde is this wyf ygon,
And knokketh at his countour boldely.
  "Quy la?" quod he. "Peter! it am I,"
Quod she; "What, sire, how longe wol ye faste? 215
How longe tyme wol ye rekene and caste
Youre sommes, and youre bookes, and youre thynges?
The devel have part on alle swiche rekenynges!
Ye have ynough, pardee, of Goddes sonde;
Com doun to-day, and lat youre bagges stonde. *1410
Ne be ye nat ashamed that daun John
Shal fasting al this day alenge goon?
What, lat us heere a messe, and go we dyne."
  "Wyf," quod this man, "litel kanstow devyne
The curious bisynesse that we have. 225

---

148 **Seint Martyn:** St. Martin of Tours
151 **Seint Denys:** St. Denis, patron saint of France
155 **professioun:** monastic vows
159 **Ful lief were me:** I would very much like
163 **sit nat me:** is not suitable for me
166 **shilde:** forbid
172 **nygardye:** miserliness
176 **Hardy:** vigorous **free:** generous
177 **buxom:** obedient
181 **An hundred frankes:** about fifteen pounds sterling
183 **sclaundre:** disgrace
185 **nere but:** would be (nothing else) but, would surely be

194 **Genylon:** Ganelon, who betrayed Roland; see n.
206 **chilyndre:** portable sundial
209 **pye:** magpie
213 **countour:** counting house
214 **Quy la?:** Who's there? **Peter!:** by St. Peter!
216 **caste:** calculate
219 **Goddes sonde:** what God has sent
222 **alenge:** miserable
225 **curious bisynesse:** worrisome preoccupations

For of us chapmen, also God me save,
And by that lord that clepid is Seint Yve,
Scarsly amonges twelve tweye shul thryve
Continuelly, lastynge unto oure age.
We may wel make chiere and good visage,   *1420
And dryve forth the world as it may be,
And kepen oure estaat in pryvetee,
Til we be deed, or elles that we pleye
A pilgrymage, or goon out of the weye.
And therfore have I greet necessitee   235
Upon this queynte world t'avyse me,
For everemoore we moote stonde in drede
Of hap and fortune in oure chapmanhede.
    "To Flaundres wol I go to-morwe at day,
And come agayn, as soone as evere I may.   *1430
For which, my deere wyf, I thee biseke,
As be to every wight buxom and meke,
And for to kepe oure good be curious,
And honestly governe wel oure hous.
Thou hast ynough, in every maner wise,   245
That to a thrifty houshold may suffise.
Thee lakketh noon array ne no vitaille;
Of silver in thy purs shaltow nat faille."
And with that word his countour-dore he shette,
And doun he gooth, no lenger wolde he lette.   *1440
But hastily a messe was ther seyd,
And spedily the tables were yleyd,
And to the dyner faste they hem spedde,
And richely this monk the chapman fedde.
    At after-dyner daun John sobrely   255
This chapman took apart, and prively
He seyde hym thus: "Cosyn, it standeth so,
That wel I se to Brugges wol ye go.
God and Seint Austyn spede yow and gyde!
I prey yow, cosyn, wisely that ye ryde.   *1450
Governeth yow also of youre diete
Atemprely, and namely in this hete.
Bitwix us two nedeth no strange fare;
Farewel, cosyn; God shilde yow fro care!

And if that any thyng by day or nyght,   265
If it lye in my power and my myght,
That ye me wol comande in any wyse,
It shal be doon right as ye wol devyse.
    "O thyng, er that ye goon, if it may be,
I wolde prey yow: for to lene me   *1460
An hundred frankes, for a wyke or tweye,
For certein beestes that I moste beye,
To stoore with a place that is oures.
God helpe me so, I wolde it were youres!
I shal nat faille surely of my day,   275
Nat for a thousand frankes, a mile way.
But lat this thyng be secree, I yow preye,
For yet to-nyght thise beestes moot I beye.
And fare now wel, myn owene cosyn deere;
Graunt mercy of youre cost and of youre cheere."
    This noble marchant gentilly anon   *1471
Answerde and seyde, "O cosyn myn, daun John,
Now sikerly this is a smal requeste.
My gold is youres, whan that it yow leste,
And nat oonly my gold, but my chaffare.   285
Take what yow list; God shilde that ye spare.
    "But o thyng is, ye knowe it wel ynogh
Of chapmen, that hir moneie is hir plogh.
We may creaunce whil we have a name,
But goldlees for to be, it is no game.   *1480
Paye it agayn whan it lith in youre ese;
After my myght ful fayn wolde I yow plese."
    Thise hundred frankes he fette forth anon,
And prively he took hem to daun John.
No wight in al this world wiste of this loone   295
Savynge this marchant and daun John allone.
They drynke, and speke, and rome a while and pleye,
Til that daun John rideth to his abbeye.
    The morwe cam, and forth this marchant rideth
To Flaundres-ward; his prentys wel hym gydeth
Til he came into Brugges murily.   *1491
Now gooth this marchant faste and bisily
Aboute his nede, and byeth and creaunceth.
He neither pleyeth at the dees ne daunceth,

227 **Seint Yve:** St. Ivo (?); see n.
231 **dryve forth:** endure
233 **pleye:** play or go; see n.
234 **goon out of the weye:** disappear
236 **queynte:** tricky
238 **hap:** risk (chance happening)   **chapmanhede:** business dealings
243 **curious:** diligent
246 **thrifty:** prosperous, thriving
248 **faille:** lack
259 **Seint Austyn:** St. Augustine of Hippo
262 **Atemprely:** moderately
263 **strange fare:** elaborate courtesies
264 **shilde:** protect

273 **To stoore with:** with which to stock
276 **a mile way:** by (so much as) twenty minutes
280 **Graunt mercy:** thank you
284 **whan that it yow leste:** when ever you please
285 **chaffare:** goods, merchandise
289 **creaunce:** borrow money, obtain credit
290 **no game:** no laughing matter
294 **took:** gave
295 **loone:** loan
303 **creaunceth:** obtains credit

But as a marchaunt, shortly for to telle,   305
He let his lyf, and there I lete hym dwelle.

The Sonday next the marchant was agon,
To Seint-Denys ycomen is daun John,
With crowne and berd al fressh and newe yshave.
In al the hous ther nas so litel a knave,   *1500
Ne no wight elles, that he nas ful fayn
That my lord daun John was come agayn.
And shortly to the point right for to gon,
This faire wyf acorded with daun John
That for thise hundred frankes he sholde al nyght   315
Have hire in his armes bolt upright;
And this acord parfourned was in dede.
In myrthe al nyght a bisy lyf they lede
Til it was day, that daun John wente his way,
And bad the meynee "Farewel, have good day!"   *1510
For noon of hem, ne no wight in the toun,
Hath of daun John right no suspecioun.
And forth he rydeth hoom to his abbeye,
Or where hym list; namoore of hym I seye.

This marchant, whan that ended was the faire,   325
To Seint-Denys he gan for to repaire,
And with his wyf he maketh feeste and cheere,
And telleth hire that chaffare is so deere
That nedes moste he make a chevyssaunce,
For he was bounden in a reconyssaunce   *1520
To paye twenty thousand sheeld anon.
For which this marchant is to Parys gon
To borwe of certeine freendes that he hadde
A certeyn frankes; and somme with him he ladde.
And whan that he was come into the toun,   335
For greet chiertee and greet affeccioun,
Unto daun John he first gooth hym to pleye;
Nat for to axe or borwe of hym moneye,
But for to wite and seen of his welfare,
And for to tellen hym of his chaffare,
As freendes doon whan they been met yfeere.   *1531

Daun John hym maketh feeste and murye cheere,
And he hym tolde agayn, ful specially,
How he hadde wel yboght and graciously,
Thanked be God, al hool his marchandise,   345
Save that he moste, in alle maner wise,
Maken a chevyssaunce, as for his beste,
And thanne he sholde been in joye and reste.

Daun John answerde, "Certes, I am fayn
That ye in heele ar comen hom agayn.   *1540
And if that I were riche, as have I blisse,
Of twenty thousand sheeld sholde ye nat mysse,
For ye so kyndely this oother day
Lente me gold; and as I kan and may,
I thanke yow, by God and by Seint Jame!   355
But nathelees, I took unto oure dame,
Youre wyf, at hom, the same gold ageyn
Upon youre bench; she woot it wel, certeyn,
By certeyn tokenes that I kan hire telle.
Now, by youre leve, I may no lenger dwelle;   *1550
Oure abbot wole out of this toun anon,
And in his compaignye moot I goon.
Grete wel oure dame, myn owene nece sweete,
And fare wel, deere cosyn, til we meete!"

This marchant, which that was ful war and wys,
Creanced hath, and payd eek in Parys   366
To certeyn Lumbardes, redy in hir hond,
The somme of gold, and gat of hem his bond;
And hoom he gooth, murie as a papejay,
For wel he knew he stood in swich array   *1560
That nedes moste he wynne in that viage
A thousand frankes aboven al his costage.

His wyf ful redy mette hym atte gate,
As she was wont of oold usage algate,
And al that nyght in myrthe they bisette;   375
For he was riche and cleerly out of dette.
Whan it was day, this marchant gan embrace
His wyf al newe, and kiste hire on hir face,
And up he gooth and maketh it ful tough.

306 **let his lyf:** leads (*let = ledeth*) his life, conducts himself
309 **crowne:** head
316 **bolt upright:** flat on her back
326 **repaire:** return
328 **chaffare:** merchandise
329 **chevyssaunce:** loan; see Expl. Notes on the business transaction described in lines 328–34.
330 **reconyssaunce:** formal pledge
331 **sheeld:** units of exchange
334 **A certeyn:** a certain number of
336 **chiertee:** fondness
341 **yfeere:** together

343 **ful specially:** in great detail
344 **graciously:** successfully
350 **heele:** good health
354 **kan and may:** know how and can
355 **Seint Jame:** St. James of Compostella
356 **took:** gave
359 **tokenes:** confirmatory details, proofs
366 **creanced:** obtained credit
367 **Lumbardes:** Lombard bankers   **redy in hir hond:** promptly and in cash
369 **papejay:** parrot
371 **viage:** undertaking
372 **aboven:** in addition to   **costage:** expense
379 **maketh it ful tough:** is unrelenting in his demands

"Namoore," quod she, "by God, ye have ynough!"
And wantownly agayn with hym she pleyde   *1571
Til atte laste thus this marchant seyde:
"By God," quod he, "I am a litel wrooth
With yow, my wyf, although it be me looth.
And woot ye why? By God, as that I gesse   385
That ye han maad a manere straungenesse
Bitwixen me and my cosyn daun John.
Ye sholde han warned me, er I had gon,
That he yow hadde an hundred frankes payed
By redy token; and heeld hym yvele apayed,
For that I to hym spak of chevyssaunce;   *1581
Me semed so, as by his contenaunce.
But nathelees, by God, oure hevene kyng,
I thoughte nat to axen hym no thyng.
I prey thee, wyf, ne do namoore so;   395
Telle me alwey, er that I fro thee go,
If any dettour hath in myn absence
Ypayed thee, lest thurgh thy necligence
I myghte hym axe a thing that he hath payed."

   This wyf was nat afered nor affrayed,
But boldely she seyde, and that anon,   *1591
"Marie, I deffie the false monk, daun John!
I kepe nat of his tokenes never a deel;
He took me certeyn gold, that woot I weel—
What! Yvel thedam on his monkes snowte!   405
For, God it woot, I wende, withouten doute,
That he hadde yeve it me bycause of yow

To doon therwith myn honour and my prow,
For cosynage, and eek for beele cheere
That he hath had ful ofte tymes heere.   *1600
But sith I se I stonde in this disjoynt,
I wol answere yow shortly to the poynt.
Ye han mo slakkere dettours than am I!
For I wol paye yow wel and redily
Fro day to day, and if so be I faille,   415
I am youre wyf; score it upon my taille,
And I shal paye as soone as ever I may.
For by my trouthe, I have on myn array,
And nat on wast, bistowed every deel;
And for I have bistowed it so weel   *1610
For youre honour, for Goddes sake, I seye,
As be nat wrooth, but lat us laughe and pleye.
Ye shal my joly body have to wedde;
By God, I wol nat paye yow but abedde!
Forgyve it me, myn owene spouse deere;   425
Turne hiderward, and maketh bettre cheere."

   This marchant saugh ther was no remedie,
And for to chide it nere but folie,
Sith that the thyng may nat amended be.
"Now wyf," he seyde, "and I foryeve it thee;   *1620
But, by thy lyf, ne be namoore so large.
Keep bet thy good, this yeve I thee in charge."
Thus endeth my tale, and God us sende
Taillynge ynough unto oure lyves ende. Amen

Heere endeth the Shipmannes Tale.

Bihoold the murie wordes of the Hoost to the Shipman and to the lady Prioresse.

"Wel seyd, by *corpus dominus*," quod oure Hoost,
"Now longe moote thou saille by the cost,   436
Sire gentil maister, gentil maryneer!
God yeve the monk a thousand last quade yeer!
A ha! Felawes, beth ware of swich a jape!
The monk putte in the mannes hood an ape,   *1630
And in his wyves eek, by Seint Austyn!
Draweth no monkes moore unto youre in.

"But now passe over, and lat us seke aboute,
Who shal now telle first of al this route
Another tale;" and with that word he sayde,   445
As curteisly as it had been a mayde,
"My lady Prioresse, by youre leve,
So that I wiste I sholde yow nat greve,
I wolde demen that ye tellen sholde
A tale next, if so were that ye wolde.   *1640
Now wol ye vouche sauf, my lady deere?"
   "Gladly," quod she, and seyde as ye shal heere.

---

381 **wantownly agayn:** wantonly in return
386 **straungenesse:** estrangement
390 **By redy token:** in cash (by clear evidence)   **heeld hym yvele apayed:** he considered himself ill-used
404 **took:** gave
405 **Yvel thedam** bad luck

---

435 **corpus dominus:** corpus Domini, the body of the Lord
438 **last quade yeer:** cartloads of bad years
440 The monk made a monkey of the man

408 **prow:** profit, benefit
409 **cosynage:** kinship   **beele cheere:** good cheer, hospitality
411 **disjoynt:** difficulty
413 **slakkere:** slower (to repay)   **dettours:** debtors
416 **score it upon my taille:** mark it on my tally, charge it to my account; see n.
423 **to wedde:** as a pledge
431 **large:** free-spending
434 **Taillynge:** credit

Prologue of the Prioress's Tale

The Prologe of the Prioresses Tale.

Domine dominus noster.

O Lord, oure Lord, thy name how merveillous
Is in this large world ysprad—quod she—
For noght oonly thy laude precious   455
Parfourned is by men of dignitee,
But by the mouth of children thy bountee
Parfourned is, for on the brest soukynge
Somtyme shewen they thyn heriynge.

Wherfore in laude, as I best kan or may,   *1650
Of thee and of the white lylye flour
Which that the bar, and is a mayde alway,
To telle a storie I wol do my labour;
Nat that I may encressen hir honour,
For she hirself is honour and the roote   465
Of bountee, next hir Sone, and soules boote.

O mooder Mayde, O mayde Mooder free!
O bussh unbrent, brennynge in Moyses sighte,
That ravyshedest doun fro the Deitee,
Thurgh thyn humblesse, the Goost that in th'alighte,

Of whos vertu, whan he thyn herte lighte,   *1661
Conceyved was the Fadres sapience,
Help me to telle it in thy reverence!

Lady, thy bountee, thy magnificence,
Thy vertu and thy grete humylitee   475
Ther may no tonge expresse in no science;
For somtyme, Lady, er men praye to thee,
Thou goost biforn of thy benyngnytee,
And getest us the lyght, of thy preyere,
To gyden us unto thy Sone so deere.   *1670

My konnyng is so wayk, O blisful Queene,
For to declare thy grete worthynesse
That I ne may the weighte nat susteene;
But as a child of twelf month oold, or lesse,
That kan unnethes any word expresse,   485
Right so fare I, and therfore I yow preye,
Gydeth my song that I shal of yow seye.

Explicit.

The Prioress's Tale

Heere bigynneth the Prioresses Tale.

Ther was in Asye, in a greet citee,
Amonges Cristene folk a Jewerye,
Sustened by a lord of that contree   *1680
For foule usure and lucre of vileynye,

Hateful to Crist and to his compaignye;
And thurgh the strete men myghte ride or wende,
For it was free and open at eyther ende.

A litel scole of Cristen folk ther stood   495
Doun at the ferther ende, in which ther were

455 **laude:** praise
458 **soukynge:** suckling
459 **heriynge:** praise
466 **soules boote:** remedy for the soul
468 **unbrent:** unburned   **Moyses:** Moses'
470 **Goost:** Holy Spirit

489 **Jewerye:** ghetto
491 **usure:** usury   **lucre of vileynye:** shameful (excessive) profits

476 **in no science:** not by the means of, or in the language of, any human learning

495 **scole:** school

Children an heep, ycomen of Cristen blood,
That lerned in that scole yeer by yere
Swich manere doctrine as men used there,
This is to seyn, to syngen and to rede,   *1690
As smale children doon in hire childhede.

Among thise children was a wydwes sone,
A litel clergeon, seven yeer of age,
That day by day to scole was his wone,
And eek also, where as he saugh th'ymage   505
Of Cristes mooder, hadde he in usage,
As hym was taught, to knele adoun and seye
His *Ave Marie*, as he goth by the weye.

Thus hath this wydwe hir litel sone ytaught
Oure blisful Lady, Cristes mooder deere,   *1700
To worshipe ay, and he forgat it naught,
For sely child wol alday soone leere.
But ay, whan I remembre on this mateere,
Seint Nicholas stant evere in my presence,
For he so yong to Crist dide reverence.   515

This litel child, his litel book lernynge,
As he sat in the scole at his prymer,
He *Alma redemptoris* herde synge,
As children lerned hire antiphoner;
And as he dorste, he drough hym ner and ner,   *1710
And herkned ay the wordes and the noote,
Til he the firste vers koude al by rote.

Noght wiste he what this Latyn was to seye,
For he so yong and tendre was of age.
But on a day his felawe gan he preye   525
T'expounden hym this song in his langage,
Or telle hym why this song was in usage;
This preyde he hym to construe and declare
Ful often tyme upon his knowes bare.

His felawe, which that elder was than he,   *1720
Answerde hym thus: "This song, I have herd seye,
Was maked of our blisful Lady free,
Hire to salue, and eek hire for to preye

To been oure help and socour whan we deye.
I kan namoore expounde in this mateere.   535
I lerne song; I kan but smal grammeere."

"And is this song maked in reverence
Of Cristes mooder?" seyde this innocent.
"Now, certes, I wol do my diligence
To konne it al er Cristemasse be went.   *1730
Though that I for my prymer shal be shent
And shal be beten thries in an houre,
I wol it konne Oure Lady for to honoure!"

His felawe taughte hym homward prively,
Fro day to day, til he koude it by rote,   545
And thanne he song it wel and boldely,
Fro word to word, acordynge with the note.
Twies a day it passed thurgh his throte,
To scoleward and homward whan he wente;
On Cristes mooder set was his entente.   *1740

As I have seyd, thurghout the Juerie
This litel child, as he cam to and fro,
Ful murily than wolde he synge and crie
O Alma redemptoris everemo.
The swetnesse his herte perced so   555
Of Cristes mooder that, to hire to preye,
He kan nat stynte of syngyng by the weye.

Oure firste foo, the serpent Sathanas,
That hath in Jues herte his waspes nest,
Up swal, and seide, "O Hebrayk peple, allas!   *1750
Is this to yow a thyng that is honest,
That swich a boy shal walken as hym lest
In youre despit, and synge of swich sentence,
Which is agayn youre lawes reverence?"

Fro thennes forth the Jues han conspired   565
This innocent out of this world to chace.
An homycide therto han they hyred,
That in an aleye hadde a privee place;
And as the child gan forby for to pace,
This cursed Jew hym hente, and heeld hym faste,
And kitte his throte, and in a pit hym caste.   *1761

503 **clergeon:** schoolboy
504 **wone:** custom
508 **Ave Marie:** Hail Mary
514 **Seint Nicholas:** patron of clerks
517 **prymer:** elementary school book
518 **Alma redemptoris:** "Gracious [mother] of the Redeemer"
519 **antiphoner:** book of antiphonal hymns
523 **seye:** mean
526 **T' expounden:** to interpret
529 **knowes:** knees
533 **salue:** greet

536 **kan:** know   **smal grammeere:** little grammar
540 **konne:** learn
541 **for my prymer:** for not learning my lessons   **shent:** scolded
544 **homward:** (as they went) towards home
560 **swal:** swelled
562 **boy:** brat   **hym lest:** he pleases
563 **sentence:** subject, meaning
567 **homycide:** murderer
568 **aleye:** alley
570 **hym hente:** seized him

I seye that in a wardrobe they hym threwe
Where as thise Jewes purgen hire entraille.
O cursed folk of Herodes al newe,
What may youre yvel entente yow availle?   575
Mordre wol out, certeyn, it wol nat faille,
And namely ther th'onour of God shal sprede;
The blood out crieth on youre cursed dede.

O martir, sowded to virginitee,
Now maystow syngen, folwynge evere in oon   *1770
The white Lamb celestial—quod she—
Of which the grete evaungelist, Seint John,
In Pathmos wroot, which seith that they that goon
Biforn this Lamb and synge a song al newe,
That nevere, flesshly, wommen they ne knewe.   585

This poure wydwe awaiteth al that nyght
After hir litel child, but he cam noght;
For which, as soone as it was dayes lyght,
With face pale of drede and bisy thoght,
She hath at scole and elleswhere hym soght,   *1780
Til finally she gan so fer espie
That he last seyn was in the Juerie.

With moodres pitee in hir brest enclosed,
She gooth, as she were half out of hir mynde,
To every place where she hath supposed   595
By liklihede hir litel child to fynde;
And evere on Cristes mooder meeke and kynde
She cride, and atte laste thus she wroghte:
Among the cursed Jues she hym soghte.

She frayneth and she preyeth pitously   *1790
To every Jew that dwelte in thilke place,
To telle hire if hir child wente oght forby.
They seyde "nay"; but Jhesu of his grace
Yaf in hir thoght inwith a litel space
That in that place after hir sone she cryde,   605
Where he was casten in a pit bisyde.

O grete God, that parfournest thy laude
By mouth of innocentz, lo, heere thy myght!
This gemme of chastite, this emeraude,

And eek of martirdom the ruby bright,   *1800
Ther he with throte ykorven lay upright,
He Alma redemptoris gan to synge
So loude that al the place gan to rynge.

The Cristene folk that thurgh the strete wente
In coomen for to wondre upon this thyng,   615
And hastily they for the provost sente;
He cam anon withouten tariyng,
And herieth Crist that is of hevene kyng,
And eek his mooder, honour of mankynde,
And after that the Jewes leet he bynde.   *1810

This child with pitous lamentacioun
Up taken was, syngynge his song alway,
And with honour of greet processioun
They carien hym unto the nexte abbay.
His mooder swownynge by his beere lay;   625
Unnethe myghte the peple that was theere
This newe Rachel brynge fro his beere.

With torment and with shameful deeth echon,
This provost dooth thise Jewes for to sterve
That of this mordre wiste, and that anon.   *1820
He nolde no swich cursednesse observe.
"Yvele shal have that yvele wol deserve";
Therfore with wilde hors he dide hem drawe,
And after that he heng hem by the lawe.

Upon this beere ay lith this innocent   635
Biforn the chief auter, whil the masse laste;
And after that, the abbot with his covent
Han sped hem for to burien hym ful faste;
And whan they hooly water on hym caste,
Yet spak this child, whan spreynd was hooly water,
And song O Alma redemptoris mater!   *1831

This abbot, which that was an hooly man,
As monkes been—or elles oghte be—
This yonge child to conjure he bigan,

611 **ykorven:** cut through
616 **provost:** magistrate
618 **herieth:** praises
620 **leet he bynde:** he had bound
626 **Unnethe:** hardly
627 **Rachel:** the biblical mother, who was inconsolable, weeping for her children
628 **torment:** torture   **echon:** each one (i.e., both)
629 **sterve:** die
631 **observe:** respect, observe (a practice)
634 **by:** in accordance with
636 **auter:** altar
637 **covent:** convent, the monks in the abbey
640 **spreynd:** sprinkled
644 **conjure:** ask, entreat

572 **wardrobe:** privy
574 **Herodes al newe:** new Herods
579 **sowded:** firmly united
580 **evere in oon:** always, continually
583 **Pathmos:** Patmos
585 **flesshly:** carnally
600 **frayneth:** asks
602 **oght:** at all
609 **emeraude:** emerald

And seyde, "O deere child, I halse thee,   645
In vertu of the hooly Trinitee,
Tel me what is thy cause for to synge,
Sith that thy throte is kut to my semynge?"

"My throte is kut unto my nekke boon,"
Seyde this child, "and as by wey of kynde   *1840
I sholde have dyed, ye, longe tyme agon.
But Jesu Christ, as ye in bookes fynde,
Wil that his glorie laste and be in mynde,
And for the worship of his Mooder deere
Yet may I synge *O Alma* loude and cleere.   655

"This welle of mercy, Cristes mooder sweete,
I loved alwey, as after my konnynge;
And whan that I my lyf sholde forlete,
To me she cam, and bad me for to synge
This anthem verraily in my deyynge,   *1850
As ye han herd, and whan that I hadde songe,
Me thoughte she leyde a greyn upon my tonge.

"Wherfore I synge, and synge moot certeyn,
In honour of that blisful Mayden free
Til fro my tonge of taken is the greyn;   665
And after that thus seyde she to me:
'My litel child, now wol I fecche thee,

Whan that the greyn is fro thy tonge ytake.
Be nat agast; I wol thee nat forsake.'"

This hooly monk, this abbot, hym meene I,   *1860
His tonge out caughte, and took awey the greyn,
And he yaf up the goost ful softely.
And whan this abbot hadde this wonder seyn,
His salte teeris trikled doun as reyn,
And gruf he fil al plat upon the grounde,   675
And stille he lay as he had ben ybounde.

The covent eek lay on the pavement
Wepynge, and herying Cristes mooder deere,
And after that they ryse, and forth been went,
And tooken awey this martir from his beere;   *1870
And in a tombe of marbul stones cleere
Enclosen they his litel body sweete.
Ther he is now, God leve us for to meete!

O yonge Hugh of Lyncoln, slayn also
With cursed Jewes, as it is notable,   685
For it is but a litel while ago,
Preye eek for us, we synful folk unstable,
That of his mercy God so merciable
On us his grete mercy multiplie,   *1879
For reverence of his mooder Marie. Amen

Heere is ended the Prioresses Tale.

Prologue to Sir Thopas

Bihoold the murye wordes of the Hoost to Chaucer.

Whan seyd was al this miracle, every man
As sobre was that wonder was to se,
Til that oure Hooste japen tho bigan,
And thanne at erst he looked upon me,
And seyde thus: "What man artow?" quod he;   695

"Thou lookest as thou woldest fynde an hare,
For evere upon the ground I se thee stare.

"Approche neer, and looke up murily.
Now war yow, sires, and lat this man have place!
He in the waast is shape as wel as I;   *1890

---

645 **halse:** beseech
648 **to my semynge:** as it seems to me
650 **by wey of kynde:** in the natural course of things
656 **welle:** source
658 **forlete:** lose
662 **greyn:** seed

---

691 **miracle:** tale of a miracle
694 **at erst:** for the first time

---

675 **gruf:** face down   **plat:** flat
683 **leve:** allow
684 **Hugh of Lyncoln:** a child martyr; see n.
685 **With:** by

---

700 **waast:** waist

This were a popet in an arm t'enbrace
For any womman, smal and fair of face.
He semeth elvyssh by his contenaunce,
For unto no wight dooth he daliaunce.

"Sey now somwhat, syn oother folk han sayd;   705

Telle us a tale of myrthe, and that anon."
"Hooste," quod I, "ne beth nat yvele apayd,
For oother tale certes kan I noon,
But of a rym I lerned longe agoon."   *1899
"Ye, that is good," quod he; "now shul we heere
Som deyntee thyng, me thynketh by his cheere."

Sir Thopas

Heere bigynneth Chaucers Tale of Thopas.

The First Fit

Listeth, lordes, in good entent,
And I wol telle verrayment
    Of myrthe and of solas,
Al of a knyght was fair and gent   715
In bataille and in tourneyment;
    His name was sire Thopas.

Yborn he was in fer contree,
In Flaundres, al biyonde the see,
    At Poperyng, in the place.   *1910
His fader was a man ful free,
And lord he was of that contree,
    As it was Goddes grace.

Sire Thopas wax a doghty swayn;
Whit was his face as payndemayn,   725
    His lippes rede as rose;
His rode is lyk scarlet in grayn,
And I yow telle in good certayn
    He hadde a semely nose.

His heer, his berd was lyk saffroun,   *1920
That to his girdel raughte adoun;

His shoon of cordewane.
Of Brugges were his hosen broun,
His robe was of syklatoun,
    That coste many a jane.   735

He koude hunte at wilde deer,
And ride an haukyng for river
    With grey goshauk on honde;
Therto he was a good archeer;
Of wrastlyng was ther noon his peer,   *1930
    Ther any ram shal stonde.

Ful many a mayde, bright in bour,
They moorne for hym paramour,
    Whan hem were bet to slepe;
But he was chaast and no lechour,   745
And sweete as is the brembul flour
    That bereth the rede hepe.

And so bifel upon a day,
For sothe, as I yow telle may,
    Sire Thopas wolde out ride.   *1940
He worth upon his steede gray,

707 **yvele apayd:** displeased
711 **deyntee:** excellent

701 **popet:** little doll
702 **smal:** slender
703 **elvyssh:** abstracted (literally, mysterious, not of this world)
704 **dooth he daliaunce:** is he sociable

712 **Listeth:** listen
713 **verrayment:** truly
715 **gent:** elegant (?); see n.
719 **Flaundres:** Flanders
720 **Poperyng:** a town in Flanders   **in the place:** right there(?); see n.
724 **swayn:** young gentleman; see n.
725 **payndemayn:** fine white bread
727 **rode:** complexion   **scarlet in grayn:** deep-dyed scarlet cloth
730 **saffroun:** saffron (deep yellow in color)
731 **raughte:** reached

732 **shoon:** shoes   **cordewane:** Cordovan leather
733 **Brugges:** Bruges   **hosen:** stockings
734 **syklatoun:** costly silken material
735 **jane:** a Genoese coin worth about half a penny
736 **deer:** either deer or animals
737 **for river:** to hawk for waterfowl
738 **goshauk:** a kind of hawk; see n.
741 **stonde:** stand as a prize
742 **bright in bour:** beautiful in (the ladies') chamber
743 **moorne:** yearn
746 **brembul flour:** dog-rose
747 **hepe:** (rose-)hip
751 **worth upon:** climbs on

And in his hand a launcegay,
A long swerd by his side.

He priketh thurgh a fair forest,
Therinne is many a wilde best,   755
Ye, bothe bukke and hare;
And as he priketh north and est,
I telle it yow, hym hadde almest
Bitid a sory care.

Ther spryngen herbes grete and smale,   *1950
The lycorys and the cetewale,
And many a clowe-gylofre;
And notemuge to putte in ale,
Wheither it be moyste or stale,
Or for to leye in cofre.   765

The briddes synge, it is no nay,
The sparhauk and the papejay,
That joye it was to heere;
The thrustelcok made eek hir lay,
The wodedowve upon the spray   *1960
She sang ful loude and cleere.

Sire Thopas fil in love-longynge,
Al whan he herde the thrustel synge,
And pryked as he were wood.
His faire steede in his prikynge   775
So swatte that men myghte him wrynge;
His sydes were al blood.

Sire Thopas eek so wery was
For prikyng on the softe gras,
So fiers was his corage,   *1970
That doun he leyde him in that plas
To make his steede som solas,
And yaf hym good forage.

"O Seinte Marie, benedicite!
What eyleth this love at me   785
To bynde me so soore?

Me dremed al this nyght, pardee,
An elf-queene shal my lemman be
And slepe under my goore.

"An elf-queene wol I love, ywis,   *1980
For in this world no womman is
Worthy to be my make
          In towne;
Alle othere wommen I forsake,
And to an elf-queene I me take   795
By dale and eek by downe!"

Into his sadel he clamb anon,
And priketh over stile and stoon
An elf-queene for t'espye,
Til he so longe hath riden and goon   *1990
That he foond, in a pryve woon,
The contree of Fairye
          So wilde;
For in that contree was ther noon
That to him durste ride or goon,   805
Neither wyf ne childe;

Til that ther cam a greet geaunt,
His name was sire Olifaunt,
A perilous man of dede.
He seyde, "Child, by Termagaunt,   *2000
But if thou prike out of myn haunt,
Anon I sle thy steede
          With mace.
Heere is the queene of Fayerye,
With harpe and pipe and symphonye,   815
Dwellynge in this place."

The child seyde, "Also moote I thee,
Tomorwe wol I meete with thee,
Whan I have myn armoure;
And yet I hope, *par ma fay*,   *2010
That thou shalt with this launcegay
Abyen it ful sowre.
          Thy mawe
Shal I percen, if I may,
Er it be fully pryme of day,   825
For heere thow shalt be slawe."

Sire Thopas drow abak ful faste;
This geant at hym stones caste
   Out of a fel staf-slynge.
But faire escapeth child Thopas,   *2020
And al it was thurgh Goddes gras,
   And thurgh his fair berynge.

[*The Second Fit*]

   Yet listeth, lordes, to my tale
Murier than the nightyngale,
   For now I wol yow rowne   835
How sir Thopas, with sydes smale,
Prikyng over hill and dale,
   Is comen agayn to towne.

   His myrie men comanded he
To make hym bothe game and glee,   *2030
   For nedes moste he fighte
With a geaunt with hevedes three,
For paramour and jolitee
   Of oon that shoon ful brighte.

   "Do come," he seyde, "my mynstrales,   845
And geestours for to tellen tales,
   Anon in myn armynge,
Of romances that been roiales,
Of popes and of cardinales,
   And eek of love-likynge."   *2040

   They fette hym first the sweete wyn,
And mede eek in a mazelyn,
   And roial spicerye
Of gyngebreed that was ful fyn,
And lycorys, and eek comyn,   855
   With sugre that is trye.

He dide next his white leere
Of cloth of lake fyn and cleere,
   A breech and eek a sherte;

And next his sherte an aketoun,   *2050
And over that an haubergeoun
   For percynge of his herte;

   And over that a fyn hawberk,
Was al ywroght of Jewes werk,
   Ful strong it was of plate;   865
And over that his cote-armour
As whit as is a lilye flour,
   In which he wol debate.

   His sheeld was al of gold so reed,
And therinne was a bores heed,   *2060
   A charbocle bisyde;
And there he swoor on ale and breed
How that the geaunt shal be deed,
   Bityde what bityde!

   His jambeux were of quyrboilly,   875
His swerdes shethe of yvory,
   His helm of latoun bright;
His sadel was of rewel boon,
His brydel as the sonne shoon,
   Or as the moone light.   *2070

   His spere was of fyn ciprees,
That bodeth werre, and nothyng pees,
   The heed ful sharpe ygrounde;
His steede was al dappull gray,
It gooth an ambil in the way   885
   Ful softely and rounde
      In londe.
Loo, lordes myne, heere is a fit!
If ye wol any moore of it,
   To telle it wol I fonde.   *2080

The [*Third*] Fit

   Now holde youre mouth, *par charitee*,
Bothe knyght and lady free,

829 **fel:** terrible   **staf-slynge:** sling on the end of a stick
831 **gras:** grace
835 **rowne:** tell
836 **sydes smale:** slender waist
839 **myrie men:** companions in arms
840 **game and glee:** entertainment
843 **jolitee:** pleasure
845 **Do come:** cause to come, summon   **mynstrales:** musicians
846 **geestours:** tellers of *gestes,* tales
848 **roiales:** royal
850 **love-likynge:** the joys of love
852 **mede:** mead   **mazelyn:** mazer, wooden bowl
853 **spicerye:** delicacies, titbits
854 **gyngebreed:** preserved ginger
855 **lycorys:** licorice   **comyn:** cumin
856 **sugre:** sugar   **trye:** excellent
857 **leere:** flesh
858 **cloth of lake:** fine linen
859 **breech:** pair of trousers; see Expl. Notes for the technical vocabulary in lines 859–66.

860 **aketoun:** quilted jacket worn under the armor
861 **haubergeoun:** chain-mail shirt
862 **For:** to prevent
863 **hawberk:** plate armor
866 **cote-armour:** coat of arms, worn over the armor
868 **debate:** fight, dispute
870 **bores:** boar's
871 **charbocle:** carbuncle, red gemstone; see n.
874 Come what may!
875 **jambeux:** greaves, leg-armor   **quyrboilly:** hardened leather
877 **latoun:** latten, a brass-like alloy
878 **rewel boon:** ivory
881 **ciprees:** cypress
882 **bodeth:** forebodes
885 **ambil:** slow walk
886 **rounde:** easily
888 **fit:** canto
890 **fonde:** try, attempt
891 **par charitee:** for charity's sake, please

And herkneth to my spelle;
Of bataille and of chivalry,
And of ladyes love-drury   895
    Anon I wol yow telle.

Men speken of romances of prys,
Of Horn child and of Ypotys,
    Of Beves and sir Gy,
Of sir Lybeux and Pleyndamour—   *2090
But sir Thopas, he bereth the flour
    Of roial chivalry!

His goode steede al he bistrood,
And forth upon his wey he glood
    As sparcle out of the bronde;   905

Upon his creest he bar a tour,
And therinne stiked a lilie flour—
    God shilde his cors fro shonde!

And for he was a knyght auntrous,
He nolde slepen in noon hous,   *2100
    But liggen in his hoode;
His brighte helm was his wonger,
And by hym baiteth his dextrer
    Of herbes fyne and goode.

Hymself drank water of the well,   915
As dide the knyght sire Percyvell
    So worly under wede,
Til on a day—

Heere the Hoost stynteth Chaucer of his Tale of Thopas.

"Namoore of this, for Goddes dignitee,"
Quod oure Hooste, "for thou makest me   *2110
So wery of thy verray lewednesse
That, also wisly God my soule blesse,
Myne eres aken of thy drasty speche.
Now swich a rym the devel I biteche!
This may wel be rym dogerel," quod he.   925
    "Why so?" quod I, "why wiltow lette me
Moore of my tale than another man,
Syn that it is the beste rym I kan?"
    "By God," quod he, "for pleynly, at a word,
Thy drasty rymyng is nat worth a toord! *2120
Thou doost noght elles but despendest tyme.
Sire, at o word, thou shalt no lenger ryme.
Lat se wher thou kanst tellen aught in geeste,
Or telle in prose somwhat, at the leeste,
In which ther be som murthe or som doctryne." 935
    "Gladly," quod I, "by Goddes sweete pyne!
I wol yow telle a litel thyng in prose
That oghte liken yow, as I suppose,

Or elles, certes, ye been to daungerous.
It is a moral tale vertuous,   *2130
Al be it told somtyme in sondry wyse
Of sondry folk, as I shal yow devyse.
    "As thus: ye woot that every Evaungelist
That telleth us the peyne of Jhesu Crist
Ne seith nat alle thyng as his felawe dooth; 945
But nathelees hir sentence is al sooth,
And alle acorden as in hire sentence,
Al be ther in hir tellyng difference.
For somme of hem seyn moore, and somme seyn
        lesse,
Whan they his pitous passioun expresse— *2140
I meene of Mark, Mathew, Luc, and John—
But doutelees hir sentence is al oon.
Therfore, lordynges alle, I yow biseche,
If that yow thynke I varie as in my speche,
As thus, though that I telle somwhat moore 955
Of proverbes than ye han herd bifoore
Comprehended in this litel tretys heere,
To enforce with th'effect of my mateere;
And though I nat the same wordes seye
As ye han herd, yet to yow alle I preye *2150
Blameth me nat; for, as in my sentence,

893 **spelle:** tale
895 **love-drury:** passionate love
897 **prys:** excellence
898 **Horn child:** a hero of English romance   **Ypotys:** child hero of a pious legend
899 **Beves:** Bevis of Hampton   **Gy:** Guy of Warwick
900 **Lybeux:** Lybeaus Desconus ("The Fair Unknown")   **Pleyndamour:** "Full-of-
Love," not identified; see n.
903 **bistrood:** bestrode
904 **glood:** glided
905 **bronde:** burning log

923 **aken:** ache   **drasty:** crappy, worthless
924 **biteche:** commit
930 **toord:** turd
931 **despendest:** waste
933 **geeste:** alliterating verse (?); see n.

906 **creest:** top of the helmet   **tour:** tower
908 **shonde:** harm, shame
909 **knyght auntrous:** knight errant
911 **liggen:** lie
912 **wonger:** pillow
913 **baiteth:** feeds   **dextrer:** war-horse
915 **well:** spring
916 **Percyvell:** the chaste hero of the romance of the Holy Grail
917 So worthy in his armor

939 **daungerous:** difficult, hard to please
947 **sentence:** substance, essential meaning

Shul ye nowher fynden difference
Fro the sentence of this tretys lyte
After the which this murye tale I write.

And therfore herkneth what that I shal seye,   965
And lat me tellen al my tale, I preye."

Explicit

The Tale of Melibee

⑥

Heere bigynneth Chaucers Tale of Melibee.

A yong man called Melibeus, myghty and riche, bigat upon his wyf, that called was Prudence, a doghter which that called was Sophie./

Upon a day bifel that he for his desport is went into the feeldes hym to pleye./ His wyf and eek his doghter hath he left inwith his hous, of which the dores weren faste yshette./ Thre of his olde foes han it espyed, and setten laddres to the walles of his hous, and by wyndowes been entred,/ and   *2160
betten his wyf, and wounded his doghter with fyve mortal woundes in fyve sondry places—/ this is to seyn, in hir feet, in hire handes, in hir erys, in hir nose, and in hire mouth—and leften hire for deed, and wenten awey./

When Melibeus retourned was into his hous, and saugh al this meschief, he, lyk a mad man rentynge his clothes, gan to wepe and crie./

Prudence, his wyf, as ferforth as she dorste, bisoghte hym of his wepyng for to stynte,/ but nat forthy he gan to crie and wepen evere lenger the moore./   975

This noble wyf Prudence remembred hire upon the sentence of Ovide, in his book that cleped is the Remedie of Love, where as he seith,/ "He is a fool that destourbeth the mooder to wepen in the deeth of hire child til she have wept hir fille as for a certein tyme,/ and thanne shal man doon his diligence with amyable wordes hire to reconforte, and preyen hire of hir wepyng for to stynte."/ For which resoun this noble wyf Prudence suffred hir housbonde for to wepe and crie as for a certein space,/ and whan she saugh hir tyme, she seyde hym in this wise: "Allas,

my lord," quod she, "why make ye youreself for to be lyk a fool?/ For sothe it aperteneth   *2170
nat to a wys man to maken swich a sorwe./ Youre doghter, with the grace of God, shal warisshe and escape./ And, al were it so that she right now were deed, ye ne oughte nat, as for hir deeth, youreself to destroye./ Senek seith: 'The wise man shal nat take to greet disconfort for the deeth of his children,/ but, certes, he sholde suffren it in pacience as wel as he abideth the deeth of his owene propre persone.' "/   985

This Melibeus answerde anon and seyde, "What man," quod he, "sholde of his wepyng stente that hath so greet a cause for to wepe?/ Jhesu Crist, oure Lord, hymself wepte for the deeth of Lazarus hys freend."/

Prudence answerde: "Certes, wel I woot attempree wepyng is no thyng deffended to hym that sorweful is, amonges folk in sorwe, but it is rather graunted hym to wepe./ The Apostle Paul unto the Romayns writeth, 'Man shal rejoyse with hem that maken joye and wepen with swich folk as wepen.'/ But though attempree wepyng be ygraunted, outrageous wepyng certes is deffended./   *2180
Mesure of wepyng sholde be considered after the loore that techeth us Senek:/ 'Whan that thy frend is deed,' quod he, 'lat nat thyne eyen to moyste been of teeris, ne to muche drye; although the teeris come to thyne eyen, lat hem nat falle;/ and whan thou hast forgoon thy freend, do diligence to gete another

---

978 **reconforte:** comfort

982 **warisshe:** recover
985 **propre persone:** own self
987 **Lazarus:** see John 11.35.
988 **attempree:** moderate

freend; and this is moore wysdom than for to wepe for thy freend which that thou hast lorn, for therinne is no boote.'/ And therfore, if ye governe yow by sapience, put awey sorwe out of youre herte./ Remembre yow that Jhesus Syrak seith, 'A man that is joyous and glad in herte, it hym conserveth florissynge in his age; but soothly sorweful herte maketh his bones drye.'/ He seith eek thus, that sorwe in   995 herte sleeth ful many a man./ Salomon seith that right as motthes in the shepes flees anoyeth to the clothes, and the smale wormes to the tree, right so anoyeth sorwe to the herte./ Wherfore us oghte, as wel in the deeth of oure children as in the los of oure othere goodes temporels, have pacience./ Remembre yow upon the pacient Job. Whan he hadde lost his children and his temporeel substance, and in his body endured and receyved ful many a grevous tribulacion, yet seyde he thus:/ 'Oure Lord hath yeve it me; oure Lord hath biraft it me; right as oure Lord hath wold, right so it is doon; blessed be the name   *2190 of oure Lord!'"/

To thise forseide thynges answerde Melibeus unto his wyf Prudence: "Alle thy wordes," quod he, "been sothe and therto profitable, but trewely myn herte is troubled with this sorwe so grevously that I noot what to doone."/

"Lat calle," quod Prudence, "thy trewe freendes alle and thy lynage whiche that been wise. Telleth youre cas, and herkneth what they seye in conseillyng, and yow governe after hire sentence./ "Salomon seith, 'Werk alle thy thynges by conseil, and thou shalt never repente.'"/"

Thanne, by the conseil of his wyf Prudence, this Melibeus leet callen a greet congregacion of folk,/ as surgiens, phisiciens, olde folk and yonge, and somme of his olde enemys reconsiled as by hir semblaunt to his love and into his grace;/   1005 and therwithal ther coomen somme of his neighebores that diden hym reverence moore for drede than for love, as it happeth ofte./ Ther coomen also ful many subtile flatereres and wise advocatz lerned in the lawe./

And whan this folk togidre assembled weren, this Melibeus in sorweful wise shewed hem his cas./ And by the manere of his speche it semed that in herte he baar a crueel ire, redy to doon vengeaunce upon his foes, and sodeynly desired that the werre sholde bigynne;/ but nathelees, yet axed he hire conseil upon this matiere./ A surgien, by licence and   *2200 assent of swiche as weren wise, up roos and to Melibeus seyde as ye may heere:/

"Sire," quod he, "as to us surgiens aperteneth that we do to every wight the beste that we kan, where as we been withholde, and to oure pacientz that we do no damage,/ wherfore it happeth many tyme and ofte that whan twey men han everich wounded oother, oon same surgien heeleth hem bothe;/ wherfore unto oure art it is nat pertinent to norice werre ne parties to supporte./ But certes, as to the warisshynge of youre doghter, al be it so that she perilously be wounded, we shullen do so ententif bisynesse fro day to nyght that with the grace of God she shal be hool and sound as soone as is possible."/   1015

Almoost right in the same wise the phisiciens answerden, save that they seyden a fewe woordes moore:/ that right as maladies been cured by hir contraries, right so shul men warisshe werre by vengeaunce./

His neighebores ful of envye, his feyned freendes that semeden reconsiled, and his flatereres/ maden semblant of wepyng, and empeireden and agreggeden muchel of this matiere in preisynge greetly Melibee of myght, of power, of richesse, and of freendes, despisynge the power of his adversaries,/ and seiden outrely that he anon sholde wreken hym on his foes and bigynne werre./   *2210

Up roos thanne an advocat that was wys, by leve and by conseil of othere that were wise, and seide:/ "Lordynges, the nede for which we been assembled in this place is a ful hevy thyng and an heigh matiere,/ by cause of the wrong and of the wikkednesse that hath be doon, and eek by resoun of the grete damages that in tyme comynge been possible to fallen for this same cause,/ and eek by resoun of the grete richesse and power of the parties bothe,/ for the whiche resouns it were a ful greet peril to

---

1014 **norice:** nourish
1015 **warisshynge:** cure
1019 **maden semblant:** feigned, pretended   **empeireden:** made (matters) worse
agreggeden: aggravated
1023 **by resoun of:** because of

---

995 **Jhesus Syrak:** the author of Ecclesiasticus
997 **motthes:** moths   **flees:** fleece   **anoyeth:** do injury

erren in this matiere./ Wherfore, Melibeus,   1025
this is oure sentence: we conseille yow
aboven alle thyng that right anon thou do thy diligence in kepynge of thy propre persone in swich a
wise that thou ne wante noon espie ne wacche thy
persone for to save./ And after that, we conseille that
in thyn hous thou sette sufficeant garnisoun so that
they may as wel thy body as thyn hous defende./ But
certes, for to moeve werre, ne sodeynly for to doon
vengeaunce, we may nat demen in so litel tyme that it
were profitable./ Wherfore we axen leyser and espace
to have deliberacion in this cas to deme./ For the
commune proverbe seith thus: 'He that soone
deemeth, soone shal repente.'/ And eek men   *2220
seyn that thilke juge is wys that soone understondeth a matiere and juggeth by leyser;/ for al be it
so that alle tariyng be anoyful, algates it is nat to
repreve in yevynge of juggement ne in vengeance
takyng, whan it is sufficeant and resonable./ And that
shewed oure Lord Jhesu Crist by ensample, for whan
that the womman that was taken in avowtrie was
broght in his presence to knowen what sholde be
doon with hire persone, al be it so that he wiste wel
hymself what that he wolde answere, yet ne wolde
he nat answere sodeynly, but he wolde have deliberacion, and in the ground he wroot twies./ And by
thise causes we axen deliberacioun, and we shal
thanne, by the grace of God, conseille thee thyng that
shal be profitable."/

Up stirten thanne the yonge folk atones, and the
mooste partie of that compaignye han
scorned this olde wise man, and bigonnen to   1035
make noyse, and seyden that/ right so as whil
that iren is hoot men sholden smyte, right so men
sholde wreken hir wronges whil that they been
fresshe and newe; and with loud voys they criden
"Werre!/

Up roos tho oon of thise olde wise, and with his
hand made contenaunce that men sholde holden hem
stille and yeven hym audience./ "Lordynges," quod
he, "ther is ful many a man that crieth 'Werre, werre!'

that woot ful litel what werre amounteth./ Werre at
his bigynnyng hath so greet an entryng and so large
that every wight may entre whan hym liketh and
lightly fynde werre;/ but certes what ende that
shal therof bifalle, it is nat light to knowe./   *2230
For soothly, whan that werre is ones bigonne,
ther is ful many a child unborn of his mooder that
shal sterve yong by cause of thilke werre, or elles
lyve in sorwe and dye in wrecchednesse./ And therfore, er that any werre bigynne, men moste have greet
conseil and greet deliberacion."/ And whan this olde
man wende to enforcen his tale by resons, wel ny alle
atones bigonne they to rise for to breken his tale, and
beden hym ful ofte his wordes for to abregge./ For
soothly, he that precheth to hem that listen nat heeren
his wordes, his sermon hem anoieth./ For Jhesus
Syrak seith that "musik in wepynge is a noyous
thyng"; this is to seyn: as muche availleth to speken
bifore folk to which his speche anoyeth as it is
to synge biforn hym that wepeth./ And whan   1045
this wise man saugh that hym wanted audience, al shamefast he sette hym doun agayn./ For
Salomon seith: "Ther as thou ne mayst have noon
audience, enforce thee nat to speke."/ "I see wel,"
quod this wise man, "that the commune proverbe is
sooth, that 'good conseil wanteth whan it is moost
nede.' "/

Yet hadde this Melibeus in his conseil many folk
that prively in his eere conseilled hym certeyn thyng,
and conseilled hym the contrarie in general audience./

Whan Melibeus hadde herd that the gretteste partie of his conseil weren accorded that he sholde
maken werre, anoon he consented to hir conseillyng and fully affermed hire sentence./   *2240
Thanne dame Prudence, whan that she saugh
how that hir housbonde shoop hym for to wreken
hym on his foes and to bigynne werre, she in ful
humble wise, whan she saugh hir tyme, seide to hym
thise wordes:/ "My lord," quod she, "I yow biseche,
as hertely as I dar and kan, ne haste yow nat to faste
and, for alle gerdons, as yeveth me audience./ For

1026 **propre persone:** own self   **wacche:** watchman
1027 **garnisoun:** body of armed men
1028 **moeve werre:** begin or provoke war
1029 **espace:** space, opportunity
1033 **avowtrie:** adultery
1037 **made contenaunce:** signaled

1043 **breken his tale:** interrupt his speech   **beden:** prayed
1045 **noyous:** annoying, bothersome
1046 **hym wanted:** he lacked

Piers Alfonce seith, 'Whoso that dooth to thee oother good or harm, haste thee nat to quiten it, for in this wise thy freend wole abyde and thyn enemy shal the lenger lyve in drede.'/ The proverbe seith, 'He hasteth wel that wisely kan abyde,' and 'in wikked haste is no profit.' "/

This Melibee answerde unto his wyf Prudence: "I purpose nat," quod he, "to werke by thy conseil, for many causes and resouns. For certes, every wight wolde holde me thanne a fool;/ this is   1055 to seyn, if I, for thy conseillyng, wolde chaungen thynges that been ordeyned and affermed by so manye wyse./ Secoundely, I seye that alle wommen been wikke, and noon good of hem alle. For 'of a thousand men,' seith Salomon, 'I foond o good man, but certes, of alle wommen, good womman foond I nevere.'/ And also, certes, if I governed me by thy conseil, it sholde seme that I hadde yeve to thee over me the maistrie, and God forbede that it so weere!/ For Jhesus Syrak seith that 'if the wyf have maistrie, she is contrarious to hir housbonde.'/ And Salomon seith: 'Nevere in thy lyf to thy wyf, ne to thy child, ne to thy freend ne yeve no power over thyself, for bettre it were that thy children aske of thy persone thynges that hem nedeth than thou see thy-self in the handes of thy children.'/ And also if   *2250 I wolde werke by thy conseillyng, certes, my conseil moste som tyme be secree, til it were tyme that it moste be knowe, and this ne may noght be./ [Car il est escript, la genglerie des femmes ne puet riens celler fors ce qu'elle ne scet./ Apres, le philosophre dit, en mauvais conseil les femmes vain-quent les hommes; et par ces raisons je ne dois point user de ton conseil.]"/

Whanne dame Prudence, ful debonairly and with greet pacience, hadde herd al that hir housbonde liked for to seye, thanne axed she of hym licence for to speke, and seyde in this wise:/ "My lord," quod she, "as to youre firste resoun, certes it may lightly been answered. For I seye that it is no folie to chaunge conseil whan the thyng is chaunged, or elles whan the thyng semeth ootherweyes than it was

biforn./ And mooreover, I seye that though   1065 ye han sworn and bihight to perfourne youre emprise, and nathelees ye weyve to perfourne thilke same emprise by juste cause, men sholde nat seyn therfore that ye were a liere ne forsworn./ For the book seith that 'the wise man maketh no lesyng whan he turneth his corage to the bettre.'/ And al be it so that youre emprise be establissed and ordeyned by greet multitude of folk, yet thar ye nat accomplice thilke ordinaunce but yow like./ For the trouthe of thynges and the profit been rather founden in fewe folk that been wise and ful of resoun than by greet multitude of folk ther every man crieth and clatereth what that hym liketh. Soothly swich multitude is nat honest./ And as to the seconde resoun, where as ye seyn that alle wommen been wikke; save youre grace, certes ye despisen alle wommen in this wyse, and 'he that al despiseth, al displeseth,' as seith the book./ And Senec seith that 'whoso wole have   *2260 sapience shal no man dispreyse, but he shal gladly techen the science that he kan withouten pre-sumpcion or pride;/ and swiche thynges as he noght ne kan, he shal nat been ashamed to lerne hem, and enquere of lasse folk than hymself.'/ And, sire, that ther hath been many a good womman may lightly be preved./ For certes, sire, oure Lord Jhesu Crist wolde nevere have descended to be born of a womman, if alle wommen hadden been wikke./ And after that, for the grete bountee that is in wommen, oure Lord Jhesu Crist, whan he was risen fro deeth to lyve, appeered rather to a womman than to his Apostles./ And though that Salomon seith that   1075 he ne foond nevere womman good, it folweth nat therfore that alle wommen ben wikke./ For though that he ne foond no good womman, certes, many another man hath founden many a womman ful good and trewe./ Or elles, per aventure, the entente of Salomon was this: that, as in sovereyn bounte, he foond no womman—/this is to seyn, that ther is no wight that hath sovereyn bountee save God allone, as he hymself recordeth in hys Evaungelie./ For ther

---

1053 **Piers Alfonce:** Petrus Alphonsus, author of the popular *Disciplina clericalis*
1062–63 **Car il est,** *etc.*: For it is written that the chattering of women can hide noth-ing except what she does not know. Moreover, the philosopher (i.e., Aristotle) says, in evil counsel women conquer men; and for these reasons I must not use any of your counsel.

1066 **perfourne:** perform, carry out   **emprise:** enterprise   **weyve:** abandon, leave off
1069 **clatereth:** babbles foolishly
1078 **per aventure:** by chance

nys no creature so good that hym ne wanteth
somwhat of the perfeccioun of God, that is his
makere./ Youre thridde reson is this: ye seyn   *2270
that if ye governe yow by my conseil, it
sholde seme that ye hadde yeve me the maistrie and
the lordshipe over youre persone./ Sire, save youre
grace, it is nat so. For if it so were that no man sholde
be conseilled but oonly of hem that hadden lordshipe
and maistrie of his persone, men wolden nat be conseilled so ofte./ For soothly thilke man that asketh
conseil of a purpos, yet hath he free choys wheither
he wole werke by that conseil or noon./ And as to
youre fourthe resoun, ther ye seyn that the janglerie
of wommen kan hyde thynges that they wot noght,
as who seith that a womman kan nat hyde that she
woot;/ sire, thise wordes been understonde of
wommen that been jangleresses and wikked;/   1085
of whiche wommen men seyn that thre thynges dryven a man out of his hous—that is to seyn,
smoke, droppyng of reyn, and wikked wyves;/ and
of swiche wommen seith Salomon that 'it were bettre dwelle in desert than with a womman that is
riotous.'/ And sire, by youre leve, that am nat I,/ for
ye han ful ofte assayed my grete silence and my grete
pacience, and eek how wel that I kan hyde and hele
thynges that men oghte secreely to hyde./ And
soothly, as to youre fifthe resoun, where as ye seyn
that in wikked conseil wommen venquisshe men,
God woot, thilke resoun stant heere in no
stede./ For understoond now, ye asken conseil   *2280
to do wikkednesse;/ and if ye wole werken
wikkednesse, and youre wif restreyneth thilke
wikked purpos, and overcometh yow by reson and
by good conseil,/ certes youre wyf oghte rather to be
preised than yblamed./ Thus sholde ye understonde
the philosophre that seith, 'In wikked conseil wommen venquisshen hir housbondes.'/ And ther as ye
blamen alle wommen and hir resouns, I shal shewe
yow by manye ensamples that many a womman hath
ben ful good, and yet been, and hir conseils
ful hoolsome and profitable./ Eek som men   1095
han seyd that the conseillynge of wommen is
outher to deere or elles to litel of pris./ But al be it so
that ful many a womman is badde and hir conseil vile
and noght worth, yet han men founde ful many a good
womman, and ful discret and wis in conseillynge./
Loo, Jacob by good conseil of his mooder Rebekka
wan the benysoun of Ysaak his fader and the lordshipe
over alle his bretheren./ Judith by hire good conseil
delivered the citee of Bethulie, in which she dwelled,
out of the handes of Olofernus, that hadde it biseged
and wolde have al destroyed it./ Abygail delivered
Nabal hir housbonde fro David the kyng, that wolde
have slayn hym, and apaysed the ire of the
kyng by hir wit and by hir good conseillyng./   *2290
Hester by hir good conseil enhaunced greetly
the peple of God in the regne of Assuerus the kyng./
And the same bountee in good conseillyng of many
a good womman may men telle./ And mooreover,
whan oure Lord hadde creat Adam, oure forme fader,
he seyde in this wise:/ 'It is nat good to been a man
alloone; make we to hym an helpe semblable to hymself.'/ Heere may ye se that if that wommen
were nat goode, and hir conseils goode and   1105
profitable,/ oure Lord God of hevene wolde
nevere han wroght hem, ne called hem help of man,
but rather confusioun of man./ And ther seyde oones
a clerk in two vers, 'What is bettre than gold? Jaspre.
What is bettre than jaspre? Wisedoom./ And what is
better than wisedoom? Womman. And what is bettre
than a good womman? Nothyng.'/ And, sire, by
manye of othre resons may ye seen that manye wommen been goode, and hir conseils goode and profitable./ And therfore, sire, if ye wol triste to my
conseil, I shal restoore yow youre doghter
hool and sound./ And eek I wol do to yow so   *2300
muche that ye shul have honour in this
cause."/

Whan Melibee hadde herd the wordes of his wyf
Prudence, he seyde thus:/ "I se wel that the word of
Salomon is sooth. He seith that 'wordes that been
spoken discreetly by ordinaunce been honycombes,
for they yeven swetnesse to the soule and hoolsomnesse to the body.'/ And, wyf, by cause of thy sweete

1080 **wanteth:** lacks
1084 **janglerie:** chatter
1087 **riotous:** dissolute
1089 **hele:** conceal
1090 **stant . . . in no stede:** has no value, is useless

1098 **benysoun:** blessing
1099 **beseged:** besieged
1103 **forme fader:** forefather
1104 **semblable:** similar
1113 **hoolsomnesse:** healthfulness

wordes, and eek for I have assayed and preved thy grete sapience and thy grete trouthe, I wol governe me by thy conseil in alle thyng."/

"Now, sire," quod dame Prudence, "and syn ye vouche sauf to been governed by my conseil, I wol enforme yow how ye shul governe yourself in chesynge of youre conseillours./ Ye shul   1115
first in alle youre werkes mekely biseken to the heighe God that he wol be youre conseillour;/ and shapeth yow to swich entente that he yeve yow conseil and confort, as taughte Thobie his sone:/ 'At alle tymes thou shalt blesse God, and praye hym to dresse thy weyes, and looke that alle thy conseils been in hym for everemoore.'/ Seint Jame eek seith: 'If any of yow have nede of sapience, axe it of God.'/ And afterward thanne shul ye taken conseil in yourself, and examyne wel youre thoghtes of swich thyng as yow thynketh that is best for youre   *2310
profit./ And thanne shul ye dryve fro youre herte thre thynges that been contrariouse to good conseil;/ that is to seyn, ire, coveitise, and hastifnesse./

"First, he that axeth conseil of hymself, certes he moste been withouten ire, for manye causes./ The firste is this: he that hath greet ire and wratthe in hymself, he weneth alwey that he may do thyng that he may nat do./ And secoundely, he that is irous and wrooth, he ne may nat wel deme;/   1125
and he that may nat wel deme, may nat wel conseille./ The thridde is this, that he that is irous and wrooth, as seith Senec, ne may nat speke but blameful thynges,/ and with his viciouse wordes he stireth oother folk to angre and to ire./ And eek, sire, ye moste dryve coveitise out of youre herte./ For the Apostle seith that coveitise is roote of alle harmes./ And trust wel that a coveitous man   *2320
ne kan noght deme ne thynke, but oonly to fulfille the ende of his coveitise;/ and certes, that ne may nevere been accompliced, for evere the moore habundaunce that he hath of richesse, the moore he desireth./ And, sire, ye moste also dryve out of youre herte hastifnesse; for certes,/ ye ne may nat deeme for the beste by a sodeyn thought that falleth in youre herte, but ye moste avyse yow on it ful ofte./ For, as

ye herde her biforn, the commune proverbe is this, that 'he that soone deemeth, soone   1135
repenteth.'/ Sire, ye ne be nat alwey in lyk disposicioun;/ for certes, somthyng that somtyme semeth to yow that it is good for to do, another tyme it semeth to yow the contrarie./

"Whan ye han taken conseil in youreself and han deemed by good deliberacion swich thyng as you semeth best,/ thanne rede I yow that ye kepe it secree./ Biwrey nat youre conseil to no persone, but if so be that ye wenen sikerly that thurgh youre biwreyyng youre condicioun shal be to yow the moore profitable./ For Jhesus Syrak seith,   *2330
'Neither to thy foo ne to thy frend discovere nat thy secree ne thy folie,/ for they wol yeve yow audience and lookynge and supportacioun in thy presence and scorne thee in thyn absence.'/ Another clerk seith that 'scarsly shaltou fynden any persone that may kepe conseil secrely.'/ The book seith, 'Whil that thou kepest thy conseil in thyn herte, thou kepest it in thy prisoun,/ and whan thou biwreyest thy conseil to any wight, he holdeth thee in   1145
his snare.'/ And therfore yow is bettre to hyde youre conseil in youre herte than praye him to whom ye han biwreyed youre conseil that he wole kepen it cloos and stille./ For Seneca seith: 'If so be that thou ne mayst nat thyn owene conseil hyde, how darstou prayen any oother wight thy conseil secrely to kepe?'/ But nathelees, if thou wene sikerly that the biwreiyng of thy conseil to a persone wol make thy condicion to stonden in the bettre plyt, thanne shaltou tellen hym thy conseil in this wise./ First thou shalt make no semblant wheither thee were levere pees or werre, or this or that, ne shewe hym nat thy wille and thyn entente./ For trust wel that comunli thise conseillours been flatereres,/ namely the conseil-   *2340
lours of grete lordes,/ for they enforcen hem alwey rather to speken plesante wordes, enclynynge to the lordes lust, than wordes that been trewe or profitable./ And therfore men seyn that the riche man hath seeld good conseil, but if he have it of hymself./

And after that thou shalt considere thy freendes and thyne enemys./ And as touchynge thy freendes, thou shalt considere which of hem been moost feithful

---

1117 **Thobie:** Tobias (Tobias 4.10)
1118 **dresse:** direct
1119 **Seint Jame:** James 1.5
1127 **blameful:** blameworthy

1142 **supportacioun:** support

and moost wise and eldest and most approved
in conseillyng;/ and of hem shalt thou aske   1155
thy conseil, as the caas requireth./ I seye that
first ye shul clepe to youre conseil youre freendes that
been trewe./ For Salomon seith that 'right as the herte
of a man deliteth in savour that is soote, right so the
conseil of trewe freendes yeveth swetnesse to the
soule.'/ He seith also, "Ther may no thyng be likned
to the trewe freend,/ for certes gold ne silver ben nat
so muche worth as the goode wyl of a trewe
freend.'/ And eek he seith that 'a trewe freend   *2350
is a strong deffense; who so that it fyndeth,
certes he fyndeth a greet tresour.'/ Thanne shul ye eek
considere if that youre trewe freendes been discrete
and wise. For the book seith, 'Axe alwey thy conseil
of hem that been wise.'/ And by this same resoun shul
ye clepen to youre conseil of youre freendes that been
of age, swiche as han seyn and been expert in manye
thynges and been approved in conseillynges./ For the
book seith that 'in olde men is the sapience, and in
longe tyme the prudence.'/ And Tullius seith that
'grete thynges ne been nat ay accompliced by
strengthe, ne by delivernesse of body, but by good
conseil, by auctoritee of persones, and by science; the
whiche thre thynges ne been nat fieble by age, but
certes they enforcen and encreescen day by
day.'/And thanne shul ye kepe this for a gen-   1165
eral reule: First shul ye clepen to youre conseil a fewe of youre freendes that been especiale;/
for Salomon seith, 'Manye freendes have thou, but
among a thousand chese thee oon to be thy conseillour.'/ For al be it so that thou first ne telle thy conseil
but to a fewe, thou mayst afterward telle it to mo folk
if it be nede./ But looke alwey that thy conseillours
have thilke thre condiciouns that I have seyd bifore—
that is to seyn, that they be trewe, wise, and of oold
experience./ And werke nat alwey in every nede by
oon counseillour allone; for somtyme
bihooveth it to been conseilled by manye./ For   *2360
Salomon seith, 'Salvacion of thynges is
where as ther been manye conseillours.'/

"Now, sith that I have toold yow of which folk ye
sholde been counseilled, now wol I teche yow which
conseil ye oghte to eschewe./ First, ye shul eschue the
conseillyng of fooles;for Salomon seith, 'Taak no
conseil of a fool, for he ne kan noght conseille but
after his owene lust and his affeccioun.'/ The book
seith that 'the propretee of a fool is this: he troweth
lightly harm of every wight, and lightly troweth alle
bountee in hymself.'/ Thou shalt eek eschue the conseillyng of alle flatereres, swiche as enforcen hem
rather to preise youre persone by flaterye than
for to telle yow the soothfastnesse of thyn-   1175
ges./ Wherfore Tullius seith, 'Amonges alle
the pestilences that been in freendshipe the gretteste
is flaterie.' And therfore is it moore nede that thou
eschue and drede flatereres than any oother peple./
The book seith, 'Thou shalt rather drede and flee fro
the sweete wordes of flaterynge preiseres than fro the
egre wordes of thy freend that seith thee thy sothes.'/
Salomon seith that 'the wordes of a flaterere is a
snare to cacche with innocentz.'/ He seith also that
'he that speketh to his freend wordes of swetnesse
and of plesaunce setteth a net biforn his feet to cacche hym.'/ And therfore seith Tullius, 'Enclyne nat
thyne eres to flatereres, ne taak no conseil of
the wordes of flaterye.'/ And Caton seith,   *2370
'Avyse thee wel, and eschue the wordes of
swetnesse and of plesaunce.'/ And eek thou shalt
eschue the conseillyng of thyne olde enemys that
been reconsiled./ The book seith that 'no wight
retourneth saufly into the grace of his olde enemy.'/
And Isope seith, 'Ne trust nat to hem to whiche thou
hast had som tyme werre or enemytee, ne telle hem
nat thy conseil.'/ And Seneca telleth the cause why:
'It may nat be,' seith he, 'that where greet fyr hath
longe tyme endured, that ther ne dwelleth
som vapour of warmnesse.'/ And therfore   1185
seith Salomon, 'In thyn olde foo trust
nevere.'/ For sikerly, though thyn enemy be reconsiled, and maketh thee chiere of humylitee, and
lowteth to thee with his heed, ne trust hym nevere./
For certes he maketh thilke feyned humilitee moore
for his profit than for any love of thy persone, by
cause that he deemeth to have victorie over thy persone by swich feyned contenance, the which victorie
he myghte nat have by strif or werre./ And Peter
Alfonce seith, "Make no felawshipe with thyne olde

1177 **egre:** sharp
1184 **Isope:** Ysopus, the Latin version of Aesop's *Fables*
1189 **Peter Alfonce:** Petrus Alphonsus

1165 **Tullius:** Cicero   **delivernesse:** agility

enemys, for if thou do hem bountee, they wol per-
verten it into wikkednesse.'/ And eek thou most
eschue the conseillyng of hem that been thy servantz
and beren thee greet reverence, for peraventure they seyn it moore for drede than for   *2380
love./ And therfore seith a philosophre in this
wise: 'Ther is no wight parfitly trewe to hym that he
to soore dredeth.'/ And Tullius seith, 'Ther nys no
myght so greet of any emperour that longe may
endure, but if he have moore love of the peple than
drede.'/ Thou shalt also eschue the conseiling of folk
that been dronkelewe, for they ne kan no conseil
hyde./ For Salomon seith, 'Ther is no privetee ther
as regneth dronkenesse.'/ Ye shul also han in suspect
the conseillyng of swich folk as conseille yow o
thyng prively and conseille yow the contrarie
openly./ For Cassidorie seith that 'it is a   1195
manere sleighte to hyndre, whan he sheweth
to doon o thyng openly and werketh prively the contrarie.'/ Thou shalt also have in suspect the conseillyng of wikked folk. For the book seith, 'The
conseillyng of wikked folk is alwey ful of fraude.'/
And David seith, 'Blisful is that man that hath nat folwed the conseilyng of shrewes.'/ Thou shalt also
eschue the conseillyng of yong folk, for hir conseil
is nat rype./

   "Now, sire, sith I have shewed yow of which folk
ye shul take youre conseil and of which folk
ye shul folwe the conseil,/ now wol I teche   *2390
yow how ye shal examyne youre conseil, after
the doctrine of Tullius./ In the examynynge thanne
of youre conseillour ye shul considere manye thynges./ Alderfirst thou shalt considere that in thilke
thyng that thou purposest, and upon what thyng thou
wolt have conseil, that verray trouthe be seyd and
conserved; this is to seyn, telle trewely thy tale./ For
he that seith fals may nat wel be conseilled in that
cas of which he lieth./ And after this thou shalt considere the thynges that acorden to that thou purposest for to do by thy conseillours, if resoun
accorde therto,/ and eek if thy myght may   1205
atteine therto, and if the moore part and the
bettre part of thy conseillours acorde therto, or noon./
Thanne shaltou considere what thyng shal folwe of

that conseillyng, as hate, pees, werre, grace, profit, or
damage, and manye othere thynges./ And in alle thise
thynges thou shalt chese the beste and weyve alle othere thynges./ Thanne shaltow considere of what roote
is engendred the matiere of thy conseil and what fruyt
it may conceyve and engendre./ Thou shalt eek considere alle thise causes, fro whennes they
been sprongen./ And whan ye han examyned   *2400
youre conseil, as I have seyd, and which partie is the bettre and moore profitable, and han
approved it by manye wise folk and olde,/ thanne
shaltou considere if thou mayst parfourne it and
maken of it a good ende./ For certes resoun wol nat
that any man sholde bigynne a thyng but if he myghte
parfourne it as hym oghte;/ ne no wight sholde take
upon hym so hevy a charge that he myghte nat bere
it./ For the proverbe seith, 'He that to muche
embraceth, distreyneth litel.'/ And Catoun   1215
seith, 'Assay to do swich thyng as thou hast
power to doon, lest that the charge oppresse thee so
soore that thee bihoveth to weyve thyng that thou hast
bigonne.'/ And if so be that thou be in doute wheither thou mayst parfourne a thing or noon, chese
rather to suffre than bigynne./ And Piers Alphonce
seith, 'If thou hast myght to doon a thyng of which
thou most repente, it is bettre "nay" than "ye." '/ This
is to seyn, that thee is bettre holde thy tonge stille
than for to speke./ Thanne may ye understonde by
strenger resons that if thou hast power to parfourne a
werk of which thou shalt repente, thanne is it
bettre that thou suffre than bigynne./ Wel seyn   *2410
they that defenden every wight to assaye a
thyng of which he is in doute wheither he may parfourne it or noon./ And after, whan ye han examyned
youre conseil, as I have seyd biforn, and knowen wel
that ye may parfourne youre emprise, conferme it
thanne sadly til it be at an ende./

   "Now is it resoun and tyme that I shewe yow
whanne and wherfore that ye may chaunge youre
counseil withouten youre repreve./ Soothly, a man
may chaungen his purpos and his conseil if the cause
cesseth, or whan a newe caas bitydeth./ For the lawe

1196 **Cassidorie:** Cassiodorus
1198 **David:** Psalms 1.1

1208 **weyve:** abandon, waive
1212 **parfourne:** perform, carry out
1215 **distreyneth:** holds, keeps
1222 **conferme:** prosecute, pursue

seith that 'upon thynges that newely bityden
bihoveth newe conseil.'/ And Senec seith, 'If   1225
thy conseil is comen to the eeris of thyn
enemy, chaunge thy conseil.'/ Thou mayst also
chaunge thy conseil if so be that thou fynde that by
errour, or by oother cause, harm or damage may
bityde./ Also if thy conseil be dishonest, or ellis
cometh of dishonest cause, chaunge thy conseil./ For
the lawes seyn that 'alle bihestes that been dishoneste
been of no value';/ and eek if so be that it be
inpossible, or may nat goodly be parfourned   *2420
or kept./

"And take this for a general reule, that every conseil that is affermed so strongly that it may nat be
chaunged for no condicioun that may bityde, I seye
that thilke conseil is wikked."/

This Melibeus, whanne he hadde herd the doctrine
of his wyf dame Prudence, answerde in this wyse:/
"Dame," quod he, "as yet into this tyme ye han wel
and covenably taught me as in general how I shal governe me in the chesynge and in the withholdynge of
my conseillours./ But now wolde I fayn that ye wolde
condescende in especial/ and telle me how liketh yow,
or what semeth yow, by oure conseillours that
we han chosen in oure present nede."/   1235

"My lord," quod she, "I biseke yow in al
humblesse that ye wol nat wilfully replie agayn my
resouns, ne distempre youre herte, thogh I speke
thyng that yow displese./ For God woot that, as in
myn entente, I speke it for youre beste, for youre honour, and for youre profite eke./ And soothly, I hope
that youre benyngnytee wol taken it in pacience./
Trusteth me wel," quod she, "that youre conseil as in
this caas ne sholde nat, as to speke properly, be called
a conseillyng, but a mocioun or a moevyng of folye,/
in which conseil ye han erred in many a
sondry wise./   *2430

"First and forward, ye han erred in
th'assemblynge of youre conseillours./ For ye sholde
first have cleped a fewe folk to youre conseil, and
after ye myghte han shewed it to mo folk, if it hadde
been nede./ But certes, ye han sodeynly cleped to
youre conseil a greet multitude of peple, ful
chargeant and ful anoyous for to heere./ Also ye han
erred, for theras ye sholden oonly have cleped to
youre conseil youre trewe frendes olde and wise,/ ye
han ycleped straunge folk, yonge folk, false flatereres, and enemys reconsiled, and folk that
doon yow reverence withouten love./ And eek   1245
also ye have erred, for ye han broght with yow
to youre conseil ire, coveitise, and hastifnesse,/ the
whiche thre thinges been contrariouse to every conseil honest and profitable;/ the whiche thre thinges ye
han nat anientissed or destroyed hem, neither in youreself, ne in youre conseillours, as yow oghte./ Ye han
erred also, for ye han shewed to youre conseillours
youre talent and youre affeccioun to make werre anon
and for to do vengeance./ They han espied by
youre wordes to what thyng ye been enclyned;/   *2440
and therfore han they rather conseilled yow to
youre talent than to youre profit./ Ye han erred also,
for it semeth that yow suffiseth to han been conseilled
by thise conseillours oonly, and with litel avys,/
whereas in so greet and so heigh a nede it hadde been
necessarie mo conseillours and moore deliberacion to
parfourne youre emprise./ Ye han erred also, for ye ne
han nat examyned youre conseil in the forseyde
manere, ne in due manere, as the caas requireth./ Ye
han erred also, for ye han maked no division bitwixe
youre conseillours—this is to seyn, bitwixen youre
trewe freendes and youre feyned conseillours—/ ne ye han nat knowe the wil of youre   1255
trewe freendes olde and wise,/ but ye han cast
alle hire wordes in an hochepot, and enclyned youre
herte to the moore part and to the gretter nombre, and
there been ye condescended./ And sith ye woot wel
that men shal alwey fynde a gretter nombre of fooles
than of wise men,/ and therfore the conseils that been
at congregaciouns and multitudes of folk, there as
men take moore reward to the nombre than to the
sapience of persones,/ ye se wel that in
swiche   conseillynges   fooles   han   the   *2450
maistrie."/

Melibeus answerde agayn, and seyde, "I graunte
wel that I have erred;/ but there as thou hast toold

1228 **dishonest:** unjust
1233 **covenably:** fittingly   **withholdynge:** retention
1234 **condescende in especial:** get down to particulars
1236 **distempre:** upset
1241 **First and forward:** first of al

1243 **chargeant:** burdensome
1248 **anientissed:** annihilated
1249 **talent:** desire, inclination
1257 **hochepot:** mixture   **there been ye condescended:** to that you have yielded (R.)

me heerbiforn that he nys nat to blame that chaungeth his conseillours in certein caas and for certeine juste causes,/ I am al redy to chaunge my conseillours right as thow wolt devyse./ The proverbe seith that 'for to do synne is mannyssh, but certes for to persevere longe in synne is werk of the devel.' "/

To this sentence answered anon dame Prudence, and seyde,/ "Examineth," quod she,   1265 "youre conseil, and lat us see the whiche of hem han spoken most resonably and taught yow best conseil./ And for as muche as that the examynacion is necessarie, lat us bigynne at the surgiens and at the phisiciens, that first speeken in this matiere./ I sey yow that the surgiens and phisiciens han seyd yow in youre conseil discreetly, as hem oughte,/ and in hir speche seyden ful wisely that to the office of hem aperteneth to doon to every wight honour and profit, and no wight for to anoye,/ and after hir craft to doon greet diligence unto the cure of hem which that they han in hir governaunce./ And, sire,   *2460 right as they han answered wisely and discreetly,/ right so rede I that they been heighly and sovereynly gerdoned for hir noble speche,/ and eek for they sholde do the moore ententif bisynesse in the curacion of youre doghter deere./ For al be it so that they been youre freendes, therfore shal ye nat suffren that they serve yow for noght,/ but ye oghte the rather gerdone hem and shewe hem youre largesse./ And as touchynge the proposicioun   1275 which that the phisiciens encreesceden in this caas—this is to seyn,/ that in maladies that oon contrarie is warisshed by another contrarie—/ I wolde fayn knowe hou ye understonde thilke text, and what is youre sentence."/

"Certes," quod Melibeus, "I understonde it in this wise:/ that right as they han doon me a contrarie, right so sholde I doon hem another./ For   *2470 right as they han venged hem on me and doon me wrong, right so shal I venge me upon hem and doon hem wrong;/ and thanne have I cured oon contrarie by another."/

"Lo, lo," quod dame Prudence, "how lightly is every man enclined to his owene desir and to his owene plesaunce!/ Certes," quod she, "the wordes of the phisiciens ne sholde nat han been understonden in thys wise./ For certes, wikkednesse is nat contrarie to wikkednesse, ne vengeance to vengeaunce, ne wrong to wrong, but they been semblable./   1285 And therfore o vengeaunce is nat warisshed by another vengeaunce, ne o wroong by another wroong,/ but everich of hem encreesceth and aggreggeth oother./ But certes, the wordes of the phisiciens sholde been understonden in this wise:/ for good and wikkednesse been two contraries, and pees and werre, vengeaunce and suffraunce, discord and accord, and manye othere thynges;/ but certes, wikkednesse shal be warisshed by goodnesse, discord by accord, werre by pees, and so forth of othere thynges./ And heerto accordeth   *2480 Seint Paul the Apostle in manye places./ He seith, 'Ne yeldeth nat harm for harm, ne wikked speche for wikked speche,/ but do wel to hym that dooth thee harm and blesse hym that seith to thee harm.'/ And in manye othere places he amonesteth pees and accord./ But now wol I speke to yow of the conseil which that was yeven to yow by the men of lawe and the wise folk,/ that seyden   1295 alle by oon accord, as ye han herd bifore,/ that over alle thynges ye shal doon youre diligence to kepen youre persone and to warnestoore youre hous;/ and seyden also that in this caas yow oghten for to werken ful avysely and with greet deliberacioun./ And, sire, as to the firste point, that toucheth to the kepyng of youre persone,/ ye shul understonde that he that hath werre shal everemoore mekely and devoutly preyen, biforn alle thynges,/ that   *2490 Jhesus Crist of his mercy wol han hym in his proteccion and been his sovereyn helpyng at his nede./ For certes, in this world ther is no wight that may be conseilled ne kept sufficeantly withouten the kepyng of oure Lord Jhesu Crist./ To this sentence accordeth the prophete David, that seith,/ 'If God ne kepe the citee, in ydel waketh he that it kepeth.'/ Now, sire, thanne shul ye committe the kepyng of youre persone to youre trewe freendes that been approved and yknowe,/ and of hem shul ye   1305

1269 **anoye:** cause trouble
1272 **sovereynly:** chiefly
1273 **curacion:** cure
1275 **gerdone:** to reward

1287 **aggreggeth:** aggravates
1294 **amonesteth:** recommends
1297 **warnestoore:** garrison
1304 **waketh:** keeps watch

axen help youre persone for to kepe. For Catoun
seith, 'If thou hast nede of help, axe it of thy freendes,/ for ther nys noon so good a phisicien as thy
trewe freend.'/ And after this thanne shul ye kepe yow
fro alle straunge folk, and fro lyeres, and have alwey
in suspect hire compaignye./ For Piers Alfonce seith,
'Ne taak no compaignye by the weye of a straunge
man, but if so be that thou have knowe hym of a
lenger tyme./ And if so be that he falle into
thy compaignye paraventure, withouten thyn   *2500
assent,/ enquere thanne as subtilly as thou
mayst of his conversacion, and of his lyf bifore, and
feyne thy wey; seye that thou [wolt] thider as thou
wolt nat go;/ and if he bereth a spere, hoold thee on
the right syde, and if he bere a swerd, hoold thee on
the lift syde.'/ And after this thanne shul ye kepe yow
wisely from all swich manere peple as I have seyd
bifore, and hem and hir conseil eschewe./ And after
this thanne shul ye kepe yow in swich manere/ that,
for any presumpcion of youre strengthe, that ye ne
dispise nat, ne accompte nat the myght of youre
adversarie so litel that ye lete the kepyng of
youre persone for youre presumpcioun,/ for   1315
every wys man dredeth his enemy./ And
Salomon seith, 'Weleful is he that of alle hath drede,/
for certes, he that thurgh the hardynesse of his herte
and thurgh the hardynesse of hymself hath to greet
presumpcioun, hym shal yvel bityde.'/ Thanne shul
ye everemoore contrewayte embusshementz and alle
espiaille./ For Senec seith that 'the wise man
that dredeth harmes, eschueth harmes,/ ne he   *2510
ne falleth into perils that perils eschueth.'/
And al be it so that it seme that thou art in siker place,
yet shaltow alwey do thy diligence in kepynge of thy
persone;/ this is to seyn, ne be nat necligent to kepe
thy persone nat oonly fro thy gretteste enemys but fro
thy leeste enemy./ Senek seith, 'A man that is well
avysed, he dredeth his leste enemy.'/ Ovyde seith that
'the litel wesele wol slee the grete bole and
the wilde hert.'/ And the book seith, 'A litel   1325
thorn may prikke a kyng ful soore, and an

hound wol holde the wilde boor.'/ But nathelees, I sey
nat thou shalt be so coward that thou doute ther wher
as is no drede./ The book seith that "somme folk han
greet lust to deceyve, but yet they dreden hem to be
deceyved.'/ Yet shaltou drede to been empoisoned
and kepe the from the compaignye of scorneres./ For
the book seith, 'With scorneres make no compaignye, but flee hire wordes as venym.'/   *2520
   "Now, as to the seconde point, where as
youre wise conseillours conseilled yow to
warnestoore youre hous with gret diligence,/ I wolde
fayn knowe how that ye understonde thilke wordes
and what is youre sentence."/
   Melibeus answerde and seyde, "Certes, I understande it in this wise: That I shal warnestoore myn
hous with toures, swiche as han castelles and othere
manere edifices, and armure, and artelries,/ by
whiche thynges I may my persone and myn hous so
kepen and deffenden that myne enemys shul been in
drede myn hous for to approche."/
   To this sentence answerde anon Prudence:
"Warnestooryng," quod she, "of heighe toures and
of grete edifices apperteyneth somtyme to
pryde./ And eek men make heighe toures,   1335
[and grete edifices] with grete costages and
with greet travaille, and whan that they been accompliced, yet be they nat worth a stree, but if they be
defended by trewe freendes that been olde and wise./
And understoond wel that the gretteste and strongeste
garnysoun that a riche man may have, as wel to kepen
his persone as his goodes, is/ that he be biloved with
hys subgetz and with his neighebores./ For thus seith
Tullius, that 'ther is a manere garnysoun that no man
may venquysse ne disconfite, and that is/ a
lord to be biloved of his citezeins and of his   *2530
peple.'/
   Now, sire, as to the thridde point, where as youre
olde and wise conseillours seyden that yow ne oghte
nat sodeynly ne hastily proceden in this nede,/ but
that yow oghte purveyen and apparaillen yow in this
caas with greet diligence and greet deliberacioun;/
trewely, I trowe that they seyden right wisely and
right sooth./ For Tullius seith, 'In every nede, er thou

1311 **conversacion:** way of life
1315 **lete the kepyng:** neglect the protection (R.)
1317 **Weleful:** happy, prosperous
1319 **contrewayte:** watch out for   **embusshementz:** ambushes   **espiaille:** spies
1325 **wesele:** weasel

1327 **doute:** fear
1333 **artelries:** artillery (catapults and cannons)
1336 **costages:** expenditures
1337 **garnysoun:** protection

bigynne it, apparaille thee with greet diligence.'/
Thanne seye I that in vengeance-takyng, in
werre, in bataille, and in warnestooryng,/ er   1345
thow bigynne, I rede that thou apparaille thee
therto, and do it with greet deliberacion./ For Tullius
seith that 'longe apparaillyng biforn the bataille
maketh short victorie.'/ And Cassidorus seith, 'The
garnysoun is stronger whan it is longe tyme avysed.'/

But now lat us speken of the conseil that was
accorded by youre neighebores, swiche as doon yow
reverence withouten love,/ youre olde enemys
reconsiled, youre flatereres,/ that conseilled   *2540
yow certeyne thynges prively, and openly
conseilleden yow the contrarie;/ the yonge folk also,
that conseilleden yow to venge yow and make werre
anon./ And certes, sire, as I have seyd biforn, ye han
greetly erred to han cleped swich manere folk to
youre conseil,/ which conseillours been ynogh
repreved by the resouns aforeseyd./ But nathelees, lat
us now descende to the special. Ye shuln first
procede after the doctrine of Tullius./Certes,   1355
the trouthe of this matiere, or of this conseil,
nedeth nat diligently enquere,/ for it is wel wist
whiche they been that han doon to yow this trespas
and vileynye,/ and how manye trespassours, and in
what manere they han to yow doon al this wrong and
al this vileynye./ And after this, thanne shul ye examyne the seconde condicion which that the same Tullius addeth in this matiere./ For Tullius put a thyng
which that he clepeth 'consentynge'; this is to
seyn,/ who been they, and whiche been they   *2550
and how manye that consenten to thy conseil
in thy wilfulnesse to doon hastif vengeance./ And lat
us considere also who been they, and how manye
been they, and whiche been they that consenteden to
youre adversaries./ And certes, as to the firste poynt,
it is wel knowen whiche folk been they that consenteden to youre hastif wilfulnesse,/ for trewely, alle tho
that conseilleden yow to maken sodeyn werre ne
been nat youre freendes./ Lat us now considere
whiche been they that ye holde so greetly
youre freendes as to youre persone./ For al be   1365
it so that ye be myghty and riche, certes ye
ne been but allone,/ for certes ye ne han no child but

a doghter,/ ne ye ne han bretheren, ne cosyns germayns, ne noon oother neigh kynrede,/ wherfore that
youre enemys for drede sholde stinte to plede with
yow or to destroye youre persone./ Ye knowen also
that youre richesses mooten been dispended
in diverse parties,/ and whan that every wight   *2560
hath his part, they ne wollen taken but litel
reward to venge thy deeth./ But thyne enemys been
thre, and they han manie children, bretheren, cosyns,
and oother ny kynrede./ And though so were that thou
haddest slayn of hem two or three, yet dwellen ther
ynowe to wreken hir deeth and to sle thy persone./
And though so be that youre kynrede be moore siker
and stedefast than the kyn of youre adversarie,/ yet
nathelees youre kynrede nys but a fer
kynrede; they been but litel syb to yow,/ and   1375
the kyn of youre enemys been ny syb to hem.
And certes, as in that, hir condicioun is bet than
youres./ Thanne lat us considere also if the conseillyng of hem that conseilleden yow to taken sodeyn
vengeaunce, wheither it accorde to resoun./ And
certes, ye knowe wel 'nay.'/ For, as by right and
resoun, ther may no man taken vengeance on no
wight but the juge that hath the jurisdiccioun of it,/
whan it is graunted hym to take thilke
vengeance hastily or attemprely, as the lawe   *2570
requireth./ And yet mooreover of thilke word
that Tullius clepeth 'consentynge,'/ thou shalt considere if thy myght and thy power may consenten and
suffise to thy wilfulnesse and to thy conseillours./
And certes thou mayst wel seyn that 'nay.'/ For sikerly, as for to speke proprely, we may do no thyng
but oonly swich thyng as we may doon rightfully./
And certes rightfully ne mowe ye take no
vengeance, as of youre propre auctoritee./   1385
Thanne mowe ye seen that youre power ne
consenteth nat, ne accordeth nat, with youre wilfulnesse./

"Lat us now examyne the thridde point, that Tullius
clepeth 'consequent.'/ Thou shalt understonde that the
vengeance that thou purposest for to take is the consequent;/ and therof folweth another vengeaunce,
peril, and werre, and othere damages withoute nombre, of whiche we be nat war, as at this tyme./

1368 **cosyns germayns:** first cousins
1375 **syb:** related, kin
1386 **ne consenteth:** is not consistent with

And as touchynge the fourthe point, that
Tullius clepeth 'engendrynge,'/ thou shalt   *2580
considere that this wrong which that is doon
to thee is engendred of the hate of thyne enemys,/ and
of the vengeance-takynge upon that wolde engendre
another vengeance, and muchel sorwe and wastynge
of richesses, as I seyde./

"Now, sire, as to the point that Tullius clepeth
'causes,' which that is the laste point,/ thou shalt
understonde that the wrong that thou hast receyved
hath certeine causes,/ whiche that clerkes clepen
Oriens and *Efficiens,* and *Causa longinqua* and
Causa propinqua; this is to seyn, the fer
cause and the ny cause./ The fer cause is   1395
almyghty God, that is cause of alle thynges./
The neer cause is thy thre enemys./ The cause accidental was hate./ The cause material been the fyve
woundes of thy doghter./ The cause formal is the
manere of hir werkynge that broghten laddres
and cloumben in at thy wyndowes./ The cause   *2590
final was for to sle thy doghter. It letted nat
in as muche as in hem was./ But for to speken of the
fer cause, as to what ende they shul come, or what
shal finally bityde of hem in this caas, ne kan I nat
deeme but by conjectynge and by supposynge./ For
we shul suppose that they shul come to a wikked
ende,/ by cause that the Book of Decrees seith,
'Seelden, or with greet peyne, been causes ybroght to
good ende whanne they been baddely bigonne.'/

"Now, sire, if men wolde axe me why that God suffred men to do yow this vileynye, certes, I kan
nat wel answere, as for no soothfastnesse./ For   1405
th'apostle seith that 'the sciences and the juggementz of oure Lord God almyghty been ful depe;/
ther may no man comprehende ne serchen hem suffisantly.'/ Nathelees, by certeyne presumpciouns and
conjectynges, I holde and bileeve/ that God, which
that is ful of justice and of rightwisnesse, hath suffred
this bityde by juste cause resonable./

"Thy name is Melibee; this is to seyn, 'a
man that drynketh hony.'/ Thou hast ydronke   *2600
so muchel hony of sweete temporeel

richesses, and delices and honours of this world/ that
thou art dronken and hast forgeten Jhesu Crist thy
creatour./ Thou ne hast nat doon to hym swich honour
and reverence as thee oughte,/ ne thou ne hast nat wel
ytaken kep to the wordes of Ovide, that seith,/ 'Under
the hony of the goodes of the body is hyd the
venym that sleeth the soule.'/ And Salomon   1415
seith, 'If thou hast founden hony, ete of it that
suffiseth,/ for if thou ete of it out of mesure, thou
shalt spewe' and be nedy and povre./ And peraventure
Crist hath thee in despit, and hath turned awey fro
thee his face and his eeris of misericorde,/ and also he
hath suffred that thou hast been punysshed in the
manere that thow hast ytrespassed./ Thou hast
doon synne agayn oure Lord Crist,/ for certes,   *2610
the three enemys of mankynde—that is to
seyn, the flessh, the feend, and the world—/ thou hast
suffred hem entre in to thyn herte wilfully by the
wyndowes of thy body,/ and hast nat defended thyself
suffisantly agayns hire assautes and hire temptaciouns, so that they han wounded thy soule in fyve
places;/ this is to seyn, the deedly synnes that been
entred into thyn herte by thy fyve wittes./ And in the
same manere oure Lord Crist hath woold and suffred
that thy three enemys been entred into thyn
house by the wyndowes/ and han ywounded   1425
thy doghter in the forseyde manere."/

"Certes," quod Melibee, "I se wel that ye enforce
yow muchel by wordes to overcome me in swich
manere that I shal nat venge me of myne enemys,/
shewynge me the perils and the yveles that myghten
falle of this vengeance./ But whoso wolde considere
in alle vengeances the perils and yveles that myghte
sewe of vengeance-takynge,/ a man wolde
nevere take vengeance, and that were harm;/   *2620
for by the vengeance-takynge been the
wikked men disseuered fro the goode men,/ and they
that han wyl to do wikkednesse restreyne hir wikked
purpos, whan they seen the punyssynge and
chastisynge of the trespassours."/

1401 **letted nat:** did not delay
1402 **conjectynge:** conjecture
1404 **Book of Decrees:** the decrees of Gratian (*Decretum Gratiani*)
1408 **presumpciouns:** assumptions

1411 **delices:** pleasures
1417 **spewe:** vomit
1418 **misericorde:** mercy
1424 **fyve wittes:** five senses
1425 **woold:** willed

[*Et a ce respont dame Prudence, "Certes,"dist elle, "je t'ottroye que de vengence vient molt de maulx et de biens;/ Mais vengence n'appartient pas a un chascun fors seulement aux juges et a ceulx qui ont la juridicion sur les malfaitteurs.*]/ And yet seye I moore, that right as a singuler persone syn-neth in takynge vengeance of another man,/   1435 right so synneth the juge if he do no vengeance of hem that it han disserved./ For Senec seith thus: 'That maister,' he seith, 'is good that proveth shrewes.'/ And as Cassidore seith, 'A man dredeth to do outrages whan he woot and knoweth that it displeseth to the juges and the sovereyns.'/ And another seith, 'The juge that dredeth to do right maketh men shrewes.'/ And Seint Paul the Apostle seith in his Epistle, whan he writeth unto the Romayns, that 'the juges beren nat the spere withouten cause,/ but they   *2630 beren it to punysse the shrewes and mysdo-ers and for to defende the goode men.'/ If ye wol thanne take vengeance of youre enemys, ye shul retourne or have youre recours to the juge that hath the jurisdiccion upon hem,/ and he shal punysse hem as the lawe axeth and re-quireth."/

"A," quod Melibee, "this vengeance liketh me no thyng./ I bithenke me now and take heede how Fortune hath norissed me fro my childhede and hath holpen me to passe many a stroong paas./ Now   1445 wol I assayen hire, trowynge, with Goddes help, that she shal helpe me my shame for to venge."/

"Certes," quod Prudence, "if ye wol werke by my conseil, ye shul nat assaye Fortune by no wey,/ ne ye shul nat lene or bowe unto hire, after the word of Senec,/ for 'thynges that been folily doon, and that been in hope of Fortune, shullen nevere come to good ende.'/ And, as the same Senec seith, 'The moore cleer and the moore shynyng that Fortune is, the moore brotil and the sonner broken she is.'/   *2640 Trusteth nat in hire, for she nys nat stidefast ne stable,/ for whan thow trowest to be moost seur or

siker of hire help, she wol faille thee and deceyve thee./ And where as ye seyn that Fortune hath norissed yow fro youre childhede,/ I seye that in so muchel shul ye the lasse truste in hire and in hir wit./ For Senec seith, "What man that is norissed by Fortune, she maketh hym a greet fool.'/   1455 Now thanne, syn ye desire and axe vengeance, and the vengeance that is doon after the lawe and bifore the juge ne liketh yow nat,/ and the vengeance that is doon in hope of Fortune is perilous and uncertein,/ thanne have ye noon oother remedie but for to have youre recours unto the sovereyn Juge that vengeth alle vileynyes and wronges./ And he shal venge yow after that hymself witnesseth, where as he seith,/ 'Leveth the vengeance to me, and I shal do it.' "/   *2650

Melibee answerde, "If I ne venge me nat of the vileynye that men han doon to me,/ I sompne or warne hem that han doon to me that vileynye, and alle othere, to do me another vileynye./ For it is writen, 'If thou take no vengeance of an oold vileynye, thou sompnest thyne adversaries to do thee a newe vileynye.'/ And also for my suffrance men wolden do me so muchel vileynye that I myghte nei-ther bere it ne susteene,/ and so sholde I been put and holden overlowe./ For men seyn, 'In   1465 muchel suffrynge shul manye thynges falle unto thee whiche thou shalt nat mowe suffre.' "/

"Certes," quod Prudence, "I graunte yow that over-muchel suffraunce is nat good./ But yet ne fol-weth it nat therof that every persone to whom men doon vileynye take of it vengeance,/ for that aperteneth and longeth al oonly to the juges, for they shul venge the vileynyes and injuries./ And therfore tho two auctoritees that ye han seyd above been oonly understonden in the juges,/ for   *2660 whan they suffren over-muchel the wronges and the vileynyes to be doon withouten pun-ysshynge,/ they sompne nat a man al oonly for to do newe wronges, but they comanden it./ Also a wys man seith that 'the juge that correcteth nat the syn-nere comandeth and biddeth hym do synne.'/ And the juges and sovereyns myghten in hir land so muchel suffre of the shrewes and mysdoeres/ that they

1433–34 **Et a ce,** *etc.*: And to this dame Prudence answered, "Certainly," she said, "I grant you that from vengeance come many evils and many goods; but (taking) vengeance does not appertain to an individual person but solely to judges and to those who have jurisdiction over evil-doers."
1435 **singuler:** private
1437 **proveth:** reproves
1445 **bithenke me:** consider   **paas:** passage, difficult situation

1462 **sompne:** invite, summon   **warne:** announce

sholden, by swich suffrance, by proces of tyme
wexen of swich power and myght that they sholden
putte out the juges and the sovereyns from hir
places,/ and atte laste maken hem lesen hire   1475
lordshipes./

"But lat us now putte that ye have leve to venge
yow./ I seye ye been nat of myght and power as now
to venge yow,/ for if ye wole maken comparisoun
unto the myght of youre adversaries, ye shul fynde
in manye thynges that I have shewed yow er this that
hire condicion is bettre than youres./ And therfore
seye I that it is good as now that ye suffre and
be pacient./   *2670

"Forthermoore, ye knowen wel that after
the comune sawe, 'it is a woodnesse a man to stryve
with a strenger or a moore myghty man than he is
hymself,/ and for to stryve with a man of evene
strengthe—that is to seyn, with as strong a man as
he is—it is peril,/ and for to stryve with a weyker
man, it is folie.'/ And therfore sholde a man flee
stryvynge as muchel as he myghte./ For Salomon
seith, 'It is a greet worshipe to a man to kepen
hym fro noyse and stryf.'/ And if it so bifalle   1485
or happe that a man of gretter myght and
strengthe than thou art do thee grevaunce,/ studie and
bisye thee rather to stille the same grevaunce than
for to venge thee./ For Senec seith that 'he putteth
hym in greet peril that stryveth with a gretter man
than he is hymself.'/ And Catoun seith, 'If a man of
hyer estaat or degree, or moore myghty than thou,
do thee anoy or grevaunce, suffre hym,/ for he that
oones hath greved thee, may another tyme
releeve thee and helpe.'/ Yet sette I caas ye   *2680
have bothe myght and licence for to venge
yow,/ I seye that ther be ful manye thynges that shul
restreyne yow of vengeance-takynge/ and make yow
for to enclyne to suffre, and for to han pacience in the
wronges that han been doon to yow./ First and foreward, if ye wole considere the defautes that been in
youre owene persone,/ for whiche defautes God hath
suffred yow have this tribulacioun, as I have
seyd yow heer-biforn./ For the poete seith that   1495
'we oghte paciently taken the tribulacions that
comen to us, whan we thynken and consideren that
we han disserved to have hem.'/ And Seint Gregorie

seith that 'whan a man considereth wel the nombre of
his defautes and of his synnes,/ the peynes and the
tribulaciouns that he suffreth semen the lesse
unto hym;/ and in as muche as hym thynketh   *2690
his synnes moore hevy and grevous,/ in so
muche semeth his peyne the lighter and the esier unto
hym.'/ Also ye owen to enclyne and bowe youre herte
to take the pacience of oure Lord Jhesu Crist, as seith
Seint Peter in his Epistles./ 'Jhesu Crist,' he seith,
'hath suffred for us and yeven ensample to every man
to folwe and sewe hym,/ for he dide nevere synne,
ne nevere cam ther a vileyns word out of his mouth./
Whan men cursed hym, he cursed hem noght, and
whan men betten hym, he manaced hem noght.'/ Also
the grete pacience which the seintes that been in
Paradys han had in tribulaciouns that they han
ysuffred, withouten hir desert or gilt,/ oghte   1505
muchel stiren yow to pacience./ Forthermoore
ye sholde enforce yow to have pacience,/ considerynge that the tribulaciouns of this world but litel
while endure and soone passed been and goon,/ and
the joye that a man seketh to have by pacience in
tribulaciouns is perdurable, after that the Apostle
seith in his epistle./ 'The joye of God,' he
seith, 'is perdurable'— that is to seyn, evere-   *2700
lastynge./ Also troweth and bileveth stedefastly that he nys nat wel ynorissed, ne wel ytaught,
that kan nat have pacience or wol nat receyve
pacience./ For Salomon seith that 'the doctrine and
the wit of a man is knowen by pacience.'/ And in
another place he seith that 'he that is pacient governeth hym by greet prudence.'/ And the same Salomon
seith, 'The angry and wrathful man maketh noyses,
and the pacient man atempreth hem and stilleth.'/ He
seith also, 'It is moore worth to be pacient
than for to be right strong;/ and he that may   1515
have the lordshipe of his owene herte is
moore to preyse than he that by his force or strengthe
taketh grete citees.'/ And therfore seith Seint Jame
in his Epistle that 'pacience is a greet vertu of perfeccioun.' "/

"Certes," quod Melibee, "I graunte yow, dame
Prudence, that pacience is a greet vertu of perfeccioun;/ but every man may nat have the perfeccioun
that ye seken;/ ne I nam nat of the nombre of right

1477 **putte**: suppose

1510 **perdurable:** eternal
1514 **atempreth:** moderates
1515 **worth:** worthy

parfite men,/ for myn herte may nevere been   *2710
in pees unto the tyme it be venged./ And al
be it so that it was greet peril to myne enemys to do
me a vileynye in takynge vengeance upon me,/ yet
tooken they noon heede of the peril, but fulfilleden
hir wikked wyl and hir corage./ And therfore me
thynketh men oghten nat repreve me, though I putte
me in a litel peril for to venge me,/ and though I do a
greet excesse; that is to seyn, that I venge oon
outrage by another."/   1525

"A," quod dame Prudence, "ye seyn youre
wyl and as yow liketh,/ but in no caas of the world a
man sholde nat doon outrage ne excesse for to vengen hym./ For Cassidore seith that 'as yvele dooth
he that vengeth hym by outrage as he that dooth the
outrage.'/ And therfore ye shul venge yow after the
ordre of right; that is to seyn, by the lawe and noght
by excesse ne by outrage./ And also, if ye wol venge
yow of the outrage of youre adversaries in
oother manere than right comandeth, ye syn-   *2720
nen./ And therfore seith Senec that 'a man
shal nevere vengen shrewednesse by shrewednesse.'/
And if ye seye that right axeth a man to defenden violence by violence and fightyng by fightyng,/ certes ye
seye sooth, whan the defense is doon anon withouten
intervalle or withouten tariyng or delay,/ for to deffenden hym and nat for to vengen hym./ And it
bihoveth that a man putte swich attemperance
in his deffense/ that men have no cause ne   1535
matiere to repreven hym that deffendeth hym
of excesse and outrage, for ellis were it agayn resoun./
Pardee, ye knowen wel that ye maken no deffense as
now for to deffende yow, but for to venge yow;/ and so
seweth it that ye han no wyl to do youre dede attemprely./ And therfore me thynketh that pacience is
good. For Salomon seith that 'he that is nat pacient
shal have greet harm.' "/

"Certes," quod Melibee, "I graunte yow that whan
a man is inpacient and wrooth of that that toucheth
hym noght and that aperteneth nat unto hym,
though it harme hym, it is no wonder./ For the   *2730
lawe seith that 'he is coupable that entremetteth hym or medleth with swych thyng as aperteneth

nat unto hym.'/ And Salomon seith that 'he that
entremetteth hym of the noyse or strif of another man
is lyk to hym that taketh an hound by the eris.'/ For
right as he that taketh a straunge hound by the eris is
outherwhile biten with the hound,/ right in the same
wise is it resoun that he have harm that by his inpacience medleth hym of the noyse of another man,
wheras it aperteneth nat unto hym./ But ye knowen
wel that this dede—that is to seyn, my grief
and my disese—toucheth me right ny./ And   1545
therfore, though I be wrooth and inpacient, it
is no merveille./ And, savynge youre grace, I kan nat
seen that it myghte greetly harme me though I tooke
vengeaunce./ For I am richer and moore myghty than
myne enemys been;/ and wel knowen ye that by moneye and by havynge grete possessions been alle the
thynges of this world governed./ And
Salomon seith that 'alle thynges obeyen to   *2740
moneye.' "/

Whan Prudence hadde herd hir housbonde avanten
hym of his richesse and of his moneye, dispreisynge
the power of his adversaries, she spak and seyde in
this wise:/ "Certes, deere sire, I graunte yow that ye
been riche and myghty/ and that the richesses been
goode to hem that han wel ygeten hem and wel konne
usen hem./ For right as the body of a man may nat
lyven withoute the soule, namoore may it lyve withoute temporeel goodes./ And by richesses
may a man gete hym grete freendes./ And   1555
therfore seith Pamphilles: 'If a net-herdes
doghter,' seith he, 'be riche, she may chesen of a
thousand men which she wol take to hir housbonde,/
for, of a thousand men, oon wol nat forsaken hire ne
refusen hire.'/ And this Pamphilles seith also, 'If
thow be right happy—that is to seyn, if thou be right
riche—thou shalt fynde a greet nombre of felawes
and freendes./ And if thy fortune change that thou
wexe povre, farewel freendshipe and felaweshipe,/
for thou shalt be alloone withouten any compaignye, but if it be the compaignye of povre   *2750
folk.'/ And yet seith this Pamphilles moreover
that 'they that been thralle and bonde of lynage
shullen been maad worthy and noble by the
richesses.'/ And right so as by richesses ther comen

manye goodes, right so by poverte come ther manye harmes and yveles,/ for greet poverte constreyneth a man to do manye yveles./ And therfore clepeth Cassidore poverte the mooder of ruyne;/ that is to seyn, the mooder of overthrowynge or fallynge doun./ And therfore seith Piers Alfonce, 'Oon   1565 of the gretteste adversitees of this world is/ whan a free man by kynde or of burthe is constreyned by poverte to eten the almesse of his enemy,'/ and the same seith Innocent in oon of his bookes. He seith that 'sorweful and myshappy is the condicioun of a povre beggere;/ for if he axe nat his mete, he dyeth for hunger;/ and if he axe, he dyeth for shame; and algates necessitee constreyneth hym to   *2760 axe.'/ And seith Salomon that 'bet it is to dye than for to have swich poverte.'/ And as the same Salomon seith, 'Bettre it is to dye of bitter deeth than for to lyven in swich wise.'/ By thise resons that I have seid unto yow and by manye othere resons that I koude seye,/ I graunte yow that richesses been goode to hem that geten hem wel and to hem that wel usen tho richesses./ And therfore wol I shewe yow hou ye shul have yow, and how ye shul bere yow in gaderynge of richesses, and in what manere ye shul usen hem./   1575

"First, ye shul geten hem withouten greet desir, by good leyser, sokyngly and nat over-hastily./ For a man that is to desirynge to gete richesses abaundoneth hym first to thefte, and to alle othere yveles;/ and therfore seith Salomon, 'He that hasteth hym to bisily to wexe riche shal be noon innocent.'/ He seith also that 'the richesse that hastily cometh to a man soone and lightly gooth and passeth fro a man,/ but that richesse that cometh litel and litel wexeth alwey and multiplieth.'/ And, sire, ye   *2770 shul geten richesses by youre wit and by youre travaille unto youre profit,/ and that withouten wrong or harm doynge to any oother persone./ For the lawe seith that 'ther maketh no man himselven riche, if he do harm to another wight.'/ This is to seyn, that nature deffendeth and forbedeth by right that no man make hymself riche unto the harm of another persone./ And Tullius seith that 'no sorwe,

ne no drede of deeth, ne no thyng that may falle unto a man,/ is so muchel agayns nature   1585 as a man to encressen his owene profit to the harm of another man./ And though the grete men and the myghty men geten richesses moore lightly than thou,/ yet shaltou nat been ydel ne slow to do thy profit, for thou shalt in alle wise flee ydelnesse.'/ For Salomon seith that 'ydelnesse techeth a man to do manye yveles.'/ And the same Salomon seith that 'he that travailleth and bisieth hym to tilien his land shal eten breed,/ but he that is ydel and   *2780 casteth hym to no bisynesse ne occupacioun shal falle into poverte and dye for hunger.'/ And he that is ydel and slow kan nevere fynde covenable tyme for to doon his profit./ For ther is a versifiour seith that 'the ydel man excuseth hym in wynter by cause of the grete coold, and in somer by enchesoun of the greete heete.'/ For thise causes seith Caton, 'Waketh and enclyneth nat yow over muchel for to slepe, for over-muchel reste norisseth and causeth manye vices.'/ And therfore seith Seint Jerome, 'Dooth somme goode dedes that the devel, which is oure enemy, ne fynde yow nat   1595 unocupied.'/ For the devel ne taketh nat lightly unto his werkynge swiche as he fyndeth occupied in goode werkes./

"Thanne thus in getynge richesses ye mosten flee ydelnesse./ And afterward, ye shul use the richesses which ye have geten by youre wit and by youre travaille/ in swich a manere that men holde yow nat to scars, ne to sparynge, ne to fool-large—that is to seyen, over-large a spendere./ For right as men blamen an avaricious man by cause of his scarsetee and chyncherie,/ in the same wise is he to   *2790 blame that spendeth over-largely./ And therfore seith Caton: 'Use,' he seith, 'thy richesses that thou hast geten/ in swich a manere that men have no matiere ne cause to calle thee neither wrecche ne chynche,/ for it is a greet shame to a man to have a povere herte and a riche purs.'/ He seith also, 'The goodes that thou hast ygeten, use hem by mesure;' that is to seyn, spende hem mesurably,/ for they that

---

1568 **myshappy:** unfortunate
1575 **hou ye shul have yow:** how you should behave
1576 **sokyngly:** slowly, gradually
1577 **abaundoneth hym:** devotes himself
1584 **no man:** any man

1590 **tilien:** till
1592 **covenable:** suitable
1599 **scars:** niggardly
1600 **scarsetee:** niggardliness   **chyncherie:** miserliness
1603 **chynche:** miser
1605 **mesurably:** moderately

folily wasten and despenden the goodes that   1606
they han,/ whan they han namoore propre of
hir owene, they shapen hem to take the goodes of
another man./ I seye thanne that ye shul fleen
avarice,/ usynge youre richesses in swich manere that
men seye nat that youre richesses been yburyed/ but
that ye have hem in youre myght and in youre
weeldynge./ For a wys man repreveth the   *2800
avaricious man, and seith thus in two vers:/
'Wherto and why burieth a man his goodes by his
grete avarice, and knoweth wel that nedes moste he
dye?/ For deeth is the ende of every man as in this
present lyf.'/ And for what cause or enchesoun
joyneth he hym or knytteth he hym so faste unto his
goodes/ that alle hise wittes mowen nat disseveren hym or departen hym from his   1615
goodes,/ and knoweth wel, or oghte knowe,
that whan he is deed he shal no thyng bere with hym
out of this world?/ And therfore seith Seint Austyn
that 'the avaricious man is likned unto helle,/ that
the moore it swelweth the moore desir it hath to
swelwe and devoure.'/ And as wel as ye wolde
eschewe to be called an avaricious man or chynche,/
as wel sholde ye kepe yow and governe yow
in swich a wise that men calle yow nat fool-   *2810
large./ Therfore seith Tullius: 'The goodes,' he
seith, 'of thyn hous ne sholde nat been hyd ne kept
so cloos, but that they myghte been opened by pitee
and debonairetee'/ (that is to seyn, to yeven part to
hem that han greet nede),/ 'ne thy goodes shullen nat
been so opene to been every mannes goodes.'/ Afterward, in getynge of youre richesses and in usynge
hem ye shul alwey have thre thynges in youre herte/
(that is to seyn, oure Lord God, conscience,
and good name)./ First, ye shul have God in   1625
youre herte,/ and for no richesse ye shullen do
no thyng which may in any manere displese God, that
is youre creatour and makere./ For after the word of
Salomon, 'It is bettre to have a litel good with the
love of God/ than to have muchel good and tresour
and lese the love of his Lord God.'/ And the prophete
seith that 'bettre it is to been a good man and
have litel good and tresour/ than to been   *2820
holden a shrewe and have grete richesses.'/

And yet seye I ferthermoore, that ye sholde alwey
doon youre bisynesse to gete yow richesses,/ so that
ye gete hem with good conscience./ And th'Apostle
seith that 'ther nys thyng in this world of which we
sholden have so greet joye as whan oure conscience
bereth us good witnesse.'/ And the wise man seith,
'The substance of a man is ful good, whan
synne is nat in mannes conscience.'/ After-   1635
ward, in getynge of youre richesses and in
usynge of hem,/ yow moste have greet bisynesse and
greet diligence that youre goode name be alwey kept
and conserved./ For Salomon seith that 'bettre it is
and moore it availleth a man to have a good name
than for to have grete richesses.'/ And therfore he
seith in another place, 'Do greet diligence,' seith
Salomon, 'in kepyng of thy freend and of thy goode
name;/ for it shal lenger abide with thee than
any tresour, be it never so precious.'/ And   *2830
certes he sholde nat be called a gentil man
that after God and good conscience, alle thynges left,
ne dooth his diligence and bisynesse to kepen his
goode name./ And Cassidore seith that 'it is signe of
a gentil herte whan a man loveth and desireth to han
a good name.'/ And therfore seith Seint Austyn that
'ther been two thynges that arn necessarie and nede-
fulle,/ and that is good conscience and good loos;/
that is to seyn, good conscience to thyn owene persone inward and good loos for thy neighebor
outward.'/ And he that trusteth hym so muchel   1645
in his goode conscience/ that he displeseth,
and setteth at noght his goode name or loos, and
rekketh noght though he kepe nat his goode name,
nys but a crueel cherl./

"Sire, now have I shewed yow how ye shul do in
getynge richesses, and how ye shullen usen hem,/ and
I se wel that for the trust that ye han in youre
richesses ye wole moeve werre and bataille./ I conseille yow that ye bigynne no werre in trust of youre
richesses, for they ne suffisen noght werres to
mayntene./ And therfore seith a philosophre,   *2840
'That man that desireth and wole algates han
werre, shal nevere have suffisaunce,/ for the richer
that he is, the gretter despenses moste he make, if he
wole have worshipe and victorie.'/ And Salomon

1634 **th'Apostle:** St. Paul
1641 **alle thynges left:** all other things left aside
1644 **loos:** reputation

seith that 'the gretter richesses that a man hath, the mo despendours he hath.'/ And, deere sire, al be it so that for youre richesses ye mowe have muchel folk,/ yet bihoveth it nat, ne it is nat good, to bigynne werre whereas ye mowe in oother manere have pees unto youre worshipe and profit./ For the vic-   1655
torie of batailles that been in this world lyth nat in greet nombre or multitude of the peple, ne in the vertu of man,/ but it lith in the wyl and in the hand of oure Lord God Almyghty./ And therfore Judas Machabeus, which was Goddes knyght,/ whan he sholde fighte agayn his adversarie that hadde a gretter nombre and a gretter multitude of folk and strenger than was this peple of Machabee,/ yet he reconforted his litel compaignye, and seyde right in this wise:/ 'Als lightly,' quod he, 'may oure Lord   *2850
God Almyghty yeve victorie to a fewe folk as to many folk,/ for the victorie of a bataile comth nat by the grete nombre of peple,/ but it cometh from oure Lord God of hevene.'/ And, deere sire, for as muchel as ther is no man certein if he be worthy that God yeve hym victorie [*ne plus que il est certain se il est digne de l'amour de Dieu*] or naught, after that Salomon seith,/ therfore every man sholde greetly drede werres to bigynne./ And by   1665
cause that in batailles fallen manye perils,/ and happeth outher while that as soone is the grete man slayn as the litel man;/ and as it is writen in the seconde Book of Kynges, 'The dedes of batailles been aventurouse and nothyng certeyne,/ for as lightly is oon hurt with a spere as another';/ and for ther is gret peril in werre, therfore sholde a man flee and eschue werre, in as muchel as a man may goodly./ For Salomon seith, 'He that loveth   *2860
peril shal falle in peril.' "/

After that Dame Prudence hadde spoken in this manere, Melibee answerde and seyde,/ "I see wel, dame Prudence, that by youre faire wordes and by youre resouns that ye han shewed me, that the werre liketh yow no thyng;/ but I have nat yet herd youre conseil, how I shal do in this nede."/

"Certes," quod she, "I conseille yow that ye accorde with youre adversaries and that ye have pees with hem./ For Seint Jame seith in   1675
his Epistles that 'by concord and pees the smale richesses wexen grete,/ and by debaat and discord the grete richesses fallen doun.'/ And ye knowen wel that oon of the gretteste and moost sovereyn thyng that is in this world is unytee and pees./ And therfore seyde oure Lord Jhesu Crist to his apostles in this wise:/ 'Wel happy and blessed been they that loven and purchacen pees, for they been called children of God.' "/   *2870

"A," quod Melibee, "now se I wel that ye loven nat myn honour ne my worshipe./ Ye knowen wel that myne adversaries han bigonnen this debaat and bryge by hire outrage,/ and ye se wel that they ne requeren ne preyen me nat of pees, ne they asken nat to be reconsiled./ Wol ye thanne that I go and meke me, and obeye me to hem, and crie hem mercy?/ For sothe, that were nat my wor-shipe./ For right as men seyn that 'over-greet   1685
hoomlynesse engendreth dispreisynge,' so fareth it by to greet humylitee or mekenesse."/

Thanne bigan dame Prudence to maken semblant of wratthe and seyde:/ "Certes, sire, sauf youre grace, I love youre honour and youre profit as I do myn owene, and evere have doon;/ ne ye, ne noon oother, seyn nevere the contrarie./ And yit if I hadde seyd that ye sholde han purchaced the pees and the recon-siliacioun, I ne hadde nat muchel mystaken me ne seyd amys./ For the wise man seith,   *2880
'The dissensioun bigynneth by another man, and the reconsilyng bygynneth by thyself.'/ And the prophete seith, 'Flee shrewednesse and do good-nesse;/ seke pees and folwe it, as muchel as in thee is.'/ Yet seye I nat that ye shul rather pursue to youre adversaries for pees than they shuln to yow./ For I knowe wel that ye been so hardherted that ye wol do no thyng for me./ And Salomon seith,   1695
'He that hath over-hard an herte, atte laste he shal myshappe and mystyde.' "/

1653 **despendours:** officials who disburse money
1664 **ne plus que ... de Dieu:** no more than it is certain that he is worthy of the love of God
1668 **seconde Book of Kynges:** AV 2 Samuel 11.25.   **aventurouse:** subject to chance

1676 **Seint Jame:** a misattribution; actually from Seneca
1682 **bryge:** strife
1684 **meke me:** humble myself
1686 **hoomlynesse:** familiarity
1690 **purchaced:** brought about
1694 **shuln** = *shullen*, should (offer peace)
1696 **mystyde:** misbetide, be unlucky

Whanne Melibee hadde herd dame Prudence
maken semblant of wratthe, he seyde in this wise:/
"Dame, I prey yow that ye be nat displesed of thynges
that I seye,/ for ye knowe wel that I am angry and
wrooth, and that is no wonder;/ and they that been
wrothe witen nat wel what they don ne what
they seyn./ Therfore the prophete seith that   *2890
'troubled eyen han no cleer sighte.'/ But
seyeth and conseileth me as yow liketh, for I am redy
to do right as ye wol desire;/ and if ye repreve me of
my folye, I am the moore holden to love yow and to
preyse yow./ For Salomon seith that 'he that repreveth
hym that dooth folye,/ he shal fynde gretter
grace than he that deceyveth hym by sweete   1705
wordes.' "/

Thanne seide dame Prudence, "I make no semblant
of wratthe ne anger, but for youre grete profit./ For
Salomon seith, 'He is moore worth that repreveth or
chideth a fool for his folye, shewynge hym semblant
of wratthe,/ than he that supporteth hym and preyseth
hym in his mysdoynge and laugheth at his folye.'/ And
this same Salomon seith afterward that 'by the sorweful visage of a man' (that is to seyn by the sory and
hevy contenaunce of a man)/ 'the fool correcteth and amendeth hymself.' "/   *2900

Thanne seyde Melibee, "I shal nat konne
answere to so manye faire resouns as ye putten to me
and shewen./ Seyeth shortly youre wyl and youre
conseil, and I am al redy to fulfille and parfourne it."/

Thanne dame Prudence discovered al hir wyl to
hym and seyde,/ "I conseille yow," quod she, "aboven
alle thynges, that ye make pees bitwene God and
yow,/ and beth reconsiled unto hym and to his
grace./ For, as I have seyd yow heer biforn,   1715
God hath suffred yow to have this tribulacioun and disese for youre synnes./ And if ye do as I
sey yow, God wol sende youre adversaries unto yow/
and maken hem fallen at youre feet, redy to do youre
wyl and youre comandementz./ For Salomon seith,
'Whan the condicioun of man is plesaunt and likynge
to God,/ he chaungeth the hertes of the mannes adversaries and constreyneth hem to biseken hym
of pees and of grace.'/ And I prey yow lat me   *2910
speke with youre adversaries in privee place,/

for they shul nat knowe that it be of youre wyl or of
youre assent./ And thanne, whan I knowe hir wil and
hire entente, I may conseille yow the moore seurely."/

"Dame," quod Melibee, "dooth youre wil and
youre likynge;/ for I putte me hoolly in youre
disposicioun and ordinaunce."/   1725

Thanne dame Prudence, whan she saugh
the goode wyl of hir housbonde, delibered and took
avys in hirself,/ thinkinge how she myghte brynge
this nede unto a good conclusioun and to a good
ende./ And whan she saugh hir tyme, she sente for
thise adversaries to come unto hire into a pryvee
place/ and shewed wisely unto hem the grete goodes
that comen of pees/ and the grete harmes and
perils that been in werre,/ and seyde to hem in   *2920
a goodly manere hou that hem oughten have
greet repentaunce/ of the injurie and wrong that they
hadden doon to Melibee hir lord, and unto hire, and
to hire doghter./

And whan they herden the goodliche wordes of
dame Prudence,/ they weren so supprised and
ravysshed and hadden so greet joye of hire that wonder was to telle./ "A, lady," quod they, "ye han shewed
unto us the blessynge of swetnesse, after the
sawe of David the prophete,/ for the reconsi-   1735
lynge which we been nat worthy to have in
no manere,/ but we oghte requeren it with greet contricioun and humylitee,/ ye of youre grete goodnesse
have presented unto us./ Now se we wel that the science and the konnynge of Salomon is ful trewe./ For
he seith that 'sweete wordes multiplien and
encreescen freendes and maken shrewes to be
debonaire and meeke.'/   *2930

"Certes," quod they, "we putten oure dede
and al oure matere and cause al hoolly in youre goode
wyl/ and been redy to obeye to the speche and
comandement of my lord Melibee./ And therfore,
deere and benygne lady, we preien yow and biseke
yow as mekely as we konne and mowen/ that it lyke
unto youre grete goodnesse to fulfillen in dede youre
goodliche wordes,/ for we consideren and knowelichen that we han offended and greved my
lord Melibee out of mesure,/ so ferforth that   1745

1707 **worth:** worthy
1711 **konne:** be able to

1723 **seurely:** surely
1726 **delibered:** considered
1734 **supprised:** taken (by it)
1739 **science:** knowledge

we be nat of power to maken his amendes./ And therfore we oblige and bynden us and oure freendes for to
doon al his wyl and his comandementz./ But peraventure he hath swich hevynesse and swich wratthe
to us-ward by cause of oure offense/ that he wole
enjoyne us swich a peyne as we mowe nat bere ne
susteene./ And therfore, noble lady, we biseke
to youre wommanly pitee/ to taken swich   *2940
avysement in this nede that we ne oure freendes be nat desherited ne destroyed thurgh oure
folye."/

"Certes," quod Prudence, "it is an hard thyng and
right perilous/ that a man putte hym al outrely in the
arbitracioun and juggement, and in the myght and
power of his enemys./ For Salomon seith, 'Leeveth
me, and yeveth credence to that I shal seyn: I seye,'
quod he, 'ye peple, folk and governours of hooly
chirche,/ to thy sone, to thy wyf, to thy freend,
ne to thy broother/ ne yeve thou nevere myght   1755
ne maistrie of thy body whil thou lyvest.'/
Now sithen he deffendeth that man sholde nat yeven
to his broother ne to his freend the myght of his body,/
by a strenger resoun he deffendeth and forbedeth a
man to yeven hymself to his enemy./ And nathelees I
conseille you that ye mystruste nat my lord,/ for I woot
wel and knowe verraily that he is debonaire
and meeke, large, curteys,/ and nothyng   *2950
desirous ne coveitous of good ne richesse./ For
ther nys nothyng in this world that he desireth, save
oonly worshipe and honour./ Forthermoore I knowe
wel and am right seur that he shal nothyng doon in
this nede withouten my conseil,/ and I shal so werken
in this cause that by the grace of oure Lord God ye
shul been reconsiled unto us."/

Thanne seyden they with o voys, "Worshipful lady,
we putten us and oure goodes al fully in youre
wil and disposicioun,/ and been redy to   1765
comen, what day that it like unto youre
noblesse to lymyte us or assigne us,/ for to maken
oure obligacioun and boond as strong as it liketh unto
youre goodnesse,/ that we mowe fulfille the wille of
yow and of my lord Melibee."/

Whan dame Prudence hadde herd the answeres of
thise men, she bad hem goon agayn prively;/ and she

retourned to hir lord Melibee, and tolde hym
how she foond his adversaries ful repentant,/   *2960
knowelechynge ful lowely hir synnes and
trespas, and how they were redy to suffren all peyne,/
requirynge and preiynge hym of mercy and pitee./

Thanne seyde Melibee: "He is wel worthy to have
pardoun and foryifnesse of his synne, that excuseth
nat his synne/ but knowelecheth it and repenteth hym,
axinge indulgence./ For Senec seith, 'Ther is the
remissioun and foryifnesse, where as the confessioun is,'/ for confessioun is neighebor to   1775
innocence./ And he seith in another place that
'he that hath shame of his synne and knowlecheth [it
is worthy remissioun].' And therfore I assente and
conferme me to have pees;/ but it is good that we do
it nat withouten the assent and wyl of oure freendes."/

Thanne was Prudence right glad and joyeful and
seyde:/ "Certes, sire," quod she, "ye han wel
and goodly answered,/ for right as by the con-   *2970
seil, assent, and help of youre freendes ye han
been stired to venge yow and maken werre,/ right so
withouten hire conseil shul ye nat accorden yow ne
have pees with youre adversaries./ For the lawe seith,
'Ther nys no thyng so good by wey of kynde as a
thyng to be unbounde by hym that it was ybounde.' "/

And thanne dame Prudence withouten delay or
tariynge sente anon hire messages for hire kyn and
for hire olde freendes which that were trewe and
wyse,/ and tolde hem by ordre in the presence of
Melibee al this mateere as it is aboven
expressed and declared,/ and preyden hem   1785
that they wolde yeven hire avys and conseil
what best were to doon in this nede./ And whan
Melibees freendes hadde taken hire avys and deliberacioun of the forseide mateere,/ and hadden examyned it by greet bisynesse and greet diligence,/ they
yave ful conseil for to have pees and reste,/ and that
Melibee sholde receyve with good herte his
adversaries to foryifnesse and mercy./   *2980

And whan dame Prudence hadde herd the
assent of hir lord Melibee, and the conseil of his
freendes/ accorde with hire wille and hire entencioun,/ she was wonderly glad in hire herte and
seyde:/ "Ther is an old proverbe," quod she, "seith
that 'the goodnesse that thou mayst do this day, do it,/

1747 **oblige**: pledge
1757 **nat yeven**: i.e., give
1767 **obligacioun**: surety, pledge

and abide nat ne delaye it nat til tomorwe.'/   1795
And therfore I conseille that ye sende youre
messages, swiche as been discrete and wise,/ unto
youre adversaries, tellynge hem on youre bihalve/
that if they wole trete of pees and of accord,/ that they
shape hem withouten delay or tariyng to comen
unto us."/ Which thyng parfourned was in
dede./ And whanne thise trespassours and   *2990
repentynge folk of hire folies— that is to
seyn, the adversaries of Melibee—/ hadden herd
what thise messagers seyden unto hem,/ they weren
right glad and joyeful, and answereden ful mekely
and benignely,/ yeldynge graces and thankynges to
hir lord Melibee and to al his compaignye,/ and
shopen hem withouten delay to go with the
messagers and obeye to the comandement of   1805
hir lord Melibee./

And right anon they tooken hire wey to the court
of Melibee,/ and tooken with hem somme of hire
trewe freendes to maken feith for hem and for to been
hire borwes./ And whan they were comen to the presence of Melibee, he seyde hem thise wordes:/ "It
standeth thus," quod Melibee, "and sooth it is, that
ye,/ causelees and withouten skile and
resoun,/ han doon grete injuries and wronges   *3000
to me and to my wyf Prudence and to my
doghter also./ For ye han entred into myn hous by
violence,/ and have doon swich outrage that alle men
knowen wel that ye have disserved the deeth./ And
therfore wol I knowe and wite of yow/ wheither ye
wol putte the punyssement and the chastisynge and
the vengeance of this outrage in the wyl of me
and of my wyf Prudence, or ye wol nat?"/   1815

Thanne the wiseste of hem thre answerde
for hem alle and seyde,/ "Sire," quod he, "we knowen
wel that we been unworthy to comen unto the court of
so greet a lord and so worthy as ye been./ For we han
so greetly mystaken us, and han offended and agilt
in swich a wise agayn youre heigh lordshipe/ that
trewely we han disserved the deeth./ But yet, for the
grete goodnesse and debonairetee that al the
world witnesseth of youre persone,/ we sub-   *3010
mytten us to the excellence and benignitee of
youre gracious lordshipe,/ and been redy to obeie to

alle youre comandementz,/ bisekynge yow that of
youre merciable pitee ye wol considere oure grete
repentaunce and lowe submyssioun/ and graunten us
foryevenesse of oure outrageous trespas and offense./
For wel we knowe that youre liberal grace and mercy
strecchen hem ferther into goodnesse than doon oure
outrageouse giltes and trespas into wikkednesse,/ al be it that cursedly and dampnablely   1825
we han agilt agayn youre heigh lordshipe."/

Thanne Melibee took hem up fro the ground ful
benignely,/ and receyved hire obligaciouns and hir
boondes by hire othes upon hire plegges and borwes,/
and assigned hem a certeyn day to retourne unto his
court/ for to accepte and receyve the sentence and
juggement that Melibee wolde comande to be
doon on hem by the causes aforeseyd./   *3020
Whiche thynges ordeyned, every man
retourned to his hous./

And whan that dame Prudence saugh hir tyme, she
freyned and axed hir lord Melibee/ what vengeance
he thoughte to taken of his adversaries./

To which Melibee answerde and seyde, "Certes,"
quod he, "I thynke and purpose me fully/ to desherite
hem of al that evere they han and for to putte
hem in exil for evere."/   1835

"Certes," quod dame Prudence, "this were
a crueel sentence and muchel agayn resoun./ For ye
been riche ynough and han no nede of oother mennes
good,/ and ye myghte lightly in this wise gete yow a
coveitous name,/ which is a vicious thyng, and oghte
been eschued of every good man./ For after the sawe of
the word of the Apostle, 'Coveitise is roote
of alle harmes.'/ And therfore it were bettre   *3030
for yow to lese so muchel good of youre
owene than for to taken of hir good in this manere,/
for bettre it is to lesen good with worshipe than it is to
wynne good with vileynye and shame./ And everi
man oghte to doon his diligence and his bisynesse to
geten hym a good name./ And yet shal he nat oonly
bisie hym in kepynge of his good name,/ but he shal
also enforcen hym alwey to do somthyng by which he

1807 **maken feith:** stand surety   **borwes:** guarantors
1815 **punyssement:** punishment

1828 **plegges:** pledges
1832 **freyned:** asked

may renovelle his good name./ For it is writen   1845
that 'the olde good loos or good name of a
man is soone goon and passed, whan it is nat newed
ne renovelled.'/ And as touchynge that ye seyn ye
wole exile youre adversaries,/ that thynketh me
muchel agayn resoun and out of mesure,/ considered
the power that they han yeve yow upon hemself./ And
it is writen that 'he is worthy to lesen his privilege
that mysuseth the myght and the power that
is yeven hym.'/ And I sette cas ye myghte   *3040
enjoyne hem that peyne by right and by lawe,/
which I trowe ye mowe nat do;/ I seye ye mighte nat
putten it to execucioun peraventure,/ and thanne were
it likly to retourne to the werre as it was biforn./ And
therfore, if ye wole that men do yow obeisance, ye moste deemen moore curteisly;/ this   1855
is to seyn, ye moste yeven moore esy sentences and juggementz./ For it is writen that 'he that
moost curteisly comandeth, to hym men moost
obeyen.'/ And therfore I prey yow that in this necessitee and in this nede ye caste yow to overcome youre
herte./ For Senec seith that 'he that overcometh his
herte overcometh twies.'/ And Tullius seith,
'Ther is no thyng so comendable in a greet   *3050
lord/ as whan he is debonaire and meeke, and
appeseth him lightly.'/ And I prey yow that ye wole
forbere now to do vengeance,/ in swich a manere that
youre goode name may be kept and conserved,/ and
that men mowe have cause and mateere to preyse
yow of pitee and of mercy,/ and that ye have
no cause to repente yow of thyng that ye   1865
doon./ For Senec seith, 'He overcometh in an
yvel manere that repenteth hym of his victorie.'/
Wherfore I pray yow, lat mercy been in youre herte,/

to th'effect and entente that God Almighty have mercy
on yow in his laste juggement./ For Seint Jame seith
in his Epistle: 'Juggement withouten mercy shal be
doon to hym that hath no mercy of another wight.' "/

Whanne Melibee hadde herd the grete skiles and
resouns of dame Prudence, and hire wise
informaciouns and techynges,/ his herte gan   *3060
enclyne to the wil of his wif, considerynge hir
trewe entente,/ and conformed hym anon and
assented fully to werken after hir conseil,/ and
thonked God, of whom procedeth al vertu and alle
goodnesse, that hym sente a wyf of so greet discrecioun./ And whan the day cam that his adversaries
sholde appieren in his presence,/ he spak unto
hem ful goodly, and seyde in this wyse:/ "Al be   1875
it so that of youre pride and heigh presumpcioun and folie, and of youre necligence and unkonnynge,/ ye have mysborn yow and trespassed unto
me,/ yet for as muche as I see and biholde youre grete
humylitee/ and that ye been sory and repentant of
youre giltes,/ it constreyneth me to doon yow
grace and mercy./ Wherfore I receyve yow to   *3070
my grace/ and foryeve yow outrely alle the
offenses, injuries, and wronges that ye have doon
agayn me and myne,/ to this effect and to this ende,
that God of his endelees mercy/ wole at the tyme of
oure diynge foryeven us oure giltes that we han trespassed to hym in this wrecched world./ For doutelees,
if we be sory and repentant of the synnes and giltes
which we han trespassed in the sighte of oure
Lord God,/ he is so free and so merciable/ that   1885
he wole foryeven us oure giltes/ and bryngen
us to the blisse that nevere hath ende." Amen.

Heere is ended Chaucers Tale of Melibee and of Dame Prudence.

1845 **renovelle:** renew
1858 **caste yow:** endeavor
1861 **appeseth him:** calms himself

1870 **informaciouns:** counsels
1877 **mysborn yow:** misbehaved yourselves

The Prologue of the Monk's Tale

ⓢ

The murye wordes of the Hoost to the Monk.

Whan ended was my tale of Melibee,
And of Prudence and hire benignytee,   *3080
Oure Hooste seyde, "As I am feithful man,
And by that precious corpus Madrian,
I hadde levere than a barel ale
That Goodelief, my wyf, hadde herd this tale!
For she nys no thyng of swich pacience   1895
As was this Melibeus wyf Prudence.
By Goddes bones, whan I bete my knaves,
She bryngeth me forth the grete clobbed staves,
And crieth, 'Slee the dogges everichoon,
And brek hem, bothe bak and every boon!'   *3090
    "And if that any neighebor of myne
Wol nat in chirche to my wyf enclyne,
Or be so hardy to hire to trespace,
Whan she comth hoom she rampeth in my face,
And crieth, 'False coward, wrek thy wyf!   1905
By corpus bones, I wol have thy knyf,
And thou shalt have my distaf and go spynne!'
Fro day to nyght right thus she wol bigynne.
'Allas,' she seith, 'that evere I was shape
To wedden a milksop, or a coward ape,   *3100
That wol been overlad with every wight!
Thou darst nat stonden by thy wyves right!'
    "This is my lif, but if that I wol fighte;
And out at dore anon I moot me dighte,
Or elles I am but lost, but if that I   1915
Be lik a wilde leoun, fool-hardy.
I woot wel she wol do me slee som day
Som neighebor, and thanne go my way;
For I am perilous with knyf in honde,
Al be it that I dar nat hire withstonde,   *3110
For she is byg in armes, by my feith:

That shal he fynde that hire mysdooth or seith—
But lat us passe awey fro this mateere.
    "My lord, the Monk," quod he, "be myrie of
          cheere,
For ye shul telle a tale trewely.   1925
Loo, Rouchestre stant heer faste by!
Ryde forth, myn owene lord, brek nat oure game.
But, by my trouthe, I knowe nat youre name.
Wher shal I calle yow my lord daun John,
Or daun Thomas, or elles daun Albon?   *3120
Of what hous be ye, by youre fader kyn?
I vowe to God, thou hast a ful fair skyn;
It is a gentil pasture ther thow goost.
Thou art nat lyk a penant or a goost:
Upon my feith, thou art som officer,   1935
Som worthy sexteyn, or som celerer,
For by my fader soule, as to my doom,
Thou art a maister whan thou art at hoom;
No povre cloysterer, ne no novys,
But a governour, wily and wys,   *3130
And therwithal of brawnes and of bones
A wel farynge persone for the nones.
I pray to God, yeve hym confusioun
That first thee broghte unto religioun!
Thou woldest han been a tredefowel aright.   1945
Haddestow as greet a leeve as thou hast myght
To parfourne al thy lust in engendrure,
Thou haddest bigeten ful many a creature.
Allas, why werestow so wyd a cope?
God yeve me sorwe, but, and I were a pope,   *3140
Nat oonly thou, but every myghty man,

1891 **As I am feithful man:** on my faith as a Christian
1892 **corpus Madrian:** the body of Madrian; see n.
1893 **barel ale:** barrel of ale
1898 **clobbed:** club-shaped
1904 **rampeth:** shakes her fist
1905 **wrek:** avenge
1906 **corpus bones:** God's bones
1907 **distaf:** a small staff used for spinning thread
1911 **overlad:** overborne, browbeaten
1914 **me dighte:** hasten
1917 **do me slee:** cause me to slay
1921 **byg:** strong

1922 **mysdooth or seith:** the prefix *mys-* goes with both words
1926 **Rouchestre:** Rochester, about thirty miles from London; see n.
1927 **brek nat oure game:** do not interrupt our game
1929 **daun John:** sir John
1934 **penant:** penitent
1936 **sexteyn:** the officer in charge of the sacred vessels, vestments, and relics
celerer: the officer in charge of kitchen and cellar and of the provision of food and drink
1939 **novys:** novice
1942 **wel farynge:** handsome
1944 **unto religioun:** into a religious order
1945 **tredefowel aright:** excellent copulator of fowls, good breeding stock; cf. EpiNPT VII.3451.
1950 **but:** unless   **and:** if

Though he were shorn ful hye upon his pan,
Sholde have a wyf; for al the world is lorn!
Religioun hath take up al the corn
Of tredyng, and we borel men been shrympes.   1955
Of fieble trees ther comen wrecched ympes.
This maketh that oure heires been so sklendre
And feble that they may nat wel engendre.
This maketh that oure wyves wole assaye
Religious folk, for ye mowe bettre paye   *3150
Of Venus paiementz than mowe we;
God woot, no lussheburghes payen ye!
But be nat wrooth, my lord, though that I pleye.
Ful ofte in game a sooth I have herd seye!"
   This worthy Monk took al in pacience,   1965
And seyde, "I wol doon al my diligence,
As fer as sowneth into honestee,
To telle yow a tale, or two, or three.
And if yow list to herkne hyderward,
I wol yow seyn the lyf of Seint Edward;   *3160
Or ellis, first, tragedies wol I telle,

Of whiche I have an hundred in my celle.
Tragedie is to seyn a certeyn storie,
As olde bookes maken us memorie,
Of hym that stood in greet prosperitee,   1975
And is yfallen out of heigh degree
Into myserie, and endeth wrecchedly.
And they ben versified communely
Of six feet, which men clepen *exametron*.
In prose eek been endited many oon,   *3170
And eek in meetre in many a sondry wyse.
Lo, this declaryng oghte ynogh suffise.
   "Now herkneth, if yow liketh for to heere.
But first I yow biseeke in this mateere,
Though I by ordre telle nat thise thynges,   1985
Be it of popes, emperours, or kynges,
After hir ages, as men writen fynde,
But tellen hem som bifore and som bihynde,
As it now comth unto my remembraunce,
Have me excused of myn ignoraunce."   *3180

Explicit

The Monk's Tale

Heere bigynneth the Monkes Tale
De Casibus Virorum Illustrium.

I wol biwaille in manere of tragedie
The harm of hem that stoode in heigh degree,
And fillen so that ther nas no remedie
To brynge hem out of hir adversitee.
For certein, whan that Fortune list to flee,   1995
Ther may no man the cours of hire withholde.
Lat no man truste on blynd prosperitee;
Be war by thise ensamples trewe and olde.

Lucifer

   At Lucifer, though he an angel were
And nat a man, at hym wol I bigynne.   *3190

For though Fortune may noon angel dere,
From heigh degree yet fel he for his synne
Doun into helle, where he yet is inne.
O Lucifer, brightest of angels alle,
Now artow Sathanas, that mayst nat twynne   2005
Out of miserie, in which that thou art falle.

Adam

   Loo Adam, in the feeld of Damyssene
With Goddes owene fynger wroght was he,
And nat bigeten of mannes sperme unclene,
And welte al paradys savynge o tree.   *3200
Hadde nevere worldly man so heigh degree

1952 **pan:** skull
1955 **borel men:** laymen   **shrympes:** shrimps, puny creatures
1956 **wrecched ympes:** weak offshoots
1959 **wol assaye:** want to try out
1962 **lussheburghes:** inferior coins; see n.
1967 **sowneth into honestee:** is conducive to propriety
1970 **Seint Edward:** St. Edward the Confessor

DeCasibus, *etc.*: concerning the falls (fates) of famous men

---

1979 **exametron:** hexameters, the meter of Latin heroic poetry

---

2001 **dere:** harm
2005 **twynne:** escape
2007 **Damyssene:** Damascus
2010 **welte:** ruled   **o:** one, a single

As Adam, til he for mysgovernaunce
Was dryven out of hys hye prosperitee
To labour, and to helle, and to meschaunce.

Sampson

    Loo Sampsoun, which that was annunciat   2015
By th'angel longe er his nativitee,
And was to God Almyghty consecrat,
And stood in noblesse whil he myghte see.
Was nevere swich another as was hee,
To speke of strengthe, and therwith hardynesse; *3210
But to his wyves toolde he his secree,
Thurgh which he slow hymself for wrecchednesse.

Sampsoun, this noble almyghty champioun,
Withouten wepen save his handes tweye,
He slow and al torente the leoun,   2025
Toward his weddyng walkynge by the weye.
His false wyf koude hym so plese and preye
Til she his conseil knew; and she, untrewe,
Unto his foos his conseil gan biwreye,
And hym forsook, and took another newe.   *3220

Thre hundred foxes took Sampson for ire,
And alle hir tayles he togydre bond,
And sette the foxes tayles alle on fire,
For he on every tayl had knyt a brond;
And they brende alle the cornes in that lond,   2035
And alle hire olyveres, and vynes eke.
A thousand men he slow eek with his hond,
And hadde no wepen but an asses cheke.

Whan they were slayn, so thursted hym that he
Was wel ny lorn, for which he gan to preye   *3230
That God wolde on his peyne han some pitee
And sende hym drynke, or elles moste he deye;
And of this asses cheke, that was dreye,
Out of a wang-tooth sprang anon a welle,
Of which he drank ynogh, shortly to seye;   2045
Thus heelp hym God, as *Judicum* can telle.

By verray force at Gazan on a nyght,
Maugree Philistiens of that citee,
The gates of the toun he hath up plyght,
And on his bak ycaryed hem hath hee   *3240
Hye on an hill whereas men myghte hem see.
O noble, almyghty Sampsoun, lief and deere,
Had thou nat toold to wommen thy secree,
In al this world ne hadde been thy peere!

This Sampson nevere ciser drank ne wyn,   2055
Ne on his heed cam rasour noon ne sheere,
By precept of the messager divyn,
For alle his strengthes in his heeres weere.
And fully twenty wynter, yeer by yeere,
He hadde of Israel the governaunce.   *3250
But soone shal he wepe many a teere,
For wommen shal hym bryngen to meschaunce!

Unto his lemman Dalida he tolde
That in his heeris al his strengthe lay,
And falsly to his foomen she hym solde.   2065
And slepynge in hir barm upon a day,
She made to clippe or shere his heres away,
And made his foomen al his craft espyen;
And whan that they hym foond in this array,
They bounde hym faste and putten out his yen. *3260

But er his heer were clipped or yshave,
Ther was no boond with which men myghte him
        bynde;
But now is he in prison in a cave,
Where-as they made hym at the queerne grynde.
O noble Sampsoun, strongest of mankynde,   2075
O whilom juge, in glorie and in richesse!
Now maystow wepen with thyne eyen blynde,
Sith thou fro wele art falle in wrecchednesse.

The ende of this caytyf was as I shal seye.
His foomen made a feeste upon a day,   *3270
And made hym as hire fool biforn hem pleye;
And this was in a temple of greet array.
But atte laste he made a foul affray,
For he two pilers shook and made hem falle,
And doun fil temple and al, and ther it lay—   2085
And slow hymself, and eek his foomen alle.

2012 **mysgovernaunce:** misconduct
2015 **which that was annunciat:** who (i.e., whose birth) was foretold
2018 **whil he myghte see:** as long as he preserved his eyesight (see line 2070)
2025 **torente:** tore to pieces
2026 while he was walking toward his wedding
2034 **brond:** burning piece of wood
2035 **cornes:** grain crops
2036 **olyveres:** olive trees
2038 **cheke:** jawbone
2039 **so thursted hym:** he was so thirsty
2044 **wang-tooth:** molar
2046 **Judicum:** the Book of Judges

2047 **Gazan:** Gaza
2048 **Philistiens:** Philistines
2055 **ciser:** strong drink
2056 **sheere:** scissors
2063 **Dalida:** Delilah
2066 **barm:** lap
2074 **queerne:** mill
2083 **foul affray:** terrifying assault

This is to seyn, the prynces everichoon,
And eek thre thousand bodyes, were ther slayn
With fallynge of the grete temple of stoon.
Of Sampson now wol I namoore sayn.   *3280
Beth war by this ensample oold and playn
That no men telle hir conseil til hir wyves
Of swich thyng as they wolde han secree fayn,
If that it touche hir lymes or hir lyves.

Hercules

    Of Hercules, the sovereyn conquerour,   2095
Syngen his werkes laude and heigh renoun;
For in his tyme of strengthe he was the flour.
He slow and rafte the skyn of the leoun;
He of Centauros leyde the boost adoun;
He Arpies slow, the crueel bryddes felle;   *3290
He golden apples rafte of the dragoun;
He drow out Cerberus, the hound of helle;

He slow the crueel tyrant Busirus
And made his hors to frete hym, flessh and boon;
He slow the firy serpent venymus;   2105
Of Acheloys two hornes he brak oon;
And he slow Cacus in a cave of stoon;
He slow the geant Antheus the stronge;
He slow the grisly boor, and that anon;
And bar the hevene on his nekke longe.   *3300

Was nevere wight, sith that this world bigan,
That slow so manye monstres as dide he.
Thurghout this wyde world his name ran,
What for his strengthe and for his heigh bountee,
And every reawme wente he for to see.   2115
He was so stroong that no man myghte hym lette.
At bothe the worldes endes, seith Trophee,
In stide of boundes he a pileer sette.

A lemman hadde this noble champioun,
That highte Dianira, fressh as May;   *3310
And as thise clerkes maken mencioun,

2098 **rafte:** despoiled, took away
2099 **Centauros:** centaurs; for another account of the labors enumerated here see Bo 4.m7.28–62.
2100 **Arpies:** Harpies
2103 **Busirus:** a king of Egypt
2104 **frete:** devour
2106 **Acheloys:** Achelous, a river god, who took the form of a bull in his fight with Hercules
2107 **Cacus:** a monster
2108 **Antheus:** a giant whom Hercules wrestled
2117 **bothe the worldes endes:** the eastern and western ends of the world   **Trophee:** unidentified; see n.
2118 **boundes:** boundary markers   **pileer:** pillar

She hath hym sent a sherte, fressh and gay.
Allas, this sherte—allas and weylaway!—
Envenymed was so subtilly withalle
That er that he had wered it half a day   2125
It made his flessh al from his bones falle.

But nathelees somme clerkes hire excusen
By oon that highte Nessus, that it maked.
Be as be may, I wol hire noght accusen;
But on his bak this sherte he wered al naked   *3320
Til that his flessh was for the venym blaked.
And whan he saugh noon oother remedye,
In hoote coles he hath hymselven raked,
For with no venym deigned hym to dye.

Thus starf this worthy, myghty Hercules.   2135
Lo, who may truste on Fortune any throwe?
For hym that folweth al this world of prees
Er he be war is ofte yleyd ful lowe.
Ful wys is he that kan hymselven knowe!
Beth war, for whan that Fortune list to glose,   *3330
Thanne wayteth she her man to overthrowe
By swich a wey as he wolde leest suppose.

Nabugodonosor

    The myghty trone, the precious tresor,
The glorious ceptre, and roial magestee
That hadde the kyng Nabugodonosor   2145
With tonge unnethe may discryved bee.
He twyes wan Jerusalem the citee;
The vessel of the temple he with hym ladde.
At Babiloigne was his sovereyn see,
In which his glorie and his delit he hadde.   *3340

The faireste children of the blood roial
Of Israel he leet do gelde anoon,
And maked ech of hem to been his thral.
Amonges othere Daniel was oon,
That was the wiseste child of everychon,   2155
For he the dremes of the kyng expowned,
Whereas in Chaldeye clerk ne was ther noon
That wiste to what fyn his dremes sowned.

2129 **Be as be may:** however it may be
2131 **blaked:** blackened
2133 **raked:** covered by raking
2135 **starf:** died
2136 **any throwe:** for any time
2137 **this world of prees:** this dangerous, difficult world
2140 **glose:** beguile, deceive
2145 **Nabugodonosor:** Nebuchadnezzar
2148 **vessel:** plate, vessels
2149 **see:** throne
2152 **leet do gelde:** had castrated
2157 **Chaldeye:** Chaldea, Babylonia
2158 **fyn:** end

This proude kyng leet maken a statue of gold,
Sixty cubites long and sevene in brede,   *3350
To which ymage bothe yong and oold
Comanded he to loute, and have in drede,
Or in a fourneys, ful of flambes rede,
He shal be brent that wolde noght obeye.
But nevere wolde assente to that dede   2165
Daniel ne his yonge felawes tweye.

This kyng of kynges proud was and elaat;
He wende that God, that sit in magestee,
Ne myghte hym nat bireve of his estaat.
But sodeynly he loste his dignytee,   *3360
And lyk a beest hym semed for to bee,
And eet hey as an oxe, and lay theroute
In reyn; with wilde beestes walked hee
Til certein tyme was ycome aboute.

And lik an egles fetheres wax his heres;   2175
His nayles lyk a briddes clawes weere;
Til God relessed hym a certeyn yeres,
And yaf hym wit, and thanne with many a teere
He thanked God, and evere his lyf in feere
Was he to doon amys or moore trespace;   *3370
And til that tyme he leyd was on his beere
He knew that God was ful of myght and grace.

Balthasar

His sone, which that highte Balthasar,
That heeld the regne after his fader day,
He by his fader koude noght be war,   2185
For proud he was of herte and of array,
And eek an ydolastre was he ay.
His hye estaat assured hym in pryde;
But Fortune caste hym doun, and ther he lay,
And sodeynly his regne gan divide.   *3380

A feeste he made unto his lordes alle
Upon a tyme and bad hem blithe bee;
And thanne his officeres gan he calle:
"Gooth, bryngeth forth the vesseles," quod he,
"Whiche that my fader in his prosperitee   2195
Out of the temple of Jerusalem birafte;
And to oure hye goddes thanke we
Of honour that oure eldres with us lafte."

Hys wyf, his lordes, and his concubynes
Ay dronken, whil hire appetites laste,   *3390
Out of thise noble vessels sondry wynes.
And on a wal this kyng his eyen caste
And saugh an hand, armlees, that wroot ful faste,
For feere of which he quook and siked soore.
This hand that Balthasar so soore agaste   2205
Wroot *Mane, techel, phares*, and namoore.

In all that land magicien was noon
That koude expoune what this lettre mente;
But Daniel expowned it anoon,
And seyde, "Kyng, God to thy fader lente   *3400
Glorie and honour, regne, tresour, rente;
And he was proud and nothyng God ne dradde,
And therfore God greet wreche upon hym sente,
And hym birafte the regne that he hadde.

"He was out cast of mannes compaignye;   2215
With asses was his habitacioun,
And eet hey as a beest in weet and drye
Til that he knew, by grace and by resoun,
That God of hevene hath domynacioun
Over every regne and every creature;   *3410
And thanne hadde God of hym compassioun,
And hym restored his regne and his figure.

"Eek thou, that art his sone, art proud also,
And knowest alle thise thynges verraily,
And art rebel to God, and art his foo.   2225
Thou drank eek of his vessels boldely;
Thy wyf eek, and thy wenches, synfully
Dronke of the same vessels sondry wynys;
And heryest false goddes cursedly;
Therefore to thee yshapen ful greet pyne ys.   *3420

"This hand was sent from God that on the wal
Wroot *Mane, techel, phares,* truste me;
Thy regne is doon; thou weyest noght at al.
Dyvyded is thy regne, and it shal be
To Medes and to Perses yeven," quod he.   2235
And thilke same nyght this kyng was slawe,
And Darius occupieth his degree,
Thogh he therto hadde neither right ne lawe.

2160 **brede:** breadth
2162 **loute:** bow down   **have in drede:** venerate
2166 **tweye:** two (an error for three); see n.
2167 **elaat:** arrogant
2169 **bireve:** deprive
2170 **dignytee:** high office
2177 **a certeyn yeres:** a certain (number of) years
2183 **Balthasar:** Belshazzar
2187 **ydolastre:** idolator
2188 **assured hym:** made him confident

2208 **expoune:** explain
2212 **nothyng God ne dradde:** feared God not at all
2213 **wreche:** vengeance
2229 **heryest:** worship
2233 **weyest noght:** are of no account
2235 **Perses:** Persians
2237 **Darius:** Darius the Mede (Dan. 5.30)

Lordynges, ensample heerby may ye take
How that in lordshipe is no sikernesse,   *3430
For whan Fortune wole a man forsake,
She bereth awey his regne and his richesse,
And eek his freendes, bothe moore and lesse.
For what man that hath freendes thurgh Fortune,
Mishap wol maken hem enemys, I gesse;   2245
This proverbe is ful sooth and ful commune.

Cenobia

   Cenobia, of Palymerie queene,
As writen Persiens of hir noblesse,
So worthy was in armes and so keene
That no wight passed hire in hardynesse,   *3440
Ne in lynage, ne in oother gentillesse.
Of kynges blood of Perce is she descended.
I seye nat that she hadde moost fairnesse,
But of hir shap she myghte nat been amended.

From hire childhede I fynde that she fledde   2255
Office of wommen, and to wode she wente,
And many a wilde hertes blood she shedde
With arwes brode that she to hem sente.
She was so swift that she anon hem hente;
And whan that she was elder, she wolde kille   *3450
Leouns, leopardes, and beres al torente,
And in hir armes weelde hem at hir wille.

She dorste wilde beestes dennes seke,
And rennen in the montaignes al the nyght,
And slepen under a bussh, and she koude eke   2265
Wrastlen, by verray force and verray myght,
With any yong man, were he never so wight.
Ther myghte no thyng in hir armes stonde.
She kepte hir maydenhod from every wight;
To no man deigned hire for to be bonde.   *3460

But atte laste hir freendes han hire maried
To Odenake, a prynce of that contree,
Al were it so that she hem longe taried.
And ye shul understonde how that he
Hadde swiche fantasies as hadde she.   2275
But natheless, whan they were knyt in-feere,
They lyved in joye and in felicitee,
For ech of hem hadde oother lief and deere,

Save o thyng: that she wolde nevere assente,
By no wey, that he sholde by hire lye   *3470
But ones, for it was hir pleyn entente
To have a child, the world to multiplye;
And also soone as that she myghte espye
That she was nat with childe with that dede,
Thanne wolde she suffre hym doon his fantasye   2285
Eft-soone, and nat but oones, out of drede.

And if she were with childe at thilke cast,
Namoore sholde he pleyen thilke game
Til fully fourty [wikes] weren past;
Thanne wolde she ones suffre hym do the same.   *3480
Al were this Odenake wilde or tame,
He gat namoore of hire, for thus she seyde:
It was to wyves lecherie and shame,
In oother caas, if that men with hem pleyde.

Two sones by this Odenake hadde she,   2295
The whiche she kepte in vertu and lettrure.
But now unto oure tale turne we.
I seye, so worshipful a creature,
And wys therwith, and large with mesure,
So penyble in the werre, and curteis eke,   *3490
Ne moore labour myghte in werre endure,
Was noon, though al this world men sholde seke.

Hir riche array ne myghte nat be told,
As wel in vessel as in hire clothyng.
She was al clad in perree and in gold,   2305
And eek she lafte noght, for noon huntyng,
To have of sondry tonges ful knowyng,
Whan that she leyser hadde; and for to entende
To lerne bookes was al hire likyng,
How she in vertu myghte hir lyf dispende.   *3500

And shortly of this storie for to trete,
So doghty was hir housbonde and eek she,
That they conquered manye regnes grete
In the orient, with many a fair citee
Apertenaunt unto the magestee   2315
Of Rome, and with strong hond held hem ful faste,

2245 **Mishap:** misfortune
2247 **Cenobia:** Zenobia   **Palymerie:** Palmyra, a city in Syria
2252 **Perce:** Persia
2256 **Office:** function, duty
2261 **torente:** tear to pieces
2262 **weelde:** wield, handle
2267 **wight:** active, agile
2272 **Odenake:** Odenathus, ruler of Palmyra

2286 **Eft-soone:** again   **nat but:** only   **out of drede:** without doubt
2287 **cast:** time, circumstance
2296 **lettrure:** learning
2300 **penyble:** indefatigable
2305 **perree:** precious stones
2306 **lafte:** neglected
2308 **entende:** strive, endeavor
2315 **Apertenaunt:** appertaining, belonging to

Ne nevere myghte hir foomen doon hem flee,
Ay whil that Odenakes dayes laste.

Hir batailles, whoso list hem for to rede,
Agayn Sapor the kyng and othere mo,   *3510
And how that al this proces fil in dede,
Why she conquered and what title had therto,
And after, of hir meschief and hire wo,
How that she was biseged and ytake—
Lat hym unto my maister Petrak go,   2325
That writ ynough of this, I undertake.

Whan Odenake was deed, she myghtily
The regnes heeld, and with hire propre hond
Agayn hir foos she faught so cruelly
That ther nas kyng ne prynce in al that lond   *3520
That he nas glad, if he that grace fond,
That she ne wolde upon his lond werreye.
With hire they maden alliance by bond
To been in pees, and lete hire ride and pleye.

The Emperour of Rome, Claudius   2335
Ne hym bifore, the Romayn Galien,
Ne dorste nevere been so corageus,
Ne noon Ermyn, ne noon Egipcien,
Ne Surrien, ne noon Arabyen,
Withinne the feeld that dorste with hire fighte, *3530
Lest that she wolde hem with hir handes slen,
Or with hir meignee putten hem to flighte.

In kynges habit wente hir sones two,
As heires of hir fadres regnes alle,
And Hermanno and Thymalao   2345
Hir names were, as Persiens hem calle.
But ay Fortune hath in hire hony galle;
This myghty queene may no while endure.
Fortune out of hir regne made hire falle
To wrecchednesse and to mysaventure.   *3540

    Aurelian, whan that the governaunce
Of Rome cam into his handes tweye,
He shoop upon this queene to doon vengeaunce.
And with his legions he took his weye
Toward Cenobie, and shortly for to seye,   2355

2320 **Sapor:** Shapur I, king of Persia c. 240–72 A.D.
2325 **Petrak:** Petrarch; see n.
2335–36 **Claudius, Galien:** the emperors Claudius Gothicus (268–70 A.D.), Gallienus
(253–68 A.D.)
2338 **Ermyn:** Armenian
2339 **Surrien:** Syrian
2351 **Aurelian:** the emperor Aurelianus

He made hire flee, and atte laste hire hente,
And fettred hire, and eek hire children tweye,
And wan the land, and hoom to Rome he wente.

Amonges othere thynges that he wan,   *3549
Hir chaar, that was with gold wroght and perree,
This grete Romayn, this Aurelian,
Hath with hym lad, for that men sholde it see.
Biforen his triumphe walketh shee,
With gilte cheynes on hire nekke hangynge.
Coroned was she, as after hir degree,   2365
And ful of perree charged hire clothynge.

Allas, Fortune! She that whilom was
Dredeful to kynges and to emperoures,
Now gaureth al the peple on hire, allas!
And she that helmed was in starke stoures   *3560
And wan by force townes stronge and toures,
Shal on hir heed now were a vitremyte;
And she that bar the ceptre ful of floures
Shal bere a distaf, hire cost for to quyte.

De Petro Rege Ispannie

    O noble, O worthy Petro, glorie of Spayne, 2375
Whom Fortune heeld so hye in magestee,
Wel oghten men thy pitous deeth complayne!
Out of thy land thy brother made thee flee,
And after, at a seege, by subtiltee,
Thou were bitraysed and lad unto his tente,   *3570
Where as he with his owene hand slow thee,
Succedynge in thy regne and in thy rente.

The feeld of snow, with th'egle of blak therinne,
Caught with the lymrod coloured as the gleede,
He brew this cursednesse and al this synne.   2385
The wikked nest was werker of this nede.
Noght Charles Olyver, that took ay heede

2360 **chaar:** chariot
2363 **triumphe:** triumphal procession
2369 **gaureth al the peple:** everyone stares
2370 **helmed was:** wore a helmet (i.e., fought)   **starke:** violent   **stoures:** battles
2372 **vitremyte:** probably a particular kind of woman's headdress; see n.
2374 **hire cost for to quyte:** to pay for her keep
2375 **Petro:** Pedro of Castile; see n.
2380 **bitraysed:** betrayed
2384 **lymrod:** lime-rod   **gleede:** burning coal; see n.
2385 **He:** Bertrand du Guesclin   **brew:** brewed, contrived
2386 **wikked nest:** a play on the name of Oliver Mauny (see n.)   **nede:** violence, crisis
2387 **Charles Olyver:** Charlemagne's Oliver, faithful friend of Roland

Of trouthe and honour, but of Armorike
Genylon-Olyver, corrupt for meede,
Broghte this worthy kyng in swich a brike.   *3580

De Petro Rege de Cipro

O worthy Petro, kyng of Cipre, also,
That Alisandre wan by heigh maistrie,
Ful many an hethen wroghtestow ful wo,
Of which thyne owene liges hadde envie,
And for no thyng but for thy chivalrie   2395
They in thy bed han slayn thee by the morwe.
Thus kan Fortune hir wheel governe and gye,
And out of joye brynge men to sorwe.

De Barnabo de Lumbardia

Off Melan grete Barnabo Viscounte,
God of delit and scourge of Lumbardye,   *3590
Why sholde I nat thyn infortune acounte,
Sith in estaat thow cloumbe were so hye?
Thy brother sone, that was thy double allye,
For he thy nevew was and sone-in-lawe,
Withinne his prisoun made thee to dye—   2405
But why ne how noot I that thou were slawe.

De Hugelino Comite de Pize

Off the Erl Hugelyn of Pyze the langour
Ther may no tonge telle for pitee.
But litel out of Pize stant a tour,
In which tour in prisoun put was he,   *3600
And with hym been his litel children thre;
The eldest scarsly fyf yeer was of age.
Allas, Fortune, it was greet crueltee
Swiche briddes for to putte in swich a cage!

Dampned was he to dyen in that prisoun,   2415
For Roger, which that bisshop was of Pize,
Hadde on hym maad a fals suggestioun,
Thurgh which the peple gan upon hym rise
And putten hym to prisoun in swich wise   *3609
As ye han herd, and mete and drynke he hadde

So smal that wel unnethe it may suffise,
And therwithal it was ful povre and badde.

And on a day bifil that in that hour
Whan that his mete wont was to be broght,
The gayler shette the dores of the tour.   2425
He herde it wel, but he spak right noght,
And in his herte anon ther fil a thoght
That they for hunger wolde doon hym dyen.
"Allas!" quod he, "Allas, that I was wroght!"
Therwith the teeris fillen from his yen.   *3620

His yonge sone, that thre yeer was of age,
Unto hym seyde, "Fader, why do ye wepe?
Whanne wol the gayler bryngen oure potage?
Is ther no morsel breed that ye do kepe?
I am so hungry that I may nat slepe.   2435
Now wolde God that I myghte slepen evere!
Thanne sholde nat hunger in my wombe crepe;
Ther is no thyng, but breed, that me were levere."

Thus day by day this child bigan to crye,
Til in his fadres barm adoun it lay,   *3630
And seyde, "Farewel, fader, I moot dye!"
And kiste his fader, and dyde the same day.
And whan the woful fader deed it say,
For wo his armes two he gan to byte,
And seyde, "Allas, Fortune, and weylaway!   2445
Thy false wheel my wo al may I wyte."

His children wende that it for hunger was
That he his armes gnow, and nat for wo,
And seyde, "Fader, do nat so, allas!
But rather ete the flessh upon us two.   *3640
Oure flessh thou yaf us, take oure flessh us fro,
And ete ynogh"—right thus they to hym seyde,
And after that, withinne a day or two,
They leyde hem in his lappe adoun and deyde.

Hymself, despeired, eek for hunger starf;   2455
Thus ended is this myghty Erl of Pize.
From heigh estaat Fortune awey hym carf.
Of this tragedie it oghte ynough suffise;
Whoso wol here it in a lenger wise,

2388 **Armorike:** Armorica (ancient name of coastal Brittany and Normandy)
2389 **Genylon-Olyver:** i.e., a traitor like Ganelon, who betrayed Roland
2390 **brike:** plight
2391 **Petro:** Pierre de Lusignan; see n.   **Cipre:** Cyprus
2392 **Alisandre:** Alexandria
2399 **Melan:** Milan   **Barnabo Viscounte:** Bernabo Visconti; see n.
2401 **acounte:** recount
2403 **brother:** brother's   **allye:** kinsman
2404 **nevew:** nephew
2407 **Hugelyn of Pyze:** Ugolino of Pisa; see n.   **langour:** suffering
2416 **Roger:** Ruggieri degli Ubaldini

2421 **unnethe:** scarcely
2425 **gayler:** jailer
2433 **potage:** soup
2443 **deed:** dead   **say:** saw
2446 **wyte:** blame
2448 **gnow:** gnawed
2455 **starf:** died; see Expl. Notes to line 2407.
2457 **carf:** cut

Redeth the grete poete of Ytaille   *3650
That highte Dant, for he kan al devyse
Fro point to point; nat o word wol he faille.

Nero

    Although that Nero were as vicius
As any feend that lith ful lowe adoun,
Yet he, as telleth us Swetonius,   2465
This wyde world hadde in subjeccioun,
Bothe est and west, [south], and septemtrioun.
Of rubies, saphires, and of peerles white
Were alle his clothes brouded up and doun,
For he in gemmes greetly gan delite.   *3660

Moore delicaat, moore pompous of array,
Moore proud was nevere emperour than he;
That ilke clooth that he hadde wered o day,
After that tyme he nolde it nevere see.
Nettes of gold threed hadde he greet plentee   2475
To fisshe in Tybre, whan hym liste pleye.
His lustes were al lawe in his decree,
For Fortune as his freend hym wolde obeye.

He Rome brende for his delicasie;
The senatours he slow upon a day   *3670
To heere how that men wolde wepe and crie;
And slow his brother, and by his suster lay.
His mooder made he in pitous array,
For he hire wombe slitte to biholde
Where he conceyved was—so weilaway   2485
That he so litel of his mooder tolde!

No teere out of his eyen for that sighte
Ne cam, but seyde, "A fair womman was she!"
Greet wonder is how that he koude or myghte
Be domesman of hire dede beautee.   *3680
The wyn to bryngen hym comanded he,
And drank anon—noon oother wo he made.
Whan myght is joyned unto crueltee,
Allas, to depe wol the venym wade!

In yowthe a maister hadde this emperour   2495
To teche hym letterure and curteisye,
For of moralitee he was the flour,

As in his tyme, but if bookes lye;
And whil this maister hadde of hym maistrye,
He maked hym so konnyng and so sowple   *3690
That longe tyme it was er tirannye
Or any vice dorste on hym uncowple.

This Seneca, of which that I devyse,
By cause Nero hadde of hym swich drede,
For he fro vices wolde hym ay chastise   2505
Discreetly, as by word and nat by dede—
"Sire," wolde he seyn, "an emperour moot nede
Be vertuous and hate tirannye—"
For which he in a bath made hym to blede
On bothe his armes, til he moste dye.   *3700

This Nero hadde eek of acustumaunce
In youthe agayns his maister for to ryse,
Which afterward hym thoughte a greet grevaunce;
Therefore he made hym dyen in this wise.
But natheless this Seneca the wise   2515
Chees in a bath to dye in this manere
Rather than han another tormentise;
And thus hath Nero slayn his maister deere.

Now fil it so that Fortune liste no lenger
The hye pryde of Nero to cherice,   *3710
For though that he were strong, yet was she strenger.
She thoughte thus: "By God! I am to nyce
To sette a man that is fulfild of vice
In heigh degree, and emperour hym calle.
By God, out of his sete I wol hym trice;   2525
Whan he leest weneth, sonnest shal he falle."

The peple roos upon hym on a nyght
For his defaute, and whan he it espied,
Out of his dores anon he hath hym dight
Allone, and ther he wende han been allied   *3720
He knokked faste, and ay the moore he cried
The fastere shette they the dores alle.
Tho wiste he wel, he hadde himself mysgyed,
And wente his wey; no lenger dorste he calle.

The peple cried and rombled up and doun,

2461 **Dant:** Dante Alighieri
2465 **Swetonius,** author of *The Lives of the Caesars*
2467 **septemtrioun:** north
2469 **brouded:** embroidered
2473 **ilke clooth:** same robe
2479 **delicasie:** pleasure
2486 **of . . . tolde:** esteemed
2490 **domesman:** judge
2494 **wade:** penetrate, go in
2495 **maister:** teacher (Seneca)
2496 **letterure:** literature

2500 **sowple:** compliant
2502 **on hym uncowple:** attack (unleash themselves on) him
2507 **nede:** necessarily
2511 **of acustumaunce:** the custom of
2517 **tormentise:** form of torment
2525 **sete:** throne   **trice:** snatch
2528 **defaute:** wickedness
2533 **mysgyed:** misguided, deluded

That with his erys herde he how they seyde,   2536
"Where is this false tiraunt, this Neroun?"
For fere almoost out of his wit he breyde,
And to his goddes pitously he preyde
For socour, but it myghte nat bityde.   *3730
For drede of this hym thoughte that he deyde,
And ran into a gardyn hym to hyde.

And in this gardyn foond he cherles tweye
That seten by a fyr, greet and reed.
And to thise cherles two he gan to preye   2545
To sleen hym and to girden of his heed,
That to his body, whan that he were deed,
Were no despit ydoon for his defame.
Hymself he slow, he koude no bettre reed,
Of which Fortune lough, and hadde a game.   *3740

De Oloferno

Was nevere capitayn under a kyng
That regnes mo putte in subjeccioun,
Ne strenger was in feeld of alle thyng,
As in his tyme, ne gretter of renoun,   2554
Ne moore pompous in heigh presumpcioun
Than Oloferne, which Fortune ay kiste
So likerously, and ladde hym up and doun
Til that his heed was of, er that he wiste.

Nat oonly that this world hadde hym in awe
For lesynge of richesse or libertee,   *3750
But he made every man reneyen his lawe.
"Nabugodonosor was god," seyde hee;
"Noon oother god sholde adoured bee."
Agayns his heeste no wight dorst trespace,
Save in Bethulia, a strong citee,   2565
Where Eliachim a preest was of that place.

But taak kep of the deth of Oloferne:
Amydde his hoost he dronke lay a-nyght,
Withinne his tente, large as is a berne,
And yet, for al his pompe and al his myght,   *3760
Judith, a womman, as he lay upright
Slepynge, his heed of smoot, and from his tente
Ful pryvely she stal from every wight,
And with his heed unto hir toun she wente.

De Rege Antiocho illustri

What nedeth it of kyng Anthiochus   2575
To telle his hye roial magestee,
His hye pride, his werkes venymus?
For swich another was ther noon as he.
Rede which that he was in Machabee,
And rede the proude wordes that he seyde,   *3770
And why he fil fro heigh prosperitee,
And in an hill how wrecchedly he deyde.

Fortune hym hadde enhaunced so in pride
That verraily he wende he myghte attayne
Unto the sterres upon every syde,   2585
And in balance weyen ech montayne,
And alle the floodes of the see restrayne.
And Goddes peple hadde he moost in hate;
Hem wolde he sleen in torment and in payne,
Wenynge that God ne myghte his pride abate.   *3780

And for that Nichanore and Thymothee
Of Jewes weren venquysshed myghtily,
Unto the Jewes swich an hate hadde he
That he bad greithen his chaar ful hastily,
And swoor, and seyde ful despitously   2595
Unto Jerusalem he wolde eftsoone
To wreken his ire on it ful cruelly;
But of his purpos he was let ful soone.

God for his manace hym so soore smoot
With invisible wounde, ay incurable,   *3790
That in his guttes carf it so and boot
That his peynes weren importable.
And certeinly the wreche was resonable,
For many a mannes guttes dide he peyne.
But from his purpos cursed and dampnable,   2605
For al his smert, he wolde hym nat restreyne,

But bad anon apparaillen his hoost;
And sodeynly, er he was of it war,
God daunted al his pride and al his boost.

2579 **Machabee:** Book of Maccabees (apocryphal in the Authorized Version)
2586 **weyen:** weigh
2590 **abate:** reduce
2591 **Nichanore and Thymothee:** Nicanor and Timotheus, generals defeated by Judas Maccabeus
2594 **greithen:** prepare
2598 **let:** prevented
2601 **boot:** bit
2602 **importable:** intolerable
2603 **wreche:** vengeance
2607 **apparaillen:** prepare
2609 **daunted:** conquered

2538 **breyde:** started, went
2546 **girden of:** cut off
2556 **Oloferne:** Holofernes
2557 **likerously:** wantonly
2560 **For lesynge:** for fear of losing
2561 **reneyen:** renounce
2566 **Eliachim:** Joachim in the Authorized Version

For he so soore fil out of his char   *3800
That it his limes and his skyn totar,
So that he neyther myghte go ne ryde,
But in a chayer men aboute hym bar,
Al forbrused, bothe bak and syde.

The wreche of God hym smoot so cruelly   2615
That thurgh his body wikked wormes crepte,
And therwithal he stank so horribly
That noon of al his meynee that hym kepte,
Wheither so he wook or ellis slepte,
Ne myghte noght the stynk of hym endure.   *3810
In this meschief he wayled and eek wepte,
And knew God lord of every creature.

To al his hoost and to hymself also
Ful wlatsom was the stynk of his careyne;
No man ne myghte hym bere to ne fro.   2625
And in this stynk and this horrible peyne,
He starf ful wrecchedly in a monteyne.
Thus hath this robbour and this homycide,
That many a man made to wepe and pleyne,
Swich gerdoun as bilongeth unto pryde.   *3820

De Alexandro

The storie of Alisaundre is so commune
That every wight that hath discrecioun
Hath herd somwhat or al of his fortune.
This wyde world, as in conclusioun,
He wan by strengthe, or for his hye renoun   2635
They weren glad for pees unto hym sende.
The pride of man and beest he leyde adoun,
Wherso he cam, unto the worldes ende.

Comparisoun myghte nevere yet been maked
Bitwixe hym and another conquerour;   *3830
For al this world for drede of hym hath quaked.
He was of knyghthod and of fredom flour;
Fortune hym made the heir of hire honour.
Save wyn and wommen, no thing myghte aswage
His hye entente in armes and labour,   2645
So was he ful of leonyn corage.

What pris were it to hym, though I yow tolde
Of Darius, and an hundred thousand mo
Of kynges, princes, dukes, erles bolde   *3839
Whiche he conquered, and broghte hem into wo?
I seye, as fer as man may ryde or go,
The world was his—what sholde I moore devyse?
For though I write or tolde yow everemo
Of his knyghthod, it myghte nat suffise.

Twelf yeer he regned, as seith Machabee.   2655
Philippes sone of Macidoyne he was,
That first was kyng in Grece the contree.
O worthy, gentil Alisandre, allas,
That evere sholde fallen swich a cas!
Empoysoned of thyn owene folk thou weere;   *3850
Thy sys Fortune hath turned into aas,
And for thee ne weep she never a teere.

Who shal me yeven teeris to compleyne
The deeth of gentillesse and of franchise,
That al the world weelded in his demeyne,   2665
And yet hym thoughte it myghte nat suffise?
So ful was his corage of heigh emprise.
Allas, who shal me helpe to endite
False Fortune, and poyson to despise,
The whiche two of al this wo I wyte?   *3860

De Julio Cesare

By wisedom, manhede, and by greet labour,
From humble bed to roial magestee
Up roos he Julius, the conquerour,
That wan al th'occident by land and see,
By strengthe of hand, or elles by tretee,   2675
And unto Rome made hem tributarie;
And sitthe of Rome the emperour was he
Til that Fortune weex his adversarie.

O myghty Cesar, that in Thessalie
Agayn Pompeus, fader thyn in lawe,   *3870
That of the orient hadde al the chivalrie
As fer as that the day bigynneth dawe,
Thou thurgh thy knyghthod hast hem take and slawe,

2611 **totar:** tore apart
2613 **chayer:** sedan chair
2614 **forbrused:** badly bruised
2615 **wreche:** vengeance
2622 **knew:** acknowledged
2624 **wlatsom:** loathsome   **careyne:** body
2631 **Alisaundre:** Alexander the Great   **commune:** widespread
2636 **for pees unto hym sende:** to send envoys to him to sue for peace
2641 **quaked:** trembled

2647 **pris:** praise
2648 **Darius:** king of the Medes
2653 **write:** should write
2656 **Macidoyne:** Macedonia
2661 Fortune has turned your six (the highest throw of a die) into an ace (the lowest)
2665 **demeyne:** control
2667 **emprise:** knightly courage
2673 **he Julius:** this Julius (Caesar)
2677 **sitthe:** afterwards
2680 **Pompeus:** Pompey the Great

Save fewe folk that with Pompeus fledde,
Thurgh which thou puttest al th'orient in awe.   2685
Thanke Fortune, that so wel thee spedde!

    But now a litel while I wol biwaille
This Pompeus, this noble governour
Of Rome, which that fleigh at this bataille.
I seye, oon of his men, a fals traitour,   *3880
His heed of smoot, to wynnen hym favour
Of Julius, and hym the heed he broghte.
Allas, Pompeye, of th'orient conquerour,
That Fortune unto swich a fyn thee broghte!

    To Rome agayn repaireth Julius   2695
With his triumphe, lauriat ful hye;
But on a tyme Brutus Cassius,
That evere hadde of his hye estaat envye,
Ful prively hath maad conspiracye
Agayns this Julius in subtil wise,   *3890
And caste the place in which he sholde dye
With boydekyns, as I shal yow devyse.

This Julius to the Capitolie wente
Upon a day, as he was wont to goon,
And in the Capitolie anon hym hente   2705
This false Brutus and his othere foon,
And stiked hym with boydekyns anoon
With many a wounde, and thus they lete hym lye;
But nevere gronte he at no strook but oon,
Or elles at two, but if his storie lye.   *3900

So manly was this Julius of herte,
And so wel lovede estaatly honestee,
That though his deedly woundes soore smerte,
His mantel over his hypes caste he,
For no man sholde seen his privetee;   2715
And as he lay of diyng in a traunce,
And wiste verraily that deed was hee,
Of honestee yet hadde he remembraunce.

    Lucan, to thee this storie I recomende,
And to Swetoun, and to Valerius also,   *3910

That of this storie writen word and ende,
How that to thise grete conqueroures two
Fortune was first freend, and sitthe foo.
No man ne truste upon hire favour longe,
But have hire in awayt for everemoo;   2725
Witnesse on alle thise conqueroures stronge.

Cresus

    This riche Cresus, whilom kyng of Lyde,
Of which Cresus Cirus soore hym dradde,
Yet was he caught amyddes al his pryde,
And to be brent men to the fyr hym ladde.   *3920
But swich a reyn doun fro the welkne shadde
That slow the fyr, and made hym to escape;
But to be war no grace yet he hadde,
Til Fortune on the galwes made hym gape.

Whanne he escaped was, he kan nat stente   2735
For to bigynne a newe werre agayn.
He wende wel, for that Fortune hym sente
Swich hap that he escaped thurgh the rayn,
That of his foos he myghte nat be slayn;
And eek a sweven upon a nyght he mette,   *3930
Of which he was so proud and eek so fayn
That in vengeance he al his herte sette.

Upon a tree he was, as that hym thoughte,
Ther Juppiter hym wessh, bothe bak and syde,
And Phebus eek a fair towaille hym broghte   2745
To dryen hym with; and therfore wax his pryde,
And to his doghter, that stood hym bisyde,
Which that he knew in heigh sentence habounde,
He bad hire telle hym what it signyfyde,
And she his dreem bigan right thus expounde: *3940

"The tree," quod she, "the galwes is to meene,
And Juppiter bitokneth snow and reyn,
And Phebus, with his towaille so clene,
Tho been the sonne stremes for to seyn.

2689 **fleigh:** fled
2697 **Brutus Cassius:** Brutus and Cassius are here considered one person; see n.
2702 **boydekyns:** daggers
2703 **Capitolie:** capitol
2706 **foon:** enemies
2709 **gronte:** groaned
2712 **estaatly honestee:** dignified decorum
2716 **of diyng:** a-dying
2719 **Lucan:** author of the *Pharsalia,* which narrates the wars between Caesar and Pompey   **recomende:** commend, submit
2720 **Swetoun:** Suetonius   **Valerius:** Valerius Maximus, whose *Facta et dicta memorabilia* contains stories about the Caesars

2721 **word and ende:** beginning and end
2725 **in awayt:** under observation (i.e., keep an eye on her)
2727 **Cresus:** Croesus, last king of Lydia
2728 **Cirus:** Cyrus the Great
2731 **welkne:** sky
2734 **galwes:** gallows
2740 **sweven:** dream   **mette:** dreamed
2745 **towaille:** towel
2748 **in heigh sentence habounde:** to abound in good judgment, wisdom
2751 **is to meene:** is to be interpreted, signifies

Thou shalt anhanged be, fader, certeyn;   2755
Reyn shal thee wasshe, and sonne shal thee drye."
Thus warned hym ful plat and ek ful pleyn
His doghter, which that called was Phanye.

Anhanged was Cresus, the proude kyng;
His roial trone myghte hym nat availle   *3950

Tragediës noon oother maner thyng
Ne kan in syngyng crie ne biwaille
But that Fortune alwey wole assaille
With unwar strook the regnes that been proude;
For whan men trusteth hire, thanne wol she faille,
And covere hire brighte face with a clowde.   2766

Explicit Tragedia.

Heere stynteth the Knyght the Monk of his tale.

The Prologue of the Nun's Priest's Tale

⑤

The prologe of the Nonnes Preestes Tale.

"Hoo!" quod the Knyght, "good sire, namoore of
        this!
That ye han seyd is right ynough, ywis,
And muchel moore; for litel hevynesse
Is right ynough to muche folk, I gesse.   *3960
I seye for me, it is a greet disese,
Whereas men han been in greet welthe and ese,
To heeren of hire sodeyn fal, allas!
And the contrarie is joye and greet solas,
As whan a man hath been in povre estaat,   2775
And clymbeth up and wexeth fortunat,
And there abideth in prosperitee.
Swich thyng is gladsom, as it thynketh me,
And of swich thyng were goodly for to telle."   *3969
    "Ye," quod oure Hooste, "by Seint Poules belle!
Ye seye right sooth; this Monk he clappeth lowde.
He spak how Fortune covered with a clowde
I noot nevere what; and als of a tragedie
Right now ye herde, and pardee, no remedie
It is for to biwaille ne compleyne   2785
That that is doon, and als it is a peyne,
As ye han seyd, to heere of hevynesse.

"Sire Monk, namoore of this, so God yow blesse!
Youre tale anoyeth al this compaignye.
Swich talkyng is nat worth a boterflye,   *3980
For therinne is ther no desport ne game.
Wherfore, sire Monk, daun Piers by youre name,
I pray yow hertely telle us somwhat elles;
For sikerly, nere clynkyng of youre belles
That on youre bridel hange on every syde,   2795
By hevene kyng that for us alle dyde,
I sholde er this han fallen doun for sleep,
Althogh the slough had never been so deep;
Thanne hadde your tale al be toold in veyn.
For certeinly, as that thise clerkes seyn,   *3990
Whereas a man may have noon audience,
Noght helpeth it to tellen his sentence.
    "And wel I woot the substance is in me,
If any thyng shal wel reported be.
Sir, sey somwhat of huntyng, I yow preye."   2805
    "Nay," quod this Monk, "I have no lust to pleye.
Now lat another telle, as I have toold."

2778 **gladsom:** pleasing
2780 **Seint Poules belle:** the bell of St. Paul's Cathedral, London
2781 **clappeth lowde:** talks noisily
2783 **noot** = *ne woot,* do not know

2764 **unwar strook:** unexpected stroke

2794 **nere** = *ne were,* were it not for
2798 **slough:** mud, mire
2803 **the substance is in me:** I have the capacity of understanding, appreciating (it)

Thanne spak oure Hoost with rude speche and boold,
And seyde unto the Nonnes Preest anon,   *3999
"Com neer, thou preest, com hyder, thou sir John!
Telle us swich thyng as may oure hertes glade.
Be blithe, though thou ryde upon a jade.
What thogh thyn hors be bothe foul and lene?
If he wol serve thee, rekke nat a bene.

Explicit.

Looke that thyn herte be murie everemo."   2815
   "Yis, sir," quod he, "yis, Hoost, so moot I go,
But I be myrie, ywis I wol be blamed."
And right anon his tale he hath attamed,
And thus he seyde unto us everichon,
This sweete preest, this goodly man sir John.   *4010

The Nun's Priest's Tale

Heere bigynneth the Nonnes Preestes Tale of the Cok and Hen, Chauntecleer and Pertelote.

A povre wydwe, somdeel stape in age,
Was whilom dwellyng in a narwe cotage,
Biside a grove, stondynge in a dale.
This wydwe, of which I telle yow my tale,
Syn thilke day that she was last a wyf   2825
In pacience ladde a ful symple lyf,
For litel was hir catel and hir rente.
By housbondrie of swich as God hire sente
She foond hirself and eek hir doghtren two.
Thre large sowes hadde she, and namo,   *4020
Three keen, and eek a sheep that highte Malle.
Ful sooty was hire bour and eek hir halle,
In which she eet ful many a sklendre meel.
Of poynaunt sauce hir neded never a deel.
No deyntee morsel passed thurgh hir throte;   2835
Hir diete was accordant to hir cote.
Repleccioun ne made hire nevere sik;
Attempree diete was al hir phisik,
And exercise, and hertes suffisaunce.
The goute lette hire nothyng for to daunce,   *4030

N'apoplexie shente nat hir heed.
No wyn ne drank she, neither whit ne reed;
Hir bord was served moost with whit and blak—
Milk and broun breed, in which she foond no lak,
Seynd bacoun, and somtyme an ey or tweye,   2845
For she was, as it were, a maner deye.
   A yeerd she hadde, enclosed al aboute
With stikkes, and a drye dych withoute,
In which she hadde a cok, hight Chauntecleer.
In al the land, of crowyng nas his peer.   *4040
His voys was murier than the murie orgon
On messe-dayes that in the chirche gon.
Wel sikerer was his crowyng in his logge
Than is a clokke or an abbey orlogge.
By nature he knew ech ascencioun   2855
Of the equynoxial in thilke toun;
For whan degrees fiftene weren ascended,

2810 **sir John:** contemptuous name for a priest
2812 **jade:** nag

2821 **stape:** advanced
2829 **foond:** provided for
2831 **keen:** cows
2832 **bour:** bedchamber
2834 **poynaunt:** spicy, piercing
2836 **cote:** small shed for livestock
2837 **Repleccioun:** overeating
2838 **Attempree:** moderate
2840 **lette:** prevented

2816 **Yis:** yes indeed
2818 **attamed:** begun

2844 **lak:** lack or fault; see n.
2845 **Seynd:** broiled or smoked   **ey:** egg
2846 **deye:** dairywoman
2847 **yeerd:** enclosed garden
2848 **stikkes:** palings
2851 **orgon:** organ; see n.
2853 **logge:** dwelling
2854 **orlogge:** timepiece
.2855–56 **ascencioun Of the equynoxial:** the time (once each hour) when each of the twenty-four imaginary points on the celestial equator rises on the horizon

Thanne crew he that it myghte nat been amended.
His coomb was redder than the fyn coral,
And batailled as it were a castel wal;   *4050
His byle was blak, and as the jeet it shoon;
Lyk asure were his legges and his toon;
His nayles whitter than the lylye flour,
And lyk the burned gold was his colour.
This gentil cok hadde in his governaunce   2865
Sevene hennes for to doon al his plesaunce,
Whiche were his sustres and his paramours,
And wonder lyk to hym, as of colours;
Of whiche the faireste hewed on hir throte
Was cleped faire damoysele Pertelote.   *4060
Curteys she was, discreet, and debonaire,
And compaignable, and bar hyrself so faire
Syn thilke day that she was seven nyght oold
That trewely she hath the herte in hoold
Of Chauntecleer, loken in every lith;   2875
He loved hire so that wel was hym therwith.
But swich a joye was it to here hem synge,
Whan that the brighte sonne gan to sprynge,
In sweete accord, "My lief is faren in londe!"—
For thilke tyme, as I have understonde,   *4070
Beestes and briddes koude speke and synge.

    And so bifel that in a dawenynge,
As Chauntecleer among his wyves alle
Sat on his perche, that was in the halle,
And next hym sat this faire Pertelote,   2885
This Chauntecleer gan gronen in his throte,
As man that in his dreem is drecched soore.
And whan that Pertelote thus herde hym roore,
She was agast and seyde, "Herte deere,
What eyleth yow, to grone in this manere?   *4080
Ye been a verray sleper; fy, for shame!"

    And he answerde, and seyde thus: "Madame,
I pray yow that ye take it nat agrief.
By God, me mette I was in swich meschief
Right now that yet myn herte is soore afright.   2895

Now God," quod he, "my swevene recche aright,
And kepe my body out of foul prisoun!
Me mette how that I romed up and doun
Withinne our yeerd, wheer as I saugh a beest
Was lyk an hound, and wolde han maad areest   *4090
Upon my body, and wolde han had me deed.
His colour was bitwixe yelow and reed,
And tipped was his tayl and bothe his eeris
With blak, unlyk the remenant of his heeris;
His snowte smal, with glowynge eyen tweye.   2905
Yet of his look for feere almoost I deye;
This caused me my gronyng, doutelees."

    "Avoy!" quod she, "fy on yow, hertelees!
Allas," quod she, "for, by that God above,
Now han ye lost myn herte and al my love!   *4100
I kan nat love a coward, by my feith!
For certes, what so any womman seith,
We alle desiren, if it myghte bee,
To han housbondes hardy, wise, and free,
And secree—and no nygard, ne no fool,   2915
Ne hym that is agast of every tool,
Ne noon avauntour, by that God above!
How dorste ye seyn, for shame, unto youre love
That any thyng myghte make yow aferd?
Have ye no mannes herte, and han a berd?   *4110
Allas! And konne ye been agast of swevenys?
Nothyng, God woot, but vanitee in sweven is.
Swevenes engendren of replecciouns,
And ofte of fume and of complecciouns,
Whan humours been to habundant in a wight.   2925
Certes this dreem, which ye han met to-nyght,
Cometh of the greete superfluytee
Of youre rede colera, pardee,
Which causeth folk to dreden in hir dremes
Of arwes, and of fyr with rede lemes,   *4120
Of rede beestes, that they wol hem byte,
Of contek, and of whelpes, grete and lyte;

2860 **batailled:** notched with crenelations
2861 **byle:** beak **jeet:** jet, a gemlike coal
2862 **asure:** azure **toon:** toes
2867 **paramours:** concubines
2870 **damoysele:** young lady, maiden
2871 **debonaire:** gracious
2872 **compaignable:** sociable
2874 **hoold:** possession, keeping
2875 **loken in every lith:** locked in every limb (i.e., completely)
2879 **My lief is faren in londe:** "My love has departed to the country," a popular song; see n.
2887 **drecched:** troubled
2888 **roore:** roar
2893 **agrief:** amiss

2896 **swevene:** dream **recche aright:** interpret correctly or favorably (in an auspicious manner)
2900–01 **maad areest Upon:** seized
2908 **Avoy!:** shame! **hertelees:** coward
2915 **secree:** discreet **nygard:** miser
2916 **tool:** weapon
2917 **avauntour:** boaster
2919 **aferd:** afraid
2920 **berd:** beard; see n.
2923 **replecciouns:** overeating
2924 **fume:** vapor rising from the stomach **complecciouns:** balance of the bodily fluids (*humours*), blood, phlegm, red or yellow bile, and black bile, which produce the sanguinary, phlegmatic, choleric, and melancholy complexions, respectively
2928 **rede colera:** red choleric humor
2930 **lemes:** flames
2932 **contek:** strife **whelpes:** dogs

Right as the humour of malencolie
Causeth ful many a man in sleep to crie
For feere of blake beres, or boles blake,   2935
Or elles blake develes wole hem take.
Of othere humours koude I telle also
That werken many a man sleep ful wo;
But I wol passe as lightly as I kan.   *4129
    "Lo Catoun, which that was so wys a man,
Seyde he nat thus, 'Ne do no fors of dremes'?
    "Now sire," quod she, "whan we flee fro the
        bemes,
For Goddes love, as taak som laxatyf.
Up peril of my soule and of my lyf,
I conseille yow the beste—I wol nat lye—   2945
That bothe of colere and of malencolye
Ye purge yow; and for ye shal nat tarie,
Though in this toun is noon apothecarie,
I shal myself to herbes techen yow
That shul been for youre hele and for youre prow;
And in oure yeerd tho herbes shal I fynde   *4141
The whiche han of hire propretee by kynde
To purge yow bynethe and eek above.
Foryet nat this, for Goddes owene love!
Ye been ful coleryk of compleccioun;   2955
Ware the sonne in his ascencioun
Ne fynde yow nat repleet of humours hoote.
And if it do, I dar wel leye a grote,
That ye shul have a fevere terciane,
Or an agu that may be youre bane.   *4150
A day or two ye shul have digestyves
Of wormes, er ye take youre laxatyves
Of lawriol, centaure, and fumetere,
Or elles of ellebor, that groweth there,
Of katapuce, or of gaitrys beryis,   2965
Of herbe yve, growyng in oure yeerd, ther mery is;

Pekke hem up right as they growe and ete hem yn.
Be myrie, housbonde, for youre fader kyn!
Dredeth no dreem; I kan sey yow namoore."
    "Madame," quod he, "graunt mercy of youre loore.
But nathelees, as touchyng daun Catoun,   *4161
That hath of wysdom swich a greet renoun,
Though that he bad no dremes for to drede,
By God, men may in olde bookes rede
Of many a man moore of auctorite   2975
Than evere Caton was, so moot I thee,
That al the revers seyn of this sentence,
And han wel founden by experience
That dremes been significaciouns
As wel of joye as of tribulaciouns   *4170
That folk enduren in this lif present.
Ther nedeth make of this noon argument;
The verray preeve sheweth it in dede.
    "Oon of the gretteste auctour that men rede
Seith thus: that whilom two felawes wente   2985
On pilgrimage, in a ful good entente,
And happed so, they coomen in a toun
Wher as ther was swich congregacioun
Of peple, and eek so streit of herbergage,
That they ne founde as muche as o cotage   *4180
In which they bothe myghte ylogged bee.
Wherfore they mosten of necessitee,
As for that nyght, departen compaignye;
And ech of hem gooth to his hostelrye,
And took his loggyng as it wolde falle.   2995
That oon of hem was logged in a stalle,
Fer in a yeerd, with oxen of the plough;
That oother man was logged wel ynough,
As was his aventure or his fortune,
That us governeth alle as in commune.   *4190
    "And so bifel that, longe er it were day,
This man mette in his bed, ther as he lay,
How that his felawe gan upon hym calle,
And seyde, 'Allas, for in an oxes stalle
This nyght I shal be mordred ther I lye!   3005
Now help me, deere brother, or I dye.
In alle haste com to me!' he sayde.
This man out of his sleep for feere abrayde;
But whan that he was wakened of his sleep,

2933 **humour of malencolie:** melancholy humor
2941 **Ne do no fors of dremes:** Attach no importance to dreams.
2950 **hele:** good health   **prow:** profit, benefit
2955 **coleryk:** dominated by the choleric humor
2956 **in his ascencioun:** when it is high in the sky
2957 **repleet of:** filled with
2958 **leye a grote:** bet a groat (a silver coin worth four pence)
2959 **fevere terciane:** a fever that recurs every third day; see Expl. Notes to lines 2942–67.
2960 **agu:** acute fever   **bane:** killer
2961 **digestyves:** medicines to aid the digestion
2963 **lawriol:** spurge laurel; the herbs named in these lines are nearly all hot, dry, and foul tasting; see n.   **centaure:** centaury.   **fumetere:** fumaria, fumitory
2964 **ellebor:** hellebore
2965 **katapuce:** caper-spurge, euphorbia   **gaitrys beryis:** rhamus
2966 **herbe yve:** ground ivy   **ther mery is:** where it is pleasant (i.e., in the garden)

2976 **so moot I thee:** as I may prosper (I swear)
2983 **preeve:** proof
2984 **Oon of the gretteste auctour:** one of the greatest authors; see n.
2989 **streit of:** scanty, short of   **herbergage:** lodging
2991 **ylogged:** lodged
3008 **abrayde:** awakened suddenly

He turned hym and took of this no keep.   *4200
Hym thoughte his dreem nas but a vanitee.
Thus twies in his slepyng dremed hee;
And atte thridde tyme yet his felawe
Cam, as hym thoughte, and seide, 'I am now slawe.
Bihoold my bloody woundes depe and wyde!   3015
Arys up erly in the morwe tyde,
And at the west gate of the toun,' quod he,
'A carte ful of dong ther shaltow se,
In which my body is hid ful prively;
Do thilke carte arresten boldely.   *4210
My gold caused my mordre, sooth to sayn,'
And tolde hym every point how he was slayn,
With a ful pitous face, pale of hewe.
And truste wel, his dreem he foond ful trewe,
For on the morwe, as soone as it was day,   3025
To his felawes in he took the way;
And whan that he cam to this oxes stalle,
After his felawe he bigan to calle.
    "The hostiler answerede hym anon,
And seyde, 'Sire, your felawe is agon.   *4220
As soone as day he wente out of the toun.'
    "This man gan fallen in suspecioun,
Remembrynge on his dremes that he mette,
And forth he gooth—no lenger wolde he lette—
Unto the west gate of the toun, and fond   3035
A dong-carte, wente as it were to donge lond,
That was arrayed in that same wise
As ye han herd the dede man devyse.
And with an hardy herte he gan to crye
Vengeance and justice of this felonye: *4230
'My felawe mordred is this same nyght,
And in this carte he lith gapyng upright.
I crye out on the ministres,' quod he,
'That sholden kepe and reulen this citee.
Harrow! Allas! Heere lith my felawe slayn!'   3045
What sholde I moore unto this tale sayn?
The peple out sterte and caste the cart to grounde,
And in the myddel of the dong they founde
The dede man, that mordred was al newe.
    "O blisful God, that art so just and trewe,   *4240
Lo, how that thou biwreyest mordre alway!

Mordre wol out; that se we day by day.
Mordre is so wlatsom and abhomynable
To God, that is so just and resonable,
That he ne wol nat suffre it heled be,   3055
Though it abyde a yeer, or two, or thre.
Mordre wol out, this my conclusioun.
And right anon, ministres of that toun
Han hent the carter and so soore hym pyned,
And eek the hostiler so soore engyned,   *4250
That they biknewe hire wikkednesse anon,
And were anhanged by the nekke-bon.
    "Heere may men seen that dremes been to drede.
And certes in the same book I rede,
Right in the nexte chapitre after this—   3065
I gabbe nat, so have I joye or blis—
Two men that wolde han passed over see,
For certeyn cause, into a fer contree,
If that the wynd ne hadde been contrarie,
That made hem in a citee for to tarie   *4260
That stood ful myrie upon an haven-syde;
But on a day, agayn the even-tyde,
The wynd gan chaunge, and blew right as hem leste.
Jolif and glad they wente unto hir reste,
And casten hem ful erly for to saille.   3075
But herkneth! To that o man fil a greet mervaille:
That oon of hem, in slepyng as he lay,
Hym mette a wonder dreem agayn the day.
Hym thoughte a man stood by his beddes syde,
And hym comanded that he sholde abyde,   *4270
And seyde hym thus: 'If thou tomorwe wende,
Thow shalt be dreynt; my tale is at an ende.'
He wook, and tolde his felawe what he mette,
And preyde hym his viage for to lette;
As for that day, he preyde hym to byde.   3085
His felawe, that lay by his beddes syde,
Gan for to laughe, and scorned him ful faste.
'No dreem,' quod he, 'may so myn herte agaste
That I wol lette for to do my thynges.
I sette nat a straw by thy dremynges,   *4280
For swevenes been but vanytees and japes.
Men dreme alday of owles and of apes,
And of many a maze therwithal;

3020 **Do . . . arresten:** have (it) seized
3029 **hostiler:** innkeeper
3034 **lette:** delay
3036 **donge:** spread dung, fertilize
3042 **upright:** face up
3043 **crye out on:** complain to   **ministres:** magistrates
3049 **al newe:** very recently, just now

3053 **wlatsom:** disgusting, nauseating
3055 **heled:** concealed
3057 **this** = *this is*
3059 **pyned:** tortured
3060 **engyned:** tortured
3061 **biknewe:** acknowledged, confessed
3066 **gabbe:** lie
3072 **agayn:** shortly before
3078 **agayn the day:** shortly before dawn
3084 **viage:** journey   **lette:** give up
3093 **maze:** source of amazement, bewilderment

Men dreme of thyng that nevere was ne shal.
But sith I see that thou wolt heere abyde,   3095
And thus forslewthen wilfully thy tyde,
God woot, it reweth me; and have good day!'
And thus he took his leve, and wente his way.
But er that he hadde half his cours yseyled,
Noot I nat why, ne what myschaunce it eyled,   *4290
But casuelly the shippes botme rente,
And ship and man under the water wente
In sighte of othere shippes it bisyde,
That with hem seyled at the same tyde.
And therfore, faire Pertelote so deere,   3105
By swiche ensamples olde maistow leere
That no man sholde been to recchelees
Of dremes; for I seye thee, doutelees,
That many a dreem ful soore is for to drede.
    "Lo, in the lyf of Seint Kenelm I rede,   *4300
That was Kenulphus sone, the noble kyng
Of Mercenrike, how Kenelm mette a thyng.
A lite er he was mordred, on a day,
His mordre in his avysioun he say.
His norice hym expowned every deel   3115
His sweven, and bad hym for to kepe hym weel
For traisoun; but he nas but seven yeer oold,
And therfore litel tale hath he toold
Of any dreem, so hooly was his herte.
By God! I hadde levere than my sherte   *4310
That ye hadde rad his legende, as have I.
    "Dame Pertelote, I sey yow trewely,
Macrobeus, that writ the avisioun
In Affrike of the worthy Cipioun,
Affermeth dremes, and seith that they been   3125
Warnynge of thynges that men after seen.
And forthermoore, I pray yow, looketh wel
In the olde testament, of Daniel,
If he heeld dremes any vanitee.
Reed eek of Joseph, and ther shul ye see   *4320
Wher dremes be somtyme—I sey nat alle—
Warnynge of thynges that shul after falle.
Looke of Egipte the kyng, daun Pharao,

His bakere and his butiller also,
Wher they ne felte noon effect in dremes.   3135
Whoso wol seken actes of sondry remes
May rede of dremes many a wonder thyng.
Lo Cresus, which that was of Lyde kyng,
Mette he nat that he sat upon a tree,
Which signified he sholde anhanged bee?   *4330
Lo heere Andromacha, Ectores wyf,
That day that Ector sholde lese his lyf,
She dremed on the same nyght biforn
How that the lyf of Ector sholde be lorn,
If thilke day he wente into bataille.   3145
She warned hym, but it myghte nat availle;
He wente for to fighte natheles,
But he was slayn anon of Achilles.
But thilke tale is al to longe to telle,
And eek it is ny day; I may nat dwelle.   *4340
Shortly I seye, as for conclusioun,
That I shal han of this avisioun
Adversitee; and I seye forthermoor
That I ne telle of laxatyves no stoor,
For they been venymes, I woot it weel;   3155
I hem diffye, I love hem never a deel!
    "Now let us speke of myrthe, and stynte al this.
Madame Pertelote, so have I blis,
Of o thyng God hath sent me large grace;
For whan I se the beautee of youre face,   *4350
Ye been so scarlet reed aboute youre yen,
It maketh al my drede for to dyen;
For al so siker as *In principio*,
Mulier est hominis confusio—
Madame, the sentence of this Latyn is,   3165
"Womman is mannes joye and al his blis.'
For whan I feele a-nyght your softe syde—
Al be it that I may nat on yow ryde,
For that oure perche is maad so narwe, allas—
I am so ful of joye and of solas,   *4360
That I diffye bothe sweven and dreem."
    And with that word he fley doun fro the beem,
For it was day, and eke his hennes alle,
And with a chuk he gan hem for to calle,

3096 **forslewthen:** slothfully waste
3101 **casuelly:** by chance
3110 **Seint Kenelm:** See n.
3111 **Kenulphus:** Cenwulf's
3112 **Mercenrike:** Mercia
3114 **avysioun:** a prophetic dream, sent as a warning (MED)
3117 **For:** to prevent, against
3118–19 **litel tale hath he toold Of:** he had little regard for
3123 **Macrobeus:** Macrobius (fl. c. 400 A.D.), author of a commentary on the *Dream of Scipio*
3124 **Cipioun:** Scipio; for his dream see PF 29–84.
3128 **Daniel:** The book of Daniel describes Daniel's prophetic visions.
3130 **Joseph:** famous as the interpreter of Pharoah's dreams
3133 **Pharao:** Pharaoh

3134 **butiller:** steward
3135 **effect:** significance
3136 **seken:** examine   **actes:** histories   **remes:** realms
3138 **Cresus:** Croesus; for his dream see MkT VII.2727–60.
3141 **Ectores:** Hector's
3150 **dwelle:** delay
3154 **telle of . . . no stoor:** regard as worthless
3156 **diffye:** renounce
3163 **In principio:** In the beginning (the opening words of Genesis 1 and John 1); see n.
3164 **Mulier est hominis confusio:** woman is man's ruin
3172 **fley:** flew   **beem:** beam, roost
3174 **chuk:** cluck

For he hadde founde a corn, lay in the yerd.
Real he was, he was namoore aferd.   3176
He fethered Pertelote twenty tyme,
And trad hire eke as ofte, er it was pryme.
He looketh as it were a grym leoun,
And on his toos he rometh up and doun;   *4370
Hym deigned nat to sette his foot to grounde.
He chukketh whan he hath a corn yfounde,
And to hym rennen thanne his wyves alle.
Thus roial, as a prince is in his halle,
Leve I this Chauntecleer in his pasture,   3185
And after wol I telle his aventure.

   Whan that the month in which the world bigan,
That highte March, whan God first maked man,
Was compleet, and passed were also,
Syn March [was gon], thritty dayes and two,   *4380
Bifel that Chauntecleer in al his pryde,
His sevene wyves walkynge by his syde,
Caste up his eyen to the brighte sonne,
That in the signe of Taurus hadde yronne
Twenty degrees and oon, and somwhat moore,   3195
And knew by kynde, and by noon oother loore,
That it was pryme, and crew with blisful stevene.
"The sonne," he seyde, "is clomben up on hevene
Fourty degrees and oon, and moore ywis.
Madame Pertelote, my worldes blis,   *4390
Herkneth thise blisful briddes how they synge,
And se the fresshe floures how they sprynge;
Ful is myn herte of revel and solas!"
But sodeynly hym fil a sorweful cas,
For evere the latter ende of joye is wo.   3205
God woot that worldly joye is soone ago;
And if a rethor koude faire endite,
He in a cronycle saufly myghte it write
As for a sovereyn notabilitee.
Now every wys man, lat him herkne me;   *4400
This storie is also trewe, I undertake,
As is the book of Launcelot de Lake,

That wommen holde in ful greet reverence.
Now wol I torne agayn to my sentence.
   A col-fox, ful of sly iniquitee,   *4415
That in the grove hadde woned yeres three,
By heigh ymaginacioun forncast,
The same nyght thurghout the hegges brast
Into the yerd ther Chauntecleer the faire
Was wont, and eek his wyves, to repaire;   *4410
And in a bed of wortes stille he lay
Til it was passed undren of the day,
Waitynge his tyme on Chauntecleer to falle,
As gladly doon thise homycides alle
That in await liggen to mordre men.   3225
O false mordrour, lurkynge in thy den!
O newe Scariot, newe Genylon,
False dissymulour, o Greek Synon,
That broghtest Troye al outrely to sorwe!
O Chauntecleer, acursed be that morwe   *4420
That thou into that yerd flaugh fro the bemes!
Thou were ful wel ywarned by thy dremes
That thilke day was perilous to thee;
But what that God forwoot moot nedes bee,
After the opinioun of certein clerkis.   3235
Witnesse on hym that any parfit clerk is,
That in scole is greet altercacioun
In this mateere, and greet disputisoun,
And hath been of an hundred thousand men.
But I ne kan nat bulte it to the bren   *4430
As kan the hooly doctour Augustyn,
Or Boece, or the Bisshop Bradwardyn,
Wheither that Goddes worthy forwityng
Streyneth me nedely for to doon a thyng—
"Nedely" clepe I symple necessitee—   3245
Or elles, if free choys be graunted me
To do that same thyng, or do it noght,
Though God forwoot it er that I was wroght;

3175 **corn:** grain
3176 **Real:** royal
3177 **fethered:** clasped with his wings
3178 **trad:** copulated with
3179 **leoun:** lion
3182 **chukketh:** clucks
3185 **pasture:** feeding place
3189 **compleet:** completed; the action takes place on May 3; see n.
3194 **Taurus:** the Bull, second sign of the zodiac
3196 **kynde:** instinct
3197 **stevene:** voice
3206 **ago:** gone
3207 **rethor:** rhetorician, master of eloquence
3209 **sovereyn notabilitee:** notable fact
3212 **book of Launcelot de Lake:** the romance of Lancelot and Guinevere

3215 **col-fox:** fox with black-tipped feet, ears, and tail
3216 **woned:** dwelt
3217 Foreseen by the exalted imagination or planned ahead with skillful forethought (?);
see n.
3218 **hegges:** hedges (serving as a fence)   **brast:** broke
3221 **wortes:** cabbages
3222 **undren:** the third hour, about 9 A.M.
3224 **gladly:** habitually
3227 **Scariot:** Judas Iscariot, who betrayed Christ   **Genylon:** Ganelon, who betrayed
Roland
3228 **dissymulour:** deceiver   **Synon:** The story is briefly told in HF 152–56.
3231 **flaugh:** flew
3234 **forwoot:** foreknows
3240 **bulte it to the bren:** bolt (sift) it to the husks (separate completely the valid
from the invalid arguments)
3241–42 **doctour:** teacher (doctor of the church)   **Augustyn, Boece, Bradwardyn:**
St. Augustine, Boethius, Thomas Bradwardyne; see n.
3243 **forwityng:** foreknowledge
3244 **Streyneth:** constrains   **nedely:** of necessity
3245 **symple necessitee:** plain or ordinary necessity; see n.
3248 **forwoot:** foreknew

Or if his wityng streyneth never a deel
But by necessitee condicioneel.   *4440
I wol nat han to do of swich mateere;
My tale is of a cok, as ye may heere,
That tok his conseil of his wyf, with sorwe,
To walken in the yerd upon that morwe
That he hadde met that dreem that I yow tolde.   3255
Wommennes conseils been ful ofte colde;
Wommannes conseil broghte us first to wo
And made Adam fro Paradys to go,
Ther as he was ful myrie and wel at ese.
But for I noot to whom it myght displese,   *4450
If I conseil of wommen wolde blame,
Passe over, for I seyde it in my game.
Rede auctours, where they trete of swich mateere,
And what they seyn of wommen ye may heere.
Thise been the cokkes wordes, and nat myne;   3265
I kan noon harm of no womman divyne.

   Faire in the soond, to bathe hire myrily,
Lith Pertelote, and alle hire sustres by,
Agayn the sonne, and Chauntecleer so free
Soong murier than the mermayde in the see   *4460
(For Phisiologus seith sikerly
How that they syngen wel and myrily).
And so bifel that, as he caste his ye
Among the wortes on a boterflye,
He was war of this fox, that lay ful lowe.   3275
Nothyng ne liste hym thanne for to crowe,
But cride anon, "Cok! cok!" and up he sterte
As man that was affrayed in his herte.
For natureelly a beest desireth flee
Fro his contrarie, if he may it see,   *4470
Though he never erst hadde seyn it with his ye.

   This Chauntecleer, whan he gan hym espye,
He wolde han fled, but that the fox anon
Seyde, "Gentil sire, allas, wher wol ye gon?
Be ye affrayed of me that am youre freend?   3285
Now, certes, I were worse than a feend,
If I to yow wolde harm or vileynye!
I am nat come youre conseil for t'espye,
But trewely, the cause of my comynge

Was oonly for to herkne how that ye synge.   *4480
For trewely, ye have as myrie a stevene
As any aungel hath that is in hevene.
Therwith ye han in musyk moore feelynge
Than hadde Boece, or any that kan synge.
My lord youre fader—God his soule blesse!—   3295
And eek youre mooder, of hire gentillesse,
Han in myn hous ybeen to my greet ese;
And certes, sire, ful fayn wolde I yow plese.
But, for men speke of syngyng, I wol seye—
So moote I brouke wel myne eyen tweye—   *4490
Save yow, I herde nevere man so synge
As dide youre fader in the morwenynge.
Certes, it was of herte, al that he song.
And for to make his voys the moore strong,   3304
He wolde so peyne hym that with bothe his yen
He moste wynke, so loude he wolde cryen,
And stonden on his tiptoon therwithal,
And strecche forth his nekke long and smal.
And eek he was of swich discrecioun
That ther nas no man in no regioun   *4500
That hym in song or wisedom myghte passe.
I have wel rad in 'Daun Burnel the Asse,'
Among his vers, how that ther was a cok,
For that a preestes sone yaf hym a knok
Upon his leg whil he was yong and nyce,   3315
He made hym for to lese his benefice.
But certeyn, ther nys no comparisoun
Bitwixe the wisedom and discrecioun
Of youre fader and of his subtiltee.
Now syngeth, sire, for seinte charitee;   *4510
Lat se; konne ye youre fader countrefete?"

   This Chauntecleer his wynges gan to bete,
As man that koude his traysoun nat espie,
So was he ravysshed with his flaterie.

   Allas, ye lordes, many a fals flatour   3325
Is in youre courtes, and many a losengeour,
That plesen yow wel moore, by my feith,
Than he that soothfastnesse unto yow seith.
Redeth Ecclesiaste of flaterye;
Beth war, ye lordes, of hir trecherye.   *4520

   This Chauntecleer stood hye upon his toos,
Strecchynge his nekke, and heeld his eyen cloos,

3250 **necessitee condicioneel:** inferential necessity; see n. to lines 3245–50.
3253 **with sorwe:** to his sorrow
3256 **colde:** fatal
3260 **noot** = *ne woot,* know not
3262 **Passe over:** let it be
3266 **kan noon:** am not able or do not know; see n.
3267 **soond:** sand
3269 **Agayn:** facing toward
3271 **Phisiologus:** the bestiary; see n.
3274 **wortes:** cabbages
3278 **affrayed:** frightened

3291 **stevene:** voice
3294 **Boece:** Boethius wrote a textbook on music.
3300 **brouke:** use
3303 **of:** from the
3306 **wynke:** close both eyes
3312 **Daun Burnel the Asse:** *Brunellus,* or the *Speculum Stultorum* (a satiric work of the late twelfth century by Nigel Wireker)
3320 **for seinte charitee:** by holy charity, for the love of God
3326 **losengeour:** flatterer
3329 **Ecclesiaste:** the book of Ecclesiasticus, Ecclesiastes, or possibly even Proverbs; see n.

And gan to crowe loude for the nones.
And daun Russell the fox stirte up atones,
And by the gargat hente Chauntecleer,   3335
And on his bak toward the wode hym beer,
For yet ne was ther no man that hym sewed.

O destinee, that mayst nat been eschewed!
Allas, that Chauntecleer fleigh fro the bemes!
Allas, his wyf ne roghte nat of dremes!   *4530
And on a Friday fil al this meschaunce.

O Venus, that art goddesse of plesaunce,
Syn that thy servant was this Chauntecleer,
And in thy servyce dide al his poweer,
Moore for delit than world to multiplye,   3345
Why woldestow suffre hym on thy day to dye?

O Gaufred, deere maister soverayn,
That whan thy worthy kyng Richard was slayn
With shot, compleynedest his deeth so soore,
Why ne hadde I now thy sentence and thy loore,
The Friday for to chide, as diden ye?   *4541
For on a Friday, soothly, slayn was he.
Thanne wolde I shewe yow how that I koude pleyne
For Chauntecleres drede and for his peyne.

Certes, swich cry ne lamentacion   3355
Was nevere of ladyes maad whan Ylion
Was wonne, and Pirrus with his streite swerd,
Whan he hadde hent kyng Priam by the berd,
And slayn hym, as seith us *Eneydos*,
As maden alle the hennes in the clos,   *4550
Whan they had seyn of Chauntecleer the sighte.
But sovereynly dame Pertelote shrighte
Ful louder than dide Hasdrubales wyf,
Whan that hir housbonde hadde lost his lyf
And that the Romayns hadde brend Cartage.   3365
She was so ful of torment and of rage
That wilfully into the fyr she sterte
And brende hirselven with a stedefast herte.

O woful hennes, right so criden ye
As whan that Nero brende the citee   *4560
Of Rome cryden senatoures wyves
For that hir husbondes losten alle hir lyves—

Withouten gilt this Nero hath hem slayn.
Now wole I turne to my tale agayn.

This sely wydwe and eek hir doghtres two   3375
Herden thise hennes crie and maken wo,
And out at dores stirten they anon,
And syen the fox toward the grove gon,
And bar upon his bak the cok away,
And cryden, "Out! Harrow and weylaway!   *4570
Ha, ha! The fox!" and after hym they ran,
And eek with staves many another man.
Ran Colle oure dogge, and Talbot and Gerland,
And Malkyn, with a dystaf in hir hand;
Ran cow and calf, and eek the verray hogges,   3385
So fered for the berkyng of the dogges
And shoutyng of the men and wommen eeke
They ronne so hem thoughte hir herte breeke.
They yolleden as feendes doon in helle;
The dokes cryden as men wolde hem quelle;   *4580
The gees for feere flowen over the trees;
Out of the hyve cam the swarm of bees.
So hydous was the noyse— a, benedicitee!—
Certes, he Jakke Straw and his meynee
Ne made nevere shoutes half so shrille   3395
Whan that they wolden any Flemyng kille,
As thilke day was maad upon the fox.
Of bras they broghten bemes, and of box,
Of horn, of boon, in whiche they blewe and powped,
And therwithal they skriked and they howped.
It semed as that hevene sholde falle.   *4591

Now, goode men, I prey yow herkneth alle:
Lo, how Fortune turneth sodeynly
The hope and pryde eek of hir enemy!
This cok, that lay upon the foxes bak,   3405
In al his drede unto the fox he spak,
And seyde, "Sire, if that I were as ye,
Yet sholde I seyn, as wys God helpe me,
'Turneth agayn, ye proude cherles alle!
A verray pestilence upon yow falle!   *4600
Now I am come unto the wodes syde;
Maugree youre heed, the cok shal heere abyde.
I wol hym ete, in feith, and that anon!' "

3335 **gargat:** throat
3337 **sewed:** pursued
3347 **Gaufred:** Geoffrey of Vinsauf, author of a standard textbook on rhetoric containing a lament on the death of King Richard I (*kyng Richard*)
3349 **With shot:** by the shot of an arrow
3356 **Ylion:** Ilium, the citadel at Troy
3357 **Pirrus:** Pyrrhus; see n.   **streite swerd:** drawn sword
3359 **Eneydos:** the *Aeneid*
3360 **clos:** enclosure, yard
3362 **sovereynly:** supremely
3363 **Hasdrubales wyf:** Her story is briefly told in FranT V.1399–1404.
3370 **Nero:** For his story see MkT VII.2463–2550.

3386 **fered for:** frightened by   **berkyng:** barking
3388 **breeke:** would break
3389 **yolleden:** yelled
3390 **quelle:** kill
3394 **Jakke Straw:** a supposed leader in the Peasants' Revolt of 1381
3398 **bemes:** trumpets   **box:** boxwood
3399 **powped:** puffed
3400 **skriked:** shrieked   **howped:** whooped
3412 **Maugree youre heed:** in spite of all you can do

The fox answerde, "In feith, it shal be don."
And as he spak that word, al sodeynly   3415
This cok brak from his mouth delyverly,
And heighe upon a tree he fleigh anon.
And whan the fox saugh that the cok was gon,
"Allas!" quod he, "O Chauntecleer, allas!
I have to yow," quod he, "ydoon trespas,   *4610
In as muche as I maked yow aferd
Whan I yow hente and broghte out of the yerd.
But, sire, I dide it in no wikke entente.
Com doun, and I shal telle yow what I mente;
I shal seye sooth to yow, God help me so!"   3425
   "Nay thanne," quod he, "I shrewe us bothe two.
And first I shrewe myself, bothe blood and bones,
If thou bigyle me ofter than ones.
Thou shalt namoore thurgh thy flaterye
Do me to synge and wynke with myn ye;   *4620

For he that wynketh, whan he sholde see,
Al wilfully, God lat him nevere thee!"
   "Nay," quod the fox, "but God yeve hym
                                      meschaunce,
That is so undiscreet of governaunce
That jangleth whan he sholde holde his pees."   3435
   Lo, swich it is for to be recchelees
And necligent, and truste on flaterye.
   But ye that holden this tale a folye,
As of a fox, or of a cok and hen,
Taketh the moralite, goode men.   *4630
For Seint Paul seith that al that writen is,
To oure doctrine it is ywrite, ywis;
Taketh the fruyt, and lat the chaf be stille.
Now, goode God, if that it be thy wille,
As seith my lord, so make us alle goode men,   3445
And brynge us to his heighe blisse! Amen.

Heere is ended the Noones Preestes Tale.

[Epilogue to the Nun's Priest's Tale

"Sire Nonnes Preest," oure Hooste seide anoon,
"I-blessed be thy breche, and every stoon!
This was a murie tale of Chauntecleer.
But by my trouthe, if thou were seculer,   *4640
Thou woldest ben a trede-foul aright.
For if thou have corage as thou hast myght,
Thee were nede of hennes, as I wene,
Ya, moo than seven tymes seventene.

See, whiche braunes hath this gentil preest,   3455
So gret a nekke, and swich a large breest!
He loketh as a sperhauk with his yen;
Him nedeth nat his colour for to dyen
With brasile ne with greyn of Portyngale.
Now, sire, faire falle yow for youre tale!"   *4650
   And after that he, with ful merie chere,
Seide unto another, as ye shuln heere.]

3416 **delyverly:** nimbly
3426 **shrewe:** beshrew, curse

3448 **breche:** buttocks   **stoon:** testicle
3451 **trede-foul:** treader (copulator) of fowls, rooster   **aright:** excellent

3432 **thee:** prosper
3435 **jangleth:** chatters
3443 **chaf:** husk, chaff

3457 **sperhauk:** sparrow hawk
3459 **brasile:** a red dye   **greyn of Portyngale:** a red dyestuff imported from Portugal

The Second Nun's Prologue

🌀

The Prologe of the Seconde Nonnes Tale.

The ministre and the norice unto vices,
Which that men clepe in Englissh Ydelnesse,
That porter of the gate is of delices,
To eschue, and by hire contrarie hire oppresse—
That is to seyn, by leveful bisynesse—   5
Wel oghten we to doon al oure entente,
Lest that the feend thurgh ydelnesse us hente.

For he that with his thousand cordes slye
Continuelly us waiteth to biclappe,
Whan he may man in ydelnesse espye,   10
He kan so lightly cache hym in his trappe,
Til that a man be hent right by the lappe,
He nys nat war the feend hath hym in honde.
Wel oghte us werche and ydelnesse withstonde.

And though men dradden nevere for to dye,   15
Yet seen men wel by resoun, doutelees,
That ydelnesse is roten slogardye,
Of which ther nevere comth no good n'encrees;
And syn that slouthe hire holdeth in a lees
Oonly to slepe, and for to ete and drynke,   20
And to devouren al that othere swynke,

And for to putte us fro swich ydelnesse,
That cause is of so greet confusioun,
I have heer doon my feithful bisynesse
After the legende in translacioun   25
Right of thy glorious lif and passioun,
Thou with thy gerland wroght with rose and lilie—
Thee meene I, mayde and martyr, Seint Cecilie.

Invocacio ad Mariam

And thow that flour of virgines art alle,
Of whom that Bernard list so wel to write,   30
To thee at my bigynnyng first I calle;
Thou confort of us wrecches, do me endite
Thy maydens deeth, that wan thurgh hire merite
The eterneel lyf and of the feend victorie,
As man may after reden in hire storie.   35

Thow Mayde and Mooder, doghter of thy Sone,
Thow welle of mercy, synful soules cure,
In whom that God for bountee chees to wone,
Thow humble, and heigh over every creature,
Thow nobledest so ferforth oure nature,   40
That no desdeyn the Makere hadde of kynde
His Sone in blood and flessh to clothe and wynde

Withinne the cloistre blisful of thy sydis
Took mannes shap the eterneel love and pees,
That of the tryne compas lord and gyde is,   45
Whom erthe and see and hevene out of relees
Ay heryen; and thou, Virgine wemmelees,
Baar of thy body—and dweltest mayden pure—
The Creatour of every creature.

Assembled is in thee magnificence   50
With mercy, goodnesse, and with swich pitee
That thou, that art the sonne of excellence
Nat oonly helpest hem that preyen thee,
But often tyme of thy benygnytee
Ful frely, er that men thyn help biseche,   55
Thou goost biforn and art hir lyves leche.

---

3 **delices:** pleasures
9 **biclappe:** trap suddenly
12 **lappe:** hem (of a garment)
14 **werche:** work
15 **dradden nevere:** were never to dread
17 **slogardye:** sluggishness, laziness
19 **in a lees:** on a leash
21 **swynke:** earn by working
26 **passioun:** suffering (of a saint)

Invocacio ad Mariam: Invocation to Mary
35 **after:** hereafter
38 **wone:** dwell
40 **nobledest:** ennobled
41 **kynde:** nature (humankind)
45 **That:** he who   **tryne compas:** the threefold universe (earth, heaven, sea)
46 **out of relees:** unceasing
47 **heryen:** praise   **wemmelees:** without blemish
56 **leche:** physician

Now help, thow meeke and blisful faire mayde,
Me, flemed wrecche, in this desert of galle;
Thynk on the womman Cananee, that sayde
That whelpes eten somme of the crommes alle   60
That from hir lordes table been yfalle;
And though that I, unworthy sone of Eve,
Be synful, yet accepte my bileve.

And, for that feith is deed withouten werkis,
So for to werken yif me wit and space,   65
That I be quit fro thennes that most derk is!
O thou, that art so fair and ful of grace,
Be myn advocat in that heighe place
Theras withouten ende is songe "Osanne,"
Thow Cristes mooder, doghter deere of Anne!   70

And of thy light my soule in prison lighte,
That troubled is by the contagioun
Of my body, and also by the wighte
Of erthely lust and fals affeccioun;
O havene of refut, O salvacioun   75
Of hem that been in sorwe and in distresse,
Now help, for to my werk I wol me dresse.

Yet preye I yow that reden that I write,
Foryeve me that I do no diligence
This ilke storie subtilly to endite,   80
For bothe have I the wordes and sentence
Of hym that at the seintes reverence
The storie wroot, and folwen hire legende,
And pray yow that ye wole my werk amende.

Interpretacio nominis Cecilie quam ponit Frater
Jacobus Januensis in Legenda

First wolde I yow the name of Seint Cecilie   85
Expowne, as men may in hir storie see.
It is to seye in Englissh "hevenes lilie,"

For pure chaastnesse of virginitee;
Or, for she whitnesse hadde of honestee,
And grene of conscience, and of good fame   90
The soote savour, "lilie" was hir name.

Or Cecilie is to seye "the wey to blynde,"
For she ensample was by good techynge;
Or elles Cecile, as I writen fynde,
Is joyned, by a manere conjoynynge   95
Of "hevene" and "Lia"; and heere, in figurynge,
The "hevene" is set for thoght of hoolynesse,
And "Lia" for hire lastynge bisynesse.

Cecile may eek be seyd in this manere,
"Wantynge of blyndnesse," for hir grete light   100
Of sapience and for hire thewes cleere;
Or elles, loo, this maydens name bright
Of "hevene" and "leos" comth, for which by right
Men myghte hire wel "the hevene of peple" calle,
Ensample of goode and wise werkes alle.   105

For "leos" "peple" in Englissh is to seye,
And right as men may in the hevene see
The sonne and moone and sterres every weye,
Right so men goostly in this mayden free
Seyen of feith the magnanymytee,   110
And eek the cleernesse hool of sapience,
And sondry werkes, brighte of excellence.

And right so as thise philosophres write
That hevene is swift and round and eek brennynge,
Right so was faire Cecilie the white   115
Ful swift and bisy evere in good werkynge,
And round and hool in good perseverynge,
And brennynge evere in charite ful brighte.
Now have I yow declared what she highte.

Explicit

58 **flemed wrecche:** banished exile   **galle:** bitterness
59 **womman Cananee:** Canaanite woman in the New Testament story (cf. Matt. 15.22)
60 **crommes:** crumbs
65 **space:** time, space of time
66 **quit:** free
73 **wighte:** weight
75 **refut:** refuge
82 **at:** from, out of (reverence for)
Interpretacio, *etc.*: The interpretation of the name Cecilia that Brother Jacob of Genoa put in the Legend
86 **Expowne:** expound, explain

89 **honestee:** chastity
96 **in figurynge:** symbolically
100 **Wantynge:** lack
101 **thewes:** morals
109 **goostly:** spiritually
110 **Seyen:** saw
117 **perseverynge:** constancy
119 **highte:** was called

The Second Nun's Tale

⊛

Here bigynneth the Seconde Nonnes Tale of the lyf of Seinte Cecile.

This mayden bright Cecilie, as hir lif seith, 120
Was comen of Romayns and of noble kynde,
And from hir cradel up fostred in the feith
Of Crist, and bar his gospel in hir mynde.
She nevere cessed, as I writen fynde,
Of hir preyere and God to love and drede, 125
Bisekynge hym to kepe hir maydenhede.

And whan this mayden sholde unto a man
Ywedded be, that was ful yong of age,
Which that ycleped was Valerian,
And day was comen of hir marriage, 130
She, ful devout and humble in hir corage,
Under hir robe of gold, that sat ful faire,
Hadde next hire flessh yclad hire in an haire.

And whil the organs maden melodie,
To God allone in herte thus sang she: 135
"O Lord, my soule and eek my body gye
Unwemmed, lest that I confounded be."
And for his love that dyde upon a tree
Every seconde and thridde day she faste,
Ay biddynge in hire orisons ful faste. 140

The nyght cam, and to bedde moste she gon
With hire housbonde, as ofte is the manere,
And pryvely to hym she seyde anon,
"O sweete and wel biloved spouse deere,
Ther is a conseil, and ye wolde it heere, 145
Which that right fayn I wolde unto yow seye,
So that ye swere ye shul it nat biwreye."

Valerian gan faste unto hire swere
That for no cas ne thyng that myghte be,
He sholde nevere mo biwreyen here; 150
And thanne at erst to hym thus seyde she:
"I have an aungel which that loveth me,

That with greet love, wher so I wake or sleepe,
Is redy ay my body for to kepe.

"And if that he may feelen, out of drede, 155
That ye me touche, or love in vileynye,
He right anon wol sle yow with the dede,
And in youre yowthe thus ye shullen dye;
And if that ye in clene love me gye,
He wol yow loven as me, for youre clennesse, 160
And shewen yow his joye and his brightnesse."

Valerian, corrected as God wolde,
Answerde agayn, "If I shal trusten thee,
Lat me that aungel se and hym biholde;
And if that it a verray angel bee, 165
Thanne wol I doon as thou hast prayed me;
And if thou love another man, for sothe
Right with this swerd thanne wol I sle yow bothe."

Cecile answerde anon-right in this wise:
"If that yow list, the angel shul ye see, 170
So that ye trowe on Crist and yow baptize.
Gooth forth to Via Apia," quod shee,
"That fro this toun ne stant but miles three,
And to the povre folkes that ther dwelle,
Sey hem right thus, as that I shal yow telle. 175

"Telle hem that I, Cecile, yow to hem sente
To shewen yow the goode Urban the olde,
For secree nedes and for good entente.
And whan that ye Seint Urban han biholde,
Telle hym the wordes whiche I to yow tolde; 180
And whan that he hath purged yow fro synne,
Thanne shul ye se that angel, er ye twynne."

Valerian is to the place ygon,
And right as hym was taught by his lernynge,
He foond this hooly olde Urban anon 185

---

133 **haire:** hair shirt
136 **gye:** preserve
137 **Unwemmed:** undefiled   **confounded:** damned
140 **biddynge:** praying
145 **conseil:** secret
147 **biwreye:** betray

160 **clennesse:** purity
172 **Via Apia:** the Appian Way
181 **purged:** cleansed you (by baptism)
182 **twynne:** depart

Among the seintes buryeles lotynge.
And he anon withouten tariynge
Dide his message; and whan that he it tolde,
Urban for joye his handes gan up holde.

The teeris from his eyen leet he falle.   190
"Almyghty Lord, O Jhesu Crist," quod he,
"Sower of chaast conseil, hierde of us alle,
The fruyt of thilke seed of chastitee
That thou hast sowe in Cecile, taak to thee!
Lo, lyk a bisy bee, withouten gile,   195
Thee serveth ay thyn owene thral Cecile.

"For thilke spouse that she took but now
Ful lyk a fiers leoun, she sendeth heere,
As meke as evere was any lomb, to yow!"
And with that word anon ther gan appeere   200
An oold man, clad in white clothes cleere,
That hadde a book with lettre of gold in honde,
And gan bifore Valerian to stonde.

Valerian as deed fil doun for drede
Whan he hym saugh, and he up hente hym tho,   205
And on his book right thus he gan to rede:
"O Lord, o feith, o God, withouten mo,
O Cristendom, and Fader of alle also,
Aboven alle and over alle everywhere."
Thise wordes al with gold ywriten were.   210

Whan this was rad, thanne seyde this olde man,
"Leevestow this thyng or no? Sey ye or nay."
"I leeve al this thyng," quod Valerian,
"For sother thyng than this, I dar wel say,
Under the hevene no wight thynke may."   215
Tho vanysshed this olde man, he nyste where,
And Pope Urban hym cristned right there.

Valerian gooth hoom and fynt Cecilie
Withinne his chambre with an angel stonde.
This angel hadde of roses and of lilie   220
Corones two, the which he bar in honde;
And first to Cecile, as I understonde,
He yaf that oon, and after gan he take
That oother to Valerian, hir make.

"With body clene and with unwemmed thoght   225
Kepeth ay wel thise corones," quod he;
"Fro paradys to yow have I hem broght,

Ne nevere mo ne shal they roten bee,
Ne lese hir soote savour, trusteth me;
Ne nevere wight shal seen hem with his ye,   230
But he be chaast and hate vileynye.

"And thow, Valerian, for thow so soone
Assentedest to good conseil also,
Sey what thee list, and thou shalt han thy boone."
"I have a brother," quod Valerian tho,   235
"That in this world I love no man so.
I pray yow that my brother may han grace
To knowe the trouthe, as I do in this place."

The angel seyde, "God liketh thy requeste,
And bothe with the palm of martirdom   240
Ye shullen come unto his blisful feste."
And with that word Tiburce his brother coom.
And whan that he the savour undernoom,
Which that the roses and the lilies caste,
Withinne his herte he gan to wondre faste,   245

And seyde, "I wondre, this tyme of the yeer,
Whennes that soote savour cometh so
Of rose and lilies that I smelle heer.
For though I hadde hem in myne handes two,
The savour myghte in me no depper go.   250
The sweete smel that in myn herte I fynde
Hath chaunged me al in another kynde."

Valerian seyde: "Two corones han we,
Snow white and rose reed, that shynen cleere,
Whiche that thyne eyen han no myght to see;   255
And as thou smellest hem thurgh my preyere,
So shaltow seen hem, leeve brother deere,
If it so be thou wolt, withouten slouthe,
Bileve aright and knowen verray trouthe."

Tiburce answerde, "Seistow this to me   260
In soothnesse, or in dreem I herkne this?"
"In dremes," quod Valerian, "han we be
Unto this tyme, brother myn, ywis.
But now at erst in trouthe oure dwellyng is."
"How woostow this?" quod Tiburce, "and in what
          wyse?"   265
Quod Valerian, "That shal I thee devyse.

"The aungel of God hath me the trouthe ytaught

186 **buryeles:** burial places (in the catacombs)   **lotynge:** in hiding
192 **hierde:** shepherd
208 **Cristendom:** baptism
214 **sother:** truer

243 **undernoom:** perceived
261 **soothnesse:** truth

Which thou shalt seen, if that thou wolt reneye
The ydoles and be clene, and elles naught."
And of the myracle of thise corones tweye   270
Seint Ambrose in his preface list to seye;
Solempnely this noble doctour deere
Commendeth it, and seith in this manere:

"The palm of martirdom for to receyve,
Seinte Cecile, fulfild of Goddes yifte,   275
The world and eek hire chambre gan she weyve;
Witnesse Tyburces and [Valerians] shrifte,
To whiche God of his bountee wolde shifte
Corones two of floures wel smellynge,
And made his angel hem the corones brynge.   280

"The mayde hath broght thise men to blisse above;
The world hath wist what it is worth, certeyn,
Devocioun of chastitee to love."
Tho shewed hym Cecile al open and pleyn
That alle ydoles nys but a thyng in veyn,   285
For they been dombe, and therto they been deve,
And charged hym his ydoles for to leve.

"Whoso that troweth nat this, a beest he is,"
Quod tho Tiburce, "if that I shal nat lye."
And she gan kisse his brest, that herde this,   290
And was ful glad he koude trouthe espye.
"This day I take thee for myn allye,"
Seyde this blisful faire mayde deere,
And after that she seyde as ye may heere:

"Lo, right so as the love of Crist," quod she,   295
"Made me thy brotheres wyf, right in that wise
Anon for myn allye heer take I thee,
Syn that thou wolt thyne ydoles despise.
Go with thy brother now, and thee baptise,
And make thee clene, so that thou mowe biholde   300
The angels face of which thy brother tolde."

Tiburce answerde and seyde, "Brother deere,
First tel me whider I shal, and to what man?"

"To whom?" quod he, "com forth with right good
          cheere,
I wol thee lede unto the Pope Urban."   305
"Til Urban? Brother myn Valerian,"
Quod tho Tiburce, "woltow me thider lede?
Me thynketh that it were a wonder dede.

"Ne menestow nat Urban," quod he tho,
"That is so ofte dampned to be deed,   310
And woneth in halkes alwey to and fro,
And dar nat ones putte forth his heed?
Men sholde hym brennen in a fyr so reed
If he were founde, or that men myghte hym spye,
And we also, to bere hym compaignye;   315

"And whil we seken thilke divinitee
That is yhid in hevene pryvely,
Algate ybrend in this world shul we be!"
To whom Cecile answerde boldely,
"Men myghten dreden wel and skilfully   320
This lyf to lese, myn owene deere brother,
If this were lyvynge oonly and noon oother.

"But ther is bettre lif in oother place,
That nevere shal be lost, ne drede thee noght,
Which Goddes Sone us tolde thurgh his grace.   325
That Fadres Sone hath alle thyng ywroght,
And al that wroght is with a skilful thoght;
The Goost, that fro the Fader gan procede,
Hath sowled hem, withouten any drede.

"By word and by myracle heigh Goddes Sone,   330
Whan he was in this world, declared heere
That ther was oother lyf ther men may wone."
To whom answerde Tiburce, "O suster deere,
Ne seydestow right now in this manere,
Ther nys but o God, lord in soothfastnesse?   335
And now of three how maystow bere witnesse?"

"That shal I telle," quod she, "er I go.
Right as a man hath sapiences three—
Memorie, engyn, and intellect also—
So in o beynge of divinitee,   340
Thre persones may ther right wel bee."

---

268 **reneye:** deny, renounce
271 **preface:** preface to the canon of the Mass
272 **doctour:** Doctor of the Church
276 **weyve:** abandon, give up
277 **shrifte:** confession; see n.
278 **shifte:** provide
282 **worth:** worthy
286 **deve:** deaf
288 **a beest:** i.e., lacking human understanding
292 **allye:** kinsman

311 **halkes:** hiding places
315 **we also:** us as well
320 **skilfully:** reasonably
327 **skilful:** discerning
329 **sowled hem:** endowed them with souls
332 **wone:** dwell
338 **sapiences three:** three mental faculties—memory, imagination (*engyn*), judgment

Tho gan she hym ful bisily to preche
Of Cristes come, and of his peynes teche,

And manye pointes of his passioun;
How Goddes Sone in this world was withholde 345
To doon mankynde pleyn remissioun,
That was ybounde in synne and cares colde;
Al this thyng she unto Tiburce tolde.
And after this Tiburce in good entente
With Valerian to Pope Urban he wente, 350

That thanked God, and with glad herte and light
He cristned hym and made hym in that place
Parfit in his lernynge, Goddes knyght.
And after this Tiburce gat swich grace
That every day he saugh in tyme and space 355
The aungel of God; and every maner boone
That he God axed, it was sped ful soone.

It were ful hard by ordre for to seyn
How manye wondres Jhesus for hem wroghte;
But atte laste, to tellen short and pleyn, 360
The sergeantz of the toun of Rome hem soghte,
And hem biforn Almache, the prefect, broghte,
Which hem apposed, and knew al hire entente,
And to the ymage of Juppiter hem sente,

And seyde, "Whoso wol nat sacrifise, 365
Swape of his heed; this my sentence heer."
Anon thise martirs that I yow devyse,
Oon Maximus, that was an officer
Of the prefectes, and his corniculer,
Hem hente, and whan he forth the seintes ladde, 370
Hymself he weep for pitee that he hadde.

Whan Maximus had herd the seintes loore,
He gat hym of the tormentoures leve,
And ladde hem to his hous withoute moore,
And with hir prechyng, er that it were eve, 375
They gonnen fro the tormentours to reve,
And fro Maxime, and fro his folk echone,
The false feith, to trowe in God allone.

Cecile cam, whan it was woxen nyght,
With preestes that hem cristned alle yfeere; 380
And afterward, whan day was woxen light,
Cecile hem seyde with a ful stedefast cheere,
"Now, Cristes owene knyghtes leeve and deere,
Cast alle awey the werkes of derknesse,
And armeth yow in armure of brightnesse. 385

"Ye han for sothe ydoon a greet bataille,
Youre cours is doon, youre feith han ye conserved.
Gooth to the corone of lif that may nat faille;
The rightful Juge, which that ye han served,
Shal yeve it yow, as ye han it deserved." 390
And whan this thyng was seyd as I devyse,
Men ledde hem forth to doon the sacrefise.

But whan they weren to the place broght
To tellen shortly the conclusioun,
They nolde encense ne sacrifise right noght, 395
But on hir knees they setten hem adoun
With humble herte and sad devocioun,
And losten bothe hir hevedes in the place.
Hir soules wenten to the Kyng of grace.

This Maximus, that saugh this thyng bityde, 400
With pitous teeris tolde it anonright,
That he hir soules saugh to hevene glyde
With aungels ful of cleernesse and of light,
And with his word converted many a wight;
For which Almachius dide hym so bete 405
With whippe of leed til he his lif gan lete.

Cecile hym took and buryed hym anon
By Tiburce and Valerian softely
Withinne hire buriyng place, under the stoon;
And after this, Almachius hastily 410
Bad his ministres fecchen openly
Cecile, so that she myghte in his presence
Doon sacrifice and Juppiter encense.

But they, converted at hir wise loore,
Wepten ful soore, and yaven ful credence 415
Unto hire word, and cryden moore and moore,
"Crist, Goddes Sone, withouten difference,
Is verray God—this is al oure sentence—

343 **Cristes come:** Christ's coming
345 **withholde:** compelled to remain
347 **colde:** painful
361 **sergeantz:** officers of the law
363 **apposed:** questioned
366 **Swape:** strike **this** = *this is*
367 **devyse:** tell, narrate
369 **corniculer:** subordinate officer, assistant to a centurion, prefect, etc.
376 **gonnen fro . . . to reve:** took away from

398 **hevedes:** heads
405 **dide . . . bete:** had him beaten
406 **whippe of leed:** scourge with leaden balls attached **gan lete:** gave up
415 **yaven:** gave
417 **withouten difference:** without difference in rank or authority

That hath so good a servant hym to serve.
This with o voys we trowen, thogh we sterve!"   420

Almachius, that herde of this doynge,
Bad fecchen Cecile, that he myghte hire see,
And alderfirst, lo, this was his axynge.
"What maner womman artow?" tho quod he.
"I am a gentil womman born," quod she.   425
"I axe thee," quod he, "though it thee greeve,
Of thy religioun and of thy bileeve."

"Ye han bigonne youre questioun folily,"
Quod she, "that wolden two answeres conclude
In o demande; ye axed lewedly."   430
Almache answerde unto that similitude,
"Of whennes comth thyn answeryng so rude?"
"Of whennes?" quod she, whan that she was
      freyned,
"Of conscience and of good feith unfeyned."

Almachius seyde, "Ne takestow noon heede   435
Of my power?" And she answerde hym this:
"Youre myght," quod she, "ful litel is to dreede,
For every mortal mannes power nys
But lyk a bladdre ful of wynd, ywis.
For with a nedles poynt, whan it is blowe,   440
May al the boost of it be leyd ful lowe."

"Ful wrongfully bigonne thow," quod he,
"And yet in wrong is thy perseveraunce.
Wostow nat how oure myghty princes free
Han thus comanded and maad ordinaunce   445
That every Cristen wight shal han penaunce
But if that he his Cristendom withseye,
And goon al quit, if he wole it reneye?"

"Yowre princes erren, as youre nobleye dooth,"
Quod tho Cecile, "and with a wood sentence   450
Ye make us gilty, and it is nat sooth.
For ye, that knowen wel oure innocence,
For as muche as we doon a reverence
To Crist, and for we bere a Cristen name,
Ye putte on us a cryme and eek a blame.   455

"But we that knowen thilke name so
For vertuous, we may it nat withseye."

420 **with o voys:** unanimously
423 **alderfirst:** first of all
429 **conclude:** include
431 **similitude:** statement (comparison)
433 **freyned:** asked
447 **withseye:** deny
448 **quit:** free
455 **cryme:** accusation

Almache answerde, "Chees oon of thise two:
Do sacrifice, or Cristendom reneye,
That thou mowe now escapen by that weye."   460
At which the hooly blisful faire mayde
Gan for to laughe, and to the juge sayde:

"O juge, confus in thy nycetee,
Woltow that I reneye innocence,
To make me a wikked wight?" quod shee.   465
"Lo, he dissymuleth heere in audience;
He stareth, and woodeth in his advertence!"
To whom Almachius, "Unsely wrecche,
Ne woostow nat how fer my myght may strecche?

"Han noght oure myghty princes to me yiven,   470
Ye, bothe power and auctoritee
To maken folk to dyen or to lyven?
Why spekestow so proudly thanne to me?"
"I speke noght but stedfastly," quod she;
"Nat proudly, for I seye, as for my syde,   475
We haten deedly thilke vice of pryde.

"And if thou drede nat a sooth to heere,
Thanne wol I shewe al openly, by right,
That thou hast maad a ful gret lesyng heere.
Thou seyst thy princes han thee yeven myght   480
Bothe for to sleen and for to quyken a wight;
Thou, that ne mayst but oonly lyf bireve,
Thou hast noon oother power ne no leve.

"But thou mayst seyn thy princes han thee maked
Ministre of deeth; for if thou speke of mo,   485
Thou lyest, for thy power is ful naked."
"Do wey thy booldnesse," seyde Almachius tho,
"And sacrifice to oure goddes er thou go!
I recche nat what wrong that thou me profre,
For I kan suffre it as a philosophre;   490

"But thilke wronges may I nat endure
That thou spekest of oure goddes heere," quod he.
Cecile answerde, "O nyce creature!
Thou seydest no word syn thou spak to me
That I ne knew therwith thy nycetee   495
And that thou were in every maner wise
A lewed officer and a veyn justise.

463 **nycetee:** foolishness
466 **dissymuleth:** dissembles
467 **woodeth:** raves, rages   **advertence:** mind
479 **lesyng:** lying
481 **quyken:** give life to
497 **veyn:** idle, foolish

"Ther lakketh no thyng to thyne outter yen
That thou n'art blynd; for thyng that we seen alle
That it is stoon—that men may wel espyen—   500
That ilke stoon a god thow wolt it calle.
I rede thee, lat thyn hand upon it falle
And taste it wel, and stoon thou shalt it fynde,
Syn that thou seest nat with thyne eyen blynde.

"It is a shame that the peple shal   505
So scorne thee and laughe at thy folye,
For communly men woot it wel overal
That myghty God is in his hevenes hye;
And thise ymages, wel thou mayst espye,
To thee ne to hemself mowen noght profite,   510
For in effect they been nat worth a myte."

Thise wordes and swiche othere seyde she,
And he weex wroth, and bad men sholde hir lede
Hom til hir hous, and "In hire hous," quod he,
"Brenne hire right in a bath of flambes rede."   515
And as he bad, right so was doon the dede;
For in a bath they gonne hire faste shetten,
And nyght and day greet fyr they under betten.

The longe nyght, and eek a day also,
For al the fyr and eek the bathes heete   520
She sat al coold and feelede no wo.
It made hire nat a drope for to sweete.
But in that bath hir lyf she moste lete,
For he Almachius, with ful wikke entente,
To sleen hire in the bath his sonde sente.   525

Thre strokes in the nekke he smoot hire tho,
The tormentour, but for no maner chaunce
He myghte noght smyte al hir nekke atwo;
And for ther was that tyme an ordinaunce
That no man sholde doon man swich penaunce   530
The ferthe strook to smyten, softe or soore,
This tormentour ne dorste do namoore,

But half deed, with hir nekke ycorven there,
He lefte hir lye, and on his wey he went.
The Cristen folk, which that aboute hire were,   535
With sheetes han the blood ful faire yhent.
Thre dayes lyved she in this torment,
And nevere cessed hem the feith to teche
That she hadde fostred; hem she gan to preche,

And hem she yaf hir moebles and hir thyng,   540
And to the Pope Urban bitook hem tho,
And seyde, "I axed this of hevene kyng,
To han respit thre dayes and namo
To recomende to yow, er that I go,
Thise soules, lo, and that I myghte do werche   545
Heere of myn hous perpetuelly a cherche."

Seint Urban with his deknes prively
The body fette and buryed it by nyghte
Among his othere seintes honestly.
Hir hous the chirche of Seint Cecilie highte;   550
Seint Urban halwed it, as he wel myghte;
In which, into this day, in noble wyse,
Men doon to Crist and to his seint servyse.

Heere is ended the Seconde Nonnes Tale.

498–99 **Ther lakketh no thyng . . . blynd:** Your bodily eyes lack nothing to make you blind (i.e., you are completely blind).
511 **myte:** a small Flemish coin of little value
513 **weex:** grew, became
515 **bath:** cauldron
518 **betten:** fed
522 **sweete:** sweat
525 **sonde:** messenger, servant

527 **for no maner chaunce:** in no way
530 **penaunce:** suffering
540 **moebles:** personal property   **thyng:** things
541 **bitook:** entrusted
544 **recomende:** commend
545 **do werche:** have my house made (into a church)
547 **deknes:** deacons
551 **halwed:** consecrated

The Canon's Yeoman's Prologue

⑨

The Prologe of the Chanouns Yemannes Tale.

Whan ended was the lyf of Seinte Cecile,
Er we hadde riden fully fyve mile,   555
At Boghtoun under Blee us gan atake
A man that clothed was in clothes blake,
And undernethe he hadde a whyt surplys.
His hakeney, that was al pomely grys,
So swatte that it wonder was to see;   560
It semed as he had priked miles three.
The hors eek that his yeman rood upon
So swatte that unnethe myghte it gon.
Aboute the peytrel stood the foom ful hye;
He was of foom al flekked as a pye.   565
A male tweyfoold on his croper lay;
It semed that he caried lite array.
Al light for somer rood this worthy man,
And in myn herte wondren I bigan
What that he was til that I understood   570
How that his cloke was sowed to his hood,
For which, whan I hadde longe avysed me,
I demed hym som chanoun for to be.
His hat heeng at his bak doun by a laas,
For he hadde riden moore than trot or paas;   575
He hadde ay priked lik as he were wood.
A clote-leef he hadde under his hood
For swoot and for to keep his heed from heete.
But it was joye for to seen hym swete!
His forheed dropped as a stillatorie   580
Were ful of plantayne and of paritorie.
And whan that he was come, he gan to crye,
"God save," quod he, "this joly compaignye!
Faste have I priked," quod he, "for youre sake,
By cause that I wolde yow atake,   585
To riden in this myrie compaignye."

His yeman eek was ful of curteisye,
And seyde, "Sires, now in the morwe-tyde
Out of youre hostelrie I saugh yow ryde,
And warned heer my lord and my soverayn,   590
Which that to ryden with yow is ful fayn
For his desport; he loveth daliaunce."
    "Freend, for thy warnyng God yeve thee good
        chaunce,"
Thanne seyde oure Hoost, "for certein it wolde seme
Thy lord were wys, and so I may wel deme.   595
He is ful jocunde also, dar I leye!
Can he oght telle a myrie tale or tweye,
With which he glade may this compaignye?"
    "Who, sire? My lord? Ye, ye, withouten lye,
He kan of murthe and eek of jolitee   600
Nat but ynough; also, sire, trusteth me,
And ye hym knewe as wel as do I,
Ye wolde wondre how wel and craftily
He koude werke, and that in sondry wise.
He hath take on hym many a greet emprise,   605
Which were ful hard for any that is heere
To brynge aboute, but they of hym it leere.
As hoomly as he rit amonges yow,
If ye hym knewe, it wolde be for youre prow.
Ye wolde nat forgoon his aqueyntaunce   610
For muchel good, I dar leye in balaunce
Al that I have in my possessioun.
He is a man of heigh discrecioun;
I warne yow wel, he is a passyng man."   614
    "Wel," quod oure Hoost, "I pray thee, tel me than,
Is he a clerk, or noon? Telle what he is."
    "Nay, he is gretter than a clerk, ywis,"
Seyde this Yeman, "and in wordes fewe,
Hoost, of his craft somwhat I wol yow shewe.
    "I seye, my lord kan swich subtilitee—   620
But al his craft ye may nat wite at me,
And somwhat helpe I yet to his wirkyng—
That al this ground on which we been ridyng,

556 **Boghtoun under Blee:** Boughton under the Blean Forest, about five miles from
Canterbury   **gan atake:** overtook
558 **surplys:** surplice (ecclesiastical gown)
559 **hakeney:** small riding horse   **pomely grys:** dapple grey
560 **swatte:** sweated
564 **peytrel:** horse collar
565 **flekked:** spotted   **pye:** magpie
566 **male tweyfoold:** a double bag
568 **Al light:** lightly clothed
575 **paas:** walk
577 **clote-leef:** burdock leaf
578 **For swoot:** to avoid sweat (running into his eyes)
580 **stillatorie:** still, vessel for distillation
581 **plantayne:** the herb plantain   **paritorie:** pellitory (also a herb)
585 **atake:** overtake

590 **soverayn:** master
596 **leye:** bet
601 **Nat but ynough:** more than enough
611 **leye in balaunce:** wager
614 **passyng:** outstanding
621 **wite at:** learn from

Til that we come to Caunterbury toun,
He koude al clene turnen up-so-doun,   625
And pave it al of silver and of gold."

      And whan this Yeman hadde this tale ytold
Unto oure Hoost, he seyde, "*Benedicitee!*
This thyng is wonder merveillous to me,
Syn that thy lord is of so heigh prudence,   630
By cause of which men sholde hym reverence,
That of his worshipe rekketh he so lite.
His overslope nys nat worth a myte,
As in effect, to hym, so moot I go,
It is al baudy and totore also.   635
Why is thy lord so sluttissh, I the preye,
And is of power bettre clooth to beye,
If that his dede accorde with thy speche?
Telle me that, and that I thee biseche."   639
      "Why?" quod this Yeman, "wherto axe ye me?
God help me so, for he shal nevere thee!
(But I wol nat avowe that I seye,
And therfore keepe it secree, I yow preye.)
He is to wys, in feith, as I bileeve.
That that is overdoon, it wol nat preeve   645
Aright, as clerkes seyn; it is a vice.
Wherfore in that I holde hym lewed and nyce.
For whan a man hath over-greet a wit,
Ful oft hym happeth to mysusen it.
So dooth my lord, and that me greveth soore,   650
God it amende! I kan sey yow namoore."
      "Ther-of no fors, good Yeman," quod oure Hoost;
"Syn of the konnyng of thy lord thow woost,
Telle how he dooth, I pray thee hertely,
Syn that he is so crafty and so sly.   655
Where dwelle ye, if it to telle be?"
      "In the suburbes of a toun," quod he,
"Lurkynge in hernes and in lanes blynde,
Whereas thise robbours and thise theves by kynde
Holden hir pryvee fereful residence,   660
As they that dar nat shewen hir presence;
So faren we, if I shal seye the sothe."
      "Now," quod oure Hoost, "yit lat me talke to the.

Why artow so discoloured of thy face?"
      "Peter!" quod he, "God yeve it harde grace,   665
I am so used in the fyr to blowe
That it hath chaunged my colour, I trowe.
I am nat wont in no mirour to prie,
But swynke soore and lerne multiplie.
We blondren evere and pouren in the fir,   670
And for al that we faille of oure desir,
For evere we lakken oure conclusioun.
To muchel folk we doon illusioun,
And borwe gold, be it a pound or two,
Or ten, or twelve, or manye sommes mo,   675
And make hem wenen, at the leeste weye,
That of a pound we koude make tweye.
Yet is it fals, but ay we han good hope
It for to doon, and after it we grope.
But that science is so fer us biforn,   680
We mowen nat, although we hadden it sworn,
It overtake, it slit awey so faste.
It wole us maken beggers atte laste."
      Whil this Yeman was thus in his talkyng,   684
This Chanoun drough hym neer and herde al thyng
Which this Yeman spak, for suspecioun
Of mennes speche evere hadde this Chanoun.
For Catoun seith that he that gilty is
Demeth alle thyng be spoke of hym, ywis.
That was the cause he gan so ny hym drawe   690
To his Yeman, to herknen al his sawe.
And thus he seyde unto his Yeman tho:
"Hoold thou thy pees and spek no wordes mo,
For if thou do, thou shalt it deere abye.
Thou sclaundrest me heere in this compaignye,   695
And eek discoverest that thou sholdest hyde."
      "Ye," quod oure Hoost, "telle on, what so bityde.
Of al his thretyng rekke nat a myte!"
      "In feith," quod he, "namoore I do but lyte."
      And whan this Chanon saugh it wolde nat bee,   700
But his Yeman wolde telle his pryvetee,
He fledde awey for verray sorwe and shame.
      "A!" quod the Yeman, "heere shal arise game;
Al that I kan anon now wol I telle.

---

625 **up-so-doun:** topsy turvy
632 **worshipe:** honor
633 **overslope:** outer garment, cassock
634 **As in effect, to hym:** Really, for him; cf. 847.
635 **baudy:** dirty   **totore:** tattered
636 **sluttissh:** slovenly
645 **overdoon:** overdone
645–46 **preeve Aright:** turn out right, succeed
648 **over-greet:** excessive
655 **sly:** expert
658 **hernes:** hiding places

665 **Peter!:** by St. Peter (I swear)!   **harde grace:** misfortune
668 **prie:** look, peer
669 **multiplie:** transmute (base metals to gold and silver)
670 **blondren:** blunder   **pouren:** stare, pore
681 **although we hadden it sworn:** though we had sworn the contrary
682 **slit** = *slideth*, slips away
688 **Catoun:** Cato
691 **sawe:** speech
696 **discoverest that:** reveal what
698 **thretyng:** threatening

Syn he is goon, the foule feend hym quelle!   705
For nevere heerafter wol I with hym meete
For peny ne for pound, I yow biheete.
He that me broghte first unto that game,
Er that he dye, sorwe have he and shame!
For it is ernest to me, by my feith;   710
That feele I wel, what so any man seith.
And yet, for al my smert and al my grief,

For al my sorwe, labour, and meschief,
I koude nevere leve it in no wise.
Now wolde God my wit myghte suffise   715
To tellen al that longeth to that art!
But nathelees yow wol I tellen part.
Syn that my lord is goon, I wol nat spare;
Swich thyng as that I knowe, I wol declare.

Heere endeth the Prologe of the Chanouns Yemannes Tale.

The Canon Yeoman's Tale

Heere bigynneth the Chanouns Yeman his Tale.

[PRIMA PARS]

With this Chanoun I dwelt have seven yeer,   720
And of his science am I never the neer.
Al that I hadde I have lost therby,
And, God woot, so hath many mo than I.
Ther I was wont to be right fressh and gay
Of clothyng and of oother good array,   725
Now may I were an hose upon myn heed;
And wher my colour was bothe fressh and reed,
Now is it wan and of a leden hewe—
Whoso it useth, soore shal he rewe!—
And of my swynk yet blered is myn ye.   730
Lo, which avantage is to multiplie!
That slidynge science hath me maad so bare
That I have no good, wher that evere I fare;
And yet I am endetted so therby
Of gold that I have borwed, trewely,   735
That whil I lyve I shal it quite nevere.
Lat every man be war by me for evere!
What maner man that casteth hym therto,
If he continue, I holde his thrift ydo.
For so helpe me God, therby shal he nat wynne,   740
But empte his purs and make his wittes thynne.
And whan he thurgh his madnesse and folye

Hath lost his owene good thurgh jupartye,
Thanne he exciteth oother folk therto,
To lesen hir good as he hymself hath do.   745
For unto shrewes joye it is and ese
To have hir felawes in peyne and disese.
Thus was I ones lerned of a clerk.
Of that no charge; I wol speke of oure werk.
Whan we been there as we shul exercise   750
Oure elvysshe craft, we semen wonder wise,
Oure termes been so clergial and so queynte.
I blowe the fir til that myn herte feynte.
What sholde I tellen ech proporcion
Of thynges whiche that we werche upon—   755
As on fyve or sixe ounces, may wel be,
Of silver, or som oother quantitee—
And bisye me to telle yow the names
Of orpyment, brent bones, iren squames,
That into poudre grounden been ful smal;   760
And in an erthen pot how put is al,
And salt yput in, and also papeer,
Biforn thise poudres that I speke of heer;
And wel ycovered with a lampe of glas;
And of muche oother thyng which that ther was;   765
And of the pot and glasses enlutyng

---

705 **quelle:** kill
707 **biheete:** promise

---

721 **never the neer:** no closer to the goal, no better off
728 **leden:** lead-colored
730 **blered is myn ye:** my eye is bleary, I have been deluded
732 **bare:** impoverished
734 **endetted:** in debt
738 **casteth hym:** applies himself.
739 **thrift ydo:** prosperity, or welfare, done for

743 **jupartye:** taking risks
749 **no charge:** no matter
751 **elvysshe:** strange, mysterious
752 **clergial:** scholarly, learned   **queynte:** complex
753 **feynte:** grows faint
759 **orpyment:** arsenic trisulphide (auripigmentum); the scientific terms in this passage are discussed in the Expl. Notes.   **squames:** flakes, scales
762 **papeer:** pepper
764 **lampe:** lamp-shaped vessel
766 **enlutyng:** sealing with "lute," clay

That of the eyr myghte passe out nothyng;
And of the esy fir, and smart also,
Which that was maad, and of the care and wo
That we hadde in oure matires sublymyng, 770
And in amalgamyng and calcenyng
Of quyksilver, yclept mercurie crude?
For alle oure sleightes we kan nat conclude.
Oure orpyment and sublymed mercurie,
Oure grounden litarge eek on the porfurie, 775
Of ech of thise of ounces a certeyn—
Noght helpeth us; oure labour is in veyn.
Ne eek oure spirites ascencioun,
Ne oure materes that lyen al fix adoun,
Mowe in oure werkyng no thyng us availle, 780
For lost is al oure labour and travaille;
And al the cost, a twenty devel waye,
Is lost also, which we upon it laye.
      Ther is also ful many another thyng
That is unto oure craft apertenyng. 785
Though I by ordre hem nat reherce kan,
By cause that I am a lewed man,
Yet wol I telle hem as they come to mynde,
Thogh I ne kan nat sette hem in hir kynde:
As boole armonyak, verdegrees, boras, 790
And sondry vessels maad of erthe and glas,
Oure urynales and oure descensories,
Violes, crosletz, and sublymatories,
Cucurbites and alambikes eek,
And othere swiche, deere ynough a leek— 795
Nat nedeth it for to reherce hem alle—
Watres rubifiyng, and boles galle,
Arsenyk, sal armonyak, and brymstoon;
And herbes koude I telle eek many oon,

As egremoyne, valerian, and lunarie, 800
And othere swiche, if that me liste tarie;
Oure lampes brennyng bothe nyght and day,
To brynge aboute oure purpos, if we may;
Oure fourneys eek of calcinacioun,
And of watres albificacioun; 805
Unslekked lym, chalk, and gleyre of an ey,
Poudres diverse, asshes, donge, pisse, and cley,
Cered pokkets, sal peter, vitriole,
And diverse fires maad of wode and cole;
Sal tartre, alkaly, and sal preparat, 810
And combust materes and coagulat;
Cley maad with hors or mannes heer, and oille
Of tartre, alum glas, berme, wort, and argoille,
Resalgar, and oure materes enbibyng,
And eek of oure materes encorporyng, 815
And of oure silver citrinacioun,
Oure cementyng and fermentacioun,
Oure yngottes, testes, and many mo.
      I wol yow telle, as was me taught also,
The foure spirites and the bodies sevene, 820
By ordre, as ofte I herde my lord hem nevene.
      The firste spirit quyksilver called is,
The seconde orpyment, the thridde, ywis,
Sal armonyak, and the ferthe brymstoon.
The bodyes sevene eek, lo, hem heere anoon: 825
Sol gold is, and Luna silver we threpe,
Mars iren, Mercurie quyksilver we clepe,
Saturnus leed, and Juppiter is tyn,
And Venus coper, by my fader kyn!

768 **smart:** brisk
770 **sublymyng:** sublimation, purifying
771 **amalgamyng:** blending, usually of quicksilver with another metal   **calcenyng:** calcination, reducing a substance to powder by heat
772 **crude:** raw, unrefined
773 **conclude:** succeed
774 **orpyment:** arsenic trisulphide   **sublymed:** purified
775 **litarge:** litharge, lead monoxide   **porfurie:** marble, porphyry (used as a mortar)
776 **a certeyn:** a certain amount of
778 **spirites ascencioun:** vaporization of volatile spirits
779 **fix:** stable, nonvolatile   **adoun:** below, in the bottom of the flask after the vaporization
790 **boole armonyak:** Armenian bole (a styptic)   **verdegrees:** verdigris, copper acetate (a greenish pigment)   **boras:** borax
792 **urynales:** glass flasks   **descensories:** retorts, vessels for distillation
793 **Violes:** vials   **crosletz:** crucibles   **sublymatories:** vessels used for sublimation
794 **Cucurbites:** gourd-shaped vessels (for distillation)   **alambikes:** alembics
795 **deere ynough a leek:** expensive enough at the price of a leek (i.e., worthless)
797 **Watres rubifiyng:** liquids that cause reddening   **boles galle:** bull's gall
798 **Arsenyk:** an arsenic compound (orpiment?)   **sal armonyak:** sal ammoniac, ammonium chloride   **brymstoon:** sulphur

800 **egremoyne:** agrimony, an aromatic herb   **valerian:** valerian, a medicinal herb   **lunarie:** moonwort (Botrychium lunaria)
804 **fourneys:** furnace   **calcinacioun:** calcination (reducing a substance to powder)
805 **watres albificacioun:** whitening by liquids (?); see n.
806 **Unslekked lym:** unslaked lime (a caustic)   **gleyre of an ey:** white of an egg
807 **cley:** clay
808 **Cered pokkets:** waxed (waterproofed) small bags   **sal peter:** saltpeter, potassium nitrate   **vitriole:** sulphate of metal, usually iron or copper
809 **wode and cole:** wood and coal
810 **Sal tartre:** *argoille,* potassium carbonate   **alkaly:** *sal alkaly,* an alkaline from ashes of plants   **sal preparat:** purified salt
811 **combust:** burnt, calcined   **coagulat:** solidified, cohesive
812–13 **oille Of tartre:** cream of tartar
813 **alum glas:** potash alum, crystallized alum   **berme:** barm, brewer's yeast   **wort:** unfermented beer   **argoille:** argol, tartar from fermenting wine, a crude potassium bitartrate
814 **Resalgar:** arsenic disulphide (ratsbane)   **enbibyng:** absorption of fluid, soaking
815 **encorporyng:** forming an amalgam or compound
816 **citrinacioun:** turning to a lemon color
817 **cementyng:** combining, fusing by heat   **fermentacioun:** fermenting, a process causing effervescence
818 **yngottes:** ingots, molds for casting metal   **testes:** cupels, crucibles for trying gold or silver
820 **spirites:** volatile substances, substances easily vaporized by heat   **bodies:** metals
821 **nevene:** name
824 **Sal armonyak:** sal ammoniac
826 **Sol:** the sun   **Luna:** the moon   **threpe:** assert, affirm positively

This cursed craft whoso wole excercise,   830
He shal no good han that hym may suffise,
For al the good he spendeth theraboute
He lese shal; therof have I no doute.
Whoso that listeth outen his folie,
Lat hym come forth and lerne multiplie;   835
And every man that oght hath in his cofre,
Lat hym appiere and wexe a philosophre.
Ascaunce that craft is so light to leere?
Nay, nay, God woot, al be he monk or frere,
Preest or chanoun, or any oother wyght,   840
Though he sitte at his book bothe day and nyght
In lernyng of this elvysshe nyce loore,
Al is in veyn, and parde, muchel moore.
To lerne a lewed man this subtiltee—
Fy! Spek nat therof, for it wol nat bee.   845
And konne he letterure or konne he noon,
As in effect, he shal fynde it al oon.
For bothe two, by my savacioun,
Concluden in multiplicacioun
Ylike wel, whan they han al ydo;   850
This is to seyn, they faillen bothe two.
    Yet forgat I to maken rehersaille
Of watres corosif, and of lymaille,
And of bodies mollificacioun,
And also of hire induracioun;   855
Oilles, ablucions, and metal fusible—
To tellen al wolde passen any bible
That owher is; wherfore, as for the beste,
Of alle thise names now wol I me reste,
For, as I trowe, I have yow toold ynowe   860
To reyse a feend, al looke he never so rowe.
    A! Nay! Lat be; the philosophres stoon,
Elixer clept, we sechen faste echoon;
For hadde we hym, thanne were we siker ynow.
But unto God of hevene I make avow,   865
For al oure craft, whan we han al ydo,
And al oure sleighte, he wol nat come us to.
He hath ymaad us spenden muchel good,
For sorwe of which almoost we wexen wood,

But that good hope crepeth in oure herte,   870
Supposynge evere, though we sore smerte,
To be releeved by hym afterward.
Swich supposyng and hope is sharp and hard;
I warne yow wel, it is to seken evere.
That futur temps hath maad men to dissevere,   875
In trust therof, from al that evere they hadde.
Yet of that art they kan nat wexen sadde,
For unto hem it is a bitter sweete—
So semeth it—for nadde they but a sheete   879
Which that they myghte wrappe hem inne a-nyght,
And a brat to walken inne by daylyght,
They wolde hem selle and spenden on this craft.
They kan nat stynte til no thyng be laft.
And everemoore, where that evere they goon,
Men may hem knowe by smel of brymstoon.   885
For al the world they stynken as a goot;
Hir savour is so rammyssh and so hoot
That though a man from hem a mile be,
The savour wole infecte hym, trusteth me.
Lo, thus by smellyng and threedbare array,   890
If that men liste, this folk they knowe may.
And if a man wole aske hem pryvely
Why they been clothed so unthriftily,
They right anon wol rownen in his ere,
And seyn that if that they espied were,   895
Men wolde hem slee by cause of hir science.
Lo, thus this folk bitrayen innocence!
    Passe over this; I go my tale unto.
Er that the pot be on the fir ydo,
Of metals with a certeyn quantitee,   900
My lord hem trempeth, and no man but he—
Now he is goon, I dar seyn boldely—
For, as men seyn, he kan doon craftily.
Algate I woot wel he hath swich a name;
And yet ful ofte he renneth in a blame.   905
And wite ye how? Ful ofte it happeth so
The pot tobreketh, and farewel, al is go!
Thise metals been of so greet violence
Oure walles mowe nat make hem resistence,
But if they weren wroght of lym and stoon;   910
They percen so, and thurgh the wal they goon.
And somme of hem synken into the ground—
Thus han we lost by tymes many a pound—

834 **outen:** make public
837 **appiere:** appear   **wexe:** become   **philosophre:** alchemist
838 **Ascaunce:** do you imagine (literally, *as if*)   **light to leere:** easy to learn
842 **elvysshe:** strange, mysterious
846 **letterure:** book learning
849 **multiplicacioun:** transmutation
852 **rehersaille:** enumeration
853 **corosif:** acidic   **lymaille:** metal filings
854 **mollificacioun:** softening
855 **induracioun:** hardening
856 **ablucions:** cleansings   **fusible:** capable of being melted
857 **bible:** book
858 **owher:** anywhere
861 **rowe:** rough, ugly
863 **Elixer:** substance that transmutes base metals to gold or silver, the "philosophers' stone"

874 **to seken evere:** always to be sought; i.e., never to be found
875 **temps:** tense   **dissevere:** separate, be separated
877 **wexen sadde:** attain stability, be satisfied
881 **brat:** cloak of rough cloth
887 **rammyssh:** like a ram, strong (in odor)
889 **infecte:** pollute
893 **unthriftily:** poorly
901 **trempeth:** mixes
907 **tobreketh:** shatters
913 **by tymes:** quickly, straightway

And somme are scatered al the floor aboute;
Somme lepe into the roof. Withouten doute,   915
Though that the feend noght in oure sighte hym
     shewe,
I trowe he with us be, that ilke shrewe!
In helle, where that he is lord and sire,
Nis ther moore wo, ne moore rancour ne ire.
Whan that oure pot is broke, as I have sayd,   920
Every man chit and halt hym yvele apayd.
    Somme seyde it was long on the fir makyng;
Somme seyde nay, it was on the blowyng—
Thanne was I fered, for that was myn office.
"Straw!" quod the thridde, "ye been lewed and nyce.
It was nat tempred as it oghte be."   926
"Nay," quod the fourthe, "stynt and herkne me.
By cause oure fir ne was nat maad of beech,
That is the cause and oother noon, so thee'ch!"
I kan nat telle wheron it was long,   930
But wel I woot greet strif is us among.
    "What," quod my lord, "ther is namoore to doone;
Of thise perils I wol be war eftsoone.
I am right siker that the pot was crased.
Be as be may, be ye no thyng amased;   935
As usage is, lat swepe the floor as swithe,
Plukke up youre hertes and beeth glad and blithe."
    The mullok on an heep ysweped was,
And on the floor ycast a canevas,
And al this mullok in a syve ythrowe,   940
And sifted, and ypiked many a throwe.
    "Pardee," quod oon, "somwhat of oure metal
Yet is ther heere, though that we han nat al.
And though this thyng myshapped have as now,
Another tyme it may be well ynow.   945
Us moste putte oure good in aventure.
A marchant, pardee, may nat ay endure,
Trusteth me wel, in his prosperitee.
Somtyme his good is drowned in the see,
And somtyme comth it sauf unto the londe."   950
    "Pees!" quod my lord, "the nexte tyme I wol fonde

To bryngen oure craft al in another plite,
And but I do, sires, lat me han the wite.
Ther was defaute in somwhat, wel I woot."
    Another seyde the fir was over-hoot—   955
But, be it hoot or coold, I dar seye this,
That we concluden everemoore amys.
We faille of that which that we wolden have,
And in oure madnesse everemoore we rave.
And whan we been togidres everichoon,   960
Every man semeth a Salomon.
But al thyng which that shineth as the gold
Nis nat gold, as that I have herd told;
Ne every appul that is fair at eye
Ne is nat good, what so men clappe or crye.   965
Right so, lo, fareth it amonges us:
He that semeth the wiseste, by Jhesus,
Is moost fool, whan it cometh to the preef;
And he that semeth trewest is a theef.
That shul ye knowe, er that I fro yow wende,   970
By that I of my tale have maad an ende.

Explicit prima pars.

Et sequitur pars secunda.

    Ther is a chanoun of religioun
Amonges us, wolde infecte al a toun,
Thogh it as greet were as was Nynyvee,
Rome, Alisaundre, Troye, and othere three.   975
His sleightes and his infinite falsnesse
Ther koude no man writen, as I gesse,
Though that he myghte lyve a thousand yeer.
In al this world of falshede nis his peer,
For in his termes he wol hym so wynde,   980
And speke his wordes in so sly a kynde,
Whanne he commune shal with any wight,
That he wol make hym doten anonright,
But it a feend be, as hymselven is.
Ful many a man hath he bigiled er this,   985
And wole, if that he lyve may a while;
And yet men ride and goon ful many a mile
Hym for to seke and have his aqueyntaunce,
Noght knowynge of his false governaunce.

---

921 **chit** = *chideth,* chides   **halt hym yvele apayd:** considers himself ill-used (*halt = holdeth,* holds)
922 **long on:** owing to
926 **tempred:** mixed
929 **so thee'ch** = *so thee ich,* as I may prosper
930 **wheron it was long:** what caused it
934 **crased:** cracked
935 **amased:** dismayed
938 **mullok:** rubbish   **ysweped:** swept
939 **canevas:** canvas
941 **ypiked:** picked through, sorted
944 **myshapped have:** may have turned out badly

952 **plite:** condition
953 **wite:** blame
964 **at eye:** to look at
Explicit, *etc.*: Here ends the first part.
Et sequitur, *etc.*: Here follows the second part.
972 **chanoun of religioun:** a canon regular (not a secular canon of a cathedral or large church)
980 **hym so wynde:** so wrap himself
981 **sly a kynde:** expert a manner
982 **commune:** have conversation with
983 **doten:** behave foolishly
989 **governaunce:** behavior

And if yow list to yeve me audience,   990
I wol it tellen heere in youre presence.
    But worshipful chanons religious,
Ne demeth nat that I sclaundre youre hous,
Although that my tale of a chanoun bee.
Of every ordre som shrewe is, pardee,   995
And God forbede that al a compaignye
Sholde rewe o singuleer mannes folye.
To sclaundre yow is no thyng myn entente,
But to correcten that is mys I mente.
This tale was nat oonly toold for yow,   1000
But eek for othere mo; ye woot wel how
That among Cristes apostelles twelve
Ther nas no traytour but Judas hymselve.
Thanne why sholde al the remenant have a blame
That giltlees were? By yow I seye the same,   1005
Save oonly this, if ye wol herkne me:
If any Judas in youre covent be,
Remoeveth hym bitymes, I yow rede,
If shame or los may causen any drede.
And beeth no thyng displesed, I yow preye,   1010
But in this cas herkneth what I shal seye.
    In Londoun was a preest, an annueleer,
That therinne dwelled hadde many a yeer,
Which was so plesaunt and so servysable
Unto the wyf, where as he was at table,   1015
That she wolde suffre hym no thyng for to paye
For bord ne clothyng, wente he never so gaye,
And spendyng silver hadde he right ynow.
Therof no fors; I wol procede as now,
And telle forth my tale of the chanoun   1020
That broghte this preest to confusioun.
    This false chanon cam upon a day
Unto this preestes chambre, wher he lay,
Bisechynge hym to lene hym a certeyn
Of gold, and he wolde quite it hym ageyn.   1025
"Leene me a marc," quod he, "but dayes three,
And at my day I wol it quiten thee.
And if so be that thow me fynde fals,
Another day do hange me by the hals!"   1029
    This preest hym took a marc, and that as swithe,
And this chanoun hym thanked ofte sithe,
And took his leve, and wente forth his weye,

And at the thridde day broghte his moneye,
And to the preest he took his gold agayn,
Wherof this preest was wonder glad and fayn.   1035
    "Certes," quod he, "no thyng anoyeth me
To lene a man a noble, or two, or thre,
Or what thyng were in my possessioun,
Whan he so trewe is of condicioun
That in no wise he breke wole his day;   1040
To swich a man I kan never seye nay."
    "What!" quod this chanoun, "sholde I be untrewe?
Nay, that were thyng yfallen al of newe.
Trouthe is a thyng that I wol evere kepe
Unto that day in which that I shal crepe   1045
Into my grave, and ellis God forbede.
Bileveth this as siker as your Crede.
God thanke I, and in good tyme be it sayd,
That ther was nevere man yet yvele apayd
For gold ne silver that he to me lente,   1050
Ne nevere falshede in myn herte I mente.
And sire," quod he, "now of my pryvetee,
Syn ye so goodlich han been unto me,
And kithed to me so greet gentillesse,
Somwhat to quyte with youre kyndenesse   1055
I wol yow shewe, and if yow list to leere,
I wol yow teche pleynly the manere
How I kan werken in philosophie.
Taketh good heede; ye shul wel seen at ye
That I wol doon a maistrie er I go."   1060
    "Ye," quod the preest, "ye, sire, and wol ye so?
Marie, therof I pray yow hertely."
    "At youre comandement, sire, trewely,"
Quod the chanoun, "and ellis God forbeede!"
    Loo, how this theef koude his service beede!
Ful sooth it is that swich profred servyse   1066
Stynketh, as witnessen thise olde wyse,
And that ful soone I wol it verifie
In this chanoun, roote of al trecherie,
That everemoore delit hath and gladnesse—   1070
Swiche feendly thoghtes in his herte impresse—
How Cristes peple he may to meschief brynge.
God kepe us from his false dissymulynge!

997 **singuleer:** individual
999 **mys:** amiss
1005 **By:** concerning
1008 **bitymes:** soon, quickly
1012 **annueleer:** chantry priest, who sings masses for the dead
1014 **plesaunt:** pleasing   **servysable:** willing to serve, attentive
1017 **wente he never so gaye:** however well he dressed
1024 **a certeyn:** a certain amount
1026 **marc:** mark, two-thirds of a pound
1029 **hals:** neck
1030 **as swithe:** immediately

1034 **took . . . agayn:** gave back
1040 **breke . . . his day:** fail to pay on the day he promised
1043 **al of newe:** for the first time
1048 **in good tyme be it sayd:** fortunately it may be said
1054 **kithed:** shown
1055 **to quyte with:** with which to requite
1058 **philosophie:** alchemy
1060 **doon a maistrie:** perform a wonderful work requiring great knowledge
1062 **Marie:** by St. Mary
1066 **profred servyse:** favors not asked for

Noght wiste this preest with whom that he delte,
Ne of his harm comynge he no thyng felte.   1075
O sely preest! O sely innocent!
With coveitise anon thou shalt be blent!
O gracelees, ful blynd is thy conceite,
No thyng ne artow war of the deceite
Which that this fox yshapen hath to thee!   1080
His wily wrenches thou ne mayst nat flee.
Wherfore, to go to the conclusion,
That refereth to thy confusion,
Unhappy man, anon I wol me hye
To tellen thyn unwit and thy folye,   1085
And eek the falsnesse of that oother wrecche,
As ferforth as that my konnyng wol strecche.

     This chanon was my lord, ye wolden weene?
Sire hoost, in feith, and by the hevenes queene,
It was another chanoun, and nat hee,   1090
That kan an hundred foold moore subtiltee.
He hath bitrayed folkes many tyme;
Of his falsnesse it dulleth me to ryme.
Evere whan that I speke of his falshede,
For shame of hym my chekes wexen rede.   1095
Algates they bigynnen for to glowe,
For reednesse have I noon, right wel I knowe,
In my visage; for fumes diverse
Of metals, whiche ye han herd me reherce,
Consumed and wasted han my reednesse.   1100
Now taak heede of this chanons cursednesse!

     "Sire," quod he to the preest, "lat youre man gon
For quyksilver, that we it hadde anon;
And lat hym bryngen ounces two or three;
And whan he comth, as faste shal ye see   1105
A wonder thyng, which ye saugh nevere er this."

     "Sire," quod the preest, "it shal be doon, ywis."
He bad his servant fecchen hym this thyng,
And he al redy was at his biddyng,
And wente hym forth, and cam anon agayn   1110
With this quyksilver, shortly for to sayn,
And took thise ounces thre to the chanoun;
And he hem leyde faire and wel adoun,
And bad the servant coles for to brynge,
That he anon myghte go to his werkynge.   1115

The coles right anon weren yfet,
And this chanoun took out a crosselet
Of his bosom, and shewed it to the preest.
"This instrument," quod he, "which that thou seest,
Taak in thyn hand, and put thyself therinne   1120
Of this quyksilver an ounce, and heer bigynne,
In name of Crist, to wexe a philosofre.
Ther been ful fewe to whiche I wolde profre
To shewen hem thus muche of my science.
For ye shul seen heer, by experience,   1125
That this quyksilver I wol mortifye
Right in youre sighte anon, withouten lye,
And make it as good silver and as fyn
As ther is any in youre purs or myn,
Or elleswhere, and make it malliable;   1130
And elles holdeth me fals and unable
Amonges folk for evere to appeere.
I have a poudre heer, that coste me deere,
Shal make al good, for it is cause of al
My konnyng, which that I yow shewen shal.   1135
Voyde youre man, and lat hym be theroute,
And shette the dore, whils we been aboute
Oure pryvetee, that no man us espie,
Whils that we werke in this philosophie."

     Al as he bad fulfilled was in dede.   1140
This ilke servant anonright out yede,
And his maister shette the dore anon,
And to hire labour spedily they gon.

     This preest, at this cursed chanons biddyng,
Upon the fir anon sette this thyng,   1145
And blew the fir, and bisyed hym ful faste.
And this chanoun into the crosselet caste
A poudre, noot I wherof that it was
Ymaad, outher of chalk, outher of glas,
Or somwhat elles, was nat worth a flye,   1150
To blynde with this preest; and bad hym hye
The coles for to couchen al above
The crosselet. "For in tokenyng I thee love,"
Quod this chanoun, "thyne owene handes two   1154
Shul werche al thyng which that shal heer be do."

     "Graunt mercy," quod the preest, and was ful glad,
And couched coles as the chanoun bad.
And while he bisy was, this feendly wrecche,

1077 **blent:** blinded, tricked
1078 **gracelees:** lacking (God's) favor, unfortunate   **conceite:** mind
1081 **wrenches:** tricks
1083 **refereth:** applies
1084 **Unhappy:** unfortunate
1085 **unwit:** lack of prudence
1088 **weene:** suppose (this)
1096 **Algates:** at least

1117 **crosselet:** crucible
1126 **mortifye:** harden, make nonvolatile
1131 **unable:** worthless
1136 **Voyde:** send away
1152 **couchen:** arrange
1153 **in tokenyng:** as a sign that
1156 **Graunt mercy:** many thanks

This false chanoun—the foule feend hym fecche!—
Out of his bosom took a bechen cole,   1160
In which ful subtilly was maad an hole,
And therinne put was of silver lemaille
An ounce, and stopped was, withouten faille,
This hole with wex, to kepe the lemaille in.
And understondeth that this false gyn   1165
Was nat maad ther, but it was maad bifore;
And othere thynges I shal tellen moore
Herafterward, whiche that he with hym broghte.
Er he cam there, hym to bigile he thoghte,
And so he dide, er that they wente atwynne;   1170
Til he had terved hym, koude he nat blynne.
It dulleth me whan that I of hym speke.
On his falshede fayn wolde I me wreke,
If I wiste how, but he is heere and there;
He is so variaunt, he abit nowhere.   1175
    But taketh heede now, sires, for Goddes love!
He took his cole of which I spak above,
And in his hand he baar it pryvely.
And whiles the preest couched bisily
The coles, as I tolde yow er this,   1180
This chanoun seyde, "Freend, ye doon amys.
This is nat couched as it oghte be;
But soone I shal amenden it," quod he.
"Now lat me medle therwith but a while,
For of yow have I pitee, by Seint Gile!   1185
Ye been right hoot; I se wel how ye swete.
Have heere a clooth, and wipe awey the wete."
And whiles that the preest wiped his face,
This chanoun took his cole—with sory grace!—
And leyde it above upon the myddeward   1190
Of the crosselet, and blew wel afterward
Til that the coles gonne faste brenne.
    "Now yeve us drynke," quod the chanoun thenne;
"As swithe al shal be wel, I undertake.
Sitte we doun, and lat us myrie make."   1195
And whan that this chanounes bechen cole
Was brent, al the lemaille out of the hole
Into the crosselet fil anon adoun;
And so it moste nedes, by resoun,
Syn it so evene above couched was.   1200

But therof wiste the preest nothyng, alas!
He demed alle the coles yliche good,
For of that sleighte he nothyng understood.
And whan this alkamystre saugh his tyme,   1204
"Ris up," quod he, "sire preest, and stondeth by me;
And for I woot wel ingot have ye noon,
Gooth, walketh forth, and bryngeth a chalk stoon;
For I wol make it of the same shap
That is an ingot, if I may han hap.
And bryngeth eek with yow a bolle or a panne   1210
Ful of water, and ye shul se wel thanne
How that oure bisynesse shal thryve and preeve.
And yet, for ye shul han no mysbileeve
Ne wrong conceite of me in youre absence,
I ne wol nat been out of youre presence,   1215
But go with yow and come with yow ageyn."
The chambre dore, shortly for to seyn,
They opened and shette, and wente hir weye.
And forth with hem they carieden the keye,
And coome agayn withouten any delay.   1220
What sholde I tarien al the longe day?
He took the chalk and shoop it in the wise
Of an ingot, as I shal yow devyse.
    I seye, he took out of his owene sleeve
A teyne of silver—yvele moot he cheeve!—   1225
Which that ne was nat but an ounce of weighte.
And taaketh heede now of his cursed sleighte!
    He shoop his ingot in lengthe and in breede
Of this teyne, withouten any drede,
So slyly that the preest it nat espide,   1230
And in his sleve agayn he gan it hide,
And fro the fir he took up his mateere,
And in th'yngot putte it with myrie cheere,
And in the water-vessel he it caste,   1234
Whan that hym luste, and bad the preest as faste,
"Loke what ther is; put in thyn hand and grope.
Thow fynde shalt ther silver, as I hope."
What, devel of helle, sholde it elles be?
Shaving of silver silver is, pardee!
He putte his hand in and took up a teyne   1240
Of silver fyn, and glad in every veyne
Was this preest, whan he saugh it was so.
"Goddes blessyng, and his moodres also,

1160 **bechen cole:** charcoal made of beechwood
1162 **lemaille:** metal filings
1165 **gyn:** contrivance
1170 **atwynne:** apart
1171 **terved:** skinned (robbed him of everything)   **blynne:** cease
1175 **variaunt:** changeable   **abit** = *abideth*, remains
1179 **couched:** arranged
1189 **with sory grace!:** bad luck to him!
1190 **myddeward:** middle

1204 **alkamystre:** alchemist
1210 **bolle:** bowl
1212 **preeve:** succeed
1213 **mysbileeve:** skepticism
1214 **conceite:** opinion
1225 **teyne:** small metal rod   **cheeve:** fare
1228 **breede:** breadth

And alle halwes, have ye, sire chanoun,"
Seyde the preest, "and I hir malisoun, 1245
But, and ye vouche-sauf to techen me
This noble craft and this subtilitee,
I wol be youre in al that evere I may."

　　Quod the chanoun, "Yet wol I make assay
The seconde tyme, that ye may taken heede 1250
And been expert of this, and in youre neede
Another day assaye in myn absence
This disciplyne and this crafty science.
Lat take another ounce," quod he tho,
"Of quyksilver, withouten wordes mo, 1255
And do therwith as ye han doon er this
With that oother, which that now silver is."

　　This preest hym bisieth in al that he kan
To doon as this chanoun, this cursed man,
Comanded hym, and faste blew the fir, 1260
For to come to th'effect of his desir.
And this chanon, right in the meene while,
Al redy was this preest eft to bigile,
And for a contenaunce in his hand he bar
An holwe stikke—taak kep and be war!— 1265
In the ende of which an ounce, and namoore,
Of silver lemaille put was, as bifore
Was in his cole, and stopped with wex weel
For to kepe in his lemaille every deel.
And whil this preest was in his bisynesse, 1270
This chanoun with his stikke gan hym dresse
To hym anon, and his poudre caste in
As he dide er—the devel out of his skyn
Hym terve, I pray to God, for his falshede!
For he was evere fals in thoght and dede— 1275
And with this stikke, above the crosselet,
That was ordeyned with that false jet,
He stired the coles til relente gan
The wex agayn the fir, as every man,
But it a fool be, woot wel it moot nede, 1280
And al that in the stikke was out yede,
And in the crosselet hastily it fel.

　　Now, good sires, what wol ye bet than wel?
Whan that this preest thus was bigiled ageyn,
Supposynge noght but treuthe, sooth to seyn, 1285
He was so glad that I kan nat expresse
In no manere his myrthe and his gladnesse;

And to the chanoun he profred eftsoone
Body and good. "Ye," quod the chanoun soone,
"Though poure I be, crafty thou shalt me fynde.
I warne thee, yet is ther moore bihynde. 1291
Is ther any coper herinne?" seyde he.
　　"Ye," quod the preest, "sire, I trowe wel ther be."
　　"Elles go bye us som, and that as swithe;
Now, goode sire, go forth thy wey and hy the." 1295
　　He wente his wey, and with the coper cam,
And this chanon it in his handes nam,
And of that coper weyed out but an ounce.

　　Al to symple is my tonge to pronounce,
As ministre of my wit, the doublenesse 1300
Of this chanoun, roote of alle cursednesse!
He semed freendly to hem that knewe hym noght,
But he was feendly bothe in werk and thoght.
It weerieth me to telle of his falsnesse,
And nathelees yet wol I it expresse, 1305
To th'entente that men may be war therby,
And for noon oother cause, trewely.

　　He putte this ounce of coper in the crosselet,
And on the fir as swithe he hath it set, 1309
And caste in poudre, and made the preest to blowe,
And in his werkyng for to stoupe lowe,
As he dide er—and al nas but a jape;
Right as hym liste, the preest he made his ape!
And afterward in the ingot he it caste,
And in the panne putte it at the laste 1315
Of water, and in he putte his owene hand,
And in his sleve (as ye biforen-hand
Herde me telle) he hadde a silver teyne.
He slyly took it out, this cursed heyne,
Unwityng this preest of his false craft, 1320
And in the pannes botme he hath it laft;
And in the water rombled to and fro,
And wonder pryvely took up also
The coper teyne, noght knowynge this preest,
And hidde it, and hym hente by the breest, 1325
And to hym spak, and thus seyde in his game:
"Stoupeth adoun. By God, ye be to blame!
Helpeth me now, as I dide yow whileer;
Putte in youre hand, and looketh what is theer."

1244 **halwes:** saints'
1245 **malisoun:** curse
1265 **holwe:** hollow
1271 **hym dresse:** address himself, go
1274 **terve:** skin, flay
1277 **ordeyned:** prepared　　**jet:** contrivance
1278 **relente:** soften, melt
1281 **yede:** went

1297 **nam:** took
1300 **doublenesse:** duplicity
1304 **weerieth:** wearies, tires
1313 **ape:** dupe
1319 **heyne:** wretch
1320 **Unwityng . . . of:** ignorant of
1322 **rombled:** groped noisily about
1327 **to blame:** blameworthy
1328 **whileer:** just now

This preest took up this silver teyne anon,   1330
And thanne seyde the chanoun, "Lat us gon
With thise thre teynes, whiche that we han wroght,
To som goldsmyth and wite if they been oght,
For, by my feith, I nolde, for myn hood,
But if that they were silver fyn and good,   1335
And that as swithe preeved it shal bee."
　　Unto the goldsmyth with thise teynes three
They wente and putte thise teynes in assay
To fir and hamer; myghte no man seye nay,
But that they weren as hem oghte be.   1340
　　This sotted preest, who was gladder than he?
Was nevere brid gladder agayn the day,
Ne nyghtyngale, in the sesoun of May,
Was nevere noon that luste bet to synge;
Ne lady lustier in carolynge,   1345
Or for to speke of love and wommanhede,
Ne knyght in armes to doon an hardy dede,
To stonden in grace of his lady deere,
Than hadde this preest this soory craft to leere.
And to the chanoun thus he spak and seyde: 1350
"For love of God, that for us alle deyde,
And as I may deserve it unto yow,
What shal this receite coste? Telleth now!"
　　"By oure Lady," quod this chanon, "it is deere,
I warne yow wel; for save I and a frere,   1355
In Engelond ther kan no man it make."
　　"No fors," quod he, "now, sire, for Goddes sake,
What shal I paye? Telleth me, I preye."
　　"Ywis," quod he, "it is ful deere, I seye.
Sire, at o word, if that thee list it have,   1360
Ye shul paye fourty pound, so God me save!
And nere the freendshipe that ye dide er this
To me, ye sholde paye moore, ywis."
　　This preest the somme of fourty pound anon
Of nobles fette, and took hem everichon   1365
To this chanoun for this ilke receite.
Al his werkyng nas but fraude and deceite.
　　"Sire preest," he seyde, "I kepe han no loos
Of my craft, for I wolde it kept were cloos;
And, as ye love me, kepeth it secree.   1370
For, and men knewen al my soutiltee,
By God, they wolden han so greet envye

To me by cause of my philosophye
I sholde be deed; ther were noon oother weye."
　　"God it forbeede," quod the preest, "what sey ye?
Yet hadde I levere spenden al the good   1376
Which that I have, and elles wexe I wood,
Than that ye sholden falle in swich mescheef."
　　"For youre good wyl, sire, have ye right good
　　　preef,"
Quod the chanoun, "and farwel, grant mercy!"   1380
He wente his wey, and never the preest hym sy
After that day; and whan that this preest shoolde
Maken assay, at swich tyme as he wolde,
Of this receit, farwel! It wolde nat be.
Lo, thus byjaped and bigiled was he!   1385
Thus maketh he his introduccioun,
To brynge folk to hir destruccioun.
　　Considereth, sires, how that, in ech estaat,
Bitwixe men and gold ther is debaat
So ferforth that unnethes is ther noon.   1390
This multiplying blent so many oon
That in good feith I trowe that it bee
The cause grettest of swich scarsetee.
Philosophres speken so mystily
In this craft that men kan nat come therby,   1395
For any wit that men han now-a-dayes.
They mowe wel chiteren as doon jayes,
And in hir termes sette hir lust and peyne,
But to hir purpos shul they nevere atteyne.
A man may lightly lerne, if he have aught,   1400
To multiplie, and brynge his good to naught!
　　Lo! swich a lucre is in this lusty game,
A mannes myrthe it wol turne unto grame,
And empten also grete and hevye purses,
And maken folk for to purchacen curses   1405
Of hem that han hir good therto ylent.
O, fy, for shame! They that han been brent,
Allas, kan they nat flee the fires heete?
Ye that it use, I rede ye it leete,
Lest ye lese al; for bet than nevere is late.   1410
Nevere to thryve were to long a date.
Though ye prolle ay, ye shul it nevere fynde.
Ye been as boold as is Bayard the blynde,
That blondreth forth and peril casteth noon.

1333 **oght:** anything, worth anything
1341 **sotted:** besotted, foolish
1342 **agayn the day:** in the sunlight (dawn)
1349 **soory:** wretched
1352 **deserve it unto yow:** repay you
1353 **receite:** recipe, formula
1362 **And nere:** if it were not for
1368–69 **I kepe han no loos Of:** I don't care to have fame for

1384 **receit:** recipe
1385 **byjaped:** tricked
1386 **introduccioun:** introductory gambit
1394 **mystily:** obscurely
1397 **chiteren:** chatter
1402 **lucre:** profit
1403 **grame:** sorrow
1409 **leete:** let (it) alone, abandon (it)
1411 **date:** time
1412 **prolle ay:** search or prowl forever
1414 **blondreth:** blunders   **casteth:** considers, reckons

He is as boold to renne agayn a stoon   1415
As for to goon bisides in the weye.
So faren ye that multiplie, I seye.
If that youre eyen kan nat seen aright,
Looke that youre mynde lakke noght his sight.
For though ye looken never so brode and stare, 1420
Ye shul nothyng wynne on that chaffare,
But wasten al that ye may rape and renne.
Withdraweth the fir, lest it to faste brenne;
Medleth namoore with that art, I mene,
For if ye doon, youre thrift is goon ful clene.   1425
And right as swithe I wol yow tellen heere
What philosophres seyn in this mateere.
    Lo, thus seith Arnold of the Newe Toun,
As his Rosarie maketh mencioun;
He seith right thus, withouten any lye: 1430
"Ther may no man mercurie mortifie
But it be with his brother knowlechyng";
How [be] that he which that first seyde this thyng
Of philosophres fader was, Hermes;
He seith how that the dragon, doutelees,   1435
Ne dyeth nat but if that he be slayn
With his brother; and that is for to sayn,
By the dragon, Mercurie, and noon oother
He understood, and brymstoon by his brother,
That out of Sol and Luna were ydrawe.   1440
"And therfore," seyde he—taak heede to my sawe—
"Lat no man bisye hym this art for to seche,
But if that he th'entencioun and speche
Of philosophres understonde kan;
And if he do, he is a lewed man.   1445
For this science and this konnyng," quod he,
"Is of the secree of the secretes, pardee."
    Also ther was a disciple of Plato,

That on a tyme seyde his maister to,
As his book Senior wol bere witnesse,   1450
And this was his demande in soothfastnesse:
"Telle me the name of the privee stoon."
    And Plato answerde unto hym anoon,
"Take the stoon that Titanos men name."   1454
    "Which is that?" quod he. "Magnasia is the same,"
Seyde Plato. "Ye, sire, and is it thus?
This is *ignotum per ignocius*.
What is Magnasia, good sire, I yow preye?"
    "It is a water that is maad, I seye,
Of elementes foure," quod Plato.   1460
    "Telle me the roote, good sire," quod he tho,
"Of that water, if it be youre wil."
    "Nay, nay," quod Plato, "certein, that I nyl.
The philosophres sworn were everychoon
That they sholden discovere it unto noon,   1465
Ne in no book it write in no manere.
For unto Crist it is so lief and deere
That he wol nat that it discovered bee,
But where it liketh to his deitee
Men for t'enspire, and eek for to deffende   1470
Whom that hym liketh; lo, this is the ende."
    Thanne conclude I thus, sith that God of hevene
Ne wil nat that the philosophres nevene
How that a man shal come unto this stoon,
I rede, as for the beste, lete it goon.   1475
For whoso maketh God his adversarie,
As for to werken any thyng in contrarie
Of his wil, certes, never shal he thryve,
Thogh that he multiplie terme of his lyve.
And there a poynt, for ended is my tale.   1480
God sende every trewe man boote of his bale!

Heere is ended the Chanouns Yemannes Tale.

1422 **rape and renne:** seize and run; see n.
1424 **mene:** say
1425 **thrift:** prosperity, welfare
1428 **Arnold of the Newe Toun:** Arnaldus of Villanova, author of the *Rosarie,* an alchemical treatise
1432 **his brother knowlechyng:** his brother's (sulphur's) help
1434 **Hermes:** Hermes Trismegistus, legendary founder of alchemy
1440 **Sol:** the sun (gold)   **Luna:** the moon (silver)

1450 **book Senior:** an alchemical treatise attributed to Senior Zadith
1454–55 **Titanos, Magnasia:** probably gypsum and magnesium oxide, but used as "cover names," intended to conceal the identity of the materials
1457 **ignotum per ignocius:** explaining the unknown by the more unknown
1470 **t'enspire:** to enlighten
1473 **nevene:** name
1477 **any thyng:** at all
1481 **boote of his bale:** remedy for his suffering

❂

The Manciple's Prologue

❂

Heere folweth the Prologe of the Maunciples Tale.

Woot ye nat where ther stant a litel toun
Which that ycleped is Bobbe-up-and-doun,
Under the Blee, in Caunterbury Weye?
Ther gan oure Hooste for to jape and pleye,
And seyde, "Sires, what! Dun is in the myre!   5
Is ther no man, for preyere ne for hyre,
That wole awake oure felawe al bihynde?
A theef myghte hym ful lightly robbe and bynde.
See how he nappeth! See how, for cokkes bones,
That he wol falle fro his hors atones!   10
Is that a cook of Londoun, with meschaunce?
Do hym come forth, he knoweth his penaunce;
For he shal telle a tale, by my fey,
Although it be nat worth a botel hey.   14
Awake, thou Cook," quod he, "God yeve thee sorwe!
What eyleth thee to slepe by the morwe?
Hastow had fleen al nyght, or artow dronke?
Or hastow with som quene al nyght yswonke,
So that thow mayst nat holden up thyn heed?"

This Cook, that was ful pale and no thyng reed,   20
Seyde to oure Hoost, "So God my soule blesse,
As ther is falle on me swich hevynesse,
Noot I nat why, that me were levere slepe
Than the beste galon wyn in Chepe."

"Wel," quod the Manciple, "if it may doon ese   25
To thee, sire Cook, and to no wight displese,
Which that heere rideth in this compaignye,
And that oure Hoost wole, of his curteisye,
I wol as now excuse thee of thy tale.
For, in good feith, thy visage is ful pale,   30
Thyne eyen daswen eek, as that me thynketh,

And, wel I woot, thy breeth ful soure stynketh:
That sheweth wel thou art nat wel disposed.
Of me, certeyn, thou shalt nat been yglosed.
See how he ganeth, lo, this dronken wight,   35
As though he wolde swolwe us anonright.
Hoold cloos thy mouth, man, by thy fader kyn!
The devel of helle sette his foot therin!
Thy cursed breeth infecte wole us alle.
Fy, stynkyng swyn! Fy, foule moote thee falle!   40
A, taketh heede, sires, of this lusty man.
Now, sweete sire, wol ye justen atte fan?
Therto me thynketh ye been wel yshape!
I trowe that ye dronken han wyn ape,
And that is whan men pleyen with a straw."   45
And with this speche the Cook wax wrooth and wraw,
And on the Manciple he gan nodde faste
For lakke of speche, and doun the hors hym caste,
Where as he lay, til that men hym up took.
This was a fair chyvachee of a cook!   50
Allas, he nadde holde hym by his ladel!
And er that he agayn were in his sadel,
Ther was greet showvyng bothe to and fro
To lifte hym up, and muchel care and wo,
So unweeldy was this sory palled goost.   55
And to the Manciple thanne spak oure Hoost:

"By cause drynke hath dominacioun
Upon this man, by my savacioun,
I trowe he lewedly wolde telle his tale.
For, were it wyn or oold or moysty ale   60
That he hath dronke, he speketh in his nose,
And fneseth faste, and eek he hath the pose.

"He hath also to do moore than ynough
To kepen hym and his capul out of the slough;

---

2 **Bobbe-up-and-doun:** Harbledown, two miles from Canterbury; see n.
3 **the Blee:** Blean Forest
5 **Dun is in the myre:** Things are at a standstill; see n.
8 **lightly:** easily
9 **nappeth:** dozes **cokkes bones:** cock's bones (euphemism for God's bones)
14 **botel hey:** small bundle of hay (i.e., worthless)
17 **fleen:** fleas
18 **quene:** trollop, whore
22 **hevynesse:** drowsiness
24 **galon wyn:** gallon of wine
31 **daswen:** are dazed

33 **nat wel disposed:** indisposed, unwell
35 **ganeth:** yawns
42 **justen atte fan:** joust at the quintain; see n.
44 **dronken han wyn ape:** have reached an advanced stage of drunkenness
46 **wraw:** angry
47 **nodde:** shake his head
50 **chyvachee:** feat of horsemanship
51 **ladel:** long-handled spoon
55 **unweeldy:** feeble **palled:** grown pale
60 **oold or moysty ale:** old or new ale; see n.
62 **fneseth:** sneezes **pose:** head cold
64 **slough:** mud, mire

And if he falle from his capul eftsoone, 65
Thanne shal we alle have ynogh to doone
In liftyng up his hevy dronken cors.
Telle on thy tale; of hym make I no fors.
    "But yet, Manciple, in feith thou art to nyce,
Thus openly repreve hym of his vice. 70
Another day he wole, peraventure,
Reclayme thee and brynge thee to lure;
I meene, he speke wole of smale thynges,
As for to pynchen at thy rekenynges,
That were nat honest, if it cam to preef." 75
    "No," quod the Manciple, "that were a greet
        mescheef!
So myghte he lightly brynge me in the snare.
Yet hadde I levere payen for the mare
Which he rit on, than he sholde with me stryve.
I wol nat wratthen hym, also moot I thryve! 80
That that I spak, I seyde it in my bourde.
And wite ye what? I have heer in a gourde
A draghte of wyn, ye, of a ripe grape,
And right anon ye shul seen a good jape.

This Cook shal drynke therof, if I may. 85
Up peyne of deeth, he wol nat seye me nay."
    And certeynly, to tellen as it was,
Of this vessel the Cook drank faste, allas!
What neded hym? He drank ynough biforn.
And whan he hadde pouped in this horn, 90
To the Manciple he took the gourde agayn;
And of that drynke the Cook was wonder fayn,
And thanked hym in swich wise as he koude.
    Thanne gan oure Hoost to laughen wonder loude,
And seyde, "I se wel it is necessarie, 95
Where that we goon, good drynke with us carie;
For that wol turne rancour and disese
T'acord and love, and many a wrong apese.
    "O Bacus, yblessed be thy name,
That so kanst turnen ernest into game! 100
Worshipe and thank be to thy deitee!
Of that mateere ye gete namoore of me.
Telle on thy tale, Manciple, I thee preye."
    "Wel, sire," quod he, "now herkneth what I seye."

The Manciple's Tale

Heere bigynneth the Maunciples Tale of the Crowe.

Whan Phebus dwelled heere in this erthe adoun,
As olde bookes maken mencioun, 106
He was the mooste lusty bachiler
In al this world, and eek the beste archer.
He slow Phitoun, the serpent, as he lay
Slepynge agayn the sonne upon a day; 110
And many another noble worthy dede
He with his bowe wroghte, as men may rede.
    Pleyen he koude on every mynstralcie,
And syngen that it was a melodie

To heeren of his cleere voys the soun. 115
Certes the kyng of Thebes, Amphioun,
That with his syngyng walled that citee,
Koude nevere syngen half so wel as hee.
Therto he was the semelieste man
That is or was sith that the world bigan. 120
What nedeth it his fetures to discryve?
For in this world was noon so faire on-lyve.
He was therwith fulfild of gentillesse,
Of honour, and of parfit worthynesse.
    This Phebus, that was flour of bachilrie, 125
As wel in fredom as in chivalrie,
For his desport, in signe eek of victorie
Of Phitoun, so as telleth us the storie,
Was wont to beren in his hand a bowe. 129

65 **capul:** horse   **eftsoone:** again
66 **have ynogh to doone:** have our hands full
72 Recall you with a lure (as a hawk)
74 **pynchen at:** find fault with
80 **wratthen:** anger
81 **bourde:** jest
82 **gourde:** gourd-shaped flask

105 **Phebus:** Phoebus Apollo
109 **Phitoun:** Python; see n.
110 **agayn the sonne:** in front of or in the sun
113 **mynstralcie:** musical instrument

90 **pouped:** blown
91 **took . . . agayn:** gave back
98 **apese:** remedy
99 **Bacus:** Bacchus, god of wine

121 **fetures:** features, appearance
125 **bachilrie:** knighthood

Now hadde this Phebus in his hous a crowe
Which in a cage he fostred many a day,
And taughte it speken, as men teche a jay.
Whit was this crowe as is a snow-whit swan,
And countrefete the speche of every man
He koude, whan he sholde telle a tale.   135
Therwith in al this world no nyghtyngale
Ne koude, by an hondred thousand deel,
Syngen so wonder myrily and weel.
Now hadde this Phebus in his hous a wyf
Which that he lovede moore than his lyf,   140
And nyght and day dide evere his diligence
Hir for to plese and doon hire reverence,
Save oonly, if the sothe that I shal sayn,
Jalous he was, and wolde have kept hire fayn.
For hym were looth byjaped for to be,   145
And so is every wight in swich degree;
But al in ydel, for it availleth noght.
A good wyf, that is clene of werk and thoght,
Sholde nat been kept in noon awayt, certayn;
And trewely the labour is in vayn   150
To kepe a shrewe, for it wol nat bee.
This holde I for a verray nycetee,
To spille labour for to kepe wyves:
Thus writen olde clerkes in hir lyves.
But now to purpos, as I first bigan: 155
This worthy Phebus dooth al that he kan
To plesen hire, wenynge for swich plesaunce,
And for his manhede and his governaunce,
That no man sholde han put hym from hir grace.
But God it woot, ther may no man embrace   160
As to destreyne a thyng which that nature
Hath natureelly set in a creature.
Taak any bryd, and put it in a cage,
And do al thyn entente and thy corage
To fostre it tendrely with mete and drynke   165
Of alle deyntees that thou kanst bithynke,
And keep it al so clenly as thou may,
Although his cage of gold be never so gay,
Yet hath this brid, by twenty thousand foold,
Levere in a forest that is rude and coold   170
Goon ete wormes and swich wrecchednesse.
For evere this brid wol doon his bisynesse
To escape out of his cage, yif he may.
His libertee this brid desireth ay.

Lat take a cat, and fostre hym wel with milk   175
And tendre flessh, and make his couche of silk,
And lat hym seen a mous go by the wal,
Anon he weyveth milk and flessh and al,
And every deyntee that is in that hous,
Swich appetit hath he to ete a mous.   180
Lo, heere hath lust his dominacioun,
And appetit fleemeth discrecioun.
A she-wolf hath also a vileyns kynde.
The lewedeste wolf that she may fynde,
Or leest of reputacioun, wol she take,   185
In tyme whan hir lust to han a make.
Alle thise ensamples speke I by thise men
That been untrewe, and nothyng by wommen.
For men han evere a likerous appetit
On lower thyng to parfourne hire delit   190
Than on hire wyves, be they never so faire,
Ne never so trewe, ne so debonaire.
Flessh is so newefangel, with meschaunce,
That we ne konne in nothyng han plesaunce
That sowneth into vertu any while.   195
This Phebus, which that thoghte upon no gile,
Deceyved was, for al his jolitee.
For under hym another hadde shee,
A man of litel reputacioun,
Nat worth to Phebus in comparisoun.   200
The moore harm is, it happeth ofte so,
Of which ther cometh muchel harm and wo.
And so bifel, whan Phebus was absent,
His wyf anon hath for hir lemman sent.
Hir lemman? Certes, this is a knavyssh speche!   205
Foryeveth it me, and that I yow biseche.
The wise Plato seith, as ye may rede,
The word moot nede accorde with the dede.
If men shal telle proprely a thyng,
The word moot cosyn be to the werkyng.   210
I am a boystous man, right thus seye I:
Ther nys no difference, trewely,
Bitwixe a wyf that is of heigh degree,
If of hir body dishonest she bee,
And a povre wenche, oother than this—   215

139 **wyf:** woman
145 **byjaped:** tricked
149 **kept in . . . awayt:** watched suspiciously
158 **manhede:** qualities of a good man   **governaunce:** behavior
161 **destreyne:** restrain
164 And give all your attention, take all pains
166 **bithynke:** imagine
167 **clenly:** carefully
169–170 **hath . . . Levere:** would rather

175 **Lat take:** assume that one takes
178 **weyveth:** refuses
182 **fleemeth:** drives out
183 **vileyns:** churlish, evil
193 **newefangel:** fond of novelty
195 **sowneth into:** tends toward, is conducive to
197 **jolitee:** attractiveness
198 **under:** in addition to
204 **lemman:** lover
205 **knavyssh:** churlish
211 **boystous:** plain
214 **dishonest:** unchaste
215 **wenche:** low-class woman

If it so be they werke bothe amys—
But that the gentile, in estaat above,
She shal be cleped his lady, as in love;
And for that oother is a povre womman,
She shal be cleped his wenche or his lemman.   220
And, God it woot, myn owene deere brother,
Men leyn that oon as lowe as lith that oother.

    Right so bitwixe a titlelees tiraunt
And an outlawe or a theef erraunt,
The same I seye: ther is no difference.   225
To Alisaundre was toold this sentence,
That, for the tirant is of gretter myght
By force of meynee for to sleen dounright,
And brennen hous and hoom, and make al playn,
Lo, therfore is he cleped a capitayn;   230
And for the outlawe hath but smal meynee,
And may nat doon so greet an harm as he,
Ne brynge a contree to so greet mescheef,
Men clepen hym an outlawe or a theef.
But for I am a man noght textueel,   235
I wol noght telle of textes never a deel;
I wol go to my tale, as I bigan.
Whan Phebus wyf had sent for hir lemman,
Anon they wroghten al hire lust volage.

    The white crowe, that heeng ay in the cage,   240
Biheeld hire werk, and seyde never a word.
And whan that hoom was come Phebus, the lord,
This crowe sang "Cokkow! Cokkow! Cokkow!"

    "What, bryd?" quod Phebus. "What song
      syngestow?
Ne were thow wont so myrily to synge   245
That to myn herte it was a rejoysynge
To heere thy voys? Allas, what song is this?"

    "By God," quod he, "I synge nat amys.
Phebus," quod he, "for al thy worthynesse,
For al thy beautee and thy gentilesse,   250
For al thy song and al thy mynstralcye,
For al thy waityng, blered is thyn ye
With oon of litel reputacioun,
Noght worth to thee, as in comparisoun,
The montance of a gnat, so moote I thryve!   255
For on thy bed thy wyf I saugh hym swyve."

    What wol ye moore? The crowe anon hym tolde,

By sadde tokenes and by wordes bolde,
How that his wyf had doon hire lecherye,
Hym to greet shame and to greet vileynye,   260
And tolde hym ofte he saugh it with his yen.

    This Phebus gan aweyward for to wryen,
And thoughte his sorweful herte brast atwo.
His bowe he bente, and sette therinne a flo,
And in his ire his wyf thanne hath he slayn.   265
This is th'effect; ther is namoore to sayn;
For sorwe of which he brak his mynstralcie,
Bothe harpe, and lute, and gyterne, and sautrie;
And eek he brak his arwes and his bowe,
And after that thus spak he to the crowe: 270

    "Traitour," quod he, "with tonge of scorpioun,
Thou hast me broght to my confusioun;
Allas, that I was wroght! Why nere I deed?
O deere wyf! O gemme of lustiheed!
That were to me so sad and eek so trewe,   275
Now listow deed, with face pale of hewe,
Ful giltelees, that dorste I swere, ywys!
O rakel hand, to doon so foule amys!
O trouble wit, O ire recchelees,
That unavysed smyteth gilteles!   280
O wantrust, ful of fals suspecion,
Where was thy wit and thy discrecion?
O every man, be war of rakelnesse!
Ne trowe no thyng withouten strong witnesse.
Smyt nat to soone, er that ye witen why,   285
And beeth avysed wel and sobrely
Er ye doon any execucion
Upon youre ire for suspecion.
Allas, a thousand folk hath rakel ire
Fully fordoon, and broght hem in the mire.   290
Allas! For sorwe I wol myselven slee!"

    And to the crowe, "O false theef!" seyde he,
"I wol thee quite anon thy false tale.
Thou songe whilom lyk a nyghtyngale;
Now shaltow, false theef, thy song forgon,   295
And eek thy white fetheres everichon,
Ne nevere in al thy lif ne shaltou speke.
Thus shal men on a traytour been awreke;
Thou and thyn ofspryng evere shul be blake,

---

228 **force of meynee:** power of his retinue, size of his army
235 **textueel:** learned in authoritative texts
239 **volage:** flighty, foolish
243 **Cokkow:** cuckoo (i.e., you are a cuckold)
246 **rejoysynge:** joy
252 **blered is thyn ye:** you have been tricked, deluded
255 **montance:** value
256 **swyve:** copulate with

258 **sadde tokenes:** strong confirmatory details, proofs
262 **wryen:** turn, go
264 **flo:** arrow
268 **gyterne:** cithern   **sautrie:** psaltry, a lute-like instrument
274 **lustiheed:** delight
275 **sad:** stable
278 **rakel:** rash, hasty
280 **unavysed:** recklessly
281 **wantrust:** distrust
283 **rakelnesse:** rashness, haste
290 **fordoon:** undone
295 **forgon:** lose
298 **awreke:** avenged

Ne nevere sweete noyse shul ye make,   300
But evere crie agayn tempest and rayn,
In tokenynge that thurgh thee my wyf is slayn."
And to the crowe he stirte, and that anon,
And pulled his white fetheres everychon,
And made hym blak, and refte hym al his song,   305
And eek his speche, and out at dore hym slong
Unto the devel, which I hym bitake;
And for this caas been alle crowes blake.

    Lordynges, by this ensample I yow preye,
Beth war, and taketh kep what that ye seye: 310
Ne telleth nevere no man in youre lyf
How that another man hath dight his wyf;
He wol yow haten mortally, certeyn.
Daun Salomon, as wise clerkes seyn,
Techeth a man to kepen his tonge weel.   315
But, as I seyde, I am noght textueel.
But nathelees, thus taughte me my dame:
"My sone, thenk on the crowe, a Goddes name!
My sone, keep wel thy tonge, and keep thy freend.
A wikked tonge is worse than a feend;   320
My sone, from a feend men may hem blesse.
My sone, God of his endelees goodnesse
Walled a tonge with teeth and lippes eke,
For man sholde hym avyse what he speeke.
My sone, ful ofte, for to muche speche   325
Hath many a man been spilt, as clerkes teche,
But for litel speche avysely
Is no man shent, to speke generally.
My sone, thy tonge sholdestow restreyne
At alle tymes, but whan thou doost thy peyne   330
To speke of God, in honour and preyere.

The firste vertu, sone, if thou wolt leere,
Is to restreyne and kepe wel thy tonge;
Thus lerne children whan that they been yonge.
My sone, of muchel spekyng yvele avysed,   335
Ther lasse spekyng hadde ynough suffised,
Comth muchel harm; thus was me toold and taught.
In muchel speche synne wanteth naught.
Wostow wherof a rakel tonge serveth?
Right as a swerd forkutteth and forkerveth   340
An arm a-two, my deere sone, right so
A tonge kutteth freendshipe al a-two.
A jangler is to God abhomynable.
Reed Salomon, so wys and honurable;
Reed David in his psalmes; reed Senekke.   345
My sone, spek nat, but with thyn heed thou bekke.
Dissimule as thou were deef, if that thou heere
A janglere speke of perilous mateere.
The Flemyng seith, and lerne it if thee leste,
That litel janglyng causeth muchel reste.   350
My sone, if thou no wikked word hast seyd,
Thee thar nat drede for to be biwreyd;
But he that hath mysseyd, I dar wel sayn,
He may by no wey clepe his word agayn.
Thyng that is seyd is seyd, and forth it gooth, 355
Though hym repente, or be hym nevere so looth.
He is his thral to whom that he hath sayd
A tale of which he is now yvele apayd.
My sone, be war, and be noon auctour newe
Of tidynges, wheither they been false or trewe. 360
Whereso thou come, amonges hye or lowe,
Kepe wel thy tonge and thenk upon the crowe."

Heere is ended the Maunciples Tale of the Crowe.

❁

The Parson's Prologue

❁

Heere folweth the Prologe of the Persouns Tale.

By that the Maunciple hadde his tale al ended,
The sonne fro the south lyne was descended
So lowe that he nas nat, to my sighte,
Degreës nyne and twenty as in highte.
Foure of the clokke it was tho, as I gesse, 5
For ellevene foot, or litel moore or lesse,
My shadwe was at thilke tyme, as there,
Of swiche feet as my lengthe parted were
In sixe feet equal of proporcioun.
Therwith the moones exaltacioun— 10
I meene Libra—alwey gan ascende
As we were entryng at a thropes ende;
For which oure Hoost, as he was wont to gye,
As in this caas, oure joly compaignye,
Seyde in this wise: "Lordynges everichoon, 15
Now lakketh us no tales mo than oon.
Fulfilled is my sentence and my decree;
I trowe that we han herd of ech degree;
Almoost fulfild is al myn ordinaunce.
I pray to God, so yeve hym right good chaunce, 20
That telleth this tale to us lustily.
"Sire preest," quod he, "artow a vicary?
Or arte a person? Sey sooth, by thy fey!
Be what thou be, ne breke thou nat oure pley;
For every man, save thou, hath toold his tale. 25
Unbokele and shewe us what is in thy male;
For trewely, me thynketh by thy cheere
Thou sholdest knytte up wel a greet mateere.
Telle us a fable anon, for cokkes bones!"
This Persoun answerde, al atones, 30
"Thou getest fable noon ytoold for me,
For Paul, that writeth unto Thymothee,
Repreveth hem that weyven soothfastnesse

And tellen fables and swich wrecchednesse.
Why sholde I sowen draf out of my fest, 35
Whan I may sowen whete, if that me lest?
For which I seye, if that yow list to heere
Moralitee and vertuous mateere,
And thanne that ye wol yeve me audience,
I wol ful fayn, at Cristes reverence, 40
Do yow plesaunce leefful, as I kan.
But trusteth wel, I am a Southren man;
I kan nat geeste 'rum, ram, ruf,' by lettre,
Ne, God woot, rym holde I but litel bettre;
And therfore, if yow list—I wol nat glose— 45
I wol yow telle a myrie tale in prose
To knytte up al this feeste and make an ende.
And Jhesu, for his grace, wit me sende
To shewe yow the wey, in this viage,
Of thilke parfit glorious pilgrymage 50
That highte Jerusalem celestial.
And if ye vouche sauf, anon I shal
Bigynne upon my tale, for which I preye
Telle youre avys; I kan no bettre seye.
"But nathelees, this meditacioun 55
I putte it ay under correccioun
Of clerkes, for I am nat textueel;
I take but the sentence, trusteth weel.
Therfore I make protestacioun
That I wol stonde to correccioun." 60
Upon this word we han assented soone,
For, as it seemed, it was for to doone—
To enden in som vertuous sentence,
And for to yeve hym space and audience,
And bade oure Hoost he sholde to hym seye 65
That alle we to telle his tale hym preye.
Oure Hoost hadde the wordes for us alle;
"Sire preest," quod he, "now faire yow bifalle!

---

3 **to my sighte:** from my point of view
7 **as there:** in that place
10 **exaltacioun:** zodiacal sign in which a planet has its strongest influence
12 **thropes ende:** the edge of a village
22 **vicary:** vicar
24 **breke . . . oure pley:** spoil our game
26 **Unbokele:** unbuckle, open up   **in thy male:** i.e., what you have to tell
28 **knytte up:** conclude
29 **cokkes bones:** cock's bones (euphemism for God's bones)
33 **weyven:** turn aside from

35 **draf:** chaff
39 **that:** if
41 **leefful:** lawful, legitimate
42 **Southren:** That is, not from the north, where much alliterative poetry was written
43 **geeste . . . by lettre:** tell a story in alliterative verse
57 **textueel:** learned in authoritative texts
58 **sentence:** substance, essential meaning
64 **space:** time
67 **hadde the wordes for us alle:** was our spokesman
68 **faire yow bifalle:** good luck to you

Telleth," quod he, "youre meditacioun.
But hasteth yow; the sonne wole adoun;   70
Beth fructuous, and that in litel space,

And to do wel God sende yow his grace!
Sey what yow list, and we wol gladly heere."
And with that word he seyde in this manere.

Explicit prohemium.

The Parson's Tale

Heere bigynneth the Persouns Tale.

Jer. 6°. State super vias, et videte, et interrogate de viis antiquis que sit via bona, et ambulate in ea; et invenietis refrigerium animabus vestris, etc.

Oure sweete Lord God of hevene, that no man wole perisse but wole that we comen alle to the knoweleche of hym and to the blisful lif that is perdurable,/ amonesteth us by the prophete Jeremie, that seith in thys wyse:/ "Stondeth upon the weyes, and seeth and axeth of olde pathes (that is to seyn, of olde sentences) which is the goode wey,/ and walketh in that wey, and ye shal fynde refresshynge for youre soules, etc."/ Manye been the weyes espirituels that leden folk to oure Lord Jhesu Crist and to the regne of glorie./ Of whiche weyes ther is a ful noble wey and a ful covenable, which may nat fayle to man ne to womman that thurgh synne hath mysgoon fro the righte wey of Jerusalem celestial;/ and this wey is cleped Penitence, of which man sholde gladly herknen and enquere with al his herte/ to wyten what is Penitence, and whennes it is cleped Penitence, and in how manye maneres been the acciouns or werkynges of Penitence,/ and how manye speces ther been of Penitence, and whiche thynges apertenen and bihoven to Penitence, and whiche thynges destourben Penitence./

Seint Ambrose seith that Penitence is the pleynynge of man for the gilt that he hath doon, and namoore to do any thyng for which hym oghte to pleyne./ And som doctour seith, "Penitence is the waymentynge of man that sorweth for his synne and pyneth hymself for he hath mysdoon."/ Penitence, with certeyne circumstances, is verray repentance of a man that halt hymself in sorwe and oother peyne for his giltes./ And for he shal be verray penitent, he shal first biwaylen the synnes that he hath doon, and stidefastly purposen in his herte to have shrift of mouthe, and to doon satisfaccioun,/ and nevere to doon thyng for which hym oghte moore to biwayle or to compleyne, and to continue in goode werkes, or elles his repentance may nat availle./ For, as seith Seint Ysidre, "He is a japere and a gabbere and no verray repentant that eftsoone dooth thyng for which hym oghte repente."/ Wepynge, and nat for to stynte to do synne, may nat avayle./ But nathelees, men shal hope that every tyme that man falleth, be it never so ofte, that he may arise thurgh Penitence, if he have grace; but certeinly it is greet doute./ For, as seith Seint Gregorie, "Unnethe ariseth he out of his synne, that is charged with the charge of yvel usage."/ And therfore repentant folk, that stynte for to synne and forlete synne er that synne forlete hem, hooly chirche holdeth hem siker of hire savacioun./ And he that synneth and verraily repenteth hym in his laste, hooly chirche yet hopeth his savacioun, by the grete mercy of oure Lord Jhesu Crist, for his repentaunce; but taak the siker wey./

And now, sith I have declared yow what thyng is Penitence, now shul ye understonde that ther been

85

89

90

---

71 **fructuous:** fruitful

State super vias, *etc.*: translated in lines 77–78
76 **amonesteth:** admonishes
77 **sentences:** teachings, opinions
80 **covenable:** suitable
83 **apertenen:** belong to

85 **som:** a certain   **waymentynge:** lamenting   **pyneth:** punishes
89 **Ysidre:** Isidore of Seville   **gabbere:** foolish talker

three acciouns of Penitence./ The firste is that   95
if a man be baptized after that he hath
synned./ Seint Augustyn seith, "But he be penytent
for his olde synful lyf, he may nat bigynne the newe
clene lif."/ For, certes, if he be baptized withouten
penitence of his olde gilt, he receyveth the mark of
baptesme but nat the grace ne the remission of his
synnes, til he have repentance verray./ Another
defaute is this: that men doon deedly synne after that
they han receyved baptesme./ The thridde defaute is
that men fallen in venial synnes after hir
baptesme fro day to day./ Therof seith Seint   100
Augustyn that penitence of goode and humble
folk is the penitence of every day./

The speces of Penitence been three. That oon of
hem is solempne, another is commune, and the
thridde is privee./ Thilke penance that is solempne is
in two maneres; as to be put out of hooly chirche in
Lente for slaughtre of children, and swich maner
thyng./ Another is, whan a man hath synned openly,
of which synne the fame is openly spoken in the contree, and thanne hooly chirche by juggement
destreyneth hym for to do open penaunce./ Commune
penaunce is that preestes enjoynen men communly in
certeyn caas, as for to goon peraventure
naked in pilgrimages, or barefoot./ Pryvee   105
penaunce is thilke that men doon alday for
privee synnes, of whiche we shryve us prively and
receyve privee penaunce./

Now shaltow understande what is bihovely and
necessarie to verray parfit Penitence. And this stant
on three thynges:/ Contricioun of Herte, Confessioun
of Mouth, and Satisfaccioun./ For which seith Seint
John Crisostom, "Penitence destreyneth a man to
accepte benygnely every peyne that hym is enjoyned,
with contricioun of herte, and shrift of mouth, with
satisfaccioun, and in werkynge of alle manere
humylitee."/ And this is fruytful penitence agayn
three thynges in which we wratthe oure Lord
Jhesu Crist;/ this is to seyn, by delit in   110
thynkynge, by reccheleesnesse in spekynge,
and by wikked synful werkynge./ And agayns thise
wikkede giltes is Penitence, that may be likned unto a
tree./

The roote of this tree is Contricioun, that hideth
hym in the herte of hym that is verray repentaunt,
right as the roote of a tree hydeth hym in the erthe./
Of the roote of Contricioun spryngeth a stalke that
bereth braunches and leves of Confessioun, and fruyt
of Satisfaccioun./ For which Crist seith in his gospel,
"Dooth digne fruyt of Penitence"; for by this fruyt
may men knowe this tree, and nat by the roote that is
hyd in the herte of man, ne by the braunches,
ne by the leves of Confessioun./ And therfore   115
oure Lord Jhesu Crist seith thus: "By the
fruyt of hem shul ye knowen hem."/ Of this roote eek
spryngeth a seed of grace, the which seed is mooder
of sikernesse, and this seed is egre and hoot./ The
grace of this seed spryngeth of God thurgh remembrance of the day of doom and on the peynes of
helle./ Of this matere seith Salomon that in the drede
of God man forleteth his synne./ The heete of this
seed is the love of God and the desiryng of
the joye perdurable./ This heete draweth the   120
herte of a man to God and dooth hym haten
his synne./ For soothly ther is nothyng that savoureth
so wel to a child as the milk of his norice, ne nothyng
is to hym moore abhomynable than thilke milk whan
it is medled with oother mete./ Right so the synful
man that loveth his synne, hym semeth that it is to
him moost sweete of any thyng;/ but fro that tyme
that he loveth sadly oure Lord Jhesu Crist, and
desireth the lif perdurable, ther nys to him no thyng
moore abhomynable./ For soothly the lawe of God is
the love of God; for which David the prophete seith:
"I have loved thy lawe and hated wikkednesse and
hate"; he that loveth God kepeth his lawe and
his word./ This tree saugh the prophete Daniel   125
in spirit, upon the avysioun of the kyng Nabugodonosor, whan he conseiled hym to do penitence./
Penaunce is the tree of lyf to hem that it receyven,
and he that holdeth hym in verray penitence is
blessed, after the sentence of Salomon./

In this Penitence or Contricioun man shal understonde foure thynges; that is to seyn, what is Contricioun, and whiche been the causes that moeven a
man to Contricioun, and how he sholde be contrit,

---

95 **acciouns**: effects
104 **destreyneth**: constrains, compels
107 **bihovely**: necessary
110 **wratthe**: anger

115 **digne**: worthy
117 **egre**: bitter
122 **medled**: mixed
124 **perdurable**: eternal

and what Contricioun availleth to the soule./ Thanne is it thus: that Contricioun is the verray sorwe that a man receyveth in his herte for his synnes, with sad purpos to shryve hym, and to do penaunce, and neveremoore to do synne./ And this sorwe shal been in this manere, as seith Seint Bernard: "It shal been hevy and grevous, and ful sharp and poynaunt in herte."/ First, for man hath agilt his Lord   130 and his Creatour; and moore sharp and poynaunt for he hath agilt hys Fader celestial;/ and yet moore sharp and poynaunt for he hath wrathed and agilt hym that boghte hym, that with his precious blood hath delivered us fro the bondes of synne, and fro the crueltee of the devel, and fro the peynes of helle./

The causes that oghte moeve a man to Contricioun been sixe. First a man shal remembre hym of his synnes;/ but looke he that thilke remembraunce ne be to hym no delit by no wey, but greet shame and sorwe for his gilt. For Job seith, "Synful men doon werkes worthy of confusioun."/ And therfore seith Ezechie, "I wol remembre me alle the yeres of my lyf in bitternesse of myn herte."/ And God seith in   135 the Apocalipse, "Remembreth yow fro whennes that ye been falle"; for biforn that tyme that ye synned, ye were the children of God and lymes of the regne of God;/ but for youre synne ye been woxen thral, and foul, and membres of the feend, hate of aungels, sclaundre of hooly chirche, and foode of the false serpent, perpetueel matere of the fir of helle;/ and yet moore foul and abhomynable, for ye trespassen so ofte tyme as dooth the hound that retourneth to eten his spewyng./ And yet be ye fouler for youre longe continuyng in synne and youre synful usage, for which ye be roten in youre synne, as a beest in his dong./ Swiche manere of thoghtes maken a man to have shame of his synne, and no delit, as God seith by the prophete Ezechiel,/   140 "Ye shal remembre yow of youre weyes, and they shuln displese yow." Soothly synnes been the weyes that leden folk to helle./

The seconde cause that oghte make a man to have desdeyn of synne is this: that, as seith Seint Peter, "whoso that dooth synne is thral of synne"; and synne put a man in greet thraldom./ And therfore seith the prophete Ezechiel: "I wente sorweful in desdayn of myself." Certes, wel oghte a man have desdayn of synne and withdrawe hym from that thraldom and vileynye./ And lo, what seith Seneca in this matere? He seith thus: "Though I wiste that neither God ne man ne sholde nevere knowe it, yet wolde I have desdayn for to do synne."/ And the same Seneca also seith, "I am born to gretter thynges than to be thral to my body, or than for to maken of my body a thral."/ Ne a fouler thral may no man   145 ne womman maken of his body than for to yeven his body to synne./ Al were it the fouleste cherl or the fouleste womman that lyveth, and leest of value, yet is he thanne moore foul and moore in servitute./ Evere fro the hyer degree that man falleth, the moore is he thral, and moore to God and to the world vile and abhomynable./ O goode God, wel oghte man have desdayn of synne, sith that thurgh synne ther he was free now is he maked bonde./ And therfore seyth Seint Augustyn: "If thou hast desdayn of thy servant, if he agilte or synne, have thou thanne desdayn that thou thyself sholdest do synne."/   150 Tak reward of thy value, that thou ne be to foul to thyself./ Allas, wel oghten they thanne have desdayn to been servauntz and thralles to synne, and soore been ashamed of hemself/ that God of his endelees goodnesse hath set hem in heigh estaat, or yeven hem wit, strengthe of body, heele, beautee, prosperitee,/ and boghte hem fro the deeth with his herte-blood, that they so unkyndely, agayns his gentilesse, quiten hym so vileynsly to slaughtre of hir owene soules./ O goode God, ye wommen that been of so greet beautee, remembreth yow of the proverbe of Salomon. He seith,/ "Likneth a   155 fair womman that is a fool of hire body lyk to a ryng of gold that were in the groyn of a soughe."/ For right as a soughe wroteth in everich ordure, so wroteth she hire beautee in the stynkynge ordure of synne./

The thridde cause that oghte moeve a man to Contricioun is drede of the day of doom and of the horrible peynes of helle./ For as Seint Jerome seith, "At

---

130 **poynaunt:** piercing
131 **agilt:** sinned against
133 **causes:** considerations or topics for meditation that will lead one to contrition
135 **Ezechie:** Hezekiah
138 **spewyng:** vomit

149 **bonde:** bondsman, slave
151 **Tak reward of:** have regard for
153 **heele:** health
154 **agayns:** in return for   **vileynsly:** cruelly   **to slaughtre:** to the slaughter
156 **groyn of a soughe:** snout of a sow
157 **wroteth:** roots

every tyme that me remembreth of the day of doom
I quake;/ for whan I ete or drynke, or what so that I
do, evere semeth me that the trompe sowneth
in myn ere:/ 'Riseth up, ye that been dede, and   160
cometh to the juggement.' "/ O goode God,
muchel oghte a man to drede swich a juggement,
"ther as we shullen been alle," as Seint Poul seith,
"biforn the seete of oure Lord Jhesu Crist";/ whereas
he shal make a general congregacioun, whereas no
man may been absent./ For certes there availleth noon
essoyne ne excusacioun./ And nat oonly that oure
defautes shullen be jugged, but eek that alle
oure werkes shullen openly be knowe./ And,   165
as seith Seint Bernard, "Ther ne shal no pledynge availle, ne no sleighte; we shullen yeven
rekenynge of everich ydel word."/ Ther shul we han
a juge that may nat been deceyved ne corrupt. And
why? For, certes, alle oure thoghtes been discovered
as to hym, ne for preyere ne for meede he shal nat
been corrupt./ And therfore seith Salomon, "The
wratthe of God ne wol nat spare no wight, for preyere
ne for yifte"; and therfore, at the day of doom ther
nys noon hope to escape./ Wherfore, as seith Seint
Anselm, "Ful greet angwyssh shul the synful folk
have at that tyme;/ ther shal the stierne and wrothe
juge sitte above, and under hym the horrible pit of
helle open to destroyen hym that moot biknowen his
synnes, whiche synnes openly been shewed
biforn God and biforn every creature;/ and in   170
the left syde mo develes than herte may
bithynke, for to harye and drawe the synful soules to
the peyne of helle;/ and withinne the hertes of folk
shal be the bitynge conscience, and withouteforth
shal be the world al brennynge./ Whider shal thanne
the wrecched synful man flee to hiden hym? Certes,
he may nat hyden hym; he moste come forth and
shewen hym."/ For certes, as seith Seint Jerome, "the
erthe shal casten hym out of hym, and the see also,
and the eyr also, that shal be ful of thonder-clappes
and lightnynges."/ Now soothly, whoso wel remembreth hym of thise thynges, I gesse that his synne shal
nat turne hym into delit, but to greet sorwe for
drede of the peyne of helle./ And therfore   175
seith Job to God, "Suffre, Lord, that I may a

while biwaille and wepe, er I go withoute returnyng
to the derke lond, covered with the derknesse of
deeth,/ to the lond of mysese and of derknesse,
whereas is the shadwe of deeth, whereas ther is noon
ordre or ordinaunce but grisly drede that evere shal
laste."/ Loo, heere may ye seen that Job preyde respit
a while to biwepe and waille his trespas, for soothly
oo day of respit is bettre than al the tresor of this
world./ And forasmuche as a man may acquiten hymself biforn God by penitence in this world, and nat
by tresor, therfore sholde he preye to God to yeve
hym respit a while to biwepe and biwaillen his trespas./ For certes, al the sorwe that a man myghte make
fro the bigynnyng of the world nys but a litel
thyng at regard of the sorwe of helle./ The   180
cause why that Job clepeth helle the "lond of
derknesse":/ understondeth that he clepeth it "lond"
or erthe, for it is stable and nevere shal faille; "derk,"
for he that is in helle hath defaute of light material./
For certes, the derke light that shal come out of the
fyr that evere shal brenne shal turne hym al to peyne
that is in helle for it sheweth him to the horrible develes that hym tormenten./ "Covered with the derknesse
of deeth"—that is to seyn, that he that is in helle shal
have defaute of the sighte of God, for certes the
sighte of God is the lyf perdurable./ "The derknesse
of deeth" been the synnes that the wrecched man hath
doon, whiche that destourben hym to see the face of
God, right as dooth a derk clowde bitwixe us
and the sonne./ "Lond of misese," by cause   185
that ther been three maneres of defautes,
agayn three thynges that folk of this world han in this
present lyf; that is to seyn, honours, delices, and
richesses./ Agayns honour, have they in helle shame
and confusioun./ For wel ye woot that men clepen
honour the reverence that man doth to man, but in
helle is noon honour ne reverence. For certes,
namoore reverence shal be doon there to a kyng than
to a knave./ For which God seith by the prophete
Jeremye, "Thilke folk that me despisen shul been in
despit."/ Honour is eek cleped greet lordshipe; ther
shal no wight serven other, but of harm and torment.
Honour is eek cleped greet dignytee and heighnesse,
but in helle shul they been al fortroden of
develes./ And God seith, "The horrible deve-   190
les shulle goon and comen upon the hevedes
of the dampned folk." And this is for as muche as the

162 **seete:** throne
164 **essoyne:** legal excuse for failure to appear at court
171 **harye:** drag
172 **withouteforth:** outside

178 **biwepe:** weep over, mourn
182 **light material:** physical light
190 **fortroden of:** trod upon by, trampled by

hyer that they were in this present lyf, the moore
shulle they been abated and defouled in helle./
Agayns the richesse of this world shul they han
mysese of poverte, and this poverte shal been in foure
thynges:/ In defaute of tresor, of which that David
seith, "The riche folk, that embraceden and oneden al
hire herte to tresor of this world, shul slepe in the
slepynge of deeth; and nothyng ne shal they fynden
in hir handes of al hir tresor."/ And mooreover the
myseyse of helle shal been in defaute of mete and
drinke./ For God seith thus by Moyses: "They shul
been wasted with hunger, and the briddes of helle
shul devouren hem with bitter deeth, and the galle of
the dragon shal been hire drynke, and the
venym of the dragon hire morsels."/ And   195
forther over, hire myseyse shal been in
defaute of clothyng, for they shulle be naked in body
as of clothyng, save the fyr in which they brenne, and
othere filthes;/ and naked shul they been of soule, as
of alle manere vertues, which that is the clothyng of
the soule. Where been thanne the gaye robes, and the
softe shetes, and the smale shertes?/ Loo, what seith
God of hem by the prophete Ysaye: that "under hem
shul been strawed motthes, and hire covertures shulle
been of wormes of helle."/ And forther over, hir
myseyse shal been in defaute of freendes. For he nys
nat povre that hath goode freendes; but there is no
frend,/ for neither God ne no creature shal been
freend to hem, and everich of hem shal haten
oother with deedly hate./ "The sones and the   200
doghtren shullen rebellen agayns fader and
mooder, and kynrede agayns kynrede, and chiden and
despisen everich of hem oother bothe day and nyght,"
as God seith by the prophete Michias./ And the
lovynge children, that whilom loveden so flesshly
everich oother, wolden everich of hem eten oother if
they myghte./ For how sholden they love hem togidre
in the peyne of helle, whan they hated everich of hem
oother in the prosperitee of this lyf?/ For truste wel,
hir flesshly love was deedly hate, as seith the
prophete David: "Whoso that loveth wikkednesse,

he hateth his soule."/ And whoso hateth his owene
soule, certes, he may love noon oother wight
in no manere./ And therfore, in helle is no solas   205
ne no freendshipe, but evere the moore
flesshly kynredes that been in helle, the moore
cursynges, the more chidynges, and the moore deedly
hate ther is among hem./ And forther over, they shul
have defaute of alle manere delices. For certes,
delices been after the appetites of the fyve wittes, as
sighte, herynge, smellynge, savorynge, and
touchynge./ But in helle hir sighte shal be ful of derknesse and of smoke, and therfore ful of teeres; and hir
herynge ful of waymentynge and of gryntynge of
teeth, as seith Jhesu Crist./ Hir nosethirles shullen
be ful of stynkynge stynk; and, as seith Ysaye the
prophete, "hir savoryng shal be ful of bitter galle";/
and touchynge of al hir body ycovered with "fir that
nevere shal quenche and with wormes that nevere
shul dyen," as God seith by the mouth of
Ysaye./ And for as muche as they shul nat   210
wene that they may dyen for peyne, and by hir
deeth flee fro peyne, that may they understonden by
the word of Job, that seith, "ther as is the shadwe of
deeth."/ Certes, a shadwe hath the liknesse of the
thyng of which it is shadwe, but shadwe is nat the
same thyng of which it is shadwe./ Right so fareth the
peyne of helle; it is lyk deeth for the horrible
angwissh, and why? For it peyneth hem evere, as
though they sholde dye anon; but certes, they shal nat
dye./ For, as seith Seint Gregorie, "To wrecche caytyves shal be deeth withoute deeth, and ende withouten ende, and defaute withoute faillynge./ For hir
deeth shal alwey lyven, and hir ende shal everemo bigynne, and hir defaute shal nat faille."/   215
And therfore seith Seint John the Evaungelist,
"They shullen folwe deeth, and they shul nat fynde
hym; and they shul desiren to dye, and deeth shal flee
fro hem."/ And eek Job seith that in helle is noon
ordre of rule./ And al be it so that God hath creat alle
thynges in right ordre, and no thyng withouten ordre,
but alle thynges been ordeyned and nombred; yet,
nathelees, they that been dampned been nothyng in
ordre, ne holden noon ordre,/ for the erthe ne shal
bere hem no fruyt./ For, as the prophete David seith,
"God shal destroie the fruyt of the erthe as fro hem;
ne water ne shal yeve hem no moisture, ne the eyr

193 **oneden:** united
197 **smale:** delicate
198 **strawed:** strewn   **motthes:** maggots   **covertures:** bedclothes, covers
201 **Michias:** Micah

209 **nose-thirles:** nostrils

no refresshyng, ne fyr no light."/ For, as seith   220
Seint Basilie, "The brennynge of the fyr of
this world shal God yeven in helle to hem that been
dampned,/ but the light and the cleernesse shal be
yeven in hevene to his children," right as the goode
man yeveth flessh to his children and bones to his
houndes./ And for they shullen have noon hope to
escape, seith Seint Job atte laste that "ther shal hor-
rour and grisly drede dwellen withouten ende."/ Hor-
rour is alwey drede of harm that is to come, and this
drede shal evere dwelle in the hertes of hem that been
dampned. And therfore han they lorn al hire hope, for
sevene causes./ First, for God, that is hir juge, shal
be withouten mercy to hem; and they may nat plese
hym ne noon of his halwes; ne they ne may
yeve no thyng for hir raunsoun;/ ne they have   225
no voys to speke to hym; ne they may nat fle
fro peyne; ne they have no goodnesse in hem, that
they mowe shewe to delivere hem fro peyne./ And
therfore seith Salomon: "The wikked man dyeth, and
whan he is deed, he shal have noon hope to escape fro
peyne."/ Whoso thanne wolde wel understande thise
peynes and bithynke hym weel that he hath deserved
thilke peynes for his synnes, certes, he sholde have
moore talent to siken and to wepe than for to syngen
and to pleye./ For, as that seith Salomon, "Whoso that
hadde the science to knowe the peynes that been
establissed and ordeyned for synne, he wolde make
sorwe."/ "Thilke science," as seith Seint
Augustyn, "maketh a man to waymenten in   230
his herte."/

   The fourthe point that oghte maken a man to have
contricion is the sorweful remembraunce of the good
that he hath left to doon heere in erthe, and eek the
good that he hath lorn./ Soothly, the goode werkes
that he hath lost, outher they been the goode werkes
that he wroghte er he fel into deedly synne or elles
the goode werkes that he wroghte while he lay in
synne./ Soothly, the goode werkes that he dide biforn
that he fil in synne been al mortefied and astoned and
dulled by the ofte synnyng./ The othere goode
werkes, that he wroghte whil he lay in deedly synne,
thei been outrely dede, as to the lyf perdurable in
hevene./ Thanne thilke goode werkes that been

mortefied by ofte synnyng, whiche goode werkes he
dide whil he was in chari/tee, ne mowe nevere
quyken agayn withouten verray penitence./   235
And therof seith God by the mouth of
Ezechiel, that "if the rightful man returne agayn from
his rightwisnesse and werke wikkednesse, shal he
lyve?"/ Nay, for alle the goode werkes that he hath
wroght ne shul nevere been in remembraunce, for he
shal dyen in his synne./ And upon thilke chapitre
seith Seint Gregorie thus: that "we shulle understonde this principally;/ that whan we doon deedly
synne, it is for noght thanne to rehercen or drawen
into memorie the goode werkes that we han wroght
biforn."/ For certes, in the werkynge of the deedly
synne, ther is no trust to no good werk that we han
doon biforn; that is to seyn, as for to have
therby the lyf perdurable in hevene./ But   240
nathelees, the goode werkes quyken agayn,
and comen agayn, and helpen, and availlen to have
the lyf perdurable in hevene, whan we han contricioun./ But soothly, the goode werkes that men doon
whil they been in deedly synne, for as muche as they
were doon in deedly synne, they may nevere quyke
agayn./ For certes, thyng that nevere hadde lyf may
nevere quykene; and nathelees, al be it that they ne
availle noght to han the lyf perdurable, yet availlen
they to abregge of the peyne of helle, or elles to geten
temporal richesse,/ or elles that God wole the rather
enlumyne and lightne the herte of the synful man to
have repentaunce;/ and eek they availlen for to usen
a man to doon goode werkes, that the feend
have the lasse power of his soule./ And thus   245
the curteis Lord Jhesu Crist ne wole that no
good werk be lost, for in somwhat it shal availle./
But, for as muche as the goode werkes that men doon
whil they been in good lyf been al mortefied by synne
folwynge, and eek sith that alle the goode werkes that
men doon whil they been in deedly synne been outrely dede as for to have the lyf perdurable,/ wel may
that man that no good werk ne dooth synge thilke
newe Frensshe songbk, *"Jay tout perdu mon temps et
mon labour."* / For certes, synne birevith a man bothe
goodnesse of nature and eek the goodnesse of grace./

---

221 **Seint Basilie:** St. Basil
228 **talent:** desire
230 **waymenten:** lament
233 **mortefied:** killed   **astoned:** paralyzed, rendered lifeless

235 **quyken:** revive
243 **abregge:** shorten
248 **Jay tout . . . labour:** I have altogether wasted my time and effort.

For soothly, the grace of the Hooly Goost fareth lyk fyr, that may nat been ydel; for fyr fayleth anoon as it forleteth his wirkynge, and right so grace fayleth anoon as it forleteth his werkynge./   250
Then leseth the synful man the goodnesse of glorie, that oonly is bihight to goode men that labouren and werken./ Wel may he be sory thanne, that oweth al his lif to God as longe as he hath lyved, and eek as longe as he shal lyve, that no goodnesse ne hath to paye with his dette to God to whom he oweth al his lyf./ For trust wel, "He shal yeven acountes," as seith Seint Bernard, "of alle the goodes that han be yeven hym in this present lyf, and how he hath hem despended,/ [in] so muche that ther shal nat perisse an heer of his heed, ne a moment of an houre ne shal nat perisse of his tyme, that he ne shal yeve of it a rekenyng."/

The fifthe thyng that oghte moeve a man to contricioun is remembrance of the passioun that oure Lord Jhesu Crist suffred for oure synnes./   255
For, as seith Seint Bernard, "Whil that I lyve I shal have remembrance of the travailles that oure Lord Crist suffred in prechyng:/ his werynesse in travaillyng, his temptacious whan he fasted, his longe wakynges whan he preyde, hise teeres whan that he weep for pitee of good peple,/ the wo and the shame and the filthe that men seyden to hym, of the foule spittyng that men spitte in his face, of the buffettes that men yaven hym, of the foule mowes, and of the repreves that men to hym seyden,/ of the nayles with whiche he was nayled to the croys, and of al the remenant of his passioun that he suffred for my synnes, and no thyng for his gilt."/ And ye shul understonde that in mannes synne is every manere of ordre or ordinaunce turned up-so-doun./   260
For it is sooth that God, and resoun, and sensualitee, and the body of man been so ordeyned that everich of thise foure thynges sholde have lordshipe over that oother,/ as thus: God sholde have lordshipe over resoun, and resoun over sensualitee, and sensualitee over the body of man./ But soothly, whan man synneth, al this ordre or ordinaunce is turned up-so-doun./ And therfore thanne, for as muche as the resoun of man ne wol nat be subget ne obeisant to God, that is his lord by right, therfore leseth it the

lordshipe that it sholde have over sensualitee, and eek over the body of man./ And why? For sensualitee rebelleth thanne agayns resoun, and by that way leseth resoun the lordshipe over sensualitee and over the body./ For right as resoun is rebel   265
to God, right so is bothe sensualitee rebel to resoun and the body also./ And certes this disordinaunce and this rebellioun oure Lord Jhesu Crist aboghte upon his precious body ful deere, and herkneth in which wise./ For as muche thanne as resoun is rebel to God, therfore is man worthy to have sorwe and to be deed./ This suffred oure Lord Jhesu Crist for man, after that he hadde be bitraysed of his disciple, and distreyned and bounde so that his blood brast out at every nayl of his handes, as seith Seint Augustyn./ And forther over, for as muchel as resoun of man ne wol nat daunte sensualitee whan it may, therfore is man worthy to have shame; and this suffred oure Lord Jhesu Crist for man, whan they spetten in his visage./ And forther over,   270
for as muchel thanne as the caytyf body of man is rebel bothe to resoun and to sensualitee, therfore is it worthy the deeth./ And this suffred oure Lord Jhesu Crist for man upon the croys, where as ther was no part of his body free withouten greet peyne and bitter passioun./ And al this suffred Jhesu Crist, that nevere forfeted. And therfore resonably may be seyd of Jhesu in this manere: "To muchel am I peyned for the thynges that I nevere deserved, and to muche defouled for shendshipe that man is worthy to have."/ And therfore may the synful man wel seye, as seith Seint Bernard, "Acursed be the bitternesse of my synne, for which ther moste be suffred so muchel bitternesse."/ For certes, after the diverse [disordinaunces] of oure wikkednesses was the passioun of Jhesu Crist ordeyned in diverse thynges./ As thus: Certes, synful mannes soule is   275
bitraysed of the devel by coveitise of temporeel prosperitee, and scorned by deceite whan he cheseth flesshly delices; and yet is it tormented by inpacience of adversitee and bispet by servage and subjeccioun of synne; and atte laste it is slayn fynally./ For this disordinaunce of synful man was

267 **disordinaunce**: rebelliousness against order   **aboghte upon**: purchased with
270 **daunte**: subdue, restrain   **spetten**: spat
273 **forfeted**: sinned   **shendshipe**: shame
276 **bispet**: spat upon

Jhesu Crist first bitraysed, and after that was he bounde, that cam for to unbynden us of synne and peyne./ Thanne was he byscorned, that oonly sholde han been honoured in alle thynges and of alle thynges./ Thanne was his visage, that oghte be desired to be seyn of al mankynde, in which visage aungels desiren to looke, vileynsly bispet./ Thanne was he scourged, that no thyng hadde agilt; and finally, thanne was he crucified and slayn./ Thanne was acompliced the word of Ysaye, "He was wounded for oure mysdedes and defouled for oure felonies."/ Now sith that Jhesu Crist took upon hymself the peyne of alle oure wikkednesses, muchel oghte synful man wepen and biwayle, that for his synnes Goddes sone of hevene sholde al this peyne endure./

The sixte thyng that oghte moeve a man to contricioun is the hope of three thynges; that is to seyn, foryifnesse of synne, and the yifte of grace wel for to do, and the glorie of hevene, with which God shal gerdone man for his goode dedes./ And for as muche as Jhesu Crist yeveth us thise yiftes of his largesse and of his sovereyn bountee, therfore is he cleped *Jhesus Nazarenus rex Judeorum./ Jhesus* is to seyn "saveour" or "salvacioun," on whom men shul hope to have foryifnesse of synnes, which that is proprely salvacioun of synnes./ And therfore seyde the aungel to Joseph, "Thou shalt clepen his name Jhesus, that shal saven his peple of hir synnes."/ And heerof seith Seint Peter: "Ther is noon oother name under hevene that is yeve to any man, by which a man may be saved, but oonly Jhesus."/ *Nazarenus* is as muche for to seye as "florisshynge," in which a man shal hope that he that yeveth hym remissioun of synnes shal yeve hym eek grace wel for to do. For in the flour is hope of fruyt in tyme comynge, and in foryifnesse of synnes hope of grace wel for to do./ "I was atte dore of thyn herte," seith Jhesus, "and cleped for to entre. He that openeth to me shal have foryifnesse of synne./ I wol entre into hym by my grace and soupe with hym," by the goode werkes that he shal doon, whiche werkes been the foode of God; "and he shal soupe with me" by the

280

285

grete joye that I shal yeven hym./ Thus shal man hope, for his werkes of penaunce that God shal yeven hym his regne, as he bihooteth hym in the gospel./

Now shal a man understonde in which manere shal been his contricioun. I seye that it shal been universal and total. This is to seyn, a man shal be verray repentaunt for alle his synnes that he hath doon in delit of his thoght, for delit is ful perilous./ For ther been two manere of consentynges: that oon of hem is cleped consentynge of affeccioun, whan a man is moeved to do synne, and deliteth hym longe for to thynke on that synne;/ and his reson aperceyveth it wel that it is synne agayns the lawe of God, and yet his resoun refreyneth nat his foul delit or talent, though he se wel apertly that it is agayns the reverence of God. Although his resoun ne consente noght to doon that synne in dede,/ yet seyn somme doctours that swich delit that dwelleth longe, it is ful perilous, al be it nevere so lite./ And also a man sholde sorwe namely for al that evere he hath desired agayn the lawe of God with parfit consentynge of his resoun, for therof is no doute, that it is deedly synne in consentynge./ For certes, ther is no deedly synne that it nas first in mannes thought and after that in his delit, and so forth into consentynge and into dede./ Wherfore I seye that many men ne repenten hem nevere of swiche thoghtes and delites, ne nevere shryven hem of it, but oonly of the dede of grete synnes outward./ Wherfore I seye that swiche wikked delites and wikked thoghtes been subtile bigileres of hem that shullen be dampned./ Mooreover, man oghte to sorwe for his wikkede wordes as wel as for his wikkede dedes. For certes, the repentaunce of a synguler synne, and nat repente of alle his othere synnes, or elles repenten hym of alle his othere synnes and nat of a synguler synne, may nat availle./ For certes, God almyghty is al good, and therfore he foryeveth al or elles right noght./ And heerof seith Seint Augustyn,/ "I wot certeynly that God is enemy to everich synnere." And how thanne? He that observeth o synne, shal he have foryifnesse of the remenaunt of his othere synnes? Nay./ And further over, contricioun sholde be wonder

290

295

300

278 **byscorned:** scorned
279 **vileynsly:** rudely
280 **scourged:** whipped
281 **Ysaye:** Isaiah   **mysdedes:** sins
284 **Jhesus Nazarenus rex Judeorum:** Jesus the Nazarene, king of the Jews
290 **soupe:** sup

294 **refreyneth:** restrains   **apertly:** clearly
299 **bigileres:** deceivers

sorweful and angwissous; and therfore yeveth hym
God pleynly his mercy; and therfore, whan my soule
was angwissous withinne me, I hadde remembrance
of God that my preyere myghte come to hym./
Forther over, contricioun moste be continueel, and
that man have stedefast purpos to shriven
hym, and for to amenden hym of his lyf./ For   305
soothly, whil contricioun lasteth, man may
evere have hope of foryifnesse; and of this comth
hate of synne, that destroyeth synne, bothe in himself and eek in oother folk at his power./ For which
seith David: "Ye that loven God, hateth wikkednesse." For trusteth wel, to love God is for to love that
he loveth, and hate that he hateth./

The laste thyng that men shal understonde in contricioun is this: wherof avayleth contricioun. I seye
that somtyme contricioun delivereth a man fro
synne;/ of which that David seith, "I seye," quod
David (that is to seyn, I purposed fermely) "to shryve
me, and thow, Lord, relessedest my synne."/ And
right so as contricion availleth noght withouten sad
purpos of shrifte, if man have oportunitee, right so

litel worth is shrifte or satisfaccioun withouten contricioun./ And mooreover contricion   310
destroyeth the prisoun of helle, and maketh
wayk and fieble alle the strengthes of the develes, and
restoreth the yiftes of the Hooly Goost and of alle
goode vertues;/ and it clenseth the soule of synne,
and delivereth the soule fro the peyne of helle, and
fro the compaignye of the devel, and fro the servage
of synne, and restoreth it to alle goodes espirituels,
and to the compaignye and communyoun of hooly
chirche./ And further over, it maketh hym that
whilom was sone of ire to be sone of grace; and alle
thise thynges been preved by hooly writ./ And therfore, he that wolde sette his entente to thise thynges,
he were ful wys; for soothly he ne sholde nat thanne
in al his lyf have corage to synne, but yeven his body
and al his herte to the service of Jhesu Crist, and
therof doon hym hommage./ For soothly oure sweete
Lord Jhesu Crist hath spared us so debonairly in oure
folies that if he ne hadde pitee of mannes
soule, a sory song we myghten alle synge./   315

Explicit prima pars Penitentie; Et sequitur secunda pars eiusdem.

The seconde partie of Penitence is Confessioun,
that is signe of contricioun./ Now shul ye understonde what is Confessioun, and wheither it oghte
nedes be doon or noon, and whiche thynges been
covenable to verray Confessioun./

First shaltow understonde that Confessioun is verray shewynge of synnes to the preest./ This is to seyn
"verray," for he moste confessen hym of alle the
condiciouns that bilongen to his synne, as ferforth as
he kan./ Al moot be seyd, and no thyng excused ne
hyd ne forwrapped, and noght avaunte thee
of thy goode werkes./ And further over, it is   320
necessarie to understonde whennes that
synnes spryngen, and how they encreessen, and
whiche they been./

Of the spryngynge of synnes seith Seint Paul in
this wise: that "Right as by a man synne entred first
into this world, and thurgh that synne deeth, right so
thilke deeth entred into alle men that synneden."/ And

this man was Adam, by whom synne entred into this
world, whan he brak the comaundementz of God./
And therfore, he that first was so myghty that he
sholde nat have dyed, bicam swich oon that he moste
nedes dye, wheither he wolde or noon, and al his
progenye in this world, that in thilke man synneden./
Looke that in th'estaat of innocence, whan Adam and
Eve naked weren in Paradys, and nothyng ne
hadden shame of hir nakednesse,/ how that   325
the serpent, that was moost wily of alle othere
beestes that God hadde maked, seyde to the womman, "Why comaunded God to yow ye sholde nat
eten of every tree in Paradys?"/ The womman
answerde: "Of the fruyt," quod she, "of the trees in
Paradys we feden us, but soothly, of the fruyt of the
tree that is in the myddel of Paradys, God forbad us
for to ete, ne nat touchen it, lest per aventure we
sholde dyen."/ The serpent seyde to the womman,
"Nay, nay, ye shul nat dyen of deeth; for sothe, God
woot that what day that ye eten therof, youre eyen
shul opene and ye shul been as goddes, knowynge
good and harm."/ The womman thanne saugh that the

---

304 **angwissous:** anxious
Explicit, *etc.*: Here ends the first part of Penance; and its second part follows.

320 **forwrapped:** concealed

tree was good to feedyng, and fair to the eyen, and delitable to the sighte. She took of the fruyt of the tree, and eet it, and yaf to hire housbonde, and he eet, and anoon the eyen of hem bothe openeden./ And whan that they knewe that they were naked, they sowed of fige leves a maner of breches to hiden hire membres./ There may ye seen that deedly synne hath, first, suggestion of the feend, as sheweth heere by the naddre; and afterward, the delit of the flessh, as sheweth heere by Eve; and after that, the consentynge of resoun, as sheweth heere by Adam./ For trust wel, though so were that the feend tempted Eve—that is to seyn, the flessh— and the flessh hadde delit in the beautee of the fruyt defended, yet certes, til that resoun—that is to seyn, Adam—consented to the etynge of the fruyt, yet stood he in th'estaat of innocence./ Of thilke Adam tooke we thilke synne original, for of hym flesshly descended be we alle, and engendred of vile and corrupt mateere./ And whan the soule is put in oure body, right anon is contract original synne; and that that was erst but oonly peyne of concupiscence is afterward bothe peyne and synne./ And therfore be we alle born sones of wratthe and of dampnacioun perdurable, if it nere baptesme that we receyven, which bynymeth us the culpe. But for sothe, the peyne dwelleth with us, as to temptacioun, which peyne highte concupiscence./ And this concupiscence, whan it is wrongfully disposed or ordeyned in man, it maketh hym coveite, by coveitise of flessh, flesshly synne, by sighte of his eyen as to erthely thynges, and eek coveitise of hynesse by pride of herte./

Now, as for to speken of the firste coveitise, that is concupiscence, after the lawe of oure membres that weren lawefulliche ymaked and by rightful juggement of God,/ I seye, forasmuche as man is nat obeisaunt to God, that is his lord, therfore is the flessh to hym disobeisaunt thurgh concupiscence, which yet is cleped norrissynge of synne and occasioun of synne./ Therfore, al the while that a man hath in hym the peyne of concupiscence, it is impossible but he be tempted somtime and moeved in his flessh to synne./ And this thyng may nat faille as longe as he lyveth; it may wel wexe fieble and faille by vertu of baptesme

330

335

and by the grace of God thurgh penitence,/ but fully ne shal it nevere quenche, that he ne shal som tyme be moeved in hymself, but if he were al refreyded by siknesse, or by malefice of sorcerie, or colde drynkes./ For lo, what seith Seint Paul: "The flessh coveiteth agayn the spirit, and the spirit agayn the flessh; they been so contrarie and so stryven that a man may nat alway doon as he wolde."/ The same Seint Paul, after his grete penaunce in water and in lond—in water by nyght and by day in greet peril and in greet peyne; in lond, in famyne and thurst, in coold and clootthlees, and ones stoned almoost to the deeth/—yet seyde he, "Allas, I caytyf man! Who shal delivere me fro the prisoun of my caytyf body?"/ And Seint Jerome, whan he longe tyme hadde woned in desert, where as he hadde no compaignye but of wilde beestes, where as he ne hadde no mete but herbes, and water to his drynke, ne no bed but the naked erthe, for which his flessh was blak as an Ethiopeen for heete, and ny destroyed for coold,/ yet seyde he that "the brennynge of lecherie boyled in al his body."/ Wherfore I woot wel sykerly that they been deceyved that seyn that they ne be nat tempted in hir body./ Witnesse on Seint Jame the Apostel, that seith that "every wight is tempted in his owene concupiscence"; that is to seyn, that everich of us hath matere and occasioun to be tempted of the norissynge of synne that is in his body./ And therfore seith Seint John the Evaungelist, "If that we seyn that we be withoute synne, we deceyve us selve, and trouthe is nat in us."/

340

345

Now shal ye understonde in what manere that synne wexeth or encreesseth in man. The firste thyng is thilke norissynge of synne of which I spak biforn, thilke flesshly concupiscence./ And after that comth the subjeccioun of the devel—this is to seyn, the develes bely, with which he bloweth in man the fir of flesshly concupiscence./ And after that, a man bithynketh hym wheither he wol doon or no thilke thing to which he is tempted./ And thanne, if that a man withstonde and weyve the firste entisynge of his flessh and of the feend, thanne is it no synne; and if it so be that he do nat so, thanne feeleth he anoon a flambe of delit./ And thanne is it

350

---

330 **membres:** genitals
335 **bynymeth:** takes away from   **culpe:** guilt
338 **disobeisaunt:** disobedient

341 **refreyded:** cooled   **malefice:** evildoing
351 **bely:** bellows

good to be war and kepen hym wel, or elles he wol falle anon into consentynge of synne; and thanne wol he do it, if he may have tyme and place./ And of this matere seith Moyses by the devel in this manere: "The feend seith, 'I wole chace and pursue the man by wikked suggestioun, and I wole hente hym by moevynge or stirynge of synne. And I wol departe my prise or my praye by deliberacioun, and my lust shal been acompliced in delit. I wol drawe my swerd in consentynge'"—/ for certes, right as a swerd departeth a thyng in two peces, right so consentynge departeth God fro man—" 'and thanne wol I sleen hym with myn hand in dede of synne'; thus seith the feend."/ For certes, thanne is a man al deed in soule. And thus is synne acompliced by temptacioun, by delit, and by consentynge; and thanne is the synne cleped actueel./   355

For sothe, synne is in two maneres; outher it is venial or deedly synne. Soothly, whan man loveth any creature moore than Jhesu Crist oure Creatour, thanne is it deedly synne. And venial synne is it, if man love Jhesu Crist lasse than hym oghte./ For sothe, the dede of this venial synne is ful perilous, for it amenuseth the love that men sholde han to God moore and moore./ And therfore, if a man charge hymself with manye swiche venial synnes, certes, but if so be that he somtyme descharge hym of hem by shrifte, they mowe ful lightly amenuse in hym al the love that he hath to Jhesu Crist;/ and in this wise skippeth venial into deedly synne.   360
For certes, the moore that a man chargeth his soule with venial synnes, the moore is he enclyned to fallen into deedly synne./ And therfore lat us nat be necligent to deschargen us of venial synnes. For the proverbe seith that "Manye smale maken a greet."/ And herkne this ensample. A greet wawe of the see comth som tyme with so greet a violence that it drencheth the ship. And the same harm doon som tyme the smale dropes of water, that entren thurgh a litel crevace into the thurrok, and in the botme of the ship, if men be so necligent that they ne descharge hem nat by tyme./ And therfore, although ther be a difference bitwixe thise two causes of drenchynge,

algates the ship is dreynt./ Right so fareth it somtyme of deedly synne, and of anoyouse veniale synnes, whan they multiplie in a man so greetly that [the love of] thilke worldly thynges that he loveth, thurgh whiche he synneth venyally, is as greet in his herte as the love of God, or moore./ And therfore, the love of every thyng that is nat biset in God, ne doon principally for Goddes sake, although that a man love it lasse than God, yet is it venial synne;/ and deedly synne whan the love of any thyng weyeth in the herte of man as muchel as the love of God, or moore./ "Deedly synne," as seith Seint Augustyn, "is whan a man turneth his herte fro God, which that is verray sovereyn bountee, that may nat chaunge, and yeveth his herte to thyng that may chaunge and flitte."/ And certes, that is every thyng save God of hevene. For sooth is that if a man yeve his love, the which that he oweth al to God with al his herte, unto a creature, certes, as muche of his love as he yeveth to thilke creature, so muche he birieveth fro God;/ and therfore dooth he synne. For he that is dettour to God ne yeldeth nat to God al his dette; that is to seyn, al the love of his herte./   365   370

Now sith man understondeth generally which is venial synne, thanne is it covenable to tellen specially of synnes whiche that many a man peraventure ne demeth hem nat synnes, and ne shryveth him nat of the same thynges, and yet natheless they been synnes / soothly, as thise clerkes writen; this is to seyn, that at every tyme that a man eteth or drynketh moore than suffiseth to the sustenaunce of his body, in certein he dooth synne./ And eek whan he speketh moore than it nedeth, it is synne. Eke whan he herkneth nat benignely the compleint of the povre;/ eke whan he is in heele of body and wol nat faste whan other folk faste, withouten cause resonable; eke whan he slepeth moore than nedeth, or whan he comth by thilke enchesoun to late to chirche, or to othere werkes of charite;/ eke whan he useth his wyf withouten sovereyn desir of engendrure to the honour of God or for the entente to yelde to his wyf the dette of his body;/ eke whan he wol nat visite the sike and the prisoner, if he may; eke if he love wyf or child, or oother worldly thyng, moore than resoun requireth; eke if he flatere or blan-   375

---

355 **departe**: separate (as a single sheep from a flock)   **prise**: prize, what is to be captured
360 **amenuse**: diminish
363 **thurrok**: bilge (of a ship)

368 **flitte**: pass away

dise moore than hym oghte for any necessitee;/ eke if he amenuse or withdrawe the almesse of the povre; eke if he apparailleth his mete moore deliciously than nede is, or ete it to hastily by likerousnesse:/ eke if he tale vanytees at chirche or at Goddes service, or that he be a talker of ydel wordes of folye or of vileynye, for he shal yelden acountes of it at the day of doom;/ eke whan he biheteth or assureth to do thynges that he may nat parfourne; eke whan that he by light-nesse or folie mysseyeth or scorneth his neighebor;/ eke whan he hath any wikked suspecioun of thyng ther he ne woot of it no soothfastnesse:/ 380 thise thynges, and mo withoute nombre, been synnes, as seith Seint Augustyn./

Now shal men understonde that, al be it so that noon erthely man may eschue alle venial synnes, yet may he refreyne hym by the brennynge love that he hath to oure Lord Jhesu Crist, and by preyeres and con-fessioun and othere goode werkes, so that it shal but litel greve./ For, as seith Seint Augustyn, "If a man love God in swich manere that al that evere he dooth is in the love of God and for the love of God verraily, for he brenneth in the love of God,/ looke how muche that a drope of water that falleth in a fourneys ful of fyr anoyeth or greveth, so muche anoyeth a venial synne unto a man that is parfit in the love of Jhesu Crist."/ Men may also refreyne venial synne by receyvynge worthily of the precious body of Jhesu Crist;/ by 385 receyvynge eek of hooly water, by almesdede, by general confessioun of *Confiteor* at masse and at complyn, and by blessynge of bisshopes and of preestes, and by oothere goode werkes./

Explicit secunda pars Penitentie.

Sequitur de septem peccatis mortalibus et eorum dependenciis, circumstanciis, et speciebus.

Now is it bihovely thyng to telle whiche been the sevene deedly synnes, this is to seyn, chieftaynes of synnes. Alle they renne in o lees, but in diverse man-neres. Now been they cleped chieftaynes, for as muche as they been chief and spryng of alle othere synnes./ Of the roote of thise sevene synnes, thanne, is Pride the general roote of alle harmes. For of this roote spryngen certein braunches, as Ire, Envye, Accidie or Slewthe, Avarice or Coveitise (to com-mune understondynge), Glotonye, and Lecherye./ And everich of thise chief synnes hath his braunches and his twigges, as shal be declared in hire chapitres folwynge./

De Superbia.

And thogh so be that no man kan outrely telle the nombre of the twigges and of the 390 harmes that cometh of Pride, yet wol I shewe a partie of hem, as ye shul understonde./ Ther is inobedience, avauntynge, ypocrisie, despit, arro-gance, inpudence, swellynge of herte, insolence, ela-cioun, inpacience, strif, contumacie, presumpcioun, irreverence, pertinacie, veyneglorie, and many another twig that I kan nat declare./ Inobedient is he that disobeyeth for despit to the comandementz of God, and to his sovereyns, and to his goostly fader./ Avauntour is he that bosteth of the harm or of the bountee that he hath doon./ Ypocrite is he that hideth to shewe hym swich as he is and sheweth hym swich as he noght is./ Despitous is he that hath desdeyn of his neighebor—that is to seyn, of his evene-Cristene—or hath despit to doon that hym oghte to do./ Arrogant is he that thynketh that he hath 395 thilke bountees in hym that he hath noght, or weneth that he sholde have hem by his desertes, or elles he demeth that he be that he nys nat./ Inpudent is he that for his pride hath no shame of his synnes./

---

376 **blandise:** blandish, fawn upon
378 **tale:** talk

Explicit, *etc.*: Here ends the second part on Penance. Now follows the section on the seven deadly sins and their subdivisions, circumstances, and species.
387 **bihovely:** useful, necessary   **Alle they renne in o lees:** they all run on one leash; see n.   **spryng:** wellspring
De Superbia: Concerning pride.

---

382 **refreyne:** bridle, restrain
384 **anoyeth:** damages
386 **Confiteor:** I confess, first word of the general confession of sins   **complyn:** compline, the last service sung before retiring

---

391 **elacioun:** defined at 400   **contumacie:** defined at 402   **pertinacie:** defined at 404
395 **evene-Cristene:** fellow Christian

Swellynge of herte is whan a man rejoyseth hym of harm that he hath doon./ Insolent is he that despiseth in his juggement alle othere folk, as to regard of his value, and of his konnyng, and of his spekyng, and of his beryng./ Elacioun is whan he ne may neither suffre to have maister ne felawe./   400
Inpacient is he that wol nat been ytaught ne undernome of his vice, and by strif werreieth trouthe wityngly, and deffendeth his folye./ *Contumax* is he that thurgh his indignacioun is agayns everich auctoritee or power of hem that been his sovereyns./ Presumpcioun is whan a man undertaketh an emprise that hym oghte nat do, or elles that he may nat do; and this is called surquidrie. Irreverence is whan men do nat honour there as hem oghte to doon, and waiten to be reverenced./ Pertinacie is whan man deffendeth his folie and trusteth to muchel to his owene wit./ Veyneglorie is for to have pompe and delit in his temporeel hynesse, and glorifie hym in this worldly estaat./ Janglynge is whan a man   405
speketh to muche biforn folk, and clappeth as a mille, and taketh no keep what he seith./

And yet is ther a privee spece of Pride that waiteth first to be salewed er he wole salewe, al be he lasse worth than that oother is, peraventure; and eek he waiteth or desireth to sitte, or elles to goon above hym in the wey, or kisse pax, or been encensed, or goon to offryng biforn his neighebor,/ and swiche semblable thynges, agayns his duetee, peraventure, but that he hath his herte and his entente in swich a proud desir to be magnified and honoured biforn the peple./

Now been ther two maneres of Pride: that oon of hem is withinne the herte of man, and that oother is withoute./ Of whiche, soothly, thise forseyde thynges, and mo than I have seyd, apertenen to Pride that is in the herte of man; and that othere speces of Pride been withoute./ But natheles that oon of   410
thise speces of Pride is signe of that oother, right as the gaye leefsel atte taverne is signe of the wyn that is in the celer./ And this is in manye thynges: as in speche and contenaunce, and in outrageous array

of clothyng./ For certes, if ther ne hadde be no synne in clothyng, Crist wolde nat so soone have noted and spoken of the clothyng of thilke riche man in the gospel./ And, as seith Seint Gregorie, that "precious clothyng is cowpable for the derthe of it, and for his softenesse, and for his strangenesse and degisynesse, and for the superfluitee, or for the inordinat scantnesse of it."/ Allas, may man nat seen, as in oure dayes, the synful costlewe array of clothynge, and namely in to muche superfluite, or elles in to desordinat scantnesse?/   415

As to the first synne, that is in superfluitee of clothynge, which that maketh it so deere, to harm of the peple;/ nat oonly the cost of embrowdynge, the degise endentynge or barrynge, owndynge, palynge, wyndynge or bendynge, and semblable wast of clooth in vanitee,/ but ther is also costlewe furrynge in hir gownes, so muche pownsonynge of chisels to maken holes, so muche daggynge of sheres;/ forthwith the superfluitee in lengthe of the forseide gownes, trailynge in the dong and in the mire, on horse and eek on foote, as wel of man as of womman, that al thilke trailyng is verraily as in effect wasted, consumed, thredbare, and roten with donge, rather than it is yeven to the povre, to greet damage of the forseyde povre folk./ And that in sondry wise; this is to seyn that the moore that clooth is wasted, the moore moot it coste to the peple for the scarsnesse./ And forther over, if so be that   420
they wolde yeven swich pownsoned and dagged clothyng to the povre folk, it is nat convenient to were for hire estaat, ne suffisant to beete hire necessitee, to kepe hem fro the distemperance of the firmament./ Upon that oother side, to speken of the horrible disordinat scantnesse of clothyng, as been thise kutted sloppes, or haynselyns, that thurgh hire shortnesse ne covere nat the shameful membres of

---

399 **konnyng:** understanding
401 **undernome of:** reproved for
403 **surquidrie:** arrogance, presumption
405 **glorifie hym:** exult
407 **pax:** an object made of wood or metal and used during the Mass for the kiss of peace
408 **agayns his duetee:** beyond what is due or owed to him
411 **leefsel:** bush for a tavern sign   **celer:** storeroom

414 **derthe:** costliness   **strangenesse:** exotic style   **degisynesse:** elaborateness
415 **costlewe:** excessively expensive   **desordinat:** excessive
417 **embrowdynge:** embroidering   **degise endentynge:** ostentatious notching of the borders   **barrynge:** ornamenting with decorative strips   **owndynge:** undulating stripes   **palynge:** vertical stripes   **wyndynge:** folding   **bendynge:** decorative borders   **semblable:** similar
418 **furrynge:** fur trimming   **pownsonynge of chisels:** punching designs with blades   **daggynge of sheres:** slitting with shears
421 **pownsoned:** punched with ornamental holes   **dagged:** ornamented with cutouts   **beete:** provide for   **distemperance of the firmament:** disturbance of the heavens (bad weather)
422 **disordinat:** excessive   **kutted sloppes:** loose outer coats cut short   **haynselyns:** short jackets

man, to wikked entente./ Allas, somme of hem shewen the boce of hir shap, and the horrible swollen membres, that semeth lik the maladie of hirnia, in the wrappynge of hir hoses;/ and eek the buttokes of hem faren as it were the hyndre part of a she-ape in the fulle of the moone./ And mooreover, the wrecched swollen membres that they shewe thurgh disgisynge, in departynge of hire hoses in whit and reed, semeth that half hir shameful privee membres weren flayne./ And if so be that they departen hire 425 hoses in othere colours, as is whit and blak, or whit and blew, or blak and reed, and so forth,/ thanne semeth it, as by variaunce of colour, that half the partie of hire privee membres were corrupt by the fir of Seint Antony, or by cancre, or by oother swich meschaunce./ Of the hyndre part of hir buttokes, it is ful horrible for to see. For certes, in that partie of hir body ther as they purgen hir stynkynge ordure,/ that foule partie shewe they to the peple prowdly in despit of honestitee, which honestitee that Jhesu Crist and his freendes observede to shewen in hir lyve./ Now, as of the outrageous array of wommen, God woot that though the visages of somme of hem seme ful chaast and debonaire, yet notifie they in hire array of atyr likerousnesse and pride./ I sey nat that 430 honestitee in clothynge of man or womman is uncovenable, but certes the superfluitee or disordinat scantitee of clothynge is reprevable./ Also the synne of aornement or of apparaille is in thynges that apertenen to ridynge, as in to manye delicat horses that been hoolden for delit, that been so faire, fatte, and costlewe;/ and also in many a vicious knave that is sustened by cause of hem; and in to curious harneys, as in sadeles, in crouperes, peytrels, and bridles covered with precious clothyng, and riche barres and plates of gold and of silver./ For which God seith by Zakarie the prophete, "I wol confounde the rideres of swiche horses."/ This folk taken litel reward of the ridynge of Goddes sone of hevene, and of his harneys

whan he rood upon the asse, and ne hadde noon oother harneys but the povre clothes of his disciples; ne we ne rede nat that evere he rood on oother beest./ I speke this for the synne of super- 435 fluitee, and nat for resonable honestitee, whan reson it requireth./ And forther over, certes, pride is greetly notified in holdynge of greet meynee, whan they be of litel profit or of right no profit,/ and namely whan that meynee is felonous and damageous to the peple by hardynesse of heigh lordshipe or by wey of offices./ For certes, swiche lordes sellen thanne hir lordshipe to the devel of helle, whanne they sustenen the wikkednesse of hir meynee./ Or elles, whan this folk of lowe degree, as thilke that holden hostelries, sustenen the thefte of hire hostilers, and that is in many manere of deceites./ Thilke 440 manere of folk been the flyes that folwen the hony, or elles the houndes that folwen the careyne. Swich forseyde folk stranglen spiritually hir lordshipes;/ for which thus seith David the prophete: "Wikked deeth moote come upon thilke lordshipes, and God yeve that they moote descenden into helle al doun, for in hire houses been iniquitees and shrewednesses and nat God of hevene."/ And certes, but if they doon amendement, right as God yaf his benysoun to [Laban] by the service of Jacob, and to [Pharao] by the service of Joseph, right so God wol yeve his malisoun to swiche lordshipes as sustenen the wikkednesse of hir servauntz, but they come to amendement./ Pride of the table appeereth eek ful ofte; for certes, riche men been cleped to festes, and povre folk been put awey and rebuked./ Also in excesse of diverse metes and drynkes, and namely swich manere bake-metes and dissh-metes, brennynge of wilde fir and peynted and castelled with papir, and semblable wast, so that it is abusioun for to thynke./ And eek in to greet pre- 445 ciousnesse of vessel and curiositee of mynstralcie, by whiche a man is stired the moore to delices of luxurie,/ if so be that he sette his herte the

---

423 **boce:** bulge　**hirnia:** hernia　**hoses:** leggings
424 **hyndre:** back
425 **disgisynge:** style of clothing　**flayne:** stripped of skin
427 **fir of Seint Antony:** erysipelas, an acute inflammation of the skin
430 **notifie:** make known　**array of atyr:** appearance of their dress
431 **uncovenable:** unseemly　**reprevable:** blameworthy
432 **aornement:** adornment　**costlewe:** expensive
433 **to:** too　**crouperes:** covers for the hindquarters of a horse　**peytrels:** horse collars
434 **Zakarie:** Zechariah

437 **notified:** made known
438 **felonous:** felonius, criminal　**damageous:** injurious
441 **careyne:** carrion
442 **shrewednesses:** wicked deeds
443 **benysoun:** blessing　**malisoun:** curse
444 **cleped:** invited
445 **bake-metes:** pies of meat, fowl, or fish　**dissh-metes:** stews
castelled with papir: adorned with battlements of paper　**abusioun:** absurdity
446 **curiositee:** intricate, skillful performances　**luxurie:** lechery

lasse upon oure Lord Jhesu Crist, certeyn it is a synne; and certeinly the delices myghte been so grete in this caas that man myghte lightly falle by hem into deedly synne./ The especes that sourden of Pride, soothly whan they sourden of malice ymagined, avised, and forncast, or elles of usage, been deedly synnes, it is no doute./ And whan they sourden by freletee unavysed, and sodeynly withdrawen ayeyn, al been they grevouse synnes, I gesse that they ne been nat deedly./

Now myghte men axe wherof that Pride sourdeth and spryngeth, and I seye, somtyme it spryngeth of the goodes of nature, and somtyme of the goodes of fortune, and somtyme of the goodes of grace./ Certes, the goodes of nature stonden   450 outher in goodes of body or in goodes of soule./ Certes, goodes of body been heele of body, strengthe, delivernesse, beautee, gentrice, franchise./ Goodes of nature of the soule been good wit, sharp understondynge, subtil engyn, vertu natureel, good memorie./ Goodes of fortune been richesse, hyghe degrees of lordshipes, preisynges of the peple./ Goodes of grace been science, power to suffre spiritueel travaille, benignitee, vertuous contemplacioun, withstondynge of temptacioun, and semblable thynges./ Of whiche forseyde goodes,   455 certes it is a ful greet folye a man to priden hym in any of hem alle./ Now as for to speken of goodes of nature, God woot that somtyme we han hem in nature as muche to oure damage as to oure profit./ As for to speken of heele of body, certes it passeth ful lightly, and eek it is ful ofte enchesoun of the siknesse of oure soule. For, God woot, the flessh is a ful greet enemy to the soule, and therfore, the moore that the body is hool, the moore be we in peril to falle./ Eke for to pride hym in his strengthe of body, it is an heigh folye. For certes, the flessh coveiteth agayn the spirit, and ay the moore strong that the flessh is, the sorier may the soule be./ And over al this, strengthe of body and worldly hardynesse causeth ful ofte many a man to peril and meschaunce./ Eek for to pride hym of his   460 gentrie is ful greet folie; for ofte tyme the gentrie of the body binymeth the gentrie of the soule; and eek we ben alle of o fader and of o mooder; and alle we been of o nature, roten and corrupt, bothe riche and povre./ For sothe, o manere gentrie is for to preise, that apparailleth mannes corage with vertues and moralitees, and maketh hym Cristes child./ For truste wel that over what man that synne hath maistrie, he is a verray cherl to synne./

Now been ther generale signes of gentillesse, as eschewynge of vice and ribaudye and servage of synne, in word, in werk, and contenaunce,/ and usynge vertu, curteisye, and clennesse, and to be liberal—that is to seyn, large by mesure, for thilke that passeth mesure is folie and synne./   465 Another is to remembre hym of bountee that he of oother folk hath receyved./ Another is to be benigne to his goode subgetis; wherfore seith Senek, "Ther is no thing moore covenable to a man of heigh estaat than debonairetee and pitee./ And therfore thise flyes that men clepen bees, whan they maken hir kyng, they chesen oon that hath no prikke wherwith he may stynge."/ Another is, a man to have a noble herte and a diligent to attayne to heighe vertuouse thynges./ Now certes, a man to pride hym in the goodes of grace is eek an outrageous folie, for thilke yifte of grace that sholde have turned hym to goodnesse and to medicine, turneth hym to venym and to confusioun, as seith Seint Gregorie./   470 Certes also, whoso prideth hym in the goodes of fortune, he is a ful greet fool; for somtyme is a man a greet lord by the morwe, that is a caytyf and a wrecche er it be nyght;/ and somtyme the richesse of a man is cause of his deth; somtyme the delices of a man ben cause of the grevous maladye thurgh which he dyeth./ Certes, the commendacioun of the peple is somtyme ful fals and ful brotel for to triste; this day they preyse, tomorwe they blame./ God woot, desir to have commendacioun eek of the peple hath caused deeth to many a bisy man./

Remedium contra peccatum Superbie.

Now sith that so is that ye han understonde what is Pride, and whiche been the speces of it, and whennes Pride sourdeth and spryngeth,/ now   475 shul ye understonde which is the remedie

448 **especes:** species, kinds   **sourden of:** arise, originate from   **ymagined:** plotted
forncast: premeditated
452 **delivernesse:** agility   **gentrice:** gentle (aristocratic) birth
464 **eschewynge:** avoidance   **ribaudye:** debauchery
465 **large by mesure:** reasonably generous
468 **flyes:** insects
Remedium, *etc.*: The remedy against the sin of Pride.
475 **sourdeth:** arises

agayns the synne of Pride; and that is humylitee, or mekenesse./ That is a vertu thurgh which a man hath verray knoweleche of hymself, and holdeth of hymself no pris ne deyntee, as in regard of his desertes, considerynge evere his freletee./ Now been ther three maneres of humylitee: as humylitee in herte; another humylitee is in his mouth; the thridde in his werkes./ The humilitee in herte is in foure maneres. That oon is whan a man holdeth hymself as noght worth biforn God of hevene. Another is whan he ne despiseth noon oother man./ The thridde is whan he rekketh nat, though men holde hym noght worth. The ferthe is whan he nys nat sory of his humiliacioun./   480 Also the humilitee of mouth is in foure thynges: in attempree speche, and in humblesse of speche, and whan he biknoweth with his owene mouth that he is swich as hym thynketh that he is in his herte. Another is whan he preiseth the bountee of another man, and nothyng therof amenuseth./ Humilitee eek in werkes is in foure maneres. The firste is whan he putteth othere men biforn hym. The seconde is to chese the loweste place over al. The thridde is gladly to assente to good conseil./ The ferthe is to stonde gladly to the award of his sovereyns, or of hym that is in hyer degree. Certein, this is a greet werk of humylitee./

Sequitur de Invidia.

After Pride wol I speken of the foule synne of Envye, which that is, as by the word of the Philosophre, "sorwe of oother mannes prosperitee"; and after the word of Seint Augustyn, it is "Sorwe of oother mennes wele, and joye of othere mennes harm."/ This foule synne is platly agayns the Hooly Goost. Al be it so that every synne is agayns the Hooly Goost, yet nathelees, for as muche as bountee aperteneth proprely to the Hooly Goost, and Envye comth proprely of malice, therfore it is proprely agayn the bountee of the Hooly Goost./   485 Now hath malice two speces; that is to seyn, hardnesse of herte in wikkednesse, or elles the flessh of man is so blynd that he considereth nat that he is in synne or rekketh nat that he is in synne, which is the hardnesse of the devel./ That oother spece of mal-

ice is whan a man werreyeth trouthe, whan he woot that it is trouthe; and eek whan he werreyeth the grace that God hath yeve to his neighebor; and al this is by Envye./ Certes, thanne is Envye the worste synne that is. For soothly, alle othere synnes been somtyme oonly agayns o special vertu,/ but certes Envye is agayns alle vertues and agayns alle goodnesses. For it is sory of alle the bountees of his neighebor, and in this manere it is divers from alle othere synnes./ For wel unnethe is ther any synne that it ne hath som delit in itself, save oonly Envye, that evere hath in itself angwissh and sorwe./ The speces of   490 Envye been thise. Ther is first, sorwe of oother mannes goodnesse and of his prosperitee; and prosperitee is kyndely matere of joye; thanne is Envye a synne agayns kynde./ The seconde spece of Envye is joye of oother mannes harm, and that is proprely lyk to the devel, that evere rejoyseth hym of mannes harm./ Of thise two speces comth bakbityng; and this synne of bakbityng or detraccion hath certeine speces, as thus: Som man preiseth his neighebor by a wikked entente,/ for he maketh alwey a wikked knotte atte laste ende. Alwey he maketh a "but" atte laste ende, that is digne of moore blame than worth is al the preisynge./ The seconde spece is that if a man be good and dooth or seith a thing to good entente, the bakbitere wol turne al thilke goodnesse up-so-doun to his shrewed entente./ The thridde is   495 to amenuse the bountee of his neighebor./ The fourthe spece of bakbityng is this: that if men speke goodnesse of a man, thanne wol the bakbitere seyn, "Parfey, swich a man is yet bet than he," in dispreisynge of hym that men preise./ The fifte spece is this: for to consente gladly and herkne gladly to the harm that men speke of oother folk. This synne is ful greet and ay encreesseth after the wikked entente of the bakbitere./ After bakbityng cometh gruchchyng or murmuracioun; and somtyme it spryngeth of inpacience agayns God, and somtyme agayns man./ Agayn God it is whan a man gruccheth agayn the peyne of helle, or agayns poverte, or los of catel, or agayn reyn or tempest; or elles gruccheth that shrewes han prosperitee, or elles for that goode men han adversitee./ And alle thise thynges sholde man   500 suffre paciently, for they comen by the rightful juggement and ordinaunce of God./ Somtyme comth

---

477 **deyntee:** dignity, worth
481 **amenuseth:** diminishes
483 **award of his sovereyns:** decision of his rulers   **Sequitur,** *etc.*: Now follows the section on envy.
484 **the Philosophre:** Aristotle
485 **platly:** flatly, directly

499 **murmuracioun:** grumbling

grucching of avarice; as Judas grucched agayns the Magdaleyne whan she enoynted the heved of oure Lord Jhesu Crist with hir precious oynement./ This manere murmure is swich as whan man gruccheth of goodnesse that hymself dooth, or that oother folk doon of hir owene catel./ Somtyme comth murmure of Pride, as whan Simon the Pharisee gruchched agayn the Magdaleyne whan she approched to Jhesu Crist and weep at his feet for hire synnes./ And somtyme grucchyng sourdeth of Envye, whan men discovereth a mannes harm that was pryvee or bereth hym on hond thyng that is fals./ Mur-   505
mure eek is ofte amonges servauntz that grucchen whan hir sovereyns bidden hem doon leveful thynges;/ and forasmuche as they dar nat openly withseye the comaundementz of hir sovereyns, yet wol they seyn harm, and grucche, and murmure prively for verray despit;/ whiche wordes men clepen the develes *Pater noster,* though so be that the devel ne hadde nevere *Pater noster,* but that lewed folk yeven it swich a name./ Somtyme it comth of Ire or prive hate that norisseth rancour in herte, as afterward I shal declare./ Thanne cometh eek bitternesse of herte, thurgh which bitternesse every good dede of his neighebor semeth to hym bitter and unsavory./   510
Thanne cometh discord that unbyndeth alle manere of freendshipe. Thanne comth scornynge of his neighebor, al do he never so weel./ Thanne comth accusynge, as whan man seketh occasioun to anoyen his neighebor, which that is lyk the craft of the devel, that waiteth bothe nyght and day to accusen us alle./ Thanne comth malignitee, thurgh which a man anoyeth his neighebor prively, if he may;/ and if he noght may, algate his wikked wil ne shal nat wante, as for to brennen his hous pryvely, or empoysone or sleen his beestes, and semblable thynges./

Remedium contra peccatum Invidie.

Now wol I speke of remedie agayns this foule synne of Envye. First is the love of God principal and lovyng of his neighebor as hymself, for soothly that oon ne may nat been withoute that oother./   515
And truste wel that in the name of thy neighebor thou shalt understonde the name of thy brother;

for certes alle we have o fader flesshly and o mooder— that is to seyn, Adam and Eve—and eek o fader espiritueel, and that is God of hevene./ Thy neighebor artow holden for to love and wilne hym alle goodnesse; and therfore seith God, "Love thy neighebor as thyselve"—that is to seyn, to salvacioun bothe of lyf and of soule./ And mooreover thou shalt love hym in word, and in benigne amonestynge and chastisynge, and conforten hym in his anoyes, and preye for hym with al thyn herte./ And in dede thou shalt love hym in swich wise that thou shalt doon to hym in charitee as thou woldest that it were doon to thyn owene persone./ And therfore thou ne shalt doon hym no damage in wikked word, ne harm in his body, ne in his catel, ne in his soule, by entissyng of wikked ensample./ Thou shalt nat desiren   520
his wyf ne none of his thynges. Understoond eek that in the name of neighebor is comprehended his enemy./ Certes, man shal loven his enemy, by the comandement of God; and soothly thy freend shaltow love in God./ I seye, thyn enemy shaltow love for Goddes sake, by his commandement. For if it were reson that man sholde haten his enemy, for sothe God nolde nat receyven us to his love that been his enemys./ Agayns three manere of wronges that his enemy dooth to hym, he shal doon three thynges, as thus:/ Agayns hate and rancour of herte, he shal love hym in herte. Agayns chidyng and wikkede wordes, he shal preye for his enemy. Agayns the wikked dede of his enemy, he shal doon hym bountee./ For   525
Crist seith, "Loveth youre enemys, and preyeth for hem that speke yow harm, and eek for hem that yow chacen and pursewen, and dooth bountee to hem that yow haten." Loo, thus comaundeth us oure Lord Jhesu Crist to do to oure enemys./ For soothly, nature dryveth us to loven oure freendes, and parfey, oure enemys han moore nede to love than oure freendes; and they that moore nede have, certes to hem shal men doon goodnesse;/ and certes, in thilke dede have we remembraunce of the love of Jhesu Crist that deyde for his enemys./ And in as muche as thilke love is the moore grevous to parfourne, so muche is the moore gret the merite; and

---

514 **wante:** be lacking
Remedium, *etc.*: The remedy against the sin of Envy.

517 **wilne:** wish
518 **amonestynge:** admonishment
526 **pursewen:** persecute

therfore the lovynge of oure enemy hath confounded the venym of the devel./ For right as the devel is disconfited by humylitee, right so is he wounded to the deeth by love of oure enemy./ Certes,   530 thanne is love the medicine that casteth out the venym of Envye fro mannes herte./ The speces of this paas shullen be moore largely declared in hir chapitres folwynge./

Sequitur de Ira.

After Envye wol I discryven the synne of Ire. For soothly, whoso hath envye upon his neighebor, anon he wole comunly fynde hym a matere of wratthe, in word or in dede, agayns hym to whom he hath envye./ And as wel comth Ire of Pride as of Envye, for soothly he that is proud or envyous is lightly wrooth./ This synne of Ire, after the discryvyng of Seint Augustyn, is wikked wil to been avenged by word or by dede./ Ire, after the Philosophre, is   535 the fervent blood of man yquyked in his herte, thurgh which he wole harm to hym that he hateth./ For certes, the herte of man, by eschawfynge and moevynge of his blood, wexeth so trouble that he is out of alle juggement of resoun./ But ye shal understonde that Ire is in two maneres; that oon of hem is good, and that oother is wikked./ The goode Ire is by jalousie of goodnesse, thurgh which a man is wrooth with wikkednesse and agayns wikkednesse; and therfore seith a wys man that Ire is bet than pley./ This Ire is with debonairetee, and it is wrooth withouten bitternesse; nat wrooth agayns the man, but wrooth with the mysdede of the man, as seith the prophete David, *"Irascimini et nolite peccare."*/ Now   540 understondeth that wikked Ire is in two maneres; that is to seyn, sodeyn Ire or hastif Ire, withouten avisement and consentynge of resoun./ The menyng and the sens of this is that the resoun of a man ne consente nat to thilke sodeyn Ire, and thanne is it venial./ Another Ire is ful wikked, that comth of felonie of herte avysed and cast biforn, with wikked wil to do vengeance, and therto his resoun consenteth; and soothly this is deedly synne./ This Ire is so

displesant to God that it troubleth his hous and chaceth the Hooly Goost out of mannes soule, and wasteth and destroyeth the liknesse of God—that is to seyn, the vertu that is in mannes soule—/ and put in hym the liknesse of the devel, and bynymeth the man fro God, that is his rightful lord./   545 This Ire is a ful greet plesaunce to the devel, for it is the develes fourneys, that is eschawfed with the fir of helle./ For certes, right so as fir is moore mighty to destroyen erthely thynges than any oother element, right so Ire is myghty to destroyen alle spiritueel thynges./ Looke how that fir of smale gleedes that been almost dede under asshen wollen quike agayn whan they been touched with brymstoon; right so Ire wol everemo quyken agayn whan it is touched by the pride that is covered in mannes herte./ For certes, fir ne may nat comen out of no thyng, but if it were first in the same thyng natureelly, as fir is drawen out of flyntes with steel./ And right so as pride is ofte tyme matere of Ire, right so is rancour norice and kepere of Ire./ Ther is a   550 maner tree, as seith Seint Ysidre, that whan men maken fir of thilke tree and covere the coles of it with asshen, soothly the fir of it wol lasten al a yeer or moore./ And right so fareth it of rancour; whan it is ones conceyved in the hertes of som men, certein, it wol lasten peraventure from oon Estre day unto another Estre day, and moore./ But certes, thilke man is ful fer fro the mercy of God al thilke while./ In this forseyde develes fourneys ther forgen three shrewes: Pride, that ay bloweth and encreesseth the fir by chidynge and wikked wordes;/ thanne stant Envye and holdeth the hoote iren upon the herte of man with a peire of longe toonges of long   555 rancour;/ and thanne stant the synne of Contumelie, or strif and cheeste, and batereth and forgeth by vileyns reprevynges./ Certes, this cursed synne anoyeth bothe to the man hymself and eek to his neighebor. For soothly, almoost al the harm that any man dooth to his neighebor comth of wratthe./ For certes, outrageous wratthe dooth al that evere the devel hym comaundeth, for he ne spareth neither

532 **paas:** passage, process (?); see n.
Sequitur, *etc.:* Now follows the section on Anger.
536 **fervent:** hot   **yquyked:** stirred, enlivened
537 **eschawfynge:** heating
539 **jalousie of goodnesse:** zeal for the good
540 **mysdede:** sin   **Irascimini et nolite peccare:** Be angry and do not sin.

546 **eschawfed:** heated
551 **a maner tree:** a kind of tree, the juniper   **Ysidre:** Isidore of Seville
556 **Contumelie:** contentiousness   **cheeste:** quarrelling

Crist ne his sweete Mooder./ And in his outrageous anger and ire—allas, allas!—ful many oon at that tyme feeleth in his herte ful wikkedly, bothe of Crist and eek of alle his halwes./ Is nat this a cursed vice? Yis, certes. Allas! It bynymeth from man his wit and his resoun, and al his debonaire lif espiritueel that sholde kepen his soule./ Certes, it   560 bynymeth eek Goddes due lordshipe, and that is mannes soule and the love of his neighebores. It stryveth eek alday agayn trouthe. It reveth hym the quiete of his herte and subverteth his soule./

Of Ire comen thise stynkynge engendrures: First, hate, that is oold wratthe; discord, thurgh which a man forsaketh his olde freend that he hath loved ful longe;/ and thanne cometh werre and every manere of wrong that man dooth to his neighebor, in body or in catel./ Of this cursed synne of Ire cometh eek manslaughtre. And understonde wel that homycide, that is manslaughtre, is in diverse wise. Som manere of homycide is spiritueel, and som is bodily./ Spiritueel manslaughtre is in sixe thynges. First by hate, as seith Seint John: "He that hateth his brother is an homycide."/ Homycide is eek   565 by bakbitynge, of whiche bakbiteres seith Salomon that "they han two swerdes with whiche they sleen hire neighebores." For soothly, as wikke is to bynyme his good name as his lyf./ Homycide is eek in yevynge of wikked conseil by fraude, as for to yeven conseil to areysen wrongful custumes and taillages./ Of whiche seith Salomon, "Leon rorynge and bere hongry been like to the cruel lordshipes" in withholdynge or abreggynge of the shepe (or the hyre), or of the wages of servauntz, or elles in usure, or in withdrawynge of the almesse of povre folk./ For which the wise man seith, "Fedeth hym that almoost dyeth for honger"; for soothly, but if thow feede hym, thou sleest hym; and alle thise been deedly synnes./ Bodily manslaughtre is, whan thow sleest him with thy tonge in oother manere, as whan thou comandest to sleen a man or elles yevest hym conseil to sleen a man./ Manslaughtre in dede is in foure   570 maneres. That oon is by lawe, right as a justice dampneth hym that is coupable to the deeth. But lat the justice be war that he do it rightfully, and that

he do it nat for delit to spille blood but for kepynge of rightwisnesse./ Another homycide is that is doon for necessitee, as whan o man sleeth another in his defendaunt and that he ne may noon ootherwise escape from his owene deeth./ But certeinly if he may escape withouten slaughtre of his adversarie, and sleeth hym, he dooth synne and he shal bere penance as for deedly synne./ Eek if a man, by caas or aventure, shete an arwe, or caste a stoon with which he sleeth a man, he is homycide./ Eek if a womman by necligence overlyeth hire child in hir slepyng, it is homycide and deedly synne./ Eek whan   575 man destourbeth concepcioun of a child, and maketh a womman outher bareyne by drynkynge venenouse herbes thurgh which she may nat conceyve, or sleeth a child by drynkes wilfully, or elles putteth certeine material thynges in hire secree places to slee the child,/ or elles dooth unkyndely synne, by which man or womman shedeth hire nature in manere or in place ther as a child may nat be conceived, or elles if a woman have conceyved, and hurt hirself and sleeth the child, yet is it homycide./ What seye we eek of wommen that mordren hir children for drede of worldly shame? Certes, an horrible homicide./ Homycide is eek if a man approcheth to a womman by desir of lecherie, thurgh which the child is perissed, or elles smyteth a womman wityngly, thurgh which she leseth hir child. Alle thise been homycides and horrible deedly synnes./ Yet comen ther of Ire manye mo synnes, as wel in word as in thoght and in dede; as he that arretteth upon God, or blameth God of thyng of which he is hymself gilty, or despiseth God and alle his halwes, as doon thise cursede hasardours in diverse contrees./ This   580 cursed synne doon they, whan they feelen in hir herte ful wikkedly of God and of his halwes./ Also whan they treten unreverently the sacrement of the auter, thilke synne is so greet that unnethe may it been releessed, but that the mercy of God passeth alle his werkes; it is so greet, and he so benigne./ Thanne comth of Ire attry angre. Whan a man is sharply amonested in his shrifte to forleten his synne,/ thanne wole he be angry, and answeren hokerly and angrily,

572 **in his defendaunt:** in defending himself
575 **overlyeth:** lies upon
577 **unkyndely:** unnatural
579 **perissed:** killed
580 **arretteth upon:** blames
583 **attry:** poisonous
584 **hokerly:** disdainfully

560 **bynymeth:** takes away
567 **areysen:** impose   **custumes:** duties (customary rents, services, or tolls)
taillages: taxes
568 **abreggynge:** reduction   **shepe:** payment   **usure:** usury

and deffenden or excusen his synne by unstedefast-
nesse of his flessh; or elles he dide it for to holde
compaignye with his felawes; or elles, he seith, the
feend enticed hym;/ or elles he dide it for his youthe;
or elles his compleccioun is so corageous that he may
nat forbere; or elles it is his destinee, as he seith, unto
a certein age; or elles, he seith, it cometh hym of gentillesse of his auncestres; and semblable thynges./ Alle thise manere of folk so wrappen   585
hem in hir synnes that they ne wol nat delivere hemself. For soothly, no wight that excuseth hym
wilfully of his synne may nat been delivered of his
synne til that he mekely biknoweth his synne./ After
this, thanne cometh sweryng, that is expres agayn the
comandement of God; and this bifalleth ofte of anger
and of Ire./ God seith, "Thow shalt nat take the name
of thy Lord God in veyn or in ydel." Also oure Lord
Jhesu Crist seith, by the word of Seint Mathew,/ "Ne
wol ye nat swere in alle manere; neither by hevene,
for it is Goddes trone; ne by erthe, for it is the bench
of his feet; ne by Jerusalem, for it is the citee of a
greet kyng; ne by thyn heed, for thou mayst nat make
an heer whit ne blak./ But seyeth by youre word 'ye,
ye,' and 'nay, nay'; and what that is moore, it
is of yvel"—thus seith Crist./ For Cristes   590
sake, ne swereth nat so synfully in dismembrynge of Crist by soule, herte, bones, and body. For
certes, it semeth that ye thynke that the cursede Jewes
ne dismembred nat ynough the preciouse persone of
Crist, but ye dismembre hym moore./ And if so be
that the lawe compelle yow to swere, thanne rule yow
after the lawe of God in youre sweryyng, as seith
Jeremye, *quarto capitulo:* Thou shalt kepe three
condicions: thou shalt swere "in trouthe, in doom,
and in rightwisnesse."/ This is to seyn, thou shalt
swere sooth, for every lesynge is agayns Crist; for
Crist is verray trouthe. And thynk wel this: that
"every greet swerere, nat compelled lawefully to
swere, the wounde shal nat departe from his hous"
whil he useth swich unleveful swerying./ Thou shalt
sweren eek in doom, whan thou art constreyned by
thy domesman to witnessen the trouthe./ Eek thow
shalt nat swere for envye, ne for favour, ne for meede,

but for rightwisnesse, for declaracioun of it, to the
worshipe of God and helpyng of thyne evene-
Cristene./ And therfore every man that taketh   595
Goddes name in ydel, or falsly swereth with
his mouth, or elles taketh on hym the name of Crist,
to be called a Cristen man and lyveth agayns Cristes
lyvynge and his techynge, alle they taken Goddes
name in ydel./ Looke eek what Seint Peter seith,
Actuum quarto, Non est aliud nomen sub celo, etc.,
"Ther nys noon oother name," seith Seint Peter,
"under hevene yeven to men, in which they mowe be
saved"; that is to seyn, but the name of Jhesu Crist./
Take kep eek how precious is the name of Crist, as
seith Seint Paul, *ad Philipenses secundo, In nomine
Jhesu, etc.,* "That in the name of Jhesu every knee of
hevenely creatures, or erthely, or of helle sholde
bowe," for it is so heigh and so worshipful that the
cursede feend in helle sholde tremblen to heeren it
ynempned./ Thanne semeth it that men that sweren so
horribly by his blessed name, that they despise it
moore booldely than dide the cursede Jewes or elles
the devel, that trembleth whan he heereth his name./

Now certes, sith that sweryng, but if it be lawefully
doon, is so heighly deffended, muche worse is
forsweryng falsly, and yet nedelees./   600
What seye we eek of hem that deliten hem
in sweryng, and holden it a gentrie or a manly dede to
swere grete othes? And what of hem that of verray
usage ne cesse nat to swere grete othes, al be the
cause nat worth a straw? Certes, this is horrible
synne./ Sweryng sodeynly withoute avysement is
eek a synne./ But lat us go now to thilke horrible
sweryng of adjuracioun and conjuracioun, as doon
thise false enchauntours or nigromanciens in bacyns
ful of water, or in a bright swerd, in a cercle, or in a
fir, or in a shulderboon of a sheep./ I kan nat seye but
that they doon cursedly and dampnably agayns Crist
and al the feith of hooly chirche./
What seye we of hem that bileeven on divynailes,
as by flight or by noyse of briddes, or of beestes, or by
sort, by nigromancie, by dremes, by chirkynge of
dores or crakkynge of houses, by gnawynge of rattes,

---

585 **corageous:** ardent
592 **Jeremye:** Jeremiah   **quarto capitulo:** in the fourth chapter
593 **unleveful:** unlawful
594 **doom:** a case at law   **domesman:** judge

597 **Actuum quarto:** Acts, chapter four
598 **ad Philipenses secundo:** (Epistle) to the Philippians, second chapter
600 **forsweryng falsly:** perjury
603 **adjuracioun:** exorcism   **conjuracioun:** conjuring up spirits
nigromanciens: necromancers
605 **divynailes:** divinations   **sort:** divination   **chirkynge:** squeaking
crakkynge: creaking

and swich manere wrecchednesse?/ Certes, al   605
this thyng is deffended by God and by hooly
chirche. For which they been acursed, til they come to
amendement, that on swich filthe setten hire bileeve./
Charmes for woundes or maladie of men or of
beestes, if they taken any effect, it may be peraventure that God suffreth it, for folk sholden yeve the
moore feith and reverence to his name./

Now wol I speken of lesynges, which generally is
fals signyficaunce of word, in entente to deceyven his
evene-Cristene./ Som lesynge is of which ther comth
noon avantage to no wight; and som lesynge turneth
to the ese and profit of o man, and to disese and damage of another man./ Another lesynge is for to saven
his lyf or his catel. Another lesynge comth of delit for
to lye, in which delit they wol forge a long tale and
peynten it with alle circumstaunces, where al
the ground of the tale is fals./ Som lesynge   610
comth for he wole sustene his word; and som
lesynge comth of reccheleesnesse withouten avisement; and semblable thynges./

Lat us now touche the vice of flaterynge, which
ne comth nat gladly but for drede or for coveitise./
Flaterye is generally wrongful preisynge. Flatereres
been the develes norices, that norissen his children
with milk of losengerie./ For sothe, Salomon seith
that "Flaterie is wors than detraccioun." For somtyme
detraccion maketh an hauteyn man be the moore
humble, for he dredeth detraccion; but certes flaterye,
that maketh a man to enhauncen his herte and his
contenaunce./ Flatereres been the develes enchauntours; for they make a man to wene of hymself be lyk that he nys nat lyk./ They been lyk   615
to Judas that bitraysen a man to sellen hym
to his enemy; that is to the devel./ Flatereres been the
develes chapelleyns, that syngen evere *Placebo*./ I
rekene flaterie in the vices of Ire, for ofte tyme if o
man be wrooth with another, thanne wole he flatere
som wight to sustene hym in his querele./

Speke we now of swich cursynge as comth of irous
herte. Malisoun generally may be seyd every maner
power of harm. Swich cursynge bireveth man fro the
regne of God, as seith Seint Paul./ And ofte tyme

swich cursynge wrongfully retorneth agayn to hym
that curseth, as a bryd that retorneth agayn to
his owene nest./ And over alle thyng men   620
oghten eschewe to cursen hire children, and
yeven to the devel hire engendrure, as ferforth as in
hem is. Certes, it is greet peril and greet synne./

Lat us thanne speken of chidynge and reproche,
whiche been ful grete woundes in mannes herte, for
they unsowen the semes of freendshipe in mannes
herte./ For certes, unnethes may a man pleynly been
accorded with hym that hath hym openly revyled and
repreved and disclaundred. This is a ful grisly synne,
as Crist seith in the gospel./ And taak kep now, that he
that repreveth his neighebor, outher he repreveth hym
by som harm of peyne that he hath on his body, as
"mesel," "croked harlot," or by som synne that he
dooth./ Now if he repreve hym by harm of peyne,
thanne turneth the repreve to Jhesu Crist, for peyne is
sent by the rightwys sonde of God, and by his suffrance, be it meselrie, or maheym, or maladie./ And if he repreve hym uncharitably of   625
synne, as "thou holour," "thou dronkelewe
harlot," and so forth, thanne aperteneth that to the
rejoysynge of the devel, that evere hath joye that men
doon synne./ And certes, chidynge may nat come but
out of a vileyns herte. For after the habundance of the
herte speketh the mouth ful ofte./ And ye shul understonde that looke, by any wey, whan any man shal
chastise another, that he be war from chidynge or
reprevynge. For trewely, but he be war, he may ful
lightly quyken the fir of angre and of wratthe, which
that he sholde quenche, and peraventure sleeth hym
which that he myghte chastise with benignitee./ For as
seith Salomon, "The amyable tonge is the tree of
lyf"—that is to seyn, of lyf espiritueel—and soothly, a
deslavee tonge sleeth the spirites of hym that repreveth
and eek of hym that is repreved./ Loo, what seith Seint
Augustyn: "Ther is nothyng so lyk the develes child as
he that ofte chideth." Seint Paul seith eek, "The
servant of God bihoveth nat to chide."/ And   630
how that chidynge be a vileyns thyng bitwixe
alle manere folk, yet is it certes moost uncovenable

614 **hauteyn:** haughty
617 **Placebo:** "I shall please"
618 **querele:** dispute

622 **unsowen:** unravel, undo   **semes:** seams
624 **mesel:** leper   **croked harlot:** crippled rascal
625 **rightwys:** just   **sonde:** dispensation   **meselrie:** leprosy
maheym: bodily injury
626 **holour:** lecher
629 **deslavee:** unbridled
631 **uncovenable:** unsuitable

bitwixe a man and his wyf, for there is nevere reste. And therfore seith Salomon, "An hous that is uncovered and droppynge and a chidynge wyf been lyke."/ A man that is in a droppynge hous in manye places, though he eschewe the droppynge in o place, it droppeth on hym in another place. So fareth it by a chydynge wyf; but she chide hym in o place, she wol chide hym in another./ And therfore, "Bettre is a morsel of breed with joye than an hous ful of delices with chidynge," seith Salomon./ Seint Paul seith, "O ye wommen, be ye subgetes to youre housbondes as bihoveth in God, and ye men loveth youre wyves." *Ad Colossenses tertio.*/

Afterward speke we of scornynge, which is a wikked synne, and namely whan he scorneth a man for his goode werkes./ For certes,   635 swiche scorneres faren lyk the foule tode, that may nat endure to smelle the soote savour of the vyne whanne it florissheth./ Thise scorneres been partyng felawes with the devel; for they han joye whan the devel wynneth and sorwe whan he leseth./ They been adversaries of Jhesu Crist, for they haten that he loveth—that is to seyn, salvacioun of soule./

Speke we now of wikked conseil, for he that wikked conseil yeveth is a traytour. For he deceyveth hym that trusteth in hym, *ut Achitofel ad Absolonem.* But nathelees, yet is his wikked conseil first agayn hymself./ For, as seith the wise man, "Every fals lyvynge hath this propertee in hymself, that he that wole anoye another man, he anoyeth first hymself."/ And men shul understonde that   640 man shal nat taken his conseil of fals folk, ne of angry folk, or grevous folk, ne of folk that loven specially to muchel hir owene profit, ne to muche worldly folk, namely in conseilynge of soules./

Now comth the synne of hem that sowen and maken discord amonges folk, which is a synne that Crist hateth outrely. And no wonder is, for he deyde for to make concord./ And moore shame do they to Crist than dide they that hym crucifiede, for God loveth bettre that freendshipe be amonges folk, than he dide his owene body, the which that he yaf for

unitee. Therfore been they likned to the devel, that evere is aboute to maken discord./

Now comth the synne of double tonge, swiche as speken faire byforn folk and wikkedly bihynde, or elles they maken semblant as though they speeke of good entencioun, or elles in game and pley, and yet they speke of wikked entente./

Now comth biwreying of conseil, thurgh which a man is defamed; certes, unnethe may he restoore the damage./   645

Now comth manace, that is an open folye, for he that ofte manaceth, he threteth moore than he may parfourne ful ofte tyme./

Now cometh ydel wordes, that is withouten profit of hym that speketh tho wordes, and eek of hym that herkneth tho wordes. Or elles ydel wordes been tho that been nedelees or withouten entente of natureel profit./ And al be it that ydel wordes been somtyme venial synne, yet sholde men douten hem, for we shul yeve rekenynge of hem bifore God./

Now comth janglynge, that may nat been withoute synne. And, as seith Salomon, "It is a sygne of apert folye."/ And therfore a philosophre seyde, whan men axed hym how that men sholde plese the peple, and he answerde, "Do manye goode werkes, and spek fewe jangles."/   650

After this comth the synne of japeres, that been the develes apes, for they maken folk to laughe at hire japerie as folk doon at the gawdes of an ape. Swiche japeres deffendeth Seint Paul./ Looke how that vertuouse wordes and hooly conforten hem that travaillen in the service of Crist, right so conforten the vileyns wordes and knakkes of japeris hem that travaillen in the service of the devel./ Thise been the synnes that comen of the tonge, that comen of Ire and of othere synnes mo./

Sequitur remedium contra peccatum Ire.

The remedie agayns Ire is a vertu that men clepen mansuetude, that is debonairetee; and eek another vertu, that men callen pacience or suffrance./

---

631 **droppynge:** leaking
634 **Ad Colossenses tertio:** (Epistle) to the Colossians, chapter three
636 **tode:** toad
637 **partyng felawes:** partners
639 **ut Achitofel ad Absolonem:** as Achitophel (did) to Absalom
641 **grevous:** hostile

643 **aboute to:** busied with
644 **maken semblant:** feign, pretend
649 **apert:** clear
650 **jangles:** idle words
651 **japeres:** mockers   **gawdes:** tricks
652 **knakkes:** tricks
Sequitur remedium, *etc.:* Now follows the remedy against the sin of Anger.
654 **mansuetude:** meekness

Debonairetee withdraweth and refreyneth the sti-rynges and the moevynges of mannes corage in his herte, in swich manere that they ne skippe nat out by angre ne by ire./ Suffrance suffreth   655 swetely alle the anoyaunces and the wronges that men doon to man outward./ Seint Jerome seith thus of debonairetee, that "it dooth noon harm to no wight ne seith; ne for noon harm that men doon or seyn, he ne eschawfeth nat agayns his resoun."/ This vertu somtyme comth of nature, for, as seith the Philosophre, "A man is a quyk thyng, by nature debonaire and tretable to goodnesse; but whan debonairetee is enformed of grace, thanne is it the moore worth."/

Pacience, that is another remedie agayns Ire, is a vertu that suffreth swetely every mannes goodnesse, and is nat wrooth for noon harm that is doon to hym./ The Philosophre seith that pacience is thilke vertu that suffreth debonairely alle the outrages of adversitee and every wikked word./ This   660 vertu maketh a man lyk to God, and maketh hym Goddes owene deere child, as seith Crist. This vertu disconfiteth thyn enemy. And therfore seith the wise man, "If thow wolt venquysse thyn enemy, lerne to suffre."/ And thou shalt understonde that man suf-freth foure manere of grevances in outward thynges, agayns the whiche foure he moot have foure manere of paciences./

The firste grevance is of wikkede wordes. Thilke suffrede Jhesu Crist withouten grucchyng, ful paciently, whan the Jewes despised and repreved hym ful ofte./ Suffre thou therfore paciently; for the wise man seith, "If thou stryve with a fool, though the fool be wrooth or though he laughe, algate thou shalt have no reste."/ That oother grevance outward is to have damage of thy catel. Theragayns suffred Crist ful paciently, whan he was despoyled of al that he hadde in this lyf, and that nas but his clothes./   665 The thridde grevance is a man to have harm in his body. That suffred Crist ful paciently in al his passioun./ The fourthe grevance is in outrageous labour in werkes. Wherfore I seye that folk that maken hir servantz to travaillen to grevously or out of

tyme, as on haly dayes, soothly they do greet synne./ Heer-agayns suffred Crist ful paciently and taughte us pacience, whan he baar upon his blissed shulder the croys upon which he sholde suffren despitous deeth./ Heere may men lerne to be pacient, for certes noght oonly Cristen men been pacient for love of Jhesu Crist and for gerdoun of the blisful lyf that is perdurable, but certes, the olde payens that nevere were Cristene commendeden and useden the vertu of pacience./

A philosophre upon a tyme, that wolde have beten his disciple for his grete trespas, for which he was greetly amoeved, and broghte a yerde to scoure with the child;/ and whan this child   670 saugh the yerde, he seyde to his maister, "What thenke ye do?" "I wol bete thee," quod the maister, "for thy correccioun."/ "For sothe," quod the child, "ye oghten first correcte youreself, that han lost al youre pacience for the gilt of a child."/ "For sothe," quod the maister al wepynge, "thow seyst sooth. Have thow the yerde, my deere sone, and correcte me for myn inpacience."/ Of pacience comth obedience, thurgh which a man is obedient to Crist and to alle hem to whiche he oghte to been obedient in Crist./ And understond wel that obedience is parfit whan that a man dooth gladly and hastily, with good herte entierly, al that he sholde do./ Obedi-   675 ence generally is to parfourne the doctrine of God and of his sovereyns, to whiche hym oghte to ben obeisaunt in alle rightwisnesse./

Sequitur de Accidia.

After the synne of Envye and of Ire, now wol I speken of the synne of Accidie. For Envye blyndeth the herte of a man, and Ire troubleth a man, and Acci-die maketh hym hevy, thoghtful, and wraw./ Envye and Ire maken bitternesse in herte, which bitternesse is mooder of Accidie, and bynymeth hym the love of alle goodnesse. Thanne is Accidie the angwissh of troubled herte; and Seint Augustyn seith, "It is anoy of goodnesse and joye of harm."/ Certes, this is a dampnable synne, for it dooth wrong to Jhesu Crist,

---

655 **refreyneth:** restrains
657 **eschawfeth:** becomes inflamed (with emotion)
658 **the Philosophre:** Aristotle
667 **outrageous labour in werkes:** forced labor, service demanded beyond the customary obligations

670 **yerde:** stick, rod   **scoure:** punish
Sequitur, *etc.*: Now follows the section on Sloth.
677 **wraw:** fretful
678 **anoy:** vexation

in as muche as it bynymeth the service that men oghte doon to Crist with alle diligence, as seith Salomon./ But Accidie dooth no swich diligence. He dooth alle thyng with anoy, and with wrawnesse, slaknesse, and excusacioun, and with ydelnesse, and unlust; for which the book seith, "Acursed be he that dooth the service of God necligently."/ 680 Thanne is Accidie enemy to everich estaat of man, for certes the estaat of man is in three maneres./ Outher it is th'estaat of innocence, as was th'estaat of Adam biforn that he fil into synne, in which estaat he was holden to wirche as in heriynge and adowrynge of God./ Another estaat is the estaat of synful men, in which estaat men been holden to laboure in preiynge to God for amendement of hire synnes, and that he wole graunte hem to arysen out of hir synnes./ Another estaat is th'estaat of grace, in which estaat he is holden to werkes of penitence. And certes, to alle thise thynges is Accidie enemy and contrarie, for he loveth no bisynesse at al./ Now certes this foule synne Accidie is eek a ful greet enemy to the liflode of the body, for it ne hath no purveaunce agayn temporeel necessitee, for it forsleweth and forsluggeth and destroyeth alle goodes temporeles by reccheleesnesse./ 685

The fourthe thyng is that Accidie is lyk hem that been in the peyne of helle, by cause of hir slouthe and of hire hevynesse, for they that been dampned been so bounde that they ne may neither wel do ne wel thynke./ Of Accidie comth first that a man is anoyed and encombred for to doon any goodnesse, and maketh that God hath abhomynacion of swich Accidie, as seith Seint John./

Now comth Slouthe, that wol nat suffre noon hardnesse ne no penaunce. For soothly, Slouthe is so tendre and so delicaat, as seith Salomon, that he wol nat suffre noon hardnesse ne penaunce, and therfore he shendeth al that he dooth./ Agayns this roten-herted synne of Accidie and Slouthe sholde men exercise hemself to doon goode werkes, and manly and vertuously cacchen corage wel to doon, thynkynge that oure Lord Jhesu Crist quiteth every good dede, be it never so lite./ Usage of labour is a greet thyng, for it

maketh, as seith Seint Bernard, the laborer to have stronge armes and harde synwes; and slouthe maketh hem feble and tendre./ Thanne comth 690 drede to bigynne to werke anye goode werkes. For certes, he that is enclyned to synne, hym thynketh it is so greet an emprise for to undertake to doon werkes of goodnesse,/ and casteth in his herte that the circumstaunces of goodnesse been so grevouse and so chargeaunt for to suffre, that he dar nat undertake to do werkes of goodnesse, as seith Seint Gregorie./

Now comth wanhope, that is despeir of the mercy of God, that comth somtyme of to muche outrageous sorwe, and somtyme of to muche drede, ymaginynge that he hath doon so muche synne that it wol nat availlen hym, though he wolde repenten hym and forsake synne,/ thurgh which despeir or drede he abaundoneth al his herte to every maner synne, as seith Seint Augustin./ Which dampnable synne, if that it continue unto his ende, it is cleped synnyng in the Hooly Goost./ This horrible synne is 695 so perilous that he that is despeired, ther nys no felonye ne no synne that he douteth for to do, as shewed wel by Judas./ Certes, aboven alle synnes thanne is this synne moost displesant to Crist, and moost adversarie./ Soothly, he that despeireth hym is lyk the coward champioun recreant, that seith "creant" withoute nede. Allas, allas, nedeles is he recreant and nedelees despeired./ Certes, the mercy of God is evere redy to the penitent, and is aboven alle his werkes./ Allas, kan a man nat bithynke hym on the gospel of Seint Luc, 15, where as Crist seith that "as wel shal ther be joye in hevene upon a synful man that dooth penitence, as upon nynty and nyne rightful men that neden no penitence."/ Looke 700 forther, in the same gospel, the joye and the feeste of the goode man that hadde lost his sone, whan his sone with repentaunce was retourned to his fader./ Kan they nat remembren hem eek that, as seith Seint Luc, 23, how that the theef that was hanged bisyde Jhesu Crist seyde, "Lord, remembre of me, whan thow comest into thy regne"?/ "For sothe," seyde Crist, "I seye to thee, to-day shaltow been with me in paradys."/ Certes, ther is noon so horrible

---

680 **wrawnesse:** fretfulness　**slaknesse:** slowness, idleness　**excusacioun:** making excuses　**unlust:** disinclination
685 **liflode:** livelihood, sustenance　**forsleweth:** loses by delaying　**forsluggeth:** spoils through sluggishness
689 **quiteth:** rewards

692 **chargeaunt:** burdensome
693 **wanhope:** despair
695 **in:** against
698 **recreant:** cowardly, confessing himself defeated (*creant*)

synne of man that it ne may in his lyf be destroyed
by penitence, thurgh vertu of the passion and of the
deeth of Crist./ Allas, what nedeth man thanne to
been despeired, sith that his mercy so redy is
and large? Axe and have./ Thanne cometh   705
sompnolence, that is sloggy slombrynge,
which maketh a man be hevy and dul in body and in
soule, and this synne comth of Slouthe./ And certes,
the tyme that, by wey of resoun, men sholde nat
slepe, that is by the morwe, but if ther were cause resonable./ For soothly, the morwe tyde is moost covenable a man to seye his preyeres, and for to thynken on
God, and for to honoure God, and to yeven almesse to
the povre that first cometh in the name of Crist./ Lo,
what seith Salomon: "Whoso wolde by the morwe
awaken and seke me, he shal fynde."/ Thanne cometh
necligence, or reccheleesnesse, that rekketh of no
thyng. And how that ignoraunce be mooder of
alle harm, certes, necligence is the norice./   710
Necligence ne dooth no fors, whan he shal
doon a thyng, wheither he do it weel or baddely./

Of the remedie of thise two synnes, as seith the wise
man, that "He that dredeth God, he spareth nat to doon
that him oghte doon."/ And he that loveth God, he wol
doon diligence to plese God by his werkes and abaundone hymself, with al his myght, wel for to doon./
Thanne comth ydelnesse, that is the yate of alle harmes.
An ydel man is lyk to a place that hath no walles; the
develes may entre on every syde, or sheten at hym at discovert, by temptacion on every syde./ This ydelnesse is
the thurrok of alle wikked and vileyns thoghtes,
and of alle jangles, trufles, and of alle ordure./   715
Certes, the hevene is yeven to hem that wol
labouren, and nat to ydel folk. Eek David seith that
"they ne been nat in the labour of men, ne they shul nat
been whipped with men"—that is to seyn, in purgatorie./ Certes, thanne semeth it they shul be tormented
with the devel in helle, but if they doon penitence./

Thanne comth the synne that men clepen *tarditas,*
as whan a man is to laterede or tariynge er he wole
turne to God, and certes that is a greet folie. He is
lyk to hym that falleth in the dych and wol nat arise./

And this vice comth of a fals hope, that he thynketh
that he shal lyve longe; but that hope faileth ful ofte./

Thanne comth lachesse; that is he that whan he
biginneth any good werk anon he shal forleten it and
stynten, as doon they that han any wight to governe
and ne taken of hym namoore kep anon as
they fynden any contrarie or any anoy./ Thise   720
been the newe sheepherdes that leten hir
sheep wityngly go renne to the wolf that is in the
breres, or do no fors of hir owene governaunce./ Of
this comth poverte and destruccioun, bothe of spiritueel and temporeel thynges. Thanne comth a
manere cooldnesse, that freseth al the herte of a
man./ Thanne comth undevocioun, thurgh which a
man is so blent, as seith Seint Bernard, and hath
swich langour in soule that he may neither rede ne
singe in hooly chirche, ne heere ne thynke of no
devocioun, ne travaille with his handes in no good
werk, that it nys hym unsavory and al apalled./
Thanne wexeth he slough and slombry, and soone
wol be wrooth, and soone is enclyned to hate and to
envye./ Thanne comth the synne of worldly sorwe,
swich as is cleped *tristicia,* that sleeth man,
as seith Seint Paul./ For certes, swich sorwe   725
werketh to the deeth of the soule and of the
body also; for therof comth that a man is anoyed of his
owene lif./ Wherfore swich sorwe shorteth ful ofte the
lif of man, er that his tyme be come by wey of kynde./

Remedium contra peccatum Accidie.

Agayns this horrible synne of Accidie, and the
branches of the same, ther is a vertu that is called *fortitudo* or strengthe, that is an affeccioun thurgh which
a man despiseth anoyouse thinges./ This vertu is so
myghty and so vigerous that it dar withstonde
myghtily and wisely kepen hymself fro perils that
been wikked, and wrastle agayn the assautes of the
devel./ For it enhaunceth and enforceth the soule,
right as Accidie abateth it and maketh it fieble. For
this *fortitudo* may endure by long suf-
frauncethe travailles that been covenable./   730
This vertu hath manye speces; and the
firste is cleped magnanimitee, that is to seyn, greet

---

706 **sloggy:** sluggish   **slombrynge:** sleeping
713 **abaundone:** devote
714 **discovert:** an exposed position
715 **thurrok:** bilge, storage place   **trufles:** trifles, idle jests
718 **laterede:** tardy, sluggish

720 **lachesse:** laziness
722 **freseth:** freezes
723 **undevocioun:** lack of devotion   **apalled:** faded
724 **slough:** slow, sluggish   **slombry:** sleepy
Remedium, *etc.*: The remedy against the sin of Sloth.
728 **anoyouse:** noisome, harmful
730 **abateth:** reduces

corage. For certes, ther bihoveth greet corage agains Accidie, lest that it ne swolwe the soule by the synne of sorwe, or destroye it by wanhope./ This vertu maketh folk to undertake harde thynges and grevouse thynges, by hir owene wil, wisely and resonably./ And for as muchel as the devel fighteth agayns a man moore by queyntise and by sleighte than by strengthe, therfore men shal withstonden hym by wit and by resoun and by discrecioun./ Thanne arn ther the vertues of feith and hope in God and in his seintes to acheve and acomplice the goode werkes in the whiche he purposeth fermely to continue./ Thanne comth seuretee or sikernesse, and that is whan a man ne douteth no travaille in tyme comynge of the goode werkes that a man hath bigonne./   735 Thanne comth magnificence; that is to seyn, whan a man dooth and parfourneth grete werkes of goodnesse; and that is the ende why that men sholde do goode werkes, for in the acomplissynge of grete goode werkes lith the grete gerdoun./ Thanne is ther constaunce, that is stablenesse of corage, and this sholde been in herte by stedefast feith, and in mouth, and in berynge, and in chiere, and in dede./ Eke ther been mo speciale remedies against Accidie in diverse werkes, and in consideracioun of the peynes of helle and of the joyes of hevene, and in the trust of the grace of the Holy Goost, that wole yeve hym myght to parfourne his goode entente./

Sequitur de Avaricia.

After Accidie wol I speke of Avarice and of Coveitise, of which synne seith Seint Paul that "the roote of alle harmes is Coveitise." *Ad Thimotheum Sexto.*/ For soothly, whan the herte of a man is confounded in itself and troubled, and that the soule hath lost the confort of God, thanne seketh he an ydel solas of worldly thynges./   740 Avarice, after the descripcioun of Seint Augustyn, is a likerousnesse in herte to have erthely thynges./ Som oother folk seyn that Avarice is for to purchacen manye erthely thynges and no thyng yeve to hem that han nede./ And understoond that Avarice ne stant nat oonly in lond ne catel, but somtyme in science and in glorie, and in every manere of outrageous thyng is Avarice and Coveitise./ And the difference

bitwixe Avarice and Coveitise is this: Coveitise is for to coveite swiche thynges as thou hast nat; and Avarice is for to withholde and kepe swiche thynges as thou hast, withoute rightful nede./ Soothly, this Avarice is a synne that is ful dampnable, for al hooly writ curseth it and spekketh agayns that vice, for it dooth wrong to Jhesu Crist./ For it bireveth hym the   745 love that men to hym owen, and turneth it bakward agayns alle resoun,/ and maketh that the avaricious man hath moore hope in his catel than in Jhesu Crist, and dooth moore observance in kepynge of his tresor than he dooth to the service of Jhesu Crist./ And therfore seith Seint Paul *Ad Ephesios quinto,* that an avaricious man is the thraldom of ydolatrie./

What difference is bitwixe an ydolastre and an avaricious man, but that an ydolastre, per aventure, ne hath but o mawmet or two, and the avaricious man hath manye? For certes, every floryn in his cofre is his mawmet./ And certes, the synne of mawmettrie is the firste thyng that God deffended in the ten comaundementz, as bereth witnesse in *Exodi capitulo vicesimo:*/ "Thou shalt have no false   750 goddes bifore me, ne thou shalt make to thee no grave thyng." Thus is an avaricious man, that loveth his tresor biforn God, an ydolastre,/ thurgh this cursed synne of avarice. Of Coveitise comen thise harde lordshipes, thurgh whiche men been distreyned by taylages, custumes, and cariages, moore than hire duetee or resoun is. And eek taken they of hire bonde-men amercimentz, whiche myghten moore resonably ben cleped extorcions than amercimentz./ Of whiche amercimentz and raunsonynge of boondemen somme lordes stywardes seyn that it is rightful, for as muche as a cherl hath no temporeel thyng that it ne is his lordes, as they seyn./ But certes, thise lordshipes doon wrong that bireven hire bondefolk thynges that they nevere yave hem. *Augustinus, De Civitate libro nono.*/ "Sooth is that the condicioun of thraldom and the firste cause of thraldom is for

---

733 **queyntise:** cunning trickery
Sequitur, *etc.:* Now follows the section on Avarice.
739 **Ad Thimotheum Sexto:** (Epistle) to Timothy, chapter six

748 **Ad Ephesios quinto:** (Epistle) to the Ephesians, chapter five
749 **ydolastre:** idolater   **mawmet:** idol
750 **mawmettrie:** idolatry   **Exodi capitulo vicesimo:** twentieth chapter of Exodus
752 **taylages:** taxes   **custumes:** duties (customary rents, services, or tolls)
cariages: services of providing transportation for the lord, or payments in lieu of the same   **bonde-men:** serfs   **amercimentz:** fines imposed at the mercy of the court
753 **raunsonynge of:** forcing payment from
754 **Augustinus, De Civitate libro nono:** St. Augustine, *City (of God),* in the ninth book

synne. *Genesis nono.*/ Thus may ye seen that   755
the gilt disserveth thraldom, but nat nature."/
Wherfore thise lordes ne sholde nat muche glorifien
hem in hir lordshipes, sith that by natureel condicion
they been nat lordes over thralles, but that thraldom
comth first by the desert of synne./ And forther over,
ther as the lawe seith that temporeel goodes of
boonde-folk been the goodes of hir lordshipes, ye,
that is for to understonde, the goodes of the emperour, to deffenden hem in hir right, but nat for to
robben hem ne reven hem./ And therfore seith
Seneca, "Thy prudence sholde lyve benignely with
thy thralles."/ Thilke that thou clepest thy thralles
been Goddes peple, for humble folk been Cristes
freendes; they been contubernyal with the
Lord./   760

Thynk eek that of swich seed as cherles
spryngen, of swich seed spryngen lordes. As wel may
the cherl be saved as the lord./ The same deeth that
taketh the cherl, swich deeth taketh the lord. Wherfore I rede, do right so with thy cherl, as thou woldest that thy lord dide with thee, if thou were in his
plit./ Every synful man is a cherl to synne. I rede
thee, certes, that thou, lord, werke in swich wise with
thy cherles that they rather love thee than drede./ I
woot wel ther is degree above degree, as reson is, and
skile is that men do hir devoir ther as it is due, but
certes, extorcions and despit of youre underlynges is
dampnable./

And forther over, understoond wel that thise con-
querours or tirauntz maken ful ofte thralles of hem
that been born of as roial blood as been they
that hem conqueren./ This name of thraldom   765
was nevere erst kowth til that Noe seyde that
his sone Canaan sholde be thral to his bretheren for
his synne./ What seye we thanne of hem that pilen
and doon extorcions to hooly chirche? Certes, the
swerd that men yeven first to a knyght, whan he is
newe dubbed, signifieth that he sholde deffenden
hooly chirche, and nat robben it ne pilen it; and
whoso dooth is traitour to Crist./ And, as seith Seint
Augustyn, "They been the develes wolves that stranglen the sheep of Jhesu Crist," and doon worse than

wolves./ For soothly, whan the wolf hath ful his
wombe, he stynteth to strangle sheep. But soothly, the
pilours and destroyours of the godes of hooly chirche
ne do nat so, for they ne stynte nevere to pile./

Now as I have seyd, sith so is that synne was first
cause of thraldom, thanne is it thus: that thilke tyme
that al this world was in synne, thanne was al
this world in thraldom and subjeccioun./ But   770
certes, sith the time of grace cam, God
ordeyned that som folk sholde be moore heigh in
estaat and in degree, and som folk moore lough, and
that everich sholde be served in his estaat and in his
degree./ And therfore in somme contrees, ther they
byen thralles, whan they han turned hem to the feith,
they maken hire thralles free out of thraldom. And
therfore, certes, the lord oweth to his man that the
man oweth to his lord./ The Pope calleth hymself servant of the servantz of God; but for as muche as the
estaat of hooly chirche ne myghte nat han be, ne the
commune profit myghte nat han be kept, ne pees and
rest in erthe, but if God hadde ordeyned that som
men hadde hyer degree and som men lower,/ therfore was sovereyntee ordeyned, to kepe and maynetene
and deffenden hire underlynges or hire subgetz in
resoun, as ferforth as it lith in hire power, and nat to
destroyen hem ne confounde./ Wherfore I seye that
thilke lordes that been lyk wolves, that devouren the
possessiouns or the catel of povre folk wrongfully, withouten mercy or mesure,/ they shul   775
receyven by the same mesure that they han
mesured to povre folk the mercy of Jhesu Crist, but
if it be amended./ Now comth deceite bitwixe marchaunt and marchant. And thow shalt understonde
that marchandise is in manye maneres; that oon is
bodily, and that oother is goostly; that oon is honest
and leveful, and that oother is deshonest and unleveful./ Of thilke bodily marchandise that is leveful and
honest is this: that, there as God hath ordeyned that
a regne or a contree is suffisaunt to hymself, thanne is
it honest and leveful that of habundaunce of this contree, that men helpe another contree that is moore
nedy./ And therfore ther moote been marchantz to
bryngen fro that o contree to that oother hire
marchandises./ That oother marchandise, that men

755 **Genesis nono:** Genesis, in the ninth chapter
760 **contubernyal:** on familiar terms
764 **underlynges:** inferiors, thralls
766 **Noe:** Noah   **Canaan:** Ham
767 **pilen:** rob

769 **pilours:** thieves

haunten with fraude and trecherie and deceite, with lesynges and false othes, is cursed and dampnable./ Espiritueel marchandise is proprely symonye, that is ententif desir to byen thyng espiritueel; that is, thyng that aperteneth to the seintuarie of God and to cure of the soule./ This desir, if so be that a man do his diligence to parfournen it, al be it that his desir ne take noon effect, yet is it to hym a deedly synne; and if he be ordred, he is irreguleer./ Certes symonye is cleped of Simon Magus, that wolde han boght for temporeel catel the yifte that God hadde yeven by the Hooly Goost to Seint Peter and to the apostles./ And therfore understoond that bothe he that selleth and he that beyeth thynges espirituels been cleped symonyals, be it by catel, be it by procurynge, or by flesshly preyere of his freendes, flesshly freendes or espiritueel freendes:/ Flesshly in two maneres; as by kynrede, or othere freendes. Soothly, if they praye for hym that is nat worthy and able, it is symonye, if he take the benefice; and if he be worthy and able, ther nys noon./ That oother manere is whan men or wommen preyen for folk to avauncen hem, oonly for wikked flesshly affeccioun that they han unto the persone, and that is foul symonye./ But certes, in service, for which men yeven thynges espirituels unto hir servantz, it moot been understonde that the service moot been honest and elles nat; and eek that it be withouten bargaynynge, and that the persone be able./ For, as seith Seint Damasie, "Alle the synnes of the world, at regard of this synne, arn as thyng of noght." For it is the gretteste synne that may be, after the synne of Lucifer and Antecrist./ For by this synne God forleseth the chirche and the soule that he boghte with his precious blood, by hem that yeven chirches to hem that been nat digne./ For they putten in theves that stelen the soules of Jhesu Crist and destroyen his patrimoyne./ By swiche undigne preestes and curates han lewed men the lasse reverence of the sacramentz of hooly

780

785

790

chirche, and swiche yeveres of chirches putten out the children of Crist and putten into the chirche the develes owene sone./ They sellen the soules that lambes sholde kepen to the wolf that strangleth hem. And therfore shul they nevere han part of the pasture of lambes, that is the blisse of hevene./ Now comth hasardrie with his apurtenaunces, as tables and rafles, of which comth deceite, false othes, chidynges, and alle ravynes, blasphemynge and reneiynge of God, and hate of his neighebores, wast of goodes, mysspendynge of tyme, and somtyme manslaughtre./ Certes, hasardours ne mowe nat been withouten greet synne whiles they haunte that craft./ Of Avarice comen eek lesynges, thefte, fals witnesse, and false othes. And ye shul understonde that thise been grete synnes and expres agayn the comaundementz of God, as I have seyd./ Fals witnesse is in word and eek in dede. In word, as for to bireve thy neighebores goode name by thy fals witnessyng, or bireven hym his catel or his heritage by thy fals witnessyng, whan thou for ire, or for meede, or for envye, berest fals witnesse, or accusest hym or excusest hym by thy fals witnesse, or elles excusest thyself falsly./ Ware yow, questemongeres and notaries! Certes, for fals witnessyng was Susanna in ful gret sorwe and peyne, and many another mo./ The synne of thefte is eek expres agayns Goddes heeste, and that in two maneres, corporeel or spiritueel./ Corporeel, as for to take thy neighebores catel agayn his wyl, be it by force or by sleighte, be it by met or by mesure;/ by stelyng eek of false enditementz upon hym, and in borwynge of thy neighebores catel, in entente nevere to payen it agayn, and semblable thynges./ Espiritueel thefte is sacrilege; that is to seyn, hurtynge of hooly thynges, or of thynges sacred to Crist, in two maneres: by reson of the hooly place, as chirches or chirche-hawes,/ for which every vileyns synne that men doon in swiche places may be cleped sacrilege, or every violence in the semblable places; also, they that withdrawen falsly the rightes that longen to hooly chirche./ And pleynly and

795

800

782 **ordred:** ordained **irreguleer:** in violation of the rules of his religious order
784 **symonyals:** simoniacs **procurynge:** procuring a benefice for someone or soliciting it
785 **able:** suitable
787 **bargaynynge:** fraud
788 **Damasie:** Pope Damasus I (366–84)
789 **forleseth:** loses completely
790 **patrimoyne:** inheritance
791 **undigne:** unworthy

791 **yeveres:** givers
793 **hasardrie:** gambling **tables:** backgammon **rafles:** game played with three dice **ravynes:** robberies **mysspendynge:** waste
797 **questemongeres:** conductors of inquests, jurymen
799 **Corporeel:** bodily, natural **met:** measurement
800 **of false:** by means of false
801 **by reson of:** because of **chirche-hawes:** churchyards

generally, sacrilege is to reven hooly thyng fro hooly place, or unhooly thyng out of hooly place, or hooly thing out of unhooly place./

Relevacio contra peccatum Avaricie.

Now shul ye understonde that the releevynge of Avarice is misericorde, and pitee largely taken. And men myghten axe why that misericorde and pitee is releevynge of Avarice./ Certes, the avricious man sheweth no pitee ne misericorde to the nedeful man, for he deliteth hym in the kepynge of his tresor, and nat in the rescowynge ne releevynge of his evene-Cristen. And therfore speke I first of miseri-corde./ Thanne is misericorde, as seith the   805 Philosophre, a vertu by which the corage of a man is stired by the mysese of hym that is mysesed./ Upon which misericorde folweth pitee in par-fournynge of charitable werkes of misericorde./ And certes, thise thynges moeven a man to the miseri-corde of Jhesu Crist, that he yaf hymself for oure gilt, and suffred deeth for misericorde, and forgaf us oure originale synnes,/ and therby relessed us fro the peynes of helle, and amenused the peynes of purga-torie by penitence, and yeveth grace wel to do, and atte laste the blisse of hevene./ The speces of miseri-corde been, as for to lene and for to yeve, and to foryeven and relesse, and for to han pitee in herte and compassioun of the meschief of his evene-Cristene, and eek to chastise, there as nede   810 is./ Another manere of remedie agayns avarice is resonable largesse; but soothly, heere bihoveth the consideracioun of the grace of Jhesu Crist, and of his temporeel goodes, and eek of the goodes perdurables that Crist yaf to us;/ and to han remembrance of the deeth that he shal receyve, he noot whanne, where, ne how; and eek that he shal for-gon al that he hath, save oonly that he hath despended in goode werkes./

But for as muche as som folk been unmesurable, men oghten eschue fool-largesse, that men clepen wast./ Certes, he that is fool-large ne yeveth nat his catel, but he leseth his catel. Soothly, what thyng that he yeveth for veyne glorie, as to mynstrals and to folk for to beren his renoun in the world, he hath synne

therof and noon almesse./ Certes, he leseth foule his good that ne seketh with the yifte of his good nothyng but synne./ He is lyk to an hors that   815 seketh rather to drynken drovy or trouble water than for to drynken water of the clere welle./ And for as muchel as they yeven ther as they sholde nat yeven, to hem aperteneth thilke malisoun that Crist shal yeven at the day of doom to hem that shullen been dampned./

Sequitur de Gulâ.

After Avarice comth Glotonye, which is expres eek agayn the comandement of God. Glotonye is unmesurable appetit to ete or to drynke, or elles to doon ynogh to the unmesurable appetit and desor-deynee coveitise to eten or to drynke./ This synne corrumped al this world, as is wel shewed in the synne of Adam and of Eve. Looke eek what seith Seint Paul of Glotonye:/ "Manye," seith Saint Paul, "goon, of whiche I have ofte seyd to yow, and now I seye it wepynge, that been the enemys of the croys of Crist; of whiche the ende is deeth, and of whiche hire wombe is hire god, and hire glorie in confu-sioun of hem that so savouren erthely thynges."/   820 He that is usaunt to this synne of glotonye, he ne may no synne withstonde. He moot been in ser-vage of alle vices, for it is the develes hoord ther he hideth hym and resteth./ This synne hath manye speces. The firste is dronkenesse, that is the horrible sepulture of mannes resoun; and therfore, whan a man is dronken, he hath lost his resoun; and this is deedly synne./ But soothly, whan that a man is nat wont to strong drynke, and peraventure ne knoweth nat the strengthe of the drynke, or hath feblesse in his heed, or hath travailed, thurgh which he drynketh the moore, al be he sodeynly caught with drynke, it is no deedly synne, but venyal./ The seconde spece of glotonye is that the spirit of a man wexeth al trouble, for dronke-nesse bireveth hym the discrecioun of his wit./ The thridde spece of glotonye is whan a man devoureth his mete and hath no rightful manere   825 of etynge./ The fourthe is whan, thurgh the grete habundaunce of his mete, the humours in his

---

Relevacio, *etc.*: The relief against the sin of Avarice.
804 **misericorde:** mercy
806 **mysese:** distress
813 **unmesurable:** immoderate

816 **drovy:** dirty
Sequitur, *etc.*: Now follows the section on Gluttony.
818 **desordeynee:** excessive
819 **corrumped:** corrupted
821 **usaunt:** accustomed

body been distempred./ The fifthe is foryetelnesse by to muchel drynkynge, for which somtyme a man foryeteth er the morwe what he dide at even, or on the nyght biforn./

In oother manere been distinct the speces of Glotonye, after Seint Gregorie. The firste is for to ete biforn tyme to ete. The seconde is whan a man get hym to delicaat mete or drynke./ The thridde is whan men taken to muche over mesure. The fourthe is curiositee, with greet entente to maken and apparaillen his mete. The fifthe is for to eten to gredily./ Thise been the fyve fyngres of the develes hand, by whiche he draweth folk to synne./   830

Remedium contra peccatum Gule.

Agayns Glotonye is the remedie abstinence, as seith Galien; but that holde I nat meritorie, if he do it oonly for the heele of his body. Seint Augustyn wole that abstinence be doon for vertu and with pacience./ "Abstinence," he seith, "is litel worth but if a man have good wil therto, and but it be enforced by pacience and by charitee, and that men doon it for Godes sake, and in hope to have the blisse of hevene."/

The felawes of abstinence been attemperaunce, that holdeth the meene in alle thynges; eek shame, that eschueth alle deshonestee; suffisance, that seketh no riche metes ne drynkes, ne dooth no fors of to outrageous apparailynge of mete;/ mesure also, that restreyneth by resoun the deslavee appetit of etynge; sobrenesse also, that restreyneth the outrage of drynke;/ sparynge also, that restreyneth the delicaat ese to sitte longe at his mete and softely, wherfore some folk stonden of hir owene wyl to eten at the lasse leyser./   835

Sequitur de Luxuria.

After Glotonye thanne comth Lecherie, for thise two synnes been so ny cosyns that ofte tyme they wol nat departe./ God woot, this synne is ful displesaunt thyng to God, for he seyde hymself, "Do no lecherie." And therfore he putte grete peynes agayns this synne in the olde lawe./ If womman thral were taken in this synne, she sholde be beten with staves to the deeth; and if she were a gentil womman, she sholde be slayn with stones; and if she were a bisshoppes doghter, she sholde been brent, by Goddes comandement./ Forther over, by the synne of lecherie God dreynte al the world at the diluge. And after that he brente fyve citees with thonder-leyt, and sank hem into helle./

Now lat us speke thanne of thilke stynkynge synne of Lecherie that men clepe avowtrie of wedded folk; that is to seyn, if that oon of hem be wedded, or elles bothe./ Seint John seith that avowtiers   840 shullen been in helle, in a stank brennynge of fyr and of brymston—in fyr for hire lecherye, in brymston for the stynk of hire ordure./ Certes, the brekynge of this sacrement is an horrible thyng. It was maked of God hymself in paradys, and confermed by Jhesu Crist, as witnesseth Seint Mathew in the gospel: "A man shal lete fader and mooder and taken hym to his wif, and they shullen be two in o flessh."/ This sacrement bitokneth the knyttynge togidre of Crist and of hooly chirche./ And nat oonly that God forbad avowtrie in dede, but eek he comanded that thou sholdest nat coveite thy neighebores wyf./ "In this heeste," seith Seint Augustyn, "is forboden alle manere coveitise to doon lecherie." Lo, what seith Seint Mathew in the gospel, that "whoso seeth a womman to coveitise of his lust, he hath doon lecherie with hire in his herte."/   845 Heere may ye seen that nat oonly the dede of this synne is forboden, but eek the desir to doon that synne./ This cursed synne anoyeth grevousliche hem that it haunten. And first to hire soule, for he obligeth it to synne and to peyne of deeth that is perdurable./ Unto the body anoyeth it grevously also, for it dreyeth hym, and wasteth him, and shent hym, and of his blood he maketh sacrifice to the feend of helle. It wasteth eek his catel and his substaunce./ And certes, if it be a foul thyng a man to waste his catel on wommen, yet is it a fouler thyng whan that, for swich

---

826 **distempred:** out of balance
827 **foryetelnesse:** forgetfulness
829 **curiositee:** elaborate preparation
Remedium, *etc.*: The remedy against the sin of Gluttony.
831 **Galien:** Galen, the Greek authority on medicine   **meritorie:** meritorious
833 **deshonestee:** dishonor, shameful acts
834 **deslavee:** uncontrolled   **sobrenesse:** sobriety   **outrage:** excess
835 **sparynge:** moderation, frugality
Sequitur, *etc.*: Now follows the section on Lechery.

839 **thonder-leyt:** lightning bolts
841 **stank:** pond, pool
848 **dreyeth:** drains (dries)

ordure, wommen dispenden upon men hir catel and substaunce./ This synne, as seith the prophete, bireveth man and womman hir goode fame and al hire honour, and it is ful plesaunt to the devel, for therby wynneth he the mooste partie of this world./ And right as a marchant deliteth hym   850
moost in chaffare that he hath moost avantage of, right so deliteth the fend in this ordure./

This is that oother hand of the devel with fyve fyngres to cacche the peple to his vileynye./ The firste fynger is the fool lookynge of the fool womman and of the fool man; that sleeth, right as the basilicok sleeth folk by the venym of his sighte, for the coveitise of eyen folweth the coveitise of the herte./ The seconde fynger is the vileyns touchynge in wikkede manere. And therfore seith Salomon that "whoso toucheth and handlith a womman, he fareth lyk hym that handlith the scorpioun that styngeth and sodeynly sleeth thurgh his envenymynge"; as whoso toucheth warm pych, it shent his fyngres./ The thridde is foule wordes, that fareth lyk fyr, that right anon brenneth the herte./ The four-   855
the fynger is the kissynge; and trewely he were a greet fool that wolde kisse the mouth of a brennynge oven or of a fourneys./ And moore fooles been they that kissen in vileynye, for that mouth is the mouth of helle; and namely thise olde dotardes holours, yet wol they kisse, though they may nat do, and smatre hem./ Certes, they been lyk to houndes; for an hound, whan he comth by the roser or by othere [bushes], though he may nat pisse, yet wole he heve up his leg and make a contenaunce to pisse./ And for that many man weneth that he may nat synne for no likerousnesse that he dooth with his wyf, certes, that opinion is fals. God woot, a man may sleen hymself with his owene knyf, and make hymselve dronken of his owene tonne./ Certes, be it wyf, be it child, or any worldly thyng that he loveth biforn God, it is his mawmet, and he is an ydolastre./   860
Man sholde loven hys wyf by discrecioun, paciently and atemprely, and thanne is she as though it were his suster./ The fifthe fynger of the develes hand is the stynkynge dede of Leccherie./ Certes, the

fyve fyngres of Glotonie the feend put in the wombe of a man, and with his fyve fingres of Lecherie he gripeth hym by the reynes for to throwen hym into the fourneys of helle,/ ther as they shul han the fyr and the wormes that evere shul lasten, and wepynge and wailynge, sharp hunger and thurst, [and] grymnesse of develes, that shullen al totrede hem withouten respit and withouten ende./ Of Leccherie, as I seyde, sourden diverse speces, as fornicacioun, that is bitwixe man and womman that been nat maried, and this is deedly synne and agayns nature./ Al that is   865
enemy and destruccioun to nature is agayns nature./ Parfay, the resoun of a man telleth eek hym wel that it is deedly synne, for as muche as God forbad leccherie. And Seint Paul yeveth hem the regne that nys dewe to no wight but to hem that doon deedly synne./ Another synne of Leccherie is to bireve a mayden of hir maydenhede, for he that so dooth, certes, he casteth a mayden out of the hyeste degree that is in this present lif/ and bireveth hire thilke precious fruyt that the book clepeth the hundred fruyt. I ne kan seye it noon ootherweyes in Englissh, but in Latyn it highte *Centesimus fructus*./ Certes, he that so dooth is cause of manye damages and vileynyes, mo than any man kan rekene; right as he somtyme is cause of alle damages that beestes don in the feeld, that breketh the hegge or the closure, thurgh which he destroyeth that may nat been restoored./ For certes, namoore may mayden-   870
hede be restoored than an arm that is smyten fro the body may retourne agayn to wexe./ She may have mercy, this woot I wel, if she do penitence; but nevere shal it be that she nas corrupt./ And al be it so that I have spoken somwhat of avowtrie, it is good to shewen mo perils that longen to avowtrie, for to eschue that foule synne./ Avowtrie in Latyn is for to seyn approchynge of oother mannes bed, thurgh which tho that whilom weren o flessh abawndone hir bodyes to othere persones./ Of this synne, as seith the wise man, folwen manye harmes. First, brekynge of feith, and certes in feith is the keye of Cristendom./

---

853 **basilicok:** basilisk, a fabulous serpent
854 **pych:** pitch
857 **holours:** lechers   **smatre hem:** defile or besmatter themselves
858 **roser:** rosebush
860 **mawmet:** idol   **ydolastre:** idolater

863 **reynes:** loins or kidneys (seat of the passions)
864 **grymnesse:** fierceness   **totrede:** trample upon
865 **sourden:** arise, originate
869 **Centesimus fructus:** hundredfold fruit; see n.
870 **right as he:** he (i.e., the deflowerer of virgins) is like beasts in the field
closure: fence
874 **abawndone:** yield, give over

And whan that feith is broken and lorn, soothly Cristendom stant veyn and withouten fruyt./ This synne is eek a thefte, for thefte generally is for to reve a wight his thyng agayns his wille./ Certes, this is the fouleste thefte that may be, whan a womman steleth hir body from hir housbonde and yeveth it to hire holour to defoulen hire, and steleth hir soule fro Crist and yeveth it to the devel./ This is a fouler thefte than for to breke a chirche and stele the chalice, for thise avowtiers breken the temple of God spiritually, and stelen the vessel of grace, that is the body and the soule, for which Crist shal destroyen hem, as seith Seint Paul./ Soothly, of this thefte douted gretly Joseph, whan that his lordes wyf preyed hym of vileynye, whan he seyde, "Lo, my lady, how my lord hath take to me under my warde al that he hath in this world, ne no thyng of his thynges is out of my power, but oonly ye, that been his wyf./   880 And how sholde I thanne do this wikkednesse, and synne so horribly agayns God and agayns my lord? God it forbeede!" Allas, al to litel is swich trouthe now yfounde./ The thridde harm is the filthe thurgh which they breken the comandement of God, and defoulen the auctour of matrimoyne, that is Crist./ For certes, in so muche as the sacrement of mariage is so noble and so digne, so muche is it gretter synne for to breken it, for God made mariage in paradys, in the estaat of innocence, to multiplye mankynde to the service of God./ And therfore is the brekynge therof the moore grevous; of which brekynge comen false heires ofte tyme, that wrongfully ocupien folkes heritages. And therfore wol Crist putte hem out of the regne of hevene, that is heritage to goode folk./ Of this brekynge comth eek ofte tyme that folk unwar wedden or synnen with hire owene kynrede, and namely thilke harlotes that haunten bordels of thise fool wommen, that mowe be likned to a commune gong, where as men purgen hire ordure./ What seye we eek of putours that   885 lyven by the horrible synne of putrie, and constreyne wommen to yelden hem a certeyn rente of hire bodily puterie, ye, somtyme of his owene wyf or his child, as doon thise bawdes? Certes, thise been cursede synnes./ Understoond eek that Avowtrie is set gladly in the ten comandementz bitwixe thefte and manslaughtre; for it is the gretteste thefte that may be, for it is thefte of body and of soule./ And it is lyk to homycide, for it kerveth atwo and breketh atwo hem that first were maked o flessh. And therfore, by the olde lawe of God, they sholde be slayn./ But nathelees, by the lawe of Jhesu Crist, that is lawe of pitee, whan he seyde to the womman that was founden in avowtrie, and sholde han been slayn with stones, after the wyl of the Jewes, as was hir lawe, "Go," quod Jhesu Crist, "and have namoore wyl to synne," or, "wille namoore to do synne."/ Soothly the vengeaunce of Avowtrie is awarded to the peynes of helle, but if so be that it be destourbed by penitence./ Yet been ther mo speces of this   890 cursed synne; as whan that oon of hem is religious, or elles bothe; or of folk that been entred into ordre, as subdekne, or dekne, or preest, or hospialiers. And evere the hyer that he is in ordre, the gretter is the synne./ The thynges that gretly agreggen hire synne is the brekynge of hire avow of chastitee, whan they receyved the ordre./ And forther over, sooth is that hooly ordre is chief of al the tresorie of God and his especial signe and mark of chastitee to shewe that they been joyned to chastitee, which that is the moost precious lyf that is./ And thise ordred folk been specially titled to God, and of the special meignee of God, for which, whan they doon deedly synne, they been the special traytours of God and of his peple; for they lyven of the peple, to preye for the peple, and while they ben suche traitours, here preyer avayleth nat to the peple./ Preestes been aungels, as by the dignitee of hir mysterye; but for sothe, Seint Paul seith that Sathanas transformeth hym in an aungel of light./ Soothly, the preest   895 that haunteth deedly synne, he may be likned to the aungel of derknesse transformed in the aungel of light. He semeth aungel of light, but for sothe he is aungel of derknesse./ Swiche preestes been the sones

---

879 **breke:** break into
880 **warde:** custody
885 **bordels:** brothels   **gong:** latrine
886 **putours:** pimps

886 **puterie:** prostitution
887 **gladly:** fittingly
891 **religious:** in a religious order   **subdekne:** subdeacon   **hospialiers:** Knights Hospitallers
892 **agreggen:** aggravate, make worse
893 **tresorie:** treasury
894 **ordred:** ordained   **titled:** dedicated

of Helie, as sheweth in the Book of Kynges, that they weren the sones of Belial—that is, the devel./ Belial is to seyn, "withouten juge." And so faren they; hem thynketh they been free and han no juge, namoore than hath a free bole that taketh which cow that hym liketh in the town./ So faren they by wommen. For right as a free bole is ynough for al a toun, right so is a wikked preest corrupcioun ynough for al a parisshe, or for al a contree./ Thise preestes, as seith the book, ne konne nat the mysterie of preesthod to the peple, ne God ne knowe they nat. They ne helde hem nat apayd, as seith the book, of soden flessh that was to hem offred, but they tooke by force the flessh that is rawe./ Certes, so thise shrewes ne   900 holden hem nat apayed of roosted flessh and sode flessh, with which the peple feden hem in greet reverence, but they wole have raw flessh of folkes wyves and hir doghtres./ And certes, thise wommen that consenten to hire harlotrie doon greet wrong to Crist, and to hooly chirche, and alle halwes, and to alle soules; for they bireven alle thise hym that sholde worshipe Crist and hooly chirche and preye for Cristene soules./ And therfore han swiche preestes, and hire lemmanes eek that consenten to hir leccherie, the malisoun of al the court Cristien, til they come to amendement./ The thridde spece of avowtrie is somtyme bitwixe a man and his wyf, and that is whan they take no reward in hire assemblynge but oonly to hire flesshly delit, as seith Seint Jerome,/ and ne rekken of nothyng but that they been assembled; by cause that they been maried, al is good ynough, as thynketh to hem./ But in swich   905 folk hath the devel power, as seyde the aun- gel Raphael to Thobie, for in hire assemblynge they putten Jhesu Crist out of hire herte and yeven hemself to alle ordure./ The fourthe spece is the assemblee of hem that been of hire kynrede, or of hem that been of oon affynytee, or elles with hem with whiche hir fadres or hir kynrede han deled in the synne of lecherie. This synne maketh hem lyk to houndes, that

taken no kep to kynrede./ And certes, parentele is in two maneres, outher goostly or flesshly; goostly, as for to deelen with his godsibbes./ For right so as he that engendreth a child is his flesshly fader, right so is his godfader his fader espiritueel. For which a wom- man may in no lasse synne assemblen with hire god- sib than with hire owene flesshly brother./ The fifthe spece is thilke abhomynable synne, of which that no man unnethe oghte speke ne write; nathelees it is openly reherced in holy writ./ This   910 cursednesse doon men and wommen in diverse entente and in diverse manere; but though that hooly writ speke of horrible synne, certes hooly writ may nat been defouled, namoore than the sonne that shyneth on the mixne./ Another synne aperteneth to leccherie, that comth in slepynge, and this synne cometh ofte to hem that been maydenes, and eek to hem that been corrupt; and this synne men clepen polucioun, that comth in foure maneres./ Somtyme of langwissynge of body, for the humours been to ranke and to habundaunt in the body of man; somtyme of infermetee, for the fieblesse of the vertu retentif, as phisik maketh mencion; somtyme for surfeet of mete and drynke;/ and somtyme of vileyns thoghtes that been enclosed in mannes mynde whan he gooth to slepe, which may nat been withoute synne; for which men moste kepen hem wisely, or elles may men syn- nen ful grevously./

Remedium contra peccatumy Luxurie.

Now comth the remedie agayns Leccherie, and that is generally chastitee and continence, that restreyneth alle the desordeynee moevynges that comen of flesshly talentes./ And evere the   915 gretter merite shal he han that moost restreyneth the wikkede eschawfynges of the [ardour] of this synne. And this is in two maneres—that is to seyn, chastitee in mariage, and chastitee of widwe- hod./ Now shaltow understonde that matrimoyne is leeffull assemblynge of man and of womman that receyven by vertu of the sacrement the boond thurgh

---

898 **juge:** yoke? see n.   **free bole:** bull allowed to run free with the village herd
900 **mysterie:** office (ministerium)   **soden:** boiled, cooked
902 **harlotrie:** lechery
903 **court Cristien:** ecclesiastical court
904 **reward:** regard (of the proper purpose)
906 **Thobie:** Tobias
907 **affynytee:** relationship between persons, other than the spouses themselves, established by marriage, as distinguished from **kynrede,** consanguinity

908 **parentele:** kinship   **godsibbes:** children of one's godparents or those for whom one's parents are godparents
911 **mixne:** dunghill
913 **langwissynge:** weakness   **vertu retentif:** body's power to retain fluids
phisik: science of medicine
Remedium, *etc.*: The remedy against the sin of Lechery.
916 **eschawfynges:** inflaming with passion

which they may nat be departed in al hir lyf—that is to seyn, whil that they lyven bothe./ This, as seith the book, is a ful greet sacrement. God maked it, as I have seyd, in paradys, and wolde hymself be born in mariage./ And for to halwen mariage he was at a weddynge, where as he turned water into wyn, which was the firste miracle that he wroghte in erthe biforn his disciples./ Trewe effect of mariage clenseth fornicacioun and replenysseth hooly chirche of good lynage, for that is the ende of mariage; and it chaungeth deedly synne into venial synne bitwixe hem that been ywedded, and maketh the hertes al oon of hem that been ywedded, as wel as the bodies./ 920 This is verray mariage, that was establissed by God, er that synne bigan, whan natureel lawe was in his right poynt in paradys; and it was ordeyned that o man sholde have but o womman, and o womman but o man, as seith Seint Augustyn, by manye resouns./

First, for mariage is figured bitwixe Crist and holy chirche. And that oother is for a man is heved of a womman; algate, by ordinaunce it sholde be so./ For if a womman hadde mo men than oon, thanne sholde she have moo hevedes than oon, and that were an horrible thyng biforn God; and eek a womman ne myghte nat plese to many folk at oones. And also ther ne sholde nevere be pees ne reste amonges hem, for everich wolde axen his owene thyng./ And forther over, no man ne sholde knowe his owene engendrure, ne who sholde have his heritage; and the womman sholde been the lasse biloved fro the tyme that she were conjoynt to many men./

Now comth how that a man sholde bere hym with his wif, and namely in two thynges; that is to seyn, in suffraunce and reverence, as shewed Crist whan he made first womman./ For he ne made 925 hire nat of the heved of Adam, for she sholde nat clayme to greet lordshipe./ For ther as the womman hath the maistrie, she maketh to muche desray. Ther neden none ensamples of this; the experience of day by day oghte suffise./ Also, certes, God ne made nat womman of the foot of Adam, for she ne sholde

nat been holden to lowe; for she kan nat paciently suffre. But God made womman of the ryb of Adam, for womman sholde be felawe unto man./ Man sholde bere hym to his wyf in feith, in trouthe, and in love, as seith Seint Paul, that a man sholde loven his wyf as Crist loved hooly chirche, that loved it so wel that he deyde for it. So sholde a man for his wyf, if it were nede./

Now how that a womman sholde be subget to hire housbonde, that telleth Seint Peter. First, in obedience./ And eek, as seith the decree, a 930 womman that is wyf, as longe as she is a wyf, she hath noon auctoritee to swere ne to bere witnesse withoute leve of hir housbonde, that is hire lord; algate, he sholde be so by resoun./ She sholde eek serven hym in alle honestee, and been attempree of hire array. I woot wel that they sholde setten hire entente to plesen hir housbondes, but nat by hire queyntise of array./ Seint Jerome seith that "wyves that been apparailled in silk and in precious purpre ne mowe nat clothen hem in Jhesu Crist." Loke what seith Seint John eek in thys matere?/ Seint Gregorie eek seith that "No wight seketh precious array but oonly for veyne glorie, to been honoured the moore biforn the peple."/ It is a greet folye, a womman to have a fair array outward and in hirself be foul inward./ A wyf sholde eek be mesurable 935 in lookynge and in berynge and in lawghynge, and discreet in alle hire wordes and hire dedes./ And aboven alle worldly thyng she sholde loven hire housbonde with al hire herte, and to hym be trewe of hir body./ So sholde an housbonde eek be to his wyf. For sith that al the body is the housbondes, so sholde hire herte been, or elles ther is bitwixe hem two, as in that, no parfit mariage./ Thanne shal men understonde that for thre thynges a man and his wyf flesshly mowen assemble. The firste is in entente of engendrure of children to the service of God, for certes that is the cause final of matrimoyne./ Another cause is to yelden everich of hem to oother the dette of hire bodies, for neither of hem hath power of his owene body. The thridde is for to eschewe leccherye and vileynye. The ferthe is for sothe deedly synne./ As to the firste, it is 940

---

918 **as I have seyd**: at 842 and 883
920 **replenysseth**: fills
921 **right poynt**: proper condition, true state
922 **figured**: symbolized
927 **desray**: disorder

932 **queyntise of array**: finery
933 **purpre**: rich purple cloth
936 **mesurable**: modest

meritorie; the seconde also, for, as seith the decree, that she hath merite of chastitee that yeldeth to hire housbonde the dette of hir body, ye, though it be agayn hir likynge and the lust of hire herte./ The thridde manere is venyal synne; and, trewely, scarsly may ther any of thise be withoute venial synne, for the corrupcion and for the delit./ The fourthe manere is for to understonde, as if they assemble oonly for amorous love and for noon of the foreseyde causes, but for to accomplice thilke brennynge delit, they rekke nevere how ofte. Soothly it is deedly synne; and yet, with sorwe, somme folk wol peynen hem moore to doon than to hire appetit suffiseth./

The seconde manere of chastitee is for to been a clene wydewe, and eschue the embracynges of man, and desiren the embracynge of Jhesu Crist./ Thise been tho that han been wyves and han forgoon hire housbondes, and eek wommen that han doon leccherie and been releeved by penitence./   945 And certes, if that a wyf koude kepen hire al chaast by licence of hir housbonde, so that she yeve nevere noon occasion that he agilte, it were to hire a greet merite./ Thise manere wommen that observen chastitee moste be clene in herte as wel as in body and in thought, and mesurable in clothynge and in contenaunce, and been abstinent in etynge and drynkynge, in spekynge, and in dede. They been the vessel or the boyste of the blissed Magdelene, that fulfilleth hooly chirche of good odour./ The thridde manere of chastitee is virginitee, and it bihoveth that she be hooly in herte and clene of body. Thanne is she spouse to Jhesu Crist, and she is the lyf of angeles./ She is the preisynge of this world, and she is as thise martirs in egalitee; she hath in hire that tonge may nat telle ne herte thynke./ Virginitee baar oure Lord Jhesu Crist, and virgine was hymselve./   950

Another remedie agayns Leccherie is spe-cially to withdrawen swiche thynges as yeve occasion to thilke vileynye, as ese, etynge, and drynkynge. For certes, whan the pot boyleth strongly, the beste reme-die is to withdrawe the fyr./ Slepynge longe in greet quiete is eek a greet norice to Leccherie./

Another remedie agayns Leccherie is that a man or a womman eschue the compaignye of hem by whiche he douteth to be tempted, for al be it so that the dede be withstonden, yet is ther greet temptacioun./ Soothly, a whit wal, although it ne brenne noght fully by stikynge of a candele, yet is the wal blak of the leyt./ Ful ofte tyme I rede that no man truste in his owene perfeccioun, but he be stronger than Sampson, and hoolier than David, and wiser than Salomon./   955

Now after that I have declared yow, as I kan, the sevene deedly synnes, and somme of hire braunches and hire remedies, soothly, if I koude, I wolde telle yow the ten comandementz./ But so heigh a doctrine I lete to divines. Nathelees, I hope to God, they been touched in this tretice, everich of hem alle./

Sequitur secunda pars Penitencie.

Now for as muche as the seconde partie of Peni-tence stant in confessioun of mouth, as I bigan in the firste chapitre, I seye, Seint Augustyn seith,/ "Synne is every word and every dede, and al that men cov-eiten, agayn the lawe of Jhesu Crist; and this is for to synne in herte, in mouth, and in dede, by thy fyve wittes, that been sighte, herynge, smellynge, tastynge or savourynge, and feelynge."/ Now is it good to understonde the circumstances that agreggen muchel every synne./ Thou shalt considere   960 what thow art that doost the synne, wheither thou be male or femele, yong or oold, gentil or thral, free or servant, hool or syk, wedded or sengle, ordred or unordred, wys or fool, clerk or seculeer;/ if she be of thy kynrede, bodily or goostly, or noon; if any of thy kynrede have synned with hire, or noon; and manye mo thinges./

Another circumstaunce is this: wheither it be doon in fornicacioun or in avowtrie or noon, incest or noon, mayden or noon, in manere of homicide or noon, horrible grete synnes or smale, and how longe thou hast continued in synne./ The thridde circum-staunce is the place ther thou hast do synne, whei-ther in oother mennes hous or in thyn owene, in feeld or in chirche or in chirchehawe, in chirche

---

954 **leyt:** flame
957 **divines:** theologianst
Sequitur, *etc.*: Now follows the second part of Penance.
960 **agreggen:** aggravate, make more serious
961 **sengle:** single

dedicaat or noon./ For if the chirche be halwed, and man or womman spille his kynde inwith that place by wey of synne or by wikked temptacioun, the chirche is entredited til it be reconsiled by the bysshop./ And the preest sholde be enterdited that dide swich a vileynye; to terme of al his lif he sholde namoore synge masse, and if he dide, he sholde doon deedly synne at every time that he so songe masse./ The fourthe circumstaunce is by whiche mediatours, or by whiche messagers, as for enticement, or for consentement to bere compaignye with felaweshipe; for many a wrecche, for to bere compaignye, wol go to the devel of helle./ Wherfore they that eggen or consenten to the synne been parteners of the synne, and of the dampnacioun of the synnere./

The fifthe circumstaunce is how manye tymes that he hath synned, if it be in his mynde, and how ofte that he hath falle./ For he that ofte falleth in synne, he despiseth the mercy of God, and encreesseth hys synne, and is unkynde to Crist; and he wexeth the moore fieble to withstonde synne, and synneth the moore lightly,/ and the latter ariseth, and is the moore eschew for to shryven hym, and namely, to hym that is his confessour./ For which that folk, whan they falle agayn in hir olde folies, outher they forleten hir olde confessours al outrely or elles they departen hir shrift in diverse places; but soothly, swich departed shrift deserveth no mercy of God of his synnes./ The sixte circumstaunce is why that a man synneth, as by which temptacioun, and if hymself procure thilke temptacioun, or by the excitynge of oother folk; or if he synne with a womman by force, or by hire owene assent;/ or if the womman, maugree hir hed, hath been afforced, or noon. This shal she telle: for coveitise, or for poverte, and if it was hire procurynge, or noon; and swich manere harneys./ The seventhe circumstaunce is in what manere he hath doon his synne, or how that she hath suffred that folk han doon to hire./ And the same shal the man telle pleynly with alle circumstaunces; and wheither he hath synned with

965

970

975

comune bordel wommen or noon,/ or doon his synne in hooly tymes or noon, in fastyng tymes or noon, or biforn his shrifte, or after his latter shrifte,/ and hath peraventure broken therfore his penance enjoyned, by whos help and whos conseil, by sorcerie or craft; al moste be toold./ Alle thise thynges, after that they been grete or smale, engreggen the conscience of man. And eek the preest, that is thy juge, may the bettre been avysed of his juggement in yevynge of thy penaunce, and that is after thy contricioun./ For understond wel that after tyme that a man hath defouled his baptesme by synne, if he wole come to salvacioun, ther is noon other wey but by penitence and shrifte and satisfaccioun,/ and namely by the two, if ther be a confessour to which he may shriven hym, and the thridde, if he have lyf to parfournen it./

980

Thanne shal man looke and considere that if he wole maken a trewe and a profitable confessioun, ther moste be foure condiciouns./ First, it moot been in sorweful bitternesse of herte, as seyde the kyng Ezechias to God, "I wol remembre me alle the yeres of my lif in bitternesse of myn herte."/ This condicioun of bitternesse hath fyve signes. The firste is that confessioun moste be shamefast, nat for to covere ne hyden his synne, for he hath agilt his God and defouled his soule./ And herof seith Seint Augustyn, "The herte travailleth for shame of his synne"; and for he hath greet shamefastnesse, he is digne to have greet mercy of God./ Swich was the confessioun of the publican that wolde nat heven up his eyen to hevene, for he hadde offended God of hevene; for which shamefastnesse he hadde anon the mercy of God./ And therof seith Seint Augustyn that swich shamefast folk been next foryevenesse and remissioun./ Another signe is humylitee in confessioun, of which seith Seint Peter, "Humbleth yow under the myght of God." The hond of God is myghty in confessioun, for therby God foryeveth thee thy synnes, for he allone hath the power./ And this humylitee shal been in herte and in signe outward, for right as he hath humylitee to God in his herte, right so sholde he humble his body

985

---

964 **dedicaat:** consecrated
965 **kynde:** semen   **entredited:** under an interdict, prohibited from use
968 **eggen:** incite
971 **eschew:** disinclined, reluctant
974 **afforced:** violated   **procurynge:** contrivance   **harneys:** trappings (circumstances)

976 **bordel wommen:** prostitutes
979 **engreggen:** burden
983 **Ezechias:** Hezekiah
984 **shamefast:** made with a sense of shame

outward to the preest, that sit in Goddes place./ For which in no manere, sith that Crist is sovereyn, and the preest meene and mediatour bitwixe Crist and the synnere, and the synnere is the laste by wey of resoun,/ thanne sholde nat the synnere   990 sitte as heighe as his confessour, but knele biforn hym or at his feet, but if maladie destourbe it. For he shal nat taken kep who sit there, but in whos place that he sitteth./ A man that hath trespased to a lord, and comth for to axe mercy and maken his accord, and set him doun anon by the lord, men wolde holden hym outrageous, and nat worthy so soone for to have remissioun ne mercy./ The thridde signe is how that thy shrift sholde be ful of teeris, if man may, and if man may nat wepe with his bodily eyen, lat hym wepe in herte./ Swich was the confession of Seint Peter, for after that he hadde forsake Jhesu Crist, he wente out and weep ful bitterly./ The fourthe signe is that he ne lette nat for shame to shewen his confessioun./ Swich was the con-   995 fessioun of the Magdalene, that ne spared for no shame of hem that weren atte feeste, for to go to oure Lord Jhesu Crist and biknowe to hym hire synne./ The fifthe signe is that a man or a womman be obeisant to receyven the penaunce that hym is enjoyned for his synnes, for certes, Jhesu Crist, for the giltes of o man, was obedient to the deeth./

The seconde condicion of verray confession is that it be hastily doon. For certes, if a man hadde a deedly wounde, evere the lenger that he taried to warisshe hymself, the moore wolde it corrupte and haste hym to his deeth, and eek the wounde wolde be the wors for to heele./ And right so fareth synne that longe tyme is in a man unshewed./ Certes, a man oghte hastily shewen his synnes for manye causes; as for drede of deeth, that cometh ofte sodeynly, and no certeyn what tyme it shal be, ne in what place; and eek the drecchynge of o synne draweth in another;/ and eek the lenger that he tarieth,   1000 the ferther he is fro Crist. And if he abide to his laste day, scarsly may he shryven hym or remembre hym of his synnes or repenten hym, for the grevous maladie of his deeth./ And for as muche as

he ne hath nat in his lyf herkned Jhesu Crist whanne he hath spoken, he shal crie to Jhesu Crist at his laste day, and scarsly wol he herkne hym./ And understond that this condicioun moste han foure thynges. Thi shrift moste be purveyed bifore and avysed; for wikked haste dooth no profit; and that a man konne shryve hym of his synnes, be it of pride, or of envye, and so forth with the speces and circumstances;/ and that he have comprehended in hys mynde the nombre and the greetnesse of his synnes, and how longe that he hath leyn in synne;/ and eek that he be contrit of his synnes, and in stidefast purpos, by the grace of God, nevere eft to falle in synne; and eek that he drede and countrewaite hymself, that he fle the occasiouns of synne to whiche he is enclyned./   1005 Also thou shalt shryve thee of alle thy synnes to o man, and nat a parcel to o man and a parcel to another; that is to understonde, in entente to departe thy confessioun, as for shame or drede, for it nys but stranglynge of thy soule./ For certes Jhesu Crist is entierly al good; in hym nys noon imperfeccioun, and therfore outher he foryeveth al parfitly or elles never a deel./ I seye nat that if thow be assigned to the penitauncer for certein synne, that thow art bounde to shewen hym al the remenaunt of thy synnes, of whiche thow hast be shryven of thy curaat, but if it like to thee of thyn humylitee; this is no departynge of shrifte./ Ne I seye nat, ther as I speke of divisioun of confessioun, that if thou have licence for to shryve thee to a discreet and an honest preest, where thee liketh, and by licence of thy curaat, that thow ne mayst wel shryve thee to him of alle thy synnes./ But lat no blotte be bihynde; lat no synne been untoold, as fer as thow hast remembraunce./   1010 And whan thou shalt be shryven to thy curaat, telle hym eek alle the synnes that thow hast doon syn thou were last yshryven; this is no wikked entente of divisioun of shrifte./

Also the verray shrifte axeth certeine condiciouns. First, that thow shryve thee by thy free wil, noght constreyned, ne for shame of folk, ne for maladie, ne swiche thynges. For it is resoun that he that trespaseth

---

990 **meene:** agent, instrument
999 **unshewed:** unconfessed
1000 **drecchynge:** continuance

1005 **countrewaite:** watch
1006 **parcel:** portion
1008 **penitauncer:** a priest with special powers granted by a pope or bishop to hear confession, give dispensations, or absolve from particular sins
1010 **untoold:** unconfessed

by his free wyl, that by his free wyl he confesse his trespas,/ and that noon oother man telle his synne but he hymself; ne he shal nat nayte ne denye his synne, ne wratthe hym agayn the preest for his amonestynge to lete synne./ The seconde condicioun is that thy shrift be laweful; that is to seyn, that thow that shryvest thee and eek the preest that hereth thy confessioun been verraily in the feith of hooly chirche,/ and that a man ne be nat despeired of the mercy of Jhesu Crist, as Caym or Judas./ And   1015 eek a man moot accusen hymself of his owene trespas, and nat another; but he shal blame and wyten hymself and his owene malice of his synne, and noon oother./ But nathelees, if that another man be occasioun or enticere of his synne, or the estaat of a persone be swich thurgh which his synne is agregged, or elles that he may nat pleynly shryven hym but he telle the persone with which he hath synned, thanne may he telle it,/ so that his entente ne be nat to bakbite the persone, but oonly to declaren his confessioun./

Thou ne shalt nat eek make no lesynges in thy confessioun, for humylitee, peraventure, to seyn that thou hast doon synnes of whiche thow were nevere gilty./ For Seint Augustyn seith, "If thou, by cause of thyn humylitee, makest lesynges on thyself, though thow ne were nat in synne biforn, yet artow thanne

in synne thurgh thy lesynges."/ Thou most eek   1020 shewe thy synne by thyn owene propre mouth, but thow be woxe dowmb, and nat by no lettre; for thow that hast doon the synne, thou shalt have the shame therfore./ Thow shalt nat eek peynte thy confessioun by faire subtile wordes, to covere the moore thy synne; for thanne bigilestow thyself, and nat the preest. Thow most tellen it platly, be it nevere so foul ne so horrible./ Thow shalt eek shryve thee to a preest that is discreet to conseille thee; and eek thou shalt nat shryve thee for veyne glorie, ne for ypocrisye, ne for no cause but oonly for the doute of Jhesu Crist and the heele of thy soule./ Thow shalt nat eek renne to the preest sodeynly to tellen hym lightly thy synne, as whoso telleth a jape or a tale, but avysely and with greet devocioun./ And generally, shryve thee ofte. If thou ofte falle, ofte thou arise by confessioun./ And though thou shryve thee   1025 ofter than ones of synne of which thou hast be shryven, it is the moore merite. And, as seith Seint Augustyn, thow shalt have the moore lightly relessyng and grace of God, bothe of synne and of peyne./ And certes, oones a yeere atte leeste wey it is laweful for to been housled, for certes, oones a yeere alle thynges renovellen./

Now have I toold yow of verray Confessioun, that is the seconde partie of Penitence./

Explicit secunda pars Penitencie, et sequitur tercia pars eiusdem.

The thridde partie of Penitence is Satisfaccioun, and that stant moost generally in almesse and in bodily peyne./ Now been ther thre manere of almesse: contricion of herte, where a man offreth hymself to God; another is to han pitee of defaute of his neighebores; and the thridde is in yevynge of good conseil and comfort, goostly and bodily, where men han nede, and namely in sustenaunce of mannes foode./ And tak kep that a man hath nede of   1030 thise thinges generally: he hath nede of foode, he hath nede of clothyng and herberwe, he hath nede of charitable conseil and visitynge in prisone and in maladie, and sepulture of his dede body./ And if thow

mayst nat visite the nedeful with thy persone, visite hym by thy message and by thy yiftes./ Thise been general almesses or werkes of charitee of hem that han temporeel richesses or discrecioun in conseilynge. Of thise werkes shaltow heren at the day of doom./

Thise almesses shaltow doon of thyne owene propre thynges, and hastily and prively, if thow mayst./ But nathelees, if thow mayst nat doon it prively, thow shalt nat forbere to doon almesse though men seen it, so that it be nat doon for thank of the world, but oonly for thank of Jhesu Crist./ For, as   1035 witnesseth Seint Mathew, *capitulo quinto,* "A

1013 **nayte:** disclaim

Explicit, *etc.:* Here ends the second part of Penance, and its third part follows.

1027 **laweful:** decreed by (Church) law   **housled:** given communion
renovellen: renew themselves
1036 **capitulo quinto:** in the fifth chapter

citee may nat been hyd that is set on a montayne, ne men lighte nat a lanterne and put it under a busshel, but men sette it on a candle-stikke to yeve light to the men in the hous./ Right so shal youre light lighten bifore men, that they may seen youre goode werkes, and glorifie youre fader that is in hevene."/

Now as to speken of bodily peyne, it stant in prey-eres, in wakynges, in fastynges, in vertuouse techyn-ges of orisouns./ And ye shul understonde that orisouns or preyeres is for to seyn a pitous wyl of herte, that redresseth it in God and expresseth it by word outward, to remoeven harmes and to han thyn-ges espirituel and durable, and somtyme temporele thynges; of whiche orisouns, certes, in the orison of the *Pater noster* hath Jhesu Crist enclosed moost thynges./ Certes, it is privyleged of thre thynges in his dignytee, for which it is moore digne than any oother preyere, for that Jhesu Crist hymself maked it;/ and it is short, for it sholde be koud the   1040 moore lightly, and for to withholden it the moore esily in herte, and helpen hymself the ofter with the orisoun,/ and for a man sholde be the lasse wery to seyen it, and for a man may nat excusen hym to lerne it, it is so short and so esy, and for it com-prehendeth in it self alle goode preyeres./ The exposi-cioun of this hooly preyere, that is so excellent and digne, I bitake to thise maistres of theologie, save thus muchel wol I seyn; that whan thow prayest that God sholde foryeve thee thy giltes as thou foryevest hem that agilten to thee, be ful wel war that thow ne be nat out of charitee./ This hooly orison amenuseth eek venyal synne, and therfore it aperteneth specially to penitence./

This preyere moste be trewely seyd, and in verray feith, and that men preye to God ordinatly and dis-creetly and devoutly; and alwey a man shal put-ten his wyl to be subget to the wille of God./   1045 This orisoun moste eek been seyd with greet humblesse and ful pure, honestly and nat to the anoy-aunce of any man or womman. It moste eek been continued with the werkes of charitee./ It availeth eek agayn the vices of the soule, for, as seith Seint Jerome, "By fastynge been saved the vices of the flessh, and by preyere the vices of the soule."/

After this, thou shalt understonde that bodily peyne stant in wakynge, for Jhesu Crist seith, "Waketh and preyeth, that ye ne entre in wikked temptacioun."/ Ye shul understanden also that fastynge stant in thre thyn-ges: in forberynge of bodily mete and drynke, and in forberynge of worldly jolitee, and in forberynge of deedly synne; this is to seyn, that a man shal kepen hym fro deedly synne with al his myght./

And thou shalt understanden eek that God ordeyned fastynge, and to fastynge apperte-nen foure thinges:/ largenesse to povre folk,   1050 gladnesse of herte espirituel, nat to been angry ne anoyed, ne grucche for he fasteth, and also resonable houre for to ete; ete by mesure; that is for to seyn, a man shal nat ete in untyme, ne sitte the lenger at his table to ete for he fasteth./

Thanne shaltow understonde that bodily peyne stant in disciplyne or techynge, by word, or by writynge, or in ensample; also in werynge of heyres, or of stamyn, or of haubergeons on hire naked flessh, for Cristes sake, and swiche manere penances./ But war thee wel that swiche manere penaunces on thy flessh ne make nat thyn herte bitter or angry or anoyed of thyself, for bettre is to caste awey thyn heyre, than for to caste awey the swetenesse of Jhesu Crist./ And therfore seith Seint Paul, "Clothe yow, as they that been chosen of God, in herte of misericorde, debonairetee, suffraunce, and swich manere of clothynge," of whiche Jhesu Crist is moore apayed than of heyres, or haubergeouns, or hauberkes./

Thanne is discipline eek in knokkynge of thy brest, in scourgynge with yerdes, in knelyn-ges, in tribulacions,/ in suffrynge paciently   1055 wronges that been doon to thee, and eek in pacient suffraunce of maladies, or lesynge of worldly catel, or of wyf, or of child, or othere freendes./

Thanne shaltow understonde whiche thynges des-tourben penaunce; and this is in foure maneres: that is, drede, shame, hope, and wanhope, that is despera-cion./ And for to speke first of drede, for which he weneth that he may suffre no penaunce;/ ther-agayns is remedie for to thynke that bodily penaunce is but short and litel at regard of the peyne of helle, that is so cruel and so long that it lasteth withouten ende./

1039 **pitous:** pious **redresseth it:** directs itself toward
1040 **privyleged of:** endowed with
1045 **ordinatly:** in an orderly manner

1051 **largenesse:** generosity
1052 **heyres:** hair shirts **stamyn:** coarse woolen cloth **haubergeons:** coats of mail
1055 **scourgynge:** whipping
1057 **desperacion:** despair

Now again the shame that a man hath to shryven hym, and namely thise ypocrites that wolden been holden so parfite that they han no nede to shryven hem;/ agayns that shame sholde a   1060 man thynke that, by wey of resoun, that he that hath nat been shamed to doon foule thinges, certes hym oghte nat been ashamed to do faire thynges, and that is confessiouns./ A man sholde eek thynke that God seeth and woot alle his thoghtes and alle his werkes, to hym may no thyng been hyd ne covered./ Men sholden eek remembren hem of the shame that is to come at the day of doom to hem that been nat penitent and shryven in this present lyf./ For alle the creatures in hevene, in erthe, and in helle shullen seen apertly al that they hyden in this world./

Now for to speken of the hope of hem that been necligent and slowe to shryven hem, that stant in two maneres./ That oon is that he hopeth   1065 for to lyve longe and for to purchacen muche richesse for his delit, and thanne he wol shryven hym; and, as he seith, hym semeth thanne tymely ynough to come to shrifte./ Another is of surquidrie that he hath in Cristes mercy./ Agayns the firste vice, he shal thynke that oure lif is in no sikernesse, and eek that alle the richesses in this world ben in aventure and passen as a shadwe on the wal;/ and, as seith Seint Gregorie, that it aperteneth to the grete rightwisnesse of God that nevere shal the peyne stynte of hem that nevere wolde withdrawen hem fro synne, hir thankes, but ay continue in synne; for thilke perpetuel wil to do synne shul they han perpetuel peyne./

Wanhope is in two maneres: the firste wanhope is in the mercy of Crist; that oother is that they thynken that they ne myghte nat longe persevere in goodnesse./ The firste wanhope comth of that   1070 he demeth that he hath synned so greetly and so ofte, and so longe leyn in synne, that he shal nat be saved./ Certes, agayns that cursed wanhope sholde he thynke that the passion of Jhesu Crist is moore strong for to unbynde than synne is strong for to bynde./ Agayns the seconde wanhope he shal thynke that as ofte as he falleth he may arise agayn by penitence. And though he never so longe have leyn in synne, the mercy of Crist is alwey redy to receiven hym to mercy./ Agayns the wanhope that he demeth that he sholde nat longe persevere in goodnesse, he shal thynke that the feblesse of the devel may nothyng doon, but if men wol suffren hym;/ and eek he shal han strengthe of the help of God, and of al hooly chirche, and of the proteccioun of aungels, if hym list./   1075

Thanne shal men understonde what is the fruyt of penaunce; and, after the word of Jhesu Crist, it is the endelees blisse of hevene,/ ther joye hath no contrarioustee of wo ne grevaunce; ther alle harmes been passed of this present lyf; ther as is the sikernesse fro the peyne of helle; ther as is the blisful compaignye that rejoysen hem everemo, everich of otheres joye;/ ther as the body of man, that whilom was foul and derk, is moore cleer than the sonne; ther as the body, that whilom was syk, freele, and fieble, and mortal, is inmortal, and so strong and so hool that ther may no thyng apeyren it;/ ther as ne is neither hunger, thurst, ne coold, but every soule replenyssed with the sighte of the parfit knowynge of God./ This blisful regne may men purchace by poverte espiritueel, and the glorie by lowenesse, the plentee of joye by hunger and thurst, and the reste by travaille, and the lyf by deeth and mortificacion of synne./   1080

1064 **apertly:** clearly
1067 **surquidrie:** arrogance

1077 **contrarioustee:** opposite
1078 **apeyren:** injure
1079 **replenyssed:** filled

Heere taketh the makere of this book his leve.

Now preye I to hem alle that herkne this litel tretys or rede, that if ther be any thyng in it that liketh hem, that therof they thanken oure Lord Jhesu Crist, of whom procedeth al wit and al goodnesse./ And if ther be any thyng that displese hem, I preye hem also that they arrette it to the defaute of myn unkonnynge and nat to my wyl, that wolde ful fayn have seyd bettre if I hadde had konnynge./ For oure book seith, "Al that is writen is writen for oure doctrine," and that is myn entente./ Wherfore I biseke yow mekely, for the mercy of God, that ye preye for me that Crist have mercy on me and foryeve me my giltes;/ and namely of my translacions and enditynges of worldly vanitees, the whiche I revoke in my retrac-   1085 ciouns:/ as is the book of Troilus; the book also of Fame; the book of the XXV. Ladies; the book of the Duchesse; the book of Seint Valentynes day of the Parlement of Briddes; the tales of Caunterbury, thilke that sownen into synne;/ the book of the Leoun; and many another book, if they were in my remembrance, and many a song and many a leccherous lay, that Crist for his grete mercy foryeve me the synne./ But of the translacion of Boece de Consolacione, and othere bookes of legendes of seintes, and omelies, and moralitee, and devocioun,/ that thanke I oure Lord Jhesu Crist and his blisful Mooder, and alle the seintes of hevene,/ bisekynge hem that they from hennes forth unto my lyves ende sende me grace to biwayle my giltes and to studie to the salvacioun of my soule, and graunte me grace of verray penitence, confessioun and satisfaccioun to doon in this present lyf,/ thurgh the benigne   1090 grace of hym that is kyng of kynges and preest over alle preestes, that boghte us with the precious blood of his herte,/ so that I may been oon of hem at the day of doom that shulle be saved. *Qui cum Patre et Spiritu Sancto vivit et regnat Deus per omnia secula. Amen.*

Heere is ended the book of the tales of Caunterbury, compiled by Geffrey Chaucer,
of whos soule Jhesu Crist have mercy. Amen.

1081 **this litel tretys:** the preceding tale; see n.
1082 **arrette:** attribute
1086 **book of the XXV. Ladies:** The Legend of Good Women   **sownen into synne:** tend toward, are conducive to, sin.

1087 **book of the Leoun:** a lost work; see n.
1092 **Qui cum Patre . . . Amen:** He who lives and reigns with the Father and Holy Spirit, God, world without end. Amen.

Appendix

General Bibliography

THE EXPLANATORY NOTES provide bibliographical references, but they are necessarily concerned with specific problems in the individual texts. The following brief bibliography is intended to provide guidance for more general studies and for studies of particular background and ancillary matters. These, of course, are intended for relatively advanced students. Beginning readers should turn first to the explanatory notes in this volume or to one of the several good introductions to Chaucer, notably Helen Cooper, *The Canterbury Tales,* 2nd ed., 1996, the relevant chapters in *The Cambridge Chaucer Companion,* ed. Piero Boitani and Jill Mann, 1986, and Derek Brewer, *A New Introduction to Chaucer,* 2nd ed., 1998.

BIBLIOGRAPHIES AND SURVEYS OF SCHOLARSHIP

General Bibliographies

Chaucer: A Bibliographical Manual, by Eleanor Prescott Hammond, 1908 (new ed. 1933). (Covers scholarship to 1908.)

A Chaucer Bibliography, 1925–1933, by Willard E. Martin, Jr., 1935 (rpt. 1973).

Bibliography of Chaucer, 1908–1953, by Dudley David Griffith, 1955.

Bibliography of Chaucer, 1954–63, by William R. Crawford, 1967.

A Bibliography of Chaucer, 1964–1973, by Lorrayne Y. Baird-Lange, 1977.

A Bibliography of Chaucer, 1974–1985, by Lorrayne Y. Baird-Lange and Hildegard Schnuttgen, 1988.

Hammond covers nineteenth-century Chaucer scholarship, and the other volumes listed above cover the periods specified, usually with a survey of the development of scholarship and critical opinion. For the years since 1985, see *Studies in the Age of Chaucer,* which prints an annual annotated bibliography (beginning in 1975–76), currently edited by Mark Allen and Bege K. Bowers. This bibliography is now conveniently available online from the University of Texas at San Antonio, at the site maintained as a searchable database by Mark Allen.

The Year's Work in English Studies, ed. Valerie Allen and Margaret Connolly, also provides an annotated yearly bibliography. Other general bibliographies are *The Annual Bibliography of English Language and Literature* (Modern Humanities Research Association) and the *MLA International Bibliography* (published by the Modern Language Association).

Selected General Bibliographies

The Essential Chaucer: An Annotated Bibliography of Major Modern Studies, ed. Mark Allen and John H. Fisher, 1987 (available on line).

Chaucer, A Bibliographical Introduction, ed. John Leyerle and Anne Quick, 1986.

The Canterbury Tales

By far the most useful sources are *The Chaucer Bibliographies,* published by the University of Toronto Press in association with the University of Rochester, under the general editorship of Thomas Hahn. These are fully annotated. Those published thus far in the series are:

Chaucer's General Prologue to the Canterbury Tales: An Annotated Bibliography, 1900 to 1984, ed. Caroline D. Eckhardt, 1990.

Chaucer's Knight's Tale: An Annotated Bibliography, 1900 to 1985, ed. Monica E. McAlpine, 1991.

Chaucer's Miller's, Reeve's, and Cook's Tales, 1900–1992, ed. T. L. Burton and Rosemary Greentree; annotations by David Briggs et al., 1997.

Chaucer's Wife of Bath's Prologue and Tale: An Annotated Bibliography, 1900–1995, ed. Peter G. Beidler and Elizabeth M. Biebel, 1998.

The volumes in the *Variorum Edition of the Works of Geoffrey Chaucer* (Paul G. Ruggiers, gen. ed.; Donald C. Baker, assoc. ed.; vol. 2, *The Canterbury Tales,* 1983–) are likewise very useful. Those published thus far are:

The General Prologue, ed. Malcolm Andrew, Daniel J. Ransom, et al., 1993 (vol. 2, parts 1A–1B).

The Miller's Tale, ed. Thomas W. Ross, 1983 (vol. 2, part 9).

The Summoner's Tale, ed. John F. Plummer III, 1975 (vol. 2, part 7).

The Squire's Tale, ed. Donald C. Baker, 1990 (vol. 2, part 12).

The Physician's Tale, ed. Helen Storm Corsa, 1987 (vol. 2, part 17).

The Prioress's Tale, ed. Beverly Boyd, 1987 (vol. 2, part 20).

The Nun's Priest's Tale, ed. Derek Pearsall, 1984 (vol. 2, part 9).

The Manciple's Tale, ed. Donald C. Baker, 1984 (vol. 2, part 10).

Surveys of Scholarship and Critical Opinion

Spurgeon, Caroline F. E., *Five Hundred Years of Chaucer Criticism and Allusion (1357–1900),* 2nd ed., 3 vols., 1925. This is a fascinating collection of early allusions to Chaucer and his work (and hence provides a glimpse of shifting critical opinions over the centuries).

Brewer, Derek S., ed., *Chaucer: The Critical Heritage,* 2 vols., 1978. This is an anthology of generous excerpts from many of the works Spurgeon quotes or cites and goes beyond 1900 to 1933, the year Robinson's *Chaucer* first appeared.

Hammond's *Chaucer: A Bibliographical Manual* surveys scholarship in the nineteenth century. The first half of the twentieth century is well covered by Albert C. Baugh in "Fifty Years of Chaucer Scholarship," Spec 26, 1951, 159–72. See also L. D. Benson, "A Reader's Guide to Writings on Chaucer," in *Geoffrey Chaucer: Writers and their Backgrounds,* ed. D. S. Brewer, 1974 (2nd ed., 1990), 321–72. For more recent years, the bibliographies listed above—the general bibliographies, the Chaucer bibliographies, and the volumes in the Variorum series—all include useful surveys of scholarship and criticism.

LANGUAGE

The Glossarial Concordance to the Riverside Chaucer, ed. Larry D. Benson, 1993, provides a full dictionary of Chaucer's language. The best resource for the study of his language is *The Middle English Dictionary,* now edited by Robert E. Lewis; its fascicles began to appear in 1956, and the project is now nearing conclusion. For the final part of the alphabet, not yet covered by the *Middle English Dictionary,* see *The Oxford English Dictionary,* 2nd ed., ed. J. A. Simpson and E. S. C. Weiner, 1989. All three of these are now available on the Internet, and *The Oxford English Dictionary* is also available as a CD-ROM.

The glossary in Skeat's *Oxford Chaucer,* vol. 6, remains a useful resource, as does *A Chaucer Glossary,* ed. Norman Davis, Douglas Gray, Patricia Ingham, and Anne Wallace-Hadrill, 1979. For proper names, most of which are not covered in the standard dictionaries, see:

A Chaucer Gazeteer, by Francis P. Magoun, Jr., 1961.

Chaucer Name Dictionary: A Guide to Astrological, Biblical, Historical, Literary, and Mythological Names in the Works of Geoffrey Chaucer, by Jacquelin de Weever, 1987.

For an index of rhyming words, see:

A New Rime Index to the Canterbury Tales Based on Manly and Rickert's Text of the Canterbury Tales, ed. Michio Masui, 1988.

For a general introduction to Chaucer's language, see:

Baugh, Albert C., *A History of the English Language,* 3rd ed. rev. Thomas Cable, 1979 (for the state of the English language in Chaucer's time).

Burnley, J. David, *A Guide to Chaucer's Language,* 1983.

Cannon, Christopher, *The Making of Chaucer's English: A Study of Words,* 1998.

Mossé, Fernand, *A Handbook of Middle English,* tr. James A. Walker, 5th printing, corr. and augm., 1968.

Mustanoja, Tauno, *A Middle English Syntax,* 1: Parts of Speech, Mémoires de la Société Néophilologue de Helsinki, 23, 1960.

For hearing the pronunciation of Chaucer's Middle English, a number of good recordings are now available. For a survey, see:

Bowden, Betsy, *Listeners' Guide to Medieval English: A Discography,* 1988.

Gaylord, Alan T., "Imagining Voices: Chaucer on Cassette," SAC 12, 1990, 215–38 (reviews cassettes and videotapes that appeared after Bowden's Guide).

Not listed in Gaylord's review are more recent tape recordings of a number of the *Tales,* available from the Chaucer Studio, Provo, Utah.

For the meter of Chaucer's verse, see (in addition to pp. xxxvi–xxxviii) the full survey of the problem, with bibliography, by Tauno Mustanoja, 65–94, in *The Companion to Chaucer Studies,* ed. Beryl Rowland, rev. ed., 1979, and Arthur W. Glowka, *A Guide to Chaucer's Meter,* 1991.

STYLE AND RHETORIC

Most general studies of Chaucer touch on matters of style, as do most of the studies of language cited above. Among more specialized studies are:

Baum, Paull F., "Chaucer's Puns," PMLA 71, 1956, 225–46; see also "Chaucer's Puns: A Supplemental List," PMLA 73, 1958, 167–70.

Birney, Earle, "The Beginnings of Chaucer's Irony," PMLA 54, 1939, 637–55; "Is Chaucer's Irony a Modern Discovery?" JEGP 41, 1942, 303–19.

Bloomfield, Morton W., "Authenticating Realism and the Realism of Chaucer," *Thought* 29, 1964, 335–58 (rpt. in his *Essays and Explorations,* 1970).

Brewer, Derek S., *Toward A Chaucerian Poetic,* Sir Israel Gollancz Lecture, PBA 60, 1974, 54–79.

Crosby, Ruth, "Chaucer and the Custom of Oral Delivery," Spec 13, 1938, 413–32.

Donaldson, E. Talbot, "Chaucer the Pilgrim," PMLA 69, 1954, 928–36 (rpt. in his *Speaking of Chaucer,* 1970).

Fichte, Jörg O., *Chaucer's "Art Poetical": A Study in Chaucerian Poetics,* 1980.

Howard, Donald R., "Chaucer the Man," PMLA 80, 1965, 337–43.

Muscatine, Charles, *Chaucer and the French Tradition: A Study in Style and Meaning,* 1957 (rpt. 1965).

Wenzel, Siegfried, "Chaucer and the Language of Contemporary Preaching," SP 73, 1976, 138–61.

RHETORIC

On the general influence of the rhetorical tradition on medieval literature, see James J. Murphy, *Rhetoric in the Middle Ages,* 1974. Stephen Knight, *Rymyng Craftily,* 1973, provides a list of rhetorical figures illustrated by examples from Chaucer's poetry. Among other important studies are:

Everett, Dorothy, "Some Reflections on Chaucer's 'Art Poetical,'" PBA 36, 1950, 149–74 (rpt. in her *Essays on Middle English Literature,* ed. Patricia Kean, 1955).
Kökeritz, Helge, "Rhetorical Word Play in Chaucer," PMLA 59, 1954, 937–52.
Manly, John M., *Chaucer and the Rhetoricians,* Warton Lecture on English Poetry, 17 (PBA 12, 1926, 95–113; rpt. in Richard J. Schoeck and Jerome Taylor, *Chaucer Criticism: The Canterbury Tales,* 1960).
Murphy, James J., "A New Look at Chaucer and the Rhetoricians," RES n.s. 15, 1964, 1–20.
Payne, Robert O., *The Key of Remembrance: A Study of Chaucer's Poetics,* 1963.

CHAUCER'S LIFE

Indispensable to the study of Chaucer's biography is *Chaucer Life-Records,* ed. Martin M. Crow and Clair C. Olson from materials compiled by John M. Manly and Edith Rickert with the assistance of Lilian J. Redstone and others, 1966. All known contemporary records appear in this volume (for a description of the project see Crow, Univ. Texas Studies in English 31, 1952, 1–12). This supersedes the *Life Records of Chaucer,* ed. W. D. Selby, F. J. Furnivall, E. A. Bond, and R. E. G. Kirk (Ch Soc, 2nd ser. 12, 14, 21, 32; 1875–1900), though that work remains useful for a number of supplementary documents necessarily omitted from the *Chaucer Life-Records.* For an index, see E. P. Kuhl, MP 10, 1913, 527–52.

The early lives of Chaucer are examined by Thomas R. Lounsbury, *Studies in Chaucer,* 1892 (rpt. 1962), vol. 1, chs. 1–2; Hammond, *Chaucer: A Bibliographical Manual,* 1–39 (where the early brief lives are printed); and, especially valuable, Clair C. Olson, *The Emerging Biography of a Poet,* 1953. For modern lives, see Derek S. Brewer, *Chaucer,* 3rd rev. ed., 1973; Donald R. Howard, *Chaucer: His Life, His Works, His World,* 1987 (lively, but often criticized for being too speculative); and Derek A. Pearsall, *The Life of Geoffrey Chaucer: A Critical Biography,* 1992.

HISTORICAL AND SOCIAL CONTEXTS

C. S. Lewis, *The Discarded Image: An Introduction to Medieval Literature,* 1964 (rpt. 1971), remains a useful introductory discussion of the medieval worldview, and Derek S. Brewer, *Chaucer and His World,* 1992, provides a good introduction to Chaucer's social milieu. For a lively contemporary account of the noble life, see Jean Froissart, *Chronicles,* tr. Geoffrey Brereton, 1978 (selections). For the general historical background, see:

Barnie, John, *War in Medieval Society: Social Values and the Hundred Years War 1377–99,* 1974.
Bisson, Lillian M., *Chaucer and the Late Medieval World,* 1998.
Bumke, Joachim, *Courtly Culture: Literature and Society in the High Middle Ages,* tr. Thomas Dunlap, 1991.
Coulton, G. G., *The Medieval Panorama: The English Scene from Conquest to Reformation,* 1938 (rpt. 1974).
———, *Chaucer and His England,* with a new bibliography by T. W. Craik, 1963 (rpt. 1968).
Du Boulay, F. R. H., *The Age of Ambition: English Society in the Late Middle Ages,* 1970.
Jusserand, J. J., *English Wayfaring Life in the Middle Ages,* rev. and enl. ed., tr. Lucy Toulmin Smith, 1920 (4th ed. rpt. 1977).
McKisack, May, *The Fourteenth Century, 1307–1399,* Vol. 5 of the *Oxford History of England,* 1959 (rpt. 1976).
Myers, Alec R., *London in the Age of Chaucer,* 1972.
Rickert, Edith, *Chaucer's World,* ed. Clair C. Olson and Martin M. Crow, 1948 (rpt. 1968). (A collection of documents illustrative of contemporary life.)
Robertson, D. W., Jr., *Chaucer's London,* 1968.
Strutt, Joseph, *Sports and Pastimes of the People of England,* enl. and corr. ed. J. Charles Cox, 1903 (rpt. 1968).
Thrupp, Sylvia L., *The Merchant Class of Medieval London (1300–1500),* 1948 (rpt. 1989).
Whitmore, Sister M. Ernestine, *Medieval English Domestic Life and Amusements in the Works of Chaucer,* 1937.

ART, RELIGION, AND LEARNING

Reproductions of the art of Chaucer's time are found in most of the works listed below and in Maurice Hussey, *Chaucer's World: Pictorial Companion,* 1968, as well as in such richly illustrated studies as Derek S. Brewer, *Chaucer and His World,* 1978 (rpt. 1992); D. W. Robertson, *Preface to Chaucer,* 1962; and V. A. Kolve, *Chaucer and the Imagery of Narrative,* 1984, an exemplary study of the interrelations of art and literature.

Evans, Joan, *English Art, 1307–1461,* 1949.
Kolve, V. A., "Chaucer and the Visual Arts," in *Geoffrey Chaucer: Writers and Their Background,* ed. D. S. Brewer, 1974 (2nd ed., 1990), 290–320.
Loomis, Roger Sherman, *A Mirror of Chaucer's World,* 1965.
Gordon, Dillian, Lisa Monnas, and Caroline Elan, eds., *The Royal Image of Richard II and the Wilton Diptych,* 1997.
Pevsner, Nicholas, "Late English Medieval Architecture," in *The Age of Chaucer,* ed. Boris Ford, Pelican Guide to English Literature 1, 1982, 229–51.
Rickert, Margaret, *Painting in England: The Middle Ages,* 2nd ed., 1965.
Stone, Lawrence, *Sculpture in Britain: The Middle Ages,* 1955.
Wilkins, Nigel E., *Music in the Age of Chaucer,* 2nd ed., 1998. (Contains Chaucer songs.)
Wood, Margaret, *The English Medieval House,* 1965.

For religious and philsophical setting, see:

Bloomfield, Morton W., "Fourteenth Century England: Realism and Rationalism in Wyclif and Chaucer," *English Studies in Africa* 16, 1973, 59–70.

Courtenay, William J., "The Dialectic of Divine Omnipotence in the Age of Chaucer: A Reconsideration," in *Nominalism and Litereray Discourse: New Perspectives,* ed. Hugo Keiper, Christopher Bode, and Richard J. Utz, 1997, 111–21. (The notes provide a good brief survey of studies of Chaucer's philosophical background.)

Hudson, Anne, *The Premature Reformation: Wycliffite Texts and Lollard History,* 1988.

Knowles, Dom David, *The Religious Orders in England,* 3 vols., 1961–62.

Leff, Gordon, *The Dissolution of the Medieval Outlook: An Essay on Intellectual and Spiritual Change in the Fourteenth Century,* 1976.

Oberman, Heiko A., "Fourteenth-Century Religious Thought: A Premature Profile," Spec 53, 1978, 80–93.

Pantin, William A., *The English Church in the Fourteenth Century,* 1955 (rpt. 1980).

Shepherd, Geoffrey, "Religion and Philosophy in Chaucer," in *Geoffrey Chaucer: Writers and Their Background,* ed. D. S. Brewer, 1974 (2nd ed., 1990), 262–89.

Szitya, Penn R., *The Antifraternal Tradition in Medieval Literature,* 1986.

Utz, Richard J., ed., *Literary Nominalism and the Theory of Rereading Late Medieval Texts: A New Research Paradigm,* 1995.

On scientific learning:

On the Properties of Things: John Trevisa's Translation of Bartholomaeus Anglicus' De proprietatibus rerum (ed. M. C. Seymour et al., 1975), provides a convenient and fascinating compendium of the general scientific knowledge of Chaucer's time. For studies of popular lore in Chaucer's works, see Beryl Rowland, *Blind Beasts: Chaucer's Animal World,* 1971, and Bartlett J. Whiting, *Chaucer's Use of Proverbs,* 1934 (rpt. 1973). For general studies of Chaucer's learning, see Thomas R. Lounsbury, *Studies in Chaucer,* vol. 2, 1892. (rpt. 1962), ch. 5, and R. W. V. Elliot, "Chaucer's Reading," in *Chaucer's Mind and Art,* ed. A. C. Cawley, 1969, 46–68. Among the many special studies, see:

Astell, Ann W., *Chaucer and the Universe of Learning,* 1996.

Curry, Walter Clyde, *Chaucer and the Mediaeval Sciences,* rev. ed., 1960.

Manzalaoui, M., "Chaucer and Science," in *Geoffrey Chaucer: Writers and Their Background,* ed. D. S. Brewer, 1974 (2nd ed., 1990), 224–61.

Plimpton, George A., *The Education of Chaucer: Illustrated from the English Schoolbooks in Use in His Time,* 1935.

Pratt, Robert A., "The Importance of Manuscripts for the Study of Medieval Education, as Revealed by the Learning of Chaucer," *Progress of Renaissance and Medieval Studies* 20, 1949, 509–30.

Rickert, Edith, "Chaucer at School," MP 29, 1932, 257–74.

On astronomy:

Eade, J. C., "'We ben to lewed or to slowe': Chaucer's Astronomy and Audience Participation," SAC 4, 1982, 53–85.

North, John David. *Chaucer's Universe,* 1988.

Smyser, Hamilton M., "A View of Chaucer's Astronomy," Spec 45, 1970, 359–73.

Wedel, Theodore O., *The Medieval Attitude toward Astrology, Particularly in England,* 1920 (rpt. 1968).

Wood, Chauncey A., *Chaucer and the Country of the Stars: Poetic Uses of Astrological Imagery,* 1970.

CHAUCER'S LITERARY ENVIRONMENT

For Chaucer's audience and the literary milieu of London and the court, see:

Fisher, John H., *John Gower: Moral Philosopher and Friend of Chaucer,* 1964.

Giffin, Mary E., *Studies on Chaucer and His Audience,* 1956.

Green, Richard F., *Poets and Princepleasers: Literature and the English Court in the Late Middle Ages,* 1980.

Hanawalt, Barbara A., ed., *Chaucer's England: Literature in Historical Context,* 1992.

Mathew, Gervase, *The Court of Richard II,* 1968.

McFarlane, Kenneth B., *The Nobility of Later Medieval England,* 1973.

Middleton, Anne, "Chaucer's 'New Men' and the Good of Literature," in *Literature and Society, Selected Papers from the English Institute 1978,* ed. Edward W. Said, 1980, 15–56.

Robertson, Durant W., "London as an Intellectual Center," in his *Chaucer's London,* 1968, 179–222.

Strohm, Paul, "Chaucer's Audience," *Literature and History* 5, 1977, 26–41.

———, *Social Chaucer,* 1989.

Tout, T. F., "Literature and Learning in the English Civil Service in the Fourteenth Century," Spec 4, 1929, 365–89.

On the general literary temper and varying attitudes toward literature at the time, see:

Allen, Judson B., *The Friar as Critic: Literary Attitudes in the Later Middle Ages,* 1971.

Bruyne, Edgar, de, *The Aesthetics of the Middle Ages,* tr. Eileen Hennessey, 1969.

Carruthers, Mary, *The Book of Memory: A Study of Memory in Medieval Culture,* 1990 (rpt. 1992).

Huizinga, Johan, *The Waning of the Middle Ages,* tr. R. Hopman, 1924 (rpt. 1954); newly trans. by Rodney J. Payton and Ulrich Mammitzsch as *The Autumn of the Middle Ages,* 1996. (This is an an important work, though some of its basic assumptions are now questioned.)

Jordan, Robert M., *Chaucer's Poetics and the Modern Reader,* 1987.

Justice, Stephen, *Writing and Rebellion: England in 1381,* 1994.

Minnis, Alistair J., *Medieval Theory of Authorship: Scholastic Literary Attitudes in the Later Middle Ages,* 1988.

Olson, Glending, *Literature as Recreation in the Later Middle Ages,* 1982.

Robertson, Durant W., Jr., *A Preface to Chaucer: Studies in Medieval Perspective,* 1962.

Smalley, Beryl, *English Friars and Antiquity in the Early Fourteenth Century,* 1960.

Strohm, Paul, *Hochon's Arrow: The Social Imagination of Fourteenth-Century Texts,* 1992.

For two contemporary views of the literary environment, see:

The Goodman of Paris (Le Ménagier de Paris): A Treatise on Moral and Domestic Economy by a Citizen of Paris, c. 1393, tr. (with omissions) Eileen Power, 1928. This shows, along with fascinating glimpses of contemporary life, the literary tastes of an educated citizen of the late fourteenth century (and includes versions of the tales Chaucer used for his Melibee and Clerk's tales).

The Love of Books: The Philobiblion of Richard de Bury, tr. E. C. Thomas, 1888 (rpt. 1966), a charming work by a learned contemporary.

SOURCES AND INFLUENCES

Detailed discussions of Chaucer's literary sources are given in the introductory notes to each tale, with relevant bibliographies. For texts of the sources and analogues, see:

Bryan, W. F., and Germaine Dempster, *Sources and Analogues of the Canterbury Tales,* 1941. (Now being revised under the general editorship of Robert M. Correale and Mary Hamel.)

Cooper, Helen, "Sources and Analogues of Chaucer's Canterbury Tales: Reviewing the Work," SAC 19, 1997, 183–210. (Chapter 1 of the new version described above.)

Havely, N. R., *Chaucer's Boccaccio: Sources of Troilus, The Knight's and Franklin's Tale,* 1980.

Miller, Robert P., *Chaucer: Sources and Backgrounds,* 1977.

The English Context

Benson, Larry D., "The Beginnings of Chaucer's English Style," in Theodore M. Anderson and Stephen A. Barney, eds., *Contradictions: From "Beowulf" to Chaucer,* 1995, 243–65, and in Lawrence Besserman, ed., *The Challenge of Periodization,* 1996.

Boitani, Piero, *English Medieval Narrative in the Thirteenth and Fourteenth Centuries,* tr. Joan Krakover Hall, 1982.

Brewer, Derek S., "The Relationship of Chaucer to the English and European Traditions," in his *Chaucer and Chaucerians,* 1966, 1–38.

Burrow, John A., *Ricardian Poetry: Chaucer, Gower, Langland, and the Gawain-Poet,* 1971.

Muscatine, Charles, *Poetry and Crisis in the Age of Chaucer,* 1972.

Kean, Patricia M., *Chaucer and the Making of English Poetry,* 2 vols., 1972 (a shortened, 1-vol. ed., 1982).

Salter, Elizabeth, *Fourteenth-Century English Poetry,* 1983.

Wallace, David, ed., *The Cambridge History of Medieval English Literature: Writing in Britain, 1066–1547,* 1999.

The Bible

Besserman, Lawrence L., *Chaucer and the Bible: A Critical Review of Research,* 1988.

———, *Chaucer's Biblical Poetics,* 1998.

Landrum, Grace W., "Chaucer's Use of the Vulgate," PMLA 39, 1924, 75–100.

Thompson, W. Meredith, "Chaucer's Translation of the Bible," in *English and Medieval Studies Presented to J. R. R. Tolkien,* ed. Norman Davis and C. L. Wrenn, 1962, 183–99.

The Latin Poets

Ayres, Harry M., "Chaucer and Seneca," RomR 10, 1919, 1–15. (See Pratt, Spec 41, below.)

Baswell, Christopher, *Virgil in Medieval England: Figuring the Aeneid from the Twelfth Century to Chaucer,* 1995.

Clogan, Paul M., "Chaucer's Use of the *Thebaid,*" English Miscellany 18, 1967, 9–31.

Curtius, Ernst Robert, *European Literature and the Latin Middle Ages,* tr. Willard R. Trask, 1953 (rpt. 1967). [A survey of the literary "topoi" (commonplaces) available to Chaucer.]

Fyler, John M., *Chaucer and Ovid,* 1979.

Hazelton, Richard, "Chaucer and Cato," Spec 35, 1960, 357–80.

McCall, John F., *Chaucer Among the Gods,* 1979.

Minnis, Alistair J., *Chaucer and Pagan Antiquity,* 1982.

Pratt, Robert A., "Chaucer's Claudian," Spec 22, 1947, 419–29.

———, "Chaucer and the Hand that Fed Him," Spec 41, 1966, 619–42. (Chaucer's debt to John of Wales.)

Shannon, Edgar F., *Chaucer and the Roman Poets,* 1929.

Wise, Boyd A., *The Influence of Statius upon Chaucer,* 1911 (rpt. 1967).

Wrenn, C. L., "Chaucer's Knowledge of Horace," MLR 18, 1923, 286–92.

Boethius

Jefferson, Bernard L., *Chaucer and the Consolation of Philosophy of Boethius,* 1917 (rpt. 1968).

Minnis, A. J. *Chaucer's Boethius and the Medieval Tradition,* 1993.

The French Poets

Calin, William, *The French Tradition and the Literature of Medieval England,* 1994.

Fansler, Dean S., *Chaucer and the Roman de la Rose,* 1914 (rpt. 1965).

Lowes, John L., "Chaucer and the Ovid Moralisé," PMLA 33, 1918, 302–25.

Olson, Glending, "Deschamps' *Art de Dictier* and Chaucer's Literary Environment," Spec 48, 1973, 714–23.

Wimsatt, James I., *Chaucer and his French Contemporaries: Natural Music in the Fourteenth Century,* 1991.

Wimsatt, James I., ed., *Chaucer and the Poems of "Ch" in University of Pennsylvania MS French 15,* 1982. (French poems of the sort the young Chaucer would have known and perhaps written.)

The Italian Poets

Boitani, Piero, *Chaucer and Boccaccio,* 1977.
Lowes, John L., "Chaucer and Dante," MP 16, 1916–17, 705–35.
Pratt, Robert A., "Chaucer's Use of the *Teseida,*" PMLA 66, 1947, 419–29.
Schless, Howard, *Chaucer and Dante: A Revaluation,* 1984.
Wallace, David, *Chaucer and the Early Writings of Boccaccio,* 1985.
———, *Chaucerian Polity : Absolutist Lineages and Associational Forms in England and Italy,* 1997.

COURTLY LOVE

The subject of courtly love, the style of aristocratic courtship that informs much of Chaucer's poetry, has long been an important concern in criticism, beginning with C. S. Lewis's influential *The Allegory of Love: A Study in Medieval Tradition,* 1936 (rpt. 1973), which derived its basic ideas from Andrew the Chaplain: *Andreas Capellanus: De Amore,* ed. and tr. P. G. Walsh, 1982. For more recent studies, see:

Benson, Larry D., "Courtly Love in the Later Middle Ages," in *Fifteenth Century Studies,* ed. Robert Yeager, 1984, 237–57; rpt. in Theodore M. Anderson and Stephen A. Barney, eds., *Contradictions: From "Beowulf" to Chaucer,* 1995.
Benton, John F., "Clio and Venus: An Historical View of Medieval Love," in *The Meaning of Courtly Love,* ed. F. X. Newman, 1968, 19–42.
Boase, Roger, *The Origin and Meaning of Courtly Love: A Critical Study of European Scholarship,* 1977.
Burnley, J. David, *Courtliness and Literature in Medieval England,* 1998.
Donaldson, E. Talbot, "The Myth of Courtly Love," in *Speaking of Chaucer,* 1970 (rpt. 1983), 154–63 (rpt. of essay in *Ventures: Magazine of the Yale Graduate School* 5, 1968, 1–33).
Kelly, Henry Ansgar, *Love and Marriage in the Age of Chaucer,* 1975.
Robertson, Durant W., Jr., "Courtly Love as an Impediment to the Understanding of Medieval Texts," in *The Meaning of Courtly Love,* ed. F. X. Newman, 1968, 1–18.

CRITICAL APPROACHES

Scholarship on Chaucer in the early part of the twentieth century was primarily historical in approach, dealing mainly with the search for his sources and the study of the biographical details of his life. Interpretation was informed by this approach (as in John M. Manly's *Some New Light on Chaucer,* 1926) or by an appreciation for Chaucer's realism (best exemplified in George L. Kittredge's *Chaucer and His Poetry,* first pub. 1915). The work of these critics is still useful, as the Explanatory Notes show. If their aesthetic preference for Chaucer's cheerful realism sometimes led them to ignore or condemn those works that did not embody that quality, they nevertheless illuminated much and defined many of the problems (for instance, the dramatic qualities of Chaucer's poetry; the "Marriage Group" in *The Canterbury Tales*) that still concern critics and readers.

By the 1960s and 1970s studies of Chaucer could be said to be dominated by three approaches, the old historical, the New Critical, and the new historical or "exegetical" schools (see William R. Crawford, *A Bibliography of Chaucer 1954–1963,* xiv–xl). The New Criticism in theory flatly "eschewed the historical approach" and was "reluctant to invoke historical data from outside the poem to explain what is in it" (Donaldson, *Chaucer's Poetry,* 2nd ed., 1975, vi). In the hands of its most distinguished practitioners, such as E. Talbot Donaldson, the New Criticism's aim was not to ban historical considerations from criticism but "to make history serve Chaucer's poetry rather than be served by it." The older historical critics were less historical than the critical disputes of the 1950s made them seem: at their worst their criticism was merely appreciative and uninformed by historical considerations; at their best—in Kittredge's genial criticism, for example—they concentrated on the text at hand and seldom invoked historical data as a means of interpretation, though the qualities they sought in the text were not those ironies, ambivalences, and verbal complexities that fascinated the New Critics and are today widely accepted as characteristic of Chaucer's works. The historical approach today is at once more historical and more aesthetic than that exemplified in the works of Kittredge or even in Manly's still useful *Some New Light on Chaucer.* Derek S. Brewer, who modestly classifies himself with "the traditional or even naive reader within the English tradition" (*Chaucer,* 3rd ed., 1973, 1), is now perhaps the foremost exponent of the historical approach, and the attempt to understand Chaucer in his time (the title of one of Brewer's books) remains a lively concern of Chaucerian studies.

Charles Muscatine's *Chaucer and the French Tradition,* 1957, provided a powerful impulse to a different form of historical study—the history of style and aesthetics—by showing that convention and originality, which once seemed the touchstones of literary merit, had a much different function in Chaucer's time than in the nineteenth century. Muscatine's work was at least the indirect inspiration for the important new studies of Chaucer's poems, treated in the light of medieval rhetoric, which began to appear in the 1960s and 1970s (see the section on Style and Rhetoric above, and especially Robert O. Payne, *The Key of Remembrance: A Study of Chaucer's Poetics,* 1963). The same impetus is evident in studies such as Robert M. Jordan's *Chaucer and the Shape of Creation,* 1967; Patricia M. Kean's *Chaucer and the Making of English Poetry,* 1972; Alfred David's *Strumpet Muse,* 1976; Donald R. Howard's *Idea of The Canterbury Tales,* 1976; and Robert B. Burlin's *Chaucerian Fiction,* 1977. Many other works might be cited; all attempt in their various ways to come to an understanding of Chaucer's poetics and to read his works in the light of that understanding.

The new historical or exegetical criticism likewise attempted to define a Chaucerian poetic. It was first exemplified in an article by Durant W. Robertson, Jr., "The Doctrine of Charity in Mediaeval Literary Gardens: A Topical Approach through Symbolism and Allegory," Spec 26, 1951, 24–49 (rpt. in his *Essays in Medieval Culture,* 1980, and fully developed in his *Preface to Chaucer,* 1962). In this learned survey of medieval art, mythography, and biblical exegesis, Robertson attempts to define a "medieval aesthetic," allegorical and iconographic, derived from late classical allegorists and Pauline interpretations of the Scriptures. Chaucer, he argues, employs a literary iconography by which the reader can discover the *sentence* of the texts, which is always some aspect of *caritas*—love of the divine—or its aberrations. This approach and the allegorical readings of Chaucer it produced had a considerable impact on Chaucer studies, especially in America, and generated a good deal of controversy (see Lawrence Besserman, "Glossyng Is a Glorious Thyng: Chaucer's Biblical Exegesis," in *Chaucer and Scriptural Tradition,* ed. David L. Jeffrey, 1984, 65–73; *Critical Approaches to Medieval Literature: Selected Papers from the English Institute 1958–59,* ed. Dorothy Bethurum, 1960).

Interest in Robertson's approach has waned (but by no means disappeared—it is invoked along with much more contemporary theoretical maneuvers in Dolores Frees' *An Ars legendi for Chaucer's Canterbury Tales,* 1991). However, "new historicism" today refers to a much different critical enterprise—that best exemplified in the works of Lee Patterson (*Negotiating the Past,* 1987; *Chaucer and the Subject of History,* 1991) and Paul Strohm (*Social Chaucer,* 1989; *Hochon's Arrow: The Social Imagination of Fourteenth-Century Texts,* 1992). Whereas the "old historicists" concentrated on literary and intellectual history, the new studies concentrate mainly on social history, drawing on sources—tax records, court pleadings, parish registers, minor controversial literary works—that were largely ignored by previous generations of historians, and they use these sources not as "influences" but as a means of defining power relationships and social discourse in which the text itself participates.

An equally impressive body of criticism has developed on the themes of feminism—most notably in the quite different works by Carolyn Dinshaw (*Chaucer's Sexual Poetics,* 1989) and Jill Mann (*Geoffrey Chaucer,* Feminist Readings series, 1991)—and gender (Susan Crane, *Gender and Romance in Chaucer's Canterbury Tales,* 1994; *Masculinities in Chaucer,* ed. Peter G. Beidler, 1998).

New historicist and feminist concerns are apparent in almost all criticism in the past two decades. Nevertheless, a rich variety of interdisciplinary and theoretical approaches to Chaucer has been developed in these years—Marxist, as in the works of David Aers (e.g., *Chaucer,* 1986); deconstructionist, as exemplified in the works of H. Marchall Leicester (e.g., his argument that Chaucer himself is a deconstructionist in Laurie A. Finke and Martin B. Shichtman, eds., *Medieval Texts and Contemporary Readers,* 1987, 15–26; and his book *The Disenchanted Self,* 1990); Bakhtinian (John Ganim, *Chaucerian Theatricality,* 1990); Freudian (exemplified in the works of Louise O. Fradenburg, such as "'Fulfild of Fairye': The Social Meaning of Fantasy in the Wife of Bath's Prologue and Tale," in Peter G. Beidler, ed., *Geoffrey Chaucer: "The Wife of Bath,"* 1996, 205–20). (Beidler's volume provides a good introduction to modern critical approaches.) For a survey of recent critical trends (rather unsympathetic to them), see S. H. Rigby. *Chaucer in Context: Society, Allegory, and Gender,* 1996. Over the same years, more traditional approaches to Chaucer have also flourished, in works such as C. David Benson's *Chaucer's Drama of Style,* 1986, Derek A. Pearsall's *The Canterbury Tales,* 1993, and Derek S. Brewer's *New Introduction to Chaucer,* 2nd ed., 1998.

Chaucer's works seem suitable for almost any critical approach (see John H. Fisher, "Chaucer's Prescience," SAC 5, 1983, 3–15), perhaps because, as some modern theorists hold, the text is as much a creation of the reader as of the poet (see Chauncey Wood, "Affective Stylistics and the Study of Chaucer," SAC 6, 1984, 21–40). However that may be, the variety and volume of such works testify to the continuing vigor of Chaucer criticism and to the appeal of the poet to readers of all critical persuasions.

Abbreviations

EDITIONS OF CHAUCER'S CANTERBURY TALES

Only editions frequently cited in the Explanatory and Textual Notes are included here; other editions are listed in the notes to the individual works.

Baugh Albert C. Baugh, ed., *Chaucer's Major Poetry,* 1963.

Donaldson E. Talbot Donaldson, ed., *Chaucer's Poetry: An Anthology for the Modern Reader,* 2nd ed., 1975.

Fisher John H. Fisher, ed., *The Complete Poetry and Prose of Geoffrey Chaucer,* 1977.

Manly, CT John M. Manly, ed., *Canterbury Tales by Geoffrey Chaucer,* 1928.

Manly-Rickert, M-R John M. Manly and Edith Rickert, eds., *The Text of* The Canterbury Tales, *Studied on the Basis of All Known Manuscripts,* 1940. 8 vols.

Partridge, Glosses in CT Stephen Bradford Partridge, *Glosses in the Manuscripts of Chaucer's Canterbury Tales: An Edition and Commentary* (Harvard thesis, 1992).

Pratt, Tales Robert A. Pratt, ed., *The Tales of Canterbury*, 1974.

Robinson F. N. Robinson, ed., *The Works of Geoffrey Chaucer*, 2nd ed., 1957.

Skeat Walter W. Skeat, ed., *The Complete Works of Geoffrey Chaucer*, 1894. 6 vols., with a Supplementary vol. 7, containing the apocryphal works, 1897 (The Oxford Chaucer).

Tyrwhitt Thomas Tyrwhitt, ed., *The Canterbury Tales*, 1775–78. 5 vols. (rpt. with revised text, 1868).

JOURNALS AND SERIES

ABR	*American Benedictine Review*
Acad	*The Academy* (London)
AMN&Q	*American Notes and Queries*
Anglia	*Anglia: Zeitschrift für englische Philologie*
AnM	*Annuale mediaevale*
Archiv	*Archiv für das Studium der neueren Sprachen und Literaturen*
Athenaeum	*The Athenaeum* (London)
CCSL	Corpus Christianorum, Series Latina
CE	*College English*
CFMA	Classiques français du moyen âge
ChauR	*Chaucer Review*
Ch Soc	Chaucer Society, London
Criticism	*Criticism: A Quarterly for Literature and the Arts*
E&S	*Essays and Studies*
EETS	Early English Text Society (Original Series)
EETS e.s.	Early English Text Society, Extra Series
EETS, SS	Early English Text Society, Supplementary Series
EIC	*Essays in Criticism*
ELH	*ELH* (English Literary History)
ELN	*English Language Notes*
ES	*English Studies*
ESt	*Englische Studien*
Expl	*The Explicator*
FFC	Folklore Fellows Communications (Helsinki)
HLQ	*Huntington Library Quarterly*
JEGP	*Journal of English and Germanic Philology*
JMRS	*Journal of Medieval and Renaissance Studies*
LeedsSE	*Leeds Studies in English*
Loeb	The Loeb Classical Library
M&H	*Medievalia et Humanistica*
MÆ	*Medium Ævum*
MLN	*MLN* (Modern Language Notes)
MLQ	*Modern Language Quarterly*
MLR	*Modern Language Review*

MP	*Modern Philology*
MS	*Mediaeval Studies* (Toronto)
MSE	*Massachusetts Studies in English*
N&Q	*Notes and Queries*
Neophil	*Neophilologus*
NM	*Neuphilologische Mitteilungen*
PBA	*Proceedings of the British Academy*
PL, Patrologia Latina	*Patrologia Cursus Completus, Series Latina*, ed. J.-P. Migne
PLL	*Papers on Language and Literature*
PLPLS-LHS	*Proceedings of the Leeds Philosophical and Literary Society, Literary and Historical Section*
PMASAL	*Papers of the Michigan Academy of Science, Arts, and Letters*
PMLA	*PMLA* (Publications of the Modern Language Association)
PQ	*Philological Quarterly*
RBPH	*Revue belge de philologie et d'histoire*
RES	*Review of English Studies*
Rolls Series	Rerum Brittanicarum Medii Aevi Scriptores
Romania	*Romania*
RomR	*Romanic Review*
RPh	*Romance Philology*
RUO	*Revue de l'université d'Ottawa*
SAC	*Studies in the Age of Chaucer*
SATF	Société des Anciens Textes Français
SHF	Société d'histoire de France
SMed	*Studi Medievali*
SN	*Studia neophilologica*
SP	*Studies in Philology*
Spec	*Speculum: A Journal of Medieval Studies*
STS	Scottish Text Society
TEAMS	Consortium for the Teaching of the Middle Ages
TLF	Textes littèraires française
TLS	*Times Literary Supplement* (London)
TPS	*Transactions of the Philological Society* (London)
TRHS	*Transactions of the Royal Historical Society*
TSE	*Tulane Studies in English*
TSL	*Tennessee Studies in Literature*
TSLL	*Texas Studies in Literature and Language*
TWA	*Transactions of the Wisconsin Academy of Sciences, Arts, and Letters*
UTQ	*University of Toronto Quarterly*
YES	*Yearbook of English Studies*

DICTIONARIES AND OTHER REFERENCE WORKS

Aarne-Thompson Antti Aarne, *Types of the Folk Tale*, tr. and enl. by Stith Thompson, FFC 3, 2nd revision, 1964.

Butler's Lives of the Saints ed. David Hugh Farmer, Paul Burns; general intro. David Hugh Farmer, 1995–.

Chaucer Name Dictionary *A Guide to Astrological, Biblical, Historical, Literary, and Mythological Names in the Works of Geoffrey Chaucer,* ed. Jacqueline De Weever, 1987.

Davis, Ch Glossary *A Chaucer Glossary,* ed. Norman Davis, Douglas Gray, Patricia Ingham, and Anne Wallace-Hadrill, 1979.

Dict. of M. A. *The Dictionary of the Middle Ages,* gen. ed. Joseph R. Strayer, 1982–89.

Hassell James Woodward Hassell, *Middle French Proverbs, Sentences, and Proverbial Phrases,* 1982.

Magoun, Ch Gazetteer Francis P. Magoun, Jr., *A Chaucer Gazetteer,* 1961.

Manual ME *A Manual of the Writings in Middle English, 1050–1100,* gen. ed. J. Burke Severs and Albert E. Hartung, 1967–.

MED *Middle English Dictionary,* ed. Hans Kurath, Sherman M. Kuhn, John Reidy, and Robert E. Lewis (Editor in Chief), 1954–.

OED *Oxford English Dictionary,* 2nd ed., prepared by J. A. Simpson and E. S. C. Weiner. 1989.

Thompson, Motif-Index Stith Thompson, *Motif-Index of Folk Literature: A Classification of Narrative Elements in Folk-Tale, Ballads, Myths, Fables, Medieval Romances, Exempla, Jest-Books and Local Legends,* rev. and enl. ed., 1955–58 (rpt. 1975). 6 vols.

Tilley Morris P. Tilley, *A Dictionary of the Proverbs in England in the Sixteenth and Seventeenth Centuries,* 1950.

Walther Hans Walther, *Proverbia sententiaeque Latinitatis medii aevi,* 1963–69. 9 vols. (Vols. 7–9 ed. Paul Gerhard Schmidt.)

Whiting Bartlett J. and Helen W. Whiting, *Proverbs, Sentences, and Proverbial Phrases from English Writings Mainly Before 1500,* 1968.

PRIMARY TEXTS

Collections of Texts

The Babee's Book *The Babee's Book: Early English Meals and Manners,* ed. Frederick J. Furnivall, EETS 32, 1868.

Benson and Andersson, Lit. Context Larry D. Benson and Theodore M. Andersson, eds., *The Literary Context of Chaucer's Fabliaux: Texts and Translations,* 1971.

Child, Ballads Francis J. Child, *The English and Scottish Popular Ballads,* 1883–98. 5 vols. in 10 (rpt. 1965).

Ch Life Records *Chaucer Life Records,* ed. Martin M. Crow and Clair C. Olson, 1966.

Curye on Inglysch *Curye on Inglysch: English Culinary Manuscripts of the Fourteenth Century (Including the Forme of Cury),* ed. Constance B. Hieatt and Sharon Butler, EETS SS 8, 1985.

EHD *English Historical Documents, 1327–1485,* ed. Alec R. Myers, 1969.

English Medieval Lapidaries J. Evans and M. S. Serjeantson, eds., *English Medieval Lapidaries,* EETS 190, 1933.

Faral, Les arts poètiques Edmund A. Faral, *Les arts poètiques du XIIe et du XIIIe siècle: Recherches et documents sur la technique littéraire du moyen âge,* 1924.

Hammond, Engl. Verse Eleanor P. Hammond, *English Verse Between Chaucer and Surrey,* 1927 (rpt. 1965).

Harley Lyrics, ed. Brook *The Harley Lyrics,* ed. George L. Brook, 4th ed., 1968.

Hist. Poems, ed. Robbins *Historical Poems of the XIVth and XVth Centuries,* ed. Rossell Hope Robbins, 1959.

Horstmann, Altenglische Legenden Carl Horstmann, *Altenglische Legenden,* Neue Folgen, 1881.

Memorials of London Henry Thomas Riley, ed., *Memorials of London Life,* 1868.

Miller, Ch: Sources Robert P. Miller, Jr., ed., *Chaucer: Sources and Backgrounds,* 1977.

Originals and Analogues *Originals and Analogues of Some of Chaucer's Canterbury Tales,* ed. F. J. Furnivall, E. Brock, and W. A. Clouston, Ch Soc. 2nd ser. 7, 10, 15, 20, 22; 1872–87.

Rickert, Ch's World Edith Rickert, *Chaucer's World,* ed. Clair C. Olson and Martin M. Crow, 1948.

S&A, Sources and Analogues *Sources and Analogues of Chaucer's Canterbury Tales,* ed. W. F. Bryan and Germaine Dempster, 1941 (rpt. 1958).

Sec. Lyrics, ed. Robbins *Secular Lyrics of the XIVth and XVth Centuries,* ed. Rossell Hope Robbins, 2nd ed., 1955.

Two Fifteenth-Cent. Cookery-Bks *Two Fifteenth-Century Cookery-Books,* ed. Thomas Austin, EETS 91, 1888 (rpt. 1964).

Wycliffite Writings, ed. Hudson *Selections from English Wycliffite Writings,* ed. Anne Hudson, 1997.

Individual Authors and Works

ADVERSUS JOVINIANUM *See Jerome.*

AENEID *See Virgil.*

ALANUS DE INSULIS (ALAIN DE LILLE, 1125/30–1203)

De planctu naturae ed. Nikolaus Häring, SMed, 3rd ser., 19.2, 1979. Trans. as *The Plaint of Nature,* James J. Sheridan, 1980.

ALBERTANUS (ALBERTANUS BRIXIENSIS, ALBERTANUS OF BRESCIA, C. 1193–1270)

De arte loquendi et tacendi ed. Thor Sundby in *Brunetto Latinos levnet og skrifter,* 1869.

De amore Dei *Liber de amore et dilectione Dei,* Coni, 1507. See also *Liber de amore et dilectione Dei et proximi et aliarum rerum et de forma vitae,* ed. Sharon Lynn Hiltz, diss., U. of Pennsylvania, 1980.

Liber Cons. *Liber consolationis et consilii,* ed. Thor Sundby, Ch Soc., 2nd ser. 8, 1873 (rpt. 1973).

AMIS AND AMILOUN

Amis and Amiloun, Robert of Cisyle, and Sir Amadace, ed. Edward E. Foster, TEAMS, 1997.

ANCRENE RIWLE (ANCRENE WISSE)

The English Text of the Ancrene Riwle, ed. from MS Corpus Christi College 402, ed. J. R. R. Tolkien, EETS 249, 1962. Trans. as *The Ancrene Riwle,* Mary B. Salu, 1955.

ANDREAS CAPELLANUS (C. 1174–1233)

De amore ed. and trans. P. G. Walsh as André le chapelain, *De amore et amoris remedio,* 1982.

AQUINAS (THOMAS AQUINAS, SAINT, 1224/25–1274)

Summa theol. *Summa theologica,* vols. 4–12 in *Opera omnia iussu Leonis XIII P. M. edita,* 1882–. Tr. by the Fathers of the English Dominican Province, rev. Daniel J. Sullivan, 1955.

ARISTOTLE (384–322 B.C.)

Meteorologica *Meteorologica,* tr. H. D. P. Lee, Loeb, 1952.
Rhetoric *The "Art" of Rhetoric,* tr. John Henry Freese, Loeb, 1926.
De Anima *On the Soul,* tr. W. S. Hett, rev. ed., 1957.
On Interpretation *The categories; On interpretation* [tr. Harold P. Cooke.], *Prior analytics* [tr. Hugh Tredennick], Loeb, 1973.

AUGUSTINE (AURELIUS AUGUSTINUS, SAINT, BISHOP OF HIPPO, 354–430)

De Civ. Dei *The City of God against the Pagans,* tr. George McCracken et al., Loeb, 1957–72. 7 vols.
Confessions *Confessions,* ed. and tr. W. Watts, Loeb, 1950–51. 2 vols.
De Trinitate "The Trinity," tr. Stephen McKenna in *The Fathers of the Church,* vol. 45, 1963.
For other works see *Opere,* CCSL, 1954–81, tr. *The Works of Saint Augustine: A Translation for the 21st Cent.,* ed. and tr. John E. Rotelle, 1990–.

AYENBITE OF INWIT *See Dan Michel.*

BARTHOLOMAEUS ANGLICUS (FL. 13TH CENTURY)

Barth. Angl. *De proprietatibus rerum,* London, 1601 (rpt. in facs. 1964). Trans. as *On the Properties of Things: John Trevisa's Translation of Bartholomaeus Anglicus' De proprietatibus rerum: A Critical Text,* ed. M. C. Seymour et al., 1975. 2 vols.

BENEDICT (BENEDICT OF NURSIA [BENEDICTUS CASSIENSIS], SAINT, C. 480–550)

Rule *The Rule of St. Benedict in Latin and English,* ed. Timothy Fry et al., 1981.

BERNARDUS SILVESTRIS (BERNARD SILVESTRIS, FL. 1136)

Megacosmos In *Cosmographia,* ed. Peter Dronke, 1978. Trans. as *The Cosmographia,* Winthrop Wetherbee, 1973.

BERYN, TALE OF BERYN

Ed. John M. Bowers in *The CT: Fifteenth-Cent. Continuations and Additions,* TEAMS, 1992.

BIBLE

Biblia sacra iuxta vulgatam versionem, ed. Robertus Weber et al., 2nd rev. ed., 1975. See the Douai version for a translation. The King James translation of the Bible (AV) is usually cited in the notes.

BOCCACCIO (GIOVANNI BOCCACCIO, 1313–75)

Ameto ed. Antonio E. Quaglio in vol. 2 of *Tutte le opere di Giovanni Boccaccio,* gen. ed. V. Branca, 1964. Tr. Judith Serafini-Sauli, 1985.
De casibus virorum illustrium Paris, 1520 (rpt. in facs., ed. Louis B. Hall, 1962). Trans. as *The Fates of Illustrious Men,* Louis B. Hall, 1965.
De claris mulieribus ed. V. Zaccaria in vol. 10 of *Tutte le opere.* Trans. as *Concerning Famous Women,* by Guido A. Guarino, 1963.
Decameron *Il Decamerone,* ed. V. Branca, 1958. Tr. G. H. McWilliam, 1972; rpt. 1995.
Il Filocolo ed. Antonio E. Quaglio in vol. 1 of *Tutte le opere.* Tr. (selections) in N. R. Havely, *Chaucer's Boccaccio: Sources of Troilus and the Knight's and Franklin's Tales,* 1980.
Teseida, Tes *Il Teseida,* ed. A. Limentani in vol. 2 of *Tutte le opere.* Trans. as *The Book of Theseus,* Bernadette M. McCoy, 1974; and (selections) in N. R. Havely, *Chaucer's Boccaccio.*

BOETHIUS (ANICIUS MANLIUS SEVERINUS BOETHIUS, 480–524)

Consolation, Cons. *Tractates and Consolation of Philosophy,* ed. H. F. Stewart and E. K. Rand, rev. H. F. Stewart, Loeb, 1968.

BOOK OF THE KNIGHT OF LA TOUR LANDRY

Ed. Thomas Wright, EETS 33, rev. ed. 1868; as tr. by William Caxton, *The Book of the Knight of the Tower,* ed. M. Y. Offord, EETS SS 2, 1971. (ME tr. of *Le Livre du chevalier de La Tour Landry pour l'enseignement de ses filles,* ed. A. de Montaiglon, 1854.)

JOHN BROMYARD (JOHANNES DE BROMYARD, FL. 1390)

Summa praedicantium Venice, 1586. 2 vols.

CATO (ATTR. MARCUS PORCIUS CATO, 234–149 B.C.; FORMERLY ATTR. TO "DIONYSIUS CATO")

Distichs, Dicta Catonis *Dicta Catonis,* in *Minor Latin Poets,* tr. J. Wight Duff and Arnold M. Duff, Loeb, 1934.

CHRÉTIEN DE TROYES (CHRESTIEN DE TROYES, CHRISTIAN OF TROY, FL. LATE 12TH CENTURY)

Cligés ed. Alexander Micha, CFMA, 1958 (rpt. 1970).
Erec et Enide ed. Mario Roques, CFMA, 1952 (rpt. 1970).
Lancelot *Le Chevalier de la charette,* ed. Mario Roques, CFMA, 1958 (rpt. 1972).
Tr. David Staines, *The Complete Romances of Chrétien de Troyes,* 1990.

CICERO (MARCUS TULLIUS CICERO, 106–43 B.C.)

De amicitia *De senectute, De amicitia, De divinatione,* tr. William A. Falconer, Loeb, 1933.
De divinatione as above.
De inventione *De inventione,* ed. and tr. H. M. Hubbell, Loeb, 1949.
De nat. deorum *De natura deorum; Academica,* tr. H. Rackham, Loeb, 1933.
De oratore *De oratore,* tr. E. W. Sutton and H. Rackham, rev. ed., Loeb, 1948. 2 vols.
De officiis *De Officiis,* tr. Walter Miller, Loeb, 1913.
De re publica *De re publica,* ed. and tr. Clinton W. Keyes, Loeb, 1928.
Epist. *Letters to His Friends,* ed. and tr. W. Glynn Williams, Loeb, 1927. 3 vols.
Somnium Scipionis in *De re publica,* as above.

CLAUDIAN (CLAUDIUS CLAUDIANUS, D. C. 408)

De raptu Proserpinae in *Claudian,* ed. and tr. Maurice Platnauer, Loeb, 1922 (rpt. 1956). 2 vols.

CONF. AMAN., CONFESSIO AMANTIS *See Gower.*

CYRURGIE OF GUY DE CHAULIAC

Ed. Margaret S. Ogden, EETS 265, 1971. (ME translation of Guy de Chauliac (1300–68), *La grande chirurgie,* ed. E. Nicaise, 1890.)

DANTE (DANTE ALIGHIERI, 1265–1321)

Convivio ed. Maria Simonelli, 1966. Tr. Richard H. Lansing, 1990.
Divine Comedy *La divina commedia,* ed. G. H. Grandgent, rev. Charles S. Singleton, 1972. Tr. Charles S. Singleton, 1970–73. 3 vols.

DESCHAMPS (EUSTACHE DESCHAMPS, C. 1340–C. 1406)

Œuvres complètes, ed. Auguste H. E. Queux de Saint-Hilaire and Gaston Raynaud, SATF, 1878–1903. 11 vols.

Miroir *Miroir de mariage,* in vol. 9 of Œuvres.

DICTA CANTONIS, DISTICHS *See Cato.*

DIVES AND PAUPER

Ed. Priscilla H. Barnum, EETS 275, 280, 1977–80. 1 vol. in two parts.

EARLY SOUTH ENGLISH LEGENDARY

Ed. Carl Horstmann, EETS 87, 1887. (See also South English Legendary.)

EPISTOLA VALERII AD RUFINUM *See Walter Map.*

THE FLOURE AND THE LEAFE AND THE ASSEMBLY OF LADIES

Ed. Derek A. Pearsall, 1962.

FROISSART (JEAN FROISSART, C. 1338–C. 1410)

Chronicles, Chroniques *Chroniques,* ed. Siméon Luce, Gaston Raynaud, Léon Mirot, SHF, 1869–1931. 12 vols. in 14. Trans. as *The Chronicles of Froissart,* Thomas Johnes, 1803–05, rev. ed., 1901. 4 vols. Selections trans. as Froissart, *Chronicles,* Geoffrey Brereton, 1978.

FULGENTIUS (FABIUS PLANCIADES FULGENTIUS, FL. C. 500)

Mythologies in *Opera,* ed. Rudolphus Helm; new ed. with additions ed. Jean Préaux, 1970. Tr. as *Fulgentius the Mythographer,* Leslie G. Whitbread, 1971.

GAMELYN, TALE OF GAMELYN

Ed. Stephen Knight and Thomas H. Olgren in *Robin Hood and Other Outlaw Tales,* TEAMS, 1997.

GAWAIN, SIR GAWAIN

Sir Gawain and the Green Knight, in *Poems of the Pearl Manuscript,* ed. Malcolm Andrew and Ronald Waldron, 1978.

GEOFFREY OF MONMOUTH (GALFRIDUS MONEMUTENSIS, BISHOP OF ST. ASAPH, C. 1100–1155)

Historia regum Britanniae *The Historia regum Britannie of Geoffrey of Monmouth,* 1985. 5 vols. Trans. as *History of the Kings of Britain,* Lewis Thorpe, 1966.

GEOFFREY OF VINSAUF (D. 1210)

Documentum *Documentum de modo et arte dictandi et versificandi,* ed. in Edmond Faral, *Les arts poétiques du XII.* Trans. as *Instruction in the Method and Art of Speaking and Versifying,* Roger P. Parr, 1968.

Poetria nova ed. in Faral, as above. Tr. Margaret F. Nims, 1967.

GESTA ROMANORUM

Ed. H. Oesterle, 1872. Modernized vers. Charles Swan, rev. W. Hooper, 1876, rpt. 1959. For ME translations see *The Early English Versions of the Gesta Romanorum,* ed. Sidney H. Herrtage, EETS e.s. 33 (re-ed. of 1833 ed. by Sir Frederic Madden), 1879.

GIRALDUS CAMBRENSIS (GERALD OF WALES, GERALD DE BARRI, C. 1146–C. 1223)

Itinerarium Cambriae in vol. 6 of *Giraldi Cambrensis opera,* ed. J. S. Brewer et al., Rolls Series, 1861–91. 8 vols. (rpt. 1964–66). Tr. Lewis Thorpe, *The Journey through Wales and The Description of Wales,* 1978.

Gemma ecclesiastica in *Opera,* above; tr. John J. Hagen as *The Jewel of the Church,* 1979.

GOWER (JOHN GOWER, C. 1325–C. 1408)

Conf. aman *Confessio amantis* in *Complete Works of John Gower,* ed. G. C. Macaulay, 1899–1902. 4 vols.
Mirour *Mirour de l'omme,* in *Works,* above. Tr. William Burton Wilson, 1992.
Vox clam *Vox clamantis,* in *Works,* above. Tr. in *The Major Latin Works of John Gower: The Voice of One Crying* and *The Tripartite Chronicle,* Eric W. Stockton, 1952.

GRATIAN (GRATIANUS, 1ST HALF OF 12TH CENTURY)

Decretum ed. Emil Friedberg, Corpus Iuris Canonici, 1, 1879. Selections trans. as *The treatise on laws (Decretum DD. 1–20),* Augustine Thompson, James Gordley, intro. Katherine Christensen, 1993.

GREGORY (POPE GREGORY I, SAINT, "GREGORY THE GREAT," C. 540–604)

Opera in PL 75–79.
Past. Care *Cura pastoralis,* PL 77. Trans. as *Pastoral Care,* Henry Davis, 1950.
Morals *Morals on the Book of Job,* tr. James Bliss, 1844–50. 3 vols.

GUIDO DELLE COLONNE (13TH CENTURY)

Historia destructionis Troiae, ed. Nathaniel E. Griffin, 1936. Tr. Mary Elizabeth Meek, 1974.

GUILLAUME DE LORRIS (FL. 1230)

Roman See *Le Roman de la rose.*

GUY OF WARWICK

Guy of Warwick *Guy of Warwick,* ed. Julius Zupitza, EETS e.s. 42, 49, 59, 1883–91.

HIGDEN (RANULPH HIGDEN, D. 1364)

Polychronicon *Polychronicon Together with the English Translations of John Trevisa [1387] and an Unknown Writer of the Fifteenth Century,* ed. Churchill Babington (vols. 1–2) and Joseph R. Lumby (vols. 3–9), Rolls Series, 1865–86 (rpt. 1964). 9 vols.

HORACE (QUINTUS HORATIUS FLACCUS, 65–8 B.C.)

Odes and Epodes tr. C. E. Bennett, Loeb, rev. ed. 1927.
Satires, Epistles, Ars poetica tr. H. Rushton Fairclough, Loeb, rev. ed. 1929.

INF., INFERNO *See Dante,* Divine Comedy.

INNOCENT III (LOTARIO DEI SEGNI, POPE, 1160/61–1216)

De Miseria, De contemptu mundi Lotario dei Segni, *De miseria condicionis humane,* ed. and tr. Robert E. Lewis, Chaucer Library, 1978.

ISIDORE OF SEVILLE (ISIDORUS, SAINT, BISHOP OF SEVILLE, C. 570–636)

Etymologies *Etymologiae,* ed. Wallace M. Lindsay, 1911. 2 vols. Selections trans. as *An Encyclopedist of the Dark Ages,* Ernest Brehaut, 1912 (rpt. 1964).

JACK UPLAND

Jack Upland; Friar Daw's reply; and, Upland's rejoinder, ed. P. L. Heyworth, 1968.

JANKYN'S BOOK

Jankyn's Book of Wikked Wyves, ed. Ralph Hanna III and Traugott Lawler, 1997.

JACOBUS DE VORAGINE, LEGENDA AUREA

Ed. Th. Graesse, 1850. Trans. as *The Golden Legend: Readings on the Saints,* by William Granger Ryan, 1993. 2 vols.; ME trans.: *The Golden Legend, or Lives of the Saints,* by William Caxton, ed., in modern spelling, F. S. Ellis, 1900.

JEAN DE MEUN (JEHAN DE MEUN, CALLED CLOPINEL; D. C. 1305)

Roman See *Le Roman de la rose.*

Testament *Le testament maistre Jehan de Meun,* ed. Silvia Buzzetti Gallarati, 1989.

JEROME (EUSEBIUS HIERONYMUS, SAINT, 350–420)

Ad Rusticum See *Selected Letters,* below.
Adversus Jovinianum, Adv. Jov. in *Opera,* CCSL, 1958–. The whole text is tr. by W. H. Fremantle, *St. Jerome: Letters and Select Works,* pp. 346–416, in *A Select Library of Nicene and Post-Nicene Fathers of the Christian Church,* Second Series, Vol. 6. Extracts are in *Ch: Sources and Backgrounds,* 1977, ed. and tr. Robert P. Miller, and in *Jankyn's Book of Wikked Wyves,* ed. and tr. Ralph Hanna III and Traugott Lawler, 1997.
Ep. *Selected Letters of St. Jerome,* tr. F. A. Wright, Loeb, 1933.

JOHN OF SALISBURY (JOHANNES SARISBURIENSIS, C. 1115–80, BISHOP OF CHARTRES)

Policraticus *Ioannis Saresberiensis episcopi Carnotensis Policratici sive De nvgis cvrialivm et vestigiis philosophorvm libri VIII,* ed. Clemens C. I. Webb, 1909. Selections translated as *Policraticus: Of the Frivolities of Courtiers and the Footprints of Philosophers,* ed. and tr. Cary J. Nederman, 1990; *Frivolities of Courtiers and Footprints of Philosophers, Being a Translation of the First, Second, and Third Books and Selections from the Seventh and Eighth Books of the Policraticus of John of Salisbury,* tr. Joseph B. Pike, 1938 (rpt. 1972); *The Statesman's Book of John of Salisbury; Being the Fourth, Fifth, and Sixth Books, and Selections from the Seventh and Eighth Books, of the Policraticus,* tr. John Dickinson, 1927 (rpt. 1963).

JUVENAL (DECIMUS JUNIUS JUVENALIS, A.D. C. 50– C. 127)

Satires in *Juvenal and Persius,* ed. and tr. G. G. Ramsay, Loeb, rev. ed., 1940 (rpt. 1950).

KALENDARIUM *See Nicholas of Lynn.*

KEMPE (MARGERY KEMPE, C. 1373–C. 1440)

The Book of Margery Kempe, ed. Lynn Staley, TEAMS, 1996.

KNIGHT OF LA TOUR LANDRY *See* Book of the Knight of La Tour Landry.

LANGLAND (WILLIAM LANGLAND, C. 1330–C. 1400)

The Vision of William Concerning Piers the Plowman: in Three Parallel Texts, Together with Richard the Redeless, ed. Walter W. Skeat, 1886; rpt. 1969.
PP A *Piers Plowman, The A Text,* ed. Walter W. Skeat, as above.
PP B *Piers Plowman, The B Text: The Vision of Piers Plowman: A Critical Edition of the B-text,* ed. A. V. C. Schmidt, 2nd ed., 1995. Tr. A. V. C. Schmidt, *Piers Plowman: A New Translation of the B-text,* 1992.

PP C *Piers Plowman, The C Text,* ed. Derek Pearsall, corr. ed., 1994.

BRUNETTO LATINI (BRUNETTO LATINI DI BUONACCORSO, 1220–1295)

Il tesoretto (The Little Treasure), ed. and tr. Julia B. Holloway, 1981.

LAY FOLKS MASS BOOK

Ed. Thomas F. Simmons, EETS 71, 1879 (rpt. 1968).

THE PRYMER OR LAY FOLKS PRAYER BOOK

Ed. Henry Littlehales, EETS 105, 109, 1895–97. 2 vols.

LEGENDA AUREA *See Jacobus de Voragine.*

LIBER ALBUS

The White Book of the City of London; Compiled 1419 by John Carpenter [and] Richard Whittington, ed. and tr. Henry T. Riley, 1861.

LOTARIO DEI SEGNI *See Innocent III.*

LUCAN (MARCUS ANNEAUS LUCAN, A.D. 39–65)

Pharsalia [The Civil War], tr. J. D. Duff, Loeb, 1957.

LYDGATE (JOHN LYDGATE, 1370–C. 1451)

The Fall of Princes ed. Henry Bergen, EETS e.s. 121–24, 1924–27. 4 vols.
Minor Poems ed. Henry N. McCracken, EETS e.s. 107, 192, 1911–34. 2 vols.
The Siege of Thebes ed. Axel Erdmann, EETS e.s. 108, 125, 1911–30. 2 vols.
The Troy Book ed. Henry Bergen, EETS e.s. 97, 103, 106, 126, 1906–35. 4 vols. See also *Troy Book Selections,* ed. Robert R. Edwards, TEAMS, 1998.

MACHAUT (GUILLAUME DE MACHAUT, D. 1377)

Œuvres de Guillaume de Machaut ed. Ernest Hoepffner, SATF, 1908–21. 3 vols.
La prise d'Alexandrie; ou, Chronique du roi Pierre Ier de Lusignan ed. M. L. de Mas Latrie, 1877.
Livre du voir-dit *Le livre dou voir dit [The book of the true poem],* ed. Daniel Leech-Wilkinson; tr. R. Barton Palmer, 1998.
Poésies lyriques ed. Vladimir Fedorovich Chichmaref, 1909. 2 vols.
Roy de Navarre *The Judgement of the King of Navarre,* ed. and tr. R. Barton Palmer, 1988.

MACROBIUS (AMBROSIUS MACROBIUS THEODOSIUS, FL. A.D. 400)

Commentarii in somnium Scipionis ed. James Willis, 1970. Trans. as *Commentary on the Dream of Scipio,* William H. Stahl, 1952.

MALORY (SIR THOMAS MALORY, FL. C. 1470)

Le Morte Darthur ed. as *Works of Sir Thomas Malory,* Eugène Vinaver, 3rd ed. rev. P. J. C. Field, 1990. 3 vols.

MANDEVILLE (SIR JOHN MANDEVILLE, D. 1372)

Mandeville's Travels ed. P. Hamelius, EETS 153, 159, 1919–23; ed. Michael C. Seymour, EETS 253, 1963. Modern English version: *The Travels of Sir John Mandeville,* tr. C. W. R. D. Moseley, 1983.

ROBERT MANNYNG (ROBERT MANNYNG OF BRUNNE, C. 1288–1338)

Handlyng Synne ed. Frederick J. Furnivall, EETS, 119, 123, 1901–03. 2 vols. Rpt. 1973.

WALTER MAP (C. 1140–1209)

Epistola Valerii ad Rufinum in *De nugis curialium,* below. (Also ed. and tr. in *Jankyn's Book of Wikked Wyves,* q.v.)
Latin Poems, ed. Wright Latin Poems Commonly Attributed to Walter Mapes, ed. Thomas Wright, Camden Society 16, 1841.
De nugis curialium: Courtier's Trifles ed. and tr. M. R. James, rev. C. N. L. Brooke and R. A. B. Mynors, 1983.

MARCO POLO (C. 1254–C. 1324)

The Book of Sir Marco Polo ed. and tr. Henry Yule, 1871 (3rd ed., 1926; rpt. 1989). 3 vols.

MARIE DE FRANCE (12TH CENTURY)

Fables ed. and tr. Harriet Spiegel, 1987.
Lais ed. Karl Warnke, 3rd ed., 1925. Trans. as *The Lais of Marie de France,* Robert Hanning and Joan Ferrante, 1978.

MATHEOLUS (FL. LATE 13TH CENTURY)

Lamentations *Les Lamentations de Matheolus et le Livre de leesce de Jehan le Fèvre: Edition critique accompagnée de l'original latin des Lamentations,* ed. A. G. van Hamel, 1892–1905. 2 vols. Rpt. 1983. Selections trans. in *Woman Defamed and Woman Defended,* ed. Alcuin Blamires, with Karen Pratt and C. W. Marx, 1992.

LE MÈNAGIER DE PARIS

Ed. Georgina E. Brereton and Janet M. Ferrier, 1981. Tr. (with omissions) as *The Goodman of Paris* by Eileen Power, 1928, and (selections) as *A Medieval Home Companion: Housekeeping in the Fourteenth Century,* ed. and tr. Tania Bayard, 1991.

MET., METAMORPHOSES *See Ovid.*

DAN MICHEL OF NORTHGATE (FL. 1386)

Ayenbite of Inwit, or Remorse of Conscience ed. Richard Morris, EETS 23, 1866; Vol. 2 (intro. and notes) ed. Pamela Gradon, EETS 278, 1979.

MIRK (JOHN MYRC OR MIRK, JOHANNES MIRKUS, FL. 1403)

Festial *A Collection of Homilies by Johannes Mirkus,* EETS e.s. 96, ed. Theodore Erbe, 1905.
Instructions for Parish Priests ed. Edward Peacock, EETS 31, rev. ed., 1902; new ed. Gillis Kristenson, 1974.

MIROIR DE MARIAGE *See Deschamps.*

ALEXANDER NECKAM (1157–1215)

De naturis rerum ed. Thomas Wright, Rolls Series, 1863.

NICHOLAS OF LYNN (FL. 1386)

Kalendarium *The Kalendarium of Nicholas of Lynn,* ed. Sigmund Eisner, tr. Gary Mac Eoin and Sigmund Eisner, Chaucer Library, 1980.

OVID (PUBLIUS OVIDIUS NASO, 43 B.C.– A.D. 17/18)

Amores ed. Showerman (see *Heroides* below).
Ars amatoria, Ars am. in *The Art of Love and Other Poems,* ed. and tr. J. H. Mozley, Loeb, rev. ed., 1957.
Fasti ed. and tr. James George Frazer, 2nd ed. revised by G. P. Goold, Loeb, 1989.
Heroides and Amores ed. and tr. Grant Showerman, 2nd ed. rev. G. P. Goold, Loeb, 1977.
Metamorphoses ed. and tr. Frank J. Miller, Loeb, 3rd ed. rev. G. P. Goold, 1957.
Remedia amoris in *The Art of Love and Other Poems,* tr. J. H. Mozeley, 2nd ed. rev. by G. P. Goold, Loeb, 1979.
Tristia tr. Arthur Leslie Wheeler, Loeb, 1924.

OVIDE MORALISÉ

Poème de commencement du quatorzième siècle, ed. C. de Boer et al., 1915–38. 5 vols.

PAMPHILUS

Prolegomena zum Pamphilus (de amore) und kritische Textausgabe, ed. Franz G. Becker, 1972, and ed. Keith Bate, in *Three Latin Comedies,* 1976. Tr. (from ed. of Jacobus

Ulrich, 1893) Thomas J. Garbàty, ChauR 2, 1968, 108–34; and in *The Book of the Archpriest of Hitta,* tr. Mark Singleton, 1975.

PAR., PARADISO *See Dante,* Divine Comedy.

PARLEMENT OF THE THRE AGES

Ed. Thorlac Turville-Petre, *Alliterative Poetry of the Later M. A.: An Anthology,* 1989.

PEARL

In *Poems of the Pearl Manuscript,* ed. Malcolm Andrew and Ronald Waldron, 1978.

PERVIGILIUM VENERIS

(The Vigil [or Eve] of Venus) in Catullus, *Works,* ed. and tr. J. W. Mackail, 2nd ed. rev. G. P. Goold, Loeb, 1988.

PETER LOMBARD (PETRUS LOMBARDUS, BISHOP OF PARIS, C. 1095–1160)

Sentences *Sententiae in IV libris distinctae,* ed. Patres Colegii S. Bonaventurae, 3rd ed., Editiones Colegii S. Bonaventurae ad Claras Aquas (Quaracchi), 1977–81.

PETRARCH (FRANCESCO PETRARCA, 1304–74)

Prose ed. G. Martellotti et al., 1955.
Rime e trionfi ed. Ferdinando Neri, 2nd ed., 1966. Tr. as *Triumphs,* Ernest H. Wilkins, 1962.

PETRUS ALPHONSUS (1062–1110)

Disciplina clericalis ed. Alfons Hilka and Werner Söderhjelm, 1911. For trans., see *The Disciplina clericalis of Petrus Alfonsi,* ed. and tr. by Eberhard Hermes; translated into English [from the German and the Latin] by P. R. Quarrie, 1977.

PETER COMESTOR (P. MANDUCATOR; C. 1100–C. 1179)

Historia scholastica in *Opera* in PL 198, 1053–1844.

PHARSALIA *See Lucan.*

PLINY (GAIUS PLINIUS SECUNDUS, "THE ELDER," A.D. 23–79)

Hist. Nat. *Historia naturalis,* ed. and tr. H. Rackham (vols. 1–5, 9) and W. H. S. Jones (vols. 6–8), Loeb, 1938–63. 9 vols.

PP, PIERS PLOWMAN *See Langland.*

PROMPTORIUM PARVULORUM

Ed. A. L. Mayhew, EETS e.s. 102, 1908. (Fifteenth-century Latin-English dictionary by Galfridus Anglicus, fl. 1440.)

PRUDENTIUS (BORN 348)

Psychomachia in *Works,* ed. and tr. H. J. Thomson, Loeb, 2 vols., 1949–53.

PTOLEMY (CLAUDIUS PTOLEMAIOS, C. A.D. 100–179)

Almagest In *Claudii Ptolomaei opera quae extant omnia,* ed. J. L. Heiberg, 1898–1919. 3 vols. Tr. G. J. Toomer as *Ptolemy's Almagest,* 1984.

PURG., PURGATORIO *See Dante.*

RAYMOND OF PENNAFORTE (RAIMUNDO DE PEÑAFORT, SAINT, C. 1180–1275)

Summa *Summa de poenitentia et matrimonio,* Rome, 1603 (rpt. 1967).

REYNARD THE FOX

William Caxton, *Hist. of Reynard the Fox,* ed. Norman F. Blake, EETS 263, 1970.

ROMAN DE THÈBES

Ed. Leopold Constans, SATF, 1890. 2 vols. Tr. John Smartt Coley, *The Story of Thebes,* 1986.

RR, ROMAN DE LA ROSE

Guillaume de Lorris and Jean de Meun, *Le Roman de la rose,* ed. Ernest Langlois, SATF, 1914–24. 5 vols. Trans. as *The Romance of the Rose,* Charles Dahlberg, 1971.

THE SARUM MISSAL

Ed. J. W. Legg, 1916. Selections tr. in Miller, *Ch: Sources.*

SECRETA SECRETORUM

Lydgate and Burgh's *Secrees of Olde Philisoffres,* ed. Robert Steele, EETS e.s. 66, 1894. *Secretum secretorum,* ed. Mahmoud A. Manazaouli, EETS 276, 1977 (other ME versions of the above). *Secreta Secretorum* (ed. Robert Steele, EETS e.s. 74, 1898.

SENECA (LUCIUS ANNEAUS SENECA, A.D. 3/4–65)

Epist. *Epistulae morales ad Lucilium,* tr. Richard M. Gummere, Loeb. 3 vols., 1917–25
Moral Essays [*Dialogi:*] *Moral Essays,* ed. and tr. John W. Basore, Loeb, rev. ed., 1951. 3 vols.

SENESCHAUCY *See Walter of Henley.*

THE SEVEN SAGES OF ROME

Ed. Karl Brunner, EETS 191, 1933 (rpt. 1971).

SIR GAWAIN *See Gawain.*

SOUTH ENGLISH LEGENDARY

Ed. Charlotte D'Evelyn and Anna J. Mill, EETS 235–36, 244, 1956. 3 vols.

STATIUS (PUBLIUS PAPINIUS STATIUS, C. A.D. 45–96)

Theb., Thebaid In *Statius,* ed. and tr. J. H. Mozley, Loeb, rev. ed., 1955–57.

TALE OF BERYN, TALE OF GAMELYN *See Beryn, Gamelyn*

THEOPHRASTUS

Liber aureolus de nuptiis in Jerome, *Adversus Jovinianum* (see Jerome).

VALERIUS MAXIMUS (1ST HALF OF 1ST CENTURY A.D.)

Facta et dicta memorabilia ed. John Briscoe, 1998. 2 vols. Tr. D. Wardle, *Memorable Deeds and Sayings,* Book I, 1998.

VINCENT OF BEAUVAIS (VINCENTIUS BELLOVACENSIS, 1184/95–C. 1264)

Spec. Nat. *Speculum naturale,* in *Bibliotheca Mundi Vincenti Burgundi,* Douay, 1624. 4 vols. (rpt. 1964). Tr. William Caxton, *Mirrour of the World,* ed. Oliver H. Prior, EETS e.s. 110, 1966.
Spec. Hist. *Speculum historiale,* in *Bibliotheca,* above.

VIRGIL (PUBLIUS VERGILIUS MARO, 70–19 B.C.)

P. Vergilii Maronis opera, ed. Roger A. B. Mynors, corr. rpt., 1972. Tr. H. Rushton Fairclough, Loeb, rev. ed., 1935. 2 vols.
Aeneid *Aeneid,* in *Opera,* above.
Eclogues *Eclogues,* in *Opera,* above.
Georgics *Georgics,* in *Opera,* above.

WALTER OF HENLEY (FL. 1250)

Seneschaucy *Walter of Henley and Other Treatises on Estate Management and Accounting,* ed. Dorothea Oschinsky, 1971.

WALSINGHAM (THOMAS WALSINGHAM, C. 1360–1420)

Historia Anglicana ed. Henry T. Riley, Rolls Series, 1863–64. 2 vols. (rpt. 1965).

WYCLIF (JOHN WYCLIFFE, C. 1320–84)

English Works *English Works of Wyclif, Hitherto Unprinted,* ed. F. D. Matthew, EETS 74, 2nd ed. rev., 1902 (rpt. 1973).
Sel. English Works *Select English Works,* ed. Thomas Arnold, 1869–71. 3 vols.

CRITICAL STUDIES

The following book-length studies and collections of essays, with their shortened and abbreviated forms, are those frequently cited in the Explanatory Notes.

Aers, Ch, Langland David Aers, *Chaucer, Langland and the Creative Imagination,* 1980.
Allen and Moritz, A Distinction of Stories Judson B. Allen and Theresa A. Moritz, *A Distinction of Stories: The Medieval Unity of Chaucer's Fair Chain of Narratives for Canterbury,* 1981.
Baum, Ch: A Crit. Appreciation Paull F. Baum, *Chaucer: A Critical Appreciation,* 1958.
Bennett, Ch at Oxford Jack A. W. Bennett, *Chaucer at Oxford and at Cambridge,* 1974.
Benson, Ch's Drama of Style C. David Benson, *Chaucer's Drama of Style: Poetic Variety and Contrast in* The Canterbury Tales, 1986.
Blair, European Armour Claude Blair, *European Armour circa 1066 to circa 1700,* 1959.
Bloomfield, Seven Deadly Sins Morton W. Bloomfield, *The Seven Deadly Sins: An Introduction to the History of a Religious Concept,* 1952.
Boitani, Ch and Boccaccio Piero Boitani, *Chaucer and Boccaccio,* 1977.
Boitani, Engl. Med. Narrative Piero Boitani, *English Medieval Narrative in the 13th and 14th Centuries,* tr. Joan Krakover Hall, 1982.
Bowden, Comm. on GP Muriel A. Bowden, *A Commentary on the General Prologue to* The Canterbury Tales, 2nd ed., 1973.
Braddy, Geoffrey Ch Haldeen Braddy, *Geoffrey Chaucer: Literary and Historical Studies,* 1971.
Brewer, Chaucer Derek S. Brewer, *Chaucer,* 3rd ed., 1973.
Brewer, Ch in His Time Derek S. Brewer, *Chaucer in His Time,* 3rd rev. ed., 1973.
Brewer, Crit. Heritage Derek S. Brewer, *Chaucer: The Critical Heritage,* 1978. 2 vols.
Brewer, New Intro. to Ch Derek S. Brewer, A *New Introduction to Chaucer,* 2nd ed., 1998.
Brusendorff, Ch Trad. Aage Brusendorff, *The Chaucer Tradition,* 1925 (rpt. 1967).
Burlin, Ch Fiction Robert B. Burlin, *Chaucerian Fiction,* 1977.
Burnley, Ch's Language J. David Burnley, *Chaucer's Language and the Philosophers' Tradition,* 1979.

Burrow, Ages of Man John A. Burrow, *The Ages of Man: A Study in Medieval Writing and Thought,* 1986.

Burrow, Ricardian Poetry John A. Burrow, *Ricardian Poetry: Chaucer, Gower, Langland, and the Gawain-Poet,* 1971.

Cambridge Ch Companion *The Cambridge Chaucer Companion,* ed. Piero Boitani and Jill Mann, 1986.

Cannon, Making of Ch's English Christopher Cannon, *The Making of Chaucer's English: A Study of Words,* 1998.

Ch and Chaucerians *Chaucer and Chaucerians: Critical Studies in Middle English Literature,* ed. Derek S. Brewer, 1966.

Ch Problems *Chaucerian Problems and Perspectives: Essays Presented to Paul E. Beichner,* ed. Edward Vasta and Zacharias P. Thundy, 1979.

Ch: Writers and Background *Geoffrey Chaucer: Writers and Their Background,* ed. Derek S. Brewer, 1974. Rpt. 1990.

Chaucer's Religious Tales ed. C. David Benson and Elizabeth Robertson, 1990.

Coulton, Life in the M. A. George Gordon Coulton, *Life in the Middle Ages,* 1967 [first published as *A Medieval Garner,* 1910].

Crane, Gender and Romance Susan Crane, *Gender and Romance in Chaucer's Canterbury Tales,* 1994.

Curry, Ch and Science Walter Clyde Curry, *Chaucer and the Mediaeval Sciences,* rev. ed., 1960.

Curtius, European Lit. Ernst Robert Curtius, *European Literature and the Latin Middle Ages,* tr. Willard R. Trask, 1953 (rpt. 1990).

David, Strumpet Muse Alfred David, *The Strumpet Muse: Art and Morals in Chaucer's Poetry*, 1976.

Donaldson, Speaking of Ch E. Talbot Donaldson, *Speaking of Chaucer,* 1970.

Eliason, Lang. of Ch Norman E. Eliason, *The Language of Chaucer's Poetry: An Appraisal of the Verse, Style, and Structure,* Anglistica 17, 1972.

Elliott, Ch's English Ralph W. V. Elliott, *Chaucer's English,* 1974.

Fansler, Ch and RR Dean S. Fansler, *Chaucer and the Roman de la rose,* 1914 (rpt. 1965).

Fichte, Ch's Frame Tales Jörg O. Fichte, ed., *Chaucer's Frame Tales,* 1987.

Fisher, John Gower John H. Fisher, *John Gower, Moral Philosopher and Friend of Chaucer,* 1964.

French, Ch Handbook Robert D. French, *A Chaucer Handbook,* 2nd ed., 1947.

Furnivall, Temp. Pref. F. J. Furnivall, *A Temporary Preface to the Chaucer Society's Six-Text Edition of Chaucer's Canterbury Tales,* Ch Soc, 2nd ser., 3, 1868.

Ganim, Ch Theatricality John M. Ganim, *Chaucerian Theatricality,* 1990.

Gerould, Ch Essays Gordon Hall Gerould, *Chaucerian Essays,* 1952.

Hammond, Engl. Verse See under Collections of Texts, above.

Hansen, Ch and Gender Elaine Tuttle Hansen, *Chaucer and the Fictions of Gender,* 1992.

Haskell, Ch's Saints Ann S. Haskell, *Essays on Chaucer's Saints,* 1976.

Hinckley, Notes on Ch Henry B. Hinckley, *Notes on Chaucer: A Commentary on the Prologue and Six Canterbury Tales,* 1907.

Hoffman, Ovid and CT Richard L. Hoffman, *Ovid and* The Canterbury Tales, 1966.

Howard, Idea of CT Donald R. Howard, *The Idea of* The Canterbury Tales, 1976.

Huppé, Reading of CT Bernard F. Huppé, *A Reading of* The Canterbury Tales, 1964.

Jordan, Ch and the Shape of Creation Robert M. Jordan, *Chaucer and the Shape of Creation: The Aesthetic Possibilities of Inorganic Structure,* 1967.

Kean, Ch and Poetry Patricia M. Kean, *Chaucer and the Making of English Poetry,* 1: *Love Vision and Debate;* 2: *The Art of Narrative,* 1972; shortened one-vol. ed., 1982.

Kellogg, Ch, Langland Alfred L. Kellogg, *Chaucer, Langland, Arthur: Essays in Middle English Literature,* 1972.

Kelly, Love and Marriage Henry Ansgar Kelly, *Love and Marriage in the Age of Chaucer,* 1975.

Kittredge, Ch and His Poetry George L. Kittredge, *Chaucer and His Poetry,* 55th Anniversary Edition, with an intro. by Bartlett J. Whiting, 1970.

Kolve, Ch and Imagery of Narrative V. A. Kolve, *Chaucer and the Imagery of Narrative: The First Five Canterbury Tales,* 1984.

Lawler, One and the Many Traugott Lawler, *The One and the Many in* The Canterbury Tales, 1980.

Learned and Lewed *The Learned and the Lewed: Studies in Chaucer and Medieval Literature,* ed. Larry D. Benson, 1974.

Leicester, Disenchanted Self H. Marshall Leicester, Jr., *The Disenchanted Self: Representing the Subject in* The Canterbury Tales, 1990.

Lounsbury, Sts. in Ch Thomas R. Lounsbury, *Studies in Chaucer,* 1892 (rpt. 1962). 3 vols.

Lowes, Geoffrey Ch John L. Lowes, *Geoffrey Chaucer and the Development of His Genius,* 1934 (rpt. as *Geoffrey Chaucer,* 1958).

Lumiansky, Of Sondry Folk Robert M. Lumiansky, *Of Sondry Folk: The Dramatic Principle in* The Canterbury Tales, 1955.

M. Madeleva, Lost Language Sister Mary Madeleva, *A Lost Language and Other Essays on Chaucer,* 1951.

Mandel, Building the Fragments Jerome Mandel, *Geoffrey Ch: Building the Fragments of* The Canterbury Tales, 1992.

Manly, New Light John M. Manly, *Some New Light on Chaucer: Lectures Delivered at the Lowell Institute,* 1926.

Mann, Ch and Estates Jill Mann, *Chaucer and Medieval Estates Satire: The Literature of Social Classes and the General Prologue to* The Canterbury Tales, 1973.

Mann, Geoffrey Ch Jill Mann, *Geoffrey Chaucer,* Feminist Readings Series, 1991.

McCall, Ch among the Gods John P. McCall, *Chaucer among the Gods: The Poetics of Classical Myth,* 1979.

McGerr, Ch's Open Books Rosemarie McGerr, *Chaucer's Open Books: Resistance to Closure in Medieval Discourse,* 1988.

Minnis, Med. Theory of Authorship A. J. Minnis, *Medieval Theory of Authorship: Scholastic Literary Attitudes in the Later Middle Ages,* 2nd ed., 1988.

Muscatine, Ch and Fr Trad. Charles Muscatine, *Chaucer and the French Tradition: A Study in Style and Meaning,* 1957 (rpt. 1965).

Mustanoja, ME Syntax Tauno F. Mustanoja, *A Middle English Syntax*, 1: *Parts of Speech*, Mémoires de la Société Néophilologique de Helsinki, 23, 1960.

Neilson, Origins of the Court of Love William A. Neilson, *The Origins and Sources of the Court of Love*, Harvard Studies and Notes in Philology and Literature 6, 1899.

New Perspectives *New Perspectives in Chaucer Criticism*, ed. Donald H. Rose, 1981.

Norton-Smith, Geoffrey Ch John A. Norton-Smith, *Geoffrey Chaucer*, 1974.

Orme, English Schools Nicholas Orme, *English Schools in the Middle Ages*, 1973.

Owen, Pilgrimage and Storytelling Charles A. Owen, Jr., *Pilgrimage and Storytelling*, 1977.

Owst, Lit and Pulpit Gerald R. Owst, *Literature and the Pulpit in Medieval England*, 2nd rev. ed., 1961.

Owst, Preaching in Med. Engl. Gerald R. Owst, *Preaching in Medieval England*, 1926 (rpt. 1965).

Partridge Stephen Bradford Partridge, *Glosses in the Manuscripts of Chaucer's* Canterbury Tales: *An Edition and Commentary* (diss., Harvard University, 1992).

Patterson, Ch and Hist Lee Patterson, *Chaucer and the Subject of History*, 1991.

Patterson, Negotiating the Past Lee Patterson, *Negotiating the Past: The Historical Understanding of Medieval Literature*, 1987.

Payne, Ch and Mennipian Satire F. Anne Payne, *Ch and Menippean Satire*, 1981.

Pearsall, CT Derek A. Pearsall, *The Canterbury Tales*, 1993.

Pearsall, Life of Ch Derek A. Pearsall, *The Life of Geoffrey Chaucer: A Critical Biography*, 1992.

Richardson, Blameth Nat Me Janette Richardson, *"Blameth Nat Me": A Study of Imagery in Chaucer's Fabliaux*, 1970.

Robertson, Ch's London Durant W. Robertson, Jr., *Chaucer's London*, 1968.

Robertson, Pref to Ch Durant W. Robertson, Jr., *A Preface to Chaucer: Studies in Medieval Perspectives*, 1962 (rpt. 1973).

Rowland, Blind Beasts Beryl Rowland, *Blind Beasts: Chaucer's Animal World*, 1971.

Rowland, Companion to Ch Sts Beryl Rowland, *Companion to Chaucer Studies*, rev. ed. 1979.

Ruggiers, Art of CT Paul G. Ruggiers, *The Art of* The Canterbury Tales, 1965.

Salter, Ch: KnT and ClT Elizabeth Salter, *Chaucer: "The Knight's Tale" and "The Clerk's Tale,"* 1962.

Scanlon, Narrative, Authority, and Power Larry Scanlon, *Narrative, Authority, and Power: The Medieval Exemplum and the Chaucerian Tradition*, 1994.

Seznec, Survival of the Pagan Gods Jean Seznec, *Survival of the Pagan Gods: The Mythological Tradition and Its Place in Renaissance Humanism and Art*, tr. Barbara F. Sessions, 1953 (rpt. 1972).

Shannon, Ch and Roman Poets Edgar F. Shannon, *Chaucer and the Roman Poets*, 1929.

Sklute, Virtue of Necessity Larry Sklute, *Virtue of Necessity*, 1984.

Strohm, Social Ch Paul Strohm, *Social Chaucer*, 1989.

Strutt, Sports and Pastimes Joseph Strutt, *Sports and Pastimes of the People of England*, enl. and corr. ed. J. Charles Cox, 1903 (rpt. 1968).

Sts. in Hon. of Baugh *Studies in Medieval Literature in Honor of Professor Albert Croll Baugh*, ed. MacEdward Leach, 1961.

Sts. in Hon. of Schlauch *Studies in Language and Literature in Honour of Margaret Schlauch*, ed. Mieczyslaw Brahmer, Stanislaw Helsztynski, Julian Krzyzanowski, 1966.

Sumption, Pilgrimage Jonathan Sumption, *Pilgrimage: An Image of Medieval Religion*, 1975.

Tatlock, Dev. and Chron. John S. P. Tatlock, *The Development and Chronology of Chaucer's Works*, Ch Soc, 2nd ser. 37, 1907 (rpt. 1963).

Thompson, Ch, Boccaccio N. S. Thompson, *Chaucer, Boccaccio, and the Debate of Love*, 1966.

Thorndike, Hist. of Magic Lynn Thorndike, *The History of Magic and Experimental Science*, 1923–64. 6 vols.

Thrupp, Merchant Class Sylvia L. Thrupp, *The Merchant Class of Medieval London (1300–1500)*, 1948; rpt. 1989.

Tuve, Seasons and Months Rosemond Tuve, *Seasons and Months: Studies in a Tradition of Middle English Poetry*, 1933.

Wallace, Ch Polity David Wallace, *Chaucerian Polity: Absolutist Lineages and Associational Forms in England and Italy*, 1997.

Weisl, Conquering the Reign Angela Jane Weisl, *Conquering the Reign of Femeny: Gender and Genre in Chaucer's Romances*, 1995.

Whittock, A Reading of CT Trevor Whittock, *A Reading of* The Canterbury Tales, 1968.

Winternitz, Musical Instruments Emanuel Winternitz, *Musical Instruments and Their Symbolism in Western Art*, 2nd ed., 1979.

Wisdom of Poetry *The Wisdom of Poetry: Essays in Early English Literature in Honor of Morton W. Bloomfield*, ed. Larry D. Benson and Siegfried Wenzel, 1982.

Wood, Ch and the Stars Chauncey Wood, *Chaucer and the Country of the Stars: Poetical Uses of Astrological Imagery*, 1970.

Explanatory Notes

THE EXPLANATORY NOTES are adapted from those in *The Riverside Chaucer*; they have been brought up to date and edited to make the material somewhat more easily accessible to beginning readers without sacrificing their usefulness to the more advanced. They are intended to provide the reader with the information needed for understanding Chaucer's text. Grammatical constructions not dealt with in the glosses are explained, sources noted, difficult passages explicated, and, as space allows, illustrative materials are quoted. Bibliographical references are supplied so that the interested reader can explore the problems of the texts in greater detail. Where relevant, the more important critical interpretations are noted, and the state of critical opinion is described. There is, however, no attempt to provide full bibliographies of the sort that Robinson gave in his 1933 edition. The number of bibliographical aids now available both in print and on the Internet has rendered that unnecessary, and the volume of critical publication has so increased as to make it impossible.

The emphasis in the notes differs according to the nature

of each work, but in general the notes concentrate on the factual rather than the speculative and on the historical rather than the interpretative; the intent is to record what is known and to provide references necessary for further study, so that readers can arrive at their own interpretations of Chaucer's often elusive works.

In citing illustrative materials, proximate rather than ultimate sources of Chaucer's ideas are emphasized and, wherever possible, the most accessible texts are cited. References in foreign languages are translated. Middle English texts are cited with regularized spellings of "u" and "v," and with modern forms for thorn and yogh. "U" and "v" are likewise usually regularized in the Latin texts quoted in the notes. Abbreviated forms of citation are used for critical books and primary texts that most often appear in the notes; full bibliographical references are provided in the list of frequently cited works.

Occasionally Robinson's notes are retained or quoted; these are identified by the notation "Robinson."

The Canterbury Tales

The work that Chaucer and his early scribes called *The Tales of Canterbury* (ParsT X.1086 and Robert A. Pratt, PQ 54, 1975, 19–25) was begun in the late 1380s and occupied Chaucer's attention until at least the late 1390s, perhaps until the end of his life. Information on the probable dates of composition of the individual tales is in the explanatory notes to each.

Collections of stories were common, and the idea of a collection of tales framed by a narrative could have come to Chaucer from a great variety of sources (Pratt and Young, in S&A, 1–11; Cooper, Structure of CT, 8–26). The closest parallel to Chaucer's work is Boccaccio's *Decameron* (see N. S. Thompson, Ch, Boccaccio, and the Debate of Love, 1996, esp. 1–6 and notes): the two works share the use of a framing narrative, a number of different narrators, a leader of the narrative (Harry Bailey and, in the *Decameron,* a "King" or "Queen" chosen each day), and they contain similar stories

(RvT and Day 9.6; ClT and 10.10; MerT and 7.9; FranT and 10.5; ShipT and 8.1); see Donald McGrady (ChR 12, 1977, 1–26). Yet, except for The Clerk's Tale (which is based on Petrarch's Latin version of Boccaccio's Italian tale), there are no very convincing examples of direct quotation or close parallels in action of the sort that would offer proof of "borrowing." Early scholars were therefore doubtful about Chaucer's knowledge of the *Decameron:* Hubertis B. Cummings (Indebtedness of Ch's Wks to the Italian works of Boccaccio, 1916 [rpt. 1965] 180) concluded that the chances were that Chaucer did not know the *Decameron;* J. S. P. Tatlock (Anglia 37, 1913, 69–117), believing the similarities between the two works required an explanation, argued that Chaucer had seen but did not own a copy of the *Decameron,* and the similarities are "such as might be remembered for years after a hasty reading." More recently some (e.g., Peter G. Beidler, Italica 50, 1973,

266–83) have argued for Chaucer's direct knowledge of the *Decameron,* and that Chaucer owed something to the *Decameron* seems now to be the majority view, though some remain skeptical (Robin Kirkpatrick in Piero Boitani, ed., Chaucer and the Italian Trecento, 1983, 201–30). For a review of the state of this question, see Helen Cooper (SAC, 1997, 192–99), who concludes that some direct influence is necessary to explain the many parallels between the two works. This is most likely the case; yet the differences between the two works are considerable, and the *Decameron* could have offered Chaucer little more than the general idea (a group of travelers engaged in organized storytelling) for his plan (Pratt and Young, S&A, 19–20).

The *Novelle* of Giovanni Sercambi (ed. Giovanni Sinicropi, 1972; summary in S&A, 36–81) provides a somewhat closer analogue to the framing narrative—a pilgrimage-like journey (like that in the *Decameron,* a journey to avoid the plague) set in February 1374; the travelers are a diverse group and Sercambi himself serves as leader and tells all the tales. It was once believed that this work was first written in 1374 and that Chaucer may have known and drawn upon it. However, it now seems clear that Sercambi's realistic framework and exact date are fictional and that the work must date from after 1400 (see Sinicropi's edition, 779–86).

Helen Cooper (SAC 19:199–209) surveys other literary influences on the framing narrative of the *Tales,* and she notes the importance of the genre of debate, poetic contests, and the practices of the *Puis* (a kind of fraternal guild of amateur poets; see D. W. Robertson, Jr., The Lit. of Med. England, 1970, 295–97).

Chaucer may have drawn the suggestions for his pilgrimage directly from life. Pilgrimages were common (Jonathan Sumption, Pilgrimage, 1975; Ronald C. Finucane, Miracles and Pilgrims, 1977) and telling tales was an ordinary pastime for travelers (cf. GP I.771–74 and Beatrice Daw Brown, MLN 52, 1937, 28–31). Chaucer may also have been influenced by the travel literature and accounts of pilgrimages then becoming popular (Christian K. Zacher, Curiosity and Pilgrimage, 1976; Donald R. Howard, Writers and Pilgrims, 1980). Nevertheless, Chaucer makes little attempt to depict an actual pilgrimage (Howard, Idea of CT, 159–62), and most critics today assume that his pilgrimage, like Sercambi's, is intended as a metaphor rather than a direct reflection of life.

The assumption that Chaucer did attempt to portray an actual pilgrimage spurred efforts by earlier scholars to determine the precise date and itinerary of his pilgrims' journey. The traditional date, 1387, was established by Skeat (3:373–74), who assumed that 18 April (IntrMLT II.5–6) was the second day of a four-day journey and consulted calendars for the years 1386–90 (having ruled out 1385 as too early and 1391 as too late). He eliminated 1386, when 18 April fell in Holy Week (and the Parson would have been needed at home); 1388 and 1390, which would have necessitated Sunday travel and, at the least, attendance at Mass would have prevented an early start; and 1389, when 18 April was Easter, a day unsuitable for telling tales. This left only 1387, which was also the year to which Skeat assigned The Knight's Tale. However, the Introduction to The Man of Law's Tale may belong to the first day rather than the second (Martin Stevens, LeedsSE n.s. 1, 1967, 1–5); Sunday Mass need not have prevented an early start (see

the itinerary of the Count of Ostrevant printed by Ewald Flügel, Anglia 23, 1901, 239–41); and religious festivals were no bar to "honest mirthes" (Dives and Pauper, EETS 275, 296–97). Most important, there is no indication in the text that Chaucer had any particular actual day in mind.

F. J. Furnivall in 1868 (Temp. Pref., 12–18, 26, and 39–41), influenced by Henry Bradshaw (see Donald C. Baker, Ch Newsletter 3, 1981, 2–6), first advanced the theory that Chaucer's pilgrimage to Canterbury took three to four days. The roads, he explained, were a "swampy mess" in April, and three royal itineraries all showed a four-day journey (Temp. Pref., 119–32). Flügel (Anglia 23:239–41) gathered itineraries from Froissart that showed the journey between London and Canterbury ranged from one to four days, though the one-day journey was the dowager queen's flight from Jack Straw's rebellion. To these should be added the journey of the Londoner, cured by Becket and "so pleased that he walked fifty miles to Canterbury in one day, so the registrar wrote, to strip, show himself cured, and challenge all comers to a foot race" (Finucane, Miracles, 101).

A three- to four-day journey is still widely assumed (e.g., Baugh, 233, and French, Ch Handbook, 196–98). Shorter itineraries were possible: in 1415 two Aragonese ambassadors made a comfortable one-night, two-day journey (F. J. Furnivall and R. E. G. Kirk, Analogues to Ch's Pilgrimage, Ch Soc., 2nd ser., 36, 1908). The reference to "prime" in The Squire's Tale seems to indicate that more than one day was intended; the time of The Manciple's Prologue seems also to have been early morning (IX.15–16). One could argue that the pilgrims spend two nights and three days on the road, which fits the usual rate of fourteenth-century travel, twenty to thirty miles a day (James E. Thorold Rogers, Hist. of Agriculture and Prices in Eng., 1866, 1:506–7, 2:610–14). However, it is not clear that Chaucer paid much attention to this matter. The related question of the stopping places on the journey cannot be answered with certainty either, since it hinges on the order of the tales (see The Order of the Tales, p. 3).

Speculation about the proper sequence of the tales is based on the assumption that Chaucer left his work unfinished, the apparent fact that he made changes in plan and arrangement as he worked, and the inference that other changes were intended but never effected. Initially, the Host's plan (GP I.790–801) calls for 120 stories, two from each of the thirty pilgrims (twenty-nine plus Chaucer) on the way to Canterbury and two on the return trip; in The Franklin's Prologue, the plan has apparently been reduced to "a tale or two" (V.698), and by the time of The Parson's Prologue another pilgrim has been added, the Canon's Yeoman, and the plan now calls for but one tale each (X.16, 24). Apparently the return trip has been abandoned. Some critics assume that a homeward journey was still intended (Charles A. Owen, Jr., Pilgrimage and Storytelling, 1977). The continuations of *The Canterbury Tales* in Lydgate's *Siege of Thebes* and in the anonymous *Tale of Beryn* are both set in Canterbury and initiate a homeward journey, as if both authors assumed that Chaucer intended his pilgrimage to extend that far and were attempting to complete the plan announced in the General Prologue (see John M. Bower, SAC 7, 1985, 23–50).

Chaucer apparently also made changes in the order and assignment of the tales. At an early stage of the composition, the Man of Law evidently told The Tale of Melibee and the

Wife of Bath told what is now The Shipman's Tale (Germaine Dempster, PMLA 68, 1953, 1142–59; Robert A. Pratt, in Sts. in Hon. of Baugh, 45–79). Some believe that The Merchant's Tale was originally assigned to another pilgrim (see introductory note to MerT) and other revisions have been suspected.

Nineteenth-century criticism sometimes treated *The Tales of Canterbury* as a mere collection of tales whose main interest lay in the framework rather than in the stories "patched up by fits and starts during such broken leisure as this man of the world could afford for indulging his poetic fancies" (G. G. Coulton, Ch and His England, 3rd ed., 1908, 144). Kittredge's discussion of the "Marriage Group" (MP 9, 1912, 435–67) helped focus attention on the interplay among the tales, and his emphasis on the dramatic relation between tale and teller (Ch and His Poetry, 146–218) encouraged a dramatic reading of the work as a whole, most thoroughly in Robert M. Lumiansky, Of Sondry Folk, 1955.

Lumiansky's study led him to the conclusion that, though unfinished, the work is nearly complete as it stands (TSE 6, 1956, 5–13). Ralph W. Baldwin, while rejecting the "roadside drama" approach, likewise argued for the integrity of the work as it stands: its narrative frame is essentially complete, with a clearly defined beginning and end and with a primarily metaphoric, rather than dramatic or narrative, function (Unity of CT, Anglistica 5, 1955). These views signaled a striking change in critical thinking about the *Tales*. There was a new appreciation of the fact that modern ideas of literary form do not necessarily apply to medieval works (Robert M. Jordan, Ch and the Shape of Creation, 1967, 111–31, and Ch's Poetics and the Modern Reader, 1987), a shift of attention away from the dramatic interplay among the pilgrims, where the unfinished character of the *Tales* is most obvious, and a tendency instead to treat the work as a thematically unified whole. Paul G. Ruggiers (Art of CT, 1965), P. M. Kean (Ch and Poetry, 1972, 2:153–75), and Judson B. Allen and Theresa A. Moritz (A Distinction of Stories, 1981) all find some degree of thematic unity in the work. That they do so, even though none treats the tales in a sequential order, may be explained by the theory that the tales are organized not as a straightforward story of pilgrimage but in the "interlaced" manner of medieval romance (John F. Leyerle, E&S, 1976, 107–21; Howard, Idea of CT, 210–332; Cooper, Structure of CT, 69–72).

Many critics do treat the tales in the sequence in which they appear in the "Ellesmere order" (that observed in this edition) and thus consider the tales in the immediate context of the fragments in which they appear (e.g., Derek Brewer, A New Intro. to Ch, 261–397; David, Strumpet Muse, 1976). Some recent criticism even regard the sequence of the tales (in the Ellesmere order) as an integral part of Chaucer's meaning (David R. Pischke, Movement of CT, 1977; Dolores Warwick Frese, An Ars Legendi for Chaucer's CT, 1991). Given these tendencies, it is not surprising that some critics regard the work as complete and finished as it stands. John Norton-Smith argues that the *Tales* was intended to be an "imperfect work" (Geoffrey Ch, 1974, 79–159); Howard emphasizes that the plan for four tales is the Host's rather than Chaucer's and that the "unfinished quality" of the *Tales* "is a feature of its form, not a fact of its author's career" (Idea of CT, 1 and 162); Traugott Lawler likewise argues that the apparently unfinished quality is calculated, that Chaucer intended but one tale for

each pilgrim from the beginning, and that the Host's ambitious plan is part of a "pattern of diminishment" (One and the Many, 1980, 118). This shift to the consideration of the *Tales* as an artistically unified work was one of the most remarkable features of Chaucerian criticism in the last few decades.

At the same time, there has been a strong attack on the whole assumption that the tales are dramatic in any way (Robertson, Pref to Ch), and some critics have stressed variety rather than unity (Payne, Ch and Menippean Satire), while, as the following notes show, much of the most valuable criticism of the *Tales* treats each tale in isolation, as parts of a single fragment, or as expressions of themes independent of any particular order or theory of a unified whole. Moreover, a number of recent studies have emphasized the fragmentary nature of the *Tales* and argued that the apparent unity of the work is most likely the achievement of an early editor or literary executor (see N. F. Blake, E&S 32, 1979, 1–18, and ed. CT Edited from the Hengwrt MS, 1980; Doyle and Parkes, in Med. Scribes, MSS and Libraries: Essays Presented to N. R. Ker, ed. M. B. Parkes and Andrew G. Watson, 1978, 163–210; and cf. Charles A. Owen, Jr., PMLA 97, 1982, 237–50). This tendency has gained great strength in recent years, and a number of important critics have elected to treat the individual tales in relative isolation (C. D. Benson, Ch's Drama of Style, 1986; H. Marshall Leicester, Jr., The Disenchanted Self, 1990) or group them for consideration by genre or thematic relationships rather than in the contexts of their fragments (Derek A. Pearsall, CT, 1993; Piero Boitani and Jill Mann, eds., Cambridge Ch Companion, 1986).

Studies of individual tales are cited in the notes that follow, which provide references to interpretative commentary. Perhaps the earliest commentaries on the tales are to be found in the marginal Latin glosses in such manuscripts as the Hengwrt and Ellesmere; they are especially frequent in The Wife of Bath's Prologue and Tale, The Tales of the Man of La, Summoner, Clerk, Merchant, Franklin, and The Pardoner's Prologue. At least some of these glosses are most likely Chaucer's own (M-R 3:483–587; Daniel S. Silvia, Jr., SP 62, 1965, 28–39). For a full account, see Stephen Bradford Partridge, Glosses in the Manuscripts of Chaucer's Canterbury Tales: an Edition and Commentary (Harvard thesis, 1992). The more important marginal glosses (almost all those from the Ellesmere manuscript) are quoted or translated from Partridge's text and included in the notes.

FRAGMENT I

The General Prologue and the tales of the Knight, Miller, Reeve, and Cook form a dramatically unified group which, though unfinished, is so tightly knit that it was almost never broken up in the scribal rearrangements. In addition to its obvious dramatic unity, critics have found a variety of unifying themes—most notably "herbergage" (Gerhard Joseph, ChauR 5, 1970, 83–96), time, space, and "privitee" (E. D. Blodgett, Spec 51, 1977, 477–93), male competitiveness (Emily Jenson, ChauR 24, 1990, 320–28), and ideals of civil conduct (Howard, Idea of CT, 227–47). Kolve (Ch and the Imagery of Narrative) sees the thematic unity extending to Fragment II, The Man of Law's Tale, and considers the first five tales as a sequence, dealing with, respectively, pagan Greece, four-teenth-century England, and the transitional period of sixth-century Europe, and exploring the genres of romance, fabliau, and chronicle.

General Prologue

The date at which Chaucer began writing the General Prologue cannot be precisely determined. The only clear historical reference, to the sea route between Middelburg and Orwell, is of little help (see 276, 277 below). Probably Chaucer began work on the *Tales* in 1387–88, but we cannot know whether he first composed a number of tales or began with the General Prologue. Nor can we determine when Chaucer finished the Prologue, since it is likely that he revised it from time to time. No completely convincing case has been made for any specific revision: it has been suggested that the Miller, Manciple, Reeve, Summoner, and Pardoner were added in a later draft, that the Squire and the Five Guildsmen are later additions, that the Wife of Bath's portrait was not given its final form until her present prologue was finished, and that Chaucer intended to compose portraits of the Second Nun and Nun's Priest. Any or all of these assumptions could be true and thus provide some reason to believe that Chaucer did indeed revise the General Prologue over a number of years and that the Prologue as we have it therefore contains some of his most mature work.

The form of the General Prologue is original with Chaucer, though it owes much to the convention of the dream vision (compare lines 1–12 to *Romaunt of the Rose*, 71–83). The portraits are indebted to the medieval rhetorical tradition (Haselmayer, in S&A, 3–5), as transmitted both by rhetorical treatises (such as Geoffrey of Vinsauf, *Poetria nova*) and by previous poetry (such as the *Roman de la rose*), as well as to conventional descriptions of Vices and Virtues (Howard R. Patch, MLN 40, 1925, 1–14). Chaucer also drew on his knowledge of the medieval sciences (Curry, Ch and Science) and on life itself (Manly, New Light). Laura C. and Robert T. Lambdin, eds., An Historical Guide to the Pilgrims in the CT, 1996, provide essays, with bibliographies, on each of the pilgrims from the historical standpoint of their occupations. The most valuable study of the literary and historical background of the portraits is Jill Mann's Ch and Med. Estates Satire, 1973, which considers them from the standpoint of "estates satire"—satire of the estates (occupations) of medieval society. This is a mode rather than a genre, best exemplified for students of Chaucer by John Gower's *Mirour de l'omme* (Mirror of Mankind, tr. William B. Wilson). Mann provides a useful analysis of the methods by which Chaucer employed such traditional materials to create characters "to whom we respond as individuals" (Ch and Estates, 189).

Jill Mann's resolution of the old problem of whether the portraits represent "individuals" or "types" (for which she provides a useful bibliography, 289 n. 1) has been challenged (Gerald Morgan ES 58, 1977, 481–93). Indeed, the question was greatly broadened by D. W. Robertson's vigorous advocacy of his theory that Chaucer does not create characters in the ordinary sense: such a character as the Wife of Bath, he maintains, is not intended to be individualized but is rather an "elaborate iconographic figure designed to show the manifold implications of an attitude," a philosophical rather than a psychological construct (Preface to Ch, 330–31). In more recent

years this question has seemed less pressing, since so many critics have moved away from "roadside drama" to a tendency to treat the tales as largely independent of their tellers (e.g., C. D. Benson, Ch's Drama of Style, 1986, 3–6).

Likewise, attention has recently shifted away from the question of how the narrator of the Prologue is related to Chaucer himself. Few, if any, today accept the old assumption that Chaucer was writing autobiographically (cf. Manly, CT, 497) or the even older idea of Chaucer as a cheerful "naif." "A naif Collector of Customs," wrote Kittredge, "would be a paradoxical monster" (Ch and His Poetry, 45). Still much disputed but widely accepted is E. T. Donaldson's thesis that the narrator is an ironic literary persona—"Chaucer the Pilgrim"—distinct from the author (PMLA 69, 1954, 928–36, rpt. in Speaking of Ch). It has been widely influential, though Donaldson himself was more cautious in applying this approch than many who have adopted his thesis. For an objection to the multiplication of personae, see H. Marshall Leicester, Jr., Disenchanted Self, 1990, 1–13.

Muriel Bowden's Commentary on GP (supplemented by the Lambdins' Historical Guide) remains the most useful compendium of information on the historical background of Chaucer's pilgrims, and Mann's Ch and Estates the best treatment of their literary backgrounds. The celebrated Ellesmere portraits are well reproduced in Ellesmere Miniatures of Cant. Pilgrims, ed. Theo Stemmler, 1977, which also contains a useful discussion and bibliography. For full bibliographies and reviews of scholarship, see Caroline D. Eckhardt, Chaucer's General Prologue to the Canterbury Tales: An Annotated Bibliography, 1900 to 1984; The Chaucer bibliographies, 1990; and see the Variorum edition of The General Prologue, ed. Malcolm Andrew, Daniel J. Ransome, et al., Variorum, vol. 2, pts. 1A–1B, 1993.

1–14   Chaucer apparently had no one model or source for the form of the General Prologue, though Skeat (5:1–2) noted the striking similarities of the opening lines to Guido delle Colonne, *Historia destructionis Troiae* (History of the Destruction of Troy, tr. Meek, 33–34), a work that Chaucer knew well (he made use of it in his *Troilus*): "It was the time when the aging (*maturans*) sun in its oblique circle of the zodiac had already entered (*cursum suum*) into the sign of Aries, in which the equal length of nights and days is celebrated in the Equinox of Spring; when the weather begins to entice eager mortals into the pleasant air; when the ice has melted and breezes (*Zephiri*) ripple the flowing streams; when the springs burst forth in fragile bubbles; when moistures exhaled from the bosom of the earth are raised up to the tops of trees and branches, for which reason the seeds sprout, the crops grow, and the meadows bloom, embellished with flowers of various colors; when the trees on every side are decked with renewed leaves; when earth is adorned with grass, and the birds sing and twitter in music of sweet harmony. Then almost the middle of the month of April had passed when . . . the aforesaid kings, Jason and Hercules, left port with their ship."

Numerous parallels have been found in other works—from the *Pervigilium veneris* (The Vigil [or Eve] of Venus) (in Catullus, Works, ed. and tr. J. W. Mackail), a second-century

Latin poem celebrating an April festival (J. E. Hankins, MLN 49, 1934, 80–83), to Middle English romance (see *Kyng Alisaunder,* ed. Smithers, EETS, 117, 237, 1952–57), for the description of Spring was a literary commonplace. (See James J. Wilhelm, The Cruelest Month: Spring, Nature, and Love, 1965.) Chaucer most likely owed the idea of beginning his narrative with a description of Spring to the dream vision; cf. RomA 49–89, BD 291–303, PF 183–210, ProLGW, and see J. V. Cunningham, MP 49, 1952, 173–74. The series of portraits may have been inspired by the series of allegorical portraits in the *Roman de la rose* (RomA 146–474) or by the "Dance of Death," with its portraits of various estates (though in neither case is there any very direct resemblance).

2 droghte of March: A dry March, necessary for sowing, promised a good crop; cf. Whiting B611: "A bushel of March dust is worth a king's ransome."

7–8 The sun is **yonge** (Guido: *maturans*) because the solar year has just begun with the vernal equinox (then 12 March). Aries, **the Ram,** is the first sign of the zodiac, through which the sun passed from 12 March to 11 April. On the face of it, these lines fix the time at the beginning of April, when the sun was a bit more than halfway through Aries. However, since 18 April is specified in the IntrMLT II.5–6, **halve cours** is usually taken to mean the second half of the sun's course through Aries, which falls in April. By 16 or 17 April the sun was five or six degrees into Taurus. Sigmund Eisner (ChauR 28, 1994, 330–43) argues that the reference to the Ram is to the constellation Aries rather than the zodiacal sign and specifies the time at 17 April.

Chaucer first uses the specification of time by astronomical periphrasis (chronographia) in *Troilus,* influenced by Boccaccio, Statius, and perhaps mainly Dante, who was very fond of the device (Curtius, European Lit., 275–76). Chaucer uses it frequently in the *Tales:* IntrMLT II. 1–6; MerT IV.1885–87, 2219–24; SqT V.48–51, 263–65; FranT V.1245–49; ParsPro X.2–12; cf. FranT V.1017–18.

10 open ye: That birds sleep with open eyes is apparently original with Chaucer. If Chaucer refers to nightingales, **slepen . . . with open ye** may be a sort of litotes meaning "sleep not at all," since nightingales were said to sing continuously day and night in the mating season (see 98 below). R. C. Paynter of the Museum of Comparative Zoology, Harvard University, kindly informs us that one can rarely see a bird with its eyes closed, since most birds have two sets of eyelids, and the set that they use for blinking is transparent.

11 Nature: The personified goddess Natura. In PF Nature represents the forces of both generation and order in the world: "Nature, the vicaire of the almyghty Lord" (PF 379). On medieval treatments of Nature, see Curtius, European Lit., ch. 6, and George Economou, The Goddess Natura in Med. Lit., 1972.

13 palmeres: So called because they carried a palm branch as a sign they had been to the Holy Land. Many were perpetual pilgrims, sworn to poverty, who journeyed from one shrine to another, often as paid substitutes for deceased persons or for those who could not find time to go themselves (Sumption, Pilgrimage: An Image of Medieval Religion, 1975, 298–99).

17 martir: Thomas Becket was martyred in 1170, canonized in 1173. His shrine at Canterbury was rivaled only by Walsingham as an object of pilgrimage until the Reformation. St. Thomas was especially associated with healing, and the water from a miraculous well near his shrine was highly prized for its curative powers; see Ronald C. Finucane, Miracles and Pilgrims: Popular Beliefs in Med. Eng., 1977, 153–72.

17–18 seke . . . seeke: A *rime riche,* or identical rhyme of homophones (identical in sound but different in meaning), much admired in ME and OF poetry; see Machui Masui, Structure of Ch's Rime Words, 1964, 28–30. For other examples see MLT II.102–3, SqT V.105–6. The scribe glosses the words involved at CkT I.4339–40, SqT V.145–46, PhyT VI.173–74, SNT VIII.477–79.

20 Southwerk: A borough south of London, across London Bridge at the beginning of the road to Canterbury. It was known not only for its many inns but also for its numerous brothels (Alec R. Myers, London in the Age of Chaucer 1972, 11; cf. 719 below). The **Tabard** was an inn so called from its sign, shaped like a tabard, a sleeveless smock embroidered with armorial bearings (the word was also applied to a laborer's smock; see GP I.541).

24 nyne and twenty: On the number of pilgrims, see 164 below.

33 The subject of **made** is "we," implied in the preceding line. When the context makes the subject clear, the pronoun is frequently omitted (cf. lines 529, 786, 811).

37 resoun: Probably used here in its technical sense of "ordo" (proper order, suitable arrangement); MED s.v. resoun n2 2(c) takes *acordaunt to resoun* rather as "sensible, reasonable, proper."

The Knight

The Notes on the Knight are adapted from those written by Vincent J. DiMarco for The Riverside Chaucer.

The Knight is usually considered an experienced and distinguished professional man-of-arms, motivated by religious ideals. William Blake (Desc. Catalogue [1809] in Compl. Writings, ed. Keynes, 1966, 566) took him as the universal "guardian of man against the oppressor." Some recent critics judge him more harshly: Terry Jones (Ch's Knight, 1980) regards him as a mere mercenary adventurer (though there is little support for this position; see John A. Pratt, ChauR 22, 1987, 8–27).

Most often the knight is viewed as an anachronism, a representative of the old crusading ideal now well out of fashion. However, the records of the controversy between Sir Richard Scrope and Sir Robert Grosvenor (ed. Nicolas, 1832; excerpts in Rickert, Ch's World, 147–50) show a number of knights and squires who campaigned in the same places as Chaucer's Knight, and attempts have been made to identify a real-life prototype (see Manly, New Light, 104–6) among the deponents at the Scrope-Grosvener trial or in the career of Henry of Derby, later Henry IV. As Mann notes (Ch and Estates, 110–11), attempts to identify a real-life prototype for the Knight have failed not because there are too few likely candidates but because there are too many.

45–46 chivalrie: Probably "prowess" as well as the ethical code of knighthood. **Trouthe** (modern "troth") means fidelity to one's pledged word (cf. FranT V.1479). **Honour** means good reputation, the opposite of shame (ParsT X.187), as well as good character. **Fredom** means generosity of goods and spirit; Brunetto Latini, *Il Tesoretto* (ed. and tr. Holloway, ll. 1445–46) relates this virtue to gentle speech: "Generosity commands, 'Do not say anything villainous/ or any curse-words there.'" **Curteisie** denotes refinement of manners and spirit as well as a command of courtly usages.

47 his lordes werre: Though Chaucer specifies that the Knight has fought in Christendom as well as in heathendom, only campaigns against Muslims, schismatics (Russian Orthodox), and pagans are enumerated.

49 Apparently a line of eleven syllables (the second "in" is omitted in some MSS and editions). Christopherson (ES 45, Suppl. 1964, 146–47) suggests phonetic shortening of *cristendom* to two syllables, but elsewhere in Chaucer's verse it is trisyllabic. The construction "As wel in . . . as in" is common in Chaucer, rare in most other ME writers.

51 Alisaundre: Alexandria (in Egypt) was conquered by Peter I (Lusignan) of Cyprus on 10 October 1365 and abandoned a week later, after great plundering and a massacre of its inhabitants; see MkT VII.2392n. The campaigns against *Satalye* and *Lyeys* (GP I.58) were also led by Peter of Cyprus, the foremost crusader of the century; see MkT VII.2391–96.

53 Pruce: Prussia, the area along the Baltic shore roughly between the Vistula and the Niemen; by Chaucer's time it was largely used as a base of operations by the Teutonic Order for its *reysen* ("raids"; cf. *reysed,* GP I.54) into Lithuania and Russia. The Knight's campaigns in the Baltic are usually considered his most recent, from which he has just returned, though Vincent J. DiMarco (RBPH 46, 1978, 654–55) notes an English ban on all travel to the Baltic in 1385–88.

54 Lettow: Lithuania, a large area south of present-day Latvia, including part of Ukraine (Magoun, Ch Gazetteer, 101).

> **Ruce** (Russia) is perhaps used here to mean the principalities of Pskov, on the Livonian frontier, and Novgorod, on the Volkhov. In 1378 Pope Urban VI authorized indulgences for those aiding the crusade against the Russian Orthodox, but no increase in crusading resulted.

57 Algezir: Algeciras, a seaport of the kingdom of Granada (*Gernade,* GP I.56), near Gibraltar. Its conquest in 1344 by Christians led by Alphonso IX of Castile ended the influence in Spain of the Muslim Merenid dynasty (*Belmarye*).

> **Belmarye:** Belmarin, Banu Merin, in the fourteenth century the powerful Berber dynasty ruling what is now Morocco, here called by the dynasty's name.

58 Lyeys: Ayash, a seaport near Antioch, in the medieval kingdom of Cilicia, or Lesser Armenia, was captured by Peter of Cyprus (see MkT VII.2391–97 and 2391n) in 1367.

> **Satalye:** Antalya (the ancient Attaleia), an independent Turcoman principality in southern Anatolia, which Peter of Cyprus attacked on 23–24 August 1361.

63 Duels between champions of opposing Christian and Muslim armies were fought as late as the sixteenth century: Captain John Smith claimed to have killed three Saracens in the lists on three successive days (General Historie of Virginia, etc., 1907, 2:128–30).

66 Palatye: Balat, near the site of ancient Miletus on the southwest coast of Turkey, was an independent emirate ruled by a Seljuk Turk. The "Lord of Palatye" paid homage to Peter of Cyprus in 1365 but is not known to have campaigned with him against other Turks.

68 worthy . . . wys: A common collocation (cf. Tr 2.180: "a wis and worthi wight"); *worthy* may mean "distinguished" here, but more probably means "brave" (as in MLT II.579). The paired terms reflect the commonplace "fortitudo et sapientia," bravery and wisdom (see Curtius, Europ. Lit. 176–80, and cf. KnT I.865).

The Squire

The Notes on the Squire are adapted from those written by Vincent J. DiMarco for The Riverside Chaucer.

The Squire is generally considered an attractive figure, and some critics, noting that Chaucer himself had been a squire and fought in Artois and Picardy (GP I.86) and that the Squire is the only pilgrim said to write poetry (GP I.95), have suggested autobiographical overtones (Bowden, Comm. on GP, 74–75). But the portrait owes much to the *Roman de la rose,* especially the descriptions of Mirth and Love (RomA 817–46, 885–917) and the catalogue of courtly accomplishments (RomB 2311–30). Rosamund Tuve (Seasons and Months, 186–88) notes similarities to MS illustrations of the month of May (92). On the Squire as a type of youth, see J. A. Burrow (The Ages of Man, 170–72), who notes he is the only pilgrim described as "young."

The Squire's youthful, romantic enthusiasms, many critics have believed, will later develop into his father's sober virtues. Some critics have been less admiring, seeing him as a representative of a degenerate chivalry. Donaldson (883) and Mann (Ch and Estates, 106, 116–19) view the portraits of the Squire and the Knight as alternative formulations of the romantic and religious aspects of chivalry, with prejudice to neither.

79–80 A squire held the first degree of knighthood, with the privileges of a **bacheler** but not those of a banneret, who could lead knights under his own banner. The Squire serves as an attendant to his father, who has perhaps instructed him in chivalry, as advised by Ramon Lull (Mann, Ch and Estates, 115).

85 in chyvachie has no article because it is an anglicized imitation of OF *en chevaucie* (A. A. Prins, ES 30, 1949, 42–44).

86 The reference is probably to the "crusade" of 1383, led by Henry Despencer, bishop of Norwich, against the largely orthodox Flemish and their schismatic French overlords. The expedition, which was a failure, was widely criticized.

90 floytynge: Probably "playing the flute" rather than "whistling," which is an uncertain medieval usage. MED s.v. *flouten.*

93 sleeves longe and wyde: ParsT X.416–30 criticizes such extravagance, but Amor in *Roman de la rose* distinguishes the pursuit of respectable elegance from Pride; RomB 2253–54: "For fresh array, as men may see,/ Withouten pride may ofte be."

96 purtreye: Nicholas Orme (From Childhood to Chivalry, 1984, 175) argues that the term is here used in the sense of "representing in speech or writing," since noble education made no provision for training in art.

98 Nightingales were believed to sing all night in the mating season: they "synge plesauntly day and night . . . whanne they have rejoysed thaire amerous desyre and plesaunces, thei make abace melodye [grow silent], for thei synge no more" (Book of the Knight of La Tour Landry, EETS 33, 156).

99–100 Squires customarily carved for their knights; cf. SumT III.2243–45 and MerT IV.1772–73. It was an honorable duty (see Froissart's account of the Black Prince serving the captive King John of France, in Chronicles, tr. Brereton, 144).

The Yeoman

A yeoman was a free servant, ranking in feudal households next below a squire. This yeoman is a forester (*forster*), a gamekeeper charged with guarding his lord's game (cf. PhyT VI.83–85), skilled in *wodecraft* and the ceremonies of the hunt: cf. Sir Gawain and the Green Knight, 1605, "Then a wyghe [man] that was wis upon wodcraftes/ To unlace [cut up] this bor lufly biginnes" [regularized]. He is dressed in the *cote and hood of grene* appropriate to a huntsman (cf. FrT III.1380–82 and KnT 1684–86; Oliver F. Emerson, RomR 13, 1922, 141). Though Earle Birney (REL 1, 1960, 9–18) finds the Yeoman overly elegant and his portrait therefore ironic, he seems clearly admirable. Manly (CT, 503) conjectured that Chaucer intended to adapt for him the Tale of Gamelyn, found in some MSS of the *Tales* (and assigned to the Cook), but there is little basis for this supposition.

101–2 he: The Knight, who leads the minimum knightly retinue ("a squire and servant that may take heede to his horse," Wm. Caxton, Bk of the Ordre of Chyvalry, ed. Byles, EETS 168, 1926, 19).

hym liste ride so: His small entourage is a matter of choice. His yeoman is a forester, which could be an important office. William B. McColly (ChauR 20, 1985, 14–27) argues that his presence reflects the high status of the Knight.

104 pecock arwes: Peacock feathers were prized for arrows (Bowden, Comm. on GP, 86–87), and still are by modern archers (George A. Test, AMN&Q 2, 1964, 67–68).

107 fetheres lowe: See Roger Ascham, *Toxophilus* [1545], ed. Arber, rpt. 1966, 132: [if the rib of the feather is improperly trimmed] "the fether shall faule and droupe downe."

115 The image of St. Christopher is a talisman against death, injury, and weariness (Waller, Surrey Archeol. Soc., Collections 6, 1874, 60–64, 296). The saint has no special associations with foresters, though Waller finds a tenuous connection with archers in the sixteenth century. The sumptuary law of 1363, which attempted to regulate the degree of luxury in clothing allowed to each class, forbade the wearing of silver ornaments by yeomen. The law, however, was widely ignored, never enforced, and repealed the next year (see Francis E. Baldwin, Sumptuary Legislation in Engl., 1926, esp. 55).

The Prioress

The Notes on the Prioress are adapted from those written by Florence H. Ridley for The Riverside Chaucer.

The Prioress has attracted more critical commentary and controversy than almost any other character in the General Prologue. She has the appearance and manners of a traditional courtly lady, though she is a bit large for the ideal beauty (156) and a bit too provincial to attain *cheere of court.* Yet she is a nun, professing *love celestial,* and though many of the attributes of the ideal secular lady-love were incorporated in the ideal nun, the bride of Christ (Mann, Ch and Estates, 128–37), the exact degree of "the engagingly imperfect submergence of the feminine in the ecclesiastical" (John L. Lowes, Convention and Revolt in Poetry, 1919, 60–61) has been the subject of much debate. She seems to violate many of the rules of her order (Rule of St. Benedict, tr. McCann); yet such rules were frequently ignored or waived by dispensation, and M. Madeleva (A Lost Language, 31–60) defends, not altogether convincingly, all of the Prioress's apparent violations of religious discipline. Henry Ansgar Kelly makes a much better case for her in his "neorevisionist" view of Chaucer's nuns (ChauR 31, 1996, 115–132).

The Prioress is associated with an actual Benedictine nunnery, St. Leonard's, adjoining *Stratford atte Bowe,* about two miles from London. Chaucer knew this nunnery (he lived only two miles from it; see H. M. Smyser, MLN 56, 1941, 205–7) and had gone there as a boy when the Countess of Ulster and her husband, Prince Lionel, visited the prince's aunt, the queen's sister Elizabeth of Hainault (cf. Manly, New Light, 204–6). Like the neighboring nunnery at Barking, it may have served as a kind of finishing school for daughters of rich London merchants (Manly, New Light, 204–5). Though not so aristocratic as Barking (where Chaucer's sister or daughter, Elizabeth, was a nun; see p. xiv), it was relatively prosperous, with thirty nuns in 1354 and probably at least that many when Chaucer was writing (see Marie P. Hamilton, in Philologica, ed. Thomas A. Kirby, 1949, 179–90). Manly (CT, 504) suggests that Chaucer's Prioress was modeled on an actual person, but no such model has been found. The prioress of St. Leonard's at this time was Mary Syward (or Suhard); see Manly, TLS, 10 Nov. 1927, 817.

Many critics today take a much harsher view of the Prioress than did Robinson, Lowes, and Kittredge. The primary cause is the anti-Semitism of her tale, which, though long recognized (Wordsworth noted her "fierce bigotry," Works, ed. A. J. George, 1932, 263–66), has become an important critical issue (see introductory note to PrT).

119 symple and coy: The phrase is common in French courtly poetry (cf. RomC 7321 "chere of symplenesse," translating Fr. "simple e quie"), though in religious verse "symple, coye" was also applied to ideal nuns (Mann, Ch and Estates, 136, 272 n. 48). *Coy* has no coquettish connotations.

120 ooth: Even a mild oath would have earned the disapproval of a strict moralist, though swearing was common (see EpiMLT II.1171n.). Skeat (5:14) cites a tradition that to swear by St. Loy, who refused to take an oath, became no oath at all. **Seinte Loy** is generally agreed to be St. Eligius

(588–629) (French Eloi, English Loy), a goldsmith and master of the royal mint who became bishop of Noyan and later the patron saint of metalworkers, carters, and farriers (cf. FrT III.1564n.). On his legend, see Andrew Breeze, Reading Med. Studies 17, 1991, 103–19. Manly suggests (CT, 505) that there was a cult of St. Loy at the royal court. That may be the reason the Prioress swears by St. Loy, though Kittredge (Ch and His Poetry, 177) believes the saint was chosen because his soft, ladylike name did not distort the lips.

121 Eglentyne: "briar rose" (MED, s.v. *eglentin*). The name connotes heroines in romance though it is curiously similar to Argentyn, the name of an actual nun at St. Leonard's (Manly, New Light, 204–11). R. T. Davies (MLN 67, 1952, 400–402) cites an actual nun with the romantic name Idoine.

122 service dyvyne: Liturgy of the canonical hours: Matins (cf. WBT III.876), Lauds (MilT I.3655), Prime (PardT VI.662), Sext, Nones, Vespers, and Compline (RvT I.4171).

123 Entuned . . . ful semely: A nasal intonation was commonly employed to avoid straining the throat in singing long liturgies (Thomas A. Kirby, in Sts. Pres. to W. A. Read, 1940, 33), but see Maynard J. Brennan, MLQ 10, 1949, 455, citing the *Tyrocinium Benedictinum*, which emphatically states that the office is to be chanted *non . . . de naribus sonando."* Cf. Kelly, ChauR 31:125.

124–26 The Prioress's French is apparently Anglo-Norman, as opposed to the **Frenssh of Parys** spoken at the royal court. Ian Short (RPh 33, 1980, 467–79) discusses English attitudes toward native French and notes that the author of the *Vie d'Edouard le Confesseur* (ed. Sodergard, 1948), a nun, apologizes because "I know only the false French of England" (vv. 7–8). Walter Map (Courtiers' Trifles, ed. and tr. James, 496–97) tells of a school ("fons," lit. spring) at Marlborough that taught its students a barbarous French, "Gallicum Merleburgae." Manly (New Light, 219–20) suggests that the French at St. Leonard's was the Flemish-tinged dialect of Hainault, introduced by Elizabeth of Hainault (and presumably spoken by Chaucer's wife). Ernest P. Kuhl (PQ 2, 1923, 306–8) believes a contrast is intended with the better dialect at the wealthy convent of Barking. On the whole question, see W. Rothwell, Bull. of the John Rylands Univ. Lib. of Manchester 74, 1992, 3–28. Cf. SumT III.1832n.

127–36 The Prioress's table manners are modeled directly on the advice of La Vieille (the Old Woman) in *Roman de la rose,* in a speech derived from Ovid's *Ars amatoria* (Art of Love), advising a young woman how to attract men (*Roman de la rose* 13408–32; tr. Dahlberg, 231). However, the manners are those of a well-bred lady prescribed in courtesy books of the time (Manly, CT, 504), and are perhaps a necessary part of a nun's caring for her habit (M. Madeleva, Lost Language, 39). Nothing the Prioress consumes is explicitly forbidden by her rule, though the care with which her eating and drinking are described suggests improper concern with food and drink, as well as with manners.

132 curteisie: This word has associations with faithfulness to a way of life ordained by God (cf. the poem "Cleanness") as well as with an aristocratic refinement of manners and spirit (see 45–46 above), though it frequently connotes merely ceremonious behavior or affability (see Burnley, Ch's Language and the Philosopher's Trad., 153), as its restriction here to table manners suggests.

141 digne of reverence: The Rule of St. Benedict (tr. Fry, 2.1, 171–73) specifies: "To be worthy of the task of governing a monastery, the abbot must always remember what his title signifies and act as a superior should."

142–50 conscience: Both "moral sense, awareness of right and wrong" and "solicitude, anxiety" (MED s.v. *conscience* 2, 4). Mice and dogs are obviously inadequate objects of a nun's compassion and may indicate that her conscience is mere sentimentalism (R. E. Kaske, ELH 30, 1963, 175–92).

146 smale houndes: Dogs were common as pets of fashionable ladies of the time (cf. Bk. of the Knight of La Tour Landry, EETS 33, 28–29). Nuns also had pets, subject to some regulation (see Kelly, ChauR 31:121; and cf. *Ancrene Riwle,* tr. Salu, 185, which allows only a cat), though the Prioress's hounds are usually taken as an indication of the discrepancy between her profession and her inclinations.

147 rosted flessh: The Benedictine Rule forbade meat (*flesh*) except to the ill or infirm (cf. The Ancrene Riwle, tr. Salu, 183). Whether she fed the dogs from her own table or had their food specially prepared, such expensive fare was not for animals (cf. ParsT X.222).

wastel-breed: The most expensive bread in ordinary use, half the price of the special *payndemayn* (Thop VII.725) but more expensive than the third-grade *Fraunceis* or *pouf* and the fourth-grade *tourte,* the dark bread eaten by the poor widow in NPT VII.2843–44. See Liber Albus, tr. Riley, 1:lxvii, as cited by Kuhl, PQ 2:302–3.

151 The Ancrene Riwle (tr. Salu, 186) warns nuns against wearing a **wympul:** "There are some anchoresses who sin in their wearing of a wimple no less than women of the world." M. Madeleva (Lost Language, 41) notes that it was a customary part of the Benedictine habit, but the emphasis on its being **semyly pynched** (elegantly pleated) relates this to traditional satiric criticisms of nuns' concern with worldly fashions (Mann, Ch and Estates, 130 and cf. Ancrene Riwle, tr. Salu, 88).

152–56 The Prioress is described in the "descending (head-to-toe) catalogue" conventional for beautiful women in courtly poetry, here left incomplete, perhaps out of deference to her calling. Her features—well-proportioned nose, grey eyes, pretty mouth, fair forehead—are those of standard romance beauties (cf. RomA 539–74, BD 855–865).

152 greye: A favorite color for the eyes of beautiful women (RomA 546, 862) and men (RomA 822) in Chaucer's time and later (cf. Shakespeare, Two Gentlemen of Verona, 4.4.192: "Her eyes are grey as glass, and so are mine"). The color intended is uncertain. Chaucer first uses it in RomA 862 to translate Fr. *vair* (variable, flecked). Middle English poets describe eyes as black, brown, green, or grey, never blue. It may be that *greye* includes shades of blue, though Arthur K. Moore (PQ 26, 1947, 307–12) makes a good case for hazel, greyish.

155 spanne brood: The high and broad forehead, which should have been covered by the Prioress's wimple, may be that of a courtly beauty (S. T. Knight, Neophil 52, 1968, 178–80), though a *spanne* is about seven to nine inches. She is a very large woman (cf. 156).

158 coral: Deemed a protection against "the feendes gyle" and various other evils (Barth. Angl., 16.32; tr. Trevisa 2:842). Such coral rosaries were fashionable; see John B.

Friedman, MÆ 39, 1970, 301–5, who also notes the reputed powers of coral.

159 The rosary has large green dividers (**gauds**), marking the Paternosters and separating sets of ten Ave Marias, or meditations on Mary. The modern "gaudy," which Baum (PMLA 73, 1958, 168) uses to detect a pun here, is not attested in Middle English.

160 brooch of gold: Nuns were forbidden to wear brooches (Kuhl, PQ 2:305).

161 crowned A: A flat capital "A" surmounted by a crown was a contemporary emblem for Queen Anne (John L. Lowes, PMLA 23, 1908, 285–99). The queen died in 1394 and presumably such emblems went out of style thereafter.

162 Amor vincit omnia: "Love conquers all." The motto is secular in origin (Virgil, Eclogue 10.69) and application (*Roman de la rose* 21332; tr. Dahlberg, 348: "O fair son, Love conquers everything"), but was sometimes used by monastics (M. Madeleva, Lost Language, 43). Its ambiguity has occasioned much commentary. Amor could be God's love, "love celestial," or it could be secular, in keeping with the romantic overtones of the portrait. Still applicable is Lowes's comment: "Which of the two loves does 'amor' mean to the Prioress? I do not know; but I think she thought she meant love celestial" (Convention and Revolt, 66).

The Second Nun and Nun's Priest

The Notes on the Second Nun and Nun's Priest are adapted from those written by Florence H. Ridley for The Riverside Chaucer.

Neither the Second Nun nor the Nun's Priest is described, though each is later assigned a tale. Critics usually assume that Chaucer intended in a final revision to add portraits of these characters.

164 chapeleyne: A nun serving her prioress as secretary, amanuensis, and attendant at festivals; see MED s.v. *chapelain* 2 (b).

preestes thre: This phrase has occasioned much comment. In line 24 Chaucer specifies that *Wel nine and twenty* pilgrims arrived at the Tabard. If three priests accompany the Prioress, the number of pilgrims listed in the GP is thirty-one; if Chaucer meant the Prioress to have but one attendant priest, the total is twenty-nine. It is usually believed that Chaucer left the line unfinished after *chapeleyne* and that, as Bradshaw suggested, the text was carelessly patched by someone else. Rickert (M–R 3:428) suggested that *and the preest is thre* was added first, then *preest is* was miscopied as *preestis,* which would remove the extra priests and make *chapelayn* refer to the one remaining. But the MED does not record this meaning of *is* ("adds up to"), and in both the Hengwrt and Ellesmere MSS the marginal notation reads "Nonne Chapelayne."

The Monk

The Notes on the Monk are adapted from those written by Susan H. Cavanaugh for The Riverside Chaucer.

The older view that Chaucer admired and lightly satirized his Monk is still current, but many now regard the portrait as heavily

ironic or even bitterly satiric (e.g., Robertson, Pref. to Ch, 253–56). Beichner provides a lively defense of the Monk as a successful administrator (Spec 34, 1959, 611–19). His vices are those commonly attacked by satirists and reformers (Bowden, Comm. on GP, 107–18; Mann, Ch and Estates, 17–37), but his worldliness, lordly air, and love of horses, hounds, and hunting are faults that Gower attributes specifically to monastic officers and "keepers" (cf. GP I.172), whose duties take them outside the monastery (Mirour, 20953–21158; tr. Wilson 280–83).

The hunting cleric was a familiar figure; see Gower, Vox Clam. 3.1490–1512; tr. Stockton; Wyclif, Eng. Works, 249: "Thei maken large kechenes, holden fatte hors & houndis and haukis & strompetis gaiely arraied, & suffren ooure men to starve for myschief." The visitation of Selborne Abbey in 1387 by William Wykeham, bishop of Winchester, found monastics of the time keeping hounds, hunting, and indulging in rich food and clothing (see Gilbert White, Nat. Hist. and Antiq. of Selborne, ed. Buckland, 1875, 509–15). The pious and affable William de Clowne, abbot of Leicester (1345–78), has been suggested as a model for the Monk. Clowne was the most famous hare hunter in England; each year he held a hare hunt for Edward III and such nobles as John of Gaunt and, in 1363, Peter of Cyprus (MkT VII.2391–98). See David Knowles, Religious Orders in Engl., 1955, 2:185–86, 365–66.

166 outridere: A monk with permission regularly to leave the cloister for monastic business (overseeing monastic properties, buying supplies, etc.). Cf. ShipT VII.65–66n.

venerie: Baum (PMLA 71, 1956, 245–46) detects a pun on "hunting" (OF *venerie*) and "sexual activity" (Med. Lat. *veneria*), but the OED does not record the latter meaning until 1497.

167 manly: manly, generous, virile; Cf. ShipT VII.43n.

168 many a deyntee hors: On monks as collectors of fine horses (the "fat horses" criticized by Wycliffites in the next note), see Mann Ch and Estates, 23–24 and cf. ParsT X.432.

169–70 Bridles adorned with bells were fashionable; see Sir Gawain and the Green Knight, 195: "mony belles ful bright of brende gold rungen" [regularized]; Wyclif, Sel. Eng. Wks, 3:520 [a worldly priest] "with fatte hors, and jolye and gaye sadeles, and bridles ringing by the weye, and himself in costly robes and pelure." Canterbury pilgrims often had clusters of bells on their bridles; the Lollard William Thorpe scornfully described the "jangling of their Canterbury bells" (in Eng. Garner, ed. Alfred W. Pollard, 1903, 97–104; rpt. Rickert, Ch's World, 264–65); cf. ProNPT VII.2794–97. These bells later gave their name to the flowers called Canterbury Bells (Bowden, Comm. on GP, 111).

172 celle: A monastic establishment subordinate to a great monastery or abbey and governed by a prior or *custos cellae* (keeper of the cell; see Huling E. Ussery, TSE 17, 1969, 1–30). Cf. ProMkT, VII.1935–38.

173 reule: The Benedictine Rule (tr. McCann), written by **Beneit,** St. Benedict (480–c. 550), who was regarded as the father of Western monasticism. His disciple **Maure,** St. Maurus, was believed to have brought the Benedictine Rule to France in 543.

175   Since the construction begun in 173–74 is left unfinished, various interpretations have been offered to avoid the anacoluthon. However, such constructions are common in colloquial speech; cf. CkT I.4391–94.

176 space: Probably "course, direction" (Lat. *spatior,* "to walk"); see MED s.v. *space* 13. Given the possible contrast with *streit* (174), *space* may have one of its more common meanings: "room, space." F. Th. Visser glosses it as "greater liberty" (ES 30, 1949, 84).

177 text: The most likely of a number of possible sources is the *Decretum* of Gratian (cf. Emerson, MP 1, 1904, 105–10), based on St. Jerome's comment on Psalm 90.3 (91.3 in AV): "Esau was a hunter because he was a sinner. And indeed we do not find in holy scripture any virtuous hunter. We do find virtuous fishermen."

   pulled hen: Such indications of worthlessness, most often in the form of a negative comparison (e.g. *nat worth an hen,* WBT III.1112; *nat worth a flye,* FranT V.1132), are common in Chaucer and throughout Middle English; see the index to Whiting, Proverbs, s.v. *not worth.* The construction was influenced by French; see Frederick H. Sykes, Fr. Elements in ME, 1899, 24–39, and note the French parallel to *nat worth an oystre* quoted below (182). For the similar *dere ynough a myte, jane,* etc., see CYT VIII.795n.

180 fissh that is waterlees: A commonplace; cf. Langland, PP C 5.148–51: "Ryht as fisches in the floed whan hem fayleth water/ Dyen for drouthe . . . Ryth so religioun roteth and sterveth/ That out of covent coveteth to dwelle"; Gower, Vox Clam. 4.281–82; tr. Stockton, pp.171–72: "A fish ought not to be out of the water nor ought a monk to be away from his cloister"; Mirour, 20845–51; tr. Wilson, 279; and Whiting F233. Langland attributes it to Pope Gregory I, Gower to Augustine. Ellershaw (Acad, 6 Dec. 1890, 531) finds its earliest use in the *Life of St. Anthony,* which is ascribed to St. Athanasius (c. 296–373).

181–82 cloystre . . . oystre: Skeat (5:22) notes the resemblance, with the meaning reversed, to Jean de Meun, Testament, 1165–67: "Let whosoever wishes to find them [monks] seek them in their cloister . . . . For they do not reckon this world at the value of an oyster."

187 Austyn: St. Augustine of Hippo (354–430) was the reputed author of a monastic rule used by Augustinian canons, though Gower applies it to monks (Mirour, 20845–92; tr. Wilson, 279).

   How shal the world be served: Clergymen frequently took secular employment, a practice too worldly for the Clerk (GP I.292) and condemned by Gower (Mirour, 20245–56; tr. Wilson, 270); see Wyclif, Eng. Works, 212–13: "But an ydiot & a lecherous wrecche shal be sett to kepe the soulis for litel pris, & the more lorel [*greater rascal*] goo on haukynge & hunting, & serve in lordis courtis, in worldly offices." In 1395 a group of Lollards petitioned Parliament to abolish this practice (Engl. Hist. Doc., 4:849). "Chaucer ironically asks how these valuable services are to be rendered if the clergy confine themselves to their religious duties and manual labor" (Robinson).

191 prikyng: Tracking a hare by its pricks, or footprints (OED s.v. *pricking* vb. sb., 2). Baum (PMLA 71:242) finds an obscene pun here. The MED offers no support, and the OED records no obscene meaning of the verb and none of

the noun until 1592 (s.v. *prick* sb. V.17). RvT I.4231 offers no support. Robertson, Pref to Ch, 255, finds an even less likely association with "hare," a traditional symbol of lechery; see FrT III.1327n. Hare hunting was highly esteemed (Manly, CT, 510, cites Machaut, Roy de Navarre, 510–12) and Chaucer refers to it in ShipT VII.104, ProThop VII.696; for a description see Edward, Duke of York, Master of Game, ed. W. A. and F. Baillie-Grohman, 1909, 181–86; rpt. Rickert, Ch's World, 221–23.

194 grys: An expensive gray squirrel fur that was expressly forbidden to all cloistered clergy (Bowden, Commentary on GP, 114; but see also Laura F. Hodges, ChauR 26, 1991, 136–38). See Gower, Mirour 21018; tr. Wilson, 281: "He [a monk] seeks for his use not the hair shirt, but rather the finest woolen materials together with furs vair and gray."

197   The use of such expensive pins by monks was frequently attacked (Bowden, Comm. on GP, 113; Gower, Mirour, 21020–22; tr. Wilson, 281: "Enamelled silver jewelry . . . hangs gaily from his [a monk's] hood in front of his breast").

200 in good poynt: This translates the OF *en bon point.* Manly (CT, 510) compares Mod. Fr. *embonpoint* (stoutness).

201 stepe: Either "large, prominent" (Robinson)—cf. MED s.v. *steōpe* adj. 1 (c.)—or "bright" (Skeat). The Ashmole version of the *Secretum secretorum* (EETS 276, 97) takes eyes "sette high and bolnyng [bulging] out" as a bad sign; if "whirlyng about," they show one to be impatient and "to women and belly plesaunce and lustis all yoven." However, they could also be considered an attractive feature; see 753 below.

203   On monks' fondness for elegant footwear, see Mann, Ch and Estates, 21–23, and Alphabet of Tales, ed. Mary M. Banks, EETS 126, 1904, 9 (an abbot rebuked by a king for his costly shoes).

206 swan: A chicken cost two and a half pence, "but a swan for the earl's dinner cost 6s., and for the judge's dinner 7s." (Ramona Bressie, MLN 54, 1939, 488). The Benedictine Rule forbade monks to eat the flesh of quadrupeds (Heinrich Gilmeister, NM 69, 1968, 224–25).

207 broun as is a berye: Cf. CkT I.4368 and Whiting B259.

The Friar

The Notes on the Friar are adapted from those written by Janette Richardson for The Riverside Chaucer.

The mendicant orders founded in the first half of the thirteenth century are represented by the friar of The Summoner's Tale as well as the pilgrim Hubert. Both reflect common charges directed against the orders in the extended controversy that resulted from the friars' early modification of their founders' ideal of apostolic poverty and from their competition with the secular clergy as preachers and confessors. See Arnold Williams, Spec 28, 1953, 499–513.

Manly's identification of the Friar as a Franciscan (New Light, 104) has been questioned by John Fleming (JEGP 65, 1966, 688–700), who is probably correct in asserting that Chaucer's satire is not limited to a specific order. That Faus Semblant in the *Roman de la rose* (see RomC 6082–7696) is a literary ancestor of the Friar has long been recognized, and such matters as the Friar's winning speech and fine clothing, as well as his abuses of his office, were traditional in later satire of the orders (Mann, Ch and Estates, 37–54; Bowden, Comm. on GP, 119–45).

208 wantowne: "jovial, light-hearted." Later references to the Friar's association with women, however, suggest that "lascivious" is also appropriate.

209 lymytour: Each convent had its own assigned limits (for begging), and these districts were sometimes subdivided into smaller "limitations."

210 ordres foure: The four orders were the Carmelites, Augustinians, Jacobites or Iacobites (Dominicans), and Minorites (Franciscans), the first letters of which formed, according to antifraternal satirists, the word CAIM (the medieval spelling of Cain). Skeat, PP Creed, EETS 17, 1866, 47–48.

212–13 Although providing dowry was a charitable act (N. R. Havely, ChauR 13, 1979, 339–40), these lines are generally thought to refer to finding husbands for victims of the Friar's own seduction; cf. WBT III.880–81.

214 Cf. the phrase, "a pillar of the church," MED s.v. *pilere* n. 1.(b), and Galatians 2.9: "James and Cephas and John, who were acknowledged pillars." Richardson (Blameth Nat Me, 71) and others find a phallic pun on **post.**

216 For **frankeleyns,** see GP I.331–60.

219 power of confessioun: Friars were sometimes given special penitential commissions not entrusted to local parish priests (Williams, SP 57:477); cf. RomC 6364–65: "I may assoile and I may shryve,/ That no prelat may lette me."

220 licentiat: A papal bull of 1300, Boniface VIII's *Super cathedram,* required the orders to specify which of their friars could be licensed as confessors.

233–34 Wycliffites (Wyclif, Eng. Works, 638) complained that friars carry knives, pins, and other small goods "for women . . . to gete love of hem, and to have many giftis for little good or nought." Max Förster, Archiv 135, 1916, 401, prints a scrap of verse: "Fratres cum knyvis goth about and swivyt [=swiveth, copulate with] mens wyvis."

237 yeddyng: defined in the *Promptorium parvulorum* (EETS e.s. 102, 548) as "geeste (romawnce)." See RomC 7457–58: "Her order wickedly they beren,/ Suche mynstrelles if they weren."

239 champioun: In certain cases in English law a final appeal could be made to a trial by battle, in which the two parties or their representatives (champions) would determine the case by the ordeal of battle. The theory was that God would assure victory to the rightful side. Such judicial duels were common in the fourteenth century, and Chaucer frequently alludes to them; cf. KnT I.1713, MLT II.631, FrT III.1662, ParsT X.698. The right to an appeal to arms remained a part of English law, at least in theory, until the early nineteenth century. See William A. Nielson, Trial by Battle, 1890.

241–42 In **tappestere** and probably in **beggestere** the suffix *stere* (OE *estre*) has its proper feminine signification, as in the Modern English "spinster"; so also doubtless in *hoppesteres* (KnT I.2017), *chidestere* (MerT IV.1535), and *tombesteres* and *frutesteres* (PardT VI.477–78). But the distinction of gender was often lost in early English (Robinson).

244–45 By contrast, ministering to *lazars* (lepers) specifically was what St. Francis practiced (Bowden, Comm. on GP, 129).

250 The line echoes line 99 almost exactly.

252a–b This couplet is found in only a few MSS. Williams (SP 57:478) suggests that it may have been canceled because of inaccuracy: No English records show that friars paid a fee (*ferme*) for rights, exclusive or otherwise, to operate within a district, or "limitation."

254 In principio: Gen. 1.1 ("In the beginning God created Heaven and earth") and John 1.1 ("In the beginning was the Word"). Here the reference is to the latter, since the first fourteen verses of this Gospel were popular for devotions (Robert A. Law, PMLA 37, 1922, 208–13) and were often used by friars when entering a home. The verses were also thought to have magical power, especially against demons (Morton W. Bloomfield, MLN 70, 1955, 559–65).

256 purchase, rente: A proverbial comparison (Whiting P438; cf. RomC 6838: "My purchace is bettir than my rente"), implying ill-gotten gains. Cf. FrT III.1451.

257 rage: The word has sexual connotations; see Douglas Moffat, NM 94 (1993), 167–84, and cf. MilT I.3273 and RvT I.3958.

258 love-dayes: Occasions for reconciliation and settlement of disputes out of court. For historical instances and protests against abuses practiced by the arbitrators, see Josephine Waters Bennett, Spec 33, 1958, 351–70, and Thomas J. Heffernan, ChauR 10, 1975, 174–76.

261 maister: Presumably Master of Arts (cf. SumT III.2185–88), a degree that was "of considerable dignity and was obtained only after lavish expenditure of money" (Robinson), but see introductory note to the portrait of the Clerk.

262 semycope: This vestment was a specific topic in the dispute of the early 1380s between Richard Maidstone, a Carmelite, and John Ashwardby, a Wycliffite (Arnold Williams, MP 54, 1956, 117–18).

264 he lisped: Laura Kendrick (Bulletin des Anglicistes Medievistes 50, 1996, 37–57) attributes the lisp to an attempt to produce a "francophone lisp," though the use of *th* for *s* is not involved.

269 Huberd: According to Manly (Tales, 513), the name is not common in English records of the fourteenth century. Why it was chosen for the only pilgrim named in the Prologue besides the Prioress is unknown. It has been suggested that the association of St. Hubert with hunting lends resonance to the name, particularly in relation to the Monk (see Warren Ginsberg, ChauR 21, 1986, 53–57, and Gaye Thiek, Paragon 10, 1992, 95–101).

The Merchant

The Notes on the Merchant are adapted from those written by M. Teresa Tavormina for The Riverside Chaucer.

In Chaucer's day, the term *merchant* applied primarily to wholesale exporters and importers, dealers in such commodities as wool, cloth, and wine. The Merchants of the Staple, exporters of wool, woolfells, and skins, were perhaps the most important single group of fourteenth-century English merchants, but the

Merchant Adventurers, who dealt in cloth and other items, were gaining power throughout the period. The activities of English merchants in international trade involved them in the flow of bullion into and out of the country—a matter of special concern to the Crown, given its frequent need of capital for the Hundred Years War and the rapid inflation and growing money economy of the time. The large scale of the merchants' operations also enabled them to act as moneylenders to the king and other magnates. See Edith Rickert (MP 24, 1926, 111–19, 249–56), who supplies details drawn from the account book of Gilbert Maghfeld, a powerful London merchant from whom Chaucer apparently borrowed money and whom she proposes as a possible model for the Merchant. Other links between Chaucer's personal background and his description of the Merchant have also been noted: Chaucer's father was himself a merchant with family roots in Ipswich, near Orwell, the English port mentioned in the portrait, and Chaucer's own work at the custom house would have brought him into close contact with many important merchants.

The portrait also matches traditional satiric and homiletic descriptions of the merchant class (Mann, Ch and Estates, 99–103). Typical elements in such descriptions are accusations of avarice, deceit, and usury; to a lesser extent, one finds allegations of self-important behavior and of the concealment of debts. Opinions on how sharp or explicit a critique Chaucer intends in the Merchant's portrait have ranged from defenses of the Merchant's financial dealings as normal business operations to suggestions that even his garb and bearing may signify moral flaws. Compare Chaucer's characterization of the merchant of Saint Denis in The Shipman's Tale.

270 **forked berd:**   A mark of fashion; the portraits of Chaucer show him wearing such a beard (see frontispiece). Beards were, however, going out of fashion with younger men (see MerT IV.1825).

271 **mottelee:** Variegated or parti-colored cloth, often in a figured design. Thomas A. Knott (PQ 1, 1922, 9–10) shows that parti-colored and figured garments were customarily worn by members of various London guilds and companies on such occasions and notes that the Merchants of the Staple wore a distinctive livery.

    hye on horse: Perhaps implying ostentation; see MED, s.v. *heighe* adv. 1b.

272 **Flaundryssh bever hat:**   Beaver-skin hats were sufficiently elegant to have been worn by the upper nobility and by important officials in formal processions (Rickert, MP 24:249; Manly, CT, 514). Kenneth S. Cahn (SAC 2, 1980, 93–94) argues that the hat suggests the Merchant's familiarity with Flanders, where he probably engaged in trade and foreign exchange.

275 Constant talk of one's profits was a fault stereotypically attributed to merchants; Mann (Ch and Estates, 101) quotes Gower, Mirour 25360–63; tr. Wilson: "[Fraud] has a very keen nose when he checks the staple of the wool, for he is now dealing with and talking of his own profit."

276 **kept for any thyng:** Pirates and foreign privateers were a genuine threat to English sea trade, and powerful merchants such as Gilbert Maghfeld were sometimes charged with the "keeping of the sea" (Rickert, MP 24:112).

277 **Middelburgh:** A Dutch port on the island of Walcheren, opposite the English port of Orwell. Middelburg was the foreign staple port (the port through which wool was allowed to be exported) from 1384 to 1388. If Chaucer's Merchant is a Merchant of the Staple, this line suggests a date of composition for the portrait not much later than 1388 (John W. Hales, Folia Litteraria, 1893, 100), though Knott (PQ 1:6) observes that wool could be and was exported to Middelburg by royal license in other years as well. Moreover, Chaucer's character may be one of the Merchant Adventurers, who made Middelburg their headquarters from 1384 to 1444 (Manly, New Light, 186–90; see also DiMarco, RBPH 56:650–55). Middelburg was near Bruges, the Flemish banking center, where the Merchant could have carried out some of his transactions.

278 **sheeldes:**   = OF *escu.* but here it probably refers to the Flemish *ecu,* a fictional "money of account," valued at 24 silver groats in real Flemish currency (Cahn, SAC 2:85). The Merchant's sale or exchange of foreign currency was for a long time taken as an illegal activity (Knott, PQ 1:10–11). B. A. Park, however, observes that some forms of exchange were lawful and in fact common in international commercial circles (ELN 1, 1964, 168–70). Seemingly legal exchanges could conceal usury, and it is still often argued that traffic in foreign currency, even when technically legal, was associated with dubious business practices (Mann, Ch and Estates, 100).

280 Cahn (SAC 2:118) notes that a regular seller of shields would regularly be in debt, and would thus need to take special care to seem like a good credit risk—prosperous, dignified, and debt-free (cf. ShipT VII.289–90). See ShipT VII.230–34 and n. for merchants who go on pilgrimages to escape their creditors (though that is not necessarily the case here).

282 **bargaynes . . . chevyssaunce:**   Although the literal senses of these words are value-neutral, the terms can connote improper financial dealings; *chevyssaunce* is often associated with usury, though the *Promptorium parvulorum* (EETS e.s. 102, 80) glosses it as *providencia* (resource, remedy, shift; cf. MED s.v. *chevisaunce* n. 2, 6).

284 The Merchant's anonymity has been taken as a sign of Chaucer's tact or scorn (Manly, CT, 515), but it may be an authenticating detail: for the author not to know a pilgrim's name implies that he in fact has one.

The Clerk

The Notes on the Clerk are adapted from those written by Warren S. Ginsberg for The Riverside Chaucer.

The word *clerk* generally denoted any man who could read or write, that is, any man of learning, and specifically an ecclesiastic, whether a student or a man in holy orders; see MED s.v. *clerk.* Education at Oxford and Cambridge was primarily intended as preparation for the priesthood; ultimately, however, many graduates were not ordained (see 291–92 below).

A student normally entered the university at fourteen or fifteen and completed his undergraduate studies about four years later (see 286 below). The student, now called a bachelor, could study three more years and receive the M. A. He would be twenty or twenty-one years old when he became a master.

Bachelors and masters were expected to teach as well as study; for the curriculum, privileges, and duties of both undergraduates and advanced students at Oxford, as well as other relevant matters, see James A. Weisheipl, MS 26, 1964, 143–85. On life at medieval Oxford, see Rickert, Ch's World, 128–36, and Bennett, Ch at Oxford.

The Clerk is usually taken as an ideal figure, though some (e.g., Warren S. Ginsberg, Criticism 20, 1978, 307–23) find a note of ambiguity amid the general approbation. The Clerk certainly does not indulge in the vices exemplified by the Clerk in The Miller's Tale (I.3200–20). Chaucer stresses the Clerk's devotion to learning, even if we hear nothing of the ultimate purpose of that study, knowledge of how to please God (Mann, Ch and Estates, 76).

The Clerk has often been identified with well-known schoolmen of Chaucer's time. Most possible models were associated with Merton College, probably including Ralph Strode (whom Chaucer names at the end of *Troilus;* see Bennett, Ch at Oxford, 58–85).

286 logyk: The most important course of study of the Trivium (grammar, rhetoric, logic), the basic curriculum of the (generally) four-year undergraduate education. The Quadrivium (arithmetic, geometry, astronomy, music) provided the basic curriculum that led, usually in three years, to the master of arts. Both curricula stressed the study of Aristotle and logic.

290 thredbare: Cf. GP I.260.

291–92 The Clerk has not been offered an ecclesiastical living (**benefice**), which would require him to perform the pastoral duties of a priest, yet he would not accept secular employment (**office**) as a secretary or member of a government office. Benefices were of two kinds, ecclesiastical and academic. The ecclesiastical benefice required its recipient to be in orders; many logicians at Oxford, however, put off entering even minor orders until a benefice was assured. After the Black Death the pattern of distributing ecclesiastical livings worsened for university graduates (William J. Courtenay, Spec, 1980, 712). Some ecclesiastical livings were available, partly because priests who had benefices flocked "in Londoun to dwelle/ And synge ther for symonye while selver is so swete" (PP B Pro 83–84). They would hire substitute curates to discharge the parish duties and pay them as little as possible, in order to keep the rest of the parish income for themselves; cf. the Parson, who would *sette nat his benefice to hyre* (GP 507). Such positions were available, but to accept one (see Wyclif, Eng. Works, 250) effectively ended one's intellectual activity: "& whan thei schulen most profit in her lernynge than schulle thei be clepid hom at the prelates will." Mann (Ch and Estates, 83) suggests that the Clerk is waiting for an academic benefice. Academic benefices were given for study leading to the doctorate of divinity (ten years after the master's) or of canon law (eight years) (William A. Pantin, Eng. Church in the 14th cent., 1955, 108). To be eligible, the Clerk would have to have studied more than Aristotle and his logic, whether he acquired that knowledge at Oxford or at Padua.

294 Twenty bookes: Because large personal libraries were unusual, the size of the Clerk's collection has drawn much

comment, even though Chaucer says (Pro LGW G 273) he owned "sixty bokes olde and newe." Prices of books varied greatly, but the average cost of a volume of Aristotle was about two pounds; each book might have cost the Clerk three times his annual income (Wilbur Lang Schramm, MLN 48, 1933, 145). The Clerk, however, does not have twenty books; he would "rather have them."

clad in blak or reed: Perhaps a tag meaning "of all forms," "in any kind of cover," rather than sumptuously bound volumes (cf MED s.v. *blak,* adj. 2b: *blak and broun;* also *blak or whit,* adj. lb). Bennett (Ch at Oxford, 13) says that by the turn of the fourteenth century, Oxford bindings were usually white.

296 gay sautrie: Cf. MilT I.3213.

297 philosophre: Chaucer puns on "philosopher" and the other sense of the word, "alchemist" (CYT VIII. 1427). The study of philosophy has not brought the Clerk the "philosopher's stone," which transmutes base metals into gold. This is one of the few puns in Chaucer that Robinson accepted; he noted "other more or less clear cases of word-play" in line 514 below, SumT III.1916–17, 1934, WBPro III.837–38, SqT V.105–6, CYT VIII.730. Critics have since found many more (cf. Paull F. Baum, PMLA 71, 1956, 225–46, and PMLA 73, 1958, 167–70). However, many of the puns proposed depend on meanings not attested in Chaucer's time and it is often difficult to determine whether or not a pun is intentional. See Archibald A. Hill (66–78 in Caroline Duncan-Rose and Theo Vennemann, eds., On Language: Rhetorica, Phonologica, Syntactica, 1988), who advises caution: "Puns are usually to be rejected unless there is evidence supporting them. That is, meaning is innocent unless proved double."

299–302 Students who were aided by contributions from friends and family were familiar figures. See MilT I.3220, PP C 6.36 ("My fader and my frendes foende [=found, provided the means] me to scole"). Clerks who received support were obliged to pray for the souls of their benefactors (Mann, Ch and Estates, 81–82).

305 forme and reverence: The word *forme* would have particular resonance for a schoolman. Requirements at Oxford were *pro forma* or *secundam formam.* The term, borrowed from Roman law, here conveyed the idea of a legal norm, pattern, or standard of specification. The Clerk's speech conforms to the established rules.

307 Sownynge in moral vertu: Candidates for both the B. A. and the M. A. were examined on their "knowledge and their morals" (Weisheipl, MS 26:157, 163).

308 gladly . . . lerne and gladly teche: Similar expressions are common in Latin, e.g., Seneca: "gaudeo discere, ut doceam" (I rejoice to learn, that I might teach; Chandler B. Beale, ELN 13, 1974, 81–86). Chauncey Wood (ELN 4, 1967, 166–72) cites *Roman de la rose* (7099–7103; tr. Dahlberg, 135), where Plato is said to have taught that man was given speech "to make our desires known, for teaching, and for learning."

The Sergeant of the Law

The Notes on the Sergeant of the Law are adapted from those written by Patricia J. Eberle for The Riverside Chaucer.

Sergeants were the most prestigious and powerful lawyers of Chaucer's time; they ranked above esquires and were the equals of knights. Their group, called the Order of the Coif, was small (only twenty-one sergeants were created during Richard II's reign), chosen from among the most accomplished apprentices who had spent at least sixteen years studying and practicing law. They had exclusive rights to plead cases in the Court of Common Pleas, and all judges were chosen from this group. Their lengthy education presupposed a wealthy background, and their profession was lucrative. Although satirists such as Gower (Mirour 24181–24624; tr. Wilson, 316–22; Vox Clam. 6.1–5) attack their wealth as evidence of greed, Sir John Fortescue (1394–1476), in his classic account of the order of sergeants, *De laudibus legum Angliae* (1.468–71 Ch.L, ed. S. B. Chrimes, 1942 [rpt.1979], trans. as *On the Laws and Governance of England,* ed. Shelley Lockwood, 1997, 72), cites their prosperity as evidence of the preeminence justly accorded to their expert knowledge of English common law.

Critical opinion has traditionally viewed the portrait as satiric (Bowden, Comm. on GP, 165–72, citing parallels with Wyclif, Eng. Works, 234, 237–38, and Langland, PP C 2.63–64). However, Isobel McKenna (RUO 45, 1975, 244), citing evidence from legal history, sees the sergeant as a "model of excellence" for his profession. Mann (Ch and Estates, 86–91) points out that Chaucer omits traditional censures of greed or dishonesty and instead notes lesser faults, such as the sergeant's desire to appear *bisi* (321) and *wise* (313).

Chaucer may have studied law at the Inner Temple (see p. xvi and the introductory note on the Manciple, below). He certainly had first-hand experience with sergeants in the course of various kinds of litigation in which he was involved.

Manly suggests (New Light, 147–57) that the word *pynche* (326) involves a pun on the name of Thomas Pynchbek, a sergeant who often served as justice of assize between 1376 and 1388 and who was known for his acquisition of land, as well as for his learning; in 1388, as chief baron of the Exchequer, he signed a writ for Chaucer's arrest in a case of debt. (See also W. F. Bolton, MP 84, 1987, 401–7).

310 Parvys: The portico of a church (cf. RomC 7108: "Biforne Oure Lady, at parvys") but here usually understood to mean the portico in front of St. Paul's Cathedral. Fortescue (On the Laws, tr. Lockwood, 75) says that clients were accustomed to consult sergeants "at the Parvys" (Lat. *ad pervisam*); cf. Robbins, Sec. Lyrics, No. 59: "If thou have aut to do with the lawe to plete/ At London at the parvis many on will the rehete [help you]."

314 justice . . . in assise: Only a sergeant of law could serve as justice in the assizes (Edward H. Warren, Va. Law Rev. 28, 1942, 914). These were originally courts held in the various counties to determine questions of land tenure, but by Chaucer's time assizes heard all civil cases originating in the counties over which they had jurisdiction.

315 patente: (Lat. *patere,* to be open). An open letter of appointment from the king; **pleyn commissioun** authorizes jurisdiction in all cases (Bowden, Comm. on GP, 167); see also McKenna (RUO 45:53–54), who argues that **patente** refers to special status as king's sergeant, ranked above the solicitor general and with special powers as counsel to the king.

317 fees and robes: The phrase reflects the Latin formula, *cum robes et feodis,* used to designate recurrent payments of clothing and money; cf. MED *robe* n. 1.(c). A king's sergeant typically received from the king a salary of twenty pounds yearly, plus a robe at Christmas (McKenna, RUO 45:256).

318–20 Transactions involving property were a special province of sergeants, who were often engaged as *purchasours* of land for a client. Purchasing land required obtaining a writ, and the process often involved litigation to remove entails, or legal conditions, limiting the right to dispose of a property (David Mellinkoff, Lang. of Law, 1963, 108). The most desirable writ was **fee symple** (Lat. *infeodo simpliciter*), which granted the right to sell, transfer, or bequeath property directly. Moralists such as Gower charged that sergeants often purchased land for themselves (Vox Clam., 6.2; Mirour, 24537–40; tr. Wilson, 321: "Nowadays the lawyer—however poor he may be at first—will very soon thereafter have so much wealth that everything appears too limited for him to purchase for himself alone"). Mann (Ch and Estates, 88–89) argues (against Manly, New Light, 131–57) that lines 318–20 leave ambiguous whether the Sergeant is acting for his client or for himself.

323–24 Reports of cases in the Court of Common Pleas (now called Year Books), probably made for the use of sergeants, were called **termes,** because the reports were ordered under headings according to law terms, the main divisions of the legal year. Although popular opinion may have assumed that the Year Books extended as far back as William I's reign (1066–87), extant manuscripts begin with Edward I (1272).

326 pynche: Cases could be dismissed because of a flaw in the wording of a writ (Albert K. R. Kiraify, A Source Book of Eng. Law, 1957, 49). Manly believed this was a pun on the name Pynchbek (see introductory note).

327 Although this is doubtless an exaggerated description of his memory, sergeants were, nevertheless, regarded as the preeminent authorities on the statutes; they were frequently summoned to Parliament to resolve difficult questions of law (Warren, Va. Law Rev. 28:914).

328 medlee: A cloth of one color or of different tones of one color, made of wool dyed before being spun, it was usually not worn by classes above the rank of knight (M. C. Linthicum, JEGP 34, 1935, 39–41). The Sergeant's *hoomly,* unpretentious dress does not indicate his official status; no mention is made of the white coif (a close-fitting cap) characteristic of his order, though the Ellesmere illumination depicts his white coif and a short, parti-colored gown, which seems to have been the official traveling costume for sergeants (see McKenna, RUO 45:258).

The Franklin

The Notes on the Franklin are adapted from those written by R T. Lenaghan for The Riverside Chaucer.

The Franklin was a provincial gentleman, an early example of the English country squire. His offices and appointments were commonly held by men of that rank (Noel Denholm-Young, Country Gentry in 14th Cent., 1969; Kenneth B. McFarlane,

Nobility of Later Med. Eng., 1973, 268–78). For a thorough discussion of the Franklin's particular situation, see Henrik Specht, Ch's Franklin in CT, Pubs. of the Dept. of Eng., Univ. of Copenhagen 10, 1981, though his conclusions have been challenged (see introductory note to the Franklin's Tale).

John M. Manly proposes a Lincolnshire knight, Sir John Bussy, as the possible historical model for Chaucer's Franklin (New Light, 162–68). Bussy was a neighbor of Thomas Pynchbek, whom Manly proposes as the historical model for the description of the Franklin's companion, the Man of Law (New Light, 151–57). Caroline D. Eckhardt (MP 87, 1990, 239–48) shows that Vavasour was a family name, probably known to Chaucer, and she speculates that the Franklin may to some degree reflect a contemporary member of that family.

Bowden presents the Franklin as a straightforward exemplar of the social type (Comm. on GP, 172–77), but there is disagreement about his social and intellectual sophistication, mainly based on the critic's interpretation of The Franklin's Tale. In one reading he is intelligent and dignified, linked by some of the biographical details with Chaucer himself (Roland Blenner-Hasset, Spec 28, 1953, 791–92); in another, satiric reading he is ignorant, even corrupt, like others of the moneyed "middle class" (Robertson, Pref. to Ch, 276), and insecure in his social position (Robert B. Burlin, Neophil 51, 1967, 55–59). Mann considers the details of the Franklin's description in the context of a number of satiric texts and differentiates Chaucer's treatment as nonsatiric (Ch and Estates, 152–59).

332 dayesye: The English daisy (*Bellis perennis*) often affords marked contrasts of red and white (cf. Pro F LGW 42–43: "Thanne love I most thise floures white and rede,/ Swiche as men callen daysyes"), which make it especially appropriate for the ruddy, white-bearded Franklin.

333 Complexioun: An individual's temperament, or "complexion," was thought to be formed by the four humors of the body (see 420 below). The idea of medieval medicine was to keep the humors in balance, but in each individual one humor tends to dominate. A **sangwyn** person (cf. KnT I.2168) like the Franklin is ruddy in complexion, dominated by blood, and loves "Joye and laghynge . . . he shal be . . . of good will and wythout malice . . . he shall haue a good stomake, good dygescion . . . he shall be fre and liberall." The phlegmatic temperament (dominated by phlegm) is "slowe sadde . . . piteuouse, chaste, and [shall] lytill desyre company of women." The choleric (cf. 587 below), dominated by choler or red bile, is "lene of body . . . hasty of worde and of answere; he lovyth hasty vengeaunce; Desyrous of company of women moore than hym nedyth." The melancholy temperament, dominated by black bile, "sholde bene pensyf and slowe . . . of sotile ymagynacion as of hand-werkys" (Secreta secretorum, EETS e.s. 74, 219–20).

334 sop in wyn: A light breakfast consisting of bits of bread in wine; cf. MerT IV.1843.

336 Epicurus owene sone: "He was, as we should say, an epicure. The philosophy of Epicurus was associated (somewhat unjustly) then as now with luxurious living" (Robinson). Cf. Bo 3.pr2.78–80 ("Epicurus . . . juggid/ and establissyde that delyt is the soverayn good") and MerT

IV.2021–25. On medieval ideas of Epicureanism, see Robert P. Miller, Medievalia 6, 1980, 151–86.

340 Seint Julian: Julian the Hospitaller, a mythical saint associated with hospitality (see Legenda aurea, tr. Ryan I:126–30).

347 sondry sesons: Medieval medical theory held that seasonal adjustment of the diet would maintain a healthy balance of the humors (cf. 435–37 below): Barth. Angl., 6.20; tr. Trevisa 1:324: "Also in fedinge men take hede to covanabilnesse of tyme, for men nedeth gretter and largere diete in winter thanne in somer." Mann, on the other hand, sees this as a gourmet's pleasure in seasonal variety (Ch and Estates, 279 n. 30). She notes (p. 279, n. 29), "Nearly all Chaucer's uses of the word 'sauce' seem to occur in a context of gluttony satire: CT VI.545 VII.2834, Former Age 16."

351–52 As a context for such a cuisine and for sauces in particular, see Two Fifteenth-Cent. Cookery-Bks., EETS 91, viii and index. John Russell's *Book of Nurture* lists the menu for a Franklin's feast (The Babee's Book, EETS 235, 32–37).

353 table dormant: A table left in place and thus differentiated from a table set up in the hall and taken down after use. The Franklin takes his meals in the hall; Peter J. Lucas, N&Q 232, 1987, 291–92, notes that it was becoming common for lords to take their meals in private; he cites Piers Plowman B 10.98–100: "Now hath eche riche [*rich man*] a reule—to eten by hymselve/ In a pryvee parlor for povre mennes sake [*to avoid poor men*]/ Or in a chambre with a chimnee and leve the chief halle." Lucas suggests the Franklin is here praised for retaining the old-fashioned ways.

355 sessiouns ther . . . lord and sire: He presided at judicial sessions, presumably as a justice of the peace. It is also possible, since *sessioun* has a more general sense and the sessions were *ther* in the Franklin's hall, that he presided as a feudal lord like the one in the SumT III.2162–67. Chaucer was a justice of the peace in Kent in 1386–89 (see p. xx).

356 knyght of the shire: Member of Parliament. Chaucer was knight of the shire for Kent in 1386 (see pp. xx–xxi).

357 anlaas and . . . gipser: Sumptuary legislation (see 115 above) and church monuments indicate that the dagger and purse marked a gentleman's social standing (Specht, Ch's Franklin, 119–23).

359 shirreve: The sheriff was the principal officer of the Crown in a shire.

contour: An officer charged as an accountant to oversee the collecting and auditing of taxes in a shire. (The term can also refer to one who pleads in court, a lawyer, but that is not the case here.)

360 vavasour: A term of feudal tenancy, literally the vassal of vassals, in Romance usage the lowest rank of nobility (Marc Bloch, Feudal Society, tr. L. A. Manyon, 1961, 177, 322). P. R. Coss reviews both literary and legal use of the term (Lit. and Soc. Terminology: The Vavasour, in Soc. Relations and Ideas. ed. T. H. Aston et al., 1983, 109–50). The primary reference may be literary. In romances vavasours often have a status appropriate to provincial gentlemen (see Roy J. Pearcy, ChauR 8, 1973, 33–59, and the study by Specht cited above). Eckhardt (MP 87:239–48) notes it is the name of a family known to Chaucer.

The Five Guildsmen

Each Guildsman represents a different trade, chosen tactfully, Ernest P. Kuhl argues (TWA, 18, 1916, 652–75), from trades that remained neutral in the political struggles among the London crafts at this time. Their great *fraternitee* is probably not one of the craft guilds, which were usually composed of practitioners of a single trade. Instead, they are probably members of one of the parish guilds, fraternal and charitable organizations that were then gaining power. Thomas Jay Garbáty (JEGP 69, 1960, 691–709) makes a strong case for identifying this fraternity with the guild of St. Botolph's in Aldersgate, but such identifications can be only speculative.

Some critics read the description of the Guildsmen as a satiric attack on middle-class pretensions (e.g., Gerald Morgan, ES 59, 1978, 481–98). Mann notes that the Guildsmen have none of the traditional mercantile vices, such as fraud, usury, and avarice (Ch and Estates, 104). Chaucer seems more amused than indignant at their bustling self-importance.

363 lyveree: The members of each guild were entitled to wear its distinctive attire, usually a cape and hood, on ceremonial occasions.

366–67   Skeat (5:36) noted that the sumptuary law of 1363 (see 115 above) forbade the use of silver ornamentation to ordinary tradesmen, and Morgan (ES 59:494) regards the Guildsmen's silver-mounted knives as a satiric detail. However, the law (which had been repealed) specifically allowed such ornamentation to "Merchants, Citizens and Burgesses, artificers, people of handy-craft" who had property to the value of five hundred pounds, a criterion these prosperous would-be aldermen probably met.

370 a yeldehalle: The guildhall was the seat of municipal government; the mayor and aldermen, the highest ranking civic officials, sat on the **deys** (dais). The use of the indefinite article *a* indicates that the reference is not necessarily to the Guildhall in London.

371–73   An alderman was required to be "wise and discreet in mind, rich, honest, trustworthy, and free" (*Liber Albus,* 29). None of the trades of these Guildsmen was represented in the aldermancy of London for another hundred years (Kuhl, TWA 18:652–757).

376 "madame":   Aldermen's wives were accorded this title (see Thrupp, Merchant Class, 18). The *Liber Albus* styles aldermen "barons" (45) and claims that as late as 1350 aldermen were buried with baronial honors (29).

377 vigilies: Skeat (5:37) quotes Speght's note: "It was the manner in time past, upon festival events, called vigiliae, for parishioners to meet in their church-houses or church-yards and there to have a drinking fit for the time.... Hither came the wives in comely manner, and they that were of the better sort had their mantles carried before them, as well for show as to keep them from cold at the table." Cf. WBPro III.555–59.

   goon ... bifore: cf. 449–51 below.

The Cook

The Notes on the Cook are adapted from those written by Douglas Gray for The Riverside Chaucer.

The Cook's portrait is "a concoction of culinary superlatives," telling us nothing of his personality, "except what is suggested by his knowledge of London ale" (Donaldson, 891). The reference to his ulcerous sore is startlingly dramatic. Langland (PP B Pr 225–26) gives a vivid picture: "Cokes and hire knaves cryden 'Hote pies, hote!/ Goode gees and gris [piglets]! Go we dyne, go we!'" Mann (Ch and Estates, 163) thinks this may have been a stimulus for Chaucer's description.

In his prologue (I.4336) the Cook calls himself *Hogge* (a nickname for Roger; see CkPro I.4345). Edith Rickert (TLS, 20 Oct. 1932, 761) discovered a contemporary Roger Knight de Ware of London, Cook. He may be the same Roger Knight de Ware, Cook, named in a plea of debt in 1384–85. Earl D. Lyon (MLN 52, 1937, 491–94) finds a reference (probably 1373) to a Roger de Ware, Cook, accused of being a common night-walker, i.e., one who broke curfew. On cooks in medieval England, see Bowden, Comm. on GP, 185–89. Curry (Ch and Science, 37–53) discusses the medical aspects of the characterization.

379 for the nones: Probably "for the occasion." He was a shopkeeper (cf. CkPro I.4352), who had been engaged to cook meals for the Guildsmen on their pilgrimage.

381 poudre-marchant tart: A sharp spice or flavoring powder (Two Fifteenth-Cent. Cookery-Bks, EETS 91, 25; Curye on Inglysch, EETS, SS 8, 208).

   galyngale: A sweet spice, the powdered root of sweet cyperus (a sedge of the genus *Cyperus*), resembling ginger; see Curye on Inglysch, EETS, SS 8, 190.

382   London ale was stronger and more expensive than other varieties. An ability to judge its quality was important, and each London ward elected "the Aleconners of the ward" to determine if each batch brewed was "so good as it was wont to be" (*Liber Albus,* 277, 312).

384 mortreux: These could be "mortrewes de Fleyssh" (meat) or "mortrewes of Fysshe" (Two Fifteenth-Cent. Cookery-Bks, 14, xliii). The first is made of finely ground pork seasoned with saffron, salt, and ginger mixed with ale, egg yolks, and bread, the other of chopped boiled fish seasoned with sugar, salt, and ginger.

386 mormal: (Fr. *mortmal*), defined in the Cyrurgie of Guy de Chauliac, EETS 265, 333, as "a filthy scabbe." It is a species of dry scabbed ulcer, gangrenous rather than cancerous. Curry, Ch and Science, 47–52, quotes Bernardus de Gordon: "*Malum mortuum* is a species of scabies, which arises from corrupted natural melancholia . . . the marks of it are large pustules of a leaden or black color, scabbed, and exceedingly fetid. . . . In appearance it is most unsightly, coming out on the hip-bone and often on the shin-bones." The authorities Curry cites attribute mormals to generally intemperate or unclean habits. See also Haldeen Braddy, who argues that it is a runny, not a dry, sore (MLQ 7, 1946, 265–67). Bennett (Ch at Oxford, 8) finds a reference to a cook with a mormal in the early rolls of Merton College.

387 blankmanger: A kind of thick stew or mousse made of chopped chicken or fish, richly spiced (cf. Two Fifteenth-Cent. Cookery-Bks., EETS 91, 85).

The Shipman

The Notes on the Shipman are adapted from those written by J. A. Burrow and V. J. Scattergood for The Riverside Chaucer.

Shipmen are rare in previous literature, and in the absence of any obvious literary stereotype, scholars have sought to identify the Shipman with individual fourteenth-century sailors from the *weste* of England (388), particularly from *Dertemouthe* (389), though Chaucer perhaps mentions Dartmouth (Devon) simply because it was a notorious haunt of pirates (Bowden, Comm. on GP, 192–93). P. Q. Karkeek (Essays on Chaucer 5, Ch Soc, 1884) pointed out records of a ship called the *Maudelayne* (410), sailing out of Dartmouth; in 1391 the master was Peter Risshenden. Manly identified Risshenden with Piers Risselden, involved with the famous buccaneer John Hawley in the controversial capture of three foreign wine-ships in 1386, an action that resulted in a court case lasting until 1394 (New Light, 169–81). But Margaret Galway (MLR 34, 1939, 497–514) noted the Shipman's similarities in career and character to John Piers, who lived *fer by weste* (though at Teignmouth, not Dartmouth), went on expeditions to Bordeaux, and in 1383 captured a ship called the *Magdeleyn*.

390 rouncy: Perhaps "hackney" or "nag,"; MED s.v. *rounci* n. (c.) "pack horse, work horse." The Ellesmere MS portrait shows the Shipman riding something similar to a cart horse.

395 good felawe: The phrase means "drinking companion," "regular guy" (MED s.v. *felaue* n.) but is used by Chaucer with connotations of rascality; cf. GP I.650 and 648, and FrT III.1385.

396–97 The Shipman apparently stole wine, perhaps by drawing some from each barrel in the cargo or, as Margaret R. Stobie (PMLA 64, 1949, 565–69) holds, by misappropriation of the "courtesy-wine" merchants were required to supply for crews. A Latin poem laments the thieving habits of sailors: "Sailors and peasants, who used to be honest, are so corrupted by fraud that hardly one of them is upright" (Mann, Ch and Estates, 171). Bordeaux (**Burdeux**), in English Gascony, was a great source of imported wine.

399–400 "He drowned his prisoners" (Robinson). Bowden notes that Edward III drowned the crew of a captured ship and does not seem to have been criticized for doing so (Comm. on GP, 194).

401–9 For a comparable list of the skills required by a good seaman, see Vegetius in his popular treatise on military training: *De re militari* 4.43; tr. Milner, 147: "It is the responsibility of sailors and pilots to acquaint themselves with the places in which they are going to sail, so as to avoid dangerous waters with projecting or hidden rocks, shallows, and sandbanks."

404 Hull is on the Yorkshire coast. **Cartage** is Carthage elsewhere in Chaucer (e.g., FranT V.1400, NPT VII.3365), but here may possibly be Cartagena in Spain (Magoun, Ch Gazetteer, 46).

408 Gootlond: Probably Gotland, an island off the Swedish coast (Magoun, Ch Gazetteer, 80–81), though Danish Jutland is another possibility.

    Fynystere: Probably Cape Finisterre, Galicia, Spain (Magoun, Ch Gazetteer, 72–73), rather than Finistere in Brittany.

410 barge: If Chaucer is using the word precisely, he probably had in mind a vessel such as that described by Alan Moore from the reign of Edward III: single-masted, but with oars, undecked but with fore- and after-castles and perhaps a top-castle, about eighty feet long on the keel with raked bows and stern, and about twenty feet wide (Mariner's Mirror 6, 1920, 229–42; also 4, 1914, 169–70).

The Doctor of Physic

The Notes on the Doctor of Physic are adapted from those written by C. David Benson for The Riverside Chaucer.

The most complete accounts of the Physician in relation to fourteenth-century medical theory and practice are Curry, Ch and Science, 3–36, and Huling E. Ussery, Ch's Physician, TSE 19, 1971. The portrait is a mixture of apparent praise and satiric hints, with the result that "we cannot be absolutely sure about anything in the Doctor's character" (Curry, 36). As with the portrait of the Sergeant of Law, this complexity is caused by Chaucer's "transforming the features which other writers attack into evidence of professional skill" (Mann, Ch and Estates, 91). A few critics have found Chaucer's attitude toward the Physician essentially admiring (Manly, CT, 524; Ussery, TSE 19:102–17); some others take an equally negative view, seeing the pilgrim as, e.g., a "society doctor" (Lumiansky, Of Sondry Folk, 195) or irreligious quack (Robertson, Ch's London, 207–8). Most critics, while conceding the pilgrim's professional competence, follow Curry in emphasizing the elements of satire, especially a love of gold and concern with only the physical (e.g., Bowden, Comm. on GP, 199–213; Donaldson, 1053–54; Howard, Idea of CT, 335).

Manly suspected that the portrait was based on a real person but could supply no name (New Light, 260–61); Ussery (TSE 19:61–89) dismisses earlier suggestions that Chaucer may have had in mind John of Gaddesden (H. H. Bashford, Nineteenth Century 104, 1928, 247–48) or John Arderne (Bowden, Comm. on GP, 208). There is no need for an actual model since so much of the portrait is conventional (Mann, Ch and Estates, 91–99).

Ussery (TSE 19:29–31, 95) argues that the Physician is a cleric, since most fourteenth-century physicians, especially eminent ones, were secular clerics, and cites the Host's comment that the Doctor is *lyk a prelat* (PardT VI.310). Clerics were forbidden to draw blood, and if the Doctor is also a surgeon (see line 413 and n.), he is probably a layman. However, Robert S. Gottfried (Doctors and Medicine in Medieval England, 1340–1530, 1986) shows there was a "gap between clerical prescription and actual practice," and he cites the case of William Hammond, a Benedictine who was royal surgeon from 1341 to 1367 (p. 139).

411 Doctour of Phisik: The Physician is one of the relatively few holders of an advanced degree, which at this period required years of study and residence at a university, four to seven years for the baccalaureate and another four to seven for the doctorate (Gottfried, Doctors and Medicine, 172).

413 phisik and of surgerye: Physic and surgery were two distinct professions and only rarely practiced by the same person. But Guy de Chauliac styles himself "Cirurgien, doctoure of phisik" (Cyrurgie of Guy de Chauliac, EETS 265, 9), and others in England so designated themselves (Ussery TSE 19:59–60).

414 astronomye: Astronomy was an important part of medieval medical practice. Some critics suggest that the Physician's reliance on astronomy is intended pejoratively (Bowden, Comm. on GP, 204; Robertson, Ch's London, 207–8), but the following lines do not describe "judicial astronomy" (what we call "astrology" and Chaucer called "the rites of payens in whiche my spirit hath no feith," Astr 2.4.59) but rather the use of astronomy to foretell physical events, as in meteorology or medicine, which was regarded as legitimate by Thomas Aquinas (Summa Theol. 2.2.95.5; tr. Fathers of the Dominican Province, 1603–4) and many others (though some churchmen were uncomfortable even with this; cf. Dives and Pauper 1:141). In the *Astrolabe*, Chaucer notes that each of the twelve zodiacal signs "hath respect to a certeyn parcel of the body of a man, and hath it in governaunce" (Astr 1.21.71–73). Some medical writers ignore planetary influences, but most stress its importance: "As Galian the full wise leche saith, and Isoder the gode clerk, hit witnessith that a man may not perfitely can [know] the sciens and crafte of medessin but yef he be an astonomoure" (Secreta secretorum, EETS e.s. 74, 195). In the lines that follow, Chaucer seems to derive much of his information about the use of astronomy in medicine from the *Kalendarium* of Nicholas of Lynn, which he knew and used (cf. Intro MLT II.1–14n. and see C. David Benson, AMN&Q 22, 5–6, 1984, 66–70). In Canons 11 and 12 of the *Kalendarium* especially, Nicholas makes clear the importance of the position of the moon when letting blood or giving medicine: "And if a physician should neglect to look at these things [the sign in which the moon is] when giving medicine, he will be deprived very often of a cure, because the power of heaven will work to the contrary" (*Kalendarium*, 211; see Laurel Braswell, SAC 8, 1986, 145–56).

415–16 The **houres** during which the Physician watched over (**kepte**) his patient probably refer to the twenty-four astrological hours, which varied according to the time of year, in which different planets reigned (cf. KnT I.2217n.) and to the six-hour periods of the day in which one of each of the four humors was dominant (see 420 below). Nicholas of Lynn provides a table (*Kalendarium*, 176–77) by which this information can be determined "for each hour of the day and night" (60).

416 magyk natureel: As opposed to black magic; cf. FranT V.1125. See Gower, who uses similar terms in Conf. aman. 6.1338 ("naturiens," as opposed to "magiciens") and 7.1301 ("Magike naturel").

417 fortunen the ascendant: Calculate the planetary positions, in order to make the **ymages** (talismanic images) when the planets are in a favorable position; cf. HF 1265–70: "And clerkes eke, which konne wel/ Al this magik naturel,/ . . . make, in certeyn ascendentes,/ Ymages, lo, thrugh which magik/ To make a man ben hool or syk." Nicholas of Lynn (*Kalendarium*, 164–75) provides a chart for determining the ascendant (eighth canon) and explains (twelfth canon) the making of such talismans: "For, as Thebith says, images and sculptures are made in stones so that they might receive the worth of precious stones from the influence of heaven. However, they do not have the power except from the aspect of the planets at the time when they were sculpted. . . . the supercelestial power gives them the power they possess" (210).

420 hoot, or coold, or moyste, or drye: The four qualities, or contraries, linked to the four elements, air (hot and moist), fire (hot and dry), earth (cold and dry), water (cold and moist). According to the theory popularized by Galen (see 429–34 below) from ideas he attributed to Aristotle and Hippocrates, the body is composed of these four elements, which correspond to the four humors (bodily fluids): blood, phlegm, choler (yellow or red bile), and melancholy (black bile). "The blood is hot and moist to the likeness of the air; phlegm is cold and moist after the kind of the water; choler hot and dry after kind of fire; melancholy cold and dry after kind of earth" (Secreta secretorum, EETS e.s. 74, 219–20; modernized). The humors of an individual could be affected by the planets and signs of the zodiac, each of which is characterized by elemental qualities (thus Aries is a fiery hot and dry sign, Mars a hot and dry planet), by seasons of the year (spring is hot and moist, like blood; summer hot and dry, like choler; autumn cold and dry, like melancholy; winter cold and moist, like phlegm), by the time of day (see 415–16 above), and by diet. An imbalance of the humors was thought to cause illness, and the physician's task was to keep the humors "in evene proporcioun in quantite and qualite" (Barth. Angl., 4.6; tr. Trevisa 1:148). If the humors were out of balance, the physician attempted to determine the nature of the imbalance and its origin (see line 421) and offered compensating treatment with medicines of the proper elemental qualities: "Also therfore [the physician] nedith to knowe the qualitees of herbes and of othir medicinal thinges and diversite of degrees, what is hote and drye, what is colde and moiste, in what degree, yif he wil nought erre in his office" (Barth. Angl., 7.69; tr. Trevisa 1:435).

425–28 The implication of collusion between druggists and doctors is traditional (see Gower, Mirour, 25645–46; tr. Wilson, 337: "The physician and Fraud the apothecary know how to get along together; the one empties your belly more than necessary, and the other knows how to empty your purse").

426 letuaries: Electuaries, medicine in the form of paste or syrup (MED s.v. *letuarie*), often mixed with honey (Lanfrank's Science of Cirurgie, ed. Robert von Fleischhacker, EETS 102, 1894, 263). Chaucer also refers to electuaries at PardT VI.307 and (as aphrodisiacs) at MerT IV.1809.

429–34 This list of eminent medical authorities contains more names than similar lists in *Roman de la rose* (15959–61; tr. Dahlberg, 271) or Dante, Inf. IV.143–44. **Esculapius** (Aesculapius) is the legendary founder of medicine, **Deyscorides** (Dioscorides, fl. 50–70 A.D.) is the author of *Materia medica*, a pharmaceutical guide. **Rufus** (of Ephesus, probably fl. c. 25 B.C. to 50 A.D.) wrote widely on medical topics. **Ypocras** (Hippocrates, born c. 460 B.C.) moved Greek medicine from superstition toward science.

Haly is almost certainly Haly Abbas (Ali ibn Abbas, d. 994), a Persian authority on medical theory and practice. **Galyen** (Galen, c. 129–99 A.D.) wrote works that were central to the curriculum of medieval medical schools. Chaucer refers to him in ParsT X.831 and (with Hippocrates) in BD 571–72 ("no phisicien,/ Noght Ypocras ne Galyen"). **Serapion** could be the Alexandrian Sempion (c. 200–150 B.C.), Serapion the Elder (Yahya ibn Sarafyun, ninth century), a Christian of Damascus whose works were translated into Latin, or Serapion the Younger (probably twelfth century), to whom is attributed the popular *Liber de Medicamentis simplicibus*. **Razis** (Rhazes, c. 854–930) wrote the comprehensive medical manual known in the West as "Continens." **Avycen**, Avicenna (Ibn Sina, 980–1037), is the author of the encyclopedic *Book of the Canon of Medicine* (cf. PardT VI.889–90). **Averrois** (Averroes, 1126–98) wrote the influential medical work that was translated into Latin as "Colliget." John of Damascus (**Damascien**) was a Syrian theologian of the eighth century, but the name Johannes (or Janus) Damascenus was given to works by Serapion the Elder and Yuhanna ibn Masawayn (Mesue, d.857). **Constantyn** (Constantine the African, fl. 1065–85) wrote a number of works on medicine, including *De coitu* (hence called the "cursed monk" in MerT IV.1810). **Bernard** (of Gordon, fl. 1283–1309) wrote the famous *Lilium mediciniae*. The last two authorities are English: **Gatesden** (John of Gaddesden, died c. 1349), author of the *Rosa anglica*, and **Gilbertyn** (Gilbertus Anglicus, fl. 1250), author of the *Compendium medicinae*.

No single source for this list has been found. "Chaucer's list contains just those names that an educated doctor of his day would have cited" (R. H. Robbins, in Sts. Lang. and Lit. in Hon. of Margaret Schlauch, 1966, 335–41).

435–37 The importance of such a diet for health is repeatedly stressed (cf. Langland, PP B 6.259–74, GP I.347–48, NPT VII.2838). Mann (Ch and Estates, 252, n. 41) suggests that the actual vocabulary of these lines may be drawn from Gower, Mirour, 8338–43; tr. Wilson, 115, on Gluttony. Mann translates: "without digesting, without swallowing, lets her meat come back again—it returns the way it entered. The right name of the sin is superfluity, which is the enemy of moderation (*mesure*)."

438 The conventional association of medicine with atheism can be found in Petrarch's *Invective contra medicum*. Curry (Ch and Science, 30) cites John of Salisbury's charge in Policraticus 2.29 (tr. Pike, 149): "Physicians, however, placing undue emphasis on nature, in general encroach upon the rights of the author of nature by their opposition to faith." This has influenced some interpretive criticism; see, e.g., Richard L. Hoffman, ChauR 2, 1967, 20–31.

439–40 For other examples of doctors clad in rich clothing, see Langland, PP B 6.269–70 ("furred hoods" and "cloaks of Calabria with gold ornaments") and B 20.176 ("A phisicien with a furred hood"); and Henryson, Testament of Cresseid, ed. Denton Fox, 1968, lines 250–51 ("cladd in a scarlet gown/ and furred well").

443–44 "Among metalle is nothing so effectuelle in vertue as golde" for, among many other medical uses, it "helpeth . . . agens cardeakle passioun" (Barth. Angl. 16.4; tr. Trevisa 2:829). Both Arnaldus of Villanova (Thorndike, Hist.

Magic 2:864) and Raymond Lully (Ramon Lull) (John L. Lowes, MP 2, 1914, 30) give directions for preparing "aurum potabile" (drinkable gold). The irony of the last line depends on the still common belief in the greediness of doctors. John Arderne stresses the importance of arranging for the fee before performing an operation (Treatises of Fistula in Ano, ed. D'Arcy Power, EETS 139, 1910, 5–6): "Asketh he boldly more or lesse but ever be he ware of skarse askingis. . . . Therfore, for the cure . . . ask he competently of a worthi man and a gret an hundred marke or fourty pounde, with robes and fees of an hundred shillyng terme of lyfe be yere . . . nevere in al my lyfe toke I lesse than an hundred shillyng for cure of that sekenes."

The Wife of Bath

The Notes on the Wife of Bath are adapted from those written by Christine Ryan Hilary for The Riverside Chaucer.

The portrait of the Wife is expanded by the Wife herself in the prologue to her tale. Chaucer knew the city of Bath, through which he would have passed to North Petherton as forester in 1391 and later. Manly (New Light, 225–34) believes that Chaucer may have based the portrait on an actual woman of St. Michael's parish there, in which cloth-weaving was a principal occupation (see 447–48 below) and which had an unusual number of women named Alison. However, her portrait is shaped by a number of literary sources, principally La Vieille's (the Old Woman's) monologue in the *Roman de la rose* (echoed in GP I.461 and 476). Chaucer also drew on Jankyn's *Book of Wikked Wyves* (cf. WBPro III.669–75), other Latin and French anti-feminist texts, estates satire (Mann, Ch and Estates, 121–27), and astrological and physiognomical lore (Curry, Ch and Science, 91–118; Wood, Ch and the Stars, 172–80). On the rich critical literature the Wife has inspired, see the notes to her Prologue.

445 biside Bathe: Probably the parish of St. Michael's "juxta Bathon," just outside the north gate of the walls of Bath (Magoun, Ch Gazetteer, 29–30).

446 somdeel deef: See WBPro III.668.

447–48 Weaving and spinning are the occupations traditionally assigned to women in medieval estates literature, and, since nothing more is said of the Wife's occupation, Mann suggests this traditional association as the chief reason for mentioning **clooth-makyng** (Ch and Estates, 121–22). However, many women of the time were engaged in the trade of weaving, which was the principal occupation in St. Michael's "juxta Bathon" (Manly, New Light, 227–29).

448 Ypres . . . Gaunt: Ypres and Ghent were celebrated for their cloth; Edward III persuaded Flemish weavers from this area to settle in England (Magoun, Ch Gazetteer, 78 and 92). Manly suggests that Chaucer's praise of the Wife's weaving is exaggerated, "perhaps ironical," since West-country weavers were not in good repute; a statute of Richard II notes that some of their cloth was so bad that English merchants abroad were in danger of their lives (Manly, CT, 527).

449–51   At the **offrynge** (Offertory) of the Mass, the wor-shipers went individually to the altar to give their offerings to the priest or (as in MilT I.3350) the clerk; see The Lay Folks Mass Book, EETS 71, 232–44. Worshipers went to the altar in order of rank, and arguments over precedence were common; see the Book of the Knight of La Tour Landry, EETS 33, 150 (on women who "be envyeusis whiche shalle go furst up on the offerande"); cf. ParsT X.407, GP I.377.

452 out of alle charitee: Taken by Richard L. Hoffman (ELN 11, 1974, 165–67) as indicative of the Wife's spiritual state (cf. ParsT X.1043); Elliott (Ch's English, 291) finds it merely idiomatic and compares KnT I.1623.

453 coverchiefs: Possibly kerchiefs, more likely linen cov-erings for the head, worn severally over a wire framework. Women's headdresses were frequent objects of satire (Mann, Ch and Estates, 124–25). For an illustration of the Wife's headgear, see A Facsimile of Cambridge MS Gg.4.27, ed. Parkes and Beadle.

456 scarlet reed: See RvT I.3954–55n.

460 at chirche dore: From the tenth century until the six-teenth, marriage was a two-part ceremony. The legally binding pledge took place at the church door, in the pres-ence of witnesses, and was followed by a nuptial Mass in the church; cf. MerT IV.1700–08n. In the ceremony at the church door, the wife was legally endowed by the hus-band to protect her financially in the event of his death. The frequently widowed Wife thus accumulated substantial assets with which to attract subsequent husbands, who then had the legal right to control but not to own her property; see Cecile S. Margulies, MS 24, 1962, 210–16, and D. W. Robertson, Jr., ChauR 14, 1984, 403–20.

461 Withouten: John S. P. Tatlock (Flügel Memorial Vol-ume, 1916, 229 n. 8) notes that "*Withouten,* generally meaning *without,* means *as well as, besides, except, not to mention,*" and concludes that Chaucer "leaves us guessing whether or not the Wife of Bath had lovers before she mar-ried." Cf. Tr 2.236 ("Withouten paramours").

oother compaignye: Cf. *Roman de la rose* 12781; tr. Dahlberg, 222: [I often failed to keep my promises to my lovers] "for I had other company [*autre compaigne*].

463–67   A love of pilgrimages for illicit purposes is typical of women in estates satire (Mann, Ch and Estates, 123). In her Prologue (III.551–62), the Wife makes clear that her pil-grimages were not for devotional purposes. On the pilgrim-age to Jerusalem, see Wayne Shumacher (ELH 18, 1951, 77–89), who compares the Wife's itinerary with the contem-porary account in the Book of Margery Kempe (ed. Staley, ch. 28–29) and Bowden (Comm. on GP, 224–25), who com-pares it with Mandeville's Travels, EETS 153, 48–66.

465 Rome: For the objects of pilgrimage in fourteenth-cen-tury Rome, see the Stacions of Rome, ed. F. J. Furnivall, EETS 25, 1–34.

Boloigne: At Boulogne-sur-Mer, on the French Atlantic coast, a miraculous image of the Virgin, which had arrived in a rudderless vessel, was a popular object of pil-grimage (Magoun, Ch Gazetteer, 35–36).

466 Galice at Seint-jame: The shrine of St. James at Com-postela in Galicia, in northwestern Spain, then a part of the kingdom of Castile. It was, with Jerusalem and Rome,

one of the three most important objects of pilgrimage in Christendom. For a description of medieval Compostela, see *Liber quartus sancti Jacobi Apostoli,* partially summa-rized by Bowden, Comm. on GP, 222–23.

Coloigne: At Cologne, on the Rhine, pilgrims visited the shrines of the three Magi and of St. Ursula and the Eleven Thousand Virgins, said to have been massacred there (Magoun, Ch Gazetteer, 57).

468 Gat-tothed: "with teeth set wide apart" (Robinson); *gap-tothed* in some MSS. The word is derived from OE *get,* gate, rather than *gat,* goat, as Skeat held (5.44). In medieval physiognomy such teeth indicated an envious, irreverent, luxurious, bold, faithless, and suspicious nature (Curry, Ch and Science, 109), and the Wife's red face (458) indicates immodesty, loquaciousness, and drunkenness (Curry, 108–9).

469 amblere: A pacing horse lifts both feet on a side simul-taneously (unlike a trotter) and is therefore comfortable for riding long distances. The Ellesmere illustration shows the Wife riding astride, as did most women in her day. The Prioress and the Second Nun are shown riding side-saddle; the side-saddle was "used only by a limited court circle" (A. A. Dent, PLPLS–LHS, 1959, 9).

475 remedies of love: means of remedying (curing or satis-fying) love-sickness (cf. KnT I.1355–76n.), with a probable reference to Ovid's *Remedia amoris.*

476 art: This is sometimes taken as a reference to Ovid's *Ars amatoria* (e.g., Richard L. Hoffman, N&Q 209, 1964, 287–88), but it may mean simply "craft," as in RomB 4289: "Hadde lerned of loves art."

the olde daunce: "la vieille daunce" *Roman de la rose* 3938 (RomB 4300, "For she knew all the olde daunce"). In French the phrase implies artfulness and skillfulness and was not originally restricted to sexual matters. Chaucer was apparently the first to use it in English (Whiting L535), and he always applies it to matters of love, courtship, or sex; cf. PhyT VI.79.

The Parson

The Notes on the Parson are adapted from those written by Siegfried Wenzel for The Riverside Chaucer.

Chaucer's portrait of the Parson is usually understood to depict an ideal priest. It is devoid of irony, and what satire can be found in it is directed against those common failings of the profession from which the Parson is free. Some early critics (e.g., Doris Ives, MLR 27, 1932, 144–48) argued that the por-trait reflects Wycliffite (Lollard) ideals, but though the Host accuses the Parson of Lollardy (EpiMLT II.1173 and n.), all the elements of the portrait can be found in contemporary dis-cussions of the ideal requirements and failings of spiritual shepherds. See Robert N. Swanson, SAC 13, 1991, 41–80.

486 cursen for his tithes: The practice could be abused; Wycliffites attacked "worldly clerkis" who "cruely" curse for tithes (Wyclif, Eng. Works, 145), but so too does the orthodox Robert Mannyng, Handlyng Synne, EETS 119, 10881–82: "The prest wote neuer what he menes,/ That for lytel, curseth his parysshens."

The Lambeth Constitutions of 1281, reiterating decrees of earlier synods, required every parish priest to pronounce the great sentence of excommunication before his congregation four times a year; see John Mirk, Instr. for Parish Priests, ed. Peacock, EETS 31, 60; "great sentence" includes those who withhold tithes. Mirk (64–65) specifies what is to be included in the tithes.

497–98 Cf. Matt. 5.19 " . . . whoever does [the commandments] and teaches [them] shall be called great." Cf. Gower, Conf Aman. 5.1825: "Crist wroghte ferst and after tawhte."

500 A commonplace based on Lam. 4.1 ("How the gold has become dim!") and its use by Gregory, Pastoral Care, tr. Henry Davis, 70–71. Chaucer's wording is exactly paralleled in French: Le Renclus de Moiliens (late twelfth century), Romans de carité, ed. van Hamel, 1885 (rpt. 1987), st. 62: "Se ors enrunge, queus ert fers?"

504 The thought of this alliterative line is a commonplace, but most parallels lack its forceful diction (e.g., Gower, Vox Clam. 3.1063; tr. Stockton, 140: "The sheep becomes tainted with the shepherd's stains").

507–14 Absenteeism was a major topic of late medieval criticism directed at the clergy; cf. Gower, Mirour, 20209–832; tr. Wilson, 270 (20209–12: "He who is in charge of a parish brings us a bad example when he leaves it uncared for"), and ParsT X.721.

510 chaunterie: A provision for a priest to chant the office for the dead or to say or sing Mass for the repose of a soul, usually that of the founder of a chantry. Such endowments were especially numerous at St. Paul's, London. Cf. Robertson, Ch's London, 110; Langland (PP B Pro 85–86) complains of those priests who seek "licence and leve at London to dwelle/ To syngen for symonie for silver is swete."

511 bretherhed: Chantries were often founded by wealthy guilds. See J. S. P. Tatlock, MLN 31, 1916, 139–42.

514 mercenarie: Cf. John 10.12. "He is a hireling (mercenarius) not a shepherd" who "leaves the sheep and flees." "There is perhaps further reference to the title 'chappelain mercenaire,' which was applied to priests who made their living entirely by saying masses" (Robinson).

523–24 nonys: noon ys: The rhyming of two words with one, a variety of "rime riche" (see note 17–18 above), is sometimes called "broken rhyme" and was a regular feature of ME verse; for other examples see GP I.671–72, KnT I.1323–24, IntrMLT II.102–3, SqT V.675–76, Tr I.4–5. On such rhymes see Helge Kökeritz, PMLA, 1969, 937–52, and Elliott, Ch's English, 85.

526 spiced conscience: Cf. WBPro III.435. The basic meaning of spiced as "seasoned" has been variously interpreted in relation to the Parson's character, mostly variations on Robinson's definition: "overscrupulous . . . The Parson was reasonable and not too fastidious in his dealings with his flock."

528 Cf. Acts 1.1 ("all that Jesus began both to do and to teach").

The Plowman

The Plowman is apparently a free skilled laborer who owns some property (catel). In the labor shortage following the Black Death, such laborers sometimes demanded high wages and incurred criticism for doing so. Contemporary preachers attacked the laborer "that goth to the plow" and formerly worked for ten or twelve shillings a year but now "musten have xx or thritti and his liverei also" (Owst, Lit and Pulpit, 369). Gower complains of the laziness of "servants of the plow" (Vox Clam. 5.9) and of the peasantry in general (Mirour 26425–508; tr. Wilson, 347–48). Chaucer's treue swynkere has thus been seen as a tacit criticism of contemporary peasants (David, Strumpet Muse, 91). However, "the trewe laborer" was also a traditional symbol of the ideal Christian (Stephen A. Barney, MS 35, 1973, 261–93). The Plowman's resemblance to Piers Plowman has often been remarked (Nevill Coghill, MÆ 4, 1935, 89–94), and it may be that Chaucer was influenced by Langland's work. On the figure of the Plowman in Langland and Chaucer, see Elizabeth D. Kirk, Yearbook of Langland Sts 2, 1988, 1–21.

530 Coghill (MÆ 4:93) compares PP B 4.147: "Lawe shal ben a laborer and lede afelde [carry afièld] donge."

533 Cf. Matt. 22.37: "Thou shalt love the lord thy God with all thy heart."

534 thogh him gamed or smerte: One of a number of phrases denoting "in all circumstances." On such "merisms" in ME, see Lawrence L. Besserman, AnM 17, 1976, 58–69.

536 In the Seneschaucy, it is specified that plowmen "ought to dig, make enclosures, and thresh; they ought to remove earth or dig trenches to dry the land and drain off the water" (Walter of Henley, ed. Oschinsky, 282–83). **Dyke and delve** is also a common collocation meaning "work hard" (MED s.v. dichen la).

541 mere: The mare is commonly said to be a humble mount, but few of the pilgrims would have ridden stallions, since for inexperienced riders mares and geldings are usually much easier to control.

The Miller

The Notes on the Miller are adapted from those written by Douglas Gray for The Riverside Chaucer.

The ruggedness, brutal strength, and grossness of the Miller are evident from the details of his portrait; the account that the Reeve gives in his tale of the miller Simkin alludes to and develops these characteristics. Curry (Ch and Science, 81–90) notes that the Miller's short-shouldered, broad, and thick figure, red beard, nose with a wart, and wide mouth were believed by the physiognomists to denote variously a shameless, talkative, lecherous, and quarrelsome character. Chaucer may have been drawing on familiar physiognomical notions rather than the learned scientific treatises cited by Curry. As Mann observes, "the redhead is a widespread figure of deceit and treachery," and his characteristics appear in conventional descriptions of ugliness (Ch and Estates, 162). On the popular image of millers, see George F. Jones, MLQ 16, 1955, 3–15. There is much information on millers and mills in J. A. W. Bennett, Ch at Oxford, especially ch. 4 and app. B. Attempts to find a possible historical model for Chaucer's Miller, for Robin in MilT and Simkin in RvT (Manly, New Light, 94–101; Margaret Galway, N&Q 195, 1950, 486–88) are unconvincing.

545 for the nones: "Here apparently in the intensive sense" (Robinson); cf. GP I.379n.

548 ram: The prize in a wrestling match; cf. Thop VII.740–41 and The Tale of Gamelyn (ed. Knight and Ohlgren, 171–72: "Ther was bisiden cride a wrastelinge/ And therfor ther was sett a ramme and a ring").

550–51   Individuals who excelled in breaking doors with their heads from the fourth to the nineteenth century (including, in the fourteenth, Thomas Heyward of Berkeley) are listed in B. J. Whiting, MLN 52, 1937, 417–19, and MLN 69, 1954, 309–10; Autrey N. Wiley, MLN 53, 1938, 505–7; and Francis L. Utley, MLN 56, 1941, 534–36.

554–57   On the iconography of the Miller's nose, see Alfred David, in Jane Chance and R. O. Wells, Jr., eds., *Mapping the Cosmos,* 1985, 76–97.

559 greet forneys: A number of critics and editors detect a suggestion of the gaping hell-mouths depicted in medieval painting. The physiognomists regarded a large mouth as a sign of a "glotonous and bold" personality (Secretum secretorum, EETS 276, 105).

560 janglere: Mann (Ch and Estates, 161) notes that the Ancrene Wisse (tr. Salu, 39: "From mill and from market, from smithy and from anchor-house one hears the news") hints that tale telling was traditionally connected with millers. The mill itself is used as a figure for a wagging tongue in ClT IV.1200 and ParsT X.406).

A **goliardeys** is a "buffoon" (MED s.v. *goliardeis*) or "a windbag, teller of dirty stories" (Fisher, 559). It is recorded elsewhere only in PP B Pro 139 ("a goliardeis, a gloton of wordes") and in Robert Mannyng, Handlyng Synne, EETS 119, 4701 (a "mynstralle," a "gulardous").

562 tollen thries: The toll (a fraction of the grain ground) was exacted in addition to the usual money payment. It might range from a twentieth to a twenty-fourth or a sixteenth part; see H. S. Bennett, Life on the Eng. Manor, 1948, ch. 6.

563 thombe of gold: Possibly an ironic reference to a proverb "an honest miller hath a golden thumb" (i.e., there are no honest millers), though it is not recorded until after Chaucer's time (Whiting M559–61; Tilley M954–59); Skeat notes that the Miller's thumb may be called golden in reference to the profit that comes from his skill in judging grain by feeling samples with the thumb and forefinger. Lines 562–63 may be taken together as "The miller was a thief yet he had the mark of honest millers, the reputation of being honest."

565 baggepipe: Essentially a folk instrument; see Winternitz, Musical Instruments, especially 66–85 and 129–36. The medieval bagpipe inherited from antiquity the Dionysiac associations of wind instruments with passion and drunkenness (Winternitz, 153, 156–62), but the symbolic associations of bagpipes were not rigidly fixed; as Winternitz notes, angels sometimes played them. When the accused Lollard William Thorpe attacked pilgrims and the noise they made as they went through towns—some, he said, would have bagpipes—Archbishop Arundel defended this sort of "solace" (D. Gray, ed., Oxford Bk. of Late Med. Verse and Prose, 1985, 17–18).

The Manciple

The Notes on the Manciple are adapted from those written by V. J. Scattergood for The Riverside Chaucer.

A manciple was a subordinate official who purchased provisions for a college or "inn of court" (law school); the temple was either the Inner or Middle Temple near the Strand. The manciple does not appear in traditional estates satire, and it may be that Chaucer is here drawing on his own personal experience (see p. xvi). The tradition that both Chaucer and Gower studied at the Inner Temple derives from Speght: "It seemeth that both these learned men were at the Inner Temple . . . " (Works of Chaucer, 1598, rpt. in Brewer, Ch: The Crit. Heritage, 1:142–43). The manciple "may be linked with the dishonesty Langland assigns to manorial officials, lawyers, and those who . . . look after provisions" (Mann, Ch and Estates, 174).

570 by taille: On a tally stick the amount of a debt was kept in notches and the stick then split, with debtor and creditor each retaining half as a record.

573–75   Perhaps based on an ironic reversal of the proverb "Many wits are better than a man's wit" (Whiting W409).

579 stywardes: Stewards, or seneschals, were the managers of estates, and usually had direct responsibility to the lord of the manor.

586 sette hir aller cappe: Deceived them all. Cf. MilPro I.3143, RvPro I.3911. Apparently the phrase occurs only in Chaucer (Whiting C32); the idea seems to be tilting somebody's cap or hood to make him seem foolish.

The Reeve

The Notes on the Reeve are adapted from those written by Douglas Gray for The Riverside Chaucer.

"A reeve acted as a kind of general foreman on a manor, seeing to the condition of fields, woods, and pastures, responsible for all work done, for collecting his lord's dues, and for presenting the annual account" (Phyllis Hodgson, ed. GP). May McKisack (The Fourteenth Cent., 1959, 317–19) points out that the social status of reeves had improved in Chaucer's time, and that they were usually capable men, holding positions of importance and trust.

In some respects (e.g., in cheating his lord without detection), the Reeve resembles the Manciple; they are "two characters of the most consummate worldly wisdom" (William Blake, Compl. Writings, ed. Keynes, 1966, 601). In physique and in personality, the Reeve is in complete contrast to the Miller, with whom he later has an altercation. The description should be compared with that which he gives in his own prologue (RvPro I.3867–98). The physical characteristics of the Reeve are those the physiognomists regularly attributed to the choleric complexion and associated with a sharp wit, a quick temper, and wanton disposition (Curry, Ch and Science, 71–90). Astuteness and fraudulence were often attributed to a choleric person; cf. Sec. Lyrics, ed. Robbins, no. 76.11: "Fraudulent & suttyll, ful cold & dry,/ Yellowe of collour, colloryke am y." Deborah S. Ellis (ChauR 27, 1992, 150–61) argues that Chaucer draws on the iconography of the medieval devil for these characteristics.

Reeves had a reputation for thieving, but Mann (Ch and Estates, 165) notes the ambiguity of Chaucer's treatment: "The suggestion of dishonesty runs right through the portrait, but its phraseology is constantly as ambiguous as the statement that the Reeve could please his lord 'subtilly.'"

The description is highly individualized (we are given not only the name of the Reeve's town but the situation of his house), and this has suggested to some that Chaucer based his portrait on an actual official: *Baldeswelle* (620), the modern Bawdeswell in northern Norfolk, lay partly in the manor of Foxley, which belonged to the earls of Pembroke. Chaucer certainly had connections with Sir William de Beauchamp, cousin of the second earl, who had the custody of the estates in Kent. There is evidence that some of the Pembroke estates were mismanaged, and Beauchamp's own management was investigated in 1386–87. Manly (New Light, 70–94) speculates that through his connections with Beauchamp Chaucer may have learned about this rascally Norfolk reeve. However, as Mann points out (Ch and Estates, 166), Norfolk people had a reputation for being crafty and treacherous; she quotes a medieval Latin poem characterizing them as "the basest of people, full of tricks, deceitful and malicious."

587 colerik: Dominated by the humor choler (yellow or red bile). See 333 and 420 above.

589 ful round yshorn: Close-cut hair is probably not a sign of a servile station (Curry, Ch and Science, 72) but rather, as Mann notes (Ch and Estates, 284 n. 70), it makes him look like a "clerk."

594 auditour: On the careful accounting a reeve was required to make to his auditors, see Seneschaucy, ch. 73, in Walter of Henley, ed. Oschinsky, 290–91.

605 the deeth: Probably "the plague," but possibly "death" in general. On the occasional use in ME of the definite article in constructions similar to French "la mort," see Mustanoja, ME Syntax, 257, and cf. Language and Versification, p. xxxiii.

606–7 His wonyng: A dwelling at the cost of the lord and a robe (cf. the **cote and hood** in line 612) were apparently regular perquisites of the bailiff, in addition to his salary (Robinson). Vincent B. Redstone (TLS 1932, 789–90) noted that there was still a heath at Bawdeswell shaded by the trees of Bylaugh Wood.

616 Scot: Apparently a common name for a horse; Manly (CT, 533) notes its occurrence in a fourteenth-century inventory (Oxf. Hist. Soc. Collectanea, 3, 1896, 60 n. 12). It is the name of a horse in FrT III.1543.

621 Tukked: Skeat notes that the Ellesmere illustrations show both the Reeve and the Friar with girdles and rather long coats (cf. SumT III.1737).

622 hyndreste: "Whether the Reeve rode last out of cowardice or instinctive craftiness, he at any rate chose the place farthest away from the Miller" (Robinson). Some critics believe that the quarrel between them is an old one, and Frederick Tupper (JEGP 14, 1915, 265) argues that millers and reeves were traditional enemies. But Mann (Ch and Estates, 284–85) remarks that the evidence shows only that a clash of interests was likely, not that it was proverbial. Donaldson (1057) suggests that the Reeve rides last because of his "habitual watchfulness," for the rear is "the best position from which to watch what is going on among any band of travellers."

The Summoner

The Notes on the Summoner are adapted from those written by Janette Richardson for The Riverside Chaucer.

The summoner, or apparitor, was a minor nonclerical officer of the ecclesiastical courts who delivered citations for people to appear before the tribunal and acted as usher, or bailiff, while sessions were in progress. Louis A. Haselmayer (Spec 12, 1937, 43–57) found that historical documents in England contain only minimal evidence for the corrupt practices that Chaucer attributes to his pilgrim and the summoner of The Friar's Tale. But see Thomas Hahn and Richard W. Kaeuper, SAC, 1983, 67–101. According to Mann (Ch and Estates, 274, n. 60), the office does not appear in estates satire much before Langland, who links summoners with Lady Meed and refers scornfully to them in various contexts (e.g., PP B 2.169–71: "Somonours shold be sadled . . . Sire Symonye hymself shal sitte upon hir bakkes"). However, attacks on the venality of the ecclesiastical courts in general were numerous in sermons and moral literature, as well as in popular poetry (Bowden, Comm. on GP, 269–72; Mann, Ch and Estates, 139–40).

624 fyr-reed cherubynnes face: Red was the conventional color for seraphs, and blue the color for cherubs, until the end of the fifteenth century. Some confusion about the hierarchy apparently existed in popular thinking, but since the color symbolism was based on the idea of being inflamed with divine love, the ironic intention of the image is nonetheless evident.

625 saucefleem: With pimples caused by an excess of phlegm in the system (Skeat 5.53), which makes the face red. The condition, also called *gutta rosacea*, was diagnosed as a symptom of leprosy (Cyrurgie of Guy de Chauliac, EETS 265, 435). The **eyen narwe,** swollen eyelids, accompany that form of leprosy called alopecia, according to Gilbertus Anglicus (see 429–34 above and Curry, Ch and Science, 44).

626   One afflicted with *gutta rosacea* should abstain "fro lecherie and fro all excessive hete" (Cyrurgie of Guy de Chauliac, 435). The sparrow is a "ful hoot bridde and lecherous" (Barth. Angl., 12:33; tr. Trevisa 1:639). Cf. PF 351, "The sparwe, Venus sone."

627   Loss of eyebrows and beard is listed as a symptom of *alopicia* by Arnaldus de Villanova (see CYT VIII.1428n., and Curry, Ch and Science, 43).

629–30   All these remedies were recommended by medieval physicians for the Summoner's malady; see Cyrurgie of Guy de Chauliac, 435, which lists all that are here mentioned.

631 oynement: A caustic ointment composed chiefly of arsenic (Curry, Ch and Science, 47).

634   The Summoner should abstain "fro alle sharpe thinges, as fro garlik, fro onions, fro pepper" (Cyrurgie of Guy de Chauliac, 435).

635   Skeat (5:53) cites Prov. 23.31 ("Look not upon the wine when it is red") and quotes The Book of the Knight of La Tour Landry, EETS 33, 116: wine "maketh the visage salce flemed [misprinted: falce flemed] rede and full of white welkes."

637–38   For the notion of speaking Latin when intoxicated, see the fabliau "Du prestre et de la dame" (Of the Priest and the Lady) in Benson and Andersson, Lit. Context, lines 103–107: "Then quickly he was dead drunk./ He was worth a thousand pounds more than he was in the morning./ Then he began to speak Latin/ And gibberish and German."

643 clepen "Watte":   Caged jays were taught to imitate

human speech. Cf. Gower, Vox Clam. 1.679–92 (tr. Stockton, 65 and 352 n.).

646 Questio quid iuris: This is a phrase the Summoner would have frequently heard in court; see Leofranc Holford-Strevens, N&Q 240, 1995, 164–65.

650–51 Chaucer's contemporary, the Dominican John Bromyard, in his *Summa praedicantium* tells of a certain man who gave "twenty pounds annually to a certain great prelate, so that for the whole year he remained with his concubine . . . secure from interference" (Owst, Lit and Pulpit, 253). On **good felawe**, see 395 above.

652 Kittredge's explanation (MP 7, 1910, 475–77) of "to pull (i.e., pluck) a finch" as a crude expression for the Summoner's own lecherous behavior is generally accepted (reference to a woman as a bird of some sort is still current in slang usages), but various other explanations have been offered; MED (s.v. *finch*) defines the phrase as "to do something with cunning, to pull a clever trick."

656–57 For the image of being punished in the purse, cf. Gower, Mirour, 20108–9; tr. Wilson, 268: "Provided the purse be blessed, the body shall be exempt to that extent"; Vox Clam. 3.197–98 (tr. Stockton, 121): "The priest's newfangled decisions declare that because the body has sinned, the sinner's purse should pay."

662 Significavit: The first word of the writ that authorized civil officers to imprison a person who had not made reparation within forty days after being excommunicated. In the approximately ten thousand writs preserved from the thirteenth to the fifteenth century, nonpayment of tithes is the most common offense specified, followed by matrimonial and testamentary cases, fornication, adultery, perjury, and defamation (R. C. Fowler, TRHS, 3rd ser., 8, 1914, 113–17). Cf. FrT III.1304–12.

664 girles: The term is used for youths of both sexes, but young women, perhaps prostitutes, may be intended here, as in MilT I.3769 (see Morton W. Bloomfield, PQ 28, 1949, 503–7).

667 ale-stake: See PardPro VI.321–22n.

The Pardoner

The Notes on the Pardoner are adapted from those written by Christine Ryan Hilary for The Riverside Chaucer.

The Pardoner (officially, *questor*) was a churchman, usually a cleric, empowered to transmit "indulgences" to the faithful. The forgiveness of sin requires penance, which consists of "Contricioun of herte, Confessioun of Mouth, and Satisfaccioun" (ParsT X.108). Contrition and confession remove the moral guilt (*culpa*) of sin, but the need for punishment (*poena*) must also be satisfied, either on earth or in purgatory. This satisfaction can be achieved, the Parson says, by giving alms or performing such penitential acts as going "naked in pilgrimages, or barefot" (X.105). The church, however, is guardian of a "treasury of merit" (earned by Christ and the saints), on which the pope and bishops may draw to provide dispensations from a part of purgatorial punishment to the truly penitent. The giving of alms to the church was the required evidence of true penitence. Thus funds could be raised for the maintenance of hospitals, the building of churches, the repair of bridges, and other worthy causes.

To raise such money, religious foundations would hire professional fund-raisers, pardoners, who would undertake to obtain pardons, and, with the permission of the archdeacons of the dioceses (who required a fee), travel about a given area, appearing in churches to offer their indulgences to those willing and able to pay. The system was easily abused, as detailed in the following lines and in The Pardoner's Prologue, and both church and state attempted, without much success, to control the more flagrant abuses. See J. J. Jusserand, Ch's Pardoner and the Pope's Pardoner, Ch Soc Essays 5:13, 421–36; Alfred L. Kellogg and Louis A. Haselmayer, PMLA 66, 1951, 251–77.

Pardoners were frequent objects of satire, though Bowden (Comm. on GP, 283) notes that this is the only fully developed and individualized satiric portrait of a Pardoner in the fourteenth century (cf. the much briefer sketches in Langland, PP B Pro 68–82, 2.219–23, 5.639–42). Chaucer's Pardoner is in the employ of the Hospital of St. Mary Rouncesval at Charing Cross in London, a dependency (cell) of the Augustinian Hospital of Our Lady of Roncesvalles, in Spain on the pilgrim road to Compostela (see 466 above). The Charing Cross cell was deeply involved in the sale of indulgences, and pardoners of "Runcevale" were suspect; see Friar Daw's Reply in Six Ecclesiastical Satires, ed. James Dean, TEAMS, 1991, 483–84: "I trowe thou menys the pardonysters of Seint Thomas of Acres,/ Of Antoun, or of Runcevale, that rennen so fast aboute." In 1382 and 1387 unauthorized sales of pardons were made by those professing to be working for this house; in the 1390s the house was raising money through the sales of indulgences for a building fund; see James Galloway, Hospital and Chapel of St. Mary Roncevall, 1913; and David K. Maxfield, ChauR 28, 1993, 148–63.

Manly believed Chaucer had some particular pardoner in mind (New Light, 122–30), and Kellogg and Haselmayer point out that the carrying of false relics was an abuse so rare that it may suggest some particular individual (PMLA 66:275). However, satirizing false relics was common (Mann, Ch and Estates, 150).

Pardoners were customarily clerics, and this Pardoner's participation in the Mass (line 708) seems to indicate that he has clerical status, but his exact status is unclear. He assumes a priestly role during parts of the Mass (Clarence H. Miller and Roberta B. Bosse, ChauR 6, 1972, 173); and the Pardoner himself seems to suggest that he is a friar (PardPro VI.416; see also 683 below).

A great deal of critical attention has been devoted to the Pardoner's sexual nature. Curry (Ch and Science, 59–70) argued that the Pardoner was a born eunuch, "eunuchus ex nativitate," a position widely accepted until recent years. Robert P. Miller (Spec 30, 1955, 180–99) regards him as spiritually and morally sterile, the opposite of the "eunuchus Dei" (Matt 19.12). Beryl Rowland (Neophilol 48, 1964, 56–60) draws on modern medical texts to define him as a "testicular pseudo-hermaphrodite of the feminine type." Recent critics have tended to see him as a homosexual (Monica E. McAlpine, PMLA 95, 1980, 8–22), who, unlike the eunuch, was a frequent figure of medieval satire (Mann, Ch and Estates, 145–48). Carolyn Dinshaw (Ch's Sexual Poetics, 156–84) takes him as a eunuch ("a figurative one, if not in fact a literal one as well"). In two mutually supporting articles in Mediaevalia 1985 (for 1982), C. D. Benson and R. F. Green present a strong case for the idea that the Pardoner is an effeminate heterosexual like Absolom in The Miller's Tale (cf. PardT

VI.948n.). It should be noted that a eunuch would have been ineligible for holy orders (Deut. 23.1) and that, as C. D. Benson notes, in the fifteenth-century Prologue to the Tale of Beryn (ed. Bowers) the Pardoner is depicted as the lecherous (but woefully unsuccessful) seducer of the barmaid Kit. McAlpine (PMLA 95:8–22) summarizes recent criticism.

670 Rouncivale: The Hospital of St. Mary of Rouncesval at Charing Cross (see introductory note).

671 court of Rome: Only the pope would grant the highly prized, and therefore expensive, plenary indulgence, which freed the recipient from all punishment.

672 "Com hider, love, to me!": Skeat (5:55) compares Pearl (ed. Gordon, 1953), lines 763–64: "Com hider to me, my lemman swete,/ for mote ne spot is not in thee" [regularized], which echoes Cant. 4.7 ("Thou art all fair, my love; there is no spot in thee").

On the rhyme **Rome : to me,** see Language and Versification, p. xxxvii.

673 stif burdoun: In musical terms, the bass (*cantus firmus*) part; cf. RvT I.4165. *Burdoun* has also been taken to mean phallus (though neither MED nor OED records any such meaning), and many critics find a pun here, following a suggestion by Baum, Ch: A Crit. Appreciation, 218 n. 20. The pun (if one exists) has led some to the assumption of a homosexual relationship between the Summoner and the Pardoner, though the text offers no further support for this interpretation.

675–79 The "Ashmole" version of the *Secretum secretorum* notes: "Heres yelow and whitissh untechable and wild maners thei shewen. . . . And the thynner the heeres ben, the more gileful, sharp, ferefull, and of wynnyng covetous, it sheweth" (EETS 276, 92). Clerics were forbidden long hair; Marie P. Hamilton (JEGP 40, 1941, 60) quotes the archbishop of Canterbury in 1342 complaining of clerics who dress fancily and scorn the tonsure, "making themselves conspicuous by hair spreading almost to the shoulders in feminine fashion."

683 cappe: Hamilton (JEGP 40:62) argues that this is the "biretta" worn by Augustinian canons, who were supposed to wear their hoods on journeys.

684 glarynge eyen: Such eyes indicate "a man given to folly, a glutton, a libertine, and a drunkard," according to the physiognomist Palemon (Curry, Ch and Science, 57; cf. *Secreta secretorum,* EETS e.s. 66, 82). The **hare** was believed to sleep with its eyes open and thought to be hermaphroditic: "it is yseid that he gendreth withoute male and hath both sexes, male and femele" (Barth. Angl., 18.68; tr. Trevisa 2:1221).

685 vernycle: A medal struck with a representation of St. Veronica's veil, upon which an image of Christ's face was said to have been imprinted. Such medals were a badge of the pilgrimage to Rome (Sumption, Pilgrimage, 222, 249–56).

688–89 A high (**smal**) voice and beardlessness were signs of eunuchry: if the testicles are cut away, "mannes strengths passith and manly complexioun chongith into femel complexioun . . . [they lose their hair . . . their voices] beth as voys of wommen" (Barth. Angl., 5.48; tr. Trevisa, 1:261). The goat was, and still popularly is, considered a lecherous

beast: Gower (Miroir 929–30; tr. Wilson, 16) describes Lechery mounted on a "goat, which is lecherous, and in which wantoness is not restrained." In Cambridge MS GG.4.27 (Facsimile, ed. Parkes and Beadle) the illustrator (in the Parson's Tale) shows Lechery riding side-saddle on a goat (see color plates in vol. 3).

691 geldyng, mare: *geldyng* suggests a eunuch, while *mare* may imply a homosexual—a somewhat unusual meaning, but see Mann, Ch and Estates, 146, who compares Walter of Chatillon's "Equa fit equus" (the horse becomes a mare); and Doreen M. E. Gillam, NM 88, 1987, 192–99, who finds that OF and ON usage shows it means "effeminate homosexual." As McAlpine points out (PMLA 95:8–22), the narrator avoids specifying the Pardoner's condition too precisely.

692 fro Berwyk into Ware: From Berwick-upon-Tweed (the northernmost spot in England) to Ware in Hertfordshire or in Kent; i.e., from one end of the Great North Road in England to the other. Cf. Whiting B260 and Magoun, Ch Gazetteer, 31–32. See also WBPro III.824n.

696–98 Cf. Matt. 14.25–31 for Christ's calling Peter.

699 latoun: A metal (*auricalum*) alloy "of copper and of tynne and of auripigment and with other metalles" that has the appearance of gold but not its value or durability (Barth. Angl., 16.5; tr. Trevisa, 2:830). It was used for ornaments (MilT I.3251) and for decorative armor (Thop VII.877).

701–4 On legislation against the use of false relics by pardoners, see Owst, Preaching, 109–10, who also quotes preachers' complaints against those who go about "with fals letters and seles, with crosses, and reliques that thei bere abowten them, and sei that thei be of seyntes bones or of holy mens clothing." Mann (Ch and Estates, 150–52) compares Boccaccio's story of Fra Cipolla (Decameron 6.10), who claims to have one of the angel Gabriel's feathers, though actually it is a parrot's.

706 made . . . apes: cf. MilT I.3389, ShipT VII.440, CYT VIII.1313. Proverbial (Whiting A148).

709 lessoun: An excerpt from the Bible or other sacred writings, perhaps here the Epistle (see Lay Folks Mass Book, EETS 71, 96–97). **Storie** has a variety of liturgical meanings but here is probably a series of lessons "covering a story in the Bible or the life of a saint" (Robinson).

710 offertorie: That part of the Mass, sung by the priest "with his ministers" (Lay Folks Mass Book, 98–99), while the faithful make their offerings. In England, unlike the continental usage, the sermon ordinarily followed either the Offertory or the Bidding Prayer, or Prayer of the Faithful (Lay Folks Mass Book, 317–19).

712 affile his tonge: Proverbial (Whiting T378) and see Tr 2.1681: "This Pandarus gan newe his tong affile." Cf. Prov. 139:4 (AV 140:3): "They have sharpened their tongues like a serpent."

719 the Belle: Southwark contained over half a dozen taverns and inns called the Bell; William Rendle and P. Norman note that one stood across from the Tabard, though there is no record of its existence before 1600 (Inns of Old Southwark, 1888, 420).

725–42 The apology offered here is similar to that in *Roman de la rose* (7103–20 and 15159–92; tr. Dahlberg, 135 and 258). For a second apology which relates to subject matter, see MilPro I.3167–86 and cf. MancT IX.207–10 and n., and, for the same general idea, Lak of Stedfastnesse 4–5 (Now "word and deed .../ ben nothing lyk"). In 741–42 Chaucer seems to quote Plato (Timaeus, tr. R. G. Bury, Loeb, 1929, 29 B: "Accordingly, in dealing with a copy and its model, we must affirm that the accounts given will themselves be akin to the diverse objects which they serve to explain"). However, like most of his contemporaries, he knew Plato only indirectly and he probably derived the quotation from Boethius (Bo 3. pr12.205–7: "The sentence of Plato that nedes the wordis moot be cosynes to the thinges of whiche thei speken"). The expression (word and deed must accord) became proverbial (Whiting W645).

746 The topos of "affected modesty," in which an author disclaims any skill or protests inadequacy to the subject, is common in classical and medieval literature (Curtius, Europ. Lit., 83–85) and frequently used by Chaucer (e.g., MerT IV.1736–37, SqT V.105–6, and FranPro V.716–27).

The Host

The Host is called Herry Bailly in The Cook's Prologue (I.4358); the Subsidy Rolls for Southwark in 1380–81 list "Henri Bayliff ostlyer" (innkeeper) and his wife "Christian." He was a man of substance who represented his borough in Parliament in 1376–77 and 1378–79 and held other public offices (Manly, New Light, 79–83).

The Host has been the subject of considerable comment. See, in addition to most general studies of the *Tales*, B. Page, ChauR 4, 1969, 1–13 (with summary of previous opinions), C. C. Richardson, TSLL 12, 1970–71, 325–44 (on the Host as representative of an uncritical contemporary audience), David R. Pichaske and Laura Sweetland, ChauR 11, 1977, 179–200 (on the Host as governor), and E. D. Higgs, MHLS 2, 1979, 28–43 (on the relation of the Host to the narrator).

752 marchal in an halle: The marshall had the exacting task of managing protocol and directing the service at feasts; see A Fifteenth-Century Courtesy Book, ed. Chambers, EETS 148, 1914.

753 eyen stepe: Either "bright" or "large, prominent" eyes (see 201 above); William P. Keen shows that the phrase is frequently used of bold, attractive heroes in ME romances (Topic 17, 1969, 9–10). Cf. MED s.v. *steōp(e* adj.1.(c).

754 Chepe: The modern Cheapside, where the most prosperous shops were located (Alec R. Myers, London in the Age of Ch, 1972, 23–24).

785 make it wys: Raise difficulties. The idiom *make it* plus adjective is common in Middle English (MED s.v. *maken* 14) and in Chaucer (RvT I.3980, FranT V.1223, ShipT VII.379n.)

791 to shorte with: For the construction, cf. MilPro I.3119, PardPro VI.345, ShipT VII.273.

796–801 Laila Gross of Fairleigh Dickinson University notes that a free dinner was the prize for the best poem at the festivals of the London "Pui" (an association of amateur poets) in the thirteenth century; excerpts from its regulations are translated by D. W. Robertson, Jr., The Lit. of Med. England, 1970, 285–87.

811 "We" is the understood subject of **preyden**, perhaps also of **swore** in the preceding line. Cf. 33 above.

817 In heigh and lough: "In every respect," a translation of the Lat. legal formula *in alto et basso* (Henry B. Hinckley, PMLA 46, 1931, 98–99). On similar expressions, see 534 above.

819 Wine was drunk as a nightcap; cf. Tr 3.671–72: "The wyn anon, and whan so that yow leste,/ So go we slepe."

826 the Waterynge of Seint Thomas: A brook at the second milestone on the Old Kent Road from London to Canterbury.

830 even-song and morwesong: Proverbial (Whiting E160).

843 shortly for to tellen: A common formula; cf. KnT I.875–88n.

844 aventure: This word, meaning "chance," regularly contrasts with words such as **cas** ("destiny"); cf. ClT IV.812, MerT IV.1967. **Sort** may mean something more like "luck." The words are, however, near synonyms and thus emphasize the inexplicability of what has happened. Many critics (e.g., Donaldson, 1061) suspect that Harry Bailey rather than these mysterious forces arranged that the **cut** should fall to the knight.

849 what nedeth wordes mo: A rhetorical formula (*occupatio*); cf. KnT I.1029, 1715, and the similar formula in PhyT VI.230.

The Knight's Tale

The explanatory notes to The Knight's Tale are adapted from those written by Vincent J. DiMarco for The Riverside Chaucer.

A reference in the Prologue to *The Legend of Good Women* to the "love of Palamon and Arcite/ Of Thebes, thogh the storye ys knowen lyte" (F 420–21) shows that Chaucer made a version of The Knight's Tale sometime before that prologue was composed (1386–88). However, the old theory of a lost version in rime royal stanzas (Bernhard ten Brink, Ch Studien, 1870, 36–69) was proven both needless and improbable by detailed arguments (not all of equal worth) by Tatlock (Dev. and Chron., 45–66), and most likely The Knight's Tale as we have it does not essentially differ from the earlier "Palamon and Arcite." A few lines do show revision to accommodate the earlier version to the *Tales* (see KnT I.875–92 and n.), and occasionally a detail different from Boccaccio seems particularly appropriate to the Knight as narrator (e.g., I.2630; cf. GP I.57), but not much can be made of this.

The tale cannot be dated precisely. Line 884 is often taken as an allusion to Queen Anne's arrival in England on 18 December 1381, but this is by no means certain (see 884 below). D. W. Robertson, Jr., (SP 84, 1987, 418–39) argues from other supposed historical references that the Knight's portrait in the General Prologue and his tale must date between 1393 and 1396, most likely "the summer of 1394." He regards both portrait and tale as "late additions" to the *Tales*.

That the tale of Palamon and Arcite was *knowen lyte* when the Prologue to *The Legend of Good Women* was written may indicate that it was a recent work. Manly (CT, 540, 549–50) argued for 1381, before the *Troilus*. Robert A. Pratt (PMLA 62, 1947, 618–19) shows that lines 1491–96 are original and replace *Teseida* 4.73, which Chaucer had used in *Troilus*

(2.64–70), and he argues that the tale must therefore date after *Troilus* (written 1385–86) and before the F Prologue to *The Legend of Good Women* (written 1386–88). The fact that The Knight's Tale shares a number of lines with both *Troilus* (see notes 1010 and 1101 below) and *The Legend of Good Women* (1035–36, 1223, 1502, 1761) lends some support to such a date.

Skeat (5:70, 75–76) attempted to date the work by reference to the calendar: Arcite escapes from prison on the night of 3 May (I.1462–67); he meets Palamon the next day, a Friday (I.1528–38), and their duel is on the next day, Saturday, 5 May. In 1386, 5 May was a Saturday. The tournament is held a year later on Tuesday, 7 May, according to Skeat's calculations, and in 1387, 7 May was a Tuesday. The other years in the decade that fit the supposed calendrical references are 1380–81. J. D. North (RES n.s. 20, 1969, 149–54) accepts Skeat's date of 1387, since Saturn was in the sign of Leo (I.2461–62) during this decade only in 1387 and 1389, and only in 1387 was either 3 May or 4 May a Friday.

The Knight's Tale is a free adaptation of Boccaccio's *Il Teseida delle nozze d'Emelia* (The Story of Theseus Concerning The Nuptials of Emily), written around 1339–41. Chaucer could have obtained a manuscript of this work on either of his trips to Italy in 1372–73 and 1378, though it is usually held that he did not know Boccaccio's work until the later trip (see Robert A. Pratt, SP 42, 1945, 762–63). William E. Coleman (MÆ 51, 1982, 92–101) notes that many MSS of the *Teseida,* including Pavia MS 881 (representing the tradition Chaucer may have known), lack any attribution to Boccaccio (whose name never appears in Chaucer's works).

The *Teseida* is a poem of 9904 lines (9896 lines, the exact length of the *Aeneid,* in the family of manuscripts known to Chaucer), written in an elaborate, pseudo-classical style and divided in epic fashion into twelve books. Boccaccio wrote copious glosses to the work (printed in Limentani's edition and translated by McCoy, *The Book of Theseus*) but they seem not to have been in the manuscript family available to Chaucer and it is not clear that he knew them. The case for his knowledge of Boccaccio's glosses is made by Piero Boitani (Ch and Boccaccio, 1977, 190–97; see 2895 below). The glosses are of some interest for interpretation but represent, on the whole, conventional learning such as Chaucer might well have possessed or have acquired from various other sources (Pratt, SP 42:745–63).

Chaucer handled his source freely, omitting much of Boccaccio's narrative and adding much of his own. Of the 2249 lines in The Knight's Tale, only about 700 correspond, even loosely, to lines in the *Teseida*. For comparisons of the two narratives, see Boitani, Ch and Boccaccio, esp. 76–189, and Ch and Trecento, 1983, 194–99. The line-by-line relation of the two poems is shown by H. L. Ward's marginal notations in the Six-Text Edition (Ch Soc 1, n.d.; minor corrections by Boyd A. Wise, Infl. of Statius upon Ch, 1911 [rpt. 1967], 78). Chaucer almost certainly had direct access to a glossed manuscript of Statius's *Thebaid;* see Wise, 46–54, 78–115, and Paul M. Clogan, SP 61, 1964, 599–603. He may also have used the Roman de Thèbes (Wise, 129–36), and he made extensive use of Boethius's *Consolation of Philosophy,* which he himself had translated (see Bernard L. Jefferson, Ch and the Consolation of Philosophy of Boethius, 1917 [rpt.], 130–32, 142–44, and F. Anne Payne, Ch and Menippean Satire, 1981, 223–40; see 2987–3089 below).

Chaucer's condensation, even elimination, of much of Boc-caccio's epic machinery suggests to many readers that The Knight's Tale is best considered a chivalric romance of a philosophical complexion (though the usefulness of generic categories such as "romance" is thoughtfully questioned by Robert M. Jordan, in Ch at Albany, ed. R. H. Robbins, 1983, 83–86), and none of the romances in the *Tales* (WBT, SqT, Thopas, FrankT, KnT) fits neatly into the confines of the genre (cf. J. A. Burrow in Cambridge Ch Companion, ed. Boitani and Mann, 109–24). See also Susan Crane, Gender and Romance in Ch's CT, 1994, 8–26; John Finlayson, ChauR 27, 1992, 126–49; Angela Jane Weisl, Conquering the Reign of Femeny, 1995. Elements of realism and contemporary courtly practices, many introduced into the tale by Chaucer, are collected by Stuart Robertson (JEGP 14, 1915, 226–55), though Chaucer also seems to attempt to "distance" the story from his audience by using a pre-Christian setting with occasional archaic features (Bruce K. Cowgill, PQ 54, 1975, 670–77).

The traditions available to Chaucer regarding Theseus (who also appears in *The House of Fame, Anelida and Arcite,* and *The Legend of Good Women*) are summarized by Walter Scheps (LeedsSE 9, 1976–77, 19–34). The Theseus of The Knight's Tale is usually seen as an idealized ruler characterized by wisdom and justice (e.g., Robertson, Pref. to Ch, 260–66). Some critics, however, have seen him as a cruel conqueror and tyrannical autocrat (Terry Jones, Ch's Knight, 1980, 192–202) or as a figure of glamorized violence (Aers, Ch, Langland, 174–95). Emphasizing Theseus's development and education in the course of the story, John Reidy (in Epic in Med. Soc., ed. Harald Scholler, 1977, 391–408) justly assesses the seemingly contradictory elements in Theseus's character; see also Georgia R. Crampton, Condition of Creatures, 1974, 45–75; and McCall, Ch among the Gods, 64–68, 72–86.

Most interpretative criticism of the tale has turned on the problems of order in an apparently unjust universe. Charles Muscatine, in an influential article (PMLA 65, 1950, 911–29; see also Ch and Fr Trad., 175–90), discusses the relation of cosmic order to the ordering function of ritual, ceremony, noble ideals, and the formal symmetries of the poem. Others (e.g., Elizabeth Salter, Ch: KnT and ClT, 9–36; Kathleen A. Blake, MLQ 34, 1973, 3–19) have in varying ways argued that the impulses toward order are frustrated and that the encouraging philosophy of Theseus's great speech on order is belied by reality; yet others (e.g., Robert W. Hanning, Lit. Rev. 23, 1980, 519–41) explain the tensions in the story as symptomatic of the split between the ideals and the realities of fourteenth-century chivalry. On this, see esp. Lee Patterson, Ch and Hist., 165–230, with extensive and useful notes (165–67 contain a good summary of critical disputes over this tale). For a selection of critical essays, see Harold Bloom, ed., Geoffrey Ch's Knight's Tale, 1988. For a very useful survey and bibliography of critical studies, see Monica E. McAlpine, Chaucer's Knight's Tale: An Annotated Bibliography, 1900 to 1985, The Chaucer Bibliographies, 1991.

PART ONE

The motto, *Iamque domos patrias, Scithice post aspera gentis prelia, laurigero, &c,* found in many MSS of all groups and perhaps included as a gloss by Chaucer himself (Manly-Rickert 2:484–85, 527), is from Statius, Theb. 12.519–20, which likewise describes the hero's victorious return to Athens. An expanded form of the motto is found in three MSS of *Anelida and Arcite,* before the stanza beginning at Anel 22, also dependent on Statius. Cf. Tes. 2.19–24.

860   Theseus, properly speaking king of Athens, is called duke by Dante (Inf. 12.17), by Boccaccio (Tes. 1 13.3–4), and elsewhere by Chaucer in Anel 29 ("this duke") and LGW 2442 ("For of Athenes duk and lord was he"). This is not an anachronism. There was a duke of Athens: the title was established by Louis IX of France, c. 1260. See Nicolas Cheetham, Med. Greece, 1981, 166–88.

875–92   Tatlock (Dev. and Chron., 66) suggests this entire passage was added when the original Palamon and Arcite was revised into The Knight's Tale. Willis J. Wager (MLN 50, 1935, 296–307) finds support for the suggestion in a tense system different from that of the immediate context, as well as a repetition of rhymes (I.865–66/877–78; 867–68/881–82) that one might not expect if the passages had been written continuously.

875–88   The rhetorical figure here employed is *occupatio* or *praeteritio,* a refusal to describe or narrate that often has the effect of describing or narrating (see Geoffrey of Vinsauf, Poetria nova, 1159–62; tr. Nims, 58). Other examples in this tale of the figure—described by Manly (PBA 12, 1926, 106) along with the absolute construction as one of Chaucer's two favorite methods of abbreviation—are I.994–99, 2197–207, 2919–66 (the account of Arcite's funeral). Robert S. Haller (MP 62, 1965, 288) sees the use of the device in The Knight's Tale as wholly functional, in introducing matters that must, for the sake of brevity, be dispensed with; Stephen T. Knight (Rymyng Craftily, 136–45) distinguishes degrees of rhetorical elaboration and heightening of style—sometimes speeding up the action, sometimes intensifying the emotion. He notices a matter-of-fact use of the device, along with that of *continuatio* (pithy expression of a thought) and *dubitatio* (doubting what to say or how to say it) in I.1187–89, 1199–201, 1216–18, 1340–42, 1353–54, 1377–80, 1417–18, and 1459–61.

884 tempest: Neither Statius nor Boccaccio mentions a storm on Theseus's homecoming. John L. Lowes (MLN 19, 1904, 240–43) sees here a reference to the storm that destroyed the ship that had brought Anne of Bohemia, fiancée of Richard II, to England on 18 December 1381 (Walsingham, Historia Anglicana, 2:46). Others (e.g., Walter C. Curry, MLN 36, 1921, 272–74) argue instead that the word is used metaphorically to describe the excitement of the Athenians (cf. *tomolto,* Tes. 2.24); see MED, s.v. *tempest,* n. 3 (a).

894   Both Statius and Boccaccio place the Temple of Clemence (I.928) within the city; and both introduce the suffering widows in the narrative before Theseus arrives.

912–13 The eldeste lady: Identified by Boccaccio as Evadne. She does not swoon in either Theb. or Tes.

915   The idea that Fortune grants victory is wholly conventional. For comprehensive treatments of the medieval idea of Fortune, see Howard R. Patch, Goddess Fortuna in Med. Lit., 1939; Jefferson, Ch and the Consolation, 49–60; Barbara Bartholomew, Fortuna and Natura, 1966, 9–45; see also 1663–72 below.

924 caytyves: Miserable wretches, perhaps from the Roman de Thèbes, 9994 (*chaitives*). For the word as a motif in the tale, see Crampton, Condition of Creatures, 92–104.

925–26   For **Fortune** and her **wheel,** see Patch, Goddess Fortuna, and Whiting F506.

932   The impious Cappaneus, one of the "Seven against Thebes" (see Tr 5.1485–1510), was struck with a thunderbolt from Zeus (Tr 5.1504–5: "Capaneus the proud/ With thonder-dynt was slayn").

938 the olde Creon: As Wise (Infl. of Statius, 130) notes, this is a familiar epithet in the Roman de Thèbes (tr. Coley, 5190: "The old and hoary Creon," 5799, 8341, etc.); cf. Anel 64: "the olde Creon." In Tes. 2.61 Creon is of mature age, but he is nowhere described by Boccaccio as old.

949–57   Wise (Infl. of Statius, 131–32) notes similarities to the Roman de Thèbes: Theseus's arrival on a horse (instead of in a chariot); the suppliants falling prostrate to make their plea; Theseus raising them to their feet. Cf. I.949 and Thèbes 9944: "And falls at his feet very humbly"; I.952 and Thèbes 9946: "He descends from his horse"; I.957 and Thèbes 9997–98: "He takes King Adrastus by the hand,/ Raises him from the ground."

952 This gentil duc: On the use of *this,* see Language and Versification, p. xxxiii.

966 His baner he desplayeth: To display one's banner before an enemy was formally to declare war (Maurice Keen, Laws of War in the MA, 1955, 106) and proclaim martial law (Howard Schless, ChauR 25, 1990, 80–81).

969–70   Statius, but not Boccaccio, includes the detail of a night-march to Thebes (Theb. 12.661: "Night too and the quiet shades they add to their toil"). Clogan (SP 61:611) suggests that Chaucer's phrasing shows knowledge of the gloss on this line in the *Thebaid.*

975   The description of Mars as red is from Tes. 1.3 (*rubicondo,* ruddy); see also I.1747, 1969, Anel 1 ("Thou ferse god of armes, Mars the rede"), and LGW 2589 ("The rede Mars"). The planet in the skies has a reddish cast.

980 Mynotaur: Not mentioned in Tes., the minotaur is depicted as defeated by Theseus on the hero's shield in Theb. 12.668–73. Chaucer recounts the exploit in LGW 1886–2150.

989   The wholesale destruction of the captured city, apparently consistent with fourteenth-century practice (Stuart Robertson, JEGP 14:227–28), finds a macabre analogue in Tes. 2.81.7–8; tr. McCoy, 68: "Since they [the widows] were unable to take any further revenge, they set fire to [Thebes]."

1006–7   By the laws of medieval warfare, "reasonable pillage" of a defeated enemy was permitted (Keen, Laws of War, 135–55); Gower (Mirour, 24037–49; tr. Wilson, 314) distinguishes those who fight primarily for the love of justice from those motivated by hope of material gain. However, "Chaucer omits Teseo's courteous dispatch of men to bury the dead and treat the wounded" (Robinson).

1010   Almost identical with Tr 4.627: "Thorugh-girt with many a wid and blody wownde."

1013–14   An example of *commutatio,* a repetition of words or phrases in reverse order (Geoffrey of Vinsauf, Poetria nova, 4.1174–75; tr. Nims, 58: "O how holy the grace of Christ! O how gracious the holiness"). See also I.1736, 2843–44.

1013–24 The names **Palamon** and **Arcite** are derived from Boccaccio's *Palemone* and *Arcita. Palaemon* occurs in Statius: he is the son of Ino, hence the grandson of Cadmus, founder of the "dreadful race" of Thebes (Theb. 1.12–14, 115–22). Boccaccio's *Arcita* may derive ultimately from the Greek poem *Digenes Akrites.*

1024 he nolde no raunsoun: Theseus's refusal to ransom his captives (like his later release of Arcite *withouten any raunsoun,* I.1205) is proof of his unmercenary character (Stuart Robertson, JEGP 14:229), not, as Palamon says (I.1111), of his tyranny. Perpetual imprisonment for prisoners who have not surrendered and who pose a threat of further war was an acceptable practice; see Reidy, in Epic in Med. Soc., 399–402. The topic of ransom is not raised by Boccaccio.

1035–36 Cf. LGW 2425–26: "Ligurges doughter, fayrer on to sene/ Than is the flour ageyn the bryghte sonne."

1039 The rhetorical device of *dubitatio* (see 875–88 above). Cf. I.1459–60 (mixed with *interrogatio,* a question) and I.2227–32.

1047 For May-day and maytime customs depicted here and in I.1500–12, see John Brand, Observations on the Pop. Antiq. of Gt. Brit., ed. Ellis, 1849, repr. 1969, 212–34; Edward R. Mitchell, MLN 71, 1956, 560–64; Floure and the Leafe, ed. Pearsall, 24–26: "And up I rose, three houres after twelfe/ About the very springing of the day,/ And on I put my geare and mine array."

1049–50 In Tes. 3.10.2 Emilia "had wound her blond tresses about her head," rather than *broyded* it into a braid; cf. Tr 5.808–12: Criseyde's manner was "To gon ytressed with hire heres clere/ Doun by hire coler at hire bak byhynde,/ Which with a thred of gold she wolde bynde."

1053–54 Emelye makes her garland of flowers, Arcite makes his of leaves (I.1508). This may be an allusion to the fashionable courtly debates between the adherents of the flower and of the leaf; see ProLGW 61–80, and Pearsall, ed., The Floure and the Leafe, 22–23.

1074–79 In Tes. 3.11–14 (tr. McCoy, 77) Arcita spies Emilia first; and both he and Palemone think "Venus has truly come down here."

1077–97 The motif of love's fatal glance was probably founded upon the Empedoclean theory of vision accepted by Plato, whereby the eye transmits light through beams that join the eye to the viewed object, and the eyes, as agents (not merely perceivers), strike through the eyes of the beloved into the heart. The motif passed from Greek literature into medieval vernaculars through the agency of the Arabs. It is hardly known in classical Latin literature. See Ruth H. Cline, RPh 25, 1972, 263–97; and Lance K. Donaldson-Evans, Neophil 62, 1978, 202–11. In Tes. 3.15–16, Boccaccio associates the "Aggressive Eyes" topos with the iconography of Cupid's arrows. Cf. KnT I.1567, Tr 2.533–35 ("so soore hath she me wounded/ . . . with lokyng of hire eyen"), MercB 1 ("Your yen two wol slee me sodenly"), Compl d'Am 41–42 ("two thinges doon me dye,/ That is to seyn, hir beautee and myn yë").

1077–79 In Tes. 3.18–19 (tr. McCoy, 80) Emilia is aware of the young men: "At that 'Alas!' . . . her eyes moved immediately to that little window . . . she rose to her feet with the flowers she had gathered . . . and as she left she was not oblivious of that 'Alas!'"

1087–91 For medieval "astrologizing" of the classical gods, see Seznec, Survival of the Pagan Gods, 37–83, 149–83. On the astrology of The Knight's Tale, see Curry, Ch and Science, 119–38; also Douglas Brooks and Alistair Fowler, MÆ 39, 1970, 123–46. Chaucer's attitude toward astrology, or "judicial astronomy," is not altogether clear. See MLT II.313–14n. For **Saturne** see 2443–78 below.

1101 Cf. Tr 1.425–26: "But whither goddesse or womman, iwis,/ She be, I not, which that ye do me serve."

1129–32 For these lines and 1169–70 and 1172–76, Chaucer draws from the conversation of Arcita and Palemone in the grove (Tes. 5.53ff.), where the jealousy motif is allowed to surface more gradually.

1132 Palamon and Arcite are not only cousins, but "sworn brothers"; i.e., united through oath in a legally binding relationship, ordinarily for the duration of the lives of the contracting parties, in which each pledged to the other military assistance in time of danger, ransom in the event of capture, the right to share in the spoils of war, the duty to avenge the other's death, and even the privilege of marrying his widow.

The relationship of Arcite and Palamon is extraordinary in that its primary aim (I.1135–39) is the furtherance of a brother's love-suit; ordinarily, romantic concerns are much subordinated to "feudal" or heroic impulses. More representative of the institution as practiced in the OF chansons de geste and the ME romances is the assumption (I.1134) of the duration of the bond; the formal abrogation of the oath (I.1604–5) when one party recognizes treacherous behavior in the other; and even the renewal of the compact (I.2783–97; cf. Amis and Amiloun, ed. MacEdward Leach, Intro.) when such alleged treachery has been proven to rest on a misunderstanding.

1155 For paramour: As a mistress, hence, opposed to Palamon's love of Emelye as a goddess (I.1157).

1163–64 Translates the marginal gloss "Quis legem det amantibus?" From Boethius, Cons. 3.ml2.52–55: "But what is he that may yeven a lawe to loverys? Love is a grettere lawe and a strengere to hymself thanne any lawe that men mai yyven." The sentiment is proverbial (Whiting L579; Walther 25383). Cf. Tr 4.618 ("Thorugh love is broken al day every lawe") and I.1606 below. Boethius quotes the proverb in his account of Orpheus and Eurydice, which he takes as a fable about the "sovereign good" versus "earthly things"; Boethius thus clearly intends the proverb as a criticism of lovers.

1165 by my pan: Elliott (Ch's English, 247, 252) remarks upon Arcite's predilection for swearing. Swearing by one's head (I.2670), crown (RvT I.4041), or *pan* is common.

1167 positif lawe: Human, legislated law (*lex civilis*), as opposed to natural law (*lex naturalis*). We are disposed by natural law to love; and any human law that tries to prevent our obeying natural law, Arcite argues, will be broken. Cf. Tr 1.236–38: "For evere it was, and evere it shal byfalle,/ That Love is he that alle thing may bynde,/ For may no man fordon the lawe of kynde."

1177–80 Similar fables are common; see Thompson, Motif-Index, K348. Siegfried Wenzel (SP 73, 1976, 145) cites a comparison of foolish lovers fighting over a corpse, from a treatise for preachers which Chaucer seems to have known (Wenzel, Traditio 30, 1974, 351–78).

1181–82 Proverbial after Chaucer; Whiting M73.

1191–1208 The friendship of Theseus and Pirithous was legendary; their daring but unsuccessful attempt to bring Proserpina from the Underworld to be Pirithous's bride is mentoned in Theb. 1.475–76 and 8.53–54, where the description of Theseus as *iuratus amico* (sworn to [his] friend) may have suggested Chaucer's describing them as *felawes*; i.e., sworn brothers (see 1132 above). That Theseus sought his dead companion in hell (1200) follows no classical account, and is most likely from the *Roman de la rose* (8148–51; tr. Dahlberg, 151: "Theseus had loved him [Pirithous] so much . . . that after his death . . . he went alive to seek him in hell").

1196 Cf. SNT VIII.236 (almost identical).

1201 Sometimes considered a line unaltered from the original Palamon and Arcite; Manly, however, compares WBPro III.224–25 as a similar violation of narrative decorum.

1223 Cf. LGW 658: "Allas," quod he, "the day that I was born!"

1238 The figure of dice was commonly applied to the vicissitudes of Fortune. Cf. MkT VII.2661.

1242 Fortune is chaungeable: Proverbial; Whiting F523.

1247 erthe, water, fir, ne eir: On the four elements, see GP I.333 and n.

1251–67 Arcite's lament is derived from Boethius (Bo 3.pr2), who asserts that true happiness can be found only in the possession of the Supreme Good; but men, driven by folly and error, mistake such transitory goods as power, fame, and riches for the Supreme Good. Arcite speaks only of the vanity of human wishes. His failure adequately to distinguish between Providence and Fortune should be compared with Bo 4.pr6; pr7; and Dante, Inf. 7.70–96. I.1255 may echo Bo 3.pr2.25–28 ("Of the whiche men, some of hem wenen that sovereyn good be to lyven withoute nede of any thyng, and travaylen hem to ben habundaunt of rychesses"). I.1258–59 may echo Bo 2.pr5.90–94 ("But also a long route of meyne, maketh that a blisful man? The whiche servantz yif thei ben vicyous of condyciouns, is a gret charge and a destruccioun to the hous, and a gret enemy to the lord hymself"). I.1260 is probably an echo of Romans 8.26 ("We know not what we should pray for as we ought").

1261 dronke . . . as a mous: Proverbial; cf. WBPro III.246 and Whiting M731.

1261–67 Cf. Bo 3.pr2.84–88, in which the soul that no longer recognizes the true good fares "ryght as a dronke/ man not nat by whiche path he may retourne/ hom to his hous."

1272 exiled fro my wele: Cf. Bo 1.pr6.75–76: "thow art exiled [and] [despoyled] of thy propre goodes."

1299 jalousie In Tes. 3.77–79, Palemone's envy of Arcita's freedom is tempered by sincere fellow-feeling, and at this point stops well short of jealousy.

1301–2 For the comparison of the (yellowish) color of the boxtree (*Buxus sempervirens*), cf. LGW 866 ("And pale as box she was"); from Ovid, Met 4.134–35; tr. Miller, "paler than boxwood").

1303–27 Palamon's lament echoes the sentiments of the imprisoned Boethius (Bo 1.m5), who takes the suffering of the innocent as a contradiction of God's otherwise benevolent governance of the universe, a position that Lady Philosophy then refutes. Cf. MLT II.813–16: FranT V.865–93;

Mars 218–26; Tr 3.1016–19; and LGW 2228–35; and see Jefferson, Ch and the Consolation, 69–71.

1305 atthamaunt: Cf. 1990 below.

1307–9 The figure of the sheep cowering in the fold is not in Boethius; Chaucer's inspiration here may have been Eccles. 2.18–19 ("They themselves are beasts,/ For that which befalleth the sons of men, as the one dieth so dieth the other"), quoted by Innocent III, De miseria condicionis humanae, 1.2.10–15; tr. Lewis.

1313–14 Cf. Tr 3.1016–19: "O auctour of nature,/ Is this an honour to thi deyte,/ That folk ungiltif suffren hire injure,/ And who that giltif is, al quyt goth he?" Chaucer draws on Bo 1.m5. both here and in *Troilus*.

1315–21 Cf. Bo 3.pr7.14–16: "Thanne by the same cause moten thise beestis ben clepid blisful, of whiche beestis al the entencioun hasteth to fulfille here bodily jolyte." Hinckley compares the Dialogue between the Body and Soul in Latin Poems Attr. to Walter Map, ed. Wright, 103, lines 227–30: "O happy condition of brute beasts! Their spirits die with their bodies, and they do not go down to the place of torments—would that such were the end of the impious."

1323 Cf. ParsT X.957: "But so heigh a doctrine I lete to divines."

1323–24 For the rhyme *dyvynys : pyne ys* cf. GP I.523n.

1329–31 The anger of Juno against Thebes was due to Jupiter's adultery with the Theban women Semele and Alcmena.

1331 Cf. Statius, Theb., 12.704; tr. Mozley: "The city walls are all agape."

1347 This is a typical love-problem (*demande d'amour* or *questione d'amore*), of the sort familiar in French, Provençal, and Italian literature of the Middle Ages. For other examples, see WBT III.904–5 and FranT V.1621–22 (from Boccaccio's *Filocolo,* tr. Donald Cheney, 1985, bk. 4). For its prevalence as a topic of literature, see Neilson, Origins of the Court of Love, 246, and John Stevens, Music and Poetry, 154–64. Manuals apparently designed to teach the art of amorous conversation in court (see I.2203) and containing series of such questions (with responses) were very popular. See *Les adevineaux amoureux,* ed. James W. Hassell, Jr., 1974; and The Demaundes off Love, ed. W. L. Braekman, Scripta: Med. and Ren. Texts and Sts. 7, 1982.

PART TWO

1355–76 Chaucer here elaborates upon Tes. 4.26–29, adding such symptoms as Arcite's chronic swooning and his changing complexion, while omitting the fearsome appearance rendered by Arcita's thick brows and shaggy hair. Both Boccaccio and Chaucer describe the malady as melancholic; John L. Lowes (MP 11, 1914, 491–546) shows that the symptoms Chaucer adds are those of the **loveris maladye of Hereos** (from Gr. *eros,* love, but influenced in form and meaning by Lat. *heros,* hero, and *herus,* master); as a mental disease (love sickness), it was regularly recognized and discussed by medieval medical authorities. Robertson (Pref to Ch, 456–60) translates relevant portions of Bernard of Gordon's Lillium medicinae (see GP 1.429–34 and n.). The Third Partition of Robert Burton's *Anatomy of Melancholy* is an encyclopedic discussion of "heroick love."

1374–76 manye: Mania is a form of madness to which *amor hereos* could lead; it could be fatal. The brain was thought to have three cells: in the front is the **celle fantastik,** which controls the imagination; in the middle cell, judgment; and in the rear, memory (cf. Bartholomaeus Anglicus 5.3; tr. Trevisa, 1:173). The **humour malencolik** (cf. GP 1.333n.), engendered in some cases by passions of the soul such as "grete thoughtes of sorwe, and of to grete studie and of drede" (in this instance, love), could lead to melancholia, which affects the middle cell and deprives one of judgment and reason; or to mania, which deprives one of the imagination (i.e., one can perceive no new images but thinks continually of his beloved); see Barth. Angl., 7.6; tr. Trevisa, 1:349: "Madness is infeccioun of the further celle of the heed with privacioun of ymaginacioun, as melancholia is infeccioun of the middle celle of the heed with privacioun of resoun [regularized]."

1379 daun: A title of respect, derived from Lat. *dominus,* lord or master, but used very loosely and applied to priests, who were also called "sir" (cf. ProNPT VII.2820), to monks (cf. ShipT VII.43 and the modern title Dom, used for Benedictines), to historical figures, authors, poets, and classical gods. In MilT I.3761 it is used for the blacksmith Gervays, in NPT VII.3334 for the fox, and in VII.3312 for "Daun Burnel the Asse." Spenser was apparently the first to apply the title "Dan" to Chaucer (OED s.v. dan).

1384–98 In Tes. 4.31–34, Arcita is motivated to return to Athens when a crewman of a ship bound there speaks to him of Emilia. A variety of sources has been proposed for Chaucer's version; closest perhaps is Mercury's appearance to the sleeping Aeneas in Aeneid 4.556–70 (W. Bryant Bachman, ELN 13, 1976, 168–73), though Ann M. Taylor (Classical Folia, 30, 1976, 40–56) suggests parallels with Laius's nighttime visit to Eteocles in Theb. 2.102–27, and argues for Chaucer's dependence upon the larger epic tradition of the descent of an other-worldly figure to exhort a hesitant hero to action.

1387 slepy yerde: Mercury's *somniferam virgam,* with which he put the hundred-eyed Argus to sleep and then killed him (Ovid, Met. 1.670; tr. Miller: "Without delay Mercury puts on his winged sandals, takes in his potent hand his sleep-producing wand, and dons his magic cap"). Mercury's command perhaps absolves Arcite of breaking his parole by returning to Athens.

1400–1 Cf. Tr 4.864–65: "Hire face, lik of Paradys the ymage,/ Was al ychaunged in another kynde."

1422 Cf. Joshua 9.21: "Let them be hewers of wood and drawers of water."

1426–43 Arcite's promotion from *page of the chambre* of a lady, to squire of the chamber of a duke—not paralleled in the *Teseida*—has been explained autobiographically with reference to Chaucer's having served while as a youth, perhaps as a page, in the household of Elizabeth, Countess of Ulster, in the time around 1357–59, then in 1368 as a squire attached to the household of Edward III (see D. S. Brewer, Spec 43, 1968, 290–91); but the autobiographical correspondence is doubted, with good reason, by Richard Firth Green (ELN 18, 1981, 251–57), who sees in Arcite's meteoric rise an idealization of a court that recognized true merit, perhaps with the implication of the venality of court life as Chaucer knew it.

1428 In the *Teseida,* Arcita assumes the name Penteo; Chaucer took the name **Philostrate** from Boccaccio's Filostrato, the primary source of the *Troilus. Philostrato,* from the Greek, means "army lover," but Boccaccio, and probably Chaucer, took it to mean "overthrown by love" (Lat. *stratus,* past participle of *sterno*).

1442–45 broghte hym . . . his rente: There is nothing in Tes. to correspond with this realistic touch.

1459–60 Chaucer frequently refers to his lack of **Englyssh**: cf. MLT II.778–79; SqT V.37–38; BD 898–99 ("Me lakketh both Englyssh and wit/ For to undo hyt at the fulle"); LGW ProF 66–67 ("Allas, that I ne had Englyssh, ryme or prose,/ Suffisant this flour to preyse aryght!"); Ven 79–80 ("And eke to me it ys a gret penaunce,/ Syth rym in Englissh hath such skarsete"). These contexts are highly rhetorical and the references may be merely variants on the "modesty" or "inexpressibility" topos (cf. GP I.746n.) but they may also reflect a concern about the state of literary English.

1460 *Roman de la rose* and LGW regularly refer to those who die for love in the language of martyrdom. See also I.1562.

1462–64 of May/ The thridde nyght: Boccaccio says only that the action took place when the moon was in Sagittarius. Chaucer specifies 3 May here and in NPT VII.3187–91 (when Chauntecleer encounters the fox) and in Tr 2.50–56 (when Pandarus suffers a *teene* for love). Manly, who takes *thridde nyght* as referring to the night of 2 May and thus specifying 3 May as the day of the duel, notes the occurrence of 3 May on lists of "Egyptian" or "dismal" days (see John C. Hirsch, ELN 13, 1975, 86–90; BD 1206–7: "I trowe hyt was in the dismal,/ That was the ten woundes of Egipte"). A variety of other explanations have been offered for the inauspiciousness of 3 May (e.g., John P. McCall, MLN 76, 1961, 201–5, and Alfred K. Kellogg and Robert C. Cox in Kellogg, Ch, Langland, 155–98). George Clark (RUO 52, 1982, 257–65) notes that since Palamon escapes after midnight (I.1467) the duel is on 4 May (the day on which Pandarus visits Criseyde) and argues that the reference is not specifically to May but to the lunar month. In medieval lunaria such as Pandarus apparently consults (Tr 2.74: "knew in good plight was the moone"), the third day of the month is inauspicious, the fourth favorable for a new beginning. Clark quotes John Metham's *Days of the Moon* (in Works, ed. Hardin Craig, EETS 132, 1916, 149): "The thryd day of the mone ys noght fortunat to begynne ony werke upon" and "The fourthe day is gode to begynne euery worldly occupacioun." On medieval moon-books or *lunaria,* see Thorndike, Hist. of Magic 1:680–82, and cf. MLT II.306–8, MilT I.3515n.

1465 adventure or destynee: Cf. GP I.844 and n.

1466 thyng is shapen: Proverbial; Whiting T171.

1470–74 Schless (ChauR 25:82) cites a real-life analogue of such an escape from Ralph Pugh, Imprisonment in Medieval England, 1968, 221–22: "In 1323 Roger Mortimer escaped also from the Tower. He and one of his servants made a *potum ingeniosum . . .* with which they drugged the guards to sleep. While the *potum* was having an effect, Mortimer and his companions smashed a wall, which connected their prison with the king's privy kitchen."

1471 clarree: Clary, a spiced, sweetened wine; see also

MerT IV.1807. Skeat's recipe (5:70), from London, British Library MS Sloane 2584, fol. 173, calls for mixing one gallon boiled honey to eight gallons of red wine, then adding one pound of cinnamon, half a pound of powdered ginger, and a quarter pound of pepper. See Curye on Inglysch, EETS, SS 8, 178–79, which notes that *claree* is sweetened with honey, *ypocras* with sugar.

1472 opie of Thebes: The reference is to Egyptian Thebes (Hg and El gloss "Opium Thebaicum"). Palamon may have had the drug with him because it was one of the recognized remedies for the *loveris maladye of Hereos* (Oliver F. Emerson, MP 17, 1919, 287–91). See also Burton's Anat. of Melancholy, 3.2.5.1 (1977 ed., 194).

1479 With dredful foot: Cf. LGW 811: "And in a cave with dredful fot she sterte."

1491   Priscilla Bawcutt (YES 2, 1972, 5–12) traces the idea of the lark greeting the dawn to Alexander Neckam, *De naturis rerum*, ed. Wright, 1863, 1.68 (115). Often understood in a moral sense as a type of zeal and industry, the lark is frequently turned into an amorous symbol, as in I.2209–15.

1494   Cf. Dante, Purg., 1.20 ("[Venus] was making the whole east smile"), which J. A. W. Bennett (MÆ 22, 1953, 114–15) suggests was associated in Chaucer's mind with Tes. 3.5–8; tr. McCoy, 78: "Venus stepped forth . . . and all the heaven of Ammon smiled."

1502 courser: A hunting horse, invariably used by Chaucer in knightly contexts. This line is nearly identical with LGW 1204: "Upon a courser stertlynge as the fyr."

1506–7   On the observance of May, see 1047 above.

1509   Cf. SqT V.53 and Tr 2.920: "Ful loude song ayein the moone shene."

1522 feeld . . . wode: Proverbial; Whiting F127; and in a Latin form, "The field has an eye, and the wood has a sharp ear," Walther 2272.

1524 men . . . steven: Proverbial; Whiting M210; for the use of *men* as the singular indefinite pronoun (as in Mod. German *Man sagt*), cf. GP I.149 and see Language and Versification, p. xxxiii.

1529 roundel: The lines quoted from Arcite's song, 1510–12, rhyming *abb,* could conceivably be the beginning of a roundel. For an example of the form, see PF 682–92.

1533 Now up, now doun: Proverbial; Whiting B575.

1534–39 Friday: For proverbial and folk wisdom that Friday is different from the other days of the week, see Neckam, De nat. rerum 1.7, ed. Wright, 42: "The sixth day, which Venus dominates, seems almost always to take a different form from the other days of the week"; John L. Lowes, MLR 9, 1914, 94; and Whiting F622. Cf. NPT VII.3341.

1542   Besserman, Ch and the Bible, 63, compares Job 3:3 ("Let the day perish wherein I was born") and Jer. 20:14 ("Cursed be the day wherein I was born"); cf. I.1073.

1545 confusioun: Theb. 1.17 calls the Theban dynasty a "confusa domus" (cursed house) of Oedipus.

1546–49 Cadme: Cadmus, father of Semele (see 1329–31 above) was said to have founded Thebes with the warriors produced when he sowed the teeth of a dragon he had slain. **Amphioun** was said to have built the walls of Thebes with the sound of his lyre; see MerT IV.1716n.

1566   Cf. Tr 3.733–34: "O fatal sustren which, er any cloth/

Me shapen was, my destine me sponne." LGW 2629–30: "Syn fyrst that day that shapen was my sherte,/ Or by the fatal systren had my dom." See Whiting D106.

1598 fiers as leon: A commonplace; Whiting L311.

1606 love is free: Proverbial after Chaucer (Whiting L516) and cf. FranT V.767.

1625–26 love ne lordshipe/Wol: Proverbial in English after Chaucer (Whiting L495), and a common sentiment in classical literature, e.g. Ovid, Met. 2.846–47; tr. Miller: "Majesty and love do not go well together nor tarry long in the same dwelling-place." See also *Roman de la rose* (8449–54; tr. Dahlberg, 156: "They knew well the saying . . . that love and lordship never kept each other company nor dwelt together"), and Tes. 5.13, where Boccaccio refers to the desire for dominance as "the poison that has power to divide." Cf. FranT V.764–66.

1626 his thankes: Adverbial genitive of *thank* in the primary sense of "thought," hence "will," "wish." Cf. I.2107, I.2114, WBPro III.272, RomB 2463 ("nevere thou woldest, thi thankis, lete"). Cf. Language and Versification, p. xxxii.

1633 allone as he was born: Perhaps proverbial (Whiting B465), though the phrase is found only in Chaucer, in WBT III.885 and Tr 4.298: "Allone as I was born."

1659 wilde bores: Cf. the duel between Eteocles and Polynices, in Theb. 11.530–31: "As when rage has sent lightening—swift boars rushing headlong to the fight and raised bristles erect on their backs." The simile is not in Tes. See Whiting B405.

1660 Up to the ancle . . . in hir blood: Pearsall (Life of Geoffrey Ch, 46) notes this is not mere hyperbole: "They are not up to their ankles in blood in a field that is all ankle-deep in blood, but up to their ankles in blood in their *chausses* or metal shoes." Pearsall cites Froissart, tr. Brereton, 343: Sir Ralph Percy (in the Battle of Chevy Chase) accepts the terms of his surrender: "I agree. But have me seen to. I am very badly wounded. My chausses and greaves [leg armor] are full of blood already."

1663–72   The distinction that Chaucer here makes between **destinee** and **purveiaunce,** Providence, is dependent on Boethius 4.pr6: Providence is the government of all mutable nature as it exists in the mind of God; Destiny is that plan as it is worked out on changeable things in time. Chaucer also seems indebted to Dante, Inf. 7.73–96, where Fortune, described in terms analogous to Destiny, is referred to as "general ministra" of Providence; cf. **minestre general** (I.1663; no corresponding term in Boethius). In Tes. 6.1–51 Boccaccio discusses the inexplicability of Fortune, without suggesting God's providential plan.

1668   From Tes. 5.77.1–2; tr. McCoy, 133: "But just as we see something that has not happened in a thousand years suddenly come to pass in a moment." The idea is proverbial (Whiting D56).

1697 Under the sonne: "Theseus looked under the low lying sun, perhaps (as Professor Child used to suggest) shielding his eyes as he swept the field in his observation" (Robinson). But cf. the fifteenth-century Robin and Gandeleyn (Child Ballad 115), 35: "Loked him est and lokyd west/ And sowt vnder the sunne," where the meaning is "in every direction" (cited by Roland M. Smith, MLN 51, 1936, 318).

1712 juge: Theseus objects to the irregularity of the duel, which should be conducted by the rules for judicial combat or for duels of honor; for a set of such rules, see those drawn up by Thomas of Woodstock, Constable of England, in Chaucer's time (ed. Henry Arthur, Viscount Dillon, Archaeologia 57, 1900, 61–66) and cf. Maurice Keen, Laws of War, 1965, 54–59.

1724 In Tes. 5.86–87, each of the young knights confesses his identity to Teseo.

1742–60 There is nothing in Tes. to correspond to the intercession of the ladies at this point. Teseo, though angry, has pledged his word that the youths will not be harmed if they identify themselves. Johnstone Parr (PMLA 60, 1945, 314–17) sees an allusion to Queen Anne's intercession for Sir Simon Burley (1388); Hinckley (Notes on Ch, 75) suggests Queen Philippa's successful appeal to Edward III on behalf of six condemned citizens of Calaise (Froissart, tr. Brereton, 109).

1747 Mars the rede: See 975 and n. above.

1761 pitee renneth soone: Chaucer's favorite line; see MerT IV.1986; SqT V.479; LGW F 503 (G 491); and cf. MLT II.660. It became proverbial after Chaucer (Whiting P243). John H. Lowes (MP 14, 1917, 718) proposed as Chaucer's source Dante, Inf. 5.100 ("Love, which is quickly kindled in the gentle heart"), but the immediate context (the sinful passion of Paolo and Francesca) and the fact that Dante is describing love, not pity, make more likely Shannon's suggestion (Ch and the Roman Poets, 178) that here the source is Ovid, Trist. 3.5.31–32: "The greater a man, the more his wrath can be appeased; a noble mind is easily capable of kindly impulses." Most of the other uses of this line are in amatory contexts, to which Dante's line might apply. For Chaucer's *pitee*, see Douglas Gray, in J. R. R. Tolkien, ed. Mary Salu and Robert T. Farrell, 1979, 173–203.

1774–81 Loomis (Essays and Studies . . . Carleton Brown, 1940, 147) sees here a suggestion of Chaucer's counsel that King Richard exercise magnanimity and mercy. Paolo Cherchi (MP 76, 1978, 46–48) traces the sentiments as a topos from *Aeneid* 6.851–53; tr. Fairclough: "Remember then, O Roman, to rule the nations with thy sway—these shall be thine arts—to crown Peace with Law, to spare the humbled, and to tame in war the proud."

1785–1825 The speech is Chaucer's addition.

1785 benedicite: A mild oath, meaning something like "bless us" or "bless my soul," etc.; from the 2nd pl. imper. of Lat. *benedicere,* to bless. *Benedicite* was usually pronounced with three syllables but could have as few as two (*benste*) or as many as five, as in this case, unique in Chaucer's works.

1799 See Whiting F459; and cf. Walther 918: "To love and be wise is hardly granted by God."

1810 cokkow or an hare: Some MSS have *cokkow of an hare* (i.e., knows nothing about it). The reference is to the foolishness of the cuckoo (cf. PF 610–16 and Alexander Neckam, *De naturis rerum,* ed. Wright, 393, lines 865–66: "The cuckoo plays the fool in vain so many times by always repeating the empty trifles of a ridiculous sound") and the proverbial madness of the hare (cf. SumT III.1327 and n., and Whiting H116). The figure is not in the *Teseida.*

1817 laas: Cf. I.1951; LGW 599–600 ("But love hadde brought this man in swich a rage/ And hym so narwe

bounden in his las"); *Roman de la rose* 15108–9; tr. Dahlberg, 257 ("I, who was captured in the net where love binds others").

1838 Cf. Tr 5.1433 ("Pipe in an ivy lef, if that the lest!") and MilT I.3387. Proverbial after Chaucer (Whiting 172, Tilley I110).

1850 fifty wykes, fer ne ner: A full year is probably intended (Tes. 5.98: "un anno intero").

PART THREE

1884 From his treatment of Boccaccio's amphitheater (Tes. 7.108–10), Chaucer has omitted the marble walls and the number of rows of seats (**degrees,** I.1890, etc.) specified as 500; he has retained, however, the colossal dimensions of a mile in circumference, and has thus produced accommodations for upwards of 200,000 spectators (Magoun, Gazetteer, 25–27). The population of London in 1377 is estimated at 35,000 (J. C. Russell, Brit. Med. Pop., 1948, 285). Unlike that in the Tes., the theater in The Knight's Tale is constructed especially for the tournament. As clerk of the works, Chaucer was commissioned to have scaffolds constructed for the jousts at Smithfield, May 1390; Margaret Hallissy, ChauR 32, 1998, 239–59, shows that this passage reflects the actualities of Chaucer's experience with building projects, and suggests an effect on the poem as a whole.

1912 Dyane of chastitee: The chaste Diana. The genitive is used as an adjective (the genitive of description or quality; see Mustanoja, ME Syntax, 80–81 and Language and Versification, p. xxxii). The construction is common in ME, both with the inflected genitive (*any lyves creature,* any living being, I.2395) and with the analytical (as here and in *diluge of pestilence,* pestilential deluge, Scog 14).

1918–66 The description of the Temple of Venus is derived from Tes. 7.51–62, a passage which, along with Tes. 7.63–66, furnished the source of PF 183–294. For the tradition of the "children" of a planetary deity, i.e., those engaging in the trades, professions, and activities that come under its influence and patronage, see Seznec, Survival of the Pagan Gods, 70–76; and Kolve, Ch and the Imagery of Narrative, 114–26.

1925–35 Chaucer derives from Boccaccio **Ydelnesse,** who becomes, under the influence of *Roman de la rose* 515–82 (RomA 531–83), porter of the house, **Foolhardynesse, Beautee, Youthe, Bauderie, Richesse, Lesynges** and **Flaterye** (both from "Lusinghe"?), and **Jalousye.** Boccaccio's "Arte" may have become Chaucer's **Charmes; Hope** and **Bisynesse,** not in *Teseida,* are probably from *Roman de la rose.* Omitted from Chaucer's version are "Memoria," "Leggiardia" (Grace, Loveliness), "Affabilitate," "Pace" (Peace), "Pazienza," "Gentilezza," and "Cortesia."

1929 gooldes: Marigolds (St. Mary's Gold). The yellow color here symbolizes jealousy (cf. *Roman de la rose* 21772–73; tr. Dahlberg, 354: "Jealousy, crowned with her marigolds of solicitude"). Cf. the use of red for anger (KnT I.1997), blue for fidelity (SqT V.644 and cf. azure, which symbolizes faithfulness in Anel 330–32 "Clad in asure . . . to be trewe"), green for disloyalty (SqT V.646), and white for virtue (SNT VIII.115, Tr 2.1062: "Minerva, the white"). Cf. the use of blue and green in Wom Unc.

1930 cokkow: A symbol of cuckoldry; see MancT IX.243n.

1936–37 Citheroun: The confusion of the island Cythera and the mountain Cithaeron, Robinson notes, may be partly due to *Aeneid* 10.51 ("high Paphus and Cythera") or 86 ("high Cythera"), and is found also in *Roman de la rose* 15660; tr. Dahlberg, 265 ("Cytherea") and Boccaccio's *Ameto* ("Citerea").

1941 For Narcissus (not in Boccaccio's treatment), see *Roman de la rose* 1439–1614 (RomA 1471–1538); Ovid, Met. 3.407–510; and Hoffman, Ovid and the CT, 79–81.

1942 folye of . . . Salomon: See WBPro III.35 and n.

1943 Ercules: Hercules is mentioned as a victim of love in Tes. 7.62. Cf. MkT VII.2095–142.

1944 Medea and Circes: Perhaps a reminiscence of *Roman de la rose* (14404–6; tr. Dahlberg, 246): "Medea could never hold Jason with any enchantment, any more than Circe could keep Ulysses."

1945 Turnus: Leader of the Italians and Aeneas's rival for the hand of Lavinia (*Aeneid* 8.1 and passim).

1946 Cresus: Croesus was not a victim of love; see MkT VII.2727–66. J. A. W. Bennett (ed., PF, 1957, 101n.) suggests that Chaucer's inspiration here is Alanus de Insulis, *De planctu naturae*, m.5, where Croesus serves as an example of character traits changing to their opposites, through love's power.

1951 Cf. LGW 600: "And hym so narwe bounden in his las."

1955–66 With this description, and that of HF 132–39, compare PF 260–79, which is translated directly from Tes. 7.64–66. In his gloss Boccaccio (Bk of Theseus, tr. McCoy) explains that "Venus is twofold, since one can be understood as every chaste and licit desire, as in the desire to have a wife in order to have children, and such like. This Venus is not discussed here. The second is that through which all lewdness is desired, commonly called the goddess of love." On this mythographic tradition, see Robert Hollander, Boccaccio's Two Venuses, 1977, 158–60. Chaucer's Venus has been read as both the lascivious goddess (see Robertson, Pref. to Ch, 124–27) and the "good" and "lawful" Venus (Bennett, ed. PF, 95–98). Boitani (Ch and Boccaccio, 89–95) sees the deity in both Tes. and KnT as incorporating both the honorable and the voluptuous traditions. On the multiple nature of Venus see Theresa Tinkle, Med. Venuses and Cupids, 1996, 27–31.

1958 brighte as any glas: Cf. Bo I.m7.6–7: "wawes, that whilom weren clere as glas and lyk to the fayre bryghte dayes."

1959 citole: The substitution of a citole for the traditional conch has been explained by John M. Steadman (Spec 34, 1959, 620–24) with reference to Ovidius Moralizatus of Bersuire, who draws a comparison of Venus to the harlot of Isaiah 23.16 ("Take an harp, go about the city, thou harlot"). However, Meg Twycross (Med. Anadyomene, 1958, 51–68) presents numerous examples of the astrological Venus playing a stringed instrument and argues that Chaucer need not have been carrying over Bersuire's interpretation.

1963–65 Cupid is traditionally represented as blind here and in MerT IV.1598; HF 137–38 ("daun Cupido/ Hir blynde sone"), 617 ("Hys blynde nevew Cupido"); Tr 3.1808 ("Thy blynde and wynged sone ek, daun Cupide"). For other

examples, see Whiting C634 and for the tradition see Erwin Panofsky, Studies in Iconology, 1939, 95–128; Theresa Tinkle, Med. Venuses and Cupids, 89–94.

1967–2050 The account of the Temple of Mars is derived mainly from Tes. 7.29–37, with occasional details taken from Boccaccio's source, Theb. 7.34–73.

1972 Trace: In his gloss on Tes. 1.15 Boccaccio explains: "The men of Magna are under a cold sky and are full-blooded and wild and eager for war; for this reason the poets excellently conceived that the house of Mars, that is the appetite for war, is in Thrace" (Bk of Theseus, tr. McCoy, 49).

1979 Boitani (Ch and Boccaccio, 84) notes that these sounds, like those of I.1985–86, are literally impossible to have been represented in a painting. He compares Dante, Purg. 10.28–96.

1985 veze: An extremely rare word in ME (MED, s.v. *fese*, cf. *bewese*). Glossed "impetus," violent motion, in seven MSS (including Hg and El), probably with reference to Theb. 7.47: "From the outer gate wild Passion leaps."

1987 northren lyght: Not the aurora borealis but rather derived from Theb. 7.45 ("the brightness of the sun opposite"), indicating that the temple is oriented toward the north.

1990 adamant: The adamant was thought to be the hardest of stones (Barth. Angl., 16.8; tr. Trevisa, 2:833: "Nothing overcometh it, nother yren nor fyre"), and later came to be identified with the diamond.

1995–2041 From Tes. 7.33–35 (cf. Theb. 7.47–54), Chaucer derived Ire, Dread, Conflict (**Contek**), Menace, Misfortune (**Meschaunce**), Madness, and Death. He omits "cieco Peccare" (Blind Sin), "ogni Omei" (Every Alas), "Differenza" (Difference), and "Stupore" (Bewilderment). **Conquest** seems to be Chaucer's own addition.

1995 Ther saugh I: This formula, probably derived from the first-person account in Boccaccio ("vedivi") and frequently used here (I.2011, 2017, 2028, 2062, 2067, 2073), is literally inappropriate for a third-person narrator but seems, like *maystow* se (I.1918), a device for achieving vividness of expression rather than a survival of an earlier, more literal version of Boccaccio's story, the "Palamon and Arcite," as Skeat believed.

1999 knyf under the cloke: Skeat (5:79) suggests the possible influence of the description of Fals Semblant, *Roman de la rose* 12093–94 (RomC 7417–18: "But in his sleve he gan to thringe/ A rasour sharp and wel bytynge").

2005–6 sleer of hymself: For the association of wrath with suicide, see Prudentius, (Psychomachia 1.145–53; tr. Thomson: "Wrath is beside herself . . . and wild passion fires her to slay herself") and Arieh Sachs, MS 26, 1964, 239–40.

2007 nayl . . . shode: Cf. the killing of Sisera by Jael in Judges 4.21: "Then Jael, Heber's wife, took a nail of the tent, and took a hamer in her hand, and went softly to him, and smote the nail into his temples, and fastened it into the ground; for he was fast asleep and weary. And so he died."

2012 Chaucer's **Compleint** and **Outhees** (Outcry), which are not in Theb., may have been derived from Lactantius (Clogan, SP 61:612).

2017 shippes hoppesteres: Dancing ships (*hoppestre,* a

female dancer). Chaucer apparently mistook "bellatricesque carinae" (Theb. 7.57: "and ships of war") or "le navi bellatrici" (Tes. 7.37) as a form of "ballatrices" or "ballatrici." OED, s.v. *dance*, v.3, cites ships dancing on the water from the sixteenth century; on the suffix -*ster* cf. GP 1.241–42n.

2022–24 Cf. Theb. 7.58–59: "And empty chariots and faces ground by chariot wheels, ay, almost even their groans!"

2029 swerd over his heed: Perhaps an allusion to the sword of Damocles, which Chaucer knew from Boethius (3.pr5.23–27: "A tyraunt, that was kyng of Sysile, that hadde assayed the peril of his estat, schewede by symylitude the dredes of remes by gastnesse of a swerd that heng over the heved of his familyer").

2031–34 Cf. MLT II.190–203n., where the glosses refer to Bernardus Silvestris, Megacosmos.

2031–32 The death of Julius Caesar (**Julius**) is related in MkT VII.2695–726; that of **Nero** in MkT VII.2519–50; and that of **Antonius** (Marc Antony) in LGW 624–62. R. H. Nicholson (ELN 25:3, 1988, 16–22) argues that *Antonius* is to be understood as Caracalla, the emperor, rather than Marc Antony.

2041–50 The figure of Mars, in a chariot, accompanied by a wolf, reflects the iconographical tradition of Albricus Philosophus, *De deorum imaginibus* (1681), 2.302; qtd. by Skeat, 5:82), with the detail of the wolf devouring a man perhaps suggested by Albricus's etymology "Mavors" (Mars) from "mares vorans" (devouring males). For the iconography, see Seznec, Survival of the Pagan Gods, 190–94.

2045 **Puella** and **Rubeus** are figures in geomancy, or divination by means of lines and figures. One would quickly jot down four rows of dots, then count the dots in each row to determine whether the number of dots is odd or even; the rows would then be represented by one dot for an odd-numbered row and two dots for an even-numbered row. Sixteen possible figures can thus be drawn, each with its name and each with astrological significance, and the resulting figures can then be used to cast a horoscope for predicting the future. One figure, *Rubeus,* consistently signifies Mars direct (a fortunate aspect). Another, *Puella,* sometimes indicates Mars retrograde (unfortunate), as in MS Bodley 581, prepared for Richard II in March 1393 (illustrated in Manly, CT, after p. 552), though sometimes she indicates Venus (W. W. Skeat, Acad, 2 March 1889, 150–51). For geomantic procedures, see Lynn Thorndike, Hist. of Magic 2:837–88.

2053–88 Tes. 7.72 (tr. McCoy, 180) says merely that the temple of Diana was "clean and adorned with beautiful hangings."

2056–61 Calistopee: The story of how Diana punished Callisto is related by Ovid, Fasti 2.156–82; Met. 2.409–507; and by Boccaccio, in his gloss to Tes. 7.50 (tr. McCoy, 203). According to the usual account, Callisto was transformed into Arctus, Ursa Major and her son, Arcas, into Bötes, sometimes (incorrectly) identified with Ursa Minor, where the **loode-sterre** (2059), or Polestar, is located. Bötes is a constellation, rather than, as Chaucer may be implying, a star. Skeat (5:83) took Chaucer's use of the word **sterre** to refer to a constellation, as in Boece 4.m5 and 4.m6, where

he follows Boethius in correctly distinguishing Bötes and Ursa Major.

2062–64 Dane: Chaucer's source for the legend of Daphne, turned into a laurel tree by her father, the river deity Peneus, is Ovid, Met. 1.452–567.

2063–64 With the Knight's insistence on being correctly understood, cf. the Pardoner's careful distinction between *Samuel* and *Lamuel* in PardT VI.585. The figure is similar to "expeditio" (Geoffrey of Vinsauf, Poetria nova, 1187–1201; tr. Nims, 59), in which the writer presents several choices, only to reject all but one; cf. BD 855–58: "Soth to seyne, hit was not red,/ Ne nouther yelowe ne broun hyt nas;/ Me thoghte most lyk gold hyt was." For the use of **I mene,** see MLT II.261n.

2065 Attheon: For the story of Actaeon, the grandson of Cadmus, see Ovid, Met., 3.138–252. In the corresponding passage in Tes. 7.79.3–8, Emilia herself invokes Actaeon in praising Diana (tr. McCoy, 182): "[You are] the avenger of your wrath, as Acteon realized when, more youthful than fortunate, he was smitten by your anger [and] . . . changed into a deer."

2070–72 Atthalante, Meleagre: For Atalanta and Meleager, see Ovid, Met. 8.260–444, where the former is referred to as Tegeaea (but cf. Heroides 4.99–100; tr. Showerman, "The son of Oenus, too, took fire with love for Maenilian Atalanta; she has the spoil of the wild beast as the pledge of his love"). For the story of the Calydonian boar, see Tr 5.1464–84.

2085 Lucyna: Lucina, a title given to Juno and Diana in their character as goddesses of childbirth through identification or confusion with a goddess of that same name, the daughter of Jupiter and Juno, who was born without her mother's feeling pain. Chaucer uses the name to refer to Diana (signifying the moon) in FranT V.1045 and Tr 4.1591 ("Phebus suster, Lucina the sheene").

2125 no newe gyse: Proverbial; see Whiting G494.

2129 Lygurge: Lycurgus of Nemea (Tes. 6.14). Chaucer apparently confuses this Lycurgus with Lycurgus of Thrace, mentioned in Theb. 4.386 and 7.180, and explicitly referred to as king of that region in the *Thebaid* glosses (Clogan, SP 61:613). Chaucer and Gower make Lycurgus the father of Phyllis (LGW 2425: "Lygurgus doughter" and Conf. aman. 4.738: "dowhter of Ligurgius"), deserted by Theseus's son Demophoon. Curry (Ch and Science, 134–37) argues his physiognomy suggests he is a type of Saturn, who has taken up Palamon's cause, but this is refuted by Theresa Tinkle (Viator 18, 1987, 303–5).

2133 grifphon: The griffin, a beast with the head of an eagle, wings, and the body of a lion, renowned for its ferocity and said to dwell in Sicia (far Northern Europe); Barth. Angl. 18.56; tr. Trevisa, 2:1207. Sir Thomas Browne (Pseudodoxia epidemica [1666], 3.9) says the beast is especially appropriate for generals and heroic commanders.

2148 alauntz: The alan (or alaunt), a large hunting dog, was so called because the breed was supposedly introduced into Western Europe by the Alani in the fourth century. See Master of Game, ed. William A. and F. Baillie-Grohman, 1919, 116–19, 202–3.

2155–66 Emetreus, the kyng of Inde: Not in Boccaccio or Statius. Curry (Ch and Science, 131–34) sees his physiognomy as wholly Martian; Brooks and Fowler (MÆ 39:132–33) find both Martian and Solar attributes in his description, representative of the choleric personality of the years between twenty and forty. Even the **frakenes** (freckles, 2169), which Albert S. Cook (Trans. Conn. Acad. 20, 1916, 16) saw as a specific reference to the pock-marks of Henry, Earl of Derby, are paralleled in the astrological descriptions of the planet-deities (Brooks and Fowler, MÆ 39:130–34).

2178 egle: Another white eagle appears in Tr 2.926 ("an egle, fethered whit as bon"); they are not generally believed to exist in nature, but Marco Polo (ed. and tr. Yule, 2.347) describes white eagles in the kingdom of Mutfili, in India.

2217 hir houre: Each of the twenty-four *houres inequal* (see 2271 below) was thought to be dominated by one of the planets "by ordir as they sitten in the hevene (Astr 2.12.21–22)," from the outmost inward—Saturn, Jupiter, Mars, Sun, Venus, Mercury, Moon (see Astr 2.12), with the hour beginning at sunrise assigned to the planet for which the day was named. Thus on Sunday the first hour after sunrise was that of the Sun, the second that of Venus, and the twenty-third (when Palamon arose) was again Venus's hour. The twenty-fourth hour was Mercury's, and the first hour of Monday, when Emelye arose (1.2273), belonged to the moon; the fourth hour of Monday belonged to Mars, and it was then that Arcite went to pray (I.2367). The *Kalendarium* of Nicholas of Lynn (176–77) contains a table showing the planetary hours.

2224 Adoon: Adonis, loved by Venus; see Ovid, Met. 10. and cf. Tr 3.721. ("Adoun, that with the boor was slawe").

2236 Venus is traditionally at war with chastity; see Seznec, Surv. of the Pagan Gods, 109.

2271 houre inequal: Hours by the clock are "equal," since each has sixty minutes. When night and day are each divided into their twelve planetary hours, the hours of the day and those of the night are of differing lengths—*inequal*—save at the equinox. See Astr 2.10–11.

2273–94 Chaucer is here dependent on Tes. 7.71–76, though his attribution to Statius (**Stace,** I.2294) may reflect his knowledge of what was probably Boccaccio's model for the passage, the description of the rites of Tiresias and his daughter Manto in Theb. 4.43–72.

2273 An example of the rhetorical device *compar* (Geoffrey of Vinsauf, Poetria nova, 1128–29; tr. Nims, 57), the use of clauses or phrases of similar length and structure; and *repetitio* (Poetria nova, 1098–99; tr. Nims, 56), repeating a word or phrase at the beginning of successive clauses: e.g., "Deed so evil! Deed more evil than others! Deed most evil of all deeds!" Cf. CIT IV.540–43 and n.

2281 Smokynge the temple: It is usually assumed that Chaucer read *Fumando il tempio* for Boccaccio's *Fu mondo il tempio* (The temple was clean); Bennett (ed. KnT) suggests that Chaucer's line represents an intentional abbreviation of Boccaccio's longer, more detailed account (Tes. 7.71–76).

2313 The **thre formes** of the goddess (cf. Lat. triformis dea) are those of Luna, in the heavens; Diana, on earth; and Proserpina, in the underworld (FranT V.1074–75).

2333–37 There is no indecent pun on *queynt(e)* here, as some suppose (e.g., W. F. Bolton, ChauR 1, 1967, 224); see L. D.

Benson, SAC, Proceedings 1, 1984, 23–47, esp. 45–46. For a counterargument, see Susan Crane, SAC, 1990, 55–56.

2339–40 The conception of the bleeding twigs (Tes. 7.92,1; tr. McCoy, 184: "The enkindled brands seemed like blood") is derived ultimately from the Polydorus episode in Virgil's *Aeneid*, 3.19–76. The gloss to Tes. 7.91 (Bk of Theseus, tr. McCoy, p. 209) explains the action of the fires as the rekindling of Palemone's hopes after the accident that befell Arcita.

2367 nexte houre of Mars folwynge: The next planetary hour ruled by Mars, the fourth after sunrise on this day (see n. 2217 above).

2388–90 Boccaccio refers to Mars as "rinchiuso," trapped, by Vulcan. Chaucer could have derived the idea of the **las** from the account in *Roman de la rose*, 13835–74 (tr. Dahlberg, 237), especially 13860, "prise et laciee," captured and netted. Cf. KnT I.1951.

2397 synk or flete: Proverbial (Whiting F268).

2399 in the place: As opposed to the *lystes,* which refer to the entire structure, Christopher Dean (N&Q 211, 1966, 90–92) argues that *place* here and elsewhere corresponds to Lat. *platea* and refers to the specific space where the action took place.

2410–17 The vows of Arcite (from Tes.7.28) have parallels in Theb. 2.732–43; 6.193–200, 607–13; 8.491–94.

2432–33 For murmurynge/ Ful lowe and dym: Tes. 7.40.6 has "con dolce romore" (with a pleasing sound).

2437 fayn as fowel: Proverbial; Whiting B292; F561, 566; cf. ShipT VII.51; CYT VIII.1342; Tr 5.425 ("For was ther nevere fowel so fayn of May"); and RomA 74–77 ("in May for the sonne brighte/ So glade . . . / That they [birds] mote syngen and be light"). V. J. Scattergood (ChauR 11, 1977, 211) notes that in Chaucer the phrase "almost always connotes a trust that turns out to be misplaced."

2443–78 pale Saturnus the colde: Cf. *olde colde Saturnus* in Bo 4.m1.12. On the hostile (*colde*) aspects of Saturn (a "wicked planete," Ast 2.4.35), see Gower, Conf. aman. 7.935–46. But Saturn was often interpreted as signifying wisdom and prudence born of experience and time (see Kean, Ch and Poetry 2:28–33; Gower (Vox clam. 2.5) held that man's conformance with divine law would result in Saturn's becoming beneficial to mankind. The deity is Chaucer's addition. Theresa Tinkle (Viator 18:289–307) surveys various medieval traditions on which Chaucer drew.

2447–48 elde hath greet avantage: A commonplace (Whiting E61 and cf. Whiting M118).

2449 olde atrenne: Proverbial (Whiting O29); cf. Tr 4.1456: "Men may the wise atrenne, and naught atrede."

2453 doghter: Chaucer knows that Venus is the daughter of Jupiter, not of Saturn; see I.2222. *Doghter* is used here, as in I.2346–48, as a term of address.

2454 Saturn's **cours,** orbit, was the largest known in the Middle Ages.

2459 cherles rebellyng: Perhaps a reference to the Peasants' Revolt of 1381 (cf. NPT VII.3393), although Parr (MLN 69:393–94) notes that some authorities on astronomy—Albohazen Haly (1485 ed.) and Guido Bonatus (1491 ed.)—ascribe to Saturn influence over rebellion and discord.

2462 leoun: Liddell (ed. CT in Globe Chaucer, 1898) quotes a paraphrase of Ptolemy to the effect that Saturn caused destruction by felling buildings while the planet passed through the signs of the quadrupeds (i.e., Leo, Taurus). Skeat quotes Hermetis Aphorismorum Liber, no. 66: "Leo works terrible evils with evils; for he increases their badness."

2466 Sampsoun: Samson; see Judges 16.29–30; cf. MkT VII.2015–94. He is introduced in a similar context of astrological determinism in MLT II.201.

2475 compleccioun: See GP I.333 and n.

PART FOUR

2491–656 For tournaments involving opposing troops of combatants (melees), which were perhaps more in vogue in the thirteenth century than in Chaucer's time, see Cowgill (PQ 54:670–77). For parallels with the 1390 Smithfield tournament, see S. Robertson, JEGP 14:239–40, and Johnstone Parr, PMLA 60, 1945, 317–19.

2491 In the ME Partonope of Blois, EETS e.s. 109, 3070–72, a day of battle is set "upon a Twysday,/ Whych yn olde tyme, I wolde noght lye/ The day of batayle doth signify" [regularized]. Tuesday, Mars's day, should have been propitious to Arcite.

2528–29 The comparison of Theseus to a god is original with Chaucer; in Tes. 7.1–2 the duke remains in the theater with the visiting warriors.

2549 sharpe ygrounde spere: Teseo prohibits the more injurious lances, but allows swords, maces, and two-edged hatchets.

2558 Gooth forth: Joseph Strutt, Sports and Pastimes, 119, quoting British Library MS Harley 69, notes the traditional call of the heralds to "come forth" (*hors chevaliers*) as a prelude to the tournament; equally traditional is the heralds' call *Do now youre devoir* (I.2598).

2568 sarge: Serge, a woolen fabric apparently held in low esteem, was used primarily for hangings, covers, etc. Cf. the disparaging reference in Chrétien de Troyes, *Erec et Enide,* ed. Michel Rouse, 1994, 6667–72; tr. Staines: "Wealthy and generous was the king: he presented cloaks made not of serge or rabbit fur or light wool, but of ermine and samite."

2601–16 Although the Parson disparages alliterating poetry (X.43), Chaucer frequently uses alliterating phrases (cf. *holt and heeth,* GP I.6); here and in the account of the Battle of Actium in LGW 629–653, the only other extended account of a battle in his work, he uses alliteration heavily. Elliott (Ch's English, 103) notes that though only I.2605, 2612, and 2615 are regular alliterative lines, **shyveren** as a verb (I.2605), **herte-spoon** (I.2606), and **tronchoun** (2615) are not ordinary Chaucerian usages, and that the passage is remarkable for its syntactic inversions.

2614 as dooth a bal: The game of football was well established from at least the time of Edward II; see F. P. Magoun, AHR 35, 1929, 33–45; and Strutt, Sports and Pastimes, 93–97, which mentions a 1389 statute forbidding the game.

2621 tyme . . . to reste: Such pauses for rest and refreshment are not uncommon in depictions of medieval tournaments; see Malory's Tournament of Winchester (Works, ed. Vinaver, Bk 18, 625).

2626–28 Chaucer's figure of the tiger bereft of her whelp was probably inspired by Tes. 8.26, which compares Diomed, hearing that Ulisse has been captured, to a lioness that has lost her cub.

2626 Galgopheye: Probably a distortion of Lat. *Gargaphia,* a valley near Plataea in Boeotia, sacred to Diana, where Actaeon (see I.2065) was slain (Ovid, Met. 3.156; tr. Miller: "Gargaphie, the sacred haunt of high-girt Diana").

2630 Belmarye: Roughly corresponding to present-day Morocco; cf. GP I.57 and n.

2636 ende . . . of every dede: Proverbial (Whiting T87); and cf. I.3026, LGW 651 ("Tyl at the laste, as every thyng hath ende"), and Tr 3.615 ("But at the laste, as every thyng hath ende").

2638–42 Jones, Ch's Knight, 180–1, sees the conditions of Palamon's capture as a violation of the rules of fair play; but cf. S. Robertson, JEGP 14:240.

2652–53 These lines are echoed in MilT I.3747–49; see MilT I.3119n.

2664–66 Cf. Scog 11–12, where Venus's tears are also rain: "But now so wepith Venus in hir spere/ That with hir teeres she wol drenche us here."

2680–83 In Tes. 8.124–27, Emilia's change of heart takes place as soon as Palemone is indisposed, even before the tournament is concluded.

2681–82 favour of forune: Robert E. Jungman (Explicator 55, 1997, 190–92) suggests Chaucer here echoes Juvenal's Tenth Satire ("And what does the mob of Remus say? It follows fortune, as it always does"), though the Juvenal's subject is the "Roman mob" rather than *wommen.*

2683 al his chiere, as in his herte: The interpretation is problematic. Perhaps (with Skeat and Robinson), "she was all his delight, as regarded his heart." Bennett (ed. KnT) plausibly suggests that in Tes. 8.124, "l'animo suo sanza dimoro/a lui voltò" (her heart forthwith turned towards him), Chaucer may have understood *volto,* countenance, for *voltò,* turned.

2685 The **furie** here and in Tes. 9.4 is from Theb. 6.495–506, where a similar being is sent by Phoebus to frighten Arion, one of the horses drawing Polynices's chariot. Polynices is flung backward, head over heels, and barely survives. Chaucer adds the detail (I.2676–79) that Arcite rides bareheaded, looking up at Emelye, when the accident occurs.

2689 Skeat (5:90) cites from Walsingham's Historia Anglicana (2:177) an account of an accident rather similar to Arcite's, which occurred in Cambridge, 1388: "... the horse falls, and almost all the interior organs of the rider are torn asunder; nevertheless, he prolongs his life until the morrow."

2712 salves: Sage (Lat. *salvia*) was a respected remedy for paralysis, convulsions, and nervous disorders; see Med. Health Handbook, ed. Luisa C. Arano, 1976, no. 36, and cf. Walther 4696: "Why should a man die when sage grows in the garden?"

2743–56 According to the physiology developed from Galen, there were three kinds of virtues (otherwise called spirits) that operate most of the body's vital processes: the **natural,** situated in the liver; the *vital,* localized chiefly in the heart; and the **animal,** operating through the brain (Barth. Angl., 3.14; tr. Trevisa, 1:103).

2745 lechecraft: Mark H. Infusino and Ynez V. O'Neill (SAC Proc 1, 1984, 221–30) note that the medical practice reflected in the account of Arcite's death is the "New Surgery" as opposed to the "Ancient" practices reflected in Boccaccio.

2747 veyne-blood: Drawing off the blood by opening a vein (Cyrurgie of Guy de Chauliac, EETS 265, 534).

ventusynge: Bleeding by means of a cupping glass, partially evacuated by heating, locally applied to the skin (Guy de Chauliac, 545).

2749   Corrupted blood must be expelled from the body or it turns into venom (Barth. Angl. 4.7; tr. Trevisa 1:151). The **vertu expulsif,** which expels what is grievous (Barth. Angl., 3.8; tr. Trevisa, 1:97), is a function of the natural virtue, which "moves the humors of the body" (Barth. Angl. 3.12; tr. Trevisa 1:99), but is here controlled by the animal virtue which governs the motions of breathing (Pauline Aiken, PMLA 51, 1936, 361–69) or coughing (Curry, Ch and Science, 138–45). Since Arcite's lungs are infected (I.2752–54), he cannot effect such a purgation, and this impairment of the lungs prevents them from expelling the smoky air from the blood and tempering the heat of the heart. The venom accordingly spreads through his body; neither emetics nor laxatives avail, and death results.

2759–60 fare wel phisik! Proverbial; Whiting N30.

2768   Cf. Tr 4.785–87: "Myn herte and ek the woful goost therinne/ Byquethe I with youre spirit to compleyne/ Eternaly."

2775 wyf: In Tes. 9.83, Arcita and Emilia are wed in a formal ceremony. Chaucer here and in I.3062 uses *wyf* merely as a term of endearment, as in Tr 3.106 ("O wommanliche wif"), 1296 ("fresshe wommanliche wif").

2779 Allone, withouten any compaignye: A regular formula in both ME and OF poetry; cf. MilT I.3264 and Mel VII.1560. Eleanor P. Hammond (Engl. Verse, 471) lists examples from Gower, Machaut, Christine de Pisan, Dante, and Petrarch.

2780 sweete foo: The use of such oxymorons is common in medieval love poetry. See, e.g., Tr 1.411: "O quike deth, O swete harm so queynte." Such expressions are characteristic of the "Petrarchan" amorous lyric, but Petrarch builds on earlier tradition.

2789–91 Bennett (ed. KnT) notes that these qualities, representing a considerable expansion of Boccaccio's "gentile e bello e grazioso" (Tes. 10.63), are almost all attributed to the Knight in GP.

2801 And yet mooreover: And still further. Chaucer may have seen *ed ancor* in Tes. 10.3 for the MS reading *e acciò.* Robinson compares Bo 2.pr6.79 where *And yit mooreover* translates "ad haec" and RomB 4493 where it corresponds to "ensurquetot."

2809–15 The narrator's remarks on the destination of Arcite's soul replace the description by Boccaccio (Tes. 11.1–3) of Arcita's journey through the spheres, his disparagement of worldly vanities, and his arrival at the place chosen for him by Mercury the psychopomp, which Chaucer used in his account of the death of Troilus (Tr 5.1807–27). Tatlock and Robinson both held that the passage from Boccaccio was rejected as inappropriate to the spirit of The Knight's Tale. Mary E. Thomas, Med. Skepticism and Ch, 1950, 64–71, 104–7, suggests Chaucer's decision not to incorporate this material indicates his reluctance to decide categorically on

a controversial topic of the times, the salvation of the righteous heathen; but this hardly explains his use of the passage in the *Troilus.*

The tone of these lines is lightly derisive. It is characteristic of Chaucer's attempts throughout the story to forestall, even undercut, high pathos, or, perhaps, of the Knight's grim humor. Such anticlimactic moments in The Knight's Tale, often humorous, are discussed by Howard (Idea of CT, 229–34) as a satire of knightly mentality; see also Edward E. Foster, ChauR 3, 1968, 88–94.

2817 Shrighte . . . howleth: See John Brand, Observ. on the Pop. Antiq. of Gt. Brit., 1849 ed., repr. 1970, 2:269: "It is an usual matter amongst [the Irish], upon the burial of their dead, to hire a company of women . . . [to] follow the corpse and furnish out the cry with such howling and barbarous outcries that he that should but heare them, and did not know the ceremony, would rather thinke that they did sing than weep."

2837–52 In Tes. 11.9–11, Boccaccio tells how no one could console the Greek heroes but, because Egeo was a wise man who well understood the vicissitudes of the world, he was able to restrain his grief and offer eternal truths, "that one sees deaths, changes, sorrows, and songs, one after the other." No one pays heed, however. Chaucer is able to introduce the more comprehensive, elevated Boethian speech of Theseus (I.2987–3089) by moving some of the platitudinous comments of Teseo's later speech (Tes. 12.6) to Aegeus (I.2843–49) and by emphasizing the consolation Aegeus's remarks bring about.

2841 Joye after wo: Cf. I.3068; and see Whiting J6L, MLT II.1161, NPT VII.3205.

2847 thurghfare ful of wo: Commonplace (Whiting W663).

2848 pilgrimes: The widespread idea of life as a pilgrimage to death was suggested by biblical passages such as Hebrews 11.13 ("They were strangers and pilgrims on the earth"); see Truth 18–20: "Forth, pilgrim, forth! . . . / Know thy contree, look up, thank God of al;/ Hold the heye wey." See also Whiting P200, and for a general treatment of pilgrimage as idea and metaphor, see Gerhart B. Ladner, Spec 42, 1967, 233–59.

2849 Deeth is an ende: Whiting D94.

2874 gloves white: This detail, not in the *Teseida,* may reflect the use of white garments for mourning; see Brand, Pop. Antiq. 2:282–83, where he notes that Henry VIII is said to have worn white at Anne Boleyn's funeral.

2895 bowe Turkeys: The Turkish bow is a powerful, short, composite, flexed bow. See Stephen J. Herben, Jr., Spec 12, 1937, 485. One appears in RomA 923 ("Turke bowes two had he [the God of Love]") (*Roman de la rose* 907; tr. Dahlberg, 43). They are frequently mentioned (cf. MED s.v. *Turkeis* adj.). However, this may be the evidence that Chaucer saw some of Boccaccio's glosses, for as Boitani (Ch and Boccaccio, 195–96) shows, Boccaccio glosses Tes. 11.35.7 "farete" as "turcassi" (both meaning quivers). Chaucer, if he had seen the gloss, might have thought that "turcassi" referred to "archi," bows. By Caxton's time, *tarcays* meant quiver (OED s.v. Tarcays).

2919–62 This is said to be the longest sentence in Chaucer's poetry (though editors determine punctuation); for other extended sentences, see Tr 1.22–51, 3.127–47.

2919–24 For the rhetorical topos of the catalogue of trees see Curtius, Europ. Lit, 195. Cf. the catalogue in PF 176–82, and on Chaucer's use of such catalogues see Barney, Wisdom of Poetry, 189–223. Chaucer's immediate source in The Knight's Tale is probably Tes. 11.22–24.

2921 holm: Although *holm* is the medieval word for holly bush (genus *Ilex*), this most probably refers to the holm-oak (*Quercus ilex*), so named because of the resemblance of its dark evergreen foliage to that of the holly.

2986 he seyde his wille: Lawler (One and the Many, 87) suggests "spoke as his desire moved him," rather than "pronounced his decision (royal will)."

2987–3089 In place of the sentiments that he has transferred from Teseo's speech to that of Aegeus (I.2843–49), in I.2987–3016, 3035–40 Chaucer draws on Bo 2.m8, 4.pr6; and 3.pr10. For the fair chain of divine love, joining together the potentially discordant universe, see specifically Bo 2.m8 and cf. PF 379–81 ("the almyghty Lord,/ That hot, cold, hevy, lyght, moyst, and dreye/ Hath knyt by evene noumbres of acord"). For the guarantee such ordered change based on love provides (I.3111–16), as well as the necessity of each thing returning to its source in God's love and guidance, see Bo 4.m6. The entire concept is analyzed in detail by Arthur O. Lovejoy, Great Chain of Being, 1950; see also Nature's confession in *Roman de la rose* (16707–81; tr. Dahlberg, 271–72), especially 16786–87, "the beautiful golden chain that binds the four elements."

The examples of the oak, the stone, and the river (I.3017–24) are from Tes. 12.7, with Chaucer adding that of the **grete tounes** (3025), perhaps from Met. 15.287–306. From Boccaccio also is the catalogue of ways in which one can die (I.3031–33; cf. Tes. 12.10), the emphasis on the folly of opposing the fact of death, and the value of a life of fame, though Chaucer wisely suppresses Teseo's disparagement of living to "an obscure old age full of misfortunes."

2994 quod he: So too in PrT VII.581 Chaucer calls attention to the speaker, even at the expense of dramatic consistency. In I.3075, *quod he,* thus inserted, has the effect of breaking up an extended monologue.

2994–3015 Cf. Bo 4.pr6.42–47: "The engendrynge of alle thinges," quod sche, "and alle the progressiouns of muable nature, and al that moeveth in any manere, taketh hise causes, his ordre, and his formes, of the stablenesse of the devyne thought."

3000–3002 auctoritee... experience: Cf. WBPro III.1–2n.

3005–10 Cf. Bo 3.pr10.25–30: "For the nature of thinges ne took nat hir begynnynge of thinges amenused and inparfit, but it procedith of thinges that ben alle hole and absolut, and descendith so doun into uttereste thinges and into thinges empty and withouten fruyt."

3011–15 Cf. Bo 4.pr6.149–53: "And thilke same ordre neweth ayein alle thinges growynge and fallynge adoun, by semblable progressions of sedes and of sexes (that is to seyn, male and femele)."

3025 The ruin of **grete tounes** (not found in Tes.) is a conventional topic of consolation; see J. E. Cross, Neophil 45, 1961, 68–69.

3030 kyng as shal a page: See Whiting D101.

3031–32 Som: Singular (i.e., one [of them]).

3034 al... mot deye: Proverbial; Whiting D243.

3035–38 Cf. Bo 4.m6.47–54: "For yif that he ne clepide nat ayein the ryght goynge of thinges, and yif that he ne constreynede hem nat eftsones into roundnesses enclyned, the thinges that ben now contynued by stable ordenaunce, thei scholden departen from hir welle (that is to seyn, from hir bygynnynge), and failen (that is to seyn, tornen into noght)"; 3.m9.40–41: "and graunte hym to enviroune the welle of good."

3041–42 Chaucer's source is Tes. 12.11.1–2; tr. McCoy, p. 315 ("And it is wisdom therefore to make a virtue of necessity when one must"), but the phrase is proverbial. It is not recorded in English before Chaucer (Whiting V43) but was common in French (Hassell V49). See Jerome, Epistula adversus Rufinum 2.11.1 ("Make a virtue of necessity"); and cf. SqT V.593 and Tr 4.1586 ("Thus maketh vertu of necessite").

3061 prisoun of this lyf: Cf. SNPro VIII.71–74n.

3064–65 For the folk-belief that excessive mourning harms the departed, see F. J. Child's notes to "The Unquiet Grave"; Ballads, no. 78 (2:234–36).

3089 mercy... passen right: Proverbial (Whiting M508); cf. Tr 3.1282 ("mercy passeth right"); LGW Pro F 162 ("made Mercy passen Ryght"). Robinson notes the underlying notion of the Christian doctrine of grace in the familiar courtly idea that the lover is dependent on his lady's mercy.

The Miller's Prologue

The explanatory notes to The Miller's Prologue and Tale are adapted from those written by Douglas Gray for The Riverside Chaucer.

The continuation of Fragment I from The Miller's Prologue through the Cook's fragment is a consecutive composition clearly written for the place it occupies after The Knight's Tale. There is no external evidence of the date of its composition, and attempts to date it on internal and aesthetic grounds may be challenged. However, the sophisticated adaptation of The Miller's Tale and The Reeve's Tale to the dramatic framework of the *Tales* has inclined many scholars to place them in the later years of Chaucer's work on the *Tales*.

3115 unbokeled is the male: Cf. ParsPro X.26 and MED s.v. *mal(le)* n (2) 1.c.

3119 Somwhat to quite with the Knyghtes tale: That is, a story that will "repay" or "match" the Knight's tale (for the word order see GP I.791n.). The tale is often taken as an elaborate burlesque of its predecessor (see introductory note below).

3120 for dronken: Some editors (e.g., Skeat, Baugh) have taken this as *fordronken,* a past participle with intensive *for-*. In such constructions it is difficult to determine whether *for* is a preposition or an intensive prefix. See Language and Versification, p. xxxiv, and cf. KnT *for old* and *for blak* I.2142–44 above.

3124 Pilates voys: A voice like that of the ranting Pilate in some mystery plays; cf. his entry in the Towneley scourging, ed. Martin Stevens and A. C. Cawley, EETS SS 13–14, 1994, I:270. Skeat (5:95) quotes Udall's translation of Erasmus's *Apothegms* (1542): "speaking out of measure loude and high, and altogether in Pilates voice." See Whiting P196 for other sixteenth-century examples.

3125 By armes: See PardT VI.651n.

3129 Robyn: Cf. "Robin the rybaudour" and his "rusty wordes" in Langland, PP B 6.73. See RomC 6337 "Now am I Robert, now Robyn." See MED s.v. Robin n. 1,(a): "as a designation for a robber, vagabond, or lowly person."

3134 a devel wey: A common oath: (Whiting D219); for the variant *a twenty devel way,* see below I.3713, RvT I.4257; CYT VIII.782, and cf. MED s.v. *devel* 6.

3141 a legende and a lyf. This phrase suggests a saint's life (cf. SNPro VIII.25–26) and, perhaps, a playful challenge to the Monk, who has been displaced (Coffman, MLN 50, 1935, 311–12).

3143 set the wrightes cap: Cf. GP I.586 and n.

3144–48 Cf. RvPro I.3860–81. The Reeve is a carpenter.

3152 no wyf … no cokewold: The idea is proverbial; Whiting M321. Skeat quotes Manning, Handlyng Synne, 1893–94: "Men sey, ther a man ys gelous/ That ther ys a kokewolde at hous." Cf. *Roman de la rose* 9129–35, tr. Dahlberg 165: "Saint Ernoul, the patron saint of cuckolds, from whom no man with a wife, to my knowledge, can be safe."

3154–56 thousand goode ayens oon badde: Cf. ProLGW G 276–77: "Of sundry wemen . . . / And evere a hundred goode ageyn oon bad."

3164 pryvetee: There is possibly a play on the differing senses: "mysteries" and "privy parts" (Paull F. Baum, PMLA 71. 1956, 242). Paula Neuss (EIC 24, 1974, 325–40) argues that double-entendre of this kind is sustained throughout tale (cf. I.3200–01, 3454, 3493, 3558). Frederick M. Biggs and Laura L. Howes (MÆ 65, 1996, 269–79) develop these ideas in relation to "the limits of human knowledge."

3165 Goddes foyson: Proverbial (Whiting G228).

3170–86 There is a similar apology by Boccaccio at the end of the *Decameron* (760–64; tr. McWilliam, 798–802): "If any of these stories is lacking in restraint, this is because of the nature of the story itself . . . I could not have related [it] in any other way without distorting it out of all recognition" (798).

3186 ernest of game: Proverbial (Whiting E18); cf. ClT IV.609, HF 822: "Take yt in ernest or in game."

The Miller's Tale

No direct source for this tale is known; its three principal motifs—the man who is made to fear a prophesied second flood, the misdirected kiss, and the branding with a hot iron—are widely distributed in medieval and modern anecdotes, occurring both individually and in combination. Chaucer may have found them combined in a single source, perhaps a French fabliau, or he may have combined them himself from various other versions, written or oral. For discussions of the analogues, see S&A, 106–23 (with copious references and texts of a number of versions) and Benson and Andersson, Lit. Context, 3–77 (with texts and translations of eleven versions).

The Miller's Tale is the first fabliau (in order of appearance) in *The Canterbury Tales.* The Reeve's Tale, The Shipman's Tale, and probably The Cook's Tale belong to this genre; and the influence of the genre is clear on a number of other tales, including the tales of the Friar, Summoner, Merchant, and the Wife of Bath's Prologue. A fabliau is basically "a versified short story designed to make you laugh, and its subject matter is most often indecent, concerned with sexual or excretory functions. The plot is usually in the form of a practical joke carried out for love or revenge" (D. S. Brewer, "The Fabliaux" in Rowland, Companion to Ch Sts, 296–97). It is a form that flourished in France in the thirteenth century; by Chaucer's time it was long out of fashion in French literature. See Charles Muscatine, The OF Fabliaux, 1986; R. Howard Bloch, The Scandal of the Fabliaux, 1986; Janette Richardson, Blameth Nat Me; Thomas D. Cooke and Benjamin Honeycutt, eds., The Humor of the Fabliaux: A Collection of Critical Essays, 1974. For selections of fabliaux see Benson and Andersson (above), R. C. Johnson and D. R. Owen, Fabliaux, 1966; Fabliaux Fair and Foul, intro. Raymond Eichmann, tr. John DuVal, 1992.

Most critics find that Chaucer "transformed" the fabliaux, especially in the Miller's and Reeve's Tales. Donald M. McGrady, ChauR 12, 1977, 1–16) argues that Chaucer knew the *Decameron* and constructed these tales by combining motifs in the manner of the Italian *novellieri*. The treatment of the Miller's and Reeve's Tales is so ambitious and individual that some have wondered if they can still be called fabliaux (see, e.g., Norton-Smith, Geoffrey Ch, 144).

The Miller's Tale is often taken as an intentional and elaborate parody of The Knight's Tale (such parody is common in the fabliaux; see Per Nykrog in The Humor of the Fabliaux, 59–73). Donaldson, 906–7, explains: "The Miller takes the same triangle [as in KnT] and transfers it to contemporary Oxford; he retains, however, some of the conventions of the courtly romance—though, of course, he does so only to make them ridiculous." Others see the tale as a fundamental criticism of the values of The Knight's Tale, most notably Peggy Knapp, Ch and the Social Context, 32–44; Lee Patterson in his discussion of "peasant consciousness" in The Miller's Tale (Lit. Practice and Social Change in Britain, 1380–1539, 113–55); and Ch and History, 244–79.

Charles Muscatine's Ch and the French Trad. (223–30) remains the best general treatment of The Miller's Tale, though a great variety of critical approaches have been employed in recent years—new historicist (Patterson, as above), psychoanalytical (H. Marshall Leicester, ELH 81, 1994, 473–79), feminist (Elaine Tuttle Hansen, Ch and the Fictions of Genre, 223–40), as well as more traditional approaches such as V. A. Kolve's useful account of the tale in the light of traditional iconography and visual imagery (Ch and Imagery of Narrative, 158–216). For a full bibliography and survey of scholarship, see Chaucer's Miller's, Reeve's, and Cook's Tales: An Annotated Bibliography 1900–1902, by T. L. Burton and Rosemary Greentree, 1997, and the Variorum edition (vol. 2, pt. 3) of the Miller's Tale, ed. Thomas W. Ross, 1983.

3188 gnof: "Churl, boor, lout" (OED compares the Frisian word **gnuffig,** "Ill mannered, coarse"). It is not recorded elsewhere in Middle English and is probably a colloquialism (Davis, Ch Glossary). R. T. Lambdin, Explicator 47, 1989, 4–6, suggests reading "gnos" (suggestive of live coal or ember), but this is not convincing.

3189 a carpenter: Cf. I.3144–48. On Oxford carpenters, see

Bennett, Ch at Oxford, 26–31 (figs. 2a and 2b reconstruct John's house [see 36–39]: he is rich enough to afford both a serving-boy or apprentice for himself and a maid for his wife).

3190 poure scoler: Probably formulaic (see RvT I.4002 and n.); Nicholas "is not too poor to have a room to himself" (Bennett, Ch at Oxford, 31). Students in academic halls regularly shared rooms, though the early fifteenth-century regulations of King's College, Cambridge, specified that each scholar "shall have a separate bed" (Rickert, Ch's World, 131). Nicholas's shelf full of books, psaltery, and astrolabe give us "the fullest inventory of a scholar's belongings before the sixteenth century" (Bennett, Ch at Oxford, 32–34).

3193 conclusiouns: The technical term for propositions or problems. Here the reference is to astrological operations undertaken to obtain answers to horary questions.

3195 certein houres: astronomically determined; cf. GP I.415–16n.

3199 hende Nicholas: Chaucer plays on the various meanings of *hende*, repeated eleven times: "courteous, gracious," "gentle," "nice," and perhaps "handy, near at hand" (P. E. Beichner, MS 14, 1952, 151–53); the word *hende* was conventional in earlier English poetry but had become worn (Donaldson, Speaking of Ch, 17–18) and was now rarely used in sophisticated poetry.

Nicholas was the patron saint of clerks; see PrT VII.514n.

3200 deerne love: The "secret" love of courtly tradition. Donaldson, Speaking of Ch, 125–27, notes that it was a common phrase in earlier verse (cf. MED s.v. *derne* 5) but that Chaucer uses it only here and in I.3278 and 3297, which suggests that Nicholas's aptitude parodies an ideal already devalued through misuse in the vernacular.

3204 The line is identical with KnT I.2779 (see n.).

3205 herbes swoote: Bennett (Ch at Oxford, 33) quotes Burton's remark that juniper "is in great request with us at Oxford, to sweeten our chambers."

3207 cetewale: Bennett (Ch at Oxford, 8) mentions a payment for "zedewaude" in the early records of Merton College.

3208 Almageste: (OF *almageste*, from Arabic "the greatest") was the name given to the great astronomical treatise of the Greek astronomer Ptolemy (Claudius Ptolomaios, c. 100–170), and was applied loosely to other textbooks of astrology. Cf. MLT II.295–301n.

3209 astrelabie: Astrolabes were not cheap: "even the Fellows of Merton had at this time only three between them" (Bennett, Ch at Oxford, 33–34).

3210 augrym stones: Stones or counters with the numerals of algorism (Arabic numerals) and intended for use upon an abacus.

3213 sautrie: Psaltery, a harp-like instrument, triangular or trapezoidal in shape, held against the breast or on the lap and plucked with quills. For illustrations, see Winternitz, pl. 41 b, 61 a; F. W. Galpin, Old Eng. Instruments of Music, 4th ed. rev. Thurston Dart, 1965, 42–48, pls. 11, 12, and 52. The Clerk of the General Prologue would rather have books than a psaltery (GP I.296). Such musical instruments were forbidden to the clergy though frequently used by the goliardic clerks (Mann, Ch and Estates, 75, citing Helen Waddell, The Wandering Scholars, 1927, app. E.). For varying interpretations of the musical imagery, see Jesse M.

Gellrich, JEGP 73, 1974, 176–88; Robertson, Pref. to Ch, 127–33; and David, Strumpet Muse, 96–97.

3216 Angelus ad virginem (The Angel to the Virgin): A song on the Annunciation, beginning "The angel, secretly entering her chamber, softly overcoming the virgin's fear, says to her 'Hail!'" For a full account of this text and its music, see John Stevens, in Med. Studies for J. A. W. Bennett, ed. P. L. Hetworth, 1981, 207–328. Nicholas might be expected to respond with particular relish to the song's delicately erotic undertones (cf. Douglas Gray, Themes and Images in the ME Religious Lyric, 1972, 104).

3217 the Kynges Noote: This piece has not been identified (for attempts see Fletcher Collins, Spec 8, 1933, 195–97; George L. Frost, Spec 8, 1933, 526–28).

3218 To anyone who has had to live in the proximity of students, this line seems clearly ironical.

3219–20 In contrast to the Clerk of the General Prologue (cf. I.301–2), Nicholas squanders his friends' or family's money, as do the students in Deschamps, Miroir de mariage, 2081–89 (Bennett, Ch at Oxford, 31).

3225 he was old: He is a *senex amans;* cf. introductory note to MerT.

3226 lik: Perhaps "like," i.e., "considered himself to be like a cuckold" (Atcheson L. Hench, ELN 3, 1965, 88–90, following Skeat), rather than "likely to be."

3227 Catoun: "Dionysius" Cato, the supposed author of a collection of Latin maxims, usually called *Disticha de moribus ad filium* (but also known as *Liber Catonis, Dicta Catonis*). It was widely current in the Middle Ages and was used in elementary school (see Curtius, Europ. Lit., 1953, 48–51; Nicholas Orme, Eng. Schools, 102–3). The proverb referred to here does not form part of the *Disticha* proper, but similar maxims are found in other collections (*Disticha diversorum*, etc.) associated with Cato (Aage Brusendorff, in Studies in Engl. Philol . . . in Hon. of Frederick Klaeber, ed. Kemp Malone and Martin B. Ruud, 1929, 337–38. For a full study of Chaucer's use of Cato, see Richard Hazelton, Spec 35, 1960, 357–80.

3231 snare: This word is used of love in Tr 1.507 ("O fool, now artow in the snare"), Tr 1.663 ("bounden in a snare"), Tr 5.748 ("er I was in the snare"), and RomA 1647 ("in the snare I fell anoon"). In MerPro IV.1227, it has distinctly misogynistic overtones; it is an image which is frequently and sardonically used in the *Quinze joies de mariage* (ed. J. Crow, 1969; tr. Brent A. Pitts, The Fifteen Joys of Marriage, 1985). There may be a hint of this here.

3233–70 Critics have often praised and analyzed the portraits of Alison and Absolon (cf., e.g., John L. Lowes, Art of Ch, 1930, 176–79). Louis A. Haselmayer (RES 14, 1938, 310–15) discusses the portraits in the French fabliaux (usually brief and conventionalized) and in the Latin *comoedia*, where the full formal rhetorical description (of the sort in Geoffery of Vinsauf's Poetria Nova, tr. Nims) is used. Chaucer's treatment here is different: the conventional description (now a bit old fashioned; Chaucer uses it after *Troilus and Criseyde* only for comic effect) is employed and translated into a naturalistic "Oxford context" (Muscatine, Ch and the Fr Trad., 229). See also D. S. Brewer, MLR 50, 1955, 267–68, who notes resemblances to "The Fair Maid of Ribbesdale" (Harley Lyrics, No. 7).

3234 gent: Possibly "a stale adjective" (Donaldson, Speaking of Ch, 22); cf. 3199 above and Thop VII.715.

3248 pere-jonette: Early-ripening pear. Skeat compares Piers Plowman C 12.220–22, where "pere-Ionettes" are mentioned as fruit that "litel while dureth,/ And that rathest rypeth rotieth most sonnest" (and what earliest ripens most soon becomes rotten). It is a succulent and swelling fruit and (not surprisingly) appears elsewhere with erotic suggestions, in the lyric "I have a new garden" (Secular Lyrics, ed. Robbins, No. 21). Cf. MerT IV.2217n.

3251 latoun: See GP I.699n.

3256 noble: A gold coin worth 6 shillings, 8 pence (see PardT VI.907n.). The principal London mint was in the Tower. Pratt (Tales, 81) notes that Chaucer had charge of the upkeep of the Tower in 1389–91.

3258 The Pardoner, in his Prologue (VI.397), compares the movement of his neck and head to a dove *sittynge on a berne*. The swallow is proverbially swift of flight and associated with summer (see Whiting 5923,5924).

3261 bragot: Bragger (Welsh *bragaud*), a drink made of ale and honey fermented together.

3268 a prymerole, a piggesnye: Both words are endearments, and both seem to be flower names, although the identification of the flowers is difficult. **Prymerole** is variously glossed a "primrose," "cowslip," or "daisy"; the evidence from early usage is inconclusive. In a Harley lyric (No. 3, 13) it is one of the flowers that the beauty of Annot surpasses. This is the only appearance of **piggesnye** in Middle English; if it is a flower it may be the cuckoo-flower (called "pig's eyes" in Essex, EDD) or the hyophthalmos (Betty Hill, NM 74, 1973, 669–70), known as "swine's eye," "sow's eye." As a term of endearment it is commonly recorded from the time of Skelton on. The early uses (cf. OED s.v. *pigsney*) suggest that it is a "low," or at least a very familiar, term of endearment, suitable no doubt for a *wenche* (3254; cf. MancT IX.212–20). (Later, in the nineteenth century, the EDD records it once in Devon as a term of contempt for an immodest woman.)

3274 Oseneye: There was an abbey of Augustinian canons at Osney, now part of Oxford, but then some distance from the city. The site is now occupied by the cemetery near the Oxford railway station. See 3659 below.

3276 queynte: A euphemism, the absolute adjective, "elegant, pleasing (thing)," used here for pudendum, with a pun on the obscenity, which was the same in Middle English as in modern speech. For a fourteenth-century illustration (from the Taymouth Hours) of this lecherous and distinctly uncourteous gesture, see Robertson, Pref to Ch, plate 5.

3280 Lemman: Cf. MancT IX.204–6n.

3291 Seint Thomas of Kent: St. Thomas Becket (cf. GP I.17 and n.). Ruth H. Cline (HLQ 26, 1963, 135) suggests that the oath, which is also used twice by the carpenter (I.3425, 3461), may have a local appropriateness, because of the parish church of St. Thomas in Osney.

3312 parissh clerk: His liturgial duties, such as bearing the pax to individual parishioners, provided "an ideal opportunity for an infatuated clerk to hint his desires and cast a loving look" (Bennett, Ch at Oxford, 43).

3312–38 Absolon: The name is rare (Bennett, Ch at Oxford, 42). The OT Absolon was a traditional example of male beauty (2 Kings [AV 2 Sam] 14.25: "Now in all Israel there was no one to be praised so much as Absolon"), especially because of his beautiful hair (2 Kings [2 Sam AV] 14.26: "When he cut the hair of his head . . . he weighed the hair of his head two hundred shekels"). The color of his hair is not specified in the OT but was taken as golden in the Middle Ages (cf. *Roman de la rose* 13870; tr. Dahlberg, p. 238: "Absolon, with his blond locks") and LGW 249 "Hyd, Absolon, thy gilte tresses clere." Cline (HLQ 26:140–45) says that a surpliced clerk should have been tonsured, though the practice seems to have been lax; cf. the archbishop of Canterbury's complaint quoted in GP I.675–79n.

3318 His shoes were "windowed," i.e., the uppers were cut in open-work patterns so that they resembled the windows of St. Paul's Cathedral in London. Cf. RomA 842–43: "And shod he was . . ./ With shoon decoped, and with laas." For illustrations, see Frederick W. Fairholt, Costume in England, 3rd ed., 1885, 2:64–65.

3326 Being a parish clerk was a part-time occupation, and Absolon was also a barber-surgeon. There was a guild of university barbers ("a shave was an expensive luxury, and few university men shaved more than once a week"; Bennett, Ch at Oxford, 45–46). A barber was often a blood-letter, though clerics were forbidden to draw blood (see introductory note on Physician in GP).

3327 maken a chartre: See Bennett (Ch at Oxford, 46) for references to conveyancing and business teaching in Oxford: "Absolon might earn substantial fees for engrossing, and perhaps too for procuring witnesses."

3329 after the scole of Oxenforde: It is not clear whether this is to be taken satirically, like the Prioress's French (GP I.125).

3331 rubible: See the illustrations in F. W. Galpin, Old Eng. Instruments of Music, fig. 14 and plates 15, 16, 43 (cf. 59–63).

3333 giterne: For illustrations, see Galpin, fig. 15, plate 7 (cf. 16–19).

3339 jolif: This adjective is applied to Absolon seven times and functions as a defining epithet, as *hende* does for Nicholas (see 3199 above) and *seli* for old John (see 3404 below). It is also used of the clerk Jankyn in a popular song describing a similar scene, involving an Alisoun, at church: "Kyrie, so kyrie, Jankyn syngyt merie, with aleyson" (a pun on Alisoun and *Kyrie eleison,* Lord have mercy) (R. L. Greene, Early English Carols, 2nd ed., Oxford, 1977, No. 457).

3349 love-longynge: Another idiom of popular verse, now out of style; cf. 3199 above and Thop VII.772n.

3369 Yis: The emphatic form of assent. The modern *yes* is equivalent to Chaucer's *ye* (Robinson).

3377 Bennett compares the carol cited in 3339 above, where Jankyn "cracks" his notes, and the Wycliffite criticism of "smale brekynge, that stireth vain men to daunsynge more than to mornynge" (Sisam, Fourteenth Cent. Verse and Prose, 123). Cf. MerT IV.1850.

3379 wafres: Thin, crisp cakes baked in wafer irons over an open flame. They were made "of cheese, eggs, milk, sugar, ginger, and the belly of a pike" (Bennett, Ch at Oxford, 45) and sold by waferwomen, who, according to the OED, were often employed in amatory intrigues (cf. PardT VI.479n.).

3382 Some MSS have the marginal gloss "Unde Ovidus: Ictibus Agrestis," but the quotation is not from Ovid. One glossator finishes the line "Overcome the rustic with blows, the townsman with a gift, the noble in conversation with a suitable argument." (Manly-Rickert 3:490), though this may have been suggested by Chaucer's line.

3384 Herodes: The part of Herod in a mystery play, the role of the blustering tyrant. In a Coventry play (Two Coventry Corpus Christi Plays, ed. H. Craig, EETS e.s. 87, 1957, 27) a rubric says "here Erode ragis in the pagond [pageant] and in the strete also" (cf. "out-herods Herod," Hamlet 3.2.15). The **scaffold hye** is probably the upper story of a pageant wagon (Bennett) rather than a simple outdoor stage (Baugh, Fisher). The Ludus Coventriae (The N-Town Play, ed. Stephen Spector, EETS SS, 11–12, 1991, p. 310) has "Herowdys scafald xal [shall] un-close shewynge Herowdes in astat," i.e., seated on a throne above the crowd. There were enough guilds in Oxford to stage a complete cycle of mystery plays, but no text has survived.

3387 blowe the bukkes horn: "Go whistle." Cf. the phrase *Pipe in an ivy lef* (Tr 5.1433) and see KnT I.1838 and n.

3389 ape i. e., she made a fool of Absolon. Cf. GP I.706n.

3392–93 nye slye . . . ferre leeve: Proverbial (Whiting S395). Cf. the modern "out of sight, out of mind."

3396 stood in his light: Also proverbial (Whiting L264).

3404 sely: Mary Brookbank Reed (PQ 41, 1962, 768–69) notes that this adjective is used of the carpenter five times (cf. *hende*, see 3199 above, and *jolif*, see 3339 above) and that Chaucer plays ironically on its different senses. Theodore I. Silar (PQ 69, 1990, 409–17) explores various meanings. In MED, s.v. *seli* adj., they range from "blessed, happy" to "innocent, foolish, hapless" and "wretched."

3429–30 An expansion of the proverbial "here today, gone tomorrow" (Whiting T351).

3449 Seinte Frydeswyde: The virgin saint (d. eighth cent.) was noted for her healing powers, especially the casting out of devils (Cline, MLN 60:480–81; A. Leyland, N&Q 219, 1974, 126–27). There was a monastery of St. Frideswide in Oxford; its church became the present cathedral.

3451–54 For the popular belief that those who follow the craft of astronomy are trying to pry into **Goddes pryvetee**, see Dives and Pauper (EETS 275, 117): "They will be of God's privy counsel, will God, nill God, and rule His judgement, His deeds, His works" [trans.]; and 140, which quotes Acts 1.7 ("It is not for you to know the times or the seasons, which the Father has put in his own power"). Cf. Whiting G198 for further examples.

3451 astromye: The form is sometimes taken as a malapropism (cf. *Nowelis flood* I.3818). However, the form *astromien* (found, for instance, in *Kyng Alisaunder*) is a genuine one, and astromye may have been a genuine variant form. See J. R. R. Tolkien, TPS, 1934, 3n.; N. F. Blake, N&Q 224, 1979, 110–11.

3457–61 A familiar fable, usually told of a philosopher; cf. Aesop's Fables, ed. E. Chambry, 1925, 1960, No. 65; and Cento Novelle Antiche, no. 38, both telling it of an astrologer. Bennett (Ch at Oxford, 53) suggests that Chaucer has substituted a "marl-pit" for the well into which the Greek astronomer fell, because he has in mind the "Campus Pits" of marl or clay at the east end of Milham

Ford, beside the Cherwell (where the present St. Hilda's College stands).

3478 thenk on Cristes passioun: Recalling Christ's passion is a traditional remedy against despair (I.3474). (It is used thus in the Ars Moriendi or Craft of Dying, ed. F. M. Comper, London, 1917, 12–14.) John quickly slips into the practices of popular religion by making the sign of the cross against **elves** and **wightes**. The sign of the cross was traditionally of great spiritual efficacy, and in popular belief it was regarded as having magical power (Alan J. Fletcher, MÆ 61, 1992, 96–105).

3480–86 nyght-spel: A magic charm against the demons of the night. (The carpenter makes the boundaries of the house secure by saying it at the four sides and at the threshold.) The **white pater-noster** survives into modern times; e. g., in the nursery-rhyme "Matthew, Mark, Luke, and John/ Bless the bed that I lie on"—still implying a protective "marking" of the corners; see I. and P. Opie, Oxf. Dict. of Nursery Rhymes, 1951, 303–5 (with full references). It is *white* because it is not in any way connected with the black magic of the devil (cf. ParsT X.508 and Skeat 5:106). **Seinte Benedight** is presumably St. Benedict (cf. GP 173n.). A Latin charm involving both the saint and the cross—"Vade retro Satana; nunquam suade mihi vana" (Englished as "Avaunt foul fiend, vain are thy tempting charms;/ The cross shall ward me from thy poysonous harms" in The Effects and Virtues of the Crosse or Medal of the Great Patriarch St. Benedict, 1660) is often engraved on St. Benedict medals and crosses (it is popular from the seventeenth century, but seems to go back to the Middle Ages). It is also possible that he has been manufactured here out of the word *benedight* ("blessed"; see OED). The nearest equivalent in ME to the night-spell is probably that spoken by the third shepherd in the Towneley First Shepherd's Play (EETS SS 13–14, 1:117): "For ferde we be fryght/ A crosse lett vs kest —/ Cryst-crosse, benedyght/ Eeest and west —/ ffor drede./ *Iesus onazarus/ Crucyefixus/ Morcus, Andreus,/* God be oure spede!"

3485 For nyghtes verye: The meaning is uncertain. The best suggestion is "against the evil spirits of the night" (Skeat and others); possibly the mysterious **verye** is a derivative or a corruption of OE *we(ar)g* "evil spirit." It would not be surprising to find an old word preserved in a charm. E. T. Donaldson (MLN 69, 1959, 310–13) suggests an emendation to another old form, **nerye** "save." Paleographically, this change is an easy one, but the resulting syntax seems awkward.

3486 Seinte Petres soster: St. Peter's brother appears in a White Paternoster quoted by J. White, The Way to the True Church, 1610, c. 2 (cf. N&Q 8, 1853, 612–13). St. Peter's sister appears in a charm quoted by Grosseteste: "Grene pater noster/ Petres leve soster" (Siegfried Wenzel, N&Q 215, 1970, 449–50).

3512 by hym that harwed helle: The story of the Harrowing of Hell (from the apocryphal Gospel of Nicodemus, ed. H. C. Kim, Toronto, 1973) was immensely popular in the Middle Ages. John would have been familiar with it from wall-paintings and from mystery plays.

3515 in the moone: On prognostication by the moon, of "the days of the moon," Willard E. Farnham, SP 20, 1923,

70–82. Sometimes recourse was had to astronomical calculations of the position of the moon; sometimes the mere day of the moon was considered as being favorable or unfavorable for an undertaking. Cf. Tr 2.7475: "And caste and knew in good plit was the moone/ To doon viage." See KnT I.1462–64n. John C. Hirsh (ELN 13, 1975, 86–90) argues that the tale's emphasis on Monday (I.3430, 3516, 3633, 3659) is significant: Nicholas's choice of the day is partly determined by his interest in the moon; the moon is the ruling planet of Monday and shares its reputation for instability. On the astrological background to the tale, see O'Connor, Spec 31, 1956, 120–25; cf. Wood, Ch and the Stars, 170–72. There was a tradition that Noah was a skillful astrologer who was aware of the approaching deluge through his study of the stars as well as through divine revelation. For Noah's esoteric knowledge, see also Francis Lee Utley, Spec 16, 1941, 450.

3530   See Ecclus. 32.24: "My son, do nothing without counsel, and you will not repent later." It is a very common proverb (Whiting C470). The form and attribution to Solomon here and in MerT IV.1483–86 are due to Albertanus of Brescia, *Lib. consolationis et consilii,* translated in Mel VII.1003.

3538–43   This is a clear reference to the comic scenes in the mystery plays in which Noah's wife refuses to enter the ark (**Noe with his felaweshipe**, Noah and his sons). For an illustration (from a window in Malvern Priory), see M. D. Anderson, Drama and Imagery in Eng. Med. Churches, 1963, pl. 14a (a ladder, like those which are to figure in the tale, can be seen clearly in the background). There are delicate hints of parallels in matters both small and great: Noah was frequently pictured as a carpenter (see Paul A. Olson, SP 59, 1962, 4n.) (and the play about him was sometimes performed by the shipwrights), and the Flood was regarded as an apocalyptic event, a typological anticipation of the end of the world and the Last Judgment. It may be noted that Noah's Flood took place (Gen. 7:11) on the seventeenth day of the second month: 17 April (March being the first month; cf. NPT VII.3187–88), the date traditionally assigned to the first day of the Canterbury pilgrimage.

3590–91 no synne: An allusion to the traditional teaching that there was no copulation on the ark. See Francis Lee Utley, Germanic Rev. 16, 1941, 242–44.

3598 sende the wise: Proverbial; cf. "a word to the wise" and Whiting W399.

3611–13 affeccioun . . . impressioun: On the idea of perception through the *affeccioun,* see MerT IV.1577–87n. (El here has the marginal gloss "Auctor.")

3637 furlong way: A measure of time, 2½ minutes, one-eighth of a *mile wey* (twenty minutes).

3645 corfew-tyme: At dusk, probably 8 P.M. (fires were then covered for the night).

3655 laudes: The second of the seven canonical hours (services), following matins and preceding prime (cf. GP I.122n.); some time, then, before day had broken (I.3731).

3659 Oseneye: Probably Osney Mead or Bulstake Mead, which was held by the Abbey (Bennett, Ch at Oxford, 54). See 3274 above.

3682–83   Absolon's interpretation follows popular tradition: divination from involuntary itching, burning ears, etc., was

a widespread practice (Skeat 5:109). To itch, then as now, could also mean "to have an irritating desire or uneasy craving provoking to action" (OED s.v. *itch* v. 2.A).

3690 greyn: Grain of Paradise, or cardamom seed (a sweetener of the breath).

3692 trewe-lof: a four-leafed sprig of herb paris (*Paris quadrifolia*) in the shape of a fourfold true-love knot. On its implications see Susanna Greer Fein, ChauR 25, 1991, 302–17.

3698–707   R. E. Kaske (SP 59, 1962, 479–500, esp. 481–83) notices in Absolon's speech some parodic echoes of the Song of Songs (e.g., **hony-comb, bryd:** "thy lips, O my spouse, drop as the honeycomb," 4.11; **my sweete cynamome:** "cinnamon," 4.14). Not all of the parallels he adduces are convincing, however, and it is far from certain that Chaucer had the Song of Songs in mind in the earlier descriptions of Alison and Absolon. Cf. the more obvious parody in MerT IV.2138–45.

3703 swelte and swete: Cf. RomB 2480: "Though thou for love swelte and swete."

3709 "com pa me":   *Pa* or *ba* is a rarely recorded word but one that was perhaps a familiar affectionate term for "kiss," possibly originating in the nursery (OED s.v. *ba*) or as a playful adaptation of Fr. *baiser* (MED s.v. *ba*). It is probably used mockingly here (perhaps echoing Absolon's more childish remarks; cf. e.g. I.3704); cf. WBPro III.433.

3713 twenty devel wey: Cf. KnT I.3134n.

3718–22   Peter G. Beidler (ChauR 12, 1977, 90–102) discusses the differences between the Flemish version and Chaucer's of this episode (for the text and trans. see S&A, 112–18). Chaucer is unique among early tellers of the story in having the woman execute the trick; he also intensifies the affront to Absolon by stressing his sensitivity to smells and sounds (I.3337–38). The episode, and particularly the roles of Gervase and of the fart, has been the subject of much symbolic and moralizing criticism (see Beidler's notes) and, more recently, psychologizing.

3723 This Absolon: For the use of *this* (and the plural *thise,* RvT I.4100), "mainly a feature of vivid, colloquial and often chatty style" (Mustanoja, ME Syntax, 174), see Language and Versification, p. xxxiii.

3725   Cf. *Roman de la rose* 3403–8 (RomB 3674–76: "For who therto may wynnen . . . / He of the surplus of the pray/ May lyve in hope to get som day") and cf. Ovid, Ars Am.; tr. Mosely, 1.669: "He who takes kisses, if he takes not the rest. . . ."

3726 Lemman . . . oore: The whole line may be meant to sound hackneyed (see Donaldson, Speaking of Ch, 26–27): **bryd** and *oore* were common in earlier verse (cf. "ledy, thyn ore," Harley Lyrics, No. 32, 16–17, and the refrain of a love song quoted by Giraldus Cambrensis, Rolls Series, 2.120), but by Chaucer's time they were now out of fashion (this is Chaucer's only use).

3742   For **berd** in the sense of "delude, hoodwink" (in the phrase *make one's beard*), see WBPro III.361 and—in what seems to be a deliberate echo of this line—RvT I.4096.

3747–49   Jonathan Wordsworth, MÆ 27, 1958, 21, notes a possible parodic echo of the rhetorical questions found in KnT (I.1454–56, 1870–71, 2652–53).

3755–58   An effective and instantaneous remedy for the

loveris maladye/ Of Hereos (KnT I.1355–76 and n.); see Edward C. Schweitzer in Julian N. Wasserman and Robert J. Blanch, eds., Ch in the Eighties, 1986, 223–33.

3761–63 An entertaining alliterative poem (ed. Sisam, Fourteenth Cent. Verse and Prose, 169–70) complains about the noise blacksmiths make at night. E. P. Kuhl (MLN 29, 1914, 156) draws attention to a reference in 1394 to the nuisance, noise, and alarm experienced by the neighbors of blacksmiths in London. Perhaps Gervase is preparing a plough or ploughs for use in the morning, which would suggest that his smithy is near the edge of town.

3761 daun: The title was used very loosely, though only here is it applied to a lower-class character. (It is used for the fox *daun Russell* in NPT VII.3334.) See KnT I.1379n.

3770 viritoot: The word is unique to Chaucer and the meaning is obscure. Many interpretations have been advanced (most recently Jeffrey L. Singman, ELN 31:2, 1993, 1–7, who suggests it is a top used in a game), but Skeat's solution "astir" (5:110–11) still seems most likely.

3771 Seinte Note: Apparently St. Neot, a ninth-century saint. Why Gervase swears by this obscure saint is not clear, though there is a town, St. Neot's, near Cambridge. It is just possible that Chaucer might have heard of the tradition (Cline HLQ 26:131–35) associating St. Neot with King Alfred's legendary founding of Oxford University.

3774 moore tow on his distaf: Proverbial (Whiting T432). There may be a more specific allusion here: Carter Revard (ELN 17, 1980, 168–70) points out (*Liber Albus*, 1:459) that in London the carrying of a distaff with a tow in it was statutory punishment for a person guilty of crimes of sex and violence. So too "Brawlers (male scolds) and scolds were to be taken in procession to the thews, holding a distaff with flax on it in the right hand" (Robertson, Ch's London, 103).

3782 Cristes foo: Probably "the devil" rather than an intentional substitution for foot (as Robinson held) to avoid open profanity (as in *cokkes bones,* MancPro IX.9).

3818 Nowelis: This seems to be a malapropism, implying a confusion of "Noe" and "Nowel," Christmas. However, "Noels" for "Noe" does appear in Froissart's Chroniques, ed. George T. Diller, TLF, 1972, 37.

3821–22 Cf. the Fr. "ne trouva point de pain a vendre" (found no bread to sell; i.e., did not stop; Tyrwhitt, quoted by Skeat), which appears in the fabliau Aloul, 591–92 in Fabliaux, Fair and Foul, tr. DuVal.

3822–23 That is, John falls from the roof of the hall to the floor (**celle** [=*selle*], "flooring"). The tubs hang from the *balkes* (I.3626), beams of squared timber, which serve as tie beams.

The Reeve's Prologue

The explanatory notes to The Reeve's Prologue and Tale are adapted from those written by Douglas Gray for The Riverside Chaucer.

3857 Chaucer may have derived the phrase, which he uses also at MLT II.211, MerT IV.1469, SqT V.202, from *Roman de la rose,* 10684; tr. Dahlberg, 189: "Diverse diverses choses distrent" (Different ones said different things). N. S.

Thompson (Ch, Boccaccio, 18–19) notes a similar line in the *Decameron:* "diversamente da diversi fu intesa" (at the end of Day 3, commenting on Lauretta's song). The expression is proverbial (Whiting M202) and the play on *diverse* is common; see Gower, Conf. aman. 5.217–18: "And thus upon the pointz diverse/ Diverseliche he gan reherce" (see Thompson, 37, n. 27).

3860 Osewold: The name, Manly says (CT, 560), was rare in fourteenth-century Norfolk, "though common enough farther north." St. Oswald (d. 642) was a Northumbrian saint.

3864 So theek: The suffixed *ik,* "I" (cf. I.3867), is a Northern and East Midland form, appropriate to a Norfolk man. Although Chaucer took great care with the dialect of the students in the tale (see 4022 below), he does not consistently represent the speech of the Reeve in his own person; only a few indications of pronunciation (e.g., *lemes, abegge*) suggest East Anglia (Norman Davis, rev. of Bennett, Ch at Oxford and Cambridge, RES 27, 1976, 336–37).

3865 With bleryng of . . . ye: A common expression; cf. I.4049 below, CYT VIII.730, MancT IX.252, and Whiting E217.

3868 Gras time: "The time when a horse feeds himself in the field" (Skeat 5:113). Bennett (Ch at Oxford, 87) notes that the Reeve, whose business keeps him constantly in the saddle, talks "in 'horsly' terms"; cf. I.3888. However, Carol A. Everest (ChauR 31, 1996, 99–114) notes the metaphor is also biblical: "As for man, his days are as grass; as a flower of the field, so he flourisheth," Psalm 102.15. She argues that the presentation of old age here is in keeping with contemporary medical theories on aging.

3873 mullok: Bennett (Ch at Oxford, 90) notes this is "an earthy dialect word." It is recorded in Middle English (MED s.v. *mollok(e)* only here and in CYT VIII.938. It emphasizes the strong impression of ripeness passing into rottenness that is given by many words in this speech.

3876 Cf. Luke 7.31–32: ". . . we have piped unto you and you have not danced."

3877 Possibly an echo of 2 Cor. 12.7 ("stimulus carnis mea," a thorn in my flesh).

3878 hoor heed . . . grene tayl: Exactly this image is put in the mouth of an old man in the *Decameron,* Introduction to the Fourth Day (tr. McWilliam, 288: "Though the leek's head is white, it has a green tail"). It may have been proverbial—it certainly was after Chaucer's time: see Whiting H240.

3882–85 Robert A. Pratt (Speculum 41, 1966, 636) compares John of Wales's *Communiloquium:* "The four fires are the four sins that consume the world. The first of these is the fire of lying . . . the second is the fire of greed . . . the third is the fire of wrath that inflames men. The fourth is [the fire of] impiety."

3882 fyr yreke: Proverbial (Whiting F185).

3884 coveitise: cf. Tr 4.1369: "elde is ful of coveytise."

3888 coltes tooth: Proverbial (Whiting C377). Cf. WBPro III.602.

3890–97 In a medieval cask (**tonne**), the **tappe** was a tapered stick used to plug the tap-hole, located on the head of the cask somewhere close to the **chymbe** (the rim, formed by the ends of staves protruding beyond the head). A new cask would require the boring of a tap-hole for the insertion of the tap; there is therefore probably a pun on the word **bore,** "born" (Robert A. Pratt, recorded in PMLA 73, 1958, 167). There is possibly (Pratt, *ibid.*) another word play in 3895–96 on **rynge** and **chymbe,** and probably on **tonge** (with the "tongue" of a bell); A. H. MacLaine (MÆ 31, 1962, 129–31) explains that when the cask is full "the stream of wine flows silently and strongly, but at the end it splashes on the rim, just like the foolish tongue of a garrulous old man." Pratt (Spec 41:637) believes the metaphor was suggested by John of Wales (quoting Seneca, Epistulae Morales, 108.26): "Just as the purest wine flows from the top of the jar and the thickest dregs settle at the bottom."

3904 Cf. Phaedrus, Fables (ed. Ben Edward Perry, Loeb, 1965) 1.14: "Ex sutore medicus" [from a cobbler a doctor], a story about a cobbler who tried to pass himself off as a physician).

3906 half-wey pryme: Usually taken to mean about 7:30 A.M. Edward A. Block (Spec 32, 1957, 826–33) argues that it is 6:30 A.M. (according to monastic time).

3907 Grenewych: Greenwich, about half a mile past Deptford. Chaucer was living there in the 1390s, possibly since 1385 (Pearsall, Life of Geoffrey Ch, 225).

3912 with force force of-showve: In the Ellesmere MS this is glossed by the Latin equivalent, "vim vi repellere" (to repel force with force; given in its full form in other MSS, "licitum est vim vi repellere," it is legitimate to repel force with force), which is a well-known legal maxim (see Franz Montgomery, PQ 10, 1931, 404–5; Louis McCorry Myers, MLN 49, 1934, 222–26).

3919 stalke: Cf. Matt. 7.3: "And why beholdest thou the mote (Lat. *festucam*) in thy brother's eye, but considerest not the beam that is in thine own eye?" It was proverbial (Whiting M710).

The Reeve's Tale

The Reeve's Tale is based on a traditional fabliau story (the "cradle-trick") that is especially widespread; see Aarne-Thompson, No. 1363. No precise source has been found, but there are some close analogues, six of them early (five of these are printed with translations and discussion in Benson and Andersson, Lit. Context, 79–201; two French texts of *Le meunier et les ii clers* are printed in S&A 124–47). Of these, two French fabliaux, *Le meunier et les ii clers,* and, to a lesser extent, *De Gombert et les ii clers* by Jean Bodel (d. 1210), are especially close to Chaucer. Peter G. Beidler (ChauR 26, 1992, 283–92) shows that the Flemish analogue (Een bispel van .ii. clerken, tr. in the article) accounts for a good many important details not found in the French versions. There are also some close similarities to Boccaccio's *Decameron,* Ninth Day, 6 (see Donald McGrady, ChauR 12, 1977, 9–10). The analogues account for every part of the plot, but none for Chaucer's masterful characterization and skillful union of plot and character. On fabliaux in general, see the introductory note to The Miller's Tale.

The Reeve's Tale has attracted much less critical attention than has The Miller's Tale, perhaps because it seems more bitter in tone (Stephen Knight, Poetry of the CT, 1973) and because it "quits" the Miller (see I.4324) in a much less subtle manner than the Miller "quits" the Knight's Tale. Yet it has

its own virtues—notably a superb use of the "low style" and "narrative speed" (Helen Cooper, CT, Oxford Guides to Ch, 1989, 108–16; see the close analysis of the style by D. S. Brewer, New Intro. to Ch, 290–91). Most criticism has concerned the character of the teller as revealed in his prologue (see Susanna Greer Fein, Rebels and Rivals: The Contestive Spirit in the CT, 1991, 73–104, on thematic relations between the prologue and the tale) and the relation of the tale to the fabliaux, beginning with Walter Morris Hart's still useful article on the RvT and the fabliaux (PMLA 23, 1908, 1–44). There is useful critical comment in the edition by A. C. and J. E. Spearing, 1979, and in V. A. Kolve, Ch and the Imagery of Narrative, 217–56. For a full bibliography see T. L. Burton and Rosemary Greentree, Ch's Miller's, Reeve's, and Cook's Tale: An Annotated Bibliography 1900 to 1992.

3921–23 The topographical details are accurate. At **Trumpyngtoun** (Trumpington), three miles from Cambridge (**Cantebrigge**), the Rhee River becomes the Cam; it is "something more than a brook" but here is "joined by the Bourn, which has always been called a brook" (Bennett, Ch at Oxford, 110–14). The bridge was perhaps higher up than the present bridge (built in 1790). There was a mill at the place now called "Byron's Pool," but previously "Old Mills" (Bennett, 111–13, and App. B). Cf. 4065n. Bennett (109) notes that Trumpington was then a small village that probably had no inn (hence the clerks' need for lodging) but only an ale-house or two (thus the Miller can send Malin to buy ale). Chaucer may have had some local knowledge through Sir Roger de Trumpington, who was in the King's household (Manly, New Light, 97–101); he was responsible for the last of Edward III's annuities to Phillipa Chaucer; John of Gaunt gave New Year gifts to Phillipa and "Blanche de Trompyngton" (Ch Life Records, 90).

3925–41 The correspondence of some details in the Reeve's description (e.g., the references to playing the bagpipe, wrestling) with those in the description of the pilgrim Miller in the GP is no doubt deliberate and provocative.

3928 turne coppes: Usually explained as "make wooden cups in a turning-lathe." Robert A. Pratt (JEGP 59, 1960, 208–11) raises the attractive possibility that this refers to some country drinking-game similar to that with a communal chant "The cup is turned over," recorded in Sussex in 1862.

3933 Sheffield (**Sheffeld**) was already famous for its steel. The word **thwitel** is poorly attested, but there are examples in fourteenth-century records, which "all concern brawls (one actually at Trumpington)" (Bennett, Ch at Oxford, 5).

3936 market-betere: One who loiters around a marketplace (MED s.v. *market* n. [1].4a), probably with the implication of quarrelsomeness; cf. Minot 2.25 (in Sisam, Fourteenth Cent. Verse and Prose, 153): "the Skottes gase [*go*] in Burghes [*towns*] and betes the stretes," where the implication is that Scots are quarrelsome swaggerers.

3941 hoote: "Called." Paull F. Baum (PMLA 71, 1956, 239) claims that there is a pun with *hoot* "hot."

Symkyn: Joseph E. Grennen (JMRS 14, 1984, 245–59) finds puns on *simus* (having a flattened nose), *simia* (monkey, ape), and *simonia* (simony).

3943 She was an illegitimate daughter of the parson, who consequently paid her dowry. On priests and concubinage, see P. Heath, The Eng. Parish Clergy on the Eve of the Reformation, 1969, 104–8. Cf. Piers Plowman B 5.160–61: "dame Peronelle, a prestes file [daughter]." One of the parsons of Trumpington, Ricardus dictus Berde de Ledbury, was in 1343 succeeded by his son (and a similar situation is recorded at nearby Grantchester). See Bennett, Ch at Oxford, 109–10.

3954–55 gyte of reed: For evidence (mainly from French and German) that the wearing of red hose was thought to be inappropriate to the lower classes, see the discussion of sartorial symbolism by George Fenwick Jones, MÆ 25, 1956, 65–66. Absolon, in the MilT (I.3319), and the Wife of Bath (GP I.456) also affect red hose; the Wife of Bath wears scarlet *gytes* (WBPro III.559).

3964 digne as water in a dich: Proverbial (Whiting D268).

3974 kamus nose: She is her father's daughter. For an attempt to explain the significance of this physiognomic detail (cf. Curry, Ch and Science, 85), see W. Arthur Turner (N&Q 199, 1954, 232), who quotes the remark (from *Scriptores Physiognomici,* ed. R. Foerster, 1893, 2:203) "whoever has a snub-nose is lustful and loves intercourse."

3987 sokene: the right of a mill-owner, in exchange for a fixed rent, to grind and take toll of all grain of the manor or town in which the mill stands; cf. MED s.v. *soken(e)* n. 2.(d).

3990 Soler Halle: A name for King's Hall, an important college that grew out of a society of scholars founded by Edward II; it was later merged into Trinity College. See A. B. Cobban, The King's Hall, 1969; and D. S. Brewer, ChauR 5, 1971, 311–17. The name *Soler Hall* (referring to the number of solars [rooms admitting sunlight] it contained) is not found in a King's Hall document; Bennett (Ch at Oxford, 94–96) suggests that Chaucer's phrase *men clepen* may indicate that it is not the official name, and that by choosing an apt, but noncommittal, epithet the poet is avoiding any risk of libel (he notes similar obfuscations in the choice of the titles *wardeyn* and *manciple*).

3991 malt: Colleges brewed their own ale (Bennett, Ch at Oxford, 6, 106).

4002 povre scolers: Probably formulaic (they can offer silver for a night's lodging): "they are called poor simply because scholars without exhibitions or benefices were assumed to be so" (Bennett, Ch at Oxford, 98–99). Cf. MilT I.3190 above. Their equivalents in the two French fabliaux are actually poor.

4014 Strother: The town cannot be identified with certainty. There is a Castle Strother in Northumberland, "The name, both as a simplex and as an element, is now found only north of the Tees" (Bennett, Ch at Oxford, 101). Cf. MED s.v. *strother* n. (1) (b).

4022 Chaucer clearly wished the language of the two clerks to sound Northern. It is apparently the first case of this kind of joking imitation of a dialect recorded in English literature. Bennett (Ch at Oxford, 99–100) notes that no college in Cambridge drew so many members from the North as King's Hall did. On the dialect forms, see J. R. R. Tolkien, TPS, 1934, 1–70; R. W. V. Elliott, Ch's English, 390–93; Jeremy J. Smith, NM 95, 1994, 433–37. The most distinctive features are: the reflex of OE ā appears as *a/aa* instead of Chaucer's usual *o/oo* (gas, sua, ham); the OE consonant

group -*lc* (usually -*lch,* -*ch*) appears as -*lk* in *swilk, whilk;* the initial consonant of *shall* appears as *sal;* the 3rd singular and plural present indicative of verbs appears as -*(e)s.* The pronominal form *thair,* which Chaucer uses only here, although it later became accepted in London English, was presumably still felt to be Northern. Also suggestive of the North are a number of words, for instance: *heythyng, heythen, ille, ymel, lathe* (all of Scandinavian origin), and *boes, pit* (for *put*), *gif* (for *if*) and *taa* (for *take*).

4026 nede has na peer: Proverbial (Whiting N51, N52; cf. "Necessity knows no law").

4027 The remark sounds proverbial, but this is the only ME example (Whiting S919).

4029 hope: "Expect" but possibly with a pun on "hope for"; both meanings are well attested (MED s.v. *hopen* v. (1) 1 and 2).

4030 wanges: Probably "back teeth, molars" (cf. OED, EDD s.v. *wang*). Bennett (Ch at Oxford, 103) cites *A Fifteenth-Century Schoolbook,* ed. W. A. Nelson, Oxford, 1956, 29: "It were better to eny of us all to be dede than to suffre such thynge as the maister hath sufferyde these thre dais agone in the totheache."

4038 by my fader kyn: Spearing (ed. RvT) notes the appropriateness of the common oaths here (the Miller's pride in ancestry); in 4041 *by my croun* (a reference to the Clerk's tonsure), in 4049 *by my thrift* (since the Miller prospers by dishonesty), in 4099 *by my croun* (the Miller's baldness, recalling the Clerk's tonsure).

4054 clerkes been noght wisest: Proverbial (Whiting C291). See Burnely, Ch's Language and Phil. Trad., 56–57: the greater prudence governs man's relation to God and is appropriate to clerks, the lesser governs worldly (primarily) economic concerns and is appropriate to merchants and millers.

4055 The mare told the wolf, who wanted to buy her foal, that the price was written on her hind foot. When he tried to read it she kicked him. The fable and its variants are fully discussed by Paull F. Baum, MLN 37, 1922, 150–53; cf. Aarne-Thompson, No. 47B. The proverb quoted in 4054 is found in the later versions of the fable by Caxton, Hist. of Reynard the Fox, EETS 263, 59; and Henryson, ed. Fox, Fables, 1064.

4065 fen: Probably Lingay Fen, a stretch of open country to the south of Trumpington, then frequently flooded (I.4106–7); this was before the fens were drained. Horses abounded in the wilds of Cambridgeshire (Bennett, Ch at Oxford, 113–14).

4066 "wehee": "The whinny of sexual desire" (Bennett, Ch at Oxford, 114; cf. Langland, PP B 7.91–92: "Thei ne wedde no women that thei with deele,/ But as wilde bestes with 'wehee' worthen up and werchen"). However, Sandy Feinstein, ChauR 26, 1991, 99–106, makes a good case that the horse is a gelding.

4096 make a clerkes berd: Proverbial (Whiting B116). Cf. MilT I.3742 above.

4101 Jossa: Recorded only here in ME. EDD s.v. *joss* records it in Suffolk as a "command to a horse to sidle up to a block or gate that the rider may easier mount." Skeat (5:124) compares OF *jos, jus* and quotes Cotgrave, "jus, down on the ground."

4122–26 ye han larned art: i.e., you have studied the arts curriculum. The Miller has no compunction about "rubbing in" his advantage. His satirical scorn for the schools seems to have been a fairly common joke at the expense of university students (cf. the Cook's repetition of *argument,* I.4329). Siegfried Wenzel (Anglia 97, 1979, 310) quotes a jest by John Waldeby about an Oxford student who wanted "to prove to his father that his room had two doors. So the father closed the one door and started to beat him until he could find the other." Wenzel (SP 73, 1976, 144) cites another such joke, appearing in Giraldus Cambrensis's *Gemma ecclesiastica* II.350 (tr. Hagen) and in The Hundred Merry Tales, ed. Paul M. Zall, 1963 (No. 69): "Of the scholar of Oxford that proved by sophistry two chickens three." On the treatment of **space** in the tale, see Peter Brown, ChauR 14, 1980, 225–36.

4127 Cutberd: St. Cuthbert, bishop of Lindisfarne (d. 686); his remains were buried in Durham Cathedral. He was a well-known saint throughout England, but his connection with the North makes him an appropriate figure for John to swear by. The form *Cutberd* is sometimes taken to represent a comic mispronunciation or malapropism (like the carpenter's *Nowelis* in MilT), but it is probably a current form (Bennett, Ch at Oxford, 101n., notes it in a Godstow document).

4129–30 slyk as he fyndes: Proverbial (cf. "Take as one finds," Whiting T15), but the saying turns out to have unexpected application, since the students do indeed take both what they find and what they bring (Spearing, ed. RvT).

4134 empty hand: Proverbial (Whiting H89); see WBPro III.415 and FrT III.1340n.

4140 chalons: Blankets, taking their name from Chalons in France, where they were manufactured. See F. P. Magoun, MS 17, 1955, 124.

4149 vernysshed his heed: The phrase is closely associated with drunkenness (cf. Fr. *être verni*) and may be virtually a synonym for being "well oiled." We should probably think of the literal meaning as well: his bald head shines with perspiration and later reflects the moonlight (Spearing, ed. RvT).

4155 The expression "to wet one's whistle" is still heard. For examples from Chaucer on, see Whiting W225 and OED s.v. *whistle* sb., 2.

4171 complyn: Compline, the last canonical hour, the service sung before retiring (and appropriately here bringing the musical passage to a conclusion).

4172 wilde fyr: Usually taken to be erysipelas, an infectious disease with inflammation of the skin, as in MerT IV.2252, but it is just possible that as in other uses of the word in imprecations (see OED s.v. *wild* 5b), the allusion is more generally to the inflammable "wild fire" used in medieval warfare (see WBPro III.373n.).

4181–82 In the margin of MSS Ha4 and Ht is noted the equivalent Latin legal maxim: "Qui in uno gravatur in alio debet relevari" (translated in the text). This legal phrase, and the use of words such as *amendement* and *esement,* support Bennett's conjecture (Ch at Oxford, 105) that the two clerks were reading law (books of civil law made up half of the library of King's Hall).

4210 unhardy is unseely: Proverbial (Whiting U3; cf. also Whiting F519, N146) and Cf. Tr 4.600–601: "Fortune . . . Helpeth hardy man unto his enprise."

4231 priketh: On the supposed obscene pun noted by Baum (PMLA 71:242), see GP I.191n. Even the metaphoric usage of this verb for the sexual act is rare (see Robbins, Sec. Lyrics 28.28: "He prikede & he pransede").

4233 the thridde cok: Near dawn. Skeat (5:109) notes that Tusser's Husbandrie, Engl. Dialect Soc., 1878, 165, says that cocks crow at midnight, at three o'clock, and an hour before day.

4235–40 It seems likely (R. E. Kaske, ELH 26, 1959, 295–310) that this exchange is parodying the courtly tradition of the "aube," the parting of lovers by the dawn, of which Chaucer offers a notable example in Tr 3.1422–1533.

4239 I is thyn awen clerk: H. A. Kelley (Love and Marriage, 198–201) notes how close these words come to contracting a valid "clandestine marriage."

4253 toty: This is the first recorded occurrence, and the only one in Chaucer. It is perhaps colloquial (Davis, Ch Glossary); MED s.v. *toti* adj., derives it from *toteren* v., "to sway, waver."

4257 a twenty devel way: Cf. I.3134n.

4264 Seint Jame: St. James the Great, one of the Apostles. He was a popular saint in the Middle Ages (especially because of his relics at Santiago de Compostela in Spain, a great place of pilgrimage).

4271 disparage: "Dishonor," but the word probably also has its more specific (and etymological) sense of being dishonorably matched to someone of inferior rank (cf. WBT III.1069); the Miller's main concern is not the seduction but the low social rank of the seducer (Muscatine, Ch and the Fr Trad., 204).

4278 pigges in a poke: Proverbial (Whiting P190).

4286 hooly croys of Bromeholm: A supposed relic of the true cross, known as the Rood of Bromholm, was famed for its miraculous powers, and was an object of pilgrimage; see Francis Wormald, Jnl. of the Warburg and Courtauld Institutes 1, 1937, 31–45 (with examples of popular prayers and illustrations [plates 7a, b] of the kind of representations of it that were sold to pilgrims); Langland's Avarice (PP B 5.226–27) says that he will "wenden to Walsyngham . . . And bidde the Roode of Bromholme brynge me out of dette."

4287 In manus tuas: Luke 23.46 ("And when Jesus had cried with aloud voice, he said, Father into thy hands I commend my spirit: and having said this, he gave up the ghost"). The formula was used as a prayer before sleep, or at the hour of death (cf. Havelok the Dane, ed. Skeat, rev. K. Sisam, 1929; 228–31: "'In manus tuas, loverde,' he seyde . . . And deyede biforn his heymen alle").

4320–21 It was a common rhetorical convention to end a tale with a proverb or *sentencia* or a general moral idea ("moral," sometimes in a rather popular, fabliau-like way; cf. Gombert, in Benson and Andersson, Lit. Context, 99: "This tale shows us by its example that a man who has a pretty wife should never allow . . . a clerk to sleep in his house, for he will do this same thing. The more one trusts them, the more one loses"). Cf. ShipT, MancT. Here we are given two proverbs: "He that does evil need not expect well" (see Whiting E185; cf. PrT VII.632) and "the guiler is beguiled" (see Whiting G491 and RomB 5759: "Bigiled is the gilere").

The Cook's Prologue

The explanatory notes to The Cook's Prologue and Tale are adapted from those written by Douglas Gray for The Riverside Chaucer.

There is an apparent inconsistency between The Cook's Prologue and that of the Manciple (IX.1–55) where, as Tyrwhitt noticed, "when the Coke is called upon to tell a tale, there is no intimation of his having told one before" (Canterbury Tales, Intro. Discourse, 1775, 4:144). The problem remains unsolved. R. M. Lumiansky (MS 17, 1955, 208–9) attempts to defend the status quo, arguing that the antagonism there expressed between the Cook and the Host would have seemed natural to Chaucer's audience, and that his question (IX.11) "Is that a cook of Londoun," etc., does not imply that he has just noticed him, but is simply a "japing" reference—"can it be this man, a London cook, is overcome by drink?" Nevertheless it remains odd that there is no reference in the Manciple's Prologue either to "another tale" by the Cook (which would imply that Chaucer was thinking of the plan that each pilgrim should tell two tales) or to an unfinished attempt at a tale. A more probable explanation seems to be that either the MancPro was composed later and Chaucer meant to cancel the Cook's fragmentary tale and perhaps to introduce the Cook later, or that it was written after the MancPro and Chaucer intended to adjust that. There is no sure way to decide the priority of composition. Possibly "the business may be the result of scribal reluctance to abandon one or the other of the passages (whichever Chaucer canceled) knowing it to be genuine and not wishing to lose any part of Chaucer's writings" (E. G. Stanley, Poetica 5, 1976, 45).

4327 For Cristes passion: Spearing (ed. RvT) compares John's oath (I.4084) and remarks that Chaucer almost invariably puts such overemphatic (and apparently vulgar) oaths in the mouths of lower-class characters. See Elliott, Ch's English, 253, and ch. 5.

4328–29 conclusioun/ Upon his argument: The joking use of the technical language of the schools suggests that the Cook has the Miller's words in I.4122–24 in mind. On the theme of **herbergage** in Fragment I, see Gerhard Joseph, ChauR 5, 1970, 83–96.

4331 Ecclus. 11.31: "Bring not every man into thine house; for many are the plots of the deceitful man." For the attribution of Ecclesiasticus to Solomon, see MilT I.3530n.

4332 herberwynge by nyghte: See the conclusion to the fabliau Gombert and the Two Clerks, quoted in MilT I.4320–21n.

4336 Hogge of Ware: See note on the portrait of the Cook in GP. Ware is a town in Hertfordshire, some thirty miles from London.

4339–40 heere : heere: A rime riche, which the Ellesmere scribe verifies by writing "hic" over the first *heere,* "audire" over the next. See GP 17–18n.

4345–52 Frederick Tupper (JEGP 14, 1915, 256–70) suggests that there is a reference here to the professional enmity between cooks and hostelers.

4347 Jakke of Dovere: The meaning is not certain; Magoun (NM 77, 1976, 79) explained it as "Dover sole," but the expression is usually explained as a twice-cooked pie, i.e., one that is stale and has been warmed up. Skeat compares "Jack of Paris," used in this sense by More (Works, London, 1557, 675E), and Fr. *jacques.* For references to ordinances against warmed-over or bad food pies "not befitting, and sometimes stinking," see Bowden, Comm. GP, 188, and Constance B. Hieatt, in Ch's Pilgrims, ed. Lambdin, 199–209.

4355 sooth in game: Proverbial (Whiting S488); cf. ProMkT VII.1964.

4357 'sooth pley, quaad pley': Proverbial (Whiting P257). The use of the Flemish adjective *quaad* (bad) may suggest that Chaucer knew the proverb in Flemish form (although *quade* appears in ProPrT VII.438). For another Flemish proverb, see MancT IX.349–50. There were many Flemings in London (cf. D. W. Robertson, Ch's London, 22), and Chaucer's wife was the daughter of a Flemish knight.

4358 Herry Bailly: It is only now that we hear the name of the Host. It corresponds to that of an actual innkeeper of Southwark, "Henri Bayliff, Ostyler." See introductory note on the portrait of the Host in GP (before 752).

The Cook's Tale

The Cook's Tale suddenly stops, apparently in mid-career. The Hengwrt MS leaves the rest of the page blank (perhaps to accommodate a continuation of the tale, should it be found) and notes, "Of this cokes tale maked Chaucer na moore" (as if a search had been made and ended when the scribe's director determined Chaucer did not finish the tale). However, Stephen B. Partridge (in an article to appear in Medieval English Manuscripts and Books: Essays in Memory of Jeremy Griffiths) shows that the note and even the blank space appear in other manuscript traditions; both antedated the Hengwrt MS and may be due to Chaucer himself.

The tale is long enough to show that, had it been finished, it was likely to have been of the same general type as the Miller's and the Reeve's (and apparently with a firmly established London setting to match those of Oxford and Cambridge), but it is too short to disclose the plot, or consequently, the source. See the discussion by Earl D. Lyon in S&A 148–54, who suggest that Chaucer may have had no literary source, but rather started out to fictionalize contemporary persons and events.

A number of MSS have inserted after The Cook's Tale the Tale of Gamelyn, also ascribed to the Cook (ed. Stephen Knight and Thomas H. Ohlgren, in Robin Hood and Other Outlaw Tales, TEAMS, 1997). Gamelyn is certainly not by Chaucer and does not seem at all appropriate to the Cook. It is often assumed, without evidence, that this tale was among Chaucer's papers and that he intended to work it over for one of the other pilgrims. The inconsistency between the Cook's Prologue (see introductory note) and the Manciple's may also suggest that Chaucer had not finally decided what he wished to do at this point.

There are a number of ways in which the incompleteness of The Cook's Tale may be accounted for: that more of it existed, but has been lost; that Chaucer was by some circumstance or other prevented from completing it, or that for some reason he decided not to do so. Stanley (Poetica 5:36–59) argues persuasively that the tale is complete as it stands. The Cook, he notes, reduces all to its lowest essentials: he sees the three pre-ceding tales simply as "consequences of incautious herber-gage," which he answers by the formula of the situation at the end of his tale ("the recipe for carefree herbergage"); hence, "there is no more for him to say on the subject."

Yet it might be argued that the careful setting of the London scene, as well as the obvious interest in a number of forms of "riot," suggests the story was meant to continue. M. C. Sey-mour (ChauR 24, 1990, 259–62) holds that the tale was com-plete but the rest of it was lost early in the manuscript tradition. Kolve, Ch and Imagery of Narrative, 257–85, questions the assumption that the tale has to be a fabliau and points out that there are other latent narrative possibilities in the fragment (e.g., of a prodigal son story). Paul Strohm likewise finds non-fabliau elements, arguing (in Robert R. Edwards, ed., Art and Context in Late Medieval English Narrative: Essays in Hon. of Robert Worth Frank, Jr., 1994, 163–76) that the tale has echoes of social unease following the Peasants' Revolt of 1381 and that its seemingly innocuous images of revelry "carried a heavy symbolic weight." See also Woods's article cited in 4366 below.

Some scribes did supply brief endings for the tale, most notably in Bodley 686 (ed. John M. Bowers in The CT: Fif-teenth-Century Continuations and Additions, TEAMS, 1992): forty-five new lines are added, and the tale ends with: "The tone [one] y-dampned to presoun perpetually,/ The tother to deth for he couthe not of clergye."

4365 prentys: A young person bound by a legal contract to serve a craftsman for from seven to nineteen years and to receive in turn lodging, board, and instruction in the trade (see Robertson, Ch's London, 77, 79).

4366 vitaillers: The victualers (sellers of foodstuffs) were the most wealthy and powerful of the London guilds; led by Nicholas Brembre, mayor of London, they engaged in a bit-ter struggle with the other guilds for political dominance of London, culminating in an appeal to Parliament by the non-victualers in 1386. William F. Woods, PLL 32, 1996, 189–205, reads the tale in light of this political struggle.

4377 Chepe: Cheapside, a busy thoroughfare, with many shops; cf. GP 1.754n. It was a favorite place for processions and festivals; see W. Kelly, Notices . . . of Leicester, 1865, 38–51; W. Herbert, Hist. of the Twelve Great Livery Com-panies, London, 1834, 1:90–99. Perhaps the kind of **ridyng** most likely to attract Perkin would have been the proces-sions of "summer kings" or Lords of Misrule, which were sometimes accompanied by riotous behavior.

4394–96 he in 4394 refers to the master, and it seems likely (Baugh, 312) that **he** in 4396 also does: the master has no share in the "minstrelsy" even though he may know how to play a guitar or a rebec (see MilT I.3331n.; possibly this is the Cook's adaptation of the musical imagery of the MilT).

4399 Apprentices regularly lived in their masters' houses.

4402 lad with revel: Disorderly persons, when carried off to prison, were preceded by minstrels, to proclaim their dis-grace. See MilT I.3774n. A dishonest gambler was thus sentenced to the pillory: "the said false dice being hung from his neck; and after that, he was to be taken to New-gate, and from thence, on the two following days, with trumpets and pipes, to be taken again to the said pillory" (Riley, Memorials of London, 582).

4404 his papir: Probably his written certificate of service and release; see R. Blenner-Hassett, MLN 57, 1942, 34–35; Reginald Call, MLQ 4, 1943, 167–76. Skeat took **papir** to refer to the master's accounts (where the results of Perkin's wickedness would appear).

4406–7 apple . . . rotie: Proverbial (Whiting A167).

4415 no theef withoute a lowke: Proverbial (Whiting T73).

4421–22 heeld for contenaunce/ A shoppe: Robertson, Ch's London, 103 (citing Riley, Memorials of London, 484–86) notes, "In 1385 Elizabeth, wife of Henry Moring, was brought before Mayor Brembre and the aldermen for pretending to maintain women in the craft of broidery in her house in Broad Street in the parish of All Hallows. She was actually hiring her women out to 'friars, chaplains, and other men' as whores."

4422 The scribe of Hengwrt writes in the margin: "Of this cokes tale maked Chaucer na moore." Stephen B. Partridge (as cited in the intro. note above) shows that similar notes appear in a number of otherwise unrelated manuscripts (e.g., "Of this Cookes Tale makith Chaucer namore" in MS Royal College of Physicians 13). Cf. SqT V.672n.

FRAGMENT II

Fragment II occurs immediately following Fragment I in almost all the manuscripts, and all editors (except Norman Blake, who follows the Hengwrt MS in all particulars) print it in that position. Though it has no explicit link to Fragment I, it continues themes set forth in The Knight's Tale. See Kolve, Ch and Imagery of Narrative, 293–94, who considers it "a new beginning of The Canterbury Tales" after the low ending of the first fragment.

Introduction to The Man of Law's Tale

The explanatory notes to The Man of Law's Introduction, Pro-logue, and Tale are adapted from those written by Patricia J. Eberle for The Riverside Chaucer.

The Man of Law's Introduction, Prologue, and Tale appear together consistently in the MSS, but their relationships have seemed problematic. The Man of Law says *I speke in prose* (II.96), though both his prologue and tale are in rime royal. Mar-tin Stevens (PMLA 94, 1979, 62–76) argues that *prose* can refer to stanzas of equal length, but neither MED (s.v. *prose* n.) nor Chaucer's own usage (VII.937, X.46) supports this. Most schol-ars believe that the reference to prose indicates that originally a prose tale, Melibee, was to follow (see Robert A. Pratt, PMLA 66, 1951, 1141–67; Robert E. Lewis, PMLA 81, 1966, 488). Some references in the Epilogue to The Man of Law's Tale have been taken to support this view (see 1188–90 and n.). On the other hand, Maria Wickert (Anglia 69, 1950, 89–104) holds that the Introduction was written for the present tale, on the basis of the references to *The Legend of Good Women* (see 61–76 below). The supposed references to Gower may also indicate a link between the Introduction and the Tale, since Gower also tells the story of Constance in his *Confessio amantis* 2.587–1598.

The date of the Introduction is uncertain. The use of the *Kalendarium* of Nicholas of Lynn (see II.1–14 and n.) makes 1386 the earliest possible date. The references to Canacee and Tyro Apollonius are usually taken as allusions to Gower's *Confessio amantis* (see 77–89 below). This would suggest a date after 1390, when Gower's poem was completed (Fisher, John Gower, 116), although since Gower and Chaucer were friends Chaucer might well have known about the *Confessio* and its contents while it was in progress.

The references to the stories of incest in the *Confessio* are thought by most scholars to be joking. Tatlock believed that Gower saw them as negative criticisms and reacted by removing a flattering reference to Chaucer from his own poem (Confessio amantis 8.2941*–57*) in a revised version dated c. 1391. The grounds for this hypothesis are not firm, however; there is no other evidence for the supposed quarrel between Chaucer and Gower (Fisher, John Gower, 27–32, 117–21; Pearsall, Life of Geoffrey Ch, 132–33).

Opinions differ on the significance of the attitudes toward literature expressed in the Introduction. The view that the Man of Law speaks for Chaucer in censuring tales of incest, perhaps as an indirect defense of Chaucer's own fabliaux (Fisher, John Gower, 289), is contested by Alfred David (PMLA 82, 1967, 217–25), who sees the Man of Law as representative of self-appointed critics of poetry with whom Chaucer disagreed. (On the incest motif, see Dinshaw, Ch's Sexual Politics, 89–122, and Elizabeth Scala, ChauR 30, 1996, 15–37.)

On one matter, it seems likely that the Man of Law's views are not Chaucer's own: the disparaging remarks on Chaucer's versification (II.47–49) presage Herry Bailly's comments on Sir Thopas (VII.919–31). However, the pose here, like that in the Prologue to Sir Thopas, is in the vein of sly self-deprecation apparent throughout Chaucer's works.

1–14 The Host's calculations of time, purportedly "off-hand and empty handed," could only have been made with astronomical instruments and tables; here and in NPT VII.3187–97 and ParsPro X.5–11, Chaucer used the *Kalendarium* of Nicholas of Lynn (ed. Eisner, 29–34). It showed that on 18 April at precisely 10 A.M. the shadow of a six-foot-tall man would be exactly six feet long (Kalendarium, 86–87), a neat congruence so rare (it occurs again only at 9 A.M., 28 June) that North (RES 20, 1969, 424) believes that for that reason Chaucer chose 18 April as the date of his pilgrims' departure for Canterbury.

The Host's other means of calculating time, by reference to the **artificial day** (the time the sun is above the horizon) presents problems. On 18 April the sun rose at 4:47 and the artificial day had 14 hours 26 minutes (Kalendarium, 83, 86), and **The ferthe part and half an houre and moore** would be closer to nine than to **ten of the clokke** (see J. C. Eade, SAC 4, 1982, 82–85). It is unlikely that many of Chaucer's listeners noticed the error.

11 Seint John: the Evangelist, known as the apostle of truth (Skeat 5:385) because of 1 John 3:19 ("By this we will know that we are from the truth").

20–31 The remarks on time are mostly proverbial and literary commonplaces. The continual passage of time (20–21) echoes RomA 369–71: "The tyme that passeth nyght and day,/ And resteles travaylleth ay,/ And steleth from us so

prively" (*Roman de la rose* 361–65; tr. Dahlberg, 35); see also ClT IV.118–19. The comparison with falling water echoes RomA 383–84: "As watir that doun renneth ay,/ But never drope retourne may" (*Roman de la rose* 371–74). The idea that lost time cannot be recovered is proverbial (Whiting T307; cf. HF 1257–58: "For tyme ylost, this knowen ye,/ Be no way may recovered be"; and Tr 4.1283: "For tyme ylost may nought recovered be").

25–29 Senec: Seneca the Younger, *Epistulae morales*, tr. Gummere, 1.3, according to Skeat; for a closer parallel see Conf. aman. 4.1485–87: "Men mai recovere lost of good,/ Bot so wys man yit nevere stod,/ Which mai recovere time lore."

30 The comparison of lost time to **Malkynes maydenhede** (30) combines several proverbial elements. *Malkin,* a diminutive of Maud (ME *Malde,* Lat. *Matilda*), was often used for a woman of the lower classes (NPT VII.3384) or of loose morals (MED s.v. *malkin*). In this sense, Malkin's maidenhead, as used in Langland, PP B 1.183–84, stands for something no one wants: "Ye ne have na moore merite . . . / Than Malkyn of hire maydenhede that no man desireth"; see Whiting M511. Here, however, the reference is to the proverb that virginity, once lost, cannot be recovered; Whiting M20 cites Conf. aman. 5.5647–49: "Beraft hire such thing as men sein/ Mai neveremor be yolde ayein,/ And that was the virginite." Martin Stevens (LeedsSE n.s. 1, 1967, 1–5) takes this as an allusion to *Malyne* in RvT (I.4236).

32 ydelnesse: Pratt (PMLA 66:1147) notes the parallel with ParsT X.715 and suggests that the word may refer to the tales told by the Miller, Reeve, and Cook.

33–38 In addressing the Man of Law, the Host uses a number of legal terms: *forward, submytted, cas, juggement, acquiteth, biheeste, devoir* (Elliott, Ch's English, 357).

39 depardieux: *De par* (OF *de part,* on the side of) is a common formula in French legal language (Skeat 5:135–36).

41 Biheste is dette: Proverbial (Whiting B214); especially appropriate to a Sergeant, who had exclusive right to plead cases of debt in the Court of Common Pleas (see intro. to portrait of the Man of Law in GP).

43–45 swich lawe . . . sholde hymselven usen: Proverbial (Whiting L107), but **oure text** may refer to the Digesta of Justinian, tr. Watson), 2.2 rubric: "That same rule which anyone maintains against another is to be applied to him."

61 Seintes Legende of Cupid: Chaucer's *Legend of Good Women.*

61–76 This catalogue of Cupid's saints omits two of the figures in *The Legend of Good Women* (Cleopatra and Philomela) and includes others whose tales are not in LGW although they are in Ovid's *Heroides* (Chaucer's major source for LGW): **Dianire** (Deianira, wife of Hercules), **Hermyon** (Hermione, lover of Orestes), **Erro** (Hero, lover of Leander), **Eleyne** (Helen of Troy, lover of Paris), **Ladomya** (Laodamia, lover of Protesilaus), **Penelopee** (Penelope, wife of Ulysses), **Brixseyde** (Briseis, a Trojan girl captured by Achilles, ultimate source of Chaucer's Criseyde). All the others do appear in LGW: **Alceste** (Alcestis, wife of Admetus; LGW F511–16, G499–504), **Lucresse** (Lucrece, LGW 1680–1885), **Babilan Tesbee** (Babylonian Thisbe, LGW 706–923), **Dido** (LGW 924–1366), **Phillis**

(LGW 2394–2561), **Adriane** (Ariadne, LGW 1886–2227), **Isiphilee** (Hypsipyle, LGW 1368–1579), **Medea** (LGW 1580–1679), and **Ypermystra** (Hypermnestra, LGW 2562–2733). Almost all are also in Gower's *Confessio amantis*. It is notable that the tale the Man of Law is about to tell is also included in the *Confessio*.

63 **Lucresse** (Lucretia) committed suicide out of shame over her rape (LGW 1854–55); **Tesbee** (Thisbe) killed herself for love of Pyramus (LGW 913–15 and 893).

64–65 **Dido** killed herself with the sword of Aeneas (LGW 1351), and **Phillis** hanged herself from a **tree** (not mentioned in LGW or Heroides; see Conf. aman. 4.856–60).

66–67 pleinte: The reference is to a formal complaint against a faithless lover, a regular feature of the *Heroides*. This account of the complaints in LGW is misleading: only **Adriane** (Ariadne) has a complaint in LGW (2185–2217); no complaint is given **Isiphilee** (Hypsipyle) in LGW (although 1564–74 refer to one); and **Deianira** and **Hermione** do not appear in LGW at all.

68 The bareyne yle: Naxos, the island where Theseus abandoned Ariadne (LGW 2163–77).

69 The dreynte Leandre: This lover of **Erro** (Hero), who drowned while swimming the Hellespont to join his love, is the only male in this list; Hero (*Herro*) is listed among the good women in LGW ProF 263.

72–74 The reference to Medea's hanging her children **by the hals** has no parallel, neither in LGW (which stresses her *kyndenesse*, 1664) nor in Heroides 12 (but there is a prophecy that she will murder them in Heroides 6.159–60 and LGW 1574). In Gower's version (Conf. aman. 5.3246–4242) Medea slays her children, but the means are not specified; in *Le Roman de la rose* (13229–62; tr. Dahlberg, 228–29) she strangled them. See also BD 726–27: "Medea. . . . That slough hir children for Jasoun."

77–89 Because the stories of **Canacee** and **Tyro Appollonius** (Apollonius of Tyre), which are scorned by the Man of Law, are included in Gower's *Confessio amantis* (Canace, 3.143–336; Apollonius, 8.271–2028), this passage has been viewed as a slighting (or playful) reference to Gower (see the note to The Man of Law's Introduction). However, the reference need not be to the *Confessio;* both *cursed stories* of incest were widely available in other versions: the Apollonius story is extant in over 100 MSS in Latin, and the tale of Canace is told by Ovid (Heroides 2) as well as Gower. Chaucer himself may once have planned to include the story of Canacee in LGW, since her name appears in the list of good women in LGW ProF 265, ProG 219.

91–92 Pierides: The nine Muses, so called from their birthplace, Pieria (Ovid, Tristia 5.3–10), are here confused with the daughters of King Pierus, who unsuccessfully challenged the Muses to a singing contest and were changed into magpies (Ovid, Met. 5.293–678).

96 prose: See introductory note above.

The Man of Law's Prologue

Lines 99–121 are a condensed translation of a part of *De miseria condicionis humane* (1.14; tr. Lewis, 114–16) by Pope Innocent III (late twelfth cent.). Chaucer's additions are the

image of the wound of need (102–3), the imagined speech of the poor man (110–12), and the caution against poverty (119).

The denunciation of riches that concludes the section in Innocent is replaced here with praise of wealthy merchants (122–32), a passage that demonstrates a habit of thought Innocent condemns, whereby "a person is valued according to his wealth." Manly-Rickert note parallels with Mel VII.1567–71; Robert P. Miller (Costerus 3, 1975, 49–71) notes a similar denunciation of poverty in *Le Roman de la rose* (7921–8206; tr. Dahlberg, 148–49). Both the praise of merchants and the passage from Innocent link the Prologue with The Man of Law's Tale. The Tale opens with an account of merchants (134–40), as well as passages in it, as well as glosses to these passages in many MSS, are based on Innocent's treatise. The use of *De miseria* in both the Prologue and the Tale argues that they are contemporaneous compositions (on the date, see introductory note to the Tale, below).

Nevertheless, the connections of the Prologue to the Tale and to the Man of Law are problematical. Manly-Rickert find the Prologue unnecessary since the Introduction (II.98) implies that The Man of Law's Tale begins with the next line. Alfred David (PMLA 82:221) notes that the rime-royal verse form suggests the Prologue and Tale were meant to be joined but agrees with Tatlock (Dev. and Chron., 188) that the praise of wealth in the Prologue sorts oddly with a tale of Custance's material deprivations (Strumpet Muse, 127).

102–3 woundid : wounde hid: On the rhyme of two words with one (a type of *rime riche*), see GP I.17–18n.

110–12 Besserman, Ch and the Bible, 72, compares Luke 16.19–26 (the story of Lazarus and the rich man) as cited by Innocent, *De miseria* 2.18, 37, tr. Lewis, 166 and retold by Gower, Conf. aman. 6.970–1109.

114 Bet is to dyen: Ecclus. 40.29 ("it is better to die than to beg"), as cited by Innocent (De miseria 1.14; tr. Lewis, 114); also quoted in Mel VII.1571–72.

115 neighebor wol thee despise: Prov. 14.20: "The poor is hated even of his own neighbour" (cited by Innocent, *De miseria* 1.14; tr. Lewis, 114.

118 dayes . . . ben wikke: Prov. 15.15: "All the days of the poor are evil" (Innocent, De miseria 1.14; tr. Lewis, 114).

120–21 brother hateth . . . freendes fleen: Prov. 19.7 ("All the brethren of the poor do hate him: how much more do his friends go far from him?"); cf. Mel VII.1559 and Whiting P295; Innocent, *De miseria* 1.14; tr. Lewis, 114.

124–25 The references are to the game of **hazard** played with dice (see PardT VI.653 and n.). Cf. Gower (Mirour 24226–28; tr. Wilson, 317), discussing the covetousness of lawyers: "For you will never maintain a just cause against a six if you have a double ace (*ambes as*)." See also MkT VII.2661n.

The Man of Law's Tale

Though earlier scholars believed The Man of Law's Tale was a youthful composition, most scholars now agree with Tatlock (Dev. and Chron., 172–88) that Chaucer's use of Innocent III's *De miseria* and of Gower's *Confessio amantis* (see below) indicate a "rather late date (about 1390)" (Robinson). The use of the *De miseria* is especially significant. In his revision of the

Prologue to *The Legend of Good Women* (G 414–15), Chaucer adds to the list of his works in the F Prologue the title "Of the Wreched Engendrynge of Mankynde/ As man may in pope Innocent yfynde." Apparently Chaucer translated this work sometime after the F Prologue was written (1387 or so). Robert E. Lewis (ed. *De miseria*, 1978, 16–31) reviews the evidence and argues that Chaucer was working simultaneously on a translation of *De miseria* (since lost) and The Man of Law's Prologue and Tale during the period from 1390 to 1394–95.

Chaucer's principal source for his tale is Nicholas Trevet's Anglo-Norman chronicle of world history, written around 1334. The relevant section is printed by Margaret Schlauch in S&A, 165–81, with an English summary, along with other analogues, including Gower's Tale of Constance. For a Middle English translation of Trevet's version, see Originals and Analogues, ed. Furnivall, Brock, and Clouston, 221–50.

Trevet's account is based on a widely popular story derived from two tale types: the princess exiled for refusing to marry her father, and the queen exiled for giving birth to a monster (Margaret Schlauch, Ch's Constance and Accused Queens, 1927, and S&A, 155–62). The story appears in several versions in Middle English (see Lilian Hornstein, Manual ME 1:120–32), and there is a version in the *Decameron* (Fifth day, 2nd Tale); it is quite distant from Chaucer's version, but David Wallace makes some interesting comparisons (Chaucerian Polity, 205–11).

Most scholars agree that Chaucer knew the adaptation of Trevet's tale in Gower's *Confessio amantis* (2.587–1598). Though Skeat and Macaulay (ed. Conf. aman. 1:482–84) believed that Chaucer's work was written first, Schlauch (Ch's Constance, 132–34, and S&A, 155–56) and Edward A. Block (PMLA 68, 1953, 600–2) argue convincingly for Gower's priority. According to Block, Chaucer's direct borrowings from Gower are limited to a few passages (nine in all); to these should be added the pathetic scene with Custance and her child as she leaves Northumberland (see 834–68 and n.). Peter Nicholson (ChauR 26, 1991, 153–74) argues for a greater debt to Gower's tale of Constance than is generally allowed.

Only one-third of The Man of Law's Tale is based closely on Trevet (Block, PMLA 68:572–616). Although Chaucer adopts all the main episodes from Trevet and adds none of his own, very few lines are direct translations. He omits about two-thirds of Trevet's version, including most of the historical and circumstantial details and all of the episodes not directly involving Custance. He also changes the order of the narrative so that the episode of the renegade Christian (II.915–45) comes just before Custance returns to Rome.

The sources for many of Chaucer's additions are indicated by the marginal glosses that appear in several manuscripts, including Ellesmere and Hengwrt (printed here from Partridge's edition). Partridge, along with most scholars who have considered the problem (e.g., Robert E. Lewis, SP 64, 1967, 1–16), holds that the marginal Latin glosses from Innocent III's *De miseria* are most likely Chaucer's.

In genre The Man of Law's Tale is sometimes called a "secular saint's life," though it ends happily rather than with the martyrdom of a saint; Morton W. Bloomfield (PMLA 87, 1972, 384–90) argues rather that the poem is a "Christian Tragedy" that delicately balances comedy and tragedy. Clearly it belongs with the genre of romance, with the romance motif

of "exile and return," the rudderless boat (as in the romance of Tristan), and the characterization of the noble heroine (which Paul M. Clogan finds typical of "hagiographical romance"; M&H 8, 1977, 217–33).

The tale of Custance has not attracted a great deal of critical attention, though there have been helpful studies on a number of matters: rhetoric (Thomas Bestul, ChauR 9, 1974–75, 216–26); the relation of the tale to the teller (Roger S. Loomis, in Ch Problems, 207–20); pathos in the characterization of Custance (Barry Windeatt, M&H 9, 1979, l43–69); and the attitude toward women in the tale (Sheila Delany, ChauR 9, 1974–75, 63–72), which some see as the dramatic cause of the Wife of Bath's vigorous assertion of female rights. For a survey of criticism, see A. S. G. Edwards, in Ch's Religious Tales, 85–94. V. A. Kolve (Ch and the Imagery of Narrative, 297–358, 360–71) has been one of its warmest admirers in recent years, and his study remains most useful.

161 Lat. gloss: "Europe is the third part of the world." On the three parts of the world (Europe, Asia, Africa), see Conf. aman. 7.520–86.

162–68 Michael R. Paull (ChauR 5, 1970–71, 181–82) notes similarities with descriptions of romance heroines.

190–203 Lat. gloss: "in the stars [appear] the sceptre of Phoroneus, the discord of the Theban brothers, the flames of Phaeton, [the flood] of Deucalion, as well as Priam's pomp, the boldness of Turnus, the cleverness of Ulysses, and the strength of Hercules" (Bernardus Silvester, Megacosmos, in Cosmographia, 3.39–44; tr. Wetherbee, 76). Chaucer takes over Barnardus's image of the heavens as a book (Megacosmos 3.33–34) in which future events are written, but he changes the emphasis so that only evil fates, **strif** and **deeth,** are foretold. Chaucer omits from his catalogue the good fortunes listed by Bernardus, and changes those references he does adopt from a positive to a negative emphasis: e.g., Bernardus stresses the "boldness" of Turnus, the "strength" of Hercules; Chaucer stresses their deaths. Other deaths in the catalogue are Chaucer's additions, sometimes suggested by a line in Bernardus: **Ector** (Hector), **Pompei,** and **Julius** (the Roman generals Pompey and Julius Caesar), **Sampson** (the Biblical Samson, see MkT VII.2015–94); and **Socrates.** Chaucer's conclusion (202–3) that men cannot read what is written in the stars is a marked change from Bernardus's conclusion: "Thus the Creator wrought, that ages to come might be beheld in advance, signified by starry ciphers" (Megacosmos 3.58–59, tr. Wetherbee, 76).

211 Diverse men . . . seyden: Proverbial; see RvPro I.3857 and n.

220–21 diversitee/ Bitwene hir bothe lawes: A loose translation of Lat. *disparitas cultus,* a term in canon law referring to the difference in religion between the baptized and the unbaptized, which created an impediment to marriage (Paul E. Beichner, Spec 23, 1948, 70–75).

224 Mahoun: Mohammed (570?–632 A.D.), prophet and founder of Islam.

236 mawmettrie: In ParsT X.750, this word (OF *Mahumet,* Mohammed) is a synonym for *ydolatrie,* despite the fact that the Koran, like the Bible, forbids idolatry.

261 I seye: For the use of this and similar expressions (e.g.,

I mene, KnT I.2063), see Hammond, Engl. Verse, 447. "Sometimes they serve merely for emphatic repetition, sometimes they are rather a scholastic formula (like Dante's use of 'dico' in Inf. 4.66 and elsewhere)" (Robinson).

281 the Barbre nacioun: Probably equivalent to "the pagan world" (cf. FranT V.1452). See Magoun, Ch Gazetteer, 29.

285–87   Custance probably uses **wrecche** (OE **wrecca**), in its original sense, "outcast or exile"; her next words echo God's reproach to Eve before casting her out of Eden (Genesis 3:16: "and thy desire shall be to thy husband, and he shall rule over thee"). In Bo 1.pr5.6, *wrecche* translates Lat. "exilium."

288 Pirrus: Pyrrhus, son of Achilles and Deidamia; his breach of the walls of Troy and the ensuing loud laments are vividly described in Aeneid 2.469–90. See NPT VII.3355–59.

289 Ilion: Ilium, the Greek name for Troy, but used by Chaucer and other medieval writers for the citadel of Troy; see Magoun, Ch Gazetteer, 91, and cf. NPT VII.3356.

290 Hanybal: Hannibal (c. 247–183 B.C.), the great Carthaginian general, invader of Italy during the Second Punic War.

295–301   Lat. gloss: "Whence Ptolemy in Book I, Chapter 8: 'the primary motions of the heavens are two, of which the first is that which continually moves the whole from east to west in one way, above the spheres' etc. 'Moreover, there is indeed a second motion which moves the sphere of the stars that run contrary to the first motion [i.e., the planets], that is to say, from west to east above the two other poles,' etc." The gloss is a paraphrase of a passage from Bk. 1, ch. 8 of the Almagest of Ptolemy (tr. Toomer, 45–46). See MilT I.3208 and WBPro III.183, 324–25.

In the Ptolemaic system of the universe there are nine concentric spheres surrounding a stationary earth: the first seven spheres bear the planets—moon, Mercury, Venus, sun, Mars, Jupiter, Saturn (the "moving stars"). The eighth sphere bears the "fixed stars" (apparently unmoving stars and constellations). The ninth is the *primum mobile,* the **firste moevyng** (first, if counting from outward to the earth), which moves all the others from east to west (hence the rising and setting of the sun and all the other stars). However, the eighth sphere also imparts a very slow movement from east to west: "All the planets move by double moving: by their own nature [*kynde*] moving from the west into the east against the moving of the firmament; and by another moving out of the east, and that by ravishing of the firmament. By violence of the firmament they are ravished every day out of the east into the west" (Barth. Angl., tr. Trevisa, 1:473 [modernized]). That is, though the individual stars are **naturelly** inclined to move west to east (by the eighth sphere), the movement of the *firste moevyng* compels all to revolve in the opposite direction. The stanza thus laments the daily revolution of the *primum mobile*—the **dirurnal sweigh**—which is responsible for the configuration of the heavens, and makes it possible for Mars to doom Custance's marriage from the moment she sets out. Cf. Bo 1.m5.1–5: "O thow makere of the wheel that bereth the sterres, whiche that art festnyd to thi perdurable chayer, and turnest the hevene with a ravysschynge sweighe, and constreynest the sterres to suffren thi lawe."

301 crueel Mars: Mars is a "malevolent" planet; cf. Lydgate, Sege of Thebes, 2553: "O cruel Mars/ ful of malencholy."

302–8   This stanza gives a more particular account of the unfavorable configuration of the heavens at Custance's departure. The **ascendent** is the "house" that is rising on the eastern horizon. A "house" is one of the twelve divisions of the "ecliptic" (the annual pathway of the sun) which corrrespond to the twelve signs of the zodiac. The rising sign may be an **angle,** which rises directly—Aries, Cancer, Libra, Capricorn, which are at the cardinal points of the compass—or a **tortuous** sign, which rises at an oblique angle. A planet in the ascendent sign is "**lord** of the ascendent" (see Astr 2.4) and has special power. Each planet has two signs of the zodiac that are its "houses" or "domiciles," signs in which it has added power: the houses of Mars are Aries and Scorpio. Aries (in the east) is the ascendent sign, "*his* [Mars's] *angle.*" Most scholars hold that Mars is **falle** into the twelfth house, **the derkeste hous,** where its power is weakened (304). Skeat (5:150) argues that Mars has moved into Scorpio, a dire event since Scorpio is "the house of death and of dread, of debt and of travail, of harm and damage" (Barth. Angl., tr. Trevisa. 1:471 [tr.].) See North, Ch's Universe, 488–90.

305 atazir: Mars is Custance's *significator nativitatis,* defined by John Walter as "the planet which is the characteristic sign of a nativity." Walter, an Oxford master in 1383, compiled a set of tables for determining astrological houses, which Chaucer may have known (J. D. North, RES n.s. 20, 1969, 430–31).

306 fieble moone: The moon is *fieble* because her power is thwarted by her location, having, like Mars, been **weyved** (moved) from a place where she had power (was **weel**) to a place where she is **nat receyved**—i.e., she is in a sign that weakens her power. The moon was thought to have a special influence on travel, particularly by sea, over which it had control as "minister and lady of the sea" (Barth. Angl., tr. Trevisa, 1:489 [tr.]).

309 eleccioun . . . roote: Lat. gloss: "All are agreed that elections are defective except in the case of the rich; indeed, it is permissible [to make an election] for these people because they, even if their elections be weak, have a "root," i.e., their nativities, which reinforces every planet that is weak in respect to the journey, et cetera." The gloss, as Tyrwhitt first noted, is the incipit of *De electionibus* (On Elections) by the Jewish authority on astrological elections, Zahel Benbriz (d. c. 822–50).

313–14   "The plain meaning is that the stars were unfavorable to her going, and this ought to have been known to the 'philosphers'" [i.e., astronomers] (Manly, CT, 568).

According to Hamilton M. Smyser (Spec 45, 1970, 371–72), this passage is evidence of Chaucer's own "real commitment to astrology," an "avowal of faith" in the use of astrology to make elections; see Loomis (Ch Problems, 207) for a similar view. Astr 2.4, however, contains Chaucer's explicit denunciation of the astrological uses of the ascendant for making *eleccions of tymes,* as "rytes of payens, in which my spirit hath no feith," and which are, moreover, too imprecise to be fully accurate. It is worth noting, following Curry (Ch and Science, 188–90) and Wood

(Ch and the Stars, 192–244), that the Man of Law's astrologically inspired dire predictions are not fully accurate— Custance does survive her voyage—and they do not take into account the workings of the divine providence in which Custance places her faith. North, Ch's Universe, 500, argues that Chaucer's own beliefs are not the issue: "It is not customary to insist that he believed in the truth of all that he told . . . and there is no earthly reason why the astronomical element in a tale should be judged any differently from the rest."

321–22   Paull (ChauR 5:179–94) notes that passages of abrupt transition like this (cf. II.897–900, 953–54, 1124–25) characterize Chaucer's reshaping of Trevet and call attention to Custance as the main focus; Ruth Crosby (Spec 13, 1938, 413–32) takes them as marks of oral delivery.

358   In the Ellesmere MS a marginal note *auctor* (either "author" or "authority") appears at this point. Robinson suggests that its purpose is to call attention to a "noteworthy utterance," called an *auctoritee* (see MerT IV.1783n., NPT VII.3050n.).

359 Semyrame: Semiramis, the militant queen of Babylon (cf. LGW 706–9), who was celebrated for her lust and her usurpation of the throne, rightfully that of her husband (*Bibliotheca historica* of Diodorus Siculus, ed. Charles Henry Oldfather, Loeb, 1933, 349–424) or son (Boccaccio, *De mulieribus claris,* chap. 2). Cf. MkT VII.2477n.

Virago is probably to be understood in the sense defined by Gavin Douglas, describing Juturna in his translation of the *Aeneid,* "a woman exersand a mannis office" (12.8.56–58, Aeneid, ed. Coldwell, STS, 1960, 4:107); cf. the similar censure of Donegild as *mannysh* (II.782). However, MED s.v. *virago* n. (a) cites only Chaucer's usage as unambiguously negative; it was the name that Adam gave to his wife.

360–61   According to a tradition transmitted by Petrus Comestor (*Historia scolastica libri Genesis,* chap. 21; PL 198:1072), Satan "chose a certain type of serpent (as Bede says) having the face of a maiden" for the temptation of Eve. The snake in Paradise is frequently so depicted in late medieval art. Cf. Langland, PP B 18.336–38: Satan, "in person of an adder . . . Thus like a lizard, with a lady's visage" [translated].

361 in helle ybounde: Cf. Apoc. 20.1–2 ("I saw an angel . . . and a great chain in his hand. And he laid hold of the dragon, that old serpent, which is the Devil, and Satan, and bound him a thousand years"). See II.634 and Buk 9–10: "The cheyne/ Of Sathanas, on which he gnaweth evere."

365 envious: On the envy of Satan, see Morton W. Bloomfield (Seven Deadly Sins, 382 n. 16), who cites Wisdom 2.24: "By the envy of the devil, death came into the world." Cf. ParsT X.492.

383   Chaucer adds to Trevet the gesture of the Sultan's kneeling to show devotion to his mother. On this and other key gestures added by Chaucer, see Windeatt, M&H 9:143–69, and Robert G. Benson, Med. Body Lang., Anglistica 21, 1980, 61–62, 130–33.

400–401 Lucan: in his *Pharsalia* (Civil Wars) does not make a **boost** (clamor) about the triumph Julius Caesar held after his defeat of Pompey, because Caesar did not hold one

(Pharsalia, tr. Braund, 3.73–79). Lucan does, however, record Caesar's own boast about the triumph he is planning (Pharsalia 4.358–62 and 5.328–34; see Shannon, Ch and Roman Poets, 114–15).

404 scorpioun: A common symbol of treachery; cf. BD 638–40: "With his hed he maketh feste,/ . . . With hys tayle he wol stynge." See also MerT IV.2058–65, MancT IX.271, and Whiting S96, who quotes a gloss on Ecclus 26.10 in the Wycliffite Bible: "A scorpion that maketh fair semblant with the face and pricketh with the tail; so a wickid woman draweth by flateryngis, and prickith til deth."

421   Lat. gloss (largely translated in the text): "Note concerning unexpected pain: sudden sorrow always follows earthly happiness. Therefore earthly felicity is strewn with much bitterness; affliction invades the extremes of joy. [Prov. 14.13] Therefore heed good counsel: 'On a day of blessings [**thy glade day**] do not be unmindful of evils' [Ecclus. 11.27]." (Innocent, De contemptu mundi 1.23 [actually 1.21; tr. Lewis, 128–30].) The gloss is preceded by the notation "Auctor." The sentiments are commonplace. See, e.g., KnT I.2841, NPT VII.3205, Tr 4.836 ("The ende of blisse ay sorwe it occupieth").

449–62   Skeat (5:155) quotes from a hymn of Venantius Fortunatus, "Lustra sex qui iam peregit" (He who has lived through thirty years), as a source for the description of the Cross red with the blood of the Lamb (452) and alone worthy to bear the King of Heaven (457–58).

463–90   Robert T. Farrell (NM 71, 1970, 239–43) notes that except for a reference to Noah (for whom Chaucer substitutes Jonas, 486) this passage is not based on Trevet. The figures cited—Daniel in the lions' den (Dan. 6.16–24), Jonah in the whale (Jon. 2.11), the passage through the Red Sea (Exod. 14.21–23)—are often found together in early Christian art and in the liturgy, as part of the rites administered to those near death. In art, the group is often joined by the figure of a woman praying. Margaret Schlauch (Kwartalnik Neofilologiczny 20, 1973, 305–6) notes that some versions of the *Gesta Romanorum* make parallels between Jonah and heroines like Custance.

482 clerkes: Skeat (5:156) cites Boethius, Bo 4.pr6.166–68 ("For whiche it es that alle thingis semen to ben confus and trouble to us men, for we ne mowen nat considere thilke ordenaunce") and 219–23 ("Lo, herof comyth and herof is don this noble miracle of the ordre destynal, whan God, that al knoweth, dooth swiche thing, of whiche thing unknowynge folk ben astonyd").

491–94   On the **foure spirites,** see Apoc. 7.1–3: "I saw four angels standing at the four corners of the earth, holding the four winds of the earth, that the wind should not blow on the earth . . . Saying, Hurt not the earth, neither the sea, nor the trees."

500 Egipcien Marie: St. Mary the Egyptian, a prostitute in fifth-century Alexandria who repented and lived in the desert for forty-seven years, subsisting on weeds and grasses, having taken only two and one-half loaves of bread into the desert with her (South Eng. Legendary, EETS 235, 1:136–48). Her legend was widespread in literature and in visual art. See Clogan, M&H 8:217–31.

502–3   For the miracle of the loaves and fishes, see Matt. 14.14–21, Mark 6.30–44, Luke 9.10–17, and John 6.11–13.

507–8 Roland M. Smith (JEGP 47, 1948, 347–48) argues that Chaucer suppresses Trevet's "castle . . . near the Humber" because it might have suggested John of Gaunt's Pontefract and given rise to comparisons between Custance and Constance of Castile; Block (PMLA 68:599 n. 73) holds that the omission is part of a larger pattern of omissions of circumstantial details in Chaucer's adaptation of Trevet.

519 Trevet, who notes that Constance had learned many languages, says she spoke Saxon. Chaucer's **Latyn corrupt** is probably used here as it is in the Alliterative Morte Arthure, where it seems to mean "Italian" (Benson ed., 3478–79: "The king, lordly himself of, language of Rome,/ Of Latin corrumped all, full lovely him menes [*speaks*]"). J. A. Burrow (MÆ30, 1961, 33–37, cites Isidore of Seville, Etymologiae 9.1.6–7, tr. Brehaut, 209: "There are four Latin languages; namely the early, the Latin, the Roman, the corrupted . . . The corrupted Latin, which, after the empire was extended more widely, burst into the Roman state along with customs and men, corrupting the soundness of speech by solecisms and barbarisms."

532 ClT IV.413 and Tr 1.1078 ("That ecch hym loved that loked on his face") are nearly identical.

609 Cf. Tr 4.357: "For verray wo his wit was neigh aweye."

610–68 Marie P. Hamilton (in Stud. in Lang. and Lit. in Hon. of M. Schlauch, 153–63) notes that unlike Trevet and Gower, Chaucer makes the trial a formal judicial inquest before the king.

617 as the lomb: Besserman, Ch and the Bible, 76, compares Isaiah 53.7 ("He is brought as a lamb to the slaughter"). Cf. Whiting L42.

620 Berth hire on hond: accuses her falsely; the phrase is common in Middle English. See MED s.v. *beren* v. 13; Whiting H65; cf WBPro III.226, 232 and n., 380, Anel 158 ("bar her on hande"), Tr 4.1404 ("beren hym on honde").

631–43 These lines suggest the custom of trial by the ordeal of battle; cf. GP I.239n. Hamilton (in Stud . . . in Hon. of M. Schlauch, 153–66) notes in the breviary (in the order for the last rites; see "Ordo commendationis animae" in Breviarum monasticum, 1880, 260) a parallel reference to Susannah's divine rescue from a false charge (**Susanne**); this Ordo was also used in rituals associated with ordeals.

634 Cf. Apoc 20.1–2 (see 361 above). The idea of Christ's binding Satan is developed in the apocryphal Gospel of Nicodemus. See Theodore Spencer, Spec 2, 1927, 187–88.

639 Susanne: see Daniel 33 (Historia Susannae, apocryphal in AV).

641 Seinte Anne: the mother of the Virgin Mary. See Ann W. Astell (SP 94, 1997, 385–416) on the cult of St. Anne, and the reference in and at SNPro VIII.70. Cf. also FrT III.1613.

641–42 synge Osannne: Cf. SNT VIII.69–70.

660 gentil herte: See KnT I.1761n.

666 Britoun book: Skeat (5:157–58) took this to be "a copy of the Gospels in Welsh or 'British'"; Andrew Breze (ChauR 32, 1998, 335–38) argues it is rather a book of Gospels "in Latin, written and illuminated in the Celtic manner."

676 Trevet (S&A, 172): "These things hast thou done, and I was silent," quoting Ps 49.21 (AV 50:21).

701–2 chaff . . . corn: See NPT VII.3443n., ParsPro X.35–36.

754 elf: "An evil spirit in the form of a woman" (Trevet, S&A, 173). Cf. *Promptorium parvulorum*, EETS e.s. 102, 144: "*Elf, spyryt:* lamia-e." Elves, however, could also be male; cf. WBT III.873–74 and III.880n.

771–77 Lat. gloss (preceded by "Auctor"): "What is worse than a drunk, in whose mouth is a stench, in whose body a trembling; who utters foolish things, betrays secrets; whose mind is gone, whose face is transformed? For there is no secret where drunkenness reigneth." (Innocent III, *De miseria,* 2.19; tr. Lewis, 166–68), quoting Prov. 31.4, also quoted in Mel VII.1194). See also PardT VI.560–61 and Whiting D425.

778–79 noon English digne: Cf. KnT I.1459–60n.

782 mannysh: That is, devoid of feminine virtues; cf. MerT IV.1536n. and 359 above.

784 Dante refers to a similar tradition that the souls of those who betray friends or guests go to Hell while their bodies continue to live (Inf. 33.124–32); see also LGW 2066–67: "And that my spirit by nyghte mote go,/ After my deth, and walke to and fro."

786 the kynges moodres court: A. C. Edwards (PQ 19, 1940, 306–9) and Smith (JEGP 47:343–51) suggest that Chaucer omits the name Knaresborough, which occurs in Trevet and Gower, because it belonged to John of Gaunt and was associated with his difficulties with his wife, Constance of Castile; as noted above, Block (PMLA 68:594 n. 58) argues that Chaucer suppresses most of the place names and circumstantial details in Trevet.

813–16 Echoes Bo 1.m5.34–46 and 4.prl.19–31.

834–68 This pathetic scene between Custance and her child owes nothing to Trevet, whose brief, sardonic note sets another tone altogether: "Then, on the fourth day she was exiled with Maurice her dear son, who (thus) learned sailing at a tender age" (S&A, 175). It was probably inspired by a similarly pathetic scene of mother and child in Gower's version (Conf. aman. 2.1054–83).

837–38 coverchief . . . eyen: Andrew Brunt (N&Q n.s. 214, 1969, 87–88) cites Barth. Angl., 6.4; tr. Trevisa 1:299: children should be protected from bright light, "for a place that is to bright departith and todelith the sight of the smale eiye that bes right ful tendre." Anne Lancashire (ChauR 9, 1975, 324) notes that in many of the cycle plays Abraham covers Isaac's eyes as he prepares to sacrifice him.

841 Mooder . . . and mayde: Cf. ProPrT VII.467.

847 any wo man: John C. Hirsch (ChauR 21, 1985, 68–69) argues for reading "any woman"; A. A. MacDonald (ChauR 22, 1988, 246–49) offers strong objections.

852 haven of refut: Cf. SNPro VIII.75n.

896 with meschance: Cf. FrT III.1334n.

925–31 Lat. gloss (preceded by "Auctor"): "O extreme foulness of lust, which not only weakens [*effeminat*] the mind but also enervates the body; sorrow and repentance always follow afterwards" (Innocent III, De miseria 2.21; tr. Lewis, 170).

934 Golias: The Philistine giant Goliath, killed by David's slingshot (1 Sam. 17.4–51).

940 Olofernus: See MkT VII.2571–74.

946–47 Septe: the ridge of seven peaks, opposite Gibraltar in Morocco, called "the seven brothers" (*septem fratres*); cf. Magoun, Ch Gazetteer, 142–43.

981 aunte: In Trivet the senator's wife is Constance's first cousin. Chaucer may have misunderstood Trevet's use of "nece" for "cousin."

1009 In both Gower and Trevet, Constance tells the child how to act before Alia at the feast.

1126 olde Romayn geestes: Apparently a reference to Roman history in general, as used in WBPro III.642 and MerT IV.2284, rather than the *Gesta Romanorum,* where the life of Maurice does not appear.

1132–38 Lat. gloss: "From the morning until the evening the time shall be changed" [Ecclus. 18.26]. "They take the timbrel and rejoice at the sound of the organ" [Job 21.12]. At 1135, Lat. gloss: "Who has ever passed an entire delightful day in his own pleasure, whom, in some part of the day, the guilt of conscience or the impulse of anger or the agitation of concupiscence has not disturbed? Or the spite of envy or the burning of avarice or the swelling of pride has not vexed? Whom some loss or offense or passion has not upset, etc." Both glosses are from Innocent, *De miseria,* 1.20; tr. Lewis, 128.

1140–41 litel while in joye: Cf. BD 211: "To lytel while oure blysse lasteth!"

1142 Deeth . . . rente: Cf. ParT X.762. Proverbial (Whiting D101).

1161 joye after wo: Proverbial (Whiting J61, Hassell D47). Cf. KnT I.2841; Tr 1.4: "Fro wo to wele, and after out of joie." Fortune, line 2: "As wele or wo, now povre and now honour."

The Man of Law's Epilogue

The Epilogue, or Endlink, of The Man of Law's Tale appears in 35 MSS; it is omitted from 22 MSS, including the Hengwrt, the Ellesmere, and all those with the "Ellesmere" arrangement. In those MSS in which the Epilogue does appear, it almost invariably follows The Man of Law's Tale and it usually introduces The Squire's Tale. It was apparently composed at the same time as the Introduction to MLT, which it echoes in the repeated *thrifty tale* (46, 1165). As noted above (introductory note to IntrMLT), the Man of Law's announcement that he speaks in prose has been explained by the plausible theory that he was originally assigned the prose tale of Melibee, and certain lines in the Epilogue (see 1188–90 below) do seem more suitable to Melibee than to the tale of Custance. It thus seems likely that the Epilogue was composed to follow The Man of Law's (then) Tale of Melibee. It is also probable that it was composed to introduce what is now The Shipman's Tale. The speaker who interrupts the Parson refers to *my joly body,* a phrase that is echoed in ShipT VII.423 and that seems to imply a female speaker (Pratt, PMLA 66:1141–67), and The Shipman's Tale was almost certainly written for a female speaker, most likely the Wife of Bath (see introductory note to ShipT below). There is, moreover, some evidence that the speaker in II.1179 was originally the Wife of Bath (see Pratt in Sts. in Hon. of Baugh, 45–79). The Man of Law's Epilogue thus seems to bear witness to an early stage in the composition of the *Tales* when this sequence appeared: IntrMLT–Melibee–EpiMLT–ShipT. First the Wife of Bath was assigned a new tale and her name erased from II.1179. Then the Melibee was reassigned, and

the Man of Law was given the Tale of Constance. Editors differ on what happened next. One school (Furnivall, Skeat, Pollard, Baugh, Pratt) holds that Chaucer's final intention was to use the passage as a link to The Shipman's Tale; accordingly, they read *Shipman* in line 1179, and in their editions Fragment VII immediately follows. The other school believes that the passage was canceled. Manly (ed. CT) printed it in an appendix; Robinson printed it as it stands here, in brackets. Fisher, while believing the Epilogue was canceled (81), prints it with *Wif of Bath* in line 1179, thus using it as a link to her Prologue. Donaldson had previously adopted that solution, noting that it "does not represent Chaucer's final intention—if he had one" (1074).

1169 Can moche good: "Literally 'know much good,' a phrase of general application, meaning 'to be capable or competent, to know one's profit or advantage.' Cf. WBPro III.231; BD 998 ('koud no good'), 1012 ('she koude good'); LGW 1175 ('And therwithal so moche good he can'). Essentially the same idiom occurs in English as early as the Beowulf (nát he þára góda, line 681)" (Robinson's note).

1171 swere: Swearing was endemic, even, as Manly notes (CT, 505), among Church dignitaries such as Sampson, the abbot of Bury St. Edmunds, who swore "By the face of God" (Jocelyn of Brakelond, Camden Soc, 1844, 35, 169). The Host assumes that the Parson's objection to swearing indicates he is a Lollard, but though the Lollards raised objections to the taking of oaths, orthodox preachers were equally opposed to casual swearing and cursing, "as the moste part of pepull dose now-adaies" (Owst, Lit. and Pulpit, 416; cf. VI.629–59; X.587–99). The Host is the most enthusiastic swearer on the pilgrimage (Elliott, Ch's English, 256–59). Frederick Tupper (Types of Soc. in Med. Lit., 1926, 50) offers little evidence for his suggestion that innkeepers were traditionally given to swearing, but the Pardoner does associate swearing with taverns (VI.472–76).

1172 Jankin: The diminutive of Sir John (cf. ProNPT VII.2810n.), a derisive name for a priest; MED s.v. *Jon.*

1173 Lollere: Lollard, a heretical follower of John Wyclif's doctrines; see Gordon Leff, Heresy in the Later Middle Ages, 1967. "The Twelve Conclusions of the Lollards," setting forth their program, are printed in EHD, 848–50. Religious zealots of whatever persuasion were frequently accused of Lollardy; cf. Poems of John Audelay, ed. Whiting, EETS 184, 1939, 15: "Yif ther be a pore prest and spirituals in spiryt . . . thay likon him to a lollere and to an epocryte." Chaucer had friends who were Lollards, and he may have been sympathetic to some aspects of the movement (Brewer, Ch in His Time, 236; Pearsall, Life of Geoffrey Ch, 132–33). Loomis (in Essays and St. in Hon. of Carleton Brown, 1940, 141–44) and Bowden (Comm. on GP, 238) argue that the Parson is meant to be an actual Lollard. The Parson's Tale, however, is perfectly orthodox and, since Lollards were almost unanimously opposed to pilgrimages (cf. the eighth of the "Twelve Conclusions"), an actual Lollard would probably not have been on the pilgrimage. On the general question of the Parson's "Lollardy," see Douglas J. Wurtele, Mediaevalia 11, 1989, 151–68.

1179 Shipman: Of the thirty-five MSS in which the EpiMLT appears, six read "Sommonour/Sompnour," twenty-eight "Squier," and one (the late Selden) "Shipman," which most editors have taken as the most probable reading. All three readings, however, are most likely scribal inventions (see Pratt, Sts. in Hon. of Baugh, 45–47).

1180 glosen: Cf. SumT III.1792–94. The speaker is more worried about the prospect of hearing a sermon than being informed about Lollardry; Wyclif and his followers were much opposed to "glossing," preferring literal interpretation of the Bible (Eng. Wks. 284: "many false gloseris maken goddis lawe derk & letten [prevent] seculere men to systeyn & kepen it"). See Lawrence Besserman, Ch's Biblical Poetics, 1998, 138–59.

1183 cokkel: A common pun was made on *Lollard,* Lat. *lollium* (weed), and the tares sown among the wheat in the parable of the tares (Matt. 13.24–30); cf. Gower, Conf. aman. 5.1880–83: "To sowe cokkel with the corn/ . . . Which Crist sew ferst his oghne hond."

1186–87 belle . . . waken: Cf. ProNPT VII.2794–98.

1188–90 It has often been noted that the references to philosophy, legal terminology, and Latin are more descriptive of Melibee than of the tale of Constance (e.g., Manly, CT, 572). Some scribes may have agreed; in a number of MSS line 1188 is changed to "Ne of art ne of astronomye," probably referring to lines 190–203, 295–315 in MLT.

1189 phislyas: The word (which does not appear elsewhere in English) apparently puzzled the scribes, who produced many variants (see Manly-Rickert 3:453). Manly and more recently Fisher have accepted the suggestion by R. C. Goffin (MLR 18, 1923, 335–36) that *phislyas* represents an uneducated speaker's attempt to use the legal term *filace,* "files" or "cases to contain files" (OED s.v. *filace* records first use in English in 1424). The MED, s.v. *phislias,* takes it as a mock-learned nonce word, "probably the science of medicine."

FRAGMENT III

The Wife of Bath's Prologue and Tale are generally regarded as the beginning of a "Marriage Group": her views on marriage provoke the responding tales of the Clerk, Merchant, and Franklin, with the intervening tales of the Friar, Summoner, and Squire serving as "interludes" in the continuing debate (Kittredge, MP 8, 1912, 435–67). This theory has had a powerful influence on criticism, though few critics accept it without qualification, and it has been rejected by some; e.g., Allen and Moritz (A Distinction of Stories, 106–7 and 116 n.43), who place the Clerk's and Merchant's Tales in a "moral" group and put the rest in a group of tales dealing with magic. Those who accept the "Bradshaw shift," by which Fragment VII precedes Fragments III–IV–V, would extend the "Marriage Group" so that it begins with the Melibee and Nun's Priest's Tale (W. W. Lawrence, Ch and CT, 1950, 125–36; Germaine Dempster, PMLA 68, 1953, 1142), or would read The Second Nun's Tale as its conclusion (Preston, Chaucer, 1952, 279–80; see also Donald R. Howard, MP 57, 1960, 223–32, though he modified his position in Idea of CT, 247 n. 36). Those who read the Tales in the order in which they appear in this edition some-times argue that the group begins with The Man of Law's Tale (see, e.g., Huppé, A Reading of CT, 107). Recently the problem has received less attention as many critics move away from the assumption that the tales are meaningfully ordered (see, e.g., Derek Pearsall, CT).

That Fragment III has a unity independent of the concerns of the "Marriage Group" is argued by W. G. East (ChauR 12, 1977, 78–82), who sees the three tales as explorations of the problems of experience versus authority posed by the Wife, and by J. N. Wasserman (Allegorica 7, 1982, 65–99), who finds a thematic unity in the philosophic opposition of the Wife of Bath and Summoner to the Friar. Jill Mann, PBA 76, 1990, 203–23, discusses anger and glossing in the Friar's and Summoner's Tales, as a counterpart to the patience that is one of the main themes of the "Marriage Group."

The Wife of Bath's Prologue

The explanatory notes to The Wife of Bath's Prologue and Tale are adapted from those written by Christine Ryan Hilary for The Riverside Chaucer.

The exact date of composition of this prologue cannot be determined, for Chaucer's conception of the Wife of Bath apparently changed over time, and he may have revised the Prologue when he changed the tale assigned to her (see introductory note to The Shipman's Tale). A reference in the lyric Lenvoy de Chaucer a Bukton (Buk 29: "The Wyf of Bathe I pray yow that ye rede") indicates her prologue was in existence (and in some sort of circulation) when that Envoy was written. The Envoy is usually dated in 1396, but that is not certain. The references to the Wife in The Merchant's Tale (IV.1685) and in the conclusion to The Clerk's Tale (IV.1170) show that her prologue preceded the final versions of these tales, but their dates are likewise uncertain.

The heavy use of Jerome's *Epistola adversus Jovinianum* here and in the Merchant's and Franklin's Tales may help indicate a date, since Chaucer's earlier works show no direct knowledge of Jerome (the quotations in the Melibee come from its source in Albertanus of Brescia). Jerome, who is not mentioned in the first version of the Prologue to *The Legend of Good Women* (c. 1386–88), is cited directly (LGW G 281: "What seith Jerome agayns Jovynyan?") in the revised Prologue (c. 1395–96). A date later than 1386–88 and probably before 1395–96 is thus indicated. John L. Lowes (MP 8, 1911, 305–34) would narrow that further on the basis of Chaucer's use of Deschamps's *Miroir de mariage,* a copy of which, Lowes believed, Chaucer obtained in 1393. Chaucer's use of the *Miroir* has been seriously questioned by Thundy (see below), and that Chaucer obtained a copy of that work in 1393 is only conjecture. Yet a date in the early to mid-1390s seems probable and is accepted by most scholars.

The character of the Wife is principally derived from that of La Vieille (the Old Woman) in *Le Roman de la rose,* one of the most influential of Chaucer's sources throughout the Prologue (see Fansler, Ch and RR, 168–74). La Vieille is one of the numerous "old bawds" in Western literature, and Chaucer may have been influenced by some of her ancestors, such as Ovid's Dipsas (see William Matthews, Viator 5, 1974, 413–43) and characters such as the preaching bawd, Gilote, in the Anglo-French Gilote et Johane in Harley 2253 (see Carter Revard, SP 79, 1982, 122–46).

Most of Chaucer's other sources for the Prologue come from antifeminist literature, most notably Jerome's *Adversus Jovinianum* (which is quoted frequently and at length in the marginal Latin Glosses), but also *Le Roman de la rose,* Theophrastus's *Liber aureolis de nuptiis* (preserved in Jerome, Adv. Jov. 1.47), Walter Map's *Epistola ad Rufinum de non ducenda uxore* (in *De nugis curialium* 4.3–5), and, perhaps, Deschamps's *Miroir de mariage* (Lowes, MP 8:329). Zacharias Thundy (in Ch Probs, 49–53) denies that Chaucer knew the *Miroir* and argues that the resemblances between Deschamps's work and The Wife of Bath's Prologue derive from their common source, the *Lamentationes* of Matheolus, which Chaucer probably used in Jehan Le Fèvre's French translation (see van Hamel's intro. to his edition). Thundy overstates his case but does show direct borrowing from Matheolus in a number of instances, thereby casting some doubts on Chaucer's knowledge of the *Miroir*.

The most important passages from Chaucer's antifeminist sources are collected, with other analogues and bibliographical notes, by Whiting in S&A, 207–22. (See also Woman Defamed, ed. Blamires, and *Jankyn's Book of Wikked Wyves,* ed. and tr. Hanna and Lawler.) On Chaucer's use of medieval antifeminist writings, see Lee Patterson, Spec 58, 1983, 656–95.

The form of the prologue is that of a literary confession (see Samuel McCracken, MP 68, 1971, 289–91; Lee Patterson, Ch and the Subj. of History, 1991, 367–68) like those of the Pardoner and the Canon's Yeoman, a form Chaucer perhaps based on the confession of La Vieille in *Le Roman de la rose.* The Pardoner and Friar seem to regard the Wife's performance as a kind of sermon (III.165, 1277), and she does draw on pulpit rhetoric (Charles E. Shain, MLN 70, 1955, 241), pulpit literature (Owst, Lit. and Pulpit, 389), and exempla (Robert P. Miller, ELH 32, 1965, 442–56). Patterson makes a good case that the prologue is a mock sermon, a "sermon joyeux" (Spec 58:674–80). This is questioned by Andrew Galloway (SAC 14, 1992, 3–30), who argues that the prologue has many of the characteristics of sermons on marriage and of polemical sermons of the time, including Lollard sermons.

The character of the Wife of Bath has elicited a considerable volume of critical literature. Alisoun explains herself by reference to astrological influences, and these have been studied in detail (Curry, Ch and Science, 91–118; Wood, Ch and the Stars, 172–80; North, Ch's Universe, 289–303). Since 1912, however, the major approach to the study of her character has been from the standpoint of, or in reaction to, Kittredge's theory of the "Marriage Group" (see note on Fragment III). Alisoun, with great gusto, champions the doctrine that the wife should rule the husband, a position that is surely unorthodox (on the wife and Lollardy, see Alcuin Blamires, MÆ 58, 1989, 224–42), perhaps heretical (see Robertson, Preface to Ch, 317–31). Yet Howard notes that she is less radical than she has been made out to be (Idea of CT, 248–52), and David argues that her basic position is one that many of the time would have accepted, that indeed it represents Chaucer's own feelings (Strumpet Muse, 158). Such criticism takes the Wife as a sympathetic figure, characterized by energy, good humor, and a Falstaffian vitality (Harold Bloom,

The Western Canon: The Books and School of the Ages, 1994, 105–26), yet with a touch of the tragic (Robert K. Root, Poetry of Ch, 236) and all the more human for her frailties and inconsistencies (Jordan, Ch and the Shape of Creation, 208). To such critics she offers a positive alternative to the rigidly class-based worldviews of the Knight and Man of Law.

Not all critics have been so admiring; D. W. Robertson (Pref to Ch, 317–30) regarded her not as a character but as an allegorical construct representing the "Synagogue," or the Old Law, and some critics have found her monstrous—an androgynous figure, spiritually corrupt (Jewel P. Rhodes, Jnl. of Women's Studies in Lit. 1, 1979, 348–52)—or a "sociopath" (Donald B. Sands, ChauR 12, 1978, 171–82). Indeed, in recent years some have attempted to revive the theory—first advanced as an elegant joke by Vernon Hall, Jr. (Baker Street Journal 3, 1948, 84–93)—that she murdered her fourth husband; for a witty refutation, see Robert W. Frank, Jr., SAC 11, 1989, 8–19.

One of the most important developments in the interpretation of the Wife of Bath has been in feminist criticism (see Dinshaw, Sexual Politics, ch.4). Mary Carruther's study (PMLA 94, 1979, 209–22) remains essential to understanding this aspect of the Wife's character, and Jill Mann, Geoffrey Ch: Feminist Readings, 70–86, provides a most useful discussion. For an excellent review of the criticism, see Peter G. Beidler and Elizabeth M. Biebel, Ch's Wife of Bath's Pro and Tale: An Annotated Bibliography 1900–1995, The Chaucer Bibliographies, 1998. Beidler has also published a very useful edition of The Wife of Bath's Prologue and Tale, 1996, with representative essays from a variety of critical approaches— Marxist (Laurie Finke, 171–88), psychoanalytical (Louise O. Fradenburg, 205–20), feminist (Elaine Tuttle Hansen, 273–89), deconstructive (H. Marshall Leicester, Jr., 234–54), and new historicist (Lee Patterson, 133–54).

1–2 Cf. *Roman de la rose* 12804–5: "Je sais tout par la pratique:/ Esperiment m'en on fait sage" (I know all by practice: Experience has made me wise"); see KnT I.3000–1. Chaucer frequently appeals to experience (e.g., FrT III.1517, SumT III.2057, ParsT X.927, HF 876–78 ("Thou shalt have yet . . . A preve by experience").

4 twelve yeer: In canon law, the minimum age of marriage for young women (Manly, CT, 575); cf. ClT IV.736.

6 chirche dor: Cf. GP I.460n.

9–24 The Wife closely follows the argument of Jerome, Adv. Jov. 1.14 (S&A, 209; tr. Miller, Ch: Sources, 424–25, Fremantle, 58–59).

11 Lat. gloss: "In Cana of Galilee" (John 2.1, from Jerome, Adv. Jov. 1.40; tr. Miller, Ch: Sources, 431, Fremantle, 379). The argument in lines 11–34 is from Adv. Jov. 1.14 (S&A 209, tr. Miller, Ch: Sources, 424–25, Fremantle, 358–59).

13 Lat. gloss: "For by going once to a marriage he taught that men should marry only once" (Jerome, Adv. Jov. 1.40; tr. Miller, Ch: Sources, 431, Fremantle, 379).

15 Samaritan: John 4.7, 18: "There cometh a woman of Samaria to draw water . . . [Jesus said] 'Thou has had five husbands, and he whom thou now hast is not thy husband.'"

23 Lat. gloss: "The number of wives is not defined since, according to Paul, those who have wives are as though they had none," alluding to Jerome, Adv. Jov. 1.15, and quoting

1 Cor. 7.30 as in Adv. Jov. 1.13 (tr. Miller, Ch: Sources, 422–25, Fremantle, 340–41).

28   Lat. gloss: "Increase and multiply" (Gen. 1.28, from Jerome, Adv. Jov. 1.3; tr. Fremantle, 347). For the history of the understanding of this text, see Jeremy Cohen, Be Fertile and Increase, 1989. This was the text on which the Brothers and Sisters of Free Love, a continental heretical sect known in England, based their pantheistic doctrines of sexual license; see John Mahoney, Criticism 6, 1964, 144–55. Critics have often noted that the Wife is apparently childless; cf. NPT VII.3344–45.

30–31 lette fader and moder: Matt. 19.5, as cited by Jerome, Adv. Jov. 1.5 (tr. Fremantle, 348).

33 bigamye and octogamye: Successive (second and eighth) marriages (from Jerome, Adv. Jov. 1.15, S&A 209; tr. Miller, Ch: Sources, 425, Fremantle, 359). Jerome specifically allows widows remarriage, but clerics (such as the Wife's fourth and fifth husbands) who married widows were guilty of bigamy; see Matheolus, Lamentationes, 1–8 (Le Fèvre 1.59–60), and Dives and Pauper, EETS 280, 2:112–16.

35 Salomon: Cf. 3 Kings (AV 1 Kings) 11.3: "And he had seven hundred wives, princesses, and three hundred concubines."

44A–F   These lines are not in the Ellesmere, Hengwrt, and some other good manuscripts. Chaucer may have been meant to cancel them, though Manly and Rickert argue that the most reasonable hypothesis concerning these and lines 575–84, 605–12, 619–26, and 717–20 is that Chaucer inserted them in a later revision. Beverly Kennedy (in Women, the Book, and the Worldly, ed. Lesley Smith and Jane H. M. Taylor, 1995, 2:85–101, and ChauR 30, 1996, 343–58) argues that all these passages (and 609–12) are inauthentic, added to besmirch Alisoun's character by making her seem promiscuous (see also John Eadie, NM 96, 1995, 169–76). The argument is not convincing, based as it is on the assumption that Hengwrt alone reflects Chaucer's own text.

44C–E   Cf. MerT IV.1427–28n.

46 chaast: The reference is to "chaste widowhood," that of the widow who does not remarry and remains celibate for the rest of her life. Nowhere is it explicitly stated that the Wife is a widow, though most critics agree that she is. See 504 below.

46   Lat. gloss: "But if they cannot contain themselves, let them marry" (Jerome, Adv. Jov. 1.9, tr. Miller, Ch: Sources, 425, Fremantle, 352; quoting 1 Cor. 7.9).

50   Lat. gloss: "Because if her husband is dead she is free to marry whom she will in the lord" (Jerome, Adv. Jov. 1.14, tr. Miller, Ch: Sources, 424, Fremantle, 358; quoting 1 Cor. 7.39).

52   Lat. gloss: "If you take a wife, you have not sinned, and if a virgin should marry she has not sinned, save those who have devoted themselves to the Lord. Thus, likewise etc." (Jerome, Adv. Jov. 1.13, tr. Miller, Ch: Sources, Fremantle, 356, quoting 1 Cor. 7.28).

54   Lat. gloss: "It is better to marry than to burn" (Jerome, Adv. Jov. 1.9, tr. Miller, Ch: Sources, 425, Fremantle, 353, quoting 1 Cor. 7.9).

54–56 Lameth, Abraham, Jacob: The Lat. gloss quotes 1 Cor. 7.9 from Jerome, Adv. Jov. 1.9 (tr. Miller, Ch: Sources,

420–21, Fremantle, 352), and notes "Lamech, a man of blood and a murderer, was the first to enter bigamy etc., Abraham trigamy, Jacob quatrigamy" This approximates (but does not echo) Jerome, Adv. Jov. 1.14, 5 (S&A 209, 208, tr. Miller, Ch: Sources, 425, Fremantle, 358). For the story of Lamech and his two wives, see Gen. 4.19–23. Cf. SqT V.550–51 and Anel 149–51: "Hit is kynde of man/Sith Lamek was . . ./To ben in love as fals as ever he can."

64–65 Th'apostel: St. Paul, 1 Cor. 7.25 ("Now concerning virgins I have no commandment of the Lord"); cf. Jerome, Adv. Jov. 1.12 (S&A, 208–9, tr. Miller, Ch: Sources, 421, Fremantle, 355). When the definite article is used with apostel, the reference is almost invariably to Paul.

67 no comandement: Proverbial (Whiting C472). Donald R. Howard points out that by undermining virginity the Wife of Bath is also undermining a medieval notion of personal perfection (MP 57, 1960, 223–32).

71–72   Jerome, Adv. Jov. 1.12 (S&A, 209; tr. Miller, Ch: Sources, 421, Fremantle, 355): "If the Lord had decreed virginity . . . he would have seemed to condemn marriage and to do away with the seed-plot of mankind, of which virginity itself is a growth."

73 Poul: St. Paul. The marginal Lat. gloss quotes 1 Cor. 7.25, as in 64–65 above (where in most MSS the gloss appears).

75 dart: Lat. gloss: "He invites candidates to the course, He holds in His hand the prize of virginity (virginitatis bravium), [saying] he that is able to receive it, let him receive it, etc.," from Jerome, Adv. Jov. 1.12 (S&A, 209, tr. Miller, Ch: Sources, 422, Fremantle, 355). Cf. 1 Cor. 9.24, whence Jerome derives bravium, a prize in a footrace. Skeat (5:293), following Tyrwhitt, suggests that a dart was a common prize in footraces and compares the similar use of spere in Lydgate, Fall of Princes 1.5108–9: "he that best hath ronne/ Doth not the spere like his desert posseede" (possess the spear he deserves).

76 Cacche whoso may: Proverbial (Whiting C112).

77–78   "Perhaps suggested by Matt. 19.11–12: 'All men cannot receive this saying . . . He that is able to receive it, let him receive it'" (Robinson).

81 every wight were swich: 1 Cor. 7.7: "Would that all men were even as I myself"; quoted in the Lat. gloss from Jerome, Adv. Jov. 1.8; tr. Miller, Ch: Sources, 419–20, Fremantle, 352.

84 indulgence: 1 Cor. 7.6: "I speak this by permission [secundum indulgentium], and not by commandment."

87   The Lat. gloss quotes 1 Cor. 7.1: "It is good for a man not to touch a woman," as in Jerome (Adv. Jov. 1.7, tr. Miller, Ch: Sources, 417, Fremantle, 350).

89 fyr and tow: Proverbial (Whiting F182).

99–101   From Jerome, Adv. Jov. 1.40 (S&A, 210, tr. Miller, Ch: Sources, 431, Fremantle, 379), echoing 2 Tim. 2.20: "But in a great house there are not only vessels of gold and silver but also of wood and of earth."

103   The Lat. glosses quote the last part of 1 Cor. 7.7 ("But every man hath his proper gift of God, one after this manner, another after that"), as in Jerome (Adv. Jov. 1.8, tr. Miller, Ch: Sources, 419–20, Fremantle, 352).

105   Lat. gloss: "The [hundred and] forty-four thousand who sing will follow the lamb," from Rev. 14.3–4, as in Jerome (Adv. Jov. 1.40; tr. Fremantle, 378).

107–12 Based on Matt. 19.21: "Jesus said unto him, If thou wilt be perfect, go and sell what thou hast, and give it to the poor, and thou shalt have treasure in heaven: and come and follow me." This is paralleled in the speech of Faux Semblant in *Le Roman de la rose* (11375–79; tr. Dahlberg, 199: "Where God commands the man of substance to sell whatever he has, give it to the poor and follow Him, He did not wish him to live in beggary in order to serve Him"). See also Jerome, Adv. Jov. 1.34 and 2.6 (tr. Fremantle, 371, 393). For a brief but lucid explication of the grades of chastity as a component of perfection—i.e., marriage, widowhood, and virginity in ascending order—see Howard, MP 57:224–25 and 67 above.

112 Almost identical with Mel VII.1088 and MerT IV.1456.

115–23 For the argument here, see Jerome, Adv. Jov. 1.36 (S&A, 210, tr. Miller, Ch: Sources, 428–29, Fremantle, 373), and *Roman de la rose* (4401–24; tr. Dahlberg, 96).

117 wright: An emendation of *wight;* Robert F. Green (N&Q 241, 1996, 259–61) makes a good argument for retaining the MS reading.

129–30 The reference is to 1 Cor. 7.3 ("The husband should render to his wife the debt [*debitum*], and likewise the wife to the husband"), quoted in the glosses of several MSS. (AV for *debitum* has "benevolence"; New and Revised Standard has "conjugal right.") See 198 below. Arthur K. Moore (N&Q 190, 1949, 245–48) finds a parallel to these lines and to lines 152–57 and 197–202 in Matheolus, Lamentationes, 2073–78 and 582–84 (Le Fèvre, 2.3277–94 and 1.1337–43).

132 sely instrument: Thundy (in Ch Probs, 36) compares Le Fèvre 2.1879 "beauls instrumens," sexual organ (of either sex).

135–41 Cf. Jerome, Adv. Jov. 1.36 (S&A, 210, tr. Miller, Ch: Sources, 428–29, Fremantle, 373–74).

144–45 It is not **Mark** (6.34–42) but John (6.9) who mentions barley loaves in the miracle of the loaves and fishes. Cf. Jerome, Adv. Jov. 1.7 (S&A, 208, tr. Miller, Ch: Sources, 428; Fremantle, 350). Robertson, Pref to Ch, 328–29, would take **barly-breed** as an identification of the Wife with the Old Law. It is mentioned as humble fare, fit for horses, asses, and beggars in 1 Kings 4.28 and 2 Kings 4.42. RomC 2755–57 suggests that it was prison food: "Glad, as man in prisoun sett,/ And may not geten for to eat/ But barly breed and watir pure." David Leon Higdon (PLL 8, 1972, 199–201) notes the miracle of the loaves and fishes is read as the Gospel for "Dominica Refectionis," mid-Lent Sunday, known also as "Refreshment Sunday." He argues that this, along with Jerome's use of white and barley breads as metaphors for chastity and incontinence, suggested *refresshed* in lines III.37–38.

147 Cf. 1 Cor. 7.20 ("Let every man abide in the same calling wherein he was called"), quoted from Jerome (Adv. Jov. 1.11, tr. Fremantle, 353) in the marginal Lat. gloss.

152–60 The Wife of Bath throughout misuses Paul's notion of the conjugal **dette** (see 129–30 above) and his ideas on the subordination of wives (see 158 below).

155 Lat. gloss: "He who has a wife is regarded as a debtor, and is said to be uncircumcised, to be the servant of his wife, and like bad servants to be bound" (Jerome, Adv. Jov. 1.12; tr. Miller, Ch: Sources, 422, Fremantle, 356).

156 tribulacion: See gloss at 158 below.

158 Lat. gloss: "And although you are the slave of a wife, do not on account of this grieve. Likewise: if you marry you have not sinned, but such shall have tribulation in the flesh, etc. [1 Cor. 7.28]. Likewise: he does not have power over his own body, but his wife (does) [1 Cor. 7.4]. Likewise: husbands, love your wives" [Eph. 5.25 or the identical Col. 3.19]. From Jerome, Adv. Jov. 1.13, 16 (tr. Miller, Ch: Sources, 422–23, Fremantle, 356).

161–62 this sentence: Eph. 5.25 ("Husbands, love your wives"; see 158 above).

170 another tonne: Cf. Bo 2.pr2.74–76: "in the entre or in the seler of Juppiter ther ben cowched two tonnes, the toon is ful of good, and the tother is ful of harm." From these, Fortune serves all with sweet or bitter drinks. The idea was common (see, e.g., Gower, Conf. aman. 6.330–48 and 8.2253–58). The ultimate source is Homer, Iliad 24.527: "For two urns are set upon the floor of Zeus of gifts that he giveth, the one of ills, the other of blessings." For another possible explanation, see 199 below.

180–81 Proverbial; Whiting A118, M170; cf. Tr 3.329: "For wyse ben by foles harm chastised."

182–83 Ptholomee: His **Almageste** originally contained neither this proverbial saying nor the quotation in lines 326–27. They appear in a collection of apothegms used as a preface to Gerard of Cremona's Latin translation of the *Almagest* and are to be found in other collections. (Karl Young, SP 34, 1937, 1–7.) Cf. MilT I.3208.

198 the statut: The *debitum*, the conjugal debt (see 129–30 above), whereby sexual relations were acknowledged as legitimately due both marriage partners (cf. ParsT X.375, 940; MerT IV.2048). Cf. ShipT VII.413–17n. The Wife of Bath, however, would ordinarily forfeit her right to sexual relations in view of the elderly or otherwise disabled or abused condition of her husbands; on *debitum*, see Elizabeth M. Makowski, Equally in God's Image: Women in the Middle Ages, ed. Julia Bolton Holloway et al., 1990, 129–43, and Kelly, Love and Marriage, 40.

198–202, 213–16 Cf. Miroir de mariage, 1576–84 (S&A, 217).

199 Lat. gloss: "It is customary to this day for the high priests of Athens to be gelded by a drink of hemlock" (Jerome, Adv. Jov. 1.49; tr. Hanna and Lawler, *Jankyn's Book of Wikked Wyves,* 186; Fremantle, 386). Daniel S. Silvia, Jr. (SP 62, 1965, 28–39) suggests that this gloss may have been a note by Chaucer to himself as a reminder to amplify the Wife's veiled threat to the Pardoner in lines 169–78.

202 swynke: Compare *labour* in MerT IV.1842, ShipT VII.108.

218 "At Dunmow, near Chelmsford in Essex, a flitch [a side] of bacon was offered to any married couple who lived a year [and a day] without quarrelling or repenting of their marriage"; the practice survived well into the twentieth century (Robinson).

222–34 Lowes (MP 8:317–18) finds a parallel in Miroir de mariage, 3634–35 ("Ask your chambermaid if I have been in an evil place") and 3544–55 (S&A, 221–22).

227–28 This is almost literally from *Le Roman de la rose* 18136–37: "Certainly they swear and lie more boldly than any man." It is glossed in MS Cambridge Dd., "Verum est" (It is true!).

232 beren hym on honde: Deceive him (cf. III.226 and 393), a variant of *bere on honde*, accuse falsely (see MLT II.620n.). For a study of its use here and elsewhere, see Edward H. Duncan, TSL 11, 1966, 19–33.

cow: An allusion to the widespread tale of the talking bird; when it tells a husband of his wife's adultery, the wife, usually with the collusion of the maid (cf. III.233), persuades him that the bird is mad. Chaucer may have known the version in the *Seven Sages of Rome* (cf. Benson and Andersson, Lit. Context, 366–71); he tells a somewhat similar tale in the MancT.

233–47 Cf. Miroir de mariage, 1589–1611 (S&A, 217–18), which is based in turn upon Theophrastus, *Liber de nuptiis,* preserved in Jerome, Adv. Jov. 1.47 (tr. Hanna and Lawler, Jankyn's Book, 150; Fremantle, 383–84). See also Matheolus, Lamentationes, 1107–14 (Le Fèvre, 2.1452–59).

246 dronken as a mous: Cf. KnT I.1261n.

248–75 This passage is paralleled in Deschamps's *Miroir de mariage,* 1625–48, based on Theophrastus, *Liber de nuptiis,* and supplemented by *Le Roman de la rose* 8579–8600; tr. Dahlberg, 157–58. In the passage parallel to lines 257–61, Theophrastus tells by what means men attract women: "One man tempts by his shape, another by his brains, another by his jokes, and yet another by his generosity" (tr. Hanna and Lawler, Jankyn's Book, 152; Fremantle, 383), but the Wife of Bath gives reasons why men desire women. Robert A. Pratt (MLN 74, 1959, 293–94) suggests Chaucer was reminded of the reasons men desire women listed by Isidore of Seville (Etymologies 9.7.29): "Beauty, family, wealth, manners."

253–56 Cf. *Roman de la rose* 8587–92; tr. Dahlberg, 157–58: "And if . . . she is beautiful, everybody will run after her . . . and they will all surround her, beg her."

263–64 Cf. *Roman de la rose* 8595–96; tr. Dahlberg, 158: "For a tower besieged on all sides can hardly escape being taken."

265–70 Cf. *Roman de la rose* 8597–8600; tr. Dahlberg, 158: "If, on the other hand, she is ugly, she wants to please everybody; and how could anyone guard something that everyone makes war against or who wants all those who see her?" The sentiment is ultimately from Theophrastus (ed. and tr. in Hanna and Lawler, Jankyn's Book, 150–55; Fremantle, 383).

269–70 Possibly proverbial (Whiting G382), though not recorded before Chaucer.

271–72 From Theophrastus as quoted by Jerome (Adv. Jov. 1.47; S&A 211; tr. Hanna and Lawler, Jankyn's Book, 152; Fremantle, 383).

272 his thankes: On the construction, see KnT I.1626n.

278 Proverbial; cf. Mel VII.1086n.

282–92 Chaucer is again following Theophrastus (in Jerome, Adv. Jov. 1.47, S&A, 211; tr. Hanna and Lawler, Jankyn's Book, 150; Fremantle, 383) along with *Le Roman de la rose* 8667–82 (tr. Dahlberg, 159) and either Deschamps's Miroir, 1538–59, 1570–75 (S&A, 216–17), or, more likely, Matheolus, Lamentationes, 2425–34 and 800–811 (Le Fèvre 3:265–68 and 2:393–418). Lines 285–89 are very close to Theophrastus: "A horse, a donkey, a bull, and the most worthless slaves, even clothes and kettles, a wooden stool, a goblet, and an earthen pitcher are all tested first and then bought or not. Only a wife is not shown, lest she should displease before she is wed."

293–302 This passage is also from Theophrastus in Jerome, Adv. Jov. 1.47 (S&A, 211; tr. Hanna and Lawler, Jankyn's Book, 150–2; Fremantle, 383); cf. Deschamps's Miroir, 1765–77 (S&A, 219).

303 Lat. gloss: "And her curly-haired 'assistant,' etc.," from Jerome, Adv. Jov. 1.47 (S&A, 211; tr. Hanna and Lawler, Jankyn's Book, 152; Fremantle, 383).

Janekyn is a common name in ME lyrics for rustic lovers, especially clerks (since it is a diminutive of "Sir John," a contemptuous term for a priest; cf. EpiMLT II.1172 and n.).

311 Oure dame: An instance of what John S. P. Tatlock (SP 18, 1921, 425–28) termed the "'domestic our,' an extension of the ordinary possessive to cases where it involves taking the point of view of the person addressed." Cf. III.432, 595, 713, 719; SumT III.1797, 1829, 2128; FranT V.1204; ShipT VII.69, 107, 356, 363; NPT VII.3383.

312 Seint Jame: Cf. GP I.466n.

327 Lat. gloss: "Among all men he is higher [*alcior,* as in most MSS; El has *ulcior*] who does not care in whose hand rests the world." See Young (SP 34:1–7) for its ultimate source in Gerard of Cremona trans. of Ptolemy's Almagest.

332 queynte: Elegant, pleasing thing; a euphemism, here referring to either sexual activity or the female sexual organ. Cf. III.444 and MilT I.3276 and n.

333–34 The idea is proverbial (Whiting C24), but this is probably from the *Le Roman de la rose* (7410–14; tr. Dahlberg, 140), where, as here, it has sexual implications: "It is the candle in the lantern: whoever brought light with it to a thousand would never find its flame smaller." Cf. the widespread tale of Virgil's revenge on his mistress, in which fire from her private parts supplies fires for the whole city of Rome (Domenico Comparetti, Virgil in the M. A., tr. E. F. M. Benecke, 1895, 326–36).

337–39 Cf. *Miroir de mariage,* 1878–84 (S&A, 219–20): if you allow your wife to dress in rich apparel, "What will you be doing? You will nourish the vice of shamelessness which will destroy her chastity."

341 The Lat. gloss quotes 1 Tim. 2.9 ("Likewise let women adorn themselves in apparel adorned with shame-facedness and chastity; not with braided hair, or gold, or pearls, without costly clothing, etc. This from Paul"), from Jerome (Adv. Jov. 1.27, tr. Fremantle, 366).

348–54 This figure appears in Deschamps's Miroir, 3208–15 (S&A, 220), and in Matheolus, Lamentationes, 1939–44 (Le Fèvre, 2.3071–80).

357–60 Cf. *Roman de la rose* 14381–84; tr. Dahlberg, 246 ("If it were Argus himself who guarded her . . . his watch-keeping would be worth nothing"), Matheolus, Lamentationes, 1800–1801 (Le Fèvre, 2.2979–80).

Argus was the hundred-eyed son of Jupiter and Niobe, commissioned by Juno to watch over Io, whom Zeus loved (Ovid, Met. 1.622–723). He was famed for watchfulness, though the idea that women could trick him was widespread; cf. MerT IV.2111–13.

361 make his berd: cf. RvT I.4096 and n.

362–64   Lat. gloss: "And if an odious wife has a good husband etc." From Jerome (Adv. Jov. 1.28, tr. Hanna and Lawler, Jankyn's Book, 190; Fremantle, 367), quoting Prov. 30.21–23: "For three things the earth is disquieted, and for four which it cannot bear; for a servant when he reigneth; and a fool when he is filled with meat; for an odious woman when she is married; and an handmaid that is heir to her mistress."

371   Lat. gloss: "Her love is compared to hell and parched earth and fire etc. Hell and the love of a woman, and the earth which is not satisfied with water, and the fire will not say 'it is enough,' etc." From Jerome, Adv. Jov. 1.28 (S&A, 210, tr. Hanna and Lawler, Jankyn's Book, 188; Fremantle, 367), quoting Prov. 30.16. Jerome has "amor mulieris" [love of a woman], for the Vulgate's "os vulvae" [mouth of the womb] (Skeat 5:301).

373 wilde fyr: "Greek fire," a flammable preparation, composed mainly of naphtha, used as a weapon in naval warfare; it could not be quenched with water.

376   Lat. gloss: "Like a worm in wood, so an evil woman destroys her husband," from Jerome, Adv. Jov. 1.28 (Hanna and Lawler, Jankyn's Book, 186–88), echoing Prov. 25.20.

378   Lat. gloss: "No one can know better than he who has endured one what a wife or woman is" (Jerome, Adv. Jov. 1.28, tr. Hanna and Lawler, Jankyn's Book, 186; Fremantle, 367).

382–94   Cf. Matheolus, Lamentationes, 686–88 and 1045–46 (Le Fèvre, 2.77–83, 1080–84, and 1099–1106).

386   Probably proverbial, though not recorded before Chaucer (Whiting H530); cf. Anel 157: "Ryght as an hors that can both bite and pleyne."

387–92   Cf. Miroir de mariage, 3600–3608, 3620–22, 3629–32 (S&A, 220–21).

389   Proverbial; see Whiting M558 (the first use in English); it is known in Latin (Walther, 1142) and remains current in "First come, first served."

393   For the technique here, cf. Roman de la rose 13823–30; (tr. Dahlberg, 237) and Miroir 3920–35 (S&A, 222).

401   Proverbial (Whiting D120 and Walther 6751). Many MSS (not El) have the Latin gloss: "Lying, weeping, spinning God gave unto woman."

407–10   Cf. Roman de la rose 9091–96; tr. Dahlberg, 165.

414 al is for to selle: Possibly proverbial, though this is the only recorded example in Middle English (Whiting W286), aside from Lydgate (Troy Book, 3.4329), who is probably quoting it from Chaucer. The commercial imagery is notable; cf. III.447, III.478, and Carruthers, PMLA 94:209–22.

415   Proverbial; see RvT I.4134 and n.

418 bacon: Bacon may refer to old meat, and so here for old men (Robinson). Richard L. Hoffman, referring to the "Dunmow flitch" (cf. 218 above), argues that the Wife's admission that she does not delight in bacon means she has never striven for a happy marriage (N&Q 208, 1963, 9–11).

432 Wilkyn, oure sheep: Baugh (389) takes Wilkyn (a diminutive for William) as the name of a pet sheep; it is more likely the name of the husband whom the Wife addresses with a variant of the "domestic plural" (see 311 above) and to whom she uses the infantile ba for "kiss" (see MilT I.3709n.). Her William is as meek as a sheep.

435 spiced conscience: Probably "scrupulous, fastidious conscience" (cf. GP I.526 and n.) (Robinson). But K. A. Rockwell (N&Q 202, 1957, 84) interprets the phrase here as meaning "a bland, gentle disposition, to be recommended to all husbands."

455–56   Cf. MerT IV.1847–48 and n.

460   Lat. gloss: "Valerius 6.3: Because she had drunk wine, Metellius beat his wife to death with a club," referring to Valerius Maximus, Facta et dicta memorabilia. Robert A. Pratt (Spec 41, 1966, 621) shows that the immediate source is a summary of Valerius in John of Wales's Communiloquium. For Chaucer's further use of the same chapter from Valerius (via John of Wales), see 642 and 647 below.

464 after wyn on Venus: Cf. Ovid, Ars amat. 1.229–44. The association of wine and Venus is commonplace; cf., e.g., PhysT VI.58–59, PardT VI.481–82, ParsT X.836, and Whiting C125, W359.

466   Proverbial, though this is the first appearance in English (Whiting M753, Tilley T395).

467–68   Cf. Roman de la rose 13452–53, tr. Dahlberg, 232: "And when a woman gets drunk she has no defenses at all." But the idea is common; cf. Whiting C619, R92, and 464 above.

469–73   Chaucer follows Le Roman de la rose 12932–48 (tr. Dahlberg, 244) very closely: "O God! But it still pleases me when I think back on it. I rejoice in my thought and my limbs become lively again when I remember the good times and the gay life for which my heart so strongly yearns. Just to think of it and to remember it all makes my body young again. Remembering all that happened gives me all the blessings of the world, so that however they may have deceived me, at least I have had my fun."

477–78   Perhaps proverbial, though this is the only recorded instance (Whiting F299); see lines 113–14.

483 Seint Joce: St. Judocus (Josse), a seventh-century Breton saint, symbolically identified by the pilgrim's staff (see Ann S. Haskell, ChauR 1, 1966, 85–87). His relics were at Hyde Abbey, whose abbot owned the Tabard Inn and had lodgings adjacent to it; M. E. Reisner (Ch Newsletter 1, 1979, 19–20) suggests the saint is named as a "bit of local lore." The name appears in the Testament of Jean de Meun, 461ff.: "When dame Katherine sees the proof of Sir Joce, who cares not a prune for his wife's love, she is so fearful that her own husband will do her a like harm that she often makes for him a staff of a similar bit of wood (d'autel fust une croce)" (from Skeat, 5:303, who offers this as the source of the joce : croce rhyme).

487   The proverb (Whiting G443) is still current.

489–90   The notion of marriage as earthly purgatory is common enough to make ascribing it to a certain source unlikely. A particularly appropriate parallel is to be found in Matheolus, Lamentationes, 3024–29 (Le Fèvre, 3.1673–95), in which Christ appears in a dream and announces: "O, since I who am the redeemer and scourge of sinners do not desire their death—for the buyer should not destroy goods bought so dearly—I wanted to provide for them many torments so that they might purify themselves. The prescribed cure heals the sick; among these [torments] the greatest is marriage." Lines 197–98 of "Golias de conjuge non ducenda" in Latin Poems, ed. Wright, 84, have:

"What shall I say, in brief, is marriage?/ Certainly either hell or purgatory!" Cf. MerT IV.1332n.

492   The proverb (Whiting S266) is still common, but this probably echoes Jerome, who tells of the Roman sage who, blamed for divorcing his wife, said that only the wearer of an ill-fitting shoe knew where it pinched (Adv. Jov. 1.48; S&A, 212; tr. Hanna and Lawler, Jankyn's Book, 178; Fremantle, 385). The same story (to which Chaucer also alludes in MerT IV.1553) is told in John of Salisbury, Policraticus, 5.10 (tr. Cary J. Nederman, 1990, 89); and in Walter Map, De nugis curialium, 4.3 (S&A, 213; tr. James, Courtiers' Trifles).

495 Jerusalem: Cf. GP I.463–67n.

496 roode beem: "The beam, usually between the chancel and the nave, on which was placed a crucifix" (Robinson). Such burial within the church itself was reserved for the very prosperous.

498–99   Lat. gloss: "Appelles wrought a wonderful work in the tomb of Darius, in Alexandreid 6." Appelles was a Jewish craftsman to whom Darius's fictional but elaborate tomb is ascribed in lines 6.381ff. of Walter of Chatillon's twelfth-century Alexandreid (ed. Marvin L. Colker, 1978; tr. David Townsend, 1996; summary in Lounsbury, Sts. in Ch 2:354). Cf. PhyT VI.16n.

503–14   Compare this with La Vieille's more leisurely recollections of a satisfying but destructive relationship (Roman de la rose 14472–546; tr. Dahlberg, 247–48).

504   Most readers take this line to mean that Janekyn is dead. Daniel S. Silvia (N&Q 212, 1967, 8–10) is nearly alone in arguing that he is alive but that the Wife of Bath, following her pattern, has lost interest in him and is actively seeking a replacement before she becomes a widow again. See 46 above.

516–24   For the idea that something given too freely is despised, see Roman de la rose 13697–708; tr. Dahlberg, 235.

517–20   Proverbial; see Whiting W549.

522   Perhaps proverbial, though this is the only occurrence in Middle English (Whiting P368).

534–38   For women's inability to keep secrets of any kind, see Roman de la rose 16347–75 (tr. Dahlberg, 276), but the idea is commonplace. See 950 below.

543–49   James F. Cotter (PLL 7, 1971, 293–97) argues for an ironic interpretation of the Wife of Bath's violations of the spirit and letter of Lent in her sexual interest in Janekyn, her clothing, and her general demeanor. But Beverly Boyd (AMN&Q 1, 1963, 85–86) suggests the word Lente may here be used in its older sense, "springtime"; this is probably right, since the ecclesiastical season of Lent never includes May (line 546). Cf. the Harley Lyric "Lenten is com with love to town."

552   Cf. Roman de la rose 9029–30; tr. Dahlberg, 164: "They go searching through the streets in order to see, to be seen," which is based on Ovid, Ars amat., tr. Mozley, 1.99: "They come to see, they come that they may be seen."

555–58   See Roman de la rose (13522–28; tr. Dahlberg, 233: "She should often go to the principal church and go visiting, to weddings, on trips, at games, feasts, and round dances") and Matheolus, Lamentationes 988–91 (Le Fèvre 2.947–52). On **vigilies**, see GP I.377n.

559 scarlet gytes: Cf. RvT I.3954–55.

   wered upon: Upon is adverbial as are upon in III.1382 and on in III.1018. Cf. Mod. Eng. "What did she have on" (Robinson).

560–62   Cf. Matt. 6.19: "Lay not up for yourselves treasures upon earth, where moth and rust doth corrupt, and where thieves break through and steal."

570–74   For a widow thinking of a new husband at her late husband's funeral, as here and at III.587–92 and 617–29, see Matheolus, Lamentations, 862–65 and 953–55 (Le Fèvre 2.597–601, 847–52).

572–74   Chaucer echoes Le Roman de la rose (13150–52; tr. Dahlberg, 227: "The mouse who has but one hole for retreat has very poor refuge and makes a very dangerous provision for himself"), and possibly Matthieu de Vendôme, Ars versificatoria (John M. Manly, Ch and the Rhetoricians, 1926, 12). Cf. Whiting M739.

576 My dame: The reference here and in III.583 is unclear. It may be to La Vieille in Le Roman de la rose (Emil Koeppel, Anglia, 14, 1892, 253); to Dame Alys, her gossyb, in line 548 (Chauncy Wood, Expl 23, 1965, Item 73); possibly, but not likely, to Venus (Walter C. Curry, PMLA, 37, 1922, 32); or, more likely, to her own mother, as suggested by "la mère" in Chapters 34–37 of Deschamps's Miroir and Matheolus, Lamentationes, 1362. However, PardT VI.684 and MancT IX.317 seem to indicate that the phrase was of loose or general application.

581 blood bitokeneth gold: "Money corresponds to blood." From The Interpretation of Dreams: The Oneirocritica of Artemidorus, tr. Robert White, 1975, 1.33, p. 197; see Beryl Rowland (Archiv 209, 1972, 277n.).

593–99   For sentiments similar to those here and at III.627–31, see Miroir 1966–77 (S&A, 220) and Ovid, Ars amat., tr. Mozely, 3.431: "Often a husband is sought for at a husband's funeral."

602 coltes tooth: See RvPro I.3888n.

603 Gat-tothed: see GP I.468n.

604 Venus seel: Most likely a violet or purplish birthmark located upon the "loins, testicles, thighs, or perhaps upon the neck" (Curry, Ch and Science, 106, quoting Les Oeuvres de M. Jean Belot, Lyon, 1654, 225).

608 quoniam: A Lat. conjunctive adverb ("since, therefore") or a relative ("that") introducing a clause, here used as a euphemism for pudendum, as in Matheolus 1237 and as translated by Le Fèvre (2.1748–49), in which men and women rush "To make carnally acquainted their quoniam [female genitals] and quippe [male genitals]"; see Thundy, Ch Probs, 36. The phrase quoniam bonum, meaning "female genitals," appears, along with a number of the Wife's other euphemisms, in Rabelais (see the list of Erotica Verba in Vol. 3 of Œuvres, Paris, 1820).

613   At the time of the Wife's birth the zodiacal sign of Taurus, a domicile of Venus, was ascending, and the planet Mars was in it. The Lat. gloss (at 609) reads "Mansor amphorisoun [i.e., Almansoris propositiones] 14: Whenever they are in ascendance unfortunately one will bear an unseemly mark upon the face. At the nativities of women when a sign is ascending from one of the houses of Venus while Mars is in it, or vice versa, the woman will be unchaste [from Almansoris propositiones, printed in

Astrologia Aphoristica, Ptolomaei, Hermetis, . . . Alman-soris, etc., Ulm, 1641, 66]. She will be the same if she has Capricorn in ascendance; thus Hermes in his trustworthy book, the 25th aphorism."

615 inclinacioun: The Wife of Bath justifies her conduct by astrological determinism. Curry (PMLA 37:48) describes her as "a fair Venerian figure and character imposed upon and oppressed, distorted and warped by the power of Mars." The Wife's horoscope is imprecise; Wood (Ch and the Stars, 172–80) modifies Curry's analysis and holds that Mars and Venus were not in conjunction at the Wife's birth. He suggests that the Wife uses astrology to set herself against clerks, who maintain the orthodox view as set forth in Dives and Pauper (EETS 275, 125): one "is enclyned by the werkyngge of the bodyes abovyn," but by virtue may overcome this inclination and thus "every wys man is lord and mayster of the planetys." See MLT II.295–301n.

615–26 The Wife of Bath proudly claims some of the worst practices charged to women in medieval antifemi-nist literature. For a review of such literature in Middle English, see Francis Lee Utley, The Crooked Rib, 136–37; Woman Defamed and Woman Defended, ed. Alcuin Blamires, 1992; and Katharina M. Wilson and Elizabeth M. Makowski, Wykked Wyves and the Woes of Marriage: Misogamous Literature from Juvenal to Chaucer, 1990.

618 chambre of Venus: From *Roman de la rose* 13336; tr. Dahlberg, 230.

619 Martes mark: Cf. the gloss cited in 613 above. Skeat notes the more precise statement in Ptolemy, *Centum dicta,* 74 (in *Almansoris propositiones,* etc.): "Whoever has Mars ascending will indeed have a mark (*cicatricem*) on the face."

624 From *Roman de la rose* 8516 (tr. Dahlberg, 156): "It doesn't matter to you if he is short or long."

630–33 Legally, the Wife was in no way bound to surrender ownership of her property to her husband; he was, however, required to provide a dower for his wife. See Cecile Stoller Margulies, MS 24, 1962, 210–16, and GP I.460n.

642 Lat. gloss: "Valerius lib. 6.3"; i.e., Valerius Maximus, Facta et dicta memorabilia 6.3, to which the incidents here and in 647 refer. The reference comes from John of Wales (Pratt, Spec 41:622; see note 460 above). Pratt shows that the whole passage (637–55) is based on the *Communilo-quium.*

Romayn gestes does not refer to the *Gesta Romanorum*; cf. MLT II.1126n.

647 Another Romayn: P. Sempronius Sophus in Valerius Maximus 6.3., but from John of Wales's *Communiloquium,* as in preceding note.

648 someres game: Cf. Robert Mannyng, *Handlying Synne,* EETS 119 and 123, 4681–82: "Daunces, karols, somour games/ Of swich come many shames."

651–53 Ecclesiaste: Ecclesiasticus. At line 657 the Lat. gloss has "[Nor] allow a bad wife to say what she likes" (Ecclus. 25.34, in part, as in John of Wales; see Pratt Spec 41:622 and 460 above).

655–58 This has the sound of a popular jingle, though this is its first recorded appearance (Whiting H618).

662 *Roman de la rose* 9980 (tr. Dahlberg, 278) has "She hates whoever corrects her." This is perhaps based upon Ovid, *Remedia amoris,* tr. Mozley, 123–24: "The impatient . . . spirit rejects skill and holds in abhorrence words of counsel," which circulated separately as a proverb (Walther, 11556). On the Wife's possible knowledge of the *Remedia amoris,* see GP I.475 and n.

669–75 Jankyn's **book of wikked wyves** is a fictional col-lection of antifeminist and antimatrimonial works written to encourage young men to choose celibacy. Chaucer most likely created it from his own collection of similar materi-als, possibly bound in one volume according to the usage of the time. (On medieval collections of "classics" similarly preserved, see Bruce Harbert in Ch: Writers and Back-ground, 139–41.) Chaucer's volume has been conjecturally re-created in *Jankyn's Book of Wikked Wyves,* ed. and tr. Ralph Hana III and Traugott Lawler, 1997.

671 Valerie and Theofraste: Valerius, the supposed author of Walter Map's famous letter (c. 1180), *Dissuasio Valerii ad Rufinum Philosophum ne uxorem ducat* (The Advice of Valerius to Rufinus the Philosopher not to Marry, in *De nugis curialium,* 4.3; tr. Hanna and Lawler, Jankyn's Book, 122–47); and Theophrastus, the author of *Aureolus liber Theophrasti de nuptiis* (The Golden Book of Theophrastus on Marriage), a vitriolic antimarriage tract preserved only in Jerome, Adv. Jov. 1.47 (tr. Hanna and Lawler, Jankyn's Book, 150–55; tr. Fremantle, 383–84).

674–75 Jerome . . . book agayn Jovinian: Jerome's *Epistola adversus Jovinianum.* Jerome writes from the standpoint of Christian asceticism. But Philippe Delhaye (MS 13, 1951, 65–86) suggests he also draws on classical philoso-phy and particular antifeminist texts. See also Robert A. Pratt, Criticism 5, 1963, 316–22.

676 Tertulan: Tertullian (c. 150–c. 230) did not write a specific book against marriage but his *De exhortatione castitatis, De monogamia,* or *De pudicitia* could have found a place in Jankyn's imaginary book.

677 Crisippus: Probably the antifeminist writer mentioned by Jerome, Adv. Jov. 1.48 (tr. Hanna and Lawler, Jankyn's Book, 180–82; Fremantle, 385).

Trotula is probably Trotula di Ruggiero, an eleventh-century female physician of Salerno, the reputed author of treatises on gynecology (the *Trotula major*) and on cosmet-ics (the *Trotula minor*), neither of which appears in antifem-inist MS collections. There is no evidence that Chaucer knew Trotula directly.

Helowys is Heloise, the eager lover but reluctant wife of Abelard, who expressed her antimatrimonial ideas in her letters to him, which were translated by Jean de Meun (see The Letters of Abelard and Heloise, tr. Betty Radice, 1974). Chaucer probably did not know the letters directly; he could have known of Heloise and her opinions from Le Roman de la rose 8759–8832; tr. Dahlberg, 160–61.

679 Parables of Salomon: The Book of Proverbs. Owst (Lit and Pulpit, 285–86) finds the ultimate source of the Wife of Bath in Prov. 7.10–12: "And, behold, there met him a woman with the attire of a harlot, and subtil of heart. She is loud and stubborn; her feet abide not in her house: Now is she without, now in the streets, and lieth in wait at every corner."

680 Ovides art: The *Ars amatoria* was sometimes included in antifeminist manuscript collections.

688 an impossible: Perhaps simply "an impossibility" (so MED), one of the "impossibles" (*adynata:* see Curtius, European Lit., 95–98), as in Tr 3.1495–98: "That first shal Phebus fallen fro his speere,/ And everich egle ben the dowves feere,/ And everich roche out of his place sterte,/ Er Troilus oute of Criseydes herte." More likely this refers to *impossibilia,* school exercises in dialectic consisting of the logical proof of impossible propositions (e.g., "God does not exist," "The Trojan war is now in progress"). See Paul V. Spade, The Medieval Liar: A Catalogue of the Insolubilia-Literature, 1975. Cf. SumT III.2231n., FranT V.1009.

692 Latin gloss: "Who painted the lion?" The allusion is to the widely known fable of the man and the lion: a peasant shows a lion a likeness of a peasant killing a lion with an axe, and the lion asks, did a man or a lion make this likeness? See Marie de France's Fables, ed. and tr. Harriet Spiegel.

701–2 The Lat. gloss has: "The one falls where the other is exalted" and then explains at 705, quoting *Almansoris propositiones,* 2 (see 613 above): "In Book One of Mansor, the exaltation of a planet is said to be that place in which another suffers the contrary etc., as Mercury in Virgo, which is the fall ["casus," or dejection] of Venus; the one, Mercury, signifies knowledge and philosophy, the other [Venus] song, lively joys, and whatever is soothing to the body." That is, the **exaltacioun** of Venus (the sign of the zodiac in which she exerts her greatest influence), which is in Pisces, is the "dejection" (fall) of Mercury, of **diverse disposicioun** to Venus; Virgo is the "dejection" of Venus, the "exaltation" of Mercury.

715–26   Eva (Eve), **Sampson** (Samson), and **Dianyre** (Deianira) are all named in *Epistola Valerii* (*De nugis curialium,* 4.3; tr. Hanna and Lawler, Jankyn's Book, 124–26, 126, 140). For Samson, see also *Roman de la rose* (9203–6; tr. Dahlberg, 166) and MkT VII.2015–94; for Hercules and Deianira, see MkT VII.2119–35 and *Roman de la rose* 9195–98; tr. Dahlberg, 166.

727–32 This story of **Socrates** and **Xantippa** is from Jerome, Adv. Jov. 1.48 (S&A, 212; tr. Hanna and Lawler, Jankyn's Book, 176), where the dirty water ("aqua immunda") is not necessarily **pisse.** On Socrates as a model of patience, see BD 717–19: ". . . Socrates / ne counted nat thre strees/ Of noght that Fortune koude doo"); and Fort 17: "O Socrates, thou stidfast champioun."

732 thonder . . . reyn: From Adv. Jov. 1.48 (S&A, 212): "'In the future,' he said, 'I shall know that rain follows such thunder.'" Proverbial after Chaucer (Whiting T267).

733 Lat. gloss: "What shall I say about Pasiphaë, Clytemnestras, and Eriphyles? The first of them so overflowed with self-indulgence that she, the wife of a king, is said to have wanted to sleep with a bull; the second to have killed her husband on account of adulterous love; the third to have betrayed Amphiaraus and preferred a golden necklace to her husband's safety, etc.; Metellius Marrio says these things, according to Valerius" (from Jerome, Adv. Jov. 1.48; tr. Hanna and Lawler, Jankyn's Book, 180).

Pasipha: Wife of Minos of Crete and mother of the Minotaur, fathered upon her by a bull. Cf. *Ars amatoria* 1.295–326.

737 Clitermystra: Clytemnestra committed adultery in the absence of her husband, Agamemnon, whom, on his return from Troy, she murdered in his bath.

741 Amphiorax: Amphiaraus was betrayed by his wife *Eriphilem,* Eriphyle, into joining the war of the Seven against Thebes, the fatal result of which he foretold. (See Tr 5.1485–510.)

747   Lyvia and **Lucye** appear in the Epistola Valerii (*De nugis curialium* 4.3, S&A, 213; tr. Hanna and Lawler, Jankyn's Book, 138–40). The former poisoned her husband, Drusus, at the instigation of her lover, Sejanus (A.D. 23); the latter, known also as Lucilia, accidentally poisoned her husband, the poet Lucretius (d. 55 B.C.), with a love potion.

757   The story of a hanging-tree appears in the *Gesta Romanorum,* chapter 33 (tr. Swan 132); in the *Epistola Valerii* (*De nugis curialium* 4.3, S&A, 212–13, tr. Hanna and Lawler, Jankyn's Book, 136), which is notably Chaucer's source here; and in Cicero, *De oratore,* tr. Sutton and Rackham, 2.69.278, the ultimate source (where only one wife is mentioned). The original of the name **Latumyus** is not known; it appears in none of the other versions.

765–68   Possibly an allusion to the story of the Widow of Epheseus (Petronius, Satyricon, tr. Michael Heseltine, rev. E. H. Warmington, Loeb, 1960, 229–35), who succumbed to a lover's advances in the presence of her husband's corpse, though she did not murder him. Robert A. Pratt (MLN 65, 1950, 243–46) notes that this story, the one alluded to in III.769–70, and the mention of poison in 771 are all paralleled in John of Salisbury, Policraticus, 8.11 (tr. Pike, 354–65; the widow of Epheseus) and 8.20 (tr. Dickinson, 367–74; allusions in 769–70).

769–70   Probably an allusion to the story of Jael and Sisera (Judg. 4.21). Cf. KnT I.2007n.

775–77   From Ecclus. 25.23; cf. Mel VII.1087n.

778–79   Prov. 21.9–10: "It is better to dwell in a corner of the house-top than with a brawling woman in a wide house. The soul of the wicked desireth evil; his neighbor findeth no favor in his eyes."

782–83   From Jerome, Adv. Jov. 1.48 (S&A, 212, tr. Hanna and Lawler, Jankyn's Book, 180), but ultimately from Herodotus (tr. Godley, Loeb, 1920), 1.8.

784–85   Lat. gloss: "As a golden ring in a swine's nose, so is a woman who is beautiful and foolish; i.e., unchaste," quoting Prov. 11.22 and adding *.i. impudica* ("i.e., unchaste"). The same passage is quoted in ParsT X.156. Pratt (Spec 42:623–24) shows that it comes from John of Wales, *Communiloquium* 5.3.4.

794 wood leoun: A common comparison; cf. SumT III.2152 and Whiting L326, L327.

800–810 Walter Map's *De nugis curialium* 2.26 (tr. James, rev. Brooke and Mynors) contains an anecdote about a wounded man who begs his attacker to take a kiss to his wife and children. When the attacker kneels for the kiss, the wounded man stabs him. John S. P. Tatlock (MLN 29, 1914, 143) suggests that this anecdote supplied Chaucer with the Wife of Bath's stratagem.

824 Denmark unto Ynde: That is, throughout the whole world; cf. Tr 5.971 ("bitwixen Orkades and Inde"). Such collocations were common in both French and English; see Whiting C63, I36, L427) and Hassell J6: "Pareille n'a, d'Inde jusqu'a Saint Jame" (has no equal from India to Saint James [of Campostella]).

829–49   The historical enmity between mendicants and possessioners, here represented by the Friar and Summoner, was a long-standing professional rivalry. See Arnold Williams, Spec 28, 1953, 499–513, and AnM 1, 1960, 22–95.

834–36   Proverbial; Whiting F336.

847 Sydyngborne: See ProMkT VII.1926 and n.

The Wife of Bath's Tale

Most scholars agree that what is now The Shipman's Tale was originally intended for the Wife of Bath. The tale she now tells is sometimes said to differ markedly in style from her prologue, but it is just as often said to accord with the Wife's notion of female dominance in marriage and to embody her fantasies of sexual and emotional satisfaction with a young man even late in life. The opening and closing passages (III.862–81 and 1257–64), obviously written with the Wife in mind, seem to stand out from the rest of the tale for their aggressiveness and sexual preoccupation, and it may be that Chaucer never completed an intended integration of tale and teller.

The tale in its present form was probably written about the same time as the prologue, around the early to mid-1390s. It is usually classified as a romance and, though John Finlayson (ChauR 15, 1980, 168–81) argues against this, it employs some common themes and motifs of romance, and it has an episodic structure characteristic of romance and other genres of traditonal tales (Carole Koepke Brown, Chaucer Review 31, 1996, 18–35). See also Weisl, Conquering the Reign of Femeny, 85–104.

The story of the disenchantment of a "Loathly Lady" is widespread (see George H. Maynadier, WBT: Its Sources and Analogues, 1901) and was known in a variety of forms, such as that in the popular "Fair Unknown" romances, in which the lady, transformed into a serpent, can be restored to her former beauty only by the hero (the feminine version of the "frog prince" fairy tale). The particular form that Chaucer used, in which the disenchantment is connected with the theme of sovereignty, apparently originated in Ireland (Sigmund Eisner, A Tale of Wonder, 1957), though J. K. Bollard (LeedsSE 17, 1986, 41–49) raises some telling objections to the theory of Irish origin. The story is found in two brief Middle English romances, The Marriage of Sir Gawain and The Weddynge of Sir Gawen and Dame Ragnell (both have an Arthurian setting), and (without the Arthurian setting) in the ballad King Henry and in the Tale of Florent in Gower's Confessio amantis. (All four versions are printed by Whiting in S&A, 223–68.) Chaucer knew and probably echoed Gower's version (see III.1080–81 and n.). None of the analogues includes the rape with which the Wife's tale begins; Laura Hibbard Loomis (SP 38, 1941, 29–31) suggests it may come from the Middle English romance Sir Degare, in which a princess, lost in a forest, is raped by a knight from Fairyland. It could as easily have been

suggested by Gawain's casual seduction of a damsel (told in the Middle English Jeaste of Syr Gawayne), in which he fathers the hero of the "Fair Unknown" romances, or it may be Chaucer's own invention.

The majority of the analogues usually adduced concern the disenchantment of the "Loathly Lady." Joseph P. Roppolo (CE 12, 1951, 263–69) presents the plausible argument that Chaucer combined this motif with that of the "Converted Knight," since the tale concerns the knight's reformation as much as the Loathly Lady's transformation. The choice offered to the hero, a wife foul and faithful or fair and possibly faithless, is unique to Chaucer's version (fair by night and foul by day or vice versa is the usual formulation) and perhaps derives from satirical antimarriage tracts (see Margaret Schlauch, PMLA 61, 1946, 416–30, and Richard L. Hoffman, AMN&Q 3, 1965, 101). Daniel M. Murtaugh (ELH 38, 1971, 473–92) argues that Chaucer uses the tale to allow the Wife to free herself from the ungenerous notion of womanhood (beautiful and unchaste or ugly and chaste by necessity) in the satiric antifeminist tradition. Chaucer's version is also unique in that the hero grants the woman sovereignty before her transformation, swayed by her arguments rather than her beauty.

The concern with *gentillesse* and the Loathly Lady's sermon on that subject are likewise found only in Chaucer's version. Here Chaucer's principal sources are Dante, Boethius, Le Roman de la rose (see 1109 below), and John of Wales, though the ideas are commonplace; the hag's defense of her ugliness and low birth is somewhat similar to the defense offered by an ugly, middle-class man in one of the dialogues in Andreas Capellanus's De amore (tr. Walsh, 72–87).

The Wife of Bath's Prologue and Tale are linked so closely that interpretive criticism since the time of Kittredge has taken the tale as part of the Wife's total performance. Much of the criticism concerns the problem of the Wife's sovereignty or lack thereof, though some scholars have raised the question of whether the Wife really wants sovereignty after all; see especially Howard, Idea of CT, 252–55; Lee Patterson, Spec 58, 1983, 656–95; and Jill Mann Ch: Feminist Readings, 92–94 (who argues that the Wife of Bath wants not dominance but mutuality).

880 incubus: An evil spirit that appears "in manys lyknesse & womannys to don lecherye with folk"; they are called "elves" in English and *incubi* in Latin when male, *succubi* when female (Dives and Pauper, EETS 280, 2:118). Note *elf* in 873, though Chaucer also uses the word for females; cf. MLT II.754n. and Thop VII.788n.

881   "The friar brought only dishonor upon a woman; the incubus always caused conception" (Robinson). Dorothy Yamamoto (ChauR 28, 1994, 275–78) notes that an incubus could not only impregnate his victim but inflict great harm, even death.

885 allone . . . born: Cf. KnT I.1633n.

890   There is a possible pun here in **pursute**, technically meaning "prosecution," and "pursuit," the knight's having been driven to appear before the king (Paull F. Baum, PMLA 71, 1956, 243). Cf. MED s.v. *pursuit(e)* n. 1(a) and 5(a).

904–5 What thyng is it: A similar question appears as a *demande d'amour* in a ballade by Eustache Deschamps; see Glending Olson, ELN 33:1, 1995, 1–7. Cf. KnT I.1347n.

929–30 For an elaboration of this idea, see *Roman de la rose*, 9945–58; tr. Dahlberg, 177.

939–41 Proverbial; Whiting G7, H505.

950 From *Roman de la rose*, 19220; tr. Dahlberg, 317: "For a woman can hide nothing," but also proverbial; Whiting W534. Cf. Mel VII.1084.

951–82 Ovid, Met. 11.174–193, has the story of Midas, but Chaucer's version is different: in Ovid, Midas's barber knows his secret, which escapes in the wind blowing through reeds growing over a hole the barber dug in which to bury the secret—no mention is made of women as gossips.

961–63 For the general idea, see *Roman de la rose*, 16521–30; tr. Dahlberg, 279.

965–68 *Roman de la rose*, 16366–68, has: "To her thinking she would be dead if the secret did not jump out of her mouth, even if she is in danger or reproached" (tr. Dahlberg, 278).

972 bitore: The bittern, a type of crane known popularly as the "mire drum" because of the booming sound it makes in the mating season (OED s.v. *bittern*). Bartholomaeus Anglicus 12.28, tr. Trevisa 1:635, says that "The mirdrommel . . . is a bridde that maketh soun and voys in watir."

1004 olde folk kan muchel: The idea is proverbial; cf. Whiting A70, O29 and KnT I.2449.

1013 Cf. Gower, Conf. aman. 1.1587: "Have hier myn hond, I schal thee wedde."

1018 wereth on: For the adverbial usage of *on* see III.559.

1028 The setting here and the question the knight is required to answer in line 905 are reminiscent of the courts of love supposedly presided over by such ladies as Eleanor of Aquitaine and her daughter Marie of Champagne. See Neilson, Origins of the Court of Love; such a court was, so it seems, actually held in Paris in 1400; see Piaget, Romania 20, 1891, 417–54; Straub, Zeitschrift für romanische Philologie 77, 1961, 1–14; Neilson, Origins of the Court of Love, 251.

1080–81 Cf. Gower, Conf. aman. 1.1727–31: "Bot as an oule fleth be nyhte/ Out of alle othre briddes syhte,/ Riht so this knyht on daies brode/ In clos him hield, and schop his rode/ On nyhtes time."

1062 Almost identical with NPT VII.3426.

1109 gentillesse: "The doctrine that gentility depends on character, not inheritance—'virtus, non sanguis' [*virtue, not blood*] was a commonly received opinion. It might be described as the Christian democracy regularly taught by the church (cf. ParsT X.460–74), though not regularly exemplified in Christian society" (Robinson).

The immediate influences here are said to be the *canzone* preceding Dante's *Convivio* (tr. Lansing) 4 and 4.3, 10, 14, 15, but such ideas were widespead. Robert M. Lumiansky (Italica 31, 1954, 1–7) cites parallels in *Il Filostrato* 7.86–100, and Frederick Tupper (PMLA 29, 1914, 101) notes similar ideas in Wyclif (Sel. Eng. Works 3:125: "And so hit is a folye, a mon to be proude for nobley of his kynn, for alle we comen of erthe") and Gower (Mirour de l'omme 12094–96; tr. Wilson, 165: "Who is the most gentle? If I am to tell the truth, the most gentle is he who most justifies himself before God"). See the discussion of Gentilesse in Conf. aman. 4.2200–2391, and Chaucer's lyric Gentilesse.

Most of the classical examples adduced are from John of Wales's *Communiloquium* (Robert A. Pratt, Spec 41, 1966, 619–42).

1110 old richesse: Cf. Dante, *Convivio* (4.3, etc.): "antica richezza"; *Roman de la rose*, 20313: "riches anciennes." See Gent 15: "Vyce may wel be heir to old richesse."

1117–24 Cf. *Roman de la rose*, 6579–92, 18619–34; tr. Dahlberg, 128, 308.

1126 Dant: Lines 1128–30 closely parallel *Purgatorio* 7.121–23: "Rarely does human probity rise up through the branches, and this wills He who gives, so that from Him it may be prayed" (see John L. Lowes, MP 13, 1915, 19–33).

1133–38 Cf. Dante, *Convivio* 5.15.2.

1139–45 Cf. Bo 3.pr4.64–69: "Certes yif that honour of peple were a natureel yifte to dignytes, it ne myghte nevere cesen nowhere . . . to don his office; right as fyer in every contre ne stynteth nat to eschaufen and to ben hoot."

1152–58 For similar sentiments, see Dante's *Canzone* (preceding *Convivio* 4), vv.34–37 and the prose comment in *Convivio* 4.7, 87–92. However, the ideas are commonplace.

1158 Cf. RomB 2181–82: "For vilanye makith vilayn,/ And by his dedis a cherl is seyn" (*Roman de la rose*, 2083–86; tr. Dahlberg, 59).

1160–76 Cf. Bo 2.pr6.

1161 strange thyng: cf. Bo 2.pr5.69–71: "Why enbracest thow straunge [i.e. *external*] goodes as they weren thyne?" and Bo 3.pr6.42–46: "For whiche thing it folweth that yif thou ne have no gentilesse of thiself (that is to seyn, prys that cometh of thy deserte), foreyne gentilesse ne maketh the nat gentil."

1165–68 Valerius: Valerius Maximus, Facta et dicta memorabilia 3.4, as quoted in John of Wales, Communiloquium 3.3.3 (Pratt, Spec 41:624): "The childhood of Tullius Hostilius endured a rustic hut; his youth was spent in herding cattle; his mature age ruled the Roman Empire and doubled its size; and his old age shone in the highest summit of majesty, adorned with the most excellent distinctions."

1168–76 Senek: The citation of Seneca and the sentiments that follow (though commonplace) came to Chaucer from John of Wales 3.3.2–3 (see Pratt, Spec 41:625).

1177–1202 The speech on poverty is based on John of Wales's *Communiloquium* (Pratt, Spec 41:626).

1178–79 Cf. 2 Cor. 8.9: "For ye know the grace of our Lord Jesus Christ, that, though he was rich, yet for your sakes he became poor, that he through his poverty might be rich," as quoted in John of Wales (Pratt, Spec 41:625).

1183–84 Proverbial (Whiting P331); but from Seneca's Ep. 2.6, which is quoted in the Lat. gloss: "Seneca in a letter: Contented poverty is an honorable estate." The whole of III.1183–90 is a paraphrase of the Senecan passage. All come not directly from Seneca but from their use in John of Wales's *Communiloquium*.

1186 Lat. gloss: "He is poor who desires what he does not have but he who has nothing and covets nothing is rich, according to that which is said in the Apocalypse 3 [17] 'You say that I am rich . . . and know not that you are wretched and miserable and poor.'" The gloss is from John of Wales (Pratt, Spec 41:626–27).

1187 Cf. *Roman de la rose*, 18566; tr. Dahlberg, 307: "Covetousness creates poverty"; cf. Walther 1884.

1193–94 Lat. gloss: "The empty-handed traveller will whistle in the robber's face and [the wealthy traveller] will tremble at the shadow of a reed" (Juvenal, Satires, tr. Ramsey, 10.22, 21). The same line is quoted in Chaucer's gloss in Bo 2.pr5.181–84 ("As who seith, a pore man that bereth no rychesse on hym by the weie may boldely synge byforn theves, for he hath nat whereof to be robbed") and in Langland, PP B 14.305; the idea was commonplace (Whiting M266).

1195–1200 Lat. gloss: "Secundus Philosophus: poverty is a hateful blessing [cf. III.1195], the mother of health, the remover of cares [cf. 1196], restorer of wisdom [cf. 1197], a possession without calumny [cf. 1200]" (John of Wales, Communiloquium 3.4.2; see Pratt, Spec 41:626). The philosopher Secundus is the supposed author of a collection of *gnomae*. A longer version of this passage is quoted in Latin in PP B 14.275, and explained at length in the lines that follow.

1202 Lat. gloss: "Crates the famous Theban after throwing into the sea a considerable weight of gold, exclaimed, 'I will drown you that you may not drown me.'" Ultimately from Jerome, Adv. Jov. 2.9 but, as Partridge notes (Glosses to CT) it comes to Chaucer from John of Wales. Robinson observes that this note "probably indicates that Chaucer meant to add lines on Crates."

1203–4 For the idea, see *Roman de la rose,* 4949–56; tr. Dahlberg, 104 (RomB 5551–60).

1210–13 Cf. PardT VI.739–47.

1219–27 Schlauch (PMLA 61:416–30) cites for these lines Ovid's *Heroides* 16.290: "Fairness and modesty are mightily at strife." Hoffman, AMN&Q 3:101, cites *Amores* 3.4.41–42: "Why did you marry a beauty if none but a chaste would suit? Those two things can never in any wise combine." Richard Firth Green (ELN 28:4, 1991, 9–12) notes a less learned analogue in a fifteenth-century French farce. Such ideas may well have circulated orally.

1258–60 Cf. ShipT VII.173–77 and n.

The Friar's Prologue

The explanatory notes to the Friars's Prologue and Tale are adapted from those written by Janette Richardson for The Riverside Chaucer.

The Friar's Prologue and Tale, and the following Summoner's Prologue and Tale, are dramatically linked to those of the Wife of Bath and were probably written shortly after them. To explain the quarrel that develops from the Summoner's attack on the Friar (WBPro III.829–49), Robinson and others conjectured that the two were enemies before the pilgrimage began. However, their argument reflects the long-standing professional rivalry between the mendicants and secular clergy (see introductory note to the portrait of the Friar, GP I.208–69). The controversy over mendicants hearing confession is probably an adequate basis for the Summoner's hostility: as Faus Semblant (False Seeming) asserts in an interpolated passage in *Le Roman de la rose,* one who is given absolution by a friar cannot be charged again with the sin (printed in *Le Roman de la rose,* n. 11222–23; tr. Dahlberg, 394–95).

1265 lymytour: See GP I.209n.

The Friar's Tale

The tale of the heartfelt curse is probably of folk origin, and the numerous analogues found across Northern Europe indicate that any avaricious type might be used for the role here played by a summoner; see S&A, 269–74, and Benson and Andersson, Lit. Context, 362–65. Chaucer's tale most nearly resembles the extant examples from England in which the victim fails to realize his own danger (Peter Nicholson, ELN 17, 1979, 93–98), and in one of which the victim is a bailiff (Owst, Lit and Pulpit, 162–63; tr. Peter Nicholson, Ch Newsletter 3:1, 1981, 1–2). See also Siegfried Wenzel SP 73, 1976, 142–43. No exact source was needed, since so widespread a tale as this must also have circulated in oral versions.

In genre The Friar's Tale is an *exemplum*, a brief tale or anecdote used in a sermon to illustrate a preacher's point. Exempla are thus especially suited to preachers such as the Friar and the Pardoner (whose tale also belongs to this genre), and they were often gathered in anthologies such as Bromyard's Summa Praedicantium and the Gesta Romanorum (both of which Chaucer may have known) for the use of such preachers. On the exemplum and its cultural importance, see Larry Scanlon, Narrative, Authority, and Power.

Exempla are brief, realistic, and often witty; as such, they are allied in style to the fabliaux, and Chaucer transforms and transcends the exemplum in much the same way he treated the fabliaux, expanding its brief plot and producing a more leisurely narrative, with more fully realized characters and brilliant dialogue. In amplifying the anecdote, Chaucer incorporated common demonological lore (Owst, Lit and Pulpit, 112) and the uncommon theme of atheism or something very like it, as the Summoner seems more concerned with learning about demons than in saving his own soul.

On the historical context of the satire of the ecclesiastical courts, see Thomas Hahn and Richard W. Kaeuper, SAC 5, 1983, 67–101. Attempts to identify the archdeacon described in the opening lines (e.g., Manly, New Light, 102–22) are not convincing.

Criticism of The Friar's Tale is not extensive; see Richardson, Blameth Nat Me, 73–85; Wallace, Chaucerian Polity, 137–45; Paul Olson, Ch and the Good Society, 1986, 186–215; and especially V. A. Kolve (SAC 12, 1990, 5–46), who examines the tale in the context of medieval art and religious thought, taking the episode of the carter as the moral and aesthetic center of the tale. Florence H. Ridley (in James M. Dean and Christian Zacher, eds. The Idea of Med. Lit . . . in Hon. of Donald R. Howard, 1992, 160–72) provides a good survey of critical opinion and a reading from the standpoint of the Friar's hypocrisy and vengefulness.

1302 erchedeken: Archdeacons, second in rank to bishops, conducted ecclesiastical courts for assigned areas while the bishop (see III.1317) did likewise for the entire diocese.

1308 lakke of sacramentz: On the obligation to confess and take communion at least once a year, see ParsT X.1027n.

1309 usure: Collecting interest on loans, prohibited by canon law.

   symonye: Buying or selling ecclesiastical positions,

named after Simon Magus (Acts 8.9–24), who wanted to purchase the power of bestowing the Holy Ghost.

1314   That is, the archdeacon never failed to impose fines rather than other penances. Cf. GP I.656–58; Gower, Mirour, 20101–12; tr. Wilson, 268: "The deacon, who follows after his profit, puts sins on sale everywhere to any man whatever, provided he can pay the price . . . He is troubled by losing money but repents not for sin." See also the introductory note to the Summoner's portrait, GP I.622–68.

1317 hook: A bishop's staff, symbolic of the pastoral office, resembles a shepherd's crook.

1327 wood were as an hare: Proverbial (Whiting H116), often as "mad as a March hare," referring to erratic behavior during the breeding season. In iconographic representations, the hare frequently symbolized lechery. See Rowland, Blind Beasts, 65, 89–91; Robertson, Preface to Ch, 113, 255.

1330 jurisdiccioun: Friars were answerable to the superiors general of their orders, not to the ecclesiastical courts. This was a matter of considerable bitterness (see Dahlberg, tr. Roman de la rose, n. 11222–23, 394–95).

1332 styves: Skeat (5:324) explains that brothels were licensed and thus exempt from ecclesiastical interference; but see the alternate explanation advanced by Henry Ansgar Kelly, ChauR 31, 1996, 125.

1334 with myschance :   Basically "bad luck to you," but as an imprecation with myschance varies considerably in forcefulness. Cf. MLT II.896, SumT III.2215, MancPro IX.11, MancT IX.193.

1340   The lure, made of feathers to resemble a bird and attached to a thong for twirling, was a device from which hawks were fed and thus trained to return to the falconer's hand. Cf. RvT I.4134, WBPro III.415.

1346–48   Cf. Wyclif, Sel. Eng. Works, 3:166: "By their feigned summoning they draw them from their labor till the time that they have granted what silver they shall pay" (translated).

1349 atte nale: For at an ale, at an ale house. Such false word division was not uncommon, cf. Mod. Eng. "once" and "nonce" or "napkin" and "apron."

1350–51   Judas, according to John 12.6, was keeper of the disciples' purse and stole from it.

1356   Priests rather than knights may be intended here; they were often addressed as "sir" out of courtesy. See ProNPT VII.2810, 2820 and intro. to notes on Sir Thopas.

1369 dogge for the bowe: Proverbial; Whiting D303. Cf. MerT IV.2014.

1377 ribibe: Literally, a kind of fiddle, but used derisively for "old woman," perhaps because of the carved head on the instrument (Ross, Expl 34, 1975, 17); cf. the similar rebekke in III.1573.

1382 grene: The color suitable to hunters and foresters (cf. GP I.103–4). However, the green garb has been taken as a hint of the yeoman's relation to the Celtic other world (Robert Max Garrett, JEGP 24, 1925, 129) and to devils who hunt mortal souls (D. W. Robertson, Jr., MLN 69, 1954, 470–72). Earle Birney (MS 21, 1959, 21) suggests that the unusual fringes blake provide a color always associated with devils (cf. III.1622).

upon: For the adverbial use see WBPro III.559n.

1399 bretherhede: Cf. III.1528 and see KnT I.1132n.

1408 venym: Thorns upon which shrikes or butcherbirds impale their prey were believed to be poisonous thereafter (Thomas P. Harrison, N&Q 199, 1954, 189).

1413   Infernal regions in both biblical tradition and Germanic mythology were often thought of as in the north. See Isaiah 14.13: "I will sit upon the mount of the congregation, in the sides of the north"; Jer. 6.1: "evil appeareth out of the north." See Alfred L. Kellogg, Spec 24, 1949, 413–14.

1436   to hevy or to hoot Proverbial (Whiting H316).

1451 purchas . . . rente: Cf. GP I.256n.

1475   Proverbial (Whiting T88, Hassell C198), derived from Eccles. 3.1 ("To every thing there is a season, and a time to every purpose under heaven"). See also ClPro IV.6, MerT IV.1972, Tr 3.855 ("Nece, alle thyng hath tyme, I dar avowe").

1489–91 Job: Job 1.12 ("And the Lord said unto Satan, Behold, all that he hath is in thy power; only upon himself put not forth thine hand"; 2.6 is similar). Cf. PardT VI.848n.

1502   Lives of St. Dunstan, archbishop of Canterbury (d. 988), contain various instances of his power over devils (Sr. Mary Immaculate, PQ 21, 1942, 240–44).

1503   Legends showing power over devils were also told of the Apostles. For James and Bartholomew, see Early South English Legendary, EETS 87, 35–37, 369–72; see the Legenda aurea (tr. Ryan) for Andrew (tr. 1:15), Thomas (tr. 1:45), Peter (tr. 1:334–36), Simon and Jude (2:264).

1510 Phitonissa: The name in the Vulgate for the Witch of Endor. When consulted by Saul, she raised the spirit of Samuel, who foretold the victory of the Philistines; 1 Kings (AV 1 Sam.) 28.7–20.

1511 som men: Baugh notes that the theological question about whether it was Samuel who appeared goes back at least to the fourth century when Eustathius, bishop of Antioch, argued that the apparition was merely a hallucination. For other references, see Cath. Encyc. 10.736. The idea of St. Basil, and other early churchmen, that Samuel was impersonated by the devil was equally current in the late Middle Ages, e.g., John of Salisbury, Policraticus 2.27; tr. Pike, 138–40.

1518   Professors in medieval universities lectured from chairs, while their students sat on the floor. See the illustration from Aberdeen Univ. Library MS 109 in N. R. Ker, MÆ 39, 1970, 32–33.

1519–20 Virgile: Cf. the description of the underworld in Bk. 6 of the Aeneid; **Dant:** Dante's Inferno. Cf. HF 445–50, which lists Virgil, Claudian, and Dante as experts on hell.

1529 trewe brother: Cf. 1399 above.

1543 Hayt: Skeat (5:328) quotes modern and medieval examples of hayt (go) and ho (whoa) as commands to draft animals. **Scot** was apparently a common name for a horse (see GP I.616n.); **Brok** ("badger") was commonly used for gray farm animals (cf. lyard boy, III.1563).

1553   For German ballad versions of the devil appearing to take what is consigned to him, see Child, Ballads, 1:219–20.

1564 Seinte Loy: St. Eligius (see GP I.120n.), here invoked as the patron of carters; see John L. Lowes, RomR 5, 1914, 382–85.

1570 upon cariage: A feudal lord had the right to use the horses and wagons of his tenants, but he could collect a payment of "carriage" instead. Cf. ParsT X.752; Bo 1.pr4.71 ("tributz or cariages").

1573 rebekke: Like *ribibe,* the word means "fiddle" and is used derisively; cf. 1377 above.

1582 virytrate: Another term of contempt, perhaps related to "old trot"; cf. Gower's use of "viele trote" (Mirour, 8713, 17900; tr. Wilson, 120, 246).

1587 Up peyne of cursyng: Echoes of the formulas for anathema are found by James A. Work (PMLA 47, 1932, 428) and A. C. Cawley (PLPLS-LHS 8, 1957, 175) in the passage that follows.

1613 Seinte Anne: see MLT II.641n.

1630 stot: Literally a horse (see GP I.615) or a bullock, but used here as another abusive term for a woman; MED s.v. *stot* n.2(a) lists this as the first recorded use in Middle English.

1636 Pratt (Tales, xxx) notes an inverted echo here of Christ's words to the repentant thief (Luke 23.43: "Verily I say unto thee, today shalt thou be with me in Paradise").

1645–55 This concluding admonition perhaps derives from the office of compline in the Breviary (Sutherland, PQ 31, 1952, 436–39).

1657–58 See Ps. 10.8–9; 10.8 is quoted in the Latin gloss: "He sitteth in the lurking places of the villages, in the secret places doth he murder the innocent, his eyes are privily set against the poor." Robert M. Correale (ELN 2, 1965, 171–74) cites Jerome's Adv. Jov. 2.3 (tr. Fremantle, 388–90) as a source for applying the biblical phrasing to the devil and notes that the two subsequent biblical echoes are also found there. Partridge (Glosses to CT) finds that the wording shows no special debt to Jerome.

1659–60 Ecclesiasticus 2.1–2: "If you aspire to be a servant of the lord, prepare yourself for testing. Set a straight course, be resolute."

1661 1 Cor. 10.13: "God is faithful, who will not suffer you to be tempted above that ye are able."

1662 champion: See GP I.239n.

The Summoner's Prologue

The explanatory notes to the Summoner's Prologue and Tale are adapted from those written by Janette Richardson for The Riverside Chaucer.

For this scurrilous anecdote about the final abode of friars, Chaucer seems to have inverted a tale, first recorded in Caesarius of Heisterbach's *Dialogus miraculorum* (thirteenth century): a Cistercian monk in a vision is taken to heaven; seeing none of his brethren there he asks where they are, and he is shown them dwelling under the cloak of the Virgin. The concept became a common iconographic theme and was used particularly by the mendicant orders and, in the fourteenth century, by the lay confraternities associated with the Dominicans and Franciscans (John Fleming, ChauR 2, 1967, 95–107). The inversion of the story may have been suggested by a fresco in Pisa, Francisco Traini's *The Last Judgment* (showing a sinner in Satan's anus), which Chaucer could have seen when he traveled from Genoa to Florence in 1373 (Theodore Spencer, Spec 2, 1927, 196–97), or merely by vulgar jokes or curses. Alan J. Fletcher (SAC 18, 1996, 99–100) finds similarities in later Lollard writings that develop Wycliff's phrase: "Friars, who are the tail of the head [of Anti-Christ]."

1667 aspen leef: A common image; Cf. Tr 3.1200 ("Right as an aspes leef she gan to quake"), Whiting A216, and MED s.v. *aspen.*

1688 Cf. Dante's description of Satan's wings, Inf. 34.48: "Sea sails I never saw so broad."

1690 The same image appears in RomC 7575–76: "For thou shalt for this synne dwelle/ Right in the devels ers of helle." This may be the translator's erroneous reading of the Fr. "cul [var. *puis*] d'enfer," or it may derive from Chaucer's usage here.

1692 furlong wey: See MilT I.3637n.

1693 bees out swarmen: Cf. Tr 2.193 ("so thikke a swarm of been"), Tr 4.1356 ("as thikke as been fleen from an hyve"), and Whiting B167.

The Summoner's Tale

The Summoner's tale of a hypocritical friar has neither a known source nor any close analogues. Two somewhat similar narratives that involve humiliating gifts, Jacques de Basieux's "Li Dis de la Vescie a Prestre" and "How Howleglas Deceived His Ghostly Father," are printed in Benson and Andersson, Lit. Context, 339–61. See also Walter Morris Hart, S&A, 275–87. The idea for the story may have come from an orally circulated jest, as Robinson thought; if so, Chaucer's elaborate development of the characters transforms a low joke into high art. The satire of the mendicants was perhaps influenced by Wycliffite attacks on the friars (Fletcher, SAC 18:91–117), but the characterization of the Friar himself is Chaucer's own achievement.

Until quite recently, The Summoner's Tale was not much admired. The scatology was shocking to critics undisturbed by Chaucer's sexual jokes. Donald Howard found the tale childish and repulsive, a product of "anal aggression" (Idea of the CT, 257). Others were more appreciative (see e.g., Richardson, Blameth Nat Me, 147–58). For a discussion of theology and scatology in the tale, see V. A. Kolve, in Robert Taylor et al., eds., The Centre and Its Compass . . . in Hon. of John Leyerle, 1993, 265–96; on the theme of anger, see Jill Mann, PBA 76, 1990, 203–23. For a full survey of scholarship and critical opinion, see John F. Plummer, ed., The Summoner's Tale, Variorum Edition, pt. 7, 1995.

1710 Holdernesse: A rural deanery in the southeast corner of Yorkshire. Holdernesse was also the home of Sir Peter Bukton, one of the two possible addressees of Chaucer's Envoy to Bukton.

1711 lymytour: See GP I.209n.

1714 Friars could preach in parish churches only by obtaining the permission of the local priest or by being licensed by the bishop of the diocese (Arnold Williams, AnM 1, 1960, 39–41).

1717 trentals: A set of thirty masses, to be said on consecutive days (sometimes all on the same day; see 1726 below), for the benefit of a departed soul; the practice was much criticized by followers of Wyclif. See Fletcher (SAC 18:103), who quotes Jack Upland (c. 1390) attacking "golden *trentale,* sold for a certain summe of money—as five schylinges or more."

1722 possessioners: The monastic orders and the secular clergy, both of whom had income from endowments and land, whereas the friars subsisted entirely on alms.

1726 hastily ysonge: Friars sometimes assembled to perform all thirty masses in one day (see English Gilds, ed. Smith, EETS 40, 1870, 8), a practice which Friar John asserts produces speedier delivery from purgatory than a priest's singing the office over thirty consecutive days.

1730 Except for mention of fire, most descriptions of purgatorial torments are vague. This use of meathooks and awls, however, does appear in the various versions of St. Patrick's Purgatory (Mabel A. Stanford, JEGP 19, 1920, 377–81).

1734 qui cum patre: Part of the formula invoking Christ's blessing at the end of prayers and sermons ("Who with the Father and the Holy Spirit lives and reigns for ever and ever").

1737 scrippe and tipped staf: Cf. Christ's command that his disciples go into the world with neither bags nor staffs (Luke 9.3: "Take nothing for your journey, neither staves, nor script, neither bread, neither money; neither have two coats apiece," repeated at Luke 10.4, Matt. 10.9–10).

1740 His felawe: Friars traveled in pairs, in accord with Christ's direction to his disciples (Luke 10.1: "After this the Lord appointed another seventy also, and sent them two and two before his face in every city and place").

1741 peyre of tables: A folding set of writing tablets. Wax coating on the inner surfaces of the ivory could be inscribed with the point of a stylus and smoothed out with the blunt end. Such writing materials date back to classical antiquity (see E. M. Thompson, Intro. to Gr. and Lat. Paleog., 1912, 14–20).

1755 hostes man: Skeat proposed "servant to the guests at the friar's convent," but Albert E. Hartung (ELN 4, 1967, 175–80) argues well for "servant borrowed from the host at whose inn the two friars are staying" (cf. III.1779). The man's function is reminiscent of the "bursarius," or spiritual friend, who received contributions of money, which Franciscans were forbidden to touch (Arnold Williams, Spec 28, 1953, 506–7).

1768 goode man: Cf. ShipT VII.29n.

1770 Deus hic: God be here. The prescribed Franciscan blessing when entering a home was *pax huic domini* (peace to this house); Matt. 10.12: "And when ye come into an house, salute it."

1792 glose: The interpretation of the "spirit" of a biblical text in contrast to its literal meaning (see Robertson, Pref to Ch, 331–32). For Chaucer *glose* is usually pejorative: "From the original sense of 'gloss,' 'interpret,' the word passes to the idea of irrelevant or misleading comment, and so to outright deception" (Robinson). See, as examples, WBPro III.509, MancT IX.34 (to mislead verbally), MkT VII.2140, ParsPro X.45 (to mislead, deceive).

1794 lettre sleeth: El has the Latin gloss "The letter kills, etc." [but the spirit gives life] (2 Cor. 3.6).

1803–4 Although the kiss of peace was a normal greeting, the action here is rendered suspect by the comparison to the sparrow, a common symbol of lechery (see GP I.626 and n.).

1820 Cf. Matt. 4.19 ("Follow me, and I will make you fishers of men"), Luke 5.10, and RomC 7490–91: "To fysshen

synful men we go,/ For other fysshynge ne fysshe we." On Friar John's claim for apostolic stature, see Bernard S. Levy, TSL 11, 1966, 45–60; Penn R. Szittya, SP 71, 1974, 30–41.

1832 je vous dy: I tell you. Although this was a common phrase (Skeat, 5:334), ability to speak French generally indicated social or educational superiority: "Oplondysch [*provincial*] men wol lykne hamsylf to gentil-men and fondeth [*attempt*] with gret bysynes for to speke Freynsh, for to be more ytold of" (John of Trevisa's translation of Higden's *Polychronicon,* ed. C. Babington and J. R. Lumby, Rolls Series, 1865–66, 1:59). See GP I.124–26n. The use of French by the merchant in The Shipman's Tale is apparently for local color; see ShipT VII.214n.

1862 jubilee: Anniversary of fifty years of service, marked by such privileges as the right to travel without an accompanying friar.

1866 Te Deum: A song of praise that regularly concluded matins, but is supposedly sung here to honor the miraculous vision.

1872 burel: Cf. FranPro V.716n.

1877 Lazar and Dives: See Luke 16.19–31. This example and the following references to Moses, Elijah, Aaron, and Adam all appear in Jerome's Adv. Jov. 2.15 and 2.27; tr. Fremantle, 398–400. Frederick Tupper (MLN 30, 1915, 8–9) prints the parallel passages.

1880 Lat. gloss: "It is better to fatten the soul than the body"), from Jerome, Adv. Jov. 2.6 (tr. Fremantle, 393).

1881–82 Lat. gloss: "We are content with food and clothing." Cf. 1 Tim. 6.8: "If we have food and covering we may rest content."

1885–90 Moyses: Exod. 34.28: "And he [Moses] was there with the Lord forty days and forty nights; and he did neither eat bread nor drink water."

1890–93 Elye: 3 Kings (AV 1 Kings) 19.8: "And he [Elijah] arose and did eat and drink, and went in the strength of that meat forty days and forty nights into Horeb, the mount of God."

1894–99 Aaron: Lev. 10.8–9: "And the Lord spake unto Aaron, saying, Do not drink wine nor strong drink, thou, nor thy sons with thee, when ye go into the tabernacle of the congregation, lest ye die."

1915–16 Paradyse . . . glotonye: Cf. PardT VI.504–11 and 508–11n.; ParsT X.819.

1923 Matt. 5.3: "Blessed are the poor in spirit: for theirs is the kingdom of Heaven."

1929 Jovinyan: The heretical fourth-century monk who provoked Jerome's Adv. Jov. (cf. introductory note to WBPro) and is there (1.40) sarcastically described as "that handsome monk, so fat and sleek, and of bright appearance, who always walks with the air of a bridegroom" (tr. Fremantle, 378).

1934 cor meum eructavit: The opening of Ps. 44 (AV 45), "My heart has uttered [a good word]," but *eructare* also means to "belch." On the history of the pun and its use in Latin satiric writings, see Paul E. Beichner, MS 18, 1956, 135–44.

1935 foore: Cf. WBPro III.110.

1937 James 1.22 ("But be ye doers of the word, and not hearers only, deceiving your own selves"); also in Adv. Jov. 2.3, tr. Fremantle, 390 (Robert M. Correale, ELN 2, 1965, 173–74).

1943 Seint Yve: See ShipT VII.227 and n.

1944 oure brother: See 2126–28 below.

1967 ferthyng . . . parted in twelve: Cf. the final scene of the tale.

1968–69 Lat. gloss: "Each united virtue is stronger than one that is divided from itself."

1973 Lat. gloss: "The workman is worthy of his hire, etc." (Luke 10.7).

1980 Thomas lyf of Inde: A legendary account of the life of Thomas the Apostle, who is said to have converted thousands in India (see *Legenda aurea,* 32–39; tr. Ryan 1:29–35). Thomas is, of course, the "doubting" Apostle (John 20:26–30).

1989–91 Lat. gloss: "Do not be like the lion in your home, driving out your servants and oppressing those subject to you" (Ecclus. 4.35).

1994–95 Cf. *Roman de la rose* (16591–604; tr. Dahlberg, 280), where Virgil's "snake in the grass" (Eclogues 3.93) is paraphrased ("here lies the cold serpent in the grass"). Proverbial after Chaucer; Whiting S153. Cf. SqT V.512.

2001–3 Cf. *Roman de la rose,* 9800–9804; tr. Dahlberg, 175: "Nor is there any serpent as malicious, when one steps on his tail (the serpent does not enjoy being stepped on), as a woman when she finds his new mistress with her lover. She spouts fire and flame everywhere." This incorporates Ars am. 2.376–78: "nor [is] the tiny adder hurt by a careless foot [so savage], as is a woman when a rival is taken in the bed she shares; she is aflame."

2017–18 Senek: Seneca. The exemplary tale of the wrathful potentate is from *De ira* 1.18. Chaucer probably knew it, and the later anecdotes about Cambyses (De ira 3.14) and Cyrus (De ira 3.21) from the *Communiloquium* of John of Wales, rather than directly from Seneca; the whole passage, lines 2017–42, is based on the *Communiloquium* (see Robert A. Pratt, Spec 41, 1966, 627–31).

2075 Placebo: "I shall please," from Ps. 114.9 (Vulgate; 116.9 in AV), well known because of its use as an antiphon in the Office for the Dead. The word came to denote flattering complaisance. See MerT IV.1476 and n., ParsT X.617n.

2079 Cirus: Cyrus the great (see MkT VII.2728n.).

2080 Gysen: The river Gyndes, a tributary of the Tigris (Francis P. Magoun, Jr., MS 15, 1953, 119). All MSS of Seneca's *De ira* (3.21.3) have *Gigen* or *Gygen;* the form *Gysen* is from John of Wales (Pratt, Spec 41:630).

2085–88 See Prov. 22.24–25: "Make no friendship with an angry man; and with a furious man thou shalt not go: Lest thou learn his ways and get a snare to thy soul," as quoted by John of Wales (Pratt, Spec 41:631).

2090 squyre: Carpenter's square, the iconographic symbol of Thomas of India (Roy Peter Clark, ChauR 11, 1976, 168). The phrase was proverbial (Whiting S645), but note the just *squier* in III.2243–80.

2093 On the power of friars to hear confession, cf. GP I.218–20 and RomC 6362–64: "Thurgh my pryveleges, alle/ That ben in Cristendom alyve/ I may assoile and I may shryve."

2094 Seint Symoun: Possibly a reference to St. Simon, the disciple (Mark 3.18), but Simon Magus (Acts 8.9–24) may be intended (Ann S. Haskell, ChauR 5, 1971, 218–24).

2098 of myn humylitee: Cf. ParsT X.1008n.

2106 stone: St. Francis prescribed humble buildings of wood and mud (John V. Fleming, JEGP 45, 1966, 696–97). See Wyclif, Eng. Works, 5: "Thei maken profession to most hey povert . . . and with this stryuen night and day who of hem may bilde gaiest wast housis and costly places, as chirchis or castels to herberwen [provide lodging for] lordis and ladyes."

2107 harwed helle: See MilT I.3512n.

2108 bookes: The hoarding of MSS bought with profits from begging was one of FitzRalph's charges against the mendicant orders (Earle Birney, Anglia 78, 1960, 215). See also Fleming, JEGP 65:697–98.

2111–13 sonne: The image, ultimately from Cicero, *De amicitia,* 13.47, is quoted from John of Wales's *Communiloquium* (Pratt, Spec 41:631): "As Cicero said about friendship, 'They remove the sun from the world who remove friendship from life.'"

2116 Elye, Elise: Although the Carmelites received their first rule in 1209 or 1210 and were endorsed by the papacy in 1226, they claimed that their founders were Elijah, who destroyed the prophets of Baal on Mt. Carmel (3 Kings [AV 1 Kings] 18.19–40), and his disciple Elisha. See Robert A. Koch, Spec 34, 1959, 547–60; Arnold Williams, MP 54, 1956, 118–19.

2126–28 youre brother: Thomas and his wife have "letters of fraternity," as members of a lay confraternity attached to Friar John's convent. These penitential associations, sponsored by various religious and civic organizations, flourished in the late Middle Ages. A census ordered by Richard II in 1389 found 507 such confraternities in England, and Philippa Chaucer received a letter of fraternity from Lincoln Cathedral in 1386. See Fleming, ChauR 2:101–5. For Wycliffites, such letters were but another deceptive way of obtaining money. See Wyclif, Sel. Eng. Works, 3:377: "Also freris by lettris of fraternite disseyven tho puple in feyth, robben hem of temporal godis, and maken tho puple to trist more in deed parchemyne, seelid with lesynges . . . than in the help of God." Cf. Fletcher SAC 18:101–2.

2149 For the connection of this action with practices of exorcism, see Karl P. Wentersdorf, Sts. in Short Fiction 17, 1980, 249–54.

2152 wood leoun: Proverbial; cf. WBPro III.794n.

2163 Manly (New Light, 119–20) suggests identifying the lord with Michael de la Pole: the tale is set in Holdernesse (III.1710), of which the de la Poles were lords until 1386.

2186–87 that honour: That is, although Friar John has a master of arts degree, he here follows St. Francis's dictum (Mann, Ch and Estates, 39) that his followers not be called "masters" (but he allows Thomas and his wife to address him with that title: cf. 1781, 1800, 1836).

Raby: See Matt 23.8: "But be not ye called Rabbi: for one is your master, even Christ; and all ye are brethren."

2196 savour: Matt. 5.13: "Ye are the salt of the earth, but if salt hath lost his savour, wherewith shall it be salted?" The word "savour" first appears in this text in Tyndale's translation (1529): D. Thomas Hanks, Jr. (ELN 31:3, 1994, 25–29) argues that Chaucer draws not on the Bible but on Gower's Vox clamantis 3.1997–98; tr. Stockton, 161: "They are the salt of the earth, by which we on earth are seasoned; without their savor man could scarcely be seasoned."

2215 with meschaunce: Cf. FrT III.1334n.

2222 ars-metrike: Literally, art of measurement (i.e., arithmetic), but with an obvious pun.

2228 with harde grace: A common imprecation; cf. CYT VIII.1189 and MED s.v. *grace* 3(b)(d).

2231 an impossible: For the relation of the problem to the class of logical exercises known as *impossibilia* in late scholastic teaching, see WBPro III.688n.

2234 Albertus Magnus's *Liber de sensu et sensato* (in Opera, ed. A. Borgnet, 1890–95, vol. 9) may be the source for Jankyn's remarks on the spreading of sound and odor (Robert A. Pratt, PQ 57, 1978, 267–68).

2244 karf his mete: Cf. GP I.100, MerT IV.1773.

2255 cartwheel: The squire's solution seems to parody iconographic representations of the descent of the Holy Spirit to the twelve Apostles at Pentecost. See Alan Levitan UTQ 40, 1971, 236–46, with illustration. Other sources have been suggested. The cartwheel has been asssociated with the "wheel of the twelve winds" in medieval art and scientific texts; see Phillip Pulsiano, ChauR 29, 1995, 382–89, and Robert Hasenfratz, ChauR 30, 1996, 241–61. V. A. Kolve (The Centre and its Compass, 265–96) suggests that the iconography of the wheel associated with Hugh of Foilloy's "The Wheel of True and False Religion" may have influenced the means of dividing the fart.

2259 In imitation of the Apostles, convents were composed of twelve members and a principal. Larger religious houses were considered to consist of several convents (Skeat, 5:341).

2289 Ptholomee: See MilT I.3208 and n.

2294 at towne: Perhaps Sittingbourne (see WBPro III.845–47), but Stanley B. Greenfield (MLR 48, 1953, 51–52) argues that it may refer to any one of a number of small towns before Rochester, which, he maintains, removes the geographical inconsistency (see MkPro VII.1926n.).

FRAGMENT IV

In some manuscripts this fragment is broken up: The Merchant's Tale is separated from The Clerk's Tale and precedes that of the Wife of Bath, with which it is connected by a spurious link. Nevertheless, the integrity of Fragment IV has never been doubted; see Jerome Mandel (Hebrew Univ. Sts in Lit. and the Arts, 16, 1988, 27–50). David Wallace (Ch Polity, 294) argues that the two tales of Fragment IV form a narrative sequence much like that in The Knight's Tale and The Miller's Tale, with The Merchant's Tale providing a "humorous critique" of The Clerk's Tale. Fragments IV and V are tightly connected (see note on Fragment V), and the order of Fragments III, IV, and V is widely attested in the manuscripts.

The Clerk's Prologue

The explanatory notes to The Clerk's Prologue and Tale were adapted from those written by Warren S. Ginsberg for The Riverside Chaucer.

2–3 coy and stille: Cf. GP I.840–41. The Clerk's demeanor ought to be maidenly: "A maidenly simplicity is fitting for clerks" (Totum regit saeculum, 145, qtd. by Mann, Ch and Estates, 76). Cf. William of Wheatley (fl. 1305–31): "The scholar . . . ought to be so chaste and modest in word and action, that he may resemble a virgin newly spoused" (qtd. by Huling E. Ussery, TSE 15, 1967, 15).

5 sophyme: By the fourteenth century, *sophisma* had come to mean any question disputed in logic. For earlier meanings as well as the place of disputations *de sophismatibus* in the curriculum of Oxford, see James A. Weisheipl, MS 26, 1964, 154, 177–81. For a fourteenth-century collection, see John Buridan, *Sophisms on Meaning and Truth,* tr. Theodore K. Scott, 1966.

6 everything hath tyme: Eccles. 3.1: "To everything there is a season, and a time to every purpose under heaven." Cf. FrT III.1475 and n.

10–11 unto the pley assente: Skeat (5:342) compares the French proverb, "He who joins a game consents to its rules." Cf. Whiting, P256.

12–14 "This reference to friars fits the preceding tale, whether or not it was written with that in mind" (Robinson). Sermons in the fourteenth century often tended to neglect their message for the sake of rhetorical extravagance. Wyclif was the chief spokesman against such bombast (Owst, Preaching in Med. Engl., 133): preachers should "algatis beware that the peple undirstond wel, and so use commun speche in ther owne persone." Lent was the time at Oxford when undergraduates began their determination (the resolving by scholastic disputation of questions of grammar and logic) for the bachelor's degree (Weisheipl, MS 26:157–59). Harry's words may thus have had particular resonance for the Clerk.

16 colours . . . figures: Rhetorical ornaments; cf. HF 854–59: "Have y not preved thus symply,/ Withoute any subtilite/ Of speche, or gret prolixite/ Of termes of philosophie,/ Of figures of poetrie,/ Or colours of rethorike?" In general, *colours* refer to figures of speech (metaphors, similes, etc.), *figures* to patterns of thought; cf. SqT V.39n., FranPro V.723–26n. Rhetoric was one of the subjects of the Trivium.

18 Heigh style . . . kynges write: The *ars dictaminis,* the medieval art of letter writing, taught that a letter should be written in low, middle, or high style depending on its subject and on the status of its recipient. Rhetoricians taught that the high style was to be used when writing of the high nobility, the low style when treating lower-class rustics.

19 Speketh so pleyn: Karl P. Wentersdorf (MS 51, 1989, 313–28) shows that the Clerk employs a full range of rhetorical figures throughout the tale.

27 at Padowe of a worthy clerk: Oxford clerks frequently studied at Padua (Bennett, Ch at Oxford, 61). Petrarch was archdeacon of Padua and canon of Parma. From 1368 until his death in 1374, he lived in Padua or in his country house at Arqua, two miles from the city. Chaucer could have met him when he passed by on his way to Milan, but there is no evidence that he did so.

29 Nayled in his cheste: Petrarch in fact was "placed in a sarcophagus of red stone, after the ancient manner" (Albert S. Cook, RomR 8, 1917, 222–24). *Nayled in his cheste* here simply means "dead and buried."

31 Petrak . . . the lauriat poete: By 1340 both the University of Paris and the Roman Senate offered Petrarch the poet's bays. On Easter Sunday, 1341, having stood a public examination before King Robert of Naples, Petrarch was crowned laureate in Rome amid great pomp.

34 Lynyan: Giovanni da Lignano (or Legnano) (c. 1310–83), an eminent professor of canon law at Bologna, wrote on law, ethics, theology, and astronomy, but was best known in England for his defense of the election of Urban VI (whom England supported during the Great Schism).

41 heigh stile: Cf. IV.18; here almost certainly derived from the misreading of *stylo . . . alto* (the form that appears in the Latin gloss of IV.1142); Petrarch wrote *stylo . . . alio* (a different style) and this was misread by the scribe who copied the manuscript used by Chaucer and the author of the glosses, who may have been Chaucer himself; cf. Severs in S&A, 330. The Ellesmere, Hengwrt, and other MSS contain a number of marginal glosses from Petrarch's tale (Partridge, Glosses to CT), most of which are recorded below (usually in translation, but in Latin where style may be of interest). See Thomas J. Farrell, SP 86, 1989, 286–309, on the glosses as contemporary responses to the tale, emphasizing important themes and highlighting the differences between Petrarch's elevated rhetoric and the Clerk's restrained style.

43–51 prohemye: Petrarch's prohemium is as follows: "There stands in Italy, toward the western side, Mount Viso, one of the highest of the Apennines, whose summit, surpassing the clouds, thrusts itself into the pure ether. This mount, noble in its own right, is most noble as the source of the Po, which, issuing in a little spring from its side, flows eastward toward the rising sun. Descending a short distance, it soon swells with great tributaries, so much so that it is not only one of the greatest rivers, but is called king of rivers by Virgil; it cuts Liguria violently with raging waters; then, bounding Emilia, Ferrara and Venice, it finally empties through many great mouths into the Adriatic Sea." (The Lat. gloss quotes the first two sentences.) All fourteenth-century translations of Petrarch's tale lack this geographical proem; most French versions, including the one Chaucer used, substitute a passage commending the story as a model for married women. See J. Burke Severs, The Literary Relationships of Chaucer's Clerk's Tale, 1942, 22–27; S&A, 296.

54 impertinent: Warren S. Ginsberg (Criticism 20, 1978, 311–14) argues for the relevance of the prologue.

The Clerk's Tale

As Chaucer acknowledges in the prologue, the source of his Clerk's Tale is Petrarch's Latin story *De obedientia ac fide uxoria mythologia* (A Fable of Wifely Obedience and Faithfulness); this in turn is a translation of the last story of Boccaccio's Decameron (10.10). Petrarch first wrote his version in 1373 and placed it as the last letter of his final work, the Epistolae seniles (17.3). War in Italy, however, prevented this letter, which was dedicated to Boccaccio, from being delivered to him; one year later, Petrarch recopied his translation, revising it here and there, and added another letter (17.4), in which

he made some further comments on the tale. Severs (Lit. Relationships) has shown that Chaucer made use of a MS containing Petrarch's final (1374) version of the story.

Boccaccio's and Petrarch's versions of the tale served as exemplars for other Italian, Latin, and French translations in the fourteenth century: Chaucer made extensive use of one of the French translations of Petrarch; this text and Severs's edition of Petrarch's Latin are printed in S&A, 288–331. French, Ch Handbook, 291–311, translates Petrarch's Latin.

The tale of Griselda is one of the most popular stories in European literature. Boccaccio's was the first written version of the tale; he gave it the literary form by which it became known throughout Europe. But Petrarch implies that Boccaccio drew upon Italian popular tradition; many elements of the story have indeed been found widely dispersed in folklore. Dudley D. Griffith (The Origin of the Griselda Story, 1931) and Wirt A. Cate (SP 29, 1932, 389–405) associate the story with the myth of Cupid and Psyche and the fairy tale "East of the Sun and West of the Moon." See as well Aarne-Thompson, 133, no. 887; 68, no. 425A (The Monster Bridegroom). William Edwin Bettridge and Francis Lee Utley (TSLL 13, 1971, 153–208) argue that Boccaccio's source was not a variant of the "Monster Bridegroom," but rather a version of a folktale known in Turkey and Greece, "The Patience of a Princess."

The extravagant, even "monstrous," behavior of both Walter and Griselda has been the subject of much discussion. Older critics supposed it derived from the fantastic actions of supernatural characters in previous (unrecorded) versions. This approach was pretty well swept away by James A. Sledd (MP 52, 1953, 73–82). G. L. Kittredge (MP 9, 1912. 435–67) had defended the aptness of the tale to the Marriage Group, but with Sledd attempts to explain the characters turned from folklore to a variety of psychological readings of Griselda and Walter. The tale has evoked a variety of other approaches: for a survey of criticism see Charlotte C. Morse, in Ch's Religious Tales, ed. C. D. Benson and Robertson, 71–83. The tale has most often been considered some sort of allegory—or one in which allegorical meaning and realistic treatment are in conflict (e.g., Salter, Ch: KnT and ClT, 39–65), though its allegorical character has been doubted (Allen and Moritz, A Distinction of Stories, 191–92), and its exemplary rather than allegorical nature has been stressed (Charlotte C. Morse, SAC 7, 1985, 51–86). Some critics have found Griselda a bit too yielding even for an allegorical character: see Margaret Hallisey, Cleane Maids, True Wives, Steadfast Widows, 1993, 68–70.

Most such studies have attempted to read the poem in the light of the medieval concepts that inform Chaucer's telling (cf. ParsT X.930–31). Part Four of the Ancrene Riwle (tr. Salu, 97), on Temptation, presents something similar to the narrative of the ClT: "When a man has just brought home his new wife . . . he behaves cheerfully . . . doing all he can to make her love him deeply, with her whole heart. When he is quite certain that her love is really fixed upon him, then indeed he feels able to correct her faults openly. . . . He becomes very stern, and shows his displeasure in his looks, trying to see whether her love for him can be weakened. At last, when he is convinced that she has been properly trained—that, whatever he does to her, she loves him not the less . . .—then he reveals to her that he loves her tenderly, and does all she wants. Then all sorrow is turned to joy. If Jesu Christ, your husband, acts thus toward you, do not be Surprised" (cited by Elizabeth Salter, Ch: KnT and ClT, 38–39). Rodney Delasanta (ChauR 31, 1997, 209–31) has recently revived the "nominalist reading" of the ClT (Robert Stepsis, ChauR 10, 1975, 129–46), seeing Walter in the light of a God of absolute omnipotence. On this doctrine see William J. Courtenay, 112–21, in Hugo Keiper, Christopher Bode, Richard J. Utz, eds., Nominalism and Literary Discourse: New Perspectives, 1997, 111–21 (Courtenay's notes provide a good brief survey of studies of Chaucer's philosophical background). See also Wallace, Ch Polity, 261–300, Dinshaw, Ch Sexual Politics, 132–55; and Hansen, Ch and Gender, on "Griselda and the Power of Silence." On the narrative style—"a gem of narrative irony"—see Lynn Staley Johnson, Mediaevalia 11 (1989, for 1985), 121–28.

58 roote: Lat. gloss: "At the root of Vesulus (*ad radicem Vesuli*) is the land of Saluces with its [many] villages and castles" (S&A, 296; Severs, 2.14–15).

colde: The adjective is not in Petrarch nor the Fr. version. Mt. Viso (Vesulus, 12,400 ft.) is permanently covered with snow (ClT, ed. Kenneth Sisam, 48).

72 Lumbardye: Cf. IV.46, 945. Not in Chaucer's sources. Phillipa Hardman (RES 31, 1980, 172–78) has shown that fourteenth-century Lombardy was infamous for its tyrants, particularly the Visconti of Milan. See Gower, Mirour, 23233–36, tr. Wilson, 304: "Some say that in Lombardy the lords are tyrants, living according to their will, without keeping the law in an honest way of life"); ProLGW F 374 ("And nat be lyk tirauntz of Lumbardye"); and the characterization of Bernabò Visconti as "scourge of Lombardy" (MkT VII.2400).

92 Lat. gloss: " 'Tua,' inquid, 'humanitas, optime Marchio'" (S&A, 298; Severs, 1.28; tr. in text).

101 ye: Cf. IV.316–22, 483–92, 876–79, 890–93, etc. On Chaucer's subtle use of the second person pronoun in the tale, see Colin Wilcockson, Use of English 31:3, 1980, 37–43. See 508 below.

106 us likketh yow: "is inconsistent in construction, the pronoun *yow*, apparently standing as an object of the impersonal *us lyketh*" (Robinson); see Language and Versification, p. xxxv.

110–40 The Prince's marriage to the social body was a popular political metaphor in the late fourteenth century. See Lynn Staley Johnson, ChauR 10, 1975, 17–29.

155–61 With the discussion of heredity here, cf. the treatment of *gentillesse* in WBT III.1109–76.

174–75 but ye wole assente: Chaucer's addition.

Explicit prima pars: In all likelihood, Petrarch wrote his tale without divisions. The MS Severs chose as his base text for the French translation, however, coincides exactly with the first four divisions of Chaucer's rendering (the fifth starts somewhat later). Chaucer probably followed the example of his French model (Severs, Lit. Rel., 192–96).

197 Lat. gloss: "Not far from the palace, et cetera" (S&A, 302; Severs, 2.1).

207, 291–94 oxes stalle: See Luke 2.7–16 and Isa. 1.3; the image is not in Chaucer's sources. The association with Mary is clear; for Griselda's resemblance to the "mulier

fortis" (woman of valor) of Prov. 31.10–31, see Kellogg, Ch, Langland, 286–88.

215–17 of the welle . . . She drank: Chaucer's addition.

223 The Virgin Mary was often pictured both as a shepherdess and as a spinner (Francis L. Utley, ChauR 6, 1972, 220–21). Cf. WBPro III.401.

227 Petrarch has "she prepared food suited to her station," the French translation "she brought cabbages or other kinds of herbs for their sustenance" (S&A, 302; Severs, 2.12). Chaucer keeps the basic structure of Petrarch, adds details from the French, and makes the scene his own with matter of his own invention.

249–52 Chaucer's addition.

260–94 Considerably expanded in Chaucer.

262–64 On the structure and internal arrangement of houses in Chaucer's time, see Hamilton M. Smyser, Spec 31, 1956, 297–315.

266 last Ytaille: Either "to farthest Italy," taking *last* as superlative adj. (cf. Bo 4.m1.24: "the laste point of the hevene"), or "as far as Italy extends" (taking *last* as the contracted third person of *lasten,* as in PF 49: "There as joye is that last withouten ende").

276–94 The well and water are often found at the threshold of the fairy world, but the scene also recalls Rebecca and Rachel (Gen. 24.13–67; 29.1–2) and the Annunciation (Utley, ChauR 6:224).

281–82 Lat. gloss: "So that, her other duties done, she might with her friends prepare to see the wife of her lord" (S&A, 304; Severs, 2.33–35).

295 Lat. gloss: "Walter, deep in thought, drew near and addressed her by name" (S&A, 304; Severs, 2.35–36).

337 Lat. gloss: "And he found her astonished at the unexpected coming of such a guest" (S&A, 304; Severs, 2.50).

344 Lat. gloss: "'Et patri tuo placet,' inquid, 'et mihi ut uxor mea sis, et credo idipsum tibi placeat sed habeo ex te querere, et cetera'" (S&A, 304; Severs, 2.51–53; tr. in text).

350 Wol ye assente: On Griselda's assent see Linda Georgianna, Spec 70, 1995, 793–821.

yow avyse: "Consider the matter," with the implication of refusal. Compare the legal formula *le roy s'avisera* for expressing royal refusal to a proposed measure (Skeat, 5:346).

356 Lat. gloss: "Sine ulla frontis aut verbi inpugnacione" (S&A, 306; Severs, 2.56–57; tr. in text).

362–64 Lat. gloss: "I will never knowingly do or even think anything that may be contrary to your will, nor will you do anything, even though you order me to die, that I will take ill" (S&A, 306; Severs, 2.59–62).

365 ynogh: Jill Mann (SAC 5, 1983, 31–33) discusses the thematic importance of *ynogh,* noting that Griselda's ordeal begins and ends (at IV.1051) with exactly the same words.

372–76 Lat. gloss: "Then, so that she should not bring any remnant of her old fortune into her new home, he ordered her stripped" (S&A, 306; Severs, 2.65–66). Griselda's clothing and unclothing, a motif not as prominent in Chaucer's sources, has received much comment. See Kristine Gilmartin, ChauR 13, 1979, 234–46. Note also the emphasis on clothing in the Envoy (Irving N. Rothman, PLL 9, 1973, 115–27), the Clerk's own threadbare attire

(GP I.290, 296), and the Wife of Bath's constant reference to clothes.

381 corone: Dives et Pauper, EETS 280, Commandment 6.2.45–47: "Thre ornamentis longyn principaly to a wyf: a ryng on hyr fyngyr, a broche on hyr breste, & garlond on hyr hefd."

400–6   Lat. gloss: "And to all she became dear and respected beyond belief, so that those who had known her birth and lineage (*originem*) could hardly be persuaded that she was Janicola's daughter, so gracious was her life and the way she lived it, so weighty and sweet were her words, by which she had bound all the people to her with a bond of great love" (S&A, 308; Severs, 2.79–84).

413   MLT II.532 and Tr 1.1078 ("That each hym loved that loked on his face") are nearly identical.

422   Lat. gloss: "Thus Walter, in humble indeed but renowned and prosperous marriage with honor, [lived] in God's highest peace" (S&A, 308; Severs, 2.87–89).

425   Lat. gloss: "And because he had so perspicaciously discerned extraordinary virtue hiding beneath such poverty, he was held by the people to be very prudent" (S&A, 308; Severs, 2.90–92).

428   Lat. gloss: "Indeed, not only was this bride skilled at womanly and domestic duties, but even undertook public duties when affairs required it" (S&A, 308; Severs, 2.92–93).

435   Lat. gloss: "When her husband was absent, she settled and resolved the disputes of the country and the quarrels of the nobles with such grave pronouncements and with such mature and equitable judgments that everyone proclaimed her to be a woman sent from heaven for the public weal" (S&A, 308; Severs, 2.93–97).

441 people to save: Cf. Matt. 1.21: "And she shall bring forth a son . . . for he shall save people."

444 had hire levere: The phrase is a confusion of the impersonal *hire were levere* and the personal *she levere had;* see Language and Versification, p. xxxv, and Mustanoja, ME Syntax, 531–32.

449   Lat. gloss: "Meanwhile, as it happened, when the baby girl had been weaned, Walter was seized with a desire as wondrous as laudable to test more deeply the fidelity of his dear wife, already well proven, and to test it again and again" (S&A, 310; Severs, 3.1–4).

452 tempte: In ParsT X.322–57, 1054–55, Chaucer distinguishes between internal and external temptation. John R. McNamara (ChauR 7, 1973, 184–93) argues that Griselda is tested by external temptation; Walter, far more grievously, by internal temptation.

459–62   Chaucer's addition.

499   Lat. gloss: "Neither by word nor countenance et cetera" (S&A, 312; Severs, 3.15–16).

508 save oonly yee: Hengwrt and Ellesmere read *thee* with *vel yee* (or *yee*) in the margin: Petrarch: "nisi te"; Fr.: "que toy." Of the other MSS, some have *thee,* some *yee.* The scribes were perhaps confused by the fact that consistency in pronouns of address here demands the plural *you,* rhyme the singular *thee:* see Mustanoja, ME Syntax, 12a, for *ye* as a form of *you,* though this is rare in Chaucer, occurring only here and in Tr 1.5: "er that I parte fro ye."

538–39 as a lamb: Cf. Isa. 53.7: "He was oppressed, he was afflicted, yet he opened not his mouth; he is brought

as a lamb to the slaughter, and as the sheep before her shearers is dumb, he openeth not his mouth."

540–43   Lat. gloss: "Suspecta viri fama, suspecta facies, suspecta hora, suspecta erat oratio" (S&A, 313; Severs, 3.32–33; trans. in text). The rhetorical device of *repetitio* is used here; see KnT I.2273n.

554–67   Chaucer's addition.

581   Chaucer's comment.

590   Derek A. Pearsall (MLN 67, 1952, 529–31) identifies Panik as Panico, a castle and family situated 18–20 miles south of Bologna. The identification, however, is not certain.

603–6   Lat. gloss: "Par alacritas atque sedulitas solitum obsequium idem amor nulla filie mencio" (S&A, 314; Severs, 3.53–54; trans. in text).

610   Lat. gloss: "Transiverant hoc in statu anni .iiij.^{or} dum ecce gravida et cetera" (S&A, 314; Severs, 4.1; trans. in text).

621–23   Chaucer's addition.

624–25   Lat. gloss: "'Et olim,' ait, 'audisti populum meum egre nostrum ferre connubium' et cetera" (S&A, 314; Severs, 4.5–6; tr. in text; **sikly berth** = *egre . . . ferre*).

647–49   Chaucer's addition.

650–51   Cf. Petrarch: "I can neither approve nor disapprove save at your will, nor indeed have I any part in these children except the labor of childbirth [*preter laborem*]" (Severs, 4.16; tr. French, Ch Handbook, 302).

660–61   Lat. gloss: "If it would please you that I should die, I would willingly die" (S&A, 316; Severs, 4.25).

666–67   Cf. Cant. 8.6: ". . . for love is strong as death" (Kellogg, Ch, Langland, 287).

722   Lat. gloss: "Slowly an evil rumor about Walter began to spread" (S&A, 318; Severs, 4.53–54).

736 twelve yeer: The minimum age for marriage; cf. WBPro III.4n.

811–12; 839–40; 851–61:   Chaucer's additions.

812 Fortune, aventure: See GP I.844n.

834–38   Kean (Ch and Poetry, 2.126) detects an echo here of Paul's counsel on marriage, widowhood, and virginity in 1 Cor. 7.1–40. Cf. Langland, PP C 19.84–90.

871   Cf. Job 1.21: "Naked came I out of my mother's womb, and naked shall I return thither."

880–82   Chaucer's addition.

lyk a worm: A stock comparison; Whiting W672. Cf. RomA 454, "nakid as a worm" (Fr. "nu comme un ver"), but see also Ps. 21.7 (AV 22.6: "But I am a worm and no man; a reproach of men, and despised of the people"; see Kean, Ch and the Making, 2.128).

890   For Walter's switch from "ye" to "thou" from this point onward in addressing Griselda, see Wilcockson, Use of English 31:3, 37–43: Because the singular pronoun can imply both affection and alienation, Walter, by this mode of address, can simultaneously conceal and reveal his love for her.

902–3   Chaucer's addition. Cf. Job 3.3: "Let the day perish wherein I was born, and the night in which it was said: 'a manchild is conceived.'"

932–38   Chaucer's addition. James 5.11: "You have heard of the patience of Job"; cf. WBPro 436. Jonathan B. Severs (MLN 49, 1934, 461–62) reports that one Petrarch MS (Cambridge, Corpus Christi College, MS 458) refers to Job at exactly the point where the Job stanza appears in Chaucer; it is, however, the only MS that does so. On the figure of Job in medieval literature, see Lawrence Besserman, The Legend of Job in the M. A., 1979, and Ann W. Astell, Job, Boethius, and Epic Truth, 1994.

990–91 Chaucer's addition.

995–1001 peple . . . chaungyng: Cf. Bo4.m5.31–33 ("The moevable peple is astoned of alle thinges that comen seelde and sodeynly in our age") and SqT V.203–5n.

995–1008 Chaucer's addition. Several MSS have "auctor" in the margin, but IV.1002 shows that Chaucer has not interrupted the Clerk. See MLT II.358n.

999 jane: a Genovese coin worth a halfpenny. "The phrase 'not worth a jane' also appears in Provencal: 'non prezo un genoi,' in V. Crescini, Studi Romanzi, 1892, 50" (Robinson). Cf. CYT VIII.795n.

1037 Lat. gloss: "One thing I pray and advise you in all good faith: that you do not drive this woman with those goads with which you have driven another, for she is younger and more delicately nurtured, and would not, I think, be able to suffer as much as I have" (S&A, 326; Severs, 6.39–40).

1056 Some critics compare the Abraham and Isaac episode (Gen 22.12: "Now I know that thou fearest God, seeing thou hast not witheld thy son, thine only son, from me").

1079–1113 Much expanded in Chaucer's version; the Latin devotes but one sentence, the French two sentences, to Griselda's reactions (S&A, 328, lines 55–58 [Lat.], 329, lines 19–21 [Fr.]): "Almost out of her wits with joy and beside herself with maternal love, on hearing these words, Griselda rushed into her children's arms, shedding her most joyous tears. She wearied them with kisses and bedewed them with her loving tears" (French, Ch Handbook, 319).

1141–62 Lat. gloss at 1142: "This story it seemed good to weave anew in a high style [stilo alto: see note 41 above] not so much that the matrons of our time might be moved to imitate the patience of this wife, which seems to me inimitable, but that the readers might be stirred at least to imitate this woman's constancy, so that what she did for her husband they might dare to do for God, for, as says the Apostle James, 'God cannot be tempted by evil, and He tempts no man' (James 1.13); yet he tests us and often allows us to suffer grievous scourgings, not that he might know the state of our souls, for he knew that before we were created etc." (Severs 6.69–78). The gloss omits Petrarch's final sentence: "Therefore I would add to the list of constant men whosoever he be who suffers without murmur for his God what this rustic wife suffered for her mortal husband" (S&A, 330; Severs, 6.69–77).

1155 Seint Jame: James 1.13; see preceding note.

1162 The translation of Petrarch and the French version ends here.

1170 Wyves love of Bathe: The second application of the tale that follows is the Clerk's direct reply, in satirical vein, to the Wife of Bath. It was obviously written when the plan of the Marriage Group was well under way. Whether any considerable time elapsed between the writing of the tale and the addition of this ending (or, for that matter, the addition of the ClPro), is unknown. See George R. Keiser (Manuscripta 17, 1073, 159–77) for a review of critical opinion.

1170–76 In 16 MSS this stanza is omitted.

1177 "The song, as the scribe's heading **Lenvoy de Chaucer** indicates, is Chaucer's independent composition. But it belongs dramatically to the Clerk and is entirely appropriate" (Robinson). For the opposing view see Skeat (5:351) and Baugh (439). Recent critics have agreed with Robinson: see Thomas J. Farrell, ChauR 24, 1990, 329–36; and John M. Ganim (ChauR 22, 1987, 112–27), who holds that the "carnival tone" (cf. M. M. Bakhtin, Rabelais and His World, tr. Hélène Iswolski, 1984, 1–14) is appropriate to the Clerk in his "playful, ironic student" role. On the rivalry of the Clerk and the Wife of Bath see John A. Alford, ChauR 21, 1986, 108–32.

The meter changes to six-line stanzas with only three rhymes (-ence, -aille, -inde) throughout the series; it is thus a double ballade. The envoy in a ballade is a brief stanza, usually differing in form from the main body of the poem, which addresses the recipient directly (see, e.g., Womanly Noblesse); it is not necessarily the logical conclusion to the poem, but offers rather a means of connecting the action to actual life by establishing a realistic context for the abstract ideas of the poem. Chaucer also uses envoy to designate a verse epistle, as in the Envoys to Bukton and Scogan, though here it seems an ordinary envoy is meant.

1188 Chichevache: Literally, "lean cow" (perhaps a corruption of "chiche face," lean face): a cow that fed on patient wives and consequently had little to eat. Sometimes Chichevache is contrasted to Bicorne ("two-horned"), which fed on patient husbands and was "always fat and in good case" (Skeat 5:351–52). See Lydgate, Bicorne and Chichevache, Minor Poems, EETS 192, 433–38.

1191 bidaffed: Usually glossed "tricked," "made a fool of," but Stevens (ChauR 7, 1972, 124–25) plausibly suggests "deafened."

1196 camaille: Camel, but also a punning reference to aventaille in line 1204. Claude Blair, Eur. Armour, 52, notes that in fourteenth-century England the piece of armor called a ventaille was in France called the camail, though both words were occasionally used in both countries.

1200 clappeth as a mille: Proverbial (Whiting C276 and M557); see ParsT X.406.

1204 aventaille: A wide strip of chain mail that formed the lower half of the movable part of the helmet and served to protect the neck and upper chest. See Blair, Eur. Armour, 52–53.

1207–10 Cf. WBPro III.253–56 and n., 265–70 and n.

1212A–G The "Host stanza" is generally held to have been written early and canceled when Chaucer wrote new lines for The Merchant's Prologue containing an echo of 1212. It is found in Ellesmere, Hengwrt, and 20 other MSS. Cf. MkT VII.1889–94, perhaps a reworking of this canceled link. Cf. Intro. to MkPro.

The Merchant's Prologue

The explanatory notes to the Merchant's Prologue and Tale are adapted from those written by M. Teresa Tavormina for The Riverside Chaucer.

1226–27 Cf. Buk 13–16: "But thilke doted fool that eft hath levere/ Ycheyned be than out of prison crepe,/ God lete him never fro his wo disseuere"; see MilT I.3231n.

1230 Seint Thomas of Ynde: St. Thomas the Apostle. See SumT III.1980n.

The Merchant's Tale

The direct reference to the Wife of Bath (IV.1685) and the heavy use of Jerome's *Adversus Jovinianum* and other works quoted in The Wife of Bath's Prologue (e.g., Deschamps's *Miroir de mariage, Lamentations* of Matheolus) argue for a date of composition in the early 1390s, about the same time as usually assigned to The Wife of Bath's Prologue and the other tales of the "Marriage Group."

The tale has three parts; the first, the debate over marriage, draws heavily on the sources mentioned above, on Albertanus of Brescia (see the Melibee), and on the homiletic commonplaces in the discussion of *luxuria* in The Parson's Tale. These are noted below (see also Lee W. Patterson, Traditio 34, 1978, 363–66). The second section of the tale, January's marriage and love-making, may be based on Boccaccio's *Ameto* (S&A, 339–40; tr. Judith Serafini-Sauli, 1985, 79–91), which describes the aged, impotent husband of a young nymph. For the third part of the tale, the pear-tree episode, Chaucer uses a common fabliau plot: the story of the blind husband and the fruit tree (for samples, see Benson and Andersson, Lit. Context, 203–73). The nearest extant analogue, perhaps a source, of Chaucer's version is an Italian tale (S&A, 341–43). Peter G. Beidler and Thérèse Decker (ChauR 23, 1989, 236–50) suggest a fourteenth-century Middle Dutch play, *Lippijn,* as a possible source (they supply a prose translation). The possible influence of *Decameron* 2.10 and 7.9 has also been defended (Peter G. Beidler, Italica 50, 1973, 266–84; Donald McGrady, ChauR 12, 1977, 11–12). These possible sources, as well as analogous fabliaux, are written in the plain, vigorous style of their genre. Chaucer's version is notable for its rhetorical elaboration, reminiscent of the Latin "Comedy of Lydia" (see Benson and Andersson, Lit. Context, 206–37). On the elaboration of the sources, see Pearsall, CT, 193–209.

Kean (Ch and Poetry 2:156–64) suggests that January is modeled in part on Le Jaloux (the Jealous Husband) in *Le Roman de la rose* (8455–9492; tr. Dahlberg, 157–69). Both he and January reflect the familiar topos of the *senex amans,* or aged lover, also found in The Miller's Tale, The Reeve's Prologue, and The Wife of Bath's Prologue (see Burrow, The Ages of Man, 156–62). It is a common theme in fabliaux, medieval lyrics (e.g., the *chansons des malmariées*), and other satiric pieces. On Chaucer's handling of the topos here and in the MilT, see Janet Boothman, Thoth 4, 1963, 3–14.

The degree to which the tale reflects its teller has been a matter of significant critical disagreement, mainly on the basis of the use of *seculeer* in lines 1251 and 1322. Some critics have suggested that Chaucer originally intended the tale for a clerical narrator, probably the Monk or Friar, perhaps as a quitting of The Shipman's Tale, which was probably first assigned to the Wife of Bath (see introductory note to ShipT); others have argued that it was always meant for the Merchant (Dempster, MP 36, 1938). A similar issue is the degree to which the bitterness of the Prologue is to be read into the tale itself—whether the tale is a dramatic unfolding of the Merchant's character as revealed in the Prologue, newly wed and bitterly unhappy (as Kittredge held), or whether the tale is to be taken

by itself, as a a rather lighthearted jape at women and human folly. For a review of the dispute, see Robert B. Edwards (Spec 66, 1991, 342–67), and for a balanced view, see Brewer, A New Intro. to Ch, 320–27, who sees the tale as much more complex than simply a matter of the narrator's bitterness.

A related problem is raised by the tale's apparent failures of decorum, its mixing of genres, styles, voices, and tones, of pagan and Christian elements, and even of narrative levels (cf. IV.1685–87). Critics have long noted these tensions and dramatic improprieties, explaining them variously as marks of the Merchant's or Chaucer's loss of artistic control (G. L. Kittredge, MP 9, 1912, 453–56), as instances of Gothic juxtaposition (Robert M. Jordan, PMLA 78, 1963, 293–99), or as deliberate testings of the bounds of fiction (Morton W. Bloomfield, 37–50, in Med. and Ren. St. 7, ed. Siegfried Wenzel, 1978; Jay Schleusener, ChauR 14, 1980, 237–50). For a review of these scholarly controversies, see Emerson Brown, Jr., ChauR 13, 1978–79, 141–56 and 247–62. For more recent studies, see Pearsall, CT, 193–209 (with helpful references) and Peter Brown and Andrew Butcher, The Age of Saturn: Literature and History in the CT, 1991, 157–204 (they take the tale as a comment on the political crisis of 1376).

1245 Lumbardye: The Lombards were active in international trade and finance and would have been professional rivals of the Merchant; Lombardy also had a thriving commercial aristocracy by Chaucer's time, the ancestry and values of which often differed from those of the traditional feudal aristocracy represented by the Clerk's Marquis Walter (Paul A. Olson, TSLL 3, 1961, 259–63). Lombard rulers were known as well for lechery, tyranny, and avarice; see ClT IV.72n.

1246 Pavye: Pavia, a Lombard city famous at the time for usury, wealth, and amorous sensuality (Olson, TSLL 3:263; Emerson Brown, Jr., NM 71, 1970, 654–58).

1248 sixty yeer: Authorities differed on when old age began (see Burrow, The Ages of Man, 5–54); "Medill Elde" is sixty in The Parlement of the Thre Ages (EETS 246, lines 150–51). Vincent of Beauvais (Spec. nat. 31.75) quotes Avicenna, who takes the years from thirty-five or forty to sixty as "senectus," a time of diminishing powers, and sixty as the beginning of senility and the end of life ("senium et finis vitae").

1251 seculeer: This can mean either "laymen" or "of the secular clergy." Critics who favor a cleric as the original teller of the tale take the meaning "lay" as evidence for their case (Albert C. Baugh, MP 35, 1937, 16–26, esp. 20; Thomas Jay Garbáty, MP 67, 1969–70, 18–24, esp. 22–23). Those who favor the Merchant either take *seculeer* as a direct or ironic attack on the clergy or argue that a layman could gibe at lay follies as easily as a cleric (Howard, Idea of CT, 261).

1259–60 blisful lyf . . . wyf: Cf. FranT V.803–5.

1267–1392   The question of whose voice is heard in these lines, commonly called the "marriage encomium," is a major interpretative crux. A review of critical opinion on the problem and a detailed analysis of the passage are given by Donald R. Benson, ChauR 14, 1979, 48–60. See also Edwards, Spec 66:342–67, and Jill Mann, in This Noble Craft, ed. Erik Looper, 1991, 173–88.

1267 As sooth as God is king: see Whiting G196.

1294 Theofraste: Theophrastus, author of the misogynistic Golden Book of Marriage (cf. WBPro III.671n.).

1296–1306   Adv. Jov. 1.47 (S&A, 212; tr. Hanna and Lawler, Jankyn's Book, 152–54).

1296 housbondrye: "Domestic economy," with a possible play on "husband" (Baum, PMLA 71, 1956, 239; see MED, s.v. *husbondrie* n. 1b, 4).

1300 half part: Cf. WBPro III.310.

1311–14   Lat. gloss: "A wife is to be loved because she is a gift of God. Jesus son of Sirach [error for Prov. 19.14]: 'House and riches are given by parents, but a good or prudent wife is properly from the Lord'" (quoting Albertanus, De amore Dei, fol. 40r [Partridge, Glosses to CT, IV.1311]).

1315 shadwe upon a wal: Proverbial (Whiting S185); see ShipT VII.9 and ParsT X.1068n.

1319 ful greet sacrement: Cf. ParsT X.918.

1322 seculer estat: cf. 1251 above.

1325–29   Lat. gloss: "'Let us make a helpmate for him'; and having taken a rib from Adam's body, He made Eve, and said, 'For this reason shall a man leave father and mother and cleave, etc.; and they shall be two in one flesh'" (Gen. 2.18, 24, as quoted in De amore Dei, fol. 39v; cf. Mel VII.1103–4).

1332 paradys terrestre: For the notion of marriage as an earthly paradise or an earthly purgatory, cf. IV.1265, 1647, 1670–73; and WBPro III.489–90 and n. On the image of paradise in the tale, see Richardson, Blameth Nat Me, 133–35; Kenneth A. Bleeth, in Learned and Lewed, ed. Benson, 45–60. Connected with the paradisal theme are the garden images later in the tale; cf IV.2029–41 and nn. Also relevant is the common justification of marriage as the only sacrament established in paradise. Cf. ParsT X.918–21.

1334–36 O flessh . . . oon herte: Cf. *Roman de la rose* (16435–44; tr. Dahlberg, 277: "Christ . . . made one flesh of us two, and when we have only one flesh . . . there can be only a single heart on the left side of one flesh") and Gen. 2.24 (as quoted in 1325–29 above).

1341 no tonge telle: A common formula; cf. Tr 4.1695–96 ("ne tonge telle"), Tr 5.445 ("That tonge telle or herte may recorde"), Tr 5.1321 ("That tonge telle or herte may devyse"); RomB 3183 ("Noon herte may thenke, ne tunge seyn"); perhaps influenced by 1 Cor. 2.9: "Eye hath not seen nor ear heard, neither have entered into the heart of man, the things which God hath prepared for them that love him."

1343 She kepeth his good: Cf. ShipT VII.243–44.

1345 "nay" . . . "ye":   Cf. ClT IV.355.

1362   Lat. gloss: "Jacob, on the advice of his mother Rebecca" (Albertanus, Lib. cons. 5; cf. Gen. 27.1–29).

1362–74   The examples of wise womanly counsel are all from Albertanus's *Liber consolationis*. They appear also in Mel VII.1098–1102, which this passage may echo. Details not in Albertanus or Melibee may come from Deschamps (IV.1366–68 from Miroir 9107–16; IV.1371–74 from Miroir 9135–49, in S&A, 338) or directly from the Bible (**the kydes skyn** from Gen. 27.16: "And she put the skins of the kids of the goats upon his hands, and upon the smooth of his neck"; **whil he slepte** may have been suggested by Judith 13.1–9).

Because the counsels of these women were variously deceitful, many critics read the exempla as sharply satiric (e.g., L. L. Besserman, Hebrew Univ. Sts. in Lit. 6, 1978, 19–20). But some recent critics have also observed the positive typological value of these women for medieval exegetes and liturgists, and argue for reading them in a positive sense (e.g., Ruth M. Ames, 90–91, in Acta IV, ed. Paul E. Szarmach and Bernard S. Levy, 1978); for an interpretation that includes both positive and negative viewpoints, see Emerson Brown, Jr., Viator 5, 1974, 410–12.

1366   Lat. gloss: "Judith, etc. from the hands of Holofernes" (Albertanus, Lib. cons. 5; cf. Judith chapters 11–13).

1369   Lat. gloss: "And through her good counsel Abigail freed her husband Nabal from the wrath of David" (Albertanus, Lib. cons. 5; cf. 1 Kings [AV 1 Sam] 25.1–35).

1371   Lat. gloss: "Through good counsel, Esther along with Mordecai [saved] the Jews in the kingdom of Ahasuerus" (Albertanus, Lib. cons. 5; cf. Esther 7.1–10).

1375   Lat. gloss: "Seneca [error for Fulgentius, *Mythologies* 1.22]: 'As nothing is better than a humble wife, nothing is more savage than an aggressive woman'" (Albertanus, Lib. cons. 5, quoting Dicta Catonis 3.23).

1377 Catoun: "Dionysius' Cato; Dicta Cantonis 3.23, quoted in Lib. cons. 5, which appears as a marginal Lat. gloss: "Be mindful to suffer your wife's tongue, if she is worthy." On Chaucer's use of Cato, see MilT I.3227n.

1380   Lat. gloss: "A good wife is a good and faithful keeper of the household" (Albertanus, De amore Dei, fol. 40v).

1381–82 sike man: Cf. Ecclus. 36.27: "Where there is no hedge, possessions will be spoiled; and woman he who is needy (*egens*) will mourn." The change of the Bible's "needy" (*egens*) to "sick" (*eger*) betrays Chaucer's debt to Albertanus's *De amore Dei* (see introductory note to Melibee), which quotes the verse with the variant *eger* (fol. 40r).

1383   Lat. gloss: "The Apostle Paul to the Ephesians [Eph. 5.25]: 'Love your wives as Christ loved the Church, etc.'"

1385   Lat. gloss: "The Apostle [says] [Eph. 5.28–29]: 'So ought men to love their wives as their own bodies, because he that loveth his wife [loveth himself]. No man ever hated his own flesh, but nourisheth it and cherisheth it.' And later [Eph. 5.33], 'Let every man love his wife as himself.'" This selection of verses here and at 1383 was made by Albertanus in De amore Dei, fols. 39v–40r. Cf. ParsT X.929.

1393 Januarie: Chaucer's name for his *senex amans* may have been suggested by the January-April marriage in Deschamps's ballade "Contre les mariages disproportionnés" (Oeuvres 5:63–64). See Norman F. Eliason, Names 21, 1973, 140. January is etymologically connected with the two-faced god Janus, associated with gates, trade, doubleness, and other matters appropriate to the tale (Emerson Brown, Jr., Names 31, 1983, 79–87).

1401 pittes brynke: Cf. the biblical use of "pit" as a figure for death or hell, e.g., Ps. 87.5 (AV 88.4: "them that go down to the pit"), Ezek. 31.14 ("them that go down to the pit"), Rev. 9.1–3 ("he opened the bottomless pit; and there arose a smoke out of the pit, as the smoke of a great furnace").

1417 twenty: Sixteen is the reading of some MSS and editors (Donaldson, Pratt), which may add to the humor. But twenty is still young; cf. Anel 78: "Yong was this quene, of twenty yer of elde."

1418–20 Oold fissh and yong flessh: Proverbial after Chaucer (cf. Whiting F236). However, not all authorities consider an old pike better eating than a young one (Mortimer J. Donovan, PQ 31, 1952, 441).

1424 Wades boot: Robinson noted that Speght's comment on this (in his 1598 ed.) "has often been called the most exasperating note ever written on Chaucer: 'Concerning Wade and his bote called Guingelot, as also his strange exploits in the same, because the matter is long and fabulous, I passe it over.' If Speght really knew the story and understood the allusion, he was more fortunate than later editors. For though there are a number of references in medieval literature which indicate he was a famous hero, they do not suffice for the reconstruction of the narrative as it was known to Chaucer." Detailed reviews of the available evidence on Wade and speculation on this reference may be found in Karl P. Wentersdorf, JEGP 65, 1966, 274–86. Baugh (135) takes *tolde tale of Wade* in Tr 3.614 (Chaucer's only other use) to mean "told a tall story"; perhaps here the reference merely connotes deceit.

1427–28 Cf. WBPro III.44c–e; Whiting S90. On the differences between the Merchant's and the Wife's expressions of the idea, see David W. Harrington, N&Q 11, 1964, 166–67.

1430 warm wex: Robert A. Pratt (Spec 41, 1966, 637) shows that the image is suggested by John of Wales's *Communiloquium,* quoting Anselm of Canterbury: "Soft wax easily takes the impression of a seal and retains it when it is hardened. The same is true of the easily molded state of childhood."

1441–95 the cause why: Cf. ParsT X.883, 939–43, and 939n. The views of medieval theologians and canonists on the motives for marriage and intercourse are discussed in relation to the MerT by Kelly, Love and Marriage, 245–74; and Patterson, Traditio 34:363–66.

1446–47 may nat lyven chaast: Cf. 1 Cor. 7.2: "Nevertheless, to avoid fornication, let every man have his own wife."

1452 dette: See WBPro III.129–30n.

1454 as a suster: Cf. ParsT X.861.

1456 that am nat I: Cf. WBPro III.112 and Mel VII.1088 (almost identical).

1461 tree: On the iconographic contexts of the Merchant's literal and figural trees, see Anthony Annunziata, in Acta IV, ed. Paul Szarmach and Bernard Levy, 1978, 128–33.

1469 Diverse men: See RvPro I.3857 and n.

1476 Placebo: Lat. "I shall please." The word is often associated with flattery, especially in the phrase "to sing Placebo," meaning "to flatter." Cf. SumT III.2075n. and ParsT X.617n.; Whiting P248.

1485–86 Wirke alle thyng by conseil: proverbial (Whiting C470); see MilT I.3530n.

1516 hangeth on a joly pyn: Perhaps with connotations of amorous desire (Pratt, Tales, 350).

1523–25 A paraphrase of "Cui des, videto" ("Consider to whom you give," Dicta Catonis, 17). The proverb is given without attribution and followed by the sentiment of IV.1526–29 in Walter Map's letter of Valerius to Rufinus (in De nugis curialium, tr. in Hanna and Lawler, Jankyn's Book, 128). Misattribution of ethical maxims to **Senek**

(Seneca) was common in the Middle Ages; almost all of Chaucer's quotations from Seneca are from John of Wales's *Communiloquium* (Pratt, Spec 41:619–42).

1530–39 On inquiring into the qualities of a wife before marriage, see WBPro III.285–92; Adv. Jov. 1.47 (S&A, 211; tr. Hanna and Lawler, Jankyn's Book, 150); Miroir 1553–75 (S&A, 216–17).

1536 mannyssh wood: See MED, s.v. *mannish* adj. 2; and Francis Lee Utley, MLN 53, 1938, 359–62; cf. MLT II.782, Tr 1.283–84: Crisyede is so womanly "that creature/ Was nevere lasse mannyssh in semynge."

1553 wringeth me my shoo: Cf. WBPro III.492n.

1561 Cf. *Roman de la rose* 13851–52; tr. Dahlberg, 238: "He who thinks that he can keep his wife to himself has very little knowledge."

1568–69 panyer ful of herbes: Perhaps an ironic allusion to an episode in the Life of Aesop, in which Aesop's master's learning is less effective than Aesop's common sense at explaining the nature of such a basket (Nicolai von Kreisler, ChauR 6, 1971, 30–37).

1577–87 The ME term **fantasye** was applied variously to the mental faculties involved in the reception or retention of sensory impressions, or to the formation, perhaps deluded, of mental images and ideas (MED s.v. *fantasie* n. 1a). Cf. Tr 1.296–98: "So gret desir and such affeccioun,/ That in his herte botme gan to stiken/ Of hir his fixe and depe impressioun." For the mirror image here, cf. the mirrors of Bo 5.m4.26–27 ("yeldith ymages ydel and vein in the manere of a mirour") and Tr 1.365 ("Thus gan he make a mirour of his mynde").

1598 love is blynd: On Cupid's traditional blindness, see KnT I.1963–65n.

1662 right of hooly chirche: The burial service (Robert A. Wichert, Expl 25, 1966, Item 32; OED s.v. *right* sb. I 1C); or perhaps the solemnization of the marriage (so Robinson and others; MED lists *right* as a variant spelling of *rite* n.)

1670 purgatorie: Cf. 1332 above and WBPro III.489–90 and n.

1685–87 This intrusive reference to the Wife has exercised critics since Skeat (5:359); see introductory note.

1693 Mayus: "A masculine form, because the name of the month is so" (Skeat 5:359); used for the sake of the meter (Baugh 448; see also Eliason, Names 21:140).

1700–1708 While not complete, this sketch of the wedding service matches surviving fourteenth-century English marriage rites fairly well. The priest's "coming forth" refers to the wedding proper, performed at the church door before the nuptial Mass (see GP I.460 and n.). See also the Sarum Missal (tr. in Miller, Ch: Sources and Backgrounds, 374–84).

1702 the hooly sacrament: Probably marriage, but the Eucharist has also been suggested, since the bride and groom received it at the nuptial Mass (John S. P. Tatlock, MLN 32, 1917, 374).

1704 Sarra and Rebekke: Referring to the prayer in the marriage service that the wife be as "wise as Rebecca, long-lived and faithful as Sarah" (tr. in Miller, Ch: Sources and Backgrounds, 381).

1716 Orpheus: Orpheus, the famous harper, descended into the underworld, where his harping so charmed Pluto that he allowed him to take his wife Eurydice back to the land of the living (but he looked back, violating the conditions laid down by Pluto, and lost her forever). Chaucer knew the story from Boethius (Bo 3.m12), Ovid (Metamorphoses 10.1–85), and Virgil (Georgics 4.454–527). See John B. Friedman, Orpheus, 1970, 90–117.

Amphioun: Ruler of Thebes who moved rocks for the city walls by the power of his music; his story was common—in Statius (Theb. 1.9–10, 8.232–33, 10.873–77), Ovid (Met. 6.178–79), and other sources. Cf. KnT I.1546; MancT IX.116–17.

1719 Joab: See 2 Kings (AV 2 Sam.) 2.28 ("So Joab blew a trumpet, and all the people stood still and pursued after Israel no more"), 18.16, 20.22. Joab is also associated with Theodomas in HF 1245–46: "There herde I trumpe Joab also,/ Theodomas, and other mo."

1720 Theodomas: Augur for the Argive besiegers of Thebes after Amphiaraus's death. Statius does not say that he was a trumpeter, but his first prayer as augur was followed at once by the trumpets of the attacking Thebans, and more trumpets followed a raid on the Thebans that he later inspired (Thebaid, tr. Mozley, 8.275–347, 10.160–553).

1727 fyrbrond: Associated with Venus in Roman de la rose 3424–26 (RomB 3705–10: "in hir right hond/ Of brennyng fyr a blasyng brond") and PF 113–14: "Cytherea . . . / That with thy fyrbrond dauntest whom the lest"; cf. 1777 below.

1730 Ymeneus: Cf. LGW 2250 ("Imeneus that god of wedyng is"); Roman de la rose 21020; tr. Dahlberg, 343 ("Hymen and Juno are the true gods of weddings").

1732 Marcian: Martianus Capella (fifth century), who wrote De Nuptiis Philologiae et Mercurii (The Marriage of Philology and Mercury), tr. William H. Stahl, Richard Johnson, E. L. Burge, 1977.

1734 hym Mercurie: For the construction, cf. KnT I.1210. See Language and Versification, p. xxxiii.

1736–37 The rhetorical "inexpressibility" topos; cf. KnT I.1459–60n.

1744–45 Ester: Esther the biblical heroine (Book of Esther), celebrated for her beauty and meekness before King Ahasuerus. Cf. BD 985–87 ("she/ Had as moche debonairte/ As ever had Hester in the Bible"), LGW ProF 250 ("Ester, ley thou thy meknesse al adown").

1762–63 January's thoughts and words here and in IV.1855–56 parody traditional formulas in lovers' aubes, dawn songs (Robert E. Kaske, MLN 75, 1960, 1–4); cf. RvT I.4235–40.

1772 Damyan: Philip Mahone Griffith (Expl 16, 1957, Item 13) argues that St. Damian was a patron saint of physicians and suggests that by naming January's squire Damian, Chaucer may have been underlining the theme of healing in the tale. Against this view, see Eliason, Names 21:140.

1773 carf biforn the knyght: Cf. GP I.100, SumT III.2243–44.

1777 hire brond: Cf. 1727 above.

1783 The Ellesmere, Hengwrt, and several other MSS have the gloss "Auctor" in the margin here and at IV.1869, 2057, 2107, and 2125 (these last two lacking in Hengwrt), perhaps indicating scribal awareness of the narrator's intrusions at these places. Cf. MLT II.358n.

1786 naddre in bosom: Proverbial phrase based on a com-

mon fable of a man warming a snake in his bosom, only to have it turn and poison him. Whiting A42; Gesta Romanorum, ch. 174 (tr. Swan, 364–65).

1793–94 hoomly foo: For the sentiment expressed here and in IV.1784 (famulier foo), see Bo 3.pr5.68–70: "And what pestilence is more myghty for to anoye a wyght than a famylier enemy?"

1795–99 An elaborate chronographia; see GP I.7–8n. (at end).

1807 ypocras: Wine mixed with sugar and spices and drained through a strainer, called by apothecaries "Hippocrates' sleeve" (MED s.v. ipocras n.); for directions for making the beverage, see The Babees' Book, EETS 32, 125–28, and Curye on Inglysch, EETS s.s. 8, 196–97.

clarree: Wine mixed with honey and spices; see I.1471n.
vernage: "Vernaccia," a strong Italian wine; see ShipT VII.70–71 and n.

1808 t'encreessen his corage: Paul Delany notes that the spiced wines January drinks were thought to give the body heat and moisture, necessary for lusty, fertile intercourse, and to stimulate the heart, which produced a "windy spirit" responsible for erection (PQ 46, 1967, 561–62; see also Brown, NM 74:100–2).

1810–11 Constantyn: Constantinus Afer, or Africanus, eleventh-century translator of Arabic medical texts; cf. GP I.433 and I.429–34n. For his life and work, and the possible intent of the epithet cursed, see Maurice Bassan MS 24, 1962, 127–40. His treatise De coitu (tr. Paul Delany, ChauR 4, 1970, 55–65) describes the nature of intercourse and prescribes foods and potions (letuaries) for male sexual disorders, especially impotence. On the use of the title daun, see KnT I.1379n.

1819 The blessing of the wedding chamber and bed was a common though not essential feature of later medieval English weddings. See Tatlock, MLN 32:374, and the Sarum Missal (tr. in Miller, Ch: Sources and Backgrounds, 383–84).

1825 houndfyssh: The skin of the dogfish was used by medieval carpenters as a sort of sandpaper or rough polishing cloth (Burrow, Ricardian Poetry, 137). Older men at this time generally wore beards; younger men were cleanshaven; cf. Thop VII.730–31n.

1832–33 werke wel and hastily: Possibly proverbial but not recorded before Chaucer (Whiting W652).

1840 owene knyf: Cf. ParsT X.859n. On the sources of the expression, and the canonists' views on sexual sin in marriage, see Kelly, Love and Marriage, 245–85; Patterson, Traditio 34:359–60; and Malcolm Andrew, ELN 16, 1979, 273–77.

1842 laboureth: Cf. ShipT VII.108, and compare WBPro III.202.

1843 sop in fyn clarree: Bread soaked in wine; perhaps a morning-after restorative (Earle Birney N&Q 6, 1959, 347), though a sop was the usual light breakfast (cf. GP I.334).

1847–48 coltish . . . ragerye: Cf. MilT I.3263; RvPro I.3888; WBPro III.455–56, 602. On ragerye, see Douglas Moffat, NM 94, 1993, 167–84.

1862 labour . . . reste: Cf. SqT V.349, Roman de la rose 19731–32; tr. Dahlberg, 325 ("Nothing can last long without rest"); Whiting L5.

1967 destynee or aventure: Cf. GP I.844n.

1969 constellacion: See WBPro III.615n.

1972 alle thyng hath tyme: Proverbial; cf. FrT III.1475n.

1986   Chaucer's favorite line; see KnT I.1761n.

2014 dogge for the bowe: Cf. Whiting D303, and see FrT III.1369.

2021–22 felicitee . . . delit: Cf. GP I.335–38, Bo 3.pr2.77–80 ("The whiche delit oonly considered Epicurus, and juggid and establissyde that delyt is the soverayn good").

2029–37   On January's garden, and its well and laurel, see, among others, J. A. Burrow, Anglia 75, 1957, 203–5; Bleeth, in Learned and Lewed, 45–60; and Carol Falvo Heffernan, PLL 15, 1979, 346–50. The enclosed garden itself recalls the "hortus conclusus" of the Song of Songs (Cant. 4.12: "a garden enclosed is my sister, my spouse"), commonly taken as a symbol of the Virgin. It is a version of the conventional *locus amoenus* ("pleasance"), common in classical and medieval poetry (see Curtius, Europ. Lit., 195–202) and defined for the later Middle Ages by *Le Roman de la rose*.

2032 Romance of the Rose: *Le Roman de la rose* opens with an elaborate description of a walled garden which contains the fountain of Narcissus; see RomA 475–700, 1349–1444 (*Roman de la rose* 463–699, 1323–1424; tr. Dahlberg, 37–40, 48–50).

2034–35   On **Priapus,** cf. Ovid, Fasti 1.391–440, 6.319–48. The phrase **god of gardyns** could be due to Boccaccio's "(id)dio degli orti," in the "chiose" (glosses) to the *Teseida* (ed. Limentani, 403, 466), though Chaucer's knowledge of them has been questioned (see introductory note to KnT notes); Priapus was also a phallic god, associated with comically frustrated lust. Cf. PF 253–59; Ovid, Fasti, tr. Frazer, 1.425–40.

2045–46 clyket and **wyket** may be a double entendre for male and female genitalia. See John Bugge (AnM 14, 1973, 55–58), citing a number of medieval parallels.

2048   Cor. 7.3: "Let the husband render the debt [*debitum*] to the wife and likewise the wife to the husband." Cf. WBPro III.198n.

2058–60   The **scorpion** was a common symbol of treachery; see MLT II.404n.

2106 the fyn of his entente: Cf. Tr 3.125: "To telle me the fyn of his entente."

2111 Argus: The hundred-eyed guardian of Io; cf. WBPro III.357–60 and n.

2115 Passe over is an ese: Proverbial; cf. Whiting P44.

2126–27 sleighte . . . Love nyl fynde: Cf. LGW 742; "But what is that that love can nat espye?"; Ovid, Met. 4.68: "What does love not see?"

2128 Piramus and Tesbee: their story is told in LGW 706–923 and in Ovid, Met. 4.55–166.

2133   This line confused the scribes, all of whom wrote *juyl* (July) for *juyn* (June); (cf. 2222, where there is no disagreement and the time is fixed in June).

2138–48   An assemblage of phrases from the Song of Songs, the details of which derive from Jerome (Adv. Jov. 1.30–31, tr. Fremantle, 368–70). On Chaucer's use of the Song here and elsewhere in the tale, see James I. Wimsatt, in Ch the Love Poet, 84–90; Kenneth A. Bleeth, in Learned and

Lewed, ed. Benson, 54–56; and Douglas Wurtele, ChauR 13, 1978, 66–79, and AnM 21, 1981, 91–110.

2138–40   Cant. 2.10–12: "Rise up, my love, my fair one, and come away. For lo, the winter is past, the rain is over and gone; the flowers appear on the earth, the time of the singing of birds is come, and the voice of the turtle is heard in our land."

2141   Cant. 1.15:   "Behold thou art fair, my love; behold thou art fair; thou hast dove's eyes [*oculi tui columbarum*]."

2142   Cant. (AV differs) 4.10: "How beautiful are thy breasts, my sister and spouse, thy breasts are more beautiful than wine."

2143   Cant. 4.12: "A garden enclosed is my sister, my spouse." On the enclosed garden (*hortus conclusus*) see 2029–37 above.

2144–45   Cant. 4.8–9: "Come from Lebanon, my spouse . . . you have wounded my heart, sister mine, spouse, you have wounded my heart with one of your eyes."

2146   Cant. 4.7: "Thou art all fair, my love; there is no spot in thee."

2147   Cant. 2.13: "Arise, my love, my fair one, come away."

2148   Cant. 5.1: "My chosen one comes into his garden."

2176 covenant: An echo of the OT term for the union between the "jealous" Yahweh and Israel commonly used in ME biblical translations (OED, s.v. *covenant* sb. 7a; MED, s.v. *covenaunt* n. 1c).

2217 pyrie: On the phallic symbolism of the pear, see Paul A. Olson, ELH 28, 1961, 207n.; and MilT I.3248n. The lyric "I have a new garden" (Sec. Lyrics, ed. Robbins, No. 21) tells of a maiden who "preyid me/ for to gryffyn her a gryf/ of myn pery tre." Pregnancy results.

2222 Geminis: V. A. Kolve, in a paper delivered at the 1980 MLA meeting in Houston and in subsequent personal correspondence, notes that depictions of Gemini develop from pictures of two wrestling youths (as in Oxford, Bodleian Library, MS Douce 144, fol. 10r) to pictures of an embracing couple, often surrounded by trees and bushes—a posture and setting not unlike those of May and Damian later in the poem.

2225–2319   Older critics see the Pluto and Proserpina episode as a digression or intrusion (e.g., Kittredge, MP 9:455; Bertrand H. Bronson, SP 58, 1961, 595); most recent critics regard it as an integral part of the whole tale (e.g., Patterson, Ch. and Hist., 341–44). See also Elizabeth Simmons-O'Neill, MLQ 51, 1990, 389–407.

The argument between Pluto and Proserpina is sometimes read as the bitter, vindictive result of an unhappy marriage (e.g., Marcia A. Dalbey, NM 75, 1978, 408–15), but more often as an amusing, relatively good-natured squabble between a couple who have learned to disagree amicably. Their marriage began with a rape, but Jill Mann notes that "Pluto is probably the only example in literature of a henpecked rapist" (Ch: Feminist Readings, 66).

2230 Ethna: Although Proserpina was actually abducted from the fields of Enna, Claudian (see 2232 below) frequently describes those fields as the countryside or valleys of Etna.

2232 Claudyan: Claudius Claudianus (d. A.D. 408?), author of the unfinished poem, The Rape of Proserpine. On Chaucer's use of Claudian, see Robert A. Pratt, Spec 22, 1947, 419–29; Donovan, in Ch Probs, 59–69.

stories: The MSS appear to support the plural here, but it is still unclear why Chaucer would choose the plural— Donovan (in Ch Probs, 63) suggests a "loose usage" in which *stories* refers to the books or even smaller divisions into which The Rape of Proserpine is organized.

2242 Salomon: Known as the author of the Song of Songs and Proverbs and celebrated not only for his wealth and wisdom but for idolatry, magical skill (cf. SqT V.250), and lechery (cf. WBPro III.35n.). On the rhetorical strategy of this speech, see Besserman, Ch's Biblical Poetics, 128–31.

2247–48 thousand...foond I oon: Eccles. 7.29 (AV 7.28), quoted in Mel VII.1057: "For 'of a thousand men,' seith Salomon, 'I foond o good man, but certes, of alle wommen, good womman foond I nevere.'"

2250–51 Jhesus, *filius Syrak*: Ecclesiasticus, in the Vulgate OT, is ascribed to Jesus, son of Sirach; for a sample of its misogyny, see the verse quoted at Mel VII.1059.

2257 lechour: William W. Main (Expl 14, 1955, Item 13) and Philip M. Griffith (Expl 16:13) argue for a play on the word *lecher*, "healer, leacher"; however, that word is very rare, appearing in Middle English only in Chaucer's Bo 4 pr6.215 ("God, governour and lechere of thoughtes"); cf. MED s.v. *lechere* n.

2265 Saturn was the father of Ceres, Proserpina's mother. See Ovid, Fasti 6.285–86.

2277–90 Cf. Mel VII.1076–79; IV.2280–83 may recall Deschamps's Miroir 9064–67, which immediately precedes a list of virgin martyrs, followed by the references to Judith and Esther, which Chaucer may have drawn on for IV.1366–68, 1371–74; IV.2284–85 may stem from Jerome's list of virtuous Roman wives in Adv. Jov. 1.46 (tr. Hanna and Lawler, Jankyn's Book, 172–74).

2284 Romayn geestes: Cf. MLT II.1126 n.

2290 noon but God: Cf. Mark 10.18: "There is no good but one, that is, God."

2298–2302 3 Kings (AV 1 Kings) 11.1–13.

2321–22 Cf. *Roman de la rose* 10097–98; tr. Dahlberg, 180 ("gayer than parrots"); see ShipT VII.38n., Thop VII.767n.

2330–37 May's alleged craving for fruit and the pregnancy implied thereby have been compared to Mary's hunger in the Cherry-Tree Carol (Child, Ballads, no. 54). On pears and pregnancy see Carol A. Everest in Melitta Weiss Adamson, ed., Food in the Middle Ages, 1995, 161-75; however, Carol A. Everest also notes (in Muriel Whittaker, ed., Sovereign Lady: Essays on Women and M. E. Literature, 1995, 63–84) that the medical doctrine held that female orgasm was necessary for conception and, if May is pregnant, January is probably not responsible.

2367 stronge lady: Brown (Viator 5:406) sees an allusion here to the "mulier fortis" of Prov. 31.10: "A strong woman who shal fynden? For her price is far above rubies" (tr. Wyclif; AV has "virtuous woman").

stoore: Kean (Ch and Poetry 1:19–20) suggests that *strong lady stoore* ironically echoes the abusive colloquial epithet *stronge hore*, as in the Sultan of Babylon (ed. Alan Lupack in Three ME Charlemagne Romances, 1990), 2223: "A! stronge hore, god gife the sorowe!" Four MSS and some early editions in fact alter *stoore* to *hore* (Manly-Rickert 6:495). Cf. MED s.v. *strong* adj. 11(c).

Epilogue to the Merchant's Tale

2422 bisy as bees: Proverbial; see SNT VIII.195n.

2426 as trewe as any steel: Proverbial; Whiting S709. The phrase appears also in PF 395, LGW ProF 334, LGW 2582, Tr 5.831, RomB 5146.

2427–34 Cf. ClT IV.1212b–d, ProMkT VII.1889–923.

2436–38 "The reference to the Wife of Bath is sufficiently clear" (Robinson); for 2438, cf. WBPro III.521.

FRAGMENT V

Fragments IV and V form a single unit: both the Hengwrt and the Ellesmere MSS treat the epilogue to The Merchant's Tale and the introduction to The Squire's Tale (IV.2420–V.8) as one continuous speech, labeled in Ellesmere as "The Prologue to The Squire's Tale." Even though in the scribal orders The Squire's and Franklin's Tales are displaced (and the link altered accordingly), "The Merchant's Endlink and The Squire's Headlink . . . always appear as a unit" (M–R 2:284). The displacement of The Squire's and Franklin's Tales in the scribal tradition may suggest they are easily separated, but the integrity of Fragment V is offered some support by several, mostly recent, critical studies: Carol Heffernan, ChauR 32, 1997, 32–45 (on female power and the Orient in SqT and FrkT); Jennifer Goodman, in Bonnie Wheeler, ed., Feminea Medievalia I, 1993, 69–90 (on the despair that links the falcon and Dorigen); Brian S. Lee, YES 22, 1992, 190–200 (FrkT as the "rhetorical conclusion" to the SqT).

Introduction to The Squire's Tale

The explanatory notes to The Squire's Prologue and Tale are adapted from those written by Vincent J. DiMarco for The Riverside Chaucer.

2 sey somwhat of love: "On the character of the Squire and the appropriateness of the request here, see GP I.79–100" (Robinson).

The Squire's Tale

Robinson believed that The Squire's Tale was late and that the "note of time" in line 73 suggests that Chaucer "was writing with the Canterbury scheme in mind." However, some critics have argued for a pre-Canterbury version (e.g., Charles Larson, Rev. des langues vivantes 43, 1977, 598–607), and there are a number of parallels with *Anelida and Arcite* (see below), which may argue for an early date. Older scholars attempted to link the poem with some contemporary court scandal (such as the love affair of Joan of Kent and Thomas Holland, which would put it in 1385; see Margaret Galway, MLR 33, 1938, 180–81), but this is not likely. J. D. North, Ch's Universe, 274, decides on astronomical grounds that the year is 1383, though that is surely too early. There is no clear evidence to settle the matter.

Chaucer claims a source ("as the storie telleth us," line 655), but none has been discovered nor is likely to be. The tale is a miscellany of various motifs, allusions, story patterns, pseudo-scientific lore, and reminiscences of travelers and merchants.

For the details of Cambyuskan's court Chaucer may have drawn upon accounts of the Mongols by missionaries such as John of Plano Carpini and Simon of St. Quentin (included in Vincent of Beauvais, Speculum historiale, bk. 31). The famous letter of Prester John (see John L. Lowes, Wash. Univ. Sts. 1, no. 2, 1913, 3–18), which mentions a king of Arabia and India who owns a magic mirror and sends another monarch a magic ring, offers closer parallels of setting than the *Travels* of Marco Polo, which appears to have been a rare book in fourteenth-century England (John M. Manly, PMLA 11, 1896, 349–62). The *Travels* of Sir John Mandeville may have supplied some details of the Mongols' eating habits (see 67–71 below). It also provided Chaucer's audience with a convenient account of the Mameluke kingdom of Egypt, apparently identified with that of *Arabe and of Inde*. See Vincent J. DiMarco, Edebiyat, n.s. 1:2, 1989, 1–22. On the fact that Chaucer treats the eastern setting with sympathy (as opposed to the treatment of Islam in MLT and medieval Jewry in PrT), see John M. Fyler, in Donald Maddox and Sara Sturm-Maddox, eds., Literary Aspects of Courtly Culture, 1994, 257–63, and Kathryn L. Lynch (Spec 70, 1995, 530–51).

The four magic gifts of the tale are common in medieval literature (see W. A. Clouston, Magical Elements in the SqT, Ch Soc, 2nd ser. 26, 1889), but the closest analogues to the magic horse in Chaucer's tale are in the two late-thirteenth-century romances, the *Cléomadès* of Adenet le Rois (in Œuvres, ed. Albert Henry, 1951–81; excerpted in S&A, 364–74) and *Méliacin ou le Cheval de Fust* of Girart d'Amiens (ed. Antoinette Saly, 1990). The story of Canacee and her brothers is likewise without any close analogues (but see Dorothee Metlitzki, Matter of Araby in Med. Engl., 1977, 144–52).

Ultimately the story of the betrayed falcon may be of Oriental origin, but no very close analogues have been found. In situation and often phrasing, the falcon episode resembles Chaucer's own *Anelida and Arcite*: see 537, 569, 610, 644–46 below. For Chaucer's use of the story of betrayed love in The Squire's Tale and *Anelida*, see Alfred David, SAC, Proceedings 1, 1984, 105–15.

In form the poem is a romance, though many critics have found it either satiric (M. C. Seymour, ES 70, 1989, 311–15) or atypical of the genre. However, Jennifer Goodman (SAC 5, 1983, 127–36) has shown the poem's affinities in structure and matter, including even the possible incest motif, with the late "composite romances," such as Valentine and Orson, and Generides (see Lillian Hornstein, Manual ME, 1:147–67). This was the sort of romance that was to become popular in the fifteenth century. Nevertheless, Robert R. Edwards (in Ratio and Invention, 1989, 131–45) finds it an experiment that failed (see also John M. Fyler, ELH 55, 1988, 1–26). Most critics agree that the Squire somehow loses control over his material. Angela Jane Weisl, Conquering the Reign of Femeny, 50–61, sees this as an opportunity for Chaucer to explore the contrast between the tightly controlled structure of The Knight's Tale, in which the voice of Emelye is stifled, and the looser Squire's Tale, in which Canacee is heard. Ian Bishop (Narrative Art of the CT, 1984, 50) finds it Chaucer's "positive response to the elements of romance that fascinated him," encapsulated in two scenes, "the one predominantly masculine and public, the other entirely feminine and intimate." See also Crane, Gender and Romance, 66–73, who argues that The Squire's Tale draws

on *Le Roman de la rose* but "resists the complicity between courtly and misogynist constructions of the feminine that Jean de Meun's text illustrates."

The tale is notable for its heavy use of astronomy; North (Ch's Universe, 263–88) reads it as a kind of astronomical allegory. See Patterson, Ch and Subj. of Hist., 216–22, on the aristocratic "obsession" with astronomy.

With the exception of the fifteenth-century Jean of Angoulême (Paul Strohm, NM 72, 1971, 69–76), most readers of the tale until well into the twentieth century were warmly admiring, most famously Edmund Spenser (see below) and John Milton (II Penseroso, 109–10: "Or call up him who left half told/ The story of Cambuskan old"). Modern critics, until quite recently, have tended to dismiss the tale as a means of satirizing its teller and his rhetorical excesses. Critics today generally find the satire gentle and the poem at least congenial. For a full bibliography and survey of scholarship (to 1987), see the Variorum edition (vol. 2, pt. 12), The Squire's Tale, ed. Donald C. Baker, 1990.

The poem abruptly ends after a promise of a narrative that would have continued for several thousand lines, much longer even than The Knight's Tale. Chaucer probably intended the tale to remain unfinished (see William Kamowski, Style 31, 1997, 391–412). There is a spurious brief scribal conclusion in the Lansdowne MS (see M–R 2:297). Continuations were written by Spenser (Faerie Queene, IV.5) and John Lane, whose work was licensed in 1614–15 but first printed in 1887 (ed. F. J. Furnivall, Ch Soc, 2nd ser. 23). On the various endings supplied by scribes and modern writers, see John Burrow, SAC 13, 1991, 17–37 (esp. 21–28). Stephen B. Partridge in a forthcoming article (to appear in Medieval English Manuscripts and Books: Essays in Memory of Jeremy Griffiths) shows that a number of MSS have a note that Chaucer left the work unfinished (see 672 below); that note, Partridge shows, may be due to Chaucer himself.

9 Sarray: The modern Tsarev, near Volgograd in southeastern Russia; see Magoun, Ch Gazetteer, 138–39.

Tartarye: The Mongol or "Tartar" empire, though sometimes used loosely for outer Mongolia; see BD 1025 ("To Pruyse, and into Tartarye") and Magoun, Ch Gazetteer, 151.

12 Cambyuskan: In form, probably corresponding to Genghis (Chingiz) Khan, Latinized Camius Khan. Skeat (5:33) felt the description better suited Genghis's grandson Kublai, whose court at Cambaluc (Beijing) Marco Polo visited; Robinson notes that it was Batu, another grandson of Genghis, who *werreyed Russye* (see John of Plano Carpini, Hist. of the Mongols, tr. Dawson, 29–30).

16–27 On Cambyuskan as an example of a pagan who displays the noble virtues of natural (non-Christian) man, see Morton W. Bloomfield, Poetica 8, 1981, 29–30.

22 centre: For the center (of a circle) linked to the idea of stability, see Bo 4.pr6.116–29.

29–33 The names **Elpheta, Algarsyf, Cambalo,** and **Canacee** offer intriguing possibilities for an astrological allegory. Manly's suggestion that *Elpheta* corresponds in medieval starlists to alpha Coronae Borealis ("Alphecca" in Richard Hinckley Allen, Star Names, 1899 [1963], 178–79) has been endorsed by J. D. North (RES n. s. 20, 1969, 259–62) and Metlitzki (Matter of Araby, 78), who notes the "familial" aspects of the constellation. *Algarsyf* may derive from *saif al-jabbar* (Metlitzki, 79–80), "the sword of the giant," corresponding to *eta* of Orion (Allen, Star Names, 316); and, less probable, *Cambalo* may correspond (North, RES 20:257–62) to *cabalcet,* or Alpha Leonis (Allen, Star Names, 256). See North, Ch's Universe, 275–76.

Chaucer's use of the name *Canacee* may be explained by the incest motif possibly suggested in SqT V.667 (cf. IntrMLT II.77 and 77–89n.); but A. J. de H. Bushnell (Blackwood's 187, 1910, 655) notes the Mongol word for *princess* can be transliterated *kanaki.*

31 Cambalo: Cf. Cambalus (V.656), apparently referring to the same person. For the "Italian" form in *-o,* see MkT VII.2345n.

35–41 An elaborate example of the "inexpressibility" topos. See KnT I.1459–60n. and cf. 105–6 below.

39 colours: James J. Murphy (Rhet. in the M. A., 1974, 189–90) notes the use of the word *colour* as a medieval innovation, superseding *exornatio* and *figura.* He suggests that to Chaucer it meant any kind of decorated language. Cf. ClT IV.16n. and FranPro V.723–26n.

48–51 Since it is exactly 15 March (line 47), three days after the vernal equinox (12 March in Chaucer's time), the sun is about three degrees into Aries. This is an especially elaborate "chronographia" (see GP I.7–8n.), so elaborate that Wood (Ch and the Stars, 98–99) holds it is a parody. Since it is Cambyuskan's birthday, it is also a horoscope, as the use of the technical term **face** makes clear.

52–57 Cf. RomA 71–77: "The briddes . . . / Ben in May for the sonne brighte/ So glade . . . / That in her hertis is sich lykyng/ That they mote syngen and be light." For the **swerd of wynter,** cf. LGW ProF.126–27: "Wynter . . . with his swerd of cold."

67–71 European reports often mentioned the strange foods of the Mongols; see Bertold Spuler, Hist. of the Mongols, tr. Drummond and Drummond, 1972, 92–93, 176–77. On the basis of **knyghtes olde** Bennett suggests (MLN 68, 1953, 531–34) that Chaucer's source may be Mandeville's *Travels* (ed. Seymour, 1967, 180–81).

73 pryme: In ecclesiastical usage, corresponding to the first hour of the day, or sunrise (cf. PardT VI.662), but here used for the period between the first hour and tierce, which began after "full prime" or "prime large" (see V.360), or about 9:00 A.M.

80–81 In at the halle dor: A knight who rides into a hall during a feast is common in romance; cf. Sir Gawain and the Green Knight, 135–36: "[At the first course] Ther hales in at the halle dor an aghlich maister" [regularized]; B. J. Whiting (MS 9, 1947, 232) lists many other examples. Coolidge Otis Chapman (MLN 68, 1953, 521–24) noted the parallel with Sir Gawain, but there is no clear indication that Chaucer knew this romance.

90–97 The passage may be modeled on *Roman de la rose* 2087–114, tr. Dahlberg, 59–60 (RomB 2209–22); those lines praise Gawain for his courtesy (V.95) and emphasize the duty to salute nobles in a polite and courtly fashion (V.91–93).

95–96 For Gawain's reputation for courtesy, see Whiting, MS 9:189–234; for his association with the faerie-land Avalon, see Roger S. Loomis, MLN 52, 1937, 413–16. WBT III.857 similarly associates the Arthurian court with **Fairye,** there used in the general sense of magic and enchantment; Chaucer's reference here may be no more pointed.

99–104 Classical and medieval rhetorical theory described the appropriate delivery (*pronuntiatio*) of speeches with respect to voice, countenance, and gesture; see, e.g., Geoffrey of Vinsauf, *Poetria nova,* tr. Nims, 2031–66, and Tr 1.12–14: "For wel sit it . . . A woful wight to han a drery feere,/ And to a sorwful tale, a sory chere." For *pronuntiatio* in Chaucer, see Beryl Rowland, SAC 4, 1982, 33–52.

105–6 stile : style: The *rime riche* (see GP I.17–18n.) is clearly intended as a pun; cf. the Franklin's pun on *colours* (FranPro V.723–26). For the "affected modesty" topos employed here, see GP I.746n.

110 The kingdom of Arabe and of Inde refers to what was variously called India Minor or Middle India, now southern Arabia (Pratt, Tales, 375n.).

115–342 The magic **steed of bras** is described primarily as a mechanical aeronautical contrivance, controlled by the manipulation of various pegs (V.127, 314–30) and perhaps by the action of the rein (312–13) and bridle (340–42); it is no mere appearance or delusion (201, 218). There is a wide range of classical, medieval, and Renaissance speculation on flying contrivances; see Berthold Laufer, Prehist. of Aviation, 1928, 19–22. For literary parallels, see W. A. Clouston, Magical Elements, and Lowes, Univ. of Washington Sts. 1, 3–18. Vincent J. DiMarco (in Thomas Kühn and Ursula Schaefer, eds., Dialogische Strukturen/Dialogic Structures, 1996, 50–66) discusses the interrelations of "magic," "science," and the rational explanation of apparent marvels.

129–31 constellacion: Cf. KnT I.1088, WBPro III.616. One would make a **seel** (cf. GP I.417n.) when the stars were in the right position. **Bond** refers to the controlling force of the practitioner's knowledge (MED, s.v. *bond* 5[a]), unless used in a more technical sense (elsewhere unattested) related to this natural magic.

132–36 For the magic mirror, see 228–35 below.

145–46 heere : heere: The Hengwrt and Ellesmere scribe notes the *rime riche* by writing "hic" above the first *heere,* "audire" above the second. See GP 17–18n.

146–55 Canacee's ring gives her the power to understand and speak the language of birds (cf. Clouston, Magical Elements, 188, 348). It also gives her an expert knowledge of medicinal herbs. The magic ring is later associated with Moses and Solomon (see 250–51 below).

156 For the magic sword, see 236–40 below.

166 glose: lying; cf. SumT III.1792n.

171 stille as any stoon: Proverbial; Whiting S772.

184 "By no device of windlass or pulley." Just so in the *Méliacin,* lines 592–95, where the horse can be moved only by manipulating the pins.

193–95 Poilleys: Lombardian and Apulian (later known as Neapolitan) horses were held in high esteem; see Rowland (Blind Beasts, 123), who suggests that the Ellesmere illustration of the Squire may picture him on a Lombardy steed.

202 Diverse folk diversely: See RvPro I.3857 and n.

203 Proverbial (Whiting H230 and Walther 26216: "Quot homines, tot sententiae," as many opinions as men).

203–5 Chaucer elsewhere (Tr 4.183–89, ClT IV.995–1001n.) shows no great faith in the common opinion of the crowd;

Burrow (Ricardian Poetry, 122–25) sees an interest in crowd reactions as typical of the literature of the period.

207 the Pegasee: Glossed in Ellesmere and several other MSS as "equ[u]s Pegaseus, " from which adjectival form derives Chaucer's form in -ee. Pegasus was the fabulous winged horse of Bellerophon, the Muses, and Zeus.

209 Dictys Cretenses (tr. Richard M. Frazer, Jr.) agrees with Virgil that the horse was wooden, but Guido delle Colonne (Historia, tr. Mary Elizabeth Meek, 221) describes it as brass—perhaps, as Meek speculates, 305n., the result of a confusion of *abiete* (planks of fir) with *aerum* (bronze). Gower, in *Confessio amantis* 1.1131, following Guido delle Colonne, says the horse is brass, as does Caxton, *Recuyell of the historyes of Troye* [1474?], 3.28.

219 For illusionists in Chaucer's time, see FranT V.1141n.

220–23 Cf. Ovid, Tristia, tr. Wheeler, 4.2.25–26: "Some of the people will inquire the causes, the objects, the names, and others will answer though they know all too little."

224 Cf. Tr 2.271–72 ("tendre wittes wenen al be wyle/ Theras thei kan nought pleynly understonde").

228–35 The discussion of optics is based on *Le Roman de la rose,* 17993–18298 (tr. Dahlberg, 299–304), where a magic mirror like that in V.132–36 is mentioned and where both **Alocen** (Lat. Alhazen, Ibn al-Haitham, c. 965–1039, author of an influential treatise on optics) and **Aristotle** are mentioned (the latter perhaps because of his *Meteorologia* 3.2–4, where rainbows are explained as reflections). Chaucer adds **Vitulon** (Lat. Vitello), the Polish Witelo, author of a treatise on perspective (ante 1278) that drew on Alhazen's work. See Thorndike, Hist. of Magic 3:602–5, 707, and David C. Lindberg, Spec 46, 1971, 66–83.

231 in Rome was swich oon: Virgil was believed to have built a magic mirror that showed the image, whether by day or night, of approaching enemies, even if many miles distant. The story was widespread and Chaucer could have known it in Gower's *Confessio amantis* (5.2031–224) or some other version, though probably the discussion of such a mirror in *Le Roman de la rose* (see 228–35 above) accounts for this allusion. On Virgil's medieval reputation as a magician, see John Webster Spargo, Virgil the Necromancer, 1934, esp. 1–68.

235 herd: The practice of reading aloud to a group remained popular (see Tr 2.82–84: "they thre/ Herden a mayden reden hem the geste/ Of the siege of Thebes").

236–40 The sword (here **spere**) with which **Achilles** wounded **Thelophus** (Telephus) and which had the power to heal the wound it inflicted is alluded to in Ovid, Rem. Am., tr. Mozley, 44–48: "The Pelian spear, which wounded once its Herculean foe, bore relief also to the wound" (see also Met. 12.112, 13.171–72; Tristia 5.2, 15); and Dante, Inf. 31.4–6: "Thus have I heard the lance of Achilles and of his father was occasion first of sad and then of healing gift." See also Tr 4.927–28: "Beth rather to hym cause of flat than egge. And with som wisdom ye sorwe bete."

243–46 hardyng of metal: On the medicinal properties of certain prepared metals, see Pliny, Hist. Nat. 34.43–45 (Vincent J. DiMarco, ChauR 16, 1981, 178).

250–51 Moyses . . . Salomon: Moses was said to have made a Ring of Memory and, for his Egyptian wife Tharbis, a Ring of Oblivion when he wished to return to Zipporah (see

Gower, Conf. aman. 4.647–49: "such a Ring,/ As Moises thurgh his enchanting/ Som time in Ethiope made"). The legend was based on Numbers 12.1 (where the Egyptian wife is mentioned) and Moses's knowledge of Egyptian magic as reported in Acts 7.22 ("And Moses was learned in all the wisdom of the Egyptians"). Solomon was also thought to be adept in the magical sciences and to have made a magical ring (see Clouston, Magical Elements, 334–40). Moses and Solomon are mentioned together in a discussion of magic in Roger Bacon's *Opus Maius* (ed. J. H. Bridges, 1897, 1:392), and possibly this is Chaucer's immediate source (Vincent J. DiMarco, Anglia 99, 1981, 399–405).

253–61 For the idea that phenomena whose causes are known to the expert seem a wonder to others, see Bo 4.m5, and pr6.199–210.

254–58 Glass was made from the ashes of ferns; Chaucer's source may be *Le Roman de la rose* (16096–105; tr. Dahlberg 272–73), which presents the making of glass as a wonder (in a defense of alchemy) and also mentions thunder.

258–59 The phenomena listed have no obvious causes. Isidore of Seville (Etymologiae, 13.9) held that **thonder** was caused by gusts of wind splitting clouds, Aristotle that the noise was produced by the impact of forcibly ejected vapor from cooling clouds striking other clouds (see Bartholomaeus Anglicus 11.13, tr. Trevisa 1:591–92). The **ebbe and flood** were explained by Macrobius (Comm. on the Dream of Scipio, tr. Stahl, 214) as the product of the collision of ocean currents, by Aristotle (as quoted in Barth. Angl. 13.21, tr. Trevisa 1:667) as resulting from the influence of the moon. Of **gossomer,** spider web, Bartholmeus Anglicus (18.10, tr. Trevisa 2:1139) writes: "It is wonder how the matiere of the thredes that cometh of the wombe of the spithere [spider] may suffice to so gret a werk and to the weuynge of so gret a webbe." **Myst** was thought to be caused by disintegrating clouds (Barth. Angl. 11.12; tr. Trevisa 1:590).

263–65 angle meridional: The celestial sphere was divided into twelve astrological "domiciles," of which the four principals were called *angles.* The *angle meridional* is the tenth, through which the sun would pass on 15 March between 10 A.M. and noon. The constellation Leo, the **beest roial,** would also have begun its two-hour ascent above the horizon at about noon on that day. Chaucer's **Aldiran** has been variously identified; North (Ch's Universe, 269) takes it as "the southernmost of the two stars in the head of Leo."

272 Venus children: Those born under the influence of the planet Venus are, of course, lovers. See Seznec, Survival of the Pagan Gods, 70–76, and KnT I.1918–66n.

273–74 Fyssh: Pisces is the "exaltation" of Venus, the sign in which she is most powerful. See WBPro III.701–2n.

287 Launcelot: Lancelot was famous as the lover of Guinevere in Arthurian romance, but there is no apparent basis (other than the idea that a perfect knight is also a perfect courtier) for the narrative skill the Squire here attributes to him.

291–94 spices . . . wyn: Spices were mixed with wine, but *spice* could also mean spiced cakes (Skeat 2:506), and the mention of eating in 294 implies that is the case here. Cf. MerT IV.1770, Tr 5.852: "The spices and the wyn men forth hem fette"; LGW 1110–11: "And spices parted, and the wyn agon,/ Unto his chambres was he led anon."

347 norice of digestion, the sleep: Possibly proverbial (though not recorded before Chaucer); Whiting S377. The Ashmole version of the *Secretum secretorum,* EETS 276, 54, explains that sleep after a meal provides the stomach with the greatest amount of bodily heat and thus aids digestion.

349 drynke and labour . . . reste: Proverbial; see MerT IV. 1862n.

351–52 Skeat (5:382) notes that the Shepherdes Kalender (ed. 1656, ch. 29) describes the six hours after midnight as under the influence of the sanguine humor (cf. V.347).

353 Healthy blood was regarded as the source of well-being; cf. Batholomaeus Anglicus 4.7, tr. Trevisa 1:153: "And if blood is wel and temperat, he kepeth hele and helthe."

358–59 fumositee: Fumes that derive from wine drinking (cf. PardT VI.567); for the worthlessness of dreams thus produced, see NPT VII.2923–39, and cf. Macrobius, Commentary on the Dream of Scipio, 1.3.4, tr. Stahl, 88: "The physical variety [of *insomnium,* a worthless dream] might be illustrated by one who has overindulged in eating or drinking and dreams that he is choking with food or unburdening himself."

371 impressioun: Cf. HF 39–40: "That purely her impressions/ Causeth hem avisions"; Tr 5.372–74: "Ek oother seyn that thorugh impressiouns,/ As if a wight hath faste a thyng in mynde,/ That therof cometh swiche avysiouns."

386 four degrees: Nicholas of Lynn's *Kalendarium,* 77, shows that on 16 March (see 48–51 above) the sun at noon was at four degrees thirty-five minutes in Aries (the Ram); since the sun is also only four degrees above the horizon, it is about 6:15 A.M.

401 knotte: Used in the same sense in V.407 and ParsT X.494. Cf. ParsPro X.28n.

404–5 prolixitee: Cf.Tr 2.1564 ("But fle we now prolixitee best is"); based on *Roman de la rose* 18298, tr. Dahlberg, 304 ("It is a good thing to flee prolixity"). Cf. Whiting P408.

409 tree: The significance of the dry tree is not clear. Skeat suggested a reference to the *Arbre Sec* that was said to have withered at Christ's crucifixion and would bloom again only when a Christian prince conquered the Holy Land (Mandeville's Travels, EETS 253, 50–51; Yule's Book of Marco Polo, 1:119–31).

419 For the tiger as an image of cruelty, see KnT I.1657, 2626–28.

428 The **faucon peregryn,** according to Brunetto Latini (*Il Tesoretto,* tr. Holloway), is so named because the young of this species were taken while on their flight, or "pilgrimage" from their breeding place, rather than from the nest. The ME form is an anglicization of Med. Lat. *falco peregrinus.*

479 pitee . . . herte: Cf. KnT I.1761n.

491 chasted is the leon: Proverbial (Whiting W211), and cf. *Othello* II.iii.261–62: "Even so as one would beat his offenceless dog to affright an imperious lion." The actual medieval practice of teaching the lion by beating the dog is illustrated in G. G. Coulton's Life in the M. A., 2:53–54; see Calvin S. Brown, Jr., and Robert H. West, MLN 55, 1940, 209–10.

496 weep . . . water: Proverbial (Whiting W81); cf. Tr 3.115: "And Pandare wep as he to water wolde."

504 tercelet: The male hawk, especially the peregrine falcon or the goshawk. So named (Cotgrave's French and English Dictionary, 1611, s.v. *tiercelet*) because it is one-third smaller than the female, or (OED, s.v. *tercellene* [1682]) because the third egg in the nest was believed to be smaller and to produce a male bird.

511 To dye **in greyn** is to dye in a fast color; see NPT VII.3459n. **Coloures** is a pun, for the tercelet deceives through the use of his rhetorical devices ("colors").

512 serpent: Cf. SumT III.1994–95n.

514–19 Cf. Christ's denunciation of the hypocritical Pharisees, Matt. 23.27: "Woe to you, scribes and Pharisees, hypocrites! for ye are like the whited sepulchres, which indeed seem beautiful outward but are within full of dead men's bones, and of all uncleanliness."

535 herte in chaunge: Cf. Criseyde's dream of an exchange of hearts, Tr 2.925–31. For the notion of an exchange of hearts, see Leyerle in The Learned and the Lewed, ed. Benson, 127–28, 138–42.

537 trewe wight and a theef: Proverbial (Whiting W25). Cf. LGW ProF 464–65 ("a trewe man, withouten drede,/ Hath nat to parten with a theves dede") and Anel 105 ("nothing thinketh the fals as doth the trewe").

543 tigre, ful of doubleness: For the association of tigers with deceit, see Rowland, Blind Beasts, 14–15, and Melvin Storm, ELN 14, 1977, 172–74.

550 Lameth: Cf. WBPro III.54–56n.

555 unbokelen his galoche: An echo of Mark 1.7: "There cometh one greater after me, the latchet of whose shoes I am not worthy to stoop down and unloose"; see also Luke 3.16 and John 1.27 (both nearly identical). Robinson noted that "Modern taste might impose a restraint in such use of a scriptural passage . . . In Chaucer's age men spoke freely of sacred persons and things." Robinson quotes the "somewhat startling application of the proverb 'God foryaf his deth'" in Tr 3.1577 and Gower's reference to Jason (Conf. aman. 5.3824: "Bot thogh he were goddes brother"), and he notes that although some passages from the troubadours (Palmer A. Throop Spec 13, 1938, 387) may involve "real disrespect for sacred things," more often such passages "seem to show affectionate familiarity with the objects of worship."

558 an hevene for to see: Cf. Tr 2.637: "It was an heven upon hym for to see."

569 my wil obeyed his wyl: Cf. Anel 119: "Withoute bode his heste she obeyde."

593 vertu of necessite: See KnT 1.3041–42 and n.

596 Seint John to borwe: Dorothy Bethurum (ed., SqT, 1965) notes that lovers' rites were associated with St. John the Baptist's Day, 21 June, and Skeat (5:385) notes that this saint was the Apostle of truth; however, the reference may conceivably be to one of the other St. Johns. Cf. Mars 9: "Taketh your leve, and with Seint John to borowe."

602–3 ete with a feend: Proverbial after Chaucer (Whiting S639).

607–9 thilke text: Bo 3.m2.39–42: "Alle thynges seken ayen to hir propre cours, and alle thynges rejoysen hem of hir retornynge ayen to hir nature." The Lat. gloss at 608 quotes Boethius: "Reditu suo singula gaudent" (trans. in text).

610 newefangelnesse: Cf. Anel 141: "This fals Arcite, of his newfanglenesse."

610–17 briddes . . . in cages: from Bo 3.m2.21–31: "[one may cage a bird and give it 'honeyed drynkes and large meats'], yit natheles yif thilke bryd skippynge out of hir streyte cage seith the agreables schadwes of the wodes, sche defouleth with hir feet hir metes ischad, and seketh mornynge oonly the wode." See also *Roman de la rose* 13941–66; tr. Dahlberg, 239. Chaucer uses the image of the caged bird again in MancT IX.163–74 (cf. MilT I.3224).

618–20 gentillesse: Cf. WBT III.1109 and n. J. R. Osgerby (Use of Eng. 11, 1959, 102–7) takes **gentillesse** as the main theme of the story.

624 kyte: A cowardly type of hawk (cf. PF 349: "the coward kyte"); for its predatory habits, see Rowland, Blind Beasts, 51, and cf. KnT I.1177–80.

644 blewe: The color symbolizing constancy; see Whiting B384 and Hassell B112 for many examples. Chaucer so uses the color in Tr 3.885 (Criseyde gives Troilus a blue ring); cf. Against Women Unconstant: "In stede of blew, thus may ye were al grene."

644–46 blewe . . . grene: Cf. Anel 145–46: "And ryght anon he cladde him in her hewe —/ Wot I not whethir in white, rede, or grene."

648 tidyves: Cf. LGW ProF 154: "As dooth the tydif, for newfangelnesse." The word appears only in Chaucer (MED s.v. *tidif* n.) and what sort of bird it designates remains unknown (see F. P. Wilson, PQ 17, 1938, 216–18); OED, s.v. *tidife*, suggests the blue titmouse.

650 Pyes: Magpies were often thought to speak and to spread gossip and rumors. Cf. HF 703–4 ("Though that Fame had alle the pies/ In al a realme, and alle the spies") and the tale of the magpie in The Seven Sages of Rome (WBPro III.232n.).

664 Theodora: Metlitzki (Matter of Araby, 156–59) suggests this character may recall the wise maiden Tawaddud (known in the West variously as Teodor, Teodora, Theodora), who, like Canacee, knew the language of birds and the secrets of medicine. But with this Greek name, Chaucer might be announcing his intention to portray a marriage between a prince of the Golden Horde and the royal house of Byzantium, such as occurred in the 1260s between Nogay and Euphrosyne, the illegitimate daughter of Michael VIII.

667   The plot here sketched, as Robinson noted, is obscure. It is sometimes assumed that this **Cambalo** is a different character from Canacee's brother (V.31, 656), but this seems unlikely. "Chaucer may have intended that Canacee should be abducted and then won back by Cambalo . . . Spenser (Faerie Queene IV.5) represents three brothers as suitors for Canacee, fighting against Cambello her brother" (Robinson). On the form of the name Cambalo, see MkT VII.2345n.

671–72   These lines, apparently genuine, set the time in May, when (on 12 May) the sun enters Gemini, a mansion of Mercury (though Virgo, which the sun enters in August, is the other mansion of Mercury).

672   A number of otherwise unrelated MSS have a note similar to that which marks the end of The Cook's Tale (cf. I.4422n.); e.g., "Of this Squyer's Tale Chaucer makith namoore," in MS Royal College of Physicians 13. (See Partridge, Glosses to CT.)

673 wel yquit: The Franklin interrupts "by pretending to think the story is over" and thus staves off the "threatened epic" (Pearsall, CT, 143). Most critics agree, but see David M. Seaman, ELN 24:1, 1986, 12–18.

The Introduction to the Franklin's Tale

675–76   For the rhyme **yowthe : allow the,** see GP I.523n.

The Franklin's Prologue and Tale

The explanatory notes to The Franklin's Prologue and Tale are adapted from those written by Joanne Rice for The Riverside Chaucer.

The concern with mastery and marriage, the use of Jerome's *Adversus Jovinianum,* and some echoes of The Merchant's Tale (see 805–6 below) all suggest that The Franklin's Prologue and Tale were composed about the same time as the other tales in the "Marriage Group." John L. Lowes (MP 15, 1918, 689–728) argued for an earlier date on the basis of parallels to the *Teseida* and The Knight's Tale, and John D. North (Ch's Universe, 436) puts the date as after 25 December 1387 on the basis of the astrological allusions (1389 or 1392 in RES n.s. 20, 1969, 162–67). Neither is completely convincing, and though the precise date remains uncertain, most scholars continue to assign the work to the middle 1390s.

The basic story in The Franklin's Tale embodies the folklore motif of the "rash promise" (Aarne-Thompson M223), which is widespread not only in Europe but also in the Orient, and it appears frequently in Celtic tales and medieval romance. The particular form reflected in Chaucer's tale appears in Boccaccio's *Filocolo* and *Decameron* 10.5, Boiardo's *Orlando innamorato,* Juan Manuel's *Conde Lucanor* (Exemplum 50; see Jesus L. Serrano Reyes, Didactismo y moralismo, 1996), and Jean de Condé's *Chevalier à la manche*; all include the rash promise, the magician, and the ending with a *demande d'amour,* but Boccaccio's *Filocolo* resembles Chaucer's tale most closely, and it is usually regarded as Chaucer's primary source (N. R. Havely, Ch's Boccaccio, 1980), even though it does not completely account for the plot, characters, and form of Chaucer's version.

The removal of the rocks, for instance, is Chaucer's own invention, though it could have been suggested by a variety of soures—Medea's rocks at sea (Thomas A. Reisner and Mary Ellen Reisner, SP 76, 1979, 1–12); feats of magic in Ovid, Met. 7.202–5 ("living rocks and oaks I root up from their own soil"; Kenneth A. Bleeth, AMN&Q 20, 1982, 130–1); or the actual rocks off the coast of Brittany (J. S. P. Tatlock, Scene of the FranT Visited, Ch Soc, ser. 2, 51, 1914, 5–9, 44–54).

Moreover, the Franklin claims that he tells a Breton lay, and the Breton setting and names do distinguish Chaucer's version from all those versions listed above. In its brevity, apparent simplicity, idealism, and concern with love and the supernatural, Chaucer's tale does resemble the "Breton lays" written by Marie de France in the twelfth century, though Chaucer probably knew only English examples of this genre—works such as *Sir Orfeo, Lay le Freine,* and *Sir Degare,* which are all in the Auchinleck MS (see introductory note to Sir Thopas); see Mortimer J. Donovan, The Breton Lay, 1969, 44–64. Carl Lindahl, in an unpublished paper, argues that Chaucer deliberately molded the tale to conform to the structural patterns and basic plots of the Breton lay. The relevant analogues are printed by Dempster and Tatlock in S&A, 377–97.

The most striking differences between The Franklin's Tale and its analogues are Chaucer's preoccupation with marriage, *gentillesse,* and troth. Traditionally, the tale has been seen as Chaucer's resolution of the "Marriage Debate" (G. L. Kittredge, MP 9, 1912, 435–67). But this view has been questioned by critics who see the Franklin as a social climber whose "middle-class" values clash with Christian ones or who does not fully understand the implications of his own tale (e.g., Robertson, Pref to Ch, 470–72). Henrik Specht clears the Franklin of many unjust criticisms (Ch's Franklin in the CT, 1981), including the idea that he is a socially ambitious member of the "middle class." Specht's conclusions have been questioned (Nigel Saul, MÆ 52, 1983, 10–26) but, Paul Strohm writes (Social Ch, 107), "His views on gentilesse are fully and genially appropriate to the social situation he already enjoys."

The themes of *gentillesse* and *trouthe* have also proved controversial. Some critics claim that no character is gentle or honorable and that the tale ultimately focuses on delusion, illusion, or mere appearance versus reality (e.g., Alan T. Gaylord, ELH 31, 1964, 331–65). Others argue that the tale in fact reflects the values of truth and gentility as well as the Franklin's idealism (e.g., Mary J. Carruthers, Criticism 23, 1981, 283–300; and Jill Mann, New Pelican Guide to Eng. Lit., Vol. I, Part 1, ed. Ford, 1982, 133–53). A number of critics have offered a different perspective by taking into account the apparent contradictions and arguing that the multiplicities in the tale are a deliberate function of its meaning (Robert E. Kaske, in Ch the Love Poet, 62–65; Bloomfield, 189–98, in Acts of Interpretation). They especially focus on the significance of the *demande d'amour* as an invitation to debate rather than a means of resolving all the problems raised by the text. Timothy H. Flake, ES 77, 1996, 209–26, sees the tale as an expression of the power of *trouthe.*

The Franklin's views on marriage are likewise controversial. Kittredge (MP 9:435–67) held that his tale solved the problem poised by the Wife of Bath: "We need not hesitate . . . to accept the solution which the Franklin offers as that which Geoffrey Chaucer the man accepted for his own part. Certainly it is a solution that does him infinite credit. A better has never been devised or imagined." Few critics today completely agree with Kittredge's assessment of the Franklin's attempt to combine the courtly servant-in-love with the traditional Pauline image of lord-in-marriage. This has often been criticized as a faulty ideal (Robertson, Pref to Ch, 472; Howard, Idea of CT, 269) or as a utopian indulgence that the Franklin really does not intend to allow to threaten male supremacy (Aers, Chaucer, Langland, 1980, 160–69). Many critics, however, do follow Kittredge's lead and see this mutual tolerance and regard as a basis for a happy marriage (Clair C. Olson, in Ch and Med. Sts., 166), as a triumph over selfishness, weakness, or evil (Ruggiers, Art of CT, 226), as a leveling of inequalities (David, Strumpet Muse, 187), or as Chaucer's only tale in which neither mate asserts sovereignty to the disadvantage of the other (Daniel S. Silvia, Rev. des langues vivantes 33, 1967, 228–36). Mark N. Taylor (ChauR 32, 1997, 64–81) relates the tale to a tradition of "anti-adultery courtly love" which allows for marriage and "a reciprocal relationship" (his notes provide a good

review of scholarhip on this matter). Mann (Geoffrey Ch: Feminist Readings, 111–20) shows the centrality of the concept of the "necessary ideal," patience, to this and other tales, such as the Wife of Bath's and the Melibee.

The Franklin's Prologue

709 Britouns: Bretons, inhabitants of Brittany, although the word is also used for the Celtic inhabitants of Great Britain (cf. MLT II.545). The collocation of *olde, gentil* and *firste Briton tonge* may suggest a kind of golden age (Harry Berger, ChauR 1, 1966, 98–99).

710 layes: OF *lai,* originally a short lyric or song, but here as "Breton lay," a brief narrative poem (see introductory note above).

716 burel man: Unlearned man or layman (see MED, s.v. *burel* n. 1b), derived from burel, a coarse, woolen cloth. Cf. ProMkT VII.1955; SumT III.1872, 1874.

716–28   This passage fits the dramatic context following the Host's attack (Lumiansky, Of Sondry Folk, 185–86) and echoes SqT V.36–41 (Berger, ChauR 1:101). The Franklin follows the "affected modesty" topos, using the rhetorical device *diminutio;* see GP 1.746n.

721 Pernaso: Lat. gloss: "From Persius: 'I have neither wet my lips in the equine well nor do I remember having dreamed on twin-peaked Parnassus'" (Persius, ed. G. G. Ramsey, Loeb, 1940, Satires, Pro 1–3). The form of the quotation is a bit garbled, possibly showing that Chaucer did not know Persius directly. This is the only known allusion to Persius in Chaucer's work. Other references to Parnassus are all in the "high style": HF 520–22, Anel 15–18, Tr 3.1809–11.

722 Scithero: Cicero. The form *Cithero* is also found in Latin MSS, possibly reflecting confusion with Mt. Cithaeron (Robert A. Pratt, Progress of Med. and Ren. Sts. in U.S. and Canada, Bull. 20, 1949, 48). This is Chaucer's only use of "Cicero"; elsewhere he uses "Tullius" or "Marcus Tullius." Russell A. Peck interprets the Franklin's use of this form of the name as an affectation (ChauR 1, 1967, 257).

723–26 colours: Mortimer J. Donovan (JEGP 56, 1957, 52–55) suggests the description of Rhetoric in Anticlaudianus 3.3 as a source. Chaucer plays on the three meanings of **colour** in rhetoric, painting, and nature, producing the rhetorical device of *traductio* (Helge Kökeritz, PMLA 69, 1954, 950). Cf. ClPro IV.16n., SqT V.39n.

The Franklin's Tale

729 Armorik: Armorica (from *Arvor,* land by the sea), ancient name of Brittany, usually used as a conscious and scholarly archaism (Tatlock, Scene of the FranT, 17).

740 penaunce: Distress or suffering; with pain, pity, service, and obedience, it is part of the stock vocabulary of courtly love. Cf., e.g., Venus 46: "In nouncerteyn we languisshe in penaunce."

752 for shame of his degree: In order not to bring shame upon him in his status as a knight and possibly as a husband and lord (see OED, s.v. *shame,* 13).

764–66 Love wol nat ben constrayned: Cf. *Roman de la rose* 9440–42; tr. Dahlberg, 170: "Love cannot endure or live if it is not free"; Ovid, Met. 2.846–47: "Majesty and love do not go well together nor tarry long in the same dwelling place"; see KnT I.1625–26n.

767 Love . . . free: Proverbial; cf. KnT I.1606n.

768–70 Women . . . desiren libertee: Cf. *Roman de la rose* 13959–66; tr. Dahlberg, 239: "All women of every condition, whether girls or ladies, have a natural inclination to seek . . . freedom." Cf. MancT IX.148–54.

773–76 Pacience . . . venquysseth: The idea is commonplace (Whiting P61); it appears in Langland, PP B 13.135 and 14.33 and in Latin proverbs: cf. "Patientia vincit omnia" (Patience conquers all), Walther 20833; Cato, Dicta Catonis 1.38: "Of human virtues Patience is the crown." Cf. Tr 4.1584: "The suffrant overcomith."

781 constellacioun: Cf. WBPro III.615n.

782 complexioun: Cf. GP I.333n.

792–98 Cf. *Roman de la rose* 9449–54; tr. Dahlberg, 170: lovers who marry "find that love can hardly ever hold them together; for when the man loved *par amour* he would proclaim himself his sweetheart's sergeant, and she grew used to being his mistress. Now he calls himself lord and master over her whom he called his lady when she was loved *par amour.*"

801 Pedmark: Penmarch, referring to the Breton cape or the commune in the southwest corner of the department of Finistère near Quimper, south of Brest. Manly (New Light, 170–73) suggests that this locale was well known after 1386 because of a celebrated case in which John Hawley and his men seized three ships there. In the fourteenth century the village that now stands nearby was evidently a baronial seat (Tatlock, Scene of the FranT, 1–9). The description of both a high shore and the grisly, outlying rocks, however, fits no known site in Brittany. The rugged coast of Penmarch perfectly fits the description of the treacherous rocks, but the nearest high shore is at Concarneau, twenty-one miles away. If this site at Penmarch is intended, then the shoreline description must be Chaucer's invention.

805–6 Echoes MerT IV.1259–60; cf. MerT IV.1340–41.

808 Kayrrud: Welsh *Caer-rhudd,* "red house" or "red town." Although several villages with the modern name "Kerru" exist in Brittany, none fits the description in the tale. The form of the name is neither Breton nor a Breton form in French. It probably represents an English approximation of a Breton pronunciation.

Arveragus: A Latinized form of a Celtic name. See William Henry Schofield (PMLA 16, 1901, 405–49) for the story of Arviragus and Genuissa found in Geoffrey of Monmouth, Hist. Brit. 4.12. Jerome W. Archer (PMLA 65, 1950, 318–22) argues against Geoffrey of Monmouth as a source. Another Arviragus is one of the sons of Cymbeline and is mentioned in Juvenal, Satires, 4.127.

809–14 Mary Hamel (ChauR 17, 1983, 316–17) finds here a verbal echo of Chrétien de Troyes's Cligès, 14–17; tr. Staines, 87: "He was so brave and stouthearted that, to win honour and renoun, he travelled from Greece to England, which in those days was called Britain." If so, this would be the only proof in Chaucer's works that he knew directly Chrétien's romances. But the resmblance seems rather slight.

815 Dorigen: The source and pronunciation of the name are uncertain, but it has a Celtic appearance (Tatlock, Scene of the FranT, 37–41).

819 Cf. KnT I.2822–26.

829–31 Donovan (JEGP 56:55) compares Anticlaudianus 1.1: "With the sculpting of her [Nature's] own reason she may translate the ideas of her own mind into the very executions of the works themselves." This is closer than the corresponding image in *Filocolo* 2.49, which alludes to Ovid's "gutta cavat lapidem" (Drops of water hollow out the stone; Ex Ponto 4.10.5).

859 grisly rokkes blake: The rocks have been subjected to a Freudian reading (Michael Stevens, in Michael Hoy and Michael Stevens, Ch's Major Tales, 1969 [rpt. 1983], 91–93) and interpreted as Dorigen's fantasies (Kenneth A. Bleeth, ES 74, 1993, 113–23). John B. Friedman (ChauR 31, 1996, 133–44) says they are "the famous megalithic *menhirs,*" tall stones and dolmens scattered along the Breton coast and believed in the Middle Ages to have been the work of giants, sorcerers, and demons.

861 Cf. Anel 177–78: "she was so mat/ That she ne hath foot on which she may sustene."

865–93 This passage echoes Book 4 of Boece (W. Bryant Bachman, Jr., ChauR 12, 1977, 55–59) and recalls Palamon's questioning in KnT I.1303–24 (Hoy and Stevens, Ch's Major Tales, 90). Some critics see Dorigen's questioning as self-indulgence, impatience, or failure to accept the natural order (e.g., Paul E. Gray, TSLL 7, 1965, 217). Kathryn Hume (SN 44, 1972, 289–94), however, argues that the intentionally pagan setting allows a philosophy that is not necessarily Christian.

865–67 Cf. Bo 1.m5.31–32: "O thou governour, governynge alle thynges by certein ende."

879 Cf. Bo 1.m5.52–53: "We men, that ben . . . a fair parte of so greet a werk."

880 merk: Cf. Gen. 1.27 "ad imaginem suam" (in his own image).

886 al is for the beste: Cf. Whiting A93.1, FrT III.1496, and ClT IV.1161.

886–89 argumentz, causes, conclusion: technical language of the schools; Cf. CkPro I.4328–29n.

899 places delitables: Essentially a translation of Latin *locus amoenus* and used here both as a simple description and as an allusion to the rhetorical topos (J. D. Burnley, Neophil 56, 1972, 93). For the rare use of the plural adjective, see Language and Versification, p. xxxiii.

900 tables: Backgammon, a game of chance played with dice, from Latin *tabularum ludus.* The form of the game was much like the modern one (see Joseph Strutt, Sports and Pastimes, 319–22).

902–19 The May garden was a conventional setting for courtly love, derived ultimately from *Le Roman de la rose* (cf. KnT I.1505–39 and MerT IV.2029–41).

913–14 Cf. SqT V.393–96.

925–34 The conventional descriptions of a courtly lover here and later in V.943–52 echo that of the squire in the GP I.79–100 and of Arcite in Teseida 4.62. C. Hugh Holman sees a parallel to the courtly-love triangle in the Merchant's Tale (ELH 18, 1951, 241–52). Lowes (MP 15:689–728) finds several parallels in Teseida 4.60–68.

938 Aurelius: A Roman name used among the Britons (see Gildas, De excidio Brit., ch. 30; Geoffrey of Monmouth,

Hist. Brit. 6.5). James F. Royster (SP 23, 1926, 380–84) calls attention to the Latin name of Orleans ("Aurelianus") and quotes a passage from *Maniere,* a fourteenth-century handbook possibly written by an Englishman, which describes Orleans as the site for the activities of necromancy and "Colle tregetour" (an English magician mentioned in HF 1277).

942 Withouten coppe: This is usually interpreted as "copiously" but Whiting (C628) gathers examples that show that "to drink without cup" means "to suffer intensely." For the idea of drinking woe (**penaunce**), see HF 1879–80: "For what I drye [suffer], or what I thynke,/ I wil myselven al hyt drynke"; Tr 2.784: "Oure wrecche [misery] is this, oure owen wo to drynke."

947–48 layes: Loosely meaning song or lyric, rather than its specialized sense in V.710.

compleintes: A common troubadour form applied to love songs and religious poems, but later a genre used by Chaucer in several of his short poems.

roundels and virelayes: Originally French dance songs with refrains, but later also used of stanzaic poems; for an example of a roundel see the conclusion to *The Parliament of Fowls.*

950 Chaucer's conception of the Furies suffering as well as inflicting pain may be colored by Dante, *Inferno* 9.37–51 (John L. Lowes, MP 14, 1917, 719–20), but probably its source is Bo 3.m12.33–37: "And the thre goddesses, furiis and vengeresses of felonyes, that tormenten and agasten the soules by anoy, woxen sorweful and sory, and wepyn teeris for pite." See SqT V.448, FrkT V.1101, Tr 4.22–23 ("O ye Herynes, Nyghtes doughtren thre,/ That endeles compleignen evere in pyne").

951–52 Ekko . . . Narcisus: Echo, a nymph who fell in love with the unresponsive Narcissus, wasted away in grief until only her voice remained. The allusion is no doubt to Ovid's story in Met. 3.353–401, as the Latin marginal gloss, "Methamorphosios," suggests. Cf. BD 735 ("And Ecquo died for Narcisus").

989–98 Dorigen's "rash promise" is also the imposing of an impossible task since she clearly intends it as a refusal. Brewer (New Intro. to Ch, 335) explains: she playfully sets forth the impossible condition "in order to make her refusal less harsh, though no less absolute." Gaylord (ELH 31:331–65) questions the legitimacy of a promise made *in pley* and never intended as a vow, and he claims that a rash promise should not be kept, according to moral treatises and medieval law (see also Leslie K. Arnovick, in Mark C. Amodio, ed., Oral Poetics in ME Poetry, 1994, 125–47). Carol A. Pulham (ChauR 31, 1996, 76–86) argues that oral promises were binding in a largely oral culture. Dorigen's stipulation is unlike any in the other analogues: cf. *Filocolo,* in which the lady asks for a garden blooming in January.

1009 impossible: Cf. WBPro III.688n.

1017–18 it was nyght: Eleanor P. Hammond (MLN 27, 1912, 91–92) takes this as a rhetorical device similar to the prose line ("And, as I can state in very few words, it was night") following eleven flowery lines of verse in Fulgentius the Mythographer (tr. Whitbread, 46). Phyllis Hodgson (ed., FranT, 1960, 90) cites this as a humorous anticlimax after *circuitio* as in Tr 2.904–5 ("The dayes honour, and the

hevenes ye,/ The nyghtes foo—al this clepe I the sonne"). But Benjamin S. Harrison (SP 32, 1935, 58–59) argues that the line is neither burlesque nor humorous, but an example of *expolitio,* a common device to explain a preceding assertion.

1033 The sun's declination (distance from the plane of the celestial equator) determines the changes of seasons according to whether its position is low (winter) or high (summer) in the sky.

1045 Lucina: Luna, as goddess of the moon, controls the tides and belong to her. Instead of praying directly to her, Aurelius prays to Apollo, her brother, because Lucina is also Diana, goddess of virginity (William B. Hunter, MLN 68, 1953, 174).

1049–54 This passage refers not only to the moon's dependence on the sun, but also to the tide's dependence on the moon. The ideas are commonplace (cf. Bartholomaeus Anglicus 1.8, tr. Trevisa, 1:489–94).

1057–70 this opposicion: Highest tides occur when the moon is either full or new (in opposition or in conjunction with the sun). The sun would exert its greatest power in its own astrological mansion, Leo, with the moon in opposition (V.1057) in Aquarius, the zodiacal sign of water especially appropriate for this miracle. Since it is only early May (cf. 906) and the sun is in Taurus, Aurelius asks Apollo to grant his prayer that when the sun is next in Leo (1058), the moon slow her course to move at the same rate as the sun (1066) so that for two years (1068) the moon will remain full (1069), thus keeping the tides high (1070) and the highest rock covered (1059–61).

1073–74 A variation on Dorigen's own words in V.891–92. Lucina is here seen as Proserpina, goddess of the underworld. Cf. KnT I.2081–82 and I.2313n.

1110 Pamphilus: Lat. gloss: "Pamphilus to Galatea: 'I am wounded and bear the arrow deep in my breast,'" from *Pamphilus de amore,* a twelfth-century Latin poem (ed. Franz G. Becker, tr. Garbáty). Cf. Mel VII.1556 and n.

1118 Oriens: Orleans; in the fourteenth century its university was an important center of astrological studies (Royster, SP 23:383–84).

1119–28 Deschamps, Chaucer's friend, describes his own student days at Orleans in *Le Miroir de mariage,* which John L. Lowes (RomR 2, 1911, 125–26) believed was a possible influence on this passage.

1125 magyk natureel: See GP I.416n.

1130 mansiouns: Mansions or stations of the moon, referring to the twenty-eight equal divisions of the moon's path in a lunar month, often used to forecast natural phenomena and favorable times for specific human activities. See MilT I.3515n.

1133 On Chaucer's attitude toward astrology or "judicial astronomy," see MLT II.313–14n.

1141 tregetoures: Although Skeat and Robinson gloss the word as "juggler," it more likely means "illusionist"; see MED s.v. *tregetour* n. (a). Since Chaucer repeatedly refers to illusions or appearances (V.1140, 1141, 1143), A. A. Prins suggests a magician who causes "hallucinations or collective apparitions" (ES 35, 1954, 161), but Roger S. Loomis (Spec 33, 1958, 244) argues for "craftsmen, *artisans mécaniques,* who, in effective unison, produced spectacular results," and he notes (242–55) similarities to actual entertainments at the royal palace in Paris in 1378. Some parallels for V.1190–91 appear in the marvels offered as entertainment in the court of the Great Khan, as reported in Mandeville's *Travels,* EETS 156: "And than thei make to come in hunting for the hert & for the boor, with houndes rennynge with open mouth. And many other thinges thei don be craft hire enchauntementes."

1203–4 By clapping his hands, the clerk may be signaling his stage assistants or breaking the magic spell as in the epilogue of *The Tempest.* Cf. the verbal echo in *The Tempest* 4.1.148: "Our revels now are ended" (Ann Thompson, Archiv 212, 1975, 317).

1222 Gerounde . . . Sayne: The specification of these two rivers would indicate the southwest coast from Gironde to Brest and the northwest coast to Honfleur.

1228 round: That the earth is round was common knowledge; see, e.g., Early South English Legendary, ed. C. Horstmann, EETS 87, 1887, 311: "Ase an Appel the eorthe is round."

1248 Capricorn: The sun entered Capricorn on 13 December in Chaucer's time.

1250–51 Robinson compares *Teseida* 3.44.2–4; tr. McCoy: "The weather altered its look and the dew-laden air wept. The grass dried and the trees were stripped bare, and the stormy tribe of Aeolus raced about, wandering here and there through the unhappy world."

1252 Janus: The two-faced god, referred to as "double-bearded," who was the god of gates as well as of beginnings and endings (John F. Adams, Sts. in Med. Culture 4, 1974, 447). The Latin marginal note reads "Janus biceps," a reference to Ovid, Fasti 1.65: "Two-headed Janus, opener of the softly gliding year." Rosemond Tuve (Seasons and Months, 186) demonstrates the similarities between Chaucer's lines and familiar seasonal motifs found in medieval manuscript illuminations in Books of Hours and Calendars.

1254 brawen: Boar's meat, a ceremonial dish for Christmas festivities. The boar's head appeared in illuminations for January in medieval calendars.

1255 Nowel: Cf. Sir Gawain and the Green Knight, 64–65: "Loud crye was ther kest of clerkes and other,/ Nowel nayted on newe, nevened ful ofte" [regularized].

1273 tables Tolletanes: Astronomical tables adapted around 1272 for the city of Toledo, under the direction of Alphonso X, King of Castile. These Alfonsine Tables were adapted for the longitudes of London and other cities.

1275 expans yeeris: Tabulated values for a planet's position in single-year periods.

    collect: tabulated values for a planet's position in twenty-year periods from A.D. 20 to 2000. The values from these two tables could then be added to the root computation to determine a planet's position for any year.

1276 rootes: Root, the first date for which a table is given and the basis for calculating a planet's motion. Cf. MLT II.314.

1277 centris: Although Skeat and Robinson gloss "centre" as part of an astrolabe, it more likely refers to the table of centers, which shows "distances from the centre equant and centre defferent from the centre of an equatorie for each of the planets" (MED, s.v. *centre,* 7c). Thus both *centris* and

argumentz, angles or arcs used in calculating the position or motion of a planet (MED), are astronomical figures.

1278 proporcioneles convenientz: Edgar S. Laird (ELN 25:3, 1988, 23–26) explains that these correspond to the Latin "minuta proportionalia," a measure for calculating celestial positions in the Ptolemaic system. This shows, Laird adds, a quite advanced knowledge of astronomy.

1279 equacions: Method of dividing a sphere into equal houses for astrological purposes.

1280 his eighte speere: The sphere of the fixed stars, counting from earth outward. This sphere provides the second of the two motions of the heavens: "The first movement carries all the others with it in its rush about the earth once within a day and night, although they strive against it, as in the case of the eighth sphere one degree in a hundred years" (The Sphere of Sacrobosco, ed. and tr. Lynn Thorndike, 1949, 119–20). This causes the precession of the equinoxes, which could be ascertained by observing the distance from the true equinoctial point (the head of the **fixe Aries** in the ninth sphere) and the star **Alnath** (α Arietis) in the head of Aries in the eighth sphere.

1283 ninthe speere: The Primum Mobile; see MLT 295–301n.

1285 his firste mansioun: "The first mansion of the moon is called Alnath" (Lat. gloss at 1281). Cf. 1130 above.

1288 face . . . terme: Each zodiacal sign was divided equally into *faces* of ten degrees and unequally into *termes;* both divisions were assigned to particular planets.

1311–22 Skeat (5:395) notes similarities between this complaint and the complaint of Anelida, especially V.1318 with Anel 288: "As verrayly ye sleen me with the peyne."

1325 but youre grace: This idea of relying on the unmerited favor of the lady was the counterpart of the Christian doctrine of grace. Cf. KnT I.3089n.

1340 nas a drope of blood: Skeat (5:395) compares this line to Anel 173 ("Other colour then asshen hath she noon") and V.1348 to Anel 169 ("She wepith, waileth, swowneth pitously").

1354 compleynt: See 947–48 above.

1355–1456 Dorigen's complaint summarizes six chapters of Jerome, *Adversus Jovinianum* (more briefly summarized in ProLGW 281–304). Gatherings of such lists of exempla were common, though Chaucer may have been influenced by Machaut (see *Œuvres,* ed. Hoepffner, intro. lxxiii). Critics generally complain about the passage's inordinate length, rhetorical excesses, apparent disorganization, and display of learning for its own sake (e.g., John M. Manly, Ch and the Rhet., Brit. Acad., 1926, 12; and James Sledd, MP 45, 1947, 44). The complaint, however, has also been viewed as an effective narrative device for postponing the tale's denouement (Hoy and Stevens, Ch's Major Tales, 87) or as an appropriate rhetorical device generalizing Dorigen's experiences (Derek S. Brewer, PBA 60, 1974, 242).

    Though Chaucer follows Jerome closely, he places his examples in a different order. Gerald Morgan (MÆ 46, 1977, 77–97) argues that this produced a coherent exposition of chastity (V.1367–1418), fidelity (1424–41), and honor (1442–56). Donald C. Baker (JEGP 60, 1961, 56–64) argues that the exempla are organized into women who commit suicide to avoid rape (1367–1404), women who commit suicide after being raped (1405–38), and notably faithful wives (1439–56). Few critics defend the length of the complaint. Yet Chaucer may have intended to make the list of good women even longer (see 1455–59 below).

1368 thritty tirauntz: Lat. gloss: "When the thirty tyrants of Athens slew Phidon at a feast, they ordered his virgin daughters to come to them, stripped naked in the manner of prostitutes, and dance with shameless gestures on the floor stained with their father's blood. When they saw the drunken feasters, they, concealing their grief, went out as if for the needs of nature and straightway embracing one another, leapt into a cistern so that they might by death preserve their virginity" (Jerome, Adv. Jov. 1.41, tr. Fremantle, 381; S&A, 395).

1379–80 Mecene . . . Lacedomye: Lat. gloss: "When the Messenians tried to violate the 50 Lacedemonian [Spartan] maidens," [they willingly chose to die rather than consent] (Jerome, Adv. Jov. 1.41, tr. Fremantle, 380; S&A, 395).

1387 Aristoclides, Stymphalides: Lat. gloss: "Aristoclides, the tyrant of Orchomenos desired the virgin Stymphatis [Stymphalides], who when her father was killed [fled] to the temple of Diana etc." [to whose statue she clung until stabbed to death] (Jerome, Adv. Jov. 1.41, tr. Fremantle, 380; S&A, 395).

1385 Lat. gloss (at 1462 in El): "The blessed Jerome, writing against Jovinian, recounts many separate histories, combining this material in book one, chapter 39" [actually 47–49].

1399 Hasdrubales wyf: Lat. gloss: "For Hasdrubal's wife, when the city was captured and burned, perceived that she would be captured by the Romans etc." [and snatched up her children in both arms and threw herself into the burning house]. (Jerome, Adv. Jov. 1.43, tr. Fremantle, 381; S&A, 396). Cf. NPT VII.3362–68.

1405 Lucresse: Lat. gloss: "And first I put Lucretia who, unwilling to survive her shameful rape, wiped out her body's stain [*maculum*] with her own blood" (Jerome, Adv. Jov. 1.46, tr. Fremantle, 382; S&A, 397). Cf. LGW 1680–1885.

1409 sevene maydens of Milesie: Lat. gloss: "Who could pass over in silence the seven virgins of Miletus, who [when all was laid waste by the attack] of the Gauls (or Galatians) [*Gallorum*]" [escaped dishonor by death]? (Jerome, Adv. Jov. 1.41, tr. Fremantle, 380; S&A, 396).

1412–13 thousand stories: Cf. Deschamps, *Miroir de mariage*, 9153: "I have a thousand examples of the goodness [of women]."

1414 Habradate: Lat. gloss: "Xenophon in the [book on] the boyhood of great Cyrus [Cyropaedia, 7.3] writes that when Habradate [Abradates] was killed" [his wife Panthea committed suicide alongside him] (Jerome, Adv. Jov. 1.45, tr. Fremantle, 382; S&A, 396–97).

1426 Demociones doghter: Lat. gloss: "The virgin daughter of Demotion, prince of the Ariopagites" [killed herself on learning of the death of her betrothed rather than marry another, which would have seemed like bigamy to her] (Jerome, Adv. Jov. 1.41, tr. Fremantle, 380; S&A, 395).

1428 Cedasus: Lat. gloss: "By what words are to be praised the daughters of Scedasus" [who killed themselves rather than survive rape] (Adv. Jov. 1.41, tr. Fremantle, 380; S&A, 395).

1432 Nichanore: Lat. gloss: "Nichanor, when Thebes was taken, was overcome by love for a captive virgin" [who killed herself] (Jerome, Adv. Jov. 1.41, tr. Fremantle, 380; S&A, 396).

1434 Another Theban mayden: Lat. gloss: "Greek and other writers tell of a Theban virgin" [who, when violated by a Macedonian enemy, killed her rapist, then herself] (Jerome, Adv. Jov. 1.41, tr. Fremantle, 380; S&A, 396).

1437 Nicarates wyf: Lat. gloss: "What should I say of the wife of Niceratus, piously unable to bear the death of her husband" [who killed herself to escape the lust of the Thirty Tyrants] (Jerome, Adv. Jov. 1.44, tr. Fremantle, 381; S&A, 396).

1439 Alcebiades: Lat. gloss: "Alcibiades, the Socratic, vanquished, etc. [by the Athenians]" [was killed and later buried by his mistress at the risk of death] (Jerome, Adv. Jov. 1.44, tr. Fremantle, 381; S&A, 396).

1442–43 Alceste: Lat. gloss: "They made a fable of Alcestis, who died willingly for Admetus, her husband, and the poem of Homer is of chaste Penelope" (Jerome, Adv. Jov. 1.45, tr. Fremantle, 382; S&A, 397). She is the heroine of The Prologue to LGW and appears in the list of Cupid's saints in IntMLT II.75.

1445 Laodomya: Lat. gloss: "Lacedoma [for Laodamia] is also sung by the mouths of poets, she who when Protesilaus was killed at Troy" [did not wish to survive him] (Jerome, Adv. Jov. 1.45, tr. Fremantle, 382; S&A, 397). She appears in The Prologue to LGW 263 and in IntMLT II.71.

1448 Porcia: Lat. gloss: "Portia could not live without Brutus" (Jerome, Adv. Jov. 1.46, tr. Fremantle, 382; S&A, 397).

1451 Arthenesie: Lat. gloss: "Also Artemesia, the wife of Mausolus is said to have been famous for her chastity" [she built a tomb for her husband so elaborate that "to this day every precious sepulcher is called 'Mausoleum' from his name"] (Jerome, Adv. Jov. 1.44, tr. Fremantle, 381; S&A 396).

1453 Teuta: Lat. gloss: "Teuta, queen of Illirica" [was famous for her chastity] (Jerome, Adv. Jov. 1.44, tr. Fremantle, 381; S&A, 396).

1455–59 On these lines appear the Lat. glosses: "Note Strato ruler of Sidon" (referring to Adv. Jov. 1.45, tr. Fremantle, 382—his wife killed him, then herself to prevent their being shamed by their conquerors); "And see almost all the barbarians, chapter 26 of the first book" (actually Adv. Jov. 1.44, tr. Fremantle, 381): "The Indians and almost all barbarians have a plurality of wives" [and the most chaste is allowed to commit suicide at her husband's funeral]); "Item Cornelia [the chaste wife of Gracchus] et cetera" (Adv. Jov. 1.49); and "Therefore let the marriages of Theano, Cleobuline, Gorgente, Timoclia, Claudius, and Cornelias, at the end of the first book, be imitated" (Adv. Jov. 1.49; cf. Fremantle, 386). Skeat (5:399), assuming the glosses are Chaucer's, notes that "Chaucer seems to have contemplated adding more examples to the list."

1455 Bilyea: Bilia, wife of Duillius, was famed for being able to tolerate her husband's bad breath: "She said, 'I thought the mouths of all men smelled like that'" (Jerome, Adv. Jov. 1.46, tr. Fremantle, 382; S&A, 397).

1456 Rodogone: Rhodogune killed her nurse for suggesting a second marriage (Jerome, Adv. Jov. 1.45, tr. Fremantle, 382; S&A, 397).

Valeria: Another woman who refused to remarry (Jerome, Adv. Jov. 1.46, tr. Fremantle, 382–83; S&A, 397).

1462 Lat. gloss: "These stories and others concerning this matter narrates the blessed Jerome against Jovinianum in his 1st book, ch. 39." Partridge, Glosses to CT, notes that in The Chaucerian Text of *Adversus Jovinianum,* ed. John Patrick Brennan, Jr., 1967, "Chapter 39 is the long final chapter of Book I; it includes chapters 48 and 49 of the standard text as well as much of 47."

1469 Is ther oght elles, Dorigen: Usually taken to mean "Is that all?" with the implication that Averagus indulgently reassures her. Derek A. Pearsall (SAC 17, 1995, 69–78) argues that the direct, unadorned use of the proper name shows a stern assumption of authority and a demand to know all—"Have you told me everything?"

1472 let slepen that is stille: Proverbial (Whiting H569), and cf. Tr 3.764: "It is nought good a slepyng hound to wake."

1479 Trouthe is the hyeste thyng: See J. Douglas Canfield, Word as Bond in English Literature from the M.A. to the Restoration, 1989, pp. xii–xiv and 45–52.

1533 relesse: Aurelius uses the legal language of a medieval release, the legal jargon common to any quit-claim of the time, including that of Cecilia Chaumpayne, releasing Chaucer from the charge of "raptus" (see Chaucer's Life, p. xix, and Roland Blenner-Hassett, Spec 28, 1953, 796–800), Christopher Cannon, Spec 68, 1993, 79–94.

1549 wryte: Seems to be used here by oversight. Cf. KnT I.1201 and n. (Robinson).

1621–22 Some critics view this question as a kind of joke, since they see no character as noble (e.g., Chauncy Wood, PQ 45, 1966, 688–711). However, this is a common medieval device for ending a courtly narrative by calling for further discussion. Cf. KnT I.1347 and n. and *Filocolo* 2.60 (Robert R. Edwards, MP 94, 1996, 141–62). It is also a common folklore motif, "Which was the Noblest Act?" (Aarne-Thompson Type 976).

FRAGMENT VI

This fragment has no explicit connection with the tales that precede and follow it, and its position varies in the manuscripts. In some it follows The Franklin's Tale, in others The Canon's Yeoman's Tale; in such manuscripts the scribes supplied spurious links (see Manly-Rickert 4:488–89). Furnivall placed it after Fragment VII, and Skeat adopted this Chaucer Society order in his edition, though he protested that there was no good reason for this placement of VI (4:434). A. W. Pollard, editor of the Globe Chaucer, 1898 (rpt. 1953), followed this order as well. Robert A. Pratt (PMLA 66, 1951, 1141–67), however, has shown the validity of the order IV-V-VI, which has been adopted by all twentieth-century editors.

There seems little relation between The Physician's and Pardoner's Tales, but critics have argued for deliberate parallels and thematic continuities between them; see Peter G. Beidler (ChauR 3, 1968–69, 275–79) and Dewey R. Faulkner (ed., Twentieth-Century Interpretations of The Pardoner's Tale, 1973, 5–6). Katherine B. Trower (ABR 29, 1978, 67–86) finds a theme of spiritual sickness unifying the fragment; Gerhard J. Joseph (ChauR 9, 1975, 237–45) and R. Michael Haines (ChauR 10, 1976, 220–35) find the unity in the theme of the gifts of Nature and of Fortune (see VI.295 and n.). See also Marc M. Pelen, ChauR 29, 1994, 1–25, and Brian S. Lee, ChauR 22, 1987, 140–60. Stephen A. Barney (in Faulkner, ed., as above, 84–87) argues for a dramatic relation, with The Physician's Tale and the Host's comment on it providing the basis for the Pardoner's performance.

The Physician's Tale

The explanatory notes to The Physician's Tale are adapted from those written by C. David Benson for The Riverside Chaucer.

The Physician's Tale is usually assigned to a date before or at the beginning of the Canterbury period (Tatlock, Dev and Chron, 150–51; Baugh, 485; Fisher, 214). Tatlock developed the argument that its first composition was either for or under the influence of *The Legend of Good Women,* and this view has been widely accepted though it has been disputed (Pat Trefzger Overbeck, ChauR 2, 1967, 92–93). Older scholars attempted to date the poem by supposed historical allusions, none completely convincing (see 72–104 below). A date no earlier than 1386 has been assumed because the poem does not appear in the list of Chaucer's works in the Prologue to *The Legend Of Good Women,* and a date no later than 1390, because it shows no influence of Gower's version of the story (Confessio amantis 7.5131–5306), though this assumes that such influence was inevitable. Recent attempts to see the tale as a reflection of the personality of the Physician assume that the work in its present form was composed expressly for *The Canterbury Tales.*

In genre, The Physician's Tale probably belongs with the other tales of high pathos and suffering innocence (ClT, MLT, PrT, SNT), though it is the only one written in couplets (Robert W. Worth, Jr., in Cambridge Ch Companion, 143–58). Like most of the other religious tales, The Physician's Tale has been largely ignored by critics, though in this case there is widespread agreement that it is an artistic failure—at best an example of Chaucer "working rather routinely" (E. T. Donaldson, Ch's Poetry, 927). Some critics have found value in the poem's apparent failures. The disparity between the tale and its teller has been taken as a source of comedy (Robert Longsworth, Criticism 13, 1971, 223–33) or irony (Emerson Brown, Jr., PQ 60, 1981, 129–49). John C. Gardner (Poetry of Ch, 1977, 293–98) argued that the poem is an example of deliberately "bad art," intended to reveal the moral failings of the teller, and Lee Patterson dismisses it as "fraudulent or 'counterfeit' hagiography" (Patterson, Ch and History, 370). Yet the tale has its defenders among recent critics, most notably Derek Brewer (A New Intro. to Ch, 341–50), who presents a persuasive case for its value. See also Jerome Mandel, ChauR 10, 1976, 316–25, and Geoffrey Ch: Building the Fragments, 61–64, for a consideration of its religious and moral seriousness.

The principal source for the tale is the brief account of Virginia in *Le Roman de la rose,* 5589–658, tr. Dahlberg, 114. The reference to *Titus Livius* (line 1) may echo *Roman de la rose* 5594 ("According to Titus Livius"), and it thus provides no clear evidence that Chaucer knew the original account in Livy's history (Livy, Loeb, vol. 3, ed. and tr. B. O. Foster, 44–50, 56–58). Shannon (S&A, 398–407) argued that Chaucer drew directly on Livy for some details, and many have echoed this assertion, though the case for Chaucer's use of the Latin author is weak (Bruce Harbert, in Ch: Writers and Background, 142–43). The tale was popular in medieval literature (there are versions in Bersuire, in Boccaccio's *De claris mulieribus,* and in Gower's Conf. aman. 7.5131–306) and it was almost always told as an exemplum of evil government. Sheila Delany (SAC 3, 1981, 47–60) attributes the artistic failure of the tale to Chaucer's inability to deal with the political themes, especially popular revolt, implicit in the story. For a review of scholarship on the sources, see William H. Brown, Jr., in Caroline Duncan-Rose and Theo Vennemann, eds. On Language . . . Festschrift for Robert P. Stockwell, 1988, 39–51. There is no convincing evidence that Chaucer drew on any version except *Le Roman de la rose,* and, perhaps most striking in a tale not highly regarded, most of the material and treatment are original (see, especially, Fansler, Ch and RR, 31–35, and Brown, PQ 60:131–37). The minor sources are identified in the notes to specific lines below (41–71). For a full survey of critical and scholarly opinion, see Helen Storm Corsa, ed., The Physician's Tale, Variorum edition, pt. 17, 1987.

6 No children had he mo: Hoffman (ChauR 2, 1967, 24), citing Grace W. Landrum (Chaucer's Use of the Vulgate, Radcliffe Diss., 1921, 2:21–22), suggests that in making Virginia an only child, Chaucer is following the story of Jephtha's daughter (see 240 below) rather than his sources, but Virginia is also apparently an only child in Livy (see R. M. Ogilvie, Commentary on Livy, 1965, 479).

9–117 These lines are essentially original with Chaucer.

14 Lat. gloss: "Look in Metamorphoses." For the story of **Pigmalion,** see Ovid, Met. 10.243–97, and *Roman de la rose* 20817–21174, tr. Dahlberg, 340–47.

16 Lat. gloss: "Apelles made a marvelous work on the grave of Darius, see in the first book of Alexander; for Zanzis in the book of Tullius." A similar gloss occurs at WBPro III.498–99. The "book of Alexander" is Walter of Chatillon's *Alexandreid* (1178–82), a well-known medieval Latin epic (see WBPro 498–99n.). Cicero ("the book of Tullius") tells of Zeuxis's artistry in *De inventione* 2.1–3. Despite the learned allusions in the glosses, however, Chaucer's immediate source is almost certainly *Le Roman de la rose* (16177–210; tr. Dahlberg, 274), which mentions Pygmalion, Apelles, and Cicero's story of Zeuxis, in a discussion of art versus nature.

20 vicaire general: Cf. PF 379 ("Nature, the vicaire of the almyghty Lord") and *Roman de la rose* 16782 (tr. Dahlberg, 282: "constable and vicar"), 19507 (tr. Dahlberg, 322); ultimately from Alanus, De planctu Naturae (Plaint of Nature, tr. Sheraton, Prose 9, 214): "O faithful vicar of heaven's prince."

32–34 Although both Skeat and Robinson cite *Le Roman de la rose* (16242–44; tr. Dahlberg, 275: "no lily at the beginning of May, no rose on its twig nor snow on its branch is so red nor so white"), Fansler (Ch and RR, 89) notes how common these flower comparisons are in descriptions of beauty.

41–71 This detailed description of Virginia's "maidenly virtues" is unparalled in earlier versions. Many critics have noticed the greater prominence Chaucer has given Virginia in the story and her resemblance to Christian virgin martyrs. Chaucer is undoubtedly drawing on material common to medieval treatises on virginity, but no single source can be accepted unquestionably as the poet's own. A number of sources have been suggested, most notably Ambrose's *De virginibus* (see Shannon, S&A, 407–8) and Juvenal's Tenth

Satire (William Kupersmith, ELN 24:2, 1986, 20–23). Glending Olson (Spec 64, 1989, 106–10) makes a good case for the influence of the *Communiloquium* of John of Wales.

54 Sownynge in vertu: See GP I.307n.

58–60 The association of wine (**Bacus**) with sexual desire (**Venus**) is commonplace (cf. WBPro III.464n.), as is that of **wyn and youthe** (Whiting, W359).

65–66 feestes . . . occasions: cf. *Roman de la rose* 13522–28; tr. Dahlberg, 233: "She should often go . . . to weddings, on trips, at games, feasts and round dances, for in such places the God and Goddess of Love keep their schools."

72–104 This digression on the responsibilities of parents and guardians has often been regarded as unduly obtrusive, and historical explanations have been sought. George Lyman Kittredge (MP 1, 1903, 5n.) first suggested that Chaucer might have had in mind his sister-in-law, Katherine Swynford, who was governess to the daughters of John of Gaunt and also John's mistress before becoming his third wife. Tatlock (Dev and Chron, 152–55) argued for a specific allusion to the elopement in 1386 of John's second daughter, Elizabeth, then married to the young Earl of Pembroke, with John Holland. They returned to England in 1388. This explanation has been widely accepted, but there is no necessity to seek an actual event behind sentiments that are quite conventional, however awkwardly introduced.

79 olde daunce: Cf. GP I.476 and n.

83–85 theef of venysoun: Proverbial (Whiting T76).

98 chastisynge: Cf. Prov. 13.24 ("He that spareth the rod hateth his son"), proverbial then as now; see Whiting Y1, Langland, PP B 5.39–40: "Whoso spareth the spryng [*switch*] spilleth his children."

101–2 Proverbial in both English (Whiting S242) and Latin (Walther 30542). The Latin gloss in a single MS (Oxford, Christ Church 152) has the variant Lat. proverb: "Whence [the saying] of an improper man—under a soft shepherd, the wolf shits wool and the flock perishes"; that gloss also appears in Langland, PP C 9.264–66. See Whiting S241 and Walther 30541.

107–8 As in a book: Cf. 2 Cor. 3.2: "Ye are our epistle written in our hearts, known and read of all men."

114–17 The Doctour: Lat. gloss: "Augustinus." St. Augustine offers a brief definition of envy in his *Enarrationes in Psalmos* 104.17 (CCSL 40:1545): "Envy is hatred of another's good fortune." The longer definition used here was commonly attributed to Augustine; cf. ParsT X.484n.

153–54 Chaucer follows Jean de Meun in calling Appius Claudius simply *Apius* and Marcus Claudius simply *Claudius.*

155–57 historial thyng: Cf. LGW 702: "And this is storyal soth, it is no fable."

168–70 This closely follows *Roman de la rose* 5612–14: "If Virginius refuses, I am ready to prove everything I have said, for I can find good witnesses" (tr. Dahlberg, 1140).

173–74 heere : heere: The scribe of the Hengwrt and Ellesmere MSS glosses the rime riche by writing "audire" over the first *heere,* "hic" over the second. See GP I.17–18n.

207–53 Many critics are disturbed by the account of Virginia's death, which is original with Chaucer; instead of killing his daughter instantly and publicly under extreme pressure, as in Livy and *Le Roman de la rose,* Virginius deliberately plans and announces the execution, which is carried out at home. Cf. 255–76 below.

225 For love, and nat for hate: Cf. *Roman de la rose* 5635: "Car il, par amour, senz haine" (For, through love, without any hatred, he [put her to death]).

230 nat nedeth ... to telle: A common rhetorical formula; see GP I.849, FranT V.1465–66, 1593–94, BD 190 ("Hyt ys no nede reherse hyt more"); cf. *Roman de la rose* 7243–45, tr. Dahlberg, 138 ("I told you just as I heard; I will never record it again").

240 Lat. gloss: "Judges, chapter 11: In that time Jephthah the Gileadite [*Galaandes* for *Galaadites*]" (Judges 11.1). In exchange for victory, Jephtha vows to sacrifice whatever first comes out of his house on his return; the victim turns out to be his only daughter, who asks for two months' respite to bewail her wasted virginity. Allen and Moritz (Distinction of Stories, 161–62) note that Jephtha's vow was widely condemned in the Middle Ages.

255–76 This closely follows *Roman de la rose* 5635–58; tr. Dahlberg, 114. The beheading of Virginia and the presentation of her head to Apius are narrated in *Le Roman de la rose* but not in Livy.

277–86 The final moral seems inappropriate, since it could only apply to Apius, who is not the primary focus of the tale (see Kean, Ch and Poetry 2:182–83). Whatever the intended effect, Chaucer presents standard medieval thinking about sin, as expressed by Innocent III: "the worm of conscience will torture in three ways" (vermis conscientiae tripliciter lacerabit) in his *De contemptu mundi (De miseria condicionis humane)* (3.2; tr. Lewis, 208), which Chaucer translated into English (LGW ProG 413–15). Innocent warns that death may be unexpected (3.1; tr. Lewis, 204) and that the damned suffer not only physically but also inwardly from the knowledge of their sin (3.2; tr. Lewis, 208). For the Augustinian doctrine of the secret punishment that sin inflicts upon its perpetrator, see Alfred L. Kellogg (Spec 26, 1951, 465–81).

286 Forsaketh synne: Proverbial (Whiting S335; cf. ParsT X.93). In the same section of the *De miseria* cited above (3.2; tr. Lewis, 208), Innocent warns that it is too late to repent when one is no longer capable of sinning.

Introduction to the Pardoner's Tale

The explanatory notes to the Pardoner's Introduction, Prologue, and Tale are adapted from those written by Christine Ryan Hilary for The Riverside Chaucer.

288 by nayles and by blood: See 651 and n. below.

295 On the gifts (or goods) of Fortune (riches and social rank; cf. Bo3.pr2) and of Nature (endowments of the body and the soul) see ParsT X.449–56, which also includes the gifts of Grace (mental powers and spiritual strength).

305 jurdones: Glass vessels with bulbous bodies and rimmed necks, used by physicians; so called because of their resemblance to flasks of the water from the River Jordan brought from the Holy Land (see OED s.v. *jordan* 1).

306 ypocras ... galiones: Skeat (5:266) notes the resemblance to the names of the medical authorities Hippocrates

and Galen (cf. BD 571–72: "Ne hele me may no phisicien,/ Noght Ypocras ne Galyen").

Ypocras is a drink made of wine and spices (see MerT IV.1807n.). *Galiones* is not elsewhere recorded; however, Guy of Chauliac describes medicines that are "Galiens" (Cyrurgie, EETS 265, 631, 636), and perhaps the reference is to one of these.

310 Seint Ronyan: Taken by Skeat (5:266–67) as a reference to St. Ronan; the Pardoner's pronunciation in line 320 (see n.) lends this some support. Haskell (Ch's Saints, 17–25) argues for the appropriateness of this saint, a Celt venerated in Brittany. However, the name may be a popular variant pronunciation of "Ninian," a Scottish saint widely known in the fourteenth century: see James Hinton Sledd, MS 13, 1951, 226–33. The OED offers no support for Frederick Tupper's oft-repeated idea (JEGP 14, 1915, 257 n., and 15:66–67) that there is a pun on Fr. *rognan,* kidney, and *runnion,* the male sexual organ; there are no citations in the OED for this form before Shakespeare nor for this sense before 1635.

313 cardynacle: A malapropism confusing *cardinal* with *cardiacle,* "herte quakynge" (see Germaine Dempster, PMLA 68, 1953, 1152), which may be caused by melancholy and for which "comfortives" should be given (Bartholomaeus Anglicus 7.32, tr. John of Trevisa, 1:377–78). Hence, perhaps, the Host's need for a drink.

314 By corpus bones: The Host confuses "by Corpus Domini" (by Our Lord's body) with "by Corpus Cristi" (by Christ's bones). Cf. MkPro VII.1892n., VII.1906n.

318 beel amy: "Fair friend," but most often used with contemptuous or derisive overtones; see MED s.v. *bel ami* (b).

320 Ronyon is here rhymed with *anon* and is apparently to be pronounced with two syllables, like "Ronan." When the Host uses the word in 310 above, it rhymes with *man* and has three syllables.

321–22 alestake: A pole projecting from a roadside public house, decked with an evergreen garland, as a sign that strong drink is sold on the premises (see Jusserand, Eng. Wayfaring Life in the M. A., 132–33). Frederick Tupper (JEGP 13, 1914, 553–65) concluded that the Pardoner's performance takes place in a tavern. The theory was attacked by Gordon H. Gerould (Ch Essays, 1952, 57–59), who suggested that the alestake may be the Summoner's garland (see GP I.666–67) and that the cake in line 322 is one he carries as a buckler (GP I.668). Gerould's explanation has been widely accepted, though it is only speculation and has been rejected by some scholars; Robert E. Nichols, Jr. (PMLA 82, 1967, 498–504) takes the cake and ale as a foreshadowing of the theme of gluttony in the tale and an ironic reference to the Eucharist, a device, he argues, that unifies the Introduction, Prologue, and Tale.

324 Moralists frequently associated ribald tales with gluttony; see, for example, Langland, PP B 5.378 ("For love of tales in tavernes into drynke the moore I dived").

The Pardoner's Prologue and Tale

The Pardoner's Prologue and Tale clearly date from the Canterbury period. The extensive use of Jerome's *Adversus Jovinianum* associates this work with The Wife of Bath's Prologue and The Merchant's and Franklin's Tales, and it is most likely that it was composed at about the same time as those works, around the middle of the decade.

The Pardoner's Prologue, like that of the Wife of Bath and Part I of The Canon's Yeoman's Tale, has the form of a "literary confession" (see W. W. Samuel McCracken, MP 68, 1971, 289–91; Lee Patterson, Ch and Hist., 367–68) and was most likely modeled on the confession of "Faus Semblaunt" in *Le Roman de la rose* (11065–11974; tr. Dahlberg, 195–209, and in RomC 6082–7292); see 403 below. On parallels with false religious confessions, see Patterson, M&H 2nd ser. 7, 1976, 153–73.

The genre of the whole performance is problematical; the Pardoner offers it as an example of his preaching, and it has often been understood to be a sermon, including a brilliant exemplum framed by a fabliau-like situation. Manly (CT, 614) identified in the prologue and tale three or four of the six usual parts of a formal sermon: the theme (VI.334); the protheme, a kind of introduction (lacking); the dilation on the text (lacking); the exemplum or illustrative anecdote (463–903); the peroration, or application (904–15); and the closing formula (perhaps 916–18). However, such formal divisions are characteristic of learned sermons, and vernacular sermons were often looser in structure; see H. Leith Spencer, English Preaching in the Late Middle Ages, 1993, 113–15, 228–67. Alan J. Fletcher (SAC 11, 1989, 15–35) argues that the tale belongs to a genre of popular sermons loosely organized, heavy with exempla, and designed to appeal to the "lewed," a form which Chaucer's audience would have found suspect. See also Sabine Volk-Birke, in Ch and Med Preaching, 347–75, and, on the relation of exemplum and sermon, C. D. Benson, Ch's Drama of Style, ch.3.

The sins that the Pardoner denounces—false oaths, gambling, gluttony—are the "tavern sins," a popular topic in medieval sermons (Owst, Lit and Pulpit, 425–49), in which, as in this tale, the tavern is the scene of gluttony and gambling, which lead inevitably to blasphemy (471–76, 650–53). The story the Pardoner tells has the form of an exemplum (see introductory note to The Friar's Tale) and is generally regarded as one of Chaucer's most powerful narratives, a "matchless short-story" (Kittredge, Ch and His Poetry, 21). Kittredge's characterization is not altogether anachronistic, since the classic short story, the fabliau, and the exemplum are all dependent on the same sort of economy of narrative, with, in the case of the exemplum, didactic power; see Ian Bishop, MÆ 36, 1967, 15–24, and Larry Scanlon, Narrative, Authority, and Power.

The tale of the three rioters is based ultimately on an international folk tale (Aarne-Thompson, no. 763), with analogues from ancient Buddhist and Oriental texts (see Clouston in Originals and Analogues), to modern African tales (see Charles Merrill and Mary Hamel, ChauR 26, 1991, 175–83), and even to Hollywood (Thomas A. Kirby, MLN 66, 1951, 269–70, cites the John Huston movie *The Treasure of the Sierra Madre*).

The story was common in medieval novelle and exempla; Tupper (S&A, 415–23) printed several versions, and Siegfried Wenzel (N&Q 241, 1996, 134–36) identifies the earliest analogue. Though none of the surviving versions could have been Chaucer's direct source, they share enough common elements

(the quest-for-death motif, the rioters' scorn for the old man, the mention of rats when the poison is purchased) to render it probable that Chaucer knew some related version (S&A, 415–16). The setting in Flanders (see 463–84 below), the theme of the plague (Peter G. Beidler, ChauR 16, 1982, 257–69), and some aspects of the old man's character are unique to Chaucer's version.

In the analogues the figure who directs the young men to the treasure is sometimes Christ, sometimes a hermit or philosopher whose advanced age is implied but not much emphasized. Critics have associated Chaucer's old man with many figures: the Wandering Jew, old age as the messenger of Death, a personification of Death, even a realistic, individualized character, or St. Paul's "vetus homo," fallen man (Robert P. Miller, Spec 30, 1955, 180–99); for a summary of such opinions, see Elizabeth R. Hatcher, ChauR 9, 1975, 250 n.1. John A. Steadman (MÆ 33, 1964, 121–30) strikes a balance between the allegorical and literal readings, and many critics rightly warn against imposing a single narrow interpretation on the figure (e.g., A. C. Spearing, ed., PardPro and T, 1965, 40). The deliberate ambiguity of the figure is stressed by some critics, such as Lee Patterson (M&H 2nd ser., 7:153–73), who believes that the figure embodies the Pardoner's own contradictions.

The main critical problems of this prologue and tale, however, are those raised by the Pardoner's motives and character. It was once believed that the Pardoner's performance took place early in the morning in a tavern (see 321–22 above) before the travelers had resumed their journey; the Pardoner's insistence on having a drink (VI.321–28) was therefore an indication that he, like the Miller in the prologue to his tale, is drunk. Older critics frequently offered this explanation for the extraordinary degree of self-revelation in his Prologue, though the text offers no support for this idea. But see John M. Bowers (ELH 57, 1990, 757–84), who argues that he is an alcoholic who cannot function without strong drink.

Some have seen the Pardoner's confession as too excessive to be believed and have argued that the Pardoner is indulging in self-parody (Calderwood, ES 45:302–9) or an elaborate "put on" (John Halverson, ChauR 4, 1970, 185–86), or that he is an "ironized signifier par excellence" (Leicester, Disenchanted Self, 175). Paul E. Beichner argues instead that the Pardoner is simply trying to entertain his hearers (MS 25, 1963, 160–72). Yet others believe that he is motivated by a need for approval (Edward I. Condren, Viator 4, 1973, 177–205), acceptance (Leo F. McNamara, PMASAL 46, 1961, 603–4), or compassion (David, Strumpet Muse, 201).

Such psychological explanations of the Pardoner have dominated criticism since the time of Kittredge, and he has been generally regarded as "the ultimate example of Chaucer's subtle handling of human psychology" (Ruggiers, Art of CT, 123); Howard's study (Idea of CT, 339–70) is the most important representative of this approach. Objections to the excesses of the psychological approach have been raised, most cogently by Derek A. Pearsall (ChauR 17, 1983, 358–65), and the idea that medieval literature has characters in the modern sense has been vigorously attacked (Robertson, Pref. to Chaucer, 34–37; cf. Gerald Morgan, MLR 71, 1976, 241–55). In an important essay, Alfred L. Kellogg (Spec 26, 1951, 465–85) studies the Pardoner as an exemplification of the Augustinian theory of sin; see also Miller's exegetical study of the implications of the suggestion that the Pardoner is a eunuch (Spec 30:180–99).

The idea that the Pardoner is evil—the "one lost soul" on the pilgrimage (Kittredge, Ch and His Poetry, 180)—is widely accepted; to some he has seemed a personification of vice itself (Joyce E. Peterson, ChauR 10, 1976, 326–36; Walter Scheps, Acta IV, 1977, 107–23). Recent critics have been more sympathetic (e.g., James F. Rhodes, ChauR 17, 1982, 40–61). Yet the hint of evil remains: Harold Bloom (The Western Canon: The Books and School of the Ages, 1994, 105–26) compares him to Iago and finds he is the "first nihilist, at least in literature."

The question of the pardoner's sexuality has dominated much recent criticism. See esp. Monica McAlpine, PMLA 95, 1986, 8–22, and the note on the Pardoner in the General Prologue. Carolyn Dinshaw (Ch's Sexual Poetics, 156–84) argues that the Pardoner's "eunuch hermeneutics" lead beyond gender to redemption. But the question of his sexuality remains unsettled. See introductory note to his portrait in the General Prologue.

The Pardoner's Prologue

331 rynge it out: For the phrasing, cf. Tr 2.1615 ("He rong hem out a proces lik a belle") and Whiting B234.

333 theme: The biblical text for a sermon, often subdivided into three subjects (here: gluttony, gambling, swearing).

334 Radix malorum est Cupiditas: 1 Tim. 6.10 ("The love of money is the root of all evil"); cf. Mel VII.1130, 1840; ParsT X.739. Morton W. Bloomfield (The Seven Deadly Sins, 1952, 74 and 95) notes that greed was increasingly seen as the root of evil in the later Middle Ages. Albert C. Friend (MLQ 18, 1957, 305–8) argues that this is a dangerous text to choose; a secular clerk, Robert Lychlade, was arrested in 1395 for using this text in a sermon against churchmen who preached for money.

336 bulles: Bulls, papal letters (here indulgences) bearing the round leaden seal, or *bulla,* stamped with the figures of Saints Peter and Paul on the obverse and the name of the pope who gave it on the reverse. Cf. RomC 6846–47: "With hondis wille I not traveilen,/ For of the Pope I have the bulle."

337 lordes seele: Cf. Langland, PP B Pro 66–67: "Ther preched a Pardoner, as he a preest were/ And broughte forthe a bull with bishopes seles." **Oure lige lorde** is probably the bishop.

patente: letter patent ("open letter," to be shown publicly; cf. GP I.315n.), containing the Pardoner's authorization.

342–43 popes, cardynales, patriarkes, and bishops: All could grant indulgences (Alfred L. Kellogg and Louis A. Haselmayer, PMLA 66, 1951, 251–77). Patriarchs here are metropolitans such as those of Venice and Lisbon.

347–49 Owst (Preaching in Med. Engl., 109–10) quotes a contemporary sermon attacking "theves" who "with fals letters and seeles, with crosses and reliques that thei bere abowten them . . . sei that thei be of seyntes bones or of holy mens clothinge, and bihoteth myche mede that will offre to hem." Siegfried Wenzel (SAC 11, 1989, 37–41) shows that the association of pardoners with fake relics was fairly common.

347 cristal stones: Cf. GP I.700.

350 latoun: See GP I.699n.

sholder-bone: On the use of a sheep's bone in divination (spatelmancy), see ParsT X.603 and n.; David M. Andersen (NM 75, 1974, 630–39) discusses the use of relics in agrarian witchcraft, appropriate to the Pardoner's rural audience.

351 hooly Jewes: The epithet *hooly* has led to attempts to identify this Jew with one who lived before the incarnation; Skeat (5:271) suggests Jacob (Gen. 30.31–43), noting this would add force to VI.365; G. M. Rutter, MLN 43, 1928, 536, suggests Gideon (Judges 6.13–40). Leo J. Henkin (MLN 55, 1940, 254–59) argues that the reference is rather to the common association of Jews with magic.

372 miteyn: Said by Brown (ed. PardT, 28) to be a mitten worn by farmers when sowing grain.

377 For analogues to the trick of telling parishioners that sinners may not offer to his relics, see Dempster, S&A, 411–13; see also 652 below on the blood of Hayles, which was visible only to the truly penitent.

390 hundred mark: A mark was worth two-thirds of a pound (13 shillings, 4 pence). In his last years Chaucer himself had official annuities amounting to only 46 pounds, 13 shillings, 4 pence (Ch Life Records, 533), considerably less than the Pardoner's claimed income. Baugh (Ch's Maj. Poetry, xv) estimates that in his most affluent years Chaucer's annual income was about 99 pounds.

391 lyk a clerk: Beichner (MS 25:160–72) argues that this implies the Pardoner is not a cleric. His clerical status is uncertain (see introduction to the notes to his portrait in the General Prologue).

392 doun yset: Manly (CT, 614) notes that this and Gower, Mirour de l'omme 5245–56; tr. Wilson, 76 (during church services the "somnolent person . . . puts his head gently down on the footstool and sleeps and dreams . . . he hears sung the story of Troilus and fair Crisyede"), show that there were seats in English churches for the congregation, though none has survived.

403 See RomC 6837: "To wynnen is alwey myn entente" (*Roman de la rose* 11565; tr. Dahlberg, 203). Morgan (MLR 71:241–55) agrees with Brusendorff (Ch Trad, 402–4) that Chaucer followed the English Romaunt rather than *Roman de la rose* here and at 407–8 and 443–44.

406 a-blakeberyed: Kökeritz (cited in Paull F. Baum, PMLA 71, 1956, 231) finds this a pun on *beryed* (buried) (VI.405) and *blakeberyed*.

407–8 Parallel to RomB 5763–64: "For ofte good predicacioun/ Cometh of evel entencioun" (*Roman de la rose* 5113–14; tr. Dahlberg, 106). Robert E. Jungmann (Ch Newsletter 1, 1979, 16–17) compares Augustine (De doctrina 4.27.59), who says that the wicked may preach what is right and good. John Gower agreed: see Miroir 21715–20; tr. Wilson, 290 (a sinful preacher "brings great good to the listener and great misery to himself when, behind, he does the contrary of what he preaches before us"). Wyclif and his supporters denied this (so too did some orthodox believers, as in Mirk's Instructions for Parish Priests, EETS 31, 19–68). A. J. Minnis (in Of the Making of Books, ed. P. R. Robinson and Rivkah Zim, 1997, 272–79) surveys medieval opinion and its relation to Wycliffite and Lollard thought on this topic.

415–20   Cf. SumT III.2212 for another example of a preacher's using the pulpit for revenge.

416 my bretheren: This may suggest that the Pardoner is a mendicant friar (see Marie P. Hamilton, JEGP 40, 1941, 48–72); cf. 391 above and GP I.683n.

435 ensamples: Exempla, illustrative anecdotes used by preachers. See the introductory note to The Friar's Tale.

441 in poverte wilfully: see WBT III.1178–79.

443–44 labour with myne handes: Cf. RomC 6845–46: "I wole bothe preche and eke counceilen./ With hondis wille I not traveilen" (*Roman de la rose* 11571–72; tr. Dahlberg, 203).

445 ne make baskettes: Cf. Langland, PP B 15.285–86: "Paule, after his prechyng paniers [baskets] he made,/ And wan with his hondes that his womb [belly] neded." Both Chaucer's text and Langland's seem to confuse St. Paul the Apostle, a tentmaker, with St. Paul the Hermit, who appears in medieval art clad in a mat of palm leaves. However, these passages very likely derive from Jerome, *Ad Rusticum* (Ep. 125.11 in Jerome, Select Letters, tr. F. A. Wright, Loeb, 1933), advising him to "Make creels of reeds or weave baskets of pliant osiers" by way of providing for himself. See John V. Fleming, Christianity and Lit. 28:4, 1979, 21–22, who argues there is no confusion here.

447–48 moneie, wolle, ches, and whete: See Mark 6.8: "And [Jesus] commanded them [the Apostles] that they should take nothing for their journey, save a staff only: no scrip, no bread, no money in their purse."

The Pardoner's Tale

463–84   For the Flemish setting, cf. S&A, 437. Manly (CT, 619) suggests that Chaucer set the tale in Flanders because of the Flemings' reputation for drunkenness; for English attitudes toward Flanders, see Dorothy McBride Norris, PMLA 48, 1933, 636–41.

467–69   Robert A. Pratt (Spec 41, 1966, 631–32) finds a source in John of Wales's *Communiloquium* for the riotous behavior both here and in the discussion of *hasardrye* (see 591 and 603 below). Vincent DiMarco (Leeds SE 23, 1992, 105–26) argues that Chaucer also used Jerome's Letter 22, to Eustochium.

468–71 superfluytee abhominable: For the conception of gluttony in the Middle Ages and its links with blasphemy and heresy, esp. in Chaucer and Gower, see R. F. Yeager, SP 81, 1984, 42–55.

470 develes temple: "The taverne is the develys chapel" (Jacob's Well, S&A, 438). Cf. The *Ayenbite of Inwit* (S&A, 438): "The taverne is the school of the devil . . . there where he maketh his miracles . . . for when the glotoun goth in the tavern he goth upright, when he cometh again, he ne hath foot that him might sustain nor bear" [modernized].

474–75 Jewes rente hym noght ynough: Cf. ParsT X.591.

479 wafereres: Cf. MilT I.3379 and n. According to OED (s.v. *waferer*), *wafereres* were apparently employed as go-betweens and bawds.

481–82   The association of lechery and gluttony, and of wine and lust, is commonplace; cf. PF 275–76 ("And Bachus, god of wyn, sat hire [Venus] besyde,/ And Ceres next, that

doth of hunger boote") and 468–71 above. Here *lecherye/ That is annexed unto golotonye* is from the *Communiloquium* of John of Wales: "luxurie et gule que est ei annexa" (Pratt, Spec 41:635).

483 hooly writ: Lat. gloss (at 485): "And do not become drunk with wine, in which is lechery" (Eph. 5.18), perhaps quoted from Innocent III, *De miseria* 2.19.12–13 (tr. Lewis, 168). A closer parallel is John of Wales: "In vino est luxuria" (*luxurie is in wyn;* cf. Pratt, Spec 41:635).

485 Looth: See Gen. 19.30–36. Langland uses Lot as an example of drunkenness and lechery in Piers Plowman B 1.27–33. His appearance here is probably due to John of Wales (Pratt, Spec 41:635).

488 Herodes: Herod and Lot are listed together as examples of drunkenness in Piers Plowman C 10.175–77: "His [God's] grace and his tresour,/ That many a lede [men] leseth thorw likerouse drynke,/ As Lot dide and Noe, and Herodes the daffe."

   Stories may refer to the *Historia evangelica,* part of the *Historia scholastica* of Peter Comestor (Skeat 5:278). Robinson doubted this, since Peter's account of Herod does not mention his drunkenness (PL 198:1574–75).

492 Senec: Lines 493–97 roughly translate Seneca's Epistle 83.18–19, tr. Gummere: "Drunkenness is nothing but a condition of insanity voluntarily assumed. . . . Even as it is the madness is no less; it merely lasts a shorter time. John of Wales quoted part of this (Pratt, Spec 41:635), and Pratt speculates that some manuscript of the *Communiloquium* may contain the whole passage from Seneca. Harry M. Ayres (RomR 10, 1919, 5–7) argues that there are further reminiscences of Seneca (esp. from Epist. 95.19–25) in VI.513–48. Skeat finds parallels instead in Innocent's *De miseria* (esp. 2.17, 18; tr. Lewis. 164–66), which he believes reflect Chaucer's prose translation (see Skeat 3:445, where the relevant passages are printed).

504–11 Corrupt . . . for glotonye: On gluttony and the Fall, see SumT III.1915–16.

508–11   Lat. gloss: "Jeronimus contra Jovinianum: 'Quamdiu jejunavit Adam in Paradiso fuit: comedit et ejectus est statim duxit uxorem'" (Adv. Jov. 2.15, tr. Fremantle, 398), tr. in the text. Cf. ParsT X.819.

512–16   Cf. Ecclus. 37.29–31: "Do not be greedy for every delicacy nor eat without restraint. For illness is a sure result of overeating, and gluttony is next door to colic. Gluttony has been the death of many; be on your guard and prolong your life." Brown (ed., 32) compares 513–14 to Seneca, Epist. 95.19 (tr. Gummere): "It took elaborate courses to produce elaborate diseases."

517–20 the shorte throte: Cf. Jerome, Adv. Jov. 2.8 (tr. Fremantle, 394: "For the sake of a temporary gratification of the appetite, land and sea are ransacked").

522–23   Lat. gloss: "Meat for the belly, and the belly for meat, but God shall destroy both the one and the other" (1 Cor. 6.13).

527–28   Jerome, Adv. Jov. 2.12; tr. Fremantle, 397: "What sort of fasting is it, or what refreshment is there after fasting, when we are blown out with yesterday's dinner, and our stomach is made a factory for the latrine."

529–35   Lat. gloss: "Ad Philipenses capitulo 3" (Phil. 3.18–19, quoted in the text; cf. ParsT X.820).

538–39 substaunce into accident: Cf. Innocent III, *De mis-*

eria 2.17.8–10 (tr. Lewis, 164): "One grinds and strains, another minces and prepares, turns substance into accident, changes nature into art." The "substance into accident" figure *(substance* = the essential nature, and *accident* = the outward quality by which a thing is identified and apprehended) as applied to cookery appears also in Walter Map, Latin Poems, ed. Wright, page liii: "Let them become in accident what they could not be in substance." Robinson notes that Chaucer could hardly have failed to relate this to the controversy over transubstantiation, a lively topic in his time, and to have been reminded of Wyclif's facetious remark that the faithful should forbid friars to enter their cellars lest the wine be transubstantiated into nothing (Wyclif, Sermones, ed. Iohann Loserth, Wyclif Soc., 1887–90, 194). On the textual implications of this joke, see Paul Strohm, SAC 17, 1995, 23–42, and on allusions to the Eucharist, see Nichols, PMLA 82:501–2.

547–48 Lat. gloss: "[She] who lives in pleasure is dead while living" (1 Tim. 5.6). From Jerome (Adv. Jov. 2.9, tr. Fremantle, 395).

549–50 Lat. gloss (tr. in the text): "Luxuriosa res vinum et contumeliosa ebrietas" (Prov. 20.1, with "contumeliosa" [quarrelsome] for Vulgate "tumultosa" [tumultuous], as in Jerome, Adv. Jov. 2.10; tr. Fremantle, 395). Lewis notes it is also quoted by Innocent (*De miseria* 2,19,14; tr. Lewis, 168).

554–55 Sampsoun: Samson, as a Nazarite, abstained from wine (Judges 13.5 and Num. 6.3). Skeat suggests the name was chosen for its sound and that it should be pronounced with a nasal intonation.

558–59 sepulture/ Of mannes wit: nearly identical to ParsT X.822; cf. MLT II.773–74. Perhaps suggested by John of Wales (Pratt, Spec 41:635): "The dissolute man is of the living dead, but the drunkard is both dead and buried."

560–61 Proverbial (Whiting D394); cf. Mel VII.1194n., MLT II.771–77n., and 584 below.

564–66 Fysshstrete: Fish Hill Street, off Thames Street, just below London Bridge.

Chepe: probably Cheapside, one of the principal shopping streets in the London of Chaucer's day (cf. I.754 and n.), though here perhaps Eastcheap; see Magoun, Ch Gazetteer, 105–6.

565–71 crepeth subtilly/ In othere wynes: A reference to the illegal diluting of better wines with cheaper varieties, a practice common enough that in the Liber albus, 615–18, there are regulations specifying that different kinds of wine are to be kept in different cellars. Manly (CT, 619) quotes Letter Book H. 145 on the price of wines from Bordeaux (**Burdeux**) and La Rochelle (**Rochele**) set at ten pence, and wines from Spain, such as those produced at **Lepe** (northwest of Cadiz), set at eight pence.

567 fumositee: see SqT V.358–59n.

579 Attila: king of the Huns, died (453) of a nosebleed brought on by excessive drinking on a night when he had just wed a new wife; see Vincent of Beauvais, *Speculum historiale* 7.22: "Attila, drunk on his wedding night, with blood gushing from his nose in an apoplectic fit, suffocated in his bed."

584 Lamuel: Lat. gloss: "Noli vinum dare," from Prov. 31.4: "Do not to kings, O Lamuel, do not to kings give wine, for

there is no secret where drunkenness reigns." The second half of this verse is quoted above at 560–61 (see n.); the quotation of the first half and echoes of part of the next verse ("Lest they drink and pervert their judgement") are found in 586–87. Both, Pratt (Spec 41:634) argues, are due to John of Wales's *Communiloquium*.

585 not Samuel, but Lamuel: For the rhetorical device used here, see KnT I.2063–64n.

591 Lat. gloss: "Policraticus, Book 1: 'Dicing is the mother of lies and perjuries'" (John of Salisbury, Policraticus 1.5, as quoted by John of Wales; see Pratt, Spec 41:633).

603 Stilboun: Chaucer draws the story in VI.603–20 from John of Salisbury's *Policraticus* 1.5.1 (S&A, 438, tr. Pike, 28–29), via John of Wales, but substitutes **Stilboun** for Chilon. Some MSS (not in the Ellesmere or Hengwrt traditions of glossing) gloss *Stilboun* with "i.e., Mercurius," since this is the Greek name for that planet. But it has been argued that Chaucer may have been thinking of the philosopher Stilbo, mentioned in Seneca, Epist. 9.18–19, 10.1 (Ayres, RomR 10:5) or in Seneca's Moral Essays, tr. Basore, 2.5.6 (on Firmness). Pratt (Spec 41:633) suggests that a scribal error ("Stilboun" for "Chilon") in the *Communiloquium* may account for the form.

621 Demetrius: His story appears in John of Salisbury's *Policraticus* 1.5 (S&A, 438, tr. Pike, 29), immediately following that of Chilon (Chaucer's *Stilboun*).

631–32 Cf. ParsT X.600n. Swearing is associated with gluttony in Langland (PP B 2.92 "Glotonye he gaf hem eke, and grete othes togydere"). Drunkenness, a branch of gluttony, was associated with gambling. See Tupper, JEGP 13:553–65; Owst, Lit and Pulpit, 417–18.

633–34 Mathew: Lat. gloss: "Do not swear at all" (Matt. 5.34).

635 Lat. gloss: "Jeremiah 4: 'You shall swear in truth, in judgment, and in righteousness'" (Jer. 4.2, omitting "that the Lord lives" after "swear"). The same text is quoted in ParsT X.592.

639 the firste table: The first three commandments, setting forth the duties owed to God, the other seven being those owed to mankind; see Dives and Pauper, EETS 275, 1:304.

641 seconde heeste: "Thou shalt not take the Lord's name in vain" (reckoned as the third commandment in most Protestant usages).

649–50 nat parten from his hous: Ecclus. 23–11 has "A man given to swearing is lawless to the core; the scourge will never be far from his house . . . his house will be filled with trouble."

650–53 On the association of gambling and blasphemy, see ParsT X.580 and n.

651 nayles: Either Christ's fingernails or the nails of the cross, probably the latter in the light of Wyclif (Select Engl. Works 3.483): "It is not leeful to swere . . . by Godds bonys, sydus, naylus, ne arms, or by ony membre of Cristis body, as tho moste dele of men usen." As Skeat notes (5:284), the rioters were probably not concerned with the distinction.

652 Hayles: Hayles Abbey in Gloucestershire, where there was a vial containing what was said to be the blood of Christ. The blood was visible only to those with pure consciences; see Horstmann, Altenglische Legenden, 281: "For there are many who can not see that holy blood, until they have purified their consciences" [trans.].

653 chaunce: In the game of hazard (*hasard,* VI.465), which is played with two dice, the thrower calls a number (his "main") and throws the dice; if his main appears, he wins; if two aces (*ambes as*), ace-deuce, or (if seven is the main) twelve appear, he loses; if seven is the main an eleven will also win, as will a twelve if six is the main. If any other number appears on the first roll, this is the thrower's *chaunce,* and the thrower casts the dice until either his *chaunce* appears and he wins, or his main reappears and he loses (see Charles Cotton, The Compleat Gamester, 1674, ed. in Games and Gamesters of the Restoration by Cyril H. Hartman, 1930, 82–84). Obviously, modern "craps" is "hazard" with seven always the main. In this case the speaker's main was eight (*cink* and *trey*); on his first throw he cast a seven, which is now his winning number, his *chaunce,* while an eight will win for his opponent.

662 prime: The first of the canonical hours (cf. GP I.122n.); the bell is rung at 6 A.M. for the singing of the office of prime.

664–65 Skeat (5:286) notes the custom of ringing a hand-bell before a corpse on its way to burial and cites Mirk's Instructions for Parish Priests, EETS 31, lines 1851–52: "Make thy clerk before thee gynge [go]/ To bere light and belle ring."

679 pestilence: Possible reference to the plagues of 1348–50, 1361–62, 1376, and 1379, though there were minor outbreaks throughout the century. For the plague background to The Pardoner's Tale, see Beidler, ChauR 16, 1982, 257–69. For contemporary descriptions of the plague, see Boccaccio, *Decameron* 1, intro., and Langland, PP B 20.52–182.

710 Deeth shal be deed: Cf. Hosea 13.14: "I shall be your death, O Death."

713 oold man: On the literary definition of old age in Chaucer's day, see Burrow, Ages of Man, 193–94.

717–20 Scholars have attempted to find a source for the hostility of the rioters toward the old man (Richard F. Harris, Southern Folklore Qtly 33, 1969, 24–38, cites Old Norse analogues), but this may have been part of the story as Chaucer received it (cf. the contempt for the old man shown by Tagliagambe in the Rappresentazione di Sant Antonio, S&A, 423–24).

719 greet age: The contemporary Geoffrey le Baker writes "The pestilence seized especially the young and strong, commonly sparing the elderly and feeble." Other chroniclers say the same (Peter G. Beidler, ChauR 16:260).

722 into Ynde: Cf. WBPro III.824n.

727–36 The old man's desire for death is not found in any of the analogues; it is based on the first elegy of Maximian, in which the aged man knocks on the ground and pleads, "Receive me, mother, take pity on the hardships of age; I seek to warm my tired bones in your bosom" (vv. 227–28; S&A, 437). Chaucer may have read Maximian in school (George R. Coffman, Spec 9, 1934, 269–71). Alicia K. Nitecki (ChauR 16, 1981, 76–84) shows that the lament of an old man, based on Maximian's elegy, was the subject of a number of Middle English poems; she notes the closest analogue is "Le regret de Maximian," in Carleton Brown, Rel. Lyrics of XIII Cent., 1932, 92–100.

743–44 Lat. gloss: "Stand up in the presence of a gray head" (Lev. 19.32).

745 oold man: Cf. Ecclus. 8.6: "Despise no man for being old."

765 ook: The oak does not appear in the analogues. Chaucer was robbed in 1390 at a place called "fowle ok" in Kent, an execution site (Pearsall, Life of Ch, 213).

770 floryns: Either coins in general or German or Flemish florins, worth three shillings and struck in imitation of the Florentine florin, the standard gold coin of the later Middle Ages. An English florin was minted briefly in 1344 but then recalled and replaced by the "noble" (Baker, Spec 36, 1961, 282–86).

779 tresor: "Treasure is believed to be a gift of Fortune . . . of ancient time it was by natural law the property of the finder, [but] it is now by the law of nations the property of the lord king himself" (Henri de Bracton, *De legibus et consuetudinibus Angliae,* ed. George E. Woodbine, 1915–42, 2:338–39). This is quoted by Joel Roache (JEGP 64, 1965, 1–6), who shows that the rioters commit theft by keeping the treasure.

781 lightly as it comth: Proverbial (Whiting C384).

793 cut: See GP I.835–36.

845 poyson: On poison lore, see Margaret Hallissy, MSE 9, 1983, 54–63.

848 he hadde leve: On God's permitting the devil to tempt an individual, see the story of Job (1.12: "And the Lord said unto Satan, Behold, all that he hath is in thy power; only upon himself put not forth thine hand"); cf. FrT III.1482–96.

889–90 Avycen: Avicenna, the authority on medicine (see GP I.432 and 429–34 n.); in his book a chapter is called a **fen** (Arabic *fann,* a division of a science). His work treats of poisons in Bk. 4, Fen 6, in Avicenna, *Liber canonis,* 1964 (rpt. of 1507 edition).

907 nobles: First struck in the reign of Edward III, they were worth six shillings eight pence (Baker, Spec 36:284–86, with illustrations).

   sterlynges: The name is said to derive from the Easterlings, Norwegians and Danes, once brought to England to undertake the purification of the minting of English money (Drennen and Wyatt, ed. PardT, 79). The OED (s.v. *sterling* sb.) says rather that it derives from late OE "*steorling," coin with a star. (*hypothetical form)

916 oure soules leche: Cf. Psalms 146.3 (AV 147.3): "He healeth the broken in heart, and bindeth up their wounds."

919–45 The Pardoner's attempt to sell his admittedly fake relics to the Host has elicited much critical commentary: Kittredge's explanation that the Pardoner suffers from a "paroxysm of agonized sincerity" is still widely quoted, but a great many other explanations have been offered, ranging from mere forgetfulness to a cynical attempt to reduce the pilgrimage to nonsense (for a summary of earlier opinions, see Halverson, ChauR 4:189–90). Howard (Idea of CT, 353) regards the Pardoner's offer of his relics as an extravagant gamble motivated perhaps by an unconscious will to lose.

   The Host's reaction has likewise been explained in a variety of ways—disgust at the Pardoner's effrontery (Gerould, Ch Essays, 71), an expression of the reader's feelings toward the Pardoner (Brewer, Chaucer, 159), an angry reaction to a personal attack (Kean, Ch and Poetry, 2:104), and an "appropriate punishment" for the Pardoner's taunting of the Host (Patterson, Ch and Hist., 406).

948 thyn olde breech: Daniel Knapp (ELH 39, 1972, 1–26) suggests that there is an allusion here to the hair breeches worn by St. Thomas, an object of veneration at Canterbury. Richard F. Green (SAC 15, 1993, 131–45) finds an allusion to a fabliaux motif (he finds eight examples) of the trousers of an adulterer passed off as a holy relic to be kissed by the faithful. He suggests that the allusion implies the Pardoner is an excessive womanizer, not a homosexual or eunuch (cf. introductory note to the portrait of the Pardoner in GP).

951 Seint Eleyne: On St. Helen's discovery of the cross, see South English Legendary, EETS 235–36, 1:174–78.

952–53 coillons . . . relikes: Possibly an echo of Le Roman de la rose (7108–9; tr. Dahlberg, 135), where there is a word play on "coillons" and "reliques" (relikes). This is usually taken as a crude reference to the Pardoner's eunuchry (e.g., Curry, Ch and Science, 67), but cf. GP I.691 and n. Baum (Chaucer, 54) and Faulkner (Twentieth-Century Interpretations of PardT, 1973, 11) argue that this indicates that the Pardoner is not a eunuch.

953 seintuarie: Taken by the OED as "shrine," but MED s.v. seintuari(e n. 5 has rather "A holy or sacred object; also, an object thought to have healing properties; also, a relic of a saint."

968 they kiste: They exchange the kiss of peace as a formal sign of reconciliation; on the custom, see Nicholas J. Perella, The Kiss: Sacred and Profane, 1969, 130. Some critics have doubted that the Host and Pardoner are actually reconciled (see Robert A. Burlin, Ch Fiction, 1977, 169–75). Glenn Burger (PMLA 107, 1992, 1143–56) takes the kiss as part of the tale's "politics of inversion and perversion." For a response and reply, see Ann Barbeau Gardiner, PMLA 108, 1994, 333–34, and Burger, 334–35.

FRAGMENT VII

Fragment VII usually follows Fragment VI in the MSS with the Ellesmere order, but in the Chaucer Society order, which Skeat adopted for his edition, VII was joined with II, forming Fragment B (II in the present edition), to correct a geographical inconsistency (see VII.1926 and the note on the Order of the Tales, p. 3).

Fragment VII is the longest and most varied of the fragments and it lacks any very clear unifying theme. Paull F. Baum (Ch: A Crit. Appreciation, 1958, 74–84) argues that the tales of this fragment form a "Surprise Group," since, though the tellers tell stories that on reflection are seen to fit their characters, they often surprise the Host's expectations. Alan T. Gaylord (PMLA 82, 1967, 226–35) suggests instead that the tales form a "Literary Group," with Harry Bailly acting as a kind of editor. Ann W. Astell (ELH 59, 1992, 269–87) likewise takes it as a "Literary Group," in the sense, she argues, that the tales illustrate and undercut the Aristotelian "causes of Literature." Howard (Idea of CT, 271–88) finds rather a sort of "retrospective" unity supplied by The Nun's Priest's Tale read as a skeptically ironic comment on the tales that have gone before.

Though the tales that make up the fragment are of varying dates of composition, the fragment itself was assembled rather late in the composition of The Canterbury Tales (see Germaine Dempster, PMLA 68, 1953, 1142–59) and perhaps never received a final revision.

The Shipman's Tale

The explanatory notes to The Shipman's Tale are adapted from those written by J. A. Burrow and V. J. Scattergood for The Riverside Chaucer.

The Host's words to the *gentil maryneer,* which follow this tale (VII.435–42), show Chaucer intended it for the Shipman. The textual history of EpiMLT II.1179 (see n.), however, suggests that the tale was originally intended for another narrator. Furthermore, the pronouns *we, us,* and *oure* (lines 12–19) suggest a married female narrator. Most critics therefore assume the tale was originally intended for the Wife of Bath (Robert A. Pratt, Sts. in Hon. of Baugh, 45–79). If that theory is correct, it shows that the tale was composed rather early in the Canterbury period, though it provides no further evidence for dating.

The tale is a fabliau, and some consider it Chaucer's first experiment in the genre, "nearer to the pure fabliau-type" (Brewer, in Rowland, Companion to Ch Sts, 259). The setting in Saint-Denis, the snatch of French at VII.214, and several oaths suggest a French source, and the tale clearly has the structure and characteristics of a fabliau (see Fichte, Ch's Frame Tales, 51–66). However, no such source has been found, and the nearest known French analogue (Le Bouchier d'Abevile, in Benson and Andersson, Lit. Context, 282–311) is not very close.

The story belongs to a well-known folktale type, "the lover's gift regained": see John Webster Spargo, Ch's ShipT, FFC 91, 1930, and S&A, 439–46. The closest extant analogue is Boccaccio's Decameron 8.1 (8.2 is a similar story). A version preserved in Sercambi's Novella 19 (text and trans. in Benson and Andersson, Lit. Context, 312–19) perhaps gave Chaucer some ideas (see Robert A. Pratt, MLN 55, 1940, 142–45). Richard Guerin (ES 52, 1971, 412–19) suggests that Chaucer used all three Italian versions. If these were his sources, however, he altered them a great deal—particularly the ending where the merchant's wife excuses herself with a ready answer (VII.400–26); in the other versions, she is the dupe. On the superior characterization in Chaucer's version, see Carol F. Heffernan, in Keith Busby and Erik Kooper, eds., Courtly Literature: Culture and Context, 1990, 261–70.

The tale has not attracted much critical attention, perhaps because of its apparent cynicism, "an immoral tale told by an immoral man" (Howard, Idea of CT, 273), though Richardson (Blameth Nat Me, 110–22) finds "embedded in the imagery" Christian standards by which the behavior of the characters is measured and found wanting. According to Albert H. Silverman (PQ 32, 1953, 329–36), the equation in the tale between sex and money shows that in the Shipman's world human relations are reduced to the level of financial transactions. This remains the dominant view, though V. J. Scattergood (ChauR 11, 1977, 210–31) sees the tale as a sympathetic but not uncritical examination of the bourgeois mercantile ethos (see also Patterson, Ch and Hist., 344–66). Paul Strohm (Social Ch,

100–2) is harsher; he sees the "commodification" of everything in the tale, including the debasement of the ideal of sworn brotherhood (see 42 below).

1 Seint-Denys: Saint-Denis, north of Paris, famous for its abbey and fair. The cloth trade was carried on there in the fourteenth century. Perhaps the *ware* in which the merchant dealt (VII.56) was cloth: see OED s.v. *ware* sb³ 3b., though this meaning is first recorded in 1442.

4–19 Compare WBPro III.337–56 and 543–62; however, neither passage mentions cost, the main point here. On the pronouns suggesting a feminine speaker in VII.12, 14, 18, 19, see introductory note.

9 shadwe upon the wal: Proverbial; see MerT IV.1315n.

13 for his owene worship: The wife claims here and at VII.421 that she dresses richly to manifest her husband's social status; see Thrupp, Merchant Class, 147–50.

22 largesse: A noble quality not always characteristic of merchants in medieval literature. This merchant's *largesse* appears at VII.281–86, though he uses *large* reproachfully (431) and his wife complains of his *nygardye* (172).

26 a thritty wynter: About thirty years (the age of Youth in Parlement of the Thre Ages 133; cf. *yonge*, VII.28).

29 the goode man: The master of the house; see MED s.v. *god man* phr. and n. 2(a). Compare VII.33, 107, and *goode wyf* at 92 and cf. SumT III.1768. The phrase is used quite frequently in contexts of cuckoldry: "Ye shall goo . . . Onto the goodewyff when the goodeman ys owte" (Mankind, ed. M. Eccles, EETS 262, 1969, 703–4).

35 village: The word suggests humble origins for both men; compare ClT IV.483.

36 cosynage: The words *cosyn* and *cosynage* are frequent in the tale. Though Ruth M. Fisher (N&Q 210, 1965, 168–70) argues for a pun on *cozen*, "cheat," that word is not recorded before 1453 (MED s.v. *cosin* n.).

38 glad therof as fowel: A proverbial comparison (Whiting F561); cf. VII.51 and KnT I.2437n., MerT IV.2322. In Chaucer it usually "connotes a trust that turns out to be misplaced" (Scattergood, ChauR 11:211).

42 bretherhede: In KnT, Palamon and Arcite are both cousins by birth (cf. VII.36) and sworn brothers: see KnT I.1132n.

43 daun John: Practically a generic name for a cleric: compare ProMkT VII.1929 and see EpiMLT II.1172 and n.
  manly: cf. GP I.167. See E. T. Donaldson, in Brewer, ed., Geoffrey Ch, 106–7: "the adjective manly does double duty for the monk's generosity and his virility."

51 fowel is fayn: Cf. 38 above.

55 Brugges: Bruges, the great Flemish mercantile center where many alien merchants had dealings.

65–66 officer: The monk holds an office in his monastery, probably that of cellarer, which requires him to do business with the outside world (compare VII.272–73). John is, like the Monk on the pilgrimage, an *outridere* (GP I.166n.).

69 oure deere cosyn: The "domestic our" (see WBPro III.311n.) is unusually frequent in this tale; see also VII.107, 356, 363.

70–71 malvesye: Malmsey, a sweet wine originally produced at Monemvasia in the Morea (*malvesie* in French).
  vernage "generally refers to a strong, sweet Italian wine,

but there is a recipe in MS Harley 2378 for making an unsweetened spiced wine" (Curye on Inglysch, EETS, SS 8, 1985, 221).

79 thilke yeer: The merchant apparently draws up his annual accounts before setting off on his principal buying trip.

91 his thynges: See 131 below.

95–97 Like other gentlewomen, merchants' wives sometimes had a girl to wait on them. Thrupp (Merchant Class, 151) quotes the demands of a retired tailor to his son: "At all due tymes whan that I or my wyf walketh oute that my said sone shall late me have an honest man chyld to wayte upon me and an honest mayde chyld to wayte upon my wyf."

108 laboured: Compare MerT IV.1842 and n.

111 wax al reed: Compare Tr 2.652: "For of hire owen thought she wex al reed."

113 God woot al: A proverbial expression (Whiting G245), here suggesting that the truth is different.

131 portehors: A breviary that priests carry (*porte*) out (*hors*) with them. This monk has just said his devotions (*thynges*, VII.91) from it.

136 al into pieces tere: Perhaps an allusion to the fate of *Genylon of France* (194), torn apart by four warhorses for betraying Roland at Roncesvalles (Chanson de Roland). He becomes a type of the traitor. Cf. MkT VII.2389, NPT VII.3227, BD 1121: "the false Genelloun."

145 legende: Properly the story of the life and sufferings (compare VII.146) of a saint. The wife dramatizes herself as a "martyr" to her husband; see A. Booker Thro, ChauR 5, 1970, 106–8.

148 Seint Martyn: St. Martin, bishop of Tours (d. 397), founder of the first monastery in Gaul.

151 Seint Denys: St. Denis (Dionysius), bishop of Paris and patron saint of France (d. 272). His remains were preserved in the monastery at Saint-Denis, so the reference is particularly apt.

155 professioun: Monastic vows (including chastity). The monk prepares for his assignation on the Sabbath (VII.307) by having his beard and tonsure (which marked his acceptance of monastic vows) *al fressh and newe yshave* (309).

158–71 Compare WBPro III.531–42 and WBT III.961–80 (especially III.979–80 with VII.159–60).

171 value of a flye: Proverbial (Whiting F345). On the theme of male sexual inadequacy in French fabliaux, see Per Nykrog, Les fabliaux, 1973, 189. But VII.377–79 suggest that the wife is lying.

173–77 Compare NPT VII.2912–17 (2914 resembles 176 here) and WBT III.1258–60 (1259 resembles 177), and also WBT III.925–48. But none of these passages numbers the qualities desired in a husband. Perhaps the hexadic form derives indirectly from Irish lists of "the six excellences": see Roland M. Smith, Journal of Celtic Studies 1, 1949–50, 98–104.

181 An hundred frankes: About 15 pounds sterling, a considerable sum. The "franc a cheval" was first issued in 1360, and established itself as a common French gold coin in Chaucer's lifetime, valued at approximately half an English noble (i.e., 3 shillings, 4 pence). Peter G. Beidler (ChauR 31, 1996, 5–17) puts the modern equivalent of 100 francs at about 5,000 dollars, at the most conservative estimate.

194 Genylon: See 136 above.

205–6 Dinner was usually taken some time between **pryme** (9 A.M.) and noon. Monks' liking for food was a satirical commonplace; compare GP I.205–6.

214 Quy la: This is Chaucer's only use of foreign speech in a foreign setting as local color (contrast SumT III.1832, 1838).

Peter: The wife swears by St. Peter, the porter of heaven, in the face of the locked door (see 85). Compare Sir Gawain and the Green Knight, 813: "'Ye, Peter!' quoth the porter, and purely I trowe" [regularized].

224–48 Merchants were notorious worriers about their property and profits. Compare VII.76 and Winner and Waster, ed. Stephanie Trigg, EETS 297, 1990, lines 246–62; and for a preacher's disapproval, see Owst, Lit and Pulpit, 352. See also Gardiner Stillwell, RES n. s. 20, 1944, 1–18. Cf. GP I.274–75.

227 Seint Yve: More likely a reference to St. Ivo of Chartres than to St. Yves of Brittany or St. Ives of Huntingdonshire: Ruth H. Cline, MLN 610, 1945, 482. Cf. SumT III.1943.

230–34 A difficult passage. For different interpretations, see Baugh (337) and M. Copland (MÆ 35, 1962, 19). *pleye/A pilgrymage* may mean either that merchants seek relaxation on pilgrimages (some MSS read *on* for *a*), or else, if *pleye* is transitive, that they pretend to go away on pilgrimages in order to escape creditors. See Jonathan Sumption (Pilgrimage, 168) on pilgrims' immunity in courts of law.

237–38 we moote stonde in drede: Medieval merchants justified their profits by emphasizing the risks (**hap, fortune**) that they took: see Gower, Miroir de l'omme, 25201–3, tr. Wilson, 330: "The law says, and it is only right, that he who can lose in a venture should also be allowed to gain from it."

243 kepe oure good: Compare MerT IV.1343. On the responsibilities of merchants' wives, see Thrupp, Merchant Class, 169–74.

261–62 Medical authorities recommended moderation in eating during hot weather; see GP I.347n.

277–78 lat this thyng be secree: The monk, who does not want the wife to hear of the loan, seems to suggest that any disclosure of it may prejudice his impending purchase.

287 On the power of ready money, see Poem 51 in Robbins, Hist. Poems, 31–32: ("At al tymys the best ware ys/ Ever redy money"). "In fact supplies of ready money were low" (Thrupp, Merchant Class, 143).

304 Compare the dicing and dancing apprentice in CkT I.4370, 4384.

328–34 In Bruges, where merchandise proved unexpectedly dear, the merchant had spent 20,000 shields on credit. The *sheeld* was a unit of account in the Bruges money market (cf. GP I.278 and Kenneth S. Cahn, SAC 2, 1980, 81–119). Having entered into a formal pledge (**reconyssaunce**) for early repayment, he accordingly returned to Saint-Denis, collected what French francs he had there, and went to Paris to borrow the rest from **certeine freendes** in order to redeem his bond (VII.368). At the end of the fourteenth century, the London–Bruges exchange rate was 25 pence sterling to the shield, so the value of the merchant's loan would have been nearly 2,000 pounds, a very large sum. See generally R. de Roover, Money, Banking and Credit in Medieval Bruges, 1948, ch. 4.

355 Seint Jame: See RvT I.4264n.

359 tokenes: Compare MancT IX.258.

367 Lumbardes: The merchant redeems his bond (368) from the Paris branch of the Italian bank that lent him the 20,000 shields in Bruges. For a different analysis, see Cahn, SAC 2:116–17. Italian bankers "practically dominated the money market" in Bruges, according to de Roover (Money, Banking and Credit, 55).

369 murie as a papejay: cf. 38 above and MerT IV.2322.

379 maketh it ful tough: The phrase occurs in ME in various senses (see GP I.785n. and Whiting T431). In Chaucer's works it usually means "put on airs, be haughty" (BD 529–31: "Loo, how goodly spak thys knight/. . . He made hyt nouther towgh ne queynt") or "be bold, swagger" (Tr 2.1025: "As make it with thise argumentes towgh"). It is not elsewhere applied to sexual activity.

384 yow: The merchant addresses his wife with the reproachfully formal plural pronoun from here to 389, reverting at 395 to his customary *thou*. Cf. Language and Versification, p. xxxiii.

400–1 not afered: Compare MerT IV.2264–75.

413–17 The wife here uses mercantile terminology (compare VII.397–99) in its traditional Pauline application to sex: "Let the husband render unto the wife the debt [debitum], and likewise the woman unto the man" (1 Cor. 7.3). Compare WBPro III.130, 153; MerT IV.1452, 2048; ParsT X.375, 940; and cf. WBPro III.198n.

416 taille: A tally was a stick in which notches were cut to record debts (compare GP I.570). *Tail* means "sexual member" in WBPro III.466 (see MED s.v. *tail* n. 1b (c)—Chaucer's uses are the first recorded), and a pun is clearly intended here. On the interchangeability of sex and money in the tale, see especially Silverman, PQ 32:329–36. Compare VII.434.

423 my joly body: Compare EpiMLT II.1185.

432 thy: Variant readings *my* and *our* miss a subtle point. The merchant, seeing no profit in anger, accepts the wife's claim that she thought the money was given to her personally (VII.406–7), and simply suggests that she should not spend so much of her money on dress (418–19).

434 Taillynge: For the pun, see 416 above.

The Introduction to the Prioress's Tale

435 corpus dominus: The Host's blunder for *corpus Domini*, the body of the Lord. See PardT VI.314n., ProMk VII.1892n.

440–41 in the mannes hood an ape: Compare GP I.706n.

432 French fabliaux writers often draw morals of this knowing sort. The Cook draws a similar conclusion from RvT: CkPro I.4330–34. Compare the end of the fabliau Gombert, quoted in note to RvT I.4320–21.

447 youre: The Host uses *thou* to address the Shipman (436), but shifts to the formal plural when he speaks *curteisly* to the Prioress (446).

The Prioress's Prologue and Tale

The explanatory notes to The Prioress's Prologue and Tale are adapted from those written by Florence H. Ridley for The Riverside Chaucer.

The stanzaic form, the rhetorical style, and the use of Dante in the Prologue seem to place this work in Chaucer's "Italian period," but it cannot be dated precisely. Sumner Ferris (ChauR 15, 1981, 295–321) argues that the tale was written to be read on the occasion of a visit to Lincoln by Richard II and Queen Anne on 26 March 1387 (see n. 684 below) and later revised for inclusion in the Canterbury Tales. The revision of the tale must have come relatively late in the Canterbury period, after The Shipman's Tale, to which it refers (see 642–43, 643n. below), and before The Nun's Priest's Tale, which echoes it a number of times (see VII.3052, 3057 and n.). The Prologue appears to be later than The Second Nun's Prologue, from which it apparently "borrows" (see n. 474–80 below), but that does not help date the work any more precisely.

The Prologue is made up of details from Scripture and the Liturgy (cf. Boyd, Ch and the Liturgy, 68–75, and Kean, Ch and Poetry 2:195–96). Though the Tale is adapted for a female speaker (cf. VII.354, 581 and notes below), it fits the Prioress's portrait in the General Prologue only in reflecting her tenderness for small creatures; there is nothing about it of the idealized romance heroine or satirized nun.

The tale belongs to the large and varied genre of Miracles of the Virgin. These are brief religious folk tales of wonders wrought by Mary as a reward for faithful devotion to her. They are found throughout Europe, in both Latin and the vernaculars. For a survey of the genre in Middle English, with examples, see Beverly Boyd, ed., Miracles of the Virgin, 1964.

The theme of a child murdered by enemies of his faith is ancient and persists even today (Florence Ridley, Western Folklore Qtly 26, 1967, 153–56).

Carleton Brown provides a history of the story Chaucer used, classifying the many versions into three groups, assigning Chaucer's tale to Group C (A Study of The Miracle of Our Lady, Ch Soc, 2nd ser. 45, 1910; S&A, 477–85). Chaucer's version is unique in such details as the little clergeon's age (see 503 below), the friend who teaches him the antiphon, and the *greyn* that Mary puts on his tongue. The tragic ending is characteristic of Group C but may also have been influenced by other legends, such as that of St. Hugh (see 684 below), embodying the ritual murder libel (on which see Alan Dundes, ed., The Blood Libel Legend, 1991, a collection of essays on a variety of aspects of the legend).

The Miracles of the Virgin were frequently fiercely anti-Semitic (see Hardy Long Frank, ChauR 13:346–62 and Robert Worth Frank, Jr., in Wisdom of Poetry, 177–88), and Chaucer's tale shares that characteristic of his sources and his times. (The tale has little connection with English life of the time: Jews had been banished from England since 1290; see C. Roth, Hist. of the Jews in Eng., rev. ed., 1970.) On medieval anti-Semitism, see Philip S. Alexander, Bull. of the John Rylands Library of Manchester 74 1992, 109–20. The anti-Semitism has been a difficult problem for readers and critics, especially in recent years, and has deeply affected critical attitudes toward both the Prioress and her tale. Some critics, reluctant to ascribe the anti-Semitism to Chaucer himself, regard the tale as a satiric revelation of the Prioress's character and see both it and her portrait in the General Prologue as harshly satiric. But the Prioress is not the only possible anti-Semite on the pilgrimage: the Parson also regards the Jews as "cursed" and links them with the Devil (X.591, 599). The Prioress's pitiless attitude toward the murderers does not essen-

tially differ from the Man of Law's fierceness toward the unbelieving Saracens (II.960–65). Henry A. Kelly (M&H, n.s. 19, 1992, 143–44) notes the vengeful character of the liturgy of the Holy Innocents, on which Chaucer draws (see 453–59, 580–85, 627 below) and which repeatedly calls on God to avenge the children slain by Herod's soldiers. On the Prioress's anti-Semitism, see Albert B. Friedman, ChauR 9, 1974, 118–29; David, Strumpet Muse, 212–14. Florence Ridley, The Prioress and Her Critics, UC English Sts., 30, 1965, provides a useful survey of the problem; Derek Pearsall, CT, 246–52, provides a just assessment.

The apparent sentimentality of the tale has also raised problems for some modern readers (e.g., Charles Owen, Pilgrimage and Storytelling, 1977, 119–21), though this aspect of the tale has found admirers from the time of Wordsworth (who translated it into modern English). Robert O. Payne (Key of Remembrance, 1963, 164–69) regards it as a deliberate experiment (along with tales such as the Man of Law's and Physician's) in the pathetic mode. On this, see Robert Worth Frank, Jr., in Ch's Religious Tales, 39–52, and Carolyn Collette, in the same volume, 95–107 (with a useful review of criticism). For a full account of the scholarship, see Beverly Boyd, ed., The Prioress's Tale, Variorum edition, vol. 2, pt. 20, 1987.

The Prioress's Prologue

453–59   Paraphrase of Psalm 8.2–3 ([AV 8.1–2]: "O Lord our Lord, how excellent is thy name in all the earth! . . . Out of the mouths of babes and sucklings hast thou ordained strength because of thine enemies"), the opening lines of matins in the Little Office of the Virgin, though Chaucer may have had in mind the introit of the Mass of the Holy Innocents (Marie P. Hamilton, MLR 34, 1939, 3; J. C. Wenk, MS 17, 1955, 216).

454 quod she: This follows smoothly from line 451; cf. 581 and n.

458 on the brest soukynge: Perhaps an allusion to St. Nicholas (see 514 below), who as an infant would suckle but once on Wednesdays and Fridays.

461 lylye: a common symbol of purity and of Mary; cf. SNPro VIII.27. In one version of the tale a lily rather than a *greyn* is placed on the child's tongue (S&A, 457; for an illustration see Pratt, Tales).

468 bussh unbrent: See Exodus 3.2: "An angel of the Lord appeared unto him [Moses] in a flame of fire out of the midst of a bush; and he looked, and, behold, the bush burned with fire, and the bush was not consumed." This was taken as an anticipation of the Virgin birth; see Chaucer's ABC 89–94: "the bush with flawmes rede . . . Was signe of thin unwemmed maidenhede./ Thou art the bush on which ther gan descende/ The Holi Gost." On this use of Marian imagery see Piero Boitani, in Fichte, ed., Ch's Frame Tales, 83–128.

469–72   Burrow (ed., Eng. Verse 1300–1500, 1977, 223) finds an allusion to Dante, *Inferno* 3.4–6: "Justice moved my high Creator; divine Power made me, supreme Wisdom (*Sapienza*) and primal Love," which defines the Trinity: Power (Father), Wisdom (Son), Love (Holy Spirit).

474–80   Based on Dante, Par. 33.16–19 (quoted in SNT VIII.53–56n.). There are also echoes of the prayer and absolution of matins; cf. Kean, Ch and Poetry 2:188–89. Robert A. Pratt (MLQ 7, 1946, 259–61) and Robert Burlin

(Ch Fiction, 278, n. 11) argue that here Chaucer "borrows" from his own earlier use of the passage in SNT, VIII.29–77.

The Prioress's Tale

488 Asye: Most versions of the tale either leave the country unspecified or set it in some remote place (Carleton F. Brown, A Study of the Miracle of Our Lady, Ch Soc, 2nd ser., No. 45, 1910, 55).

489 Jewerye: The Jewish quarter of the city, a ghetto; see MED s.v. *jeuerie* 2 (c).

490–91 lucre of vileynye: Glossed in the Ellesmere and Hengwrt MSS with "turpe lucrum," a term in canon law (derived from 1 Tim. 3.8) meaning "shameful (excessive) profits" (John A. Yunck, N&Q 205, 1960, 165–67). Jewish communities were protected for the taxes they provided and for moneylending, **usure,** forbidden in canon law but essential for business (Roth, Hist. of the Jews, 192–97, 207).

495 litel scole: Apparently a village school (Carleton F. Brown, MP 3, 1906, 467–91), though its enrollment (*children a heep*) implies it was modeled on the song schools of London (Nicholas Orme, English Schools, 60–68) such as St. Paul's, near which Chaucer lived as a child.

503 litel clergeon: Used in the general sense of a young clerk rather than a chorister, as Skeat (5:176) suggested (Brown, MP 3:467–71). The word *litel* is heavily used throughout this part of the tale.

   seven yeer: The child is ordinarily ten in the analogues; Chaucer's change increases both the pathos and the realism. Seven "puts him just on the borderline between *infantia,* the age of innocence, and its successor, *pueritia*" (Burrow, Ages of Man, 74). See Bartholomaeus Anglicus (6.5, tr. Trevisa 1:300), who notes that seven is the age at which children entered school; the clergeon is in his first term, which ends at Christmas.

508 Ave Marie: The first prayer in the primer printed by Plimpton (517 below): "Hail mari full of grace the lord is with the. blessed be thow among women & blessid be the frute of thi wombe Jesus. Amen." Cf. Luke 1.28, 42.

512 child ... soone lere: Proverbial (Whiting C219).

514 Seint Nicholas: Bishop of Myra, first half of fourth century; for his legend, see Jacobus de Voragine, Legenda aurea, tr. Ryan 1:21–27. St. Nicholas was renowned for his infant piety (cf. 458 above) and his precocious learning, which made him the patron of schoolboys and clerks. His providing dowries for poor girls (South English Leg., 33–64) is perhaps the basis for his modern transformation into Santa Claus. His feast, 6 December, is closely related to Childermas (Hamilton, MLR 34:6). On his further appropriateness to the tale, see Haskell, Ch's Saints, 47–55.

517 prymer: An elementary school book, usually containing the alphabet, basic prayers, elements of the faith (creed, Our Father, etc.) and simple devotions such as the Hours (Little Office) of the Virgin Mary (Nicholas Orme, Eng. Schools, 62). Possibly it was of the sort represented by the fourteenth-century English primer reproduced in George A. Plimpton, Ch's Education, 1935, plates IX.1–IX.15. Plimpton also reproduces a fifteenth-century French primer that includes a selection of hymns, among which is the *Alma Redemptoris Mater* (plates XIII.1–XIII.39).

518 Alma redemptoris: An antiphon to Mary in liturgical use from Advent to Candlemas (2 February). It begins, "Alma Redemptoris Mater, quae pervia caeli/ Porta manes, et stella maris, succurre cadenti,/ Surgere qui curat, populo." This is the song usually sung in the "C" versions: "Godus Moder, Mylde and Clene/ Hevene yate and Sterre of se,/ Saue thi peple from synne and we" (woe). The frontispiece to Brown, Miracle of Our Lady, reproduces the musical notation from an early MS.

540 Cristemasse: The end of the feast of Christmas is the beginning of the next school term.

572 wardrobe: A euphemism for *pryvee* or *gong* (the more direct term used by the Parson, X.885), deriving from the practice of having one place serve as both clothes room and latrine (John W. Draper, ESt 60, 1926, 238–39).

576 Mordre wol out: Proverbial (Whiting M806); echoed in NPT VII.3052, 3057.

578 blood out crieth: Cf. Gen. 4.10 ("And he [the Lord] said [to Cain], What hast thou done? The voice of thy brother's blood crieth unto me from the ground"), referring to the ancient belief that the blood of one murdered would cry out unless it were covered (Wenk, MS 17:217).

579 O martyr, sowded to virginitee: Singled out, with VII.649–55, by Matthew Arnold to illustrate the virtue of Chaucer's poetry (Brewer, Ch: The Crit. Heritage, 2:218).

580–85 Latin gloss (in Hengwrt, not Ellesmere): "Let us look in the Apocalypse of John and there we shall find a lamb and with him 144 thousand of those with the sign, etc. who sing a new song etc." [cf. Rev. 14.1]. "These are those who have not polluted themselves with women; those indeed who have remained virgins, who follow the lamb wherever he goes, etc." [cf. Rev. 14.4]. The gloss is from Jerome's *Adversus Jovinianum* (1.40, tr. Fremantle, 378). The passage from Revelations was read at the Feast of the Holy Innocents (Beverly Boyd, Ch and the Liturgy, 1971, 69–70).

581 quod she: This suggests adaptation of the tale to its context. The phrase echoes ProPrT VII.454 and emphasizes the speaker's presence. It has been seen as a means of indicating the Prioress's limitations, questioning her tale, making clear its expression of innocent belief, or the poet's desire to dissociate himself from its anti-Semitism (Trevor Whittock, A Reading of CT, 1968, 204–5; Leo Spitzer, Traditio 2, 1944, 454; John R. Nist, TSL 15, 1966, 96–97). KnT I.2994 is similar—*quod he*—and likewise calls attention to the speaker, even at the expense of dramatic consistency (though here the speaker is the teller of the tale).

583 Pathmos: Patmos, an island in the Aegean, where the apostle **Seint John** was believed to have written the Apocalypse in a cave that is still pointed out today.

607–8 Cf. VII.453–59. Chaucer has replaced "propter inimicos tuos" of the Introit with *lo, heere thy myght,* perhaps because he is about to reveal how God confounded his enemies through the voice of a child (Wenk, MS 17:216).

609 emeraude: Cf. English Medieval Lapidaries, EETS 190, 121: "He that beres a emeraud upon him the mor shal love to kepe his body in chastite" [regularized].

610 ruby: The ruby shines in the dark (LGW 1119: "Ne ruby non, that shynede by nyghte"), and therefore betokens the light of Christ (Friedman, MÆ 39, 1970, 304).

616 provost: In reference to foreign cities, the officer charged with punishment of offenders: OED s.v. *provost* 6;

cf. MED s.v. *provost* n. (c). Since both Christians and Jews are alien in this place, Edward H. Kelly argues the murderers' punishment (628–34) is no indication of anti-Semitism (PLL 51, 1969, 368), but see Owen (Pilgrimage and Story, 230 n. 7).

627 Latin gloss: "Rachel weeping for her children would not be consoled, etc." (Matt. 2.18), part of the gospel for the Mass of the Holy Innocents (Hamilton, MLR 34:4). St. Matthew here quotes Jeremiah 31.15 and thus relates the Massacre of the Innocents to Jeremiah's prophecy. David (Strumpet Muse, 210, 212–13) argues that such reminiscence of Old Testament material suggests Chaucer's awareness that Jews were not only legendary monsters but children of the promise (Gen. 9.9, 17.1–7) and thus creates an ironic contrast between the Prioress's view and his own.

632 Yvele shal have: Proverbial (Whiting E178).

639 hooly water: The ceremonial sprinkling of the body with holy water regularly follows the Requiem Mass; here perhaps it implies the child's release from the flesh, symbolized by the filth in which he had been thrown (Wenk, MS 17:218; Boyd, Ch and Liturgy, 51).

643 As monkes ben: Apparently a reference to the monk in The Shipman's Tale rather than to the Monk in the General Prologue, whom the Prioress has no reason to reprove.

662 greyn: Unique to Chaucer's version; a lily, gem, and white pebble occur in three analogues (S&A, 457–58). The grain has been explained in a great variety of ways: Paul E. Beichner (Speculum 36, 1961, 302–7), for example, takes it as medicine a "loving mother" might administer to relieve her child's injured throat, since *greyn* is glossed in the Promptorium Parvulorum as "grain of paradise" (cardamom), used as a breath-sweetener (MilT I.3690). Albert B. Friedman surveys this and other theories, suggesting that the *greyn* is important as a prop rather than a symbol (ChauR 11, 1977, 328–33). A miracle is not meant to be understood, and perhaps *greyn* was left deliberately ambiguous (cf. Sherman Hawkins, JEGP 63, 1984, 614–17).

684 Hugh of Lyncoln: The young Hugh of Lincoln was said to have been martyred by Jews in 1255. His story is preserved in the ballad "Sir Hugh or the Jew's Daughter" (Child, Ballads, no. 155). For the legend, see Butler's Lives of the Saints 3:421–22 and Joseph Jacobs, in Dundes, The Blood Libel, 41–71. Hugh was regularly listed among martyred saints until recent times, though it is clear that the boy was not murdered by Jews (Gavin I. Langmuir, Spec 47, 1972, 459–82). Lincoln Cathedral, where a plaque commemorated his supposed martyrdom until 1959 (Lachs, Western Folklore Qtly. 19, 1960, 61–62), was the center of his cult. On 19 February 1387, Chaucer's wife, together with Henry, Earl of Derby, and other members of John of Gaunt's family, was admitted to the Fraternity of Lincoln Cathedral (Ch Life Records, 91–92). As noted above, Ferris (ChauR 15:295–321) argues the tale was written for a 26 March 1387 visit to Lincoln by Richard II and Queen Anne.

The Prologue to Sir Thopas

The explanatory notes to The Prologue and Tale of Sir Thopas are adapted from those written by J. A. Burrow for The Riverside Chaucer.

"This Prologue is noteworthy as conforming in meter to the rime royal stanza of the preceding tale. The regular meter of the headlinks, or talks by the way, is the heroic couplet, even when they connect tales in stanzaic form or in prose" (Robinson).

696–97 Alfred L. Kellogg (MÆ 29, 1960, 119–20) compares Virgil's reproach to Dante in Purg. 19.52: "Why do you keep your eyes fixed on the ground?"

700–2 Chaucer jokes about his stoutness and consequent unattractiveness to women in Scog 31–32, where he numbers himself among "alle hem that ben hoor and rounde of shap,/ That ben so lykly folk in love to spede." Compare MercB 27–28: "Sin I fro Love escaped am so fat,/ I never thenk to ben in his prison lene."

703–4 elvish: Because Chaucer seems so gregarious in GP I.30–34, Thomas A. Knott (MP 8, 1910, 135–39) took this as implying a temporary mood of seriousness induced by The Prioress's Tale. But Chaucer portrays himself as generally unsociable in HF 644–60, and VII.694–95 suggests that the Host is noticing him for the first time. J. A. Burrow (in M. Teresa Tavormina and R. F. Yeager, eds., The Endless Knot: Essays in Hon. of Marie Boroff, 1995, 105–11) studies the connotations of *elvish*—uncanny, intractable—as if Chaucer were "bent on protecting his authorial privacy against readerly intrusion" (106). On "authorial self-definition" and the contrast between the narrator of Thopas and that of Melibee, see Lee W. Patterson, SAC 11, 1989, 117–75 (on Melibee see also Seth Lerer, in Mark C. Amodio, ed., Oral Trad. and the CT, 1994, 181–205).

Sir Thopas

Sir Thopas contains no clue to its date. John M. Manly dated it before the Canterbury period, at the time of a Flemish embassy in 1383 (E&S 13, 1928, 52–73); but his reading of the whole poem as a satire on the Flemish bourgeoisie is not convincing (see 719 below). In any case, the structure of the tale, insofar as it depends on a pilgrim interrupting at 918 (see 833–35 below), shows that Chaucer had the Canterbury journey in mind.

For his own tale of Sir Thopas, Chaucer adopts the genre of the popular romance (albeit a burlesque) and pointedly departs from his normal poetic usages ("as though he himself were not the author but only the reporter of the rest," Speght, ed., 1598). He imitates the popular poetry of his day in meter, rhyme, and diction. The tail-rhyme stanza is employed in many ME romances (see A. McI. Trounce, MÆ 1, 1932, 87–108, 168–82; 2, 1933, 34–57, 189–98; 3, 1934, 30–50), but Chaucer uses it only here. Most tail-rhyme romances have a twelve-line stanza; Chaucer's basic stanza has six lines, rhyming either *a a b a a b* (18 stanzas) or *a a b c c b* (8 stanzas), as in the first part of the romance of *Bevis of Hampton* in the Auchinleck MS. The remaining five stanzas incorporate a one-stress line or "bob" (first at VII.793), perhaps in imitation of the English *Sir Tristrem,* and four of them follow the bob with an extra section of three lines, variously rhymed (797–826, 881–90). Perhaps Chaucer had in mind the pointless metrical variations to be found in romance texts (e.g., the Auchinleck *Bevis*). He also imitates the loose rhyming technique of these romances, allowing himself several uncharacteristic licenses; see 781, 806, 819, and 902 below.

The diction of Thopas has a distinct popular coloring, drawn from contemporary English romance, ballad, and song. The pilgrim-poet addresses his audience as *lordes* (712, 833), divides his narrative into *fits* (see 888–90 below), calls his hero *child Thopas* (see 810 below), and employs several other expressions (discussed in the notes below) not found elsewhere in Chaucer's work (see Walter Scheps, NM 80, 1979, 69–77). A group of words shared with The Miller's Tale (*gent* 715, *rode* 727, *love-longynge* 772, *lemman* 788, etc.) has a similar popular character (Donaldson, Speaking of Ch, 13–29).

The stereotyped style of common ME narrative verse, in tail-rhyme, short couplet, and ballad stanza, makes it difficult to determine exactly which poems Chaucer had in mind. The standard collection of parallels, taking account of all previous work, is by Laura Hibbard Loomis in S&A, 486–559. The most striking verbal similarities are indicated in the notes below. On the language of romance in Sir Thopas, see Yoshiyuki Nakao, in Michio Kawai, ed., Lang. and Style in Engl. Lit.: Essays in Hon. of Michio Masui, 1991, 343–60, and Mechthild Gretsch, Anglia 108, 1990, 113–32.

Chaucer's chief model appears to have been *Guy of Warwick* (see 899 below), the tail-rhyme version of which survives only in the Auchinleck MS (1330–40), along with *Bevis of Hampton* and the unique copy of *Horn Childe*. Loomis (S&A, 489) believed Chaucer used that MS. He could have known *Lybeaus Desconus, Sir Launfal, Sir Eglamour,* and *Ypotis* in a lost antecedent of the fifteenth-century MS B. L. Cotton Caligula A.ii, in which they all appear. Yet these two MSS cannot account for all that Chaucer knew. *Perceval of Gales* appears only, and *Thomas of Erceldoune* first, in the Lincoln Thornton MS. Chaucer had no doubt read and heard much English narrative verse (probably ballads as well as romances; see 739, 740–41, and 839 below). On the oral characteristics of these romances as reflected in Sir Thopas, see Ward Parks, in Amodio, ed., Oral Trad., 149–79.

The plot of Sir Thopas consists of several familiar motifs of romance—the adventurous knight, the hero in love, the giant adversary, the arming of the hero—combined into a deliberately inconclusive and shapeless whole. No single source is to be looked for, although Francis P. Magoun, Jr. (PMLA 42, 1927, 833–44) proposed an episode in *Lybeaus Desconus* (ed. Maldwyn Mills, EETS 261, 1969). The cowardly nature of the hero and his prosaic origins in Flanders (718–20) push the poem toward the burlesque (see J. A. Burrow, YES 14, 1984, 44–55). The burlesque genre was well understood by most early readers of Thopas; witness the imitations by Dunbar (*Schir Thomas Norny*) and Drayton (*Nimphidia*). Like Drayton, Richard Hurd in his *Letters on Chivalry and Romance,* 1765 ed., 319, compared Chaucer with Cervantes: "Sir Topaz is all Don Quixote in little."

712   The appeal for attention, here and at 833 and 893, is in the minstrel manner. See 833–35 below.

Listeth: Chaucer uses the word only here and at 833. His usual word is *hark/hearken* (e.g., GP I.788, ClT IV.1163), but *list(en)* occurs more commonly with *lord(ing)s* at the beginning of ME poems (J. A. Burrow, Essays on Med. Lit., 66–69).

entent: The rhyme with *verrayment* (a word Chaucer uses only here) requires *entent* rather than the regular Chaucerian *entente.*

715 gent: A "stale adjective," used also of Alisoun in MilT I.3234 (see n.), and in PF 558 ("the goos, with here facounde gent"), and presumably inappropriate here.

717 sire Thopas: "An excellent title for such a gem of a knight" (Skeat 5:183). The topaz, a bright gem, is used as a type of superlative excellence in the Bible (Job 28.19: "The topaz of Ethiopia shall not equal it") and in medieval French poetry, where it is applied to both men (S&A, 493) and women (Machaut, Jugement dou Roy de Behaingne, tr. Palmer, lines 1861–62: "That beautiful topaz/ who in beauty and sweetness surpasses all"). Some lapidaries credit the topaz with effect against lust; see English Medieval Lapidaries, EETS 190, page 107: "He that bereth this stone [topaz] shall the more love to leede his body in chastity" [regularized].

The title *sire,* prefixed to Thopas whenever the name occurs (except VII.830)—as also *sir Gy* (899), *sir Lybeux* (900), *sir Percyvell* (916), and even *sir Olifaunt* (808)—imitates the promiscuous use of titles in popular English romances. Except in Thopas, Chaucer avoids prefixing *sire* to a knight's name, thus following contemporary French practice, which confined the usage to wealthy bourgeois; see Burrow, Essays on Med. Lit., 69–74.

719 Flaundres: Flanders, a center of industry and trade just across the Channel, provides a comically mundane setting for knightly feats. This does not, however, imply that Thopas as a whole is to be understood as a satire on Flemings, as Manly proposed (E&S 13:52–73). Cf. Burrow, YES 14:44–55, and see PardT VI.463–84n.

720 Poperyng: A Flemish town noted for its cloth, no doubt selected by Chaucer for its comic-sounding name and commonplace associations (William W. Lawrence, PMLA 50, 1935, 86).

in the place: "Interpreted by Skeat 'in the mansion, manorhouse'; but it may be a mere rime-tag, meaning 'right there'" (Robinson).

722   Compare *Eglamour* (Cotton MS, ed. F. E. Richardson, EETS 256, 1965, 934–36): "I was born in Artas;/ Syr Prymsamour my fadyr was,/ The lord of that countre." Manly (CT, 630) notes that the lord of Poperinge was the abbot of St. Bertin, though this may not have been known to Chaucer or his audience.

724–35   For ME parallels to the description of Thopas and his dress, see Loomis, S&A, 504–7.

724 swayn: A word used in the romances of young gentlemen attendant on knights, sometimes equivalent to "squire" (e.g., *Bevis of Hampton,* Auchinleck MS, 571–72: "Beves, while thow art swain,/ Thow schalt be my chaumberlain"). But Chaucer uses it elsewhere only as a Northern word for "servant" (RvT I.4027).

725–27   Poetic praise of a pink-and-white complexion is normally reserved for women and children, as in the stock simile "red as rose" (Whiting R199), sometimes coupled with the equally common "white as (lily) flower" (Whiting L285; cf. VII.867). But the comparison with **payndemayn,** fine white bread, is unparalleled. Loomis (S&A, 504) suggests that "Punning on the word 'flour' probably led Chaucer to his own variant" (for the pun, cf. WBPro III.477–78).

rode: Complexion. A word used elsewhere by Chaucer only of Absolon (MilT I.3317) and generally applied to women (Donaldson, Speaking of Ch, 20–21).

scarlet in grayn: Deep-dyed scarlet cloth; *grayn* was the most effective and expensive of red dyes. See NPT VII.3459n.

730–31 Compare the dwarf in *Lybeaus* 127–28: "Hys berd was yelow as ony wax,/ To hys gerdell henge the plex [plaits]," and Bevis of Hampton disguised as a begging paimer: "His berd was yelw, to his brest wax,/ And to his gerdel heng his fax [hair]" [regularized] (Bevis 2243–44). Bevis's golden locks are admired (2246–47) but by the reign of Richard II long hair and long beards were no longer in fashion; see Richard Corson, Fashions in Hair, 1965, 104.

saffroun: Used in cooking for color and flavor. Compare the domestic similes in VII.725 and 727 and the romance parallel in Seven Sages 101: "His here was yelow as the safferon" (S&A 507).

Brugges: Bruges, the main commercial center in Flanders (see ShipT VII.55n.).

734 syklatoun: A fine and costly material (patterned silk?) from the East; see *Guy of Warwick*, 2835: "Gode clothes of sikelatoun & Alisaundrins."

735 jane: Cf. ClT IV.999n.

736–41 For ME parallels to the description of Thopas's pastimes, see Loomis, S&A, 508–15.

737 river: (OF *rivere,* used here in a technical sense— "hawking") is stressed on its second syllable.

738 goshauk: A kind of hawk much used in England. "Not a hawk for a knight" notes Manly, following the Boke of St. Albans, which assigns the *goshawk* to yeomen; but Hands (N&Q 216, 1971, 85–88) shows that the Boke is unreliable here, citing correspondence about a *goshawk* between Sir John Paston and a relative.

739 Archery was a pastime not practiced by knights in romance (S&A cites no parallels). It suggests rather the yeoman heroes of greenwood ballads (compare GP I.104–10). See 740–41 and 839 below.

740–41 By Chaucer's time, wrestling was not considered a knightly sport. Yeomen wrestle in the Gest of Robyn Hode (Child, Ballads, no. 117) st. 135, and, like Chaucer's Miller (GP I.548), the greenwood hero Gamelyn wrestles for the prize of a ram; see GP I.548n.

742 bright in bour: Thirty "maidens bright" fall in love with Guy of Warwick (235–53), but he cares only for Felice. The stock phrase, *bright in bour,* is found only here in Chaucer, but is common in the romances; compare Guy (Auchinleck) 11.6, where it rhymes with "par amoure," as here.

745 For this rhetorical device, *contrarium,* the reinforcement of a word by adding the negative of its opposite, see also VII.882; MancT IX.20; RomA 310 ("ful yelow and nothyng bright"); BD 143 ("ful pale and nothyng rody"). The emphasis on Thopas's chastity (compare 717 above) is unexpected in a popular English romance; Loomis, S&A, cites no convincing parallels. Donaldson (Ch's Poetry, 935) speaks of Thopas's "downright effeminacy" (see also Loomis, S&A, 504). Edmund Spenser (in the 1590 edition only) introduced Thopas into his allegory of chastity; The Faerie Queene (ed. A. C. Hamilton, 1977, 3.7.48: "Till him Chylde Thopas to confusion brought").

746–47 brembul . . . rose: The dog-rose was distinguished in ME from other kinds of "bramble" by appellations such as "red bramble" and "hip bramble"; see MED s.v. *brembel* 2(a).

748–49 Compare Amis and Amiloun, 1885–86: "So it bifel that selve day,/ With tong as y you tel may." See 918 below.

756 Deer and especially the timid hare provide an anticlimax (in the short tail-line, as often) after *many a wilde best,* though they are both technically "wild" or undomesticated (S. I. Tucker, RES n.s. 10, 1959, 54–56).

760–65 The plants (*herbes*) mentioned are all spice-bearing exotics, not to be found in Flanders: licorice, **cetewale** or zedoary (with a root like ginger), clove, and nutmeg. See Loomis (S&A, 550–55), and compare MilT I.3207n. The passage belongs to a tradition of descriptions of paradisal woods and gardens—the *plaisance* or *locus amoenus*—best represented by Le Roman de la rose, 1331–44 (RomA 1359–72), which includes all four spices mentioned here among the plants growing in Love's garden.

767 papejay: The parrot's voice is a type of ugliness in Thomas Hoccleve's Praise of His Lady, 19–20: "Hit comly body shape as a foot-bal;/ And shee syngith ful lyk a papejay," Sec. Lyrics, ed. Robbins, 223. So also in another ME burlesque, ed. Wright and Halliwell, Reliquiae antiquae, 1841–43, 182: "Tho throstyll and tho popegey notyd full clene." However, the *papejaye* also appears in lists of birds in RomA 81 ("The chelaundre and papyngay") and 913: "With popinjay, with nightingale."

770 spray: Only here in Chaucer. "On the spray" and "sing on the (a) spray" are stock poetic phrases; for examples, see MED s.v. *sprai* (1).

772 love-longynge: This compound (cf. *love-likynge,* VII.850) occurs elsewhere in Chaucer only in MilT (I.3349, 3679, 3705). It belongs to the idiom of popular poems such as Bevis 897: "Love-longing me hath be-caught" [regularized].

773 herde the thrustel synge: Bird-song provokes love-longing in several romances (S&A, 516–26), e.g., *Thomas of Erceldoune* (ed. James A. H. Murray, EETS 61, 1875), 29–33: "I herde the jay, the throstill cokke . . . Allone in longing thus as I laye" [regularized], and *Guy of Warwick,* 4519–20: "So michel he herd tho foules sing,/ That him thought he was in gret longing."

774 Pryked as he were wood: Cf. *Guy of Warwick* 181.10: "And priked right as he wer wode." See also S&A, 512–13, and RvT I.4231. Repetition of the verb *prick* eight times in Thopas, five between 754 and 779, comically suggests the limited diction of ME romance.

781 plas: Like *gras* (831), this word always has a final *-e* in rhyme elsewhere in Chaucer; but it commonly rhymes with *aas* in Guy of Warwick (S&A, 517).

783 yaf hym good forage: This "may mean 'turned him out to graze': but forage usually is 'dry fodder' and Sir Thopas was quite capable of the absurdity implied" (Manly, CT, 631). The suggestion gains support from Chaucer's two other uses of *forage,* MerT IV.1422 and especially RvPro I.3868: "Gras tyme is doon; my fodder is now forage."

784 The first fit (see 888–90 below) falls into three sections, each of six stanzas: introductory descriptions (st. 1–6), Thopas in the forest (st. 7–12), and the quest for the fairy queen (st. 13–18). Here, as at 748, the new section begins abruptly. Presumably Thopas makes this speech after waking from a night's sleep (787) in the clearing. For parallels to his forest nap, see S&A, 514–15.

788 elf-queene: Line 814 here and WBT III.872–73 show

that Chaucer made no distinction between *elf* and *fairy*. His fairy queen probably owes something to Thomas Chester's *Launfal* (see 794–95 below) and to *Thomas of Erceldoune;* in both poems the hero falls in love with a fairy woman in a forest (see S&A, 516–26). Spenser probably derived Prince Arthur's vision of the Fairy Queen from Chaucer's episode; Faerie Queene 1.9.9–15.

lemman: A common ME word for "mistress," used by the mature Chaucer only in contexts degraded morally or socially or both; see MancT IX.204–22, and 204–6n.

789 goore: Originally a triangular piece of cloth inserted in a garment, but here a cloak. See Donaldson, Speaking of Ch, 23–24.

793 Single-stress lines ("bobs") occur in two other ME romances, neither in tail-rhyme: Sir Gawain and the Green Knight, and Sir Tristrem. Chaucer perhaps knew the latter in the Auchinleck MS. Bobs often take the form of a prepositional phrase with indistinct meaning: compare *in londe* at 887 and *in toune*, Sir Gawain and the Green Knight, 614. See E. G. Stanley, NM 73, 1972, 417–26.

794–95 Chaucer is probably imitating *Launfal*, 316–18, where the fairy princess says to the hero: "Yf thou wilt truly to me take,/ And alle women for me forsake,/ Riche I will make thee" [regularized].

796 dale . . . downe: A stock alliterative phrase. The word *down*, "hill," is found only here in Chaucer.

797 clamb: "A knight would surely have leapt or vaulted, not climbed, into his saddle" (Robinson). See Bevis 1943–44: "Into the sadel a lippte [he leaped],/ That no stirop he ne drippte [touched]."

798 stile and stoon: Unlike *dale and downe* (796), this collocation is not recorded elsewhere in ME. It looks like a fake traditional phrase, created by Chaucer on the analogy of "stick and stone" and "still as stone."

804–6 Cf. *Guy of Warwick* 148.7–9: "In this warld is man non/ That ogaines him durst gon,/ Herl, baroun, no knight" (and cf. Guy 236.9–11).

805 The identical rhyme on *goon* must be deliberately bad, like that on *contree* (722).

806 childe: Outside prepositional phrases such as *with childe,* the word does not have a final -e elsewhere in Chaucer (a possible exception is MLT II.919). The form here may be a deliberate mock-poetic departure from Chaucer's normal usage.

807 greet geaunt: Giants are common in ME romances; see S&A, 530–41, and Gerald Bordman, Motif-Index of the English Metrical Romances, FFC 190, 1963, under F531. Three are especially relevant to Thopas: the Saracen Sir Amoraunt and the African Colbrond, both adversaries of the hero in *Guy of Warwick*, st. 95–133, 253–69; and Maugys in the Île d'Or episode of *Lybeaus Desconus* 1225–1395. Magoun (PMLA 42:833–44) proposes the latter work as a major source for the plot of Thopas, but the relationship of giant and lady is quite different in Chester's poem.

808 sire Olifaunt: Sir Elephant. The comic name is modeled on giants' names, such as Sir Amoraunt in Guy 98.1 (with similar promiscuous use of "sir"; see 717 above) or Guymerraunt in *Octovian Imperator* 921, both names rhyming conveniently with *geaunt* and *Tervagaunt*. Spenser borrows Chaucer's name in Faerie Queene 3.7.48, 3.11.3–6.

810 Child: "A youth of noble birth, esp. an aspirant to knighthood; also, a knight or warrior," MED s.v. *child* 6(a). The usage is common in romance and ballad, but confined in Chaucer to Thopas (also at VII.817, 830, 898).

Termagaunt: Supposed to have been a god of the Saracens, along with Apollo, Mahomet, and others. Amoraunt swears by Tervagaunt (the OF form of the name) in *Guy of Warwick* 121.2, 126.7; and the giant in *Lybeaus* 1301 "levede [believed] yn Termagaunt."

812 I sle thy steede: It was considered unsporting to set out to kill an opponent's horse. Bevis calls the act "gret vileinie" (*Bevis of Hampton,* 1891). Compare *Guy of Warwick* 101.2, 260.10 and *Lybeaus* 1316.

815 In *Thomas of Erceldoune* 257–60, the castle of the fairy mistress is full of "all manere of mynstralsye."

symphonye: Probably a hurdy-gurdy, a sort of mechanized fiddle; see Susann and Samuel Palmer, The Hurdy-Gurdy, 1980. By Chaucer's time the instrument was becoming associated with blind street entertainers and losing its former dignity. See also E. Winternitz, Musical Instruments, chap. 4.

819 armoure: Elsewhere Chaucer always uses *armure,* from OF with ü (rhyming with *cure,* and *endure* in Complaint of Mars, 129–31). Here, rhyming with *soure* (ū), *armoure* is most likely a vulgarism.

829 Unlike the mace or club (813), the **staf-slynge** does not figure in the armory of ME giants; see Bordman, Motif-Index, F531.4.5. Loomis (S&A, 531) suggests that it is transferred from the biblical David to the Chaucerian Goliath. In a larger form (such as Olifaunt might have used), the "staff-sling" was a kind of siege-engine.

831–32 The double explanation of the hero's success is most closely matched in *Bevis of Hampton* 812: "Thourgh godes grace and his virtue" (cf. 2490) [regularized] and 2003: "Thourgh godes grace and min engyn." See also Loomis, S&A, 533.

gras: An irregular form without -e, required by rhyme. Cf. 781 above.

833–35 Evidently an imitation of the opening of *Bevis of Hampton* 1–4: "Lordinges, herkneth to my tale!/ Is merier than the nightingale,/ That I shal singe;/ Of a knight ich wile yow roune [tell]" [regularized]. Chaucer's lines recall the opening of Thopas (see 712 above). They themselves open a new fit, the second. This structural division is indicated, here as at 891, by a paragraph mark or extra-large capital letter in about a quarter of the MSS, including the Ellesmere and Hengwrt. See Burrow (Essays on Med. Lit., 61–65; RES n.s. 22, 1971, 54–58), noting that the three fits contain 18, 9, and 4½ stanzas respectively, each halving the length of its predecessor until vanishing point is nearly reached.

835 rowne: A word that usually in ME and always elsewhere in Chaucer denotes private or whispered speech, but here refers to open discourse: "tell." Chaucer seems to have been amused by Bevis 4 (see previous note).

836 sydes smale: Perhaps a feminine touch (cf. VII.702), like those in the third stanza (Donaldson, Speaking of Ch, 22).

839 myrie men: OED s.v. *merry man* 1, "companion in arms." The expression occurs in Gamelyn 774, and in many early Robin Hood ballads, e.g., Gest of Robyn Hode (Child, Ballads, no. II 7), sts. 205, 281, 316, 340, 382. Here, as at

VII.739, Chaucer's burlesque seems to glance at greenwood balladry.

842 hevedes three: Many-headed giants appear in Irish and Icelandic stories (Thompson, Motif-Index, F531.1.2.2), and there is a five-headed specimen in the ballad Sir Cawline (Child, Ballads, no. 61), st. 30; but there is none in surviving ME romances. Chaucer's failure to mention the extra heads earlier may reflect either upon the narrator's competence or upon the hero's veracity.

845–46   mynstrales most often denoted musical entertainers in Chaucer's day, whereas **geestours** recited stories of stirring deeds (*gestes*, Latin *gesta*). Compare HF 1197–98: "Of alle maner of mynstralles/ And gestiours that tellen tales."

848–50 romances: The term *romance* was broadly applied in ME: see Paul Strohm, Spec 46, 1971, 348–59. The MS collections freely mix tales of chivalry and love with stories concerning religion and the church. Loomis (S&A, 488–89) points out that B. L. MS Cotton Caligula A.ii contains, besides romances such as *Lybeaus* and *Launfal,* the pious tale of *Ypotis* (898 and n. below) and also "the extraordinary Trentals of St. Gregory, and a life of St. Jerome, two fourteenth-century poems which may account, since Gregory was called a pope and Jerome was, to the contemporary mind, a cardinal, for the diverting romances of popes and cardinals." Yet Chaucer certainly intends some incongruity here.

853 spicerye: Delicacies and tidbits ("spices") were often served with sweet wines before retiring to bed (MerT IV.1807n.) or, as here, for daytime refreshment.

854 gyngebreed: For a recipe, see Curye on Inglysch, EETS SS 8, 154.

856 sugre: Sugar is mentioned, with licorice, ginger, and cumin, among the "spices" in the Harley lyric Annot and John, st. 4 (S&A, 552).

857–87   The account of the arming of Thopas is not, as Manly suggested (E&S 13:70), full of deliberate mistakes and comic absurdities. Rather it is "a fairly realistic description of the successive stages of arming. If there be any satire intended it must reside in the overelaboration of detail and in the emphasis upon the obvious" (Stephen J. Herben, Jr., Spec 12, 1937, 475–87). Accounts of arming are common in epics and romances; see Brewer, in Ch Problems, 221–43, and S&A, 526–30.

859 sherte: The arming of Lybeaus Desconus begins with "a scherte of selk" (Cotton MS, ed. Mills, 223). Such underclothing, of silk or fine linen (*cloth of lake*), was commonly worn by knights (Blair, European Armour, 53).

860 aketoun: A quilted jacket, worn under armor as an added defense and to prevent chafing (Blair, European Armour, 33, 75).

863 hawberk: Plate armor (*plate,* 865) for breast and back, worn over the chainmail shirt or haubergeoun, and providing the main body-defense in Chaucer's day. See Herben, Spec 12:480; and Blair, European Armour, 55–61, 74, and fig. 28.

864 Jewes werk: A fine Saracen hauberk in one French chanson de geste is said to have been forged by "Ysac de Barceloigne," presumably a Spanish Jew (*La Prise d'Orange,* ed. Claude Regnier, 1967, 969). H. S. Ficke's nonliterary evidence for the Jews as armorers is not impressive

(PQ 7, 1928, 82–85), nor is Loomis's attempt to derive *Jewes* from an obscure word in *Guy of Warwick* (S&A, 528). Skeat suggested an allusion to some form of decorative work, such as damascening, but this is more characteristic of later armor (Blair, European Armour, chap. 8).

866 cote-armour: A surcoat worn over the armor, often decorated with the wearer's armorial bearings (Blair, 75–76, and figs. 25 and 27).

867 whit as is a lilye: A proverbial simile (Whiting L285). No heraldic absurdity need be supposed, as by Manly. The line refers, in a general eulogistic way, to the whiteness of the fabric.

869–71   Cf. *Lybeaus* 1567–69: "Hys scheld was of gold fyn,/ Thre bores heddes ther-inne/ As blak as brond y-brent"; and also *Sir Degarré* (in ME Romances, ed A. V. C. Schmidt and Nicholas Jacobs, 1980), 1006–8. Boars' heads are a common heraldic bearing, most often in threes, as in *Lybeaus* and Degarré. The **charbocle** is probably (but see next note) the heraldic escarbuncle, a rayed bearing held to represent the precious stone carbuncle, best known as the traditional arms of the Plantagenets' county of Anjou. Cf. Allit. Morte Arthure, in King Arthur's Death, ed. Larry D. Benson, rev. Edward E. Foster, 1994, 2523: "A charbocle in the chef, changand of hewes." Thopas's escutcheon is therefore not ludicrous (quite unlike those in burlesques such as Tournament of Tottenham); but the unusual combination of boar's head and escarbuncle on a gold ground has not been traced and is doubtless fanciful.

871 charbocle: The heraldic interpretation in the previous note is not certain. John L. Melton (PQ 35, 1956, 215–17) notes the reading *by his syde* for *bisyde* in about half the MSS, and sees a reference to an actual precious stone on the hilt of the sword at the knight's side; cf. Guy, Part II, 1993–95: "the hilt . . . That richeliche was graven with gold./ Of charbukle the pomel."

872–74   For parallels to the hero's braggart vows here and at 817–26, see Loomis, S&A, 541–44. Skeat suggested that the oath on ale and bread was a "ridiculous imitation of the vows made by the swan, the heron, the pheasant, or the peacock, on solemn occasions," as in the Voeux du Paon (Vows of the Peacock) of Jacques de Longuyon. Loomis (S&A, 541) compares "familiar vows of popular phraseology, never to take meat or drink, or, specifically, never to eat bread." (Cf. BD 92: "Certes, I nil never ete breed.") The effect is in any case deliberately flat and commonplace.

875 quyrboilly: Leather hardened by soaking in heated wax (Fr. *cuir bouilli,* boiled leather), much used by fourteenth-century armorers for pieces such as Thopas's lower leg-defenses (**jambeux**). See Blair, European Armour, 19, 41.

877 latoun: Latten, a brass-like alloy (cf. I.699n.). A pair of gauntlets of gilded latten belonging to the Black Prince survives at Canterbury. See Blair, European Armour, 41, 66. Blair (171) refers to headpieces mounted in latten. It would not be unsuitable for helmets, as has been suggested.

878 rewel boon: Ivory, from walrus or whale. Ivory was employed as a luxury in saddles and sheaths (VII.876). The fairy mistress in *Thomas of Erceldoune* (line 49) has a saddle of *roelle bone.* See also *Ipomadon A* (ed. Eugen Kölbing, 1889), 6456, and, for ballad instances, the glossary to Child's Ballads, s.v. *roelle-bone.*

879 brydel . . . shoon: Compare the fairy mistress in *Thomas of Erceldoune* 63: "als clere golde hir brydill it schone." The parallels with *Thomas* hereabouts (cf. VII.878 and 884) suggest that Chaucer may have had that romance, or a lost early ballad version, in mind.

881–83 ciprees . . . sharpe ygrounde: Cf. Wars Of Alexander (ed. Hoyt Dugan and Thorlac Truville-Petre, EETS, SS 10, 1989), 790: "Al tospryngis in sprotis speris of sy[p]ris [cyprus]." Spearpoints were commonly sharpened before combat, whence the customary description "sharply ground." See KnT I.2549, Tr 4.43: "with speres sharpe igrounde"; Bevis 3401: "Though his spere wer scharp i-grounde."

884 dappull gray: Perhaps another touch of romance or ballad diction, but first recorded in English here. The palfrey of the fairy mistress in *Thomas of Erceldoune* (line 41) is "a dappill graye." Chaucer elsewhere uses more Gallic forms: *pomely grey* (GP I.616) or *pomely grys* (CYPro VIII.559).

885 ambil: Ambling is a soft gait, associated with mules and ladies' horses (GP I.469n.).

888–90 Such minstrelish indications of the ending of a fit (an ancient Germanic term for a section of a poem, equivalent to Latin *passus*) occasionally appear in romances and ballads. See Loomis, S&A, 496–503; and Albert C. Baugh, Spec 42, 1967, 24–26. *Here [is] a fit* is similarly used in *Thomas of Erceldoune* (line 307), the ballad Adam Bell (Child, Ballads, no. 116) sts. 51 and 97, and Ipomedon B 1524.

891–93 Each of the poem's three fits begins with an appeal for attention, in the minstrel manner, coupled with an announcement of subject. See 712 and 833–35 above. **holde youre mouth** is even ruder than Gamelyn 169: "Lytheneth and listeneth and holdeth your tongue."

895 love-drury: A compound unique in Chaucer (see 772 above). *Drury,* "love, courtship," itself occurs in Chaucer only here and in RomA 844: "By druery and by solas."

897–902 Other lists of heroes and romances are cited by Loomis, S&A, 556–59. Those in *Richard Coeur de Lyon* (ed. Karl Brunner, 1913), lines 7–32, and 6725–41, and Laud Troy Book (ed. J. E. Wülfing, EETS 121–22, 1902–3), lines 11–30, resemble Thopas in seeking to exalt a protagonist by preferring him to other heroes. Both, like Thopas, include Bevis and Guy (Richard, 6730; *Troy Book,* 15).

898 Horn child: The English hero Horn figures in two ME romances, *King Horn* (couplets) and *Horn Childe* (tail rhyme). He is frequently called "Horn child" in the older couplet poem; but Chaucer probably knew the inferior tail-rhyme version, preserved only in the Auchinleck MS and headed there "Horn Childe and Maiden Rimnild." For this use of *child,* see 810 above.

Ypotys: The hero of a ME verse legend *Ypotis,* in which the pious child (the name is that of Epictetus, the Stoic philosopher) instructs the emperor Hadrian in the Christian faith (ed. Horstmann, *Altenglische Legenden*). The poem appears together with romances in B. L. Cotton Caligula A.ii (see introductory note), which like the Auchinleck and Lincoln Thornton MSS freely mix romances with didactic and religious matter such as *Ypotis.* Chaucer does not imitate *Ypotis* in Thopas. The allusion may have been prompted by the hero's youth (prominent in all the romances mentioned in this stanza).

899 The English *Bevis of Hampton* (**Beves**) and *Guy of Warwick* (**Gy**) both appear in the Auchinleck MS, and their heroes are often cited together (see 897–902 above). Chaucer drew on both poems for Thopas, especially on *Guy.*

900 Lybeux: "Lybeaus Desconus" (The Fair Unknown) is the name assumed by young Guinglain, Gawain's son, in the romance of that title by Thomas Chester, an English contemporary of Chaucer. See 730–31, 807, and 869–71 above.

Pleyndamour: An obscure knight called Sir Playne de Amoris is overthrown by La Cote Male Tayle in Malory (ed. Vinaver, 472); but there is no evidence of any such romance hero worthy to rank with Guy and the rest. Passages such as "Syr Prynsamour the erle hyght;/ Syr Eglamour men call the knyght" (*Eglamour,* 19–20) may have inspired Chaucer's invention of the name.

902 Chivalry: rhymes without the regular final *-e* here, as do *chivalry* and *love-drury* at 894–95 (if the MS spellings are to be trusted).

903 A typical conventional romance line (S&A, 511–13): Guy (6411) has "His gode stede he bistrod." Chaucer's **al** is a choice example of the redundant or meaningless *all,* cultivated in Thopas: VII.715, 719, 773, 831.

905 sparcle out of brond: A common comparison (Whiting S561–69).

906 tour: Towers frequently figure in crests; see Fairbairn's Book of Crests, ed. A. C. Fox-Davies, 1892, plates 156–57.

907 lilie flour: Guy of Warwick has an unspecified flower as his crest (250.1–3). The royal house of France sported a fleur-de-lis or lily (helmet illustrated in Blair, European Armour, fig. 86). But the lily stuck in the tower is unparalleled and probably, like Thopas's escutcheon, fanciful.

909 knyght auntrous: This semitechnical phrase, frequent in romances (S&A, 547–50), involves a reduced form of the adjective *aventurous* not found elsewhere in Chaucer.

911 liggen in his hoode: To "lie in one's hood" is to sleep dressed, as knights errant do. Cf. Sir Gawain and the Green Knight 729: "Ner slain with the slete he sleped in his yrnes [irons, armor]" [regularized]. **Hoode** may refer to the coif of mail: MED s.v. *hod* 3(a).

912 Knights errant use their helmets as pillows (**wonger,** a rare word) in Malory, ed. Vinaver, 1:253, 2:563.

915–16 A clear imitation of the lines from the opening stanza of the tail-rhyme romance of *Sir Perceval of Gales* (ed. J. Campion and F. Holthausen, 1913): lines 5–8: "His righte name was Percyvell,/ He was fosterde in the felle,/ He dranke water of the welle:/ And yitt he was hye wyghte."

well: The word normally has a final *-e* in Chaucer's English, but the rhyme is carried over from Perceval, a Northern romance.

917 worly under wede: Chaucer elsewhere consistently avoids this type of alliterating phrase, very common in ME poetry ("lovely under linen," "comely under kell," etc.). The form *worly,* in place of *worthy* (which some MSS read), derives from *worthly* (also present as a MS variant). It is a rare and deliberately un-Chaucerian form; see Burrow, Essays on Med. Lit., 74–78.

918 The analogy of VII.748 and of many similar lines in ME romances suggests a phantom conclusion to this interrupted line: "Til on a day [it so bifel]."

The Prologue to Melibee

The explanatory notes to The Prologue and Tale of Melibee are adapted from those written by Sharon Hiltz Romino for The Riverside Chaucer.

933 in geeste: *Geeste* usually means "exploit," "deed," or "tale," as in III.642 and elsewhere. Here it seems to designate a literary form distinct from *ryme* or *prose*. The Parson uses the corresponding verb to designate alliterative verse ("I kan nat geeste 'rum, ram, ruf' by lettre," ParsPro X.43), which he likewise distinguishes from *rym* (X.44) and *prose* (X.46); probably here *in geeste* means "in alliterating verse" (Gavin Bone, MÆ 7, 1938, 226). Cf. Paul Strohm, Spec 46, 1971, 348–59.

937 litel: The adjective here and in 957 and 963 is a modest deprecation of the tale's importance (Glending Olson, ChauR 10, 1975, 147–53). See ParsT X.1081; Astr Pro 41–42 ("Now wol I preie mekely every discret persone that redith or herith this litel tretys"); and, for similar usages, HF 1093 ("This lytel laste bok"), Tr 5.1786 ("Go, litel bok, go, litel myn tragedye").

943–52 Robertson (Pref to Ch, 367–69) explains that all the Evangelists tell the same story "when they are read spiritually rather than literally"; assuming that *tretys* in 957 and 963 "is obviously The Canterbury Tales itself," he asserts that Melibee affords a clue to the *sentence* (meaning) of all the tales that preceded it (see also Richard L. Hoffman, Classica et Mediaevalia 45, 1969, 552–77). Few critics have agreed, though the critical climate is changing, and the importance of Melibee to the structure of the *Tales* is now often asserted.

955 somwhat moore/ Of proverbes: "Chaucer's remark about proverbs is odd, as Professor Tatlock has observed, for the French version of Melibee which he followed was considerably more condensed than the Latin original" (Robinson). See, however, Dolores Palomo (PQ 53, 1974, 314–15), who accepts Albert H. Hartung's hypothesis that Chaucer produced an earlier version of the tale of which the present tale is a revision (A Study of the Textual Affiliations of Ch's Mel Considered in Its Relation to the Fr. Source, diss., Lehigh U., 1957, 1).

On the use of proverbs in the tale (and in *Tales* as a whole), see Stephen D. Winick, Proverbium: Yearbook of International Proverb Scholarship 11, 1994, 259–81.

963–64 tretys lyte … murye tale: Though Glending Olson (ChauR 10:149–51) argues that two versions are here implied, identical terms are applied to The Parson's Tale: *myrie tale* (X.46), *litel tretys* (X.1081; cf. 943–52 above). *Tale* is apparently the more general term, comprehending treatises such as the Melibee and The Parson's Tale (Paul Strohm, MP 68, 1971, 321–28).

The Tale of Melibee

The date of the Melibee is uncertain. Nineteenth-century critics tended to assign this, along with Chaucer's other religious and didactic pieces, to an early period. However, Chaucer apparently made his translation of Innocent III's *De miseria condicionis humane* in the late 1380s (ed. Lewis, see 30–31),

and The Parson's Tale is now often assigned to his later years (see introductory note to ParsT). Tatlock, Dev. and Chron., 188–98, argued for a date after 1376 on the basis of a deliberate omission (see 1199 below), and he held that it came after *Troilus* and The Knight's Tale, which it seems to quote (see 1054 and 1560 below), and before The Man of Law's Prologue, written to introduce a tale in prose generally believed to have been the Melibee. A number of the tales echo the proverbs and sententiae in the Melibee, and the dispute between Prudence and Melibeus on women and the value of their advice is echoed in The Wife of Bath's Prologue and Tale (see, e.g., notes 1084 and 1086 below), The Clerk's Tale (999–1000), and The Merchant's Tale (1098–1102). As Pearsall notes (CT, 288), it seems most likely that "the direction of internal borrowing is from the translated [Melibee] to the independently conceived work." A date early in the Canterbury period (1388–90) seems most likely. Some critics hold to the theory that this was a revision of an earlier version (see 955 above and Lloyd J. Matthews, ChauR 20, 1986, 221–94). Various attempts to find a reflection of specific political events (see below) would help establish a date, but none is convincing.

In genre, the Melibee is a moral treatise, cast in semifictional form, offering advice on the conduct of life. See Judith Ferster, Fictions of Advice, 1996, 89–107, and Lynn Staley Johnson, SP 87, 1990, 137–55, both of whom treat the tale in the political context of the time. Carolyn P. Colette (ChauR 29, 1995, 416–33) reads it in the context of "female counsel," as a guide for real women.

Chaucer's prose has not been much admired, and many critics have dismissed the style of Melibee as an overly elaborate rhetorical style intended as parody (Palomo, PQ 53:304–20; Elliott, Ch's English, 173–74). Margaret Schlauch finds it consciously artistic (in Ch and Chaucerians, 153–56), and Diane Bornstein (ChauR 12, 1978, 236–54) argues it is an example of the sophisticated *style clergial* in vogue in the fourteenth and fifteenth centuries.

Like Chaucer's other prose works, The Tale of Melibee is a translation, in this case from the French *Livre de Melibee et de Dame Prudence*, written by Renaud de Louens sometime after 1336 (ed. Severs, S&A, 560–614). Renaud's work is in turn a translation of the *Liber consolationis et consilii* (ed. Thor Sundby, Ch Soc, 1873), written in 1246 by Albertanus of Brescia (?1193–?1270), as one of three moral treatises that he presented to each of his three sons as they came of age. The others are *De arte tacendi et loquendi* and *De amore et dilectione Dei et proximi at aliarum rerum et de forma vitae*" (ed. Sharon Hiltz, diss., U. of Pennsylvania, 1980). Renaud handled his Latin text very freely, cutting it to about two-thirds its original length (Severs, S&A, 561), though he also made some additions, drawing on *De amore Dei*. There is no evidence in Melibee that Chaucer knew any of Albertanus's works directly; he relied solely on the French (Severs, S&A, 563 and n.2), which he closely followed. His few deviations from the source, noted by Severs, are recorded in the following notes. The glosses to The Merchant's Tale apparently quote both Liber cons. and De amore Dei (see MerT V.1311–14n., 1362n., etc.).

Various attempts have been made to read the work as a political allegory, whether a specific event (e.g., John of Gaunt's campaign in Spain: Leslie J. Hotson, SP 18, 1921, 429–52; George Williams, A New View of Ch, 1965, 162) or as generally applicable to English affairs at the time (Gardiner Stillwell, Spec 19, 1944, 433–44). V. J. Scattergood, in Court and Poet, ed. Glyn S. Burgess, 1981, 287–96, argues that Sir Thopas and Melibee were written together, probably in the late 1380s, to form an antiwar tract. (On pacifism in the Melibee, see R. F. Yeager, SAC 9, 1987, 137–55.) William Askins (SAC, Proceedings 2, 1986, 103–12) holds that the Melibee may have been written as a reaction to the parliamentary disputes of 1386–88. The relevant passages, however, are nearly all in Chaucer's French original; the general concern with matters of war and peace in the text is pertinent to almost any time and place from Albertanus's time to Chaucer's to our own. Other critics have stressed the religious aspects of Melibee (Bernard F. Huppé, A Reading of the CT, 1964, 237–39), and yet others its possible relation to the themes of the "Marriage Group" (W. W. Lawrence, Ch and CT, 1950, 131–33).

Until very recent years, The Tale of Melibee has received little attention from critics. Manly, Baugh, and Donaldson all excluded it from their influential editions, and it was famously regarded as Chaucer's revenge on the Host for interrupting Sir Thopas (Lumiansky, Of Sondry Folk, 94). Raymond Preston (Ch, 1952, 212) perhaps exaggerates when he says that the Melibee can be a joke only to those who skip it, but David (Strumpet Muse, 220) is surely right in maintaining that whereas Sir Thopas is short enough to be a joke, the Melibee is simply too long to be either a parody or an intentionally dull piece intended as a characterization of its teller.

In the past few years the critical climate has greatly changed. The tale has increasingly attracted sympathetic attention (Colette, ChauR 29: 416–33, provides a useful review of the scholarship), and a good many critics now see the Melibee as having a central thematic function in the *Tales*. Celia R. Daileader (ChauR 29, 1994, 26–39) sees it as an important development of the theme of women as teachers initiated in the WBT; see also Jane Cowgill (in Ch's Religious Tales, ed. C. D. Benson and Robertson, 171–83), who extends the discussion to a "feminine style of persuasion" throughout the *Tales*. Howard (Idea of CT, 309–16) considers it a "major structural unit," part of the "address to the ruling class" that is a recurrent theme of the *Tales*. Traugott Lawler, One and the Many, 102–8, regards it as a pivotal tale, a specifically Christian complement to the philosophical Knight's Tale and an anticipation of The Parson's Tale. For a full and perceptive treatment, see David Wallace, Ch Polity, 212–66.

In the following notes, Renaud is cited by page and line number from Severs's edition in S&A, Albertanus by page and line number in Sundby's edition. Notice that the line numbers for the text of The Tale of Melibee appear at the ends of the respective lines, marked by slashes.

967 Melibeus: Explained at 1419 as *A man that drynketh hony;* a false etymology from the Lat. *mel bibens.*

   Prudence: Lat. "prudentia," prudence.

   Sophie: From the Gr. σοφια, wisdom. Melibee's wounded daughter is not named in the Latin or French texts.

968 into the feeldes: This is Chaucer's addition (Severs, S&A, 568.10). Scattergood (in Burgess, ed., Court and Poet, 288) suggests this is intended to recall Thopas VII.909–15 and thus establish the continuity between the two works.

970 thre ... olde foes: The three enemies of man: the world, the flesh, and the devil (see VII.1421).

972 feet: Fr. *piez,* an error for *yeux,* "eyes" (Lat. *oculis,* Liber cons. 2.18); Severs, S&A, 568.14.

987 Christ mourned **Lazarus** (John 11.35: "Jesus wept") and raised him from the dead (John 11.36–42).

995 Jhesus Syrak seith: Jesus, son of Sirach, author of Ecclesiasticus; this, however, is from Prov. 17.22; the error is due to the French.

996 sorwe in herte: Ecclus. 30.25 (AV 30.23).

997 mothes in the shepes flees: Prov. 25.20 (Vulg.): "Like a moth in a garment or a worm in wood, sorrow injures the heart of a man." Moths were thought to breed in the fleece of sheep (see Bartholomaeus Anglicus, tr. Trevisa 2:1266).

998 goodes temporels: The French adjective plural, *-(e)s,* is relatively rare in Chaucer except in his translated prose; see Language and Versification, p. xxxiii.

999–1000 Job: Job 1.21; cf. ClT IV.871.

1003 Salomon seith: Cf. MilT I.3530 and n., MerT IV.1485–86. From Ecclus. 32.24; Whiting C470. The confusion of Solomon and the author of Ecclesiasticus here and elsewhere derives from Albertanus (Liber cons. p. 6.11; S&A, 570.64).

1017 maladies ben cured by hir contraries: Proverbial (Whiting C414) and Walther (Nova series) 35738b. The idea is repeated at 1277 below.

1030 he that soone deemeth: A commonplace: see Mel VII.1135 and cf. Whiting D143, J78.

1031 thilke juge is wys: Proverbial (Whiting J75, Tilley J75).

1032 juggeth by leyser: Cf. Whiting T44, "In long tarrying is noys."

1033 womman that was taken in avowtrie: See John 8.3–8.

1036 iron is hoot ... smyte: Proverbial: Whiting I60, Hassell F51; cf. Tr 2.1275–76: "Pandare . . . / Felte iren hoot, and he bygan to smyte."

1047 noon audience: Ecclus. 32.6 (Vulg.): Cf. ProNPT VII.2801–2.

1048 comune proverbe: Publilius Syrus, Sententiae, 653; see Whiting C458.

1053 Piers Alfonce seith: Petrus Alphonsus, a Spanish Jew who was baptized in 1106; the reference is to his Disciplina clericalis (Ex. 24, tr. Quarrie, 146).

1054 hasteth wel ... abyde: Proverbial (Whiting H171, H166). Tr 1.956 is identical: "He hasteth wel that wisely kan abyde." Chaucer has added this sentence (S&A, 573.154).

   wikked haste: Cf. ParsT X.1003.

1057 seith Salomon: Eccles. 7.29; cf. MerT IV.2247–48.

1059 Jhesus Syrak seith: Ecclus. 25.30 (Vulg.): "If a woman has primacy, she is contrary to her husband." Cf. MerT IV.2250–51, ParsT X.927.

1062–63 Car il est ... : The French passage is omitted by Chaucer, though it is in both the French and Latin texts. Though it is necessary to the sense, the passage does not appear in any of the manuscripts and was first supplied by Tyrwhitt in the eighteenth century.

1071 Senec seith: An erroneous attribution in the Latin text; actually from Martin of Braga, *Formula vitae honestae* 4.70–71 (in Opera omnia, ed. Claude W. Barlow, 1950). The misattribution is repeated throughout (e.g., 1147 below).

1075 appeered rather to a woman: See Mark 16.9: "Now when Jesus was risen . . . he appeared first to Mary Magdalene."

1075–79 Salomon: Cf. MerT IV.2277–90n.

1076 Salomon seith: Possibly alluding to Prov. 31.10: "Who can find a virtuous woman? for her price is far above rubies." Cf. ClT IV.207n., MerT IV.2367n.

1079 no wight . . . bountee: Cf. Matt. 19.17 ("There is none good but one, that is, God"); Luke 18.19 ("None is good, save one, that is God").

1084 womman kan nat hyde that she woot: Cf. Whiting W534, W485, and WBT III.950 and n.

1086 thre thynges: This common proverb (Whiting T187) appears also in WBPro III.278–80, and though here it derives from Albertanus, Chaucer may have known it in Innocent III, *De miseria condicionis humane* (ed. Lewis, 1.16.33), or Jerome's *Epistola adversus Jovinianum* 1.28 (tr. Fremantle, 367). ParsT X.631 quotes Prov. 27.15 ("A continual dropping in a very rainy day and a contentious woman are alike"), the ultimate source of the saying, which may also conflate Prov. 10.26 ("As vinegar to the teeth, and as smoke to the eyes, so is the sluggard to them that send him") and 19.13 ("The contentions of a wife are continual droppings").

1087 bettre dwelle in desert: Cf. WBPro III.775–77; Prov. 21.19 ("It is better to live in the wilderness than with a contentious woman"); also in Adv. Jov. 1.28; tr. Fremantle, 367.

1088 Almost identical with MerT IV.1456, WBPro III.112.

1090 wikked conseil: Cf. Whiting W545.

1094 Chaucer omits the Fr. "For often when men want to work by evil counsel, women dissuade them from it and convince them," which is also in the Latin (S&A, 576.229–31).

1096 conseillynge of wommen: Cf. Whiting C473 and NPT VII.3256.

1098–1102 These examples of womanly counsel appear in the same order in MerT IV.1363–74; they derive from Gen. 27 (**Rebekke**), Judith 8 (**Judith**), 1 Kings (AV 1 Sam.) 25 (**Abygail**), Esther 7 (**Hester**).

1103–4 It is not good: Gen. 2.18. Cf. MerT IV.1325–29.

1106 confusion of man: Cf. NPT VII.3164n. and Whiting W529.

1107–8 Lat. gloss: "Quid melius auro? Jaspis./ Quid Jaspide? Sensus./ Quid Sensu? Mulier./ Quid mulier? Nihil" (translated in the text, with the addition of the qualification "good").

1117–18 Thobie: Tob. 4.20.

1121–23 thre thynges: Cf. VII.1246–48 and Whiting T184.

1124 may nat do: Chaucer omits the French "and by his own counsel overcome any force." The passage is also present in the Latin (S&A, 578.275–76). Cf. Publilius Syrus, Sententiae, 322.

1125 irous . . . may nat wel deme: Cf. Whiting I62 and Walther 12913.

1127 as seith Senec: From Publilius Syrus, Sententiae, 319; not from Seneca. Chaucer follows his source in misattributing sentences from Publilius Syrus to Seneca throughout (at lines 1185, 1449, 1450, etc.).

1130 the Apostle seith: 1 Tim. 6.10 ("Radix enim omnium malorum est cupiditas"); cf. VII.1840, PardPro VI.334, ParsT X.739, Whiting C491. *The Apostle* (with definite article) always refers to Paul.

1135 soone deemeth: See 1030 and 1054 above.

1143 Another clerk: Not identified in the source ("Et alius dixit").

1144 The book: Petrus Alphonsus, *Disciplina clericalis,* Ex. 2; tr. Quarrie, 109.

1147 Seneca seith: Not from Seneca; see Pseudo-Seneca, *De moribus* 16 (PL 72:29); cf. Whiting C462.

1153 riche man . . . conseil: Proverbial (Whiting M273).

1164 in old men: Cf. Job 12.12 ("With the ancient is wisdom; and in length of days understanding"); Whiting C452, M118.

1181 Caton seith: "Dionysius" Cato, *Dicta Catonis* 3.4. See MilT I.3227n.

1184 Isope seith: "Ysopus," the Latin version of Aesop's Fables; for the sentiment, see Walther 15973, Whiting S123.

1185 seith Seneca: Not from Seneca, but Publilius Syrus, *Sententiae,* 434; cf. Whiting F194, R77.1.

1186 seith Salomon: Ecclus. 12.10. Cf. Whiting F364, F367, C467.

1189 Peter Alfonce seith: Petrus Alphonsus, *Disciplina clericalis,* Ex. 2 (tr. Quarrie, 109).

1191 a philosophre: Unidentified in either the French or the Latin.

1194 Salomon seith: Prov. 31.4. The idea is proverbial (Whiting D425); cf. PardT VI.560–61; and see MLT II.771–77n.

1196 Cassiodorie seith: Cassiodorus (Flavius Magnus Aurelius Cassiodorus, fl. first half of sixth century), *Variae* 10.18 (ed. Å. Fridh, CCSL, vol. 96, 1973).

1199 Both the French and English versions omit about two pages of the Latin text at this point (Liber cons., 53–55). Another passage (Liber cons., 57–58) is omitted after VII.1210.

After VII.1199, Chaucer omits "And Solomon says, 'Woe to the land that has a child as a lord and whose lord dines in the morning'" (Eccles. 10.16). Tatlock (Dev. and Chron., 192) argues that Chaucer was thinking of the young king Richard II: though the middle 1380s would best fit with the omission, Tatlock argues, such a reference would have been tactless "at any time from 1376 to (say) 1395."

1200 folwe: Fr. *fuir.* This word may be the result of a confusion of *suir* ("follow") with *fuir* ("flee"); it does not appear in the Latin original (S&A, 582.385).

1215 to muche embraceth: Proverbial (Whiting M774). Cf. Chaucer's Proverbs 7–8: "Who so mochel wol embrace,/ Litel therof he shal distreyne."

1219 bettre holde thy tonge: Proverbial (Whiting T366). Cf. PF 514–16: "But bet is that a wyghtes tonge reste/ Than entermeten hym of such doinge,/ Of which he neyther rede can ne synge."

1225 upon thynges that newely: Proverbial: a legal aphorism (Walther 3180), which Albertanus quotes from no particular source. Cf. Tr 4.416: "And upon newe cas lith newe avys."

1226 Senec seith: Not identified in Seneca. Cf. Whiting C467.

1229 lawes seyn: Cf. Justinian (483–565), *Digesta* 45.1.26, ed. Mommsen, Scholl, Kroll, 1954.

1230 parfourned or kept: Chaucer omits the French "et en moult d'autres manieres" (and in many other ways), which conflates a longer passage in the Latin text (S&A, 583.428–29).

1250 They han espied . . . enclyned: Chaucer's addition, found in neither the Latin nor French texts (S&A, 584.458).

1257 cast . . . hochepot: This phrase is not found in the Latin or French versions (S&A, 585.465). *Hochepot* is a legal term meaning a gathering of properties together for equal distribution—i.e., treating all claimants as equal. See OED s.v. *hotchpot* 3.

1264 to do synne is mannyssh: Cf. Augustine, Serm. 164.14: "To err is human; to persist in error is diabolical" (Walther 11267b); Whiting S346.

1277 oon contrarie: Cf. 1017 above.

1283 how lightly is every man enclined: Cf. Whiting M75.

1291 Seint Paul . . . in many places: Cf. Rom. 12.17 ("Recompense to no man evil for evil. Provide things honest in the sight of all man"); cf. similar sentiments in 1 Pet. 3.9; 1 Thess. 5.15; 1 Cor. 4.12.

1309 Piers Alfonce: *Disciplina clericalis,* Ex. 17, tr. Quarrie, 135.

1316–17 Salomon seith: Prov. 28.14; cf. Whiting M83.

1320 Senec seith: Not from Seneca; from Publilius Syrus, *Sententiae,* 555, 594. Cf. Whiting M338.

1325–26 Ovyde seith: Rem. amor. 421–22: "The little viper will slay a huge bull with its bite/ And a dog, which is not large, holds back the wild boar." Chaucer omits the title of the reference, which is given in the Latin and French texts (S&A, 588.541; Liber cons., 71.3), and adds *and the wilde hert* and *A litel thorn may prikke a kyng ful soore.* Skeat (5:214) explains Chaucer's *wesele* as the result of a confusion of Fr. *vivre* Lat. (=*vipere,* viper) with Lat. *viverra,* a ferret.

1326 the book: Ovid's book, continuing the passage translated in 1325.

1336 olde and wise: Chaucer omits "and at great expense" (S&A, 590.588; Liber cons., 73.4–5).

1355 doctrine of Tullius: Cicero, De officiis 2.5. Cf. VII.1200–10. Chaucer departs here from both the French and the Latin, perhaps because his source was "faulty or incomprehensible at this point" (S&A, 589.581–82).

1364 ne been nat youre freendes: Chaucer's addition (S&A, 590.591–92).

1395 Oriens: Not in the Latin or French texts. Chaucer apparently uses it as the equivalent of "longinqua." Although Chaucer may have misread the French ("Deux causes ouvrères et efficiens"), he may have been responsible for the Latin terms, none of which, aside from "efficiens," is in the Latin (Liber cons., 85.5–6); cf. Manly-Rickert 4:304; S&A, 591.628–29.

1406 the apostle seith: The Latin text refers expressly to 1. Cor. 4.55 (". . . the Lord . . . will bring to light the hidden things of darkness, and will make manifest the counsels of the heart"), but Chaucer has accommodated it to Romans 11.33 ("O the depth of the riches both of the wisdom and knowledge of God! how unsearchable are his judgements, and his ways past finding out!"); cf. Skeat 5:216.

1410 See 967 above; the allegory of the opening, which had not been developed, is here resumed. See Paul Strohm, ChauR 2, 1967, 32–42, and Charles A. Owen, Jr., ChauR 7, 1973, 267–80.

1415 hony . . . venom: Ovid, Amores 1.8.104: "wicked poisons have for hiding place sweet honey."
goodes of the body: See ParsT X.452.

1416 Salomon seith: Prov. 25.16; Chaucer adds *and be nedy and povre* (S&A, 592.655–56).

1421 three enemys: See 970 above.

1424 deedly synnes: See the ParsT for a treatment of the seven deadly sins.

1433–34 [Et a ce respont . . . : Chaucer omits the French passage. The lines seem necessary to the sense, but Severs thinks it likely they were missing from Chaucer's source manuscript (S&A, 593.677–80).

1437 proveth shrewes: The Latin is "Bonis nocet qui malis parcet" (He who spares evil-doers does harm to the good; Pseudo-Seneca, *De moribus,* PL 72:29), accurately translated in the French as "Celui nuit aus bons que espargne les maufais" (S&A, 593.682–83). Perhaps, as Robinson suggested, Chaucer's source manuscript was here corrupt.

1440 spere: A mistake for *swerd* (Fr. *glaive;* Lat. *gladium*).
1440–43: Romans 13.4.

1481–83 the common sawe: cf. Whiting M86.

1496 the poete: Identified only as "le poete" in the French text, and not mentioned at all in the Latin. Skeat compares Luke 23.41 ("we receive the due rewards of our deeds"). Possibly he was a versifier of the *De duodecim utilitatibus tribulationis* ascribed to Peter of Blois (James R. Kreuzer, MLN 63, 1948, 54).

1497 Seint Gregorie seith: The passage has not been located in Gregory's works.

1509 epistle: Chaucer omits the name of the epistle (2 Cor. 4.17), which is present in the French text. The Latin original lacks the passage altogether (S&A, 597–772).

1519–20 nat . . . parfite men: Cf. WBPro III.111–12.

1524 venge oon outrage by another: Cf. Whiting O56.

1550 Salomon seith: Eccles. 10.19; Cf. Whiting M633.

1554 body . . . without a soule: Perhaps proverbial in Latin; Skeat notes that "Homo sine pecunia est quasi corpus sine anima" (A man without money is like a body without a soul) is written on the flyleaf of a MS (5:219). Cf. Whiting M235.

1556 seith Pamphilles: Hero of a twelfth-century Latin poetic dialogue, *Pamphilus de Amore,* tr. Garbáty, lines 53–54: "If she is rich, any oxherd's daughter can choose from a thousand her desired husband." Cf. FranT V.1110n.

1558 Pamphilles seith: Not from Pamphilus, though the idea is common (see Whiting R108).

1559 farewel freendshipe: Proverbial; cf. ProMLT II.120–21 n.

1560 alloone . . . compaignye: Identical to KnT I.2779 (see n.) and MilT I.3204.

1561 seith this Pamphilles: Not from Pamphilus. Cf. Petrus Alphonsus, *Disciplina clericalis* (Ex. 4, tr. Quarrie, 114): "He who is deprived of high birth will become rich and famous."

1564 Cassidore: See Cassiodorus, Variae 2.13. Chaucer has *mooder of ruyne* for the Fr. *mere de crimes,* Lat. *mater criminum;* his source MS may have been corrupt here (S&A, 600.843).

1567 eten: An accurate translation of the Fr. *mengier,* but that is a scribal error for *mendier* or *demander;* the Lat. has *postulate;* Severs, S&A, 601.845.

1568–70 seith Innocent: Innocent III, *De miseria condicionis humane* 1.16; tr. Lewis, 162–64. Cf. MLT II.99–121.

1571 seith Salomon: Ecclus. 40.28 (Vulg. 29); Cf. ProMLT II.114.

1583 the lawe seith: The source for this quotation, added by Renaud, is not known.

1587   This differs slightly from both the French and Latin texts; Chaucer's version may have been due to a corruption in his French source (S&A, 602.869).

1589 Salomon seith: Ecclus. 33.27.

1593 versifiour: Unidentified. Cf. Prov. 20.4 ("The sluggard will not plow by reason of the cold; therefore shall he beg in harvest, and have nothing"); cf. also Whiting M110.

1595 seith Seint Jerome: Ep. 125.11 ("Ad Rusticum monachum") in Select Letters, tr. Wright: "Engage in some occupation, so that the devil may always find you busy." Cf. SNPro VIII.6–7.

1611–12 a wys man repreveth: This quotation does not appear in the Latin text and has not been identified. Cf. Whiting D94.

1617 seith Seint Austyn: Not identified in Augustine's works; cf. Prov. 27.20: "Hell and destruction are never full; so the eyes of man are never satisfied."

1628 love of God: For "fear of God" (Fr. *paour*, Lat. *timore*) is probably due to an erroneous reading "amour" in Chaucer's source manuscript (Severs, S&A, 603.910).

1630 the prophet seith: Ps. 36.16 (AV 37.16). The *prophete* is David, "philosophe" in the French text.

1639–40 seith Salomon: Ecclus. 41.15 (AV 41.12). Chaucer's **freend** for *nomen* (name) apparently results from a French MS which had "ami" instead of "nom" (Manly-Rickert 4.506).

1644 And therfore seith: This explanation is not in the French or Latin and may be Chaucer's addition.

1651   The **philosophre** has not been identified.

1666–67   Cf. Whiting M42, K49 ("A king shall die as well as a knave").

1668 seconde Book of Kynges: 2 Kings (AV 2 Samuel) 11.25: "For variable is the outcome of war; the sword devours first one, then the other."

1671 Salomon seith: Ecclus. 3.27 (AV 26); here and at 995 Solomon and Jesus son of Sirach are confused.

1676 Seint Jame seith: "Saint Jaques" in Chaucer's source, an error for *Seneques* (S&A, 606–968).

1678 unytee: Manly and Rickert (4:506) suggest that the addition of *unytee* in the English text where the French has only "paix" may stem from an interest in unity in fourteenth-century England and cite Langland, PP B Passus 19.

1686 over-greet hoomlynesse: Proverbial (Whiting H426); cf. "Familiarity breeds contempt."

1691 the wise man seith: Pseudo-Seneca, De moribus 3 (PL 72:30); Whiting D265.

1701 the prophete seith: Chaucer has *prophete* for Fr. "philosopher" but no literary source of the quotation is known; Whiting E225.

1707–8 Salomon seith: An expansion of Eccles. 7.4 (AV 7.3): "Sadness is better than laughter." VII.1709–10 expand the rest of the verse: "because through sadness the countenance corrects the wayward soul" (Skeat 5:222).

1783 the lawe: Justinian, *Digesta* 50.17.35.

1794 goodnesse that thou mayst do: Proverbial (Whiting T348).

1815   Chaucer begins at this point to paraphrase the French version more freely.

1825–26   These lines are Chaucer's addition (S&A, 612.1125).

1860 lord: Fr. "seigneur," the reading of Chaucer's source MS. All other MSS have "homme"; Lat. "viro" (Liber cons., 123.11). Cf. S&A, 613.1160.

1884–88   Cf. 1 John 1.9 ("If we confess our sins, he is faithful and just to forgive us our sins, and to cleanse us from all unrighteousness"). Not in the Latin or French texts (S&A, 614.1179).

The Monk's Prologue

The explanatory notes to The Monk's Prologue and Tale *are adapted from those written by Susan H. Cavanaugh for* The Riverside Chaucer.

The opening words of the Host in The Monk's Prologue correspond closely to part of a single stanza which appears in twenty-two MSS at the end of The Clerk's Tale (see ClT IV.1212a–g note). Apparently, Chaucer first wrote the speech for the latter position, but transferred it to The Monk's Prologue when he developed at length the characterization of the Host and his wife. The words of the Host to the Monk (VII.1941–62) are similarly repeated in substance in the Epilogue to The Nun's Priest's Tale (VII.3447–62; see introductory notes to NPPro.)

1892 corpus Madrian: No St. Madrian is known, and this is probably another of the Host's malapropisms; he has trouble with any oath involving *corpus* (see 1906 below, Intr PardT VI.314, ShipT VII.435) and with saints' names (cf. Intr PardT VI.310 n.). *Madrian* means "spice, or sweetmeat" (MED). Materne and Mathurin have been proposed as the saint intended, but neither seems likely. Ann Sullivan Haskell (JEGP 67, 1968, 430–40) reviews these and other suggestions and argues instead for a reference to St. Hadrian or Adrian; two late scribes wrote *Adrian* for *Madryan* (Manly-Rickert 7:464). Haskell claims but offers no proof that Adrian was known in the fourteenth century as the patron saint of brewers.

1894 Goodelief: Printed as two words, *gode lief,* in some editions, and taken as an epithet (cf. WBPro III.431), but now accepted by many as a proper name popular in the mid-fourteenth century (Edith Rickert, MP 25, 1927, 79–82). In Southwark records, the wife of the real Harry Baily (or Bailly) is named Christian (Manly, New Light, 79–81). Rickert (MP 25:81) believes that the fictional name was chosen from "ironic malice."

1901–4   Cf. GP I.449–52.

1906 corpus bones: Another of the Host's blunders (see 1892 above), this time attributed to his wife.

1907 distaf: See 2374 below.

1926 Rouchestre: Glending Olson (ChauR 21, 1986, 246–56) notes that the reference to Rochester is appropriate to the Monk: its cathedral included a monastic house and a mural of Fortune's wheel; the bishop, Thomas Brinton, campaigned against monastic corruption.

Since Sittingbourne, mentioned in WBPro III.847, is ten miles farther on the road to Canterbury, the order of tales in the MSS, in which Fragment III precedes Fragment VII (with IV through VI intervening), has seemed to many to violate the canons of realism. This is on the assumption that the *towne* mentioned at the end of The Summoner's Tale is Sittingbourne. See SumT III.2294n.

1929 daun John: The name of the monk in The Shipman's Tale (cf. VII.43 and n.). The Host addresses the Monk by his right name, *daun Piers,* in ProNPT VII.2792. On the title *daun,* see KnT I.1379n.

1934 lyke a penant or a goost: Cf. GP I.205.

1955 borel: Cf. FranPro V.716n.

1956 wrecched ympes: The expression is proverbial (Whiting T465). Cf. Matt. 7.17 ("a corrupt tree bringeth forth evil fruit"), and see LGW 2395 ("wiked fruit cometh of a wiked tre").

1962 lussheburghes: Coins of inferior metal imported into England from Luxemburg during the reign of Edward III. Cf. Langland, PP B 15.348: "In lussheburwes is a luther alay [*false alloy*], and yet loketh he lik a sterlyng."

Robinson notes that while the Host's banter here is simply a variation on the old theme of the Goliardic poets ("A cleric knows more about pleasing a maiden than a knight"), sacerdotal celibacy was much discussed in England at the end of the fourteenth century. Wyclif and his followers were skeptical of the ban on clerical marriage, and the Lollards openly attacked the regulation: the third of the "Twelve Conclusions of the Lollards" (1395) condemned clerical celibacy "that in prejudice of women was first ordained [and] induces sodomy in Holy Church" [translated] (Anne Hudson, ed., *Selections from English Wycliffite Writings,* 1997). "The particular argument of the Host, however, seems to have been seldom used. In the century-long controversy about compulsory celibacy the opponents of the law . . . rarely referred to the effect on the population of the withdrawal of the clergy from parenthood" (Robinson). On the opinions of Wyclif and the Lollards, see Anne Hudson, *The Premature Reformation: Wycliffite Texts and Lollard History,* 1988.

1964 in game a sooth: Proverbial; cf. CkPro I.4355n.

1970 Seint Edward: Probably Edward the Confessor (c. 1004–66), king of England, who was venerated as a saint. Richard II had a special devotion to the Confessor, whom he had depicted alongside himself in the Wilton Diptych; see Shelagh Mitchell in The Regal Image of Richard II and the Wilton Diptych, ed. Dillan Gordon et al., 1997, 115–20.

1973–77 Tragedie: Cf. Bo 2.pr2.70: *Glose. Tragedye is to seyn a dite of a prosperite for a tyme, that endeth in wrecchidnesse.* Cf. also VII.1991–94 and 2761–65 and the introductory note to the tale below.

1985 by ordre telle nat: The Monk's apology for departing from chronological order is sometimes held to apply to the "Modern Instances" (see introductory note to Monk's Tale below), but it should be remarked that the ancient tragedies themselves fail to follow a strict chronological arrangement.

The Monk's Tale

The most thorough discussions of the date of The Monk's Tale and the probable circumstances of its composition remain those of Tatlock (Dev. and Chron., 164–72) and Kittredge

(Date of Tr, 1909, 38–50). The Monk's Tale, like that of the Second Nun, has usually been taken to be one of Chaucer's earlier works, written, perhaps, shortly after his first Italian journey (M. C. Seymour, ChauR 24, 1989, 163–65). The use of the eight-line "Monk's Tale Stanza" (*ababacac*) has been thought to indicate an early, pre–rime-royal stage in Chaucer's development.

However, if that is so, the work must have been revised at a later stage for its position in the *Tales.* The Bernabò stanza cannot have been written before 1386 (Bernabò died 19 December 1385), and, if the tale is early, must be a later interpolation, along with the other so-called Modern Instances— Petro of Spain (d. 1369), Petro of Cypress (d. 1369), and Hugolino of Pisa (from Dante). Tatlock, who opposes the theory of interpolation, takes the whole tale as a product of the Canterbury period, though he gives no decisive reason in support of the late date. Edward M. Socola (JEGP 49, 1950, 159–71) argues on the basis of Chaucer's developing ideas about Fortune that all the tragedies were composed at approximately the same time and therefore after the date of the latest of the Modern Instances, December 1385. Positive evidence in support of any of these theories, however, is lacking. The tragedies may have been written in the early part of Chaucer's career, perhaps in the early 1370s, when the Italian influence was first making itself evident in his works, and later revised. However, a later date cannot be ruled out.

The Monk's Tale is a collection of brief tragedies in the "Fall of Princes" tradition. Chaucer's immediate models for the general plan and some of the details were Boccaccio's *De casibus virorum illustrium* (apparently acknowledged in the subtitle) and *Le Roman de la rose* (5829–6901; tr. Dahlberg, 117–32). The Fortune motif appears to have come from *Le Roman de la rose,* where modern as well as ancient instances are used to illustrate the capricious workings of the goddess, while the prevailing tone, set out in 1973–77 of the introductory link and the first stanza of the tale, is partially indebted to certain passages of Boethius's *De consolatione philosophiae* (2.pr2; 3.pr5). Many of the tragedies themselves are so brief that establishing their sources is both impossible and unimportant, except for the light they would throw on Chaucer's reading. The particular sources known for each are cited in the notes that follow. The more important analogues have been assembled and printed by Robert K. Root in S&A, 615–44.

The Monk's tragedies center on the workings of Dame Fortune, whose capricious turnings of her great wheel were thought to govern the fates of men. It has been argued that this concept, literally applied in The Monk's Tale, reflects not a theory of tragedy as Chaucer understood it but rather the "philosophical inadequacy" of the Monk (see, e.g., Howard, Idea of CT, 280–81). R. W. Babcock (PMLA 46, 1931, 205–13) assembled an extensive list of Roman and medieval stories and collections similar to Chaucer's tale, and classified it, along with *Le Roman de la rose,* in a nonclerical medieval tradition, where the goddess Fortuna operates independently of a divine plan. Howard R. Patch (MLR 22, 1927, 377–88) detects a belief in divine providence elsewhere in the writings of Chaucer and is supported by other critics who have stressed the discrepancy between the fatalistic viewpoint of the Monk and a more genial attitude toward man's destiny expressed in Chaucer's other writings (see especially R. E. Kaske, ELH 24,

1957, 249–68). For a full discussion, see Henry A. Kelly, Chaucerian Tragedy, 1997, 39–91.

The placement of the Modern Instances, which differs in various MSS, is a major textual problem. In the Hengwrt, Ellesmere, and most of the Ellesmere's nearest relatives, the Modern Instances stand at the end. But in most of the other manuscripts they come between Zenobia and Nero. Skeat (3:429) chose that order, holding that Croesus must come last because its last stanza repeats the definition of tragedy to which the knight objects and because the Host repeats the image of Fortune's covering her face with a cloud (see VII.2766 and VII.2782). Manly and Rickert (4:508) agree, and most editors (with the exception of Donaldson, Ch's Poetry) follow Skeat's practice. However, the matter remains impossible to resolve with complete certainty. The Monk's apology for the chronological confusion (see 1985 above) does not settle the matter, and a slight inconsistency exists, on any assumption, in the final state of the text, since if the tragedy of Croesus stands at the end, as the following headlink appears to require, then the tale has so good a formal conclusion that the Knight's interruption (ProNPT VII.2767) may seem out of place (see Robert Boenig, N&Q 43, 1996, 261–64). The question is further complicated by The Nun's Priest's Prologue itself, which exists in several MSS in a short form omitting all reference to the Croesus passage (see introductory note to the Nun's Priest's Prologue). On the Modern Instances, see Wallace, Ch Polity, 313–29 (with a summary of the debate).

1999 Lucifer: "Light-bearer," the name of the morning star. It was applied to the rebel archangel on the basis of Isaiah 14.12 ("How art thou fallen from heaven, O Lucifer, son of the morning"), which was thought to apply to Satan.

2007 Damyssene: The notion that Adam was created in a field where Damascus later stood occurs in Boccaccio's De casibus, Book 1; Lydgate writes in Fall of Princes 1.500: "Of slym of th'erthe in Damascene the feeld/ God made hem fairest a-bove ech creature" [regularized].

2009 sperme unclene: The phrase was commonplace; e.g., Innocent III's De miseria condicionis humane 1.1; tr. Lewis, 94: "Man is formed . . . of most filthy sperm (de spurcissimo spermate)."

2015 The story of Samson occurs in Boccaccio's De casibus 1.17, but Chaucer appears to have based his account primarily on Judges 13–16. Robinson notes the probable influence of Le Roman de la rose (16677–688; tr. Dahlberg, 281) and Vincent of Beauvais, Spec. hist. (see Fansler, Ch and RR, 30–31, and Pauline Aiken, Spec 17, 1942, 58-59).

2044 wang-tooth: A detail taken from the Vulgate, Judg. 15.19: "And thus the Lord opened a molar tooth in the jaw of an ass."

2046 judicum: Liber judicum, the Book of Judges, where the story of Samson is told.

2091–94 telle hir conseil til hir wyves: The moral, which departs from the emphasis on Fortune in the other tragedies, is paralleled in the account of Samson in Le Roman de la rose 16700; tr. Dahlberg, 281: "Guard against women and never confide in them."

2095 The story of Hercules was widely known, but Chaucer's account appears to have been based on Boethius's Cons. 4.m7, with details perhaps from Ovid's Metamorphoses 9

or Heroides 9 (Hoffman, Ovid and CT, 186–92). Boccaccio's De claris mulieribus 22 includes a short account of Deianira (S&A, 629–30); see also Gower (Conf. aman. 2.2148–312) for a full version.

2096 The **werkes** of Hercules are taken from the list in Boethius, Cons. 4.m7.13–31 (cf. Bo 4.m7.28–62), which corresponds only in part with the traditional twelve labors.

2098 rafte: The first of the traditional twelve labors of Hercules was the slaying of the Nemean lion, whose skin Hercules afterwards wore. Cf. Bo 4.m7.30–32.

2099 Centauros: Probably a reference to the centaur Pholus, whom Hercules slew after the labor of the Erymanthian boar. He also inadvertently killed Chiron, the centaur son of Saturn and Philyra (Skeat 5:232). Cf. Bo 4.m7.29–30.

2100 Arpies: Hercules's sixth labor was the killing of the Harpies, the Stymphalian birds who ate human flesh. Cf. Bo 4.m7.32–34.

2101 dragoun: Hercules's eleventh labor was to bring back from the garden of the Hesperides the golden apples guarded by the dragon Ladon. Cf. Bo 4.m7.34–35.

2102 Cerberus: Hercules's twelfth labor was to bring to the upper world the three-headed dog Cerberus, who guarded the gates of Hades. Cf. Bo 4.m7.36–37.

2103 Busirus: Here Chaucer conflates two stories, that of Busirus, a king of Egypt who killed and sacrificed all foreigners who came to his land, and that of Diomedes, a king of Thrace who fed his mares on human flesh until Hercules killed him as his eighth labor and fed his body to the horses (cf. Bo 4.m7.37–41). Hoffman (Ovid and CT, 186–89) notes that the confusion of the two occurs in the gloss to an eleventh-century MS copy of Ovid's Ibis: "Busiris gave his guests to his horses to be eaten. Or let us say that it was Diomedes, whom Hercules killed."

2105 firy serpent: The Lernaean hydra. William C. McDermott (Classica et Medievalia 23, 1962, 216–17) notes that Chaucer's epithet, which lacks classical parallel, arose from a misreading of Aeneid 6.288, where "flammisque armata" (armed with flame) applies to Chimaera rather than Hydra. Cf. Bo 4.m7.41–42: "he, Hercules, slowh Idra the serpent, and brende the venym."

2106 Acheloys: Cf. Bo 4.m7.48–50: "Hercules brak oon of his hornes, and he for schame hidde hym in his ryver."

2107 Cacus: Hercules slew the monster Cacus to appease Evander. Cf. Bo 4.m7.52–55.

2108 Antheus: The wrestler Antaeus, giant son of Neptune and Ge, increased in strength each time his body touched the ground. Cf. Bo 4.m7.50–52.

2109 the grisly boor: As his fourth labor, Hercules captured (but did not slay) the Erymanthian boar. Cf. Bo 4.m7.55–56 ("bristlede boor").

2110 bar the hevene: the last of his labors. Cf. Bo 4.m7.58–60.

2117–18 bothe the worldes endes: On the pillars of Hercules in both the West (in the Strait of Gibraltar) and the East, see Robert A. Pratt (in Sts. in Hon. of Ullman, ed. Lillian B. Lawler et al., 1960, 118–25).

Trophee: The identity of Trophee remains uncertain. G. L. Kittredge (Putnam Anniv. Vol., 555–56, 559) conjectured that the noun tropea, trophea, "pillars," came to be misunderstood as the name of a book. Lydgate, Fall of Princes

1.283–87, takes *Trophee* as the name of a literary work, which he cites as the source of Chaucer's *Troilus*. Pratt (Sts. in Hon. of Ullman, 121–23) argues that Chaucer probably believed in the existence of a commentator named Tropheus.

Several MSS, including the Ellesmere MS and Hengwrt, are here glossed "Ille vates Chaldeorum Tropheus." But this is probably due to scribal error (Frederick Tupper, MLN 31, 1916, 11–13) and thus is of no help in determining the identity of *Trophee*.

2120 Dianira: Deianira, second wife of Hercules, gave her husband the poisoned shirt of the centaur Nessus, believing that it had the power to restore waning love. See Ovid's *Metamorphoses* (S&A, 630–31) and Gower's version (Conf. aman. 2.2148–2312).

2136 Who may trust on Fortune?: Proverbial (Whiting F546).

2139 Ful wyse is he: Proverbial (Whiting K10).

2143–2246 The accounts of **Nabugodonosor** (Nebuchadnezzar), king of Babylon (c. 605–562 B.C.), and of his son **Balthasar** are based on the Book of Daniel 1–5. For the suggestion that Chaucer used the *Bible historiale* of Guyart des Moulins, see Dudley R. Johnson, PMLA 66, 1951, 832–39. Skeat notes (5:234) that Gower and Chaucer share the same unusual spelling of the name *Nabugodonosor;* see Gower's version of the story (Conf. aman. 1.2786–3042).

2147 twyes wan Jerusalem: See 2 Kings (AV 2 Samuel) 24.11–25.9.

2152 leet do gelde: This statement does not occur in the Vulgate. Johnson (PMLA 66:834) cites Peter Comestor's more explicit statement (Hist. scholastica, Liber Danielis 1) that Nebuchadnezzar ordered the emasculation of Daniel and other youths: "After Nebuchadnezzar had led into Babylon the noblest boys of the Jews, including some of royal stock, he castrated the most beautiful and educated among those who stood in the king's palace." The statement also occurs in the *Bible historiale* of Guyart Des Moulins. On *leet do,* see Language and Versification, p. xxxv.

2155 wiseste child: Skeat glosses child as "young man," but J. A. Burrow notes (The Ages of Man, 96–97) that *child* has its modern meaning here, since Daniel is one of the most frequently cited biblical examples of the *puer senex.*

2157 in Chaldeye clerk ne was: The Chaldeans were traditionally versed in occult learning. Cf. Gower, Conf. aman. Pro 663–667: "Lo thus expoundeth Daniel . . . Wher that the wisest of Caldee/ Ne cowthen wite [could not know] what it mente."

2166 tweye: An error for three: Shadrach, Meshach, and Abednego. Daniel does not play a part in the fiery furnace episode in the Vulgate (Dan. 3).

2244–45 Proverbial (Whiting F667, cf. F635); Bo 3.pr5.66–68: "Certes swiche folk as weleful fortune maketh frendes, contraryous fortune maketh hem enemys."

2247 Cenobia, Palymerie: Zenobia was queen of Palmyra, a city in the desert just east of Syria, in the third century A.D. Chaucer based his account of her on Boccaccio's De claris mulieribus and apparently made some use also of the De casibus 6.6 (S&A, 632–36). For a feminist analysis of Zenobia, see Valerie Wayne, in Carole Levin and Jeanie Watson, eds., Ambiguous Realities, 1987, 48–64.

2248 Persiens: No Persian account of Zenobia is known.

Chaucer may have misread Boccaccio's "priscis testantibus literis" (ancient letters testifying) as "persis testantibus literis" (Persian letters testifying) (Ludeke, 98–99, in Festschrift zum 75. Geburtstag von Theodor Spira, ed. H. Viebrock and W. Erzgräber, 1961).

2252 Perce: Persia, apparently a mistake. Boccaccio says she was of the race of the Ptolemies of Egypt.

2256 From her childhede . . . she fled/ Office of wommen: The phrase closely follows Boccaccio's "a pueritia sua, spretis omnino muliebribus officiis" (S&A, 633: "Having spurned all duties of woman since her childhood").

2307 sondry tonges: Zenobia knew several languages, was familiar with Egyptian literature, and studied Greek under the philosopher Longinus (S&A, 635).

2325 Petrak: Chaucer's source was Boccaccio, not Petrarch, although Petrarch devotes ten lines to Zenobia in the Trionfo della Fama 2.107–17. "Why Chaucer refers here to Petrarch rather than to Boccaccio is unknown. From the fact that he never names Boccaccio it has even been inferred that he attributed to Petrarch (or to Lollius) all the writings of Boccaccio that he knew" (Robinson).

2345 In Boccaccio the names are "Heremianus" and "Timolaus." "Chaucer's forms in -*o* might be thought to indicate that he had a source or intermediary in Italian. But he changed a number of names in various works to an Italian form. Cf. *Cambalo,* V.667" (Robinson).

2347 in her hony galle: Proverbial (Whiting F517).

2351 Aurelian: Aurelianus, emperor of Rome, 270–75 A.D., defeated Zenobia in 272.

2372 vitremyte: Probably a woman's headdress of linen or light canvas. No other use of the word is known, and its meaning is unclear. The MED, s.v. *vitremite* n., defines it as "some type of headdress, prob. of glass but perh. of canvas." Vincent DiMarco, ELN 25:4, 1988, 15–19, relates *mitra* to the Maeonian mitra, a cloth cap worn by Greek women, a symbol of effeminacy; being forced to wear it reduces Zenobia to a "mere woman." Cf. S&A 633 (a redaction of Boccaccio's version): "She who was recently accustomed to addressing the troops and wearing a helmet is now compelled to wear a veil and listen to the fables of mere women."

2374 distaf: The staff of a hand spinning wheel, upon which the flax to be spun is placed; figuratively, women's work or occupation (OED s.v. *distaff*). Cf. ProMkt VII.1907.

2375–98 Petro . . . of Spayne: King Pedro of Castile and León was assassinated in 1369 by his illegitimate half-brother, Don Enrique of Trastamara, who was aided by Bertrand du Guesclin, Oliver de Mauny, and others. "Chaucer had various reasons for interest in Pedro of Spain. The Black Prince fought with him against Enrique in 1367. Then John of Gaunt married Constance, Pedro's daughter, in 1371, and assumed in her right the title of King of Castile and León. And for about two years after Constance came to England Chaucer's wife, Philippa, appears to have been attached to her household" (Robinson). Chaucer is now known to have traveled to Spain in 1366, and it has been conjectured that he went on an embassy to Pedro's court (see Chaucer's Life, p. xv).

Chaucer's stanzas on Pedro are generally held to be based on oral information. Braddy (Geoffrey Ch, 23–36) argues convincingly that Chaucer's informant was his friend and Pedro's partisan, Sir Guichard d'Angle. Henry Savage (Spec 24, 1949, 357–75), who gives a detailed account of the murder, suggests that his informant was Don Fernando de Castro, an eyewitness of the event who was later in the service of John of Gaunt (but see Braddy, Geoffrey Ch, 124–27).

2383–84   These lines refer to the arms of Bertrand du Guesclin, who lured Pedro into Enrique's tent, where he was murdered. Brusendorff (Ch Trad., 489) quotes a ballade attributed to Deschamps and written after the death of du Guesclin in 1380: "A silver shield with a black two-headed eagle carried on a red baton . . . the good Bertrand du Guesclin." The **feeld of snow** corresponds to the silver; the black **egle** on a **lymrod** (a stick smeared with birdlime) glowing red (**as the gleede**) corresponds to the eagle on the red baton.

2386 wikked nest: Skeat (5:239) notes a play on the name of Oliver Mauny (OF *mau ni*, i.e., *mal nid*, "bad nest"), another of Pedro's betrayers.

2388 Armorike: Armorica was the home of Oliver de Mauny.

2389 Genylon-Olyver: Cf. ShipT VII.136n., VII.194, and NPT VII.3227n.

2391 Petro, kyng of Cipre: Pierre de Lusignan, king of Cyprus, was assassinated by three of his own knights on 17 January 1369. "Like Peter of Spain he was well known to the English court, having been entertained by Edward III in 1363 and having numbered many Englishmen among his followers. His reputation for chivalry, as Chaucer says, was of the highest, but his murder can hardly be ascribed to jealousy of his fame. It was due rather to resentment at his personal misconduct and his oppressive rule" (Robinson).

Braddy (Geoffrey Ch, 23–36; 124–27) points out that Chaucer's account of Pierre's death is at variance with historical fact, and suggests that it may be derived from Machaut's fictitious account in *La prise d'Alexandrie* (see S&A, 636–67).

2392 Alisandre: Peter's celebrated victory at Alexandria on 10 October 1365 was accomplished with the aid of English knights. See GP I.51n. Donald K. Fry (JEGP 71, 1972, 356) notes that the event was well known to the English court because of the participation of Sir Stephen Scrope and Nicholas Sabraham and through Machaut's La prise d'Alexandrie, as well as Froissart's Chronicles.

2399 Bernabo Viscounte: Bernabò Visconti, lord of Milan, fell from power on 6 May 1385, when he was arrested by his nephew and son-in-law, Gian Galeazzo. In December of the same year he died suddenly in prison, and current opinion attributed his death to poison. Like the two Peters, Bernabò was a figure of special interest to Chaucer and the English court. His niece, Violante, married Chaucer's first patron, Lionel, duke of Clarence; his daughter Caterina had been offered in marriage to Richard II; and his daughter Donnina married the English condottiere, Sir John Hawkwood. Furthermore, Chaucer knew Bernabò personally, for he visited his court on an embassy to treat with him and Hawkwood in 1378. G. L. Kittredge (Date of Ch's Troilus, Ch Soc, 2nd ser., 42, 1909, 46–50) maintains that the stanza on Visconti was written as soon as news of the latter's death

reached England (January of 1386, he conjectures). Wallace (Ch Polity, 319–29) offers some support for this date.

2407 Hugelyn of Pyze: Ugolino della Gherardesca, also known as Ugolino da Pisa, conspired first with his grandson Nino and later with Nino's rival, Archbishop Ruggieri, to seize control of Pisa. For his supposed betrayal of Pisan interests he was put in prison, where he died of starvation in 1289.

Chaucer's account of Ugolino is based primarily on Dante's Inferno 33.1–90, but variations (see Theodore Spencer, Spec 9, 1934, 295–301) suggest that Chaucer either wrote from memory or had additional information. Dante makes no mention of Archbishop Ruggieri's betrayal of Ugolino, and gives the number of children imprisoned with him in the tower as four. For the suggestion that these variations originated in Chaucer's use of Villani's Chronicle 121 and 128 (quoted by Charles Singleton, ed. Inferno, 1970, 2:607–9), see Baddeley and Toynbee, N&Q, ser. 8:11, 1897, 205–6, 369–70. Chaucer omits Dante's reference to Ugolino's dream, as well as Ugolino's cannibalism, but expands the narrative in other places, emphasizing the pathos (see Spencer, Spec 9:295–301). The reference to Fortune, which brings the story into accord with the scheme of The Monk's Tale, is absent in Dante but occurs in Villani. On Chaucer's and Dante's versions, see Piero Boitani, The Tragic and the Sublime in Med. Lit., 1989, 20–55.

2416 Roger: Ruggieri degli Ubaldini, Archbishop of Pisa (1278–95), conspired with Ugolino but later betrayed him (see 2407 above).

2463 Nero: Chaucer's information on Nero appears to be based on Jean de Meun's passage on Fortune in *Le Roman de la rose* 6183–6488, which accounts for all but the second stanza of the tragedy. Chaucer names Suetonius as his source, but Fansler (Ch and RR, 24–25) notes that the reference to Suetonius may itself have been taken from *Le Roman de la rose* 6458, tr. Dahlberg, 126: "As Suetonius wrote it." Skeat notes the possible influence of Boethius (Bo 2.m6 and 3.m4), but as Fansler (Ch and RR, 26) points out, *Le Roman de la rose* follows Boethius so closely in places that it is practically impossible to determine which was Chaucer's original.

As possible sources for the second stanza, with its emphasis on Nero's extravagance, see Root (S&A, 640), who suggests Boccaccio's De casibus, Suetonius' Lives of the Caesars, and Boethius's Consolation of Philosophy; Aiken (Spec 17:60–62) maintains that all the details not accounted for in *Le Roman de la rose* occur in Vincent of Beauvais's Spec. hist. 8.7, where the material borrowed from Suetonius is duly attributed to him.

2465 Swetonius: Suetonius' Lives of the Caesars was an ultimate source for both Jean de Meun and Chaucer, but it is questionable whether either of them relied directly on this work. See 2463 above.

2475 Nettes of gold: Vincent DiMarco (ChaucR 28, 1994, 389–92) finds a source for these nets in the as yet unedited "Alphabetum narrationum" (ca. 1308), by Arnold de Liège.

2477 His lusts were al lawe: Singleton (ed. Inferno, 5.52–60n.) notes that this is a nearly direct translation from Orosius's account of Semiramis: "ut cuique libitum esset liberum fieret." Cf. MLT II.359 n.

2479–95 Skeat notes the close similarity between this passage and Boece 2.m6. Fansler (Ch and RR, 26) points out that much of the similarity is to be found in Chaucer's glosses to Boethius, which might have been derived from *Le Roman de la rose.*

2503–15 This Seneca: Chaucer describes Seneca's death twice, with a slightly different motive in each case. Baugh (365) notes that the actual reason for Seneca's death, not given by Chaucer, was an accusation against him for conspiring to assassinate Nero. DiMarco (ChauR 26:133–36) finds a source for **bothe his armes** in the "Alphabetum narrations."

2516 Chees in a bath to dye: Cf. Bo 3.pr5.47–49: "Nero constreynede Senek, his familyer and his/ mayster, to chesen on what deeth he wolde/ deye."

2550 Fortune lough: Cf. Bo 2.m1.12: "She [Fortune] is so hard that sche leygheth and scorneth/ the wepynges of hem" [whom she casts down].

  De Oloferno: For the story of Holofernes, see the Vulgate Book of Judith.

2565 Bethulia: The location of biblical Bethulia remains unidentified. Magoun (Ch Gazeteer, 32) suggests what is now Nabulus, corresponding to central Israel.

  Lat. gloss: "And the children of Israel did according to what the priest of the Lord Eliachim had decided for them" (Judith 4.7).

2575–2630 Anthiochus: Antiochus IV, king of Syria (175–163 B.C.); see 2 Macc. 9.

2591 Nichanore . . . Thymothee: Two of the generals defeated by Judas Maccabeus; see 2 Macc. 9.13: "And while he (Antiochus) was at Ecbatana, news came to him of what had happened to Nicanor and the forces of Timothy."

2631 Alisaundre: The story of Alexander the Great (356–323 B.C.), king of Macedon, was **commune** in the Middle Ages because Alexander was the hero of a popular cycle of romances as well as of a historical tradition represented by the works of Quintus Curtius, Justin, and Orosius. While Chaucer appears to be writing in the historical tradition, his account of Alexander is so brief and general that no specific source for his material has been identified. For an account of the writings on Alexander, see George Cary, The Medieval Alexander, 1956, and Lumiansky, Manual ME, 1:104–5.

2655 Machabee: 1 Macc. 1.1–7.

2660 "This account of Alexander's death, given as an alternative tradition by Diodorus Siculus 17.118, and adopted by Quintus Curtius, is usually followed by medieval writers. See, for example, Vincent of Beauvais, Spec. hist. 4.64–65" (Robinson).

2661 sys . . . aas: For the figure, see ProMLT II.124–25n.; Gower, Mirour de l'omme, 22103 ("the die with which you [Fortune] play is sometimes a six, sometimes an ace"), 23399 ("God shall change your six into an ace"); tr. Wilson, 293, 306.

2671–2726 Chaucer's account of **Julius Caesar** (c. 100–44 B.C.) is so full of generalities widely current in the Middle Ages that scholars have been unable to agree on its sources. Certain passages derive ultimately from such classical writers as Lucan, Suetonius, and Valerius Maximus (see VII.2719–20), but it is uncertain whether Chaucer relied directly upon them. Shannon (Ch and Roman Poets,

334–39) believed that Chaucer used Lucan's Pharsalia, though the two accounts differ. Robinson notes that certain features peculiar to Chaucer's tragedy: "the triumph, the epithet *lauriat,* the account of Pompey's death, are closely paralleled in the French *Li Hystore de Julius Cesar* of Jehan de Tuim" (fl. 1240; ed. F. Settegast, 1881). For a complete discussion, see Root, S&A, 642–44.

2672 From humble bed: The tradition of Caesar's humble birth, which occurs in Ranulph Higden's Polychronicon 3.42 and later English writers, is at variance with historical fact. Martha S. Waller (Indiana Soc. Sts. Qtly. 31, 1978, 48–55) shows how the tradition may have arisen by the confusion of Suetonius's account of Augustus Caesar's ancestry.

2677 of Rome the emperour: Caesar was never emperor of Rome, but in the Middle Ages he was regarded as the first of the Roman emperors. See Brunetto Latini, *Il Tesoretto,* tr. Holloway, 27.6: "Julius Caesar was the first emperor of the Romans, and after him all the other emperors of Rome were called Caesar," and 38.1: "And thus Julius Caesar was the first emperor of the Romans."

2680 Pompeus: Pompey the Great was actually Caesar's son-in-law. Baugh notes that writers before Chaucer seem to have confused Pompeius Rufus (who was Caesar's father-in-law) with Gnaeus Pompeius (Pompey the Great), who married Caesar's daughter, Julia, and was famous for his campaigns in the East. See Ranulph Higden's Polychronicon and Trevisa's translation (4:188–89, 192–93), where the same error occurs twice. Fisher cites the mistake as evidence that Chaucer was working from general knowledge.

2697 Brutus Cassius: Chaucer was not the first medieval writer to make Brutus and Cassius into one person. The error occurs in a number of earlier texts; Hammond (Eng. Verse, 450) notes Philargyrius's fifth-century commentary on Virgil: "Tiberius Caesar Julius and Antonius waged civil war against Brutus Cassius." H. Theodore Silverstein, MLN 47, 1932, 148–50.

2703 Capitolie: Capitol, the Temple of Jupiter on the Tarpeian (later Capitoline) Hill of Rome, where some medieval writers, including Vincent of Beauvais, placed the assassination of Caesar (see Aiken, Spec 17:67). Pratt notes that the assassination actually took place in the Curia of Pompey in the Campus Martius.

2727 Cresus: Croesus, last king of Lydia, reigned c. 560–546 B.C. Chaucer's primary source for his tragedy is *Le Roman de la rose* 6489–6622 (tr. Dahlberg, 126–28), though the first stanza may also echo Boethius, Bo 2.pr2.58–63: "Wystestow nat how Cresus, kyng of Lydyens, of whiche kyng Cirus was ful sore agast a lytil byforn—that this rewliche Cresus was caught of Cirus and lad to the fyer to ben brend; but that a rayn descendede down fro hevene that rescowyde hym?"

2728 Cirus: Cyrus the Great (reigned 550–530 B.C.), founder of the Persian Empire, overthrew Croesus in 547 B.C.

2740 a sweven: Croesus's dream was a medieval fabrication. It appears to have arisen by the conflation of Herodotus's accounts of Croesus (1.87) and Polycrates (3.124) and occurs in its present form in *Le Roman de la rose* and Vincent of Beauvais's Spec. hist. (S. J. Crawford, TLS, 26 June 1924, 404). Chaucer alludes to the dream in NPT

VII.3138–40 and HF 103–06: "Lo, with such a conclusion/ As had of his avision/ Cresus, that was kyng of Lyde,/ That high upon a gebet dyde."

2761 Tragediës: With the definition here, cf. VII.1973–77, 1991–94, and Bo 2.pr2.67–72: "What other thynge bywaylen the cryinges of tragedyes but oonly the dedes of Fortune, that with an unwar strook overturneth the realmes of greet nobleye? (*Glose. Tragedye is to seyn a dite of a prosperite for a tyme, that endeth in wrecchidnesse.*)"

2764 unwar strook: Note the use of this striking image in Boece (previous note), where it translates "indiscreto ictu."

The Nun's Priest's Prologue

The explanatory notes to The Nun's Priest's Prologue and Tale are adapted from those written by Susan H. Cavanaugh for The Riverside Chaucer.

The Nun's Priest's Prologue exists in two forms. The shorter and probably earlier version, which lacks lines 2771–90, survives in fourteen MSS, ten of which have the Host as interrupter of the Monk (see Manly-Rickert 4:513–14, 2:410–13). The long form of the Prologue, printed here, appears to represent Chaucer's latest intention. In it he adds the Host's echo of the Monk's definition of tragedy (lines 2766 and 2782) and makes the Knight interrupt the speaker, thereby removing what could have been a monotonous repetition of the Host's interruption of Chaucer just before the Melibee. On the dramatic fitness of the Knight as interrupter, see R. E. Kaske, ELH 24, 1957, 249–68, and Donald K. Fry, JEGP 71, 1972, 355–68.

2782 Fortune covered with a clowde: Cf. MkT VII.2766.

2785 biwaille: Cf. MkT VII.1993, 2762.

2801–2 noon audience: See Mel VII.1047 and n.

2803 substance: The meaning is obscure. MED s.v. *substance* 6 (d) has "That which gives support for an action or idea, a basis or foundation; also, the cause of something" (OED is similar). Most editors take substance as "ability" or "capacity" (to appreciate a tale); possibly the sense of "cause" may refer to the Host's duty as *reportour* (GP 814).

2810 sir John: A common and rather contemptuous designation for a priest but apparently the Nun's Priest's actual name (VII.2820); see II.1172n. The familiarity of the Host's address is shown in the use of the second person singular, **thou.** See Language and Versification, p. xxxiii.

2816 Yis: The emphatic form; cf. MilT I.3369n.

The Nun's Priest's Tale

The Nun's Priest's Tale was probably composed with its narrator in mind. The homiletic material, method, and use of exempla are highly appropriate to the teller, while the digressions on dreams, the value of the advice of women, and the problems of predestination reveal a character intimately acquainted with matters of current intellectual interest. Chaucer's deliberate pairing of the Nun's Priest's brilliant tale with the Monk's pedestrian tale is now generally acknowledged. First noted by Samuel B. Hemingway (MLN 31, 1916, 479–83), the relationship between the tales is further explored by Charles S. Watson (Sts. in Short Fiction 1, 1964, 277–88), who shows how The

Nun's Priest's Tale parallels and parodies the concept of the falls of great men, and by Rodney K. Delasanta (TSL 13, 1968, 117–32), who claims the Monk's simplistic attitude toward fortune is dramatically refuted by the Nun's Priest (see also Noel Harold Kaylor, Jr., in The Living Middle Ages, ed. Uwe Boker et al., 1989, 87–102, and Kean, Ch and Poetry, 129–39). There are also satiric allusions to The Prioress's Tale (see 3052, 3057 below) and Melibee (see 3164 below). Howard (Idea of CT, 287) believes that by such means The Nun's Priest's Tale provides a "retrospective" unity to all of Fragment VII.

This lends support to Robinson's assertion that the tale was composed "when the scheme of the Canterbury pilgrimage was well under way." There are, however, no clear indications of date. The only sure historical allusion is to Jack Straw and the revolt of 1381 (see 3394 below). Hotson's theory that the work is an allegorical representation of the duel between Mowbray and Bolingbroke in September of 1397 (see 3215 below) is now almost universally rejected. Rand (see 3123–24 below) argues for a date before 1386 because of the mistaken reference to Macrobius. On the basis of calendrical allusions, North (RES n.s. 20, 1967, 418–22; Ch's Universe, 457–58) dates the tale in 1392: Chauntecleer is seized by the fox on 3 May (VII.3190 and 3187–90 below), which is a Friday (VII.3352), and 3 May was a Friday in 1381, 1387, 1392, and 1398; North argues, on the basis of the astronomical situation on that date, that 1392 is most likely.

The Nun's Priest's Tale is a "beast fable," which ultimately derives from the fable "Del cok e del gupil," by Marie de France (Fables, ed. and tr. Harriet Spiegel, 1987 [rpt. 1994], 168–71), which Chaucer probably knew from the corresponding episode by Pierre de Saint Cloud in Branch II of the Old French beast epic, the *Roman de Renart* (Hulbert, S&A, 646–58), and perhaps from the corresponding episode by an unknown "clerc" of Troyes in Branch VI of *Renart le Contrefait* (ed. Gaston Raynaud and Henri Lemaitre, 1914). Chaucer's combining of features from both the fabular and epic traditions has led to considerable debate concerning his sources. In her classic study, On the Sources of the Nonne Prestes Tale (1898), Kate Petersen carefully analyzed the many forms of the tale and placed Chaucer's version in the beast epic tradition of the *Roman de Renart* rather than the fabular tradition of Marie. Stanley R. Maveety (College Lang. Assoc. Journ. 4, 1960, 132–37) argues for the influence of Marie, since the tale "is not so much a departure from the fable as an extension of it." Both influences are present, and, as A. Paul Shallers (ELH 42, 1975, 319–37) points out, much of the tale's dynamism arises from Chaucer's combining two genres, the moral fable and the amoral beast epic. The central episode or fabular section of the tale, beginning with Chauntecleer's crow to the sun in Taurus and ending with the *moralite*, corresponds with Marie's fable, while the overall frame, including the dream section, the hen, and the old woman on whose farm the action takes place, follows the pattern of the *Roman de Renart*. The hen's skepticism, her denunciation of fear and cowardice, the debate on woman's counsel, and the absurdly inflated and expanded style of the narrative are to be found in *Renart le Contrefait*. While earlier scholars (Petersen, Sources of NPT; Hulbert, S&A, 645–46) have postulated a lost source for the tale, all the details relevant to Chaucer's narrative are to be found in these three poems (Robert A. Pratt, Spec 47, 1972, 667).

The central episode accounts for only a small part of Chaucer's tale. The narrative is expanded with anecdotes and moral applications and is enriched with literary allusions and verbal extravagances. The use of homiletic material is discussed by Petersen, who notes that the commentary of Robert Holcot (d. 1349), *Super Sapientiam Salomonis* (On the Wisdom of Solomon), furnished much of Chaucer's information on dreams. For a full account of the influence of the Wisdom commentary on this tale, see Robert A. Pratt, Spec 52, 1977, 538–70; for the use of sermon techniques in the tale, see Susan Gallick, Spec 50, 1975, 471–76, and Sabine Volk-Birke, Ch and Medieval Preaching, 276–302.

The extent to which the moralizations in the tale are to be taken seriously is much debated, and much criticism can be categorized as "allegorical" versus "mock-heroic." Monica E. McAlpine, in Art and Context, ed. Edwards, 79–92, provides a valuable review of such interpretations and supplies her own sensible reading. The tale has been read and interpreted from a variety of other points of view: Jill Mann reads it as an epitome of Chaucer's comic undermining of the "rituals through which male and female roles are constructed" (Geoffrey Ch: Feminist Readings, 187); Edward Wheatley (SAC 18, 1996, 119–41) finds that scholastic fable commentaries, used in classrooms, underlie the structure and interpretive techniques of the tale. Stephen Manning (JEGP 59, 1960, 403–16) points out, however, that fables were controversial in the Middle Ages, particularly as a means of preaching with "fablis and lesyngis [lies]" (see Owst, Preaching in Med. Engl., 80), and he suggests that Chaucer is ridiculing the rhetorical and poetic practice of his day. It is a complex work that has attracted some of the best criticism of Chaucer. Muscatine's discussion, in Ch and the Fr. Trad., 237–43, remains an excellent starting point for exploring this literature. For a survey of the criticism and scholarship, see Derek Pearsall, ed., The Nun's Priest's Tale, Variorum edition, vol. 2, pt. 9, 1984.

2821 stape in age: Cf. MerT IV.1514 and "ronne in age" RomB 4495.

2832 Robinson finds "humorous exaggeration" in ascribing a **bour** and **halle** to the widow's cottage. Manly (CT, 637) compares Froissart's description (*Chroniques,* tr. Johnes, ch. 95) of a "small house, dirty and smoky, and as black as jet. There was in this place only one poor chamber, over which was a sort of garret that was entered by means of a ladder." The house is sooty because there is no chimney. Chaunticleer and the other chickens roost in the hall (see VII.2884).

2838 Attempre diete: Cf. PP B 6.265, 268–69: "Lat noght Sire Surfet sitten at thi borde/ . . . And if thow diete thee thus I dar legge [*wager*] myne eris/ That Phisik shal his furred hood for his fode selle." On the importance of diet in medieval medicine, see GP I.435–37.

2844 broun breed: The cheapest variety; cf. GP I.147n.

    in which she foond no lak: Either "with which she found no fault" or "of which she had no lack," since *lak* can mean either "fault" (cf. BD 958 "I knew on hir noon other lak") or "lack" (PF 87 "Berafte me my bok for lak of lyght").

2851 organ: Organs, like clavichords and virginals later on, were referred to as a pair, like scissors and trousers today (C. Clutton and A. Niland, The British Organ, 1963, 46), hence the plural verb *gon.* Ian Bishop (RES n.s. 30, 1979, 259) suggests Chaucer was distinguishing between

the high-pitched portative and the larger positive or great organ of a church. Cf. SNT VIII.134–35n.

2854 clokke: This was a recent innovation in England, and clocks were objects of wonder. The famous clock at Wells Cathedral was constructed in about 1390, and the clock at Salisbury in 1386. Their timekeeping was notoriously inaccurate (Bishop, RES n.s. 30:259–60); for a brief survey of clocks in the fourteenth century, see Lynne Mooney, SAC 15, 1993, 106–9. The cock as timekeeper and astrologer was a common metaphor; cf. PF 350 ("The kok, that orloge is of thorpes lyte"), Tr 3.1415 ("the cok, comune astrologer").

2857–58 whan degrees fiftene: It was commonly believed that the cock crowed on the hour (Hinckley, Notes on Ch, 128), and this fostered the idea of the cock's instinctive knowledge of astronomy (John M. Steadman, Isis 50, 1959, 242). See RvT I.4233n.

2859–64 Neville Coghill and J. R. R. Tolkien (eds., NPT, 1959, 17, 46) note that Chauntecleer's description follows precisely the rules for describing a beautiful woman as set forth in Geoffrey of Vinsauf's *Poetria nova,* tr. Nims, 562–99 (see 3347 below). Various allegorical interpretations have been invoked to account for Chauntecleer's colors (J. Leslie Hotson, PMLA 39, 1924, 762–81; Charles Dahlberg, JEGP 53, 1954, 286), but Lalia P. Boone (MLN 64, 1949, 78–81) put speculation to rest: the description fits an actual breed of rooster, the Golden Spangled Hamburg. A similar description of a cock occurs in a ME lyric, "My Gentle Cock" (Robbins, Sec. Lyrics, 41–42). Kathleen Ann Kelly (ELN 30:3, 1993, 1–16) suggests that the description of the phoenix in Mandeville's Travels may have influenced Chaucer's description.

2870 Pertelote: A departure from the French analogues, where the hen is called Pinte. *Pertelote* means "one who confuses (Fr. *perte*) someone's lot or fate" (Pratt, Spec 47:655).

2879 My lief is faren in londe!: A popular song: "My lefe ys faren in londe;/ Allas! why ys she so?/ And I am so sore bound/ I may nat com her to./ She hath my hert in hold/ Where euer she ryde or go,/ With trew love a thousand-fold." (Sec. Lyrics, ed. Robbins, 152).

2882 in a dawenynge: Medieval theory held that morning was a propitious time for prophetic dreams. See Curry, Ch and Science, 207–8.

2914–17 The qualities Pertelote mentions were regularly demanded of courtly lovers; cf. LGW 1528–31: "And he was wis, hardy, secre, and ryche./ Of these thre poyntes there nas non nym liche:/ Of fredom passede he, and lustyhede,/ Alle tho that lyven or been dede." See also the qualities of the ideal husband enumerated in ShipT VII.173–77 and WBT III.1258–60.

2917 Men who boast of their conquests in love were held in particular contempt by those who observed the chivalric code of conduct; cf. Tr 2.724–25: "N'avantour, seith men, certein, he is noon;/ To wis is he to doon so gret a vice."

2918–20 aferd: The cock is "ful bold and hardy, and so fighteth boldly for his wives" [regularized](Barth. Angl., 12.17; tr. Trevisa 1:627)

    berd: Alexander Neckham writes in his De naturis rerum (ed. Wright, 121) that a cock's wattles were commonly known as beards (*vulgo dicuntur barbae*); see Steadman, Isis 50:243.

2922–3157 "Chaucer's writings give abundant evidence of his interest in dreams. Several pieces, BD, HF, PF, ProLGW, purport to be the records of dreams, and though this might be a mere case of conformity to literary fashion, the poems themselves show more than a passing consideration of the dream experience. Then in at least three passages of some length, HF 1–65, Tr 5.358–85, and the present debate of Chauntecleer and Pertelote, the medieval theories on the subject are explicitly discussed" (Robinson). Information on dreams would have been available to Chaucer in such works as Macrobius's *Commentarii in somnium Scipionis* (see 3123–24 below) or one of its many borrowers, and in the standard medical treatises. Most of the discussion between Chauntecleer and Pertelote is based, however, on Robert Holcot's *Super Sapientiam Salomonis; lectiones* 103 and 202 (Pratt, Spec 52:538–70).

Medieval theory distinguished between two types of dreams, those arising from natural causes, which had no prophetic value, and those of prophetic significance. Pertelote, a skeptic like Pandarus (Tr 5.358–64), identifies Chauntecleer's dream as a *somnium naturale,* one which arises from an imbalance of humors and has no significance. Chauntecleer maintains, however, that his is a celestial or prophetic dream. See Curry, Ch and Science, 195–232; Steven F. Kruger, *Dreaming in the Middle Ages,* 1992, 17–122.

2923–32 Cf. Barth. Angl., 6.27, tr. Trevisa 1:336–37: "Somtyme such swevenes cometh of to moche replecioun . . . somtyme of complexioun, as he that is . . . colericus [dreams] of fire and firy things." Cf. HF 21–22: "folkys complexions/ Make hem dreme of reflexions."

2924 fume: Fumes were thought to be the result of overindulgence; see PardT VI.567. On the worthlessness of dreams caused by fumes, see SqT V.358–59 and n. For **complecciouns,** see GP I.333n.

2928 youre rede colera: "the cok is hoot and drie [i.e., choleric] of complexioun" (Barth. Angl. 12.17, tr. Trevisa 1:627). People with an excess of red choler dream "of fire, lighteninge, and dredful brennyng of air" [regularized] (Barth. Angl. 4.10, tr. Trevisa 1:159).

2933–36 humour of malencolie: Black choler; one with an excess of this humor dreams "dredeful swevenes and of derknes, griselych to se" (Barth. Angl. 4.11, tr. Trevisa 1:161).

2940 Ne do no fors of dremes: the Lat. gloss in some MSS (but not Ellesmere or Hengwrt) quotes "Sompnia ne cures" (Walther 30027), ultimately from the Distichs (*Dicta Catonis* 2.3), attributed to Marcus Porcius Cato (*Catoun*); see MilT I.3227.

2942–67: Pertelote's advice is in accord with her diagnosis and standard medical practice. Chauntecleer is naturally choleric (VII.2928), hot and dry, and must therefore avoid too much of the hot and dry sun which would increase his choler and lead to a **fevere terciane,** a fever caused by choler and recurring every three days. The patient must first be administered **digestyves** (VII.2961) and then **laxatyves** (2962); see Curry, Ch and Science, 226–27, and Pauline Aiken, Spec 10, 1935, 282–83.

2953 purge bynethe and eek above: Vincent of Beauvais (quoted by Aiken, Spec 10:282) recommends purging "aut superius aut inferius" (either above or below); Pertelote enthusiastically recommends both.

2961–66 In Dioscorides, De medica materia 2.72, earthworms (**wormes**) are prescribed for tertian fever (qtd by John L. Lowes, Geoffrey Ch, 26–27n.). **lawriol** (lauris nobilis) is a hot and dry herb with "virtue of purging" (Barth. Angl. 17.48, tr. Trevisa 2:942); **centuare** (centiiaria) is a "most bitter herb, hot and dry" that "unstopeth the spleen and the reins" (Barth. Angl. 17.47); **fumetere** (fumus terre), a hot and dry herb with "horrible savoure and hevy smell . . . clensith and purgith melancholia" (Barth. Angl. 17.59); **ellebor,** "a full violent herb," hot and dry, never to be used except "warly" (Barth. Angl. 17.55); **katapuce,** "setteth on fire and scorcheth the whole body" (John Gerarde, The Herball, 1597, quoted by Corinne E. Kauffman, ChauR 4, 1970, 45); **gaitrys beryis,** identified by Skeat (5:252) as the buckthorn, whose berries "purge downwards mightily flegme and choller with great force, much troubling the body" (Langham, Garden of Health, 1633, 99); **herbe yve,** an extremely nauseous herb (Manly, CT, 640), but strong "though he be bitter" (Barth. Angl. 17.53). Pertelote overprescribes: since almost all these herbs are hot and dry and taken together would increase Chauntileer's hotness and dryness, her prescription could endanger his very life (Kauffman, ChauR 4:41–48).

2967 "The conversational effect of the meter is surely intentional, and it is not necessary to regularize the line by omitting *hem* or *up*" (Robinson).

2984 Oon of the gretteste auctour: The superlative may refer to Cicero or Valerius Maximus, both of whom tell the stories (Cicero, *De divinatione* 1.27; Valerius, *Facta et dicta memorabilia* 1.7). Petersen (Sources of NPT, 109–10) argues that the latter is meant, as Chaucer appears to have found the stories in Holcot's *Super Sapientiam Salomonis,* where they are quoted from Valerius. Shio Sakanishi (MLN 47, 1942, 250–51) argues convincingly that they come rather from Giraldus Cambrensis, who also quoted Valerius. However, opposite this line in some manuscripts is the marginal gloss "Tullius" (Partridge, VII.2984), indicating, perhaps, that Cicero is intended (Pratt, Spec 52:562–63 and n. 56).

3050 The marginal gloss "auctor" is written here in the Ellesmere MS. Cf. MLT II.358n.

3052, 3057 Mordre wol out: The phrase is proverbial (Whiting M806) and echoes PrT VII.576.

3065 nexte chapitre: "This statement does not apply to Cicero, Valerius, or Holcot. Manly remarks that Chaunticleer is perhaps 'deceiving Pertelote by a pretense of scrupulous accuracy.' In 3164 he is certainly not above taking advantage of her ignorance of Latin!" (Robinson).

3078 agayn the day: See 2882 above.

3092 of owles and of apes: The owl is traditionally an evil portent. Cf. PF 343 ("The oule ek, that of deth the bode bryngeth"), Tr 5.318–20 ("I mot nedes dye./ The owle ek . . . / Hath after me shright al thise nyghtes two"), LGW 2253–54 ("The oule . . ./ That prophete is of wo and of myschaunce"). The ape is an emblem of foolish gullibility (cf. GP I.706, CYT VIII.1313). Chester L. Shaver (MLN 58, 1943, 106–7), noting later collocations of owls and apes, suggests that the phrase means something monstrous and absurd.

3110–12 Kenelm: Legend maintained that Kenelm (Cenheim), son of Kenelphus (Cenwulf, d. 821), king of Mercia, succeeded his father at the age of seven but was murdered at the instigation of his sister. Shortly before his death, Kenelm dreamed that he climbed a beautiful tree which was cut down beneath him by his attendant, whereupon his soul flew to heaven as a little bird (Early South Eng. Legendary, EETS 87, 345–55; Jacobus de Voragine, Legenda aurea, tr. Caxton 4:60–66).

3123–24 The Somnium Scipionis (**Cipioun**) was originally a chapter of the *De republica* of Cicero. It was edited with an elaborate commentary by Macrobius in about 400 A.D. Chaucer reproduces from *Le Roman de la rose* a garbled reference to the Somnium (making Scipio the dreamer) in RomA, 7–10, which he repeats and compounds (making Macrobius the author rather than commentator) in BD 264–86. Later in The Parliament of Fowls he draws directly on the Somnium, and he attributes the book correctly to Cicero in PF 31. George I. Rand (AMN&Q 7, 1969, 149–50) concludes on this basis that NPT was written before PF, but this argument is not convincing.

3128 Daniel: Dan. 7–12 describes the visions in which the fate of the Jews was revealed to Daniel.

3130–35 Joseph: Joseph as a master interpreter of dreams was a medieval commonplace; cf. BD 278–82. Chauntecleer's exempla occur in Gen. 37, 40, and 41. Lines 3130–32 closely parallel the corresponding passage in Holcot's *Super Sapientiam Salomonis,* lectio 202 ("Therefore some dreams are worthy of credence"), where the exemplum of Joseph is also used (Pratt, Spec 52:559).

3138–40 Cresus: For his dream, see MkT VII.2738–50.

3141 Andromacha: Her dream of the death of **Ector** (Hector), which has no ancient authority, is recounted in Guido delle Colonne, *Hist. destructionis Troiae,* tr. Meek, 165. Chauntecleer's anecdote may be based on Pinte's use of this exemplum in *Renart le Contrefait,* 31323–40 (Pratt, Spec 47:648).

3163 In principio: The first words of the Gospel of St. John and of the Book of Genesis. The first words of St. John's Gospel were the object of special devotion in Chaucer's time (see GP I.254n.), and the line probably means "for as sure as gospel truth." An allusion to Genesis is not, however, inappropriate in this context.

3164 Mulier est hominis confusio: Part of a comic definition of woman so widely known that it was almost proverbial. For a collection of analogues, see Carleton F. Brown, MLN 35, 1920, 479–82. Cf. Mel VII.1106.

3167 your softe syde: Cf. Barth. Angl. 12.17, tr. Trevisa 1:627, on the domestic cock: "And settith next to him on rooste the henne that is most fatte and tendre and loveth hire best and desireth most to have hire presence. In the morwetide whanne he fleeth to gete his mete, furst he leith his side to hire side and bi certeyne tokenes and beckes, as it were love tacchis, a [he] woweth and prayeth hire to tredinge."

3173–75 Cf. Barth. Angl. (as above): "And whenne he fyndeth mete he clepith his wifes togedres with a certeyn voys and spareth his owne mete to fede therwith his wifes."

3187 According to medieval belief, the world was created at the vernal equinox, the beginning of the solar year; see Bede, De ratione temporum (ed. Charles W. Jones, 1943) 6.6–7.

3187–90 This elaborate chronographia (see the end of n. at GP I.7–8n.) is meant to establish the date as 3 May, the date of Palamon's escape from prison (see KnT I.1462–64 and n.) and of Pandarus's dream the night before he woos Criseyde for Troilus (Tr 2.56).

3190 Syn March [was gon]: For *was gon* the MSS read *began;* taken literally this would set the day as 1 April (April Fool's Day, but the custom is unknown before the eighteenth century), though the day must be 3 May (see 3194–99 below). Chaucer probably wrote *was gon* and scribal miscopying from 3187 led to the mistaken repetition of *began* in 3190.

3194–99 The *Kalendarium* of Nicholas of Lynn (ed. Eisner, 89, 93), which Chaucer probably used here, shows that on 3 May the sun was at 21° 6' of Taurus (the bull, the second sign of the zodiac) and that at 9 A.M. in the latitude of Oxford the sun was at a height of 41° 17'.

3196–97 knew by kynde: See 2857–58 above.

3205–6 ende of joye is wo: A medieval commonplace, attributed to Solomon in a marginal gloss (cf. Prov. 14.13: "Even in laughter the heart is sorrowful; and the end of that mirth is heaviness"). The idea is frequent in Chaucer (KnT I.2841, MLT II.1161, Tr 1.3–4: "his aventures fellen/ Fro wo to wele, and after out of joie"; cf. MLT II.421n.).

3209 The name "Petrus Comestor," author of the widely read *Historia scholastica,* is written here in the margin of five MSS, including Ellesmere and Hengwrt, but no reference to him in the NPT has been traced.

3212 the book of Launcelot de Lake: The story of Lancelot, knight of Arthur's court and lover of Queen Guinevere. "Who" was not in use as a relative in Chaucer's time, so **that** in the following line may refer either to Lancelot or to the book. This is the story that Paolo and Francesca were reading when they were inspired to commit adultery (Dante, Inferno 5.117–38). Hinckley (Notes on Ch, 141) quotes Hugh of Rutland's *Ipomedon:* "I know nothing of the art of lying, Walter Map knows well his share of it." Map was the supposed author of the prose Book of Lancelot.

3215 col-fox: J. Leslie Hotson (PMLA 39:762–81) argued elaborately that Chaucer uses a *col-fox* instead of the usual red fox of the Reynard cycle to suggest the name of Nicholas Colfax, a supporter of Mowbray; his colors are those of Mowbray's truncheon as earl marshal; his name, *daun Russell,* suggests Sir John Russell, a minion of Richard II. Hotson takes Chauntecleer's colors as suggesting the arms of Henry Bolingbroke and sees the confrontation of the cock and the fox as representing the duel between Mowbray and Bolingbroke on 16 September 1398. The identification with Bolingbroke is very unlikely, as is the rest of the theory.

3217 By heigh ymaginacioun forncast: The line has been taken to be either a reference to Chauntecleer's dream or to God's foreknowledge, and to mean "foreseen by the exalted imagination" (i.e., in Chauntecleer's prophetic dream) or "foreordained by the high vision of God." Victor M. Hamm (MLN 69, 1954, 394–95) notes that Dante uses the phrase "alta fantasia" in connection with his ecstatic visions in Purgatorio 17.25 and Paradiso 33.142 (see also Pratt, Spec 47:666 and n. 36). However, Karl P.

Wentersdorf (SN 52, 1980, 31–34) shows convincingly that the phrase refers to the fox's cunningly premeditated attack on Chauntecleer.

3222 undren: Strictly speaking, 9 A.M., but *undren* was loosely used to cover the entire period from 9:00 until noon.

3227 Genylon: Ganelon, in the *Chanson de Roland,* betrayed Charlemagne's army at Roncesvalles; cf. MkT VII.2389, ShipT VII.194.

3228 Synon: the betrayer of Troy; see HF 152–56: "the Grek Synon,/ [That] with his false forswerynge,/ . . . Made the hors broght into Troye,/ Thorgh which Troyens loste al her joye." Cf. SqT V.209–10.

3241–50   The question of predestination versus free will and the issue of divine grace were much debated in the universities during Chaucer's time. **Augustyn,** St. Augustine (354–430), bishop of Hippo, one of the four original Doctors of the Church, was an exponent of the orthodox doctrine on the subject, which held that free will was granted to man by God to be used to the extent that God allowed. **Boece,** Boethius, discusses the problem (see Bo 4.pr6 and Bk. 5, esp. pr6.140ff.) and makes the distinction between "simple" and "conditional" necessity mentioned here. **Bradwardyn** (Thomas Bradwardine; c. 1290–1349) was an Oxford theologian who became archbishop of Canterbury. In his treatise *De causa Dei* (ed. Savile, 1618), he reaffirmed the (orthodox) doctrine of predestination and grace (VII.3242–45); see Gordon Leff, Bradwardine and the Pelagians, 1957. The subject is treated at length in Tr 4.953–1078. See Grover C. Furr, in Utz, Literary Nominalism, 135–46, on the argument over free will in the fourteenth century.

3245–50 symple necessitee . . . necessitee condicioneel: See Bo 5.pr6.178–83: *Simple* necessity is direct, as in "it byhovith by necessite that alle men ben mortal." *Conditional* necessity is inferential: "yif thou wost that a man walketh, it byhovith by necessite that he walke." God's foreknowledge, Boethius argues, is not a necessary cause of man's actions.

3256 Wommenes conseils: Proverbial (Whiting W505), cf. Mel VII.1096.

3260   Cf. *Roman de la rose,* 15195–210, tr. Dahlberg, 258–59: "If you ever find set down here any words that seem critical and abusive of feminine ways, then please do not blame me for them nor abuse my writing, which is all for our instruction. I certainly never said anything, nor ever had the wish to say anything . . . against any woman alive."

3266   Since **kan** may mean "am able" or "know," and **divyne** may be read as either a verb or an adjective, the sentence has several possible meanings. For a complete analysis of what Muscatine (Ch and the Fr. Trad., 239) calls "the most deliciously ambiguous line in Chaucer," see Lawrence L. Besserman, ChauR 12, 1977, 68–71.

3271–72 Phisiologus: "The Naturalist," the title or the supposed author of a popular compilation in which descriptions of imaginary and real animals, birds, and stones were allegorized to illustrate points of Christian doctrine. The descriptions are introduced by the formula: "Physiologus says" (*Physiologus dicit*). The Latin Physiologus circulated in numerous versions, for which see Florence McCulloch, Med. Lat. and Fr. Bestiaries, Univ. of North Carolina Sts. in the Romance Langs. and Lits., 33, revised ed., 1962.

The mermaid or siren (**mermayde**) appears in several versions of Physiologus, where she is characterized by a sweet voice that leads sailors to destruction (McCulloch, s.v. *siren* and *onocentaur*); cf. RomA 681 ("her syngyng is so clere") and Bo 1.pr1.69–70 ("ye mermaydenes, whiche/ that ben swete til it be at the laste").

3280 his contrarie: Robinson notes that according to the old philosophy every object or creature had its contrary toward which it felt a natural antipathy. Professor Jon Whitman of Hebrew University (Jerusalem), in a letter, quotes Fulgentius, Mythologies 1.6 (tr. Whitbread, 51–52): "Quarrels are brought about in a threefold fashion, that is, by nature, cause, and accident. Hate is natural, as between dogs and hares, wolves and sheep, men and snakes."

3294 Boece: Boethius's treatise *De musica* (ed. G. Friedlein, Leipzig, 1867) was a standard medieval university text. In it, he advocated a mathematical rather than instinctual approach to music (*feelynge*). Chaucer's couplet, therefore, may have an ironic meaning (David S. Chamberlain, MP 68, 1970, 188–91).

3312 Daun Burnel the Asse: *Burnellus,* or *Speculum stultorum,* a comic beast tale (c. 1180) by Nigel Wireker (ed. J. H. Mosely and R. R. Raymo, 1960; tr. as The Mirror for Fools, J. H. Mozely, 1963). For the story to which Chaucer refers, see lines 1251–1502. "A young man named Gundulfus broke a cock's leg by throwing a stone at it. Later, when Gundulfus was to be ordained and receive a benefice, the cock crowed so late that Gundulfus overslept and lost his living" (Robinson).

3325 Allas, ye lordes: This passage, which is inappropriate to the pilgrimage framework (Kenneth Sisam, ed., NPT, 1927), is taken almost verbatim from John of Wales's preaching manual, the *Communiloquium* 1.8.2 (Pratt, Spec 41, 1966, 635–36). Cf. also ProLGW F 352–54: "For in youre court ys many a losengeour,/ And many a queynte totelere accusour,/ That tabouren in youre eres many a sown."

3329 Ecclesiaste of flaterie: The exact text to which Chaucer refers has not been found. Sisam argues that Ecclesiastes may stand for Solomon in any of his works and may refer to Prov. 29.5, quoted in Chaucer's Melibee in the section on flattery (VII.1178–79).

3338 O destinee: Cf. Bo 5.pr3.189–90: "the ordenance of destyne whiche that mai nat ben enclyned" [*bent, turned aside*].

3341 Friday: Friday, Venus's day, was traditionally associated with bad luck. The Expulsion, the Deluge, the Betrayal, the Crucifixion, and the fatal wounding of Richard I all occurred on a Friday. See also KnT I.1534–39 and n.

3345 Moore for delit: Cf. *Roman de la rose,* 4385–88; tr. Dahlberg, 96: "A lover thinks of nothing else; he takes no account of bearing fruit, but strives only for delight."

3347 Gaufred: Geoffrey of Vinsauf, author of the *Poetria nova* (c. 1210), the standard text on medieval rhetoric (i.e., poetics), gives rules for writing poetry, with flamboyant illustrations of his own composition. In VII.3347–52 Chaucer parodies the most famous of these, the lamentation on the death of Richard the Lion-Hearted, which begins (*Poetria nova,* tr. Nims, 375–76): "O tearful day of Venus!

O bitter star!/ That day was your night; and that Venus your venom." In VII.3355–73 Chaucer elaborately expands a simple statement in accord with the rules set down by Geoffrey. Chaucer again quotes Geoffrey (43–45) in Tr 1.1065–71: "For everi wight that hath an hous to founde/ Ne renneth naught the werk for to bygynne/ With rakel hond, but he wol bide a stounde,/ And sende his hertes line out fro withinne/ Aldirfirst his purpos for to wynne." Both passages from Geoffrey of Vinsauf circulated independently from the *Poetria nova* (see Karl Young MP 41, 1943, 172–82, James J. Murphy, RES n.s. 15, 1964, 1–20).

3357 Pirrus: Pyrrhus, son of Achilles, seized Priam by the hair (not the beard) and killed him with his sword. The laments he caused are narrated in Aeneid 2.486–90. Cf. MLT II.288.

3359 Eneydos: Aeneid 2.533–58. Chaucer may have found the hint for his references to Troy, Carthage, and Rome in the six lines (363–68) of the Poetria nova just preceding those parodied in VII.3347–52 (Pratt, MLN 64, 1949, 76–78).

3363 Hasdrubales wyf: Hasdrubal was king of Carthage when the Romans captured and burned it in 146 B.C. Chaucer tells of his wife's suicide in FranT V.1399–1404, from Jerome, *Adversus Jovinianum* 1.43; tr. Fremantle, 381 (see V.1399n.).

3375–3401   The chase of the fox was a stock scene in medieval literature and art. An example occurs in the poem The Fals Fox (Sec. Lyrics, ed. Robbins, 44–45). See also Kenneth Varty, Reynard the Fox: A Study of the Fox in Medieval Art, 1967, 34–42, with reproductions of scenes of the chase (that from the Queen Mary Psalter being an especially fine example).

3381 Ha, ha!:   The regular cry to frighten away wolves and other marauding animals. The thirteenth-century Dominican, Nicholas Biard, says in a sermon: "There is no wolf disguised as a sheep, that will not flee if the shepherds go on shouting Ha! Ha!" (Tatlock, MLN 29, 1914, 143).

3383 Colle oure dogge: For the "domestic plural" *oure,* see WBPro III.311n. The name *Colle* appears in a list of dogs ("Colle, Grubb, Lugtrype, Slugge, Turne-bob") in a fifteenth-century poem (Robbins, ed., Hist. Poems, 189); Robbins (p. 355n.) claims "Colle" is derogatory.

   Talbot and Gerland: Dogs' names. There is a list of names of hounds in one MS of the *Roman de Renart* (S&A, 656.411–14: "Constans called his mastiff . . . Mauvoisin, 'Bardol, Travers, Humbaut, Rebors,/ Run after Renart the red!'").

3384 Malkyn: A typical name for a country girl or serving-maid; see IntroMLT II.30n. In medieval art, it was a regular feature of the chase of the fox for the woman to carry a distaff as a weapon (Kenneth Varty, Nottingham Med. Sts. 8, 1964, 62–81). Cf. 3375–3401 above.

3394 he jakke Straw: A supposed leader of the Peasants' Revolt of 1381. The Flemings, prosperous foreigners engaged in the wool trade, were the victims of a particularly ruthless attack by the mob. See R. B. Dobson, ed., The Peasants' Revolt of 1381, 1970, and Steven Justice, Writing and Rebellion: England in 1381, 1994. The reference has been the subject of much recent comment: see Paul Strohm, Social Ch, 165–68; Stephen T. Knight, Geoffrey Ch, 1986,

141–45; Peter Travis, JMRS 18, 1988, 195–220; and John Ganim, Chaucerian Theatricality, 113–15. On the use of *he,* see Language and Versification, p. xxxiii.

3426 shrewe us bothe two: Almost identical with WBT III.1062.

3441 Seint Paul seith: Rom. 15.4: "For whatever was written in former days was written for our instruction, that by steadfastness and by the encouragement of the scriptures we might have hope." Chaucer's Retraction, X.1083, is nearly identical.

3443 fruyt . . . chaf: For the familiar figure, see MLT II.701–2; ParsPro X.35–36; ProLGW G 312, G 529 ("Lat be the chaf, and writ wel of the corn"); cf. Whiting C428. The comparison derives from Matt. 3.12 ("He will thoroughly purge his floor, and gather his wheat into the garner, but he will burn up the chaf with an unquenchable fire"); so also Luke 3.17. Manning (JEGP 59:414) notes the similarity between the Nun's Priest's words and the introduction to the versified Romulus collection attributed to the twelfth-century writer, Walter of England: "If the fruit is more pleasing than the flower, gather the fruit, if the flower more than the fruit, the flower; if both, take both" (Leopold Hervieux, ed., *Les fabulistes Latins,* 1894, 2:316). See also Robertson (Pref to Ch, 58 and 316–17) on the chaff image in Augustine and other patristic writers.

3445 As seith my lord: It is uncertain who is meant. If the ascription applies to the phrase **if that it be thy wille,** there may be an allusion to the prayer of Jesus in Gethsemane (Matt. 26), but in that case *oure lord* would be more natural than *my lord.* A Lat. gloss in the Ellesmere and Hengwrt reads: "the Lord Archbishop of Canterbury," and a considerable, but so far unsuccessful, search has been made to find a similar benediction associated with that prelate (then William Courtenay). Manly observes that the Nun's Priest's "lord" was the bishop of London, Robert Braybrooke. While VII.3444–46 may echo an episcopal blessing, many ME secular compositions, including a good number of Chaucer's *Tales,* conclude with a prayer. Robert M. Correale (Expl 39, 1980, 43–45) notes the similarity between these lines and the ending of a homily for the Feast of the Conversion of St. Paul. He argues that the "lord" intended is St. Paul, mentioned in VII.3441.

The Nun's Priest's Epilogue

These lines occur in a group of nine MSS generally taken to be of inferior authority and may have been canceled by Chaucer when he wrote lines 1941–62 of The Monk's Prologue, where the same ideas are repeated (See introductory note to Monk's Prologue). Tatlock (PMLA 50, 1935, 113–15) defends retention of the link, on the grounds that repeated language and ideas are characteristic of Chaucer's style, and that in the best MSS, link passages pointing to lacunae in the text would have been suppressed to give a semblance of completeness to the work.

3451 trede-foul: Cf. ProMkT VII.1945. Roy J. Pearcy (N&Q 213, 1968, 43–45) shows the parallel between a man in a religious house and cocks in a hen-run was traditional in the Middle Ages. Cf. *Decameron,* first story of the third day (ed. Branca 1:325–26).

3459 brasile: A red dye derived from the wood of an East Indian tree (OED s.v. *brazil,* 1.2). The name was afterwards applied to Brazil in South America because a similar dye-producing tree was found there.

greyn of Portyngale: Another crimson dye-stuff, obtained from the dried bodies of the insect *Coccus ilicis,* which were thought to be seed grains; also known as "kermes berries." See Magoun, Ch Gazetteer, 129.

FRAGMENT VIII

Though editors have differed on whether Fragment VI or Fragment VII should precede Fragment VIII, none has printed the last three fragments in any order other than VIII–IX–X. Howard (Idea of CT, 305) and Lawler (One and the Many, 145–46) argue that these three fragments form a coherent group that recapitulates earlier themes of the whole work, providing a sense of closure. James Dean (PMLA 100, 1984, 746–62) argues that the three fragments share a closing sequence of transformations; and John M. Fyler (in Morse, Doob, Curry eds., The Uses of Manuscripts in Literary Studies, 1982, 193–211) traces a process of linguistic deterioration in SNT, CYT, and MancT. The two tales of Fragment VIII are explicitly linked (by line 554), though there is no other explicit relation between the tales, and the attribution of the first to the Second Nun occurs only in the rubric. Moreover, the two tales were apparently written at different times.

Nevertheless, critics have frequently remarked on the thematic unity of the two tales (e.g., Muscatine, Ch and Fr Trad., 216–17). The thematic links are most often found in the use of alchemical imagery (Jospeh E. Grennen, JEGP 65, 1966, 466–81) and in the manipulation of such contrasts as reason versus revelation, sight versus blindness, and contrasting imagery, themes, and attitudes (see, for example, Robert M. Longsworth, ChauR 27, 1992, 87–96; Russell A, Peck, AnM 8, 1967, 17–37). Glending Olson explains the unity of theme and imagery in the context of Dante's influence (ChauR 16, 1982, 222–36) and supplies a summary of commentary viewing the two tales as complementary, as does Bruce K. Cowgill (PQ 74, 1995, 343–57) and, earlier, Peter Brown (ES 64, 1983, 481–90), who found that the lesson that the Canon's Yeoman learns is the same as that which Cecilia offers to Almachius.

Patterson (Ch and History, 267–68) notes the pattern of confessional tales preceded by "tales that aspire to hagiographical authority: Man of Law–Wife of Bath, Physician–Pardoner," and especially the Second Nun's–Canon's Yeoman, which includes the only full-fledged saint's life in the *Tales.*

The Second Nun's Prologue and Tale

The explanatory notes to the Second Nun's Prologue and Tale were adapted from those written by Florence H. Ridley for The Riverside Chaucer.

The reference to the *Lyf of Seynt Cecile* in the Prologue to *The Legend of Good Women* (ProLGW F 426) shows that The Second Nun's Tale was written before 1386–87, and its borrowings from Dante (see 36–56 below) and use of rime royal show that it probably belongs to Chaucer's Italian period. Older scholars put it very early in that period, around 1373, since they regarded it as a close translation of its source (e.g., Skeat 3:485) and therefore as an immature work. But later critics have found its style evidence of poetic maturity (Knight, Poetry of CT, 175–79), and on the whole a date in the later 1370s or very early 1380s is most likely.

Some critics have thought that the prologue and tale were composed at differing times: Skeat (5:403) held that lines 36–56 of the Invocation to Mary were a later interpolation, and Judith A. Weise (Style 31, 1977, 440–79) argues on the basis of the romance vocabulary that differing parts of the tale (120–343, 344–553) were written at differing times. However, she bases her work on that of Joseph Mersand (Ch's Romance Vocabulary, 1936), now made obsolete by Christopher Cannon's The Making of Chaucer's English, 1999.

The prologue and tale are eminently suited to a nun and seem to suggest a definite personality (George J. Engelhardt, MS 37, 1975, 295–96); however, she is mentioned only in the rubric, and Norman E. Eliason (MLQ 3, 1942, 9–16) argued that she is merely a scribal invention. It is clear that the tale was never completely revised (see VIII.62, 78, 139 and nn.), and its lack of any clear integration with the *Tales* is notable. Even though recent criticism has found close thematic relationships between The Second Nun's Tale and The Canon's Yeoman's Prologue and Tale (see introductory note to Fragment VIII above), the tale was apparently taken into *The Canterbury Tales* and allowed to stand without revisions to adapt it to its context.

Chaucer's tale is a saint's life, an account of the life, sufferings, miracles, and martyrdom of a saint. The saint's life was a genre of popular literature in Chaucer's time. There are lives of Saint Cecilia in two important collections—the Northern Homily Cycle, ed. Saara Nevanlinna (Helsinki, Société néophilologique), 1972–84, and The South English Legendary, ed. D'Evelyn and Mill, EETS, 235–36, 244; see Sherry L. Reames, in M. Teresa Tavormina and R. F. Yeager, eds., The Endless Knot, 1995, 197–99. On medieval hagiography, see Hippolyte Delehaye, Legends of the Saints, tr. Donald Attwater, 1962; for Chaucer's use of the genre, see Gerould, Ch Essays, 3–32. In the Retraction, X.1087, Chaucer seems to imply that he wrote more than one saint's life, though only the life of Cecilia has survived. The use of rime royal in this work groups it with other tales of suffering innocence (MLT, ClT, PrT) and religion (cf. D. Pearsall, in Ch's Religious Tales, 11–19).

Almost nothing is known of the historical Cecilia; on the history of the legend, see Butler's Lives of the Saints (4:402–5) and Thomas Connolly, Mourning into Joy: Music, Raphael, and Saint Cecilia, 1994, a full study of the saint's history, hagiography, and traditional association with music.

The first 28 lines of the prologue, on Idleness, are conventional and may be based on a variety of sources (see 1–28 below). The Invocation to Mary (VIII.29–84) is based mainly on Dante (Par. 33.1–39), though it contains some commonplaces and echoes from other sources (see Paul M. Clogan, M&H n.s. 3, 1972, 221–31). The Interpretation of Cecilia's Name (VIII.85–119) and the tale (from VIII.120 to about 345) are drawn from the *Legenda aurea* of Jacobus de Voragine (ed. Gerould, in S&A, 671–77, tr. Ryan).

Gerould believed that the second half of the tale (from about 349 to the end) was based on a version descended from the *Passio* by Mombritus (which he printed in S&A, 677–84), and critics generally assumed that this or a similar work was Chaucer's source. However, Sherry L. Reames (MP 87, 1989, 337–51) discovered in French liturgical manuscripts a "Franciscan abridgement" of the legend remarkably close to the version that Chaucer knew; Reames prints that version in her article. This discovery negates a good deal of previous criticism, which, especially in the trial scene (VIII.421–512 and n. below), credited Chaucer's artistry in adapting his source to details he took from the "Franciscan abridgement."

Older critics found the tale dull (e.g., Donaldson, Ch's Poetry, 1108–9) and most simply ignored it, along with Chaucer's other religious tales (cf. C. D. Benson, in Ch's Religious Tales, 1–7). Recently it has received more attention; its metaphoric and thematic relations to CYT have been explored (see introductory note to Fragment VIII), as have its possible relations to Wycliffite dissent (Lynn S. Johnson, SP 89, 1992, 314–33), its subtle challenge to established values and ideologies (John Scattergood, in M. Stokes and T. L. Burton, eds., Med. Lit. and Antiquities, 1987, 145–62), and its "Christian feminism" (John C. Hirsch, in Ch's Rel. Tales, 161–70; Ruth M. Ames, God's Plenty, 1984, 171–78). On gender and narrative voice in the tale, see Leicester, Disenchanted Self, 198–231.

1–28 The idea for the stanzas on idleness may derive from the introduction to the French translation of the *Legenda aurea* by Jean de Vignay (1282/85–1348). However, the ideas are commonplace. Line 1 is proverbial: Idleness is the nurse (mother, gate) of the vices (evils, sins), Whiting I6; cf. Mel VII.1589. Whittock (A Reading of CT, 252) shows how the lines develop that proverb.

2–3 Ydelnesse: Idleness is the gate-keeper of the garden of Love in *Le Roman de la rose* (RomA 593: "Lo, sir, my name is Ydelnesse"), KnT I.1940, and ParsT X.714 (where ydelnesse is "the yate of all harmes").

4 contrarie: The principle in medicine (Mel VII.1017) was applied to the deadly sins (*vices*), each of which has as its remedy a contrasting virtue; cf. ParsT, where the remedy for *Ydelnesse* (*Accidie*) is *fortitudo or strengthe* (X.728).

4–6 bisynesse: Cecilia is the antitype of sloth (Frederick Tupper, PMLA 29, 1914, 106); cf. ParsT X.684: "Accidie [idleness] . . . loveth no bisines at al."

6–7 feend thurgh ydelnesse us hente: Cf. Mel VII.1595 and Whiting D182.

10–11 trappe: Cf. Wyclif, Sel. Eng. Works, 3:200: "Ydelness is the devilis panter to tempte men to synn" (Robinson).

14 werche: Cf. VIII.2–5, 64–66, 77, 84, 384–85. Bruce A. Rosenberg (ChauR 2, 1968, 282–91) and Joseph E. Grennen (JEGP 65, 1966, 466–81) trace the theme.

19–21 Sloth holds idleness on a **lees** (leash), causing men to sleep, eat, drink, and devour the produce of others.

25–26 legende . . . lif . . . passioun: In early Middle English, *lif* indicates a brief biography, emphasizing a saint's suffering (*passioun*); *legende* is most often applied to the lives in the *Legenda aurea*, though the word could be used satirically, as in MilPro I.3141 (Paul Strohm, ChauR 10, 1975, 161–64).

27 rose . . . lilie: The rose symbolizes martyrdom, the lily purity (see 221 below and cf. ProPrT VII.461 and n.).

29–77 Invocacio: The resemblance to ProPrT VII.467–80 and to ABC is striking; cf. ProPrT VII.474–80n.

30 Bernard: Bernard of Clairvaux (c. 1090–1153), whose prayer to the Virgin in Dante's *Paradiso* supplies the source for what follows.

36–56 Based on Dante, Par. 33.1–51; Skeat took the passage as a late addition (5:403), but Carleton Brown argues effectively for the unity of the Invocation (MP 9, 1911, 1–11).

36 Translation of Par. 33.1:" Vergine madre, figlia del tuo figlio" (Virgin mother, daughter of your son).

37 welle of mercy: Cf. ParsT 177–78: "Zacharie yow clepeth the open welle/ To wasshe sinful soule out of his gilt."

39 Translation of Par. 33.2: "Umile et alta più che creatura" (Humble and higher than any creature). Cf. Luke 1.28: "Hail, thou that art highly favoured, the Lord is with thee, blessed art thou among women."

40–41 From Par. 33.4–6: "Tu se' colei, che l'umana natura/ nobilasti che sì suo Fattore/ non disdegnò di farsi sua fattura" (You are she who so ennobled human nature that its Maker did not disdain to become its making).

43–49 Cf. Par. 33.7: "Nel ventre tuo si raccese l'amore" (In your womb was rekindled the love). The phrase **cloistre blisful** may derive from Par. 25.127 ("beato chiostro," blessed cloister), but the passage as a whole is close to the *Quem terra* by Venantius Fortunatus (*Analecta Hymnica*, ed. Guido M. Dreves and Clemens Blume, 1866–1922, II.38, No. 1, 27, 1–4): "The womb (claustrum) of Mary bears Him, ruling the threefold fabric (*trinam machinam*), Whom earth, stars, sea, honor, worship, proclaim."

50–51 Cf. Par. 33.19–20: "In te misericordia, in te pietate, In te magnificenza" (In you is mercy, in you is pity, in you is munificence).

52 sonne: At times applied to Mary (Brown, MP 9:7). Skeat (5:404) suggests it may have had a feminine reference in Chaucer's day. Robinson notes that "Another phrase, in the same underlying passage from Dante, 'meridiana face, di caritate' (Par. 33.10–11) was interpreted by Italian commentators as the noonday sun at the height of its power."

53–56 Cf. Par. 33.16–18: "La tua benignità non pur soccorre/ a chi domanda, ma molte fiate/ liberamente al domandar precorre" (Your kindness not only helps those who ask but many times generously anticipates the asking). This passage is echoed also in ProPrT VII.477–80 and (in a secular context) *Troilus* 3.1261–67.

58 flemed wrecce: Perhaps suggested by "exiled sons of Eve" in the Hours of the Virgin (see 62 below).

galle: Bitterness; Skeat (5:404) sees a possible allusion to the name "Mary" and the Heb. *mar,* fem. *marah,* "bitter"; cf. Exodus 15.23: "And when they came to Marah, they could not drink of the waters of Marah, for they were bitter; therefore the name of it was called Marah." Chaucer plays on the concept in ABC 49–51: "Glorious mayde and mooder, which that nevere/ Were bitter, neither in erthe nor in see,/ But ful of swetnesse and of merci evere."

59–61 womman Cananee: Cf. Matt. 15.22 ("mulier Chananaea," woman of Canaan), 15:27: "And she said, Truth Lord: yet the dogs eat of the crumbs that fall from their masters' table."

62 sone of Eve: This has seemed to many inappropriate to a female narrator. Tupper (MLN 30, 1915, 9–11) argues *sone of Eve* is well suited to a nun, since it occurs in the Compline service of the Hours of the Virgin as *exiled sones of Eve* (Prymer or Lay Folks Prayer Book, ed. Henry Littlehales, EETS 105, 1895, 34). Yet "filii" is the inclusive plural, and a nun would more naturally refer to herself as "doghter." The masculine singular probably is evidence that the tale was composed without thought of the Second Nun (see introductory note).

64 feith . . . withouten werkis: James 2.17: "Even so faith, if it hath not works, is dead, being alone."

69 Anne: Cf. MLT II.641n.

71–74 For the concept of the body as prison, cf. KnT I.3061; the passages are indebted to Macrobius, Som. Scip., 1.11.2–4, tr. Stahl, 131: "the body serves as fetters, and . . . it is a tomb, being the prison of the entombed."

72 contagioun: Cf. "contagione corporis" [bodily contagion] (Macrobius, Som. Scip. 1.11.11). This is the earliest use of the word in this sense in English; MED s.v. *contagion* n.

75 havene of refut: Cf. ABC 14 ("Haven of refut"), MLT II.852. There are similar scriptural expressions, e.g., Ps. 45 (AV 46).1 ("God is our refuge"), and the epithet is common in hymns from Chaucer's day to the present.

78 reden: This reference to reading material supposedly delivered orally seems obvious evidence of lack of revision, though various explanations have been offered, none very convincing.

79 Foryeve me: Chaucer frequently employs the "modesty topos" (see GP I.746n.), though it may be especially appropriate to a hagiographer, whose purpose is not to excel in narration, but to instruct (Clogan, M&H n.s. 3:216: "his main concern was edification").

84 The request for correction is an extension of the "modesty topos"; cf. Tr 5.1856–59: "O moral Gower, this book I directe/ To the and to the, philosophical Strode,/ To vouchen sauf, ther nede is, to correcte."

85–119 The *Interpretacio* is based on Jacobus (S&A, 671): "coili lilia" (**hevenes lilie**); "caecis via" (**wey to blynde**); "caelo et lya" (**hevene and Lia,** the active life); "caecilia quasi caecitate carens" (**Wantynge of blyndnesse**); "coelo et leos" (**hevene of peple**). These etymologies are all wrong, the name perhaps deriving from *caecus* (blind) (Robinson). However, such etymologies were considered a legitimate means of expressing the moral significance of words, since medieval etymologists held that the origin of a word was related to its force or function; see Isidore of Seville, *Etymologiae,* ed. Lindsey 1.1.29, tr. Brehaut, 99 ("A knowledge of etymology is often necessary for interpretation, for, when you see whence a name has come, you grasp its force more quickly"); on etymologizing, see R. Howard Bloch, Etymologies and Geneologies, 1983, ch. 1, and Curtius, Europ. Lit., 497.

96–98 hevene . . . bisynesse: Thought of heaven signifies the contemplative life, thought of Leah (**Lia**), the active life (Skeat, 5:406; for Leah, see Gen. 29.16–35).

104 leos: Greek λᾱός (people). Chaucer did not know Greek. This comes from his source.

114, 118 brennynge: The references to fire throughout symbolize the saint's later imperviousness to flames. Possibly she reflects Mary; cf. ABC 89–91: "The bush with flawmes rede/ Brenninge, of which ther never a stikke brende,/ Was signe of thin unwemmed maidenhede."

The Second Nun's Tale

134–38 The tradition of Cecilia in music apparently originated in this episode; see Butler, Lives of the Saints 4:404, and Connolly, Mourning into Joy, 211–37 (Plate 6, from a fifteenth-century MS, shows Cecilia with a small portative organ).

134–35 organs: The plural may result from translation of "cantantibus organis" (S&A, 672), but see NPT VII.2851n.

139 every second and third day: Mistranslation of "biduanis ac triduanis ieiuniis" (with two- and three-day fasts, S&A, 672). Small errors such as this indicate that Chaucer never completely, if at all, revised the tale (Sherry L. Reames, Spec 55, 1980, 55).

152 aungel: Perhaps from Ps. 90 (AV 91.11): "For he shall give his angels charge over thee, to keep thee in all thy ways" (M. Madeleva, Lost Lang., 59), but reminiscent of the demon lover of Sarah, OT Book of Tobit (Vulgate).

159 clene love: A number of saints renounced marriage, but Cecilia's marriage distinguishes her legend from that of other virgin martyrs (Marc David Glasser, TSL 23, 1978, 12). The account may have been influenced by the concept of mystical marriage (Clogan, M&H n.s. 3:237). The significance of Cecilia's continence, however, may lie in its reflection of an Augustinian tradition of moderation (Reames, Spec 55:40–41) or in asserting a theme of unity through bodily integrity (Grennen, JEGP 65:473).

172–73 Via Apia: The road, which runs past catacombs where early Christians hid, is not **miles three** from the city; Chaucer mistranslates "tercium miliarum ab urbe" (the third milepost from the city, S&A, 672). The Roman setting is taken by McCall as creating an air of historical authenticity (Ch among the Gods, 88–110); but see Boitani (Eng. Med. Narrative, 253), who finds the setting entirely romantic and fabulous.

177 Urban: Pope Urban I, 222–30 (for his legend, see Jacobus de Voragine, *Legenda aurea,* 341–42, tr. Ryan, 1:314–15). Urban VI was pope of Rome (1378–89) at the probable time of the tale's composition during the Great Schism, but the theory that Chaucer modified his sources to reflect English support of Urban and imply an allegory of the reunion of the church (John C. Hirsch, ChauR 12, 1977, 129–33) is not convincing in the light of the source more recently discovered by Reames (see introductory note above).

192–94 The saint's virtuous counsel and steadfast chastity inspired by Christ have resulted in the birth of a convert, Valerian, fruit of the **seed** sown within her.

195 bisy bee: The comparison most likely derives from of "apis argumentosa" (S&A, 672). Chaucer may have coined the English phrase, which became proverbial (Whiting B165).

201 oold man: Probably St. Paul (cf. 207–9 below). Reames takes his appearance before mention of Valerian's faith as one indication among many of Chaucer's modifying his source to lessen human participation and emphasize God's grace in conversion (Spec 55:36–57).

207–9   Cf. Ephesians 4.5–6: "One lord, one faith, one baptism. One God and father of all, who is above all, and through all, and in you all."

221 Corones two: For illustrations, see V. A. Kolve, in New Perspectives, 141, fig. 5, and Plate 7 in Connolly, Mourning into Joy. In the Life of St. Cecilia in the Early South Eng. Legendary, EETS 87, 490–96, the angel explains "the lilie betokeneth youre maydenhood . . . the rose betokeneth youre martirdom" (lines 77–78). Crowns of victory or glory are frequently mentioned in the Bible (e.g., Prov. 4.9, 1 Cor. 9.25, 2 Tim. 4.8), and the symbolism of lilies for good works and of red roses for martyrdom appears as early as the third century, in Cyprian (c. 250), The Letters of St. Cyprian of Carthage, tr. G. W. Clarke, 1984, 1:17: "In the past [the Church] was clad in white through the good works of our brothers; now she is arrayed in crimson through the blood of her martyrs. Amongst her blossoms she lacks neither the lily nor the rose." Nuptial garlands and crowns were also an ancient custom (garlands for brides were still used in England; see ClT IV.381n.). An incident in the fictitious sixth-century life of St. Amato (bishop of Auxerre, d. 418), in which nuptial garlands and celestial crowns are apparently combined (see the Bollandist Acta Sanctorum, Antwerp, 1679, 1 May, 52–53), parallels the situation involving Cecilia's and Valerian's crowns: the young Saint Amato was compelled to marry a virgin, but on their wedding night the couple took vows of virginity, "and behold an angel, who carried two garlands for them, appeared, praising their intention and exhorting them to persevere in it." Both in this episode and in the life of St. Cecilia "husband and wife each receive a garland. It seems natural to regard the crowns as celestial substitutes for the nuptial crowns of an earthly marriage" (Robinson).

229 soote savour: The repeated references to smell convey the sweetness of sanctity and contrast with the rankness in CYT VIII.885–90; cf. Paul B. Taylor, ES 60, 1979, 380–88, and Bruce K. Cowgill, PQ 74, 1995, 343–57.

236 love no man so: Closely similar to KnT I.1196.

240 palm of martirdom: Martyrdom is seen as the victor's prize; cf. PF 182, "the victor palm." The phrase is from the preface to the Ambrosian Mass for St. Cecilia's day, quoted in the Legenda aurea (S&A, 673; tr. Ryan, 2:320) and tr. in VIII.274–83.

271 Seint Ambrose: Bishop of Milan, d. 347. The reference is to the preface proper to the Mass attributed to him. For the original, see Millett Henshaw, MP 26, 1928, 16.

277 shrifte: In view of Jacobus's "Tiburcii . . . confessio" (S&A, 673), "confession" seems the correct meaning; but see Fisher, ed.: "conversion" (315).

282–83   Jacobus has "devocio castitatis" (S&A, 673). The most plausible reading is the simplest: "the world knows what chastity's devotion to love [i.e., Christ or love of him] is worth." But Clogan (M&H n.s. 3:237, 240) would translate: the world knows "what devotion to chastity is capable of effecting."

290 kisse his brest: Russell A. Peck (AnM 8, 1967, 31) suggests that with this conversion another spiritual marriage occurs, symbolized by Cecilia's gesture.

338–39   Chaucer slightly modifies Jacobus: "in una hominis sapientia sunt tria, scilicet ingenium, memoria et intellectus" (in the one human wisdom are three things, namely, imagination, memory, and judgment). The idea that the mind consisted of these three faculties (**sapiences**) was common; see Bartholomaeus Anglicus 3.10; tr. Trevisa, 1:98, and Bo 5.pr4.153–54, where the three faculties are wit, imagination, and reason, with a higher faculty, intelligence.

345–48   A summary rather than a direct translation of Jacobus (S&A, 674). The remainder of the tale is based on the "Franciscan abridgement" edited by Reames (MP 87:357–361).

353 Goddes knyght: This is a common image of the Christian; cf. 2 Tim. 2.3 ("Thou therefore endure hardness, as a good soldier of Jesus Christ") and Langland, PP B 11.312 (where "God's knights" applies to the clergy); this marks a shift to military imagery, as in 383–85 below.

369 corniculer: A subordinate officer who wears a corniculus, a horn-shaped helmet ornament, as a sign of rank. The term derives from the source "corniculario prefecti" (Reames, MP 87:359, lines 106–7).

383–85   Cf. Romans 13.12: "The night is far spent, the day is at hand; let us therefore cast off the works of darkness, and let us put on the armour of light."

386–88   Cf. 2 Tim. 4.7–8: "I have fought a good fight, I have finished my course, I have kept the faith. Henceforth there is laid up for me a crown of righteousness, which the Lord, the righteous judge shall give me at that day."

421–512   Cecilia's confrontation with Almachius is for many critics the key scene in the tale (Whittock, Reading of CT, 258–60), and, until Reames's discovery of the Franciscan redaction, this has seemed the product of Chaucer's skillful manipulation of his sources (Paul E. Beichner, ChauR 8, 1973, 198–204, an article that nonetheless remains useful).

437   In her defiance of Almachius, Cecilia resembles the "mulier fortis," valiant woman, of Prov. 31.17 ("She girdeth her loins with strength, and strengtheneth her arms"). To interpret the figure as a "spiritual Amazon or virago" and Cecilia's courage as an expression of the Second Nun's pride (Engelhardt, MS 37:295–96) is at odds with both scripture and legend. Janemarie Luecke (ABR 33, 1982, 335–48) offers a feminist interpretation, identifying Cecilia with the Second Nun as a strong-willed woman who utilizes virginity to effect freedom of action. Cf. ClT IV.207n., MerT IV.2367n.

462 laughe: The "Franciscan abridgement" (Reames, MP 87:360, line 137) has "Tunc ridens beata Cecilia dixit" (Then laughing the blessed Cecilia said), unlike the sources earlier proposed. On laughter in the tale, see Anne Eggebroten, ChauR 19, 1984, 55–61; on the semiotics of comedy in this tale, see Daniel F. Pigg, in Jean E. Jost, ed., Ch's Humor, 1994, 340–42.

463–65   A close parallel to the Sarum Breviary has been noted (Mary Virginia Rosenfeld, MLN 55, 1940, 358), but it comes directly from the "Franciscan abridgement" (Reames, MP 87:360, lines 137–3).

477–79 here : here: The scribe of Hengwrt and Ellesmere glosses the rime riche by writing "audire" above the first here, "hic" above the second. See GP I.17–18n.

490 philosophre: Also a term for medieval alchemists, one of the several links to CYT that critics have noted (see introductory note to Fragment VIII). It comes from the source: "Nam meas injurias phylosophando contempsi" (For by philosophying I disdained my injuries); Reames, MP 87:360, lines 148–49.

515 bath: A caldarium, pot for boiling water. The Roman hypocaust, bathing room heated from below, might be meant (Fisher ed., 319); such a room is preserved in the church of Santa Cecilia in Trastevere (Mary Sharp, Guide to the Churches of Rome, 1966, 65). But a medieval tradition of illustration shows the saint naked, in a cauldron, with fire blazing beneath (Kolve, in New Perspectives, 141).

521 Because of her holiness, expressed by affinity with the burning empyrean and burning charity, Cecilia is safe from physical fire (Peck, AnM 8:25–26). Kolve (New Perspectives, 152–54) draws parallels with the children in the fiery furnace (Dan. 3), who also refused to worship an idol and were thought to have been preserved by their virginity, and with St. Eulalia, who remained a virgin and, though thrown into fire, did not burn.

The Canon's Yeoman's Prologue and Tale

The explanatory notes to the Canon's Yeoman's Prologue and Tale were adapted from those written by John Reidy for The Riverside Chaucer.

The Canon and his Yeoman do not appear in the General Prologue, and we cannot know whether Chaucer had the Canon's intrusion in mind from the beginning. It is generally agreed that the tale was written late in the Canterbury period. Norman Blake's argument that the tale is spurious (ed., CT, 1980, 6, 9) depends on a rigid adherence to a textual theory (the sole authority of the Hengwrt MS) that few accept. See Ralph Hanna, Engl. MS. Sts. 1100–1700, 1989, 64–84.

Tyrwhitt (4:181) believed that the occasion for Chaucer's tale was "some sudden resentment." H. G. Richardson (TRHS 4th ser. 5, 1922, 38–40) showed that a chaplain, William de Brumley, confessed in 1374 to having made counterfeit gold pieces according to the teaching of William Shuchirch, a canon of the King's Chapel at Windsor. Shuchirch was not the only false practitioner of the time: the Prior of Binham, William of Somerton, became apostate from his order and was arrested in secular dress through trusting an alchemist (Marie P. Hamilton, Spec 16, 1941, 107, quoting Coulton, Life in the M. A., III.95–98). In 1390 Chaucer was responsible for the repairs to Windsor Chapel, and if Shuchirch was still alive and practicing, Chaucer would have known him. Manly (New Light, 245–52) was inclined to agree with Richardson that Chaucer lost money in dealings with Shuchirch; French (Ch Handbook, 328) dismisses this as "an amusing speculation" but agreed that Chaucer must have had some particular person in mind.

Manly further argues (New Light, 246–47) that the tale was not written for the Canterbury series but for an audience that included canons of Windsor. The case for separate composition is well made by Albert E. Hartung (ChauR 12, 1977, 111–28), on the basis of manuscript evidence as well as the address to *chanons religious* (see 992–1011 below). This raises the problem of the unity of the work, and some critics have found the tale imperfectly adapted to its setting (e.g., Thomas W. Craik,

Comic Tales of Chaucer, 1964, 96–97). However, the general structure of the tale is shown by Samuel McCracken (MP 68, 1971, 289–91) to be an example of a developing three-part structure (prologue, part 1, part 2) in Chaucer's "confessional narratives" (Wife of Bath, Pardoner, Canon's Yeoman); see also Lee Patterson, Ch and the Subject of Hist., 367–68. On the unity of parts 1 and 2, see Britton J. Harwood, PMLA 102, 1987, 342–43).

The problem of unity is also raised by the puzzle over the existence of two canons (the Yeoman's master and the dishonest canon of part 2). Joseph E. Grennen succeeds best in arguing a unity of theme and diction that shows the involvement of the characters in a kind of meta-alchemical process of degeneration (Criticism 4, 1962, 225–40; Journ. Hist. Ideas 25, 1964, 279–84).

No source is known for the tale, and the closest analogue so far unearthed for the tricks in part 2 is a story by Ramón Lull (d. 1315), in which a swindler adds to molten gold a mixture purporting to be an herbal electuary, but actually containing much gold, so that the amount of gold found at the end is greater than was originally melted down (see Willa Babcock Folch-Pi, N&Q 212, 1967, 10–11). John W. Spargo cites, together with other illustrative material, a somewhat similar trick from the *Novelle* of Sercambi (S&A, 685–98). Recently Jesus L. Serrano Reyes (*Didactismo y moralismo en Geoffrey Chaucer y Don Juan Manuel,* 1996, 251–368) has argued that Chaucer was influenced by Exemplum 20 of Don Juan Manuel's "El Conde Lucanor" (tr. John E. Keller and L. Clark, The Book of Count Lucanor and Patronio, 1966, 89–91). None of the analogues can match Chaucer's version for precision, specificity, or plausibility.

There was a great deal of interest in alchemy in Chaucer's time. Authorities such as Vincent of Beauvais denied that any real change could be made in metal, and Pope John XXII (1316–34) condemned it, principally because of swindling and counterfeiting (S&A, 691–92). But condemnations did not stop it; there was an outburst of writings and apparently of practice in Chaucer's time, with the inevitable swindling that the promise of gold-making would induce.

The science of alchemy—which strove to produce the "philosophers' stone," which would cure illness, prolong life, and turn "base metals" into gold—came to Europe in the twelfth century, through translations from Arabic into Latin. The Arabs in turn had received the doctine in Greek writings from Hellenistic Egypt. (For fuller accounts, see John Reidy, ed., Thomas Norton's Ordinal of Alchemy, EETS 272, 1975, lii–lxvii, and Eric J. Holmyard, Alchemy, 1957; cf. John Gower's account of the science in Conf. aman., V.2457–2632.)

The theory was that the manipulation of the constituent elements of the metals could change their natures through such procedures as *fermentacioun* (see 817 below), coloring metal alloys white or yellow with arsenic or sulphur to look like silver or gold (*silver citrinacioun;* see 816 below), adjusting the blend of sulphur and mercury, believed to be constituents of all metals (see 1438–40 below), and manipulating the elemental qualities of a base metal. This idea, first found in Arabic writings, was based on the theory of the four elements, each containing two of the four qualities, hot, cold, moist, dry. If the qualities could be calculated and isolated, mixtures or medicines could be produced to correct imbalances in sick people, or in substances. These would be elixirs, and a perfect elixir was one that would prolong life besides "curing" base or sick metals into gold (VIII.862–63).

The process usually called for *calcination* (VIII.804) of the original material by heating and pounding or by attacking with acids ("mercury") or both; this reduced the material to ash, or dead ("mortified") matter. Then repeated distillations were made to separate and purify the elements (*sublymyng*, 771), which were then to be recombined by imbibing (*enbibyng*, 814), or soaking, and successive sublimations. A color sequence of whitening and reddening was thus finally obtained.

Thus far one can follow or partially guess the operations as described in alchemical writings, but the later stages are always too vague to be understood. The final product, a red elixir for gold and a white for silver, was spoken of as a stone, a liquid, a powder, a tincture; and the phrases *watres rubifiyng* (VIII.797) and *watres albificacioun* (805) may refer to these elixirs, which finally reddened or whitened the baser metals into gold or silver.

The art was supposed originally to be a secret revelation from the Egyptian god of wisdom, Thoth, corresponding to the Greek *Hermes* (VIII.1434). The chosen few were therefore to guard its holiness from the profane; hence the numerous "cover names" (see VIII.1435–40, 1447, 1463–66, 1467–71). This tradition passed on to Western Europe, where alchemical treatises were attributed to holy men such as Moses and St. Dunstan; ancient sages such as *Plato* (VIII.1448) were alleged to have received advance revelation of Christian doctrines, as well as of the secrets of alchemy, and the alchemical process was made analogous to the Christian mysteries of the death and resurrection of Christ. There were alchemists who believed that they had been taught the true secret—and who wrote alchemical treatises—and those who were called "puffers" or "Geber's cooks" (after the author of a well-known alchemical treatise) and who, however learned, experimented forever in vain, like the Yeoman's master. There were also out-and-out swindlers like the canon of part 2.

It is not clear how much alchemical literature Chaucer knew. Pauline Aiken (SP 41, 1944, 371–89) thinks he could have obtained all he needed for The Canon's Yeoman's Tale from Vincent of Beauvais's *Speculum naturale,* but Edgar H. Duncan (Spec 43, 1968, 641–46) believes that he had read or scanned those works he names (relevant passages are printed in S&A, ed. John Webster Spargo, 685–96). In 1477 Chaucer was quoted as an alchemical authority (in Norton's Ordinal, 1162–66, referring to CYT VIII.1454–57), and in the seventeenth century Elias Ashmole printed the tale "to shew that Chaucer himself was a Master therein" (*Theatrum Chemicum Britannicum,* 1652, 467). Some modern critics (e.g., Mary-Virginia Rosenberg, Cent. Rev. of Arts and Sci. 6, 1962, 578) believe that Chaucer knew and respected the great secret. Most critics, however, believe that Chaucer is skeptical (Kittredge, Ch and His Poetry, 15) or at least holds on practical and religious grounds that the ignorant nonscientist should leave the science alone (Brewer, Geoffrey Ch, 150). Muscatine (Ch and the Fr Trad., 220) argues that the work shows a more general distrust of technology and of "that complacent faith in science that depises God." Sheila Delaney (Medieval Literary Politics, 1990, 10–17) finds elements of social protest in the tale. Mahmoud Manzalaoui (in Ch: Writers and Background,

ed. Brewer 256–57) deals succinctly with Chaucer's attitude toward alchemy, which he considers mainly satirical, and with the scholarship to 1975. For a more recent review and a significant discussion, see Lee Patterson, SAC 15, 1993, 25–57.

The Canon's Yeoman's Prologue

The character of the Yeoman has been much studied, especially since Lumiansky examined his continuing two-mindedness toward alchemy (Of Sondry Folk, 227–35). See esp. Howard, Idea of CT, 294–96; Robert Cook, ChauR 22, 1987, 28–40; and Patterson (SAC 15:25–57).

556 Boghtoun: Boughton was five miles beyond Ospring, a regular stopping place, where the pilgrims had presumably spent the night; they were now some five miles from Canterbury.

557 A man: The Canon, identified as a Canon Regular of St. Augustine, or Black Canon, by Hamilton (Spec 16:103–8); he wears the customary habit of his order: cassock, *overslope* (VIII.633), a surplice over it (558), and outermost a black cloak with hood attached (557, 571).

565 He: George R. Coffman (MLN 59, 1944, 269–71) argues that the Yeoman's horse must be meant, in view of *his croper* (566), since a crupper must be a horse's.

566 male tweyfoold: A double bag; frequently taken to imply folded over and hence almost empty.

583–86 Brewer (Geoffrey Ch, 149) finds the Canon's explanation of his arrival inadequate, and indeed it certainly does not account for his headlong speed. With a three-mile gallop, the pair would overtake the slow-moving pilgrims in about ten minutes; at a canter or even a trot they could have caught up in half an hour or less and arrived in a more decent condition. Chaucer clearly intends a dramatic and striking entrance.

587 Kittredge (Trans. Roy. Soc. Lit. 30, 1910, 88–90) sets out the received opinion that the Yeoman, in collusion with his master, here begins an attempt at a confidence trick but is exposed and broken down by the Host's skillful probing. This version has often been accepted, usually without question (e.g., Lumiansky, Of Sondry Folk, 229–30). For a different view, see John Read, Alchemist in Life, Lit. and Art, 1947, 29–35; R. G. Baldwin, JEGP 61, 1962, 234; and John Reidy, PMLA 80, 1965, 32.

612 Al that I have: For the Yeoman's possessions, see VIII.733–36.

635 baudy and totore: Cf. George Ripley, Compound, in Ashmole, Theatrum, 153: "Their Clothes be bawdy and woryn threde-bare."

636–38 For standard responses to this question—the elixir was stolen, one needs gold to start with, one must disguise his wealth—see Reidy, PMLA 80:32; the Yeoman knew at least one of these (VIII.892–97, and cf. VIII.1371–74).

645–46 The Lat. gloss quotes the common proverb (Walther 19859) "Everything that is too much turns into a vice"; cf. Whiting E199, 200, 203, and Tilley E224. Grennen (Journ. Hist. Ideas 25:284) sees in Chaucer's version an extra meaning referring to an alchemical process continued too long, so that the product fails at its final testing. For this sense of **preeve**, see MED s.v. *preven* 13(b).

664 discoloured: See 727–28 below. According to Kittredge (Trans. Roy. Soc. Lit. 30:90), it is this reminder of his lost fresh complexion that finally exasperates the Yeoman into open hostility toward his master.

673–79   The Yeoman admits to borrowing, though not necessarily to intentional fraud. For the strictness of the alchemical code with regard to borrowing, see Reidy, PMLA 80:35–36.

681 although we haden it sworn: Closely similar to KnT I.1089.

685 drough hym neer: Owen (Pilgrimage and Story, 7) thinks that here Chaucer admits the implausibility of a company on horseback all hearing a tale; if the Canon had heard **al thyng** before he came close, he would have intervened earlier.

688–89 Catoun: *Dicta Catonis* 1.17, quoted in the Lat. gloss: "The self-conscious man thinks everyone is talking about him."

695–96   The Canon accuses his Yeoman of *calumnia,* slander, and *detractio,* detraction, i.e., unnecessarily revealing truth that is detrimental to someone's reputation.

707 For peny ne for pound: For examples of such phrases, see MED s.v. *peni* 1 (c).

The Canon's Yeoman's Tale

726 an hose upon myn heed: The illustration in the Ellesmere manuscript shows the Yeoman thus adorned; Edwin F. Piper (PQ 3, 1924, 253) wonders whether Chaucer or the illuminator knew the proverb "A man's a man though he wear a hose upon his head," of which this is the first recorded version (see Whiting H549).

727–28   An important element in alchemy was the color sequence, in which a "dead" mass of "first matter" (apparently lead or an alloy heated and hence blackened with surface oxidation) was "revived" and perfected. The sequence, in Chaucer's time, was black, white, red, the final color being that of the perfected "philosophers' stone." The Yeoman's face has undergone a reverse sequence, from red to a dull leaden color (Grennen, Journ. Hist. Ideas 25:279–80).

730 blered is myn ye: Proverbial; cf. RvPro I.3865n.

746–47   Lat. gloss: "The solace of the wretched, etc.," beginning of the Latin proverb "The solace of the wretched is to have companions in grief" (Walther 29943); cf. Tr 1.708 ("Men seyn, 'to wrecche is consolacioun/ To have another felawe in hys peyne.'"); Whiting, W715.

757 silver: From the Yeoman's haphazard account, Edgar Hill Duncan (MP 37, 1940, 248–54) pieces together an account of the sublimation of orpiment and mercury, preliminary to a process of *silver citrinacioun* (VIII.816), or yellowing of silver, similar to those described by Geber and Arnaldus de Villanova (VIII.1428).

759 orpyment: Probably arsenic trisulphide; one of the four "spirits" (see 820 below) to be sublimed along with quicksilver (VIII.772).

  brent bones, iren squames: These, together with the *salt* and *papeer* (762), were "feces," which were supposed to retain the grosser earthy impurities in the "spirits" when these were sublimed (Duncan, MP 37:251).

761–66   For an account of an **erthen pot,** its **enlutyng,** and its surmounting by a **lampe of glas,** the whole constituting a vessel for sublimation, see Duncan, MP 37:250–51.

764 lampe: the definition is not wholly certain, but presumably a glass vessel placed over the *erthen pot* (761), and cemented or luted on. See MED s.v. *laumpe* (g).

768 esy fir, and smart: Fires and furnaces of different temperatures for different processes were of great importance to alchemists. See Norton's Ordinal, 2831–96, 2983–3086.

775 grounden litarge: See 907 below.

778–79 spirites ascencioun ... fix adoun: "Spirits" were volatile, that is, they vaporized when heated and were deposited on the top or lid of the vessel; the residue remaining solid at the bottom was "earthy," or "fixed."

782 a twenty devel waye: See MilT I.3134n.

795 deere ynough a leek: Expensive enough at the price of a leek (i.e., worthless). Proverbial (Whiting L182); for similar expressions, see ClT IV.999 and n.; Tr 3.1161 ("deere ynough a rysshe"); LGW 741 ("deere ynogh a myte"); and MED s.v. *dere* adj. (1) 3(d).

798 Arsenyk, sal armonyak, and brymstoon: See 820 below.

799 herbes: Many alchemists scoffed at ignorant workers who attempted to obtain the elixir or philosophers' stone from vegetable substances; see, e.g., Norton's Ordinal, 1051–58, and Duncan, MP 37:260. Roger Bacon took a different view: "a vegetable substance is better, such as fruit and parts of trees and herbs" (Notes on Pseudo-Aristotle, *Secreta secretorum,* in Robert Steele, *Opera Hactenus Inedita Rogeri Baconi* 5, 1920, 117).

800 lunarie: Moonwort; its use in alchemy and witchcraft is testified by John Gerarde (*The Herball or Generall Historie of Plantes,* London, 1636, 407). He condemns such "drowsie dreames and illusions." A poem printed by Ashmole in Theatrum, 348–49, describes the alchemical process by relating its stages to the parts of this plant.

804 fourneys ... of calcinacioun: Geber (Works, tr. Richard Russell, rev. E. J. Holmyard, 1928, 229) prescribes a rectangular furnace, four feet by three feet, for calcination.

805 watres albificacioun: Possibly "whitening by liquids" but probably a mistake for *watres albifying* (liquids which whiten metals and turn them to silver), caused by confusing the present participle form with the gerund; cf. *Watres rubifiyng* in line VIII.797.

809 wode and cole: See 768 above.

816 silver citrinacioun: This employs a process by which metal alloys were colored white or yellow with arsenic or sulphur to look like silver or gold (here yellowish or gold).

817 fermentacioun: A precious metal, gold or silver, in an alloy with base metals, was thought to act as a "ferment" to leaven base metals with its own properties.

820 foure spirites ... bodies sevene: Al-Razi (Abu Bakr Muhammad ibn Zakariyya, c. 826–925), known to the Latin West as Rhazes, divided minerals into six classes (see Holmyard, Alchemy, 89), of which the two most important for alchemists were spirits (i.e., volatile substances like camphor and the four in VIII.822–24) and bodies (i.e., the six metals: gold, silver, lead, tin, iron, and copper). The Latin Geber follows this, treating quicksilver—which boils easily—as a spirit; but he includes "Mundification" of quicksilver among his chapters on preparation of metals, or "Metallick Bodies" (Works, tr. Russell, 62, 124, 126–28, 146, 157–58; cf. Aiken, SP 41:378–79). This might lead to confusion, and the Yeoman names quicksilver in both categories (VIII.822, 827). Instead of quicksilver, some Arabic authorities have "Chinese iron," some sort of alloy; Gower, Conf. aman. 4.2472, lists brass as the seventh.

889 infecte: Grennen (Journ. Hist. Ideas 25:281–82) notes an alchemical double meaning with the technical sense of Lat. *inficere,* used of corrupting of metals and acids by inferior substances.

907 The pot tobreketh: Duncan (MP 37:253–54) suggests that the explosion is caused by adding ground-up litharge (VIII.775) to the mixture and using saltpeter for the salt required.

962–65 Lat. gloss: "Do not think that all that shines is gold nor any apple good that looks nice," from Alanus de Insulis, *Liber parabolarum* (PL 210:585–86). See also Whiting A155, G282; HF 272: "Hyt is not al gold that glareth."

967–69 wiseste: This seems to apply to the Yeoman's master, while the **trewest** who proves a thief would be the canon of part 2.

970 er that I fro yow wende: Chaucer seems not to intend retaining the Yeoman in his company of pilgrims.

971 tale: The Yeoman has not been asked to tell a tale, and he has already fulfilled his promise to the Host (VIII.717–19). The scheme of tale-telling has been only hinted to him (VIII.597–98).

992–1011 This address to **chanons religious** was a reason for Manly's suggestion that part 2 was read to an audience of canons at the King's Chapel at Windsor; see the introductory note. Robinson, however, thinks that the passage could be merely rhetorical (cf. PhyT VI.72, NPT VII.3325). Hartung (ChauR 12:111–28) argues strongly that part 2 was originally complete in itself, on the basis of certain textual variants and also of inconsistencies he finds between part 2 and the Prologue and part 1.

1048 in good tyme: A formula to avert evil consequences, similar to "touch wood." Cf. BD 370: "A Goddes half, in good time!"

1066–67 profred servyse: Proverbial (Whiting S167); cf. PF 518: "For office uncommytted ofte anoyeth."

1095 chekes waxen rede: Cf. 727–28 above. For a possible parallel in an alchemical process, see Grennen, Journ. Hist. Ideas 25:280–81.

1117 crosselet: The crucible containing one ounce of quicksilver (VIII.1120–21) is put on the fire, and the canon throws in the purported "powder of projection." The canon has the priest build up the charcoal (1157), but, pretending to correct him, sets a special piece above the crucible (1189–91). This contains silver filings in a hole stopped with wax (1160–64); when the wax melts, the silver drops into the crucible. The trick depends on the fact that the quicksilver boils and vaporizes at about 357° C., leaving only the silver, which melts at 962° C. (1196–1200). The canon pours the molten silver into an ingot or mold, which he has cut to measure out of chalk (1222–23, 1232–33), and drops it into cold water. The result is a one-ounce bar of silver, to all appearances transmuted from quicksilver.

1126 mortifye: Meaning apparently that the fluid quicksilver

will harden into silver, losing its volatile "spiritual" quality; cf. VIII.1436. The *quyk* in *quyksilver* means "alive," and the canon will "kill" (*mortifye*) it.

1185 by Seint Gile: Ann S. Haskell (ChauR 7, 1973, 221–26) explores the implications of invoking this saint, who is said to be appropriate to those stricken by misery and "driven into solitude."

1189 with sory grace: Cf. SumT III.2228 and n.

1265 An holwe stikke: This second trick is almost the same as the first, only the silver filings are now concealed in a hollow stick, with which the canon stirs the fire.

1296 The third trick is simple sleight of hand. The canon melts the copper, pours it into his ingot, immerses it in water to solidify it, and while apparently feeling for it, substitutes for it the *teyne* of silver which we know him to have had up his sleeve (VIII.1225).

1313 ape: "Dupe"; cf. GP 1.706n.

1342–49 The passage echoes the language of romance (e.g., **Nyghtyngale, lady … caroling** and **knight in armes**); see Judith Scherer Herz, MP 58, 1966, 234–35.

  brid gladder agayn the day: Proverbial; in Chaucer's usage it has a slightly ominous overtone; see KnT I.2437n.

1371–74 One of the standard responses to the question of why the alchemist does not seem rich; cf. 636–38 above.

1407–8 See Whiting C201 ("A burnt child dreads the fire (*varied*)," H53, M160. Grennen (Criticism 4:230–32) sees a reference to the alchemical understanding of "spirits" that flee from the fire while the earthly parts remain (cf. 759 above). For the perfect work, however, the spirit and body must be united and the spirit fixed with the body in the fire.

1410 bet than never is late: Proverbial (Whiting L89, T211).

1411 Nevere to thryve: Proverbial, though this is the only citation in Whiting, T256; see further references there.

1413 Bayard the blynde: See MED s.v. *baiard* n.(1), esp. (c) *as blind as Baiard;* and Whiting B71, 72, 73.

1422 rape and renne: Literally "seize and run," but then both verbs cannot be syntactically related in the same way to **al that.** Various forms of the phrase occur, perhaps all deriving by confusion of the verbs from *repen and rinen* (OE *hrepian and hrinan,* touch and seize).

1428 Arnold of the Newe Toun: Arnaldus de Villanova (c. 1240–1311), a prolific writer on scientific and technical matters.

1429–40 Rosarie: Arnaldus's Rosarium philosophorum, "Rosary (or Rose Garland) of the Philosophers"; but John L. Lowes (MLN 28, 1913, 229) shows Chaucer's source to be Arnaldus's De lapide philosophorum, "On the Philosophers' Stone," better titled "On the Secrets of Nature"; the relevant passage is given in S&A, 698.

  The **dragon** (VIII.1435) is mercury, which is not hardened (mortified) except with his **brother,** sulphur, derived from gold and silver.

1434 Hermes: Hermes Trismegistus, "Thrice-great Hermes," was the Greek name for Thoth, the Egyptian god of wisdom. Hermes was claimed by Greek alchemists as the author of their art; for Hermes's medieval reputation, see Thorndike, Hist. of Magic 2:214–20.

1438–40 Mercurie … brimstoon: Aristotle's theory that metals originated from a blend of two vapors (a perfect blend resulted in gold, an imperfect one in a base metal) led to the idea that a faulty blend might be corrected and transmuted by use of sulphur (*brimstoon*) and *mercurie*. Since real sulphur and mercury were known to combine to produce mercuric sulphide, cinnabar, alchemists claimed that the sulphur and mercury they meant were something secret and different.

1441–47   These lines derive from Arnaldus's *De lapide philosophorum* (Edgar Hill Duncan, MLN 57, 1942, 31–33); Karl Young (MLN 58, 1943, 102–5) shows that **secree of the secretes** (VIII.1447) is not the pseudo-Aristotle, *Secreta secretorum*, "Secret of Secrets" (see 799 above), but simply a phrase meaning "best of secrets," a common name for alchemy (cf. Manly, CT, 653).

1448–71   This dialogue between Plato and a disciple is based on a passage from "Zadith" printed in Lazarus Zetzner, Theatrum Chemicum 5, 1622, 249, under the title Senioris Zadith fil. Hamuelis Tabula Chimica, "The Chemical Table of Senior Zadith, Son of Hamuel," Chaucer's **book Senior** (VIII.1450). Julius Ruska (Anglia 61, 1937, 136–37) shows that Chaucer freely invented most of the dialogue, drawing on a few sentences of the Latin. Cf. S&A, 697–98.

1450 Senior: Muhammad ibn Umail (tenth century); for his works and commentary, see Ruska, Anglia 61:136n. In a paper at a meeting of the Modern Language Association in 1971, Edgar Hill Duncan pointed out that in Trinity Coll. Cambridge MS 1122, in the prologue to the work, fol. 39r, the word "senior" is annotated "i. Plato," (i.e., Plato) in a contemporary hand. At the beginning of the work, fol. 40r, a later hand wrote opposite the title "Liber hic dicitur Senior" (This book is called Senior), and further down the leaf a third hand wrote "liber Platonis" (The book of Plato). From this fourteenth-century English manuscript one can see how Chaucer may have come by both Plato and his title for the work.

1454 Titanos: From Greek, a white earth, probably gypsum, but also possibly chalk or lime; here, of course, a cover name.

1455 Magnasia: Magnesia, now magnesium oxide, but here a cover name, and variously described, but always of a brilliant whiteness. The pseudo-Lull, *Testamentum,* in Manget, Bibl. Chem. 1:727, calls it a white earth and equates it with the special alchemists' quicksilver; elsewhere it is an amalgam of tin and mercury.

1463–71   On the holiness and necessary secrecy of the art, see the introductory note.

FRAGMENT IX

Fragment IX occurs regularly before and is explicitly connected to (X.1) The Parson's Prologue and Tale in most early manuscripts. This fragment is usually taken by editors to contain the penultimate story on the journey to Canterbury, though there are difficulties, and some critics have questioned this assumption (see introductory note to Fragment X below). Charles A. Owen (JEGP 57, 1958, 449–76) has argued that The Manciple's Tale is the first story on the homeward journey. But Fragment IX is clearly involved in some of the confusions produced by the unfinished condition of The Cook's Tale: the Cook is introduced at IX.11 as if for the first time. Perhaps Chaucer intended

to cancel The Cook's Prologue and the fragmentary Cook's Tale. Despite these difficulties, a good many critics see The Manciple's Tale as thematically connected with the tales that precede (see introductory note to Fragment VIII above) and with the final, nonfictional tale that follows and thus as a suitable conclusion to the tale-telling and a fit introduction to The Parson's Tale. On this see Mark Allen, SAC 9, 1987, 77–96.

The Manciple's Prologue and Tale

The explanatory notes to The Manciple's Prologue and Tale are adapted from those written by V. J. Scattergood for The Riverside Chaucer.

The date and the relationship of The Manciple's Prologue to his Tale have provoked much discussion. The "slight story" in the tale and its "evident rhetorical padding" have seemed to many evidence of an early date of composition (S. S. Hussey, Chaucer, 2nd ed., 1981, 137). Likewise, the prologue has seemed to many to have no relation to the tale, and that problem is complicated by the appearance of the Cook, who has already told his unfinished tale (see introductory note to The Cook's Tale). However, most critics now accept Severs's contention that it is logical that the dishonest Manciple of the General Prologue should be involved in a discreditable incident with the Cook and tell a tale that "exalts expediency rather than morality" (JEGP 51, 1952, 1–16), and it is now usually assumed that both the Prologue and the Tale "issue from Chaucer's most sardonic maturity" (Coghill, in Ch and Chaucerians, ed. Brewer, 1966, 138; see also J. A. Burrow, Essays in Criticism 36, 1986, 97–119).

The Manciple's Tale consists of the fable of the "tell-tale bird" followed by a fifty-four-line moral recommending restraint in speech. The story of the talking bird is widespread; Chaucer knew probably one version as it appears in *The Seven Sages of Rome* (WBPro III.232n.). The version told by the Manciple derives ultimately from Ovid's *Metamorphoses* 2.531–632, though Chaucer concentrates only on the episode involving Phoebus and the crow, omitting much else. There are versions of this tale in the *Ovide moralisé,* 2130–2548; Machaut's *Livre du voir dit* 7773–8110 (tr. Palmer, 534–55); and Gower's *Confessio amantis* 3.768–817 (all are printed in S&A). Chaucer could have used any one or all of them. On the relation of Chaucer's tale to Gower's version, see Richard Hazelton (JEGP 62, 1963, 1–31), and for his use of Ovid's version, see Helen Cooper, in Charles Martindale, ed. Ovid Renewed, 1988, 71–81.

The exempla of the caged bird, cat, and she-wolf can be found in *Le Roman de la rose* and elsewhere (see 175–86 below), and the main sources for the concluding aphorisms seem to be the Bible and the *Dicta Catonis* (see 325–60 below).

Most interpretive criticism of the tale has concentrated on its concern with speech and language, beginning with Frederick Tupper (PMLA 29, 1914, 93–128), who stressed its concern with the "sins of the tongue"; Morton Donner (MLN 70, 1955, 245–49) and others have argued that the tale is a sermon on careless speech; and a number of scholars, such as Britten J. Harwood (ChauR 6, 1971, 268–79), think "the subject of the tale is language." V. J. Scattergood (EIC 24, 1974,

124–46) agrees, but he notes that it is a tale about a servant who has to be careful about how he tells the truth. David Raybin (JEGP 95, 1996, 190–237) sees it as a study of "voice and power," with the crow gaining his freedom by clever speech. Louise Fradenburg (ELH 52, 1985, 85–118) likewise sees it as about the problems of inferiors in their relation to authority but interprets it on more general political lines.

Many critics, such as James Dean (Texas St. in Lang. and Lit. 21, 1979, 17–33), Mark Allen (SAC 9, 1987, 77–96), and Chauncey Wood (Medievalia, 6, 1980, 209–29), interpret the tale as part of the preparation for the close of *The Canterbury Tales*: what Dean calls an "anti-tale" or a "farewell to his book" that prepares for the Parson's new direction in language and thought. See also Brewer, New Intro. to Ch, 382–91, and Strohm, Social Ch, 175–76.

For a full survey (to the early 1980s) of critical opinion, see Donald C. Baker, ed., The Manciple's Tale, Variorum ed., pt. 10, 1984.

The Manciple's Prologue

2–3 Bobbe-up-and-doun: Probably Harbledown, two miles north of Canterbury on the old road from London, though "Up and down field" in the parish of Thannington (Athenaeum 1868 II:866) and Bobbing, two miles west of Sittingbourne (N&Q 167, 1932, 26), have both been suggested (Robinson).

5 Dun is in the myre: Proverbial (Whiting D434). The reference is to a rural game that imitates the freeing of a horse (*dun* = dark-colored horse) from the mud: the participants test their ability to move some unwieldy object (for references, see Tilley D642). The Host is complaining about the Cook's slow progress (*al bihynde,* IX.7) and because the storytelling has come to a temporary halt.

6 for preyere ne for hyre: Cf. Whiting L480 ("For love or gold").

8 Richard M. Trask (Sts. in Short Fict. 14, 1977, 109–16) interprets this line symbolically: the **theef** may be the devil; but the reference could simply be to the danger from highwaymen; Chaucer himself was robbed in 1390 (PardT VI.765n.)

9 cokkes bones: Cf. ParsPro X.29 and n.

11 a cook of Londoun: Identified by Edith Rickert (TLS, 20 Oct. 1932, 761) as Roger Knight of Ware; see introductory note to Cook's portrait in the General Prologue.
   with meschaunce: Cf. FrT III.1334n.

12–13 For difficult literary composition as a **penaunce,** cf. Complaint of Venus 79: "And eke to me it [endyting] ys a gret penaunce."

14 nat worth a botel hey: Proverbial (Whiting B470); cf. GP I.177n.

20 For the rhetorical structure, see Thop VII.745n.

24 Chepe: Cheapside (see GP I.754n.).

38 "A curse; apparently with reference to the belief that the devil entered through the open mouth. See Andrae, Anglia, Beiblatt 13, 1902, 306, for a story of a lad who was held to be possessed. He had the habit of keeping his mouth open, and the women said he did so in order that the Devil might pass easily in and out" (Robinson). But Roy J. Pearcy (ELN 11, 1974, 167–75) suggests that the devil entered the Cook

through drink, and that he failed in sobriety, which should guard the mouth (cf, Gower, Mirour, 16453–56, tr. Wilson, 226: "The fourth special good that Sobriety brings us is that she guards safely the principal portal of the heart, that is our mouth").

39 breeth infecte wole: Particularly in regard to the plague, it was thought that infection was carried through foul air; see Johannes Nohl, *The Black Death: A Chronicle of the Plague,* trans. C. H. Clarke, 1961, ch. 4.

40 stynkyng swyn: An apt comparison, and not only in terms of smell. The pig was traditionally associated with the Cook's other failings, sleepiness (IX.7, 16, 22–23; cf. Whiting G467, H408, S539, S970) and drunkenness (IX.44, 57, 67; cf. Whiting S532, 534, 955, 968).

42 justen atte fan: "The vane (*fan*) or board was at one end of a cross-bar, which swung round on a pivot. At the other end hung a bag or club. The jouster had to strike the fan and avoid the stroke of the bag" (Robinson). Originally this was an exercise for knights (see 11 above), designed to sharpen military skill: the target was sometimes dressed as a Saracen. To joust at the quintain successfully demanded horsemanship and manual dexterity that were beyond the inebriated Cook.

44 wyn ape: The different stages of drunkenness, or its effects on different men, were sometimes compared to four animals: the lamb (meek), the lion (bold), the ape (foolish), and the sow (wallowing). See *Gesta Romanorum,* tr. Swan, ch. 159. To be ape-drunk was to be playful; see Lydgate, Troy Book 2.5779–81: "And with a strawe pleyeth like an ape,/ And devoutly gynneth for to gape,/ And noddeth ofte"; and cf. IX.35, 45, 47. But Norton-Smith (Geoffrey Ch, 152) argues on the basis of IX.40 that the Cook is "sow-drunk."

46–47 For the traditional enmity between cooks and manciples, see Frederick Tupper, JEGP 14, 1915, 256–70.

48 doun the hors hym caste: Cf. I.3121, where the drunken Miller can *unnethe* sit his horse.

50 fair chyvachee of a cook: Certainly ironic, this may be allusively humorous, too, if the Cook is identified with Roger Knight (see 11 above).

60 oold or moysty ale: "Old or new ale." *Moist* as an adjective could mean "damp," or as a noun refer to "must," or new wine. Cf. Sir Tristrem, 2492: "No hadde thei no wines wat [wet], No ale that was old."

72 brynge thee to lure: The *lure* was a device (see FrT III.1340 n.) by which the falconer attracted his flying bird down so that he could **reclayme** it.

74–75 thy rekenynges: Cf. GP I.586, where it is implied that the Manciple may have been deceiving his superiors over his accounts.

78 mare: "The mare was rarely the mount of a person of quality" (Rowland, Blind Beasts, 117), but cf. GP I.541n.

90 pouped in this horn: I.e., drunk from the horn-like mouth of the wine flask (**gourde,** IX.83). But the sense "blown upon this wind instrument" is also present. Paull F. Baum (PMLA 73, 1958, 168) suggests a pun on "broke wind," but neither OED (s.v. *poop* v.1) nor MED (s.v. *poupen* v.) offers any support.

97–99 Norton-Smith (Geoffrey Ch, 150–51) suggests that lines IX.97–98 derive from Ovid's *Ars amatoria,* tr. Mozley,

1.238: "Care flees and is dissolved in much wine"; and that IX.99 refers to Ars am., tr. Mozley, 1.543–44: "Lo! Druken old Silenus scarce sits his crookbacked ass, and leaning clings to the mare before him."

The Manciple's Tale

106 olde bookes: Probably Ovid's Met. 1.438–567 or 2.531–632 (S&A, 701–2).

109 Phitoun: Python, the fabled serpent sprung from the mud and stagnant waters remaining after Deucalion's flood, was killed by Phoebus with his arrows (Met. 1.438–51).

110 Slepynge agayn the sonne: Perhaps parodic, suggesting that Phoebus's exploit was not particularly magnificent; see Hazelton JEGP 62:9. But according to David F. Marshall, a serpent superimposed upon the sun illustrates the **mercurias noster**, the *prima materia* of the alchemical process (Ch Newsletter 1, 1979, 18).

116 Amphioun: See MerT IV.1716n.

121–24 In representational art Phoebus was the ideal type of young, but not immature, manly beauty. His traditional associations with music and archery (cf. IX.108–18, 129) meant that he was usually depicted with a lyre or bow. Cf. Ovid, Met., tr. Miller, 1.559; "My hair, my lyre, my quiver shall always be entwined with thee, O laurel."

139 a wyf: Coronis of Larissa (Ovid, Met., tr. Miller, 2.542: "In all Thessaly there is no fairer maid than Coronis of Larissa"). Chaucer's sources do not describe Phoebus as married to her, so *wyf* may here mean "woman" (cf. I.445; III.998, VI.71, etc.). Yet Chaucer gives this tale a very domestic setting.

148–54 A gloss appearing only in the Hengwrt MS (Partridge IX.147) suggests that the passage is based on Theophrastus's *Liber aureolus de nuptiis,* as quoted by Jerome in Adv. Jov. 1.47; see Hanna and Lawler, Jankyn's Book, 150–55. For similar sentiments, see *Roman de la rose* 14381–84, 14393–94 (tr. Dahlberg, 246: "No man can keep watch over a woman if she does not watch herself . . . Argus' watch would be worth nothing in this case") and WBPro III.357–61. Whiting (W240) says that the whole passage is proverbial, but cites only this instance. The **olde clerkes** are probably Theophrastus and Jerome.

160–62 Cf. Horace's *Epistolae,* tr. Fairclough, 1.10.24 ("You may drive out Nature with a pitchfork, yet she will ever hurry back"), which Chaucer may have known by way of *Roman de la rose* 14019–25 (tr. Dahlberg, 240).

163–74 Cf. Bo 3.m2.21–31, which Chaucer followed in SqT V.610–17; but here he probably used *Roman de la rose* 13941–58, tr. Dahlberg, 239.

175–80 Cf. *Roman de la rose* 14039–52, tr. Dahlberg, 240–41. For a fragmentary debate between "nurture" and "kynde" that uses the same exemplum, see V. J. Scattergood, N&Q 215, 1970, 244–46; for the traditional story on which this is based, see Willy L. Braekman and Peter S. Macaulay, NM 70, 1969, 690–702.

183–86 Cf. *Roman de la rose* 7761–66 (tr. Dahlberg, 146: "As the she-wolf does, whose madness makes her so much worse that she always takes the worst of the wolves"). This is the probable source, but the idea was widespread (T. B. W. Reid, MÆ 24, 1955, 16–19).

187–88 nothyng by wommen: For the general sentiment, cf. Tr 5.1779–81: "N'y sey nat this al oonly for thise men,/ But moost for wommen that bitraised be/ Thorough false folk— God yeve hem sorwe, amen!"

199 man of litel reputacioun: In some versions of the story the man is identified as Ischys, son of Elatus, an Arcadian; but Ovid (Met. 2.599) has simply "with a young Thessalian." The stress on social differences (cf. IX.253, and also 190, 211–22) led Whittock to detect "something akin to modern class bitterness" (Reading of CT, 284).

204–6 The word **lemman** was not held to be coarse, and the Manciple is the only pilgrim to apologize for it; he reuses it at 238. Chaucer used it freely in his very early Romaunt (RomA 1209, 1272, etc.) but perhaps came to regard it as part of that idiom of popular poetry that he mocks in The Miller's Tale (cf. Donaldson, Speaking of Ch, 13–29); to the provincial Nicholas and Absolon it meant "sweetheart" (cf. MilT I.328, 3700), but elsewhere it had come down in the world. David Burnley (ES 65, 1984, 195–204) notes that in a fifteenth-century glossary it appears in a section entitled "Names for blameworthy women," where it translates *concubina*. For the *lemman/lady* contrast, see Cleanness, 1351–52: "And had a wyf for to welde, a wortheliche quene/ And mony a lemman, never the later, that ladies were called" [regularized].

207–10 word . . . dede: The idea is ultimately from Plato's *Timaeus,* 29B, but Chaucer probably derived it from Boethius or from *Le Roman de la rose.* Cf. GP I.725–42n.

211–37 Cf. Reason's defense of direct speech in *Roman de la rose* 6987–7184 (tr. Dahlberg, 133–36).

220 wenche: The word is usually applied to lower-class women, especially servants; see Elliott, Ch's English, 206–8. Cf. MerT IV.2202.

222 There is an obvious pun on "lay" meaning "to have sexual intercourse"; see Thomas W. Ross, Ch's Bawdy, 1972, 130. Cf. MilT I.3269–70.

226 The anecdote about Alexander was familiar; it appears in Cicero's *De republica* 3.12 (in fragmentary form); Augustine's *De civitate Dei* 4.4 (tr. William M. Green); John of Salisbury's *Policraticus* 3.14 (tr. Pike, 204); *Gesta Romanorum* ch. 146 (tr. Swan); and elsewhere.

235 textueel: Cf. IX.316. But 314–62 are almost entirely based on "textes." Note the similar claim at ParsPro X.57.

243 Cokkow: That the cuckoo/cuckold pun was known at this time is clear from Clanvowe's Boke of Cupide, in Works of Sir John Clanvowe, ed. V. J. Scattergood, 1975, 183–85: "If thou be fer or longe fro this make,/ Thou shalt as other that be forsake,/ And then shalt thou be hoten as do I" (you shall be called as I am). See also Whiting C603. It was thought that the cuckoo laid its eggs in the nests of other birds and that its young ejected the young of their hosts; hence "The cuckow ever unkynde" in PF 358.

252 blered is thyn ye: Proverbial; cf. RvT I.3865n.

260 shame . . . vileyne: Cf. *Ovide moralisé,* 2352: "La vilonie et la grante honte."

271 The scorpion was a common symbol of treachery. See MLT II.404n.

279 O ire recchelees: For similar denunciations, see SumT III.2005–88, ParsT X.537–650.

295–99 The metamorphosis from **white** to **blake** is the point of the story in most of the analogues; but to deprive the crow of its *song* is Chaucer's innovation, as is the earlier destruction of Phoebus's bow, arrows, and musical instruments (IX.267–69); see Harwood, ChauR 6:268–79.

301 tempest: Cf. John of Garland, *Integumenta Ovidii:* "The raven is said to be sacred to Jupiter . . . because he is able to foretell tempests as Phoebus can" (S&A, 716).

311–13 Tauno Mustanoja suggests as a source *Carmen ad astralabium filium* (Song to his Son Astrolabe), attributed to Abelard: "I do not want you to tell a man about the crime of his beloved wife, because it would burden him more that it should be known"; see Franciplegius, ed. Bessinger and Creed, 1965, 250–54.

314 Salomon: Cf. Prov. 21.23: "Whoso keepeth his mouth and his tongue keepeth his soul from trouble."

317 taughte me my dame: Cf. WBPro III.576, PardT VI.684.

318 My sone: Cf. the repeated use of "My son" in Prov. 23.15, 19, 26. For this form of address in other wisdom literature, see J. S. P. Tatlock, MLN 50, 1935, 296.

319 keep wel thy tonge: Proverbial (Whiting T373). Cf. Tr 3.294: "firste vertu is to kepe tonge."

320 wikked tonge worse than a feend: Possibly proverbial; Whiting T402 (the only instance).

322–24 Possibly proverbial (Tilley T424, but not found by Whiting).

325–28 Cf. *Dicta Catonis* 1.12: "Being silent does no harm but speaking brings trouble"; Albertanus de Brescia's *De arte loquendi et tacendi,* xcviii; ed. Sundby, 98: "We have seen few or none overthrown by being silent but many by speaking." Cato and Albertanus may be the **clerkes** of IX.326.

329–31 Cf. *Roman de la rose* 7037–43 (tr. Dahlberg, 134: "He who takes trouble over what restrains his tongue is a wise man, except when he speaks of God and nothing more").

332–33 firste vertu . . . kepe wel thy tonge: The expression was widespread: *Dicta Catonis* 1.3, quoted as a gloss in some MSS (Partridge IX.332): "To rule the tongue I reckon virtue's height"; Albertanus, *De arte loquendi,* xcvi (who quotes Cato, as above); *Roman de la rose* 12179–83 (tr. Dahlberg, 212, RomC 7505–9: "Sir, the firste vertu, certayn . . . / That is his tonge to refrayne"); cf. Whiting V41.

338 Cf. Prov. 10.19 ("In the multitude of words there wanteth not sin"; quoted as a gloss in some MSS; Partridge IX.339). Cf. Mel VII.1550; Whiting S608 cites other examples.

340–42 Cf. Ps. 57.4 ("even the sons of men, whose teeth are spears and arrows, and their tongue a sharp sword"). See Whiting T385, 388.

343 In Prov. 6.16–18 a "lying tongue" is one of six things which are an abomination unto the Lord.

344 Reed Salomon: The Book of Proverbs, such as 17.20: "He that hath a froward heart findeth no good: and he that hath a perverse tongue falleth into mischief"; 26.28: "A lying tongue hateth those that are afflicted by it; and a flatering mouth worketh ruin."

345 Reed David . . . Senek: David's Psalms, such as Ps. 12.3: "The Lord shall cut off all flattering lips, and the tongue that speaketh proud things"; 119.2 (AV 120.2):

"Deliver my soul, O Lord, from lying lips and from a deceitful tongue."

Senek: Chaucer uses Seneca's *De ira* in SumT III.2017–88 (see 2017–18n.), where three exempla against anger are cited. They came to him, like almost all his borrrowings from Seneca, from John of Wales's *Communiloquium.*

350 Almost identical to the Flemish proverb "Luttel onderwinds maakt groote rust" (Grauls and Vanderheijden, RBPH 13, 1934, 745–49). For English examples, see Whiting J13, M482. Cf. CkPro IV.4357.

355–56 forth it gooth: Ultimately from Horace's Epistolae, tr. Fairclough, 1.18.71: "And the word once let slip flies beyond recall," perhaps by way of *Roman de la rose* 16545; tr. Dahlberg, 279: "Once a speech has taken wing it cannot be called back." See also Albertanus, *De arte loquendi,* cxviii, p. 98: "Words are rather like javelins; they are easy to send forth but difficult to draw back." For proverbs making similar points, see Whiting D287, H134, T198

357–58 Cf. Albertanus, *De arte loquendi,* cvi, p. 106: "When your counsel or secret is hidden it is as though enclosed in your prison; when it is revealed, truly it holds you bound in its prison."

359–60 From *Dicta Catonis* 1.12: "Flee rumors, lest you begin to be thought [their] new author." Quoted as a gloss in some manuscripts (Partridge, IX.359).

FRAGMENT X

The explanatory notes to Fragment X and to The Parson's Prologue and Tale are adapted from those written by Siegfried Wenzel for The Riverside Chaucer.

Since the first line of The Parson's Prologue explicitly links it with the preceding tale, The Manciple's and Parson's Prologues and Tales actually form a single fragment. They have traditionally been divided into two fragments because of nineteenth-century editors' doubts that Chaucer could have intended The Parson's Tale, which begins at 4:00 in the afternoon (X.5), immediately to follow the brief Manciple's Tale, which begins in the morning (IX.16). From the fact that in the early Hengwrt MS the word *Maunciple* is written over an erasure and some later manuscripts here give the names of other pilgrims (see M-R IV:527–28), it was deduced that the linking of The Manciple's Tale and The Parson's Tale was the work of some scribe. Most critics now accept the reading *Maunciple,* ignoring the temporal inconsistency (cf. Howard, Idea of CT, 165–66) and finding artistic justification for the juxtaposition of these two tales (see the introductory note to The Manciple's Tale).

A case can be made for The Parson's Tale as an independent work: Charles A. Owen, Jr., (MÆ 63, 1994, 239–49) argues from the MSS and Albert E. Hartung (in Richard E. Newhauser and John A. Alford, eds., Lit. and Religion in the Later M.A., 1995, 61–80) makes an argument from internal evidence. However, the view that the Parson's is only accidentally the last tale in an unfinished work cannot be seriously held in light of the carefully crafted Parson's Prologue, with its repeated stress that The Parson's Tale is to be the last on the fictional pilgrimage and with its seemingly deliberate use of verbal echoes and literary motifs. A convenient discussion of the latter is Siegfried Wenzel, in Europäische Lehrdichtung, ed. H. G. Rötzer and H. Waiz, 1981, 86–98. On the elements of closure in Fragment X, see Lawler, The One and the Many, 153–72. David Lawton (SAC 9, 1987, 3–40) argues that even if a "compiler" other than Chaucer added Fragment X, it provides an authentic closure, predictable from the GP.

The Parson's Prologue

2–11   For the elaborate specification of time, Chaucer again, as in IntrMLT II.1–14 (see n.), draws on the *Kalendarium* of Nicholas of Lynne, according to which the sun is descended from the meridian (**south lyne**) not quite 29° and a man's shadow is eleven times one-sixth the height of his body (cf. X.6–9) at 4:00 P.M. on 16 or 17 April. And at 4:00 P.M. on 15 through 17 April, to an observer in London, the zodiacal sign **Libra** (the Scale) was beginning to rise (**ascende**) above the horizon (J. D. North, RES 20, 1969, 424–26). This contradicts the date given in IntrMLT II.5–6, 18 April, as well as the traditional assumption that the pilgrimage began on 17 April and ended with The Parson's Tale on 20 April. Sigmund Eisner (E&S 29, 1976, 20–21) suggests Chaucer was not bothered by the temporal contradiction and chose to set The Parson's Prologue and Tale on 17 April because in 1394 that day was Good Friday.

4 nyne and twenty: Cf. GP I.24. Russell A. Peck (ES 48, 1967, 205–15) argues that in medieval number symbolism twenty-nine denotes "imperfection, concupiscence, spiritual decrepitude," from which the Parson will now lead the pilgrims.

10–11 moones exaltacioun: The moon's exaltacioun (the zodiacal sign in which a planet exerts its greatest influence) is Taurus rather than Libra, which is the exaltation of Saturn. The first of the three "faces" of Libra (the first 10°) was the "face" of the moon, and Skeat suggests Chaucer confused "exaltation" with "face" (5:445). Wood (Ch and the Stars, 272–97) argues that Chaucer mentions Libra for a symbolic allusion to divine justice.

12 at a thropes ende: No village is known to have existed between Harbledown (cf. IX.2) and Canterbury.

26 Unbokele . . . male: Cf. MilPro I.3115 and n.

28 knytte up: Possibly a rhetorical term, also in preaching; see Siegfried Wenzel, SP 73, 1976, 155–61.

29 cokkes: A euphemism for *Goddes;* Dives and Pauper (1:241) condemns those who use "'koc' for God" and swear "be cockis body"; "Yif they sweren only swiche othis for to begylyn hire evene cristene . . . they synnyn dedlyche & arn forsworn." And if they swear thus to avoid greater oaths "yit they synnyn wel grevously." Cf. MancPro IX.9 and 591 below.

32–34 Paul: See 1 Tim. 4.7 ("But refuse profane and old wives' fables") and cf. 1 Tim. 1.4 ("Neither give heed to fables and endless geneologies"), 2 Tim. 4.4 ("And they shall turn away their ears from the truth and shall be turned unto fables").

35–36 draf . . . whete: Cf. MLT II.701–2, NPT VII.3443n.

42–43 Southren man: Contemporary alliterative poetry was written mainly in the north and west of England. Parallels to **rum, ram, ruf** are listed in Skeat 5:446, and Dennis Biggins, PQ 42, 1963, 558–62. On Chaucer's use of alliteration and possible knowledge of alliterative poetry, see KnT I.2601–16n.

43 geeste: Apparently this refers to alliterative verse (cf. ProMel VII.933 and n.).

51 Jerusalem celestial: See Rev. 21.2 ("I John saw the holy city, new Jerusalem"). For life as a way "towards the high Jerusalem," beset by the beasts of the seven deadly sins, see Ancrene Riwle, tr. Salu, 86. The connection between penance, pilgrimage, and man's way to the heavenly Jerusalem is made in a sermon by Peraldus; see Wenzel, in Europ. Lehrd., 98.

57 textueel: Cf. MancT IX.235, 316.

67 hadde the wordes for us alle: Tyrwhitt notes the fourteenth-century Anglo-French description of the Speaker of Parliament as one who "avoit les paroles pur les Communes" (has the words for the Commons); see Rotuli Parliamentorum, 51 Edward III, no. 87.

69 meditacioun: On The Parson's Tale in relation to the tradition of religious meditation, see Thomas H. Bestul, Spec 64, 1989, 600–19.

The Parson's Tale

Though spoken by a parish priest to a group of listeners, The Parson's Tale is formally not a sermon or homily but a handbook on penance; see Siegfried Wenzel, ChauR 16, 1982, 248–51, and Lee Patterson, Traditio 34, 1978, 331–51. Some earlier critics were dubious about Chaucer's authorship because of the tale's style and subject matter, but most modern critics fully accept the work as Chaucer's. The problem of authorship is intimately linked with the question of sources. The Parson's Tale uses material from the *Summa de poenitentia* or *Summa casuum poenitentiae* (1222/29) by the Dominican St. Raymund of Pennaforte for lines 80–386 and 958–1080, and from the *Summa vitiorum* (1236) by the Dominican friar William Peraldus (or Peyraut) for a large part of lines 390–955. (See K. O. Petersen, The Sources of the ParsT, 1901.) The Latin *summae* of Pennaforte and Peraldus were immensely popular and were utilized in many Latin and vernacular handbooks. G. Dempster (S&A, 723–60) reproduced representative extracts from both *summae* as well as parallels from two French manuals, the Anglo-Norman *Compileison* (last quarter of thirteenth century) and Frère Laurent's *Somme le Roi* (1279), which had been suggested as possible influences on Chaucer.

The linking of material from the two *summae,* especially at X.387, was felt by some critics to be inorganic, mechanical, and crude, and led Manly and Rickert to reaffirm the possibility that The Parson's Tale is the work of someone other than Chaucer, even though they found no textual support for genuine doubt of Chaucer's authorship (Manly-Rickert 4:527, in contradiction to 2:454–55). But the linking of the treatment of the deadly sins to the discussion of penance is logical and paralleled in other handbooks. Likewise, the startling disproportion of Chaucer's section on the sins and their remedies to the remainder of the tale is neither unique nor a good argument against his authorship.

The probability is that instead of mechanically combining two Latin treatises, The Parson's Tale embodies material intelligently drawn from a larger number of sources. This has received support from Siegfried Wenzel's discovery of a source for the "remedies" for the seven deadly sins; see his article (Traditio 27, 1971, 433–53) and his edition of *Summa virtutum de remediis anime*, Chaucer Library, 1984; moreover, he has identified two redactions of Peraldus's *Summa vitiorum* (referred to as Quoniam and Primo) that are close to Chaucer (Traditio 30, 1974, 351–78); and he has found different sources or analogues for several other passages (ChauR 16:237–56). Though the possibility that the tale is but the translation of a single source that already combined all these materials remains open, it is equally possible to think that Chaucer himself made a purposeful compilation and translation from diverse sources.

The diction of the tale in general and some instances of phraseology in particular (lines 79, 572, 898) may suggest that Chaucer's immediate source was in French rather than Latin; see, e.g., H. G. Pfander, JEGP 35, 1936, 257; Norton-Smith, Geoffrey Ch, 155. But no French treatise significantly close to The Parson's Tale has been identified, and the occasional gallicisms need not be due to an immediate source.

There is no external evidence for dating the tale. Older scholars put it very early: Victor Langhans (Anglia 53, 1929, 243–68) argued a date of 1358 (he assumed Chaucer was born earlier than now believed) on purely internal grounds — vocabulary, style, and Chaucer's personal development. But comparison of specific phrases and verses not found in Chaucer's suggested sources with parallels in other parts of the *Tales* has led some scholars to the view that The Parson's Tale was composed after the other tales; thus Charles A. Owen, Jr., MLN 71, 1956, 84–87, and especially Patterson, Traditio 34:356–70.

References to Pennaforte are to *Summa de poenitentia et matrimonio*, Rome, 1603, repr. 1967. The section "De poenitentiis et remissionibus" forms title 34 of Book 3 (pp. 437–502). Notice that the line numbers for the text of The Parson's Tale follow the practice established in the Chaucer Society Six-Text edition and appear at the *end* of the respective line.

State super vias . . . : Jer. 6.16, tr. in lines 77–78. Chaucer's phrase "de viis antiquis" normally reads "de semitis antiquis" in the Vulgate Bible and medieval sermons. The verse is connected with penance in a sermon by John Felton, vicar of St. Mary Magdalen, Oxford, 1397 and after; see Wenzel, ChauR 16:251–52.

75 that no man wole perisse: Probably an awkward rendering of "nolens aliquos perire" (wishing no one to perish) of 2 Pet. 3.9, although Chaucer's clause could also mean "who wishes to destroy no one." For the following phrase, cf. 1 Tim. 2.3–4: "our Saviour, Who will have all men to be saved."

82–83 The six divisions or parts of the tale, which begin respectively at X.84 (*what is Penitence*), 86 (*whennes it is cleped*), 95 (*how manye . . . acciouns*), 102 (*how many speces*), 107 (*whiche thynges apertenen*), and 1057 (*whiche thynges destourben*), to which a seventh part on *the fruyt of penaunce* is added at 1076.

86 This sentence probably corresponds to the topic *whennes it is cleped Penitence*, announced at 82, i.e., the etymology of penitence. Pennaforte gives it at this very point: "Penitence is so called as if it were the holding of sorrow" (3.34.1).

87–88 These two sentences do not occur in Pennaforte and are stylistically different from the authorities previously quoted.

93 forlete synne er that synne forlete hem: Since one condition of true penitence and forgiveness is the penitent's firm intention not to commit again those sins of which he repents (*and namoore to do . . .*), sinners who repent at a time in their lives when they can no longer commit their former sins (that is, when "sins leave them") therefore cannot be certain (**siker**) that their repentance will be genuine. The same thought and image occur at PhyT VI.286 (see n.).

95–101 three acciouns of Penitence: Though Chaucer's wording is awkward, especially because of the shifting of terms from **gilt** (98) to **defaute** (99, 100), this section, in agreement with Pennaforte, declares that penitence, i.e., sorrow for one's personal sins, can occur in three situations: (98) before baptism received in adulthood, for any sins that were committed; (99) after baptism, for any mortal sins; and (100) further for any venial sins. **Acciouns** here means "acts" or "functions."

118 The grace of this seed: Perhaps a mistake for *the egernesse of this seed*; cf. Patterson, Traditio 34:352; see also Frances Beer (N&Q 233, 1988, 298–301), who argues that it is an error for "seed of egrece."

133 causes: Pennaforte similarly discusses "six causes that lead to contrition" (3.34.9), but they are only in part like Chaucer's, and the development is quite different. For an Anglo-Norman analogue, see Dempster, S&A, 751–56.

143 desdeyn of synne: Perhaps a reference to Job 30.28, "moerens incedebam" (I went mourning), or Ps. 42.2 (AV 43.2), "quare tristis incedo" (Why do I go in sadness). Not in Pennaforte.

145 Seneca: Epist. morales, tr. Gummere, 65.21. Pennaforte refers to "Philosophus."

151 Pennaforte quotes and attributes this sentence to Augustine.

155 The Ellesmere scribe glosses "You women, take note and beware."

155–57 Prov. 11.22; cf. WBPro III.784–85 n. The application (X.157) appears in Quoniam; see Wenzel, ChauR 16:237–38.

175–230 The discussion of fear of the suffering in hell is a homiletic exegesis of Job 10.20–22, quoted in X.176–77.

231–54 The fourth consideration that may move a person to contrition concerns the notion that mortal sin annuls the spiritual or eternal merit a person gains by performing good deeds. This has two aspects (X.232): (a) merits once gained by good works but since canceled by mortal sin may again be "activated" through penance (235–41); and (b) good works performed in the state of sin will never have spiritual merit with regard to man's eternal life, though they may be helpful in lesser ways (242–45). Pennaforte's fifth "causa," meditating on the loss of heaven, has little bearing on Chaucer's *fourthe* cause.

248 Jay tout perdu: The same line is quoted in Fortune 7. French proverbs and snatches of verse appear frequently in the Latin *Summa praedicantium* by the English Dominican John Bromyard; similarly, the English Franciscan John of Grimestone (1372) quotes a French song and several French proverbs in his commonplace book.

255–82 Christ's passion, the fifth incentive to contrition, is here presented as the consequence of a triple disorder or insubordination (X.260–63), which was the result of sin. No parallels in Pennaforte. The notion that sin consists in a disordering of man's inner faculties is taken up by the Parson again at 322–32.

261–62 Bernard L. Witlieb, N&Q 215, 1970, 202–7, presents parallels from *Ovide moralisé* to this medieval commonplace.

309 quod David: Ps. 31.5 (AV 32.5). The gloss *I purposed fermely* also occurs in Pennaforte, 3.34.11, end.

317 The parts of this division are treated as follows: (a) nature of confession, X.318–979; (b) its necessity, 980–81; (c) its conditions, 982–1027. The three topics also occur in Pennaforte, 3.34.13–27.

318–979 The definition of "confession" given in X.318 is developed in the following lines. In 321 three subtopics on "sin" are announced, whose discussion takes up 322–957. The following section, 958–79, returns to a definition of "sin" and a discussion of the circumstances of sin. Though this entire section has occasional parallels in Pennaforte, it is unlikely that Chaucer used the latter as his direct source here.

319 condiciouns: Chaucer may seem to confuse "circumstances of sin" (which he treats later, 960–79) and "conditions of (a valid) confession" (which he also treats later, separately, at 982–1027), both common topics in penitential literature; see Patterson, Traditio 34:349, n. 46. However, "circumstances" and "conditions" of sin could be used synonymously, and the terminology of X.319–20 (not in Pennaforte) may be less muddled than has been suggested; see Wenzel, ChauR 16:239–40.

320 True confession must be complete, open, and self-accusing. **Al moot be seyd** is a translation of the etymology of *con-fessio* (saying together, or all at once). Thus according to Pennaforte (3.34.13), who adds: "ille confitetur qui totum fatetur" (he confesses who says all).

322–49 the spryngynge of synnes: The origin of sin (in Adam and Eve) is meant, as well as its effect, present in all mankind (Original Sin) as concupiscence, which in scholastic terminology is called the *fomes peccati* (*norissynge of synne*, X.338), i.e., the root from which all actual sins spring. The Parson's teaching here is commonplace, based on Augustine and transmitted through Peter Lombard and many other scholastic theologians and handbooks for preachers. See 331–32 below, and Alfred L. Kellogg, Traditio 8, 1952, 424–30.

331–32 The moralization of the Fall, in which the serpent, Eve, and Adam are interpreted as the devil, the flesh, and reason, and their actions respectively as the three stages in committing a sin (suggestion, delight, and consent), is standard medieval teaching. It derives from Augustine, De trinitate 12; see Robertson, Pref to Ch, 69–75.

350–56 The Parson gives two series of steps in the progression of sin. For the second series (X.355–56), Kellogg pointed to a similar passage in the *Summa de officio sacerdotis* by Richard de Wetheringsett (before 1222): see Kellogg, Chaucer, Langland, 339–52. But Wetheringsett in fact furnishes two different lists, as does Chaucer, who retains the pattern of the earlier list, probably under the influence of the theological considerations stated by Wetheringsett in the same context; see Wenzel, ChauR 16:243–45.

351 subjeccioun: The expected word is *suggestion,* which is found in some MSS.

bely: "Bellows." The image of the devil as a blacksmith blowing his bellows of evil suggestion and eliciting *a flambe of delit* (353) also occurs in the Summa by Wetheringsett; see Wenzel, ChauR 16:245.

355–56 Quotation of Exod. 15.9 with gloss. From Wetheringsett's Summa (see 350–56 above).

358–955 Development of *whiche* (i.e., what kinds of) sins there are, as announced at X.321. The initial distinction between venial and mortal ("deadly") sins (358–70) is followed by an illustrative list of venial sins (371–81), by a series of remedies for venial sins (382–86), and then by the long discussion of the seven deadly sins and their individual remedies (387–955).

362 Manye smale maked a greet: See Whiting S397. A Latin form, "Levia multa faciunt unum grande" (many light ones make one heavy one), appears in Augustine, *Tractates in epist. Joannis ad Parthos* 1.6 (PL 35:1982; tr. John W. Rettig, Fathers of the Church, vol. 93, 1995, 129).

363–64 The example of the ship derives from Augustine, Epist. 265, 1 (PL 33:1089; tr. Sister Wilfred Parsons, Fathers of the Church, vol. 32, 1956, 281), and is frequently quoted by others; see Petersen, Sources, 7 n.1.

368 Free translation of the standard scholastic definition of sin: "aversio a bono incommutabili ad bonum commutabile" (a turning from an unchanging good to a changeable good), which is based on Augustine, De libero arbitrio 1.16 (PL 32:1240; tr. Thomas Williams, 1993, 27). See Kellogg, Traditio 8:426, and Petersen, Sources, 34–35, n. 2. The quoted formulation is used in Quoniam, where the following explanation of "bonum incommutabile" (unchanging good) as everything created (X.369) likewise appears.

387 the sevene deedly synnes: The topic of deadly sins was announced at X.359. The term "deadly sin" can refer to both mortal sins (*peccata mortalia,* as used in X.359) and the seven chief vices or sins (*vitia* or *peccata capitalia* or *principalia,* as in 387). The ambiguity, in both Latin and vernacular languages, is characteristic of some scholastic theologians and generally of preachers from the thirteenth century on. See Morton W. Bloomfield, Seven Deadly Sins, 1952, 43–44. Chaucer's rendering of *vitia capitalia* with **chieftaynes of synnes** may have been influenced either by French usage ("chevetain vice" in the *Somme le Roi;* see Wilhelm Eilers, Essays on Ch, Ch Soc, 1868, 509) or else by the common notion that these vices are captains or leaders in the army of vices ("some of them go first, like captains [*duces*]" in Gregory, Morals 31.45.87, tr. Bliss, 3:489; cf. the use of "capteyns" in Lydgate's Assembly of the Gods, *passim*).

Alle they renne in o lees: Either literally "they all run together on one leash," as hunting dogs, or figuratively in the sense of "they all are connected in one chain." For the notion that the capital vices are psychologically concatenated, see Siegfried Wenzel, Spec 43, 1968, 4–5.

388 Of the roote of thise sevene synnes: Apparently a rubric wrongly shifted into the text.

braunches: The image of the capital vices as branches of a tree whose root is pride was commonplace. See Bloomfield, Seven Deadly Sins, 70 and *passim*.

406 clappeth as a mille: Proverbial; see ClT IV.1200 and n.

407–8 Apparently without parallel in the proposed sources. John L. Lowes suggested possible models in Deschamps's *Miroir de mariage* (MP 8, 1910–11, 322n.), but the vice was common. Cf. GP I.449–51 n.

kisse pax: For the custom, see William Maskell, Ancient Liturgy of the Ch. of Engl., 3rd ed., 1882, 170–73, n. 76; for pictures of a pax, see Jospeh Braun, Das christliche Altargerät, 1932, plates 116–20.

411 leefsel: Perhaps a "leafy bower" or "arbor" as in I.4061 (Elliott, Ch's English, 148–49), but the meaning "bush for a tavern sign" (MED s.v. *lēf* n. [1] 1[b]) is substantiated by the use of a tavern sign as a symbol for pride in clothing by Peraldus and derived treatises; see Wenzel, ChauR 16:238.

415 array of clothynge: For condemnations of pride in clothing by contemporary preachers, see Owst, Lit. and Pulpit, 390–411, and his index under *costume*.

418 daggynge of sheres: Cf. Rom A 840: "And al toslytered for queyntise."

422–29 Complaint at the shortness or scantiness of clothes as a sign of pride does not occur in Peraldus or derived Latin treatises. For similar remarks in French, see Mark Harvey Liddell, Acad 49, 1896, 509.

424 According to medieval encyclopedias, in the full of the moon apes display their posteriors (Dennis Biggins, MÆ 33, 1964, 200–3). Beryl Rowland suggests a reference to estrus (ChauR 2, 1968, 159–65).

437–43 For contemporary complaints at unruly retainers, see Owst, Lit. and Pulpit, 324–26, and the Harley lyric Satire on the Retinues of the Great (Hist. Poems, ed. Robbins, 27–29).

441 houndes: Peraldus speaks of wolves instead of dogs.

450 On the gifts of fortune and nature, see PardPro VI.295n.

461 gentrie: Peraldus speaks of "nobilitas generacionis" (nobility of birth), Quoniam of "stema, idest nobilitas generis" (pedigree, that is, nobility of clan). The view here expressed is paralleled in WBT III.1109–76 and in Gentilesse (16–17: "But ther may no man, as men may wel see,/ Bequethe his heir his vertuous noblesse").

467–68 Seneca, *De clementia,* in Moral Essays, tr. Basore, 1.3.3 ("Yet of all men none is better graced by mercy [*clementia*] than a king or a prince," and 1.19.2 (tr. in text), as quoted by Peraldus. On Chaucer's substituting **pitee** for "clementia," see Burnley, Ch's Language, 100 and n. 2: "Seneca in fact commends rational *clementia* rather than affective *pietas.*"

484 the Philosophre: Robert C. Fox suggests Aristotle, Rhetoric, 2.10 (N&Q 203, 1958, 523–24); the use of **the** strengthens the suggestion (in Chaucer's usage *the philosophre* almost always means "Aristotle").

Seint Augustyn: Augustine, *Enarrationes in Ps.* 104, 17 (CCSL 40:1545: "Envy is hatred of another's good fortune"), Sermon 353.1 (Sermons, tr. Edmund Hill in The Works of St. Augustine, 1995), and elsewhere. The sorrow-joy definition is used again in ParsT X.491–92 and PhyT VI.114–17 (see n.).

494 wikked knotte: The knot image appears in John de Grimestone's commonplace book; see Wenzel, Traditio 30:359 n. 27.

508 the develes Pater noster: Perhaps suggested by Peraldus. A Pater Noster of misers or usurers is often mentioned in sermons.

509 prive hate: "Odium occultum," a species of envy in Quoniam, which also contains, at this point, a reference to the later section on wrath; see Wenzel, Traditio 30:361. Chaucer mentions hate again at X.562.

532 paas: The usual interpretation "step" or "passage, section" leaves the sentence entirely cryptic. Wenzel (ChauR 16:245–48 and notes) suggests a meaning of "way, progression, process" and relates the sentence and its context to the notion that the remedial virtues are linked as stages in a process of healing (see X.530), just as the vices are linked in a psychological concatenation (see 387 above).

536 the Philosophre: Ultimately Aristotle, *De anima* (On the Soul), tr. Hett, 1.1.24: "[Anger is] a surging of the blood and heat around the heart"; cf. A. V. C. Schmidt, N&Q 213, 1968, 327–28. Chaucer's **fervent** has cognates in the medieval Latin translations of Aristotle as well as in Seneca. Chaucer's definition actually combines the two definitions between which Aristotle distinguishes.

539 wys man: Ecclus. 7.4 (AV 7.3): "Sorrow is better than laughter."

Irascimini etc.: Psalm 4.5 (AV 4.4).

551 tree: The juniper; cf. Isidore, *Etymologiae*, ed. Lindsay, 17.7.35.

552 Perhaps a reference to the kindling of the new fire in the liturgy of the Easter vigil; or else to the mandatory annual confession, usually made before Easter Sunday; cf. X.1027.

564–79 The discussion of homicide, not in Peraldus, is ultimately derived from Pennaforte, 2.1.2–3; see Dudley R. Johnson, PMLA 57, 1942, 51–56.

565 The **sixe thynges** are: hatred, backbiting, giving evil counsel, withholding or reducing wages, usury, and withdrawing alms, as listed in X.566–69. Pennaforte lists only five kinds.

569 the wise man: Solomon; cf. Prov. 25.21 ("If thine enemy be hungry, give him bread to eat"), but probably quoting Gratian, Decretum 1.86.21 (ed. Emil Friedberg, 1876, 1:302: "Feed those who are dying of hunger").

571 The four kinds of bodily manslaughter are: by law, for necessity, by accident, and through contraception, onanism, and abortion. See Johnson, PMLA 57:55–56, and John T. Noonan, Contraception, 1965, 215–16 and 235–36.

580–653 As stated in 653, at this point Chaucer turns to "sins of the tongue." Partial parallels occur in Peraldus (Petersen, Sources, 53–61), but in a separate tractatus, "De peccato linguae," which follows upon but is not verbally linked to the tractatus on wrath. Treatises derived from Peraldus, such as Quoniam, distribute his "sins of the tongue" among various deadly sins including wrath. Chaucer seems to be aware of different traditions; see 618 and 653, and cf. R. F. Yeager, SP 81, 1984, 42–55.

580 Gambling and blasphemy are connected in both Peraldus (people "play and blaspheme" in the devil's temple, the tavern: Summa vitiorum, 9.2.1) and Quoniam, in which the punishment for blasphemy can especially be seen "de lusoribus et aleatoribus" (with regard to gamblers and dice-players): MS Durham Cathedral, B. I. 18, fol. 62r. Cf. PardT VI.650–53.

591 dismembrynge of Crist: Cf. PardT VI.472–75 and 629–59, EpiMLT II.1171n.

592   Jeremye: Jeremiah 4.2; the same text is quoted in PardT VI.635–37.

600   forsweryng falsly: Cf. PardT VI.631–32 and discussion by Patterson, Traditio 34:361–62.

603–7   Various kinds of divination and incantation are usually included in the sin of *sortilegium.* The latter is a species of avarice in Quoniam (together with swearing and lying), whereas Peraldus had treated similar sins under pride. Chaucer's subsuming *sortilegium* under swearing (603), a branch of wrath, is peculiar.

603   shulder-boon of a sheep: For this practice, see Rowland, Blind Beasts, 149–52, and cf. PardPro VI.350–70 and 350n.

605   gnawynge of rattes: For the ancient belief that the gnawing of rats can serve as an omen of the future, see Rowland, Blind Beasts, 66–67.

612–18   Largely derived from Peraldus ("adulatio"; Petersen, Sources, 55), with some parallels in Quoniam (under envy). Lines not found in either treatise are X.612, 617, 618.

614   While Peraldus and Quoniam cite in this context several verses from Proverbs that contain the milk image of X.613 (Prov. 16.29, 24.28), none of them is close to the quotation attributed to **Salomon** in 614. But Peraldus and Quoniam link flattery to backbiting as follows: "And it seems that flattery is worse than backbiting, because backbiting lowers a man, but flattery raises him up" (Peraldus, Summa vitiorum 9.2.7, not noticed by Petersen). Chaucer's "Salomon" quotation clearly indicates a misreading of Peraldian material.

617   Placebo: Lat. "I shall please"; see also SumT III.2075, and MerT IV.1476n. "To sing placebo" appears as a synonym for "to flatter" in Somme le Roi and its English translations (e.g., *Book of Vices and Virtues,* ed. W. Nelson Francis, EETS 217, 1942, 58: "The ferthe synne is whanne they syngen alwey 'Placebo'; that is seye, 'My lord seith soth, or my lady or John or William seith wel.'" [regularized]). Cf. MerT IV.1446.

619–21   cursynge,   "maledictio," derives from Peraldus (Petersen, Sources), 55–56. Chaucer's definition **Malisoun . . . harm** seems to be corrupt.

624   The examples of abuse given here and in 626 do not occur in the suggested sources.

627   a vileyns herte: Peraldus has: "rusticus est, qui rusticitatem libenter dicit" (he is truly a boor [*rusticus*] who willingly speaks boorish things) (Summa vitiorum 9.2.9, not noticed by Petersen).

631   Salomon: Prov. 27.15. Compare WBPro III.278–80 and Mel VII.1086n.

634   Paul seith: Col. 3.18. Compare WBPro III.160–61. The quotation does not appear in Peraldus or Quoniam, although the latter expands Peraldus's treatment of chiding between husband and wife with a few remarks on how a husband should chastise an unruly wife, concluding: "If she does not experience the fear of God in her frequent disturbance, he should do as Solomon orders him: 'Strike her with a hard staff!'" (MS Durham Cathedral, B. I. 18, fol. 32v.).

639   wikked conseil: For Achitophel's bad counsel, see 2 Sam. 17.

640   seith the wise man: The quoted saying is actually Peraldus's text. *Every fals lyvynge* renders "omnis injusticia" (every injustice).

650   a philosophre: unidentified, as in Peraldus.

654–76   Summa virtutum, 16–18 and 28, provides the souce of the remedy for wrath.

658   the philosphre: Aristotle, On Interpretation, 11.

661   lerne to suffre: A commonplace (Whiting S865); see FranT V.773–75, Tr 4.1584 ("Men seyn, 'The suffrant overcomith'"); Walther 16974.

678   Accidie is, properly, only **anoy of goodnesse** (*taedium boni*) according to standard scholastic definitions followed by Quoniam; see Siegfried Wenzel, *Sin of Sloth,* 1967, 218, n. 17. The expansion **joye of harm** belongs to the definition of envy (see 484 above).

679   Salomon: Probably result of a misreading of "Paral." (Chronicles) in the source text; Quoniam here quotes 2 Chron. 19.7 ("do all things with diligence").

686   The fourthe thyng: Comparison with the source text shows that the preceding three "things" are arguments for scorning the vice, here advanced without numbering in 678 (two) and 681.

696   Judas: Judas hanged himself in despair, Matt. 27.5.

698   creant: The cry of surrender in combat. Chaucer's image is of a spineless participant in judicial combat (see GP I.239n.) who surrenders (**coward champioun recreant**). "To say *creant*" is a commonplace expression in ME homiletic literature for "giving up"; see MED s.v. *creaunt* (b).

714   ydelnesse . . . yate: see SNPro VIII.2–3 and n., and KnT I.1940.

720–21   Without parallel in the suggested sources at this point, this passage has given rise to speculations that Chaucer may allude to the government takeover by Gloucester in 1388 (Robinson) or to a court scandal involving Katherine Swynford (Owen, MLN 71:84–87). But the condemnation of negligent pastors (X.721) is a homiletic commonplace: Owst, Lit. and the Pulpit, and Preaching in Med. Engl. 41–47, 139. In Peraldus and derived works, clerical absenteeism is treated under avarice.

739   roote of alle harmes: Tim. 6.10. Cf. Mel VII.1130, 1840, PardPro VI.334 and n.

749   The notion that an idolater has only one idol but an avaricious person many occurs also in Dante, Inferno 19:112–14: "You have made a god of gold and silver/ and how do you differ from the idolator/ save that he worships one and you a hundred?" See Howard Schless, Dante and Chaucer: A Revaluation, 1984, 218.

752   cariages: Cf. FrT III.1570n.

762   The same deeth: The sentiment is common; see Whiting D101, and cf. KnT I.3030, MLT II.1142.

782   "Irregularity," in canon law, is a condition that permanently prevents a person from receiving Holy Orders or from exercising them; see P. Trudel, A Dictionary of Canon Law, 1920.

783   Simon Magus: Cf. Acts 8.18–24. Cf. FrT III.1309, SumT III.2094.

795   Some of these branches, notably *lesynges,* were already treated under wrath (608). In Quoniam all occur here, under avarice.

comaundementz: the conventional seventh and eighth commandments of the Decalogue, Exod. 20.15–16 ("Thou shalt not steal; Thou shalt not bear false witness against thy neighbor").

801 hurtynge of hooly thynges: translates "sacri ledium," the supposed etymology of "sacrilegium": "sacrum laedere," to hurt something holy. The actual etymon is "sacer (sacred things) + legere (gather, steal)"; see OED s.v. *sacrilege* sb[1].

816 trouble water: Rowland refers to Aristotle's observation that the horse prefers muddy water (Blind Beasts, 125); Peraldus likens the prodigal to dirty water.

818–19 Glotonye...Adam and Eve: Cf. SumT III.1915–16, PardT VI.504–11 and PardT 508–11n.

820 seith Seint Paul: Phil. 3.18–19; quoted also in PardT VI.529–33.

822 sepulture of mannes resoun: used also in PardT VI.558–59.

831 Galien: Galen, the Greek physician (see GP I.429–34n.).

853 venym of his sighte: The basilisk "sleeth alle thing that hath life with breth and with sight" [regularized] (Bartholomaeus Anglicus 18.16, tr. Trevisa, 2:1153); cf. Beryl Rowland, Animals with Human Faces, 1973, 28–31.

858 hound...pisse: This memorable image occurs verbatim in Quoniam and was borrowed by Dunbar, *Tretis of the Tua Mariit Wemen and the Wedo*, 185–87 (Priscilla Bawcutt, N&Q 209, 1964, 332–33). Bromyard applies a very similar image to slanderers: "They lift their leg over higher and green places, wishing to foul them," *Summa praedicantium*, D.5.9 (before 1330). The reading **bushes** is weakly attested by the MSS (variants are *benches* and *beautees*) but is supported by "virgultum" in Quoniam.

859 sleen hymself with his owene knyf: Cf. MerT IV.1840n. The expression is proverbial, apparently popularized by *Somme le Roi*: Whiting M154.

861 as though it were his suster: Not in the suggested sources. Cf. MerT IV.1454 and Patterson, Traditio 34:365.

865–914 The section on the species of lechery is somewhat obscure in structure but essentially follows the five species discussed by Peraldus and Quoniam: 1. "Fornicatio" (X.865–67); 2. "stuprum" (868–72); 3. "adulterium" (873–906); 4. "incestus" (907–9); 5. "vitium contra naturam" (910–11). Quoniam adds a section on "luxuria clericorum," which furnishes material for X.891–903. The discussion of adultery here seems to be divided into three subspecies: (a) between partners one of whom or both are married to someone else (X.873–90); (b) between a man in holy orders and a married or unmarried woman (891–903); and (c) between husband and wife (904–6, already treated at 859). After the fifth species, "vitium contra naturam," Chaucer adds as another synne "pollutio nocturna" (912–14), which is not treated in the suggested sources, but is otherwise a traditional topic.

867 Seint Paul: Gal. 5.21: "They which do such things shall not inherit the kingdom of God." Chaucer's text should read: "Saint Paul denies them the reign, which is not denied to anyone but those who commit deadly sin."

869 Cf. Matt. 13.8: "But others fell to good ground and brought forth fruit, some an hundredfold, some sixtyfold, some thirtyfold." The three degrees of the parable were traditionally related to the states of virginity, widowhood, and married life.

872 Loss of virginity does not prevent people from regaining the state of grace, but the original state of inviolate virginity cannot be restored.

874 approchynge of oother mannes bed: Translates the etymology of "adulterium" given by Peraldus: "ad alterius thorum accessio."

898 withouten juge: "without judge," for the biblical "absque iugo" (without yoke) (Judg. 19.22). Chaucer's wording has been explained as a misreading of Old French *sans ioug* as *sans iuge* and has been taken as evidence that he used a French source (Skeat 5:471; Fisher). Or it may be that the form "juge" is to be taken as a variant of "yoke."

898–99 free bole: See George C. Homans, RES 14, 1938, 447–49. The image occurs in Quoniam.

907 affynytee: In canon law, the relationship between persons established by marriage, excluding that between the spouses themselves; to be distinguished from **kynrede,** or consanguinity.

911 the sonne...mixne: Proverbial, see Whiting S891 and Wenzel, Traditio 30:376, n. 117.

916 two maneres: At 948 Chaucer adds a third, virginity. His source has three species, in the same order; but the variant readings at 9.12 in the Summa virtutum may explain his mistake.

918 as I have seyd: See 842 and 883.

925–29 Cf. Gen. 2.22: "And the rib, which the Lord God had taken from man, made he a woman, and brought her unto man." This moral interpretation of Eve's being created from Adam's rib was a commonplace. See, for instance, Gower, Mirour, 17521–32, tr. Wilson, 240–41.

927 experience of day by day: Preachers' references to daily experience were commonplace in Chaucer's time; Owst, Lit. and Pulpit, 24–41, gives many examples.

939 for thre thynges: Actually four reasons for sexual intercourse are discussed. For Chaucer's position in the late medieval moral evaluation of sexual intercourse, see Noonan, Contraception, 246–57; Joseph J. Mogan, ChauR 4, 1970, 123–41; and Kelly, Love and Marriage, 245–85.

947 Magdelene: Cf. Matt. 26.7: "There came unto him a woman having an alabaster box of very precious ointment, and poured it on his head, as he sat at meat."

951–55 All special remedies are listed and the examples occur in Peraldus, *Summa vitiorum* 2.3.1 and 3.4.1–2; the material of X.953–55 also appears in Quoniam. See Wenzel, Summa virtutum, 29–30. For an Anglo-Norman analogue, see Dempster, S&A, 750–51.

956–57 The Parson's discussion of the deadly sins contains clear quotations of or allusions to the first (X.750–51), second (588), fifth (887), sixth (837, 867, 887), seventh (795, 798, 887), eighth (795), and ninth (844) commandments.

957 lete to divines: Cf. the similar expression at KnT I.1323.

958 seconde partie: See X.316, and 318–979 above.

960 agreggen: According to penitential theology, the circumstances of a sinful act may increase (or occasionally diminish) its seriousness. In discussing the circumstances, Chaucer follows the standard list formulated in the hexameter "Quis, quid, ubi, per quos, quoties, cur, quomodo, quando" (who, what, where, through whom, how often, why, how, when) quoted in Pennaforte.

977 This sentence apparently treats the circumstance of time ("quando"); see 960 above.

980–81 These lines apparently discuss the second major section of confession, whether it is necessary (cf. X.317).

982–1027   The condition for a **trewe**, i.e., valid, confession, the third topic on confession announced at X.317. Though the structure of this section is confusing, it essentially follows Pennaforte's exposition (3.34.22–26). Pennaforte announces four necessary qualities: "amara," "festina," "integra," and "frequens" (in his treatment the last two are reversed). Chaucer follows the same conditions: **sorweful** (X.983), **hastily** (998), **alle** (1006), and **ofte** (1025), but fails to introduce the last two by number. The framework taken from Pennaforte is often expanded, particularly with the **foure thynges** of 1003–5. The **certeine condiciouns** of 1012–24 correspond to Pennaforte's nine subsidiary aspects of "integra," in the same order: "voluntaria" (X.1012), "fidelis" (1014–15), "propria" and "accusatoria" (joined, 1016–18), "vera" (1019–20), "nuda" (1021–22), "discreta" (1023: **discreet**), "pura" (1023: **nat … for veyne glorie**, etc.), and "morosa" (1024). The confusing failure on Chaucer's part to label the third and fourth qualities by number also follows Pennaforte exactly, who, after introducing the first quality ("amara") with "prima," introduces the other three with "item" (also).

1003–5   The **foure thynges**, which are common requirements for a valid confession and absolution, may have been added here to qualify, or avert wrong application of, the quality of speediness (cf. X.998 and 1003).

1003 wikked haste: Cf. Mel VII.1054; proverbial after Chaucer (Whiting H166).

1008 but if it like to thee of thyn humilitee: see SumT III.2098 and the discussion by Patterson, Traditio 34:366–69.

1014–15   The two sentences translate the distinction Pennaforte makes of "fidelis" as meaning "of the true faith" and "having faith in Christ's forgiveness." Cain (**Caym**) and Judas are standard types of religious despair.

1027 laweful: "Decreed by law." Reference to the church decree that every adult Christian must confess his or her sins and receive Holy Communion at least once a year (Gratian, *Decretum*, ed. Friedberg, 2:887). Cf. FrT III.1308.

1031–33   Allusion to the conventional "seven works of mercy," not included in Pennaforte but commonly treated in religious handbooks; e.g., *Spec. Christiani,* ed. Gustaf Holmstedt, EETS 182, 1933, 40–47. Works of mercy are identified with **almesses** (almsgiving) by Thomas Aquinas, Summa theol., 2.2.32.2.

1040–44   Not in Pennaforte; for analogues see Petersen, Sources, 28 n. 1.

1044   That praying the Our Father deletes venial sins is a common teaching: Augustine, *Enchiridion,* 71 (PL 40:265), tr. J. F. Shaw, 1961, 84: "Now the daily prayer of the believer makes satisfaction for those sins of a momentary and trivial kind which are necessary incidents of this life."

1052 disciplyne: The twofold meaning of "teaching" and "mortification," both used by Chaucer, is common for medieval Latin "disciplina"; see Wenzel, ChauR 16:239. Pennaforte has the noun "flagella" instead.

1057–75   The impediments to Penance, the sixth major topic announced at X.83.

1068 passen as a shadwe: An image with a strong biblical background (Job 14.2: "fleeth also as a shadow"; 8.9: "our days upon earth are a shadow," etc.), but **on the wal** seems to be Chaucer's addition. See MerT IV.1315n.

1073 Agayns the seconde wanhope: A manifest slip. Chaucer speaks of the second cause (thinking that he has sinned *so ofte,* 1071) of the first kind of despair.

1076–80   The topic of **the fruyt of penaunce** was neither announced at X.83 nor treated by Pennaforte. Chaucer loosely uses material from the conventional Joys of Heaven (X.1076–79) and perhaps the beatitudes (1080). The former appear often at the end of religious manuals, such as Richard Rolle's *The Pricke of Conscience,* ed. Richard Morris, 7.7532–9624. The beatitudes are treated last in Peraldus's Summa virtutum.

Chaucer's Retraction

The explanatory notes to Chaucer's Retraction were written by Siegfried Wenzel.

This final section, usually referred to as Chaucer's Retractation or Retraction(s) (cf. X.1085), appears in this position in practically all manuscripts that contain The Parson's Tale complete (Manly-Rickert 2:471–72). Chaucer's authorship has often been questioned; it is supported by the manuscript evidence and by Thomas Gascoigne's report of Chaucer's death-bed repentance (between 1434 and 1457; reproduced and discussed by Douglas J. Wurtele, Viator 11, 1980, 335–59), though Gascoigne's report could, of course, have been derived from the Retraction itself. Such repentance is not without precedent; Augustine, Bede, Giraldus Cambrensis, Jean de Meun, Sir Lewis Clifford, and others down to the time of Tolstoy experienced similar conversions (G. L. Kittredge, MP 1, 1903–4, 12–13; J. S. P. Tatlock, PMLA 28, 1913, 521–29; on Augustine, esp. see Rosemarie P. McGeer, Ch's Open Books, 1998, 132–140). The alternatives to reading the Retraction as an expression of the poet's personal remorse are to see it either as an application to the poet-narrator of the Parson's call to penitence, the concluding step in a poem on the theme of the pilgrimage of life (see introductory note to Fragment X), or Chaucer's utilization of the *retractio* as a literary convention that includes establishing a canon of his authentic works (see Olive Sayce, MÆ 40, 1971, 230–48). Convenient surveys of critical opinions are James D. Gordon, in Sts. in Hon. of Baugh, 81–96, and Wurtele, Viator 11:335–59. Peter W. Travis (Exemplaria 3, 1991, 135–58) argues that the Retraction itself allows for a variety of readings, thus denying "interpretive closure." On the whole idea of closure in *The Canterbury Tales,* see McGerr, Ch's Open Books, 131–53, and Larry Sklute, Virtue of Necessity, who argues that Chaucer cultivates an "inconclusive form."

1081 Now preye I: If the title or rubric *Heere taketh the makere of this book his leve* is authentic, the speaker here is clearly Chaucer the poet, as he is in lines 1085–89. Otherwise, 1081–84 and 1090 (or 1091–92) can be read as spoken by the Parson and would thus form the expected conventional conclusion to his treatise on penance, which is lacking at 1079. In that case, 1085–90 would have to be an insertion into the original form of The Parson's Tale, made either by Chaucer or someone else. Such a reading has been accepted by a number of critics from Tyrwhitt (3:277) to Eliason (Lang. of Ch, 209–10) and Wurtele (Viator 11:431–43).

this litel tretys: The phrase, also used in ProMel VII.957 and 963, is normally taken to refer to The Parson's Tale, primarily because of the meaning of *tretys;* cf. James A. Work, MLN 47, 1932, 257–59; John W. Clark, ChauR 6, 1971, 152–56; and Wurtele, Viator 11:340–41. But critics who read the *Tales* as a work of moral instruction take the phrase to refer to the entire poem; see esp. Robertson, Pref to Ch, 268–69, for parallels. Cf. ProMel VII.943–52n.

1083 Romans 15.4; also quoted in NPT VII.3441–42.

1086 book of the XXV. Ladies: Evidently LGW (in which there are accounts of but ten good women). "XXV" may be a misreading for "XIX," a reading that appears in three manuscripts and was adopted by Skeat and Robinson in his first edition. See Eleanor Prescott Hammond, MLN 48, 1933, 514–16.

1087 book of the Leoun: Unknown and presumably lost. It could have been a redaction of Machaut's Dit dou Lyon (Victor Langhans, Anglia 52, 1928, 113–22) or of Deschamps's Dit du Lyon (Brusendorff, Ch Trad., 429–30), perhaps freely adapted as a compliment to Prince Lionel on the occasion of his marriage (F. M. Dear, MÆ 7, 1938, 105–12). Neither conjecture can be proven.

1092 Qui cum Patre . . . Amen: The conventional ending (which reads *per omnia saecula saeculorum*) of liturgical prayers and sermons.

Rubric compiled: The medieval concept of *compilatio* and notions of authorship are discussed by Malcolm B. Parkes, 115–41, in Med. Learning and Lit. Essays Pres. to Hunt, ed. Alexander and Gibson, 1976. On Chaucer as a compilator, see Minnis, Med. Theory of Authorship, 190–210.

Glossary

The glossary is adapted from that written by Larry D. Benson and Patricia J. Eberle for The Riverside Chaucer.

THIS GLOSSARY contains entries for those words in *The Canterbury Tales* that may present difficulties for beginning readers; words used only a few times (and for which a page gloss has been provided for each appearance) are excluded, as are those that have the same meaning and the same or closely similar forms in modern English. The vocabulary thus does not reflect Chaucer's full usage (for that see *A Glossarial Concordance to The Riverside Chaucer* and the Glossarial Database of Middle English, available online.)

The definitions are intended to illustrate some of the range of meanings and usages of Chaucer's words, but they are necessarily brief and, in entries for words that have survived in modern English, they emphasize those meanings and usages peculiar to Middle English. Where necessary, the definitions are divided into numbered subsections; these are intended for clarity and not as a record of the semantic development of the words. Variant spellings of the words cited are recorded, with the exception of variations of *i* and vocalic *y* (such as *him* and *hym*). Parentheses are used to indicate forms that appear both with and without final *-n* and *-e* or initial *y*.

The spelling chosen for the entry form is ordinarily that which is most common in the texts or, in some cases, that most likely to present difficulties to the modern reader. Cross-references are provided for all but the most obvious variants. Since this glossary is intended for readers unfamiliar with Middle English, inflected forms are fully recorded: genitives and plurals for nouns as well as those datives with a stem differing from that of the nominative and accusative (such as *lyve,* dative of *lyf*); comparatives and superlatives for adverbs and adjectives as well as plural and weak adjectives with forms differing from the singular or strong declension (such as *deve,* plural of *deef*). The infinitive (if it appears in the texts) is the entry form for verbs, and all other inflected forms are ordinarily listed. For reasons of space and clarity, verbal nouns (or gerunds) are ordinarily listed with the verb from which they derive.

For students who want to study Chaucer's usages in greater depth than a glossary such as this allows, the entry form of the *Middle English Dictionary* is listed at the end of each entry, so that the proper form can be quickly found in the MED or in the *Glossarial Concordance* or the Glossarial DataBase of Middle English, both of which use the MED entry forms.

Abbreviations

absol.	absolute	*esp.*	especially	*neg.*	negative	*prp.*	present participle
acc.	accusative	*fem.*	feminine	*nom.*	nominative	*pt.*	preterite
adj.	adjective	*fig.*	figurative sense	*Nth.*	Northern	*reflx.*	reflexive
adv.	adverb	*gen.*	genitive	*num.*	numeral	*rel.*	relative
art.	article	*imp.*	imperative	*obj.*	object	*sg.*	singular
astro.	astronomical, astrological	*impers.*	impersonal	*pass.*	passive	*subj.*	subjunctive
		indef.	indefinite	*phr.*	phrase	*super.*	superlative
aux.	auxiliary	*inf.*	infinitive	*pl.*	plural	*tr.*	transitive
comb.	combining form	*interj.*	interjection	*poss.*	possessive	*usu.*	usually
comp.	comparative	*intens.*	intensifier	*pp.*	past participle	*v.*	verb
conj.	conjunction	*interr.*	interrogative	*pr.*	present	*var.*	variant form
contr.	contraction	*intr.*	intransitive	*prec.*	preceded	*vbl. n.*	verbal noun
dat.	dative	*intro.*	introducing	*pred.*	predicate	*wk.*	weak
def.	definite	*masc.*	masculine	*prep.*	preposition	*1, 2, 3*	first, second, third person
demons.	demonstrative	*n.*	noun	*pro.*	pronoun		

Alphabetical Organization

Note that y (vocalic) is alphabetized as *i;* e.g., *dy-* follows *de-* rather than *dw-*. Doubled vowels are treated as if single; e.g., **beem** follows **bely** rather than **beden**. Past participles with *y-* and *i-* are alphabetized by the root; e.g., **ybete** is listed under **bete(n)**. Infinitives, adverbs, and adjectives with *y-* and *i-* (e.g., **ysee, ywis**) are alphabetized under *I*. Final *-e* in parentheses, indicating a variant form, is ignored in alphabetizing. Words that have forms both with and without final *-n,* indicated by parentheses, are alphabetized immediately following forms without such spellings (e.g., **be(n)** follows **be**; **clere(n)** follows **clere**).

A

a, an *indef. art.* (1) a, an I.43; (2) (before plurals modified by **certayn, fewe**) a, an, or untranslated VII.2177; (3) (before numerical units) untranslated **a twenty** I.3713, **a thritty** VII.26; (4) (after quantifying *adj.*) untranslated **everich a word** every word I.733, **many a myrthe** many mirths III.399. MED a *indef. art.*

a *num.* one I.4181. Cf. **on,** *num.* MED on *num.*

a, an *prep.* (1) on I.3516; **an heigh** on high I.1065, I.3571; (2) (in oaths) by, in I.854, I.3134 (see note), III.50. Cf. **on,** *prep.* MED on *prep.*

abayst, abaysed, abasshed *ppl.* abashed, embarrassed; afraid, perplexed II.568, IV.317. MED abaishen *v.*

abaundoune *v.* devote (oneself), yield X.713; *3 pr. sg.* **abaundoneth** VII.1577; *pr. pl.* **abawndone** X.874. MED abandonen *v.*

abedde *adv.* (1) in bed III.407, VII.177; (2) to bed III.1084, IV.1818. MED abedde *adv.*

abegge, abeye pay for *see* **abye(n)**.

abhomynable *adj.* (1) (physically) disgusting VI.471, X.122; (2) (morally) detestable VI.631, VII.3053, X.910. MED abhominable *adj.*

abhomynacioun, abhomynacion *n.* (1) **haven a. of** be disgusted by III.2179, X.687; (2) *pl.* **abhomynaciouns** disgusting practices II.88. MED abhominacioun *n.*

abyde(n) *v. intr.* (1) wait, be patient VII.1054; (2) remain, stay (in a place) I.927; (in a condition) III.255; *v. tr.* (3) wait for, await IV.119; (4) refrain V.1522; *3 pr. sg.* **abideth** VII.985, *(contr.)* **abit** VIII.1175; *pr. subj. pl.* **abyde** VI.747; *imp. sg.* **abyd(e)** III.169; *imp. pl.* **abideth** II.1175; *prp.* **abidyng(e)** I.3595, IV.757; *pp.* **abiden** I.2982. MED abiden *v.*

abye(n), abegge, abeye *v.* pay for I.3938, VI.756; **a. dere** pay a high price for I.3100; *3 pt. sg.* **aboughte** I.2303, **aboghte** X.267; *pp.* **aboght** redeemed VI.503. MED abien *v.*

abit remains *see* **abyden**.

able *adj.* (1) competent, qualified I.1241; **a. to been** capable of being I.167 (2) (of things) suitable III.1472. MED able *adj.*

aboght, abought(e) paid for *see* **abye(n)**.

aboundance, abounde *see* **habundance** and **habounde**.

about(e) *adv.* (1) all around I.621, I.3239; (2) in a circular course II.15; (3) on every side I.2133; (4) in the vicinity I.2579; (as *adj.*) nearby I.488; (5) from place to place III.653; (6) in turn I.890; (7) (as *adj.*) **ben a.** be diligent or

eager I.1142; be ready, about (to do something) III.166; be engaged or busy in III.1449; **bringen a.** cause to happen VI.821; **comen a.** come to pass VII.2174; **goon a.** attend to, be busy with III.1530, VI.158. MED abouten *adv.,* abouten *adv. as adj.*

aboute(n) *prep.* (1) around I.158 (2) in attendance on IV.1495; (3) here and there VIII.914; (4) approximately I.2198, I.3645; (5) concerning IV.2019. MED abouten *prep.*

above(n) *adv.* (1) above, overhead I.2663; (as *adj.*) overhead I.2479, III.207; at a higher level I.2204; (2) earlier (in discussion) VII.1470, VII.1785; (3) on top of I.1903, III.1065; (4) in the upper part VII.2953; (5) on the surface V.518; (6) in a higher rank or position V.795; **ben al a.** be successful, prosperous V.772; (7) in addition V.1155. MED aboven *adv.,* aboven *adv. as adj.*

above(n) *prep.* (1) higher up than, at a higher level, above I.1962; (2) higher in rank V.1048; (3) to a greater extent than, more than I.2769, III.1715; superior to IV.1376; (4) in addition to, besides VII.372. MED aboven *prep.*

abregge *v.* abridge, alleviate IV.1614; limit, curtail X.243; *vbl. n.* **abregginge** reduction X.568. MED abreggen *v.,* abregginge *ger.*

accidie *n.* sloth (the sin) X.388, 677. MED accidie *n.*

accompl- accomplish *see* **acomplice.**

accompte reckon *see* **acounte.**

accord, acord *n.* (1) good will VII.1289; (2) decision, agreement I.3082; **fallen of a.** come to an agreement V.741; **of, on a.** in agreement VI.25; (3) reconciliation X.992; (4) harmony VII.2879. MED accord *n.*

accordaunt, accordant, acordaunt *adj.* (with **to**) consonant with, in accord with I.37, V.103; harmonious with I.3363. MED accordaunt *adj.*

accorde, acorde(n) *v.* (1) agree IV.1792; **fille accorded** came to an agreement III.812; (2) be in agreement I.818; agree mutually, conspire I.3301; consent VII.1205, VII.1206; *3 pr. sg.* **acordeth** V.798; *pr. pl.* **acorde(n)** VII.947; *pr. subj. sg.* **accorde** VIII.638; *3 pt. sg.* **acorded** I.244; *prp.* **accordynge** III.924: *pp.* **acorded** I.818, **accorded** in agreement III.812, reconciled X.623. MED accorden *v.*

accuse(n) *v.* charge (with an offense), blame, reproach IV.2270, X.512; **a. gilt** make a formal charge I.1765; *2 pr. sg.* **accusest** X.796; *3 pt. sg.* **acused** I.1765; *vbl. n.* **accusynge** accusation X.512. MED accusen *v.,* accusinge *ger.*

accomplice, acomplice *v.* accomplish I.2864, X.734; fulfill, satisfy X.943; *pp.* **accompliced** VII.1132; *vbl. n.* **accomplissynge** accomplishment X.736. MED accomplisshen *v.*

acounte *v.* (1) reckon, evaluate VII.1315; (2) recount VII.2401; *pr. subj. sg.* **accompte** VII.1315. MED accounten *v.*

acquite(n) *v.* (1) make good II.37; (2) relieve (of an obligation) III.1599; fulfill (an obligation), acquit X.179; (3) *(reflx.)* act, behave IV.936; *imp. pl.* **acquiteth** II.37. MED aquiten *v.*

adoun, a-doun *adv.* (1) downward, down I.393, I.990; (2) below I.2023, III.2177. MED adoun *adv.*

advocat *n.* lawyer VII.1021, VIII.68; *pl.* **advocatz** VI.291. MED advocat *n.*

aferd, afered *pp.* afraid I.628, I.1518; leery I.4095. MED afered *ppl.*

affeccioun *n.* (1) emotion, feeling X.728; **of a.** with passion II.586; (2) desire VIII.74; *pl.* **affeccions** V.55. MED affeccioun *n.*

affermeth *v. 3 pr. sg* confirms,. declares valid VII.3125; *3 pt. sg.* **affermed** VII.1050; *pp.* **affermed** declared valid, VII.1231. MED affermen *v.*

affraye *v.* (1) arouse, startle IV.455; (2) frighten, disturb VII.400; *pp.* **affrayed** II.563. MED affraien *v.*(1)

after *adv.* (1) behind I.2571; (2) afterwards, I.989. MED after *adv.*

after *prep.* (1) (in space) after, behind, following VII.3381; for I.136, II.467; (2) (in time) after, following I.1008, I.1467, I.1653; (3) in order to get, for I.1266, I.2699, I.2762; (4) according to, in keeping with, as I.176, V.389; **a. oon** alike I.1781; in imitation of, according to, like I.731, I.3329; (5) in proportion to VII.657; (6) in *comb.* forms **after-dyner (-mete, -soper)** the period after dinner, supper VII.255, IV.1921, V.302. MED after *prep.*

after *conj.* (1) (in time) after I.3357, V.364; **a. that** after the time when I.2522, V.477, X.99; (2) to the degree that, insofar as IV.203. MED after *conj.*

agayn, ageyn, ayen, ayeyn *adv.* (1) again, once more I.1488; (2) back (to a former state) I.991; (3) in return, in exchange I.4274; in reply I.1092. MED ayen *adv.*

agayn, ageyn, ayeyn *prep.* against, in opposition to I.66; before, in anticipation V.53. MED ayen *prep.*

agains, against, agaynes, agayns, ayeynes, ayeyns *prep.* (1) (with *v.* of motion) toward II.391, III.1000; (2) in the presence of, before I.1509, VIII.1279; (3) in opposition to, against VII.2320; X.738; (4) with regard to, about X.1060; (5) in anticipation of, shortly before IX.301, X.685. MED ayenes *prep.*

agaste *v. 3 pt. sg. (reflx.)* was frightened I.2424, VII.2205; *pp.* **agast** I.4267, II.677, III.798. MED agasten *v.*

agilte(n) *v. pr. pl. (intr.)* do wrong, sin III.392, X.1043; *pr. subj. sg.* **agilte** V.150, X.946 *pp.* **agilt** X.984. MED agilten *v.*

ago(n), agoon *pp.* departed, gone I.1276, I.2802; (of time) ago I.1813, I.3537. MED agon *v.*

agreggeth *v. 3 pr. sg.* aggravates, makes worse VII.1287; *pr. pl.* **agreggen** X.892; *pt. pl.* **agreggeden** VII.1019; *pp.* **agregged** X.1017. MED aggreggen *v.*

agreved *pp.* harmed, injured I.4181; angered I.2057, IV.500. MED agreven *v.*

ay *adv.* (1) (of continuous action) always, forever IX.174; (2) (of recurring actions) every time I.63; (3) (of a changing action or state) progressively; **ay neer and neer** nearer and nearer I.4304; **ay newe** always IV.2204. MED ai *adv.*

aylen, ailleth ail *see* eyle(n).

al, all(e) *adv.* (1) completely, all I.682, I.1377; (2) (as *intens.*) **al only** solely VII.1472. MED al *adv.*

al *conj.* (with verb-subject word order) although, even though, even if I.744, I.2264; **al be (it, that, so)** even if, although I.297. MED al *conj.*

al, all(e) *adj.* all, the whole of I.584, I.3636; **alle thyng** every thing III.1475; **al tyme** high time I.3908; *gen.* **oure aller** of us all I.799. MED al *adj.*

al, all(e) *n.* all, everything I.319, VIII.773; **alle and some** one and all I.3136; **at al** (with *neg.*) in any way VII.170; **at al** (*intens.*) in every way IV.1222; **in al** completely III.46; *gen.* **aller** I.586. MED al *n.*

alday, al day *adv.* all day, all the time I.1380, I.3902; daily I.1168, VII.21. MED al dai *adv.*

alderfirst *adv. sup.* first of all VII.1203, VIII.423. MED alderfirst *adv.*

algate(s) *adv.* (1) in all ways, entirely V.246, VIII.318; surely III.1514; (2) all the while, at all times VII.374; continuously III.588; (3) in any event, at any rate VIII.1096; (4) nevertheless III.1431. MED al-gates *adv.*

alighte *v.* (1) descend from a position, dismount IV.981; (2) descend to a position, arrive VII.470; *3 pt. sg.* **alighte** I.983; *pp.* **alyght** I.722. MED alighten *v.*(1)

allye *n.* ally, kinsman VII.2403, VIII.297; *pl.* **allyes** III.301. MED allie *n.*

allye(n) *v.* (1) form an alliance VI.616 (2) join in marriage I.3945, IV.1414; *pp.* **allyed** VII.2350. MED allien *v.*

allone, alloone *adj.* alone I.1633, I.2725. MED al-one *adj.*

almesse *n.* (1) alms VII.1567; (2) benevolent or charitable action II.168, X.1029; (3) satisfaction made for sin X.814; *pl.* X.1033. MED almesse *n.*

als *adv. and conj.* (1) also I.4317, III.373; (2) as I.3870, VII.1661; (as *conj. intro. subj.*) as I.4177. Cf. **also, as.** MED also *adv.,* also *conj.*

also, alswa *adv. and conj.* (1) also I.64, I.4085; (2) as I.3870; (3) (*intro, subj.*) clause) as (or untranslated) IV.1226, VII.922; Cf. **als, as.** MED also *conj.*

alwey(s), alway *adv.* (1) always, continually I.185, I.275; (with *comp. adv.* or *adj.*) progressively I.4222; (2) **for a.** forever IV.1529. MED al-wei *adv.*

amende(n) *v.* (1) remedy, correct IV.441, VIII.84; (2) excel, surpass VII.2858; (3) change I.3066; (4) (*reflx.,* with **of**) mend one's ways, turn away from sin X.305; *3 pr. sg.* **amendeth** VII.1710; *pr. subj. sg.* **amende** III.1810; *pp.* **amended** I.910. MED amenden *v.*

amendement *n.* (1) correction, rectification X.683; (2) redress, compensation I.4185; **doon a.** make amends X.443; (3) **comen to a.** be converted to Christian living, X.606, X.903. MED amendement *n.*

amenuse *v. (tr.)* reduce, diminish X.377: belittle X.481; *3 pr. sg.* **amenuseth** X.1044; *pr. subj. sg.* **amenuse** X.377; *3 pt. sg.* **amenused** X.809. MED amenusen *v.*

ameved *3 pt. sg.* changed IV.498; *pp.* **amoeved** moved (emotionally) X.670. MED ameven *v.*

amydde(s) *adv. and prep.* in the middle of I.3810, III.2149. MED amidde adv., amidde *prep.*

amys *adj. and adv.* wrong, amiss I.3736, III.2172; badly V.1298. MED amis *adv.*

amonesteth *3 pr. sg.* (1) reminds, warns X.76; (2) recommends VII.1294; *pp.* **amonested** admonished X.583; *vbl. n.* **amonestynge** admonishment X.518. MED amonesten *v.,* amonestinge *ger.*

among(es) *prep.* among, in the presence of I.2349; **a. (al) this** meanwhile IV.785. MED amonges *prep.*

amorwe, a-morwe *adv.* in the morning I.822, III.593. MED amorwen *adv.*

amounteth *v. 3 pr. sg.* amounts to, means I.2362, I.3901. MED amounten *v.*

an on *see* **a** *prep.*

an *var.* of **a** *art., usu.* before vowels and *h-.*

and *conj.* (1) and I.24; (2) if VII.1950; (3) **and but** unless IV.174. MED and *conj.*

angle *n. (astro.)* a section of the zodiac II.304 (see note), V.263 (see note); *pl.* **anglis** V.230. MED angle *n.*(2)

angwissh *n.* anxiety, worry, anguish I.1030, IV.462. MED angwisshe *n.*

anhange *v.* hang VI.259; *pp.* **anhanged** VI.275. MED anhongen *v.*

any(e), eny *adj.* (1) any I.198, I.3269; (2) (as *n.*) any I.4120; (3) (as *adv. modifying adj.*) any I.1611; **withouten a. moore (mo)** without anything further, unhesitatingly I.1541, I.3970. MED ani *adj.*

anyght, a-nyght(es) *adv.* at night, by night I.2007, I.3214. MED anightes *adv.*

anoy *n.* (1) annoyance, discomfort VII.680; affliction, vexation X.678; (2) source of trouble, cause of annoyance VII.130; **do a.** cause trouble VII.1489; *pl.* **anoyes** X.518. MED anoi *n.*

anoye(n) *v.* (1) disturb II.492, VIII.1036, X.512; (2) damage, injure V.875; (3) **ben anoyed** be reluctant X.687; *3 pt. sg.* **anoyeth** V.875; *pr. pl.* **annoyen** V.884; *imp. pl.* **annoyeth** II.494; *pp.* **anoyed** III.1848. MED anoien *v.*

anoyous(e) *adj.* (1) troublesome, disturbing VII.1243; (2) harmful X.365. MED anoious *adj.*

anon, anoon *adv.* at once, straightway I.1708; **right a.** immediately I.2334; **right a.** immediately I.965; **(right) a. as (that)** as soon as V.615. MED an-on *adv.*

anon-right(es), anonright *adv.* (also two words) immediately VIII.169, V.1308. MED anon-rightes *adv.*

answere(n), answer *v.* answer I.3418, III.1077; *1 pr. sg.* **answere,** I.3911; *3 pr. sg.* **answereth** IV.1190; *1 & 3 pt. sg.* **answerde** III.1298, VII.3029, **answered(e)** X.30; *pt. pl.* **answerde(n)** V.377, VII.1016, **answereden** VII.1803; *vbl. n.* **answeryng** answer IV.512. MED answeren *v.,* answering *ger.*

apayd, apayed *pp.* pleased, satisfied V.1548, X.1054; **yvele a.** displeased IV.2392; **holde (oneself) yvele a.** consider (oneself) badly treated, ill-used VII.390, VIII.921. MED apaien *v.*

apaisen, apaysed(e) appease *see* **apese.**

apalled grown pale *see* **appalled.**

aparaunce appearance *see* **apparence.**

ape *n.* (1) ape, monkey I.3935; (2) fool, dupe I.3389, I.4202; (as *adj.*) IX.44; *pl.* **apes** I.706. MED ape *n.*

aperceyve(n) *v.* (1) perceive IV.600; (2) comprehend X.294; *3 pr. sg.* **aperveyveth** IV.1018. MED apperceiven *v.*

apere appear *see* **appere.**

apert *adj.* plain, clear X.649; **pryvee and a.** in private and public, in all circumstances III.1114, V.531; as *adv.* openly, publicly III.1136. MED apert *adj.*

aperteneth, apperteyneth *3 pr. sg.* (with **to, unto**) befits, is suitable to VII.981, VII.1012; *pr. pl.* **apertenen** X.83, **appertenen** I.1050; *prp.* **apertenyng,** pertaining VIII.785. MED appertenen *v.*

apese *v.* appease, alleviate, remedy IV.433, IX.98; *3 pr. sg.* **appeseth hym** grows calm VII.1861; *3 pt. sg.* placate VII.1100. MED appesen *v.*

apothecarie, pothecarie *n.* druggist VI.852, VI.859; *pl.* **apothecaries** I.425. MED apotecarie *n.*

appalled, apalled *pp.* grown pale V.365; (as *adj.*) enfeebled I.3053. MED apallen *v.*

apparail(l)e *n.* (1) apparel, trappings X.432; (2) personal characteristics IV.1208. MED appareil *n.*

apparaille(n) *v.* (1) prepare X.829; (2) dress, provide with clothing III.343; *(reflx.)* equip oneself, get ready VII.1344; *3 pr. sg.* **apparailleth** X.462; *pr. subj.* **apparaile** VII.1346; *imp. sg.* **apparaille thee** prepare yourself VII.1344; *pp.* **apparailled** X.933; *vbl. n.* **apparaillyng(e)** preparation I.2913. MED appareillen *v.,* appareilling *ger.*

apparence *n.* apparition or illusion raised by magic V.218, V.1157; *pl.* **apparences** V.1140. MED apparaunce *n.*

appere, apiere(n) *v.* appear I.2346, III.1030; *3 pr. sg.* **appeereth** X.444; *3 pt. sg.* **appeered** VII.1075. MED apperen *v.*(1)

appetit, appetyt *n.* (1) natural inclination, inherent drive IX.182, X.207; (2) desire or inclination I.1670, I.1680; (3) appetite (for food or drink) VI.546, X.818; sexual appetite III.623, IX.189; *pl.* **appetites** I.1670. MED appetit *n.*

approche *v.* (1) go or come near III.178, come into (a person's) presence X.579; (2) be concerned, involved V.556; *3 pr. sg.* **approcheth** I.2095; *3 pt. sg.* **approched** II.903; *pr. subj. sg.* **approche** III.178; *imp. sg.* **approche** VII.698; *pp.* **approched** II.903, *vbl. n.* **approchynge** X.874. MED approchen *v.,* approching *ger.*

approved, approved *pp.* tested, proven by experience VII.1163, IV.1349; (as *adj.*) VII.1155. MED appreven *v.*

appul *n.* apple I.4406, VIII.964; *pl.* **apples** I.3262. MED appel *n.*

aqueyntaunce, aqueyntance *n.* intimate acquaintance or familiarity I.245, III.1342; *pl.* **aqueyntaunces** friends, companions III.1991. MED aqueintaunce *n.*

argument *n.* (1) argument, disputation I.4123, I.4329; assertion II.228; **maken a.** reason, dispute II.1040, VII.2982; (2) an angle or arc used in calculating the position or motion of a planet V.1277; *pl.* **argumentes** IV.1619, **argumentz** V.886. MED argument *n.*

aright, aryght *adv.* (1) correctly, truly VIII.259; **it stondeth not a.** all is not well I.3426; **gon (faren) a.** go well I.3115; (2) straight, correctly I.4254; (3) exactly, precisely I.267; certainly I.189. MED a-right *adv.*

arise(n) *v.* (1) stand up, get up VI.744; rise from sleep I.1041; return from the grave III.1507; (2) *(fig.)* arise (from sin) X.683; (3) (of things) appear, occur, arise I.249, VIII.703; *3 pr. sg.* **ariseth** III.1802, *(contr.)* **arist** II.265; *pr. pl.* **aryse(n)** III.1507; *pr. subj. sg.* **arise** X.1025; *imp. sg.* **arys** I.1045; *pp.* **arisen** I.1041; *vbl. n.* **arisyng** V.1287. MED arisen *v.,* arising *ger.*

armes *n. pl.* (1) weapons or armor VII.2249; **in a.** armed I.874; (2) fighting, warfare V.811; heroic acts I.2238; **men of a.** armed soldiers V.1092; (3) heraldic devices I.1012, I.2891. MED armes *n.*

arn are *see* **be(n).**

array *n.* (1) preparation V.63; (2) arrangement II.299; order IV.262; (3) condition, state I.934, III.902; treatment IV.670; position I.3447; appearance II.775; (4) a crowd of people IV.273; (5) equipment, furnishings I.73, IV.2026; clothing I.1408, IV.965; **greet (riche) a.** splendid furnishings, magnificence I.2199, VII.2082. MED arrai *n.*

arraye *v.* (1) arrange IV.961, IV.980, VII.3037; treat I.1801; (2) plan, prepare II.1098; (3) equip I.2046; (4) decorate V.910; (5) provide, construct I.2090; *3 pr. sg.* **arraieth hym** dresses I.3689; *3 pt. sg.* **arrayed** I.2090; *pp.* **arrayed** I.1389, (as *adj.*) V.1187. MED arraien *v.*

arreest, arrest, areest *n.* (1) arrest, confinement; **in, under a.** under restraint, in custody I.1310, IV.1282; (2) seizure; **maken a.** seize, take into custody VII.2900; (3) lance-rest I.2602. MED areste *n.*

arryve(n) *v.* (1) come into port II.469; (2) reach one's destination I.922; *pp.* **arryved** II.386. MED ariven *v.*

art(e) *n.* (1) the arts curriculum of the university I.3191; academic learning I.4056; (2) craft, principles, and practice of any field I.2791, IV.35; art (of love) I.476, IV.1241; treatise on a craft V.1120; (3) skill, cunning I.4097; human skill (in contrast to nature) V.197; (4) clever scheme, plan I.2445; *pl.* **artes** V.1120. MED art *n.*(1)

arte, artow are you (art thou); *see* **be(n).**

arwe *n.* arrow III.2068, IV.1673; *pl.* **arwes** I.104. MED arwe *n.*

as *adv.* and *conj.* (1) as, in the way that, like I.152, I.187; **be as be may** be that as it may II.1012; (2) (with *subj.*) as if, as though I.2340; as, or (*introducing subj.* and *imp.* clauses) untranslated (e.g., **as beth,** be IV.7); (in oaths) so, as IV.136; (3) (as intensifier, with *adv.*) **as faste** very quickly VIII.1235; **as nowe (as nowthe)** right now, at present I.462, I.2264; **as swithe** immediately, quickly II.637; (with comparisons) as I.263; (4) (with clauses describing contrasting circumstance) although, in spite of the fact that III.1949; (5) (with clauses giving a reason for an action) since, because, as for, as much as X.387; (6) (of reference) as (or untranslated) **as by** I.244; so as I.39; **as of** taking into consideration I.87; **as who seith** as some say, one says VII.1084; (7) (of time) while, when, as IV.234; (8) (correlative) **also . . . as** III.2134; cf. **als, also.** MED as *conj.*

ascende *v.* *(astro.)* rise above the horizon X.11; *prp.* **ascendyng** V.264; *pp.* **ascended** VII.2857. MED ascenden *v.*

ashamed *pp.* ashamed, disgraced, embarrassed I.2667, X.152, X.1061. MED ashamed *ppl.*

asonder *adv.* (1) apart I.491, II.1157; (2) different, distinguishable III.1674. MED asonder *adv.* & *adj.*

assay *n.* (1) trial III.290, IV.621; (2) attempt, effort VIII.1249. *pl.* **assayes** IV.697. MED assai *n.*

assaye(n) *v.* (1) test IV.454; tempt VII.1446; (2) investigate, experience IV.1740; try out VII.1959; (3) try, attempt V.1567, VIII.1252; *pr. subj. sg.* **assaye** IV.1229; *imp. sg.* **assay** VII.1216; *imp. pl.* **assayeth** IV.1740; *pp.* **assayed** III.286. MED assaien *v.*

assaut *n.* attack, assault I.989; *pl.* **assautes** VII.1423. MED assaut *n.*

assemble(e) *n.* (1) assembly, gathering II.403; (2) sexual congress X.907. MED assemble *n.*

assemble(n) *v.* (1) *(intr.)* come together II.328; **a. flessly** have sexual intercourse X.939; combine VIII.50; (2) *(tr.)* bring together, combine I.1286; *pr. subj. pl.* **assemble** X.943; *pp.* **assembled** I.717; *vbl. n.* **assemblynge** assembly VII.1241; sexual congress X.904. MED assemblen *v.*(1), assemblinge *ger.*

assent *n.* (1) consent I.852, II.35; **by noon a.** not at all I.945; **by oon a.** unanimously I.777, I.852; (2) opinion I.3075; will, intent I.852; **oon of** (someone's) in league (with someone) VI.758. MED assent *n.*

assente *v.* (1) assent, agree to I.374; consent to IV.129, IV.150; (2) come to an agreement X.61; approve VI.146; **ben a.** be agreed IV.1575; (3) submit IV.494; *1 pr. sg.*

assente II.39; *pr. pl.* **assenten** II.344; *pr. subj. sg.* **assente** IV.494; *2 pt. sg.* **assentedest** VIII.233; *3 pt. sg.* **assented** VII.1872; *pt. pl.* **assenteden** IV.1570; *prp.* **assentynge** II.342; *pp.* **assented** VI.146. MED assenten *v.*

assoille *v.* absolve VI.933, VI.939; *1 pr. sg.* **assoille** VI.387; *imp. pl.* resolve, explain IV.1654. *vbl. n.* **assoillyng** absolution I.661. MED assoilen *v.*, assoiling *ger.*

assure *v.* promise, pledge IV.1983; *1 pr. sg.* **assure** IV.1983; *3 pr. sg.* **assureth** guarantees I.926; **asseureth** makes confident IV.93; *pr. pl.* **assure(n)** bind I.1924; *pr. subj. pl.* **assure** pledge IV.165; *3 pt. sg.* **assured** made confident VII.2188; *pp.* **assured** entrusted IV.2191. MED assuren *v.*

asterte *v.* escape IV.414; escape one's grasp III.1314; *3 pt. sg.* **asterted** II.437; *pp.* **astert** I.1592. MED asterten *v.*

astoned *3 pt. sing.* took by surprise IV.316; *pp.* upset VI.316; benumbed, paralyzed X.233. MED astoned *ppl.*

astrologien *n.* astronomer III.324. MED astrologien *n.*

asure *n.* azure IV.254, VII.2862. MED asur *n.*(1)

aswage *v.* (1) lessen, diminish IV.2082, V.835; (2) appease, placate VII.2644. MED asswagen *v.*

aswowne *adv.* in a faint I.3828, IV.1079. MED aswouen *adj.* & *adv.*

atones *adv.* at once, immediately II.670, IV.1178; at the same time I.1836; *(Nth.)* **atanes** I.4074. MED at-ones *adv.*

atte *prep.* and *contr.* of **at the** I.29, I.125. MED atte *prep.*

atteyne, attayne *v.* attain, achieve IV.447, V.775. MED atteinen *v.*

attemperaunce, attemperance *n.* moderation VII.1535; temperance VI.46. MED attempraunce *n.*

attempree *adj.* moderate, temperate VII.988, X.932. MED attempre *adj.*

attemprely, atemprely *adv.* moderately, in due measure VII.1380, X.861. MED attempreli *adv.*

atwo, a-two *adv.* in two I.3820; asunder X.888. MED atwo *adv.*

auctorite(e) *n.* (1) legal power VIII.471; authority IV.1597; power to inspire or convince VII.1165, VII.2975; (2) written authority, an authoritative passage or statement I.3000, IV.1658; an authoritative work III.1; *pl.* **auctoritees** III.1276. MED auctorite *n.*

auctour *n.* (1) creator, originator X.882; (2) author, authority IX.359; *pl.* **auctours** III.1212. MED auctour *n.*

audience *n.* (1) hearing, ability to hear IV.329; (2) **in a.** in the presence of an audience, aloud III.1032, VIII.466; **in open, general a.** publicly II.673; (3) opportunity to be heard IV.104, X.39. MED audience *n.*

aught, oght *pro.* anything I.1571, II.738; **for a. I woot, se** for all I know, see I.389. MED ought *pron.*

aught, oght, ought *adv.* at all, in any way I.3045, II.1034. MED ought *adv.*

auter *n.* altar I.2252, I.2292. MED auter *n.*

availle(n), avayle *v.* (1) *(tr.)* help, benefit III.1366, X.241; *(impers.)* help, be of use to I.3040, III.1324; (2) do good, be helpful, be of use IV.1194; (3) *(intr.)* be successful, prosper I.2401; **a. agayn** prevail against X.1047; *3 pr. sg.* **availleth** I.3040, **avayleth** X.308; *pr. pl.* **availle(n)** X.241, X.243. MED availen *v.*

avaunce(n) *v. tr.* promote X.786; *(intr.)* be profitable I.246; *pp.* **avaunced** advanced VI.410. MED avauncen *v.*

avaunt *n.* in phrase **make a.** dare assert, boast I.227, IV.1457, V.1576. MED avaunt *n.*

avauntage, avantage *n.* (1) supremacy, superiority I.1293, I.2447; advantage II.216; (as *pred.*) advantageous II.146; **at his a.** in the best position V.772; (2) benefit X.609; **don a.** benefit II.729; (3) monetary gain X.851. MED avauntage *n.*

avante(n) *v. (reflx.)* boast III.403, VII.1551; *1 pr. sg.* **avaunte** III.403; *imp. sg,* **avaunte** X.320; *vbl. n.* **avauntyng(e)** boasting I.3884, X.391. MED avaunten *v.,* avaunting *ger.*

avauntour *n.* boaster X.393. MED avauntour *n.*

aventure *n.* (1) fortune, chance I.1465, I.1506, I.1516; **taken a.** take one's chances I.1186, III.1224; **by (of) a.** by chance, accidentally I.1516, V.1508; (2) event, experience VII.3186; mishap I.2722, VI.934; (3) danger, risk IV.1877; **in a.** uncertain X.1068; **putten in a.** wager VIII.946; (4) exploit, adventure V.659; *pl.* **aventures** events I.795. MED aventure *n.*

avys *n.* (1) thinking, deliberation; **taken a.** ponder, think over; judgment, advice I.1868, X.54; (2) discussion, consultation I.786. MED avis **n.**

avyse *v.* (1) look at IV.238; (2) *(reflx.)* bethink oneself, consider IV.350, VIII.572; *1 pr. sg.* **avyse** IV.797; *3 pr. sg.* **avyseth** III.1228; *pr. pl.* **avyse** consider IV.1988; *imp. sg.* **avyse thee** be forewarned I.4188; *imp. pl.* **avyseth yow** be forewarned I.3185; *prp.* **avysynge** deliberating VI.124; *pp.* **avysed** considered VIII.572; **be well avysed** be forewarned, take heed I.3584; **yvele avysed** ill-considered IX.335. MED avisen *v.*

avysely *adv.* carefully VII.1298; discreetly IX.327. MED aviseli *adv.*

avysement *n.* deliberation, consultation IV.1531, X.602; **of ful a.** after careful consideration II.86; **taken a.** take thought VII.1751. MED avisement *n.*

avisioun, avision *n.* dream, vision III.1858, VII.3114; account of a dream VII.3123. MED avisioun *n.*

avow *n.* vow I.2237, I.2414. MED avoue *n.*

avowtier *n.* adulterer III.1372; *pl.* **avowtiers** X.841. MED avouter *n.*

avowtrye, avoutrie *n.* adultery III.1306, X.840. MED avoutrie *n.*

awayt *n.* ambush III.1627, VII.3225; **in a.** under surveillance VII.2725, IX.149. MED awaite *n.*

awayteth *v. 3 pr. sg.* waits, waits for V.1299, VII.586; *prp.* **awaityng(e) on** observing III.2052; waiting for I.3642. MED awaiten *v.*

awake(n) *v.* wake up, awake I.1474, V.476; *imp. sg.* **awak** I.3478; *imp. pl.* **awaketh** I.3700; *3 pt. sg.* **awaked(e)** I.2523, **awook** I.3364; *pp.* **awaked** IV.1957. MED awaken *v.*

awey(e), away *adv.* away I.1180, I.2318; (as *adj.*) gone I.4071, V.1064. MED awei *adv.*

awen *(Nth. form)* own; *see* **owen(e)** *adj.*

axe(n), asken *v.* (1) ask (a question), inquire IV.696; make a request I.2239, II.101; **a. conseil** seek advice VII.1156; (2) demand, order IV.348, VI.24; (3) (of things) require VII.1443; (4) seek VII.1162; *1 pr. sg.* **axe** I.1347; **aske** I.2420; *3 pr. sg.* **asketh** I.2777; **axeth** IV.25; *pr. pl.* **axen** VII.1029; **asken** VII.1091; *pr. subj. sg.* **aske** II.102; *imp. pl.* **axe** X.705; *1 & 3 pt. sg.* **axed** I.3661, VIII.542; **asked** V.1510; *pt. pl.* **axed** VIII.430; **asked** I.3195; *prp.* **axinge** VII.1774; *vbl. n.* **axyng(e)** request I.1826, VIII.423. MED asken *v.,* askinge *ger.*

ayen, ayeyn again *see* **agayn.**

ayeyn(s), ayen(s) against *see* **agains.**

B

bacheler, bachiler *n.* (1) young man I.80, IX.107; (2) young knight in the service of another knight I.3085; (3) **b. of lawe** holder of a first university degree in law V.1126; *pl.* **bacheleris** unmarried men IV.1274. MED bacheler *n.*

bacoun, bacon *n.* cured pork III.1753, VII.2845. MED bacoun *n.*

bad(e) asked *see* **bidde.**

badde *adj.* (1) wicked, evil I.3155, IV.1542; dishonorable IV.1593; (2) inferior, poor VII.2422; debased IV.1167; (3) inadequate, worthless IV.1608; *comp.* **badder** V.224. MED badde *adj.*

bagges *n. pl.* money-bags II.124, VII.82. MED bagge *n.*(1)

bailly, baillif *n.* steward, manager of a farm or manor I.603, II.1392. MED baillif *n.*

bak *n.* back I.1050, I.2143. MED bak *n.*

bake *v.* bake I.384; *pp.* (as *adj.*) **(y)bake** baked I.4312. MED baken *v.*

bal *n.* ball I.2614. MED bal *n.*

baner(e) *n.* personal banner I.966, I.976, I.2410. MED banere *n.*

bar(e), baar, baren bore *see* **bere(n).**

bare *adj.* (1) not covered I.683, I.1758, I.2877; (2) unadorned, simple V.720; (3) deprived (of) IV.1548; (4) empty, vacant I.4390; inadequate, useless III.1480. MED bar *adj.*

bareyne *adj.* (1) sterile, childless IV.448, X.576; (2) fruitless, leafless I.1977; bare, desolate II.68, III.372; (4) devoid I.1244. MED baraine *adj.*

barge *n.* (1) medium-sized seagoing sailing vessel I.410, V.850; (2) barge, river boat I.3550, V.1144. MED barge *n.*

barre *n.* bar I.1075; *pl.* **barres** bars I.329; strips of precious metal or silk X.433; stripes I.329. MED barre *n.*

bataille, bataile *n.* battle I.879, I.988; duel I.1609; *pl.* **batailles** I.61. MED bataille *n.*

bathe *adj. Nth. var.* of **both** both I.4087, I.4112.

baude *n.* bawd, pimp III.1354; *pl.* **bawdes** III.1339, **baudes** VI.479. MED baude *n.*

be *see* **by, be.**

bee *n.* bee, the insect; *pl.* **been** V.204; **bees** VII.3392. MED be *n.*

be(n), bee(n) *v.* to be I.813, I.2235, VIII.228; *1 pr. sg.* **am** I.767, *(Nth.)* **is** I.4031; *2 pr. sg.* **art** I.1154, (with *pro.*) **artow** I.1141, (with *pro.* unstressed) **arte** X.23, *(Nth.)* **is** I.4089; *3 pr. sg.* **is** II.260, **ys** I.524; *pr. pl.* **ar(e)** II.286, VII.350, **arn** IV.342, **been** I.887, **be(n)** I.924, I.782; *pr. subj. sg.* **be(e)** I.733, VIII.1392; **be as be may** be as it may, however it may be VII.2129, VIII.935; *pr. subj. pl.* **be** I.840; *imp. sg.* **be** IV.1052; *imp. pl.* **beeth** VII.207, **beth** IV.7; *1 & 3 pt. sg.* **was** I.116; *2 pt. sg.* **were** II.366, **weere** VII.2660; *pt. pl.* **were(n)** I.18, I.28, *pt. subj. sg.* **were** I.737; *pp.* **be(n)** I.929, **been(e)** I.359, III.7. **ybeen** VII.3297; *vbl. n.* **beynge** being VIII.340. MED ben *v.,* being *ger.*

beaute(e), beute *n.* beauty II.162, V.34. MED beaute *n.*

beede *v.* offer VIII.1065; *3 pr. sg.* **bedeth** IV.1784; *pr. pl.* **beede** IV.360; *pp.* **bode(n)** commanded III.1030. MED beden *v.*

bede(n) ask *see* **bidde.**

beye, beyeth buy *see* **bye(n).**

beek *n.* beak V.418, V.637. MED bek *n.*(3)

bely *n.* (1) belly III.2267, VI.534; **b.-naked** stark naked IV.1326; (2) a bellows X.351. MED beli *n.*

ben, been be *see* **be(n).**

beem *n.* beam, timber crosspiece VII.3172; *pl.* **bemes** VII.2942. MED bem *n.*

bene *n.* bean I.3772, II.94. MED bene *n.*(1)

benedicite(e) *interj.* (the Lord) bless you I.2115, I.3768. MED benedicite *interj.*

benygne, benigne, benyngne *adj.* (1) (of persons) gracious, kind I.518, I.2215, IV.1097; (2) (of face, expression, *etc.*) showing kindness IV.554, IV.1742; (3) (of the weather) mild V.52. MED benigne *adj.*

benignely, benyngnely *adv.* graciously IV.2093, IV.2186. MED benigneli *adv.*

benignitee, benygnytee, benyngnytee *n.* good will, kindness IV.929, X.455; goodness II.446. MED benignite *n.*

bente *v. 3 pt. sg.* bent IX.264; *pp.* **bent(e)** arched, bent I.3246. MED benden *v.*(1)

berd, beerd *n.* (1) beard I.270, I.332; (2) trick I.3742; **make a b.** delude, trick I.4096, III.361. MED berd *n.*(1)

bere *n.* bear I.1640, I.2058; *pl.* **beres** I.2018. MED bere *n.*(1)

beere *n.* bier I.2871, I.2877. MED bere *n.*(8)

bere(n) *v.* (1) bear, carry I.1422, II.457; spread abroad X.814; **b. a burdoun** carry the accompaniment (in music) I.673, I.4165; (2) wear I.158, I.3265, V.433; (3) hold up I.1387, IV.1358; (4) **b. doun** put down, overthrow I.3831; pierce I.2256; (5) bear, endure VII.1464; **b. lif** live IV.1552; **b. sikly** take ill, resent IV.625; (6) bear, give birth to IV.612; (7) *(reflx.)* conduct oneself, behave I.1405, I.1523, III.1108; (8) **b. companie** accompany VIII.315, X.967; (9) **b. on hand** accuse III.393; deceive, convince of a falsehood III.232; **b. witnesse** support, testify VIII.336; *1 pr. sg.* **bere** II.1127; *2 pr. sg.* **berest** X.796; *3 pr. sg.* **bereth** I.796, **berth** II.620; *pr. pl.* **bere(n)** V.1367; *pr. subj. sg.* **bere** I.2547; *imp. sg.* **ber(e)** I.2760, I.3397; *1 & 3 pt. sg.* **bar(e)** I.105, III.575, **baar** I.108, III.1224, **beer** VII.3336; *pt. pl.* **baren** I.721, bar VII.2613; *pp.* **bore(n)** I.378, V.178; **(y)born** I.1019, I.1073, **borne** (as *adj.*) IV.1790; *vbl. n.* **beryng(e)** conduct, bearing IV.1604, VI.47. MED beren *v.*(1), bering *ger.*

berye *n.* berry I.207, I.4368; *pl.* **beryis** VII.2965. MED berie *n.*

berie, burye(n) *v.* bury III.500, VI.884, VII.638; *3 pr. sg.* **burieth** IV.571; *3 pt. sg.* **buryed** VIII.407; *pt. pl.* **buryed** VIII.548; *pp.* **beryed** buried VI.405, **(y)buryed** I.946, IV.1178; *vbl. n.* (as *adj.*) **buryinge** VIII.409. MED birien *v.*, biriinge *ger.*

berne *n.* barn I.3258, VI.397; *pl.* **bernes** III.871. MED bern *n.*(2)

best, beest *n.* beast III.1034, V.264; *pl.* **beestes** I.2929. MED beste *n.*

best(e) *adj. sup.* (and as *n.*) (1) best I.252, I.3056; (2) (as *n.*) best person, thing, idea, etc. I.1614; **oure b.** (**my,** *etc.*) what is best for us (**me,** *etc.*) IV.1161; **atte beste** in the best way, most excellently I.29; **with the b.** ranking with the highest, among the finest II.76. MED best *adj. as n.*

best(e) *adv. sup.* most I.533; most excellently I.2201, V.932. MED beste *adv.*

bet *adj. comp.* (1) better IV.2214; (as *adv.*) more I.242; **b. is it** is better IV.1419, V.1422; **hem were b.** they should VII.722; (2) (as *n.*) **him fil no bet** he had no better luck I.744. Cf. **beter.** MED bet *adj. & adv.*

bet *adv. comp.* better I.242, I.3711; **go bet** go quickly VI.667; **the b.** the better III.1951; **what wol ye b. than wel?** why not leave well enough alone? I.3370, VIII.1283. Cf. **bettre.** MED bet *adj. & adv.*

beete *v.* (1) mend I.3927; relieve X.421; (2) kindle, feed (a fire) I.2253; *pt. pl.* **betten** kindled VIII.518. MED beten *v.*(2)

bete(n) *v.* (1) beat, flog VIII.405, X.838; (2) hammer (metal) I.2162, VI.17; (3) embroider or paint, adorn I.979; *1 pr. sg.* **bete** VII.1897; *3 pr. sg.* **beteth** V.766; *pr. pl.* **beete** I.4308; *pr. subj. sg.* **bete** VI.14; *pt. pl.* **bette(n)** I.4308, VII.971; *pp.* **bete(n)** III.511, VII.542, **ybet(e)** I.3759, III.1285, (as *adj.*) I.2162; **(y)beten** V.414, VII.542. MED beten *v.*(1)

beter, bettre, better *adj.* better, more I.256, I.1254. Cf. **bet** *adj.* MED bettre *adj.*

beth, beeth be *see* **be(n).**

betten *see* **bete(n)** *v.* (beat), a **beete** *v.* (mend)

bettre, better *adv.* I.342, I.608; Cf. **bet** *adv.* MED bettre *adv.*

by, be *prep.* (1) (location) near, by I.112, I.4036; in, in the direction of I.388; **by and by** side by side I.1011; (2) (of time) at, in, on I.334, III.755; during I.97; (3) (agency) by, by means of I.25; (4) (of reference) **as by his facultee** in view of his profession I.244; **spak (sey) by** said (say) this about III.229; (in oaths) I.120; (5) (of number) by, in groups of V.354; MED bi *prep.*

bicome(n), become *v.* (1) become III.1644, VI.698; (2) suit, befit; *3 pt. sg.* **becam** III.603; *pp.* **bicomen** IV.2098. MED bicomen *v.*

bidde *v.* (1) ask, pray, say a prayer I.3641, VIII.140; (2) demand, order III.28; (3) advise, urge I.3228; (4) **b. farwel** say goodbye VII.320; *1 pr. sg.* **bidde** IV.1387; *3 pr. sg.* **biddeth** I.3641, *(contr.)* **bit** IV.1377; *pr. pl.* **bidden** X.506; *imp. pl.* **bidde** V.321; *1 & 3 pt. sg.* **bad** V.1212, VIII.513; *pt. pl.* **bad(e)** I.787, X.65; *prp.* **biddynge** VIII.140; *pp.* **bidde** II.440; *vbl. n.* **biddyng** command, request VIII.1109. MED bidden *v.*, biddinge *ger.*

byde *v.* (1) stay, remain, linger I.4237; (2) wait I.1576; *3 pt. sg.* **bood** I.4399. Cf. **abyde(n).** MED biden *v.*

bye(n), beye *v.* buy, purchase III.167, VII.56, VII.272; **b. dere** pay a high price for II.420; *3 pr. sg.* **byeth** VII.303; **beyeth** X.784; *pr. pl.* **bye(n)** III.287, X.772; *3 pt. sg.* **boghte** I.2088, **boughte** VI.293; *pt. pl.* **boghte** II.420; *pp.* **(y)boght** I.3836, IV.1648, **boghte** X.154; *vbl. n.* **byynge** buying I.569. MED bien *v.*, biinge *ger.*

bifalle, befalle *v.* (1) befall, happen, occur I.1805; (2) **faire yow b.** good luck to you X.68; *3 pt. sg.* **bifalleth** IV.449; *pr. subj. sg.* **befalle** X.68; *3 pr. sg.* **byeth** VII.332; **bifil** (with omission of subject) it happened I.19; *pt. subj. sg.* **bifelle** IV.136; *pp.* **bifalle(n)** I.795. MED bifallen *v.*

biforn, byfore(n), bifoore *adv.* (1) (time) before, previously I.1376, II.1184, VI.393; (2) (space) in front I.371; **al b.** first IV.446; (as *conj.*) **b. that** X.233. MED biforen *adv.*, biforen *conj.*

biforn, bifore(n) *prep.* (1) (space) before, in front of I.100; ahead of II.848; (2) (time) before III.2223. MED biforen *prep.*

bigyle *v.* (1) deceive, delude I.3300, I.3404; defraud I.4048; betray VI.274; (2) lead into error or sin II.582; (3) *2 pr. sg.* (with *pro.*) **bigilestow** X.1022; *pr. subj. sg.* **bigyle** VII.3428; *pt. pl.* **bigiled** II.549; *pp.* **bigyled** I.3914. MED bigilen *v.*

bigynne *v.* (1) begin I.42, I.428; (2) **b. a question** put a question VIII.428; (3) (as *aux.*; cf. **gynne**) does, did VII.1043, VII.2682; *3 pr. sg.* **bigynneth** I.3614; *pr. pl.* **begynne(n)** VII.1650, VIII.1096; *pr. subj. sg.* **bigynne** VII.1344; *imp. sg.* **bigynne** VIII.1121; *1 & 3 pt. sg.* **bigan(ne)** I.44, I.1354; *1 pr. sg.* **bigynne** III.1175; *2 pr. sg.* **bigonne** VIII.442; *pt. pl.* **bigonne(n)** V.1015; **bigan** III.185; *pp.* **bigonne(n)** I.52, VII.682; *vbl. n.* **bigynnyng** I.3007. MED biginnen *v.*, biginninge *ger.*

bigon *v. pp.* (**wo,** *etc.*) in a woeful state, II.918, III.606. MED bigon *v.*

biheete assure *see* **byhote.**

biheste, biheeste *n.* promise II.41, V.1163; *pl.* **bihestes** VII.1229. MED biheste *n.*

bihighte(n) promised *see* **byhote.**

biholde *v. 1 pr. sg.* (1) look at, gaze on I.1301; (2) observe, notice, consider VII.1878; *imp.* **bihoold** VI.639; *3 pt. sg.* **biheeld** IX.241; *pp.* **biholde(n)** VIII.179. MED biholden *v.*

byhote *v. 1 pr. sg.* **bihote** promise I.1854; **biheete** assure VIII.707; *3 pr. sg.* **biheteth** X.379; **bihooteth** X.291; *1 & 3 pt. sg.* **bihight(e)** V.788, V.1559; *pt. pl.* **bihighten** V.1327; *pp.* **bihight** X.251. MED bihoten *v.*

bihoveth *v. 3 pr. sg.* is appropriate to, befits V.602; **bihooveth** VII.1170; (with *dat.*) **b. him** (**hire,** *etc.*) it behooves him (her, *etc.*) V.602; he (she, *etc.*) needs to, must V.1359; **boes** *(Nth.)* I.4027; *pr. pl.* **bihoven** X.83. MED bihoven *v.*

biknowe(n) *v.* make known, confess X.170; reveal II.886; *3 pr. sg.* **biknoweth** X.481; *pt. pl.* **biknewe** VII.3061. MED biknouen *v.*

bileve, bileeve *n.* belief I.3456, VIII.63. MED bileve *n.*

bileve *v.* believe I.3162; *1 pr. sg.* **bileeve** VII.1408; *pr. pl.* **bileeve(n)** III.1178, X.605; *imp. pl.* **bileveth** VII.1511, VIII.1047. MED bileven *v.*(2)

bille *n.* (1) formal document IV.1937; (2) formal plea or charge VI.166; formal petition; **putten the b.** submit a petition IV.1971; (3) **b. of somonce** a summons III.1586. MED bille *n.*

bilongeth *v. 3 pr. sg.* belongs, pertains IV.1459, VII.2630; *pr. pl.* **bilongen** X.319. MED bilongen *v.*

bynde *v.* (1) tie, bind I.4070, I.4082; fetter (a prisoner) IX.8; (2) bind (a book) III.681; assume an obligation I.2414; **ben bounde(n)** be under obligation I.1149, X.1008; *pr. pl.* **bynden** VII.1747; *pr. subj. sg.* **bynde** IV.1205; *3 pt. sg.* **bond** I.2991; **boond** I.4082; *pt. pl.* **bounde** VII.2070; *pp.* **ybounde(n)** I.1149, I.4070; (as *adj.*) I.2151; **bounde(n)** I.1316, X.686; *vbl. n.* **byndyng** I.1304. MED binden *v.*, bindinge *ger.*

bynethe(n) *prep.* and *adv.* below, beneath I.4041, III.2142. MED binethen *adv.*, binethen *prep.*

bynyme *v.* take away, remove; *3 pr. sg.* **bynymeth** X.335, X.560. MED binimen *v.*

biquethe *v.* bequeath I.2768, III.1121; *1 pr. sg.* **biquethe** I.2768; *pp.* **biquethe** III.1164. MED biquethen *v.*

bireve(n) *v.* take away, deprive; *3 pr. sg.* **bireveth** III.2059; *pr. pl.* **bireven** X.902; *3 pt. sg.* **birafte** II.83; *pp.* **biraft** I.1361; **bireved** III.2071. MED bireven *v.*

biseged *pp.* besieged VII.1099, VII.2324. MED bisegen *v.*

biseken *v.* beseech, beg VII.1116; *1 pr. sg.* **biseche** I.3600; **biseeke** III.1669; *3 pr. sg.* **bisecheth** V.1574; *pr. pl.* **biseke(n)** I.918, VII.1743; *pr. subj. pl.* **biseche** VIII.55; *3 pt. sg.* **bisoght(e)** II.516; **bisoughte** II.1094; *pt. pl.* **bisoght** I.4118; *prp.* **bisechyng(e)** II.379; **bisekynge** IV.178. MED bisechen *v.*

bisette *v. 3 pr. sg.* of **bisetten** employed I.279; *pt. pl.* **bisette** employed, used (time) VII.375; *pp.* **biset** I.3299, bestowed X.366; set, arranged I.3012; **yvel biset** ill used I.3715; **wel . . . beset** well employed I.279. MED bisetten *v.*

bisy *adj.* (1) active, busy I.321; occupied IV.1029; diligent, industrious I.1491, IV.2422; (2) attentive, solicitous IV.603; (3) intense, continual I.2320, IV.134; **b. cure** diligence I.2853; *comp.* **bisier** I.322. MED bisi *adj.*

biside(s) *adv.* (1) at the side, along with V.1241; (2) **ther b.** nearby I.1478, II.398; (3) **gon b.** go astray VIII.1416; (4) in addition, moreover IV.416, V.1241. MED bisides *adv.*

biside(s) *prep.* (1) next to, by the side of V.649, X.702; alongside of I.874, IV.777; (2) near, close to I.445, I.620; **hym bisides** near at hand I.402. MED bisides *prep.*

bisye *v. (reflx.)* concern oneself, be busy about VIII.758, VIII.1258, VIII.1442; *3 pr. sg.* **bisieth** VIII.1258; *imp. sg.* **bisye** VII.1487; *3 pt. sg.* **bisyed** VIII.1146. MED bisien *v.*

bisily *adv.* (1) diligently, carefully I.3763; intently II.1095; (2) zealously, eagerly I.1883, V.88; earnestly, anxiously I.301. MED bisili *adv.*

bisinesse *n.* (1) work, activity I.3654, VI.399; **diden b.** were occupied in, worked at I.1007; (2) task, undertaking IV.1015, VIII.1212; **doon b.** accomplish a task IV.1904; (3) diligence, effort I.520; (4) solicitude, attentiveness I.1928, III.933. MED bisinesse *n.*

bisoght(e), bisoughte *see* **biseken.**

bistowe *v.* bestow, give I.3981, III.113; *pp.* **bistowed** VII.419. MED bistouen *v.*

bit asks *see* **bidde.**

bitake, betake *v. 1 pr. sg.* (1) give, grant, hand over VIII.541; (2) entrust IV.559, X.1043; *3 pt. sg.* **bitook** VIII.541. MED bitaken *v.*

byte *v.* (1) pierce, cut I.2634, I.2640, V.153; (2) bite, sting I.3745, III.386; (3) burn, corrode I.631; *pr. pl.* **byte** I.2634; *3 pt. sg.* **boot** VII.2601; *prp.* (as *adj.*) **bitynge** piercing, sharp I.2546. MED biten *v.*(1)

bithynken *v.* (often *reflx.*) (1) think, reflect, realize X.171; (2) think of, imagine III.772; (3) remember I.4403, X.700; *1 pr. sg.* **bethenke** VII.1445; *3 pr. sg.* **bithynketh** X.352; *3 pt. sg.* **bythoughte** I.4403; *pp.* **am bythoght** have in mind I.767. MED bithinken *v.*

bityde *v.* happen I.3450; *3 pr. sg.* **bitydeth** VII.1224; *pr. pl.* **bityden** VII.1225; *pr. subj. sg.* **bytyde** IV.306; *pt. pl.* **bityden** VII.1225; *pt. sg.* **bityd** III.2191. MED bitiden *v.*

bitokeneth, bitokneth *v. 3 pr. sg.* betokens, is a sign of III.581, VII.2752. MED bitoknen *v.*

bitrayen *v. pr. pl.* **bitrayen** betray, deceive VIII.897; *pp.* **bitrayed** VIII.1092. MED bitraien *v.*

bitrayseth *3 pr. sg.* betrays VI.92; *pr. pl.* **bytrayse** X.616; *pp.* **bitraysed** VII.2380. MED bitraishen *v.*

bitwene *prep.* between I.2859, I.3105. MED bitwene *prep.*

bitwix, bitwixe(n) *prep.* between I.277, I.1180; among II.1115. MED bitwixe *prep.*

biwaille(n), biwayle(n) *v.* bewail, lament II.26, IV.1381, X.87; *pp.* **biwailled** IV.530. MED biwailen *v.*

biwreye(n) *v.* (1) betray (someone's confidence) III.974, VIII.150; (2) reveal VII.1145, VIII.147; *2 pr. sg.* **biwreyest** II.773; *imp. sg.* **biwreye** III.974; *1 pt. sg.* **biwreyed** III.533; *pp.* **biwreyed** IX.352; *vbl. n.* **biwreyyng** revealing VII.1148. MED biwreien *v.,* biwreiing *ger.*

blame *n.* (1) censure, criticism, reproach II.827; **putten out of b.** relieve (someone) of a charge I.3185; (2) guilt VIII.455; **ben to b.** be at fault, be guilty I.375, I.3710; blameworthy VIII.1327; **for b.** for fear of doing wrong II.860; **rennen in a b.** make a mistake VIII.905. MED blame *n.*

blame *v.* rebuke, blame, reproach VII.3261; *1 pr. sg.* **blame** II.372; *2 pr. sg.* **blamest** II.106; *3 pr. sg.* **blameth** X.580; *pr. pl.* **blamen** VII.1095; *imp. pl.* **blameth** I.3181; *3 pt. sg.* **blamed** I.3863; *pt. pl.* IV.1471; *pp.* **(y)blamed** VII.1093, VII.2817. MED blamen *v.*

blede *v.* bleed VII.2509; *pr. pl.* **blede** I.1801; *3 pr. sg.* **blede** V.1194, *pr. subj. pl.* **bledde** I.145; *prp.* **bledynge** VI.581. MED bleden *v.*

blent *v. 3 pt. sg. (contr.)* blinds, deceives VIII.1391; *pp.* **(y)blent** deceived I.3808, IV.2113. MED blenden *v.*(1)

blesse(n), blisse *v.* (1) bless IV.552, VII.1118; (2) *(reflx.)* cross oneself I.3448; *3 pr. sg.* **blesseth** II.449, **blisseth** II.868; *pr. subj. sg.* **blesse** I.3484; *3 pt. sg.* **blessed** IV.1916; *prp.* **blessynge** III.869; *pp.* **(y)blessed** I.3218, IV.1819; *vbl. n.* **blessyng(e)** VIII.1243, X.386. MED blessen *v.,* blessinge *ger.*

blew(e) *adj.* blue I.564, IV.2219, (as *n.*) X.426. MED bleu *adj.,* bleu *n.*

blind(e), blynd(e) *adj.* (1) blind, unable to see II.561; (2) unable to understand, heedless VII.1997 (3) blind, closed at one end VIII.658; (as *n.*) blind people VIII.92. MED blind *adj.,* blind *n.*

blis(se) *n.* (1) happiness, I.1230; (2) rejoicing I.3097; (3) source of joy VII.3166; (4) heavenly bliss III.830; **so have I (ye) b.** as I (you) may have salvation II.33, III.830; *pl.* **blisses** IV.1638. MED blisse *n.*

blisful *adj.* (1) glad, happy II.726, III.220; (2) heavenly, glorious, blessed I.17, X.1077; (3) fortunate VII.1198; fair, beautiful I.3247. MED blisful *adj.*

blisfully *adv.* happily I.1236. MED blisfulli *adv.*

blisse *see* **blesse(n).**

blood *n.* (1) blood I.635; one of the four bodily humors V.352 (see note); (2) lineage, descent I.1018; kin I.1583. MED blod *n.*(1)

blody, bloody *adj.* (1) bloody I.1010, I.1755; (2) warlike I.2512. MED blodi *adj.*

blowe *v.* (1) blow I.565; (2) spread abroad, make widely known I.2241; *1 pr. sg.* **blowe** VIII.753; *3 pr. sg.* **bloweth** II.705; *pr. pl.* **blowen** I.2512; *3 pt. sg.* **blew** VIII.1146; *pt. pl.* **blewe** VII.3399; *pp.* **blowe(n)** blown, inflated I.2241, VIII.440; *vbl. n.* **blowyng(e)** VIII.923. MED blouen *v.*(1), blouing *ger.*(1)

bood stayed *see* **byde.**

bode(n) commanded *see* **beden.**

body *n.* (1) body, object I.2283; **b. erect** upright object II.9; (2) person II.1185, VI.338; *gen.* **bodies** VIII.854; *pl.* **bodies** metals VIII.820. MED bodi *n.*

(y)boght, boghte paid for *see* **bye(n).**

boy(e) *n.* (1) servant VI.670; (2) rascal, knave III.1322. MED boie *n.*(1)

bokeler, bokeleer *n.* buckler, small shield I.112, I.3266. MED bokeler *n.*(1)

bolde, boold *adj.* (1) bold, confident VIII.1413, IX.258; (2) **ben (so) b.** dare, presume I.4271, VI.339; (3) (of persons) overconfident, brazen, rash VIII.1415; (of actions) shameless IV.2269; (as *n.*) shameless person VI.141; (4) strong, powerful I.458; (5) **b. of speche** well-spoken I.755. MED bold *adj.*

boldely, booldely *adv.* (1) bravely I.3433; (2) confidently IV.1358, V.581; (3) recklessly III.227; (4) vigorously III.1303. MED boldeliche *adv.*

boldnesse, booldnesse *n.* courage, self-assurance VI.71; arrogance VIII.487. MED boldnesse *n.*

bole *n.* bull VII.1325, X.898; *gen. sg.* **boles** VIII.797; *pl.* **boles** I.2139. MED bole *n.*(1)

bon, boon *n.* bone I.1177, III.511; *pl.* **bones** I.546, **banes** *(Nth.)* I.4073. MED bon *n.*(1)

bonde *adj.* enslaved, bound to serve another III.378, III.1660; **boonde-folk, boonde-men** serfs X.754, X.753. MED bonde *adj.*

bond, boond *n.* (1) fetter, shackle VII.2072; (2) promise, pledge V.1534, VII.368; (3) force that controls or dominates V.131 (see note), X.132; *pl.* **bondes** X.132; **boondes** VII.1828. MED bond *n.*

bone, boone *n.* request, prayer I.2669, VIII.356. MED bon *n.*(2)

bonte goodness *see* **bounte(e).**

boor *n.* boar I.2070, III.1829; *gen.* **bores** VII.870; *pl.* **bores** I.1658. MED bor *n.*

bord(e) *n.* (1) board, plank I.3440; (2) dining table III.2167, III.2243; **the heigh b.** the head table V.85; **to b.** as boarder(s) III.528; (3) **into shippes b.** aboard ship I.3585; **over b.** overboard II.922. MED bord *n.*

borel lay, not clerical *see* **burel(l).**

yborn(e), borne born *see* **bere(n).**

borwe *n.* (1) something given as a pledge VII.1828; **to b.** as a pledge I.1622, V.1234; (2) one legally responsible for another's fulfilling a pledge VII.1807; **Seint John to b.** with St. John, as a guarantor V.596; *pl.* **borwes** VII.1807. MED borgh *n.*

borwe *v.* borrow I.4417, II.105; *pr. pl.* **borwe** VIII.674; *3 pt. sg.* **borwed** VI.871; *pp.* **borwed** VIII.735; *vbl. n.* **borwynge** X.800. MED borwen v., borwing *ger.*

boost *n.* (1) boastful speech VI.764; **maken a b.** brag about II.401, III.98; (2) arrogance VII.2609; **leyen down (low) the b.** humble the pride VII.2099, VIII.441. MED bost *n.*

bosteth *3 pr. sg.* boasts III.1672, X.393. MED bosten *v.*

boot bit *see* **byte.**

boote *n.* (1) advantage, help, good III.472; (2) relief, remedy I.424; **b. of bale** deliverance from trouble VIII.1481; **soules b.** salvation of souls, savior VII.466. MED bote *n.*(1)

botel *n.* bottle III.1931, VI.886; *pl.* **botelles** VI.871; **botels** VI.877. MED botel *n.*(1)

boterflye *n.* butterfly IV.2304, VII.2790, VII.3274. MED buter-flie *n.*

both(e) *num.* (1) (as *n.*) two together, both I.1839, VI.523; (2) (as *adj.*) I.990, VII.1024; **bathe** *(Nth.)* I.4087; (3) (as *conj.*) I.4112. MED bothe *num.*

botme *n.* bottom VII.3101, VIII.1321. MED botme *n.*

bough *n.* branch, bough I.1980; *pl.* **bowes** I.1642. MED bough *v.*

(y)bounde(n) bound *see* **bynde.**

boundes *n. pl.* (1) boundary markers VII.2118; (2) limits I.2993, IV.46; restraints, moral rules V.571. MED bounde *n.*

bounte(e), bonte *n.* (1) goodness, virtue VIII.38; **sovereyn b.** perfect goodness IV.2289, VII.1079; prowess VII.2114; (2) kindness, benevolence IV.159, X.466; generosity X.284; *pl.* **bountees** good qualities X.396. MED bounte *n.*

bour *n.* inner room, bedchamber III.869; lady's chamber III.300; *gen.* **boures** I.3677; *pl.* **boures** III.869. MED bour *n.*

bowe(n), bow *v.* (1) bow or kneel X.598; (2) submit III.440; (3) bend IV.113; *imp. pl.* **boweth** IV.113. MED bouen *v.*(1)

box *n.* box tree, boxwood I.2922, VII.3398. MED box *n.*(1)

brak broke *see* **breke(n).**

branche *n.* (1) branch IV.1641; (2) line of descent III.1128; (3) species X.114, X.388; *pl.* **braunches** I.1067; **branches** X.728. MED braunch *n.*

bras *n.* brass I.366, I.3944. MED bras *n.*

brast(e) burst *see* **breste(n).**

brawen, brawn *n.* (1) muscle I.546; (2) meat III.1750; *pl.* **brawnes** VII.1941; **braunes** VII.3455. MED braun *n.*

breed *n.* (1) bread I.341, I.3628; (2) food VII.2438. MED bred *n.*(1)

bredeth *v. 3 pr. sg.* breed, grow IV.1783; *pp.* **bred** II.364, V.499. MED breden *v.*(3)

breyde *v. 1 & 3 pt. sg.* (1) *(intr.)* moved suddenly, start out (of sleep, swoon, etc.) V.477; **b. out of wit** went out of one's mind V.1027; (2) *(tr.)* snatched III.837; *pp.* **broyden** embroidered I.3238. MED breiden *v.*(1)

breke(n) *v.* (1) *(tr.)* break I.551; (2) break into, force an entry X.879; (3) violate a commandment X.883; **b. forward (biheste, trouthe)** fail to keep one's word II.40, V.1519; **b. (one's) day** fail (to pay) on the appointed day VIII.1040; (4) break off, interrupt VII.1043; (5) *(intr.)* break I.954; *3 pr. sg.* **breketh** I.1642; *pr. pl.* **breken** X.882; *pr. subj.* **breke** IV.2306; *imp. sg.* **brek** VII.1900; *3 pt. sg.* **brak** I.1468; *pt. subj. pl.* **breeke** VII.3388; *pp.* **broke(n)** I.1168, VIII.920, (as *adj.*) I.1920; *vbl. n.* **brekynge** X.884. MED breken *v.*, brekinge *ger.*

brenne(n), brynne *v.* burn III.52, III.1731; *3 pr. sg.* **brenneth** VII.2404; *pr. pl.* **brenne** X.196; *pr. subj. sg.* **brenne** VIII.1423; *imp. pl.* **brenne** VIII.515; *2 pt. sg.* **brendest** I.2384; *3 pt. sg.* **brente** I.2403; **brende** I.3812; *pt. pl.* **brende(n)** I.2425; *prp.* **brennynge** I.2000; *pp.* **(y)brent** I.946, I.2017; **(y)brend** VII.3365, VIII.318; (as *adj.*) **brend gold** refined (pure) gold I.2162, I.2896; *vbl. n.* **brennyng(e)** X.220. MED brennen *v.*, brenninge *ger.*

brere *n.* briar, thorn IV.1825; *pl.* **breres** I.1532. MED brer *n.*

brest, breest *n.* breast I.115, I.131; (as *adj.*) I.2710; *pl.* **brestes** I.3975. MED brest *n.*(1)

breste(n) *v.* break, burst I.1980, IV.1169; *3 pr. sg.* **brest** I.2610; *pr. subj. sg.* **breste** V.759; *3 pt. sg.* **brast** V.1480; *pt. pl.* **bruste** VI.234; **broste** II.671; *pt. subj. sg.* **brast(e)**

II.697; *pp.* **brosten** I.3829; *vbl. n.* **brestyng** breaking V.973. MED bresten *v.*, bresting *ger.*

breeth *n.* breath I.5, I.2806. MED breth *n.*(1)

brid *n.* bird IV.1281, V.460; *(fig.)* sweetheart I.3726; *gen. sg.* **briddes** VII.2176; *pl.* **briddes** I.2929. MED brid *n.*

brydel *n.* bridle or reins I.169; **have the b.** have control I.2376, III.813; *pl.* **bridles** X.433. MED bridel *n.*

brymston, brymstoon *n.* brimstone, sulphur I.629, VIII.798, X.841. MED brim-ston n.

brynge(n) *v.* bring I.1613; *3 pr. sg.* **bryngeth** II.974, **bringes** *(Nth.)* I.4130; *pr. pl.* **brynge** II.964; *pr. subj. sg.* **brynge** IV.1489; *2 pt. sg.* **broghtest** VII.3229; *1 & 3 pt. sg.* **broght(e)** I.566, III.426; **broughte** V.1273; *pt. pl.* **broghte(n)** I.1442, VII.1400; *pp.* **(y)broght** I.1111, I.1490, **(y)brought** I.2697, II.316. MED bringen *v.*

brynke *n.* (1) shore, coast V.858, V.1160; (2) edge, brink IV.1401. MED brinke *n.*

brynne burn *see* **brenne(n).**

Briton, Britoun *n.* (1) Breton, inhabitant of Brittany III.858; *pl.* **Britouns** V.709; (as *adj.*) V.1179; (2) Celtic inhabitant of ancient Britain; *pl.* **Britons** II.545; (as *adj.*) II.666. MED Britoun *n. & adj.*

brooch *n.* brooch, pin I.160, I.3265; *pl.* **broches** VI.908; **brooches** IV.255. MED broche *n.*(1)

brode, brood *adj.* wide, broad I.3266, I.4124, V.191; *comp.* **brodder** III.1688. MED brod *adj.*

brode *adv.* (1) frankly I.739; (2) with wide-open eyes VIII.1420. MED brode *adv.*

(y)broght, (y)brought brought *see* **brynge(n).**

brond(e) *n.* burning piece of wood, torch IV.1777; *gen.* **brondes** I.2339; *pl.* **brondes** I.2338. MED brand *n.*

broste(n) burst, broken *see* **breste(n).**

brotel, brotil *adj.* fragile IV.1279; uncertain, unreliable IV.2061. MED brotel *adj.*

brotelnesse, brotilnesse *n.* instability, undependability IV.1279; fickleness IV.2241. MED brotelnesse *n.*

broun *adj.* (1) brown, dark, or dull I.207, I.4368; **b. breed** coarse bread made of bran VII.2844; (2) (of persons) dark complexioned, tanned I.109, I.394. MED broun *adj.*

bruste burst, broken *see* **breste(n).**

buylden *v.* construct, build III.1977; *3 pr. sg.* **buyldeth** III.655; *pr. pl.* **buylde** IV.1279; *3 pt. sg.* **bulte** I.1548; *vbl. n.* **buyldynge** III.1979. MED bilden *v.*, bildinge *ger.*

bukke *n.* adult male deer VII.756; *gen. sg.* **bukkes** I.3387. MED bukke *n.*

bulle *n.* bull, i.e., papal decree IV.748, VI.388; *pl.* **bulles** IV.739. MED bulle *n.*

bulte built *see* **buylden.**

burel(l), borel *n.* coarse woolen cloth III.356; (as *adj.*) **b. man (men, folk)** layman, laymen, unlearned people III.1872, V.716. MED burel *n.*(1)

burned *pp.* (as *adj.*) burnished, polished I.1983, V.1247; glowing VI.38. MED burnen *v.*

burthe, byrthe *n.* birth II.192, II.314, III.400. MED birthe *n.*

busk, bussch *n.* (1) woods, thicket I.1517, I.2013; (2) a shrub, bush VII.468; *pl.* **buskes** I.1579, **bushes** X.858. MED bush *n.*(1)

but *conj.* (1) but, except I.1226, I.1754, II.431; unless IV.174; **b. if** unless I.656; (2) only V.638; nothing but, no more than I.2722, II.501; *(prec. by neg.)* only, nothing more than

I.2847, III.1728; **I nam (nere) b.** I am (would be) almost, as good as I.1122, VII.185; (3) (after statement of impossibility or *subj.*) that IV.1665, X.339; (4) **b. (if) it were** unless, if . . . not II.431; (5) (as *n.*) an exception X.494. MED but *conj.*

buttok *n.* buttock I.3803, III.2142; *pl.* **buttokes** I.3975. MED buttok *n.*

buxom *adj.* submissive, obedient IV.1287, VII.177. MED buxom *adj.*

C (*See also* K *and* S)

cache, cacche(n) *v.* (1) grasp, seize I.4273, X.852; (2) catch, capture VII.1178; entrap VIII.11; **c. with drynke** drunk X.823; (3) **c. a sleep** go to sleep I.4227; **c. countenance** regain composure IV.1110; get I.498, III.306; *imp. sg.* **cacche** III.76; *3 pt. sg.* **caughte** I.498; *pt. pl.* **caughte** I.4106; *pp.* **caught** I.1214, **kaught** I.145. MED cacchen *v.*

caytyf, kaytyf *n.* (1) captive, prisoner VII.2079; (2) wretched or unfortunate person I.1717, VI.728; *pl.* **caytyves** I.924, I.1717. MED caitif *n.*

caytyf, kaytyf *adj.* captive, enslaved I.1552; wretched X.271. MED caitif *adj.*

cake *n.* cake or loaf of bread I.4311, VI.322. MED cake *n.*

calle(n) *v.* call I.2085; *1 pr. sg.* **calle** I.4287; *3 pr. sg.* **calleth** IV.1081; *pr. pl.* **calle(n)** I.284, II.723; *3 pt. sg.* **called** V.1209; *prp.* **(y)called** I.4264, III.1123. MED callen *v.*

cam(e) *see* **come(n).**

can *see* **konne.**

capon *n.* capon, chicken III.1839; *pl.* **capouns** VI.856. MED capoun *n.*

capul *n.* horse I.4105, IX.65; *pl.* **caples** III.1554. MED capel *n.*

care *n.* grief, trouble, sorrow I.1321, I.1489; *pl.* **cares** V.1305. MED care *n.*(1)

carf carved *see* **kerve.**

carie *v.* carry I.130, I.3410; *pr. sg.* **carieth** I.1634; *pr. pl.* **carie(n)** VII.624, IX.96; *3 pt. sg.* **caried** VIII.567; *pt. pl.* **caryeden** I.2900; *pp.* **(y)caried** I.1021, VI.791; *vbl. n.* **cariyinge** VI.875. MED carien *v.*, cariing *ger.*

carolynge *vbl. n.* singing for a carol dance VIII.1345. MED caroling *ger.*

cart(e) *n.* (1) cart, wagon I.2022; (2) chariot, war-chariot I.2041. MED cart *n.*

carter(e) *n.* cart-driver I.2022, III.1540. MED carter *n.*

cas, caas *n.* quiver (for arrows) I.2080, I.2896. MED case *n.*(1)

cas, caas *n.* (1) situation, circumstance I.1411; **as in this (that) c.** in this (that) situation I.2357, I.3297; **for no c., in no (maner) c.** under no circumstances III.665, III.1831, VIII.149; (2) event, occurrence IV.316; (3) chance, fate I.844; **by, par, upon c.** by chance, by accident I.3661; (4) cause, reason, purpose V.1430, IX.308; (5) manner, concern I.2971; (6) case, type of situation X.105; **setten c.** suppose VII.1851; (7) a case at law II.36; *pl.* **caas** legal cases I.323, **cas** VI.163. MED cas *n.*

caste(n) *v.* (1) throw, cast I.2429, I.3712; **c. aweie** get rid of, throw away VI.542, VIII.384; **c. out** drive out X.531 (2) cast down VII.3047; (*intr.*) throw about, move quickly I.3330; (3) emit, shed VIII.244; **c. of** take off III.783; (4)

place, put I.4017, VII.2714; **c. up** lift III.1249; put (forcibly) VI.268; (5) cast, direct (eyes) I.896, I.2081; notice VIII.1414; (6) reckon, calculate I.2172; deliberate, think I.2854, X.692; (7) (*reflx.*) apply oneself to, devote oneself to VII.1591; practice VIII.738; set oneself to do VII.1858; (8) foreordain, arrange VI.880, VII.2701; *1 pr. sg.* **caste** I.2172; *3 pr. sg.* **casteth** VIII.1414, (*contr.*) **cast** III.782; *pr. pl.* **caste(n)** II.212, VI.268, *imp. sg.* **cast** VIII.384; *3 pt. sg.* **cast(e)** I.1077, I.2081; *pt. pl.* **caste(n)** I.2947, II.212; *pp.* **(y)cast** VI.880, VIII.939, **casten** VII.606. MED casten *v.*

castel *n.* castle I.1057; *pl.* **castelles** VII.1333, **castels** III.870. MED castel *n.*

catel(l) *n.* property, possessions II.27, IV.1525. MED catel *n.*

cause *n.* (1) cause, source I.419, V.260, V.451; **bi (the) c. of** because of I.174; **bi the (that) c. (that)** because I.2488; (2) occasion I.1256, VII.152; (3) the reason why I.716, I.2977; (4) motive X.142; justification IV.1185, X.707; pretext III.1378; (5) aim, purpose III.123, IV.387; (6) an affair or undertaking VII.1741; legal action or case III.1378; (7) **bi (the, that) c. (that)** because I.2488; **c. why** why V.185; *pl.* **causes** V.451. MED cause *n.*

causen *v.* cause VIII.1009; *3 pr. sg.* **causeth** I.2476; *pr. pl.* **causen** V.452; *3 pt. sg.* **caused** II.9. MED causen *v.*(1)

cercle *n.* circle (here a conjurer's magic circle) X.603; *pl.* **cercles** circles I.2131. MED cercle *n.*

certeyn(e) *adj.* (1) specified, fixed I.252a, I.815; (2) a definite but unspecified extent (of time) II.149, IV.918, (amount) II.242; (number) I.2967; (3) particular, specific I.1471, I.3494, II.481; (4) fixed, invariable V.866; (5) confident VII.1664. MED certain *adj.*

certeyn, certayn *adv.* certainly, indeed I.3495, II.884. MED certain *adv.*

certeyn, certayn *n.* (1) a fixed amount VIII.1024; a definite but unspecified number I.3193; (2) certainty, assurance X.1000; **in c.** certainly IV.1182. MED certain *n.*

certeinly *adv.* certainly I.204, I.235. MED certainli *adv.*

certes *adv.* certainly, indeed I.875, I.1237; (as *n.*) **for c.** certainly II.609. MED certes *adv.*

cesse *v.* cease, stop II.1066; *3 pr. sg.* **cesseth** V.257, *pr. pl.* **cesse** X.601; *3 pt. sg.* **cessed** VIII.538. MED cesen *v.*

chaast, chaste *adj.* chaste I.2051, I.2297; *adv.* **chaast** IV.1446. MED chaste *adj.*, chaste *adv.*

chace *v.* (1) pursue V.457; drive out, banish VII.566; **c. out** expel III.2157; **c. from (out) of** deprive II.366; (2) harass, afflict X.526; (3) pursue, go on with IV.341, IV.393; *3 pr. sg.* **chaceth** X.544; *pr. pl.* **chacen** X.526; *pt. pl.* **chaced** III.2157; *pp.* **chaced** II.366. MED chacen *v.*

chaffare *n.* (1) trade, business I.4389, VII.340; (2) merchandise, wares II.138, III.521, IV.2438. MED chaffare *n.*

chambre *n.* chamber, private room I.1065, III.618; *pl.* **chambres** I.18. MED chaumbre *n.*

champioun, champion *n.* (1) athlete (*esp.* wrestler) VII.2023; (2) defender (of one of the parties) in a judicial duel II.631, III.1662. MED champioun *n.*

chanoun, chanon *n.* canon (cleric) VIII.573, VIII.1022; *gen. sg.* **chanons** VIII.1101, **chanounes** VIII.1196; *pl.* **chanons** VIII.992. MED canoun *n.*(2)

chapeleyne *n.* chaplain I.164 (see note); *pl.* **chapelleyns** X.617. MED chapelein *n.*

chapitre *n.* (1) division of a written work VII.3065, X.238; (2) meeting of members of a religious house III.1945; session of the archdeacon's court III.1361; *pl.* **chapitres** X.389. MED chapitre *n.*

chapman *n.* merchant VII.254, VII.256; *pl.* **chapmen** VII.288. MED chap-man *n.*

char, chaar *n.* carriage or chariot I.2138, VII.2610. MED char *n.*(2)

charge *n.* (1) burden, hardship X.92; (2) duty, responsibility IV.163; order, command IV.193; **yeven in c.** order VII.432; (3) **taketh c.** be concerned III.321; **yeve litel c.** be little concerned, care little I.1284; (4) weight, significance I.1284, V.359; **no c.** it does not matter VIII.749. MED charge *n.*

charge(n) *v.* (1) load III.1539, X.361; (2) burden, weigh down IV.2211, VII.2366; (3) order, request II.802, III.2026; *1 pr. sg.* **charge** III.1992; *3 pr. sg.* **chargeth** X.361; *pr. subj. sg.* **charge** X.360; *3 pt. sg.* **charged** II.209; *pp.* **charged** IV.2211. MED chargen *v.*

charitable *adj.* benevolent; devout I.143, X.807. MED charitable *adj.*

charite(e) *n.* (1) Christian virtue of love I.532, IV.221; **out of alle c.** lacking such love, deeply upset I.452, X.1043; (2) an act of charity, good deed I.1433, X.374; **for (par seinte) c.** out of kindness, for goodness' sake I.1721, VII.3320. MED charite *n.*

chastite(e) *n.* chastity I.1912, III.94. MED chastite *n.*

chaunce *n.* event, happening I.1752; lot, fate VIII.593; **per c.** by chance; (2) winning throw at dice VI.653. MED chaunce *n.*

chaunge(n) *v.* (1) *(intr.)* change, vary V.1035; (2) *(tr.)* change (one's mind, feelings, attitude) IV.709; **c. colour** grow pale (or red) I.1400, I.1637; shift, move IV.511; (3) exchange VI.724; *3 pr. sg.* **chaungeth** I.1538, **changeth** II.1134; *pr. subj. sg.* **chaunge** VII.1559; *imp. sg.* **chaunge** VII.1226; *3 pt. sg.* **chaunged** I.348, **changed** V.370; *prp.* **chaungynge** (as *adj.*) IV.996; *pp.* **chaunged** I.1370, **changed** V.709; *vbl. n.* **chaungyng(e)** I.1647. MED chaungen *v.*, chaunginge *ger.*

cheyne *n.* (1) chain I.1343, VII.2364; (2) tie, bond I.2988, V.1356; *pl.* **cheynes** I.1343. MED chaine *n.*

cheke *n.* (1) cheek III.433, V.1078; (2) jawbone VII.2038; *pl.* **chekes** I.633. MED cheke *n.*

chere, cheere, chiere *n.* (1) face IV.238, IV.599; (2) facial expression I.913, V.103; **a c. make** assume the expression IV.535; (3) manner, bearing IV.241; manners I.139; attention, solicitude VII.6; (4) mood II.396, IV.7, IV.1211; good humor IV.1112; (5) source of pleasure I.2683. **maken c.** treat kindly, entertain VII.327. MED chere *n.*(1)

cherice *v.* hold dear, favor VII.2520; *3 pr. sg.* **cherisseth** treats V.1554; *imp. sg.* **cherisse** IV.1388; *imp. pl.* **cherisseth** take good care of, respect V.353. MED cherishen *v.*

cherl *n.* (1) common man (of nongentle birth or station) X.761; fellow, chap VI.750; peasant I.2459; slave X.763; (2) ill-mannered boor, ruffian I.3169, I.3917, III.2206; villain III.460; *gen.* **cherles** I.3169; *pl.* **cherles** VII.2543. MED cherl *n.*

cherlyssh *adj.* churlish, villainous V.1523. MED cherlish *adj.*

chese *n.* cheese III.1739, III.1747, VI.448. MED chese *n.*

chese(n), cheese *v.* (1) choose, select III.1232, III.1748; elect X.468; chosen of God, blessed X.1054; (2) decide III.1179; **c. amys** make the wrong choice I.3181; **may nat c.** have no choice III.1748; **c. rather** prefer V.1384; *1 pr. sg.* **chees** IV.2148; *3 pr. sg.* **cheseth** X.276; *pr. pl.* **chese(n)** I.3181, X.468; *imp. sg.* **ches(e)** I.3177, III.1219, **chees** I.1595; *imp. pl.* **cheseth** III.1232, **chese** III.1227; *3 pt. sg.* **chees** IV.1597; *pp.* **chosen** I.2109; *vbl. n.* **chesynge** choice, choosing IV.162. MED chesen *v.*, chesinge *ger.*

cheste, chiste *n.* (1) strongbox, chest III.317; (2) coffin III.502, IV.29. MED cheste *n.*

chevyssaunce *n.* financial arrangement (*esp.* loan) I.282, VII.329, VII.347. MED chevisaunce *n.*

chide(n) *v.* (1) *(tr.)* criticize, scold III.419, X.632; (2) *(intr.)* complain III.281, VII.428; *2 pr. sg.* **chidest** III.244; *3 pr. sg.* **chideth** VII.1707; *(contr.)* **chit** VIII.921; *pr. pl.* **chiden** III.1983; *pr. subj. sg.* **chide** X.632; *1 & 3 pt. sg.* **chidde** I.3999, III.223; *prp.* **chidyng(e)** (as *adj.*) quarrelsome III.279; *vbl. n.* **chidyng(e)** chiding. quarreling X.525, X.633; *pl.* **chidynges** X.206. MED chiden *v.*, chidinge *ger.*

chief *adj.* chief, principal I.1057, I.1730, V.1046; **c. synnes** the capital (deadly) sins X.389. MED chef *adj.*

chiere manner, solicitude *see* **chere.**

chynche *adj.* (as *n.*) miser VII.1619. MED chinche *n.*

chirche, cherche *n.* (1) church (building) I.460, I.708, VIII.546; (2) the church (as institution) I.3986, II.235; (as *adj.*) III.1307; *gen.* **chirches** I.3983; *pl.* **chirches** III.1979. MED chirche *n.*

chivalry(e) *n.* (1) knights, body of knights, VII.2681; the nobility II.235; **flour of c.** best of knights I.982, I.3059; (2) knighthood, knightly prowess I.2184, IX.126; (3) the ideal of knightly conduct I.45, I.2106. MED chevalrie *n.*

choys *n.* choice, decision IV.154, IV.170; **fre(e) c.** free will VII.3246. MED chois *n.*

circumstaunce, circumstance *n.* (1) attendant condition X.964, X.967; relevant aspect I.1932, II.152; detail, feature VI.419; **with every (alle) c.** with (attention to) all the details X.610, X.976; with due propriety, with all ceremony I.2263, II.317; with great care IV.584; (2) general condition X.692; *pl.* **circumstaunces** I.2788, **circumstances** X.86. MED circumstaunce *n.*

citee *n.* city I.939, I.989; *pl.* **citees** III.870. MED cite *n.*

clayme *v.* (1) claim, demand X.926; (2) claim, call, name VII.36; declare oneself (to be) III.1120; *3 pr. sg.* **claymeth** VII.36; *pr. pl.* **clayme** III.1120. MED claimen *v.*

clamb climbed *see* **clymbe(n).**

clappeth *3 pr. sg.* knocks III.1584; *pr. pl.* **clappen** talk noisily, chatter X.406; *pr. subj. sg.* **clappe** may say VIII.965; *imp. pl.* **clappeth** IV.1200 wag your tongue, chatter; *3 pt. sg.* **clapte** clapped V.1203; clapped shut III.1699; **c. to** slammed shut I.3740, IV.2159; *vbl. n.* **clappyng** noise, chatter IV.999. MED clappen *v.*

clause *n.* sentence, brief passage II.251; **in a c.** briefly I.715, I.1763, IV.1431. MED clause *n.*

clene *adj.* (1) clean I.504; pure, unpolluted II.1183, VI.873; (2) chaste, morally pure I.2326, III.97; (3) clear, unobstructed V.99; (4) elegant, shapely III.598. MED clene *adj.*

clene *adv.* (1) cleanly I.133; (2) brightly, splendidly I.367; (3) fully, entirely V.626; **ful (al) c.** completely, entirely II.1106, VIII.625. MED clene *adv.*

clennesse *n.* purity, chastity III.1910. MED clennesse *n.*

clense *v.* cleanse I.631; *3 pr. sg.* **clenseth** X.312. MED clensen *v.*

clepe(n) *v.* (1) speak, say, call out I.3577, V.374; (2) call (a name) I.2730, I.3956; **ben cleped** be called, named I.269, I.376; (3) ask X.289; (4) summon V.1487, VII.1157; (5) **c. ayein** recall, restore IX.354; *1 pr. sg.* **clepe** III.93; *2 pr. sg.* **clepest** X.760; *3 pr. sg.* **clepeth** III.102; *pr. pl.* **clepe(n)** I.620, II.191; *pr. subj. sg.* **clepe** III.296; *imp. sg.* **clepe** I.3432; *3 pt. sg.* **cleped** V.374; *pp.* **(y)cleped** I.376, VIII.129, **(y)clept** VIII.772, VIII.863, **clepid** VII.227. MED clepen *v.*

clere, cleer(e) *adj.* (1) bright, shining V.48, X.1078; (2) clear, free from impurity VI.914, (of sounds) IX.115, (of skies) I.1062; (3) beautiful, splendid VII.858; *comp.* **clerer** II.194. MED cler *adj.*

clere, cleere *adv.* (1) brightly I.2331, II.11; (2) loudly I.170, IV.1845. MED cler *adv.*

clerk *n.* (1) member of the clergy VI.391, X.961; minor cleric I.3312; (2) student, scholar I.480, III.673; university student III.527; learned person IV.1293, V.1105; author, writer I.1163, I.4028; *gen.* **clerkes** I.4060; *pl.* **clerkes** I.3275, **clerkis** II.480. MED clerk *n.*

cleernesse *n.* (1) brightness VIII.403, X.222; (2) splendor VIII.111. MED clernesse *n.*

clyket *n.* latch-key IV.2117. MED cliket *n.*(1)

clymbe(n) *v.* climb I.3625, IV.2210; *3 pr. sg.* **clymbeth** VII.2776; *3 pt. sg.* **clamb** VII.797; *pt. pl.* **clomben** I.3636, **cloumben** VII.1400; *pp.* **clombe(n)** II.12, VII.3198, **cloumbe** VII.2402. MED climben *v.*

cloysterer *n.* monastic I.259, I.3661. MED cloistrer *n.*

cloke *n.* cloak I.157, I.1999. MED cloke *n.*(1)

clokke *n.* clock II.14, VII.2854, X.5. MED clokke *n.*

clomben climbed *see* **clymbe(n).**

clos(e), cloos *pp.* (as *adj.*) (1) closed VII.3332, IX.37; (2) **kepen c.** keep secret, concealed VII.1146. MED closen *v.*

cloth, clooth *n.* (1) cloth, I.2158; (2) drapery I.2281; (3) garment, clothing III.1881, VII.2473; *pl.* **clothes** I.899. MED cloth *n.*

clothe(n) *v.* clothe, dress VIII.42, X.933; *imp. pl.* **clothe** X.1054; *3 pt. sg.* **cladde** I.1409; *pt. pl* **cladden** IV.864; *pp.* **(y)clothed** I.911, I.1048, **(y)clad** I.103, VIII.133; *vbl. n.* **clothing(e)** VII.2304, VII.2366. MED clothen *v.*, clothing *ger.*

cloumben climbed *see* **clymbe(n).**

cofre *n.* chest, money-chest I.298, II.26. MED cofre *n.*

cogheth coughs *see* **coughen.**

cok *n.* cock, rooster I.823, I.3687; cock-crow I.4233; *gen.* **cokkes** I.3675; *pl.* **cokkes** I.3357.

cokewold *n.* cuckold I.3226, IV.2256, VI.382. MED cokewold *n.*

cokkow *n.* cuckoo I.1930; (as *interj.*) the cry of the cuckoo IX.243. MED cokkou *n.*

cole *n.* coal I.2692, I.3731; *pl.* **coles** VIII.1114. MED col *n.*(2)

col-blak *adj.* coal-black I.2142, I.3240. MED col-blak *adj.*

colde, coold *adj.* (1) cold I.2778, I.2957; (2) cooled off V.402; chilling, painful I.1920, I.2467; fatal VII.3256; (3) dominated by cold I.2443; (as *n.*) one of the four elementary qualities I.420. MED cold *adj.*, cold *n.*

colde *v.* grow cold, chill II.879, V.1023. MED colden *v.*

coler n. collar I.3239, I.3265. MED coler *n.*

colour *n.* (1) color I.1038; (2) complexion I.1400, V.370; (3) rhetorical device IV.16, V.723; (4) pretense III.399; *pl.* **colours** VI.36, **coloures** V.511. MED colour *n.*

come(n) *v.* (1) come I.23, I.671; (2) **c. to the effect** realize VIII.1261; **c. bi** understand (something) III.984, VIII.1395; *1 pr. sg.* **come** I.3720; *2 pr. sg.* **comest** III.246; *3 pr. sg.* **cometh** I.1643, **comth** I.3818; *pr. pl.* **come(n)** I.2575, VI.477; *pr. subj. sg.* **coome** II.802; *pr. subj. pl.* **come** X.443; *imp. sg.* **com** I.3709, **com of** come on, hurry up I.3728; *imp. pl.* **cometh** I.839; *1 & 3 pt. sg.* **cam(e)** I.547, I.2810; *pt. pl.* **come(n)** II.145, **coome(n)** III.1571, V.1012, **came** IV.752; *prp.* **comyng(e)** I.2128, (as *adj.*) VII.1023; *pp.* **come(n)** I.23, I.671, **ycome(n)** I.77, I.3942; *vbl. n.* **comyng(e)** IV.912. MED comen *v.*, cominge *ger.*

commende *v.* praise, commend IV.1024; *3 pr. sg.* **commendeth** II.76; *pt. pl.* **commendeden** X.669; *prp.* **commendynge** IV.239; *pp.* **comended** IV.1349. MED commenden *v.*

commune, comune *adj.* (1) **in c.** generally I.1251, I.2681; (2) unanimous II.155, VI.601; (3) public IV.1583; **c. profit** common good, welfare of all IV.431, IV.1194; (as *n.*) land held in common IV.1313; (4) familiar VII.1481, VII.2246; notorious VI.596; (5) general, widespread V.107. MED commune *adj.*, commune *n.*

compaignye *n.* (1) group I.24; professional group II.134; (2) fellowship, companionship I.2779, I.3204, VI.63; **holden (maken, beere) c.** keep company III.1521, VII.1330; **par c.** for fellowship's sake, companionship I.4167; **c. (of man)** sexual intimacy I.461, I.2311; *pl.* **compaignyes** I.2589. MED compaignie *n.*

compleyne, complayne *v.* (1) lament IV.530; (2) complain VI.241; *pr. pl.* **compleyne** I.908; *2 pt. sg.* **compleynedest** VII.3349; *3 pt. sg.* **compleyned** VII.3349; *prp.* **compleynynge** I.1072; *pp.* **compleyned** IV.530; *vbl. n.* **compleynynge** II.929. MED compleinen *v.*, compleininge *ger.*

compleint(e) *n.* (1) lament V.920; (2) poetic lament IV.1881; *pl.* **compleintes** V.948. MED compleinte *n.*

complexioun, compleccioun *n.* constitution, temperament determined by the humors I.333 (see note), X.585; *pl.* **complecciouns** VII.2924. MED complexioun *n.*

comprehende *v.* (1) contain, include VII.957, X.1042; (2) understand V.223; *3 pr. sg.* **comprehendeth** X.1042; *pp.* **comprehended** VII.957. MED comprehenden *v.*

comune common *see* **commune.**

comunly, communely, communly *adv.* ordinarily, commonly III.2257, IV.726. MED communeli *adv.*

conceyve *v.* (1) conceive (offspring) VII.472, X.577; engender, give rise to VII.1209; (2) comprehend, understand X.552; *pp.* **conceyved** V.336. MED conceiven *v.*

conclude(n) *v.* (1) include VIII.429; (2) summarize, conclude (a speech, argument) I.1895; end VIII.849, VIII.957; succeed VIII.773; (3) deduce I.3067, III.1171; decide IV.1607; *1 pr. sg.* **conclude** III.1171; *pr. pl.* **concluden** VIII.957; *pp.* **concluded** IV.1607. MED concluden *v.*

conclusioun, conclusion *n.* (1) end II.683; purpose, goal III.115; **for (plat) c.** definitely I.1845; (2) result VIII.394; fate I.1869, I.4328; success VIII.672; (3) inference VII.3057; judgment, decision I.1743, I.3402; *pl.* **conclusiouns** mathematical propositions I.3193. MED conclusioun *n.*

condicioun, condicion *n.* (1) state, circumstances, situation II.99, II.271; social position II.313, X.755; (2) quality

X.1012; circumstance X.319; (3) character, disposition I.1431; character trait VI.41; (4) stipulation V.529; *pl.* **condiciouns** VII.1169, **condicions** X.592. MED condicioun *n.*

conferme *v. 1 pr. sg.* (1) confirm, ratify IV.1508, X.842; (2) corroborate I.2350; pursue (a course of action) VII.1222; promote VII.1222; (3) *(reflx.)* resolve VII.1777; *pp.* **confermed** affirmed I.2350, established VI.136. MED confermen *v.*

conformed *3 pt. sg. (reflx.)* obeyed, conformed VII.1872; *prp.* **conformynge** consenting IV.546. MED conformen *v.*

confort, comfort *n.* (1) consolation V.826, X.740, X.1030; (2) pleasure, delight I.773. MED comfort *n.*

conforten *v.* (1) encourage X.652; (2) console IV.1918; *3 pr. sg.* **conforteth** I.958; *pr. pl.* **conforten** V.823; *prp.* **confortynge** IV.1935; *pp.* **conforted** V.832. MED comforten *v.*

confounde *v.* harass, distress X.434, X.774; harm, destroy II.362, X.529; encumber, overcome II.100, X.740; *pp.* **confounded** VIII.137, **confoundid** II.100. MED confounden *v.*

confus *adj.* confused I.2230, VIII.463. MED confused *ppl.*

confusioun, confusion *n.* (1) destruction, ruin I.1545; cause of pain III.1958, VII.1106; damnation VII.1943; (2) humiliation X.187; (3) disorder, chaos V.869. MED confusioun *n.*

conjoynt *pp.* joined to X.924; *vbl. n.* **conjoynynge** joining together VIII.95. MED conjoinen *v.*, conjoining *ger.*

conscience *n.* (1) conscience, sense of right and wrong IV.1635, VIII.434, X.979; (2) sense of fairness III.1438; scrupulousness I.398, I.526; (3) feelings, sensibility I.150. MED conscience *n.*

conseil, counceil *n.* (1) a meeting, council I.3096; discussing an issue VII.1042; (2) body of advisers to a ruler II.204; (3) an adviser I.1147; **ben of c.** be my adviser, confidante I.1141; (4) counsel, advice VIII.192; **taken c.** deliberate VII.1121; **werken bi (with) c.** act after deliberation I.3530, IV.1485; scriptural counsel (as distinct from commandment) III.82; (5) plan, decision I.784, VII.1065; (6) secret I.665, I.3503, VIII.145; **kepen (hyden) c.** keep a secret III.980, VII.1143; **in c.** secretly III.1437, IV.2431; *pl.* **conseils** VII.3256. MED counseil n.

conseille *v.* teach, instruct III.66, VII.129; *pr. pl.* **conseille** VII.1026; *imp. pl.* **conseileth** VII.1702; *3 pt. sg.* **conseiled** X.126; *pt. pl.* **conseilled** VII.1351, **conseilleden** VII.1352; *pp.* **conseilled** VII.1082; *vbl. n.* **conseillyng** counsel, instruction III.67, VII.1002, **conseilynge** X.1033; *pl.* **conseillynges** VII.1163. MED counseilen *v.*, counseiling *ger.*

consente(n) *v.* consent, agree IV.537, VII.1382; **c. with** be consonant or consistent with VII.1386; **c. to** submit to, acquiesce in, VII.1382; *1 pr. sg.* **consente** IV.1508; *3 pr. sg.* **consenteth** consents X.543; *pr. pl.* **consenten** V.902; *3 pt. sg.* **consented** VII.1050; *pt. pl.* **consented** X.332, **consenteden** VII.1362; *vbl. n.* **consentynge** consent X.296; *pl.* consentynges X.293. MED consenten *v.*, consentinge *ger.*

considere *v.* (1) think (about) VII.1154; (2) take into account V.675, VIII.1388; realize VII.1508; **considered** *(pp.)* considering, taking into account I.2233, IV.78; (3) take an interest I.2233, IV.78; *1 pr. sg.* **considere** IV.2179; *3 pr. sg.* **considereth** VII.1497; *pr. pl.* **consideren** VII.1496; *imp. sg.* **consider(e)** I.2233; *imp. pl.* **considereth** VIII.1388; *3 pt. sg.* **considered** IV.78; *prp.* **considerynge** V.675; *pp.* **con-**

sidered (with **hath**) considered I.1763, (with **is**) observed V.1283. MED consideren *v.*

constable *n.* (1) chief steward II.716; (2) warden of a royal castle II.512, II.575. MED constable *n.*

constance, constaunce *n.* constancy IV.688, IV.2283. MED constaunce *n.*

constellacioun, constellacion *n.* configuration of the heavenly bodies I.1088, IV.1969. MED constellacioun *n.*

constreyneth *v. 3 pr. sg.* (1) (of persons) compels, forces IV.800; (of circumstances) constrain, impel VII.1570; (2) dominate, control V.764; *pr. pl.* **constreyne** force, impel X.886; *pp.* **constreyned** forced, impelled III.1071. MED constreinen *v.*

contenance, contenaunce *n.* (1) behavior, conduct IV.671, X.614; (2) self-control IV.1110; (3) outward appearance I.1916, I.4421; **maken god c.** appear composed II.320; **holden (for) c.** keep up appearances I.4421; **for c.** for show VIII.1264; (4) gesture, expression V.284; *pl.* **contenaunces** expressions V.284, courtesies VII.8. MED contenaunce *n.*

contrarie *adj.* contrary, discordant X.342; unfavorable VII.3069. MED contrarie *adj.*

contrarie *n.* (1) opposite I.1667, I.3057; **in c. (of)** in opposition (to) VIII.1477; (2) hostile act VII.1280; difficulty X.720; opponent I.1859, VII.3280; *pl.* **contraries** opposites VII.1017. MED contrarie *n.*

contrarie(n) *v.* (1) oppose, resist IV.2319; (2) antagonize, offend V.705; (3) contradict III.1044, IV.1497; *1 & 3 pt. sg.* **contraried** III.1044, IV.1497. MED contrarien *v.*

contrarious(e), contrarius *adj.* different, contrary III.698; hostile, rebellious III.780. MED contrarious *adj.*

contree *n.* (1) region I.216, III.1397; (2) nation, country I.2973; (3) countryside VI.933; *pl.* **contrees** I.2973. MED contree *n.*

conveyen *v.* (1) escort, accompany I.2737; (2) communicate IV.55; *3 pt. sg.* **conveyed** I.2737. MED conveien *v.*

convenyent *adj.* suitable, proper X.421; *pl.* **in proporcioneles convenientz** in planetary tables V.1278 (see note). MED convenient *adj.*

converte *v.* (1) (with **from**) turn aside VI.212; (2) convert to a religious faith II.686, VIII.414; *3 pr. sg.* **converteth** II.574; *3 pt. sg.* **converted** VIII.404; *prp.* **convertynge unto** turning to I.3037; *pp.* **converted** VIII.414. MED converten *v.*

cope *n.* cloak I.260, VII.1949. MED cope *n.*

coper *n.* copper VIII.829, VIII.1292. MED coper *n.*

coppe, cuppe *n.* cup I.134, V.616; *pl.* **coppes** I.2949. MED cuppe *n.*

corage *n.* (1) heart (as the source of emotions), feelings I.22, IV.787; (2) inclination, desire IV.1254; sexual desire IV.907; spiritual state X.655; (3) courage, valor II.939, X.689; bold act IV.1513; *pl.* **corages** I.11. MED corage *n.*

corageus, corageous *adj.* (1) brave VII.2337; (2) ardent X.585. MED corageous *adj.*

corde *n.* rope, cord I.3569; instrument of torture I.1746; *pl.* **cordes** snares VIII.8. MED corde *n.*

corn *n.* (1) kernel VI.863, VII.3175; (2) (collective *n.*) grain I.562, I.3939; *pl.* **cornes** grain crops VII.2035. MED corn *n.*

coroned, crouned, crowned *pp.* VII.2365; (as *adj.*) crowned I.161, sovereign, consummate V.526. MED corounen *v.*(1)

coroune, corone, croun, crowne *n.* (1) crown IV.1118; garland I.2290, IV.381; (2) top of the head I.4099, VII.309; (3) reward VIII.388; *pl.* **corones** VIII.221. MED coroune *n.*

correccioun *n.* (1) correction X.60; **under c.** subject to correction X.56; (2) punishment VI.404; **doon c.** punish III.1320; fine III.1617; (3) jurisdiction III.1329. MED correccioun *n.*

correcte(n) *v.* (1) correct V.1274; rectify, remedy VIII.999; (2) set right by rebuke or punishment III.661, X.673; direct, admonish VIII.162; *3 pr. sg.* **correcteth** VII.1473; *imp.* **correcte** X.673; *pp.* **corrected** III.181. MED correcten *v.*

corrupte *v.* corrupt X.998; *3 pr. sg.* decays I.2746; *pp.* **corrupt** corrupted X.167; (as *adj.*) corrupted II.519; infectious IV.2252; decayed X.333. MED corrupten *v.*

corrupcioun, corrupcion *n.* (1) decayed matter X.535, X.942; (2) cause of corruption X.899. MED corrupcioun *n.*

cors *n.* (1) body I.3429, IX.67; corpse VI.665; (2) (as a semipronoun in asservations) **his c.** him VII.908, **thy c.** you VI.304. MED cors *n.*

corse, corsed curse(d) *see* **cursen.**

(y)corve(n) carved *see* **kerve(n).**

cosyn *n.* blood relative, kinsman I.1093, I.1131; closely related I.742, IX.210; *pl.* **cosyns** X.836. MED cosine *n.*

cost, coost *n.* coast, region III.922; coast, shore V.995, VII.436. MED coste *n.*

costage *n.* expense, expenditure III.249, IV.1126; **doon c.** spend money VII.45; *pl.* **costages** expenditures VII.1336. MED costage *n.*

cote, coote *n.* tunic, coat I.103, I.328. MED cote *n.*(2)

couche(n) *v.* (1) *(intr.)* lie down IV.1206; (2) *(tr.)* lay something down, put down I.2933, I.3211; arrange VIII.1182; adorn I.2161; *3 pt. sg.* **couched** arranged VIII.1179; *pp.* **couched** arranged VIII.1182. MED couchen *v.*

coughen *v.* cough IV.2208; *3 pr. sg.* **cougheth** I.3697, **cogheth** I.3788. MED coughen *v.*

counte *v.* *1 pr. sg.* value at, consider I.4056, I.4192. MED counten *v.*

countrefete *v.* (1) imitate I.139, VI.13; (2) simulate, make a pretense VI.447; forge (a document) II.746, IV.743; *3 pt. sg.* **countrefeted** IV.2121; *pp.* **countrefeted** copied II.746; (as *adj.*) false, affected VI.51. MED countrefeten *v.*, countrefet *ppl.*

courser *n.* warhorse, charger I.1513, I.1704; *pl.* **courseres** I.2501. MED courser *n.*

coveite *v.* (1) covet, desire III.1187; crave III.1189, X.459; lust for sexually III.266, X.844; *3 pr. sg.* **coveiteth** III.266; *pr. pl.* **coveiten** X.959. MED coveiten *v.*

coveitise *n.* (1) covetousness, greed VIII.1077, X.336; (2) strong desire or craving X.853. MED coveitise *n.*

coveitous *adj.* covetous, greedy VII.1131, VII.1838. MED coveitous *adj.*

covenable *adj.* suitable, appropriate VII.1592, X.80. MED covenable *adj.*

covenant *n.* agreement, contract I.600; promise V.1587; *pl.* **covenantz** I.1924. MED covenaunt *n.*

covent *n.* religious house, organized group of friars or monks III.1863, VII.677. MED covent *n.*

coverchief *n.* kerchief, headscarf III.590; *pl.* **coverchiefs** I.453. MED cover-chef *n.*

covere *v.* cover VII.2766; conceal X.984; *pr. pl.* **covere** X.422;

1 & 3 pt. sg. **covered** III.590, VII.2782; *pp.* **(y)covered** I.354, I.3212. MED coveren *v.*(1)

craft *n.* (1) cleverness VIII.619; skill, art I.401; (2) cunning, guile III.1468, VI.84; (3) trade, occupation I.692, VII.1270; trade guild I.4366; *pl.* **craftes** I.2409. MED craft *n.*(1)

crafty *adj.* (1) skillful, ingenious VIII.1290; subtle VIII.1253; (2) deceitful VIII.655; (3) skilled in a craft I.1897. MED crafti *adj.*

craftyly, craftely *adv.* skillfully II.48, VIII.903. MED craftili *adv.*

creat *pp.* created VII.1103, X.218. MED creat *ppl.*

crepe(n) *v.* creep, move slowly I.4250, VII.2437; *3 pr. sg.* **crepeth** VI.565; *3 pt. sg.* **creep** I.4226, **crepte** I.4193; *pt. pl.* **crepte(n)** III.1698, VII.2616; *pp.* **cropen** I.4259. MED crepen *v.*

crie(n) *v.* (1) shout, cry out I.636, IX.301; announce I.2731, V.46; (2) **c. on, upon** complain about, blame V.650, V.1496, VII.3043; (3) **c. after** beg for I.2699, III.518; **c. upon (to)** implore I.4006, II.850; (4) *(tr.)* beg for I.3288, II.1111; (5) lament I.1221, II.919; weep VII.979; *1 pr. sg.* **crye!** I.1111; *pl.* **crye(n)** I.2835, II.850; *2 pt. sg.* (with *pro.*) **cridestow** I.1083; *3 pt. sg.* **cride** I.1078, *pt. pl.* **cride(n)** I.949, I.2562, **crieden** I.1756; *prp.* **criynge** I.2699; *pp.* **cryd** IV.563, **cried** I.2344; *vbl. n.* **criyng(e)** weeping, lamentation I.906, I.1100. MED crien *v.*, criing *ger.*

croys, croce *n.* cross I.699, III.484. MED crois *n.*

croked *pp.* (as *adj.*) (1) crooked, not straight VI.761; (2) crippled II.560, X.624. MED croked *ppl.*

cropen crept *see* **crepe.**

crosselet *n.* (alchem.) crucible VIII.1147, VIII.1153; *pl.* **crosletz** VIII.793. MED crosselet *n.*(2)

croun crown *see* **coroun(e).**

crouned crowned *see* **coroned.**

crueel, cruel *adj.* harsh, cruel, savage I.1303, II.295. MED cruel *adj.*

cuppe cup *see* **coppe.**

curat, curaat *n.* curate I.219, III.2095; *pl.* **curates** X.791, **curatz** III.1816. MED curat *n.*

cure *n.* (1) attention VI.557; **take c.** pay (no) attention to I.303; **honest c.** regard for decency VI.557; (2) **do (no) c.** take (no) pains I.1007, III.1074; **bisy c.** active diligence I.2853; (3) duty, responsibility IV.82; **have in c.** have in one's power II.230, VI.22; jurisdiction III.1333; (4) medicinal treatment V.1114, VII.1270; remedy, cure VIII.37; *pl.* **cures** duties, obligations IV.82. MED cure *n.*(1)

curious, curius *adj.* (1) (persons) skillful, expert I.577; diligent VII.243; (2) (things) skillfully made, intricate I.196; elaborate II.402; (3) (writing) arcane, difficult V.1120; (4) painstaking IV.1577, VII.225. MED curious *adj.*

curs *n.* curse, excommunication I.655, I.661, VI.946; **Cristes c.** damnation III.1347; *pl.* **curses** VIII.1405. MED curs *n.*

cursednesse *n.* (1) sinfulness, wickedness VII.631, VIII.1301; (2) perversity, malice IV.1239. MED cursednesse *n.*

cursen *v.* curse III.1624, X.621; excommunicate I.486; *3 pr. sg.* **curseth** IV.902; *pr. pl.* **cursen** IV.898; *pr. subj. sg.* **corse** IV.1308; *3 pt. sg.* **cursed** VII.1504; *pt. pl.* **cursed** VII.1504; *pp.* **corsed** I.933, (as *adj.*) **cursed(e)** II.80, X.580; *vbl. n.* **cursyng(e)** excommunication I.660, III.1587; *pl.* **cursynges** curses X.206. MED cursen *v.*, cursing *ger.*

curteis *adj.* (1) courtly, refined, courteous I.250, IV.1815; (2) generous, merciful X.246; (3) deferential I.99. MED courteis *adj.*

curteisie *n.* courtliness, good manners, courtesy as a moral ideal I.46, II.166; act of good manners VI.739; **of (for) (your) c.** if you please I.725, III.1669. MED courteisie *n.*

curteisly *adv.* politely III.1771, VII.446; discreetly I.3997. MED courteisliche *adv.*

custume *n.* custom III.682, IV.1889; *pl.* **custumes** duty, taxes X.567, X.752. MED custume *n.*

cut *n.* lot I.845, VI.795; **draw c.** draw lots I.835, VI.793. MED cut *n.*(2)

D

day(e) *n.* (1) day I.91; the light part of the day I.1040, I.1481, I.3438; **artificial d.** sunrise to sunset II.2; **by d.** in daylight V.297; **d. natureel** twenty-four-hour day V.116; (2) period of time, term I.2998; lifetime IV.1136, V.1447; (3) time agreed for a meeting I.2095, IV.1998; (4) **al d.** every day, always IV.1155; **by d.** in daylight V.297; **d. by (be) d.** daily I.1407; **fro d. to d.** daily I.3371; **on, upon a d.** on a certain day I.19, I.1414, VI.118; **upon a d.** in one day I.703; **tomorwe d.** tomorrow morning I.3784; *gen.* **dayes** I.1629; *pl.* **dayes** I.2736, **dawes** V.1180. MED dai *n.*

daliaunce, daliance *n.* (1) sociable conversation, sociability III.565, III.1406; **do d.** be friendly, sociable VII.704; (2) flirting III.565; *pl.* **daliaunces** flirtations VI.66. MED daliaunce *n.*

damage *n.* injury, harm VII.1012, X.419; *pl.* **damages** VII.1389. MED damage *n.*

dame *n.* (1) (as a form of address) a woman of rank, lady I.3956, III.296; mistress of the household III.311, III.1797, VII.356; (2) dam I.3260; mother III.576, IX.317; *gen.* **dames** mother's III.583. MED dame *n.*

dampnable *adj.* damnable, worthy of damnation VI.472, VII.2605, X.679. MED dampnable *adj.*

dampnably, dampnablely *adv.* damnably VII.1826, X.604. MED dampnableli *adv.*

dampnacioun *n.* damnation III.1067, VI.500. MED dampnacioun *n.*

dampneth *v.* *3 pr. sg.* damns, condemns X.571; *1 pt. sg.* **dampned** III.2037; *pp.* **dampned** I.1175; **damned** II.843; *pp.* (as *adj.*) **dampned** X.191. MED dampnen *v.*

dar *v.* *1 pr. sg.* dare I.1151, II.273; *2 pr. sg.* **darst** I.1140, (with *pron.*) **darstou** VII.1147; *3 pr. sg.* dar III.1019; *pr. pl.* **dar** X.507; *1 & 3 pt. sg.* **dorste** I.227, I.454, **durste** VII.805; *pt. pl.* **dorste** I.4009; *pt. subj.* **dorste** VIII.532. MED durren *v.*

dart *n.* dart, spear I.1564, III.75. MED dart *n.*

daun *n.* sir, master (as a title of respect) I.1379, I.2673. MED daun *n.*

daunce *n.* dance III.993, V.277; procession III.991; **the old d.** tricks of the trade, game of love I.476, VI.79; *pl.* **daunces** I.1931. MED daunce *n.*

daunce(n) *v.* dance I.96, I.2202; *3 pr. sg.* **daunceth** IV.1728; *pr. pl.* **daunce(n)** I.2486, V.272; *3 pt. sg.* **daunced** I.4380; *prp.* **daunsynge** IV.1778, (as *adj.*) I.2201. MED dauncen *v.*

daungerous, dangerous *adj.* (1) domineering, disdainful I.517; (2) disdainful, standoffish III.514; fastidious, hard to please VII.939; (3) niggardly, grudging III.151, III.1427. MED daungerous *adj.*

dawe *v.* dawn IV.1842; *3 pr. sg.* **daweth** I.1676; *pr. subj. sg.* **dawe** I.4249; *pp.* **dawed** III.353. MED dauen *v.*

dawenyng(e) *n.* dawn I.4234, VII.2882. MED dauninge *ger.*

debaat *n.* (1) quarrel, dispute III.822, III.1288; **at d.** in conflict I.3230; (2) conflict, warfare I.1754, II.130. MED debat *n.*

debate *v.* dispute, argue VI.412; fight VII.868. MED debaten *v.*(1)

debonaire, debonere *adj.* gracious, of good disposition VII.1760; meek, submissive I.2282. MED debonaire *adj.*

debonairely, debonairly, debonerly *adv.* courteously, graciously VII.1064, X.315; meekly X.660. MED debonaireli *adv.*

debonairete(e), debonairte(e) *n.* graciousness VII.1621, VII.1820; meekness X.1054. MED debonairete *n.*

deceite *n.* deceit, trickery III.401, VI.592; *pl.* **deceites** X.440. MED deceite *n.*

deceyve(n) *v.* deceive III.1467, IV.2423, X.608; *2 pr. sg.* **deceyvest** IV.2064; *3 pr. sg.* **deceyveth** VII.1705; *pr. pl.* **deceyve** X.349; *pp.* **deceyved** IV.1356. MED deceiven *v.*

declaracioun *n.* manifestation, evidence X.595. MED declaracioun *n.*

declare(n) *v.* (1) tell, declare I.2536, VII.482; **d. his confessioun** confess X.1018; (2) explain, make clear I.3002, II.572; elucidate X.391; (3) reveal, make known I.2356, VIII.719; **oure wittes to d.** reveal our thoughts III.1479; *3 pt. sg.* **declared** VIII.331; *pp.* **declared** II.206. MED declaren *v.*

decree *n.* (1) decretal, ecclesiastical law I.640, I.1167; judgment X.17; **in his d.** in his judgment VII.2477; (2) laws collectively, the body of canon law X.931; *pl.* **Book of Decrees** Gratian's Decretum VII.1404. MED decre *n.*

deed, dede *adj.* dead I.145, I.942; deadly, deathlike I.1578, I.3643, VI.209; **I nam but d.** I'm as good as dead III.1006. MED ded *adj.*

dede, deede *n.* (1) action, deed I.742, I.1775; military action I.2636; (2) effect, result VII.1668; **in d.** in truth, indeed I.659; in actuality VII.2321; **with the d.** immediately VIII.157; simultaneously III.70; *pl.* **dedes** I.1438, **dedis** III.1155. MED dede *n.*

deedly, dedly *adj.* mortal, destructive of the soul X.956; like death, deathly I.1082; dying, about to die V.1040. MED dedli *adj.*

deedly *adv.* (1) intensely VIII.476; (2) deathlike, deadly II.822. MED dedli *adv.*

deef *adj.* deaf I.446, III.636; *pl.* **deve** VIII.286. MED def *adj.*

defame, diffame *n.* (bad) reputation, shame IV.730, VI.612; **for his d.** to cause him dishonor VII.2548. MED defame *n.*

defame *v.* (1) disgrace, bring dishonor on (someone) X.645; (2) accuse, slander I.3147; *pp.* **defamed** VI.415. MED defamen *v.*

defaute *n.* (1) lack X.207; (2) fault, defect VIII.954; (3) misdeed, sin VI.370, X.1030; wickedness VII.2528; *pl.* **defautes** faults III.1810, sins X.165. MED defaute *n.*

defende, deffende(n) *v.* (1) prohibit, forbid VI.590; (2) restrain III.1470; (3) defend II.933; beat off VII.1532; protect VII.1441; (4) speak in support of X.584; *3 pr. sg.* **deffendeth** forbids X.651; *pr. pl.* **defenden** forbid VII.1221; *3 pt. sg.* **defended** forbade III.60; *pp.* **def-**

fended VII.988, **defended** protected VII.1336. MED defenden *v.*

defense, deffense, defence *n.* defense VII.1533; means of defense III.467, VII.1161; **at d.** on guard, ready for battle IV.1195. MED defense *n.*

deffye *v.* defy, repudiate I.3578; *1 pr. sg.* **defye** I.1604, **deffie** VII.402, **diffye** III.1928; despise, scorn III.1928; *imp. sg.* **deffie** reject IV.1310. MED defien *v.*(1)

defoulen *v.* (1) trample on X.191; (2) injure, torment X.273; (3) pollute, defile V.1418, X.878; *pr. pl.* **defoulen** X.882; *1 & 3 pt. sg.* **defouled** X.984; *pp.* **defouled** X.273. MED defoulen *v.*

degre(e) *n.* (1) status, social rank I.1434; **after (at, in)** (one's) **d.** according to one's rank I.2192, I.2856; (2) situation, condition I.3040, IV.1494, IX.146; **ech in his d.** each in turn IV.263; **in my d.** insofar as I can IV.969; (3) manner, way; **in som (swich) d.** in some way, to some extent I.2844, III.1124; **at alle d.** in every way I.3724; **in ech d.** in all respects III.404; **in no d.** in no way, not at all V.198, VII.171; (4) *(astro.)* V.386; *pl.* **degrees** tiers, rows of seats I.1890. MED degre *n.*

deye, dye(n) *v.* die I.3034, I.3048, IV.665, X.237; *1pr. sg.* **dye.** I.1568; *3 pr. sg.* **deyth** III.2039, **dyeth** IV.1876; *pr. pl.* **deie** III.1405, **dye** I.2826; *pr. subj. sg.* **dye** III.1145; *3 pt. sg.* **deyde** X.642, **dyed** I.2843; *pt. pl.* **deyde(n)** III.1901, V.1429; *pt. subj. sg.* **deyde** I.3427, **dyde** III.965; *pt. subj. pl.* **deyden** III.1901; *pp.* **deyd** VII.651; *vbl. n.* **diyng** VII.2716. MED dien *v.,* diinge *ger.*

deigned *v. 3 pt. sg.* condescended VII.3181; granted, permitted VII.2720; *(impers.)* **hym d. (nat)** (did not) seem proper to him, he disdained VII.2134. MED deinen *v.*(1)

deynte(e) *n.* (1) pleasure, delight IV.2043, V.301; **have d.** to take pleasure in, be eager II.139, V.681; (2) esteem; **holde d. (of)** esteem X.477; **tolde no d.** did not value III.208; (3) fine food or drink, delicacy I.346; *pl.* **deyntees** delicacies II.419. MED deinte *n.*

deynte(e) *adj.* excellent I.168, IV.1112. MED deinte *adj.*

deys *n.* dais, platform I.370, I.2200. MED deis *n.*

deite(e) *n.* deity, godhead VIII.1469, IX.101; godly dominion V.1047. MED deite *n.*

deel *n.* bit, part; **every d.** all I.2091; completely I.1825; **never a (no) d.** not a bit III.561; **an hondred thousand d.** one hundred thousand times IX.137; **a (full) greet d.** very much, often I.415. MED del *n.*(2)

deelen *v.* (1) (with **with**) deal with, have to do with I.247; (2) have sexual intercourse with X.908; *3 pt. sg.* **delte** VIII.1074; *pp.* **deled** portioned out, divided III.2249. MED delen *v.*

deliberacioun, deliberacion *n.* deliberation, consideration, discussion VI.139, VII.1029. MED deliberacioun *n.*(1)

delicaat, delicat *adj.* (1) delightful, pleasing IV.682; splendid X.432; choice X.828; (2) fond of luxury, self-indulgent VII.2471, X.835; (3) fastidious X.688. MED delicat *adj.*

delices *n. pl.* pleasures, luxuries X.633; delights VII.1411. MED delice *n.*

deliciously *adv.* delightfully V.79; sumptuously X.377. MED deliciousli *adv.*

delit *n.* pleasure, delight I.335, III.418; sexual intercourse VI.159; **foul d.** sexual intercourse V.1396; **bi, with d.** delightfully VI.545; *pl.* **delites** pleasures X.298. MED delite *n.*(1)

delitable *adj.* delightful, sensuously pleasing IV.62, IV.199; *pl.* **delitables** V.899. MED delitable *adj.*

delite *v. (intr.)* be delighted, enjoy (often *reflx.* with **in**) VII.2470, X.601; *3 pr. sg.* **deliteth** X.805; *pr. pl.* **deliten** X.601; *3 pt. sg.* **delited** III.2044; *prp.* **delitynge** IV.997. MED deliten *v.*

delivere(n) *v.* (1) save X.586; **d. of (fro)** save from II.518, III.1724; (2) release, set free I.1769, II.941; (3) **was d. of** gave birth to II.750; *3 pr. sg.* **delivereth** X.308; *pr. pl.* **deliveren** III.1724; *imp. sg.* **delyvere** IV.134; *imp. pl.* **delivereth** III.1729; *3 pt. sg.* **delivered** VII.1100; *pp.* **delivered** II.750. MED deliveren *v.*

demande, demaunde *n.* question VIII.430, VIII.1451; *pl.* **demandes** requests, stipulations IV.348. MED demaunde *n.*

deme(n), deeme(n) *v.* (1) make a judgment, render a verdict VI.199, VII.1855; (2) condemn, sentence III.2024, VI.271; (3) suggest VII.449; (4) form a judgment or opinion V.1498, VII.1125, VII.1402; determine I.3194; (5) think V.44; suppose V.1486, X.1071; expect VII.1188; consider I.1881, I.3161; (6) express an opinion, argue V.221, V.261; (7) perceive V.563; *1 pr. sg.* **deeme** IV.753; *3 pr. sg.* **demeth** I.1353; *pr. pl.* **demen** V.224; *pr. subj. sg.* **deme** IV.1976; *imp. pl.* **demeth** I.1353; *1 & 3 pt. sg.* **demed** I.3226; *pt. pl.* **demed(e)** V.202; *pp.* **demed** VI.271. MED demen *v.*

departe(n) *v.* (1) *(tr.)* separate, part I.1134, II.1158; (2) divide VI.812, X.356; share III.2133; break up III.1049; (3) *(intr.)* depart, leave I.3070, III.1049; *1 pr. sg.* **departe** V.1532; *3 pr. sg.* **departeth** X.356; *pr. pl.* **departe(n)** I.3070; *pr. subj. sg.* **departe** III.2133; *pp.* **departed** I.1621, (as *adj.*) divided X.972; *vbl. n.* **departyng(e)** II.260. MED departen *v.,* departinge *ger.*

depe, deep *adj.* (1) deep I.3031, V.155; (2) profound VII.1406; (as *n.*) **depe** deep water, sea II.455. MED dep *adj.,* dep *n.*

depe, deepe *adv.* (1) deep, deeply I.129, IV.1940; (2) deeply, thoroughly (of color) V.511; (3) passionately, fervently I.1132; *comp.* **depper** more deeply II.630. MED depe *adv.*

depeint, depeynted *pp.* (1) portrayed I.2027, I.2034; (2) painted, stained VI.950. MED depeinten *v.*

depper deeper *see* **depe** *adv.*

deer *n. sg. and pl.* deer or animal(s) (the two meanings are not easily distinguishable) I.2150, V.1190. MED der *n.*

deere, dere *adj.* (1) honored, dear I.1234, III.1823, VIII.272; **have (holde) d.** hold in high esteem VII.2278; *comp.* **derre** I.1448; (2) (of things) excellent, fine V.341; (of abstractions) noble, excellent I.3588, II.237, III.827; (3) (of things) expensive III.522, VI.148; **deer ynough a leek (rysshe,** *etc.***)** expensive enough at the cost of a leek, rush, *etc.* (worthless) IV.999. MED dere *adj.*(1)

deere *adv.* dearly, expensively VIII.1133; **(a)bye so (to, full) dere** gain at a (too) high price, pay for (too) dearly II.420, VI.100. MED dere *adv.*

derk(e) *adj.* (1) dark I.2082, I.3731; (2) (morally) unclean X.1078; (3) obscure, mysterious II.481; (4) deceptive, malicious I.1995; (5) gloomy V.844; *super.* **derkest** III.1139; *(astro.)* most inauspicious II.304. MED derk *adj.*

derkness(e) *n.* darkness I.1451, VIII.384. MED derknesse *n.*

dees dice *see* **dys.**

des- *For words with this prefix, see also words beginning with* **dis-**.

descende(n) *v.* (1) descend, come down IV.392; (2) decline, deteriorate I.3010; (3) derive, be descended from I.3984; *prp.* **descendynge** I.3010; *pp.* **descended** I.3984. MED descenden *v.*

descharge(n) *v. (reflx.)* unburden oneself X.362; *pr. subj. sg.* **descharge** X.360; *pr. subj. pl.* **descharge** X.363. MED dischargen *v.*

descripsioun, descripcioun *n.* (1) account VI.117, X.741; (2) design I.2053. MED descripcioun *n.*

desdeyn, desdayn *n.* (1) scorn, disdain X.143; **take (have) in d.** scorn, despise VIII.41, X.150; (2) **have (take) in d.** be indignant, take offense I.789, V.700. MED disdeine *n.*

desert(e) *n.* (1) what is deserved X.757; **after his d.** according to what he deserves V.532; (2) worthiness, merit X.396; *pl.* **desertes** X.396. MED desert *n.*(1)

desert *n.* wasteland, wilderness, desert II.501, VII.1087. MED desert *n.*(2)

deserve *v.* (1) deserve, merit I.1232, I.2379; (2) **d. it unto you** repay you VIII.1352; *3 pr. sg.* **deserveth** X.972, **disserveth** X.756; *1 pt. sg.* **deserved** X.273; *2 pt. sg.* **deservedest** VI.216; *pp.* **disserved** I.1716, **deserved** I.1726. MED deserven *v.*

desherite *v.* disinherit VII.1835; *pp.* **desherited** VII.1751, **disherited** II.2926. MED disheriten *v.*

desolaat, desolat *adj.* (1) alone, lonely IV.1321; (2) lacking II.131; destitute, powerless III.703; *(astro.)* in an unfortunate position III.703; (3) wretched VI.598. MED desolate *adj.*

desordeynee *adj.* excessive X.818, X.915. MED disordeine *adj.*

despeir, dispeir *n.* despair I.1245, X.693; **in d.** in a depression I.3474. MED despeir *n.*

despeireth *v. 3 pr. sg.* loses hope X.698; *imp. pl.* **dispeire** IV.1669; *pp.* **despeyred** in despair V.943, discouraged V.1084. MED despeiren *v.*

despise *v.* (1) despise, look down on II.115, X.201; treat with contempt VIII.298; (2) speak ill of VII.1019, X.663; blaspheme X.599; *3 pr. sg.* **despiseth** VII.1070; *pr. pl.* **despise(n)** X.189; *pr. subj. pl.* **dispise** VII.1315; *pt. pl.* **despised** X.663; *prp.* **dispisynge** VII.1019. MED despisen *v.*

despit *n.* (1) disdain, scorn X.391; **han d. of, han in d.** scorn III.1876, V.1395, X.395; **in youre d.** in scorn of you VII.563; aversion V.1395; (2) defiance, spite III.2061, X.392, X.429; affront, insult III.2176; **in (for) d.** as an insult I.941, V.1371; (3) malice, spite I.941; anger, resentment III.481. MED despit *n.*

despitous, despitus *adj.* (1) scornful, disdainful X.395; (2) disobedient, spiteful III.761; (3) hateful, malicious I.516, I.1777. MED despitous *adj.*

despitously, dispitously *adv.* angrily VII.2595; cruelly IV.535. MED despitousli *adv.*

destyne(e) *n.* destiny, fate I.1108, I.2323; Destiny (personified) I.1663. MED destine *n.*

destourbe(n), desturbe *v.* hinder, prevent VI.340; *3 pr. sg.* **destourbeth** VII.977; *pr. pl.* **destourben** X.83; *pr. subj. sg.* **destourbe** X.991; *pp.* **destourbed** X.890. MED distourben *v.*

destroye(n) *v.* (1) destroy III.2080, V.883; kill I.1330; (2) harass III.377, VI.858; (3) damage, injure V.1251, X.220; ruin VII.1751; *3 pr. sg.* **destroyeth** III.377; *pr. pl.* **destroyen** X.790; *3 pt. sg.* **destroyed** IV.630; *pp.* **destroyed** I.1330. MED destroien *v.*

destruccioun, destruccion *n.* destruction, ruin I.2538, III.2007. MED destruccioun *n.*

deeth, deth *n.* (1) death I.964, I.1134, I.1320; (2) **the d.** the plague I.605. MED deth *n.*

dette *n.* (1) debt V.1578; indebtedness I.280, VII.376; (2) obligation X.252; **biheste is d.** a promise is a binding obligation II.41; (3) the marital debt (spouse's right to sexual intercourse) III.130, X.940. MED dette *n.*

dettour *n.* debtor III.155, VII.397; *pl.* **dettours** VII.413. MED dettour *n.*

devel *n.* (1) Satan, the Devil IV.1436, X.733; (2) any malignant spirit, demon VII.2936; (3) (in curses) III.476, III.1547; **a d. (twenty) weye** in the devil's (twenty devils') name I.3134, VIII.782; *gen.* **develes** X.351; *pl.* **develes** VII.2936. MED devel *n.*

devoir *n.* duty I.2598, X.764. MED dever *n.*

devyne, divyne *v.* guess VII.224; *prp.* **dyvynynge** I.2515; *vbl. n.* **divynynge** speculation I.2521. MED divinen *v.*, divininge *ger.*

devyse(n), divyse *v.* (1) think about IV.1586; imagine I.1790, IV.108; (2) design, plan IV.2000; (3) construct I.1901; compose IV.739; (4) tell, narrate, set forth VIII.266; explain I.1425; converse V.261; (5) command I.1416; *1 pr. sg.* **devyse.** I.34; *3 pr. sg.* **devyseth** III.1904; *pr. pl.* **devyse** V.261; *vbl. n.* **devisynge** arranging, preparation I.2496. MED devisen *v.*, devisinge *ger.*

devocioun, devocion *n.* (1) reverence, piety I.2371, II.257; (2) worship, prayers I.3640; (3) earnestness III.739, IV.1447, VIII.283. MED devocioun *n.*

dye *see* **deye** *v.*

dich *n.* ditch I.3964, VII.2848. MED diche *n.*

did(e), didest, dide(n) *see* **don.**

dighte *v.* (1) prepare, arrange IV.974; get dressed I.1041; (2) furnish I.3205; (3) *(reflx.)* go, depart VII.1914; (4) have sexual relations, copulate with IX.312; *3 pt. sg.* **dighte** III.398; *pp.* **(y)dight** adorned I.3205. MED dighten **v.**

digne *adj.* (1) suitable, fitting II.778; worthy IV.411; (2) honorable II.1175, VI.695; deserving X.494; (3) proud, haughty I.3964. MED digne *adj.*

dignytee *n.* (1) worthiness VII.456; **for Goddes d.** for God's sake I.4270, VI.782; excellence X.1040; (2) high rank or office IV.470, VII.2170. MED dignite *n.*

diligence *n.* (1) persistent effort, diligence III.1818, IV.230; **don (one's) d.** exert (one's) fullest effort I.2470, III.205; (2) eagerness IV.1185, VII.44; **have d.** pay attention VII.1637. MED diligence *n.*

dyner *n.* the first full meal of the day (usually between 9 A.M. and noon) II.1094, II.1118, VII.253. MED diner *n.*

dirryveth *3 pr. sg.* derives I.3006; *pp.* **dirryved** derived I.3038. MED deriven *v.*

dis- *For words with this prefix, see also words beginning with* **des-.**

dys, dees *n. pl.* dice I.1238; the game of dice I.4420. MED de *n.*

disclaundre *v.* slander III.2212; pp. **desclaundred** X.623. MED disclaundren *v.*

disconfite *v.* overcome, defeat VII.1339; *3 pr. sg.* **disconfiteth** X.661; *pp.* **disconfited** X.530; *vbl. n.* **disconfitynge** defeat, dishonor I.2719. MED discomfiten *v.*, discomfiting *ger.*

disconfort *n.* (1) loss of courage, dismay I.2010; distress, sorrow VII.984; (2) misfortune V.896. MED discomfort *n.*

discord *n.* disagreement, strife IV.432. MED discorde *n.*

discovere *v.* (1) reveal, disclose VII.1141, VIII.1465; betray (a secret) VIII.696; (2) betray, expose (someone by betraying his secrets) IV.1942; *2 pr. sg.* **discoverest** VIII.696; *3 pr. sg.* **discovereth** X.505; *pr. subj. sg.* **discovere** IV.1942; *imp. sg.* **discovere** VII.1141; *3 pt. sg.* **discovered** VII.1713; *pp.* **discovered** VIII.1468. MED discoveren *v.*

discrecioun, discrecion *n.* sound judgment I.1779, VIII.613, IX.282; moral discernment X.824; rational perception VII.2632; **by (no) d.** (im)moderately III.622, X.861. MED discrecioun *n.*

discret(e), discreet *adj.* (1) judicious, prudent IV.1909; morally discerning VI.48; (2) courteous, respectful of decorum I.518, VII.2871. MED discrete *adj.*

discreetly *adv.* judiciously, prudently VII.1268, X.1045. MED discreteli *adv.*

discryven, descryven *v.* describe V.40; **d. of** tell about IV.1737; *3 pr. sg.* **discryveth** IV.43; *pp.* **discryved** VII.2146; *vbl. n.* **discryvyng** account X.535. MED descriven *v.,* descrivinge *ger.*

disese *n.* distress, discomfort VIII.747. MED disese *n.*

dishonest(e), deshonest *adj.* dishonorable, unjust VII.1228, X.777; shameful IV.876; unchaste, immodest IX.214. MED dishoneste *adj.*

disordinat, desordinat *adj.* excessive X.415, X.431. MED disordinate *adj.*

disordinaunce *n.* rebelliousness, disorderly behavior X.277; *pl.* **disordinaunces** X.275. MED disordinaunce *n.*

dispende, despende *v.* (1) spend X.849; waste, squander (money) V.690; (2) distribute, give out VII.1370, X.812; (3) spend, waste (one's time, *etc.*) IV.1123, VII.931, VII.2310; *2 pr. sg.* **despendest** VII.931; *pr. pl.* **despenden** VII.1606, **dispenden** X.849; *pp.* **despended** VII.80, **dispended** VII.1370. MED dispenden *v.*

dispense, dispence, despence, despense *n.* (1) outlay of money, expenditure VII.16; expense VII.5; extravagant expenditures I.1928, III.700; **fre of d.** generous in spending IV.1209; **esy of d.** careful about spending I.441; (2) living expenses II.105, III.1432; *pl.* **despenses** VII.1652. MED dispense *n.*

displesant, displesaunt *adj.* offensive X.544, X.697. MED displesaunt *adj.*

displese(n) *v.* offend, annoy VII.1438, IX.26; displease III.1222, IV.506; *1 pr. sg.* **displese** IV.1982: *3 pr. sg.* **displeseth** III.293; *pr. pl.* **displese** III.128; *pr. subj. sg.* **displese** IV.1982; *pp.* **displesed** VIII.1010. MED displesen *v.*

dispoillen *v.* undress, strip IV.374; *pp.* **despoyled** stripped, robbed X.665. MED despoilen *n.*

disport, desport *n.* (1) amusement, fun I.4043, I.4420; **don (maken) d.** amuse, give pleasure to I.775, IV.1924; (2) pleasure VII.2791; comfort, source of comfort IV.1332; (3) **greet d.** excellent deportment I.137. MED disport *n.*

disporte *v. (reflx.)* amuse oneself I.3660; *pr. pl.* **disporten** IV.2040; MED disporten *v.*

disposeth *imp. pl.* arrange, prepare III.1659; *3 pt. sg.* **disposed** decided IV.244; *pp.* **disposid** controlled, regulated X.336; decided IV.244; prepared IV.755; **wel d.** in good health IX.33. MED disposen *v.*

disposicioun *n.* (1) power to control, rule I.2364; (2) mental attitude I.1378; (3) *(astro.)* aspect, disposition (of a planet) I.1087, III.701. MED disposicioun *n.*

dispreyse *v.* disparage, criticize VII.1071; *prp.* **dispreisynge** VII.1551; *vbl. n.* **dispreisynge** VII.1686. MED dispreisen *v.,* dispreisinge *ger.*

disputisoun, disputison *n.* discussion IV.1474; scholarly, logical disputation V.890, VII.3238. MED desputeison *n.*

dissensioun, dissencion *n.* disagreement, dispute IV.747, VII.1691. MED dissencioun *n.*

dissevere(n) *v.* separate VII.1615; *pp.* **dissevered** VII.1431. MED disseveren *v.*

distaf *n.* distaff, staff for holding unspun fiber during spinning I.3774 (see note), VII.1907, VII.2374. MED distaf *n.*

distreyne, destreyne *v.* (1) restrain, confine X.269; (2) constrain, compel IX.161; (3) torment, afflict I.1816; *3 pr. sg.* **destrayneth** afflicts I.1455; *pp.* **distreyned** oppressed X.752. MED distreinen *v.*

distresse, destresse *n.* misfortune, hardship I.919; suffering, grief V.916, VIII.76. MED distresse *n.*

divers(e) *adj.* (1) differing III.701; various, sundry I.3857, II.211; (2) separate, distinct X.489. MED diverse *adj.*

diversely, diversly *adv.* (1) differently, in differing ways III.1877; (2) with differing opinions I.3857, IV.1469. MED diverseli *adv.*

diversitee *n.* difference II.220. MED diversite *n.*

divyn(e) *adj.* divine I.122, III.1719. MED divine *adj.*

dyvynytee *n.* (1) divine nature VIII.340; the Divine Being VIII.316; (2) theology III.1512. MED divinite *n.*

divyse devise *see* **devyse(n).**

divisioun, division *n.* (1) dividing up X.1009, X.1011; (2) clan, division I.2024; (3) distinction, difference I.1780; (4) dissension I.2476. MED divisioun *n.*(1)

do(o) *see* **don.**

dogge *n.* dog VII.3383; **d. for the bowe** dog trained to hunt with an archer III.1369; *pl.* **dogges** VII.1899. MED dogge *n.*

doghter, doughter *n.* daughter I.2064, I.2222; *gen. sg.* **doghter** IV.608; *pl.* **doghtren** V.1429, **doghtres** V.1370, VI.73. MED doughter *n.*

doke *n.* duck I.3576; *pl.* **dokes** VII.3390. MED doke *n.*

doom *n.* (1) judgment IV.1000; **sitten in d.** sit in judgment VI.257; **sweren in d.** take an oath in court X.592; **day of d.** the Last Judgment X.118; (2) judicial decision, sentence VI.163; case at law X.594; **to my d.** in my opinion VII.1937; *pl.* **doomes** VI.163. MED dom *n.*

dominacioun *n.* power, control I.2758, VI.560; **in his d.** dominant V.352 (see note). MED dominacioun *n.*

don, don(e), do, doo(n) *v.* (1) do, perform I.78, I.268; **d. bisynesse (cure, diligence)** take pains, work hard, be diligent I.1007, III.1074, IV.1298; **d. right** enforce the law VII.1439; **d. nedes** conduct business II.174; **d. profit** be useful, beneficial VII.1269, X.1003; **d.** (one's own) **profit (avantage)** derive benefit (for oneself) II.729, VII.1588; **is to d.** is to be done, is necessary III.2194; (2) cause, give (pleasure, ease, *etc.*) I.766, I.1248; (with *inf.*) cause (something) to be done III.1364, IV.253, V.46; **dide doon sleen hem** had them slain III.2042; **d. cryen the feeste** had the feast announced V.46; (3) place, put VIII.899; **d. wey** take away I.3287; **d. wey** be done with VIII.487; **d. up** raise I.3801; (4) act, proceed, behave VII.1648, VIII.903; (5) as auxiliary forming periphrastic *(pr.)* I.3410, (emphatic) III.853; *1 pr. sg.* **do** I.2461: *2 pr. sg.*

doost VI.312, (with *pro.*) **dostow** III.239; *3 pr. sg.* **dooth** I.98, **doth** III.1034; *pr. pl.* **doon** II.1531, **do(n)** III.438; *pr. subj. pl.* **do** VII.1012; *imp. sg.* **do** I.3287; i*mp. pl.* **dooth** VI.745, **do** I.2598; *1 & 3 pt. sg.* **did(e)** I.1004, I.268; *pt. pl.* **dide(n)** I.1007, I.1177; *pt. subj. sg.* **did(e)** I.451, VI.746; *pp.* **have do** finish up I.3728; **ydon** I.1025; **ydo(o)** VIII.899; **(y)doon** I.1083, VIII.386; *vbl. n.* **doyng(e)** VIII.421. MED don *v.*(1), doinge *ger.*

dong(e) *n.* dung, manure I.530, VI.535, VIII.807. MED dong *n.*(1)

dore *n.* door I.460, III.6; *pl.* **dores** I.1987. MED dore *n.*(1)

dorste dared *see* **dar.**

dote(n) *v.* act foolishly VIII.983; *1 pr. sg.* **dote** IV.1441 MED doten *v.*

double *adj.* double I.262; duplicitous, treacherous X.644. MED double *adj.*

doublenesse *n.* duplicity, treachery V.566. MED doublenesse *n.*

doughter *see* **doghter.**

doumb, dowmb, dombe *adj.* mute, speechless, dumb I.774, II.1055, VIII.286. MED domb *adj.*

doun *adv.* down, downward I.952, I.1103; **beren d.** overcome I.3831, IV.2270; **up and d.** all over, in every way I.977, I.2054; **up so d.** upside down I.1377, (as one word) VIII.625. MED doun *adv.*

doute *n.* (1) uncertainty, doubt, X.91; **withoute(n) (out of) d.** certainly I.487, I.1322; (2) reverence X.1023; (3) danger IV.1721; *pl.* **doutes** opinions, conjectures V.220. MED doute *n.*

doute(n) *v.* fear, be afraid VII.1327, X.880, X.953; *3 pr. sg.* **douteth** X.953; *pr. pl.* **douten** X.648; *pr. subj.* **doute** VII.1327; *3 pt. sg.* **douted** X.880. MED douten *v.*

doutelees *adv.* doubtless I.1831, I.2667. MED douteles *adv.*

dowve *n.* dove IV.2139, VI.397; *pl.* **dowves** I.1962. MED douve *n.*

dowere, dowaire *n.* dowry IV.807, IV.848. MED douere *n.*

drad, dradde(n) dreaded *see* **drede(n).**

draughte, draghte *n.* drink I.135, I.382, VI.315; *pl.* **draughtes** VI.568. MED draught *n.*

drawe(n) *v.* (1) draw, pull, drag II.339; draw water I.1416; **d. cut** draw lots I.842; **d. along** pull, tear apart VII.633; (2) bring, carry, drag I.3663; lead, entice I.519, X.121; **d. in** lead to, cause X.1000; **d. (in)to memorie** remember I.2074, X.239; get, obtain X.549; derive VIII.1440; (3) go, move, come III.1549; go toward, approach I.3633; **d. unto** agree with, come to agree IV.314; *3 pr. sg.* **draweth** I.835; *pr. pl.* **drawe(n)** IV.1817, V.252; *imp. sg.* **drawe** VI.966; *imp. pl.* **draweth** I.835; *3 pt. sg.* **drow** I.3633, **drough** I.3892; *prp.* **drawynge** III.2150; *pp.* **(y)drawe** II.339, **(y)drawen** X.549. MED drauen *v.*

drede *n.* (1) fear I.1396, II.657; personified I.1998; (2) anxiety, worry IV.134, VII.123; (3) awe, reverence; **have in d.** hold in awe VII.2162; **no d.** no doubt, without question II.869, III.1169; **withouten, out of d.** doubtless, certainly II.29, V.1544; (5) danger, peril II.657, VII.1327. MED drede *n.*

drede(n) *v.* (1) (sometimes *reflx.*) dread, be fearful I.660, VII.2929; (2) fear (something) IV.636, VIII.320; (3) hold in awe, reverence V.1312, VIII.125; (4) avoid, abhor VII.1176; (5) doubt, be in doubt I.1593, IV.1316; *1 pr. sg.* **drede** I.1593; *3 pr. sg.* **dredeth** VII.1316; *pr. pl.* **drede**

X.763; *pr. subj. sg.* **drede** VIII.477; *imp. sg.* **drede** III.1214, IV.1201; *imp. pl.* **dredeth** VII.2969, **dreed** IV.1201; *3 pt. sg.* **dradde** IV.523; *pt. pl.* **dredde** IV.181; *pt. subj. pl.* **dradden** VIII.15; *pp.* **drad** IV.69. MED dreden *v.*

dredeful, dredful *adj.* (1) timid I.1479; (2) frightening II.937, VII.2368. MED dredeful *adj.*

dreye, drye *adj.* dry I.3024, I.3730; (as *n.*) one of the elemental qualities I.420 (see note). MED drie *adj.*(1), drie *n.*(1)

dreynt(e) drowned *see* **drenche(n).**

dreem *n.* dream II.804; *pl.* **dremes** V.357. MED drem *n.*(2)

dreme *v. pr. pl.* **dreme** dream VII.3092; *1 & 3 pt. sg.* **dremed** III.582; *(impers.)* **me dremed** I dreamed VII.787; *vbl. n. pl.* **dremynges** VII.3090. MED dremen *v.*(2), dreming *ger.*(2)

drenche(n) *v.* (1) drown, be drowned I.3521, II.455; (2) sink X.363; (3) flood, inundate X.839; *3 pr. sg.* **drencheth** X.363; *3 pt. sg.* **dreynte** II.923; *pt. pl.* **dreynte** V.1378; *pp.* **dreynt(e)** I.3520, (as *adj.*) II.69, *vbl. n.* **drenchyng(e)** drowning I.2456. MED drenchen *v.*, drenchinge *ger.*

drery *adj.* sad IV.514, IV.671. MED dreri *adj.*

dresse *v.* (1) place, put IV.381; (2) arrange, put in order I.3635; (3) prepare IV.1049; *(reflx.)* get ready II.265; (4) address one's attention to V.290, VIII.77; care for, tend to I.106; (5) guide, direct VII.1118; (6) go, move II.416, V.290; (7) treat IV.2361; *3 pr. sg.* **dresseth** I.3635; *pr. pl.* **dresse(n)** I.2594, II.263; *3 pt. sg.* **dressed** I.3358; *pp.* **(y)dressed** IV.381. MED dressen *v.*

drye(n) *v.* dry VII.2746; *3 pr. sg.* **dryeth** I.1495, **dreyeth** X.848. MED drien *v.*(1)

drynke(n) *v.* drink I.635, I.750; *1 pr. sg.* **drynke** X.160: *3 pr. sg.* **drynketh** IV.1807; *pr. pl.* **drynke(n)** I.4147. II.707; *imp. sg.* **drynk** III.2053; *2 & 3 pt. sg.* **drank** II.743; *pt. pl.* **dronken** I.820; *pp.* **dronke(n)** I.135, (as *adj.*) drunk X.822, **ydronke** VII.1411; *vbl. n.* **drynkynge** X.576. MED drinken *v.*, drinkinge *ger.*

dryve *v.* (1) drive, chase I.1859, I.2727; compel X.527; (2) drive (a cart) III.1540; (3) drive (a nail) I.2007, III.769; (4) go rapidly II.505, III.1694; (5) conclude (a bargain) V.1230; (6) (with **forth**) bear up under, endure VII.231; *3 pr. sg.* **dryveth** II.505; *pr. pl.* **dryven** VII.1086; *3 pt. sg.* **droof** III.1540; *prp.* **dryvynge** II.947; *pp.* **(y)drive(n)** I.2007, I.4110. MED driven *v.*

droghte *n.* dryness, lack of rain I.2, I.595, V.118. MED droughte *n.*

dronk, dronke(n), ydronke drank *see* **drynke(n).**

dronkelewe *adj.* addicted to drink III.2043, X.626. MED dronke-leue *adj.*

droppeth *v. 3 pr. sg.* fall in drops, drip I.3895; X.632; *3 pt. sg.* **dropped** VIII.580, dripped with moisture; *prp.* **droppyng(e)** leaking X.631, (as *adj.*) leaky III.278; *pp.* **ydropped** I.2884; *vbl. n.* **droppyng(e)** dripping VII.1086. MED droppen *v.*, droppinge *ger.*

duc *n.* duke I.860, I.873, I.893; *pl.* **dukes** I.2182. MED duk *n.*

due, dewe *adj.* (1) legal, customary X.561; (2) obligatory, required X.867; payable IV.1452; (3) **in d. manere** properly VII.1254; (4) predestined I.3044. MED due *adj.*

duetee *n.* tax, fee owed to an authority III.1352, III.1391; (2) due respect I.3060. MED duete *n.*

dul(le) *adj.* dull II.202, V.279. MED dul *adj.*

dulleth *v. 3 pr. sg.* depresses VIII.1093; *pp.* **dulled** weakened X.233. MED dullen *v.*

duracioun *n.* duration, set period of time I.2996. MED duracioun *n.*

dure(n) *v.* endure I.1236, IV.166. MED duren *v.*

dwelle(n) *v.* (1) remain, stay I.512, I.973, X.223; (2) reside, dwell I.4003; inhere in I.2804; (3) continue III.947; *1 pr. sg.* **dwelle** I.2462; *3 pr. sg.* **dwelleth** I.1310; *pr. pl.* **dwelle(n)** VII.1373, VIII.656; *2 pt. sg.* **dweltest** VIII.48; *3 pt. sg.* **dwelte** I.512, **dwelled** I.2804; *pt. pl.* **dwelten** II.550; *prp.* **dwelling(e)** I.702, VII.2822; *pp.* **dwelled** I.1228, **dwelt** VIII.720; *vbl. n.* **dwellynge** abode I.1937. MED dwellen *v.*, dwellinge *ger.*

E

ech *pro.* each (one) I.427, I.791, I.1132; **ech a** every III.256; *adj.* every III.404, III.1968. MED ech *pro.*

echon(e), echoon *pro.* each one, everyone IV.124, VI.113, VI.349. MED ech on *pro.*

effect *n.* (1) result, consequence I.2989; **in e.** in fact, actually IV.721; **take e.** have an effect X.607; (2) substance I.2207, III.1451; the point I.1189; purpose I.1487; **to the e.** for this purpose, so that VII.1868; **to this e.** for this purpose VII.1883; *pl.* **effectes** I.2228. MED effect *n.*

eft *adv.* (1) again, another time II.792, II.802, IV.1227; (2) immediately V.631; (3) likewise I.3647. MED eft *adv.*

eftsoone(s), eft-soone(s) (also as two words) *adv.* (1) again III.1992; another time VII.2286, VIII.933; (2) immediately I.3489; (3) in return III.808, III.1992. MED eftsones *adv.*

Egipcien *adj.* Egyptian II.500, (as *n.*) VII.2338. MED Egipcien *n. & adj.*

egle *n.* eagle V.123; *gen.* **egles** VII.2175. MED egle *n.*

ey *interj.* oh, ah I.3768. MED ei *interj.*

eye, ye, eighe *n.* eye I.10, I.896, V.1036; *pl.* **eyen** I.152, **yen** VII.2070. MED eie *n.*(1)

eyle *v.* ail, afflict, cause trouble for I.3424; *3 pr. sg.* **What eyleth (thee, yow,** *etc.***)** What's the trouble with (you, *etc.*) I.1081, I.3769; *3 pt. sg.* **eyled** V.501. MED eilen *v.*

ek(e), eek(e) *adv.* also II.716, II.829, III.30. MED ek *adv. & conj.*

elde, eelde *n.* old age I.2448, III.1215. MED elde *n.*

elder(e) *comp.* of **old** older VII.530, VII.2260; *super.* **eldest(e)** I.912, V.30. MED olde *adj.*

eldres *n. pl.* elders, ancestors IV.65, VI.364. MED eldre *n.*

elf *n.* supernatural being, spirit (often evil) III.873; *pl.* **elves** I.3479. MED elf *n.*

elf-queene *n.* fairy queen VII.790. MED elf *n.*

elles *adj.* else, other III.1866, III.2203. MED elles *adj.*

elles, ellis *adv.* otherwise, else I.375, I.1151. MED elles *adv.*

embrace, enbrace *v.* embrace IV.1101; hold, retain IV.412; *3 pr. sg.* **embraceth** VII.1215; *pt. pl.* **embraceden** X.193; *vbl. n.* **embracynge** embrace X.944; *pl.* **embracynges** X.944. MED embracen *v.*, embracing *ger.*

empoysone *v.* poison X.514; *pp.* **empoysoned** III.751; *vbl. n.* **empoisonyng(e)** VI.891. MED empoisounen *v.*, empoisouning *ger.*

emprenteth *v. imp. pl.* impress, imprint IV.1193; *pp.*

emprented IV.2117, V.831; *vbl. n.* **emprentyng** impression V.834. MED emprenten *v.*, emprenting *ger.*

emprise, enprise *n.* (1) enterprise VII.1066; (2) chivalric exploit V.732; knightly courage VII.2667; (3) difficult task X.691. MED emprise *n.*

enchesoun *n.* cause V.456; reason, occasion VII.1593. MED enchesoun *n.*

enclyne *v.* (1) bow, accede VII.1594; condescend II.1082; (2) be inclined (to do something) X.361; *imp. sg.* **enclyne** VII.1180; *imp. pl.* **enclyneth** VII.1594; *prp.* **enclynynge** VII.1152; *pp.* **enclyned** VII.1250. MED enclinen *v.*

encombred *pp.* encumbered, burdened I.1718; hindered (by being stuck) I.508. MED encombren *v.*

encrees *n.* increase, growth I.2184, II.237. MED encres *n.*

encresse(n), encreesen *v.* increase II.1068, IV.1808; *3 pr. sg.* **encresseth** I.1315, **encreeseth** X.350; *pr. pl.* **encressen** I.1338, **encreesen** X.321, **encreescen** VII.1740; *pt. pl.* **encreesceden** VII.1276; *pp.* **encressed** IV.408. MED encresen *v.*

endelong *prep.* from end to end, along V.992; down the length of V.416; (as *adv.*) lengthwise I.1991. MED endelong *adv.*, endelong *prep.*

endite *v.* write, compose I.95, II.781; describe (in writing) I.1872; draft (a legal document) I.325; *3 pr. sg.* **enditeth** IV.41; *pr. sub. pl.* **endite** IV.17; *pp.* **endited** VII.1980; *vbl. n. pl.* **enditynges** X.1085. MED enditen *v.*, enditinge *ger.*

enforce(n) *v.* (1) force III.340; (2) strengthen, reinforce VII.958; grow stronger VII.1043; *3 pr. sg.* **enforceth** X.730; *pr. pl.* **enforcen** VII.1152; *imp. sg.* **enforce thee** try VII.1047; *pp.* **enforced** X.832. MED enforcen *v.*

engendre(n) *v.* engender, produce VII.1209; beget IV.1272; *3 pr. sg.* **engendreth** III.465; *pr. pl.* **engendren** VII.2923; *pp.* **engendred** I.4; *vbl. n.* **engendrynge** cause VII.1390. MED engendren *v.*, engendring *ger.*

engendrure *n.* (1) the act of procreation VII.1947; (2) offspring X.621; *pl.* **engendrures** offspring X.562. MED engendrure *n.*

engyn *n.* (1) intelligence, skill VIII.339; (2) contrivance V.184. MED engin *n.*

enhauncen *v.* advance I.1434; increase (pride, *etc.*) X.614; *3 pr. sg.* **enhaunceth** strengthens X.730; *pp.* **enhaunced** IV.1374. MED enhauncen *v.*

ensample, exemple *n.* (1) example I.568, III.1580; (2) illustrative story, exemplum III.179; (3) model, pattern I.505, I.520; *pl.* **ensamples** exempla, illustrative anecdotes VII.1998. MED ensaumple *n.*

entencioun, entencion *n.* intention, purpose VI.408, VIII.1443. MED entencioun *n.*

entende *v.* (1) intend, plan III.1479; strive VII.2308; (2) pay attention to V.689; take care of V.1097; attend, wait upon IV.1900; (3) listen V.689; *3 pr. sg.* **entendeth unto** strives toward III.275. MED entenden *v.*

entent(e) *n.* (1) purpose, intention II.40; plan II.206; **doon al oure e.** take care VIII.6; **in hool e.** wholeheartedly IV.861; **in (ful) good e.** willingly I.958, in good faith II.824; (2) mind, heart V.1178; **seyde (al) his e.** spoke his (whole) mind III.1733; (3) meaning, view VII.1078; **as to commune e.** in plain language V.107. MED entente *n.*

ententyf *adj.* eager X.781; diligent VII.1015. MED ententif *adj.*

envenyme *v.* poison III.474; **envenymed** infused with poison VII.2124; *vbl. n.* **envenymynge** X.854. MED envenimen *v.*, enveniming *ger.*

envye *n.* (1) ill-will, spite VIII.1372; (2) envy I.907. MED envie *n.*

er *adv.* before, formerly I.3789, VIII.1273; for *super.* cf. **erst(e)**, *adv. super.* MED er *adv.*

er *prep.* before III.1619, VII.2797. MED er *prep.*

er *conj.* before I.255, I.1040; **er that** before I.36, I.835. Cf. **or** *conj.* MED er *conj.*(1)

ere, eere *n.* ear III.636, III.1021; *pl.* **erys** I.556, **eres** IV.941, **eeris** VII.1418. MED ere *n.*(1)

erl *n.* earl III.1157, VII.2407; *pl.* **erles** I.2182. MED erl *n.*

erly, eerly *adv.* early I.33, I.809. MED erli *adv.*

ernest *n.* (1) seriousness IV.733; **in e.** seriously I.1125; (2) serious matter VIII.710; **make e. of game** take a joke seriously I.3186. MED ernest *n.*

erren *v.* wander, err VII.1025; *pr. pl.* **erren** VIII.449; *pp.* **erred** VII.1241. MED erren *v.*(1)

erst(e) *adj. super.* (as *n.*) **at e.** at first, for the first time VIII.151, VIII.264. MED erest *adj.*

erst(e) *adv. super.* before, earlier IV.144, IV.336; **e. er** before III.2220, VI.662; **e. than** before I.1566. MED erest *adv.*

erthe *n.* earth I.1246. MED erthe *n.*(1)

erthely *adj.* earthly, mortal I.1166, VI.21. MED ertheli *adj.*

eschue, eschewe *v.* forgo, eschew IV.1451, VIII.4; escape, flee from I.3043; *3 pr. sg.* **escheweth** VII.1320, **eschueth** X.833; *2 pr. subj. sg.* **eschue** X.632; *imp. sg.* **eschue** VII.1181; *pp.* **eschued** VII.1839, **eschewed** VII.3338; *vbl. n.* **eschewynge** avoiding X.464. MED escheuen *v.*, escheuinge *ger.*

ese, eyse *n.* (1) ease, comfort IV.217; **at e.** comfortable III.2101; **take (one's) e.** rest I.969; (2) relief, refreshment I.4119; (3) pleasure IV.1643; **don (someone) e.** please I.768; (4) **lith in youre e.** is convenient for you VII.291. MED ese *n.*

esen *v.* comfort, entertain I.2194; *pp.* **esed** accommodated I.29, relieved I.2670. MED esen *v.*

esy *adj.* (1) comfortable IV.1264; (2) lenient, gentle I.233; moderate I.441; **e. fir** moderate blaze VIII.768; (3) not difficult X.1042; *comp.* **esier** more tolerable VII.1500. MED esi *adj.*

esily *adv.* (1) comfortably IV.423; (2) **e. a pas** at an unhurried pace V.388; (3) easily V.115. MED esili *adv.*

especial *adj.* special, intimate VII.1166; special, particular X.893; (as *n.*) **in e.** to particulars VII.1234. Cf. **special(e)**. MED especial *adj.*

espye(n) *v.* (1) search out, discover I.1420; (2) find out II.324; **tyme (leyser) e.** find an opportunity I.3293; (3) notice, see I.1112; take notice, take the measure of I.1420; *pr. subj. sg.* **espie** I.3566; *pr. subj.pl.* **espie** I.3729; *3 pt. sg.* **espide** VIII.1230; *pp.* **espied** VIII.895. MED aspien *v.*

espiritueel *adj.* spiritual X.516; *pl.* **espirituels** X.79. MED espirituel *adj.*

est *n.* east II.297, III.1247; (as *adv.*) I.2601. MED est *n.*

estat, estaat *n.* (1) state, condition IV.610; (2) rank, social standing I.1322; class IV.123; (3) term of office III.2018. MED estat *n.*

estward *adv.* eastward I.1893, IV.50. MED estward *adv.*

ete(n) *v.* eat I.947, IV.1812; *1 pr. sg.* **ete** X.160; *3 pr. sg.* **eteth** X.372; *pr. pl.* **eten** VI.468; *imp. sg.* **ete** VII.1416; *pr. subj. sg.* **ete** VII.1417; *3 pt. sg.* **eet** I.2048; *prp.* **etyng** III.2167; *pp.* **eten** I.4351; *vbl. n.* **etynge** X.332. MED eten *v.*, etinge *ger.*

eterne *adj.* eternal I.1109, III.5. MED eterne *adj.*

evene *adj.* (1) equal I.2588; **evene-Cristen(e)** fellow Christian X.608, X.810; (2) impartial I.1864; moderate I.83; tranquil IV.811. MED even *adj.*

evene *adv.* (1) evenly I.3316; (2) directly I.1060; (3) correctly VIII.1200; (4) calmly I.1523. MED even *adv.*

ever(e), euere *adv.* (1) ever, always I.50, I.335; (2) **e. (the) lenger (the moore)** increasingly IV.687, V.404; **e. the gretter** proportionately greater X.916; (3) (as *intens.*) **as, als e.** as I.1475, I.4177; **e. in oon** continually, always VII.27; **e. sithe** ever after I.3893; **e. yet** always before this III.545. MED ever *adv.*

everemo(o), everemore, everemoore *adv.* always I.67; continually III.1086; perpetually I.1229; **e. in oon** always, continually IV.2086. MED ever-mor *adv.*

every, everiche *adj.* every, each I.15; **e. a** every single I.733; **e. maner wight** every sort of person I.1875; **in e. maner (wyse)** in all ways VII.245. MED everi *pro.*

everich *pro.* each one I.1848, VI.931. MED everi *pro.*

everichon(e), everichoon *pro.* everyone I.747, VII.1899. MED everich-on *pro.*

everydeel (also two words) *n.* everything V.1288; (also two words) *adv.* wholly, completely I.368, IV.1508. MED everi-del *n. & adv.*

execucioun, execucion *n.* performance, action; **putten in (to) e.** carry out (a plan) VII.1853; **doon e.** carry out (an intended act) IX.287, carry out (orders) IV.522, punish III.1303. MED execucioun *n.*

expounde(n), expoune, expowne *v.* explain, expound VII.535, VII.2208, VIII.86; *3 pt. sg.* **expowned** VII.2156. MED expounen *v.*

expres *adv.* clearly, explicitly III.27, VI.182; **e. agayn** explicitly opposed to X.587. MED expresse *adv.*

F

fable *n.* (1) story X.31; (2) fiction VI.155; *pl.* **fables** fictions, III.1760. MED fable *n.*

face *n.* (1) face I.199; **shrewe his f.** curse him III.2227; **in my f.** right at me VII.1904; (2) expression IV.1399; (3) (*astro.*) one-third (10 degrees) of a zodiacal sign IV.1288; *pl.* **faces** II.650. MED face *n.*

fader, fadir *n.* (1) father I.100, VIII.208; (2) forefather VI.505; *gen. sg.* **fader** I.4038, **fadres** II.861; *pl.* **fadres** II.129. MED fader n.

fay faith *see* **fey.**

fayerye, fairye *n.* (1) the realm of the supernatural IV.2227, V.96; (as collective) supernatural beings, the supernatural III.859, IV.2039; (2) something magic or enchanting IV.1743; *pl.* **fayeryes** III.872. MED fairie *n.*

faille *n.* **sanz f.** doubtless, for certain II.501; **withoute(n) f.** doubtless, for certain I.1644, I.1854. MED faile *n.*

faille(n), fayle *v.* (1) fail, disappoint I.1610, VIII.388; (2) fail to do, accomplish (with **to**) IV.1632; (with **of**) III.430, VIII.671; **f. of my day** fail to pay on the set day VII.275; (3)

lack, be lacking VII.248, VII.2462; **f. you my thankes** be lacking in gratitude VII.188; (4) grow weak I.2798, I.3887; *1 pr. sg.* **faille**, VII.415; *3 pr. sg.* **failleth** V.167, **fayleth** X.250; *pr. pl.* **faille(n)** VIII.671, VIII.851; *pr. subj. sg.* **faille** III.574, *1 & 3 pt. sg.* **failled** I.2806, V.1577. MED failen *v.*

fayn, fawe *adj.* happy, pleased II.787; eager III.220. MED fain *adj.*

fayn *adv.* gladly, eagerly II.41. MED fain *adv.*

fair(e), feir *adj.* (1) pleasing, attractive I.154, I.211; **f. at (to) eye(n)** pleasant to see IV.1168, VIII.964; (2) shining I.3976; (3) favorable I.1861, I.1874; (4) convincing VII.1711, X.1022; (5) gracious, benevolent I.1861; morally good X.1061; (6) (as form of address) dear II.245, II.319; *comp.* **fairer** I.754; *super.* fairest I.2201. MED fair *adj.*

fair(e) *adv.* (1) well I.94, I.124, III.1142; handsomely I.273; neatly I.3210; (2) courteously, pleasantly I.3289, II.1051, III.803; gently I.2697, VIII.536, V.347; (3) fully, completely VII.830; **f. and wel** very well, completely I.539, I.1826; (4) (with *prep.*) directly, squarely I.606, I.984. MED faire *adv.*

fair(e) *n.* beauty V.518; fine thing I.165; **foule or (ne) f.** all circumstances II.525, V.121. MED fair *n.*

falle(n) *v.* (1) fall, descend I.128, I.921; fall out or away from VII.2126; (2) fall into, come (to a condition) I.25, I.1418, X.1025; **f. acorded** agree III.812; (3) **f. to (unto)** belong to, be appropriate to II.149, IV.259; **as fer as reson f.** insofar as was appropriate to reason V.570; (4) befall, happen I.585, I.1668, V.134; **f. of** result from VII.1428; *2 pr. sg.* **fallest** VI.556; *3 pr. sg.* **falleth** I.1669, **falles** *(Nth.)* I.4042; *pr. pl.* **falle(n)** I.2327, X.100; *pr. subj. sg.* **falle** I.2555; *3 pt. sg.* **fil** I.845, **fel** I.1462; *pt. pl.* **fille(n)** I.949, I.2666; *pt. subj. sg.* **fille** I.131; *pp.* **(y)falle** I.25, I.324, **(y)fallen** II.909; *vbl. n.* **fallyng(e)** I.2464, I.2722. MED fallen *v.*, fallinge *ger.*

fals *adv.* untruly III.1057, VII.1204. MED fals *adv.*

fals(e) *adj.* (1) deceitful, treacherous I.925, III.1670; (2) wicked I.4268, VI.154; (3) untrue II.640, III.382; wrong IV.2380. MED fals *adj.*

false(n) *v.* falsify, misrepresent I.3175; *pp.* **falsed** broken (a promise) V.627. MED falsen *v.*

falshede *n.* falsehood VIII.979, VIII.1051. MED falshede *n.*

falsly *adv.* (1) disloyally I.1142, I.1586; deceitfully VI.654; (2) evilly III.738, VI.228; (3) untruly VI.415. MED falsli *adv.*

falsnesse *n.* deceitfulness, dishonesty VIII.976, VIII.1086. MED falsnesse *n.*

fame *n.* (1) reputation, good or bad I.3055, IV.418, VI.111; notoriety I.3148; (2) news II.995, IV.940; (as *proper n.*) **book of F.** X.1086. MED fame *n.*(1)

famulier *adj.* (1) belonging to the household IV.1784; (2) intimate I.215. MED familier *adj.*

fantasye *n.* (1) imagination IV.1577; (2) an imagined notion V.844; delusion I.3835; (3) fancy, desire I.3191; inclination I.516; **after** (one's) **f.** according to (one's) desire(s) III.190, V.205; **doon his f.** fulfill his amorous desire VII.2285; *pl.* **fantasies** VII.2275. MED fantasie *n.*

fare *n.* (1) behavior, conduct I.1809; **strange f.** elaborate courtesy, formality VII.263; (2) **made f.** caused a fuss I.3999. MED fare *n.*(1)

fare(n) *v.* (1) go II.512; (2) act, behave I.1261; **f. by** deal with, treat X.899; (3) fare, get along, do I.1265, I.4350; **how f. ye** how are you III.1801; (4) to be (well) provided for III.1773; (5) (*impers.*) happen I.4408, VIII.966; *1 pr. sg.* **fare** I.3871; *3 pr. sg.* **fareth** III.1088, **fares** *(Nth.)* I.4023; *pr. pl.* **fare(n)** I.1261, III.1094; *pr. subj. sg.* **fare** V.1579; *imp. sg.* **far(e) wel** good luck, good-bye I.2740, I.4236; *imp. pl.* **fareth wel** farewell IV.1688; *3 pt. sg.* **ferde** I.1372; *pt. pl.* **ferden** I.1647; *prp.* (as *adj.*) **well (beste) farynge** good (best) looking V.932, handsome, attractive VII.1942, *pp.* **fare(n)** I.2436, III.1773. MED faren *v.*

fast(e) *adv.* (1) tightly, closely I.2151, III.520, IV.1821; strictly III.652; (2) quickly I.1469, IV.1927; (3) close I.1478; **f. by** close to I.719, I.1476, III.970; (4) eagerly, heartily I.1266, III.672; *comp.* **fastere** more tightly VII.2532. MED faste *adv.*

faucon, faukon *n.* falcon V.411, V.424. MED faucoun *n.*

faught *see* **fighte(n).**

fee *n.* property III.630; **f. symple** unrestricted possession I.319; *pl.* **fees** payments I.1803. MED fe *n.*(2)

feble, fieble *adj.* feeble, weak I.1369, II.306, IV.1198. MED feble *adj.*

fecche(n) *v.* fetch, bring II.662, IV.276; fetch, take away II.1064; *imp. sg.* **fecche** bring I.3492; *pr. subj. sg.* **fecche** take away III.1554; *3 pt. sg.* **fette** III.2159; *pt. pl.* **fette** VII.851; *pp.* **(y)fet** I.819, V.174. MED fecchen *v.*, fetten *v.*

fey, fay *n.* faith I.1126, III.203; **by (upon)** (one's) **f.** on one's good word I.3284 (var. of **feith** below).

feyne *v.* (1) make up, invent, devise I.736, III.1378; (2) imitate, counterfeit III.1507, V.524; (3) dissemble, make false pretences V.510; (4) pretend IV.513; (*reflx.*) II.351, IV.1950; **f. thy wey** pretend to go another way VII.1311; (5) avoid (obeying a command) IV.529; *pr. pl.* **feyne** III.1507; *imp. sg.* **feyne** VII.1311; *3 pt. sg.* **feyned** IV.513; *prp.* **feynynge** III.1378; *pp.* **yfeyned** IV.529, **feyned** VI.62, (as *adj.*) I.705; *vbl. n.* **feynynge** V.556. MED feinen *v.*, feining *ger.*

feir fair *see* **fair(e)** *adj.*

feith, faith *n.* (1) religious belief I.62, VIII.644, VIII.110; (2) loyalty IV.1053; (3) pledged word III.2139; **f. to borwe** my word as a pledge V.1234; (4) **in (good) f.** truly V.673; **by (upon) my f.** on my word, certainly III.841, III.1403. Cf. **fey** above. MED feith *n.*

feithful *adj.* (1) devout VIII.24; (2) loyal IV.310, IV.343; (3) true III.1425. MED feithful *adj.*

feithfully *adv.* (1) faithfully, devotedly II.461, IV.1111; (2) truly III.1420; indeed, assuredly III.1433, IV.1066. MED feithfulli *adv.*

fel fell *see* **falle(n).**

fel, felle *adj.* fierce, cruel I.1559, I.2630. MED fel *adj.*

felawe *n.* (1) companion, comrade I.890; friend, associate I.1031; **good f.** agreeable fellow I.395 (see note), III.618; (2) equal partner I.1624, X.400; (3) fellow fighter I.2548; *gen.* **felawes** VII.3026; *pl.* **felawes** associates VII.2985, fellows of a college I.4112. MED felaue *n.*

felaweshipe, felawshipe *n.* (1) company, fellowship I.26, I.32, VI.938; household I.3539; (2) companionship, friendliness I.474; (3) equal partnership I.1626. MED felaushipe *n.*

feeld *n.* field I.886, I.984; pl. **feeldes** I.977. MED feld *n.*

feld felled *see* **felle** *adj.*

feelen *v.* (1) feel VIII.155; (2) perceive VIII.711; *1 pr. sg.*
feele I.2232; *3 pr. sg.* **feeleth** I.1220; *pr. pl.* **feelen** X.581;
1 & 3 pt. sg. **felte** I.1575, III.410, **feelede** VIII.521; *pt. pl.*
felte VII.3135; *prp.* **felynge** V.480; *pp.* **felt** V.586; *vbl. n.*
sense of touch X.959; feeling, emotion III.610. MED
felen *v.*(1), felinge *ger.*(1)

felicitee *n.* happiness I.338, I.1266. MED felicite *n.*

felle *v.* fell, cause to fall I.1702; *pp.* **feld** I.2924. MED fellen *v.*

felle fierce *see* **fel** *adj.*

felle(n) *see* **falle(n).**

felonye *n.* (1) crime, wickedness II.643; (2) ill will, malice
X.543; *pl.* **felonies** X.281. MED felonie *n.*

fend, feend *n.* (1) demon VIII.984; (2) **the f.** Satan, the Devil
I.4288, II.454; *gen. sg.* **feendes** II.571; *pl.* **feendes** II.460.
MED fend *n.*

feendly, feendlych *adj.* devilish, demoniac II.751, II.783,
V.868. MED fendliche *adj.*

fer *adj.* far, remote VII.718; **f. cause** remote cause VII.1395;
comp. **ferre** I.3393; *super.* (as *n.*) **ferreste** those farthest
away I.494. MED fer *adj.*(1)

fer *adv.* far I.491, I.1648; at a distance VII.2997; **f. ne ner**
more or less I.1850 (see note); *comp.* **ferre** I.48, I.2060,
ferrer I.835. MED fer *adv.*

fere, feere *n.* fear I.1333, VII.2906. MED fer *n.*(1)

ferde(n) fared *see* **fare(n).**

fered *pp.* frightened, afraid VII.3386, VIII.924. MED fered
ppl.

fereful *adj.* fearful, frightened VIII.660. MED ferful *adj.*

ferforth *adv.* **as f. as** insofar as, to the extent that II.1099,
III.56; **so f.** to such an extent V.567. MED fer-forth *adv.*

fermely *adv.* firmly, steadfastly X.309. MED fermeli *adv.*

ferrer farther *see* **fer** *adv.*

ferthe *num.* (as *adj.*) fourth II.17, X.943; (as *n.*) fourth
VIII.824, X.480. MED ferthe *num.*

ferther *adj.* farther, far IV.2226, VII.496. MED ferther *adj.*

ferther *adv.* farther I.36, V.1177. Cf. **forther.** MED ferther
adv.

fest *n.* fist I.4275, III.792. MED fist *n.*(1)

feste, feeste *n.* (1) festival I.2736; feast I.2197, I.3684; (2)
festivity I.2483; **make f.** make merry VII.327; (3) treat
respectfully VII.1109; *pl.* **festes** I.1931, **feestes** VI.65.
MED feste *n.*

feste, feeste *v.* feast, dine II.1007, IV.1892; *3 pr. sg.* **festeth**
entertains I.2193; *prp.* **festeiynge** entertaining V.345.
MED festen *v.*

festne *v.* fasten I.195. MED fastnen *v.*

fet(e), feet(e) feet *see* **foote.**

(y)fet fetched *see* **fecche(n).**

fethere *n.* feather I.2144; pl. **fetheres** IX.304. MED fether *n.*

fetisly *adv.* elegantly, neatly I.273, I.3319, III.1742. MED
fetisli *adv.*

fette fetched *see* **fecche(n).**

fiers(e) *adj.* fierce, dangerous I.1598, I.1945. MED fers *adj.*

fighte(n) *v.* fight I.984, I.1711; *3 pr. sg.* **fighteth** I.2559; *pr.
pl.* **fighte** I.4291; *pr. subj. pl.* **fighten** I.1836; *3 pt. sg.*
faughte I.989; *pt. pl.* **foughte(n)** I.1178, I.1699; *prp.* **fightyng** I.1661; *pp.* **foughten** I.62; *vbl. n.* **fightyng** I.1656.
MED fighten *v.,* fightinge *ger.*

figure *n.* (1) form, appearance III.1459; (human) form
VII.2222; (2) image, likeness V.831; configuration I.2043
(see note); (3) parable I.499; rhetorical ornament, figure
of speech IV.16; *pl.* **figures** VI.28. MED figure *n.*

fil, fille(n) fell *see* **falle(n).**

fille *n.* **(al)** (one's) **f.** as much as one wants I.1528, I.2559.
MED fille *n.*(1)

filthe *n.* (1) filth III.1215; (2) moral foulness, infamy
III.1393, X.258; sinfulness X.606, X.882; *pl.* **filthes** foul
things X.196. MED filth *n.*

fyn *n.* (1) end, conclusion VII.2694; (2) outcome VII.2158;
(3) object, purpose IV.2106. MED fin *n.*(2)

fyn(e) *adj.* fine, excellent IV.1843; *comp.* **fyner** I.1039; *super.*
fynest(e) I.194. MED fin *adj.*

final *adj.* final, ultimate V.987; **cause f.** ultimate cause or purpose VII.1401, X.939. MED final *adj.*

fynde(n) *v.* (1) find, discover I.648, I.736; (2) provide VI.169;
provide for VI.537, VII.2829; (3) fabricate, invent I.736; *1
pr. sg.* **fynde** I.2812; *3 pr. sg.* **fyndeth** II.1150, **fynt**
(contr.) I.4071, **fyndes** *(Nth.)* I.4130; *pr. pl.* **fynde(n)**
III.1753, IV.1275; *pr. subj. sg.* **fynde** VII.1227; *imp. sg.*
fynd I.2244; *1 & 3 pt. sg.* **foond** I.2445, **fond** I.701; *pt. pl.*
founde VI.769, **foond** VII.2069; *pt. subj. sg.* **fond**
VII.2331; *pp.* **founde** I.4059, **founden** be provided II.243;
vbl. n. **fyndyng** I.3220. MED finden *v.,* finding *ger.*

fynger finger III.1890; *pl.* **fingres** I.129, IV.380. MED finger
n.

fynt finds *see* **fynde(n).**

fyr(e) *n.* fire I.2336; one of the four elements I.1246; **wilde f.**
Greek fire III.373 (see note); erysipelas I.4172 (see note),
IV.2252; **f. of seint Antony** erysipelas X.427 (see note);
gen. **fires** VIII.1408; *pl.* **fyres** I.2292. MED fir *n.*

firy *adj.* fiery I.1493, I.1564, III.276. MED firi *adj.*

firmament *n.* (1) the sky, the heavens IV.2219; (2) celestial
sphere II.295. MED firmament *n.*

fit *n.* (1) episode, experience I.4230, III.42; (2) canto, division of a poetic narrative VII.888. MED fit *n.*(1), fit *n.*(2)

flambe *n.* flame X.353; *pl.* **flambes** VIII.515. MED flaume *n.*

flater(e) *v.* flatter X.618; *2 pr. sg.* **flaterest** IV.2059; *pr. subj.
sg.* **flatere** X.376; *prp.* (as *adj.*) **flaterynge** III.1294; *pp.*
yflatered III.930; *vbl. n.* **flaterynge** flattery, X.612, deception II.405. MED flateren *v.*(1), flattering *ger.*

flaterye *n.* flattery I.1927, III.932. MED flaterie *n.*

flatour *n.* flatterer, deceiver VII.3325. MED flatour *n.*

flaugh flew *see* **fle(e)** *v.* fly.

fle(e), fleen *v.*[1] (1) flee, run away II.121, III.279; (2) escape
I.2993, VIII.1081; (3) go away, depart I.1469, IV.119; (4)
avoid, shun VII.1484; *3 pr. sg.* **fleeth** I.1469; *pr. pl.* **fleen**
II.121; *pr. subj. sg.* **fle** X.1005; *imp. sg.* **fle** VII.1330; *3 pt.
sg.* **fledde** II.544, **fleigh** VII.2689; *pt. pl.* **fledden** I.2930;
pp. **fled** II.541. MED flen *v.*(1)

fle(e) *v.*[2] fly V.122; *3 pr. sg.* **fleeth** IV.119; *pr. pl.* **flee**
VII.2942; *3 pt. sg.* **fley** VII.3172, **fleigh** VII.3339; *2 pt. sg.*
flaugh VII.3231; *pt. pl.* **flowen** VII.3391. MED flien *v.*

fleesh, flessh *n.* (1) human flesh I.2640, VI.732; (2) body
III.157, IV.1335; (3) physical or sensual nature VII.1421,
X.336; (4) meat I.147, I.344. MED flesh *n.*

flesshly *adj.* (1) bodily, physical X.206; (2) sensual, carnal
X.204. MED fleshliche *adj.*

flesshly *adv.* (1) physically X.333; in a worldly manner

X.202; (2) carnally, sensually X.939. MED fleshliche *adv.*

fleete *v. pr. sg. subj.* swim, float I.2397; *3 pr. sg.* **fleteth** II.901, **fleet** *(contr.)* drifts II.463; *prp.* **fletynge** floating I.1956. MED fleten *v.*(1)

flye *n.* any sort of flying insect: housefly I.4352; **nat worth a f.** worthless V.1132, VII.171, VIII.1150; *pl.* **flyes** bees X.441. MED flie *n.*(1)

flood *n.* (1) flood I.3518; (2) high tide V.259; *pl.* **floodes** high tides VII.2587. MED flod *n.*

flok *n.* flock, group I.824. MED flok *n.*(1)

floryn *n.* gold coin I.2088, X.749; *pl.* **floryns** VI.770 (see note). MED floren *n.*

flour *n.* (1) flower I.4, I.2937; (2) virginity IV.2190; (3) prime of life I.3048, III.113; (4) best part I.4174; **bereth the f.** takes first place VII.901; (5) (with **of**) the model, the best I.982, IV.919, IV.2497; *pl.* **floures** I.90. MED flour *n.*(1)

flour *n.* flour, meal I.4053, I.4093, III.477. MED flour *n.*(2)

floure *v. pr. subj. sg.* **floure** flourish IV.120; *3 pt. sg.* **floured** VI.44. MED flouren *v.*(1)

flowen fled *see* **fle(e)** *v.* fly.

fo(o) *n.* foe, enemy I.63, I.1590; *pl.* **foes** VII.970, **foos** VII.2029, VII.2706. MED fo *n.*

folde *n.* times (indicating multiplication): **hundred (thousand) f.** hundred (thousand) times II.1120, VI.40. MED folde *n.*(2)

folie *n.* (1) foolishness, folly I.1798, I.3146; **doon f.** act foolishly I.3045, VII.1704; idle tale, nonsense V.1131; (2) sin, wrongdoing VI.464, X.315; lechery, fornication I.3880; *pl.* **folies** foolish thoughts V.1002, foolish deeds VII.1801. MED folie *n.*

folily *adv.* foolishly IV.1403, VIII.428. MED folili *adv.*

fool *n.* (1) fool I.1606, I.1799; (2) sinner, rascal IV.2278; **f. of hire body** promiscuous X.156; (3) jester, court fool VII.2081; *pl.* **fooles** IV.1251. MED fol **n.**

fool *adj.* (1) foolish VIII.968; (2) lecherous X.853. MED fol *adj.*

foold *n.* (1) sheepfold I.1308; (2) *(fig.)* parish I.512. MED fold *n.*(1)

fool-large *adj.* improvident, prodigal VII.1599, X.814; (as *n.*) spendthrift VII.1620. MED fol-large *adj.*

folwe(n), folowe(n) *v.* follow III.1124, IV.873; *3 pr. sg.* **folweth** II.865; *pr. pl.* **folwe(n)** I.2682, IV.897; *imp. sg.* **folwe** VII.1693; *imp. pl.* **folweth** IV.1189; *1 & 3 pt. sg.* **folwed** III.583, IV.1249; *pt. pl.* **folwed** I.2151; *prp.* **folowynge** I.2367; *pp.* **folwed** VII.1198. MED folwen *v.*

foomen *n. pl.* foes, enemies VII.2068, VII.2080. MED foman *n.*

fond, foond found *see* **fynde(n)**.

fonde *v.* try IV.283, IV.1410. MED fonden *v.*

for *prep.* (1) because of I.264, I.2144 (see note); (2) for, on behalf of I.62, I.301; (3) (with *inf.*) in order to I.17, I.73; **f. to** (with *inf.* untranslated *intens.*) I.3667, II.1067; (4) in order to (get something) I.191, I.1177, III.961; (5) to prevent, avoid VII.862; as a protection against X.607; (6) concerning, as regards I.387, I.3858, **(as) f. me** so far as I am concerned I.1619; **f. aught (ought)** so far as I.389; MED for *prep.*

for *conj.* (1) because I.4225; (2) since I.3667; (3) so that I.2879. MED for *conj.*

forasmuche, for as much(e) (muchel) *adv. phr.* inasmuch as

VII.33, VII.1267. MED for as muche *adv.*

forage *n.* (1) feed for animals VII.783 (see note); (2) dried hay, straw I.3868, IV.1422. MED forage *n.*

forbede *v.* forbid I.3508; *1 pr. sg.* **forbede** V.1481; *3 pr. sg.* **forbedeth** forbids III.652; *pr. subj. sg.* **forbede** I.3508, **forbeede** X.881; *imp.* III.519; *3 pt. sg.* **forbad** IV.570; *pp.* **forbode(n)** IV.2296, X.845. MED forbeden *v.*

forbere *v.* (1) endure, tolerate III.665; (2) forgo, refrain from I.885; *vbl. n.* **forberynge of** abstinence from X.1049. MED forberen *v.,* forbering *ger.*

forby *adv.* by, past (in space) VI.125, VI.668. MED forbi *adv.*

force *see* **fors**.

fordoon *v.* destroy, ruin II.369; *pr. subj. pl.* **fordo** VII.127; *pp.* **fordo** V.1562; **fordoon** IX.290. MED fordon *v.*

forgat forgot *see* **foryete**.

forgo(n), forgoon *v.* (1) give up III.315, VIII.610, X.812; refrain from, avoid IV.2085; (2) forfeit, lose IX.295; *pp.* **forgoon** VII.993, X.945. MED forgon *v.*

forleseth *v. 3 pr. sg.* loses X.789; *pp.* **forlore** lost I.3305, **forlorn** V.1557. MED forlesen *v.*

forlete(n) *v.* (1) leave, forsake X.583; (2) cease X.250; (3) lose VI.864; *3 pr. sg.* **forleteth** X.119; *pr. pl.* **forlete** X.93; *pr. subj. sg.* **forlete** renounce X.93. MED forleten *v.*

forme *n.* (1) shape, form V.337; appearance V.1161; (2) proper manner I.305; (3) pattern V.283; (4) lair of a hare VII.104; *pl.* **formes** I.2313 (see note). MED forme *n.*

forme *v.* form, create VI.12; *pp.* **yformed** VI.10. MED formen *v.*

forneys, fourneys *n.* (1) cauldron I.202, X.554; (2) furnace VII.2163. MED furnaise *n.*

fors, force *n.* (1) physical strength, power I.1927, I.2015; **by (of) (fyne) f.** by (sheer) compulsion, force I.2554; **by f.** by necessity VI.205; (2) importance III.2189; **(is) no f.** does not matter VI.303; **(do) make no f.** pay no attention to, care nothing for III.1512; **what f.** what does it matter IV.1295. MED force *n.*

forsake(n) *v.* (1) repudiate, disavow IV.1290; (2) refuse, reject VII.1557; (3) abandon, desert IV.1290, VII.669, VII.2241; *1 pr. sg.* **forsake** VII.794: 3 pr. sg. **forsaketh** X.562; *imp. pl.* **forsaketh** VI.286; *pr. subj. sg.* **forsake** III.1522; *3 pt. sg.* **forsook** III.644; *pp.* **forsake(n)** VI.80, X.994. MED forsaken *v.*

forseyde, foreseyde *pp.* aforesaid VII.1254, X.410. MED fore-said *ppl.*

forsweryng *vbl. n.* perjury VI.657; *pl.* **forswerynges** VI.592. MED forswering *ger.*

forth *adv.* (1) forth, onward I.825, III.1540; **mot f.** must leave II.294; **tarien f. a day** pass a day, kill time I.2820; **dryven f. the world** pass the time VII.231; (2) out, out of VII.293, VIII.312; **strecche f.** stretch out VI.395, VII.3308; (3) **heer f.** ahead, beyond III.1001; **fro this (thennes) f.** from then on, thenceforth VII.565; **and so f.** and so on III.1924; **doth f.** carry on IV.1015; **tell (spoken) f.** tell on I.2816, VI.660; (4) afterward V.1081; (5) (as *intens.* adding sense of continuation) III.1540, V.1552. MED forth *adv.*

forther *adv.* farther, onward I.4117, I.4222; **f. in age** older IV.712; **f. over** moreover X.437. Cf. **ferther** *adv.* MED further *adv.*

forthermo, forthermoor(e) *adv.* (also two words) furthermore III.783, IV.169, VI.594. MED further more *adv.*

forthy *adv.* therefore, for this reason I.1841, I.4031; **nat f.** nevertheless VII.975. MED for-thi *adv. & conj.*

forthre(n) *v.* advance, aid I.1137, I.1148. MED furtheren *v.*

forthward *adv.* forward II.263, V.1169. MED forth-ward *adv.*

fortunat, fortunaat *adj.* (1) fortunate, favored by fortune IV.1970, V.25; happy, successful IV.422; (2) *(astro.)* auspicious IV.1970. MED fortunat *adj.*

fortune *n.* (1) (personified) Fortune I.915, VI.295; (2) chance, accident VII.238; destiny I.2659, V.1497; (3) state, condition VII.1559. MED fortune *n.*

forward, foreward *n.* agreement, promise I.829; **as f. is (was)** as is (was) agreed I.2619, II.34. MED fore-ward *n.*

for-why *conj.* because VI.847. MED for-whi *conj.*

foryete *v. 1 pr. sg.* forget I.1882; **f. mynde (wit)** lose one's mind, wits II.527; *3 pr. sg.* **foryeteth** X.827; *pr. subj. sg.* **foryete** I.1882; *imp. pl.* **foryet** I.2797; *1 & 3 pt. sg.* **forgat** I.4076, VI.919; *pp.* **forgeten** I.3054, **foryeten** I.1914. MED foryeten *v.*

foryeve(n) *v.* forgive I.743, X.810; *1 pr. sg.* **foryeve** I.1818; *2 pr. sg.* **foryevest** X.1043; *3 pr. sg.* **foryeveth** IX.206; *pr. subj. sg.* **foryeve** IX.1084; *imp. sg.* **foryeve** III.807; *imp. pl.* **foryeveth** IX.206; *3 pt. sg.* **foryaf** X.808. MED foryeven *v.*

fostre *v.* raise VI.219; educate IV.593; nourish, feed IX.165, IX.1756; *3 pr. sg.* **fostreth** pampers IV.1387; *imp. sg.* **fostre** IX.175; *3 pt. sg.* **fostred** IV.222; *pp.* **(y)fostred** I.3946, (as *adj.*) V.1043; *vbl. n.* **fostryng** nourishment III.1845. MED fostren *v.,* fostring *ger.*

foot(e) *n.* (1) foot I.2509; foot (as measurement) I.4124; (2) poetic foot VII.1979; *pl.* **feet(e)** II.1104, X.8; (as *pl.,* following *num.*) **foot** I.2607, I.4124. MED fot *n.*

foul(e), fowle *adj.* (1) ugly II.764, III.265, IV.1209; frightening III.776; miserable, wretched I.3061; dirty, disgusting IV.1095, VI.536; (as *n.*) **f. or fair(e)** any circumstances V.121; (2) shameful III.963, III.2049; defiled, evil II.586; *comp.* **fouler** III.999, VI.525; *super.* **fouleste** X.147. MED foul *adj.*

foule *adv.* miserably I.4220, III.1312. MED foule *adv.*

fowel *n.* bird, foul I.190; *pl.* **foweles** I.9, **fowles** V.647. MED foul *n.*

frankeleyn *n.* landowner I.331 (see note); *pl.* **frankeleyns** I.216. MED frankelein *n.*

fraunchise, franchise *n.* (1) social status of a freeman X.452; (2) nobility of character, generosity of spirit V.1524. MED fraunchise *n.*

fre(e) *adj.* (1) free (not servile), having the social status of a noble or freeman IV.2069; (as *n.*) noble VI.35, VII.1567; generous of spirit V.1622, VII.467; (2) unrestrained, free I.1292, III.49, IV.147; unconstrained (assent, choice, will) I.852, I.1606, IV.150; without obstruction VII.494; generous, liberal (in spending) I.4387, IV.1209, VII.43. MED fre *adj.*

fre(e) *adv.* freely, without restrictions V.541, VII.3269. MED fre *adv.*

fredom, fredam *n.* nobility of character, generosity II.168, IX.126. MED fredom *n.*

freend, frend *n.* friend I.670, I.1468; *gen.* **freendes** I.3220; *pl.* **frendes** husbands I.992, friends I.1483, II.347. MED frend *n.*

frely *adv.* (1) freely, without restraint I.1207, I.1849, III.150; (2) nobly, generously VIII.55; liberally V.1604; willingly, gladly VIII.55. MED freli *adv.*

freletee *n.* frailty, moral weakness III.92; sinfulness VI.78. MED frelete *n.*

frere *n.* friar I.208, I.621, III.829; *pl.* **freres** I.232. MED frere *n.*

fressh(e) *adj.* (1) new, unfaded, young I.90; (2) blooming, lovely I.1068, I.2386; (3) vigorous IV.1173, V.23; sexually vigorous III.508, III.1259; (4) joyous V.284; *comp.* **fressher** V.927. MED fresh *adj.*

fressh *adv.* (1) **al f.** newly, recently I.2832, VII.309; (2) gaily I.1048, IV.781. MED freshe *adv.*

frete(n), freeten *v.* devour, eat (of or like an animal) I.2019; *pr. pl.* **frete** III.561; *pp.* **freeten** II.475. MED freten *v.*(1)

fro, fra *adv.* in *phr.* **to (til) and f.** back and forth I.1700, I.4039. MED from *adv.*

fro, fram, from *prep.* (1) from I.44, I.397, I.671; away from VIII.22; (2) of II.453; **ware (thee) f.** beware of VI.905. MED from *prep.*

fruyt *n.* (1) fruit I.3872, VI.510; (2) product, result III.114, VI.656; offspring VII.990; (3) profit, best part I.1282, IV.1270, V.74; essential part II.411, VI.3443. MED fruit *n.*

ful, fulle *adj.* (1) (with **of**) filled to capacity, full I.233, I.2279; (2) complete, full, entire I.3075, II.86; (3) (as *n.*) **atte (at the) f.** fully, completely I.3936. MED ful *adj.,* fulle *n.*(1).

ful *adv.* (1) completely, fully VI.25; (2) (as *intens.* with *adj.* or *adv.*) very I.132; completely I.4230, II.1106. MED ful *adv.*

fulfille(n) *v.* (1) fill (something) full III.859, X.947; (2) satisfy (lust, appetite, *etc.*) I.1318, III.1218, V.1372; (3) carry out, accomplish, execute II.284, VII.1744; *3 pr. sg.* **fulfilleth** X.947; *pt. pl.* **fulfilleden** VII.1523; *pp.* **fulfild** I.940, **fulfilled** VI.535. MED ful-fillen *v.*

fully, fulliche *adv.* fully, completely I.876, I.969. MED fulli *adv.*

furlong *n.* (1) one-eighth of a mile I.4166, V.1172; (2) (as *adj.*) **f. wey** time needed to walk a furlong (about 2½ min.), a short time IV.516, II.557 (see note). MED furlong *n.*

G

gadereth *v. 3 pr. sg.* gathers I.1053; *3 pt. sg.* **gadred(e)** I.824, I.4381; *pp.* **gadered** I.2183; *vbl. n.* **gaderyng** VII.1575. MED gaderen *v.,* gaderinge *ger.*

gay(e) *adj.* (1) joyous, merry I.3254, III.1727; attractive, good-looking I.3769, III.355; (2) bright, ornamented I.111; fine, elegant I.3323, III.221; gaily dressed, richly attired I.74; (3) pleasant sounding I.296. MED gai *adj.*

gay(e) *adv.* handsomely I.3689, VIII.1017. MED gai *adv.*

gayler *n.* jailer I.1474, VII.2433. MED gaioler *n.*

gayneth *3 pr. sg. (impers.)* helps, avails (him, us, etc.) I.1176, I.2755. MED geinen *v.*

galle *n.* (1) bile, secretion of the liver X.195, VIII.797; (2) bitterness VII.2347. MED galle *n.*(1)

galwes *n. pl.* gallows III.658, VII.2734. MED galwe *n.*

game *n.* (1) amusement, sport, revelry, I.853, I.2286, I.3117; (2) joke, jest I.4354, III.1279; **maken ernest of g.** take a joke seriously I.3186; **in (for) ernest or in (for) g.** in jest or earnest, in any case IV.609; **in** (one's) **g.** playfully, in jest VI.829; (3) scheme, trick I.3405. MED game *n.*

gan *see* **gynne.**

garnysoun *n.* body of armed men VII.1027; protection VII.1337. MED garnisoun *n.*

gauren *v.* (with **on**) stare at V.190; *3 pr. sg.* **gaureth** VII.2369. MED gauren *v.*

geant, geaunt *n.* giant VII.807, VII.828. MED geaunt *n.*

general(e) *adj.* (1) all-inclusive, universal I.1663, I.2969, X.388; (as *n.*) **in g.** without exception II.417; (2) of wide application X.464; not specifically I.2285; couched in general terms V.945; (3) (in titles) **ministre (vicaire) g.** chief servant, chief representative I.1663, VI.20. MED general *adj.*, general *n.*

gentil(e) *adj.* (1) noble, well-born I.2539, III.1153, VII.2658; (2) noble in character I.1761, IV.1919; (3) superior, refined, excellent (sometimes ironically) I.567, I.647, I.718; *super.* **gentilleste** most noble IV.72. MED gentil *adj.*

gentillesse, gentilesse *n.* (1) nobility of birth or rank III.1117, VII.2251, X.585; (2) nobility of character I.920, I.3382, II.853. MED gentilesse *n.*

gentilly, gentily *adv.* nobly, courteously, honorably, I.3104, II.1093. MED gentilli *adv.*

gentils *n. pl.* nobles VI.323. MED gentil *n.*

gentrie, genterye *n.* noble birth III.1152, X.461; noble deed X.601. MED gentrie *n.*

gerdone *v.* reward, requite VII.1275; *pp.* **gerdoned** VII.1272. MED guerdonen *v.*

gerdon, gerdoun *n.* reward, requital V.973, V.1220; *pl.* **gerdons** VII.1052. MED guerdoun *n.*

gere, geere *n.* (1) apparel, clothing IV.372; (2) armor, fighting equipment I.2180; equipment, gear I.352, I.4016; (3) behavior, conduct I.1372; *pl.* **geeris** apparatus V.1276; *pl.* **geres** manners, ways of behaving I.1531. MED gere *n.*

gerland *n.* wreath, garland I.1507, I.1961; *pl.* **gerlandes** I.2937. MED gerlond *n.*

gees *see* **goos.**

gesse *v.* (1) perceive I.2593; conclude X.175; (2) suppose, imagine II.622; *1 pr. sg.* **(as) I g.** as I believe, I suppose (often merely a tag; e.g., I.117) II.1143, V.1412. MED gessen *v.*

gest *n.* guest, visitor IV.338; *pl.* **gestes** IV.1016. MED gest *n.*

geste, geeste *n.* story, history (either true or fictitious) V.211; *pl.* **geestes** histories II.1126. MED geste *n.*(1)

gete(n) *v.* (1) get I.1512, III.210; save, preserve I.2755; (2) beget IV.1437; *2 pr. sg.* **getest** X.31; *3 pr. sg.* **geteth** I.3620; *pr. pl.* **gete(n)** I.4099, VII.1574; *pr. subj. pl.* **gete** VII.1632; *imp. sg.* **get** I.3465; *3 pt. sg.* **gat** I.703; *pp.* **(y)geten** I.291, I.3564, III.1236; *vbl. n.* **getyng(e)** acquiring VII.1597. MED geten *v.*(1), getinge *ger.*(1)

gyde *n.* guide I.804, I.4020, II.164. MED gide *n.*

gyde *v.* lead, direct IV.776; *3 pr. sg.* **gydeth** VII.300; *pr. subj.* **gyde** VII.259 *(sg.)*, II.245 *(pl.)*; *imp. pl.* **gydeth** VII.487. MED giden *v.*

gye *v.* (1) lead, guide VII.2397; (2) advise, direct X.13; (3) rule, control, govern I.3046, IV.75; (4) protect, preserve VIII.136; *pr. subj.* **gye** I.2786 *(sg.)*, VIII.159 *(pl.)*. MED gien *v.*

gif *conj.* if I.4190. Cf. **if** *conj.*

gile *n.* guile, deception VIII.195, IX.196. MED gile *n.*(3)

gilt *n.* (1) sin, offense, crime VII.1825, X.84; (2) culpability,

fault II.855; **in the g.** at fault III.244; **withouten g.** guiltless, innocent V.1039; *pl.* **giltes** sins X.1043. MED gilt *n.*(1)

giltelees, giltlees *adj.* innocent, blameless II.643. MED giltles *adj.*

giltelees *adv.* innocent, blameless I.1312, II.674. MED giltles *adv.*

gilteles *n.* innocent, blameless IX.280. MED giltles *n.*

gilty *adj.* guilty I.660, II.668, VI.429. MED gilti *adj.*

gynne *v.* (1) begin; (with **for, for to**) begin to I.3863, IV.2329; (2) as *aux.* with *inf.* *3 pr. sg.* **gynneth** forms the periphrastic present (e.g., **gynneth go** does go, goes I.4064); *3 pt. sg.* **gan** forms the past singular (e.g., **gan ryde** did ride, rode, I.2569); and *pt. pl.* **gonne(n)** forms the past plural (e.g. *pl.* **gonne crye** did cry, cried I.2955). MED ginnen *v.*

girdell *n.* belt I.3250, VII.731; *pl.* **girdles** I.368. MED girdel *n.*

gyse *n.* manner, custom I.993, I.1253; fashion I.2125; **at his owene g.** after his own fashion, as he pleased I.1789; **in his g.** in his usual manner II.790. MED gise *n.*

gyterne *n.* a cithern, guitar-like instrument I.3353; *pl.* **gyternes** VI.466. MED giterne *n.*

glad(e) *adj.* joyful, happy I.811, I.846; *comp.* **gladder** I.3051. MED glad *adj.*

glade(n) *v.* (1) gladden, comfort IV.2221; (2) entertain, please VII.2811, VIII.598; *3 pr. sg.* **gladeth** IV.1107; *pr. subj. sg.* **glaade** IV.822. MED gladen *v.*

gladly *adv.* (1) joyfully, with pleasure I.308, III.669; (2) willingly IV.665, VII.452; (3) habitually, commonly, usually, customarily V.224, fittingly X.887. MED gladli *adv.*

gleede *n.* (1) ember, glowing coal VII.2384; (2) fire II.1111; *pl.* **gleedes** I.3883. MED glede *n.*(2)

glyde *v.* glide, move, pass I.1575, V.373; *3 pt. sg.* **glood** wafted up, rose V.393; *pp.* **glyden** VII.1887. MED gliden *v.*

glyteren *v. pr. pl.* glitter I.977; *3 pt. sg.* **glytered** I.2166; *prp.* **gliterynge** I.2890. MED gliteren *v.*

glorifie(n) *v.* (*usu. reflx.*) exult, be proud X.405, X.757. MED glorifien *v.*

glose *n.* (1) gloss, interpretation III.1920; (2) deception V.166. MED glose *n.*

glose(n) *v.* (1) interpret, explain (a text) II.1180; (2) use circumlocution IV.2351; (3) flatter, cajole III.509; deceive VII.2140; *pr. subj. sg.* **glose** III.119; *pp.* **yglosed** deceived, flattered IX.34; *vbl. n.* **glosyge** interpretation III.1793. MED glosen *v.*, glosinge *ger.*

glotonye *n.* gluttony III.1916, III.1927; the sin of Gluttony X.831; *pl.* **glotonyes** greedy desires VI.514. MED glotonie *n.*

glotoun *n.* glutton VI.520. MED glotoun *n.*

go(n), goon *v.* (1) walk I.2510, VII.1907; **ryde ne (or) go** ride nor (or) walk I.1351; (2) go I.12; *(reflx.)* go, get oneself I.3434; **go (thy) wey** go away I.3712; *1 pr. sg.* **go** I.2252, **ga** *(Nth.)* I.4254; *2 pr. sg.* **goost** III.273; *3 pr. sg.* **goth** II.1097, **gooth** I.3355, **gas** (Nth.) I.4037; *pr. pl.* **goon** I.769, **go(n)** IV.1923; *pr. subj.* **go** V.1066 *(sg.)*, V.1217 *(pl.)*; *imp. sg.* **go** I.2760, **ga** *(Nth.)* I.4102; *imp. pl.* **gooth** I.2558; *3 pt. sg.* **yede** VIII.1141; *pp.* **yede** VIII.1281, **(y)go** I.286, VIII.907, **gon** II.17, **(y)goon** I.1413. MED gon *v.*

good(e) *adj.* good I.74, I.183; *comp. see* **bet** *adj.*; *super. see* **best(e).** MED god *adj.*

good(e) *n.* (1) abstract goodness, virtue VII.1289; (2) good words III.1281; (3) useful knowledge; **connen g.** have useful knowledge II.1169; **connen (one's) g.** know what is good for (one's) self III.231; (4) good thing, benefit III.1195, X.312; **don g.** be beneficial to III.580, V.875; (5) possessions, goods, wealth I.3983, III.1796, III.1952; *pl.* **goodes** VII.998, **godes** X.769. MED god *n.*(2)

goodly *adv.* (1) excellently VII.1780; (2) graciously VII.1875; gladly, willingly I.803; (3) (as *intens.*) **not g.** not easily, not at all VII.1670; **mai nat g.** can hardly VII.1230; **as g. as** as well as IV.1935. MED godli *adv.*(2)

goodliche, goodly *adj.* excellent, beautiful, pleasing, gracious V.623, VII.1731. MED godli *adj.*(2)

godsib(bes) godparent, close friend *see* **gossip.**

gonne(n) did *see* **gynne.**

goos *n.* goose I.3317, I.4137; *pl.* **gees** IV.2275. MED gos *n.*

gossip, godsib *n.* (1) godparent or parent of one's godchild X.909; (2) close friend III.529; *pl.* **godsibbes** X.908. MED god-sibbe *n.*

goost *n.* (1) spirit, mind VI.43; (2) **the (hooly) g.** the Holy Spirit VIII.328, X.250; evil spirit, demon II.404; (3) soul of a dead person, ghost I.2768. MED gost *n.*

goostly *adj.* spiritual X.392, X.962. MED gostli *adj.*

goot *n.* goat I.688, VIII.886. MED got *n.*

governaunce, governance *n.* (1) rule, control, government II.987, III.814; (2) behavior, manner IV.1603; (3) control (of a machine) V.311. MED governaunce *n.*

governe *v.* (1) govern, rule, control III.1237; (2) *(reflx.)* conduct oneself VII.994; *3 pr. sg.* **governeth** VII.3000; *pr. pl.* **governe** I.1303; *pr. subj. sg.* **governe** II.1161; *imp. pl.* **governeth** IV.322; *1 pt. sg.* **governed** III.219; *pp.* **governed** III.1262; *vbl. n.* **governyng(e)** I.599; *pl.* **governynges** VI.75. MED governen *v.,* governinge *ger.*

governour *n.* ruler, master I.813, I.861, V.1031; *pl.* **governours** VII.1754. MED governour *n.*

grace, gras *n.* (1) divine favor, grace I.573; providence I.3595, V.1508; **fair (harde, sory) g.** good (bad) fortune III.746; **with sory (harde) g.** bad luck to (him, you, *etc.*) III.2228, VI.717; (2) good will, favor, kindness, love I.1120, I.1232; **stonden in (someone's) g.** find favor with (someone) IV.1590; **do g.** be favorable to I.2322, do a favor for VI.737; **dooth yourselven g.** spare yourself V.458; (3) graciousness VIII.67; **of your (thy) g.** by your (thy) kindness I.3080, V.161; **doon so fair a g.** behaved so graciously I.1874; *pl.* **graces** thanks VII.1804. MED grace *n.*

gramercy, grant mercy, graunt mercy *interj.* thank you III.1403, IV.1088, VII.2970. MED gramerci *interj.*

gras grace *see* **grace.**

gras *n.* grass I.3868, III.774; (as *adj.*) **g. tyme** youth I.3868. MED gras *n.*

graunte(n) *v.* (1) grant, allow III.1174, IV.179; (2) agree, consent VI.327; **g. it wel** admit, agree III.95; (3) ordain, appoint IV.179; *1 pr. sg.* **graunte** I.1620; *3 pr. sg.* **graunteth** I.1828; *pr. subj.* **graunte** IV.842 *(sg.),* X.1090 *(pl.); 3 pt. sg.* **graunted** I.3290; *(3 pt. pl.)* **graunted** I.786 *(pl.); pp.* **graunted** agreed I.810; *vbl. n.* **grauntyng(e)** I.2439. MED graunten *v.,* grauntinge *ger.*

grave(n) *v.* (1) bury IV.681; (2) carve, engrave V.830; *pr. subj. sg.* **grave** carve VI.15; *pp.* **(y)grave** engraved I.3796, buried III.1065, (as *adj.*) graven X.751. MED graven *v.*(1)

greese, grece *n.* grease I.135, VI.60. MED grese *n.*

Grekes *n. pl.* Greeks I.2899, II.744. MED Grek *n.*

greyn, grayn *n.* (1) grain crop I.596, VI.374; (2) seed VII.662; cardamom seed I.3690; (3) **g. of Portyngale** a red dyestuff VII.3459; **depe in g.** deeply dyed V.511. MED grain *n.*

gret(e), greet(e), great *adj.* (1) big, large in size or quantity I.559, VII.1946; **g. and smal (lyte)** of every sort IV.382, VII.2932; coarse IV.1422; (2) great (in degree) I.84, I.137; much I.385, I.870; (3) great (in quality), excellent I.203; high (in status), important IV.1494; chief, most important III.2005; (4) diligent, active I.318, IV.1001; frequent, energetic VI.164, IX.53; great, very much I.312, I.437; consummate III.1196, IV.1501; *comp.* **gretter** I.197; *super.* **grettest(e)** I.120, III.1116. MED gret *adj.*

greete *v.* greet IV.1014; *imp. sg.* **grete** VII.363; *3 pt. sg.* **grette** II.1051; *pt. pl.* **grette** IV.1174. MED greten *v.*(2)

gretly, greetly *adv.* greatly IV.1829, X.880. MED gretli *adv.*

grevaunce *n.* annoyance, pain, sorrow V.941, VII.1486; *pl.* **grevances** X.662. MED grevaunce *n.*

greves *n. pl.* groves I.1495, branches I.1507. MED greve *n.*(1)

greve *v.* (1) cause pain, distress II.352, III.1490; (2) *(reflx.)* be annoyed, take offense I.3910; be angry I.3859; *1 pr. sg.* **greve** III.1205; *3 pr. sg.* **greveth** I.917; *pr. subj. sg.* **greeve** VI.186; *pr. subj. pl.* **greve** I.3910; *pp.* **greved** VII.1490. MED greven *v.*

grevous(e) *adj.* (1) grievous, painful I.1010, X.732; (2) hostile, malicious X.641. MED grevous *adj.*

grevously, grevousliche *adv.* painfully VII.1001, X.667; strenuously X.667. MED grevousli *adv.*

grief *n.* (1) trouble III.2174, VII.127; (2) pain VIII.712. MED gref *n.*

grym(me) *adj.* fierce, angry I.2042, I.2519. MED grim *adj.*

gripe(n) *v.* seize; *3 pr. sg.* **gripeth** seizes X.863. MED gripen *v.*

grone(n) *v.* groan, complain III.443, VII.2886; *3 pr. sg.* **groneth** I.3646; *3 pt. sg.* **gronte** VII.2709; *vbl. n.* **gronyng** VII.2907. MED gronen *v.,* grunten *v.,* groninge *ger.*

grope *v.* (1) *(intr.)* grope, feel about III.2148; (2) *(tr.)* test, examine I.644; *3 pr. sg.* **gropeth** I.4222; *pr. pl.* **grope** VIII.679; *imp. sg.* **grope** II.2141; *3 pt. sg.* **groped** I.4217. MED gropen *v.*

grot(e) *n.* groat, a silver coin worth fourpence III.1292, VI.945; *pl.* **grotes** III.1964. MED grot *n.*(3)

grucche *v.* complain, bear a grudge against III.443, IV.170; *3 pr. sg.* **gruccheth** I.3045; *pr. pl.* **grucchen** I.3058, X.507; *3 pt. sg.* **gruched** X.502, **gruchched** X.504; *vbl. n.* **gruchyng** III.406, **gruchchyng** X.499. MED grucchen *v.,* grucchinge *ger.*

H

habit(e) *n.* (1) clothing III.342, VII.2343; (2) physical condition I.1378. MED habit *n.*

habounde *v.* be full of, abound IV.1286, VII.2748. MED abounden *v.*(1)

habundaunce, habundance *n.* plenty, abundance III.1723; fullness X.627. MED aboundaunce *n.*

habundaunt, haboundant *n.* abundant VII.2925, X.913. MED aboundaunt *adj.*

had(e), hadde(n), haddes(tow) *see* **have(n).**

haf, haaf lifted *see* **heve(n).**

hayl *interj.* (greeting) good health, good fortune (to you) I.3579, III.1384; **al h.** (greeting) good day I.4022. MED heil *interj.*

haliday *n.* holy day I.3309, I.3340; *pl.* **halydayes** I.3952. MED hali-dai *n.*

hals *n.* neck II.73, IV.2379. MED hals *n.*

halt holds *see* **holde(n).**

halwen *v.* consecrate, hallow X.919; *3 pt. sg.* **halwed** VIII.551; *pp.* **halwed** X.965. MED halwen *v.*

halwes *n. pl.* saints I.14, VIII.1244. MED halwe *n.*

han *see* **have(n).**

hand(e) *see* **hond(e).**

hang *see* **honge.**

hap *n.* chance, fortune VII.2738; luck, good fortune VIII.1209. MED hap *n.*

happe(n) *v.* occur by chance, happen I.585; (*impers.* with *obj. pron.* **hit**) happens to, chances to VI.606, VI.885; *3 pr. sg.* **happeth** V.592; *pr. subj. sg.* **happe** III.1401; *3 pt. sg.* **happed(e)** I.1189, VI.606. MED happen *v.*(1)

happy *adj.* lucky, fortunate VII.1680, VII.1558. MED happi *adj.*

hard(e) *adj.* (1) hard, firm I.2135, I.3021; (2) cruel, unyielding I.229, II.857; (3) difficult III.271, III.1791. MED hard *adj.*

harde *adv.* hard, strenuously I.3279, I.3476; *comp.* **harder** more strenuously IV.1754. MED harde *adv.*

yharded *pp.* hardened V.245. MED harden *v.*

hardy *adj.* hardy, sturdy I.405; brave, audacious I.882. MED hardi *adj.*

hardily *adv.* certainly, surely III.2285, IV.25; boldly IV.2273. MED hardili *adv.*

hardynesse *n.* boldness, bravery II.939, VII.1318. MED hardinesse *n.*

hardnesse *n.* (1) obstinacy X.486; (2) rigor, self-denial X.688. MED hardnesse *n.*

harlot *n.* (1) idle rogue, rascal I.4268, X.626; (2) buffoon, jester I.647; (3) servant III.1754; *pl.* **harlotes** lechers X.885. MED harlot *n.*

harlotrie *n.* sexual misconduct, ribaldry I.3145, I.3184; *pl.* **harlotries** I.561. MED harlotrie *n.*

harm *n.* (1) injury, misfortune, evil II.836, VI.745; disease I.423; **h. of peyne** physical impairment X.624; slander IV.2310, X.498; (2) pain, grief, suffering II.479; (3) pity I.385, IV.1908; *pl.* **harmes** evils VII.1840, X.390; sorrows I.2232. MED harm *n.*

harneys *n.* (1) arms, armor I.1613, I.1634; (2) equipment III.136; (3) trappings, circumstances X.974; *pl.* **harneys** sets of armor I.1630. MED harneis *n.*

harrow *interj.* help! I.3286, I.3825; alas VI.288. MED harou *interj.*

hasard *n.* gambling, dicing VI.591, VI.608. MED hasard *n.*

hasardour *n.* gambler VI.596; *pl.* **hasardours** VI.613. MED hasardour *n.*

hasardrye *n.* gambling VI.599, X.793. MED hasardrie *n.*

hast, hastou, hath *see* **have(n).**

haste(n) *v.* (*reflx.*) hasten, hurry I.2052; (with *obj.*) VI.159; *3 pr. sg.* **hasteth** VII.1054; *imp. pl.* **hasteth** VII.157, **haste** VII.1052. MED hasten *v.*

hastif *adj.* hasty, hurried I.3545, IV.349. MED hastif *adj.*

hastifly, hastifliche *adv.* hastily II.388, II.1047. MED hastiflie *adv.*

hastifnesse *n.* hastiness, rashness VII.1122, VII.1133. MED hastifnesse *n.*

hauberk, hawberk *n.* coat of mail I.2431; plate armor VII.863; *pl.* **hauberkes** I.2500. MED hauberk *n.*

hauk *n.* hawk III.1340, III.1938; *gen.* **haukes** V.478; *pl.* **haukes** I.2204. MED hauk *n.*(1)

haunte *v.* (1) frequent a place X.885; (2) busy oneself, practice X.780; make a practice of, do habitually I.4392; *3 pr. sg.* **haunteth** VI.547; *pr. pl.* **haunte(n)** X.794, X.847; *pt. pl.* **haunteden** VI.464. MED haunten *v.*(1)

have(n), han *v.* (1) (*aux.*) have II.674; (2) have, possess I.224, I.245; **h. on hond** be engaged in, have in hand IV.1686; (3) (*reflx.*) behave VII.1575; *1 pr. sg.* **have** I.35; *2 pr. sg.* **hast** I.1094, (with *pro.*) **hastou** II.676; *3 pr. sg.* **hath** I.688, **has** (Nth.) I.4026; *pr. pl.* **have** IV.633, **han** I.1807; *pr. subj. sg.* **have** I.2792; *imp. sg.* **have** III.445; *imp. pl.* **haveth** II.654; *1 & 3 pt. sg.* **hadde** I.31, I.689, **had(e)** I.554 IV.2167; *2 pt. sg.* **haddest** IV.2066, (with *pro.*) **haddestow** VII.1946; *pt. pl.* **hadde(n)** I.2859, **had** VII.3361; *pt. subj. pl.* **hadde(n)** VIII.864, VIII.681; *pp.* **had** I.4184; *vbl. n.* **havynge** possessing VII.1549. MED haven *v.,* havinge *ger.*

he *1 sg. pro.* he I.45; as emphatic modifier (with proper *n.*) e.g., **he Moyses** this Moses V.250, VII.2673; (as *n.*) male person IV.2290; **that fellow** I.2519. MED he *pron.*(1)

hed, heed, heved *n.* head I.198, I.1054, X.502; *pl.* **heddes** I.2180, **hevedes** VII.842. MED hed *n.*(1)

hed(e), heed(e) *n.* heed, attention I.303, III.1901; **mawgree (his, her) h.** despite (his, her) care, despite all (he, she) could do I.1169, III.887. MED hed *n.*(2)

hegge *n.* hedge X.870; *pl.* **hegges** VII.3218. MED hegge *n.*

hey *n.* hay I.3262, III.1539, III.1547. MED hei *n.*

heigh(e), hey(e), hy(e) *adj.* (1) high, lofty I.2463; (2) exalted X.153; divine, holy V.773, VI.913; noble, admirable I.2537; high in rank or power VII.2698; (3) strong, vigorous, powerful III.2291, IV.1513; prominent, well-formed I.2167, I.3975; (4) lofty, elevated in thought or language I.2989, IV.18; (5) arrogant, haughty VII.2520; dire, severe II.795, II.963; (6) much, great I.2913, IV.1577; (7) (as *n.*) **an (on) h.** above, aloft I.1065; **h. and lowe** all respects, all things I.817, II.993; all classes, everyone II.1142; *comp.* **hyer** I.399; *super.* **hyeste** II.326. MED heigh *adj.*

heighe, hye *adv.* (1) high I.271, I.4322; (2) honorably, in a high social position I.3981. MED heighe *adv.*

heighly *adv.* richly VII.1272; solemnly X.600. MED heighli *adv.*

helde(n) *see* **holde(n).**

hele, heele *n.* (1) health, well-being VII.2950, X.153; (2) prosperity, happiness I.3102. MED hele *n.*(1)

hele(n), heele(n) *v.* heal IV.2372, V.641, V.471; *3 pr. sg.* **heeleth** VI.366; *pp.* **heeled** I.2706. MED helen *v.*(1)

helm *n.* helmet I.2676, VII.877; *pl.* **helmes** I.2500. MED helm *n.*

helpe(n) *v.* help I.584, I.1150; *1 pr. sg.* **helpe** VIII.622; *2 pr. sg.* **helpest** VIII.53; *3 pr. sg.* **helpeth** I.2820; *pr. pl.* **helpen** X.241; *pr. subj. sg.* **helpe** I.1127; (*pr. subj. pl.*) X.778; *imp. sg.* **help** I.2086; *imp. pl.* **helpeth** VIII.1328; *1 & 3 pt. sg.* **heelp** I.1651, I.4246; *pp.* **holpe(n)** IV.2370, V.1305; *vbl. n.* **helpyng(e)** I.1468. MED helpen *v.,* helpinge *ger.*

hem *3 pl. pro. dat. and acc.* them I.11, I.18. MED hem *pro.*

hemself, hemselven *3 pl. pro. dat. and acc.* (emphatic) themselves I.1254, V.1378. MED hem-self *pro.*

hende *adj.* courteous, gracious, pleasant III.1286; as an epithet I.3199 (see note). MED hende *adj.*

heng(e), heeng hanged *see* **honge.**

hente(n) *v.* (1) seize, grasp I.904, I.957; (2) fetch, strike I.2638; *pr. subj. sg.* **hente** VIII.7; *imp. sg.* **hent** III.1553; *1 & 3 pt. sg.* **hent(e)** I.698, VII.3422; *pt. pl.* **henten** I.904; *pp.* **(y)hent** III.1311, VI.868. MED henten *v.*

heep *n.* (1) crowd, multitude I.575; (2) heap, pile I.944, VIII.938; (3) great quantity IV.2429. MED hep *n.*

heer *n.* hair I.589; *pl.* **heeris** I.2134, **heeres** I.2883, **heres** III.953, **herys** I.555. MED her *n.*

her(e) *see* **hir(e)** *3 pl. poss. pro.* (their), **hir(e)** *3 fem. sg. pro.* (her).

her(e), heer(e) *adv.* here I.1610, I.1612; in compounds (with or without hyphen): **heer-aboute** concerning this matter I.3562; **heerafter** after this VIII.706; **herafterward** after this III.1515; **heer-agayns** against this I.3039; **heerby** by this VII.1262; **heerbiforn** before this VII.1262; **heerupon** at this, then IV.190; **heer-to** for this purpose II.243. MED her *adv.* Compound forms are listed separately in MED.

heraud *n.* herald I.2533; *pl.* **heraudes** I.2599. MED heraud *n.*

herberwe, herborwe *n.* (1) dwelling place I.4145, X.1031; *(astro.)* house, position in the zodiac V.1035; (2) harbor, anchorage I.403. MED herberwe *n.*

here(n), heere(n) *v.* hear I.169, II.349, VII.2773; *1 pr. sg.* **heere** I.3369; *2 pr. sg.* (with *pro.*) **herestow** I.3366; *3 pr. sg.* **heereth** X.599, **hereth** I.1641; *pr. pl.* **heere** V.953; *pr. subj. sg.* **heere** I.3642; *imp. sg.* **heer** I.4263; *1 & 3 pt. sg.* **herde** I.221, III.832; *2 pt. sg.* (with *pro.*) **herdestow** I.4170; *pt. pl.* **herde(n)** III.2156, VII.1135; *pp.* **herd** I.849, **herde** III.2156, VII.1135; *pp.* **herd** I.849; *vbl. n.* **herynge** X.207. MED heren *v.*, heringe *ger.*

herye(n) *v.* praise VIII.47; *2 pr. sg.* **heryest** VII.2229; *3 pr. sg.* **heryeth** II.1155; *pr. pl.* **herye(n)** IV.616, VIII.47; *prp.* **heryinge** VII.678; *pp.* **heried** II.872; *vbl. n.* **heriynge** praise II.459. MED herien *v.*(1), heriinge *ger.*

herken *v.* listen to, hear; *imp. sg.* **herke** II.425; *imp. pl.* **herketh** III.1656. MED herken *v.*

herkne(n), herkene *v.* listen, hear I.1526, I.2532; *1 pr. sg.* **herkne** VIII.261; *3 pr. sg.* **herkneth** X.373; *pr. pl.* **herkne** X.1081; *imp. sg.* **herkne** VIII.927; *imp. pl.* **herkneth** I.788; *3 pt. sg.* **herkned** I.4173; *prp.* **herknynge** V.78; *pp.* **herkned** V.403. MED herkenen *v.*

hert *n.* stag, full-grown red deer I.1689; *gen.* **hertes** I.1681; *pl.* **hertes** V.1191. MED hert *n.*

herte *n.* heart I.150, I.229; **h. roote** the bottom of one's heart III.471; (as *adj.*) **h. blod** heart's blood III.718. **herteblood** I.2006; *gen.* **hertes** IV.112; *pl.* **hertes** I.1537. MED herte *n.*

hertely *adv.* heartily, sincerely I.762, III.1801. MED hertelie *adj.*

hertly, hertely *adj.* hearty, cordial IV.176, V.5. MED hertelie *adv.*

heste, heeste *n.* (1) command I.2532, II.1013; (2) commandment VI.647, X.798; *pl.* **heestes** commands II.284. MED heste *n.*(1)

heet(e) promised *see* **hoten.**

hete, heete *n.* heat VI.38, VII.1593. MED hete *n.*(1)

heeth *n.* heath, field I.6, I.606, I.3262. MED heth *n.*

hethen *n.* heathen I.66, VII.2393. MED hethen *n.*

hethen *adj.* heathen II.378, II.549. MED hethen *adj.*

hethenesse *n.* the non-Christian world I.49, II.1112. MED hethenesse *n.*

heve(n) *v.* raise, lift, heave I.550, X.858; *2 pr. sg.* **hevest** I.3466; *3 pt. sg.* **haf** I.2428, **haaf** I.3470. MED heven *v.*

heved head *see* **hed(e)** *n.*

heven(e) *n.* heaven I.519, I.1090, I.2249; (as *adj.*) **hevene kyng** heavenly king I.3464; *gen. sg.* **hevenes** of heaven VIII.87; *pl.* **hevenes** VIII.508. MED heven *n.*

hevy(e) *adj.* (1) heavy III.1436, VIII.1404, IX.67; (2) sad VII.1709; gloomy V.822; (3) weighty, important, serious VII.1022, VII.1499; (4) sluggish, slow X.677, X.706. MED hevi *adj.*

hevynesse *n.* (1) sadness I.2348; (2) drowsiness, sluggishness X.686. MED hevinesse *n.*

hewe *n.* (1) color, complexion I.394, I.458; (2) appearance IV.377; guise, pretense V.508; *pl.* **hewes** colors I.2088.

hewe(n) *v.* hew, chop I.1422, I.2865. MED heuen *v.*(1)

hewed *pp.* hued, colored, V.1245, VII.2869. MED heuen *v.*(2)

hy(e), hyer high(er) *see* **heigh(e)** *adj.*

hyde(n) *v.* hide I.1477, I.1481; **hideth to shew** refrains from showing X.394; *2 pr. sg.* (with *pro.*) **hydestow** III.308; *3 pr. sg.* **hideth** X.113, *(contr.)* **hit** V.512; *pr. pl.* **hiden** X.1064; *1 & 3 pt. sg.* **hidde** III.745, V.595, **hyd** IV.1944; *pp.* **hid** III.2143, (as *adj.*) II.777. MED hiden *v.*

hyder *adv.* hither, here I.682, II.1041. MED hider *adv.*

hyderward *adv.* hitherward in this direction VII.426, VII.1969. MED hider-ward *adv.*

hidous(e) *adj.* hideous, terrible I.1978, I.3520, VII.3393. MED hidous *adj.*

hidously *adv.* fiercely, violently I.1701. MED hidousli *adv.*

hye *v.* hasten, hurry (often *reflx.*) VII.210, VIII.1084, VIII.1151; *imp. sg.* **hy** VIII.1295. MED hien *v.*

hye, hyer high(er) *see* **heighe** *adv.*

hight, highte(n) was called *see* **hoten.**

highte, heighte *n.* height I.1890; **(up)on h.** on high I.2607, I.2919; aloud I.1784. MED heighte *n.*

hym *3 masc. sg. pro. acc. and dat.* him I.284, I.293; *(reflx.)* himself I.87, I.703; (as emphatic modifier with proper *n.*), *e.g.,* **hym Arcite** this Arcite I.1210, **hym Daryus** that Darius III.498; (as *n.*) **hym and here** man and woman II.460. MED him *pro.*

hyndre *v.* hinder, impede I.1135, VII.1196. MED hindren *v.*

hynesse, heighnesse *n.* high rank X.190, X.336. MED heighnesse *n.*

hir(e), her *3 fem. sg. pro.* (1) *dat. and acc.* her I.163, I.1421; (2) *poss.* her, hers I.3407, III.901. MED hire *pro.*(1)

hir(e), here *3 pl. poss. pro.* their I.368, I.586. MED hire *pro.*(2)

hyre *n.* payment, wages III.1973; **quit(e)** (someone's) **h.** repay (someone) III.1008. MED hire *n.*

hirs *3 pl. poss. pro.* theirs III.1926. MED heres *pro.*

hit, it *pro.* it I.2211, X.1082. MED hit *pro.*

hitte *1 & 3 pt. sg.* hit I.2647, III.808; *pp.* **hit** I.4305. MED hitten *v.*

hood(e) *n.* hood I.103, I.195; **putte in the mannes h. an ape** made a monkey of the man VII.440. MED hod *n.*

hool(e) *adj.* (1) whole, entire I.533, X.961; (as *n.*) the whole I.3006; (2) sound, unhurt, healthy III.977, IV.1289. MED hole *adj.*(2)

hool *adv.* wholly, completely III.2033, IV.1538; **h. in al** perfectly IV.1538. MED hole *adv.*

hoold *n.* (1) possession, keeping III.599, III.1607; **in, to** (one's) **h.** in (one's) possession VII.2874; (2) stronghold, castle II.507. MED hold *n.*(2)

holde(n) *v.* (1) hold, grasp IV.1100; hold up (an object) VI.697, IX.19; restrain VII.1326; (2) maintain, continue I.2236, III.1144; hold, continue (on one's way) I.1506; hold to (one's word, *etc.*) II.41; (3) manage (household, business, *etc.*) I.4421, X.440; (4) consider, think III.572, III.1186; **h. hym (her) ypayd (apayd)** consider himself (herself) rewarded, satisfied III.1185, IV.1512; (5) *(pp.)* **holde** beholden, obligated, obliged III.135; *var. inf.* **helde** keep, possess III.272; *1 pr. sg.* **holde** II.676; *3 pr. sg.* **holdeth** IV.1189, *(contr.)* **halt** II.721; *pr. pl.* **holde(n)** III.1190, X.440; *pr. subj.* **holde** IV.287 *(sg.),* VII.1599 *(pl.);* *imp. sg.* **hoold** I.2668; *imp. pl.* **hoold** I.783, **holde** VII.891, **holdeth** consider I.1868; *1 & 3 pt. sg.* **heeld(e)** I.176, IV.818; *pt. pl.* **helde(n)** I.2517, VII.2; *pt. subj. sg.* **helde** V.916; *prp.* **holdyng(e)** I.2514; *pp.* **holde(n)** considered I.141, I.1307; kept I.1690; **hoolden** X.432, **yholde(n)** I.2374, IV.1932; **halde** *(Nth)* I.4208; *vbl. n.* **holdynge** X.437. MED holden v.(1), holdinge *ger.*

holy, hooly, haly *adj.* holy, sacred I.17, I.178; *comp.* **hoolier** X.955. MED holi *adj.*(2)

hoolly *adv.* wholly, completely I.599, III.211; **al h.** completely I.1818. MED holli *adv.*

holily, hoolily *adv.* in a holy manner III.2286, IV.1455. MED holiliche *adv.*(1)

hoolynesse *n.* holiness I.1158, I.3180. MED holinesse *n.*(2)

holpe(n) helped *see* **helpe(n).**

hoolsome *adj.* useful VII.1095. MED holsom *adj.*

hom, hoom *n.* home I.512; (as *adv.*) I.4032. MED hom *n.*

homycide *n.* (1) murder III.2009, VI.644, X.564; (2) murderer VII.2628; *pl.* **homycides** murderers VI.893. MED homicide *n.*

hoomly *adj.* (1) of the household, domestic IV.1794; (2) plain, unpretentious III.1843, IV.1785. MED homli *adj.*

hoomly *adv.* plainly, without pretension I.328, VIII.608. MED homli *adv.*

hond(e), hand(e) *n.* (1) hand I.193; **of** (someone's) **h.** feats of arms, deeds in battle I.2103, II.579; (2) **bere(n)** (someone) **on h.** falsely accuse III.393, X.505; persuade (someone of a falsehood) III.575; (3) **have in h.** have under control III.211, III.327; **have on h.** be involved or concerned with III.451, IV.1686; with verb (e.g., **come, put, fall) in (on)** (one's) **h.** (come, put, *etc.*) into possession, into the power of V.684; **redy to (in) his h.** at hand, III.1321, VII.367; (4) **biforen-h.** beforehand, earlier VIII.1317; *pl.* **hondes** I.2874, **handes** I.186. MED honde *n.*

honest(e) *adj.* honorable, respectable, decent III.1183, VI.328; honest IX.75. MED honeste *adj.*

honeste(e) *n.* honor, honorable condition III.1267; (2) propriety of behavior, decorum VII.2712, X.932; (3) chastity, moral purity VI.77, VIII.89. MED honeste *n.*

honestetee *n.* (1) virtue IV.422; (2) decency, decorum X.429; good appearance X.431. MED honeste *n.*

honestly *adv.* (1) honorably, decently VII.244, VIII.549,

X.1046; (2) properly, modestly I.1444; suitably IV.2026. MED honestliche *adv.*

honge, hange *v.* hang I.2410, I.3565; *3 pr. sg.* **hongeth** I.2415, **hangeth** IV.1516; *3 pt. sg.* **heng** I.160, **heeng** I.358; *pt. pl.* **honge** *(intr.)* I.2422, **henge** *(intr.)* I.677, **hanged** *(tr.)* III.761; *prp.* **hangynge** I.392, II.73; *pp.* **hanged** I.2568; *vbl. n.* **hangyng** I.2458. MED hongen *v.,* honginge *ger.*

hoor(e) *adj.* white III.2182; white-haired or gray with age IV.1400, IV.1461. MED hor *adj.*

hope *v.* hope, expect X.91; trust, suppose III.490; *1 pr. sg.* **hope** I.3725; *3 pr. sg.* **hopeth** III.920 MED hopen *v.*(1)

hord, hoord *n.* hoard, store I.3262, I.4406; storehouse VII.84, X.821. MED hord *n.*(1)

hors(e) *n.* horse I.94; *pl.* **hors** I.74, **horses** X.432.

hostelrye *n.* inn I.23, I.718; *pl.* **hostelryes** I.2493. MED hostelrie *n.*

hostileer, hostiler *n.* innkeeper I.4360, VII.3029, VII.3060; *pl.* **hostilers** servants at an inn X.440. MED hostiler *n.*

hoot(e) *adj.* hot I.394, VII.1036; intense I.2319, I.3754. MED hot *adj.*

hoote *adv.* hotly, passionately I.1737, II.586. MED hote *adv.*

hoten *v.* (1) to be named, be called; (2) promise, assure; (3) command; *inf.* **hoten** be called III.144; *1 pr. sg.* **heete** promise, assure II.1132; **hight(e)** I.719; *pr. subj. sg.* **heete** promise I.2398; *1 & 3 pt. sg.* **highte** was called I.1191, I.4336; *pt. pl.* **highte** were called I.2920, **highte(n)** IV.496; *pp.* **hoote** called I.3941, **heet** V.1388, **hight(e)** I.616, VII.2849, **hight** promised I.2472, III.1024; (as *inf.*) **to highte** to be called I.1557. MED hoten *v.*(1)

hour(e) *n.* hour I.3519, II.3; planetary hour I.416, I.2217, I.2367 (see note); **h. inequal** one-twelfth of the time between sunrise and sunset I.2217 (see note); *pl.* **houres** I.2211. MED houre *n.*

hous(e) *n.* (1) house I.343, I.345; **in h.** indoors III.352; household V.24, VII.20; family III.1153, VI.649; (2) religious establishment I.252, VII.1931; (3) *(astro.)* astrological house, sign of the zodiac II.304, V.672; *pl.* **houses** I.491. MED hous *n.*

housbondrye *n.* careful management I.4077, VII.2828; economy IV.1296; household goods III.288, IV.1380. MED hus-bondrie *n.*

how *interj.* (to attract attention) ho! hey! I.3437, I.3577. MED hou *interj.*(1) & (2)

how, hou *adv.* how I.187, I.284, I.1219; however I.1394; **h. that** although X.710; **h. that** how I.642, I.1385; **h. now?** what's going on? I.4025; (with *adj.*) what, what a IV.333. MED hou *adv.* & *conj.*

humblesse *n.* humility I.1781, I.2790. MED humblesse *n.*

humour *n.* bodily fluid I.421 (see note to I.420), I.1375; *pl.* **humours** VII.2925. MED humour *n.*

I (*See also* Y)

i- prefix of past participles; *see under* the root syllable (*e.g.,* **yharded** is alphabetized as **harded**).

I *see* **ey** *(interj.).*

ich, I, y, ik *1st sg. pro. nom.* I.20, II.39. MED ich *pro.*

ydel(e) *adj.* (1) futile, worthless X.740; **y. sweryng** profanity

X.378, VI.638; (as *n.*) **in (on) y.** in vain VI.642; (2) inactive I.2505, IV.217. MED idel *adj.,* idel *n.*

ydolastre *n.* idolator IV.2298, VII.2187. MED idolastre *n.*

ye(n) eye *see* **eye.**

if, yif, gif *conj.* if I.145, I.503; **if that** if I.144; **but if** unless I.1799. MED if *conj.*

yfeere *adv.* together IV.1113; **met(te) y.** met one another II.394; cf. **in-feere.** MED ifere *adv.*

yfynde *inf.* find V.470, V.1153; *pp.* **yfounde** I.1211. Cf. **finde(n)** *v.* MED ifinden *v.*

yheere *inf.* hear I.3176, IV.2154; cf. **here(n).** *v.* MED iheren *v.*

yle *n.* isle, island II.68, II.545. MED ile *n.*(1)

ylyk(e) *adj.* alike, equal I.2734; **the same** I.1539; (as *prep.*) like I.592. Cf. **lyk(e)** *adj.* MED ilich *adj.*

ylyk(e), yliche *adv.* alike, equally I.2526, III.2225; constantly, invariably IV.602, V.20. MED iliche *adv.*

ilke *pro.* as *adj.* (as *intens.* with **that, this, thise**) same, very I.175, I.3447. MED ilke *pro.*

ymaginacioun, ymaginacion *n.* (1) the imagination, fancy I.1094; (2) ingenuity III.2218. MED imaginacioun *n.*

imaginyng(e) *v. prp.* imagining, considering IV.598, X.693; plotting I.1995; *pp.* **imagined** X.448. MED imaginen *v.*

in *adv.* in, within I.3907, VIII.1164; (of clothing) I.41, VIII.881; (direction) in, into VIII.1240. MED in *adv.*

in *n.* inn, lodging I.2436, I.3547; dwelling-place III.350. MED in *n.*

in *prep.* (1) in I.298, I.4158; (2) into I.4094; (3) on IV.2137. MED in *prep.*

in-feere *adv.* together III.924, VII.2276. MED in-fere *adv.*

infortune *n.* misfortune, bad luck I.2021, VII.2401. MED infortune *n.*

ynogh, ynough, ynowe *adj.* (1) sufficient, enough I.373, I.1613; (2) plenty of, abundant I.2836, III.332; great IV.792. MED inough *adj.*

ynogh, ynough, ynow *adv.* (1) very much, extremely, a great deal IV.1781; (2) enough, sufficiently I.888; (3) **wel y.** perfectly, very well VI.79; (4) fully, completely, VII.2458. MED inough *adv.*

ynogh, ynough, ynow(e) *n.* (1) enough, a sufficiency I.3149; **this (it) is y.** no more of this IV.1051; (2) plenty, an abundance III.1681. MED inough *n.*

inpacience *n.* impatience VII.1544, X.276. MED impacience *n.*

inpacient *adj.* impatient VII.1540, X.401. MED impacient *adj.*

instrument *n.* instrument I.1367; tool, device III.132, VIII.1119; *pl.* **instrumentz** I.1931. MED instrument n.

into, in to *prep.* (1) into I.23, I.1514; (2) onto, on I.3471, I.3585; (3) to, unto I.692, VI.722; (4) until VII.1233, VIII.552. MED in-to *prep.*

inward *adv.* in, inward I.4079; inwardly, within VII.1645. MED in-ward *adv.*

inwith, in-with *prep.* within, in II.797, IV.870. MED inwith *prep.*

ypocrisye *n.* hypocrisy VI.410, X.391, X.1023. MED ipocrisie *n.*

ypocryte *n.* hypocrite V.520, X.394; *pl.* **ypocrites** X.1060. MED ipocrite *n.*

ire *n.* anger, irritability I.940, I.1560; **caught an i.** became angry III.2003; one of the Deadly Sins III.1834, X.388. MED ire *n.*

iren *n.* iron I.500, I.1076. MED iren *n.*

irous *adj.* angry III.2016, III.2043, VII.1125, X.619. MED irous *adj.*

yse *v. inf.* see IV.2402; *pp.* **yseyn** IV.2404, **ysene** I.592; cf. **se(n).** MED isen *v.*(1)

yvel(e) *n.* evil I.4320; *pl.* **yveles** VII.1428. MED ivel *n.*

yvel(e) *adj.* evil, malicious I.3173; **(with) y. preef, thedam,** *etc.* bad luck (to someone) VII.405. MED ivel *adj.*

yvel(e) *adv.* badly I.3715, IV.460; **me list ful y.** I have no desire I.1127; **y. apayd** displeased, angry IV.2392; **holden him y. apayed** consider oneself ill-used VII.390, VIII.921; **y. biseye** ill-looking IV.965; **y. avysed** ill-advised IX.335. MED ivele *adv.*

yvory *n.* ivory III.1741, VII.876. MED ivorie *n.*

ywis *adv.* indeed, surely I.3277, I.3705. MED iwis *adv.*

J

jalous(e), jelous, jelos *adj.* (1) jealous I.1329, I.1840; (2) fervent, vigorous I.2634. MED jelous *adj.*

jalousie *n.* (1) jealousy I.1299, I.1333; (2) solicitude, zeal X.539. MED jelousie *n.*

janglest *v.* 2 *pr. sg.* chatter, gossip II.774; *3 pr. sg.* **jangleth** VII.3435; *pr. pl.* **jangle** V.220; *vbl. n.* **jangelyng(e)** V.257, X.406. MED janglen *v.,* janglinge *ger.*

jangler(e) *n.* gossip, chatterer I.560, IX.348. MED janglere *n.*

jangleresse *n.* female gossip, chatterbox III.638; *pl.* **jangleresses** IV.2307. MED jangleresse *n.*

jape *n.* (1) trick I.4338; (2) joke I.3799; *pl.* **japes** tricks I.705, jokes VI.319. MED jape *n.*

jape(n) *v.* joke, jest IX.4; *pr. subj. sg.* **jape** IV.1389; *pp.* **japed** tricked I.1729. MED japen *v.*

japere *n.* jester, trickster X.89; *pl.* **japeres** X.651, **japeris** X.652. MED japere *n.*

jaspre, jasper *n.* jasper (a gem) VII.1107. MED jaspre *n.*

joyneth *v.* 3 *pr. sg.* joins, unites VII.1614; *pp.* **joyned** VIII.95. MED joinen *v.*(1)

joly, jolyf *adj.* (1) merry, cheerful I.3355, V.48; (2) spirited, playful I.3263; lusty, amorous I.3339, I.4232, VI.453; (3) pretty, attractive I.3316, III.860; *comp.* **jolyer** finer V.927. MED joli *adj.*

jolily *adv.* merrily, gracefully I.4370, VII.14. MED jolili *adv.*

jolitee, joliftee *n.* (1) merriment, cheerfulness V.278, VI.780; pleasure X.1049; (2) passion, sexual desire I.1807; (3) attractiveness IX.197. MED jolite *n.*

juge *n.* judge I.814, I.1719; *gen.* **juges** VI.175; *pl.* **juges** VI.291. MED juge *n.*(1)

juggement *n.* judgment I.778, I.805; decree X.337; *pl.* **juggementz** IV.439. MED jugement *n.*

jugeth judge, decide VII.1031; *pp.* **jugged** given judgment VI.228. MED jugen *v.*

just(e) *adj.* (1) just, fair V.20; (2) true, exact III.2090. MED juste *adj.*

juste(n) *v.* joust I.2604; *3 pr. sg.* **justeth** V.1098; *pr. pl.* **justen** I.2486; *prp.* **justyng** V.1198. MED justen *v.*

K (*See also* C)

kan, kanstow can *see* **konne.**

karf carved *see* **kerve.**

kembe *v.* comb; *3 pr. sg.* **kembeth** I.3374; *3 pt. sg.* **kembde** V.560; *pp.* **(y)kembd** I.2143. MED kemben *v.*

kene, keene\ *adj.* (1) bold, fierce VII.2249; eager IV.1759; (2) keen, sharp I.104, I.1966. MED kene *adj.*

kep, keep *n.* in **take(n) k.** (1) take heed, pay attention to VI.90; take notice, see IV.2398; (2) take care, be concerned for III.321; (3) be alert, on guard VIII.1265. MED kep *n.*

kepe(n) *v.* (1) keep I.4102, VI.798; **k. (thy) tonge** hold (your) tongue IX.319; (2) take care of, look after I.593; protect, preserve I.2329, II.454; sustain IV.229; (3) observe, hold to I.852, V.1479; (with *inf.* and *neg.*) care nothing about, be unconcerned about I.2960; **I k. han no los** I don't care to have fame VIII.1368; *1 pr. sg.* **kepe** I.2238; *2 pr. sg.* **kepest** VII.1144; *3 pr. sg.* **kepeth** IV.1133; *pr. pl.* **kepe(n)** IV.1681, V.956; *pr. subj.* **kepe** I.4247 (*sg.*), VII.1139 *(pl.)*; *3 pt. sg.* **kepe** I.512, V.26; *pt. pl.* **kepte** II.269; *imp. sg.* **kepe** IX.362, keep VII.432; *imp. pl.* **kepeth** II.764, **keepe** IV.17; *prp.* **kepyng(e)** V.571, V.651; *pp.* **kept** protected I.276; *vbl. n.* **kepyng(e)** guarding I.3851, preservation X.571. MED kepen *v.,* kepinge *ger.*

kerve *v.* carve, cut V.158; *3 pr. sg.* **kerveth** X.888; *pt. sg.* **karf** III.2244, **carf** I.100; *pp.* **corven** I.3318, **ycorve(n)** I.2013, VIII.533, **(y)korven** I.2696, VII.611; *vbl. n.* **kervyng** sculpture I.1915. MED kerven *v.,* kervinge *ger.*

kesse, keste kiss(ed) *see* **kisse.**

kyd, kidde known, revealed *see* **kythe(n).**

kyn *n.* kin, family I.3942, IV.2197; **by my (youre) fader k.** on the honor of my (your) family IV.1515, VIII.829, IX.37; on your father's side VII.1931; *gen.* **som kynnes** some kind of II.1137. MED kin *n.*

kynde *n.* (1) nature III.1149; humankind VIII.41; natural form I.1401; natural disposition V.608; manner VIII.981; **by k.** by instinct VII.3196; **by wey of k.** in the natural course of things VII.1783; **of (propre) k.** by nature, naturally V.619; (2) sort, species I.1401, VIII.252; family, descent III.1101, VIII.121; **sette in k.** classify VIII.789; (3) semen X.965. MED kinde *n.*

kynde *adj.* kind, benevolent I.647, III.823. MED kinde *adj.*

kyndely *adj.* natural X.491. MED kindeli *adj.*

kyndely *adv.* kindly, benevolently VII.353. MED kindeli *adv.*

kynrede *n.* kindred, family, lineage V.735, V.1565; *pl.* **kynredes** X.206. MED kinrede *n.*

kisse, kesse *v.* kiss I.3284, IV.1057; *3 pr. sg.* **kisseth** IV.1823; *pr. pl.* **kissen** X.857; *pr. subj. sg.* **kisse** I.3797 (*pr. subj. pl.*), VI.965; *imp. sg.* **kys** II.861; *imp. pl.* **kysse** I.3716; *3 pt. sg.* **kiste** I.3305, **keste** V.350; *pt. pl.* **kiste** VI.968; *prp.* **kissynge** IV.1083; *pp.* **kist** I.1759; *vbl. n.* **kissyng(e)** I.3683. MED kissen *v.,* kissinge *ger.*

kyte *n.* kite, vulture I.1179, V.624. MED kite *n.*

kythe(n) *v.* make known, reveal, show V.748; *3 pr. sg.* **kitheth** V.483; *pr. subj. sg.* **kithe** II.636; *imp. sg.* **kithe** III.1609; *pp.* **kyd** IV.1943, **kithed** VIII.1054. MED kithen *v.*

kitte cut *see* **kutte.**

knave *n.* (1) boy VII.310; **k. child** male baby IV.612; (2) servant I.3434, I.3469; (3) peasant X.188; churl, villain III.253, X.433; *pl.* **knaves** servants I.2728. MED knave *n.*(1)

knee *n.* knee X.598; *pl.* **knowes** V.1025, **knees** I.1103, **knes** IV292. MED kne *n.*

knede *v.* knead I.4094; *prp.* (as *adj.*) **knedyng** kneading (trough, tub) I.3548, I.3564. MED kneden *v.*

knele *v.* kneel VII.507; *3 pr. sg.* **kneleth** I.1819; *3 pt. sg.*

kneled I.897; *imp. pl.* **kneleth** VI.925; *prp.* **knelynge** II.383; *vbl. n. pl.* **knelynges** X.1055. MED knelen *v.,* knelinge *ger.*

knytte *v.* join, fasten, draw together I.1128; **k. up** conclude X.28, X.47; *2 pr. sg.* **knyttest** II.307; *3 pr. sg.* **knytteth** VII.1614; *pp.* **knyt** IV.1391, fastened, tied I.4083; *vbl. n.* **knyttynge** X.843. MED knitten *v.,* knittinge *ger.*

knokke *v.* knock I.3676; *1 pr. sg.* **knokke** VII.730 *3 pr. sg.* **knokketh** I.3764; *pr. pl.* **knokke** VI.541; *imp. sg.* **knokke** I.3432; *3 pt. sg.* **knokked** I.3436; *vbl. n.* **knokkynge** beating X.1055. MED knokken *v.,* knokkinge *ger.*

knotte *n.* (1) knot I.197; (2) gist, main point (of a tale) V.407; conclusion (of a speech) X.494. MED knotte *n.*

knowe(n) *v.* (1) know I.730; (2) recognize I.382, II.649; (3) acknowledge VII.2622, VIII.259; *1 pr. sg.* **knowe** I.1815; *2 pr. sg.* **knowest** I.1723, (with *pro.*) **knowestow** I.3156; *3 pr. sg.* **knoweth** II.50; *pr. pl.* **knowe(n)** I.642, VII.287; *1 & 3 pt. sg.* **knew(e)** I.240, I.1227; *pt. pl.* **knewe** I.1017; *pt. subj. sg.* **knewe** IV.1078; *pt. subj. pl.* **knewen** VIII.1371; *prp.* **knowynge** VIII.989; *pp.* **knowe** I.1203, I.2300; *vbl. n.* **knowyng(e)** knowledge V.301, X.1079. MED knouen *v.,* knouinge *ger.*

knoweleche, knoweliche *n.* (1) knowledge X.75; (2) acquaintance VII.30. MED knouleche *n.*

knowelecheth *v. 3 pr. sg.* acknowledges VII.1774; *pr. pl.* **knowelichen** VII.1745; *prp.* **knowelechynge** VII.1771; *vbl. n.* **knowlechyng** acknowledgment, help VIII.1432. MED knoulechen *v.,* knoulechinge *ger.*

konne *v.* (1) know I.210, I.371; know, be informed about I.3193; know by heart VI.332, VII.543; **k. no bettre red** be helpless VII.2549; **k. wit** be wise IV.2245; **k. (one's) good** know what is good for one III.231; **k. (someone's) thank** be grateful to someone I.1808; (2) have mastery of a skill I.110 I.210; **k. lettrure** know how to read VIII.846; (3) (with *inf.*) be able to, know how to I.94, I.652, III.386; *1 & 3 pr. sg.* **kan** I.643; *2 pr. sg.* **kanst** III.904, **canst** III.904; (with *pro.*) **kanstow** II.632; *pr. pl.* **can** II.1169, **kan** III.980, **konne(n)** I.4123, IV.2438; *pr. subj. sg.* **konne** I.4396; *1 & 3 pt. sg.* **koude** I.94, I.1571, **kouthe** I.390; *pt. pl.* **koude** I.4104; *pt. subj. sg.* **koude** III.1008, X.946; *prp.* (as *adj.*) **konninge** skillful VII.2500; *pp.* **koud** X.1041, **kowth** IV.942; for *vbl. n.* see **konnyng(e)** below. MED connen *v.*

korven, (y)korve(n) carved *see* **kerve.**

koude, kouthe could, knew *see* **konne.**

kouthe, kowth(e) *adj.* known I.14, IV.942, X.766. MED couth *adj.*

konnyng(e) *vbl. n.* ability, skill V.35, V.251; MED conninge *ger.*

kutte *v.* cut VI.954; *3 pr. sg.* **kutteth** IX.342; *pt. sg.* **kitte** III.722; *pp.* **kut** VII.648; (as *adj.*) **kutted** X.422. MED cutten *v.*(1)

L

labour *n.* effort, work I.2913, I.3388; **do** (one's) **l.** make an effort, take pains II.381, VII.463; trouble, hardship II.423. MED labour *n.*

laboure(n) *v.* labor, work I.186, I.2408; *3 pr. sg.* **laboureth** IV.1842; *pr. pl.* **labouren** X.251; *pp.* **laboured** put to work VII.108. MED labouren *v.*

(y)lad, ladde led *see* **lede(n).**

lady *n.* lady, gentlewoman I.839, I.912; woman IV.2367; mistress, ruler I.2231, III.1048; beloved I.1143, I.1289; **(oure) l.** Virgin Mary VI.308, VII.474; *gen. sg.* **lady** I.88, **ladyes** VII.895; *pl.* **ladyes** I.898, **ladys** I.2579. MED ladie *n.*

lafte left *see* **leve** *v.*

lay *n.* religious law, doctrine, or belief II.572, V.18. MED lei *n.*

lay *n.* song IV.1881; *pl.* **layes** V.712. MED lai *n.*(2)

lay *see* **leye** *v.,* **lye(n)** *v.*

lak, lakke *n.* (1) lack, want III.1308, IV.2271; (2) offense IV.2199. MED lak *n.*

lakketh *v. 3 pr. sg.* be lacking, is missing IV.1998; *(impers.)* **him (me,** *etc.***) l.** (something) is lacking to him (me, *etc.*), he lacks X.16; *pr. pl.* **lakken** VIII.672; *pr. subj. sg.* **lakke** VIII.1419; *3 pt. sg.* **lakked(e)** I.756, VI.41. MED lakken *v.*

langage *n.* (1) language I.4330, II.516, V.1000; (2) speech, words I.211, I.2227. MED langage *n.*

langour *n.* suffering V.1101, X.723. MED langour *n.*

langwissheth *3 pr. sg.* languishes, grows weak IV.1867, V.950; *vbl. n.* **langwissynge** weakness X.913. MED languishen *v.,* languishinge *ger.*

lappe *n.* (1) loose part of a garment, hem VIII.12; (2) fold in a garment or sleeve used as a large pocket I.686, IV.585, V.635; (3) lap VII.2454. MED lappe *n.*

large *adj.* (1) generous, open-handed X.465; bountiful VII.3159; free-spending VII.431; (2) large, ample I.472; big I.753; large, extensive I.2678; **l. quart** full quart I.3497. MED large *adj.*

large *adv.* freely I.734; **pryme l.** fully prime, nine A.M. V.360. MED large *adv.*

large *n.* (in *phr.*) **at** (one's) **l.** at (one's) liberty, free I.1292, I.1327; (as *adv. phr.*) freely I.1283. MED large *n.*

largely *adv.* fully I.1908, I.2738. MED largelie *adv.*

largesse *n.* generosity VII.22, VII.1275. MED largesse *n.*

las, laas *n.* (1) belt, cord VIII.574; (2) snare I.1951, I.2389. MED las *n.*

lasse, lesse *n.* less VII.949; **l. and moore, moore and l.** everyone, everything I.1756, III.934, III.1562. MED lesse *n.*(1), lesse *n.*(2)

lasse, lesse *adj.* less I.3519, I.4409; lower in rank VII.1072. MED lesse *adj.*

lasse, lesse *adv.* less VII.1454, X.358. MED lesse *adv.*

last *adv.* last I.2200, VII.2825. MED laste *adv.*

last(e) *super. adj.* (1) last I.2808, I.3430; farthest, most distant IV.2666; most extreme, greatest VI.221; (2) (as *n.*) **atte (at the) l.** finally, at last I.707, IV.547. MED laste *adj.*

laste(n) *v.* last, continue I.2557, X.551; *3 pr. sg.* **lasteth** II.499; *pr. subj. sg.* **laste** VII.653; *3 pt. sg.* **laste** V.574, **lasted** V.806; *pt. pl.* **laste** VII.2200; *prp.* **lastynge** enduring I.3072, (as *adj.*) VIII.98. MED lasten *v.*(1)

lat, laten let, granted *see* **lete.**

late *adj.* late III.750; *comp.* **latter** more recent, later III.765; **latter end** final outcome VII.3205. MED late *adj., latere adj.*

late *adv.* (1) late I.4196; (2) recently, lately I.77, I.690; **erly and l.** always I.4401, VI.730; *comp.* **latter** slower X.971. MED late *adv., latere adv.*

latoun, laton *n.* latten (a brass-like alloy) I.699 (see note), VI.350. MED latoun *n.*

laude *n.* praise III.1353, VII.455; *pl.* **laudes** early morning church service I.3655. MED laude *n.*(1)

laughe(n), laugh *v.* laugh I.474, I.3722; *1 pr. sg.* **laughe** III.201; *3 pr. sg.* **laugheth** I.1494; *pr. sg. subj.* **laughe** X.664; *3 pt. sg.* **lough** I.3114; *pt. pl.* **loughe** I.3858; *prp.* **laughynge** I.2011; *pp.* **laughen** I.3855; *vbl. n.* **lawghynge** X.396. MED laughen *v.,* laughinge *ger.*

launde *n.* clearing, glade I.1691, I.1696. MED launde *n.*

laurer *n.* (1) laurel tree I.2922; (2) laurel leaves I.1027, I.2175. MED laurer *n.*

lawe *n.* (1) law I.309, I.577; (2) religion II.237, II.336; *gen. sg.* **lawes** VII.564; *pl.* **lawes** II.221. MED laue *n.*

laxatyf *n.* laxative, purgative I.2756, VII.2943; *pl.* **laxatyves** VII.2962. MED laxatif *n.*

leche *n.* physician, healer III.1956, VI.916; *pl.* **leches** III.1957. MED leche *n.*(3)

lechour, lecchour *n.* lecher III.242, III.767; *pl.* **lecchours** III.468. MED lechour *n.*

leed *n.* (1) lead VIII.406, VIII.828 (see note); (2) leaden vessel, cauldron I.202. MED led *n.*

lede(n) *v.* (1) lead, bring I.2275, II.442; (2) govern, control II.434; *2 pr. sg.* **ledest** V.866; *3 pr. sg. (contr.)* **let** VII.306; *pr. pl.* **lede(n)** II.1158, V.1552; *pr. subj. sg.* **lede** II.357; *3 pt. sg.* **ladde** I.1446; *pt. pl.* **leden** V.1552, **ledde** VIII.392, **ladde** IV.390; *pp.* **(y)lad** carried I.530, I.2620. MED leden *v.*(1)

lef, leef left, stopped *see* **leve** *v.*

leef, lief, leve, leeve *adj.* (1) dear, beloved I.3501; (as *n.*) dear one, sweetheart I.3393, III.431; **have l.** love, hold dear V.572; (2) **ben l.** (with *indirect obj.*) be pleasing, desirable (to someone), (someone) likes VII.159, VIII.1467; (3) desirous I.3510, VI.760; **have l.** be willing III.1574; **l. or looth** whether one likes it or not I.1837, IV.1961; *wk. sg.* **leeve** I.1136; *wk. pl.* **leeve** V.341; *comp.* **levere** dearer V.572; **were (hadde) lever(e)** (with *indirect obj.*) (one) would prefer II.1027, III.168. MED lef *adj.*

leef *n.* (1) leaf I.1838, III.1667; (2) page I.3177, III.635, III.667; *pl.* **leves** I.1496. MED lef *n.*(1)

left(e) *see* **leve** *v.,* **lift** *adj.*

leefful lawful *see* **leveful.**

legende *n.* saint's life I.3121; tale of martyrdom I.3141, III.742, VII.145; collection of saints' lives II.61; *pl.* **legendes** III.686. MED legende *n.*

leye, legge(n) *v.* (1) lay, place I.3269; (2) wager, bet I.4009; (3) *(reflx.)* lie down I.1384; *1 pr. sg.* **leye** III.1828; *3 pr. sg.* **layth** I.4021, **leith on** works on I.4229; *pr. pl.* **leyn** IX.222, **laye** VIII.783; *imp. sg.* **ley(e)** I.841, **lay** I.4085; *3 pt. sg.* **leyde** I.1384, **layde** VI.232; *pt. pl.* **leyde(n)** II.213, VII.2454; *pp.* **leyd** I.81. MED leien *v.*(1)

leyser *n.* (1) opportunity I.3293, (2) time, leisure I.1188, III.683; **bettre l.** more time III.551. MED leiser *n.*

lemaille *n.* metal filings VIII.1164, VIII.1197, VIII.1267. MED limaille *n.*

lemes limbs *see* **lymes** *n.*

lemman *n.* loved one, sweetheart, mistress I.3280, VII.788; paramour, lover II.917, III.722; *pl.* **lemmans** III.1998, **lemmanes** X.903. MED lemman *n.*

lene, leene *adj.* thin, lean I.287, I.591. MED lene *adj.*(1)

lene *v.* lean, incline VII.1448. MED lenen *v.* (1)

lene *v.* lend I.611, VIII.1024; *imp. sg.* **lene** I.3777, **leene**

VIII.1026; *imp. pl.* **lene** I.3082; *3 pt. sg.* **lente** VIII.1050; *pt. pl.* **lente** VII.354; *pp.* **ylent** VIII.1406. MED lenen *v.*(3)

lengere *comp.* of **long(e)** *adj.* longer I.330, I.821. MED lengere *adj.*

lengere *comp.* of **long(e)** *adv.* longer I.1576, I.2354. MED lengere *adv.*

lengthe *n.* (1) length I.1970, I.2646; (2) height I.83, II.934. MED lengthe *n.*

Lente *n.* Lent III.543 (see n.), IV.12. MED lenten *n.*

leoun, leon *n.* lion I.1598; *pl.* **leouns** VII.2261. MED lioun *n.*(1)

leonesse *n.* lioness VIII.1406. MED liounesse *n.*

lepe *v.* (1) leap, jump III.267; (2) rush, run I.4079, I.4378; *pr. pl.* **lepe** VIII.915; *3 pt. sg.* **leep** I.2687; *prp.* **lepyng** I.4079. MED lepen *v.*

lere, leere *v.* learn III.982, III.1516; *pr. pl.* **leere** V.104; *pr. subj. pl.* **leere** VIII.607; *pp.* **lered** (as *adj.*) learned VI.283. MED leren *v.*

lerne(n) *v.* (1) learn I.308, I.3192, III.1978; (2) teach VIII.844; *1 pr. sg.* **lerne** VII.536; *pr. pl.* **lerne** IX.334; *imp. sg.* **lerne** IX.349; *imp. pl.* **lerneth** V.777; *1 pt. sg.* **lerned** V.719; *pt. pl.* **lerned** VII.498; *prp.* **lernynge** VII.516; *pp.* **lerned** VIII.748, (as *adj.*) I.480; *vbl. n.* **lernyng(e)** learning, education I.300. MED lernen *v.*, lerninge *ger.*

lese(n), leese *v.* lose I.1215, III.2054; *1 pr. sg.* **lese** II.225; *3 pr. sg.* **leseth** X.251; *pr. subj. sg.* **lese** II.225; *pr. subj. pl.* **leese** VIII.1410; *imp. pl.* **leseth** II.19; *3 pt. sg.* **loste** III.721; *pt. pl.* **losten** I.936; *pp.* **lorn** I.3536, **lost** I.2257, I.4314; *vbl. n.* **lesynge** loss I.1707. MED lesen *v.*(4), lesinge *ger.*(3), losen *v.* (2)

lesyng(e) *vbl. n.* lie, lying VIII.479, X.593; *pl.* **lesynges** lies VI.591, (personified) deceit I.1927. MED lesinge *ger.*(2)

leest(e) leste *super. adj.* least, smallest I.1701, IX.185; **atte (at the) l. weye** in any event, at least I.1121, I.3680, VIII.676; (as *n.*) **atte (at the) l.** at least I.3683, II.38; **meeste and l.** great and small, everyone I.2198, V.300. MED leste *adj.*(1)

leest *adv.* least VII.2142, VII.2526. MED leste *adv.*

lete, laten *v.* (1) grant, give I.1335; **l. life** die VIII.406; (2) leave I.508, III.1276, V.290; (3) (as *aux.* with *inf.*) cause, have, get (something done) VII.2159; **l. don** cause (something) to be done VI.173, VII.2152; (4) allow, permit I.128, III.767; (5) **l. blood** draw blood (as medical treatment) I.3326; (6) in exhortations, sometimes with imperative force I.855, II.170; in suppositions **l. men shette** say that men were to shut III.1141; (7) cease, stop (doing something) I.3311, I.4214; leave alone III.1289; desist from I.3145, III.242; stop I.3285, V.947; *1 pr. sg.* **lete** IV.1781; *3 pr. sg.* **lete** III.504; *(contr.)* **lat** III.2232; *pr. pl.* **lete(n)** let VII.2708, X.721; **leete(n)** V.1379; *pr. subj. sg.* **lete** III.504, **lat(e)** I.188; *pr. subj. pl.* **leete** VIII.1409; *imp. sg.* **lat** VIII.1102; **leet** VI.731; *imp. pl.* **lete** give up, abandon VI.659; *3 pt. sg.* **leet** I.128, I.175; *pt. pl.* **lete** I.4308, **leete** V.1379; *pp.* **lete** III.2151, **lat** IV.1991, **laten** I.4346. MED leten *v.*

lette *v.* (1) *(tr.)* hinder, delay, prevent II.1117; disturb VII.86; (2) *(intr.)* refrain from, desist from I.1317; *2 pr. sg.* **lettest** III.839; *3 pr. sg.* **letteth** hinders IV.1573, *(contr.)* **lette** desists X.995; *pr. subj. sg.* **lette** V.994; *3 pt. sg.* **lette** VII.2840, **letted** I.1892; *pt. pl.* **lette** V.994; *pp.* **let** VII.2598. MED letten *v.*

leve, leeve *n.* permission, leave I.1064, IV.888; **by your l.** if you please, with your permission I.3916, III.112. MED leve *n.*(2)

leve *v. pr. subj. sg.* may (God) grant III.1644, VII.683. MED leven *v.*(3)

leve *v.* (1) leave, depart I.4414; (2) give up, quit V.828, VIII.287; (3) stop, desist from IV.250; *1 pr. sg.* **leve** VII.3185; *imp. sg.* **leef** I.1614, **lef** III.2089; *imp. pl.* **leveth** VII.1460; *1 & 3 pt. sg.* **lefte** I.492, I.892, **lafte** VII.2306; *pt. pl.* **lefte(n)** I.2599, VII.972, **lafte** VI.762, VII.2198; *pp.* **left** III.528, **(y)laft** I.2016, I.2746. MED leven *v.*(1)

leve, leeve *v.* believe, trust III.319; *2 pr. sg.* (with *pro.*) **leevestow** do you believe VIII.212; *3 pr. sg.* **leeveth** IV.1001; *pr. pl.* **leven** II.1181; *imp. pl.* **leeveth** I.3088. MED leven *v.*(4)

leve, leeve dear *see* **leef** *adj.*

leveful, leefful *adj.* permitted, lawful VIII.5, X.41. MED lefful *adj.*(2)

levere dearer *see* **leef** *adj.*

leves leaves *see* **leef** *n.*

lewed *adj.* (1) ignorant, uneducated I.3455, V.221; lay, non-cleric X.791; **l. man** layman, nonprofessional V.1494; (2) stupid, foolish IV.2275, VIII.925; uncouth, boorish I.3145, IV.2149; *super.* **lewedest(e)** lowest, most uncouth IX.184. MED leued *adj.*

lewedly *adv.* unskillfully, ignorantly VIII.430, IX.59; **kan but l. on** knows little about II.47. MED leuedli *adv.*

lewednesse *n.* ignorance III.1928, V.223. MED leuednesse *n.*

lycorys *n.* licorice I.3207, I.3690, VII.761. MED licoris *n.*

licour *n.* moisture, juice, sap I.3, VI.452. MED licour *n.*

lye *n.* lie I.3015, I.3391. MED lie *n.*(1)

lye, liggen *v.* lie, recline, remain I.3651, VII.911; *1 pr. sg.* **lye** I.4206; *2 pr. sg.* (with *pro.*) **listow** IX.276; *3 pr. sg.* **lith** I.1218; *pr. pl.* **lye(n)** III.1981, VIII.779, **liggen** I.2205; *pr. subj. sg.* **lye** IV.1292; *1 & 3 pt. sg.* **lay** was staying I.20, I.538; **by his suster lay** had sexual relations with his sister VII.2482; *pt. pl.* **layen** I.3210, **leye** IV.877; *pt. subj. sg.* **lay** I.1150; *prp.* **liggynge** lying I.1011, I.2390; *pp.* **leyn** II.887. MED lien *v.*(1)

lye(n) *v.* lie, deceive I.763, I.3513; *2 pr. sg.* **lixt** III.1618, **lyest** VIII.486; *3 pr. sg.* **lyeth** V.217; *pr. subj.* **lye** IV.1741 *(sg.),* VII.2498 *(pl.);* *3 pt. sg.* **lyed** I.659. MED lien *v.*(2)

lief dear *see* **leef** *adj.*

liere *n.* liar VII.1066; *pl.* **lyeres** VII.1308. MED liere *n.*(1)

lyf *n.* life I.71, I.1172; *dat.* **on lyve** alive I.3039; **hys (here, *etc.*) lyve** during his (their, *etc.*) lifetime III.392; **eterne on l.** eternally living III.5, IV.1652; *gen.* **lyves** IV.833, I.2395; (as modifier) **lyves body (creature)** living being I.2395; *pl.* **lyves** I.1718. MED lif n.

lifly *adv.* in a lifelike manner I.2087. MED lifli *adv.*

lift, left *adj.* left I.2953, VII.1312. MED lift *adj.*

lige *adj.* liege III.1037, IV.310, V.111; *pl.* (as *n.*) **liges** subjects II.240. MED lege *adj.,* lege *n.*(2)

ligge(n) lie, recline *see* **lye** *v.*

light(e) *adj.* (1) light in weight I.2120; (2) easy (to do) VII.1040; (3) cheerful, happy I.4154, IV.1211, VIII.351; *comp.* **lighter(e)** easier VII.1500. MED light *adj.*(2)

lighte(n) v. (1) *(tr.)* illuminate I.2426; (2) ignite III.334; (3) *(intr.)* shine X.1037; *pr. pl.* **lighte** X.1036; *3 pt. sg.* **lighte** VII.471; *imp. sg.* **lighte** VIII.71; *pp.* **lighted** V.1050. MED lighten *v.*(1)

lighte v. become light V.396; *3 pr. sg. (contr.)* **lighte** alights, dismounts II.786, V.169. MED lighten *v.*(2)

lightly adv. (1) with light clothing V.390; gently, easily VII.1861; (2) with little effort, easily III.517, X.1041; (3) quickly I.4099, VI.752; (4) readily, eagerly VII.1174; naturally inclined VII.1283, X.534; (5) indifferently, not seriously X.1024. MED lightli *adv.*

lightne v. illuminate, light X.244; *vbl. n. pl.* **lightnynges** lightning bolts X.174. MED lightnen *v.*(1), lightninge *ger.*

lightnesse n. (1) agility, nimbleness I.3383; (2) frivolity X.379. MED lightnesse *n.*(2)

lyk(e) adj. like I.259, V.62; **l. to, unto** similar to, like II.361, II.1030; similar X.631; *comp.* **likker** more like III.1925. MED lik *adj.*

like(n) v. please, give pleasure (to someone) IV.506; *(impers.)* **hym (hire, etc.) lyketh** it pleases (him, her, etc.), he (she, etc.) likes III.914; *3 pr. sg.* **liketh** I.1847; *pr. subj. sg.* **lyke** III.1278; *3 pt. sg.* **lyked** I.2092; *vbl. n.* **lykyng(e)** pleasure, desire II.767, III.736. MED liken *v.*(1), likinge *ger.*(1)

likerous adj. (1) sensual, lecherous III.752, VI.540, IX.189; (2) eager V.1119; greedy, gluttonous IV.214, VI.540; (3) delicious, delightful I.3345. MED likerous *adj.*

likerousnesse n. lustfulness III.611; lecherous act X.859; self-indulgence X.430; greedy appetite VI.84, X.741. MED likerousnesse *n.*

likly adj. probable, likely I.1172, VI.64. MED likli *adj.*

liklihede n. in *phr.* **by l.** probably IV.448, VII.596. MED liklihode *n.*

lyklynesse n. in *phr.* **by l.** probable IV.396. MED liklinesse *n.*

likne v. liken, compare III.369; *2 pr. sg.* **liknest** III.371; *imp. pl.* **likneth** X.156; *pp.* **likned** II.91. MED liknen *v.*(2)

lym(e) n. (1) quicklime VIII.806; (2) mortar V.1149, VIII.910. MED lim *n.*(2)

lymes, lemes n. pl. **lymes** limbs I.2135, I.3886. MED lim *n.*(1)

lymytour n. friar licensed to beg in a given district I.269, III.874; *pl.* **lymytours** III.866. MED limitour n.

lynage n. lineage, family I.1550, I.1829; noble birth VII.2251. MED linage *n.*

lynde n. lime or linden tree I.2922, IV.1211. MED linde *n.*

list(e), lest(e) *3 pr. sg. (contr.)* (1) *(impers.* with *indirect obj.)* it pleases (him, her, etc.), he (she) pleases, likes I.1183, I.1201; **me l. ful (ryght) yvele** I have very little desire to I.1127; (2) (personal uses) wish, want, be pleased I.3176; *3 pr. sg.* (full form) **listeth** chooses V.689; *pr. pl.* **listen** choose VII.1044; *pr. subj. sg.* **leste** it please I.828; *3 pt. sg.* **lyste** I.102, **leste** I.750. MED listen *v.*(1)

lystes n. pl. enclosed grounds for a tournament I.1859; **in l.** in formal combat I.63, I.1713; **for l.** for battle I.1852. MED liste *n.*(2)

listeth *imp. pl.* listen VII.712, VII.833. MED listen *v.*(2)

lite adj. little I.2627; modest, humble VII.963, X.295; **much(e) and (or) l.** great and small, all I.494. MED lite *adj.*(1)

lite adv. little I.1520, I.1723. MED lite *adv.*

lite n. little, a small amount I.1334, I.1450. MED lite *n.*(3)

litel, litil adj. little I.87, I.298. MED litel *adj.*

litel adv. I.1489; **l. and l.** little by little III.2235. MED litel *adv.*

litel, litil n. little I.1779. MED litel *n.*

lyve(s) lives *see* **lyf.**

live(n) v. live I.335, I.506; *1 pr. sg.* **lyve** I.1295; *2 pr. sg.* **lyvest** VII.1756, (with *pro.*) **lyvestow** VI.719; *3 pr. sg.* **lyveth** I.1028; *pr. pl.* **lyve(n)** II.1157, III.1257; *pr. subj. sg.* **lyve** V.696; *3 pt. sg.* **lyved(e)** I.2844; *pt. pl.* **lyved(en)** III.141, III.1877; *prp.* **lyvyng(e)** I.532; *pp.* **lyved** I.1793; *vbl. n.* **lyvynge** III.1122, X.596. MED liven *v.*(1), livinge *ger.*

lixt lie, deceive *see* **lye(n)** *v.*

lo(o) *interj.* look! take notice! I.1791, I.1844. MED lo *interj.*

(y)logged *pp.* lodged VII.2991, VII.2996. MED loggen *v.*

looke v. (1) look (at something) I.1783, I.3344; (2) look, appear, seem I.289, III.1082; (3) consider, see, find out I.3433, IV.1371; (4) **l. (that)** see to it, take care I.4345, VIII.1419; *2 pr. sg.* **lookest** VII.696; *3 pr. sg.* **looketh** I.1499; *pr. pl.* **looken** VIII.1420; *imp. sg.* **looke** consider III.1113; *imp. pl.* **looketh** consider I.1798, **looke** VI.87; *3 pt. sg.* **looked** I.289; *prp.* **lookynge** II.1015, **lokynge** I.2679; *pp.* **looked** I.3515; *vbl. n.* **lookyng(e)** gaze, look I.2171; appearance IV.514, X.936; astrological aspect I.2469. MED loken *v.*(2), lokinge *ger.*

lokkes n. pl. locks (of hair) I.81, I.677. MED lok *n.*(1)

lomb, lamb n. lamb I.3704, II.617; *gen. sg.* **Lambes** (i.e., Christ's) II.452; *pl.* **lambes** X.792. MED lomb *n.*

lond(e), land n. (1) country, kingdom I.400, II.522; (2) landed property I.579; (3) land, the earth III.372; **upon l.** in the country I.702; *pl.* **londes** I.14, **landes** VI.443. MED lond *n.*

long(e) adj. (1) long I.93, I.354; **lange** *(Nth.)* I.4175; (2) distant in time VIII.1411. Cf. **lengere** *adj.* MED long *adj.*(1)

long(e) adv. long I.2415; for a long time I.286; *comp.* **longer** II.521. Cf. lengere adv. MED longe *adv.*

longen v. (1) be suitable, fitting I.2278; (2) be the business, concern of IV.285; **l. to (unto)** pertain to someone (as a right) VII.1469, X.802; be causally connected with V.1131; **l. to** be inherent in X.873; *3 pr. sg.* **longeth** IV.2024; *pr. pl.* **longen** I.3885; *prp.* **longynge for** pertaining to I.3209, V.39. MED longen *v.*(3)

longeth *3 pr. sg.* long for, desire IV.451; *pr. pl.* **longen** I.12; *(impers.* with *indirect obj.)* long IV.2332. MED longen *v.*(1)

lordship(e) n. (1) *(pl.)* masters, those having rule X.442, X.568; (2) sovereignty, power I.1625, IV.797; *pl.* **lordshipes** official positions VII.1476. MED lordshipe *n.*

lordynges n. pl. gentlemen, my lords (term of address) I.761, I.788, I.828. MED lordinge *n.*

loore, lore n. (1) teaching I.527, I.3527; (2) learning IV.87. MED lore *n.*(2)

lorne lost *see* **lese(n)***.*

loos, lause adj. loose I.4138, I.4352. MED los *adj.*

loos, los n. (1) reputation VII.1644; (2) praise VIII.1368; (3) infamy VIII.1009. MED los *n.*(2)

los n. loss I.2543, III.720. MED los *n.*(1)

looth adj. displeasing, hateful I.3393, IV.491 (in *impers.* constructions) **be(n) l. (hym, hire, etc.)** (he, she, etc.) does not wish I.1837; **(hym, me, etc.) were** *(subj.)* **l.** (he, I, etc.) would not wish, would hate I.486, II.91, IV.364; **l. or lef, dere** pleasant or not, whether one likes it or not I.1837, IV.1961; *super.* **lothest** most reluctant V.1313. MED loth *adj.*

lough low see **low(e)** *adj.,* **lowe** *n.*

lough(e) laughed *see* **laughe(n).**

loute *v.* bow down VII.2162; *3 pr. sg.* **lowteth** VII.1187. MED louten *v.*(1)

love *n.* love I.475, I.672; (as *proper n.*) I.1564; (in compounds) **love-dayes** days of reconciliation I.258 (see note); **love-drynke** aphrodisiac III.754; **love-drury** passionate love VII.895; **love-knotte** elaborate knot I.197; **love-likynge** love VII.850; **love-longynge** passionate, romantic love (only in comic contexts) I.3679, I.3705, VII.772; *gen. sg.* **loves** I.1815. MED love *n.*(1) (compounds listed separately)

love(n) *v.* love II.586, VIII.160; *1 pr. sg.* **love** I.1143; *2 pr. sg.* **lovest** I.1581; *3 pr. sg.* **loveth** I.1731; *pr. pl.* **love(n)** III.321, III.921; *pr. subj.* **love** I.1799 *(sg.),* III.446 *(pl.); imp. sg.* **love** I.3280; *imp. pl.* **loveth** X.526; *1 & 3 pt. sg.* **loved(e)** I.3222, I.4376; *pt. pl.* **lovede(n)** I.1198, X.202; *prp.* **lovynge** II.625, (as *adj.*) X.202; *pp.* **loved** I.2794; *vbl. n.* **lovyng(e)** X.515, X.529. MED loven *v.*(1), lovinge *ger.*(1)

lovere *n.* lover I.80, I.1164; *gen. sg.* **loveris** I.1373; *pl.* **loveres** I.1347, **loveris** II.53. MED lovere *n.*(2)

low(e), lough *adj.* (1) low I.107, VII.3265; (2) quiet, soft I.2433; (3) low in rank I.522; *comp.* **lower** more ignoble IX.190; *super.* **loweste** X.482. MED loue *adj.*

lowe *adv.* (1) low I.1111, I.2023; (2) low, quietly V.216; (3) humbly I.1405. MED loue *adv.*

lowe, logh, lough *n.* in *phr.* **in heigh and l.** in all respects, in every way I.817, II.993; **heigh and (or) l.** all classes, everyone II.1142. MED loue *n.*(3)

lowely, lowly *adj.* humble, modest I.99, I.250. MED louli *adj.*

lowely, lowly *adv.* humbly IV.421, VII.1771. MED louli *adv.*

lulleth *3 pr. sg.* soothes, caresses II.839, IV.1823; *3 pt. sg.* **lulled** IV.553. MED lullen *v.*

lust *n.* (1) desire, wish II.762, II.763; sexual desire II.925, III.611; (as *proper n.*) I.1932; (2) pleasure, delight IV.1643, V.812; sexual pleasure III.927, X.845; (3) object of desire IV.660; *pl.* **lustes** desires I.3066, pleasures IV.1679. MED lust *n.*

lusty *adj.* (1) pleasing I.2176, I.2484; (2) full of vigor, lively I.80; eager I.4004, VIII.1345; admirable, fine III.553; (3) (of land) fruitful IV.59; *comp.* **lustier** more eager VIII.1345. MED lusti *adj.*

lusten *v. 3 pr. sg.* (impersonal) it pleases him (her, etc.), he (she, etc.) wishes III.78, IV.322; *3 pt. sg.* **luste** VIII.2335. MED lusten *v.*

luxurie *n.* lechery II.925, VI.484. MED luxurie *n.*

M

mad(e), maade, ymaad *see* **make(n).**

mad *adj.* mad, crazy I.2342, I.4231. MED mad *adj.*

magestee *n.* majesty I.4322, II.1082. MED mageste *n.*

magik *n.* magic II.214; **m. natureel** natural science I.416, V.1125. MED magike *n.*

may, mayst, maistow *see* **mowe(n).**

maydenhed(e), maydenhod *n.* virginity I.2329, III.888, VII.2269. MED maidenhede *n.*

maister *n.* (1) master I.837, I.3446; teacher VII.2518; master tradesman I.4389; (2) as a title of respectful address I.3437; (3) master of arts I.261, III.2184; (4) (as *adj.*) main, chief I.2902; *gen.* **maistres** V.1220; *pl.* **maistres** I.576. MED maister *n.*

maistresse, mistresse *n.* mistress IV.823; governess V.374, VI.106; *pl.* **maistresses** governesses, VI.72. MED maistresse *n.*

maistrye *n.* (1) mastery, dominion III.818, III.1040; (2) skill I.3383; (3) admirable achievement VIII.1060; **for the m.** extremely I.165. MED maistrie *n.*

make *n.* (1) mate III.270, IV.2080; spouse IV.840, IV.1289; (2) opposite, opponent I.2556. MED make *n.*(1)

make(n) *v.* (1) make I.384; build I.1901, IV.2295; (2) compose, write (song, poems, *etc.*) I.95, I.325; (3) make a formal promise (with **assurance, vow,** *etc.*) II.341, V.1535; (4) cause, bring about a condition III.1899; **m. an ende** finish, conclude V.408, X.47; cause (with *obj.* and *inf.*) I.581, I.3092; cause to be (with *obj.* and *adj.*) I.184, I.265; *1 pr. sg.* **make** I.1733; *2 pr. sg.* **makest** VII.920, (with *pro.*) **makestow** II.371; *3 pr. sg.* **maketh** I.947; *pr. pl.* **make(n)** I.4051, VII.1974; *pr. subj. sg.* **make** III.297; *pr. subj. pl.* **make** X.1053; *imp. sg.* **make** I.3720; *imp. pl.* **maketh** IV.2173; *3 pt. sg.* **maked** I.526, **made** I.387, **maade** IV.678; *2 pt. sg.* **madest** II.368; *pt. pl.* **made(n)** I.33, III.594; *prp.* **makynge** I.1366; *pp.* **(y)maked** I.1247, VI.545, **(y)maad** I.3094, II.693; *vbl. n.* **makyng** making VIII.922. MED maken *v.*(1), makinge *ger.*

male *n.* pouch, traveling bag VI.920, VIII.566. MED male *n.*(2)

malencholi(e) *n.* (1) the humor of melancholy (black bile) VII.2933; (2) anger, rage III.252. MED malencolie *n.*

malisoun *n.* curse VIII.1245, X.443; cursing X.619. MED malisoun *n.*

man *n.* man I.228, I.477; *gen. sg.* **mannes** IV.1331; *pl.* **men** II.246; men, people in general III.326; *gen. pl.* **mennes** II.202. MED man *n.*

man *indef. pro.* one, anyone III.2002, V.553. Cf. **men** *indef. pro.* MED man *n.* & *indef. pro.*

manace *n.* menace, threat I.2003, VII.2599. MED manace *n.*

manace *v.* menace, threaten IV.1752; *3 pr. sg.* **manaceth** IV.122; *3 pt. sg.* **manaced** VII.1504; *vbl. n.* **manasynge** I.2035. MED manacen *v.,* manacinge *ger.*

maner(e) *n.* (1) manner, form V.337; **in m. of** in the shape of I.1889; **in no m.** in no way IV.818, IV.1237; (2) way, manner I.876; means, method V.187, VIII.1057; **by m. of** by reason of VI.264; (3) manner, behavior I.140, V.546; custom VIII.142; **al the m.** the whole affair II.880; (4) (as *adj.*) sort of, kind of I.71, X.103; *pl.* **maneres** ways, sorts X.358, **manneres** X.387. MED manere *n.*

manhede, manhod *n.* (1) manliness, qualities proper to a man I.1285, VII.2671; (2) gentility, courteous behavior I.756, IX.158. MED manhede *n.*

many(e) *adj.* many I.1521, II.577; (as *n.*) many II.999, VI.530; **m. a** many I.60, I.168; **m. oon** many a one I.317, I.2118. MED mani *adj.*

manly *adj.* manly, virile I.2130, V.99; proper to a man X.601; generous VII.43; *adv.* vigorously I.987; as a man should do X.689. MED manli *adj.,* manli *adv.*(1)

mannyssh, mannysh *adj.* (1) human VII.1264; (2) mannish, unwomanly II.782; (3) (as *adv.*) **m. wod** IV.1536. MED mannish *adj.*

mansioun, mansyon *v.* (1) dwelling place I.1974; (2) *(astro.)* the "domicile" of a planet V.50 (see note); position of the moon V.1285, V.1289; *pl.* **mansiouns** V.1130, **mansions** V.1154. MED mansioun *n.*(1)

marbul *n.* marble I.1893, V.500; (as *adj.*) VII.681. MED marble *n.*

marc, mark *n.* mark, a monetary unit, two-thirds of a pound (13 shillings, 4 pence) VI.390, VIII.1026, VIII.1030. MED marke *n.*(2)

marchant, marchaunt *n.* merchant I.270, X.777; *gen.* **marchauntes** II.2425; *pl.* **marchantz** X.779, **marchauntz** II.122, **merchantz** II.148. MED marchaunt *n.*

mark, merk *n.* (1) mark, birthmark III.619; (2) image V.880; **m. of Adam** image of Adam (i.e., male sex) III.696. MED marke *n.*(1)

masse *see* **messe.**

matere, mateere, matiere *n.* (1) physical matter VIII.811, X.333; material VIII.1232; (2) matter, business I.727, I.1259, II.205; subject matter II.322; (3) cause, ground VII.1536, X.491; *gen.* **matires** VIII.770, **materes** VIII.814; *pl.* **materes** VIII.779. MED matere *n.*

maugree *prep.* despite, in spite of I.2618, II.104. MED maugre *prep.*

maze *v. 2 pr. pl.* you are bewildered, dazed IV.2387; *pp.* **mazed** II.526, (as *adj.*) II.628. MED masen *v.*

mede, meede *n.* mead, meadow I.89, III.861. MED mede *n.*(2)

meede *n.* payment, reward I.770, IV.885; bribe I.3380, VI.133. MED mede *n.*(4)

medle *v.* be concerned with, take a hand in VIII.1184; *3 pr. sg.* **medleth** VII.1541; *imp. pl.* **medleth** VIII.1424; *pp.* **medled** mixed with X.122. MED medlen *v.*

meynee, meignee *n.* (1) household, household attendants I.1258, III.2156; (2) troop of followers, company I.4381, V.391. MED meine *n.*

meke, meeke *adj.* meek, gentle I.69, I.3202; *super.* **mekeste** IV.1552. MED mek *adj.*

mekely *adv.* meekly, humbly II.1079, III.432. MED mekli *adv.*

mekenesse *n.* meekness, humility VII.1686, X.476. MED meknesse *n.*

meel *n.* meal, repast III.1774, VII.2833. MED mel *n.*(2)

mele *n.* meal, ground grain I.3939, III.1739. MED mele *n.*(1)

membres *n. pl.* sexual organs, genitals X.330; members, supporters X.137. MED membre *n.*

memorie *n.* memory, consciousness I.1906; **have (in) m.** remember IV.1669; **in m.** conscious I.2698; **maken m.** remind VII.1974; **drawen (in)to m.** call to mind I.2074, X.239. MED memorie *n.*

men *indef. pro. sg.* one, someone, anyone I.149, I.2777. Cf. **man** *indef. pro.* MED men *indef. pro.*

meene *n.* (1) agent, instrument IV.1671; (2) moderation, mean (between extremes) X.833; *pl.* **meenes** II.480. MED mene *n.*(3)

meene, mene *v.* (1) mean I.1673; signify VII.2751; (2) say, speak VIII.1424; *1 pr. sg.* **mene** I.2063; *2 pr. sg.* (with *pro.*) **menestow** VIII.309; *3 pr. sg.* **meneth** I.2287; *1 & 3 pt. sg.* **mente** I.2990, VIII.999; *pt. pl.* **mente** V.399; *vbl. n.* **menyng** meaning V.151. MED menen *v.*(1), meninge *ger.*(1)

meene whil(es) *phr.* meanwhile II.546, II.668. MED menewhil *n. & adj.*

mennes men's *see* **man** *n.*

merciable *adj.* merciful V.1036, VII.688. MED merciable *adj.*

merk *see* **mark** *n.*

mervaille, merveyle, merveille *n.* marvel, wonder I.3423, II.502; *pl.* **mervaylles** V.660. MED merveille *n.*

merveillous *adj.* astonishing, marvelous IV.454, V.1206. MED merveillous *adj.*

meschaunce, meschance, myschaunce, myschance *n.* (1) misfortune, bad luck I.2009, II.602; **with m.** bad luck (to him) I.4412; (2) misconduct VI.80; *pl.* **meschaunces** evil practices V.1292, **meschances** misadventures III.367. MED mischaunce *n.*

mescheef, meschief *n.* (1) trouble, misfortune I.493, I.1326; deprivation, need VIII.1072; **at m.** in distress, at a disadvantage I.2551; (2) wrong, mischief I.1326, III.2190. MED mischef *n.*

message *n.* (1) message V.99; **don a m.** deliver a message II.1087, VIII.188; (2) emissary, diplomatic courier IV.738; *pl.* **messages** messengers VII.1784, emissaries VII.1796. MED message *n.*(1)

messager, messageer *n.* messenger I.1491, II.6; *pl.* **messagers** X.967. MED messager *n.*

messe, masse *n.* mass III.1728, IV.1894; **m. penny** offering for a mass III.1749. MED messe *n.*(1)

meeste *n.* most I.2198, V.300. Cf. **moost(e)** *adj.* MED most *n.*

mester situation *see* **myster.**

mesurable *adj.* moderate I.435, V.362; modest X.936. MED mesurable *adj.*

mesure *n.* (1) measurement IV.256, X.776; (2) moderation, restraint VII.991; **by m.** in due proportion, moderately X.465; **out of m.** immoderately VII.1417; very greatly VII.1745; cruel, without mercy VII.1848. MED mesure *n.*

mete, meete *n.* (1) food I.136, I.345; (2) meal V.173; **at m.** at dinner I.127, II.1119; **after-mete** after dinner IV.1913, IV.1921; *gen.* **metes space** dinner time II.1014; *pl.* **metes** X.445. MED mete *n.*(1)

meete *v.* meet I.4374; *3 pr. sg.* **meeteth** I.1524; *3 pt. sg.* **mette** V.1508; *pt. pl.* **mette** II.559; *pp.* **(y)met** I.1636, I.2624. MED meten *v.*(4)

meeth, mede *n.* mead (alcoholic beverage made of fermented honey) I.3378, VII.852. MED mede *n.*(1)

mette *v. 1 & 3 pt. sg.* dreamed, III.577; *(impers.)* me (him, *etc.*) **mette** I (he, *etc.*) dreamed I.3684, VII.2894; *pp.* met VII.2926, VII.3255. MED meten *v.*(3)

myght(e) *n.* power, strength I.960, I.1607; **doon his (her, *etc.*) m.** exerts his (her, *etc.*) efforts IV.1122; ability, capacity I.538, III.1188; **over your (hir) m.** beyond your (her) capacity III.1661, VI.468. MED might *n.*

myght(e), myght- *see* **mowe(n).**

myghty *adj.* (1) great, mighty I.1673, I.2536; strong, big, powerful I.108, I.1423; (2) capable X.547. MED mighti *adj.*

myghtily *adv.* strongly I.3475, II.921; by strength VII.2592. MED mightili *adv.*

myle *n.* mile I.1504; (as *adj.*) **m. wey** by a long way VII.276; *gen.* **miles** VI.928; *pl.* (with preceding *num.*) **myle** VIII.555, (with *num.* following) **miles** VIII.173. MED mile *n.*(1)

myn(e), my *1 sg. poss.* (1) *(adj.)* my, mine (*usu.* **min(e)** before vowels and **h-**) I.782, I.804, VII.1548; (*usu.* **my**

before consonants) I.718, I.837; (2) *(pro.)* mine I.1159, I.2406. MED min *pro.*

mynde *n.* (1) mind I.1402; thought, consideration II.908; (2) reason, wits VI.494, VII.594; (3) memory I.4077, IV.849; **forgat hir m.** lost her memory II.527; **out of m.** forgotten IV.2390. MED minde *n.*(1)

mynstralcye *n.* (1) music I.2197, I.2524; (2) musical instrument IX.113, IX.267; (3) entertainment I.4394. MED minstralsie *n.*

myrie, mery(e), murye(e) *adj.* merry, cheerful, pleasant I.208, I.235, I.757; *comp.* **murier** VII.834. MED mirie *adj.*

myrye, murye *adv.* merrily, cheerfully I.3575, VI.843; *comp.* **murier** IV.2322. MED mirie *adv.*

myryly, murily *adv.* merrily, cheerfully III.330, VII.110; *comp.* **murierly** I.714. MED mirili *adv.*

mirour *n.* (1) mirror I.1399, IV.1582; (2) model, exemplar II.166, V.1454; *pl.* **mirours** lens, magnifying glasses V.234. MED mirour n.

myrthe, murthe *n.* gaiety, mirth I.759, I.3654; pleasure, cause of mirth I.766, II.410. MED mirthe *n.*

mysaventure *n.* misfortune II.616; **with m.** bad luck (to him) III.1334. MED misaventure *n.*

myschaunce, myschance *see* **meschaunce.**

myschief *see* **mescheef.**

mysdooth *v. 3 pr. sg.* do wrong VII.1922; *pp.* **mysdoon** X.85; *vbl. n.* **mysdoynge** VII.1708. MED misdon *v.*, misdoinge *ger.*

misericorde *n.* mercy, pity VII.1418, X.804. MED misericorde *n.*

mysese, myseyse *n.* distress, suffering X.177, X.194. MED misese *n.*

mysgo(n), mysgoon *pp.* gone astray I.4218, I.4252. MED misgon *v.*

myshappe *v.* suffer misfortune VII.1696; *pr. subj. sg. (impers.)* **me myshappe** I should suffer misfortune I.1646; *pp.* **myshapped** turned out badly VIII.944. MED mishappen *v.*

mysse *v.* (1) miss, fail to find I.4216, III.1416; lack VII.352; (2) fail I.3679. MED missen *v.*(1)

mysseyeth *v. 3 pr. sg.* slander X.1510; *pp.* **mysseyd,** spoken out of turn IX.353, **myssayd** IV.2391. MED misseien *v.*

myster, mester *n.* (1) craft, occupation I.613; (as *adj.*) kind of I.1710; (2) difficult situation I.1340. MED mister *n.*

myte *n.* a small Flemish coin worth a farthing or half a farthing (used in expressing worthlessness) VIII.633, VIII.698. MED mite *n.*(2)

mo(o) *adj.* more I.808, I.849; **tymes mo** often IV.449 Cf. **moore** *adj.* MED mo *adj.*

mo *adv.* more I.2071, VII.413; **never(e) m.** never again I.1346, III.1099; **never the mo** in any way III.691. Cf. **moor(e)** *adv.* MED mo *adv.*

mo *n.* more, others I.1933; **other(e) mo** many others IV.1215, IV.2263; **withouten mo** without any others, alone I.2725, VIII.207. Cf. **moore** *n.* MED mo *n.*

mooder *n.* mother II.276; *gen.* **moodres** II.786; *pl.* **moodres** VI.93. MED moder *n.*

moeve *v.* move X.133; **m. werre** begin or provoke war VII.1028, VII.1649; *pr. pl.* **moeven** X.128; *3 pt. sg.* **moeved** II.1136; *pp.* **moeved** X.293; *vbl. n.* **moeving(e)**

mover II.295; *pl.* **moevynges** movements X.655. MED meven *v.,* mevinge *ger.*

moyste *adj.* (1) moist, damp VII.992; (as *n.*) moisture, one of the elemental qualities I.420; (2) fresh, new VI.315, VII.764; supple (or new) I.457. MED moiste *adj.*

moone *n.* moon I.2077, I.3352; position of the moon I.403; *gen.* **moones** V.1154. MED mone *n.*(1)

mone, moone *n.* lament, moan V.920; (with **make**) I.1366, II.656. MED mon *n.*(1)

moralite(e) *n.* (1) morality I.3180, III.2046, X.38; (2) discourse on morals VII.2497, X.1088; moral significance (of a tale) VII.3440; *pl.* **moralitees** moral qualities X.462. MED moralite *n.*

mordre, moordre *n.* murder I.1256, VII.576. MED morther *n.*(1)

mordre *v.* murder VII.3225; *pr. pl.* **mordren** X.578; *pp.* **mordred** III.801; *vbl. n.* **mordrynge** murder I.2001. MED mortheren *v.,* mortheringe *ger.*

mordrour, mordrere *n.* murderer IV.732, VII.3226. MED mortherer *n.*

moore, more *adj.* more, greater in quantity, size, or extent I.2429, VII.5; **the m. part** the greater part, the majority VII.1257. Cf. **mo(o)** *adj.* MED more *adj.*

moor(e) *adv.* more I.1307, VI.369; (with *adj.* forming the *comp.*) I.802, III.441; **ever(e) lenger the m.** the longer (an activity continues) the more (intense the activity becomes) IV.687, V.404. Cf. **mo** *adv.* MED more *adv.*

moore *n.* (1) more (in quantity) III.1871; **m. and less(e), lasse and m.** the high (in rank) and the low, everyone I.1756, II.959, VI.53; (2) **withoute(n) (any) m.** without anything else I.1541, I.2316. Cf. **mo** *n.* MED more *n.*(3)

morne, moorne *v.* mourn, complain III.848; long for, yearn I.3704; *1 pr. sg.* **moorne** I.3704; *3 pr. sg.* **moorneth** mourns V.819; *pr. pl.* **moorne** long for VII.743; *vbl. n.* **moornyng(e)** mourning II.621, longing I.3706. MED mornen *v.,* morninge *ger.*

mortal, mortel *adj.* (1) mortal IV.1150, VIII.438; (2) deadly I.61, I.1553. MED mortal *adj.*

mortifye *v.* (in alchemy) transmute VIII.1126, VIII.1431; *pp.* **mortefied** destroyed, killed X.233. MED mortifien *v.*

morwe *n.* morning I.334; **morwe-tyde** morning time IV.2225, V.901. MED morwe *n.*

morwenynge *n.* morning, dawn I.1062, V.397; *pl.* **morwenynges** III.875. MED morninge *n.*

most(e), mosten must *see* **mot.**

moost(e), most *adj. super.* most I.303, I.798; greatest, chief I.895, III.505; (as *n.*) **meeste and leeste** one and all I.2198. MED most *adj.*

moost(e), most *adv. super.* most I.2325, I.2394; (forming *super.* of *adj.* or *adv.*) most I.2203, IV.979. MED most *adv.*

moot *1 & 3 pr. sg.* (1) (as *aux.,* with *inf.*) must I.732; may I.738, I.1838; (2) (without *inf.*) must go II.294; **m. nedes** must necessarily I.1169; *2 pr. sg.* **most** II.104; *pr. pl.* **moote(n)** I.232, III.589; *pr. subj. sg.* **mote** I.832, I.3918, **moot(e)** I.4177, VII.3300; *1 & 3 pt. sg.* (often *pr.* in meaning) **most(e)** I.712, IV.1402; (as *aux.,* with *inf.*) must I.847; *(impers.)* **us** (**him,** etc.) **m.** we (he, etc.) must VIII.946; *pt. pl.* **moste(n)** IV.1334, VII.2992; *pt. subj. sg.* **most(e)** may, might II.380, VI.550. MED moten *v.*(2)

mountaigne, mountayne, montayne, monteyne *n.* mountain II.24, VII.2586, VII.2627; *pl.* **montaignes** VII.2264. MED mountaine *n.*

montance *n.* amount, value I.1570, IX.255. MED mountaunce *n.*

mowe(n) *v.* be able VII.1466; *1 & 3 pr. sg.* **may** can I.230, may IV.2337; *2 pr. sg.* **mayst** I.1285, (with *pro.*) **maistow** I.2128; *pr. pl.* **mowe(n)** I.3550, VIII.681; **may** I.1268; *pr. subj.* **mowe** may VIII.300 *(sg.)*, VI.932 *(pl.)*; *1 & 3 pt. sg.* **myghte** I.299, I.1270; *2 pt. sg.* **myghtest** I.1655; *pt. pl.* **myghte(n)** I.568, II.470; *pt. subj. sg.* **myghte** IV.638. MED mouen *v.*(3)

muche, moche *adj.* much I.1359, V.586; many III.1273, VII.2770. MED muche *adj.*

muche, moche *adv.* much, greatly I.1116, VII.992. MED muche *adj.*

muche *n.* much III.2134, IV.2292; **m. and (or) lite** great and small, everyone I.494. MED muche *n.*

muchel *adj.* much I.2352, III.811; many VIII.673. MED muchel *adj.*

muchel *adv.* much, greatly I.132, III.809. MED muchel *adv.*

muchel *n.* much I.211, I.467. MED muchel *n.*

multiplie *v.* multiply III.28, VII.1740; (2) transmute base metals into gold VIII.669, VIII.731; *3 pr. sg.* **multiplieth** VII.1580; *pr. pl.* **multiplie** VIII.1417; *pr. subj. sg.* **multiplie** VIII.1479; *vbl. n.* **multiplying** increase VI.374, transmutation of base metals VIII.1391. MED multiplien *v.*, multipliinge *ger.*

mury(e), murier merry, merrier *see* **myrie** *adj.*, **myrye** *adv.*

murily, murierly merrily *see* **myryly.**

murmur(e) *n.* murmuring, grumbling I.2459, III.406. MED murmure *n.*

murmur(e) *pr. pl.* murmur, grumble X.507; *pt. pl.* **murmureden** V.204; *vbl. n.* **murmurynge** murmur I.2432. MED murmuren *v.*, murmuringe *ger.*

murthe mirth *see* **myrthe.**

N

n' *var.* of **ne** not (before vowels) VII.2841.

na *see* **no.**

nacioun *n.* nation II.268; family III.1068; *pl.* **nacions** I.53. MED nacioun *n.*

nad, nadde *contr.* of **ne had(de)** *(sg.)* had not IX.51. Cf. **have(n)** *v.*

nadde *contr.* of **ne hadde** *(pl.),* had not VIII.879. Cf. **have(n)** *v.*

nay *interj.* no I.1126, *etc.*; (as *n.*) **it is no n.** it cannot be denied I.4183. Cf. **no** *interj.* MED nai *interj.*

nayl *n.* (1) nail I.2007; (2) fingernail X.269; *pl.* **nayles** nails III.769, claws I.2141; **by nayles** by (God's) nails VI.288, VI.651. MED nail *n.*

naille *v.* nail, fasten IV.1184; *prp.* **nailynge** I.2503; *pp.* **nayled** IV.29. MED nailen *v.*

naked *adj.* naked I.1956, I.2066; bare, unadorned X.345; unsheathed (sword) V.84; **bely-naked** stark naked IV.1326. MED naked *adj.*

nam *1 pr. sg. contr.* of **ne am**, am not I.2811; **I n. but** I am as good as (dead, lost, *etc.*) I.1122, I.1274. Cf. **be(n)** *v.*

name *n.* (1) name I.854, I.1556; (2) reputation I.1437, I.2107; (3) condition, status X.766; *pl.* **names** I.2595. MED name *n.*

namely, nameliche *adv.* namely, especially, I.1268, I.3989. MED nameli *adv.*

namo *adj.* no more, no other I.101. MED no mo *adj.*

namo *adv.* no more, never again V.573. MED no mo *adv.*

namo *n.* no others I.544, III.957. MED no mo *n.*

namoore *adj.* no more IV.2318, X.188. MED no more *adj.*

namoore *adv.* no more I.98, I.2470; no longer I.4138, VII.160; never again VII.395. MED no more *adv.*

namoore *n.* no more I.974, I.2741. MED no more *n.*

narw(e) *adj.* narrow I.625, II.946; small VII.2822. MED narwe *adj.*

narwe, narowe *adv.* (1) closely, tightly I.3224, III.1803; (2) carefully IV.1988. MED narwe *adv.*

nas *1 & 3 pr. sg. contr.* of **ne was** was not, I.251, I.288; **nas but** was as good as (lost, dead, *etc.*) II.209. Cf. **be(n)** *v.*

nat, not *adv.* not I.246, I.3679; **nat but** nothing but I.2722, VI.403, only III.1728; **n. but ynough** more than enough VIII.601. MED not *adv.*

nath *3 pr. sg. contr.* of **ne hath** has not III.100. Cf. **have(n)** *v.*

natheles(s), nathelees *adv.* nonetheless, nevertheless I.35, I.1832. MED no-the-lesse *adv.*

nativitee *n.* birth V.45, VII.2016. MED nativite *n.*

nature *n.* (1) nature (as the controlling force of life) I.2758; (as *proper n.*) VII.11; (2) nature, character (of a person or thing) X.658; natural instinct VII.2855; (3) sperm, seed X.577; *gen.* **natures** V.353. MED nature *n.*

natureel, natural *adj.* natural I.2750, III.1144; **magyk n.** science I.416, V.1125; **day n.** twenty-four hours V.116. MED natural *adj.*

naturelly, natureelly *adv.* naturally, by nature II.298, III.1134. MED naturalli *adv.*

naught, nought, noght *n.* nothing I.756, III.1549. MED nought *pro.*

naught, nought, noght *adv.* (emphatic) not, in no way, not at all I.2068, I.3298; **right n.** not at all, III.582. MED nought *adv.*

ne, n' *adv.* not (*usu.* with another negative) I.70, I.449. MED ne *adv.*

ne *conj.* nor I.179, IV.304; **ne (nat) ... ne** neither . . . nor VI.339, VII.1681. MED ne *conj.*(1)

nece *n.* (1) niece III.383, III.537; (2) kinswoman, female relative (of any degree of relation) VII.100, VII.106. MED nece *n.*

necessitee *n.* necessity I.3042, IV.94; need VII.235. MED necessite *n.*

necligence, negligence *n.* negligence I.1881, II.22; (as *proper n.*) X.711. MED necligence *n.*

necligent *adj.* negligent III.1816, VI.101. MED necligent *adj.*

nede, neede *adv.* (with **moot, mot**) necessarily, of necessity IV.531, VII.2507. MED nede *adv.*

nede, neede *n.* (1) need, necessity I.2505, I.4026; **be(n) n.** be necessary I.304, IV.461; (with *dat.*) **yow (thee,** *etc.*) **ben n.** you (thou, *etc.*) need VII.109, VII.3453; (2) moment of need, crisis II.112, VII.2386; (3) business I.3632, VII.303; affair IV.1631; *pl.* **nedes** affairs VIII.178, duties VII.76. MED nede *n.*(1)

nede *v.* (1) be necessary II.871; (2) need, require X.700; (3)

(impers.) **him** *(etc.)* **n.** is needed by (him, *etc.*), he *(etc.)* needs III.1275, III.1955; **what n.** what is the need of I.849, II.232; *3 pr. sg.* **nedeth** I.462, **needeth** I.3599; *pr. pl.* **neden** X.927; *3 pt. sg.* **neded(e)** I.4020, VI.106. MED neden *v.*(2)

nedeful(le), needfulle *adj.* (1) needy X.805; (as *n.*) the needy II.112, X.1032; (2) needed VII.1643. MED nedeful *adj.*

nedelees *adj.* needless, unnecessary X.600, X.647. MED nedeles *adj.*

nedelees, nedeles *adv.* needlessly IV.621, X.698. MED nedeles *adv.*

nedely *adv.* of necessity, necessarily III.968, VII.3244. MED nedeli *adv.*(2)

nedes *adv.* (with **mot, moste,** *etc.*) by necessity, necessarily I.1169; **n. cost** necessarily I.1477. MED nedes *adv.*

nedy *adj.* needy, poor VII.1417, X.778. MED nedi *adj.*

neigh nigh *see* **ny** *prep.,* **ny(e)** *adj.,* **ny** *adv.*

nekke *n.* neck I.238, III.277; (as *adj.*) VII.649. MED nekke *n.*

nempne(n) *v.* name II.507, V.318; *3 pt. sg.* **nempned** IV.609; *pp.* **ynempned** X.598. MED nemnen *v.*

ner, neer *adv.* near, nearby I.1439; *come n.* draw near I.839, III.433; *comp.* **neer** nearer I.968; (as *adj.*) **never the n.** no nearer, no closer to one's goal, VIII.721. MED nerre *adv.*

nere *2 pt. sg. contr.* of **ne were** were not I.875; *pt. pl.* **nere** II.547; *pt. subj. sg.* **nere** it would not be I.1129; *pt. subj. pl.* **nere** II.548. Cf. **be(n)** *v.*

net *n.* snare VII.1179; *pl.* **nettes** nets I.3927. MED net *n.*(1)

never(e) *adv.* never I.70; **n. a deel** not a bit, not at all I.3064, VII.403; **n. erst** never before IV.144, X.766; **n. mo (more)** never again I.1346, (as one word) X.129; **n. the mo** in no way, not at all II.982, III.691, (as one word) IV.2089. MED never *adv.*

newe *adj.* (1) new, fresh I.457, II.138; modern I.176, X.721; (2) (as *n.*) **of n.** recently IV.938; for the first time VIII.1043; *comp.* **newer** VI.546. MED neue *adj.*

newe *adv.* newly, recently I.365, I.2162; **al n.** just now IV.1826; **n. and n.** again and again VI.929. MED neue *adv.*

newely *adv.* recently VII.1225. MED neuli *adv.*

next(e) *adj.* nearest VI.870; **n. way** most direct route II.807; next I.2367. MED nexte *adj.*

next *adv.* the next time V.443; next VII.450. MED nexte *adv.*

next *prep.* next to IV.694. MED nexte *prep.*

ny(e) *adj.* near, close X.836; **n. cause** immediate cause VII.1395; (as *n.*) the one who is near I.3392. MED neigh *adj.*

ny, neigh *adv.* (1) near III.178; (2) nearly I.4400; close, closely I.588; **wel n.** very nearly, almost I.1330, I.1407; (3) precisely I.732. MED neigh *adv.*

ny, neigh *prep.* close to, near II.550, III.931. MED neigh *prep.*

nyce *adj.* (1) foolish II.1088, III.938; (2) scrupulous I.398, IV.2434. MED nice *adj.*

nycete(e) *n.* foolishness I.4046, VIII.463; folly IX.152; lust III.412. MED nicete *n.*

nygard *n.* miser III.333, VII.2915; *pl.* **nygardes** III.1263. MED nigard *n.*

nyl(l) *1 & 3 pr. sg. contr.* of **ne wyl** will not, do not wish to II.972, III.98; *pr. pl.* **nel** III.941. Cf. **wille** *v.*

nys *3 pr. sg. contr.* of **ne ys** is not I.901, I.1274. Cf. **be(n)** *v.*

nyst(e) *1 & 3 pt. sg. contr.* of **ne wiste** did not know I.3414, I.4225, V.502. Cf. **wite(n)** *v.*

no *interj.* no! no indeed! (more emphatic than **nay;** *usu.* in answer to a negative question) IV.819, V.1000. MED no *interj.*

no, na *adj.* no, not any I.70, I.4134; nothing II.273; **no man** anyone VII.1584. Cf. **non(e)** *adj.* MED no *adj.*

no *adv.* no VI.958, *etc;* not VIII.212. Cf. **noon** *adv.* MED no *adv.*

noble *n.* a gold coin (6 shillings, 8 pence) I.3256; *pl.* **nobles** I.3780. MED noble *n.*(2)

nobleye *n.* nobility IV.828, VIII.449. MED nobleie *n.*

noblesse *n.* (1) nobility, high rank III.1167, IV.468; nobleness, nobility of character II.185, II.248; (2) splendor, magnificence IV.782. MED noblesse *n.*

noght nothing *see* **naught** *n., adv.*

noyse *n.* (1) noise I.2492 sound I.2524; clamor I.2534; sound, song IX.300, X.605; (2) uproar, disturbance VII.1035, VII.3393; *pl.* **noyses** uproars, disturbances VII.1514. MED noise *n.*

nolde *1 & 3 pt. sg. contr.* of **ne wolde** would not, did not want to I.2704, III.665; *pt. pl.* **nolde(n)** II.917, III.1898. *See* **nyl(l)** *v.* Cf. **wille** *v.*

nombre *n.* number I.716, III.25. MED nombre *n.*

non(e), noon *adj.* no I.1787, III.415; *(Nth.)* **neen** I.4185, I.4187. Cf. **no** *adj.* MED non *adj.*

non(e), noon *pro.* none I.524, II.87. MED non *pro.*

noon *adv.* no V.387; not III.2069, V.778. Cf. **no** *adv.* MED non *adv.*(1)

nones, nonys *n.* **for the n.** for the occasion I.3126; at that time, then I.879; indeed I.545, I.1423. MED nones *n.*(1)

nonne *n.* nun I.118; *gen.* **nonnes** VII.2809. MED nonne *n.*

norice *n.* nursemaid, governess VII.3115; nourisher V.347, VIII.1; *pl.* **norices** X.613. MED norice *n.*

norice *v.* nourish VII.1014; *3 pr. sg* **norisseth** VII.1594; *pr. pl.* **norissen** X.613; *pp.* **(y)norissed** brought up, nurtured IV.399; *vbl. n.* **norissyng(e)** nourishment I.437, X.348, **norisshynge** growth I.3017, upbringing IV.1040. MED norishen *v.,* norishinge *ger.*

noot *1 & 3 pr. sg.* (*contr.* of **ne woot**) I (he) know(s) not, do(es) not know I.1101, I.1263.

note, noote *n.* (1) melody VII.521, VII.547; (2) voice I.235. MED note *n.*(3)

nothing, no thyng *n.* nothing III.633; (also as two words) I.3598; (as *adv.*) in no way, not at all V.1094. MED nothing *pro.*

notifie *v. pr. pl.* indicate X.430; *pp.* **notified** indicated X.437, made known, proclaimed II.256. MED notifien *v.*

nought nothing *see* **naught** *n., adv.*

O

o, oo *var.* of **on** *num.* one I.304, I.1891; same I.2475.

obeye *v.* obey IV.194, IV.531; (with **to, unto**) be obedient VII.1550, VII.1742; *(reflx.)* be obedient VII.1684; *1 pr. sg.* **obeye** VII.1684; *3 pr. sg.* **obeyeth** IV.1961; *pr. pl.* **obeye(n)** IV.194, VII.1550; *3 pt. sg.* **obeyed** III.1255. MED obeien *v.*

obeisant, obeisaunt *adj.* obedient IV.66, X.264, X.676. MED obeisaunt *adj.*

obeisaunce, obeisance *n.* (1) homage, act of obedience

I.2974; **do o.** obey; IV.24; (2) respectful submission, deference IV.794; *pl.* **obeisaunces** acts of respect V.515. MED obeisaunce *n.*

obligeth *v. 3 pr. sg.* **obligeth** pledge X.847; *pr. pl.* **oblige** VII.1747. MED obligen *v.*

observaunce, observance *n.* (1) duty I.1316; attention, respectful act IV.1564, V.516; (2) ceremony, rite I.1500; **don o.** perform a customary rite, fulfill a religious duty I.1045, X.747; *pl.* **observaunces, observances** ceremonies I.2264, attentions V.516, customs V.956, practices V.1291. MED observaunce *n.*

observe *v.* respect, observe (a practice) VII.631; *3 pr. sg.* **observeth** X.303; *pr. pl.* **observe** respect, practice X.947; *pt. pl.* **observede** took care X.429. MED observen *v.*

occasioun, occasion *n.* cause X.946; opportunity X.512; *pl.* **occasiouns** X.1005, **occasions** VI.66. MED occasioun *n.*

occupie *v.* occupy, take up V.64; take possession of II.424; *3 pr. sg.* **occupieth**, VII.2237; *pr. pl.* **ocupien** take X.884; *pp.* **occupied** busy with VII.1596. MED occupien *v.*

of *adv.* off III.783, VI.226; **don of** take off I.2676; **com(e) of** come on, hurry III.1602. MED of *adv.*

of, off *prep.* (1) of I.55; (2) (agency) by III.661; from I.3612, I.4253, VII.2399; because of, for V.718, VII.2992; (3) (of respect) concerning I.177, I.2812; **as of** considering I.87; (4) (partitive) some, some of I.146, III.187, VI.910; (5) (time) since IV.834, IV.964. MED of *prep.*

offende(n) *v.* (1) do wrong, injure IV.1829; (2) displease IV.2164; (3) assail, transgress upon IV.1756; *pr. pl.* **offende** injure I.3065; *pp.* **offended** injured I.2394, displeased X.986. MED offenden *v.*

offense, offence *n.* (1) offense, transgression VII.1748; **doon o.** do wrong, injure I.1083, III.2058, IV.922; (2) sense of injury II.1138; *pl.* **offenses** VII.1882. MED offense *n.*

office *n.* (1) employment I.292, III.1421; role, function VII.2256; **fil in o.** obtained employment I.1418; (2) duty III.1137, VIII.924; (3) religious rite I.2863, I.2912; (4) function III.127, III.1144; (5) place of employment III.1577; *pl.* **offices** official positions X.438; **houses of o.** storehouses, larders IV.264. MED office *n.*

officer(e) *n.* (1) a court official, servant in a great household I.1712; officer of the law VIII.497; (2) an ecclesiastical official VII.65, VII.1935; (3) an official in charge of jousts I.1712; *pl.* **officers** servants V.177, **officeres** servants VI.480. MED officer *n.*

offre(n) *v.* make an offering (religious) VI.384, VI.386; *3 pr. sg.* **offreth** X.1030; *pr. subj. sg.* **offre** VI.376; *pr. subj. pl.* **offre(n)** VI.907, VI.929; *imp. pl.* **offreth** VI.910, **offre** VI.943; *pp.* **offred** X.900; *vbl. n.* **offryng(e)** offering (at mass) I.450, X.407; gifts given at the offering I.489, III.1315. MED offren *v.,* offringe *ger.*

ofte, often *adj.* frequent, repeated X.233; **o. sithe(s), tyme(s)** very often, many times I.52, I.485, I.1312. MED ofte *adj.,* often *adj.*

oft(e), often *adv.* often I.55, I.310; **o. a day** many times I.1356; *comp.* **ofter** more often IV.215. MED ofte *adv.,* often *adv.*

oght *see* **aught** *pro.* (anything), *adv.* (at all).

oghte ought *see* **owen.**

ook *n.* oak I.1702; *pl.* **okes** I.2866. MED oke *n.*

old(e), oold *adj.* (1) old I.174, I.429; (2) (as *n.*) the aged I.2499, II.417; age 1.2142; **of o.** long since III.1615,

IV.964; *comp.* **elder** VII.530; *super.* **eldest(e)** I.912, VI.1155. MED olde *adj.*

on *adv.* on, onward I.2558, I.3134. MED on *adv.*(1)

on-lofte *adv.* on high, above II.277, IV.229. MED on-lofte *adv.*

oon, on *indef. pro.* one, someone I.148, I.3817. MED on *pro.*

on *prep.* (1) on, in (location) I.271; (time, occasion), I.19; (2) on, concerning I.438, VIII.923; about I.3478. Cf. **a, an.** *prep.* MED on *prep.*

oon *num.* (1) (as *adj.*) one I.2039, III.573; same I.1012; (2) (as *pro.*) I.1013, I.2334; **evere in o.** always alike, continually I.1771, I.3880; **many o.** many a one, many I.317, VI.435; (3) (as *intens.*) **o. the faireste** (**best,** *etc.*) the fairest (best, *etc.*) IV.212, V.734. Cf. **a** *num.* MED on *num.*

ones, onis, oones *adv.* (1) once I.1034, III.10; (2) **al o.** agreed VI.696. MED ones *adv.*

open(e) *adj.* open I.10; public, manifest II.636. MED open *adj.*

open(e) *v.* open X.170, X.328; *3 pr. sg.* **openeth** X.289; *pt. pl.* **opened(en)** VIII.1218, X.329; *pp.* **opened** IV.2152. MED openen *v.*

operacion, operacioun *n.* scientific process V.130, V.1290; **ne doon hir o.** do not behave as they should III.1148; pl. **operaciouns** V.1129. MED operacioun *n.*

oppresse *v.* oppress V.1411, VII.1216; suppress, overcome VIII.4; rape V.1385, V.1406; *pr. subj. sg.* **oppresse** VII.1216; *pp.* **oppressed** raped V.1385. MED oppressen *v.*

oppression, oppressioun *n.* wrong III.889; oppression III.1990. MED oppressioun *n.*

or *conj.* ere, before II.289; *see* **er** *conj.,* **other** *conj.* MED or *conj.*

ordeyned *v. 3 pr. pt. sg.* ordered, disposed VIII.1277; *pp.* **ordeyned** arranged I.2553, appointed V.177. MED ordeinen *v.*

ordinaunce, ordinance *n.* (1) decree, order I.2567, I.3012; law VIII.445, VIII.529; **at, in** (someone's) **o.** under (someone's) authority II.763; (2) preparation II.250, IV.961; plan II.805, X.19; (3) orderly arrangement X.260; **by, in o.** in good order, correctly IV.961, VII.1113. MED ordinaunce *n.*

ordre *n.* (1) order, arrangement I.3003, V.66; **by o.** in order, sequentially I.1934, V.92; (2) manner V.66, VII.1529; (3) rank X.891; (4) religious order I.214, III.2191; religiously sanctioned condition IV.1347; (5) rule X.177; *pl.* **ordres** I.210. MED ordre *n.*

ordred *adj.* in religious orders, ordained X.961. MED ordren *v.*

ordure *n.* (1) filth X.157, X.851; rubbish, nonsense X.715; (2) excrement X.428, X.885. MED ordure *n.*

orison, orisoun *n.* prayer I.2261, I.2372; *pl.* **orisons** II.537, **orisouns** X.1038. MED orisoun *n.*

oth, ooth *n.* oath I.120; *pl.* **othes** I.810. MED oth *n.*

other(e), othre, oother(e) *adj.* other I.113, I.759. MED other *adj.*

oother *conj.* either VII.1053. *See* **outher** *conj.* MED other *conj.*

other(e), oother *pro.* other I.2045; **o. noon** nothing else, no other III.2132, VIII.929, no other way I.1182; **noon o.** **(weyes)** not otherwise I.1085, VI.412; **ech after o.** one after another I.899; *gen.* **otheres** VI.698; *pl.* **othere** I.2885. MED other *pro.*

otherweys, ootherweyes *adv.* otherwise, differently IV.1072. MED other-weies *adv.*

ought *see* **aught** *pro.* (anything), *adv.* (at all).

ought, oughte(n) *see* **owen.**

our(e) *1 pl. poss.* (1) *(adj.)* our I.34, I.62; (2) *(pro.)* **oures** ours VI.786, VII.273. MED oure *pro.*, oures *pro.*

out *interj.* help! I.3286, I.3825. MED oute *interj.*

out(e) *adv.* out I.45, *etc.;* (with *aux.* and omission of *v.* of motion) go out, come out VII.576, VII.3052. MED oute *adv.*

out(e) of *prep. phr.* (1) outside of, out from I.181, I.4077; (2) without I.487, I.1141. MED oute *adv.*

outen *v.* display, show publicly IV.2438; make public VIII.834; *pr. pl.* **oute** display, spread out III.521. MED outen *v.*

outher *adj.* either I.2556, VII.1667. MED outher *adj.*

outher *conj.* either III.1828; **o. . . . or (outher)** either . . . or VIII.1149, neither . . . nor II.1136. *See* **other** *conj.* MED outher *conj.*

outherwhile *adv.* sometimes VII.1543, (as two words) VII.1667. MED other-while *adv.*

outrage *n.* (1) excess X.834; (2) act of violence VII.1525, VII.1527; (3) violence, excessive cruelty I.2012, VII.1536; *pl.* **outrages** acts of violence VII.1438. MED outrage *n.*

outrageous(e) *adj.* (1) excessive, inordinate IV.2087, VI.650; (2) flagrantly evil VII.1825, X.412. MED outrageous *adj.*

outrely *adv.* utterly, completely I.237, I.1154. MED outreli *adv.*

outward *adj.* external, outer IV.424, X.298, X.662. MED outwarde *adj.*

outward *adv.* externally X.656; outwardly VII.1645. MED outwarde *adv.*

over *adv.* (1) over I.3177; **forther over** furthermore VI.648; (2) too, excessively (in compounds) **over-hard** too severe VII.1696; **over-hastily** too hastily VII.1576; **over-hoot** too hot VIII.955; **over-greet** excessive VII.1686, VIII.648; **over-large** excessive VII.1599; **over-largely** excessively VII.1601; **over-lowe, overlowe** too low VII.1465; **over-muche(l)** too much, excessively VII.1467; *sup.* **overeste** outermost I.290. MED over *adv.* (compounds listed separately).

over *prep.* over I.2140, *etc.;* beyond I.2998, II.277; **o. al this** furthermore, in addition I.2850, V.137. MED over *prep.*

overal *adv.* everywhere IV.1048; in every way IV.2129. MED over-al *adv.*

overcome *v.* overcome, defeat VII.1427; *3 pr. sg.* **overcometh** VII.1092; *pp.* **overcome** II.264. MED overcomen *v.*

oversprede *v.* spread over, cover IV.1799; *3 pt. sg.* **overspradde** I.678. MED overspreden *v.*

owen(e) *adj.* (following *poss. n.* or *pro.*) own I.213; awen *(Nth.)* I.4239. MED ouen *adj.*

owen *v.* (1) *(tr.)* owe X.746; (2) *(tr.)* own VI.361; (3) *(intr.)* as *aux.* (with *inf.*) ought to, should VII.1501; *1 pr. sg.* **owe** III.425; *2 pr. sg.* **owest** III.1615; *3 pr. sg.* **oweth** X.252; *pr. pl.* **owe(n)** owe III.2106; *1 & 3 pt. sg.* (as *aux.*) **oghte** should I.505, I.1249; *(impers.)* **him (us, etc.) oghte** he (we, *etc.*) should II.1097, **ought(e)** VII.1268; *pt. pl.* **oghte(n)** VIII.6, VIII.1340, **oughte(n)** VII.983, VII.1172. MED ouen *v.*

P

pace *see* **passe(n).**

page *n.* (1) servant, serving boy I.3030, V.692; (2) boy I.3972; **p. of the chambre** personal servant I.1427. MED page *n.*(1)

paye(n) *v.* pay I.806, IV.2048, IX.78; *pr. pl.* **payen** VII.1962; *imp. sg.* **pay** III.1598; *imp. pl.* **paye** VII.291; *1 & 3 pt. sg.* **payd(e)** I.539, III.1617, VII.366; *pp.* **(y)payed** paid, rewarded I.1802, I.4315, **payd** (with **holde**) pleased, satisfied III.1185. MED paien *v.*

payen *n.* pagan *pl.* **payens** II.534. MED paien *n.*

paire *see* **peyre.**

paleys, palays *n.* palace I.2199, IV.2415. MED palais *n.*

palfrey *n.* riding horse I.207, I.4075; *pl.* **palfreys** I.2495. MED palefrei *n.*

papejay *n.* parrot IV.2322, VII.369. MED papejaie *n.*

paramour(s) *adv.* passionately I.1155, I.2112. MED par amoure *adv.*

paramour(e) *n.* lady-love, concubine III.454, III.1372; sexual desire IV.1450; wenching I.4372, I.4392; *pl.* **paramours** concubines VII.2867; courtly love-making I.3354, I.3758. MED paramoure *n.*

paraventure, peraventure, paraunter *adv.* perhaps II.190, III.893; by chance IV.234. MED paraventure *adv.*

parcel *n.* portion V.852, X.1006. MED parcel *n.*

parde(e) *interj.* by God! indeed! I.563, I.1312. MED parde *interj.*

pardoun *n.* forgiveness, pardon VI.917, VII.1773; indulgence VI.906; *pl.* **pardoun** indulgences I.687, VI.920. MED pardoun *n.*

parfay, parfey *interj.* by my faith! indeed! I.3681, II.110. MED par fei *interj.*

parfit(e) *adj.* perfect, complete I.72, VII.1520. MED parfit *adj.*

parfitly *adv.* perfectly, completely III.111, IV.690. MED parfitli *adv.*

parfourne(n), perfourne *v.* perform, carry out VII.1066, X.782; **p. up** complete III.2261; *2 pr. sg.* **parfournest** express VII.607; *3 pr. sg.* parfourneth X.736; *3 pt. sg.* **parfourned** IV.2052; *pp.* **parfourned** carried out VI.151, expressed VII.456; **parfourmed** completed III.2104, IV.1795; *vbl. n.* **parfournynge** doing X.807. MED performen *v.*, performinge *ger.*

parlement *n.* parliament, assembly I.3076; debate I.2970; decision I.1306. MED parlemente *n.*

part(e) *n.* (1) part, portion I.1178, I.3006; **the moore p.** the majority VII.1206; **an hondred (twenty) thousand p.** by a hundred (twenty) thousand times III.2062, V.553; (2) party, side I.2446, I.2582; **on every p.** on every side I.2185; (3) **have p. on (of)** take possession of I.2792, VII.218. MED part *n.*

parte(n) *v.* (1) divide, share III.1534, IV.1630; (2) separate, leave (one another) I.4362; depart, leave VI.649; *2 pr. sg.* **partest** leave VI.752; *pr. pl.* **parte** I.4362; *prp.* (as *adj.*) **partyng felawes** partners X.637; *pp.* **parted** divided III.1967, X.8. MED parten *v.*

party, partie *n.* part I.3008, II.17; partisan I.2657; *pl.* **parties** factions VII.1014. MED partie *n.*

pas, paas *n.* (1) pace, speed I.2901; walk (of a horse) I.825, VIII.575; **a p.** at a walk, slowly I.2217, I.2897; **a softe p.** quietly I.3760, at a slow gait II.399; **a sturdy p.** briskly III.2162; **esily a p., an esy p.** at an easy pace V.388; **a sory p., sorwfully a p.** sadly, at a sad (slow) pace I.3741;

(2) passage, difficult situation VII.1445; *pl.* **paas** steps II.306; (3) **pas** paces (as unit of measurement) I.1890. MED pase *n.*(1)

passe(n), pace *v.* (1) go, proceed I.2574; leave aside VII.443; (2) depart, pass by I.3578; (3) surpass IV.1417, VIII.857; surpass, excel I.3089; *3 pr. sg.* **passeth** proceeds, goes on I.1033; *1 pr. sg.* **pace** I.36, passe I.1461; *pr. pl.* **passe(n)** IV.117, VII.9; *pr. subj. sg.* **pace** IV.1092; *imp. sg.* **passe over** let it be VI.303; *3 pt. sg.* **passed** surpassed I.448; *prp.* **passyng(e)** going I.2848, surpassing I.2885, (as *adj.*) exceeding IV.1252, outstanding VIII.614; *pp.* **(y)passed** I.464, IV.1892, **past** VII.2289. MED passen *v.*

passioun, passion *n.* (1) passion, suffering I.3478, I.4327; martyrdom VIII.26; (2) feeling, emotion II.1138. MED passioun *n.*

pasture *n.* feeding place VII.1933, VII.3185; pasture land IV.1313. MED pasture *n.*

pater-noster *n.* the Lord's Prayer I.3485, I.3638. MED pater-noster *n.*

peces, pieces *n. pl.* pieces X.356, VII.136. MED pece n.

pecock *n.* peacock I.3926; (as *adj.*) I.104. MED po-cok *n.*

peyne, payne *n.* (1) punishment, penalty III.1314, VII.1749; **up p. of** on the penalty of I.1707, I.2543; **the p.** torture I.1133; (2) pain I.1297, I.1382; (3) effort V.509; **don (one's) p.** devote (one's) efforts, work diligently V.730, IX.330; *pl.* **peynes** pains I.1338, punishments X.229. MED peine *n.*

peyne *v.* (1) punish, inflict pain X.213; harm, hurt VII.2604; (2) *(reflx.)* endeavor, make an effort X.943; *1 pr. sg.* **peyne** VI.330; *3 pr. sg.* **peyneth** II.320; *3 pt. sg.* **peyned** I.139; *pp.* **peyned** tortured, punished X.273. MED peinen *v.*

peynte(n) *v.* (1) paint I.2087, VI.12; (2) adorn X.610; (3) disguise IV.2062; *pr. pl.* **peynte** V.725; *pr. sg. subj.* **peynte** VI.15; *3 pt. sg.* **peynted(e)** III.692, V.560; *pp.* **peynted** I.1934. MED peinten *v.*

peyre, paire *n.* pair X.555; set I.159, III.1741. MED paire *n.*(1)

penaunce, penance *n.* (1) penance (for sin) I.223; (2) misery, suffering I.1315, II.286; **doon p.** inflict suffering VIII.530; *pl.* **penaunces** penances X.1053, **penances** X.1052. MED penaunce *n.*

peny *n.* penny (one-twelfth of a shilling) I.4119, III.1575; **masse p.** money offered for the singing of a Mass III.1749; *pl.* **pens** VI.376. MED peni *n.*

peple, people *n.* people I.706, I.962; nation II.489, IV.995; *gen.* **peples** IV.412. MED peple *n.*

peer(e) *n.* peer, equal I.4026, V.678. MED per *n.*

peraventure perhaps, by chance *see* **paraventure.**

perce(n) *v.* pierce IV.1204, V.237; *pr. pl.* percen VIII.911; *3 pt. sg.* **perced** VII.555; *pp.* **perced** I.2; *vbl. n.* **percynge** VII.862. MED percen *v.*, percinge *ger.*

perdurable *adj.* eternal VII.1509, X.124; *pl.* **perdurables** X.811. MED perdurable *adj.*

perfourne perform *see* **parfourne(n).**

perisse *v.* perish X.75; *pr. pl. subj.* **perisse** VI.99; *pp.* **perissed** killed X.579. MED perishen *v.*

perles, peerles *n. pl.* pearls I.2161, VII.2468.

perrye, perree *n.* precious stones, jewels I.2936, III.344. MED perrie *n.*

persevere *v.* continue, persevere III.148, VII.1264; *3 pr. sg.*

persevereth lasts VI.497; *vbl. n.* **perseverynge** constancy VIII.117. MED perseveren *v.,* perseveringe *ger.*

Persyen *n.* Persian III.2079; *pl.* **Persiens** VII.2248, **Perses** VII.2235. MED persien *n.*

persone, persoun *n.* person I.521, III.1313; **propre p.** own self VII.985, VII.1026; body X.591; *pl.* **persones** VII.1165. MED persoune *n.*(1)

persoun, person, parson *n.* parson I.478, I.702. MED persoune *n.*(2)

pees *n.* (1) peace I.532, I.1447; (2) silence, quiet II.228; **hoold** (one's) **p.** be quiet I.2668, VI.462; (as *imp.*) hush, be quiet II.836, III.850. MED pes *n.*

Peter *interj.* by Saint Peter! III.446, III.1332. MED Peter *n.*

philosophie *n.* (1) learning I.645, I.4050; philosophy I.295, II.1188; (2) alchemy VIII.1058, VIII.1373. MED philosophie *n.*

philosophre, philosofre *n.* (1) philosopher, learned writer II.25, VI.620; **the p.** Aristotle X.658; (2) astrologer II.310; magician V.1561; alchemist VIII.1122; *gen.* **philosophres** VIII.862; *pl.* **philosophres** VIII.113. MED philosophre *n.*

phisik *n.* science of medicine X.913; medicine, remedy I.411, I.443. MED phisike *n.*

pye *n.* magpie I.3950, III.456; *pl.* **pyes** V.650. MED pie *n.*(1)

pieces *see* **peces.**

pyketh *v. 3 pr. sg.* makes (himself) neat IV.2011; *pp.* **(y)pyked** picked out III.44a, sorted out VIII.941. MED piken *v.*(1)

pile(n) *v.* rob, plunder III.1362; *pr. pl.* **pilen** X.767; *pp.* (as *adj.*) **piled** bald (deprived of hair) I.3935, I.4306; thin, scanty I.627. MED pilen *v.*(1)

pyler, pileer *n.* pillar I.1993, I.2466; *pl.* **pilers** VII.2084. MED pilere *n.*

pilours *n. pl.* scavengers I.1007; thieves X.769. MED pilour *n.*(1)

pyne *n.* pain I.1324, I.2382; misery, suffering II.1080. MED pine *n.*(1)

pype(n) *v.* pipe, play the pipe, whistle I.3876, I.3927; **p. in an ivy leef** go whistle (in vain) I.1838 (see note); *prp.* (as *adj.*) **pipyng** whistling, hissing I.3379. MED pipen *v.*

pit *see* **putte(n).**

pitee *n.* pity I.920; grief I.2833, II.292. MED pite *n.*

pitous *adj.* (1) merciful, compassionate I.143, I.953; (2) pitiful, sorrowful I.955, I.1919; pious X.1039. MED pitous *adj.*

pitously *adv.* piteously, sorrowfully I.949, I.1117. MED pitousli *adv.*

plat, platte *adj.* flat, blunt I.1845; blunt side of a sword V.164, (as *n.*) V.162. MED plat *adj.*

plat *adv.* flat VII.675; flatly, clearly II.886, VI.648. MED plat *adv.*

plate *n.* plate armor VII.865; plate of metal X.433; *pl.* **paire plates** set of plate armor I.2121. MED plate *n.*

platly *adv.* flatly, directly X.485, X.1022. MED platlie *adv.*

plede *v.* plead VII.1369; *vbl. n.* **pledynge** plea X.166. MED pleden *v.,* pledinge *ger.*

pley *n.* (1) amusement VI.627; (2) game IV.10; funeral game I.2964; (3) dramatic performance III.558; (4) jest, joke III.1548; **in p.** in jest, jokingly I.1125, I.4355; *pl.* **pleyes** dramatic performances III.558. MED pleie *n.*

pleye(n) *v.* (1) play, amuse oneself II.558; *(reflx.)* I.1127,

I.3660; jest, be playful I.758, VII.1963; (2) play amorously, flirt I.3273; have sexual intercourse IV.1841; (3) play (musical instrument or game) I.236; (4) act (a part), perform I.3384, V.219; (5) act, deal with (someone) III.2074, VI.654; work (tricks) V.1141; *1 pr. sg.* **pleye** III.245; *3 pr. sg.* **pleyeth** I.3306; *pr. pl.* **pleye(n)** I.2959, V.219; *imp. sg.* **pley** I.4198; *pr. subj.* **pleye** VI.654; *3 pt. sg.* **pleyde** I.4068; *pt. pl.* **pleyde** I.3858; *prp.* **pleyynge** VI.608; (as *vbl. n.*) **pleyyng(e)** I.1061, IV.1854. MED pleien *v.*(1), pleiinge *ger.*

pleyn, playn *adj.* (1) clear I.1487, VIII.284; (as *n.*) **short and p.** brief, simple account I.1091, IV.577; (2) unadorned, simple V.720, VII.2091; sincere VI.50. MED plaine *adj.*

pleyn *adj.* full, complete I.337, I.2461; open (battle) I.988. MED pleine *adj.*

pleyn, playn *adv.* (1) clearly I.790; (2) entirely I.327, I.1464. MED plaine *adv.*

pleyne *v.* (1) lament I.1320, II.1067; (2) complain III.387, V.776; *(reflx.)* III.336; **p. (up)on** make complaint, or bring an accusation, against V.1355, VI.167; *1 pr. sg.* **pleyne** V.1355; *3 pr. sg.* **pleyneth** I.4114; *pr. pl.* **pleyne(n)** I.1251, IV.97; *pr. pl. subj.* **pleyne** IV.97; *1 & 3 pt. sg.* **pleyned** III.390, V.1457; *vbl. n.* **pleynynge** lament X.84. MED pleinen *v.*, pleining *ger.*

pleynly *adv.* (1) plainly, simply I.727, I.1209; (2) fully I.1733, II.894. MED pleinli *adv.*, plainli *adv.*

pleynt(e) *n.* complaint, lament II.66, V.1029; *pl.* **pleintes** II.1068. MED pleinte *n.*

plentee *n.* plenty, abundance II.443, IV.264; **ful greet p.** in great abundance VI.811. MED plente *n.*

plesaunce, plesance *n.* (1) pleasure, amusement, delight I.1925, I.2485; (as *proper n.*) I.1925; **doon** (someone's) **p.** give pleasure to, please (someone) I.1571, III.408; (2) desire IV.501; will II.762; **doon** (someone's) **p.** do as (someone) wishes IV.658, VII.2866. MED plesaunce *n.*(1)

plesaunt, plesant(e) *adj.* pleasing, agreeable I.138, IV.991. MED plesaunte *adj.*

plese(n) *v.* please I.610, II.381; *pr. pl.* **plesen** VII.3327; *pr. subj. pl.* **plese** IV.1680; *3 pt. sg.* **plesed** II.788; *pp.* **(y)plesed** I.2446, III.930; *vbl. n. pl.* **plesynges** pleasures II.711. MED plesen *v.*, plesinge *ger.*

plighte *1 pr. sg.* (with *trouthe*) pledge (one's word) V.1537, VII.198; *imp. sg.* **plight** III.1009; *3 pt. sg.* **plighte** III.1051; *pt. pl.* **plighten** V.1328; *pp.* **plight** VI.702. MED plighten *v.*

plighte *3 pt. sg.* pulled II.15; VII.2049; *pp.* **plyght** pulled out, plucked III.790. MED plicchen *v.*

plit(e) *n.* plight, condition IV.2335, VIII.952. MED plight *n.*

plogh, plough *n.* plow I.3159, VII.288; (as modifier) **p. harneys** ploughing equipment I.3762. MED plough *n.*

poynaunt *adj.* spicy I.352, VII.2834; piercing X.130. MED poinaunt *adj.*

poynt *n.* (1) punctuation mark, period VIII.1480; (2) point in space or time I.114; (3) item, detail VIII.344; **at poynt-devys** in every detail, to perfection I.3689, V.560; **every p.** in detail VII.3022; **from p. to p.** from beginning to end, in every particular IV.577; (4) state, condition I.200, X.921; **in (o) p. to** (with *inf.*) about to, on the point of II.331, II.910; (5) point (of a spear, *etc.*) I.114; (6) *(pl.)* laces, ties I.3322; **pointz** I.2971, **pointes** VIII.344. MED pointe *n.*(1)

portreyynge *see* **purtreye.**

portreiture *n.* painting I.1968; *pl.* **portreitures** I.1915. MED portraiture *n.*

pothecarie *see* **apothecarie.**

poure *v.* pore, gaze intently I.185, III.295; peep III.1738, IV.2112; *pr. pl.* **pouren** VIII.670; *pr. subj. sg.* **poure** III.295. MED pouren *v.*(1)

povre, povere, poore, poure *adj.* poor I.225, III.1923; (as *n.*) the poor, poor people X.373, X.461; *super.* **povrest** IV.205, **povereste** VI.449. MED povre *adj.*

pray- *see* **preye(n).**

pray(e), preye *n.* prey I.2015, III.1376; *pl.* **preyes** III.1472. MED preie *n.*(2)

preche(n) *v.* preach I.481, I.712; *2 pr. sg.* **prechest** III.247; (with *pro.*) **prechestow** III.366; *3 pr. sg.* **precheth** VII.1044; *pr. pl.* **preche(n)** III.436, V.824; *imp. pl.* **precheth** IV.12; *pp.* **preched** III.1714; *vbl. n.* **prechyng** VI.401. MED prechen *v.*, prechinge *ger.*

precious(e), precius *adj.* (1) precious III.338, X.591; (2) fastidious, fussy III.148; prudish IV.1962. MED preciouse *adj.*

predicacioun *n.* sermon, preaching III.2109, VI.345. MED predicacioun *n.*

preef, preeve *n.* proof III.2272; test IV.787, VIII.968; **with yvel p.** bad luck to you III.247. MED preve *n.*

preye(n), praye(n) *v.* pray, beseech, plead I.301, II.258; *2 pr. sg.* **prayest** X.1043; *3 pr. sg.* **preyeth** II.866, **prayeth** II.866; *pr. pl.* **preye(n)** I.1260, III.1902, **praye** III.1945; *pr. subj* **preye** III.358 *(sg.),* X.1084 *(pl.)*; *imp. sg.* **preye** V.1066, *imp. pl.* **prey(e)** V.1066, VII. 687, **preyeth** X.526, **prayeth** III.1663; *3 pt. sg.* **preyde** II.391, **preyed(e)** IV.1612, VI.251; *pt. pl.* **preyeden** III.895, **preyden** I.811; *prp.* **preyynge** IV.977; *pp.* **preyed** I.2108, **(y)prayed** IV.269, VIII.66; *vbl. n.* **preiynge** X.683. MED preien *v.*(1), preiinge *ger.*

preyer(e), prayere *n.* prayer I.1204, III.1489; *pl.* **preyeres** III.1884, **prayeres** III.865. MED preiere *n.*(2)

preyse *v.* praise III.294, IV.459; *inf.* **to preyse(n)** to be praised VII.1516; *3 pr. sg.* **preyseth** IV.1854; *pr. pl.* **preyse(n)** IV.935, IV.1022; *pr. subj. sg.* **preyse** IV.1546; *pt. pl.* **preised** VI.113; *pp.* **preised** III.706; *vbl. n.* **preysinge** praise X.494, glory X.949; *pl.* **preisynges** praises X.454. MED preisen *v.*, preisinge *ger.*

presse, prees *n.* (1) crowd, throng II.393, II.646; (2) difficulties VII.2137; (3) cupboard, linen press I.3212; (4) casting mold I.263; curler I.81. MED presse *n.*

preesseth *v. 3 pr. sg.* **preesseth** push forward I.2530; *imp.* urge, entreat III.520. MED pressen *v.*

prest, preest *n.* priest I.501, II.1166; *gen.* **preestes** VIII.1023 *(sg.),* II.377 *(pl.)*; *pl.* **preestes** I.164. MED prest *n.*(3)

preve, preeve *v.* (1) test IV.699, IV.1330; (2) prove, demonstrate I.485, VI.169; (3) succeed VIII.1212; turn out IV.1000; (4) reprove VII.1437; *3 pr. sg.* **preeveth** IV.1155, **preveth** IV.2238, **proveth** V.455; *pr. subj. sg.* **preeve** IV.1152; *imp. sg.* **preeve** III.2057; *3 pt. sg.* **preved** IV.28, **proved** I.547; *pt. pl.* **preved** IV.2283; *pp.* **(y)preved** I.485, VII.1114, **preeved** I.3001. MED preven *v.*

prye(n) *v.* peer, gaze I.3458, IV.2112. MED prien *v.*

prikke *v.* (1) prick VII.1326; (2) cause pain, ache III.1594; (3) spur, ride rapidly I.2678, VII.754; stab, pierce I.4231;

(4) incite, urge I.11, I.1043; *3 pr. sg.* **priketh** III.656; *pr. subj.* **prike** VII.811 *(sg.),* IV.1038 *(pl.); 3 pt. sg.* **pryked** VII.774, **prighte** V.418; *prp.* **prikyng** VII.837; *pp.* **priked** VIII.561; *vbl. n.* **prikyng(e)** I.2599, VII.775. MED priken *v.,* prikinge *ger.*

prikke *n.* (1) point of a weapon I.2606; stinger X.468; (2) **to that p.** (come, bring) to that point II.119, II.1029. MED prike *n.*

pryme *n.* (1) the canonical hour (6 A.M.) VI.662; (2) the hours from six to nine in the morning IV.1857, V.73; (3) about 9 A.M. I.2189, I.2576; **fully p., p. large** 9 A.M. V.360; **half-wey p.** about 7:30 A.M. I.3906. MED prime *n.*

prys *n.* (1) price, value I.815, III.523; **of p.** valuable, excellent VII.897; (2) **baar the (our) p.** took the prize I.237; (3) praise III.1152, IV.1026; reputation, honor I.67, I.2241. MED pris *n.*(1)

pryve(e) *adj.* (1) secret I.2460, III.620; (2) private, confidential II.204; discreet, secretive I.3201; **p. membres** private parts, sexual members X.427. MED prive *adj.*(1)

pryvee adv. **p. and apert** secretly or publicly, in all circumstances III.1114, V.531. MED prive *adv.*

pryvely adv. secretly, discreetly I.609, I.1222; alone VII.92. MED privelie *adv.*

pryvetee *n.* (1) privacy, secrecy VII.1194; (2) secret I.3164, I.3454; **in p.** secretly I.3493, I.3623; secret counsel, private affairs I.1411, I.3603; (3) private parts, sexual members VII.2715. MED privete *n.*

procede(n) *v.* proceed IV.2020, VII.1341; come forth, originate III.328; *3 pr. sg.* **procedeth** VII.1873. MED proceden *v.*

proces, processe *n.* (1) course of events VII.2321; ordinary course V.1345; (2) story, discourse V.658; (3) passage (of time) VII.1475; **by p.** in time, at length, eventually I.2967, V.829. MED proces *n.*

profit(e) *n.* (1) profit, advantage III.214, VII.1237; **do** (one's) **p.** work for (one's) advantage VII.1588, VII.1592; good VII.1688; **commune p.** common good, welfare of the state IV.431, IV.1194; (2) profit, income I.249, III.1344. MED profite *n.* (1)

profre(n) *v.* offer VIII.1123; *3 pr. sg.* **profreth** I.1415; *pr. pl.* **profre** IV.848; *pr. subj. sg.* **profre** VIII.489; *3 pt. sg.* **profred** III.1288; *(reflx.)* pressed his suit I.3289; *pp.* **profred** IV.152. MED profren *v.*

propertee, propretee *n.* nature, essential quality VII.1174; property, characteristic X.640. MED proprete *n.*

propre *adj.* (1) own I.540, I.581; **owene p.** very own VII.985, X.1021; individual, peculiar I.3037, III.103; (2) correct VI.417; comely, well-formed I.3345, I.3972; **of p. kynde** by nature, naturally V.610, V.619. MED propre *adj.*

proprely, properly adv. (1) particularly X.485; (2) correctly, appropriately I.729, I.1459; handsomely I.3320; naturally III.1191. MED proprelie *adv.*

prow *n.* profit, benefit, advantage VI.300, VII.408. MED prou *n.*

prowesse *n.* excellence of character III.1129. MED prouesse *n.*

publiced *ppl.* made known IV.415, IV.749. MED publishen *v.*

pulle(n) *v.* (1) pluck IX.304; rob, swindle I.652 (see note); (2) pull IV.2353; *3 pt. sg.* **pulled** I.1598; *pp.* **ypulled** I.3245; (as *adj.*) **pulled** plucked I.177. MED pullen *v.*

punysse *v.* punish VII.1441, VII.1443; *pp.* **(y)punysshed** I.657, VII.1419; *vbl. n.* **punyssynge** punishment VII.1432, **punysshyng(e)** III.1304. MED punishen *v.,* punishinge *ger.*

purchace(n) *v.* purchase, acquire I.608, VIII.1405; bring about, provide VII.1690; *pr. pl.* **purchasen** bring about, provide VII.1680; *pr. subj. sg.* **God purchace** may God provide II.873; *pp.* **purchaced** brought about VII.1690; *vbl. n.* **purchasyng** legal conveyance of property I.320, acquisition of profits III.1449. MED purchasen *v.,* purchasinge *ger.*

pure *adj.* (1) pure, chaste VIII.48, X.1046; (2) very, sheer I.1279. MED pure *adj., adv.*

purge *v.* discharge, cleanse of bodily wastes III.134, VII.573; cleanse VIII.181; *pr. pl.* **purge(n)** VII.2947, X.428; *pr. subj. pl.* **purge yow** take a laxative VII.2947; *pp.* **purged** cleansed VIII.181. MED purgen *v.*(1)

purpos *n.* plan, purpose I.2542, I.3981; **in p. was** intended I.3978; **it cam hym to p.** he decided V.606; **now to p.** now to the point II.170, III.711. MED purpos *n.*

purposen *v.* intend X.87; decide IV.706; *(reflx.)* resolve VII.1834; *1 pr. sg.* **purpose** III.1055; *2 pr. sg.* **purposest** VII.1203; *3 pr. sg.* **purposeth** X.734; *1 pt. sg.* **purposed** X.309; *prp.* **purposynge** decided upon, intending V.1458; *pp.* **purposed** IV.706. MED purposen *v.*

pursue(n) *v.* (1) pursue X.355; (2) (with **to**) petition VII.1694; *pr. pl.* **pursewen** persecute X.526. MED pursueun *v.*

purtreye *v.* draw I.96; *3 pt. sg.* **purtreyed** depicted in the mind IV.1600; *vbl. n.* **portreyynge** portraiture I.1938. MED portraien *v.,* portraiinge *ger.*

purveye(n) *v.* (1) prepare IV.191, VII.1342; (2) provide III.917; *pp.* (with **of**) **purveyed** provided with III.591. MED purveien *v.*

purveiaunce, purveiance, purveaunce *n.* (1) foresight, providence I.1252, I.1665; (2) arrangement, preparations I.3566, II.247; (3) provision III.570. MED purveiaunce *n.*

putte(n) *v.* (1) put VII.763, X.1045; **p. on** impute to VIII.455; (2) suppose VII.1477; *1 pr. sg.* **put** III.1231, **putte** I.1841; *2 pr. sg.* **puttest** VII.2685; *3 pr. sg.* **putteth** I.3802, *(contr.)* **put** X.142; *pr. pl.* **putten** I.1435; *pr. subj. sg.* **putte** VII.1753; *imp. sg.* **put** III.2140; *imp. pl.* **put** I.3185, **putte** VIII.1329; *1 & 3 pt. sg.* **putte** I.3732, II.763; *2 pt. sg.* **puttest** VII.2685; *pt. pl.* **putte(n)** VII.2070, VIII.1338; *pp.* **(y)put** III.1333, IV.262; *(Nth.)* **pit** I.4088. MED putten *v.*

Q

quake *v.* tremble I.3614, V.860; *1 pr. sg.* **quake** X.159; *3 pt. sg.* **quook** I.1576; *prp.* **quakynge** IV.317; *pp.* **quaked** VII.2641. MED quaken *v.*

queynte *adj.* (1) ingenious, clever I.3275, I.4051; learned, complex II.1189, VIII.752; (2) elaborately contrived I.1531, I.3605; tricky VII.236; (3) curious I.2333, III.516; (4) strange V.239; (5) (as *n.*) elegant, pleasing thing I.3276, (sexual favors) III.332, III.444. MED queinte *adj.,* queinte *n.*

quenche(n) *v.* quench, extinguish X.628; *(intr.)* go out X.210, X.341; *3 pt. sg.* **queynte** went out I.2334; *pp.* **(y)queynt** I.2336, I.3754. MED quenchen *v.*

questioun, question *n.* (1) question I.1347, V.579; (2) problem IV.1654; logical problem III.2223; **holdynge hir q.** debating I.2514. MED questioun *n.*

quyk(e) *adj.* (1) living X.658; (2) lively V.194; vivid I.306; *super.* **quykkest** busiest V.1502. MED quik *adj.*

quyke(n) *v.* revive X.235; give life to VIII.481; *pr. pl.* **quyken** X.242; *3 pt. sg.* **quyked** rekindled I.2335; *pp.* **(y)quyked** kindled V.1050, stirred, enlivened X.536. MED quiken *v.*

quite(n) *v.* (1) pay III.1292, VII.2374; pay for I.3127; ransom I.1032; (2) recompense, requite I.3119, VII.1053; (3) pay back (revenge) I.3746, I.3916; **q.** (someone's) **hir(e), while** repay II.584, III.1008; (4) *(reflx.)* do one's duty, conduct oneself V.673; *1 pr. sg.* **quyte** VI.420; *3 pr. sg.* **quiteth** X.689; *pr. pl.* **quiten** X.154; *pr. subj. sg.* **quite** I.770; *1 pt. sg.* **quitte** III.422; *pp.* **(y)quyt** I.4324, V.673. MED quiten *v.*

quod *v. 1 & 3 pt. sg.* said I.788, VII.707. MED quethen *v.*

R

rad(de) read *see* **rede(n).**

rafte, (y)raft took (taken) away *see* **reve(n).**

rage *n.* (1) madness, violent insanity I.2011, III.2166; (2) grief V.836; (3) rush of wind I.1985. MED rage *n.*

rakel, rakle, racle *adj.* rash, hasty IX.278, IX.289. MED rakel *adj.*

ransoun, raunson *n.* ransom I.1024, I.1176; **maad his r.** paid his penalty III.411. MED raunsoun *n.*

rasour *n.* razor I.2417, VII.2056. MED rasoure *n.*

rather *adv.* (1) earlier VI.643; sooner II.335; (2) rather I.487. MED rathere *adv.*

raughte *v. 3 pt. sg.* reached I.136; reached (to) I.3696. MED rechen *v.*(1)

ravyshedest *v. 2 pt. sg.* seized, carried off VII.469; enraptured, entranced IV.1750; **r. on** be enraptured by IV.1774; *2 pt. sg.* **ravyshedest** VII.469; *3 pt. sg.* **ravysshed** IV.2230; *pp.* **ravysshed** III.1676. MED ravishen *v.*

reawme *n.* realm II.797, VII.116; *pl.* **remes** VII.3136. MED reaume *n.*

recche *v.* care, be concerned for III.329; *(impers.)* **r. me (yow,** *etc.*) I (you, *etc.*) care III.53, IV.2276; esteem V.71; *1 pr. sg.* **recche** I.1398; *2 pr. sg.* **rekkest** III.1453; *3 pr. sg.* **reccheth** I.2397, **rekketh** III.327; *pr. pl.* **recche** V.71, **rekke(n)** X.905, X.943; *3 pt. sg.* **roghte** I.3772; *pt. subj. sg.* **roghte** IV.685. MED recchen *v.*(2)

recchelees *adj.* careless, reckless IV.488, VII.3107; heedless of rules I.179 (see note); negligent II.229. MED recheles *adj.*

reccheleesnesse *n.* recklessness, carelessness X.111, X.611. MED rechelesnesse *n.*

receyve(n) *v.* (1) receive II.259, II.991; (2) *(astro.)* favorably situated, welcomed (by an auspicious planet) II.307; *1 pr. sg.* **receyve** VII.1881; *3 pr. sg.* **receyveth** II.396; *pr. pl.* **receyve(n)** X.106, X.127; *pr. subj. sg.* **receyve** II.259; *imp. pl.* **receyveth** VI.926; *3 pt. sg.* **receyved** III.1889; *pp.* **received** IV.955; *vbl. n.* **receyvynge** X.385. MED receiven *v.*, receivinge *ger.*

reconforte *v.* comfort, encourage VII.978; *(reflx.)* take heart I.2852; *3 pt. sg.* **reconforted** VII.1660. MED recomforten *v.*

record(e) *n.* reputation III.2049; **of r.** on record, recorded III.2117. MED recorde *n.*

recorde *v.* I.829; pronounce I.1745; *1 pr. sg.* **recorde.** recall, remind I.829; *3 pr. sg.* **recordeth** narrates VII.1079. MED recorden *v.*

reed *n.* (1) advice, counsel I.3527, IV.1357; adviser I.665; (2) assent, permission IV.653; (3) course of action I.1216, VII.2549; plan III.2030, VI.146. MED red *n.*(1)

rede, reed(e) *adj.* red I.90; (as *n.*) red material I.294; red wine VI.526; *comp.* **redder** VII.2859. MED red *adj.*, red *n.*(2)

rede(n) *v.* (1) read I.709, II.84; interpret I.741, II.203; (2) study V.1120; lecture (as a professor) III.1518; (3) advise I.3071; *1 pr. sg.* **rede** I.3068; *pr. pl.* **rede(n)** VIII.78; *pr. subj. pl.* **rede** IV.1154; *imp. sg.* **rede** III.183, **reed** IX.344; *imp. pl.* **redeth** III.982; *3 pt. sg.* **redde** III.714, **radde** III.791; *pp.* **rad** I.2595, **red** III.765. MED reden *v.*(1)

redy *adj.* ready I.21, I.352; **al r.** already, right IV.299; **r. token** clear evidence VII.390. MED redi *adj.*(3)

redily *adv.* readily I.2276, VII.414; quickly, soon VI.667. MED redili *adv.*(2)

redresse *v.* redress, set right, amend III.696, IV.431; *3 pr. sg. (reflx.)* **redresseth it in** turns toward, addresses itself to X.1039; *3 pt. sg.* **redressed** vindicated V.1436. MED redressen *v.*

refreyne, refrayne *v.* bridle, restrain X.382, X.385; *3 pr. sg.* **refreyneth** X.294. MED refreinen *v.*(2)

refresshe *v.* provide with food, refreshment I.2622, III.1767; *pt. sg.* **refresshed** III.146; *pp.* **refresshed** comforted, refreshed III.38; *vbl. n.* **refresshyng(e)** relief X.78, X.220. MED refreshen *v.*, refreshinge *ger.*

refte took away *see* **reve(n).**

refusen *v.* refuse VII.1557; *pt. pl.* **refuseden** IV.128. MED refusen *v.*

regard *n.* in *phr.* **at (to, in) r. of** compared to X.180, X.399. Cf. **reward.** MED regarde *n.*

regn(e) *n.* dominion, rule VII.2184; kingdom, country I.866; *pl.* **regnes** I.2373. MED regne *n.*(1)

regne *v.* reign, rule, flourish II.816; *3 pr. sg.* **regneth** II.776; *3 pt. sg.* **regned** VII.2655. MED regnen *v.*

reherce(n) *v.* narrate, repeat I.732; *prp.* **rehersynge** V.206; *pp.* **reherced** X.910; *vbl. n.* **rehersyng(e)** talk, conversation I.1650. MED rehersen *v.*, rehersinge *ger.*

reyn, rayn *n.* rain I.492, I.595; *pl.* **reynes** IV.2140. MED rein *n.*(1)

reyne *n.* rein, bridle I.4083, V.313; *pl.* **reynes** I.904. MED reine *n.*(1)

reyneth *v. 3 pr. sg.* rains I.1535. MED reinen *v.*(1)

reyse(n) *v.* (1) raise, build III.2102; raise (a fiend) VIII.861; (2) raise, gather in III.1390; *pp.* **reysed** *(astro.)* exalted III.705. MED reisen *v.*(1)

rekk- *see* **recche.**

rekene(n) *v.* (1) recount, tell I.1933, I.1954; (2) reckon, calculate I.401, VII.78; (3) consider III.367; take account of II.110; *1 pr. sg.* **rekene** X.618; *1 pt. sg.* **rekned** I.1933; *pp.* **yrekned** III.367; *vbl. n.* **rekenyng(e)** account I.600; *pl.* **rekenynges** accounts VII.218; **maad oure r.** paid our bills I.760. MED rekenen *v.*, rekeninge *ger.*

relesse *v.* release, set free from IV.153, V.1533; forgive (a debt) X.810; *1 pr. sg.* **releesse** V.1613; *1 & 3 pt. sg.*

relessed VII.2177; *2 pt. sg.* **relessedest** X.309; *pp.* **releessed** X.582; *vbl. n.* **relessyng** forgiveness X.1026. MED relesen *v.*(1), relesinge *ger.*

releeve *v.* relieve, rescue X.945, VII.1490; *pp.* **releeved** VIII.872; **releved** compensated I.4182; *vbl. n.* **releevynge** remedy X.804, relief X.805. MED releven *v.*, relevinge *ger.*

religioun *n.* (1) religious order VII.1944, VIII.972; (2) religion, faith VIII.427; religious life I.477. MED religioun *n.*

religious *adj.* monastic, in a religious order VII.1960. MED religious *adj.*

relik(e) *n.* religious relic VI.949; *pl.* **relikes** I.701. MED relik *n.*

remembraunce, remembrance *n.* memory II.187, X.1087; **have r.** remember I.1046; **make r.** remind IV.2284. MED remembraunce *n.*

remembre(n) *v.* (1) (with **on, upon**) remember VII.999; (with **of**) X.466; *(impers.)* III.469, X.133; *(reflx.)* IV.1898, X.1063; (2) remind V.1243; *1 pr. sg.* **remembre** VII.513; *3 pr. sg.* **remembreth** III.469; *pr. pl.* **remembre** V.1243; *imp. pl.* **remembreth** V.1542; *(reflx.)* **remembre yow** IV.881; *3 pt. sg.* **remembred** II.1057; *prp.* **remembrynge** I.1501. MED remembren *v.*

remes realms *see* **reawme.**

remoeven *v.* remove, move away V.1221; *pr. subj. pl.* **remoeve** V.993; *imp. pl.* **remoeveth** VIII.1008; *pt. pl.* **remoeved** V.1205. MED remeven *v.*

reneye(n) *v.* renounce II.376, VII.2561; *1 pr. sg.* **reneye** VIII.464; *pr. subj. sg.* **reneye** VIII.464; *imp. sg.* **reneye** VIII.459; *pt. pl.* **reneyed** II.340; *vbl. n.* **reneiynge** X.793. MED reneien *v.*(1), reneiinge *ger.*

renne(n) *v.* run I.3890, III.356; *3 pr. sg.* **renneth** I.1761; *pr. pl.* **renne(n)** I.2868, I.4100; *3 pt. sg.* **ran** I.509; *pt. pl.* **ronne(n)** I.2925, VII.3388; ran VII.3381; *pp.* **yronnen** I.2639, **(y)ronne** I.8, I.2693; *vbl. n.* **rennyng** run I.551. MED rennen *v.*(1), renninge *ger.*(1)

renoun *n.* fame, renown I.316, I.1432. MED renoun *n.*

renovelle *v.* renew VII.1845; *pr. pl. (intr.)* **renovellen** are renewed X.1027; *pp.* **renovelled** renewed VII.1846. MED renovelen *v.*

rente *n.* income I.256; rent I.579, III.1390; tribute II.1142, VII.2211; *pl.* **rentes** IV.1313. MED rente *n.*

rente *v. 1 & 3 pt. sg.* tore I.990, III.635; *(intr.)* split VII.3101; *pt. pl.* **rente** VI.475; *pp.* **yrent** II.844; *vbl. n.* **rentynge** I.2834. MED renden *v.*(2), rentinge *ger.*

repaire *v.* return V.589; go VII.326; *3 pr. sg.* **repaireth** II.967, **repeireth** V.339; *prp.* **repeirynge** V.608. MED repairen *v.*

repente(n) *v.* repent (often *reflx.*) III.1629, VI.431; *3 pr. sg.* **repenteth** VII.1135; *pr. pl.* **repente(n)** X.298; *pr. subj. pl.* **repente** III.1663; *imp. pl.* **repenteth** V.1321; *3 pt. sg.* **repented** III.632; *prp.* **repentynge** II.378. MED repenten *v.*

repreve *n.* reproof III.16, IV.2263; reproach VI.595; **youre r.** reproach to you VII.1223; shame III.84; *pl.* **repreves** insults X.258. MED repreve *n.*

repreve(n) *v.* reprove, blame (often with **of, for**) V.1537, VII.1536; *inf.* **to repreve** to be blamed, blameworthy VII.1032; *3 pr. sg.* **repreveth** X.33; *pr. pl.* **repreve** III.1206, **repreeve** III.1177; *pr. subj. sg.* **repreve** III.937; *pt. pl.* **repreved** X.663; *pp.* **repreved** X.623; *vbl. n.* **reprevynge**

blaming X.628; *pl.* **reprevynges** quarrels X.556. MED repreven *v.*, reprevinge *ger.*

requere(n) *v.* (1) ask, request III.1052; (2) require, need IV.430; *1 pr. sg.* **requere** III.1010; *3 pr. sg.* **requireth** X.376; *pr. pl.* **requeren** VII.1683; *3 pt. sg.* **required** IV.430; *prp.* **requirynge** asking VII.1772. MED requeren *v.*

resoun, reson *n.* (1) reason, judgment I.37, I.1766; (2) argument I.3844, II.213; (3) reason, cause V.406, VII.979; **by r. of** because VII.1024, X.801; (4) **ben r.** is reasonable, right I.847, III.2277; **by r.** reasonably, justly VI.458; *pl.* **resons** opinions I.274; **resouns** reasons, causes VII.1025. MED resoun *n.*(2)

respit *n.* respite, delay I.948, VIII.543. MED respite *n.*

rest(e) *n.* rest I.1003; **(un)to** (one's) **r.** to bed I.30, I.820; peace, tranquillity IV.160, IV.741. MED reste *n.*(1)

reste(n) *v.* (1) rest VII.109; (2) stay, remain III.1736; *3 pr. sg.* **resteth** stays X.821; *pr. subj.* **reste** V.126 (pl.); *1 pt. sg.* **rested** IV.1926. MED resten *v.*(1)

restoore *v.* restore, give back VII.1110; repair X.645; *1 pr. sg.* **restoore** IV.867; *3 pr. sg.* **restoreth** X.312; *3 pt. sg.* **restored** I.991; *pp.* **restoored** X.870. MED restoren *v.*

restreyne, restrayne *v.* restrain, hold in check VII.1432, VII.2587; *(reflx.)* VII.2606; control IX.329; prevent VII.1492; *3 pr. sg.* **restreyneth** prevents VII.1092; *pr. pl.* **restreyne** VII.1432. MED restreinen *v.*

rethorik(e) *n.* rhetoric, learned eloquence IV.32, V.719; **colours of r.** figures of speech V.726. MED rethorike *n.*

retourne *v.* return II.986; *3 pr. sg.* **retourneth** VII.1183, **retorneth** X.620; *pr. pl.* **retourne** VII.597; *pr. subj.* **returne** X.236; *imp. pl.* **retourneth** IV.809; *3 pt. sg.* **retourned** VII.1770; *pp.* **retourned** VII.973; *vbl. n.* **retournynge** return I.2095, **returnyng** X.176. MED retournen *v.*, returning *ger.*

reule, rule *n.* rule VII.1166, X.217; code of behavior for monastics I.173. MED reule *n.*

reule(n) *v.* (1) rule, govern, VII.3044; (2) *(reflx.)* conduct oneself, behave IV.237; *imp. pl.* **rule yow** X.592; *pp.* **reuled** I.816. MED reulen *v.*

reuthe pity *see* **routhe.**

reve(n) *v.* rob, steal I.4011; take away VIII.376; *3 pr. sg.* **reveth** X.561; *3 pt. sg.* **rafte** III.888, **refte** IX.305; *pp.* **(y)raft** I.2015, **reft** V.1017. MED reven *v.*

revel *n.* revelry I.2717, I.3652; merrymaking I.4402; festival, entertainment II.353; *pl.* **revels** festivals, entertainments VI.65. MED revel *n.*(1)

reverence *n.* reverence, respect I.141, I.305, I.312; honor IV.2251, V.93; ceremony I.525; **at r. of** (someone) in honor of X.40; **doon** (someone) **r.** pay honor, respect to II.1001, III.206; **have (hold) in r.** respect, honor VII.3213. MED reverence *n.*

reward *n.* regard, consideration VII.1259, VII.1371. Cf. **regard.** MED reward *n.*

rewe(n) *v.* (1) (with **on, upon**) have mercy on, feel pity for I.2382; (2) *(intr.)* repent, rue I.3530; *2 pr. sg.* **rewest** II.854; *3 pr. sg.* **me reweth of** I feel sorry for I.3462; *pr. subj.* **rewe** I.1863 *(sg.)*; *imp. sg.* **rewe** I.2233; *imp. pl.* **reweth upon** V.974. MED reuen *v.*(1)

ribaudie *n.* ribaldry, coarse jesting I.3866, VI.324; debauchery X.464. MED ribaudie *n.*

riche *adj.* rich I.311, I.479; splendid, magnificent I.296,

I.979; (as *n.*) rich people I.248; *comp.* **richer** VII.1548; *super.* **richest(e)** I.2872, IV.2242. MED riche *adj.*

riche *adv.* richly I.609; splendidly I.2577. MED riche *adv.*

richely *adv.* richly, splendidly I.1012, IV.267. MED richeli *adv.*

rychesse *n.* riches, wealth I.1255, I.1829; *pl.* **richesses** riches VII.1370. MED richesse *n.*

ryde(n) *v.* ride I.27, I.94; **r. out** ride forth on an expedition I.45, VII.750; **r. or go** ride or walk I.1351; *1 pr. sg.* **ride** I.2252; *2 pr. sg.* **rydest** III.1452, (with *pro.*) **rydestow** III.1386; *3 pr. sg.* **rideth** I.1691, *(contr.)* **rit** I.974; *pr. pl.* **ryde(n)** I.2897, II.399; *pr. subj. pl.* **ryde** VII.260; *imp. pl.* **ryde** VII.1927; *3 pt. sg.* **rood** I.169; *pt. pl.* **riden** I.825; *prp.* **ridyng(e)** I.2159, VIII.623; *pp.* **riden** I.48; *vbl. n.* **ridyng(e)** equestrian display, jousting I.4377, X.432. MED riden *v.*, riding *ger.*

right(e) *adj.* (1) proper, true V.1311; right (as opposed to left) I.1959, VII.1312; (2) just I.2718; (3) direct I.1263, II.556. MED right *adj.*

right *adv.* (1) (as *intens.*) right, (with **as**) I.554, I.659; (with *adj.*) very I.288, I.857; indeed I.257, I.757; **r. no maistrie (suspicioun,** *etc.*) no mastery (suspicion, *etc.*) at all VI.58, VII.322; **r. ynogh (ynowe)** plenty III.2, V.470; **r. naught (noght, nowthe)** not at all IV.1011; not a thing I.756, IV.2303; (with *adv.*) very I.1140; just a I.535; just now I.767; exactly I.2619, VI.765; (2) directly V.1390, VII.313; **ful r.** directly I.1691; carefully IV.243; **right anoon, anon-right** immediately I.965, IV.1656. MED righte *adv.*

right *n.* right justice I.3089, III.1049; **by r.** by law, justly II.44, VI.183; **of r.** as a right V.1324; *pl.* **rightes** X.802; **at alle rightes** in all respects I.1852, I.2100. MED right *n.*

rightful *adj.* righteous, just I.1719, II.847. MED rightful *adj.*

rightwisnesse *n.* righteousness, justice III.1909, VI.637. MED right-wisnesse *n.*

rym(e) *n.* rhyme, verse III.1127, VII.925; versified tale VII.709, VII.928; *pl.* **rymes** verses II.96. MED rime *n.*(3)

ryme *v.* versify I.1459, VII.932; *vbl. n.* **rymyng** versifying II.48, VII.930. MED rimen *v.*(1), riming *ger.*

rynge *v.* ring, reverberate I.2431; sound, proclaim VI.331; *pr. pl.* **rynge(n)** sound I.2600, I.2359; *3 pt. sg.* **rong** I.3215. MED ringen *v.*(2)

riot *n.* debauchery, wanton behavior I.4392, VI.465. MED riote *n.*

riotour *n.* debauchee, profligate VI.692, VI.876; *pl.* **riotoures** VI.661. MED riotour *n.*

ryse *v.* rise, arise I.33, I.1047; *3 pr. sg.* **riseth** I.1493, *(contr.)* **rist** I.3688; *pr. pl.* **ryse(n)** I.3768, IV.1574; *imp. sg.* **rys** IV.2138; *imp. pl.* **riseth** X.161; *1 & 3 pt. sg.* **roos** I.823, III.1863; *pp.* **risen** I.1065. MED risen *v.*

rit rides *see* **ryde(n)**.

ryver(e) *n.* (1) river I.3024, III.2080; (2) riverbank, hawking ground V.1196; riverbank III.884; **for r.** to hawk for waterfowl VII.737; *pl.* **ryveres** V.898. MED rivere *n.*

roche, rok(ke) *n.* rock V.500; *pl.* **rokkes** V.868. MED roche *n.*(2)

rood rode *see* **ryde(n)**.

roghte cared about *see* **recche**.

roial *adj.* royal I.1018, I.1497; *pl.* **roiales** VII.848; *comp.* **roialler** II.402. MED roial *adj.*

roialliche, roially *adv.* royally, splendidly I.378, I.1687,

I.1713. MED roialli *adv.*

rok(ke), rokkes rock(s) *see* **roche**.

roule *v.* wander III.653; *3 pr. sg.* **rolleth** rolls I.2614; *3 pt. sg.* **rolled** considered III.2217; *prp.* **rollynge** rolling I.201. MED rollen *v.*(2)

rombled *v. 3 pt. sg.* murmured VII.2535; rumbled VIII.1322. MED rumbelen *v.*

rome(n) *v.* roam I.1099, IV.2184; *3 pr. sg.* **rometh** I.1119; *pr. pl.* **rome** VII.297; *1 & 3 pt. pl.* **romed** I.1113; *pt. pl.* **romeden** V.1013; *prp.* **romyng(e)** I.1071; *pp.* **romed** I.1528. MED romen *v.*

rong rang *see* **rynge**.

ronne(n), (y)ronne ran *see* **renne(n)**.

roore *v.* cry out loudly, lament VII.2888; *3 pr. sg.* **roreth** echoes I.2881; *prp.* **rorynge** roaring X.568; *vbl. n.* **roryng** lamentation IV.2364. MED roren *v.*(1), roringe *ger.*(1)

roos rose *see* **ryse(n)**.

roote *n.* (1) root I.2, I.3206; essential part VIII.1461; (2) root, origin I.423, II.358; (3) radix, date from which astronomical calculations can be made II.314; (4) foot of a mountain IV.58; *pl.* **rootes** V.1276. MED rote *n.*(4)

roten *adj.* rotten I.3873, I.4406. MED roten *adj.*

route, rowte *n.* company, crowd I.622, I.3854. MED route *n.*(1)

routhe, reuthe *n.* (1) pity, compassion IV.893, VI.261; **han r. of (on, upon)** pity I.2392; **maketh r.** pities, feels sorry I.4200; (2) pitiful sight or occurrence I.914, IV.562. MED reuthe *n.*

rowne(n) *v.* whisper III.1572, VIII.894; *pr. pl.* **rowne(n)** III.241; *3 pt. sg.* **rowned** III.1021; *prp.* **rownynge** IV.2130. MED rounen *v.*

rude *adj.* (1) rough IV.916, IV.1012; rugged, wild IX.170; (2) humble III.1172; ignorant, unlearned I.3227, IV.2351; (3) boorish IV.750; crude, impolite VII.2808. MED rude *adj.*

rule *see* **reule** *n.*, **reule(n)** *v.*

rumblynge *vbl. n.* rumbling sound III.2233. MED rumbelinge *ger.*

S (*See also* C)

sad, sadde *adj.* (1) serious, sober I.2985, IV.602; (2) steadfast, firm IV.220, VIII.397; trustworthy II.135, IX.258; (as *adv.*) firmly IV.564; (3) **wexen s.** be satisfied VIII.877. MED sad *adj.*

sadly *adv.* (1) soberly VII.76; steadily II.743; (2) firmly I.2602, III.2264; tightly IV.1100. MED sadli *adv.*

sadnesse *n.* steadfastness, constancy IV.452; seriousness IV.1591, IV.1604. MED sadnesse *n.*

say saw *see* **se(n)**.

saille, sayle(n) *v.* sail II.321; *3 pr. sg.* **sailleth** II.445; *pr. pl.* **saille** IV.2108; *pt. pl.* **seyled** VII.3104; *prp.* **saillynge** II.968, **seillynge** V.851; *pp.* **yseyled** VII.3099. MED seilen *v.*

sayn saw, seen *see* **se(n)**.

sal *1 & 3 pr. sg. & pr. pl. (Nth.)* shall I.4043, I.4174, I.4185. Cf. **shal**.

saluwe, salewe *v.* greet, salute VII.533, X.407; *3 pr. sg.* **salueth** I.1492, **saleweth** V.94; *pp.* **salewed** V.1310; *vbl. n.* **saluyng** greeting I.1649. MED saluen *v.*, saluinge *ger.*

sapience *n.* wisdom IV.1481, IV.2243, VII.472; *pl.* **sapiences** the mental faculties VIII.338. MED sapience *n.*

sat(e) *see* **sitte(n)** *v.*

sauf, save *adj.* safe, secure II.343, III.1015; **s. your grace** with all respect VII.1070, VII.1082. MED sauf *adj.*

saufly *adv.* (1) safely III.878; (2) confidently, without fear of contradiction IV.870, V.761. MED saufli *adv.*

saugh saw *see* **se(n).**

salvacioun, savacion, savacioun *n.* (1) salvation (of one's soul) III.1498, X.93; (2) safety, security III.621. MED savacioun *n.*

save *conj.* except that III.998, IV.2085. MED sauf *prep.*

save *prep.* except for I.683, I.3898. MED sauf *prep.*

save(n) *v.* save I.3533, II.860; preserve, keep, maintain I.3949; *3 pr. sg.* **savith** I.661, **saveth** II.907; *pr. subj. sg.* **God save** may God preserve I.2563, I.3108; *imp. pl.* **saveth** II.229; *2 pt. sg.* **savedest** II.639; *3 pt. sg.* **saved** II.473; *pp.* **saved** III.1092; MED saven *v.*

savynge *prep.* except for, save for I.2838, I.3971; preserving, with all respect to (one's honor, worship, etc.) IV.1766. MED savinge *prep.*

savour *n.* (1) taste VII.1158; delight III.2196; (2) smell, odor III.2226, V.404. MED savour *n.*

savoure *v.* taste III.171; *3 pr. sg.* **savoureth** X.122; *pr. pl.* **savouren** enjoy X.820; *vbl. n.* **savourynge** taste X.959, **savoryng(e)** X.207, X.209. MED savouren *v.*, savouringe *ger.*

sawe *n.* saying I.1163, III.660; speech, what is said I.1526, VIII.691. MED saue *n.*(2)

sawe *see* **se(n).**

scape(n) *v.* escape I.1107, I.3608; *pr. subj. sg.* **scape** I.3800; *pp.* **scaped** II.1151. MED scapen *v.*(1)

scarsly *adv.* economically I.583; scarcely, hardly VII.228, X.1002. MED scarsli *adv.*

schal, schol- *see* **shal.**

science *n.* (1) knowledge I.316, III.699; (2) art, branch of learning VIII.680, VIII.721; (3) learned composition VII.476; *pl.* **sciences** branches of learning V.1122. MED science *n.*

sclaundre *n.* disgrace, ill fame VII.183; scandal X.137. MED sclaundre *n.*

sclaundre *v.* slander VIII.998; *2 pr. sg.* **sclaundrest** VIII.695; *pr. subj. sg.* **sclaundre** VIII.993. MED sclaundren *v.*

sclendre slender *see* **sklendre.**

scole *n.* (1) school VII.495, VII.498; "schools" of the universities III.1277, III.2186; (2) method I.125, I.3329; *pl.* **scoles** III.44c. MED scole *n.*(2)

scorne *v.* scorn, deride VII.1142, VIII.506; *3 pr. sg.* **scorneth** X.379; *3 pt. sg.* **scorned** VII.3087; *pp.* **scorned** X.276; *vbl. n.* **scornynge** scorn X.511. MED scornen *v.*, scorninge *ger.*

see *n.* sea I.276, I.698; **Grete s.** Mediterranean I.59. MED se *n.*(1)

se(n), see(n) *v.* (1) see I.831, I.1349, I.1352; (2) **s. on (upon)** look upon I.1082; **s. of** look after VII.339; (3) understand I.1947, II.938; *inf.* **to se(n), see(n)** to be seen, to be looked upon I.914, I.1035; *1 pr. sg.* **se** I.1325; *2 pr. sg.* **seest** I.2232; *3 pr. sg.* **seeth** II.266; *pr. pl.* **seen** I.3016, **se** I.3025; *pr. subj. sg.* **god you see** may God watch over you (a greeting) III.2169, VI.715; *imp. sg.* **se(e)** I.1801, IV.1789; *imp. pl.* **see** IX.9, **seeth** X.77; *1 & 3 pt. sg.* **seigh** I.193, I.1066, **say** III.645, **saugh** I.764, I.3415; *2 pt. sg.* **sawe** II.848; *pt. pl.* **sye(n)** IV.1804, VII.3378, **sawe** II.218,

sayn II.172; *pp.* **seye** III.552, **(y)sene** I.134, I.592, **seene** I.924; **seyn** II.624, **sayn** II.172. MED sen *v.*(1)

secree *adj.* (1) secret III.1871, IV.1937; (2) trusty, discreet III.946; able to keep a secret IV.1909; (as *adv.*) secretly V.1109. MED secre *adj.*

secree *n.* secret, confidential information III.1341, VII.1141. MED secre *n.*

secreely, secrely *adv.* secretly IV.763; confidentially IV.2006, VII.1143. MED secreli *adv.*

sege, seege *n.* siege I.56, V.306. MED sege *n.*(2)

seye, (y)seye saw, seen *see* **se(n).**

seyde said *see* **seyn.**

seigh saw *see* **se(n).**

seyn, seye(n), sayn *v.* say I.181, I.468, VII.3046; **herd s.** heard tell, heard it said VII.531; **men sayth** it is said I.4210; **sooth to s.** to tell the truth I.284; **(was) for to s.** (was) to mean, meant I.3605, VII.523; *1 pr. sg.* **seye** I.855; *2 pr. sg.* **seist** I.1605, (with *pro.*) **seistow** I.1125, **seystou** IV.2125; *3 pr. sg.* **seith** X.918; *pr. pl.* **seye(n)** III.935, III.1627, **seyn** III.945, **sayn** I.1198; *pr. subj.* **seye** III.119 *(sg.)*; *imp. sg.* **sey** VII.705; *imp. pl.* **sey** VII.2805, **seyeth** I.1868, **seyth** V.1526; *2 pt. sg.* **seydest** III.348, (with *pro.*) **seydestow** VIII.334; *3 pt. sg.* **seyd(e)** I.183, VII.1891, **sayd(e)** II.638, III.80; *pt. pl.* **seyde(n)** VII.1016, VIII.922; *pp.* **seyd** I.305, **(y)sayd** I.1867, V.1547. MED seien *v.*(1)

seeke sick *see* **sik(e)** *adj.*

seke(n), seche(n) *v.* (1) (*tr.*) seek, look for I.13, III.1957; examine, investigate II.60, VII.3136; (2) (*intr.*) seek, search I.2587, II.521; (with *prep.*) I.1266; **s. upon** harass III.1494; *inf.* **to seche, seken** to be looked for, sought I.784, VIII.874; *3 pr. sg.* **seketh** III.919; *pr. pl.* **seken** III.1002, **sechen** VIII.863; *imp. sg.* **seke** VII.1693; *3 pt. sg.* **sought(e)** I.1200, **soghte** I.4404; *pt. pl.* **soughten** VI.772; *pt. subj. sg.* **soghte** VI.488; *pp.* **(i)soght** VII.590. MED sechen *v.*

seel *n.* seal (on a document) II.882, III.2128. MED sele *n.*(3)

selde, seeld(e) *adv.* seldom I.1539, IV.427, VII.1153; (as *adj.*) **s. tyme** seldom IV.146. MED selde *adj.*

self *see* **selve.**

sely *adj.* (1) innocent, blessed II.682, III.132; (2) hapless, wretched I.3404, I.3423; poor VII.11. MED seli *adj.*

selle(n) *v.* sell I.278, II.140; *inf.* **to selle** to be sold, for sale III.414; *3 pr. sg.* **selleth** X.784; *pr. pl.* **sellen** X.439; *3 pt. sg.* **solde** VII.2065; *pp.* **soold** I.4347. MED sellen *v.*

selve, self *adj.* same I.2584, I.2860; very II.115; **it self** itself X.1042; *pl.* **us selven** ourselves III.812, **us self** IV.108. MED self *adj.*

semblable *adj.* similar IV.1500, VII.1104. MED semblable *adj.*

semblaunt, semblant *n.* semblance, outward appearance IV.928, V.516. MED semblaunt *n.*

seme(n), seeme *v.* (1) seem II.1092, IV.132; (2) (*impers.*) it seems, seemed (to me, you, *etc.*) III.1463, V.201; **hem semed** they seemed V.56; *3 pr. sg.* **semeth** IV.2409; *pr. pl.* **seme(n)** V.869, X.430; *pr. subj. sg.* **seme** III.1199; *3 pt. sg.* **semed** I.39, seemed X.62; *pt. pl.* **semed(en)** IV.853, VII.1018; *pp.* **semed** V.1146. MED semen *v.*(2)

semely, semly *adj.* seemly, impressive I.751; comely I.1960; *super.* **semelieste** IX.119. MED semeli *adj.*

semely *adv.* in a seemly, comely manner I.123, I.136. MED semeli *adv.*

sende(n) v. send I.426, I.2317; *3 pr. sg.* **sendeth** I.2762, (*contr.*) sent IV.1151; *pr. subj.* **sende** III.1258 *(sg.),* VII.1796 *(pl.); imp. sg.* **sende** I.3598; *imp. pl.* **sendeth** VI.614; *pt. subj. sg.* **sente** should send IV.1665; *3 pt. sg.* **sent(e)** I.400, V.1605, **sende** I.4136; *pt. pl.* **sente(n)** II.136, VII.616; *pp.* **(y)sent** II.960, II.1041. MED senden v.(2)

sentence n. (1) meaning, significance VII.952, VII.3165; substance, essential meaning VII.947, X.58; (2) contents, theme I.798, III.162; subject III.1126, III.1518; (3) opinion I.3002, IV.636; decision, verdict I.2532, IV.791; **hy (heigh) s.** good judgment I.306, IV.1507; (4) authoritative saying, maxim II.117, II.1139; *pl.* **sentences** opinions, teachings X.77. MED sentence n.

serchen v. search, analyze VII.1407; *pr. pl.* **serchen** visit, haunt III.867. MED serchen v.

sergeant n. officer of the law IV.519, IV.524; **s. of the Lawe** high-ranking lawyer I.309 (see note); *pl.* **sergeantz** VIII.361. MED sergeaunt n.

sermone v. preach VI.879; *vbl. n.* **sermonyng** discourse, argument I.3091. MED sermounen v., sermouninge ger.

servage n. bondage, servitude, captivity I.1946, II.368. MED servage n.

serve(n) v. (1) serve (someone) I.1143; (2) be of service, useful IX.339; (3) treat, deal with IV.641; *1 pr. sg.* **serve** I.1231; *3 pr. sg.* **serveth** I.1421; *pr. pl.* **serve(n)** I.1805, VII.1274; *1 & 3 pt. sg.* **served(e)** I.749, IV.640; *pp.* **(y)served** I.187, I.963. MED serven v.(1)

servyse, service n. service I.250; devotion V.628; religious service I.122, V.297. MED servise n.

seson, sesoun n. season I.19, I.1043; *pl.* **sesons** I.347. MED sesoun n.

seet sat *see* **sitte(n).**

sete, seete n. seat, throne VII.2525, X.162; *pl.* **seetes** thrones, seats I.2580. MED sete n.(2)

sete(n) sat *see* **sitte(n).**

seeth sees *see* **se(n).**

sette(n) v. (1) set, put I.815, III.726; (2) *(reflx.)* sit down I.1541, VI.207; **s. hym (hire,** etc.) **on knees** kneel I.3723, II.638; *(pass.)* be seated I.2528, VI.392; (3) arrange, set, assign I.4383; **s. a- werk** assign a job, put to work I.4337, III.215; (4) value I.1570, I.3756; **s. at nought** take no account of, reckon as worth nothing V.821; (5) **s. hir cappe, his howve** deceive them, him I.586, I.3911; *1 pr. sg.* **sette** IV.2303: *3 pr. sg.* **setteth** VII.1179, *(contr.)* **set** II.299; *pr. pl.* **sette(n)** III.129, X.606; *pr. subj. sg.* **sette** VII.1027; *imp. sg.* **sette** III.2269; *1 & 3 pt. sg.* **sette** I.507, III.215; *pt. pl.* **sette(n)** I.4383, II.1118; *pp.* **(y)set** I.132, IV.409; (as *adj.*) **tyme, day (y)set** the assigned time (day) I.1635, IV.774. MED setten v.

seur, sure adj. sure VII.1452, VII.1763. MED seur adj.

seurete(e), suretee n. (1) safety, security X.735; safeguard VI.937; assurance III.903; (2) pledge I.1604, V.528; collateral II.243; surety, guarantee (to fulfill a pledge) V.1581. MED seurte n.

seurely, surely adv. surely VII.275, VII.1723. MED seurli adv.

sewe v. follow VII.1429, VII.1502; *imp. pl.* **seweth** VII.1538; *3 pt. sg.* **sewed** pursued VII.3337. MED seuen v.(1)

shadde shed *see* **shedeth.**

yshadwed pp. shadowed I.607. MED shadwen v.

shake v. shake I.1473, IV.978; *3 pr. sg.* **shaketh** IV.1849; *3 pt.*

sg. **shook** I.2265; *pp.* **shake** I.406. MED shaken v.

shal, shall, schal *1 & 3 pr. sg.* (1) *(aux.)* (obligation) must, ought to I.731, I.792; (with ellipsis of *inf.*) must do V.750, must go II.279; (2) *(aux.)* (denoting futurity) will, shall I.187, I.500; (with ellipsis of *inf.*) I.1183, II.1078; (with v. of motion understood) I.3467; *1 & 3 pr. sg.* **shal** I.360, VIII.1155; *2 pr. sg.* **shalt** I.1145, (with *pro.*) **shaltou** I.1391; *pr. pl.* **shul** I.1821, **shuln** X.141, **shulle(n)** X.162, X.191; *1 & 3 pt. sg.* **shold(e)** I.184, I.1380; *2 pt. sg.* **sholdest** I.1137; (with *pro.*) **sholdestou** III.1944, **scholdestow** IX.329; *pt. pl.* **sholde(n)** VIII.1363, VIII.1465. MED shulen v.(1)

shame, schame n. (1) shame, disgrace II.829, VI.214; **don s.** disgrace, harm I.1555, I.3050; **it is s.** it is shameful, blameworthy I.503, VII.1604; **for s.** *(interj.)* you should be ashamed VII.2891; (2) modesty III.342, III.782; fear of disgrace III.1393, V.752; embarrassment VIII.1095; *gen.* **shames deeth** a shameful death II.819, IV.2377. MED shame n.

shame(n) v. shame V.1164, V.1565; *3 pr. sg. (impers.)* **thee shameth** you are ashamed II.101; *pp.* **shamed** ashamed X.1061. MED shamen v.

shamefast adj. modest I.2055, VI.55; embarrassed VII.1046; possessed of a sense of shame X.987. MED shamefaste adj.

shamefastnesse n. modesty I.840, VI.55; sense of shame X.986. MED shamefastnesse n.

shape(n) v. (1) fashion, create, shape III.1463; (2) devise (a plan) II.210; arrange matters I.2541, VI.813; (3) appoint II.253; destine, ordain I.1108, I.1225; (4) *(reflx.)* prepare I.809, I.3403; intend I.4179, VI.874; *pr. pl.* **shape(n)** II.966, VII.1799; *imp. pl.* **shapeth** IV.1408; *3 pt. sg.* **shoop** III.1538; *pt. pl.* **shopen** V.897; *prp.* **shapynge** directing IV.783; *pp.* **(y)shapen** I.4179, III.139, **(y)shape** I.1225, IX.43. MED shapen v.

shave v. shave I.3326; *pp.* **(y)shave** I.588, VII.2071; *vbl. n.* **shaving** shaving VIII.1239. MED shaven v., shavinge ger.

shedeth *3 pr. sg.* **sheds,** emits (a liquid) X.577; *3 pt. sg.* **shedde** shed VII.2257, **shadde** *(intr.)* poured down VII.2731. MED sheden v.

sheeld, shilde n. shield I.2122; a unit of monetary exchange (as *pl.*) VII.331; *pl.* **sheeldes** coins I.278, shields I.2499. MED sheld n.

shende v. ruin, destroy II.927; defile X.854; *3 pr. sg.* **shendeth** II.28, *(contr.)* **shent** X.848; *pr. sg.* **shende** III.376; *pr. subj. sg.* **shende** should corrupt I.4410; *3 pt. sg.* **shente** VII.2841; *pp.* **shent(e)** I.2754, II.931, **(y)shent** punished, scolded, rebuked III.1312, VII.541; ruined IV.1320. MED shenden v.

shene, sheene adj. bright I.115, I.1509. MED shene adj.

shere, sheere n. pair of shears, scissors I.2417, VII.2056; *pl.* **sheres** III.722, X.418. MED shere n.(1)

sherte n. shirt III.1186, IV.1985; nightshirt IV.1852; *pl.* **shertes** X.197. MED shirte n.

sheete n. sheet VIII.879; *pl.* **shetes** X.197, **sheetes** I.4140. MED shete n.(2)

shete(n), sheete v. shoot I.3928, X.714, *pr. subj. sg.* **shete** X.574. MED sheten v.

shette(n) v. shut III.1141, VIII.517; *imp. sg.* **shette** VIII.1137; *3 pt. sg.* **shette** I.3499, I.3634; *pt. pl.* **shette(n)** VIII.1218; *pp.* **shet** I.2597, **yshette** II.560. MED shitten v.

shewe(n), schewe(n) *v.* (1) reveal, set forth III.2093,
III.2219; (2) *(intr.)* is shown X.331, X.696; (with *inf.*) pretend, make a show of VII.1196; *1 pr. sg.* **shewe** III.1849; *3
pr. sg.* **sheweth** II.882; *pr. pl.* **shewe(n)** VII.459, X.425; *pr.
subj. sg.* **shewe** VIII.916; *imp. sg.* **shewe** III.1690; *imp. pl.*
sheweth VI.179; *3 pt. sg;* **shewed** I.2268; *prp.* **shewynge**
VII.1428; *pp.* **shewed** I.1938; *vbl. n.* **shewynge** revealing
X.318. MED sheuen *v.*(1), sheuinge *ger.*

shilde *v. pr. subj. sg.* **God shilde (shelde)** may God protect
IV.1787; **God shilde that** may God protect against, forbid
that I.3427, IV.839. MED shelden *v.*

shyneth *v. 3 pr. sg.* shines I.976; *pr. pl.* **shynen** I.2043; *3 pt.
sg.* **shoon** I.198; *prp.* **shynyng(e)** III.304, VII.1450; *vbl. n.*
shynyng I.3255. MED shinen *v.*, shininge *ger.*

sho(o) *n.* shoe I.253, III.492; *pl.* **shoos** I.3318, **shoes** I.457,
shoon VII.732. MED sho *n.*

shook *see* **shake.**

shol- *see* **shal.**

shoon *see* **shyneth** (shone), **sho(o)** (shoes).

shopen *see* **shape(n).**

yshorn *pp.* shorn I.589, VII.1952. MED sheren *v.*

shorte *v.* shorten I.791, III.1261; *3 pr. sg.* **shorteth** X.727; *pr.
subj. sg.* **shorte** III.365. MED shorten *v.*

shour *n.* shower I.3520; *pl.* **shoures** I.1, V.118. MED shour *n.*

shove *pp.* shove moved V.1281; *vbl. n.* **showvynge** shoving
IX.53. MED shouven *v.*, shouvinge *ger.*

shrewe *n.* (1) scoundrel I.3907; (2) scold, shrew IV.1222,
IV.1534; **moost s.** greatest scoundrel III.505; *pl.* **shrewes**
VI.835. MED shreue *n.*

shrewe *v. 1 pr. sg.* curse III.446, III.1062. MED shreuen *v.*

shrewed *pp.* (as *adj.*) cursed, wicked III.54, X.495. MED
shreued *adj.*

shrewednesse, schrewednesse, schrewydnesse *n.* wickedness VII.1531; malignancy III.734; *pl.* **shrewednesses**
wicked deeds X.442. MED shreuednesse *n.*

shrift(e) *n.* confession III.1818, VIII.277. MED shrift *n.*

shrighte *3 pt. sg.* shrieked, cried aloud I.2817, V.417; *pt. pl.*
skriked VII.3400. MED skriken v.

shryve(n) *v.* (1) *(reflx.)* confess X.129, X.305; *2 pr. sg.*
shryvest X.1014; *3 pr. sg.* **shryveth** X.371; *pr. pl.*
shryve(n) X.298, confess X.106; *pp.* **yshryve** I.226,
(y)shryven confessed III.1440, VI.380. MED shriven *v.*

shul- *see* **shal.**

syd(e) *n.* (1) side, I.112, I.558; **on every s.** from all sides,
everywhere IV.81, IV.1801; **upon eche s.** from all sides
III.256; (2) behalf IV.1392, IV.1410; **on every s.** for all
concerned V.1521; *pl.* **sydes** I.2635, **sydis** VIII.43. MED
side *n.*

syk, sigh *n.* sigh I.1117, V.498; *pl.* **sikes** 1.1920. MED sike *n.*

sik(e), seeke *adj.* sick I.18, I.2804; (as *n.*) sickness III.394.
MED sik *adj.*

sik(e), siken *v.* sigh I.1540, I.3488; X.228; *3 pr. sg.* **siketh**
I.3619; *3 pt. sg.* **siked** I.2985, **sighte** II.1035. MED siken
v.(2)

siker *adj.* sure, true I.3049, III.2069; assured, certain X.93;
comp. **sikerer** truer, more accurate VII.2853. MED siker
adj.

siker *adv.* truly, certainly III.465. MED siker *adv.*

sikerly, sekirly *adv.* truly, certainly I.137, III.44e. MED sik-
erli *adv.*

sikernesse *n.* security, safety II.425, IV.1280. MED sikernesse *n.*

siknesse *n.* sickness I.493, IV.651. MED siknesse *n.*

simylitude *n.* (1) equal, counterpart I.3228; (2) comparison
VIII.431. MED similitude *n.*

symonye *n.* selling or buying of ecclesiastical offices
III.1309, X.781. MED simonie *n.*

symple *adj.* simple, unaffected, modest I.119, III.1789; ordinary VII.3245; unrestricted possession I.319. MED simple
adj.

syn *conj.* since I.853; **s. that** since, since the time that I.601;
since, because I.2328, V.457. MED sin *conj.*

syn *prep.* since I.1193, II.365. MED sin *prep.*

synge(n) *v.* sing I.236; *1 pr. sg.* **synge** VII.663; *2 pr. sg.* (with
pro.) **syngestow** IX.244; *3 pr. sg.* **syngeth** I.3360; *pr. pl.*
synge(n) II.642, VII.2096; *pr. subj. sg.* **synge** II.294; *imp.
pl.* **syngeth** VII.3320; *3 pt. sg.* **soong** I.122, **song** I.1509,
sang VII.771; *2 pt. sg.* **songe** IX.294; *pt. pl.* **songe(n)**
III.216, IV.1735; *prp.* **syngynge** I.91; *pp.* **(y)songe** I.266,
III.1726, **songen** I.1529; *vbl. n.* **syngyng** VII.557. MED
singen *v.*, singinge *ger.*

singuleer, synguler *adj.* individual, private, personal
VII.1435, VIII.997; particular X.300. MED singulere *adj.*

synken *v.* (1) *(intr.)* sink I.2397; (with **in, into**) sink into,
penetrate I.951; (2) *(tr.)* cause to sink V.1073; *1 pr. sg.*
synke I.2397; *pr. pl.* **synken** VIII.912; *3 pt. sg.* **sank**
X.839; *pp.* **sonken** V.892. MED sinken *v.*

synne *n.* sin I.561; *pl.* **synnes** IV.13. MED sinne *n.*

synne(n) *v.* sin VI.138, X.914; *3 pr. sg.* **synneth** VII.1435; *pr.
pl.* **synnen** III.1530; *pr. pl.* **synned** X.136, **synneden**
X.324; *pp.* **synned** X.96; *pr. subj. sg.* **synne** X.973; *vbl. n.*
synnyng X.235. MED sinnen *v.*, sinninge *ger.*

sir(e) *n.* (1) master I.355, VIII.918; master of the house, hus-
band III.713; father I.4246; (2) (polite form of address) sir
I.1715, II.570, III.1356; (of a knight, only in Thop)
VII.717; (of a priest) VIII.1205; *gen.* **sires** father's
IV.2265; *pl.* **syres** I.3909. MED sire *n.*

sit sits *see* **sitte(n).**

sith(e), sithen, sitthe(n) *adv.* since, since that time I.3893,
II.58; **s. many yeres (a day, long while)** many years
(days), a long time ago I.1521, V.536; next, then I.2617,
VI.869, VII.2677. MED sitthe *adv.*, sitthen *adv.*

sith, sitthe *conj.* since I.930, I.1732; **s. that** since I.2102,
I.3231. MED sitthe *conj.*

sithe *n.* times II.733; **ofte(n) s.** many times I.1877, IV.233; *pl.*
sithes I.485. MED sith *n.*

sitte(n) *v.* (1) sit I.94, III.838; (2) suit, fit VIII.132; *(impers.)*
suit, befit IV.1277, IV.2315; *1 pr. sg.* **sitte** III.238; *3 pr. sg.*
sitteth I.1527, *(contr.)* **sit** I.1599; *pr. pl.* **sitten** I.2204,
VIII.1195; *pr. subj.* **sitte** VIII.841 (*sg.*), VIII.1195 (*pl.*);
imp. pl. **sit** III.2174; *3 pt. sg.* **sat** I.271, **seet** I.2075; *pt. pl.*
seten V.92; *prp.* **sittyng(e)** I.633; *pp.* **seten** I.1452; *vbl. n.*
sittyng seating arrangement IV.958. MED sitten *v.*, sit-
tinge *ger.*

skile *n.* grounds, reason VII.1810; **is s.** is reasonable II.708,
IV.1152; *pl.* **skiles** reasons, arguments V.205. MED skil *n.*

sklendre, sclendre *adj.* lean, slender I.587, IV.1602; weak,
feeble IV.1198, VII.1957; meager VII.2833. MED sclendre *adj.*

skriked shrieked *see* **shrighte.**

slake *v.* (1) *(intr.)* desist IV.705; (2) *(tr.)* slake, put an end to

IV.802; *3 pr. sg.* **slaketh** IV.1107; *pr. subj. pl.* **slake** VI.82.
MED slaken *v.*(1)

slakke *adj.* slack, loose IV.1849; slow I.2901; *comp.*
slakkere slower (to repay) VII.413. MED slak *adj.*

slawe(n), (y)slawe slew, slain *see* **sle(n).**

sle(n), slee(n) *v.* (1) slay, kill I.661, I.1222; (2) extinguish
VII.2732; *(alchemy)* mortify VIII.1436; *1 pr. sg.* **sle**
VII.812; *2 pr. sg.* **sleest** X.569; *3 pr. sg.* **sleeth** I.1118; *pr.
pl.* **sleen** II.964, **sle** V.462; *pr. subj. sg.* **sle** I.1618; *imp. sg.*
slee VII.1899; *1 & 3 pt. sg.* **slough** I.987, **slow** II.627; *pt.
pl.* **slowe** V.1430; *pp.* **(y)slayn** I.63, I.2708; **(y)slawe**
II.484, VII.826; **slawe(n)** IV.544; **slayn** VIII.1436. MED
slen *v.*

sleigh(e), sly(e) *adj.* sly, cunning I.3201, I.3940; ingenious
V.230; artful, tricky VIII.981; (as *n.*) sly one I.3392. MED
sleigh *adj.*

sleighte, slyghte *n.* (1) trickery, cunning I.604, VI.131; (2)
skill, ingenuity I.1948, I.4050; (3) ingenious plan, trick
IV.2131; *pl.* **sleightes** IV.2421. MED sleight *n.*

slep, sleep *n.* sleep I.1044, I.3643; *pl.* **slepes** I.1920. MED
slep *n.*

slepe(n) *v.* sleep I.3406, I.3685; *1 pr. sg.* **sleepe** VIII.153; *2
pr. sg.* (with *pro.*) **slepestow** I.4169; *3 pr. sg.* **slepeth**
II.597; *pr. pl.* **slepe(n)** I.10, V.360; *pr. subj. pl.* **slepe(n)**
IV.118, V.126; *1 & 3 pt. sg.* **sleep** I.98, V.721; **slepte**
I.4194; *pt. pl.* **slepte** III.770, **slepen** V.360; *prp.* **slepynge**
II.21; *vbl. n.* **slepyng(e)** sleep X.193. MED slepen *v.,*
slepinge *ger.*

slyde *v.* slip away IV.82; *3 pr. sg.* *(contr.)* **slit** VIII.682; *prp.*
(as *adj.*) **slydynge** slippery VIII.732. MED sliden *v.*

slough, slow(e) slew *see* **sle(n).**

slouthe *n.* sloth, laziness II.530, V.1232; one of the Seven
Deadly Sins X.388. MED slouthe *n.*

slow(e) *adj.* (1) slow (in wits) II.315; (2) slow, sluggish
III.1816, X.724. MED slou *adj.*

smal(e) *adj.* (1) small I.146, I.2076; little V.71, VII.536; (2)
insignificant, minor III.283, IX.73; humble IV.483; (as *n.*)
grete and s. of all ranks, everyone I.4323, VII.24, of
every variety I.3178, VII.105; (3) slim, slender I.3234,
IV.1602; delicate I.153, X.197; elegant I.158; (4) high (of
the voice) I.688, I.3360. MED smal *adj.*

smal(e) *adv.* (1) finely VIII.760; **but s.** but little III.592, V.71;
(2) delicately, elegantly I.3245, I.3320. MED smale *adv.*

smert *n.* pain I.3813, VI.2606. MED smerte *n.*

smert(e) *adj.* painful I.2225, I.2392; brisk VIII.768.
MED smert *adj.*

smerte *v.* (1) *(tr.)* inflict pain V.564; (2) *(impers.)* suffer I.230;
(3) *(intr.)* feel pain, suffer, smart III.2092, VIII.871; *pr.
subj.* **smerte** I.1394 *(sg.)*, VII.2713 *(pl.)*; *pt. subj. sg.*
smerte I.534. MED smerten *v.*

smerte *adv.* sharply, painfully I.149, VI.413. MED smerte
adv.

smyte(n) *v.* (1) strike I.1220, I.1658; (2) cut I.3569, VI.226; *3
pr. sg.* **smyteth** I.1709, *(contr.)* **smyt** IV.122; *pr. subj. pl.*
smyte V.157; *imp. pl.* **smyt** IX.285; *3 pt. sg.* **smoot** I.1704;
pt. pl. **smoot** I.149; *pp.* **smyten** X.871. MED smiten *v.*

smok, smokke *n.* shift, simple garment (over which more
elaborate clothing [sleeves, bodices, *etc.*] could be worn)
I.3238, III.783. MED smok *n.*

so *adv.* so I.11, *etc.*; so much III.215; (in *phr.*) **al so as**

IX.167; (as *intens.*) **so as** as I.39, VI.393; **wheither so**
whether VII.2619; **who so** whoever VII.1161; **what so**
whoever I.522, whatever VII.2912; **why so** why VII.926;
if so be(n) if it be, if V.564; (with *subj.* or *imp.*) as (or
untranslated) I.2237, III.823; **so that** provided that
III.125, II.625. MED so *adv.*

sobre *adj.* grave, serious II.97, IV.366; sober, abstemious
III.1902, IV.1533. MED sobre *adj.*

sobrely *adv.* gravely, seriously IV.296, V.1585. MED sobreli
adv.

socour *n.* succor, help I.918, II.644. MED socour *n.*

sodeyn *adj.* sudden, unforeseen II.421, IV.316; impetuous
X.542. MED sodein *adj.*

sodeynly, sodeynliche *adv.* suddenly I.1118, I.1575. MED
sodeinli *adv.*

soft(e) *adj.* (1) soft, tender I.153, III.1840; gentle V.907; **a s.
pas** slowly I.3760, II.399; (2) lax, negligent VI.101; *comp.*
softer I.3249. MED softe *adj.*

softe *adv.* (1) gently I.1021, I.2781; tenderly II.275; easily
VI.543; (2) quietly I.1773, I.3697. MED softe *adv.*

softely *adv.* quietly I.4058; gently V.636, VII.672; slowly
VII.886; comfortably X.835. MED softli *adv.*

soghte, (i)soght sought *see* **seke(n).**

sojourne, sojurne *v.* remain, dwell III.987, IV.1796; *pp.*
sojourned II.148. MED sojournen *v.*

solas *n.* (1) comfort, solace X.206; (for love pains) I.3200;
(2) pleasure I.798, entertainment I.3335; comfort, refreshment VII.782. MED solas *n.*

solde, soold *see* **selle(n).**

solempne *adj.* (1) splendid, impressive II.387, IV.1125; (2)
dignified, important I.209, I.364. MED solempne *adj.*

solempnely *adv.* ceremoniously, solemnly II.317, V.179; with
dignity I.274. MED solempneli *adv.*

solempnytee *n.* splendor, ceremony I.870, III.629. MED
solempnite *n.*

som(e) *adj.* some I.776, I.2844; a certain I.640, I.1088; *pl.*
somme VII.2127. MED som *adj.*

som(e), somme *pro.* some I.3175; one I.2119; **al and s.** one
and all, everyone I.2761, everything, the sum of it III.91
(also *pl.* I.2187); **som . . . som** one . . . another I.3031
(also *pl.* III.925-27). MED som *pro.*

somdel *adv.* somewhat I.446, I.3337. MED som-del *adv.*

somer *n.* summer I.394, I.1337; (as *adj.*) IV.2049; *gen.*
someres II.554. MED somer *n.*(1)

somme *n.* sum V.1220, V.1225; *pl.* **sommes** VIII.675. MED
somme *n.*(2)

somne *v.* summon III.1347, III.1577; *1 pr. sg.* **sompne** invite
VII.1462; *2 pr. sg.* **sompnest** VII.1463; *pr. pl.* **sompne**
VII.1472; *pp.* **somoned** III.1620. MED somnen *v.*

somonour, sumnour *n.* summoner I.543 (see n.), III.832; *pl.*
somonours III.1641. MED somnour *n.*

somtyme *adv.* once, formerly I.65, I.85; (as two words)
III.527; sometimes, at times I.1668, I.3383; sometime, at
some future time I.1243. MED som-time *adv.*

somwhat *adj.* (1) somewhat, a bit VII.955, VII.3195; (2) *adv.*
somewhat, a bit I.264, I.2424; (3) *pro.* something I.3119,
I.4203; **in s.** to some extent X.246. MED som-what *adj.,*
som-what *adv.,* som-what *pro.*

sond, soond *n.* sand I.3748, II.509, VII.3267. MED sand *n.*

sonde *n.* (1) dispensation (of God) decrees II.523, II.760;

God's gifts VII.219; (2) message II.388, II.1049; (3) messenger, agent, servant VIII.525. MED sonde *n.*

sondry *adj.* various, differing I.14, I.25. MED sondri *adj.*

soone *adv.* soon, quickly I.1420, I.1467; **(ful) s.** immediately I.1022, I.2270; *comp.* **sonner** VII.1450; *super.* **sonnest** VII.2526. MED sone *adv.*

song, soong, songe(n) sang, sung *see* **synge(n).**

sonken sunk *see* **synken.**

sonne *n.* sun I.7, I.30. MED sonne *n.*

soper, sopeer *n.* meal, supper I.348, V.1189. MED sopere *n.*(1)

soor(e) *n.* pain, misery I.1454, I.2233; **sore** VI.358. MED sore *n.*(1)

soor(e) *adj.* sore, painful I.2220, I.2419. MED sore *adj.*(2)

sore, soore *adv.* sorely, painfully, bitterly I.148, I.230; intensely I.2315, I.4229. MED sore *adv.*

sory, soory *adj.* (1) sad, miserable I.2004, IV.1244; **s. countenaunce (cheere)** sad facial expression I.2010, I.3618; (2) sad, feeling compassion (for someone or something) VI.115; (3) wretched II.466, VIII.1349; **s. grace** ill fortune, bad luck III.746; **with s. grace** with bad luck, unfortunately VI.876, (as imprecation) bad luck (to someone) VIII.1189; *comp.* **sorier** X.459. MED sori *adj.*

sort *n.* kind, class I.4381, I.4419; type I.4044; company II.141. MED sort *n.*(1)

sorwe *n.* sorrow I.951; lamentation I.1277, III.594; **with s.** to (his) sorrow VII.3253, (in imprecations) bad luck (to someone) I.4412, III.308; *pl.* **sorwes** I.2419. MED sorwe *n.*

sorwe *v.* grieve, repent X.296; *3 pr. sg.* **sorweth** I.2652; *pr. pl.* **sorwen** I.2824. MED sorwen *v.*

sorweful *adj.* (1) sorrowful I.1070, I.1106; (2) sad, pitiful VII.3204; *super.* **sorwefulleste** IV.2098. MED sorweful *adj.*

sorwefully *adv.* sorrowfully, sadly I.2978, III.913. MED sorwefulli *adv.*

sote, soot(e) *adj.* sweet-smelling, fragrant I.1, V.389; Cf. **swete** *adj.* and **swoote.** MED sote *adj.*

sothe, sooth *adj.* true I.4357, V.21; *comp.* **sother(e)** VIII.214. MED soth *adj.*

sooth *adv.* in sooth, truly VI.636, VII.1343. MED sothe *adv.*

sothe, sooth(e) *n.* truth I.845, I.1521; **for s.** in truth, truly I.283; **(the) s. to seyn (telle)** to tell the truth I.284, II.443; **seyn (full, right) s.** to tell the truth, to speak truly I.4356; *pl.* **sothes** VII.1177. MED soth *n.*

soothfastnesse *n.* truth VII.796, IV.934; certainty VII.1405, X.380. MED sothfastnesse *n.*

sothly, soothly *adv.* truly I.117, I.468. MED sothli *adv.*

sotil(e) subtle, crafty *see* **subtil(e).**

sotilly craftily *see* **subtilly.**

soughten *see* **seke(n).**

soun *n.* sound 1.674, 1.2881; *pl.* **sounes** 1.2512. MED soun *n.*

sound(e) *adj.* in **hoole and s.** completely healthy and well II.1150, VII.1015. MED sounde *adj.*

soupe *v.* dine V.1217; *pr. pl.* **soupen** V.297. MED soupen *v.*(2)

sourdeth *3 pr. sg.* arises, originates X.450, X.475; *pr. pl.* **sourden** X.448, X.865. MED sourden *v.*

sours *n.* (1) upward flight III.1938; (2) source IV.49. MED sours *n.*

soutil subtle, crafty *see* **subtil(e).**

soutiltee craftiness *see* **subtiltee.**

sovereyn, soverayn *adj.* best, most excellent I.67, I.2407;

supreme VI.91; *(astro.)* superior (*i.e.,* being in the western side of the zodiac) I.1974; ruling, sovereign II.276, III.1048. MED soverain *adj.*

sovereyn *n.* lord, master VIII.590; *pl.* **sovereyns** VII.1438. MED soverain *n.*

soveraynetee, sovereynetee *n.* sovereignty, mastery III.818, III.1038. MED soverainte *n.*

sowdan *n.* sultan II.177, II.436. MED soudan *n.*

sowdanesse *n.* sultaness II.358, II.958. MED soudanesse *n.*

sowne *v.* (1) play (a musical instrument) I.565, V.270; (2) imitate, repeat V.105; (3) (with **in, into**) tend toward, be consonant with V.517; *3 pr. sg.* **sowneth** IX.195; *pr. pl.* **sownen** X.1086; *pt. pl.* **sowned** VII.2158; *prp.* **sownynge** I.275. MED sounen *v.*

space *n.* (1) space of time IV.1687, VII.979; **a s.** a while I.2982, IV.918; opportunity, time I.35, V.493; (2) space, area I.4124; room, spaciousness I.176. MED space *n.*

spak spoke *see* **speke(n).**

spare *v.* (1) spare, leave unhurt III.421; economize IV.1297; (2) desist, refrain I.192, III.1328; hold back I.737, III.1543; *(reflx.)* hold oneself back, be reserved I.3966; *1 pr. sg.* **spare** III.1435; *3 pr. sg.* **spareth** X.558; *pr. pl.* **spare** III.1543; *pr. subj. pl.* **spare** VII.286; *imp. sg.* **spare** III.1763; *imp. pl.* **spareth** III.186; *3 pt. sg.* **spared** X.996; *prp.* (as *adj.*) **sparynge** frugal VII.1599; *pp.* **(y)spared** IV.2301, X.315; *vbl. n.* **sparynge** frugality X.835. MED sparen *v.,* sparinge *ger.*

spece *n.* species, kind X.407, X.486; *pl.* **speces** X.83. MED spice *n.*(2)

speche *n.* speech, talk I.307, I.517; conversation V.238, V.964; manner of speech I.3338, IX.205; language II.519, VIII.1443. MED speche *n.*

special(e) *adj.* special, particular X.488, X.738; (as *n.*) particular VII.1355; **in s.** in particular, particularly I.444. Cf. **especial.** MED speciale *adj.*

spede, speede *v.* (1) *(intr.)* succeed, prosper VI.134; (2) *(reflx.)* hasten, hurry I.3728, III.1732; (3) *(tr.)* help, give success, cause to prosper I.769, I.2258; **nedes s.** accomplish one's purpose I.4205; speed, hasten I.4033; *pr. subj. sg.* **speede** 1.769, **spede** I.2558; *imp. sg.* **speed** I.3562; *imp. pl.* **spede** III.1732; *3 pt. sg.* **spedde** I.1217; *pt. pl.* **spedde(n)** VII.253; *pp.* **(y)sped** I.4205, I.4220. MED speden *v.*

speke(n) *v.* speak I.142, I.413; *1 pr. sg.* **speke** I.727; *2 pr. sg.* **spekest** V.676, (with *pro.*) **spekestow** III.837; *3 pr. sg.* **speketh** I.2203; *pr. pl.* **speke(n)** I.4146, II.214; *pr. subj. sg.* **speeke** IX.324, **speke** X.911; *imp. sg.* **spek** IX.346; *imp. pl.* **speketh** IV.19; *1 & 3 pt. sg.* **spak** I.124, I.1858; *pt. pl.* **speeken** VII.1267, **speke** IV.932; *pp.* **yspoken** I.2972, **spoke(n)** I.31, VI.707; *vbl. n.* **spekyng(e)** IX.335. MED speken *v.,* spekinge *ger.*

spende(n) *v.* spend, expend I.4135, III.1796; pass (time) IV.391; *3 pr. sg.* **spendeth** VIII.832; *pr. pl.* **spende(n)** I.806, VI.781; *imp. sg.* **spende** VII.1605; *3 pt. sg.* **spente** I.300; *prp.* (as *adj.*) **spendyng** VIII.1018; *pp.* **spent** I.645. MED spenden *v.*

spere, speere *n.* spear I.114, I.975; *gen. pl.* **speres** I.2954; *pl.* **speres** I.1653. MED spere *n.*(1)

spices *n. pl.* spices IV.1770; spiced cakes, sweetmeats V.291. MED spice *n.*(1)

spicerye *n.* mixture of spices VI.544; delicacies, tidbits VII.853; Oriental goods (spices, cloth, *etc.*) II.136. MED spicerie *n.*

spye(n) *v.* spy III.316; espy, discover VIII.314; *3 pt. sg.* **spyed** watched for V.1506. Cf. **espye(n)**. MED spien *v.*(1)

spille *v.* (1) *(tr.)* put to death, kill III.898, III.1611; ruin III.388, spill (blood, tears) X.571; waste IX.153; (2) *(intr.)* *1 pr. sg.* **spille** die I.3278; *pr. subj. sg.* **spille** should die II.285; *pp.* **spilt** IX.326. MED spillen *v.*

(y)spoke(n) spoken *see* **speke(n).**

sprede *v.* spread VII.577; *3 pt. sg.* **spradde** IV.722; *pp.* **sprad** I.2903, **yspred** I.4140. MED spreden *v.*

sprynge(n) *v.* spring, rise up I.822, I.2173; leap 1.1871; *3 pr. sg.* **springeth** III.1939; *pr. pl.* **sprynge(n)** I.2607, V.1147; *3 pt. sg.* **sproong** I.3282, **sprong** VI.111, **sprang** IV.940; *pp.* **(y)spronge(n)** I.1437, VII.1210; *vbl. n.* **spryngyng(e)** IV.49. MED springen *v.*, springinge *ger.*

springen *v.* sprinkle, mingle II.1189, *pp.* **(y)spreynd** I.2169, II.442. MED sprengen *v.*

squier *n.* (1) young knight (knight bachelor, the first degree of knighthood) I.79, V.926; (2) squire, servant to a knight I.1410, I.2502; *pl.* **squieres** I.2502, **squiers** V.293. MED squier *n.*

stant stands *see* **stonde(n).**

starf died *see* **sterve(n).**

statut *n.* law, statute 1.327, III.198. MED statute *n.*

stede *n.* **in s. of** instead of I.231, VI.953; **stant in no s.** has no value VII.1090. MED stede *n.*(1)

steede *n.* steed, warhorse I.2157, I.2727; *pl.* **steedes** I.2495. MED stede *n.*(2)

stedefastnesse, stedfastnesse, stidefastnesse *n.* steadfastness IV.699, IV.1050; loyalty IV.2063. MED sted-fastnesse *n.*

stele(n) *v.* (1) *(tr.)* steal I.562, I.3940; (2) *(intr.)* steal away, go quietly I.3786; *3 pr. sg.* **steleth** II.21; *pr. pl.* **stelen** X.790; *3 pt. sg.* **stal** I.3995; *pp.* **stole(n)** I.2627, II.744, **stoln** I.4111; *vbl. n.* **stelyng** X.800. MED stelen *v.*, stelinge *ger.*

stent- cease *see* **stynte(n).**

sterre *n.* star I.2061, II.852; *pl.* **sterres** I.268; *gen. pl.* **sterres** IV.1124. MED sterre *n.*

sterte *v.* move suddenly or vigorously I.1044, II.335; (with **up** or **doun**) leap I.952, I.1080; *(reflx.)* move oneself, leap I.1579; tremble I.1762; rush III.573; suddenly awake I.1393; *3 pt. sg.* **sterte** I.952, **stirte** III.1046; *pt. pl.* **stirte(n)** VI.705, VII.3377; *pp.* **ystert** gone into, immersed in II.4, **stirt** leaped V.1377, **stert** awoke IV.1060. MED sterten *v.*

sterve(n) *v.* die I.1249, III.1242; *pr. subj. sg.* **sterve** I.1144; *pr. pl.* **sterve** VIII.420; *pt. sg.* **starf** I.933; *pt. pl.* **storven** VI.888; *pp.* **ystorve** II.2014. MED sterven *v.*

steven(e) *n.* voice I.2562, VII.3197. MED stevene *n.*(1)

stierne *adj.* stern, grim IV.465, X.170; cruel I.2154, I.2441; strong, violent I.2610. MED sterne *adj.*

stif *adj.* strong I.673, hard III.2267. MED stif *adj.*

stiketh *v. 3 pr. sg.* (1) *(tr.)* pierces, stabs I.3877, II.430; (2) affix, place VII.907; *3 pt. sg.* **styked** II.509 *(intr.)* stuck; *prp.* **stykynge** piercing VI.211; *pp.* **(y)stiked** I.2811, V.1476, (as *adj.*) VI.556; *vbl. n.* **stikynge** placing X.954. MED stiken *v.*, stikinge *ger.*

stikke *n.* stick, twig VIII.1265; *pl.* **stikkes** tree trunks I.2934. MED stikke *n.*

stille *adj.* still, silent I.2535, V.497. MED stille *adj.*

still(e) *adv.* still, motionless I.1003, I.1527; quietly I.2985, I.3721; still, continually, yet I.1335, I.3420. MED stille *adv.*

stille *v.* quiet, make peaceful VII.1487; *3 pr. sg.* **stilleth** makes peaceful VII.1514. MED stillen *v.*(1)

stynge *v.* sting IV.2059; *3 pr. sg.* **styngeth** III.1995; *pp.* **stongen** I.1079, **ystonge** VI.355. MED stingen *v.*

stynketh *3 pr. sg.* stinks VIII.1067; *pr. pl.* **stynken** VIII.886; *3 pt. sg.* **stank** VII.2617; *prp.* (as *adj.*) **stynkyng(e)** VI.534, X.157. MED stinken *v.*

stynte(n), stente *v.* (1) *(intr.)* stop, cease I.4339; stop talking VIII.927; cease, stop an activity I.903, IV.703; stop speaking about I.1334, I.2479; refrain VII.2735; (2) *(tr.)* stop, bring to a stop I.2450, I.2732; *1 pr. sg.* **stynte** I.2811; *3 pr. sg.* **stynteth** X.769; *(contr.)* **stynt(e)** I.2421; *pr. subj. sg.* **stynte** I.4339; *imp. sg.* **stynt** I.3144; *imp. pl.* **stynteth** I.2674; *3 pt. sg.* **stente** IV.1023; *pp.* **ystynt** III.390, **stynted** I.2968, **stent** I.1368. MED stinten *v.*

stire(n) *v.* (1) *(intr.)* stir; (with **to**) move, incite VI.346, VII.1506; (2) *(tr.)* stir, cause to move about VIII.1278; *3 pr. sg.* **stireth** VII.1128; *3 pt. sg.* **stired** VIII.1278; *prp.* **stirynge** I.3673; *pp.* **stired** X.446; *vbl. n.* **stirynge** incitement X.355; *pl.* **stirynges** X.655. MED stiren *v.*, stiringe *ger.*

stiropes *n. pl.* stirrups II.1163, III.1665. MED stirop *n.*

stirte(n) started, moved suddenly *see* **sterte.**

stole(n), stoln *see* **stele(n).**

stomak *n.* appetite III.1847; compassion III.1441. MED stomak *n.*

ston, stoon *n.* (1) stone I.774, I.1888; (2) gem I.2146, IV.1818; (3) testicle VII.3448; *pl.* **stones** 1.3210. MED ston *n.*

stonde(n) *v.* (1) stand (upright) I.3830, I.4101; stand (be placed) I.745, I.3923; **s. at, to** stand ready I.788, X.60; **s. by, at** defend II.345, IV.1195; **s. agayn** resist, deny III.1488; **s. at, to** abide by II.36; (2) **s. in** be (in grace, dread, *etc.*) I.88, IV.1091; **s. so** is thus I.1322, IV.346; **it s. with (someone)** someone's condition is I.3426; **s. on, in** consists of, depends on X.107, X.743; endure IV.2314; *1 pr. sg.* **stonde** IV.1091; *2 pr. sg.* **stondest** II.657; *3 pr. sg.* **stondeth** I.1639, **standeth** VII.257, *(contr.)* **stant** I.3677; *pr. pl.* **stonden** X.451; *imp. sg.* **stand** I.4101; *imp. pl.* **stondeth** IV.1195; *3 pt. sg.* **stood** I.354; *pt. pl.* **stode(n)** II.176, II.678, **stoode(n)** IV.1715, IV.1902; *prp.* **stondyng(e)** II.68; *pp.* **stonden** IV.1494. MED stonden *v.*(1)

stongen, ystonge stung *see* **stynge.**

stoor *n.* livestock I.598, VI.365; possessions III.2159; **in s.** in stock, in reserve IV.17; **tell(en) of no s.** regard as of no value III.203, VII.3154. MED store *n.*

storie *n.* (1) historical narrative 1.1201, I.1464; ecclesiastical narrative I.709; (2) story, tale IV.1186; *pl.* **stories** I.859. MED storie *n.*(1)

storven, ystorve died *see* **sterve(n).**

stounde *n.* time, space of time I.1212; **in a s.** once, at a certain time I.3992; moment, brief space of time II.1021; *pl.* **stoundes** III.286. MED stounde *n.*

stoupe *v.* stoop VIII.1311; *3 pr. sg.* **stoupeth** IV.2348; *imp. pl.* **stoupeth** VIII.1327; *prp.* (as *adj.*) IV.1738. MED stoupen *v.*

stout(e) *adj.* strong, sturdy I.545; bold I.2154. MED stoute *adj.*

strangle *v.* strangle, destroy X.769; *3 pr. sg.* **strangleth** X.792; *pr. pl.* **stranglen** X.768; *pp.* **strangled** destroyed I.2018; *vbl. n.* **stranglyng(e)** throttling I.2458, destruction X.1006. MED stranglen *v.,* stranglinge *ger.*

straughte stretched *see* **strecche(n).**

straunge, strange *adj.* (1) foreign I.13, I.464; strange, unknown IV.138, V.89; exotic V.67; external III.1161; (2) distant, reserved VII.263; (3) **made it s.** raised difficulties I.3980, V. 1223. MED straunge *adj.*

straungenesse, strangenesse *n.* distance, estrangement VII.386; exotic style X.414. MED straungenesse *n.*

strawe *v. pr. subj. sg.* strew V.613; *pp.* **strawed** X.198. MED streuen *v.*

stre, straw *n.* (1) straw I.2918, I.3873; (2) in expressions of worthlessness: **sette nat a s.** nothing at all, not a bit VII.3090; (as *interj.*) **s. (for)** an expression of contempt IV.1567, V.695. MED strau *n.*

strecche(n) *v.* (1) *(tr.)* stretch out VI.395, VII.3308; (2) *(intr.)* extend VIII.469, VIII.1087; *3 pr. pl.* **strecchen** VII.1825; *pt. pl.* **straughte** I.2916; *prp.* **strecchynge** VII.3332. MED strecchen *v.*

streight *adv.* directly, straightly I.671; immediately I.1650. MED streight *adv.*

streyne *v.* (1) clasp tightly IV.1753; (2) constrain IV.144; *3 pr. sg.* **streyneth** constrains VII.3244; *pr. pl.* **streyne** strain VI.538. MED streinen v.(1)

streit(e) *adj.* (1) narrow 1.1984; strict 1.174; (2) small 1.4122; scanty III.1426, VII.2989; **s. swerd** drawn sword VII.3357. MED streit *adj.*

strem, streem *n.* stream, current I.464, I.3895; *pl.* **stremes** I.402. MED strem *n.*

streng *n.* string III.2067. MED streng *n.*

strenger *see* **strong(e).**

strepe(n) *v.* strip I.1006, IV.863; *3 pr. sg.* **strepeth** IV.894; *pr. pl.* **strepen** IV.1116. MED strepen *v.*

strete, streete *n.* street, road I.2902, I.4384. MED strete *n.*(2)

strif *n.* strife I.1187, I.1282; **s. of Thebes** siege of Thebes II.200; **maken s.** cause trouble III.2000. MED strife *n.*

stryve *v.* strive, quarrel, I.3040, IV.170; *3 pr. sg.* **stryveth** VII.1488; *pr. pl.* **stryve(n)** I.1177 *pr. subj.* **stryve** X.664 *(sg.);* *imp. sg.* **stryve** III.1986; *3 pt. sg.* **stroof** I.1038; *vbl. n.* **stryvyng(e)** strife, quarreling VI.550, VII.1484. MED striven *v.,* strivinge *ger.*

strogelest struggle *see* **strugle.**

strook *n.* stroke, blow I.1701; *pl.* **strokes** I.1922. MED stroke *n.*

stronde *n.* strand, shore II.825, II.864; *pl.* **strondes** I.13. MED stronde *n.*(1)

strong(e), stroong *adj.* strong, powerful I.1056, I.2373; difficult, painful VII.1445; arrant, downright IV.2367, VI.789; *comp.* **stronger** VII.1348, **strenger** VI.825; *super.* **strongest** VII.1337, VII.2075. MED strong *adj.*

strugle *v.* struggle IV.2374, IV.2376; *2 pr. sg.* **strogelest** VI.829; *vbl. n.* **struglyng** II.921. MED strogelen *v.,* strogelinge *ger.*

sturdy *adj.* strong, obstinate III.612; stout III.1754; harsh, cruel IV.698, IV.1049; **a s. pas** angrily III.2162. MED sturdi *adj.*

subget *adj.* subject, subordinate X.264; *(pl.)* **subgetz** IV.482,

subgetes IV.634. MED subget *adj.*

subgetz, subgetis, subgitz *n. pl.* subjects, subordinates III.1990, X.467, X.774. MED subget *n.*

substaunce, substance *n.* (1) substance, essential quality VI.539; meaning VII.2803; (2) income I.489; possessions VII.999. MED substaunce *n.*

subtil(e), subtille, soutil, sotil(e) *adj.* (1) ingenious, skillful I.2049, I.3275; crafty V.285; (2) delicate I.1054; thin I.2030. MED sotil *adj.*

subtilly, sotilly *adv.* craftily, subtly I.610, IV.2003; skillfully V.222, V.1284. MED sotilli *adv.*

subtiltee, subtilitee, soutiltee *n.* craftiness VIII.620, VIII.1371; trickery, guile III.576; trick III.1420; treachery IV.691; *pl.* **subtilitees** tricks IV.2421. MED sotilte *n.*

suffisaunce, suffisance *n.* sufficiency I.490, IV.759. MED suffisaunce *n.*

suffisaunt, suffisant, sufficient *adj.* sufficient I.1631, II.243; capable VI.932; adequate VII.1027. MED suffisaunt *adj.,* sufficient *adj.*

suffise *v.* suffice, be sufficient I.4125, II.1099; be capable of, able VII.1650; *(impers.)* is enough I.2039; **s. hym** is enough for him IV.1626; *3 pr. sg.* **suffiseth** I.1953; *pr. pl.* **suffisen** III.1882; *pr. subj. sg.* **suffise** IV.740; *prp.* **suffisynge** I.3629; *pp.* **suffised** I.1233. MED suffisen *v.*

suffraunce, suffrance *n.* patience, forbearance IV.1162, X.625. MED sufferaunce *n.*

suffre(n), soffre *v.* (1) allow, permit I.649, I.945; (2) endure, suffer III.252, IV.537; *3 pr. sg.* **suffreth** I.1219; *pr. pl.* **suffre(n)** IV.1471, VII.1480; *pr. subj.* **suffre** VII.1220 *(sg.);* *imp. sg.* **suffre** IV.1377; *imp. pl.* **suffreth** III.437; *3 pt. sg.* **suffred(e)** VII.979, X.663; *pp.* **(y)suffred** I.2772, VII.1505; *vbl. n.* **suffrynge** VII.1466. MED sufferen *v.,* sufferinge *ger.*

suppose *v.* believe, think III.786, IV.1403; *1 pr. sg.* **suppose** III.1791; *1 pt. sg.* **supposed** V.575; *prp.* **supposynge** VIII.871; *pp.* **supposed** VII.595; *vbl. n.* **supposyng(e)** supposition IV.1041, VIII.873. MED supposen *v.,* supposinge *ger.*

sur- *see* **seur.**

Surrien *adj.* Syrian II.153, II.435; (as *n.*) VII.2339; *pl.* **Surryans** II.963.

suspecioun, suspecion *n.* suspicion II.681, IX.281. MED suspecioun *n.*

suspect *n.* suspicion VI.263; **have (be) in s. (of)** suspect, be suspicious of IV.905, VII.1197. MED suspect *n.*

sustene, susteene *v.* sustain, support, maintain I.1993, II.847; *pr. pl.* **sustenen** X.439; *pp.* **sustened** VII.490. MED sustenen *v.*

suster *n.* sister I.871; *pl.* **sustren** I.1019, **sustres** VII.2867. MED suster *n.*

swatte sweated *see* **swete** *v.*

swelle *v.* swell I.2752, IV.2306; *3 pr. sg.* **swelleth** I.2743; *pr. subj. sg.* **swelle** VI.354; *3 pt. sg.* **swal** III.967; *pp.* (as *adj.*) **swollen** IV.950; *vbl. n.* **swellynge** X.391. MED swellen *v.,* swellinge *ger.*

swelwe, swolwe *v.* swallow VII.1618, IX.36; *3 pr. sg.* **swelweth** VII.1618; *pr. subj. sg.* **swelwe** IV.1188, **swolwe** X.731. MED swolwen *v.*

swerd *n.* sword I.112, I.558; *gen.* **swerdes** I.2646; *pl.* **swerdes** I.1700. MED sword *n.*

swere(n) *v.* swear I.454, X.594; *1 pr. sg.* **swere** III.2137; *3*

pr. sg. **swereth** X.596; *pr. pl.* **sweren**, X.599; *pr. subj. pl.*
swere VIII.147; *imp. sg.* **swere** IV.357; *imp. pl.* **swere**
IV.357, **swereth** X.591; *1 & 3 pt. sg.* **swoor** I.959,
III.397; *pt. pl.* **swore(n)** I.1826, IV.496; *pp.* **(y)sworn**
I.1089, I.1132, **yswore** V.325, **swore(n)** IV.403, **yswore**
V.325, (as *adj.*) VI.808, **sworne** III.1405; *vbl. n.*
swerynge(e) VI.631, X.602, **swerying** X.593. MED
sweren *v.,* sweringe *ger.*

swete, sweete *adj.* sweet, pleasing, dear I.5, V.978. Cf.
swoote *adj.* MED swete *adj.*

sweete *adv.* sweetly, pleasingly, gently I.3305, I.3691. MED
swete *adv.*

swete, sweete *v.* sweat VIII.522; *1 pr. sg.* **swete** I.3702; *pr. pl.*
swete VIII.1186; *3 pt. sg.* **swatte** VIII.563. MED sweten
v.(1)

swetely *adv.* sweetly, gently I.221, I.3215. MED sweteli *adv.*

swetnesse, swetenesse *n.* sweetness VII.555, X.1053. MED
swetenesse *n.*

sweven(e) *n.* dream VII.2740, VII.2896; *pl.* **swevenes**
VII.3091, **swevenys** VII.2921. MED sweven *n.*

swich(e), suche, swilk *adj.* such I.3, I.4171; **s. oon** such a
one V.231. MED swich *adj.*

swich(e) *pro.* such, such a one V.41, V.519. MED swich *pro.*

swymme *v.* float I.3550, I.3575; *pr. pl.* **swymmen** swim in,
are surrounded by III.1926. MED swimmen *v.*

swynk *n.* work, labor I.188, I.540. MED swink *n.*

swynke(n) *v.* (1) (*intr.*) work I.186, III.202; (2) (*tr.*) earn by
working VIII.21; *pr. pl.* **swynke** I.3491; *pp.* **swonken**
I.4235, **yswonke** IX.18. MED swinken *v.*

swithe *adv.* quickly II.730; **as s.** immediately, without delay
II.637, VIII.936. MED swithe *adv.*

swyve *v.* (*tr.*) copulate with I.4178, IX.256; (2) (*intr.*) copulated, fornicated I.4422; *3 pt. sg.* **swyved** IV.2378; *pp.*
swyved I.3850. MED swiven *v.*

swolwe(n) swallow *see* swelwe.

swoote, soote *adj.* sweet, sweet-smelling I.2860, I.3205. Cf.
swete *adj.,* **sote** *adj.* MED sote *adj.*

swough, swogh *n.* swoon, faint III.799, IV.1100. MED swoue
n.

swowne *v. 3 pr. sg.* **swowneth** swoon, faint V.430; *3 pt. sg.*
swowned I.2943; *prp.* **swownynge** I.2819; *pp.* **swowned**
I.913; *vbl. n.* **swownyng(e)** IV.1080, IV.1087. MED
swounen *v.,* swouninge *ger.*

T

t' *contr.* of **to** often used before vowels (*e.g.,* **t'endite** I.1209).

table *n.* (1) tablet, surface for writing I.1305; **first t.** first set of
Commandments VI.639; (2) table I.100, VI.490; **t. dor-
mant** permanently set-up table I.353; (3) (*pl.*) backgammon
V.900, X.793; *pl.* **tables** tablets III.1741. MED table *n.*

take(n) *v.* (1) (*tr.*) take I.34, II.963; **t. kepe** take heed I.503,
VI.352; **t. on (upon) hym (me,** *etc.*) undertake I.3160,
VI.612, VIII.605; consider III.1116; **t. in desdayn (agref,**
etc.) disdain, be upset, *etc.* I.789, III.191; (2) give, bring
VII.294; give, strike III.792; (3) (*reflx.*) betake oneself, go
X.842; (4) (*intr.*) (with **to**) come III.31; *inf. (Nth.)* **taa**
I.4129; *1 pr. sg.* **take**. I.4052; *2 pr. sg.* (with *pro.*)
takestow VIII.435; *3 pr. sg.* **taketh** I.1217; *pr. pl.* **take(n)**

I.1879, II.147; *pr. subj.* **take** III.1055 *(sg.),* VII.2893 *(pl.);*
imp. sg. **taak** VII.1180; *imp. pl.* **taak** I.1084, **take** X.598,
taketh VI.74; *1 & 3 pt. sg.* **took** I.303, III.382; *pt. pl.*
tooke IV.202; *pt. subj. sg.* **tooke** would take IV.1582; *pp.*
take(n) I.1439, I.2551, **ytake(n)** I.3353; *vbl. n.* **takyng(e)**
VII.1032, VII.1435. MED taken *v.,* takinge *ger.*

tale *n.* (1) tale, narrative I.36, I.330; (2) esteem, regard
VII.3118; *pl.* **tales** tales I.792, **talys** gossip III.319. MED
tale *n.*

talent *n.* inclination, desire VI.540, VII.1249; *pl.* **talentes**
X.915. MED talent *n.*

talke(n) *v.* talk V.692, VIII.663; *vbl. n.* **talkyng** VIII.684.
MED talken *v.,* talkinge *ger.*

targe *n.* shield I.471, I.975. MED targe *n.*(1)

tarie(n) *v.* (1) (*tr.*) delay, keep (someone) waiting IV.1696,
V.73; tarry, waste (day, time, *etc.*) I.2820, I.3905; (2)
(*intr.*) tarry, delay I.3409, II.374; *3 pr. sg.* **tarieth** X.1001;
subj. pl. **tarie** V.1233 *(pl.);* *imp. sg.* **tarie** I.3905; *3 pt. sg.*
taried X.998; *pp.* **taried** V.402; *vbl. n.* delay **tarynge**
I.821. **tariyng(e)** I.3546, II.262. MED tarien *v.*(1), tariinge
ger.(1)

teche(n) *v.* teach I.308, I.654; *1 pr. sg.* **teche** VI.440; *3 pr. sg.*
techeth V.104; *pr. pl.* **teche** IX.132; *imp. sg.* **teche**
III.1418; *imp. pl.* **teche** III.187; *1 & 3 pt. sg.* **taughte**
I.497, III.1050; *pt. pl.* **taught** VI.364; *pp.* **(y)taught** I.127,
II.224; *vbl. n.* **techyng(e)** teaching, doctrine I.518,
VIII.93; *pl.* **techynges** VII.1870. MED techen *v.,* techinge
ger.

teyne *n.* flat metal rod or plate VIII.1225, VIII.1229; *pl.*
teynes VIII.1332. MED teine *n.*

telle(n) *v.* (1) tell I.38, I.73; **herd t.** heard it told III.1675; (2)
count X.390; enumerate VIII.799; (3) **t. of** respect,
account IX.236; **t. no deyntee (tale)** of have no regard for
III.208; **t. of no stoor** regard as worthless III.203,
VII.3154; *inf.* **to telle** to be told V.447; *1 pr. sg.* **telle** I.330;
3 pr. sg. **telleth** I.797; *pr. pl.* **telle(n)** I.859, V.824; *pr. subj.*
telle I.3505 *(sg.),* VII.2092 *(pl.);* *imp. sg.* **tel** III.2251,
telle V.702; *imp. pl.* **tel** I.808, **telleth** I.910; *1 & 3 pt. sg.*
toold(e) VII.2021, **tolde** I.1059, I.1160, **tald** *(Nth.)*
I.4207; *pt. pl.* **tolde(n)** I.1689, I.3184; *pt. subj. sg.* **tolde**
VII.2653; *prp.* **tellynge** VII.1797; *pp.* **(y)told** I.1584,
VIII.627, **(y)toold** I.2924, I.3109; *vbl. n.* **tellyng** VII.948.
MED tellen *v.,* tellinge *ger.*

temporel, temporeel, temporal *adj.* temporal, worldly
II.107, III.1132, VII.999; *pl.* **temporele** X.1039, **temporels** VII.998, **temporeles** X.685. MED temporal *adj.*

tempte *v.* try, test III.1661, IV.452; *3 pr. sg.* **tempteth**
IV.1153; *3 pt. sg.* **tempted** X.332; *pp.* **tempted** IV.621.
MED tempten *v.*

terme *n.* (1) period of time; **t. of** (one's) **lyf** duration of (one's)
life III.644, III.820; (2) word, expression I.3917; technical
language VI.311; (3) (*astro.*) term, a division of a zodiacal
sign V.1288; *pl.* **termes** Year Books I.323; technical words
I.639, IV.16; expressions I.3917. MED terme *n.*

than(ne), thenne *adv.* then I.12, I.42. MED thanne *adv.*

thank *n.* thanks, gratitude I.612, IV.1801; **kan** (someone) **t.**
owe thanks, be grateful I.1808, I.3064; good will, favor
X.1035; *gen.* (in *adv. phr.*) **his (hir,** *etc.*) **thankes** willingly, voluntarily I.1626, III.272; *pl.* **thankes** VII.188.
MED thank *n.*

thanke(n), thonke *v.* thank I.3069, V.557; *1 pr. sg.* **thonke** IV.830, **thanke** VII.355; *3 pr. sg.* **thanketh** II.383, **thonketh** V.1545; *pr. pl.* **thanke(n)** IV.616, V.354, **thonken** IV.188; *pr. subj. sg.* **thanke** IV.1088; *pr. subj. pl.* **thanke** VII.2197; *3 pt. sg.* **thanked** V.753, **thonked** VII.1873; *pt. pl.* **thonked** I.1876; *imp. sg.* **thanke** VII.2686; *imp. pl.* **thonketh** II.1113; *prp.* **thankyng** III.1868; *pp.* **(y)thanked** I.925, III.2118, **thonked** IV.2385; *vbl. n. pl.* **thankynges** thanks VII.1804. MED thanken *v.,* thankinge *ger.*

thar *3 pr. sg. impers.* (with *inf.*) **him t., t. thee,** *etc.* he, you must, need I.4320, III.329; *pr. pl.* **thar** VII.1068. MED thurven *v.*

that *adj.* that I.102, I.113. MED that *def. art. & adj.*

that *conj.* that I.226, I.297; so that II.262; as soon as II.1036; (after *conj.* and *rel.,* untranslated) **though that** though I.68, **if that** if I.399, **wherfore that** why I.1568, **which(e) that** which IV.1587, *etc.*; (introducing exclamations) I.1227, III.614. MED that *conj.*

that *rel. pro.* that, which, who I.43, I.344; what I.1425, VIII.642. MED that *pro., rel. pro.*

the, thee *2 sg. pro. dat.* and *acc.* you I.3728, *etc.* MED the *pro.*(2)

thee(n) *v.* prosper, thrive III.2232, VII.817; *pr. subj. sg.* **thee** VIII.929, (with *pro.*) **theek** I.3864, **theech** VI.947. MED then *v.*

theef *n.* thief I.1325, I.3791; *pl.* **theves** VI.789, **thevis** III.2173. MED thef *n.*(2)

thenke(n), thenche, thynke(n) *v.* think X.293; imagine I.346, I.3253; believe I.1767; intend VII.1834; *1 pr. sg.* **thynke** III.201, **thenke** IV.641; *3 pr. sg.* **thynketh** VII.1524; *pr. pl.* **thynke(n)** I.3701, III.2204, **thenke(n)** V.537, X.671; *pr. subj. sg.* **thynke** VII.954; *imp. sg.* **thynk** I.1606, **thenk** I.3478; *imp. pl.* **thenketh** VI.75; *1 & 3 pt. sg.* **thoughte** I.3453, **thoghte** I.1767; *pt. pl.* **thoughte(n)** III.2030; *prp.* **thynkynge** X.689; *vbl. n.* **thynkynge** X.111. MED thinken *v.*(2), thinkinge *ger.*

thennes *adv.* thence, from that place or time II.308, V.326. MED thennes *adv.*

ther(e), theer(e) *adv.* (1) there I.43, I.197; (2) where I.892; wherever I.3702; wherein III.128; **overal t.** wherever III.237; (3) (as introductory expletive) I.118; (with optative clauses of blessing or cursing, untranslated) I.2815, III.1561. MED ther *adv.*

therto(o) *adv.* to there I.48; to that VIII.738; for that purpose V.1330; moreover, in addition I.153, I.289. MED ther-to *adv.*

therwith *adv.* with that I.678; with it I.3777; whereupon, immediately I.1299. MED ther-with *adv.*

therwithal *adv.* therewith I.566; moreover I.3233; with that, immediately I.1078; simultaneously I.3788. MED ther-withal *adv.*

thewes *n. pl.* personal qualities, morals IV.409, IV.1542. MED theu *n.*(1)

thider *adv.* thither, there I.2275, I.2545. MED thider *adv.*

thikke *adj.* thick I.1056; dense, set closely together I.1579, IV.1824; **t. of** thick with, thickly set with I.1075; stout, sturdy I.549, I.3973; (as *n.*) thick I.4066; *super.* **thikkest(e)** I.2612. MED thikke *adj.,* thikke *n.*

thikke *adv.* thickly, densely I.2510, I.3322. MED thikke *adv.*

thilk(e) *dem. adj.* that, that same I.182, I.1193; *pro.* that, that one X.106. MED thilke *adj.,* thilke *pro.*

thyn(e) *poss.* (1) (as *adj.* usu. before vowel and **h-**) thy, your I.951, VII.2077; (before consonants) **thy** I.3905 (2) (as *pro.*) thine, yours I.1235, VI.653. MED thin *pro.*

thyng *n.* thing I.985; document I.325; possessions I.490; **any t., for any t.** at all costs I.276; *pl.* **thynges** I.175. MED thing *n.*

thynke(n) *see* **thenke(n).**

thynke, thenche *v. impers.* (with *dat.*) *3 pr. sg.* **me (yow,** *etc.***) thynketh** (it) seems to (me, you, *etc.*), (I, you, *etc.*) think I.37, I.1867; *pr. subj. sg.* **thynke** VII.954; *3 pt. sg.* **thoughte** I.785, **thoghte** I.3672; *pt. pl.* **thoughte** II.412. MED thinken *v.*(1).

thynne, thenne *adj.* thin, weak IV.1682; (as *n.*) thin I.4066; (as *adv.*) I.679. MED thin(ne *adv.,* thin(ne *n.*

this *adj.* this I.269, I.929; *pl.* **thise** I.1531. MED this *adj.*

this *contr.* of **this is** I.2761, VII.3057.

this *pro.* IV.785, VI.224; *pl.* **thise** IV.375. MED this *pro.*

tho *adj. pl.* those I.1123, III.195. MED tho *def. art. & adj.*(2)

tho *adv.* then I.993, I.2696. MED tho *adv.*

tho *pro. pl.* those I.2351, III.370. MED tho *pro.*(2)

thogh, though *adv.* and *conj.* though, although I.253; (with **that**) I.68, I.727; (with **as**) I.553, I.1079. MED though *adv.,* though *conj.*

thoght, thought(e) *n.* (1) thought I.479, IV.2359; (2) anxiety, care V.822, VII.589; *pl.* **thoghtes** IV.116. MED thought *n.*

thoghte *see* **thenke(n)** and **thynke** *v.*

thombe *n.* thumb I.563, V.83. MED thoume *n.*

thonder *n.* thunder I.492, III.732. MED thonder *n.*

thonk- *see* **thanke(n).**

thought- *see* **thenke(n), thynke.**

thow, thou *2 sg. pro. nom.* thou, you I.1559, *etc.* MED thou *pro.*

thral *n.* servant, slave III.155, V.769, VI.183; *pl.* **thralles** X.152. MED thral *n.*(1)

thral *adj.* enslaved, bound (as a serf) I.1552, III.1660; *pl.* **thralle** VII.1561. MED thral *adj.*(1).

thraldom *n.* slavery, servitude II.286, X.142. MED thraldom *n.*

thraste thrusted *see* **threste.**

threed *n.* thread I.2030, VII.2475. MED threde *n.*

thredbare, threedbare *adj.* threadbare I.260, I.290. MED thred-bare *adj.*

thresshfold *n.* threshold I.3482, IV.288. MED thresh-wolde *n.*

threste *v.* thrust, push I.2612; *3 pt. sg.* **threste** IV.2003; *pt. pl.* **thraste** VI.260. MED thresten *v.*

threte *v.* threaten *3 pr. sg.* **threteth** threatens X.646; *vbl. n.* **thretyng** threatening VIII.698. MED threten *v.*(1), thretinge *ger.*

thries *adv.* thrice I.63, I.463. MED thrice *adv.*

thrift *n.* prosperity, welfare VIII.739, VIII.1425; **by my t.** by my welfare (I swear) I.4049. MED thrift *n.*

thrifty *adj.* (1) useful, serviceable II.138, III.238; provident, well-managed VII.246; suitable II.46; (2) worthy II.1165, IV.1912. MED thrifti *adj.*

thriftily *adv.* properly I.105, I.3131; suitably, politely V.1174. MED thriftili *adv.*

thryve *v.* thrive, succeed I.3675, VIII.1212; *pr. subj. sg.* **thryve** III.1764. MED thriven *v.*

throop *n.* village IV.199, IV.208; *gen.* **thropes** X.12; *pl.* **thropes** III.871. MED thorp *n.*

throte *n.* throat I.2013, I.2458. MED throte *n.*

throwe *n.* (1) period of time, while III.1815; **any t.** at, for any time VII.2136; (2) short while II.953. MED throu *n.*(1)

throwe(n) *v.* throw IV.453, X.863; *3 pt. sg.* **threw** II.85; *pt. pl.* **threwe** VII.572; *pp.* **ythrowe** VIII.940. MED throuen *v.*(1)

thurgh *prep.* (1) through, throughout I.1565, I.4151; (2) by means of II.22, V.1295; because of I.920, I.1328. MED thurgh *prep.*

thurghout *prep.* throughout I.1096, II.256. MED thurgh-oute *prep.*

thurst *n.* thirst II.100, X.343. MED thirst *n.*

tyde *n.* (1) tide of the sea II.510, II.1134; (2) time V.142; *pl.* **tydes** I.401. MED tide *n.*

til *conj.* until I.698, II.791; **t. that** until I.983. MED til *conj.*

til *prep.* until I.1621, III.2012; to, into I.180, I.1132; (as *adv.*) in **t. and fro** I.4039. MED til *prep., til adv.*

tyme *n.* time I.35, I.44; **by tyme(s)** quickly, soon VIII.913, X.363; **in good t.** timely VIII.1048; **oft tyme(s)** often I.52, I.1312; **of olde t.** long ago II.50; **som t.** at some time I.2474, I.2846, sometimes I.3332; once, formerly III.527; *pl.* **tymes** I.534. MED time *n.*

to(o) *adv.* too II.420, IV.2434. MED to *adv.*(2)

to *prep.* (1) to I.30; (2) as I.1289, I.1622, IV.793; **as to** according to IV.53, V.677; (as *adv.*) **t. and fro** here and there I.2508. MED to *prep., to adv.*(1)

too *n.* toe I.2726; *pl.* **toos** VII.3180, **toon** VII.2862. MED to *n.*

to-breke *v.* break in pieces, shatter I.3918; *3 pr. sg.* **tobreketh** VIII.907; *pp.* **tobroke** III.277; (as *adj.*) I.4277; MED tobreken *v.*

tobreste *v. pr. pl.* break in pieces, shatter I.2611; *pp.* **tobrosten** I.2691. MED tobresten *v.*

toforn *prep.* before V.268. MED toforen *prep.*

togidre(s) *adv.* together I.824, VI.702. MED togeder *adv., togederes adv.*

tohewen *pr. pl.* hew in pieces I.2609; *pp.* **tohewe(n)** II.430, II.437. MED toheuen *v.*

took(e) *see* **take(n).**

token *n.* evidence VII.390; *pl.* **tokenes** proofs, confirming details VII.359, IX.258. MED tokene *n.*

tolde, toold(e), (y)told, (y)toold *see* **telle(n).**

tomorwe, to-morwe *adv.* tomorrow I.780, I.1610; (as *n.*) VII.1795. MED to-morwe *adv.*

tonge *n.* tongue I.265, I.712; *pl.* **tonges** languages VII.2307. MED tonge *n.*(1)

tonne *n.* barrel, cask I.3894, III.177. MED tonne *n.*

torente *3 pr. sg.* tore in pieces VII.2025; *pt. pl.* **torente** tore in pieces VI.709; *pp.* **torent** torn, slain VI.102; (as *adj.*) **torent(e)** tattered IV.1012, torn in pieces VII.2261. MED torenden *v.*

torment *n.* torment, suffering I.1298, II.845; torture VII.628; *pl.* **tormentz** I.2228.

tormenteth *v. 3 pr. sg.* torment, torture I.1314; *pr. pl.* **tormenten** X.183; *pp.* **tormented** II.885; *vbl. n.* **tormentynge** IV.1038. MED tormenten *v., tormentinge ger.*

tormentour *n.* tormentor, torturer II.818, VIII.527; *pl.* **tormentoures** VIII.373. MED tormentour *n.*

torne *see* **turne(n).**

totere *pr. pl.* tear in pieces VI.474; *3 pt. sg.* **totar** VII.2611; *pp.* **totore** tattered VIII.635. MED toteren *v.*(2)

touche(n) *v.* (1) *(tr.)* touch III.87, X.327; (2) touch upon, treat (a subject) III.1271; concern I.3494; (3) *(intr.)* (with **to**) concern VII.1299; *3 pr. sg.* **toucheth** I.3179; *pr. pl.* **touche** VIII.156; *pr. subj. sg.* **touche** VII.2094; *pr. subj. pl.* **touche** VIII.156; *3 pr. sg.* **touchede** I.2561; *prp.* **(as) touchyng(e)** concerning III.1988, III.2290; *pp.* **touched** III.1271; *vbl. n.* **touchynge** touch, touching X.207. MED touchen *v., touchinge ger.*

tough *adj.* tough, strong I.1992; **make it t.** be unrelenting VII.379. MED tough *adj.*

toun(e), town(e) *n.* town I.217; *gen.* **townes** III.1285; *pl.* **tounes** I.3025, **townes** VII.2371. MED toun *n.*

tour *n.* tower I.1030, I.1056; *pl.* **toures** I.2464. MED tour *n.*(1)

trad trod *see* **tret.**

traisoun treason *see* **treson.**

traunce *n.* trance I.1572, III.2216. MED traunce *n.*

travaille, travayle, travel *n.* (1) effort, work I.2406, IV.1210; (2) suffering I.3646, VIII.781; *pl.* **travailles** X.256. MED travail *n.*

travaille(n) *v.* (1) work, exert efforts III.1365, X.667; (2) suffer X.985; *3 pr. sg.* **travailleth** VII.1590; *pr. pl.* **travaillen** X.652; *prp.* **travaillynge** in childbirth I.2083; *pp.* **travailed** X.823; *vbl. n.* **travaillyng** X.257. MED travailen *v., travailinge ger.*

tree *n.* (1) tree I.2062; cross I.3767, II.456; (2) wood III.101, IV.558; *pl.* **trees** I.607. MED tre *n.*

trecherye *n.* treachery, treason VII.3330, VIII.1069. MED trecheri *n.*

trede(n) tread *see* **tret.**

tresor, tresour, tresoor *n.* treasure II.442, III.204. MED tresour *n.*

treson, traisoun *n.* treason, treachery I.2001, VII.3117; *pl.* **tresons** I.2468. MED treisoun *n.*

trespaas, trespas *n.* wrong, fault, sin I.1764, I.1818. MED trespas *n.*

trespace *v.* (1) *(intr.)* (with **to**) do wrong to IV.1828; (with **agayns**) trespass VII.2564; (2) *(tr.)* commit (sins) VII.1885; *3 pr. sg.* **trespaseth** X.1012; *pr. pl.* **trespassen** X.138; *pr. subj. sg.* **trespasse** VI.741; *pp.* **(y)trespassed** VII.1419, VII.1877, **trespased** VII.416. MED trespassen *v.*

tret *3 pr. sg. (contr.)* treads, steps III.2002; *pr. pl.* **trede(n)** I.3022; *3 pt. sg.* **trad** copulated with VII.3178; *pp. (intr.)* **troden** stepped VI.712; *vbl. n.* **tredyng** copulation VII.1955. MED treden *v., tredinge ger.*

tretable *adj.* amenable X.658. MED tretable *adj.*

tretee *n.* (1) treaty, agreement I.1288, VI.619, VII.2675; (2) discussion, negotiation IV.1692, V.1219. MED trete *n.*(2)

trete(n) *v.* (1) speak about, discuss VI.64, VI.521; tell, assert VI.630; (2) negotiate VII.1798; (3) treat X.582; *pr. pl.* **trete(n)** V.220, X.582. MED treten *v.*

tretys, tretice *n.* (1) treatise VII.957, X.957; (2) treaty II.233; (3) negotiation (for a treaty or contract) IV.331. MED tretise *n.*

treuthe truth *see* **trouth(e).**

trewe *adj.* true, faithful I.959, I.2418; honest I.1326, IV.1298; truthful I.3529, X.982; real, authentic I.531, I.3781; (as *n.*) the faithful II.456; *super.* **trewest(e)** V.1539, VIII.969. MED treu *adj.*

trewely *adv.* (1) truly, honestly I.481, I.707; (2) (as expletive) indeed I.761, I.1267. MED treuli *adv.*

triumphe *n.* triumphal procession II.400, VII.2363. MED triumph *n.*

troden trod *see* **tret.**

trompe, trumpe *n.* trumpet I.674, II.705; *pl.* **trompes.** MED trompe *n.*

trone *n.* throne 1.2529, V.275. MED trone *n.*

troubleth *v. 3 pr. sg.* troubles, disturbs X.544; *pr. pl.* **troublen** III.363; *pp.* **troubled** VIII.72; (as *adj.*) **troubled** VII.1701. MED troublen *v.*

trouble *adj.* (1) troubled IV.465; disturbed, confused IX.279, X.537; (2) murky, stirred up X.816. MED trouble *adj.*

trouth(e), treuthe *n.* (1) pledge I.763, VII.1069; loyalty to one's word, fidelity I.46, I.2789; honesty I.4397; (2) truth, truthfulness II.630, VIII.259; *pl.* **trouthes** VI.702. MED treuth *n.*

trowe *v.* (1) believe VIII.378, IX.44; (2) suppose, think I.691; *1 pr. sg.* (as a weak expletive) **I trowe,** indeed, I warrant, I.155, III.217; *1 pr. sg.* **trowe** I.524; *2 pr. sg.* **trowest** III.1557; *3 pr. sg.* **troweth** VIII.288; *pr. pl.* **trowe(n)** II.222, VIII.420; *imp. sg.* **trowe** III.1985; *imp. pl.* **trowe(th)** VII.1511, IX.284; *3 pt. sg.* **trowed** I.3416; *pt. pl.* **trowed** IV.403; *prp.* **trowynge** VII.1446; *pp.* **trowed** I.1520. MED trouen *v.*

truste(n) *v.* trust II.832, VII.1110; *1 pr. sg.* **triste** II.832, **truste** IV.149; *3 pr. sg.* **trusteth** VII.1646; *imp. sg.* **trust(e)** X.204, X.253; *imp. pl.* (used for emphasis) **trusteth me** VIII.889, IV.1561, **trust(e) wel** VII.1150, VII.3024, **trusteth wel** I.2182, II.1048. *pr. subj. sg.* **truste** X.955; *3 pt. sg.* **trusted** III.958. MED trusten *v.*

tubbe *n.* tub, vat I.3621; *pl.* **tubbes** I.3836. MED tubbe *n.*

turne(n), torne *v.* (1) turn (*intr.*) I.1488, I.2318; go I.1327, III.988; (2) turn (*tr.*) I.3928, VIII.625; transform, change (with **into, to**) IX.100; *3 pr. sg.* **turneth** I.3390; *pr. pl.* **turne(n)** VI.539, VII.2297; *imp. sg.* **turne** VI.761, **turneth** VII.3409; *3 pt. sg.* **turned** V.1011; *pt. pl.* **turned** I.3842; *pp.* **(y)turned** I.1238, I.1377. MED turnen *v.*

turtel, turtle *n.* turtledove I.3706; *gen.* **turtles** IV.2139. MED turtel *n.*

twey(e), tweyne *num.* two I.704, I.792. MED twein *num.*

twies *adv.* twice I.4348, II.1058. MED twies *adv.*

twynne(n) *v.* go, depart V.577; get away, escape VII.2005; *pr. subj. pl.* **twynne** I.835. MED twinnen *v.*(1)

twiste *v.* press upon V.566; *1 & 3 pt. sg.* **twiste** tortured III.494, squeezed IV.2005. MED twisten *v.*

U

unavysed *pp.* (as *adj.*) reckless, thoughtless IX.280; unpremeditated X.449. MED unavised *adj.*

unbynde(n) *v.* unbind, free, deliver from X.277, X.1072; *3 pr. sg.* **unbyndeth** unbinds, breaks up X.511; *pp.* **unbounde(n)** IV.1226, VII.1783. MED unbinden *v.*

under *prep.* under I.105, *etc.*; close to, next to, by I.1981, IX.3; in the direction of I.1697; along with, in addition to IX.198. MED under *prep.*

understonde, understande *v.* understand I.746, X.211; believe VII.168; *1 pr. sg.* **understonde** VII.1279; *3 pr. sg.*

understondeth VI.646; *pr. pl.* **understonde** VII.1278; *imp. pl.* **understoond** VII.1091, **understonde** X.564, **understondeth** X.541; *1 & 3 pt. sg.* **understood** V.434, VIII.570; *pp.* **understonde(n)** II.520, VII.1284; *vbl. n.* **understondyng(e)** understanding, comprehension X.388. MED understonden *v.,* understondinge *ger.*

undertake, undirtake *v.* (1) undertake, begin an enterprise I.405, V.36; (2) declare, affirm, assert I.288, I.3532; *1 pr. sg.* **undertake** I.288; *3 pr. sg.* **undertaketh** X.403. MED undertaken *v.*

unfeyned *pp.* (as *adj.*) unfeigned, sincere VIII.434. MED unfeined *adj.*

unkynde *adj.* unnatural, cruel II.88, VI.903. MED unkinde *adj.*

unkonnynge *n.* ignorance, lack of skill VII.1876, X.1082. MED unconninge *ger.*

unnethe(s) *adv.* hardly, scarcely I.3121, II.1050. MED unethe *adv.*

unreste *n.* distress, discomfort III.1104, IV.719. MED unreste *n.*

unsely, unseely *adj.* unfortunate, unhappy I.4210, VIII.468. MED unseli *adj.*

until, untill *prep.* to (direction) I.3761; until (time) II.1070. MED until *prep.*

unto *prep.* (1) (direction) to, into, unto I.71, *etc.;* (2) (respect) to I.214; for VII.1581; as I.1486; about VII.3046; (3) (time) until I.2412, II.765. MED unto *prep.*

untressed *pp.* (as *adj.*) loose, unarranged I.2289, IV.379. MED untressed *adj.*

untrewe *adj.* unfaithful IV.995, IV.1786; untrustworthy VIII.1042; (as *adv.*) inaccurately I.735. MED untreu *adj.,* untreue *adv.*

untrouthe *n.* faithlessness II.687, IV.2241; perjury II.687. MED untreuth *n.*

unwar *adj.* unexpected II.427, VII.2764. MED unwar *adj.*

unwar *adv.* (1) unexpectedly V.1356; (2) unwarily, heedlessly X.885. MED unwar *adv.*

unwemmed *pp.* (as *adj.*) spotless, undefiled II.924, VIII.225. MED unwemmed *adj.*

up *adv.* up I.681, *etc.;* **up and doun** in all respects, in every way III.119; from one end to the other I.977; **up so doun, up-so-down** topsy turvy, upside down I.1377, VIII.625. MED up *adv.*

up *prep.* on, upon I.2543, II.795. MED up *prep.*

upon *adv.* on I.617, III.559, III.1382. MED upon *adv.*

upon, uppon *prep.* (1) on, upon I.111; next to, beside I.3923; **u. land** in the countryside I.702; (2) at, upon V.1496; to I.4006; at (of sight) I.3951, VII.124; (3) concerning, about I.3632, I.4329. MED upon *prep.*

upright(e) *adv.* (1) upwards I.3444; upright I.1387, IV.1844; (2) **bolt u.** flat on one's back I.4194, I.4266. MED upright e *adv.*

us *1st person pl. objective* and *acc.* us I.411, *etc.;* **us self** ourselves IV.108. MED us *pron.*

usage *n.* custom II.998, III.589; **of (old, verray) u.** by (long) habit VI.899, X.601; experience, skill I.110, I.2448. MED usage *n.*

usen *v.* (1) use, employ II.44, III.137; practice (an art, skill) VI.428, VIII.1409; (2) be accustomed to X.245; *1 pr. sg.* **excuse** III.1611; *3 pr. sg.* **useth** VI.599; *pr. pl.* **use(n)** VII.1574, VIII.1409; *pr. subj. pl.* **use** IV.1678; *imp. sg.* **use** VII.1602; *pt. 3 pt. sg.* **used** IV.2149; *pt. subj. sg.* **used**

III.132; *2 pt. sg.* **usedest** I.2385; *pt. pl.* **useden** V.1293, **used** VII.499; *pp.* **used** III.562, (as *adj.*) accustomed VIII.666; *prp.* **usynge** using VII.1609, (as *adj.*) accustomed to III.777; *vbl. n.* **usynge** using VII.1624. MED usen *v.*, usinge *ger.*

usure *n.* usury III.1309, VII.491, X.568. MED usure *n.*

V

vanysshe *v.* vanish V.328; waste away VI.732; *1 pr. sg.* **vanysshe** VI.732; *3 pt. sg.* **vanysshed** V.342; *pp.* **vanysshed** III.996; *vbl. n.* **vanysshynge** disappearance I.2360. MED vanishen *v.*, vanishinge *ger.*

variaunce, variance *n.* variation IV.710, X.427. MED variaunce *n.*

veyn(e) *adj.* idle, foolish I.1094, I.2240; (as *n.*) **in v.** idly, in vain, V.972; **v. glorie** vainglory, empty pride I.2240, VI.411, X.934. MED vein *adj.*

veyn(e) *n.* vein (of plants) I.3; **every v.** every part VIII.1241. MED vein *n.*

venge(n) *v.* (1) (*reflx.*) revenge (oneself) VII.1281, VII.1352; (2) (*tr.*) avenge VII.1371, VII.1531; *1 pr. sg.* **venge** VII.1461; *3 pt. sg.* **vengeth** VII.1458; *pp.* **venged** VII.1281. MED vengen *v.*

vengeaunce, vengeance *n.* revenge, punishment I.2066, I.2302; *pl.* **vengeaunces** VII.1429. MED vengeaunce *n.*

venym *n.* venom, poison I.2751, II.891; *pl.* **venymes** poisons VII.3155. MED venim *n.*

venymous, venenouse *adj.* poisonous VII.2105, X.576. MED venimous *adj.*

venquysse *v.* vanquish VII.1339, X.661; *3 pr. pl.* **venquysseth** V.774; *pr. pl.* **venquisshe(n)** VII.1090, VII.1094; *pp.* **venquysshed** II.291. MED venquishen *v.*

verray, verrey *adj.* (1) true I.1551, III.423; faithful I.3609, IV.2285; genuine, arrant III.253; (2) pure, sheer I.1748, V.166; (as *intens.*) indeed I.4103; **the v. devel (hogges,** *etc.*) the devil himself, even the hogs, *etc.* VI.480, VII.3385. MED verrei *adj.*

verray *adv.* truly X.87, X.113. MED verrei *adv.*

verraily *adv.* truly II.587, II.927. MED verreilli *adv.*

vers *n.* verse, stanza VII.522; *pl.* **vers** verses VII.1107, VII.3313. MED vers *n.*

vertu *n.* (1) power I.4, V.146; **v. expulsif (retentif,** *etc.*) power of the body to expel (retain) fluids, *etc.* I.2749 (see note), X.913; ability I.1436, X.453; **by (through) v. of** by the power of X.340; (2) moral excellence, virtue I.307, II.164; **maken v. of necessity** make the best of a situation I.3042, V.593; *pl.* **vertues** X.197. MED vertu *n.*

vertuous(e) *adj.* virtuous. of good moral character I.515, X.652; capable, able I.251, V.687. MED vertuous *adj.*

viage *n.* (1) journey I.723, II.259; travel II.312; expedition I.77; (2) business, undertaking III.1569, VII.371. MED viage *n.*

vileynye *n.* (1) rudeness, churlishness I.70, I.726; (2) shame, dishonor I.942; **don thee (hym,** *etc.*) **v.** bring disgrace, shame on you (him, etc.) IV.1791, IV.2261; **him to v.** a dishonor to him IX.260; **in v.** shamefully, lecherously VIII.156, X.857; (3) reproach, disgrace III.34, IV.2303; (4) evil X.852; **lucre of v.** ill-gotten gains; (5) harm,

injury I.4191, VII.1357; *pl.* **vileynyes** VII.1458. MED vileinie *n.*

vileyns *adj.* evil, churlish III.1158, X.556, X.854; rude, churlish III.1268. MED vileins *adj.*

vitaille *n.* food, victuals I.248, I.569. MED vitaile *n.*

voyde(n) *v.* expel, remove I.2751; get rid of IV.910; empty IV.1815; move V.188; *imp. sg.* **voide** leave IV.806; *imp. pl.* **voyde** send away VIII.1136; *3 pt. sg.* **voyded** caused to disappear V.1150; *pp.* **(y)voyded** removed V.1159. MED voiden *v.*

voys *n.* (1) voice I.688, I.1371; tone of voice II.449, III.1036; **in Pilates v.** ranting loudly I.3124; (2) opinion II.155; **with o v.** unanimously VII.1765, VIII.420; esteem IV.1592; (3) report II.169. MED voice *n.*

vouche sauf *v.* grant, agree, permit I.812, II.1083; *pr. pl.* **vouche s.** VII.1115; *pr. subj. sg.* **vouche s.** IV.306; *pr. subj. pl.* **vouche s.** X.52; *imp. pl.* **voucheth s.** IV.885. MED vouchen *v.*, vouchen sauf *v.*

W

wade(n) *v.* go IV.1684; wade, walk through III.2084; go into, penetrate VII.2494. MED waden *v.*

wayk(e) *adj.* weak I.887, II.932; *compar.* **weyker** VII.1483. MED weik *adj.*

waille, wayle *v.* (1) (*intr.*) wail, lament I.3398; (2) (*tr.*) bewail, bemoan X.178; *1 pr. sg.* **wayle** I.931; *3 pr. sg.* **wayleth** I.1221, **wailleth** V.1348; *3 pt. sg.* **wayled** V.1116; *prp.* **waillynge** I.1366; *vbl. n.* **wailyng(e)** wailing, lamentation IV.1213, X.864. MED weilen *v.*, weilinge *ger.*

waymenten *v.* lament X.230; *vbl. n.* **waymentynge** lamentation I.902, X.85. MED waimenten *v.*, waimentinge *ger.*

wayte(n) *v.* (1) watch, watch for I.3302, IV.1303; await, seek an occasion I.1222, II.582; **w. bisily** watch intently V.88; (2) expect II.246; **w. after** look for, desire II.467, IV.1303; look for, expect I.525; *3 pr. sg.* **waiteth** IV.708; *pr. pl.* **waiten** X.403; *pr. subj. pl.* **wayte** I.3295; *imp. pl.* **wayte** take note of III.517; *3 pt. sg.* **wayted** I.571; *prp.* **waityng(e)** I.929, III.1376; *vbl. n.* **waityng** watching IX.252. MED waiten *v.*, waitinge *ger.*

wake(n) *v.* (1) (*tr.*) be or remain awake I.3354, I.3672; pray or meditate all night III.1847; (2) wake up IV.2397; (3) (*tr.*) awaken II.1187; *1 pr. sg.* **wake** VIII.153; *3 pr. sg.* **waketh** I.3373; *pr. pl.* **wake** IV.118; *imp. pl.* **waketh** III.1654; *3 pt. sg.* **wook** I.1393; *pp.* **waked** I.4284; *vbl. n.* **wakynge** waking hours II.22, keeping vigil X.1048; *pl.* **wakynges** vigils X.257. MED waken *v.*, wakenen *v.*, wakinge *ger.*

walke(n) *v.* walk, go, roam I.2309, III.546; *1 pr. sg.* **walke** III.1820; *2 pr. sg.* **walkest** I.1283; *3 pr. sg.* **walketh** I.1052; *pr. pl.* **walken** VI.530; *pr. subj. sg.* **walke** II.784; *imp. sg.* **walke** III.2087; *imp. pl.* **walketh** VIII.1207; *1 & 3 pt. sg.* **walked** I.3458, VI.722; *pt. pl.* **walked** III.564; *pt. subj. sg.* **walked** VI.722; *prp.* **walkynge** II.878, VII.3192; *pp.* **walked** I.2368, **was go walked** walked away, gone III.1778; *vbl. n.* **walkyng(e)** roaming III.397, V.408. MED walken *v.*(1), walkinge *ger.*

walwe *v. 1 pr. sg.* wallow, writhe III.1102; *3 pr. sg.* **walweth** III.1085; *pr. pl.* **walwe** I.4278; *prp.* **walwynge** surging, tossing about I.3616. MED walwen *v.*

wan won *see* **wynne(n).**

wan *adj.* (1) wan, sickly I.3828, *etc.*, (2) dark I.2456. MED wan *adj.*

wanhope *n.* despair I.1249, X.693. MED wanhope *n.*

wante *v.* be lacking, absent X.514; *3 pr. sg.* **wanteth** is lacking VII.1048, (*impers.*) **hym wanteth** he lacks VII.1080; *pr. subj. sg.* **wante** VII.1026; *3 pt. sg.* (*impers.*) **hym wanted** he lacked VII.1046; *vbl. n.* **wantynge** lack I.2665, VIII.100. MED wanten *v.*, wantinge *ger.*

wantownesse *n.* lasciviousness II.31; affectation I.264. MED wantouness *n.*

war *adj.* (1) aware I.157, I.896; (2) **(be) w.** beware, take care I.1218, VII.439; **be w. by** be warned by (the example of) III.180, VII.2185; (3) prudent, discreet I.309, I.3604. MED war(e *adj.*

war(e) *imp. sg.* and *pl.* beware, take notice of VII.2956; **w. that** take notice of what III.1903; **w. fro(m)** beware of III.1994, X.797; (*reflx.*) **w. him** let him beware of I.662; **w. you** look out VI.905, VII.699. MED waren *v.*(1)

wardeyn *n.* (1) master (of a college) I.3999, I.4006; (2) *pl.* **wardeyns** guardians III.1216. MED wardein *n.*

ware *n.* goods, merchandise III.522, VII.56. MED ware *n.*(2)

warisshe, warice *v.* (1) (*tr.*) cure, treat VI.906, VII.1017; (2) (*intr.*) recover VII.982; *pp.* **warisshed** V.856; *vbl. n.* **warisshynge** cure VII.1015. MED warishen *v.*, warishinge *ger.*

warne *v. 1 pr. sg.* warn, command to take heed I.3583; announce, inform VII.1462; *3 pt. sg.* **warned** VII.3146; *prp.* **warnynge** foretelling VII.3126; *pp.* **(y)warned** warned I.3535, VII.3232; *vbl. n.* **warning** information VIII.593. MED warnen *v.*, warninge *ger.*(1)

warnestoore *v.* fortify, garrison VII.1297, VII.1333; *vbl. n.* **warnestooryng** fortification VII.1335. MED warnestoren *v.*, warnestoringe *ger.*

wasshe *v.* wash, cleanse II.356, VII.2756; *imp. sg.* **wassh** VI.356; *3 pt. sg.* **wessh** I.2283, II.453; *pp.* **wasshe(n)** I.3311, VI.353. MED washen *v.*

wast *n.* wastefulness III.500, X.813. MED wast *n.*

waste(n) *v.* (1) (*tr.*) waste I.4416, X.848; (2) (*intr.*) waste away I.3023, II.20; *3 pr. sg.* **wasteth** III.2235; *pr. pl.* **wasten** VIII.1422; *pp.* **wasted** decayed I.3020, **wasted** III.1720; (as *adj.*) **waste** devastated I.1331; *vbl. n.* **wastynge** waste VII.1392. MED wasten *v.*, wastinge *ger.*

water *n.* water I.400; one of the four elements I.1246; *gen.* **watres** VIII.805; *pl.* **watres** VIII.853. MED water *n.*

wawe *n.* wave II.508, X.363; *pl.* **wawes** I.1958. MED wau *n.*

wax, waxe(n) grow *see* **wexe(n).**

wedde(n) *v.* wed I.1832, I.3228; *1 pr. sg.* **wedde** IV.346: *pr. pl.* **wedde(n)** III.1260, X.885; *pr. subj. sg.* **wedde** IV.346; *3 pt. sg.* **wedded(e)** I.868, III.1080; *pp.* **(y)wedded** I.2351, II.712; *pp.* (as *adj.*) **wedded** I.3609, *vbl. n.* **weddyng(e)** wedding, marriage I.883, VII.2026, (as *adj.*) IV.868. MED wedden *v.*, weddinge *ger.*

weder *n.* weather II.873, III.2253. MED weder *n.*(1)

wey *adv.* **do w.** take away I.3287, put aside VIII.487. MED wei *adv.*

wey(e), way(e) *n.* (1) way, path, road I.34, I.467; **go (ryden,** *etc.*) **oure (his,** *etc.*) **w.** go (ride, *etc.*) on our (his, *etc.*) way I.856, I.3601, I.3712; (2) way, manner, means I.1291, II.217; **atte leeste w.** at least I.1121, I.3680; **by (be) no (any) w.** in no (any) way II.1084, VII.2280; (3) **furlong**

(mile) w. as much time as it takes to walk a furlong (mile) I.4199, VII.276; (4) **a (twenty) devel w.** in the name of (twenty) devil(s) I.3134, I.3713; *pl.* **weyes** ways VI.214. MED wei *n.*

weyen *v.* weigh VII.2586; *2 pr. sg.* **weyest noght** count for nothing VII.2233; *3 pr. sg.* **weyeth** considers, weighs I.1781; *3 pt. sg.* **weyed out** measured VIII.1298; *pt. pl.* **weyeden** weighed I.454. MED weien *v.*(1)

weyker weaker *see* **wayk(e).**

weylaway, weylawey *interj.* alas! I.938, I.3714. MED weilawai *interj.*

weyve(n) *v.* (1) (*tr.*) abandon, give up III.1176, VIII.276; (2) (*intr.*) (with **fro, from**) deviate IV.1483; *3 pr. sg.* **weyveth** refuses IX.178; *pr. pl.* **weyve(n)** deviate VII.1066, X.33; *pr. subj.* **weyve** refuse X.353 (*sg.*), neglect VII.1066 (*pl.*); *pp.* **weyved** banished, turned away II.308. MED weiven *v.*(2)

wel, weel, well *adj.* (with **ben, seem**) well I.2109, II.308. MED wel *adj.*

wel, weel(e), well *adv.* well I.29, X.711; (as *intens.* of *adj.*) very much I.256, I.614; (as *intens.* of *adv.*) very I.1254, I.1330; (with *num.*) fully, a good I.24. MED wel *adv.*

welde, weelde *v.* control, handle VII.2262; wield (limbs), move with ease III.1947; *3 pt. sg.* **weelded** ruled VII.2665, **welte** VII.2010; *vbl. n.* **weeldynge** control VII.1610. MED welden *v.*, weldinge *ger.*

wele *n.* happiness, prosperity I.895, I.1272. MED wele *n.*(1)

well(e) *n.* (1) well, spring, source I.1533, I.2283; (2) source I.3037. MED welle *n.*

welte ruled *see* **welde.**

wenche *n.* girl, young woman (of low birth) I.3254, I.3973; servant girl I.3631; mistress, concubine VI.453; *pl.* **wenches** III.393. MED wench *n.*

wend, wende(n) supposed *see* **wene.**

wende(n) *v.* go, travel I.16, I.21; leave, depart II.253, III.915; pass away I.3025; *1 pr. sg.* **wende** IV.307; *3 pr. sg.* **wendeth** III.918; *pr. pl.* **wende** VI.927; *pr. subj. sg.* **wende** VII.3081; *1 & 3 pt. sg.* **wente** I.78, III.544; *2 pt. sg.* (with *pro.*) **wentestow** I.3486; *pt. pl.* **wente(n)** I.999, I.2148; *pp.* **went** I.3665. MED wenden *v.*

wene, weene *v.* suppose, think III.786, expect I.4320; *1 pr. sg.* **wene**; IV.1174; *2 pr. sg.* (with *pro.*) **wenestow** III.311; *3 pr. sg.* **weneth** IV.2408; *pr. pl.* **wene(n)** IV.1280, consider themselves I.1804; *pr. subj. sg.* **wene** VII.1148; *3 pt. sg.* **wende** I.1269, I.3474; *pt. pl.* **wende(n)** I.3994, IV.440; *3 pt. subj. sg.* **wende** would have thought VI.782; *pt. subj. pl.* **wenden** should think I.3962; *prp.* **wenynge** VII.2590; *pp.* **wend** IV.691. MED wenen *v.*(2)

went(e) *see* **wende(n).**

wepe(n) *v.* weep I.230, I.144; *1 pr. sg.* **wepe** I.931; *3 pr. sg.* **wepeth** I.1221; *pr. pl.* **wepen** II.529; *pr. subj. sg.* **wepe** II.294; *imp. sg.* **weep** I.2470; *1 & 3 pt. sg.* **weep** I.2345, III.588, **wepte** I.148, III.592; *pt. pl.* **wepen** II.820, **wepten** VIII.415; *prp.* **wepyng(e)** II.768, II.834; *pp.* **wopen** V.523, **wept** IV.1544; *vbl. n.* **weping(e)** weeping I.231, I.2831. MED wepen *v.*, weping *ger.*

wepen(e), wepne *n.* weapon(s) I.1591, I.1601. MED wepen *n.*

were *v.* wear IV.886, V.147; *2 pr. sg.* (with *pro.*) **werestow** VII.1949; *3 pr. sg.* **wereth** III.1018; *pr. pl.* **were** I.2948; *pt. sg.* **wered(e)** I.75, I.1388; *pp.* **wered** I.4303; *vbl. n.* **werynge** wearing X.1052. MED weren *v.*(2), weringe *ger.*

wery *adj.* I.3643, I.4107; (with *inf.*) tired of (doing something) II.1071, IV.1291; (with *pp.*) tired out by (doing something) II.596. MED weri *adj.*

werk(e) *n.* (1) work, task I.3311, II.928; deed I.479, IV.28; (2) work, creation V.879; *pl.* **werkes** I.3308, **werkis** II.478; *gen. pl.* **werkes** deeds', labors' VII.2096. MED werk *n.*

werke(n), werche(n), wirche(n) *v.* work, labor I.3430, IV.1661; do, act I.779, I.3528; cause I.2072; be effective I.2759; **do w.** make VIII.545; *3 pr. sg.* **werketh** VII.1196; *pr. pl.* **werke(n)** VII.2938, VIII.1139, **werkes** *(Nth.)* I.4030; *pr. subj. sg.* **werke** IV.1357; *imp. sg.* **werk(e)** VII.1003, VII.1170, **wirk** IV.1485; *imp. pl.* **werketh** IV.504; *3 pt. sg.* **wroghte** I.497, **wroughte** V.1202; *2 pt. sg.* **wroghtest** II.856, (with *pro.*) **wroghtestow** VII.2393; *pt. pl.* **wroghten** IV.1692; *pp.* **(y)wroght** I.196, I.367; *vbl. n.* **wirkyng(e)** III.698, X.250, **werkyng(e)** work VIII.116; deed IX.210; *pl.* **werkynges** acts X.82. MED werken *v.*, werkinge *ger.*

werre *n.* war I.47, I.1287; *pl.* **werres** VII.1650. MED werre *n.*(1)

werreye(n) *v.* wage war (on) I.1484, I.1544; *3 pr. sg.* **werreyeth** X.401; *3 pt. sg.* **werreyed** V.10. MED werreien *v.*

wers(e), wors(e) *comp. adj.* and *adv.* worse I.3174, I.3733. MED werse *adj.*

wessh washed *see* **wasshe.**

wete, weete *adj.* wet I.1280, I.4107; (as *n.*) wetness, damp weather VIII.1187. MED wet *adj.*

wette *v. 3 pt. sg.* wet, dampened I.129; *pp.* **ywet** I.4155. MED weten *v.*

wex *n.* wax IV.1430, VIII.1268. MED wax *n.*(1)

wexe(n), waxe *v.* grow, increase III.28, VI.23; become VIII.837; *1 pr. sg.* **wexe** VIII.1377; *3 pr. sg.* **wexeth** I.3024; *pr. pl.* **wexe(n)** IV.998, VIII.1095; *pr. subj. sg.* **wexe** VII.1559; *3 pt. sg.* **wex** I.1362, **weex** II.563, **wax** I.4234; *pt. pl.* **wax** III.636; *prp.* **wexyng** growing I.2078; *pp.* **(y)woxen** IV.1462, IV.1762; **woxe** X.1021. MED waxen *v.*(1)

whan(ne), when(ne) *adv.* and *conj.* (1) when I.135; **w. that** when I.1; **w. so that** whensoever V.1005; **w. that evere** whenever III.45; (2) *(interr.)* when VI.733. MED whan *adv. & conj.*

what *adj.* (1) whatever IV.10, IV.165; (2) *(interr.)* what I.905, I.1029; (3) *(rel.)* **w. thyng** what IV.1059. MED what *adj.*

what *adv.* (as *conj.*) **w. for** because of I.1453, V.54; **w. so** however much IV.1389. MED what *adv.*

what *interj.* what! indeed! I.854, I.3366. MED what *interj.*

what *pro.* (1) *(interr.)* what I.3370; **w. thogh** what (does it matter) if IV.2293, VII.2813; why III.167, III.2072; (2) *(indef.)* **w. so** whatever I.3843, IV.306; (3) *(rel.)* what, that which III.1735, IV.1460. MED what *pro.*

wheither *conj.* (1) whether I.1857; **w. that** whether I.570; **w. so** whether VIII.2619; (2) *(interr.* introducing a question with alternative answers) (tell me) whether I.1125, III.2069. Cf. **wher(e).** MED whether *conj.*

wheither *pro.* which (of two) III.1227, III.1234; whichever I.1856. MED whether *pro.*

whelp *n.* pup I.257; cub I.2627; *pl.* **whelpes** VIII.60. MED whelp *n.*

whennes *adv.* whence VI.355, VIII.432. MED whennes *adv.*

wher(e), wheer *adv.* and *conj.* (1) *(interr.)* where, in what place I.3486; (introducing a question with alternative answers) whether, VII.3131; **w. so** whether VIII.153; (2) *(conj.)* where I.421, I.1351; wherever III.318; **w. as** where I.1113, II.647; **w. that** where I.897; wherever I.1207, VIII.733; (3) *(abs.)* where II.611. Cf. **wheither.** MED wher *adv. & conj.*

wherby *adv.* by which I.2266. MED wher-bi *adv.*

wherefor(e) *adv.* why I.1568; for which reason II.1049, VII.121. MED wher-for *adv.*

wherof, whereof *adv.* from what III.72; for which VIII.1148; for what IX.339. MED wher-of *adv.*

wher-so, wherso, whereso *adv.* wherever VII.2638, IX.361. MED wher-so *adv.*

wherto *adv.* why VII.1612, VIII.640. MED wher-to *adv.*

wherwith *adv.* with which III.1718, X.468; *(interr.)* with what III.131; (as *pro.*) the wherewithal I.302. MED wherwith *adv.*

whete *n.* wheat I.3988, I.3991. MED whete *n.*

why *see* **wy** *interj.*

why *adv.* (1) why I.1083, etc.; **w. so** VII.926; **w. that** why I.717, I.911; **cause w.** the reason (for this) I.4144; (2) *(interr.)* why I.1083. MED whi *adv.*

which(e) *interr.* which V.1622; (in exclamations) what IV.2421; **w. a** what a I.2675, I.3611.

which(e) *rel.* (1) *(pro.)* which, who III.1092, III.2029; **w. that** which III.2156, VII.2006; who III.537, IV.780; *(indef.)* whichever I.796; (2) *(adj.)* which I.2972, III.676; what I.40, VI.279. MED which *adj.,* which *pro.*

while) *n.* time I.3299; **a w.** a short time I.1437, VIII.1184; **alas (weylawey) the w.** alas the time (it happened) IV.251; **any w.** for any time II.753; in any way IX.195; **the mene (meen) w.** the meantime II.546, III.1445; *pl.* **in the meene whiles** meantime II.668; (as *adv.*) **the whiles** while VI.439; *conj.* while I.35, I.1295; **w. that** while I.397. MED whil *n.*

whiles, whils *conj.* while VIII.1137, VIII.1188. MED whiles *conj.*

whilom *adv.* once, formerly I.795, I.859. MED whilom *adv.*

whit(e) *adj.* (1) white I.976, I.238; (as *n.*) white wine VI.526; (2) innocent, pure VIII.115; **never so w.** ever so purely II.355; *comp.* **whitter** VII.2863. MED whit *adj.*

who *pro.* (1) *(interr.)* who I.831; (2) *(indef.)* he who, whoever, I.4271; **w. that** who V.771; **as w. seith** as if to say VII.1084; *gen.* **whos** whose II.642; *dat.* and *acc.* **whom** whom I.501; **whom that** whom I.4334, II.665; *pro. nom.* **whoso** whoever, anyone I.644, I.3045 MED who *pro.*

wy, why *interj.* why, indeed I.3285, III.445. MED whi *interj.*

wyd(e) *adj.* wide, roomy I.28, I.93. MED wid *adj.*

wyde *adv.* widely III.1524, IV.722; **wyde-where** far and wide II.136. MED wide *adv.*

wydwe, widewe *n.* widow I.253, I.1171; *gen.* **wydwes** III.1581; *pl.* **wydwes** IV.1423. MED widwe *n.*

wyf(e) *n.* woman III.998; wife I.445, I.932; *gen.* **wyves** IV.599; *pl.* **wyves** I.234, **wyvys** IV.1651. MED wif *n.*

wyfhod *n.* womanliness IV.699; marriage III.149; fidelity as a wife II.76. MED wifhod *n.*

wyfly *adj.* womanly, having the skills or qualities proper to a woman IV.429, IV.919. MED wifli *adj.*

wyflees *adj.* without a wife, unmarried IV.1236, IV.1248. MED wifles *adj.*

wight *n.* (1) creature, person, being I.71, I.537; **no w.** no one I.280, V.1393; (2) **a litel w.** a little (while or bit) I.4283; *pl.* **wightes** I.3479. MED wight *n.*

wighte, weighte *n.* weight I.2145, VII.1226. MED weght *n.*(1)

wyke, wowke *n.* week I.1539, V.1295; *pl.* **wykes** I.1850. MED weke *n.*

wyket *n.* wicket gate, door IV.2118, IV.2152. MED wiket *n.*

wykke *adj.* wicked, evil I.1087, I.1580; miserable II.118. MED wikke *adj.*

wikked(e) *adj.* wicked, evil I.3484, II.404. MED wikked *adj.*

wikkedly *adv.* wickedly I.1735, IV.723. MED wikkedli *adv.*

wikkednesse *adj.* wickedness, evil III.695, III.715; crime, wicked deed II.623; *pl.* **wikkednesses** evil, evil deeds X.275. MED wikkednesse *n.*

wil(le) *n.* will, desire I.1104, I.1317; *gen.* **willes** V.568. MED wille *n.*

wilfully *adv.* voluntarily VI.441, VII.1422; willfully VII.3096; obstinately X.586. MED wilfulli *adv.*

wilfulnesse *n.* obstinacy I.3057; desire VII.1382. MED wilfulnesse *n.*

wille *v.* (1) wish, desire IV.721; (2) *(fut. aux.)* will I.42, I.4029; *1 pr. sg.* **wil** I.4178, **wol** I.3976; *2 pr. sg.* **wolt** I.1595, (with *pro.*) **woltow, wiltow** I.1156, VIII.307; *3 pr. sg.* **wil** II.857, **will** I.4029, **wol(e)** I.945, I.1042; *pr. pl.* **wil** I.4133, **wol** I.816, **wole** II.30, X.901, **wollen** X.548; *pr. subj. sg.* **wole** I.805; *1 & 3 pt. sg.* **wolde** I.276, I.766; *2 pt. sg.* **woldest** I.1142; (with *pro.*) **woldestow** I.2835; *pt. pl.* **wolde(n)** I.27, I.2714; *pt. subj. sg.* **wolde** I.766, III.444, **wolde she were** would that she were II.161, **wolde God** would that God (would grant) III.37, III.1103, **wolde I hadde** I wish I had III.1633, VI.952; *pt. subj. pl.* **wolde** would like to VII.1234; *pp.* **wold** desired VII.1000, **woold** willed VII.1425; *vbl. n.* **willynge** will, desire IV.319. MED willen *v.*, willinge *ger.*

wilne(n) *v.* desire, wish I.2114, X.517; *2 pr. sg.* **wilnest** I.1609; *3 pr. sg.* **wilneth** I.2564. MED wilnen *v.*

wynde *v.* wind, twist about VIII.980; clasp, wrap VIII.42; *1 pr. sg.* **wynde** III.1102; *ppl.* **wounde** I.3953; *vbl. n.* **wyndynge** folding X.417. MED winden *v.*(1), windinge *ger.*(1)

wynke *v.* close (both) one's eyes V.348, VII.3306; *3 pr. sg.* **wynketh** VII.3431. MED winken *v.*

wynne(n) *v.* win I.891, I.1486; earn III.1453, profit I.427; **w. on** get the better of I.594; *1 pr. sg.* **wynne** III.1432; *3 pr. sg.* **wynneth** X.637; *pr. subj. sg.* **wynne** I.1617 *(sg.)*; *1 & 3 pt. pl.* **wan** III.1477, V.664; *pt. pl.* **wan** V.1401; *pp.* **ywonne** III.2293, **wonne(n)** I.51, I.3381; *vbl. n.* **wynnyng** profit I.275; *pl.* **wynnynges** II.127. MED winnen *v.*, winninge *ger.*(1)

wirche(n) work *see* **werke(n)**.

wys *adv.* (in asseverations with **so, as**) surely, truly I.2786, V.1470. MED wis *adv.*

wys(e) *adj.* wise, prudent I.68, I.309; (as *n.*) wise ones I.3958; **make it w.** deliberate on it, raise difficulties I.785; *comp.* **wyser** IV.1569; *super.* **wisest(e)** I.4054, VIII.967. MED wise *adj.*

wyse *n.* manner, way I.1913, I.2370; **in every, alle (maner) w.** in every way, completely II.1098, IV.605; **in no (manner) w.** by no means, not at all III.1898, VIII.714; (as *adv.*) **double w.** doubly I.1338. MED wise *n.*(2)

wisly, wisely *adv.* certainly, surely I.4162, V.789; (in asservations with **as, so, also**) surely, truly I.1863, IV.822, V.469. MED wisli *adv.*

wist(e) knew *see* **wite(n)** *v.*

wit *n.* (1) mind II.609, X.453; intelligence, judgment III.2291, V.674; (2) **(as) to my w.** as I understand III.41, V.875; opinion V.203; (3) knowledge, wisdom I.3901, II.10, II.888; *pl.* **fyve wittes** the five senses VII.1424. MED wit *n.*

wite(n) *v.* know I.3555, IV.1740; **w. at** learn from VIII.621; *1 & 3 pr. sg.* **woot** I.389, I.886; *2 pr. sg.* **woost** I.1156, (with *pro.*) **wostow** I.1163; *pr. pl.* **wite(n)** I.1260, VIII.906, VIII.906; *2 pr. pl.* **woot** I.740; *1 & 3 pt. sg.* **wiste** I.224, III.553; *pt. pl.* **wiste(n)** VI.266; *pt. subj. sg.* **wiste if** he knew VI.513; *pp.* **wist** II.1072; *vbl. n.* **wityng** knowledge I.1611. MED witen *v.*(1), wittinge *ger.*(1)

wyte(n) *v.* blame III.806, X.1016; *1 pr. sg.* **wyte** VII.2670; *2 pr. sg.* **wytest** accuse II.108; *imp. pl.* **wyte** I.3140. MED witen *v.*(3)

with *prep.* (1) with I.10, *etc.*; **w. that word** thereupon, immediately I.856, I.1399; (2) by (agency) I.76, I.511; because of I.107; (3) concerning, with respect to IV.1499, VII.114; **w. a ren** at a run I.4079. MED with *prep.*

withal(le), with alle *adv.* withal, indeed I.127, I.283; moreover, also III.156, V.687. MED with-al *adv.*

withdrawe(n) *v.* withdraw X.143; withhold III.617, X.802; *3 pr. sg.* **withdraweth** X.655; *pr. pl.* **withdrawen** X.449; *pr. subj. sg.* **withdrawe** X.377. *imp. pl.* **withdraweth** VIII.1423; *vbl. n.* **withdrawynge** withholding X.568. MED withdrauen *v.*, withdrauinge *ger.*

withholde(n) *v.* (1) restrain, resist, hold back VII.1996; (2) retain, keep X.744, X.1041; *pp.* **withholde(n)** held, detained VIII.345; retained, in the service of I.511; *vbl. n.* **witholdynge** retention VII.1223. MED withholden *v.*, withholdinge *ger.*

withoute *adv.* outside I.1888; outwardly, on the outside V.1111. MED withouten *adv.*

withoute *prep.* without I.343, I.461. MED withouten *prep.*

withseye, withseyn *v.* deny, gainsay I.805, I.1140; *pr. subj. sg.* **withseye** deny, renounce VIII.447. MED withseien *v.*

withstonde(n) *v.* withstand, resist III.1659, X.733; *3 pr. sg.* **withstandeth** III.1497; *pr. subj. sg.* **withstonde** X.353; *pp.* **withstonden** X.953; *vbl. n.* **withstondynge** resisting X.455. MED withstonden *v.*, withstondinge *ger.*

wityng knowledge *see* **wite(n)** *v.*

wityngly *adv.* knowingly X.401, X.579. MED wittingli *adv.*

witnesse *n.* testimony, evidence II.629, VI.169; **take to w.** offer as evidence VI.483; **take (to) w.** offer as guarantor, witness III.233, IV.821.

witnessen *v.* (1) *(tr.)* testify to, provide evidence of X.594; (2) *(intr.)* prove X.842, X.1036; *3 pr. sg.* **witnesseth** VII.1459; *pr. pl.* **witnessen** VIII.1067; *imp. pl.* **witnesse on** take the evidence of, consider as a witness III.951, III.1491; *vbl. n.* **witnessyng** testimony VI.194. MED witnessen *v.*, witnessinge *ger.*

wo(o) *adj.* woeful VII.2938; (as *adv.*) **wo begon** afflicted, in distress I.3372, II.918. MED wo *adj.*, wo *adv.*

wo *n.* woe I.900; sorrow V.1027; **me (hym,** *etc.***) is wo** woe to me (him, *etc.*), I (*etc.*) regret VII.10. MED wo *n.*

wood *adj.* (1) mad, crazy I.184, I.582; foolish VIII.450; (2) angry III.1327, III.1666. MED wod *adj.*

wode *n.* wood I.1522, I.1618; *gen.* **wodes** VII.3411; *pl.* **wodes** I.2297. MED wode *n.*

woodnesse *n.* madness I.2011, I.3452. MED wodnesse *n.*

woful *adj.* woeful I.1063, II.261. *comp.* **wofuller** I.1340. MED woful *adj.*

wook woke *see* **wake(n).**

wol(e), wole(n), wollen will *see* **wille.**

wolde- would *see* **wille.**

wombe *n.* belly I.4290, VI.522; womb IV.877, VII.2484. MED wombe *n.*

wommanhede, woomanheede *n.* femininity, womanliness, having the qualities proper to a woman I.1748, II.851. MED wommanhede *n.*

wonder *adj.* wonderful, amazing I.2073, VII.3078. MED wonder *adj.*

wonder *adv.* wonderfully, amazingly I.483, I.1654. MED wonder *adv.*

wonder, wondir *n.* marvel, miracle, object or cause of wonder I.502, II.408; *pl.* **wondres** miracles II.182. MED wonder *n.*

wonderly *adv.* wondrously, amazingly I.84, VII.1793. MED wonderli *adv.*

wondre(n) *v.* wonder, be amazed IV.335, V.1514; *1 pr. sg.* **wondre** VIII.246; *3 pr. sg.* **wondreth** IV.669; *pr. pl.* **wondren** V.258; *3 pt. sg.* **wondred** I.1445; *pt. pl.* **wondred** V.225, **wondreden** V.307; *prp.* **wonderynge upon** wondering about IV.358; *pp.* **wondred** V.236; *vbl.n.* **wondryng** wondering, amazement V.305. MED wondren *v.*, wondringe *ger.*

wone *n.* custom, wont, habit I.335, I.1040. MED wone *n.*

wone *v.* dwell VIII.38, VIII.332; *3 pr. sg.* **woneth** III.1573; *3 pt. sg.* **woned** III.2163; *pt. pl.* **woneden** I.2927; *prp.* **wonynge** I.388; *pp.* **woned** dwelt VII.3216 (see **wont**); *vbl. n.* **wonyng** dwelling I.606. MED wonen *v.*(1), woninge *ger.*(1)

wonne(n), ywonne won *see* **wynne(n).**

wont, woned *pp.* accustomed I.1195, I.1557, IV.339. MED wonen *v.*(1)

word(e) *n.* word I.304, I.733; decree I.1109, I.2350; **at o w.** in a word, briefly VIII.1360; **with that w.** thereupon I.856, I.948; *pl.* **wordes** I.313, **woordes** VII.1016; **in w. fewe** briefly VIII.618; **withoute(n) wordes mo** immediately I.3408, I.3650. MED word *n.*

world *n.* world I.187, II.157; **new w.** modern times I.176; **what maner w.** what sort of carrying on III.2171; *gen.* (descriptive) **worldes** worldly, of this world VII.3200. MED world *n.*

worship(e) *n.* worship I.1904, VII.654; honor V.571; renown V.811. MED worshipe *n.*

worshipe(n) *v.* worship I.2251; honor IV.166. MED worshipen *v.*

worshipful *adj.* honorable I.1435, IV.401. MED worshipful *adj.*

worst(e), wurst *super. adj.* worst IV.83, VII.161; (as *n.*) I.1614, VI.776. MED werste *adj.*, werste *n.*

worth *adj.* worth, equivalent in value to I.182, III.572; worthy VII.1515, VII.1707; worthwhile I.785. MED worth *adj.*

worthy *adj.* (1) respectable, having worth or standing I.43, I.64; distinguished, excellent VII.3243; **w. of his hond** brave in battle II.579; (2) (with *inf.*) deserving I.2794, II.457; able I.579, I.2380; *super.* **worthieste** IV.1131. MED worthi *adj.*

worthily *adv.* honorably I.2737; deservedly IV.1022; reverently X.385. MED worthili *adv.*

worthinesse *n.* worthiness, excellence, honor I.50, I.2592. MED worthinesse *n.*

woost, wostow know *see* **wite(n).**

woot knew *see* **wite(n)** *v.*

woxe(n), ywoxen grew *see* **wexe(n).**

wrappe *v.* wrap IV.583, V.636; cover, conceal V.507; *pr. pl.* **wrappen** wrap, wallow in X.586; *pp.* **wrapped** wrapped V.1356; *vbl. n.* **wrappynge** covering X.423. MED wrappen *v.*, wrappinge *ger.*

wratthe *n.* wrath VII.1124, X.168. MED wrath *n.*

wratthe(n) *v.* anger, make angry IX.80; *(reflx.)* become angry X.1013; *pr. pl.* **wratthe** X.110; *pp.* **wrathed** X.132. MED wratthen *v.*

wrecche *adj.* wretched V.1020, X.214. MED wrecche *adj.*

wrecche *n.* (1) wretch, miserable person I.931, III.1609; (2) exile VIII.58; *pl.* **wrecches** I.1717. MED wrecch *n.*

wrecched *adj.* wretched I.921, I.950. MED wrecched *adj.*

wrecchedly *adv.* wretchedly, miserably III.2054, VII.1977. MED wrecchedli *adv.*

wrecchednesse *n.* wretchedness, misery I.3897, II.941. MED wrecchednesse *n.*

wreche *n.* vengeance II.679; punishment VII.2603. MED wrech *n.*

wreke(n) *v.* avenge I.961, VII.1036; *(reflx.)* revenge oneself VI.857, VII.1020; *pr. pl.* **wreke** V.454; *imp. sg.* **wrek** VII.1905; *pp.* **wreke(n)** III.809, V.784. MED wreken *v.*

wrynge *v.* *(tr.)* squeeze, wring VII.776; pinch III.492; *(intr.)* wring (one's hands) IV.1212; *3 pr. sg.* **wryngeth** pinches IV.1553; *3 pt. sg.* **wrong** pinched III.492; **wroong** II.606. MED wringen *v.*

write(n) *v.* write I.96, II.87; *1 pr. sg.* **write** III.1752; *2 pr. sg.* **writest** IV.1733; *3 pr. sg.* **writeth** reveals I.3869, *(contr.)* **writ** III.709; *pt. pl.* **write(n)** IV.2304, V.551; *pr. subj. pl.* may write **writen** I.2814; *3 pt. sg.* **wroot** II.725, III.1743; *pt. pl.* **writen** V.233; *pt. subj. sg.* **write** were to write VII.2653; *pp.* **(y)writen** I.2350, II.191, **ywrite** VII.3442, **written** II.666; *vbl. n.* **writyng(e)** IV.2104, X.1052. MED writen *v.*, writinge *ger.*

wroght-, wrought- *see* **werke(n).**

wrong, wroong wrung *see* **wrynge.**

wroth(e), wrooth *adj.* angry I.451, III.125. MED wroth *adj.*

Y (See also I)

y- Past participles with this prefix are ordinarily alphabetized under the root syllable; e.g., **yput** is under **putte(n).** Infinitives, adjectives, and adverbs with this prefix are alphabetized under **i-.**

yaf gave *see* **yeve(n).**

yate, gate *n.* gate I.1415, X.714. MED gate *n.*(1)

yave(n) gave *see* **yeve(n).**

ye *see* **eye.**

ye 2 *pl. pro. nom.* you I.780, II.276. MED ye *pro.*

ye *adv.* yes I.3455, II.417. MED ye *adv.*

yede, yedest went *see* **go(n).**

yelde(n) *v.* pay III.130, III.1821; yield, render X.378; surrender, give up III.912, IV.843; *3 pr. sg.* **yeldeth** pays X.941;
pr. subj. sg. **God yeelde yow** may God reward you
III.1772, III.2177; *imp. sg.* **yeld** give up, hand over VI.189,
imp. pl. **yeldeth** give back VII.1292; *prp.* **yeldynge** paying,
giving VII.1804; *pp.* **yolden** given up I.3052; *vbl. n.* **yeldynge** yielding I.596. MED yelden *v.,* yelding *ger.*

yelow, yelewe *adj.* yellow I.675, I.1929. MED yelwe *adj.*

yeman *n.* yeoman, free-born servant I.101, VIII.562; free-
born man I.3270; official III.1380, III.1387; *pl.* **yemen**
free-born servants I.2509. MED yeman *n.*

yer(e), yeer(e) *n.* year I.1203, I.1458; as *pl.* with *num.* I.82,
IV.1248; *pl.* **yeres** I.1521, **yeris** I.3869, **yeeres** I.2828,
yeeris V.1275. MED yer *n.*

yerd, yeerd *n.* yard, garden III.1798, V.1251; pen VII.2847.
MED yerd *n.*

yerde *n.* (1) stick, switch (for punishment) I.149, X.670; staff
(of authority) I.1387; **under the (yowre) y.** subject to
(your) authority IV.22, VII.97; (2) yard (measure) I.1050;
pl. **yerdes** switches X.1055. MED yerde *n.*

yeve(n), yive(n), gyve *v.* give I.223, I.225, III.78; *1 pr. sg.*
yeve IV.1527; *2 pr. sg.* **yevest** I.1284; *3 pr. sg.* **yeveth**
I.1253; *pr. pl.* **yeven** VII.1113; *pr. subj. sg.* **yeve** I.4335;
imp. sg. **yif** I.2260, **yeve** VII.1060; *imp. pl.* **yeveth**
VII.1754; *1 & 3 pt. sg.* **yaf** I.177, III.599, **yeve** X.946; *pt.
pl.* **yaf** V.302; **yave(n)** VII.1789, VIII.415; *pp.* **yeve(n)**
IV.758, VII.407; **yive(n)** III.401, VI.779; *vbl. n.* **yevynge**
giving, gift X.567. MED yeven *v.,* yevinge *ger.*

yif give *see* **yeve(n).**

yif, if *conj.* if I.3797, IX.173; **but yif** unless I.656; **yif that** if
I.763. MED if *conj.*

yifte *n.* gift III.39, IV.1311; *pl.* **yiftes** I.2198. MED yifte *n.*

yis *adv.* yes, yes indeed (more emphatic than **ye**) I.3369,
I.3526. MED yis *adv.*

yit, yet *adv.* yet I.70, V.4361. MED yet *adv.*

yive(n) give *see* **yeve(n).**

yolden yielded *see* **yelde(n).**

yond *adv.* yonder I.1099, III.1798. MED yond *adv.*

yong(e) *adj.* young I.7, I.79; *super.* **yongest(e)** IV.1559, V.33.
MED yong *adj.*

yore, yoore *adv.* long ago, formerly, II.174, II.1167; **(full) y.
ago(n)** long ago I.1813, I.1941; before, formerly II.174,
II.984; for a long time I.4230, II.272; **of tyme y.** for a long
time V.963. MED yor *adv.*

Index to Proper Names
in the Tales

THIS INDEX contains only brief identifications; in most cases full particulars are in the notes, ordinarily the note to the first line in which the name appears. The index includes names of persons, places, peoples, literary works, characters in literature and mythology, the names of stars and constellations, and a few adjectives related to proper nouns (e.g., English); most allegorical personifications and the names of days and months are not listed here (they are included in the main glossary).

Only *The Canterbury Tales* are cited in this index, though references to other works by Chaucer are given when when they have explanatory value.

The index lists all appearances of each form, except for names that appear more than three or four times in a single work (the individual prologues and tales are considered separate works); in such cases ordinarily only the first two references are listed, followed by "etc." For very high frequency names—**God** and **Crist**—only the first two uses in the *Tales* are listed. Full listings are provided in the *Glossarial Concordance to the Riverside Chaucer* and (on-line) in The Glossarial Database of Middle English.

The abbreviations used are the same as those in the Glossary, with the addition of *dim.* for "diminutive." As in the Glossary, vocalic *y* is alphabetized as *i*.

The abbreviations for Chaucer's works are those listed on p. 321.

A

Aaron Moses's brother (Ex. 28:1–4): SumT III.1894.
Abigayl wife of Nabal (1 Sam. 25): MerT IV.1369, Mel VII.1100.
Abraham the patriarch (Gen. 11.27ff.): WBPro III.55.
Absolon the parish clerk in MilT: MilT I.3313, MilT I.3339, etc.
Absolonem son of King David (2 Sam. 13–19.8): ParsT X.639.
Acheloys a river god: *gen.* MkT VII.2106.
Achilles the Greek hero of the Trojan War: MLT II.198, SqT V.239, NPT VII.3148.
Achitofel David's evil counselor (2 Sam. 15.31ff.): ParsT X.639.
Adam first man: WBPro III.696, MerT IV.1325, PardT

VI.505, Mel VII.1103, MkT VII.2007, NPT VII.3258; ParsT X.323, etc.
Adoon Adonis, loved by Venus: KnT I.2224.
Adriane Ariadne, daughter of King Minos (see LGW 1886–2227): IntMLT II.67.
Aesculapius *see* **Esculapius**.
Affrike Africa, the continent: NPT VII.3124.
Ayash *see* **Lyeys**.
Alayn *see* **Aleyn**.
Albon, daun a name the Host uses for the Monk: ProMkT VII.1930.
Alcebiades Alicibiades, the Greek general (d. 404 B.C.): FranT V.1439.
Alceste Alcestis, wife of Admetus; heroine of the Prologue of LGW (see LGW F 511–15, Tr 5.1527–33): IntMLT II.75; FranT V.1442.
Alcione Alcyone (halcyon), wife of Ceyx (see BD 63–220): IntMLT II.57.
Alexander, Alexandria *see* **Alisaundre**.
Aldiran a star: SqT V.265.
Aleyn, Alayn one of the clerks in RvT: RvT I.4013, RvT I.4016, etc.
Alfonce *see* **Peter Alfonce**.
Algarsyf son of Cambyuskan in SqT: SqT V.30, SqT V.663.
Algezir Algeciras in Spain: GP I.57.
Alhazen *see* **Alocen**.
Ali *see* **Haly**.
Alys (1) the Wife of Bath: WBPro III.320 (*see* **Alisoun**, sense (2); (2) the Wife of Bath's "gossip": WBPro III.548.
Alisaundre Alexandria, in Egypt: GP I.51; CYT VIII.975.
Alisaundre, Alisandre Alexander the Great (356–323 B.C.) of Macedon (see MkT VII.2631–70): MkT VII.2392, MkT VII.2631, MkT VII.2658; MancT IX.226.
Alisoun, Alison (1) the wife in the MilT: MilT I.3366, MilT I.3401, etc.; (2) the Wife of Bath: WBPro III.804. (3) The Wife of Bath's "gossip": WBPro III.530. *see* **Alys**.
Alla, Alle king of Northumbria in MLT: MLT II.578, MLT II.604, etc.
Almache, Almachius the prefect in SNT: SNT VIII.362, SNT VIII.405, etc.
Almageste the *Almagest* of Ptolemy: MilT I.3208; WBPro III.183, WBPro III.325. *see* **Ptholome(e)**.

Alnath   a star: FranT V.1281.

Alocen   Alhazen (c. 965–1039), writer on optics: SqT V.232.

Alphonce   *see* **Peter Alfonce**.

Amazones   the Amazons: KnT I.880.

Ambrose, Seint   St. Ambrose (c. A.D. 340–97): SNT VIII.271, ParsT X.84.

Amphiorax   Amphiaraus, an Argive hero and seer: WBPro III.741.

Amphioun   Amphion, King of Thebes and a famous harper: KnT I.1546; MerT IV.1716; MancT IX.116.

Andromacha   Andromache, wife of Hector: NPT VII.3141.

Angelus ad Virginem   a religious song (The Angel to Mary): MilT I.3216.

Anne   St. Anne, mother of the Virgin Mary: MLT II.641; FrT III.1613; SNPro VIII.70.

Anselm, Seint   St. Anselm (1033–1109): ParsT X.169.

Antecrist   the Antichrist: ParsT X.788.

Antheus   Anteus, a giant: MkT VII.2108.

Anthiochus   Antiochus Epiphanes, king of Syria (reigned 176–164 B.C. (see MkT VII.2575–2630): MkT VII.2575.

Antiochus   king of Antioch in the story of Appolonius of Tyre: IntMLT II.82.

Antonius   Marc Anthony (c. 82–30 B.C.), lover of Cleopatra (see LGW 580–705): KnT I.2032.

Antony, Seint   St. Anthony of Egypt (born c. A.D. 250): ParsT X.427.

Apelles   *see* **Appelles**.

Apennyn   the Apennines, a mountain range in Italy: ClPro IV.45.

Apia   *see* **Via Apia**.

Apius   the false judge in PhyT: PhyT VI.154, PhyT VI.178, etc.

Apocalipse   The Book of Revelation: ParsT X.136.

Appelles, Apelles   legendary sculptor: WBPro III.499; PhyT VI.16.

Appollo   the classical god and ruler of the sun: SqT V.671; FranT V.1031; *see* **Phebus**.

Appollonius   hero of the story of Appolonius of Tyre: IntMLT II.81.

Arabe   Arabia: SqT V.110.

Arcite, Arcita   one of the heroes in KnT: KnT I.1013, KnT I.1080, etc. *gen.* **Arcites** KnT I.1577.

Argus   the mythical guardian of Io: KnT I.1390, WBPro III.358; MerT IV.2111.

Ariadne   *see* **Adriane**.

Aries   the first sign of the zodiac: SqT V.51; FranT V.1282. *see* **Ram**.

Aristoclides   tyrant of Orchomenos: FranT V.1387.

Aristotle   the Greek philosopher (384–322 B.C.): GP I.295; SqT V.233.

Armorik(e)   Armorica, coastal Brittany and Normandy: FranT V.729, FranT V.1061; MkT VII.2388.

Arnold of the Newe Toun   Arnaldus of Villanova (c. 1235–1314), author of an alchemical treatise: CYT VIII.1428. *see* **Rosarie**.

Arpies   the Harpies: MkT VII.2100.

Arrius   a character cited by the Wife of Bath: WBPro III.758 (see note), WBPro III.762.

Arthemesie   Artemisia, widow of Mausolus: FranT V.1451.

Arthour   legendary king of Britain: WBT III.857, WBT III.882, etc. *gen.* **Arthures** WBT II.1089.

Artoys   a region in northern France: GP I.86.

Arveragus   Dorigen's husband in FranT: FranT V.808, FranT V.814, etc.

Asye   Asia Minor: PrT VII.488.

Assuer(e), Assuerus   Ahasuerus, king of the Persians in the Book of Esther: MerT IV.1374, MerT IV.1745; Mel VII.1101.

Atalia   *see* **Satalye**.

Atthalante   Atalanta, mother of Parthenopaeus: KnT I.2070.

Atthenes   Athens: KnT I.861, KnT I.873, etc.; FranT V.1369.

Attheon   Actaeon: KnT I.2065, KnT I.2303.

Attilla   king of the Huns (reigned A.D. 433–53): PardT VI.579.

Augustinus *see* **Austyn**.

Aurelian   Lucius Domitius Aurelianus (emperor A.D. 270–75): MkT VII.2351, MkT VII.2361.

Aurelius, Aurelie   the squire in FranT: FranT V.938, FranT V.982, etc.

Austyn, Augustin, Augustyn, Augustinus   St. Augustine of Hippo (A.D. 354–430): GP I.187; ShipT VII.259; Mel VII.1617; ParsT X.97, ParsT X.630, etc.; ParsT X.754 (Latin form).

Averrois   Averroes (1126–98), Arabic physician and commentator on Aristotle: GP I.433.

Avycen   Avicenna (980–1037), Arabic author of the *Canon of Medicine*: GP I.432; PardT VI.889.

B

Babiloigne, Babilan   Babylon: IntMLT II.63; SumT III.2082; MkT VII.2149.

Bacus   Bacchus, god of wine: MerT IV.1722; PhyT VI.58; MancPro IX.99.

Bayard   common name for a horse: RvT I.4115; CYT VIII.1413.

Bailly   *see* **Herry Bailly**.

Balat   *see* **Palatye**.

Baldeswelle   Bawdeswell, in Norfolk: GP I.620.

Balthasar   Belshazzar (Daniel 5; see MkT VII.2183–246): MkT VII.2183, MkT VII.2205.

Baptist John   John the Baptist: PardT VI.491.

Barbarie   heathendom: FranT V.1452.

Barnabo Viscounte   Bernabò Visconti of Milan (d. 1385: see MkT VII.2399–406); MkT VII.2399.

Basilie   St. Basil the Great (c. A.D. 330–379): ParsT X.221.

Bathe   a city in Somersetshire: GP I.445; ClT IV.1170; MerT IV.1685.

Belial   the devil: ParsT X.897, ParsT X.898.

Belle   the Bell, a tavern in Southwark: GP I.719.

Belmarye   Morocco (Benmarin): GP I.57; KnT I.2630.

Benedight, Beneit (Seinte)   St. Benedict (c. A.D. 480–c.550): GP I.173; MilT I.3483.

Bernard   (1) Bernard Gordon, a fourteenth-century physician: GP I.434; (2) St. Bernard of Clairvaux

(c. 1090–1153): SNPro VIII.30; ParsT X.130, ParsT X.166, ParsT X.253, etc.

Berwyk probably Berwick-on-Tweed: GP I.692.

Bethulia, Bethulie a city of the Israelites: Mel VII.1099; MkT VII.2565.

Beves hero of the romance of *Bevis of Hampton*: Thop VII.899.

Bible the Bible: GP I.438; WBPro III.650, WBPro III.687; SumT III.1845; PardT VI.578, PardT VI.586; CYT VIII.857.

Bilyea Bilia, wife of Dullius (Roman general in 256 B.C.): FranT V.1455.

Blee Blean Forest: CYPro VIII.556; MancPro IX.3.

Bobbe-up-and-down Harbledown, two miles from Canterbury: MancPro IX.2 (see n.).

Boece Anicius Manlius Severinus Boethius (c. A.D. 480–524): WBT III.1168; NPT VII.3242, NPT VII.3294; ParsT X.1088.

Boghtoun under Blee Boughton under Blean, about five miles from Canterbury: CYPro VIII.556.

Boloigne (1) Boulogne, in France: GP I.465; (2) Bologna, in Italy: ClT IV.589, ClT IV.686, etc.

Bradwardyn, Bisshop Thomas Bradwardine (c. 1290–1349): NPT VII.3242.

Briseis *see* **Brixseyde**.

Britaigne, Britayne, Briteyne (1) Brittany: GP I.409; FranT V.729, FranT V.1159, etc.; (2) Britain: FranT V.810.

Briton(s), Britoun(s) (1) (as *adj.*) Breton, inhabitant of Brittany: FranT V.711, FranT V.1179; (as *n. pl.*) FranT V.709, WBT III.858; (2) Celtic inhabitant of ancient Britain: MLT II.561; (as *adj.*) MLT II.666; (as *n. pl.*) MLT II.545, MLT II.547, etc.

Brixseyde Briseis, lover of Achilles: IntML II.71.

Brok a horse: FrT III.1543.

Bromeholm site of a shrine in Norfolk: RvT I.4286.

Brugges Bruges, in Flanders (modern Belgium): ShipT VII.55, ShipT VII.61, etc.; Thop VII.733.

Brutus Marcus Junius Brutus (78?–42 B.C.): FranT V.1449; MkT VII.2706.

Brutus Cassius Brutus and Cassius, tyrannicides, here considered one person: MkT VII.2697.

Burdeux Bordeaux, wine-growing center in France: GP I.397, PardT VI.571.

Burnel the Asse, Daun a character in a satiric work by Nigel Wireker (late 12th cent.): NPT VII.331 (see n.).

Busirus Busyrides, legendary king of Egypt: MkT VII.2103.

C

Cacus a giant: MkT VII.2107.

Cadme, Cadmus Cadmus, founder of Thebes: KnT I.1546, KnT I.1547.

Caym Cain (Gen. 4.1–16): ParsT X.1015.

Calistopee Callisto, loved by Jupiter: KnT I.2056.

Cambalo, Cambalus Cambyuskan's son in SqT: SqT V.31, SqT V.656, SqT V.667.

Cambises king of Persia (reigned 529–522 B.C.): SumT III.2043.

Cambyuskan the king in SqT: SqT V.12, SqT V.28, etc.

Campaneus *see* **Cappaneus**.

Canaan son of Ham (Gen. 9.26): ParsT X.766.

Canacee (1) the incestuous lover of her brother: Int MLT II.78; (2) the heroine in SqT: SqT V.33, SqT V.144, etc.; *gen.* **Canacees** SqT V.247.

Cananee, woman Canaanite woman (Matt. 15.22): SNPro VIII.59.

Cancre, Cancer the fourth sign of the zodiac: MerT IV.1887, MerT IV.2224.

Cane Cana (cf. John 2.1): WBPro III.11.

Cantebrigge, Cantebregge Cambridge: RvT I.3990, RvT I.3921.

Cappaneus Campaneus, one of the Seven against Thebes (cf. Tr 5.1485–510): KnT I.932.

Capitolie the Capitol in Rome: MkT VII.2703, MkT VII.2705.

Capricorn the tenth sign of the zodiac: FranT V.1248.

Cartage (1) probably Cartagena, Spain: GP I.404.; (2) Carthage, in northern Africa: FranT V.1400; NPT VII.3365.

Cassidore, Cassidorie, Cassidorus Flavius Magnus Aurelius Cassiodorus (c. A.D. 480–575): Mel VII.1196, Mel VII.1348, Mel VII.1438, etc.

Cassius *see* **Brutus Cassius**.

Caton, Catoun Dyonisius Cato, supposed author of the *Disticha, Dicta Catonis* (Distichs, couplets of Cato): MilT I.3227; MerT IV.1377; Mel VII.1181; Mel VII.1216, etc.; NPT VII.2940, NPT VII.2971, NPT VII.2976; CYPro VIII.688.

Caunterbury Canterbury: GP I.16, GP I.22, etc.; CYPro VIII.624.

Caunterbury weye the road from London to Canterbury: MancPro IX.3.

Caunterbury, Tales of Chaucer's work: ParsT X.1086.

Cecile, Cecilie St. Cecilia (d. c. A.D. 176), heroine in SNT: SNPro VIII.28, SNPro VIII.85, etc.; **the lyf of Sent Cecile**, the SNT: CYPro VIII.554.

Cedasus Scedasus of Boeotia: FranT V.1428.

Ceys and Alcione the story of Ceyx and Alcyone (see BD 62–220): IntMLT II.57.

Cenobia, Cenobie Zenobia (late 3rd cent. A.D.; see MkT VII.2247–374); MkT VII.2247, MkT VII.2355.

Centauros probably Pholos the Centaur: MkT VII.2099.

Cerberus the watchdog of Hades: MkT VII.2102.

Cesar Julius Caesar: MkT VII.2679. *see* **Julius**.

Chaldeye Chaldea (present-day Iraq): MkT VII.2157.

Charles *gen.* of Charlemagne (A.D. 768–814), chief character in the *Chanson de Roland* (Song of Roland): MkT VII.2387.

Chaucer Geoffrey Chaucer: IntMLT II.47.

Chauntecleer the cock-hero in NPT: NPT VII.2849, NPT VII.2875, etc.; *gen.* **Chauntecleres** NPT VII.3354.

Chepe Cheapside, in London: GP I.754; CkT I.4377; PardT VI.564, PardT VI.569; MancPro IX.24.

Chichevache a legendary cow: ClT IV.1188.

Cicero *see* **Tullius**.

Cipioun Scipio Africanus Minor (c. 185–129 B.C.): NPT VII.3124.

Cipre the island of Cyprus: MkT VII.2391.

Circes   Circe, the enchantress: KnT I.1944.

Cirus   Cyrus the Great (d. 529 B.C.): SumT III.2079, MkT VII.2728.

Citherea   Venus, goddess of love: KnT I.2215. **see Venus.**

Citheron, Citheroun   Mt. Cithaeron in Greece: KnT I.2223, KnT I.1936.

Civitate, De   Augustine's City of God: ParsT X.754.

Claudyan   Claudius Claudianus, a Latin author (d. A.D. 408): MerT IV.2232.

Claudius   (1) Claudius Gothicus (emperor A.D. 268–70): MkT VII.2335; (2) Appius's henchman in PhyT: PhyT VI.153, PhyT VI.179, etc.

Clemence   goddess of mercy: KnT I.928.

Clitermystra   Clytemnestra, wife of Agamemnon: WBPro III.737.

Coitu, De   *On Intercourse,* a treatise on sex: MerT IV.1811. *see* **Constantyn.**

Colle   a dog: NPT VII.3383.

Coloigne   Cologne, on the Rhine: GP I.466.

Colossenses   Colossians: ParsT X.634.

Consolaccione, Boece de   Boethius's *Consolation of Philosophy*: ParsT X.1088.

Constantyn   Constantinus Africanus (1015–87), author of *De Coitu,* q.v.: GP I.433; MerT IV.1810.

Corynthe   Corinth, in Greece: PardT VI.604.

Creon   tyrant of Thebes: KnT I.938, KnT I.961, etc.

Croesus   *see* **Cresus.**

Cresus   Croesus, king of Lydia (560–546 B.C.): KnT I.1946; MkT VII.2727, MkT VII.2728, MkT VII.2759; NPT VII.3138.

Crete   the island in the Mediterranean: KnT I.980; WBPro III.733.

Crisippus   Chrysippus (c. 280–204 B.C.), a stoic philosopher: WBPro III.677.

Crisostom   *see* **John Crisostom, Seint.**

Crist   Christ: GP I.698, GP I.739, etc.; *gen.* **Cristes** GP I.481. *see* **Jhesu(s).**

Cristendom   Christianity: GP I.49; MLT II.351, MLT II.377; SNT VIII 208, SNT VIII.447, SNT VIII.459; ParsT X.875, ParsT X.876.

Crystyanytee   Christians: MLT II.544.

Cupide, Cupido   the god of love: KnT I.1623, KnT I.1963; IntMLT II.61.

Custance, Custaunce   the heroine in MLT: MLT II.151, MLT II.184, etc. *gen.* **Custances** MLT II.1008.

Cutberd, Seint   St. Cuthbert (d. A.D. 686): RvT I.4127.

D

Dalida   the biblical Delilah (Judges 16): MkT VII.2063.

Damascien   Johannes Damascenus (d. A.D. 752), an Arabic physician: GP I.433.

Damasie, Seint   Pope Damasus I (A.D. 336–84): ParsT X.788.

Damyan   the squire in MerT: MerT IV.1772, MerT IV.1789, etc.

Damyssene   (*adj.* as *n.*) of Damascus: MkT VII.2007.

Dane   Daphne: KnT I.2062, KnT I.2064.

Daniel   the biblical prophet: MLT II.473, MkT VII.2154, MkT VII.2166, MkT VII.2209; NPT VII.3128; ParsT X.126.

Dant   Dante Alighieri (1265–1321): FrT III.1520, MkT VII.2461; WBT III.1126; *gen.* **Dantes,** WBT III.1127.

Daphne   *see* **Dane.**

Daryus   Darius III (d. 330 B.C.), king of Persia: WBPro III.498.

Darius   Darius the Mede (Daniel 5.31ff.): MkT VII.2237, MkT VII.2648.

Dartmouth   *see* **Dertemouthe.**

David, Davit   King David (1 Kings–3 Kings 2.10; AV 1 Samuel–1 Kings 2.10): MLT II.935; SumT III.1933; Mel VII.1100, Mel VII.1198, etc.; MancT IX.345; ParsT X.125, ParsT X.193, etc.

Decrees, Book of   the Decretals (*Corpus iuris canonici*) of Gratian: Mel VII.1404.

Deianira   *see* **Dianira.**

Deyscorides   Dioscorides, an authority on medicine (fl. c. A.D. 50): GP I.430.

Delphos   Delphi, in Greece: FranT V.1077.

Demetrius   king of Parthia (139–127 B.C.): PardT VI.621.

Demociones daughter   an Athenian exemplar of chastity: FranT V.1426.

Demophon   beloved of Phyllis (see LGW 2393–561): IntMLT II.65.

Denmark   Denmark: WBPro III.824.

Denys, Seint   St. Denis (d. 272), patron saint of France: ShipT VII.151.

Depeford   Deptford, near London: RvPro I.3906.

Dertemouthe   Dartmouth, on the English Channel: GP I.389.

Dyane   Diana, goddess of chastity: KnT I.1692, KnT I.1912, etc.; FranT V.1390; and of hunting: KnT I.1682. *gen.* **Dianes** FranT V.1390. *see* **Lucina.**

Dianira, Dianyre   Deianira, wife of Hercules: IntMLT II.66; WBPro III.725; MkT VII.2120.

Dido   queen of Carthage (see LGW 924–1367 and HF 239–432): IntMLT II.64.

Dioscorides   *see* **Deyscorides.**

Dives   the rich man in the parable (Luke 16.19ff.): SumT III.1877.

Donegild   mother of Alla in MLT: MLT II.695, MLT II.740, etc.

Dorigen   the heroine of FranT: FranT V.815, FranT V.919, etc.

Dover   Dover, on the English Channel: CkPro I.4347.

Dun   a horse: MancPro IX.5.

Dunmowe   Little Dunmowe, in Essex: WBPro III.218.

Dunstan, Seint   St. Dunstan (A.D. 908–88): FrT III.1502.

E

Ecclesiaste   Ecclesiasticus, a book of the Apocrypha: WBPro III.651; NPT VII.3329 (?). *see* **Jhesus (filius) Syrak.**

Ector   Hector, hero of Troy: KnT I.2832; MLT II.198; NPT VII.3142, NPT VII.3144. *gen.* **Ectores** NPT VII.3141.

Edward, Seint   St. Edward the Confessor (king of England 1043–66): ProMkT VII.1970.

Egeus Aegeus, king of Athens and father of Theseus: KnT I.2838, KnT I.2905.

Egipcien Egyptian: (as *adj.*) MLT II.500; (as *n.*) MkT VII.2338.

Egipte Egypt: NPT VII.3133.

Eglentyne the Prioress: GP I.121.

Ekko the nymph who loved Narcissus (see Rom A 1469–538): FranT V.951.

Eleyne Helen of Troy: IntMLT II.70, MerT IV.1754.

Eleyne, Seint Saint Helen (c. A.D. 247–c. 327): PardT VI.951.

Eliachim the high priest in Judith 4.7 (Joachim in A. V.): MkT VII.2556.

Elise Elisha (2 Kings 2): SumT III.2116.

Elpheta wife of Cambyuskan in SqT: SqT V.29.

Elye Elijah (1 Kings 19.8, 2 Kings 2.11): SumT III.1890, SumT III.2116.

Emelya, Emelye, Emelie sister of Hippolyta and heroine of KnT: KnT I.1077, KnT I.1567, KnT I.2658, etc.

Emetreus, kyng of Inde one of Arcite's supporters in KnT: KnT I.2156, KnT I.2638, KnT I.2645.

Enee Aeneas, hero of Virgil's *Aeneid* and faithless lover of Dido (see HF 219–433 and LGW 924–1367): IntMLT II.64.

Eneydos Virgil's *Aeneid* (summarized in HF 151–382): NPT VII.3359.

Engelond England: GP I.16, GP I.580; KnT I.2113; MLT II.1130; FrT III.1322, FrT III.1340; FranT V.810; PardT VI.921; CYT VIII.1356.

Englissh, Englyssh the English language: GP I.265; KnT I.1459; IntMLT II.49, MLT II.778; SqT V.37; SNPro VIII.2, SNPro VIII.87, SNPro VIII.106; ParsT X.869.

Ephesios Ephesians: ParsT X.748.

Epicurus *gen.* the Greek philosopher (341–270 B.C.): GP I.336.

Episteles Ovid's *Heroides*: IntMLT II.55.

Ercules, Hercules Hercules, the Greek hero (for his life see Bo 4.m7, his expedition with Jason LGW 1480–558, and his death MkT VII.2095–142): KnT I.1943; MLT II.200; WBPro III.725; MkT VII.2095, MkT VII.2135.

Eriphilem Eriphyle, wife of Amphiaraus: WBPro III.743.

Erro Hero, beloved of Leander: IntMLT II.69.

Esculapius Aesculapius, god of medicine: GP I.429.

Essex the county: WBPro III.218.

Ester, Hester the biblical Esther: MerT IV.1371, MerT IV.1744; Mel VII.1101.

Ethiopeen Ethiopian: ParsT X.345.

Ethna Mount Etna: MerT IV.2230.

Euclide Euclid, the Greek mathematician (fl. 300 B.C.): SumT III.2289.

Europe Europe, the continent: MLT II.161.

Eva, Eve the first woman: MLT II.368; WBPro III.715; MerT IV.1329; SNPro VIII.62; ParsT X.325, ParsT X.331, etc.

Evaungiles the Gospels: MLT II.666.

Exodi Exodus: ParsT X.750.

Ezechias Hezekiah (Isaiah 38.15): ParsT X.983.

Ezechie, Ezechiel the biblical prophet: ParsT X.135, ParsT X.143, ParsT X.140, ParsT X.236.

F

Fairye, Fayerye (1) the land of the fairies: SqT V.96; Thop VII.802, Thop VII.814; (2) the classical Underworld; MerT IV.2227, MerT IV.2234, MerT IV.2316.

Fame, the book of Chaucer's *House of Fame*: ParsT X.1086.

Femenye land of the Amazon women: KnT I.866, KnT I.877.

Ferrare Ferrara, in Italy: ClPro IV.51.

Fynystere Cape Finisterre, in northwest Spain: GP I.408.

Fyssh Pisces, the zodiacal sign: SqT V.273. *see* **Pisces**.

Fysshstrete a street in London: PardT VI.564.

Flaundres Flanders, part of present-day Belgium: GP I.86; PardT VI.463; ShipT VII.199, ShipT VII.239, etc.; Thop VII.719.

Flemyng Fleming: CkPro I.4357; NPT VII.3396; MancT IX.309.

Florence Florence, Italy: WBT III.1125.

France, Fraunce France: FranT V.1118; ShipT VII.116, ShipT VII.151, ShipT VII.194.

Fraynceys Petrak *see* **Petrak (Fraunceys)**.

Frydeswyde, Seinte St. Frideswide (8th cent. A.D.): MilT I.3449.

G

Galathee Galatea, heroine of the *Pamphilus de amore*: FranT V.1110. *see* **Pamphilles**.

Galgopheye probably Gargaphia, in Greece: KnT I.2626.

Galice Galicia, in Spain: GP I.466.

Galien, Galyen (1) Galen (A.D. 130?–201?), the Greek physician: GP I.431; ParsT X.831; (2) Gallienus (emperor A.D. 253–68): MkT VII.2336.

Galilee a province of Palestine: WBPro III.11.

Gallus *see* **Symplicius Gallus**.

Gatesden John of Gaddesden (b. 1280), a physician: GP I.434.

Gaufred Geoffrey of Vinsauf (early 13th cent.): NPT VII.3347.

Gaunt Ghent, the city in Belgium: GP I.448.

Gawayn Gawain, the hero of Arthurian romance: SqT V.95.

Gawle, folk of Galatians: FranT V.1411.

Gazan the biblical Gaza: MkT VII.2047.

Geminis the third sign of the zodiac: MerT IV.2222.

Genesis Genesis, the biblical book: ParsT X.755.

Genylon Ganelon, betrayer of Roland: NPT VII.3227; ShipT VII.194.

Genylon-Olyver a traitor: MkT VII.2389.

Gerland a dog: NPT VII.3383.

Gernade Granada, in Spain: GP I.56.

Gerounde the river Gironde, in France: FranT V.1222.

Gerveys a blacksmith in MilT: MilT I.3761, MilT I.3765, etc.

Ghent *see* **Gaunt**.

Gy Guy of Warwick, hero of English romance: Thop VII.899.

Gilbertyn Gilbertus Anglicus (13th cent.), a physician: GP I.434.

Gile, Seint   St. Giles (St. Aegidius, 6th or 7th cent. A.D.): CYT VIII.1185.

Gille   a maid in MilT: MilT I.3556.

Gysen   the river Gyndes, tributary of the Tigris: SumT III.2080.

God, Gode   the Deity: GP I.533, GP I.573, etc.; *gen.* **Goddes** GP I.854;   **Godes** ParsT X.832.

Golias   Goliath (1 Sam. 17): MLT II.934.

Goodelief   Herry Bailly's (q.v.) wife: ProMkT VII.1894.

Gootland   probably Gotland, an island in the Baltic: GP I.408.

Grece   Greece: KnT I.962, FranT V.1444; MkT VII.2657.

Grece, See of   the Mediterranean: MLT II.464.

Gregorie, Seint   Pope Gregory the Great (c. A.D. 540–604): Mel VII.1497; ParsT X.92, ParsT X.214, etc.

Grek   (*adj.*) Greek: NPT VII.3228.

Grekes   (*n. pl.*) Greeks: KnT I.2899, KnT I.2951, etc.; WBPro III.744; as *gen. pl.* SqT V.209.

Grenewych   Greenwich, about a half-mile past Deptford: RvPro I.3907.

Grete See   the Mediterranean: GP I.59.

Grisilde, Grisildis   heroine of ClT: ClT IV.210, ClT IV.232, etc.; MerPro IV.1224. *gen.* **Grisildis** ClT IV.576; MerPro IV.1224.

H

Habradate   Adabrates, king of the Susi: FranT V.1414; *gen.* **Hadrabates** FranT V.1416.

Haly   Hali ibn-Abbas, 10th-cent. Arabic physician: GP I.431.

Hanybal   Hannibal, the Carthaginian general (247–183 .C.): MLT II.290.

Hasdrubales wyf   wife of the king of Carthage (in 146 B.C.): FranT V.1399, NPT VII.3363.

Hayles   Hales Abbey in Gloucestershire: PardT VI.652.

Helen   *see* **Eleyne.**

Helie   Eli (1 Sam. 1–4): ParsT X.897.

Helowys   Héloise (d. 1164), lover of Abelard: WBPro III.677.

Hercules   *see* **Ercules.**

Hereos, loveris maladye of   love-sickness: KnT I.1374.

Hermanno   Heremianus, a son of Zenobia: MkT VII.2345.

Hermengyld   murdered Custance in MLT: MLT II.533, MLT II.535, etc.; *gen.* **Hermengyldes** MLT II.595.

Hermes   Hermes Trismegistus, legendary alchemist: CYT VIII.1434.

Hermyon   Hermione, lover of Orestes: IntMLT II.66.

Hero   *see* **Erro.**

Herodes   (1) Herod Antipas (Matt. 2, 14, and Mark 6.14–29): PardT VI.488; PrT VII.574; (2) the part of Herod in the mystery plays: MilT I.3384.

Herry Bailly   the Host: CkPro I.4358.

Hester   *see* **Ester.**

Hypermnestra   *see* **Ypermystra.**

Hypsipyle   *see* **Isiphile(e).**

Hogge   Hodge (*dim.* of Roger, q.v.), the Cook: CkPro I.4336.

Holdernesse   a district in Yorkshire: SumT III.1710.

Horn child   a hero of English romance: Thop VII.898.

Hostillius   *see* **Tullius Hostillius.**

Huberd   the Friar: GP I.269.

Hugelyn of Pyze   Ugolino of Pisa (d. 1299): MkT VII.2407.

Hugh of Lyncoln   a child martyr (d. 1255): PrT VII.684.

Hulle   Hull, on the Yorkshire Coast: GP I.404.

Huwe, sir   Hugh, a nickname for a priest: FrT III.1356.

I (*See also* Y)

Ilion, Ylion   Ilium, the citadel of Troy (used as a name for the city): MLT II.289; NPT VII.3356.

Ymeneus   Hymen, god of marriage: MerT IV.1730.

Inde, Ynde   India: KnT I.2156; WBPro III.824; SumT III.1980; ClT IV.1199; MerPro IV.1230; SqT V.110; PardT VI.722.

Innocent   Innocent III (pope in 1198–1216): Mel VII.1568.

Ypermystra   Hypermnestra (see LGW 2562–723): IntMLT II.75.

Ypocras   Hippocrates (5th cent. B.C.), the Greek medical authority: GP I.431.

Ypolita   Hippolyta, queen of the Amazons: KnT I.868, KnT I.881, etc.

Ypotys   child hero of a pious legend: Thop VII.898.

Ysaak   Isaac (Gen. 22, 27): Mel VII.1098.

Ysaye   Isaiah, the biblical prophet: ParsT X.198, X.209, etc.

Ysidre, Seynt   Isidore of Seville (c. A.D. 570–636): ParsT X.89, ParsT X.551.

Isiphile(e)   Hypsipyle (see LGW 1306–579): IntMLT II.67.

Isope   Ysopus, a collection of Latin fables: Mel VII.1184.

Israel   Israel: MkT VII.2060, MkT VII.2152.

Ytaille, Ytayle   Italy: MLT II.441; ClPro IV.33; ClT IV.57, ClT IV.266, etc.; MerT IV.1511, MerT IV.1714; MkT VII.2460.

Yve, Seint   St. Ives (probably St. Yvo of Chartres, c. 1140–1216): SumT III.1943; ShipT VII.227.

J

Jacob   the biblical patriarch (Gen. 24.28–34, 27): WBPro III.56; MerT IV.1362; Mel VII.1098; ParsT X.443.

Jakke   Jack, *dim.* of **John**: MilT I.3708 (see note); FrT III.1357.

Jakke Straw   Jack Straw, a leader of the revolt of 1381: NPT VII.3394.

Jame, Seint   St. James the Apostle: ClT IV.1154; Mel VII.1119, Mel VII.1517, Mel VII.1676, Mel VII.1869; ParsT X.348; (in oaths) Jame RvT I.4264; WBPro III.312; FrT III.1443; ShipT VII.355. *see* **Seint-Jame.**

Janekyn   an apprentice in WBPro: WBPro III.303, WBPro III.383.

Janicula, Janicle   father of Grisilde in ClT: ClT IV.208, ClT IV.404, etc.

Jankin   (1) derisive name for a priest (*dim.* of **John**, q.v.): EpiMLT II.1172; (2) the lord's squire in SumT: SumT III.2288, SumT III.2293. (3) the Wife of Bath's fifth husband: WBPro III.548, WBPro III.2288, etc.

Leandre Leander of Abydos, lover of Hero: IntMLT II.69.

Lente season of Lent: WBPro III.543, WBPro III.550; ClPro IV.12; ParsT X.103.

Leon, Leoun (1) the fifth sign of the zodiac: KnT I.2462: (2) the constellation Leo: SqT V.265.

Leoun, the book of the a lost work by Chaucer: ParsT X.1087.

Lepe wine-growing district in Spain: PardT VI.563, PardT VI.570.

Lettow Lithuania: GP I.54.

Lia Leah, Jacob's wife (Gen. 29:16–35): SNPro VIII.96, SNPro VIII.98.

Lybeux, sir Libeaus Desconus, hero of medieval romance: Thop VII.900.

Lyde Lydia, ancient kingdom (in present-day Turkey): MkT VII.2727, NPT VII.3138.

Lyeys Ayash in Armenia: GP I.58.

Lignano *see* **Lynyan.**

Lygurge Lycurgus, legendary king of Thrace, one of Palamon's supporters in KnT: KnT I.2129, KnT I.2644.

Lyncoln Lincoln: PrT VII.684.

Lynyan Giovanni da Lignano (c. 1310–83): ClPro IV.34.

Lithuania *see* **Lettow.**

Lyvia Livia Drusilla (d. A.D. 29): WBPro III.747, WBPro III.750.

Livius *see* **Titus Livius.**

Loy, Seinte St. Eligius (A.D. 588–659): GP I.120; FrT III.1564.

Lombardes bankers from Lombardy: VII.367.

Lollere a heretic: EpMLT II.1173, EpMLT II.1177.

Lombardy *see* **Lumbardye.**

London, Londoun London: GP I.382 (as *adj.*), GP I.509; MilT I.3632; CkPro I.4325; WBPro III.550; CYT VIII.1012; MancPro IX.11.

Looth Lot (Gen. 19.30–38): PardT VI.485.

Luc St. Luke, the evangelist: Thop VII.951, ParsT X.700, ParsT X.702.

Lucan Marcus Annaeus Lucanus (A.D. 39–65): MLT II.401; MkT VII.2719.

Lucia, Lucye Lucilia, wife of the Roman poet Lucretius: WBPro III.747, WBPro III.752.

Lucifer Satan: MkT VII.1999, MkT VII.2004; ParsT X.788.

Lucina, Lucyna a name of Diana, as goddess of childbirth: KnT I.2085; as moon: FranT V.1045; *see* **Dyane, Luna.**

Lucresse Lucretia, wife of Lucius Tarquinus Collatinus (see LGW 1680–885): FranT V.1405, IntMLT II.63.

Lumbardye Lombardy, an area in northern Italy: SqT V.193; ClPro IV.46, ClT IV.72, ClT IV.945; MerT IV.1245; MkT VII.2400.

Luna the moon (as a name for silver): CYT VIII.826, CYT VIII.1440. *see* **Lucina.**

M

Mabely the old woman in FrT: FrT III.1626.

Machabee (1) Book of Macabees (apocryphal in AV): MkT VII.2579, MkT VII.2655; (2) Judas Machabeus (q.v.): Mel VII.1659.

Machabeus *see* **Judas Machabeus.**

Macidoyne, Macidonye Macedonia: FranT V.1435, MkT VII.2656.

Macrobeus Ambrosius Theodosius Macrobius, an authority on dreams (fl. A.D. 395–423): NPT VII.3123.

Madrian identity unclear: ParsT X.996.

Magdelene, Magdeleyne St. Mary Magdelene: ParsT X.502, ParsT X.504, ParsT X.947, ParsT X.996.

Magus *see* **Simon Magus.**

Mahoun, Makomete Mohammed (c. A.D. 570–632): MLT II.224, MLT II.333, MLT II.340; *gen.* **Makometes** MLT II.336.

May the month of May: GP I.92; IntMLT II.6; KnT I.1034, KnT I.1037, etc.; WBPro III.546; MerT IV.1748; SqT V.281; FranT V.906, FranT 907, FranT 928, FranT V.928; MkT VII.2120; CYT VIII.1343.

Mayus, May the young wife in MerT: MerT IV.1693, MerT IV.1742, MerT IV.1774, etc.

Malkyn Molly (*dim. of* **Matilda**): (1) a servant girl in NPT: NPT VII.3384; (2) *gen.* **Malkynes** a lower-class woman: IntMLT II.30.

Malle a form of **Malkyn**, the name of a sheep: NPT VII.2831.

Malyne a form of **Malkyn**: the Miller's daughter in RvT: RvT I.4236.

Marcian Martianus Capella (1st half 5th cent. A.D.): MerT IV.1732.

Marcus Tullius Scithero Cicero: FranPro V.722; *see* **Tullius.**

Mardochee Mordecai, in the Book of Esther: MerT IV.1373.

Marie, Egipcien St. Mary the Egyptian (5th cent. A.D.): MLT II.500.

Marie, Seinte the Virgin Mary: MLT II.641, MLT II.841, MLT II.920; PrT VII.508, PrT VII.690; in oaths and exclamations, FrT III.1604; MerT IV.1337, MerT IV.1899; MerT IV.2418; IntPardT VI.308, PardT VI.685; ShipT VII.402; Thop VII.784; CYT VIII.1062.

Mark St. Mark, the evangelist: Thop VII.951, WBPro III.145.

Marrok, Strayte of the Strait of Gibraltar: MLT II.465.

Mars, Marte (1) the Roman god of war: KnT I.975, KnT I.1559, etc.; (2) the planet: KnT I.2021, MLT II.301, MLT II.305, WBPro III.612; *gen.* **Martes** KnT I.2024; SqT V.50; WBPro III.619; (as a name for iron) CYT VIII.827.

Martin, Seint St. Martin of Tours (c. A.D. 316–400): ShipT VII.148.

Mary *see* **Marie.**

Mathew St. Matthew, the evangelist: PardT VI.634; Thop VII.951; ParsT X.588, ParsT X.842, ParsT X.845, etc.

Maudelayne the Shipman's barge: GP I.410.

Maure St. Maurus (d. A.D. 565): GP I.173.

Maurice, Mauricius son of Constance and Alla in MLT: MLT II.723, MLT II.1063, etc.; *gen.* **Maurices** MLT II.1127.

Maxime, Maximus prefect converted by Cecilie in SNT: SNT VIII.368, SNT VIII.377, etc.

Mecene Messenia in Greece: FranT V.1379.

Medea sorceress and lover of Jason (see LGW 1580–670): IntMLT II.72, KnT I.1944.

Panik, Panyk   Panico, near Bologna in Italy: ClT IV.590, ClT IV.764, ClT IV.939.

Parables of Salomon   Prov. 10.1 to 22.16 (Vulgate): WBPro III.679.

Parys   (1) Paris, the city: GP I.126; WBPro III.678; ShipT VII.57, ShipT VII.332, ShipT VII.366; (2) Paris, the abductor of Helen of Troy: MerT IV.1754; SqT V.548.

Parlement of Briddes   Chaucer's *Parliament of Fowls*: ParsT X.1086.

Parthes   Parthians: PardT VI.622.

Parvys   the porch of St. Paul's Cathedral, London (cf. Rom C 7108): GP I.310.

Pasiphaë   *see* **Phasipha**.

Pathmos   the Mediterranean island of Patmos: PrT VII.583.

Paul   *see* **Poul**.

Pavye   Pavia, in Italy: MerT IV.1246.

Pedmark   Penmarch, in Brittany: FranT V.801.

Pegasee   the Pegasean (horse), i.e., Pegasus: SqT V.207.

Pemond   Piedmont, a province of northern Italy: ClPro IV.44.

Penalopee, Penelopee   Penelope, wife of Ulysses: IntMLT II.75; FranT V.1443.

Penmarch   *see* **Pedmark**.

Penneus   *gen.* of Peneus, river god and father of Daphne: KnT I.2064.

Perce   Persia: MkT VII.2252.

Percien   Persian: SumT III.2079; *pl.* **Persiens** MkT VII.2248, MkT VII.2346. *see* **Perses**.

Percyvell   hero of Arthurian romance: Thop VII.916.

Perkyn (Revellour)   the apprentice in CkT: CkT I.4371, CkT I.4387.

Pernaso   Mt. Parnassus, sacred to the Muses: FranPro V.721.

Perotheus   Pirithous, a friend of Arcite in KnT: KnT I.1191, KnT I.1202, KnT I.1205, KnT I.1227.

Perses   Persians: MkT VII.2235. *see* **Percien**.

Pertelote   Chauntecleer's favorite wife in NPT: NPT VII.2870, NPT VII.2885, etc.

Peter (Piers) Alfonce   Petrus Alphonsus: Mel VII.1053, Mel VII.1189, Mel VII.1218, Mel VII.1309, Mel VII.1566.

Peter, Petre   St. Peter the Apostle: GP I.697; Mel VII.1501; ParsT X.142, ParsT X.287, etc.; in oaths, WBPro III.446; FrT III.1332; ShipT VII.214; CYPro VIII.665; *gen.* **Petres** MilT I.3486; SumT III.1819.

Petrak (Frauncyes)   Petrarch, Francesco Petrarca (A.D. 1304–74): ClPro IV.31, ClT IV.1147; MkT VII.2325.

Petro   Pedro, king of Castile (d. A.D. 1369; see VII.2375–90): MkT VII.2375.

Petro, kyng of Cipre   Pierre de Lusignan, king of Cyprus (d. 1369; see VII.2391–98): MkT VII.2391.

Phanye   daughter of Croesus: MkT VII.2758.

Pharao   Pharaoh (Gen. 41): NPT VII.3133; ParsT X.443.

Phasipha   Pasiphaë, wife of King Minos of Crete: WBPro III.733.

Phebus   Phoebus Apollo, the classical god and mythological character: FranT V.1036, FranT V.1041, etc.; the main character in MancT: MancT IX.105, MancT IX.125, etc.; the sun: KnT I.1493; IntMLT II.11, etc.; *gen.* **Phebus** MancT IX.238.

Phidon   an Athenian slain by the Thirty Tyrants: FranT V.1369.

Philipenses   Philippians (in the Bible): ParsT X.598.

Philippes   *gen.* of Philip, Alexander's father: MkT VII.2656.

Philistiens   Philistines: MkT VII.2048.

Phillis   Phyllis, beloved of Demophon (see LGW 2394–561): IntMLT II.65.

Philologie   Philology (as proper noun, personified): MerT IV.1734.

Philostrate   the name assumed by Arcite in KnT: KnT I.1428, KnT I.1558, KnT I.1728.

Phisiologus   the bestiary: NPT VII.3271 (see note).

Phitonissa   the Witch of Endor (1 Chronicles 10.13, 1 Samuel 28.7): FrT III.1510.

Phitoun   the Python slain by Apollo: MancT IX.109, MancT IX.128.

Pycardie   Picardy, a province of France: GP I.86.

Pierides   the Muses, daughters of Pierus: IntMLT II.92 (see note).

Piers Alfonce   *see* **Peter (Piers) Alfonce**.

Piers, Daun   the Monk: ProNPT VII.2792.

Pigmalion   the legendary Greek sculptor: PhyT VI.14.

Pilates   *gen.* of Pontius Pilate, as a character in the mystery plays: MilPro I.3124.

Piramus   lover of Thisbe (see LGW 706–923): MerT IV.2128.

Pirithous   *see* **Perotheus**.

Pirrus   Pyrrhus, slayer of Priam: MLT II.288; NPT VII.3357.

Pisces   the twelfth sign of the zodiac: WBPro III.704; *see* **Fyssh**.

Pize   Pisa, in Italy: MkT VII.2407, MkT VII.2409, MkT VII.2416, MkT VII.2456.

Placebo   a flatterer in MerT: MerT IV.1476, MerT IV.1478, etc.

Plato   Plato, the Greek philosopher (c. 427–348 B.C.): GP I.741; CYT VIII.1448, CYT VIII.1453, etc.; MancT IX.207.

Pleyndamour   hero of an unidentified romance: Thop VII.900.

Pluto   ruler of the Underworld: KnT I.2082, KnT I.2299, KnT I.2685; MerT IV.2038, MerT IV.2227, MerT IV.2311, etc.; FranT V.1075.

Poilleys   Apulian, from Apulia in southeast Italy: SqT V.195.

Pompei, Pompeye, Pompeus   Pompey the Great, Gnaeus Pompeius (106–48 B.C.; see MkT VII.2679–94): MLT II.199; MkT VII.2680, MkT VII.2693, etc.

Poo   Po, the river in Italy: ClPro IV.48.

Poperyng   Poperinghe, a town in Flanders: Thop VII.720.

Porcia   Portia, wife of Marcus Brutus: FranT V.1448.

Portyngale   Portugal: EpiNPT VII.3459.

Poul, Paul, Paulus   St. Paul the Apostle: WBPro III.73; FrT III.1647; PardT VI.521, PardT VI.523; Mel VII.989, Mel VII.1291, Mel VII.1440; NPT VII.3441; ParsPro X.32, ParsT X.162, etc.; *gen.* **Poules** SumT III.1819; Saint Paul's Cathedral in London GP I.509; MilT I.3318; ProNPT VII.2780.

Priam   king of Troy: NPT VII.3358.

Priapus   god of gardens and fertility: MerT IV.2034.

Proserpina, Proserpyna, Proserpyne Proserpyne, wife of Pluto and queen of the Underworld: MerT IV.2039, MerT IV.2229, MerT IV.2264.

Protheselaus Protesilaus, husband of Laodamia: FranT V.1446.

Pruce Prussia: GP I.53; (as *adj.*) Prussian: KnT I.2122.

Prudence wife of Melibeus in Mel: Mel VII.967, Mel VII.974, etc.; ProMkT VII.1890, ProMkT VII.1896.

Ptholome(e) Ptolemy (Claudius Ptolomeus), the astronomical authority: WBPro III.182, WBPro III.324, SumT III.2289; *see* **Almageste**.

R

Rachel wife of Jacob (Gen. 29–35): PrT VII.627.

Ram the zodiacal sign Aries: GP I.8; SqT V.386. *see* **Aries**.

Raphael the archangel (Tobias 6.17): ParsT X.906.

Rauf Ralph, a name for a fornicator in FrT: FrT III.1357.

Razis Rhazes (A.D. 865–925), an Arabic authority on medicine: GP I.432.

Rebekka, Rebekke Rebecca, wife of Isaac (Gen. 27): MerT IV.1363, MerT IV.1704; Mel VII.1098.

Remedie of Love Ovid's *Remedia amoris* (Remedies for Love): Mel VII.976.

Rhazes *see* **Razis**.

Rhodogune *see* **Rodogone**.

Richard, kyng Richard I of England (A.D. 1157–99): NPT VII.3348.

Robert, sir a name for a fornicator in FrT: FrT III.1356.

Robyn (1) John's servant in MilT: MilT I.3466, MilT I.3555; (2) the Miller: MilPro I.3129.

Rochele, the La Rochelle, a wine-growing region in France: PardT VI.571.

Rodogone Rhodogune, daughter of Darius: FranT V.1456.

Roger (1) the Cook: CkPro I.4345, CkPro I.4353, CkPro I.4356 (*see* Hogge); (2) Ruggieri degli Ubaldini, bishop of Pisa (1278–95): MkT VII.2416.

Romance of the Rose the poem by Guillaume de Lorris and Jean de Meun: MerT IV.2032.

Rome Rome: GP I.465, GP I.671, GP I.687; MLT II.142, MLT II.145, etc.; WBPro III.673; ClT IV.737; SqT V.231; FranT V.1406; MkT VII.2316, MkT VII.2335, etc.; NPT VII.3371; SNT VIII.361; CYT VIII.975.

Ronyan, Ronyon probably St. Ronan (d. A.D. 737): Int-PardT VI.310, IntPardT VI.320.

Rosarie *Rosarium philosophorum* (Rosary [or Rose Garden] of the Philosophers), an alchemical treatise by Arnaldus of Villanova: CYT VIII.1429. *see* **Arnold of the Newe Toun**.

Rouchestre Rochester, about 30 miles from London: ProMkT VII.1926.

Rouncivale a hospital at Charing Cross: GP I.670.

Ruce, Russye Russia: GP I.54; SqT V.10.

Rufus Rufus of Ephesus (2nd cent. A.D.), a medical authority: GP I.430.

Russell, daun the fox in NPT: NPT VII.3334.

S

Sayne the river Seine: FranT V.1222.

Salomon Solomon, king of Israel (reigned 974–c. 937 B.C.): KnT I.1942; MilT I.3529; CkPro I.4330; WBPro III.35, WBPro III.679; ClPro IV.6; MerT IV.1483, MerT IV.1487, etc.; Sq V.250; Mel VII.997, Mel VII.1003, etc.; CYT VIII.961; MancT IX.314, MancT IX.344; ParsT X.119, ParsT X.127, etc.

Saluce, Saluces Saluzzo, in Northern Italy: ClPro IV.44, ClT IV.414, etc.

Samaritan, the the woman of Samaria (John 4.7–18): WBPro III.16, WBPro III.22.

Sampson, Sampsoun Samson (Judges 14–16: see MkT VII.2015–94): KnT I.2466; MLT II.201; WBPro III.721; PardT VI.554, PardT VI.572, etc.; MkT VII.2015, MkT VII.2023, etc.; ParsT X.955.

Samuel the judge of Israel (1 and 2 Samuel): FrT III.1510; PardT VI.585.

Sapor Shapur I, king of Persia (reigned c. A.D. 240–73): MkT VII.2320.

Sarra Sarah, wife of Abraham (Gen. 12–23): MerT IV.1704.

Sarray Tsarev, capital of the Mongol Empire: SqT V.9; SqT V.46.

Satalye Atalia (in present-day Turkey): GP I.58.

Sathan, Sathanas Satan, the devil (see MkT VII.1999–2006): MilT I.3750; MLT II.365, MLT II.582, MLT II.598, MLT II.634; FrT III.1526, FrT III.1655; SumPro III.1686, SumPro III.1687, SumPro III.1689; PrT VII.558; MkT VII.2005; ParsT X.895; *see* **Lucifer**, sense 1.

Saturne, Saturnus Saturn, the roman god: KnT I.1328, KnT I.2450, etc.; the planet, KnT I.1088; (as a name for lead) CYT VIII.828.

Scariot Judas Iscariot: NPT VII.3227. *see* **Judas**.

Scithero *see* **Marcus Tullius**.

Scithia Scythia: KnT I.867, KnT I.882.

Scot name of a horse: GP I.616; FrT III.1543.

Seint-Denys a suburb of Paris: ShipT VII.1, ShipT VII.59, etc.

Seint-Jame Santiago (de Compostela), in Spain: GP I.466.

Seintes Legende of Cupide *The Legend of Good Women*: IntMLT II.61.

Semyrame Semiramis, queen of Assyria (c. 800 B.C.): MLT II.359.

Senec, Senek, Seneca, Senekke Lucius Annaeus Seneca, Roman author (c. 4 B.C.–A.D. 65; see MkT VII.2495–518 and cf. Bo 3.pr5.40–56): IntMLT II.25; WBT III.1168, WBT III.1184; SumT III.2018; MerT IV.1376, MerT IV.1523, MerT IV.1567; PardT VI.492; Mel VII.984, Mel VII.991, etc.; MkT VII.2503, MkT VII.2515; MancT IX.345; ParsT X.144, ParsT X.145, ParsT X.467, ParsT X.759.

Senior an alchemical treatise: CYT VIII.1450.

Septe a mountain range in Morocco: MLT II.947.

Serapion ibn-Serabi (fl. c. A.D. 1070), an Arabic medical authority: GP I.432 (see n.).

Sheffeld Sheffield: RvT I.3933.

Sidyngborne Sittingbourne, a town between Rochester and Canterbury: WBPro III.847.

Symkyn (*dim.* of Symond) the miller in RvT: RvT I.3941, RvT I.3945, etc. *see* **Symond**.

Simon Magus   a sorcerer (Acts 8.9): ParsT X.783.
Simon the Pharisee   (Luke 1.39ff.): ParsT X.504.
Symond   Simon, the miller in RvT: RvT I.4022, RvT I.4026. *see* **Symkyn**.
Symoun, Seint   identity uncertain: SumT III.2094 (see n.).
Symplicius Gallus   Sulpicius Gallus (2nd cent. A.D.): WBPro III.643.
Synay   Mt. Sinai: SumT III.1887. *see* **Oreb**.
Synon   the betrayer of Troy: SqT V.209; NPT VII.3228.
Syrak   *see* **Jhesus (filius) Syrak**.
Socrates   the Greek philosopher (c. 469–399 B.C.): MLT II.201; WBPro III.728.
Soler Halle   King's Hall, a college at Cambridge: RvT I.3990.
Solomon   *see* **Salomon**.
Sophie   daughter of Melibeus in Mel: Mel VII.967.
Southwerk   Southwark, across the Thames from London: GP I.20, GP I.718; MilPro I.3140.
Spaigne, Spayne   Spain: GP I.409; PardT VI.565, PardT VI.570; MkT VII.2375.
Stace   Publius Papinius Statius (c. A.D. 45–96): KnT I.2294.
Stilboun   identity uncertain: PardT VI.603 (see n.).
Stymphalides   Stymphalis, murdered by Aristoclides: FranT V.1388.
Stratford atte Bowe   a town about three miles from London: GP I.125.
Straw *see* **Jakke Straw**.
Strother   a town in the north of England: RvT I.4014.
Surrye   Syria: MLT II.134, MLT II.173, etc.
Surrien, Surryen   (*adj.*) Syrian: MLT II.153; (*n.*) MLT II.435, MkT VII.2339; (*n. pl.*) **Surryens** MLT II.394, MLT II.963.
Susanne, Susanna   heroine of the apocryphal Book of Susannah (Dan. 13 in the Vulgate): MLT II.639; ParsT X.797.
Swetonius, Swetoun   Gaius Suetonius Tranquilus (c. A.D. 70–160): MkT VII.2465, MkT VII.2720.

T

Tabard   an inn in Southwark: GP I.20, GP I.719.
Talbot   a dog in NPT: NPT VII.3383.
Tarquyn   Tarquinus Sextus, son of Tarquinus Superbus (see LGW 1680–885): FranT V.1407.
Tars   Tarsia, in Chinese Turkestan: KnT I.2160.
Tartarye   Tartary, in present-day southern Russia: SqT V.9.
Taur, Tawr, Taurus   the second sign of the zodiac: WBPro III.613; MerT IV.1887; NPT VII.3194.
Termagaunt   a supposed Saracen idol: Thop VII.810.
Tertulan   Tertullian (c. A.D. 155–222): WBPro III.676.
Tesbee   Thisbe, lover of Pyramus (see LGW 706–923): IntMLT II.63; MerT IV.2128.
Teuta   queen of Ilyria (3rd cent. B.C.): FranT V.1453.
Thebes   (1) Thebes, chief city of ancient Boetia, in Greece: KnT I.933, KnT I.939, etc.; MLT II.200, MLT II.289; WBPro III.741, WBPro III.746; MerT IV.1716, MerT IV.1721; MancT IX.116; (2) ancient capital city of Upper Egypt: KnT I.1472.
Thelophus   Telephus, king of Mysia: SqT V.238.
Theodamus   Theodamas, the augur of the army at Thebes: MerT IV.1720.

Theodora   wife of Algarsif in SqT: SqT V.664.
Theofraste   Theophrastus, author of the *Liber aureolus de nuptiis* (The Golden Book of Marriage): WBPro III.671; MerT IV.1294, MerT IV.1295, MerT IV.1310.
Theseus   duke of Athens in KnT: KnT I.860, KnT I.878, etc.
Thessalie   Thessaly, in Greece: MkT VII.2679.
Thymothee   (1) a Syrian general (2 Maccabees 9): MkT VII.2591; (2) St. Timothy, recipient of Paul's Epistles: ParsPro X.32; Also **Thimotheum** *Lat.* ParsT X.739.
Thisbe   *see* **Tesbee**.
Thobie   Tobias (in the apocryphal Book of Tobias): Mel VII.1117; ParsT X.906.
Thomas   (1) the householder in the SumT: SumT III.1770, SumT III.1772, etc.; (2) a name the Host uses for the Monk in ProMkT; ProMkT VII.1930.
Thomas (of Ynde), Seint   St. Thomas, the doubting Apostle, in oaths: WBPro III.666, MerPro IV.1230; *gen.* **Thomas** SumT III.1980.
Thomas (of Kent), Seint   St. Thomas à Becket (A.D. 1118–70); in oaths: MilT I.3291, MilT I.3425, MilT I.3461.
Thopas, sire   hero of Thop: Thop VII.717, Thop VII.724, etc.
Thrace   *see* **Trace**.
Thymalao   Timolaus, son of Zenobia MkT: MkT VII.2345.
Tybre   Tiber, the river in Rome: MkT VII.2476.
Tiburce   Tiburtius, converted by Cecilie in SNT: SNT VIII.242, SNT VIII.260, etc. *gen.*, **Tyburces**, SNT VIII.277.
Tyro   Tyre: IntMLT II.81. *see* **Appollonius**.
Titus (Livius)   Livy, the Roman historian (59 B.C.–A.D. 17): PhyT VI.1.
Tolletanes   (*adj. pl.*) of Toledo, in Spain: FranT V.1273.
Trace   Thrace, a region in northern Greece: KnT I.1638, KnT I.1972, etc.
Tramyssene   Tlemcen, in Algeria: GP I.62.
Troie, Troye   the ancient city: KnT I.2833; MLT II.288; SqT V.210, SqT V.306, SqT V.548; FranT V.1446; NPT VII.3229; CYT VIII.975.
Troilus, the book of   Chaucer's *Troilus and Criseyde*: ParsT X.1086.
Trophee   unidentified: MkT VII.2117.
Trotula   probably Trotula di Ruggiero, a female medical authority (11th cent.): WBPro III.677.
Trumpyngton   Trumpington, near Cambridge: RvT I.3921.
Tsarev   *see* **Sarray**.
Tullius Hostillius   king of Rome (7th cent. B.C.): WBT III.1166.
Tullius   Tully, Marcus Tullius Cicero (106–43 B.C.): Mel VII.1165, Mel VII.1176, etc. *see* **Marcus Tullius Scithero**.
Turkye   Turkey: GP I.66.
Turnus   king of the Rutuli, defeated by Aeneas: KnT I.1945; MLT II.201.

U

Urban   Urban I, pope (A.D. 222–30): SNT VIII.177, SNT VIII.179, etc.

V

Valentynes day, book of   Chaucer's *Parliament of Fowles*: ParsT X.1086.
Valeria   wife of Servius, the Latin grammarian: FranT V.1456.
Valerian   husband of Cecilie in SNT: SNT VIII.129, SNT VIII.148, etc.; *gen.* **Valerians** SNT VIII.277.
Valerie   Valerius, supposed author of a misogynist tract: WBPro III.671.
Valerius   Valerius Maximus, Latin author (early 1st cent. A.D.): WBT III.1165, MkT VII.2720.
Venus   (1) the goddess of love: KnT I.1102, KnT I.1104, etc.; WBPro III.464, WBPro III.618, etc.; MerT IV.1723, MerT IV.1777, etc.; SqT V.272; FranT V.937, FranT V.1304; NPT VII.3342; (2) sexual desire: PhyT VI.59; (3) the planet: KnT I.1536, KnT I.2585; WBPro III.697, WBPro III.704, etc.; (as a name for copper) CYT VIII.829. *gen.* **Venus** KnT I.2487; WBPro III.604, WBPro III.708; MerT IV.1875, MerT IV.1971; SqT V.272; ProMkT VII.1961; *see* **Citherea**.
Venyse   Venice: ClPro IV.51.
Vesulus, Mount   Monte Viso, in Northern Italy: ClPro IV.47, ClT IV.58.
Via Appia   the Appian Way: SNT VIII.172.
Virgile   Publius Vergilius Maro (70–19 B.C.): FrT III.1519.
Virginia   heroine in PhyT: PhyT VI.213.
Virginius   father of Virginia in PhyT: PhyT VI.2, PhyT VI.167, etc.
Viscounte   *see* **Barnabo Viscounte**.
Vitulon   Witelo (Vitelo), thirteenth-century Polish physicist: SqT V.232.
Vulcanus   Vulcan, husband of Venus: KnT I.2222, KnT I.2389.

W

Wades   *gen.* of Wade, an obscure legendary figure: MerT IV.1424.

Walter   husband of Griselda in ClT: ClT IV.77, ClT IV.421, etc.
Walys   Wales: MLT II.544.
Ware   possibly the town in Hertfordshire: GP I.692, CkPro I.4336.
Wateryng of Seint Thomas   a spring or brook about two miles from London: GP I.826.
Watte   *dim.* of Walter: GP I.643.
Wilkyn   *dim.* of William, one of the Wife of Bath's husbands: WBPro III.432.
William, kyng   William the Conqueror (reigned 1066–97): GP I.324.
Witch of Endor   *see* **Phitonissa**.

X

Xantippa   Xantippe, wife of Socrates: WBPro III.729.

Y (*See also* I)

Yorkshire   the county in northern England: SumT III.1709.
Ypres   a city in Flanders (in present-day Belgium): GP I.448.

Z

Zakarie   Zechariah, the biblical prophet: ParsT X.434.
Zanzis   Zeuxis, an Athenian painter (5th cent. B.C.): PhyT VI.16.
Zephirus   Zephyrus, the west wind: GP I.5.

Index to the Explanatory Notes

The Index to the Explanatory Notes was compiled by Gustavo P. Secchi.

THIS INDEX is a highly selective guide to the more important subjects covered in the Explanatory Notes. It is not intended as an exhaustive analysis of the notes but rather as a convenient means of locating discussions of major topics. Most entries record the fullest discussion of the topic (usually the first) and do not record subsequent entries (which may be found by looking up the cross-references provided in the notes cited). Most proper names that occur in Chaucer's texts are not listed here; they may be found in the Index to Proper Names in the Tales (see page 549). References are to the notes on specific lines (e.g., I.161 = Fragment I, note 161) or to the unnumbered notes that introduce the particular tales, prologues, or such (cited by page number).

A

M

Madness   See Mania
Magic   See also Geomancy, *sortilegium*
   Images   I.417
   Magic ring   See Canacee, Moses, Solomon
   Natural m.   I.416
Magpies   V.650; cf. Birds
maister   I.261
   Friars not to be called   III.2186–87
Malkyn (name)   VII.3384
   M's maydenhead   II.30
Malmsey   VII.70–71; cf. Alcoholic beverages
Manciples   356
Mania   I.1374–76
Mansions   V.1130; cf. Astronomy
Manslaughter   X.571
Marc Antony   I.2031–32
March, dryness of   I.2
Marcian   IV.1732
Mare, homosexual connotation of   I.691; cf. Horses
Marigolds   I.1929; cf. Flowers
marital debt   VII.413–17
mark   VI.390; cf. Money
market-betere   I.3936
Marriage   I.460
   Blessing of wedding bed   IV.1819
   Paradise, m. as earthly   IV.1332
   Prince's m. to social body   IV.110–40
   Purgatory, m. as earthly   III.489–90
   Wedding service   IV.1700–8
Marriage encomium   IV.1267–1392
Mars   See Index to Proper Names in the Tales
   Temple of M.   I.1967–2050
   Paintings in t. of M.   I.1995–2041
Marshall   I.752
Matins   See Canonical hours
Mausoleum   V.1451
mawmettrie   II.236
May, 3rd night of   I.1462–64
May Day   I.1047
Mayor   I.370
Meat   I.147; cf. Food
Medea   I.1944, II.61–76, II.72–74
Medicine
   Doctors of Physic   351, I.411.
   Sin, medical thinking about   VI.277–86
   See Atheism, Diet, Electuaries, Gold, Herbs, *lechecraft*,
     oynement, *phisik*, Sage, *surgerye*, *ventusynge*, *vertu*
     expulsif, *veyne-blood*. See also Astronomy, Complexion,
     Elements, Leprosy, Virtues
medlee   I.328; cf. Clothing
Melancholy   I.1374–76
   See also Complexion, Love Sickness
Meleager   I.2070–72
mercenarie   I.514
Merchants
   Dealing in foreign currency   I.278
   Debt, m. constantly in   I.280
   Profits, constant talk by m. of own   I.275, VII.237–38

Mercury   I.1387
Mercy   I.3089
Mermaid   VII.3271–72
Merry Men   VII.839
Metals, medicinal use of   V.243–36
Midas   III.951–82
Middelburg   I.277
Millers   355; cf. Thumb, Miller's golden
   Honesty, m's proverbial lack of   I.563
   Janglers, m's connection with   I.560
Minorites   See Franciscans (s.v. Fraternal orders)
Minotaur   I.980
Misrule, Lords of   I.4377
Mist, cause of   V.258–59
Mohammed   II.224
Monastic orders   See Fraternal orders
Money
   See *floryn*, *frank*, *jane*, *lusshebourges*, *mark*, *noble*, *sheeld*,
     sterlyng
Mongols' food   V.67–71; cf. Food
Monks' footwear   I.203; cf. Clothing
Monks' wearing jewelry   I.197; cf. Clothing
Moon, prognostication by the   I.3515, II.305; cf. Astrology
mormal   I.386
mortreux   I.384; cf. Food
Moses's Ring   V.250–51; cf. Magic
mottelee   I.271; cf. Clothing
Mourning, excesive   I.3064–65
Mouth, as devil's gateway   IX.38
Music   See *bagpipes*, *citole*, *flute-playing*, *geestours*, *myn-*
   strales, *nasal singing*, *organs*, *psaltery*, *rebekke*, *ribibe*,
   roundel, St. Cecilia and m., *burdoun*, *symphonye*. See
   also Quadrivium
mynstrales   VII.845–46; cf. Music
Mystery plays   I.3384
   Noah in   I.3538–43

N

Nails, Christ's   VI.651
Narcissus   I.1941
Nasal singing   I.123; cf. Music
Natura   I.11
Naxos   II.68
Nero   I.2031–32, VII.2463
Night spells   I.3480–86
Nightingales   I.10, I.98; cf. Birds
Noah's Flood, date of   I.3538–43
noble   I.3256, VI.907; cf. Money
Nones   See Canonical hours
Norfolk accent   I.3864
North, location of Hell in the   III.1413
Northern dialect   I.4022
Northern light   I.1987

O

Oaths   See Swearing
occupatio   I.849, I.875–88; cf. Rhetorical figures
Offertory   I.449–51, I.710

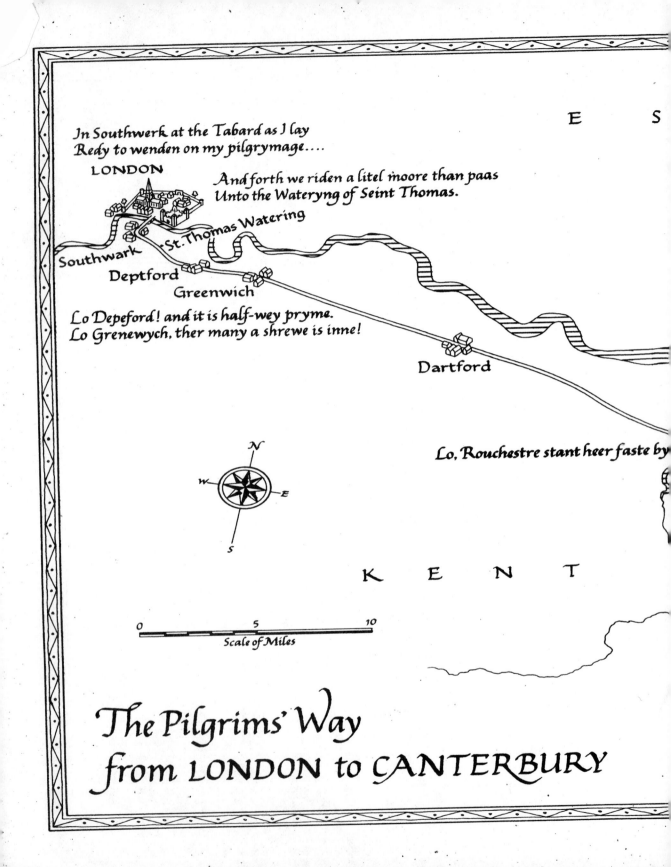

In Southwerk at the Tabard as J lay
Redy to wenden on my pilgrymage....

LONDON

And forth we riden a litel moore than paas
Unto the Wateryng of Seint Thomas.

St. Thomas Watering

Southwark

Deptford

Greenwich

Lo Depeford! and it is half-wey pryme.
Lo Grenewych, ther many a shrewe is inne!

Dartford

E S

Lo, Rouchestre stant heer faste by

N
W E
S

K E N T

0   5   10
Scale of Miles

The Pilgrims' Way
from LONDON to CANTERBURY